I'm Your Man

I'm Your Man

The Life of Leonard Cohen

Sylvie Simmons

ecco

An Imprint of HarperCollinsPublishers

To N.A., in loving memory

The way you do anything is
the way you do everything.

—TOM WAITS

FIRST EDITION

Designed by Leah Carlson-Stanisic

Library of Congress Cataloging-in-Publication Data has been applied for.

ISBN 978-0-06-199498-2

12 13 14 15 16 OV/RRD 10 9 8 7 6 5 4 3 2 1

Contents

Prologue

He is a courtly man, elegant, with old-world manners. He bows when he meets you, stands when you leave, makes sure that you're comfortable and makes no mention of the fact he's not; the discreet stroking of the Greek worry beads he carries in his pocket gives the game away. By inclination he is a private man, rather shy, but if probing is required he'll put his feet in the stirrups with dignity and humor. He chooses his words carefully, like a poet, or a politician, with a habit of precision, an ear for their sound, and a talent and a taste for deflection and mystery. He has always liked smoke and mirrors. And yet there is something conspiratorial in the way he talks, as there is when he sings, as if he were imparting an intimate secret.

He is a trim man—there's no excess to him at all—and smaller than you might think. Shipshape. You imagine that he wouldn't find it hard to wear a uniform. Right now he is wearing a suit. It is dark, pin-striped, double-breasted, and if it's off-the-rack it doesn't look it.

"Darling," says Leonard, "I was born in a suit."[1]

One

Born in a Suit

===================

When I'm with you
I want to be the kind of hero
I wanted to be
when I was seven years old
a perfect man
who kills

—"The Reason I Write," *Selected Poems 1956–1968*

The chauffeur turned off the main road by the synagogue, which took up most of the block, and headed past St. Matthias's Church on the opposite corner, and up the hill. In the back of the car was a woman—twenty-seven years old, attractive, strong featured, stylishly dressed—and her newborn baby son. The streets they passed were handsome and well-appointed, the trees arranged just so. Big houses of brick and stone you might have thought would collapse under the sheer weight of their self-importance appeared to float effortlessly up the slopes. Around halfway up, the driver took a side road and stopped outside a house at the end of the street, 599 Belmont Avenue. It was large, solid and formal-looking, English in style, its dark brick softened by a white-framed veranda at the front and at the back by Murray Hill Park, fourteen acres of lawns, trees and flower beds, with a sweeping view of the St. Lawrence River to one side and, on the other, downtown Montreal. The chauffeur stepped out of the car and opened the rear door, and Leonard was carried up the white front steps and into his family home.

Leonard Norman Cohen was born on September 21, 1934, in the Royal Victoria Hospital, a gray stone pile in Westmount, an affluent neighborhood of Montreal, Canada. According to the records, it was at six forty-five on a Friday morning. According to history, it was halfway between the Great Depression and World War II. Counting backward, Leonard was conceived between the end of Hanukkah and Christmas Day during one of the subarctic winters his hometown managed to deliver with both consistency and brio. He was raised in a house of suits.

Nathan Cohen, Leonard's father, was a prosperous Canadian Jew with a high-end clothing business. The Freedman Company was known for its formal wear, and Nathan liked to dress formally, even on informal occasions. In suits, as in houses, he favored the formal English style, which he wore with spats and tempered with a boutonniere and, when his bad health made it necessary, with a silver cane. Masha Cohen, Leonard's mother, was sixteen years younger than her husband, a Russian Jew, a rabbi's daughter and a recent immigrant to Canada. She and Nathan had married not long after her arrival in Montreal in 1927. Two years later she gave birth to the first of their two children, Leonard's sister, Esther.

Early photographs of Nathan and Masha show him to be a square-faced, square-shouldered, stocky man. Masha, slimmer and a head taller, is in contrast all circles and slopes. The expression on Masha's face is both girlish and regal, while Nathan's is rigid and taciturn. Even were this not the required camera pose for the head of a household at that time, Nathan was certainly more reserved, and more Anglicized, than his warm, emotional Russian wife. As a baby, Leonard, plump, compact and also square-faced, was the image of his father, but as he grew he took on his mother Masha's heart-shaped face, thick wavy hair and deep, dark, sloping eyes. From his father he acquired his height, his tidiness, his decency and his love of suits. From his mother he inherited her charisma, her melancholy and her music. Masha always sang as she went about the house, in Russian and Yiddish more than in English, the sentimental old folk songs she had learned as a child. In a good contralto voice, to imaginary violins, Masha would sing herself from joy to melancholy and back again. "Chekhovian" is how Leonard described his mother.[1] "She laughed and wept deeply,"[2] said Leonard, one emotion following the other in quick succession. Masha Cohen was not a nostalgic woman; she did not talk much about the country she had left. But she carried her past in songs.

The residents of Westmount were well-to-do, upper-middle-class Protestant English Canadians and second- or third-generation Canadian Jews. In a city that was all about division and separation, the Jews and Protestants had been filed together on the simple grounds of being neither French nor Catholic. Before the "Quiet Revolution" in Quebec in the sixties, and before French became the sole official language of the province, the only French in Westmount were the domestic help. The Cohens had a maid, Mary, although she was Irish Catholic. They also had a nanny, whom Leonard and his sister called "Nursie," and a gardener named Kerry, a black man, who doubled as the family chauffeur. (Kerry's brother held the same job with Nathan's younger brother Horace.) It is no secret that Leonard's background was privileged. Leonard has never denied being born on the right side of the tracks, has never renounced his upbringing, rejected his family, changed his name or pretended to be anything other than who he is. His family was well-off, although there were

certainly wealthier families in Westmount. Unlike the mansions of
Upper Belmont, the Cohens' house, though big, was semidetached,
and their car, though chauffeur driven, was a Pontiac, not a Cadillac.

But what the Cohens had that very few others came close to matching was status. The family Leonard was born into was distinguished
and important—one of the most prominent Jewish families in Montreal. Leonard's ancestors had built synagogues and founded newspapers in Canada. They had funded and presided over a lengthy list
of Jewish philanthropic societies and associations. Leonard's great-
grandfather Lazarus Cohen had been the first of the family to come
to Canada. In Lithuania, which was part of Russia in the 1840s, when
Lazarus was born, Lazarus had been a teacher in a rabbinical school
in Wylkowyski, one of the most rigorous yeshivas in the country. In
his twenties, he left his wife and their baby son behind to try for his
fortune. After a brief stay in Scotland, he took a ship to Canada, stopping in Ontario in a small town called Maberly, where he worked his
way up from lumber storeman to the owner of a coal company, L. Cohen
and Son. The son was Lyon, Nathan's father, whom Lazarus sent for,
along with his mother, two years later. The family eventually made
their way to Montreal, where Lazarus became president of a brass
foundry and started a successful dredging company.

When Lazarus Cohen first arrived in Canada in 1860, the country's Jewish population was tiny. In the middle of the nineteenth century there had been fewer than five hundred Jews in Montreal. By the
mid-1880s, when Lazarus assumed the presidency of the synagogue
Congregation Shaar Hashomayim, there were more than five thousand. The Russian pogroms had led to a wave of immigration, and by
the end of the century the number of Jews in Canada had doubled.
Montreal had become the seat of Canadian Jewry, and Lazarus, with
his long, white, biblical beard and uncovered head, was a familiar
figure among its community. Along with building a synagogue, Lazarus established and headed a number of organizations to aid Jewish

settlers and would-be immigrants, even traveling to Palestine (where Lazarus bought land as early as 1884) on behalf of the Jewish Colonization Association of Montreal. Lazarus's younger brother Rabbi Tzvi Hirsch Cohen, who joined him in Canada soon after, would become chief rabbi of Montreal.

In 1914, when Lyon Cohen took over the presidency of Shaar Hashomayim from his father, the synagogue could claim the largest congregation in a city whose Jewish population now numbered around forty thousand. In 1922, having grown too big for its old premises, the synagogue relocated to a new building in Westmount, almost a block in length, just minutes down the hill from the house on Belmont Avenue. Twelve years later Nathan and Masha added their only son to the synagogue's "Register of Births of the Corporation of English, German and Polish Jews of Montreal," giving Leonard his Jewish name, Eliezer, meaning "God is help."

Lyon Cohen, like his father, had been a very successful businessman—clothing and insurance. He also followed Lazarus into community service, being appointed secretary of the Anglo-Jewish Association while still in his teens. He would go on to establish a Jewish community center and a sanatorium, and preside over relief efforts for victims of the pogroms. Lyon held top positions in the Baron de Hirsch Institute, the Jewish Colonization Association and Canada's first Zionist organization. He went to the Vatican on behalf of his community to talk to the pope. He cofounded the first Anglo-Jewish newspaper in Canada, the *Jewish Times*, to which he contributed the occasional article. Lyon had written a play when he was sixteen years old titled *Esther*, which he produced and in which he acted. Leonard never knew his grandfather—he was two years old when Lyon died—but there was a strong connection, which intensified as Leonard grew older. Lyon's principles, his work ethic and his belief in "the aristocracy of the intellect,"[3] as Lyon always referred to it, all sat well with Leonard's own persuasion.

Lyon was also a staunch Canadian patriot, and when World War I broke out he launched a recruitment drive to encourage Montreal's Jews to enlist in the Canadian Army. The first to sign up were his sons Nathan and Horace (the third son, Lawrence, was too young). Lieutenant Nathan Cohen, number 3080887, became one of the first Jewish commissioned officers in the Canadian Army. Leonard loved the photographs of his father in uniform. But after his return from the war, Nathan suffered recurring periods of ill health, which left him increasingly invalid. This might be why Nathan, although the oldest son of the oldest son, did not continue the family tradition of holding the presidency of the synagogue, nor of much else. Although on paper he was president of the Freedman Company, the business was largely run by his brother Horace. Neither was Nathan an intellectual nor a religious scholar like his forebears. The dark wooden bookshelves in the house on Belmont Avenue held an impressive leather-bound set of the great poets—Chaucer, Wordsworth, Byron—Nathan's bar mitzvah gift, but their spines remained uncracked until Leonard took them down to read. Nathan, Leonard said, preferred the *Reader's Digest*, but "his heart was cultured; he was a gentleman."[4] As to religion, Nathan was "a Conservative Jew, not fanatical, without ideology and dogma, whose life was purely made up of domestic habit and affiliations with the community." Religion was not something that was discussed in Nathan's house, or even thought about. "It was mentioned no more than a fish mentions the presence of water."[5] It was simply there, his tradition, his people.

Masha's father, Rabbi Solomon Klonitzki-Kline, was a noted religious scholar. He had been the principal of a school for Talmudic study in Kovno in Lithuania, some fifty miles from the town where Lazarus had been born. He was also an author, whose two books, *Lexicon of Hebrew Homonyms* and *Thesaurus of Talmudic Interpretations*, would earn him the sobriquet "Sar HaDikdook," the Prince of Grammarians. When the persecution of Jews made life in Lithuania untenable, he moved to the U.S., where one of his daughters lived and had married an American. Masha had gone to Canada, where she had taken a job as a nurse. When Masha's work permit expired, he turned to his American son-in-law for help, which led to his introduction to Lyon Cohen's resettlement committee. It was through the subsequent friendship of the rabbi and Lyon that Masha and Nathan met and married.

Leonard, as a young boy, heard about Grandfather Kline more than he saw him, since the rabbi spent much of his time in the U.S. Masha would tell Leonard stories about how people came hundreds of miles to hear his grandfather speak. He also had a reputation as a great horseman, she told him, and Leonard was particularly pleased with this information. He liked it that his was a family of important people, but he was a young boy and physical prowess trumped intellect. Leonard was planning to attend the military academy once he was old enough. Nathan told him he could. Leonard wanted to fight wars and win medals—like his father had done, before he became this invalid who sometimes found it hard to even walk up stairs, who would stay home from work, nursed by Leonard's mother. Through Leonard's early childhood, Nathan had often been ill. But the boy had proof that his father had been a warrior once. Nathan still had his gun from World War I, which he kept in his bedside cabinet. One day, when no one was around, Leonard slipped into his parents' bedroom. He opened the cabinet and took out the gun. It was a big gun, a .38, its barrel engraved with his father's name, rank and regiment. Cradling it in his small hand, Leonard shivered, awed by its heft and the feel of its cold metal on his skin.

Five ninety-nine Belmont Avenue was a busy house, a house of routine, well ordered, and the center of the young Leonard's universe. Anything the boy might need or want to do orbited closely around it. His uncles and cousins lived nearby. The synagogue, where Leonard went with the family on Saturday morning, and on Sunday for Sunday school, and to Hebrew school two afternoons a week, was a short walk down the hill. So were his regular schools, Roslyn Elementary School and, later, Westmount High. Murray Hill Park, where Leonard played in the summer and made snow angels in the winter, was immediately below his bedroom window.

The Westmount Jewish community was a close-knit one. It was also a minority community in an English Protestant neighborhood. Which was itself a minority, if a powerful one, in a city and a province largely populated by the Catholic French. Who were themselves a minority in Canada. Everybody felt like some kind of outsider; everyone felt like they belonged to something important. It was "a romantic, conspiratorial mental environment," said Leonard, a place of "blood and soil and destiny." "That is the landscape I grew up in," he said, "and it's very natural to me."[6]

Leonard's community, half a city away from the working-class immigrant Jewish neighborhood around Saint-Urbain (which formed the backdrop to Mordecai Richler's novels) might have appeared to be hermetically sealed, but of course it wasn't. The Cross on the top of Mount Royal; Mary, the family maid, always crossing herself; and the Easter and Christmas celebrations at school were part of the young Leonard's landscape just as the Sabbath candles his father lit on Friday evenings were, and the imposing synagogue down the hill, from whose walls Leonard's great-grandfather and grandfather stared down at him in large, framed portraits, reminding him of the distinction of his blood.

As Leonard recalled it, it was "an intense family life."[7] The Cohens would get together regularly—at the synagogue, in the workplace and also once a week at Leonard's paternal grandmother's home. "Every Saturday afternoon, at around four o'clock, Martha, her devoted maid, would wheel in a tea trolley with tea and little sandwiches and cakes and biscuits," says David Cohen, two years older than Leonard and a cousin with whom Leonard was particularly close. "You were never invited, and you never asked if you could go, but you knew that she was 'receiving.' It sounds very archaic, but it was quite something." Leonard's grandmother had a flat in one of the grand houses on Sherbrooke Street at Atwater, which was where all the parades that were held in Montreal would end up—"Saint Jean Baptiste," says David Cohen, "that was a big one, before it became a very tough political situation in Montreal, and we'd watch from inside from the big, beautiful window in her living room." Their grandmother was very much a Victorian lady, "but, though it sounds archaic and old-fashioned, she was a pretty hip lady too." She made quite an impression on Leonard, who would later describe her tea parties in his first novel, *The Favorite Game.*

In that same book, Leonard described the older men in his family as serious and formal. Not all of them were. Among the more colorful members of the family was Cousin Lazzy, David's older brother Lazarus. Leonard thought of Lazzy as "a man about town, familiar with the chorus girls and the nightclubs and the entertainers."[8] There was also a cousin of an older generation, Edgar, Nathan's cousin, a businessman with a literary bent. Many years later Edgar H. Cohen would go on to write *Mademoiselle Libertine: A Portrait of Ninon de Lanclos,* a biography published in 1970 of a seventeenth-century courtesan, writer and muse whose lovers included Voltaire and Molière, and who, after a period in a convent, emerged to establish a school where young French noblemen could learn erotic technique. Leonard and Edgar, says David Cohen, were "very close."

Leonard's was a comfortable, secure life during an uncomfortable, insecure time. Days before Leonard's fifth birthday, Germany invaded Poland and World War II began. Closer to home, in 1942 there was an anti-Semitic rally on St. Lawrence Boulevard—the Main, as locals called it—which was the traditional dividing line between English and French Montreal. It was led by Montreal's French Nationalist movement, which included supporters of the Vichy regime in France.

One particularly risible claim of the organization was that the Jews had taken over the clothing business in order to force modest young French-Canadian girls to wear "improper gowns in New York styles."[9] During the rally, the windows of several Jewish-owned shops and delis on the Main were broken and racist slurs painted on walls. But for a seven-year-old living in Westmount, sitting in his room reading his *Superman* comics, it was another world. "Europe, the war, the social war," Leonard said, "none of it seemed to touch us."[10]

He breezed through the early years of childhood, doing all that was required—clean hands, good manners, getting dressed for dinner, good school reports, making the hockey team, keeping his shoes polished and lined up tidily under his bed at night—without showing any worrying signs of sainthood or genius. Nor of melancholy. The home movies shot by Nathan, a keen amateur cameraman, show a happy little boy, beaming as he pedals his tricycle along the street, or walks hand in hand with his sister, or plays with his dog, a black Scottish terrier named Tinkie. His mother had originally given it the more dignified name of Tovarich, the Russian word for "ally," but it was vetoed by his father. Nathan was already aware that in this small, Anglicized, Canadian Jewish community, Masha's Russianness, her accent, her imperfect English and big personality, made her stand out. "It wasn't thought to be a good idea to be passionate about anything," said Leonard, or to draw attention. "We were taught," says cousin David, "to mind our P's and Q's."

Then in January 1944, at the age of fifty-two, Leonard's father died. Leonard was nine years old. Around fourteen years later, in two unpublished stories titled "Ceremonies" and "My Sister's Birthday,"[11] Leonard described what happened: "Nursie told us the news." Seated at the kitchen table, her hands folded in her lap, Leonard's nanny informed Leonard and Esther that they would not be going to school that morning because their father had died in the night. They should be quiet, she said, because their mother was still sleeping. The funeral would take place the following day. "Then the day dawned on me," Leonard wrote. "'But it can't be tomorrow, Nursie, it's my sister's birthday.'"

At nine o'clock the next morning, six men arrived and carried the coffin into the living room. They set it down alongside the leather chesterfield sofa. Masha had the maid soap all the mirrors in the house. By noon people started arriving, shaking the snow off their boots and topcoats—family, friends, people who worked at the factory. The coffin was open, and Leonard peered inside. Nathan was wrapped in a silver prayer shawl, his face white, his mustache black. His father, Leonard thought, looked annoyed. Uncle Horace, who ran the Freedman Company with Nathan and who had served alongside him in the Great War, whispered to Leonard, "We've got to be like soldiers." Later that night, when Esther asked Leonard if he had dared to look at their dead father, each confessed that they had, and agreed that it appeared that someone had dyed his mustache. Both of these stories ended with the same line: "Don't cry, I told her. I think it was my best moment. Please, it's your birthday."

A third version of the event appeared in *The Favorite Game*. It was a more poised account, partly due to Leonard's writing having matured considerably in the time between these abandoned stories and his first novel, and partly from the distance accorded by having ascribed it in the latter to a fictional character (although Leonard has confirmed that it happened as he wrote it in the book).[12] This time the episode concludes with the young boy taking one of his father's bow ties from his bedroom, slicing it open, and hiding a small piece of paper inside it on which he had written something. The next day, in his own private ceremony, the boy dug a hole and buried it in the garden under the snow. Leonard has since described this as the first thing he ever wrote. He has also said he has no recollection of what it was and that he had been "digging in the garden for years, looking for it. Maybe that's all I'm doing, looking for the note."[13]

The act is so weighty with symbolism—Leonard having for the first time in his life made a rite of his writing—that it is tempting to take these words from a 1980 interview at face value, even if it is more likely just another of the many good lines that Leonard always gave his interviewers. Children are often drawn to the mystical and to secret ceremonies. And if Leonard has also said that as a young child he had "no particular interest in religion," except for "a couple of times when we went to hear a choir,"[14] he was also well aware that he was a Kohen, one of a priestly caste, a patrilineal descendant of Moses's brother, Aaron, and born to officiate. "When they told me I was a Kohen, I believed it. I didn't think it was some auxiliary information," he said. "I wanted to live this world. I wanted to be the one who lifted up the Torah. . . . I was this little kid, and whatever they told me in these matters resonated."[15]

Still, as a child he showed little interest in the synagogue his ancestors founded. Hebrew school, he said, "bored" him, and Wilfred Shuchat, who was appointed rabbi of Shaar Hashomayim in 1948, appears to confirm this. Leonard "was okay" as a student, says the old rabbi, "but scholarship wasn't his real interest. It was his personality, the way he interpreted things. He was very creative."

Leonard did not cry at the death of his father; he wept more when his dog Tinkie died a few years later. "I didn't feel a profound sense of loss," he said in a 1991 interview, "maybe because he was very ill throughout my entire childhood. It seemed natural that he died. He was weak and he died. Maybe my heart is cold."[16]

It is true that since the previous summer Nathan had been in and out of the Royal Victoria Hospital. If it is also true that the loss of his father had no great effect on Leonard, he was not so young at nine years old that it would not have registered on him. Somewhere inside, something would have changed—an awareness for the first time of impermanence, perhaps, or a sad wisdom, a crack where the insecurity or the solitude came in. What Leonard has said, and written, that he was most aware of during this important episode of his childhood was the change of status it bestowed on him. While his father lay in the living room in the coffin, his uncle Horace took him aside and told him that he, Leonard, was the man of the house now, and that the women—his mother and his fourteen-year-old sister, Esther— were his responsibility. "This made me proud," Leonard wrote in "Ceremonies." "I felt like the consecrated young prince of some folk-beloved dynasty. I was the oldest son of the oldest son."[17]

Two

House of Women

In his early teens Leonard developed a keen interest in hypnosis. He acquired a slim, pocket-sized, anonymously written book with the lengthy title *25 Lessons in Hypnotism: How to Become an Expert Operator* and the extravagant claim of being "the most perfect, complete, easily learned and comprehensive COURSE in the world, embracing the Science of Magnetic Healing, Telepathy, Mind Reading, Clairvoyant Hypnosis, Mesmerism, Animal Magnetism and Kindred Sciences." On the front cover, beneath a crude sketch of a Victorian lady held spellbound by a wild-haired, mustached gentleman, Leonard wrote his name in ink in his best handwriting and set about his studies.

It turned out that Leonard had a natural talent for mesmerism. Finding instant success with domestic animals, he moved on to the domestic staff, recruiting as his first human subject the family maid. At his direction, the young woman sat on the chesterfield sofa. Leonard drew a chair alongside and, as the book instructed, told her in a slow gentle voice to relax her muscles and look into his eyes. Picking up a pencil, he moved it slowly in front of her face, back and forth, back and forth, and succeeded in putting her in a trance. Disregarding (or depending on one's interpretation, following) the author's directive that his teachings should be used only for educational purposes, Leonard instructed the maid to undress.

What a moment it must have been for the adolescent Leonard. This successful fusion of arcane wisdom and sexual longing. To sit beside a naked woman, in his own home, convinced that *he* made this happen, simply by talent, study, mastery of an art and imposition of his will. When he found it difficult to awaken her, Leonard started to panic. He was terrified his mother might come home and catch them—though one imagines this would have simply added a sense of impending doom, despair and loss to the heady mix that would make it even more exquisitely Leonard Cohenesque.

Chapter Two of the hypnotism manual might have been written as career advice to the singer and performer Leonard would become. It cautioned against any appearance of levity and instructed, "Your features should be set, firm and stern. Be quiet in all your actions. Let your voice grow lower, lower, till just above a whisper. Pause a moment or two. You will fail if you try to hurry."[1]

When Leonard re-created the episode in his twenties in *The Favorite Game,* he wrote, "He had never seen a woman so naked. . . . He was astonished, happy, and frightened before all the spiritual authorities of the universe. Then he sat back to stare. This is what he had waited for so long to see. He wasn't disappointed and never has been."[2] Although it is ascribed to his fictionalized alter ego, it is hard to imagine that these sentiments were not Leonard's own. Decades later he would still say, "I don't think a man ever gets over that first sight of the naked woman. I think that's Eve standing over him, that's the morning and the dew on the skin. And I think that's the major content of every man's imagination. All the sad adventures in pornography and love and song are just steps on the path toward that holy vision."[3] The maid, incidentally, was a ukulele player, an instrument his fictional alter ego took for a lute and the girl, by extension, for an angel. And everybody knows that naked angels possess a portal to the divine.

———————

"Leonard always complained there were no girls. That he couldn't get girls," says Mort Rosengarten. "And it was always a serious complaint." Rosengarten is a sculptor and Leonard's oldest friend. He is the model for Krantz, the best friend of the protagonist of *The Favorite Game*. "You have to remember," Rosengarten says, his soft voice barely audible over the whirr of the ventilator emphysema obliges him to use, "that at that time we were raised in a totally segregated way. At school the boys were in one part of the school and the girls were in another and there was no interaction whatsoever, and because we didn't fall in with the conventional Westmount society of our peers in terms of our behavior, we didn't have access to those women either, because they were on a certain path. But I always thought that Leonard was lucky, that he knew and understood something about women, because he lived in a house of women, his sister, Esther, and his mother. I knew nothing about women; I just had a brother, and my mother wasn't giving any of her secrets away about what women were about. So we always complained."

Rosengarten's home is a small, wonky, two-story terraced house with a bathtub in the kitchen, near to the Parc du Portugal, off the Main. When he moved here forty years ago, it was a blue-collar, immigrant neighborhood. Despite the signs of gentrification—the fancy boutiques and cafés—the old Jewish delis with Formica tabletops that Mort and Leonard used to frequent are still there. It was a world away from their privileged Westmount origins. Mort grew up on Upper Belmont, five hundred yards and another economic stratum above the Cohen family's Lower Belmont home. Though the money is long gone now, the Rosengartens had been extremely wealthy; they had two Cadillacs and a country estate in the Eastern Townships, some sixty miles outside Montreal. Leonard and Mort met and became friends on neutral territory, when Mort was ten and Leonard nine years old. It was at summer camp in June 1944, five months after the death of Leonard's father.

The Cohens had long been accustomed to spending the season together at the seaside in Maine, in the U.S. But in the summers of 1940 and '41, when Canada was at war with Germany but America had not yet joined the battle, the U.S. imposition of currency restrictions made it more sensible for Canadians to take their holidays at home. A popular spot was the Laurentians, north of Montreal. The writer Mordecai Richler described it as "a veritable Jewish paradise, a minor-league Catskills,"[4] with hotels and inns where old men in yarmulkes gossiped in Yiddish across the road from the "Gentiles only" bowling green. For those at Leonard's end of the age spectrum there was a proliferation of summer camps along the lakes around Sainte-Agathe. Camp Hiawatha offered its young charges the usual menu of fresh air, cabin dorms, communal showers, arts and crafts, playing fields and biting insects, but "it was terrible," says Rosengarten, with feeling. "Their biggest concern was to reassure the parents that you would never get into any kind of adventure whatsoever. I was stuck there for a few years, though Leonard only went for one summer; his mother found a more sensible camp where they taught you to canoe and swim"—swimming being something Leonard did enthusiastically and well. An itemized bill from Camp Hiawatha in 1944 appears to confirm Rosengarten's dim view of the activities on offer: Leonard's allowance was spent on the tuck shop, stationery, stamps, a haircut and a train ticket home.[5]

Leonard and Mort had more in common than their prosperous Westmount Jewish backgrounds. Neither had much of a father figure in his life—Leonard's was dead and Mort's often absent—and each had a mother who, certainly by 1940s Westmount Jewish society standards, was unconventional. Mort's mother came from a working-class background and considered herself "modern." Leonard's was a Russian immigrant and had been considerably younger than her late husband. If Masha's accent and dramatic nature had not ensured a certain separateness from the other mothers in the young boys' small, insular community, being an attractive, strikingly dressed young widow most likely would. But Leonard and Mort's friendship would really deepen four years later, when they both attended the same junior high school.

Westmount High, a large gray stone building, with lush lawns and a crest with a Latin motto (*Dux Vitae Ratio*: "Reason Is Life's Guide"), looked like it had snuck out of Cambridge and onto a plane to Canada in the dead of night, having grown tired of spending centuries shaping the minds of well-bred British boys. In fact it was relatively young, a Protestant school founded in a far more modest building in 1873, although still among the oldest English-speaking schools in Quebec. At the time of Leonard's attendance, Jewish pupils made up between a quarter and a third of the school population. A general mood of religious tolerance, or indifference, reigned, and the two groups mixed and socialized, went to each other's parties. "We took our Jewish holidays when they came up and we celebrated the Christian holidays," says Rona Feldman, one of Leonard's classmates. "A lot of us were in the choir and the Christmas plays." Leonard's Catholic nanny, who walked him to school every morning—no matter, as Mort Rosengarten pointed out, that "it was a block away; Leonard's family was a very formal kind of scene"—had taken him to church with her in the past. "I love Jesus," Leonard said. "Always did, even as a kid." He added, "I kept it to myself; I didn't stand up in shul and say 'I love Jesus.'"[6]

At the age of thirteen, Leonard celebrated his bar mitzvah, his Jewish coming of age. Watched by his uncles and cousins, a battalion of Cohens, he climbed onto a footstool—it was the only way he could see—and read from the Torah for the first time in the synagogue his ancestors had founded and presided over. "There were lots of members of his family," recalls Rabbi Shuchat, with whom Leonard had taken his bar mitzvah class, "but it was very difficult for Leonard, because his father was not there" to speak the customary prayer of release. But since the war began, everyone seemed to have someone, or something, missing. "There was the rationing and coupons for certain things like meat," Rona Feldman remembers, "and they sold war savings stamps in the school and some of the classes competed with each other for who bought the most war savings stamps each week. There was a girl going to school with us who was part of a program of children sent to different places to keep them safe during the war, and we all knew families who had members overseas in the army or the air force." And when the war was over, there were the nightmarish photos of victims of the concentration camps. The war, said Mort Rosengarten, was "a very big thing for us," meaning Leonard and himself. "It was absolutely a very important factor in our sensibility."

The summer of 1948, the bridge between leaving Roslyn Elementary and starting at Westmount High, was once again spent at summer camp. Among the mementos from Camp Wabi-Kon in Leonard's archives are a swimming and water safety certificate, and a document written in a neat, child's hand and signed by Leonard and six other boys. A schoolboy pact, it read: "We should not fight and we must try to get along better. We should appreciate things better. We should be better sports and we should have more spirit. We shouldn't boss each other around. We must not use foul language."[7] They had even devised a list of penalties, ranging from missing supper to going to bed half an hour early.

The boyish earnestness and idealism had an almost Enid Blyton–like innocence to it. Back home in his bedroom on Belmont Avenue, though, Leonard was thinking about girls—cutting pictures of models from his mother's magazines and gazing out of the window as the wind whipped up the skirts of the women as they walked through Murray Hill Park or plastered them deliciously to their thighs. In the back pages of his comic books he would study the Charles Atlas ads that promised puny little boys like himself the kind of muscles it takes to woo a girl. Leonard was small for his age; a new use the adolescent had found for Kleenex was to wad it up and put it in his shoes to make lifts. It bothered Leonard that he was shorter than his friends—some of the girls in his high school class were a head taller—but he started to learn that girls could be won around "by stories and talk." In *The Favorite Game* his alter ego "began to think of himself as the Tiny Conspirator, the Cunning Dwarf."[8] In Rona Feldman's recollection, Leonard in fact was "extremely popular" with the girls in their class, although, due to his height, "most girls thought he was adorable more than a hunk. I just remember him being very sweet. He had that same kind of grin that he has now, a little bit of a half grin, kind of shy, and when he smiled it was so genuine, it was so satisfying to see him smile. I think he was very well liked."

———————

Since the age of thirteen Leonard had taken to going out late at night, two or three nights a week, wandering alone through the seedier streets of Montreal. Before the Saint Lawrence Seaway was built the city was a major port, the place where all the cargo destined for central North America went to be offloaded from oceangoing freighters and put on canal boats and taken up to the Great Lakes or sent by rail to the West. At night the city swarmed with sailors, longshoremen and passengers from the cruise ships that docked in the harbor, and welcoming them were countless bars, which openly flouted the law requiring that they close at three A.M. The daily newspapers carried notices for shows on Saint Catherine Street that started at four in the morning and ended just before dawn. There were jazz clubs, blues clubs, movie houses, bars where the only thing they played was Quebecois country and western, and cafés with jukeboxes whose content Leonard came to know by heart.

Leonard wrote about his night ramblings in an unpublished, undated piece from the late fifties titled "The Juke-Box Heart: Excerpt From a Journal." "When I was about 13 yrs old I did the things my friends did until they went to bed, then I'd walk miles along Saint Catherine street, a night-lover, peeking into marble-tabled cafeterias where men wore overcoats even in the summer." There was a boyish innocence to his description of his early wanderings: peering into the windows of novelty shops "to catalogue the magic and tricks, rubber cockroaches, handshake buzzers." As he walked he would imagine he was a man in his twenties, "raincoated, battered hat pulled low above intense eyes, a history of injustice in his heart, a face too noble for revenge, walking the night along some wet boulevard, followed by the sympathy of countless audiences [. . .] loved by two or three beautiful women who could never have him." He might have been describing a character from one of the comic books he read or from one of the private eye movies he had seen; Leonard was by this time already a cinephile. But, after throwing a quote from Baudelaire into the mix, he was enough of a self-critic to add, "This writing embarrasses me. I am humorist enough to see a young man stepping out of Stendhal, given to self-dramatization, walking off a comfortless erection. Perhaps masturbation would have been more effective and less tiring."[9]

Leonard walked slowly past the working girls on the street, but in spite of the need and longing in his eyes the hookers looked over his head, calling out to the men who passed, offering them what Leonard had begun to want more than anything. The world of Leonard's imagination must have grown enormously during that time, and an exhilarating sense of possibility, but also a sense of isolation, an awareness of the blues. Says Mort Rosengarten, who after a time would join his friend on his late-night adventures, "Leonard looked young, and I did too. But you could get served in bars—girls at thirteen. It was very open back then and also very corrupt. A lot of these bars were controlled by the Mafia, you had to pay someone off to get a license, and it was the same with taverns, which were bars that sold only beer and only to men, no women allowed, and there were lots of those because they were the cheapest place to drink. At six in the morning you could go in and it would be full of people. Leonard didn't have to sneak out of the house; we both came from homes where nobody really worried about that or where we were. But the Westmount Jewish community was quite small and a very protected environment, with a very strong sense of group identity, these young people who all knew each other. So he went to Saint Catherine Street to experience what we had never seen or been allowed to do."

While this was going on, Leonard's musical boundaries were also starting to expand. At his mother's encouragement he had started taking piano lessons—not because he had shown any special interest or talent in that area but because his mother encouraged Leonard in almost everything and piano lessons were what one did. Piano was not Leonard's first musical instrument—in elementary school he had played a Bakelite Tonette, a kind of recorder—and he did not stick with it for long. He found practicing the exercises that his teacher, Miss MacDougal, sent him home with a dull and solitary business. He preferred the clarinet, which he played in the high school band alongside Mort, who had escaped his own piano lessons by taking up the trombone. Leonard was involved in a number of extracurricular school activities. He had been elected president of the student council and was also on the executive of the drama club, as well as on the board of publishers responsible for the high school yearbook, *Vox Ducum*—a periodical that might claim to have been the first to publish one of Leonard's stories. "Kill or Be Killed" appeared in its pages in 1950.

Rosengarten recalls, "Leonard was always very articulate and could address groups of people." A report from Camp Wabi-Kon dated August 1949 noted that "Lenny is the leader of the cabin and is looked up to by all members of the cabin. He is the most popular boy in the unit and is friendly with everyone [and] well-liked by the entire staff."* At the same time, school friends remembered Leonard as a shy boy, engaged in the solitary pursuit of writing poetry, someone who deflected attention more than courted it. Nancy Bacal, another close friend who has known Leonard from boyhood on, remembers him during that period as "someone special, but in a quiet way. That seeming contradiction: he moves into leadership naturally, except that he remains invisible at the same time. His intensity and power operates from below the surface." A curious mix, this public and private nature, but it appears to have been workable; certainly it stuck.

———

The Big Bang of Leonard, the moment when poetry, music, sex and spiritual longing collided and fused in him for the first time, happened in 1950, between his fifteenth and sixteenth birthdays. Leonard was standing outside a secondhand book shop, browsing through the racks, when he happened upon *The Selected Poems of Federico Garcia Lorca*. Leafing through its pages, he stopped at "Gacela of the Morning Market."[10]

The poem made the hairs stand up on the back of his neck. Leonard had felt that sensation before, hearing the power and the beauty of the verses read aloud at the synagogue—another repository of secrets. Lorca was a Spaniard, a homosexual, an open anti-Fascist, who

———

* The same report described Leonard's "personal and hygiene habits" as "neat and clean. He is careful about his clothes and always appears well dressed." It also made note of his interest and abilities in sailing—"one of the best skippers in the unit"—and his "fine sense of humor."

was executed by the Nationalist militia when Leonard was two years old. But "the universe he revealed seemed very familiar" to Leonard, his words illuminating "a landscape that you thought you alone walked on."[11] Part of that landscape was loneliness. As Leonard tried to explain more than three years later, "When something was said in a certain kind of way, it seemed to embrace the cosmos. It's not just my heart, but every heart was involved, and the loneliness was dissolved, and you felt that you were this aching creature in the midst of an aching cosmos, and the ache was okay. Not only was it okay, but it was the way that you embraced the sun and the moon." He was, in his own words, "completely hooked."[12]

Lorca was a dramatist and a collector of old Spanish folk songs as well as a poet, and his poems were dark, melodious, elegiac and emotionally intense, honest and at the same time self-mythologizing. He wrote as if song and poetry were part of the same breath. Through his love for Gypsy culture and his depressive cast of mind he introduced Leonard to the sorrow, romance and dignity of flamenco. Through his political stance he introduced Leonard to the sorrow, romance and dignity of the Spanish Civil War. Leonard was very pleased to meet them both.

Leonard began writing poems in earnest. "I wanted to respond to these poems," he said. "Every poem that touches you is like a call that needs a response, one wants to respond with one's own story."[13] He did not try to copy Lorca—"I wouldn't dare," he said. But Lorca, he felt, had given him permission to find his own voice, and also an instruction on what to do with it, which was "never to lament casually."[14] Over the subsequent years, whenever interviewers would ask him what drew him to poetry, Leonard offered an earthier reason: getting women. Having someone confirm one's beauty in verse was a big attraction for women, and, before rock 'n' roll came along, poets had the monopoly. But in reality, for a boy of his age, generation and background, "everything was in my imagination," Leonard said.

"We were starved. It wasn't like today, you didn't sleep with your girlfriend. I just wanted to embrace someone."[15]

At the age of fifteen, at around the same time he discovered the poetry of Lorca, Leonard also bought a Spanish guitar for twelve Canadian dollars from a pawnshop on Craig Street. He found he could play some very rudimentary chords almost immediately on the top four strings, thanks to having previously owned (like the hypnotized maid in *The Favorite Game*) a ukulele. Leonard had taught himself to play ukulele—much as he had taught himself hypnosis—from an instruction manual, the famous 1928 book by Roy Smeck, the so-called "Wizard of the Strings." "I think I had mentioned it to cousin Lazzy, who was very kind to me after my father died—he would take me to the baseball games at the Montreal ballpark, the Montreal Royals, which was the first team that Jackie Robinson played in. He said, 'Roy Smeck is coming to El Morocco,' a nightclub in Montreal. 'Would you like to meet him?' I couldn't go hear him, because a child wasn't allowed in a nightclub, but he brought me to Roy Smeck's hotel room and I met the great Roy Smeck."[16]

In the summer of 1950, when Leonard left once again for summer camp—Camp Sunshine in Sainte-Marguerite—he took the guitar with him. Here he would begin playing folk songs, and discover for the first time the instrument's possibilities when it came to his social life.

You were still going to summer camp at age fifteen?

"I was a counselor. It was a Jewish Community Camp for kids that really couldn't afford the expensive summer camps and the director they had hired, an American, accidentally happened to be a Socialist. He was on the side of the North Koreans in the Korean War, which had just broken out. The Socialists at that time were the only people who were playing guitar and singing folk songs; they felt that they had an ideological obligation to learn the songs and repeat them. So a copy of The People's Songbook *appeared. Do you know it? A great songbook, with all the chords and tab-*

lature, and I went through that book many, many times during that sum-
mer, with Alfie Magerman, who was the nephew of the director and had
Socialist credentials—his father was a union organizer—and a guitar.
I started learning the guitar, going through that songbook from beginning
to end many many times during that summer. I was very touched by those
lyrics. A lot of them were just ordinary folk songs rewritten—"His Truth
Goes Marching On" was transformed by the Socialists into 'In our hands
is placed a power / Greater than their hoarded gold / Greater than
the might of Adam / Multiplied a million-fold / We will give birth
to a new world / From the ashes of the old / For the union makes us
strong / Solidarity Forever / Solidarity Forever / Solidarity Forever /
For the union makes us strong.' *There were a lot of the Wobbly songs—I*
don't know if you know that movement? A Socialist international workers
union. Wonderful songs. 'There once was a union maid / Who never
was afraid / Of goons and ginks and company finks / And deputy
sheriffs that made the raid . . . No you can't scare me I'm stickin' with
the union.' *Great song."*

If one can tell a man's enthusiasm by the length of an answer,
Leonard was clearly enthused. Some fifty years after his stay at Camp
Sunshine he could still sing the songbook by heart from beginning to
end.* In 1949, 1950, a guitar did not come attached to the immense
iconography and sexual magnetism it would later acquire, but Leonard learned quickly that playing one did not repel girls. A group photograph shot at summer camp shows the teenage Leonard, though
still short, slightly plump and wearing clothes no man should ever
wear in public—white shorts, white polo shirt, black shoes, white
socks—with the blondest, coolest-looking girl sitting next to him, her
knee touching his.

Back home in Westmount, Leonard continued his investigations

---

* Another song Leonard learned for the first time at Camp Sunshine was "The
Partisan," which would be the first song he recorded that was not his own.

into folk music—Woody Guthrie, Lead Belly, Canadian folksingers, Scottish border ballads, flamenco. He says, "That's when I started finding the music I loved."[17] In Murray Hill Park one day, he happened upon a young, black-haired man standing by the tennis courts, playing a lonely-sounding Spanish melody on an acoustic guitar. A cluster of women had gathered about the musician. Leonard could see that "he was courting them" with his music, in some mysterious way.[18] Leonard was also captivated. He stayed to listen and at the appropriate moment asked the young man if he would consider teaching him how to play. The young man, it turned out, was Spanish and did not understand English. Through a combination of gestures and broken French, Leonard gained the phone number of the boardinghouse downtown where the Spaniard was renting a room, and a promise that the Spaniard would come to 599 Belmont Avenue and give him a lesson.

On his first visit, the Spaniard picked up Leonard's guitar and inspected it. It wasn't bad, he said. Tuning it, he played a rapid flamenco progression, producing a sound on the instrument unlike anything Leonard had ever thought possible. He handed the guitar back to Leonard and indicated that it was his turn. Leonard had no desire after such a performance to play one of the folk songs he had learned and declined, professing that he did not know how. The young man placed Leonard's fingers on the frets and showed him how to make some chords. Then he left, promising to return the next day.

At the second lesson, the Spaniard started to teach Leonard the six-chord flamenco progression he had played the day before, and at the third lesson Leonard began learning the tremolo pattern. He practiced diligently, standing in front of a mirror, copying how the young man held the guitar when he played. His young teacher failed to arrive for their fourth lesson. When Leonard called the number of his boardinghouse, the landlady answered the phone. The guitar player was dead, she told him. He had committed suicide.

"I knew nothing about the man, why he came to Montreal, why he appeared in that tennis court, why he took his life," Leonard would say to an audience of dignitaries in Spain some sixty years later, "but it was those six chords, it was that guitar pattern, that has been the basis of all my songs, and of all my music."[19]

In Montreal in 1950, Leonard's home life had taken a new turn. His mother had remarried. Her new husband was Harry Ostrow, a pharmacist, "a very sweet, ineffectual man, a nice guy," as Leonard's cousin David Cohen recalls him, with whom Leonard seemed to have little more than a pleasant but distant relationship. By coincidence Masha's second husband would also be diagnosed with a grave illness. With his mother preoccupied with the prospect of nursing another sick man, and his sister, twenty years old now, with other things on her mind than her adolescent brother, Leonard was left to his own devices. When he was not in the classroom or involved in some after-school activity, he was in his bedroom, writing poems, or, increasingly, out cruising the streets of Montreal with Mort.

Sixteen and legally old enough to drive, Mort took one of the family's two Cadillacs and cruised down the hill to Leonard's house. "One of our favorite things was at four in the morning we would drive the streets of Montreal, especially the older part of Montreal, along the harbor and out to the east end where the oil refineries were," says Rosengarten. "We were looking for girls—on the street at four o'clock in the morning, these beautiful girls we thought would be walking around, waiting for us. Of course there was absolutely nobody." On nights when the snow was heavy and the streets were empty they would still drive, the heater on, heading east to the Townships or north to the Laurentians, the Cadillac with Mort at the wheel cutting a black line through the deep snowdrifts like Moses practicing for his trick with the Red Sea. And they would talk about girls, talk about everything.

"They were not bound to anything. They could sample all the

possibilities. They flashed by trees that took a hundred years to grow.
They tore through towns where men lived their whole lives. . . . Back
in the city their families were growing like vines. . . . They were flying from the majority, from the real bar mitzvah, the real initiation,
the real and vicious circumcision which society was hovering to inflict
through limits and dull routine," Leonard wrote, re-creating these
night rides with Mort in fiction. "The highway was empty. They
were the only two in flight and that knowledge made them deeper
friends than ever."[20]

Three

Twenty Thousand Verses

———

The streets around McGill University were named for august British men—Peel, Stanley, McTavish—its buildings constructed by solid, stony Scotsmen in solid Scottish stone. There was an Oxbridge air to the grand library and the grander Arts Building, on whose dome the McGill flag flew at half-mast when one of their number died. The spacious quadrangle was outlined by tall, thin trees whose posture remained perfectly erect even when weighed down by heavy snow. Beyond the iron gates there were Victorian mansions, some converted into boardinghouses where students lived. Had someone told you the British Empire was run from McGill, you'd be forgiven for believing them; in September 1951, when Leonard started at McGill on his seventeenth birthday, it was the most perfect nineteenth-century city-within-a-city in North America.

Three months earlier Leonard had graduated from Westmount High. *Vox Ducum*, the yearbook he had helped edit, contained two photos of him. One was a group shot in which the sixteen-year-old Leonard beamed from the center front row, above a caption that read, with unfamiliar familiarity, "Len Cohen, President of the Student Council." The other, more formal photograph, which accompanied his yearbook entry, showed Leonard wearing a suit and a faraway look. As yearbook tradition dictated, Leonard's entry opened with a stirring quote: "We cannot conquer fear yet we can yield to it in such a manner as to be greater than it." It went on to list his pet aversion ("the coke machine"), hobby ("photography"), pastimes ("leading sing-songs at intermissions") and ambition: "World Famous Orator." Under "Prototype" Leonard summed himself up as "the little man who is always there." It closed with an impressive list of his high school activities: presidency of the student council, a place on *Vox Ducum*'s publishing board, membership in the Menorah Club, the Art Club, the Current Events Club and the YMHA (Young Men's Hebrew Association) and cheerleader.[1] To all appearances this was a sixteen-year-old with a good deal of self-confidence, tempered with a large dollop of the requisite Canadian self-mockery. All in all, though, an achiever. It was only to be expected that the next step would be McGill, the foremost English-speaking university in the province.

During his first year at McGill, Leonard studied general arts, moving on to math, commerce, political science and law. More accurately, according to his own report, he read, drank, played music and missed as many lectures as possible. Judging by his average grade on graduation—56.4 percent—this was not one of his customary understatements. Leonard performed underwhelmingly in his favorite subject, English literature, and did no better in French—a class he took, according to his friend and fellow student (now chancellor of McGill) Arnold Steinberg, "because both of us had heard it was an easy course to pass. I failed the course and Leonard's French was certainly minimal. We never took it seriously." The curriculum offered no Baudelaire or Rimbaud; instead they spent the whole year studying a book about a young, aristocratic White Russian couple who had been forced to move to Paris after the revolution and work as servants for a French family. Written by the French dramatist Jacques Deval, it was titled *Tovarich*—the original name of Leonard's Scottish terrier Tinkie.*

This insensitivity to the language of half their hometown's population was by no means exclusive to Leonard and his friends. Montreal's Anglophones—particularly residents of a privileged enclave like Westmount, of which McGill was a privileged extension— had few dealings with the Francophone population other than the French-Canadian girls who had started pouring into the city from the countryside in the thirties, during the Great Depression, to get work as maids. The general attitude to bilingualism at that time was not a lot different, if less deity-specific, from that of the first female governor of Texas, Ma Ferguson: "If the English language was good enough for Jesus Christ, it's good enough for everybody." To English-speaking Montrealers of that time, French would have felt as much a foreign language as it did to any English schoolchild, and likewise would have been taught by an English-speaking teacher, because French-speaking teachers couldn't work in English-speaking schools (and vice versa).

"The French were invisible," says Mort Rosengarten. "At that time we had two school boards in Montreal, the Catholic, which was Francophone, and the Protestant, which was Anglophone, and the Jews—who had their own school board at one point—decided to throw in their lot with the Protestants. Not only were they in different schools, they had different school hours, so the kids were never on the street at the same time, so you never really had contact with them. It was very strange." Mort had already been at McGill for a year, studying art, and Steinberg studying commerce, when Leonard arrived. Where Leonard excelled at university, as he had at Westmount High, was in extracurricular activities. Like a trainee Grand-

---

* Tinkie was still alive at this time; he would expire during his sixteenth year after wandering off alone in a snowstorm.

father Lyon he amassed committee positions, society memberships and presidencies.

Along with his fellow McGill students, Leonard was enrolled automatically in the Debating Union. He shone in debate. He had a natural flair, as well as a taste, for using language with precision. He took easily to composing a statement that might or might not reflect his innermost thoughts but that, with his poet's ear, sounded convincing, or at the very least good, and could win over an audience. For a shy young man Leonard had no trouble getting onstage and talking in front of people; oration was the one subject at McGill for which he was awarded an A. In his first year at McGill Leonard won the Bovey Shield for his university's debating team; in the second year he was elected the Debating Union's secretary; in the third he rose to vice president and in his fourth and final year, president.

Leonard and Mort joined a Jewish fraternity house on the campus, Zeta Beta Tau, and Leonard became president of that too, and a good deal more swiftly. A certificate confirms his election date as January 31, 1952, only four months after his first day at McGill.[2] Like the other fraternities, ZBT had its own songbook—celebratory marching songs of the type improved by alcohol—and Leonard knew the words to all of them. Fraternities and presidencies might appear surprisingly pro-establishment for a youth who had shown himself to have Socialist tendencies and a poetic inclination, but Leonard, as Arnold Steinberg notes, "is not antiestablishment and never was, except that he has never done what the establishment does. But that doesn't make him antiestablishment. Leonard, of all the people I knew, was the most formal by far. Not formal vis-à-vis other people; he had a very winning way, very, very charming. But in his manners, his dress, his way of speaking, he had a very conventional approach to things."

Leonard's summer camp reports had described him as clean, tidy and polite, and he was. "That's how we were brought up," says David Cohen, Leonard's cousin. "We were always taught to be well mannered and say 'yes, sir,' 'thank you,' stand up when an adult came into the room and all that good stuff." As to his sartorial formality, Leonard had a reputation even then for being dressed to the nines (although, master of understatement that he was, he would have insisted he was dressed to the eights). Mort shared Leonard's love for a good suit. Both having families in the clothing business, they could indulge their tastes.

"We would design our own clothes in our teens and they were very distinctive," says Rosengarten, "and generally more conservative than the popular fashions at the time. I had access to a custom tailor who would make them according to my idea of what the suit should be and Leonard told them what he wanted. I even had my shirts made, but mostly because I had a very thin neck and couldn't get adult shirts in my size." David Cohen recalls seeing Mort hanging out in the pool room at the student union, cigarette dangling from the corner of his mouth, the sleeves of his made-to-measure shirt held up with armbands. "In some ways," Rosengarten continues, "the conformist part of the Westmount Jewish community were very hostile to the fact that we were artists and not conforming and doing the right things—but we always had a good suit. And Leonard was always impeccably dressed."

Leonard's unconventionality showed in other ways, Steinberg says. "He was always writing and drawing, even in his teens, and he never went anywhere without a notepad. He would draw sketches endlessly, but mostly he wrote. He would have ideas and he wrote them down, and he would write poems. Writing was his passion and so much a part of him. I remember sitting next to him in the French class on one of those double desk benches and there was an English woman named Shirley who we thought was the most beautiful girl. He was madly in love with this Shirley and he would write poems in class inspired by her."

Girls and writing tied for top place in Leonard's teenage preoccupations, and in each of these areas his performance showed marked improvement over Westmount High. One more markedly than the other: love was not yet the victory march he described in *The Favorite Game*, his alter ego walking home, exultant, from his first lover's arms, eager to brag about his conquest, piqued that the citizenry of Westmount hadn't risen from their beds to organize a ticker-tape parade. But this was the early fifties, a time when underwear white as a picket fence came up to the chest, where they met brassieres as impenetrable as fortresses. A boy's options were limited. "You could eventually hold a girl's hand," said Leonard. "Sometimes she would let you kiss her." Anything more was "forbidden."[3]

His writing had no such constraints and was quite promiscuous. Leonard wrote poems "all the time," Rosengarten recalls, "in a kind of journal he always carried with him, and which once in a while he would lose or leave somewhere and the next day he would frantically try to find it, very upset, because there was all this work in there and he had no copies." At home Leonard had started to use a manual typewriter, tapping away at the keys while his grandfather Rabbi Solomon Klonitzki-Kline wrote in the next room. Masha's father had moved in for the year, and he and Leonard would often sit together of an evening, going through the Book of Isaiah, which the rabbi knew by heart and which Leonard came to love for its poetry, imagery and prophecy. More than anything though, Leonard loved sitting with the old man, who would express "solidarity and pleasure"[4] that his grandson was a writer also.

Despite his poor showing in English classes (he did far better in math), it was at McGill that Leonard really became a poet—indeed was knighted a poet in a spontaneous ceremony by Louis Dudek, the Polish-Canadian Catholic poet, essayist and publisher. Dudek taught the thrice-weekly literature course that Leonard took during his third year. The class of fifty would meet Monday, Wednesday and Friday at five P.M. in the Arts Building; the curriculum included Goethe,

Schiller, Rousseau, Tolstoy, Chekhov, Thomas Mann, Dostoyevsky, Proust, T. S. Eliot, D. H. Lawrence, Ezra Pound and James Joyce.

Dudek's agenda, as described by Ruth Wisse, one of Leonard's fellow students and subsequently professor of Yiddish literature and comparative literature at Harvard, was to teach his students two important things: "The first was modern poetry and literature, which had evolved fully abroad but which had barely started in Canada, with small groups of poets having a limited audience. . . . The second program was the massive movement of European literature and thought since the eighteenth century, with its profound practical implications, which students' minds had still to experience, like buckets of cold water thrown at them from a high lectern." Leonard, she said, "was launched by the first." Confident even then of his inclusion in this world of modern Canadian poets, he "did not treat his teacher with [Wisse's] kind of deference but more like a colleague, on equal terms."[5] Leonard agreed. "Back then I was very self-confident. I had no doubts that my work would penetrate the world painlessly. I believed I was among the great."[6]

Lagging a little among Leonard's interests and pursuits, though still firmly in the race, was music. Intriguingly, considering his propensity for joining societies, Leonard was not a member of the McGill Music Club (despite the presence on the committee of an attractive blonde named Ann Peacock, whose name could also be found among the editorial staff of *The Forge*, a literary magazine). But in 1952, between his first and second years, Leonard formed his first band with two university friends, Mike Doddman and Terry Davis. The Buckskin Boys was a country and western trio (Mort had not yet taken up the banjo or it might have been a quartet), which set about cornering the Montreal square-dance market.

A square-dance band? What possessed you?

"Square dances were popular at the time. We would be hired for high school square dances and church square dances—those being the social oc-

casions that were affirmed and encouraged by the elders. There was really no slow dancing, not much touching, you just join arms and twist around for a while. Very decent. [A wry smile] And we all found out we had buckskin jackets—I had inherited mine from my father—so we called ourselves the Buckskin Boys."

The only Jewish country and western band in Montreal?

"It was actually an eclectic religious group. Mike was a neighbor of mine who played harmonica and Terry, who was a friend of Mike's, knew how to call the dances and played a bucket bass" (a washtub, rope and hockey stick). *"We played the traditional songs, like 'Red River Valley' and 'Turkey in the Straw.'"*

Were you any good?

"We never thought we were very hot, we were just happy that people hired us. I think if I heard the music now I would probably appreciate it. But there was never any sense that this would have any future, that there was anything but the moment. No sense of a career involved at all. The word 'career' always had an unattractive and burdensome resonance in my heart. My idea mostly was to avoid participating in that activity called career, and I've been pretty much able to avoid it."

The band would practice at the Davis family house, in the basement playroom. "They always seemed to have a great time together, with a lot of friendly kibitzing going on," remembers Dean Davis, the late Terry Davis's brother; Dean ran the phonograph at their shows and acted as soundman. "I know my parents thought of Leonard as being very polite and a gentleman for his age. My mother always thought it was pretty funny that their trio consisted of a Protestant, a Jew and a Catholic." Recalls Janet Davis, Terry's widow, "If she was giving them dinner, which happened to be pork on a Friday, she would say it was lamb if they asked."

Leonard also played in a second band, this time all Jewish, part of McGill's Jewish student society, Hillel. They provided the music for a play whose crew included Freda Guttman and Yafa "Bunny"

Lerner, two of Leonard's college-years girlfriends. Mostly, though, he played guitar—alone, in the quadrangle, at the frat house, or anywhere there was a party. It wasn't a performance; it was just something he did. Leonard with a guitar was as familiar a sight as Leonard with a notebook. Melvin Heft, who was at several of those teenage parties, says, "After a while, when he thought the mood was right, Leonard would take out his guitar and play songs and sing to us. He was not a braggart or trying to be a big shot—'I'm going to sing to you'—he just did it, no fuss at all; it was a natural thing for him. He was always there, singing. He was enjoying it and so were we."

On weekends the action might move to Mort's house in the Townships—half a dozen students piling into one car and heading for the countryside. Mort's parents weren't there and the place would be empty, except for a man who worked on the property and a woman who acted as concierge, neither of whom was in any position to stop their partying. The crowd might include Leonard; Arnold Steinberg; sometimes Yafa and Freda; Marvin Schulman, one of the first of their set to be openly gay; and Robert Hershorn, a close friend of Leonard's who came from an even wealthier family. They would sit around drinking and talking. When it got dark they would drive to the Ripplecove Inn on Ayer's Cliff, above Lake Massawippi, and drink and talk some more. At closing time they would go back to the house and put a record on the phonograph or play music themselves—Leonard on guitar, running through the folk songs he had learned at the Socialist camp or the pop songs he had absorbed from the jukeboxes of Saint Catherine Street.

"We used to listen to music a lot," says Rosengarten, "and Leonard, even before he started to write his own stuff, was relentless. He would play a song, whether it was 'Home on the Range' or whatever, over and over and over all day, play it on his guitar and sing it. When he was learning a song he would play it thousands of times, all day, for days and days and weeks, the same song, over and over, fast and slow, faster, this and that. It would drive you crazy. It was the same when he started to write his own stuff. He still works that way. It still takes him four years to write a lyric because he's written twenty thousand verses or something."

Sometimes the crowd would assemble at Leonard's family home on Belmont Avenue, although on these occasions his family would be there. Esther would drift in and out—mostly out; her little brother and his friends did not hold much interest—but Masha would preside over everything, making a fuss, making food, entertaining. "His mother was a dramatic lady," says Rosengarten. "She was Russian, and she could be very, very dramatically unhappy about something and then burst into laughter and send it all up. Sometimes we would be going downtown at about nine o'clock in the evening and Masha would have a fit and say that it was no time to be going out and get all upset, but other times, when we would leave a bar with eight friends at three in the morning and go to her house and start carrying on, and she would come downstairs and greet everyone and offer them food, totally at ease with it; there was no telling how she was going to react." Steinberg concurs: "Masha was very volatile, but everybody loved her because she was basically a lovely, warmhearted person and she adored Leonard. I don't think she mixed much with the other mothers, so she hadn't picked up the worrisome habits, and so it seemed to me that Leonard was very free. It was always fun just dropping in. I would sit there and listen and Leonard would play his guitar. He never thought of himself as a good musician or performer, but he was always playing, and always learning to play the guitar."

From the midfifties, the guests at Leonard's parties were starting to include poets and writers, older men, often teachers from McGill. "There were no barriers, no master/student relationships," Leonard said. "They liked our girlfriends."[7] Among the most influential of these teachers were Louis Dudek; Frank ("F. R.") Scott, McGill's dean of law, a poet and a Socialist; and Hugh MacLennan, author of

the celebrated 1945 book *Two Solitudes,* an allegory of the irrecon-
cilable differences between Canada's French- and English-speaking
populations. MacLennan joined McGill the same year as Leonard,
who took his classes in the modern novel and creative writing. But the
man who would prove the most crucial was an assistant political science teacher, a poet whom Leonard met in 1954 after inviting him to
read from his new work, *The Long Pea-Shooter,* at the fraternity house.
"There was Irving Layton and then there was the rest of us," Leonard
would say almost a lifetime later. "He is our greatest poet, our greatest
champion of poetry."[8] Irving Layton would have readily agreed, and
added even more laudatory adjectives of his own. Layton was larger,
and louder, than life, a bullish man who looked like he'd been hewn
from the same Scottish stone as McGill, only with less attention to
detail. Layton was a hothead; his eyes blazed, there was an inner fire.
Leonard, as did a succession of extraordinary women, loved him.

A dating agency would have been very unlikely to have introduced these two as potential life mates. Twenty-two years Leonard's senior, Layton's brazen, iconoclastic, self-promoting style could
hardly be more different from Leonard's modest, self-effacing demeanor. Layton, with his wild mane of hair and disheveled clothes,
looked like he had stepped out of a hurricane; Leonard looked like
his clothes had been sewn on him every morning by a team of personal tailors. Layton was proudly belligerent; Leonard, despite a long
attraction to machismo, wasn't. Layton had fought in the Canadian
Army, attaining the rank of lieutenant, the same as Leonard's father;
Leonard as a young child had hoped to go to military school, but that
dream had died with his father. Still, Leonard had his father's gun;
his mother had argued with him about it, but in the end, Leonard
won. Then there was the class difference. Layton was born in a small
town in Romania in 1912 (his name was Israel Lazarovitch before his
family emigrated to Canada) and raised in Saint-Urbain, Montreal's
working-class, Jewish immigrant neighborhood. Leonard's upper-

class Westmount background was at the opposite end of the Jewish social spectrum. What they had in common was a love of honesty, a taste for irony and a skill in the art of debate (in 1957, Layton appeared in a nationally televised debating series called *Fighting Words*, which he invariably won).

Layton openly despised bourgeois Canada and its puritanism, and so did Leonard, if more covertly—as befitted a man who considered his own family bourgeois—such as when he worked behind the scenes to overturn the rule banning women and alcohol from students' rooms at his fraternity house. Layton was powerfully sexual—which Leonard liked to think he was too, or might be, given half the chance—and so was Layton's poetry: flagrant, unabashed, happy to provide names and details. Layton was passionate about poetry and the beauty and melody of the word—as was Leonard. Layton had become a poet, he said, "to make music out of words." But he also wanted his poetry "to change the world," to which the idealist in Leonard related strongly.

As Rosengarten explains it, "The [Second World] War had been a very important factor on our sensibility; people you knew were going off and getting killed, and there was a possibility that we would lose the war and the Nazis would take over America or Canada. But the other thing was that, while this was going on, the word was that if we *did* win the war, because of the great sacrifice everybody had made, the world was going to become this wonderful utopian place, with all this collective energy that had been dissipated in the war directed toward its creation. I think for us it was somewhat disillusioning that, at the end of the war, the first thing they did was kind of repudiate the collective aspect of the society and maintain this idea that it was really good for business to produce things instead, and sell people products as substitutes for this collective spirit. And the enormous numbers of women who worked and did things during the war that were considered unfit for women were packed up after the war and sent back to the kitchen. Leonard and I, these were things we were shockingly aware of." That sense of a lost Eden, of something beautiful that did not work out or could not last, would be detectable in a good deal of Leonard's work.

"There was a very interesting poetry scene in Montreal," says Rosengarten, "and it was centered around Irving Layton and Louis Dudek, who were good friends at the time." (They fell out later; their feuds over poetry became famous.) "There were lots of parties where they would read, many of them at Irving's house in Côte-Saint-Luc," west of Montreal. It is a large suburb today, with a street named after Layton, but in the fifties the farmhouse in which Irving lived with his wife and two children stood alone, surrounded by farmland. "At these parties people would read their poems to one another and discuss them and criticize stuff; it was pretty intense, and it would go sometimes most of the way through the night. There were many times when Leonard and I might quit the bars downtown at three in the morning and go over there to Irving's, and there the scene would be going on. Leonard would show his poems at these parties. They took it seriously. They had a little magazine they mimeographed, two hundred and fifty copies, called *CIV/n*, because at that time the bookstores didn't carry Canadian poets, you couldn't buy a book with any of that contemporary poetry in a bookstore in Montreal; it was pretty grim. But, looking back on it, I realize now that that poetry scene had more influence on me in terms of aesthetics than all the art schools I attended in England with all these people who became important sculptors. I think the gang in Côte-Saint-Luc were way ahead of all of them."

"We really wanted to be great poets," said Leonard. "We thought every time we met it was a summit conference. We thought it was terribly important what we were doing."[9] He looked on these evenings as a kind of poetry boot camp, where "training was intense, rigorous, and taken very seriously." Leonard would always have an attraction to such regimens. "But the atmosphere was friendly. Once in a while there were tears, someone would leave in a rage, we would argue, but interest in the art of writing was at the center of our friendship." He considered it an apprenticeship and he was an enthusiastic learner. "Irving and I used to spend a lot of evenings studying poems by someone like Wallace Stevens. We would study the poem until we discovered the code, until we knew exactly what the author was trying to say and how he did it. That was our life; our life was poetry."[10] Layton became, if not Leonard's life coach, then his guide, his cheerleader and one of his dearest friends.

In March 1954 in the fifth issue of *CIV/n* Leonard made his debut as a published poet. Alongside poems by Layton and Dudek (who were on the editorial board) and others of the Montreal poetry scene were three works credited to Leonard Norman Cohen: "Le Vieux," "Folk Song" and "Satan in Westmount," the last of the three about a devil who quoted Dante and "sang fragments of austere Spanish songs."* The following year Leonard won first prize in McGill's Chester Macnaghten Literary Competition with his poems "Sparrows" and the four-part *Thoughts of a Landsman*, which included "For Wilf and His House," a poem that was published in 1955 in *The Forge*. A remarkably mature work, erudite and moving, it began,

> *When young the Christians told me*
> *how we pinned Jesus*
> *like a lovely butterfly against the wood*
> *and I wept beside paintings of Calvary*
> *at velvet wounds*
> *and delicate twisted feet*

and ended,

---

* Curiously, on the same page as Leonard's "Folk Song" was a line drawing, not by Leonard, of a bird on a wire.

Then let us compare mythologies.
I have learned my elaborate lie
of soaring crosses and poisoned thorns
and how my fathers nailed him
like a bat against a barn
to greet the autumn and late hungry ravens
as a hollow yellow sign.

Layton had started taking Leonard with him to his book readings, where Leonard reveled in his friend's showmanship, his grand gestures and braggadocio, and the passion that his performance induced in the audience, the women in particular. In the summer of '55 Layton brought Leonard along to the Canadian Writers Conference in Kingston, Ontario, and invited Leonard onstage, where Leonard read his own work and played a little guitar.

The guitar had done nothing to hurt Leonard's success with women—and he could offer them hospitality now that he and Mort had taken a room on Stanley Street. "We weren't really living there, we were just hanging out there, we'd have friends over," said Rosengarten of the old-fashioned double parlor in a Victorian boardinghouse. Leonard's mother was not well pleased at this development, but she found it hard not to indulge him. Their relationship appeared to be very involved, even beyond the usual mother-son attachment, let alone an archetypal Jewish mother and son—and Masha, according to no less an authority on Jewishness than Rabbi Wilfred Shuchat at Shaar Hashomayim, was "very Jewish." When Nathan died, Leonard became the object of her indulgence, castigation and utter devotion. She was a vital, passionate woman, with an infirm husband, something of an outsider in Westmount circles, so it was hardly surprising that her only son, her youngest child, became her focus.

Leonard loved his mother. If she smothered him, he smiled or made wisecracks. He learned to shrug off emotional blackmail and her insistence on feeding him and his friends at all hours of the day and night. "My mother taught me well never to be cruel to women," Leonard wrote in an unpublished piece from the seventies. But what he also learned from Masha was to count on the devotion, support and nurturing of women and, if and when it became too intense, to have permission to leave—if not always completely, and rarely without conflicting emotions.

———

Aviva Layton, née Cantor, is a vivacious blond Australian, sharp as a pin. She was raised in a "small, stifling, middle-class Jewish community" in Sydney that she couldn't wait to leave, and the minute she turned twenty-one she did. She wanted to go to New York. When they wouldn't let her in, she went to Montreal. Friends had given her the name of someone to call, Fred Cogswell, the poet and editor of the Canadian literary magazine *Fiddlehead*. Cogswell, it turned out, lived in Nova Scotia, some eight hundred miles distant. "But," she says, "he told me there was a whole covey of Montreal poets that I should look up," and he gave her the names of half a dozen of them, including Dudek, Scott and Layton. The first person she called was Layton—"I wasn't going to look up anyone whose name sounded vaguely Jewish"—who invited her to come to the house in Côte-Saint-Luc where he lived with his second wife, the artist Betty Sutherland, and their children.

Aviva arrived to find he had company. "All the big names in Canadian literature were there," including those on Cogswell's list—"except they weren't big names then, they were a small fringe group. I thought, 'This is marvelous.'" She intended to become part of the group. This intention was thwarted when, soon afterward, she and Irving began an affair. It would last twenty years and produce a son, but its more immediate result was to cut her off from everyone. "I couldn't go back to his house. This was the fifties, and you had to be very careful about scandal; Irving was teaching in a parochial school and he could easily have lost his job. So I lived in Montreal mostly in isolation, with Irving coming to visit me two or three times a week. The only person Irving ever trusted to know about us was Leonard, and he brought him to my small, basement apartment.

"Irving was in his forties then, twenty-one years older than me, and Leonard was twenty, one year younger than me. I can see myself opening the door to that apartment and there was Leonard on the other side, looking very young, slightly chubby, but there was something absolutely special about him. Irving had said, 'Somebody called Leonard Cohen is going to come and have coffee with us and he is the real thing.' I'll never forget him saying that—and with Irving 'the real thing' meant he's a real poet. And this was late in 1955; *Let Us Compare Mythologies* was about to come out."

The three met up at Aviva's apartment on a regular basis. In spite of the large age difference between Leonard and Layton—Layton was old enough to be his father—they behaved, Aviva says, "like equals. A lot of people say Leonard was Irving's student—some think he was his actual, literal student, which is absolutely incorrect—or that Irving was his mentor. No. Leonard thought, and still does, that Irving was the great writer and poet and man in his life, as well as friend, but I would not say that Leonard was the junior partner in that enterprise."

Leonard, Layton said, "was a genius from the first moment I saw him. I have nothing to teach him. I have doors to open, which I did— the doors of sexual expression, of freedom of expression and so on and so forth. Once the doors were opened, Leonard marched very confidently along a path . . . somewhat different from my own."[11] Says Aviva, "Leonard famously said that Irving taught him how to write poetry and he taught Irving how to dress. I think Leonard wrote better poetry and Irving was a better dresser, but they taught each other things." As to the class difference, she says, "That was interesting.

Leonard came from the Bel Air of Montreal, absolutely exclusive, and Irving was born in the slums, but when Irving and I came to rent a house we went to as close to where Leonard had been brought up as possible, and when Leonard wanted to buy a house or rent or live, he came right back to Irving's old part of town. Irving wanted to be where Leonard wanted to escape from, and Leonard wanted to be where Irving wanted to escape from."

Irving would later say of Leonard that "he was able to find the sadness in Westmount. That takes genius. He was able to see that not all rich people, not all comfortable people, not all plutocrats, were happy." Genius, Layton said, is "the ability—a very rare ability—to see things as they actually are. You are not fooled."[12] Leonard had taken Irving and Aviva to Belmont Avenue on several occasions. "He used to go there frequently and still had his room there and lived there I think in between places. One time when Masha wasn't around we had a huge party, one of those mad parties you had in those days, and somebody vomited on her damask, heavy curtains. The place was an absolute shambles. I remember going in the kitchen with Leonard and he would open up the kitchen drawers and show us that Masha would keep every paper clip and nail and little bit of string that had ever come through the front door."*

When Aviva first met Leonard, he told her something, she says, "which he might not remember but which I remember absolutely clearly. He said he'd been studying law at McGill, and that one day while he was studying, he looked into the mirror and it was blank. He couldn't see his own reflection. And he knew then that the academic life in whatever form whatsoever was not for him." The following year, armed with a BA degree; another literary award, the Peterson

---

* The contents of the drawer, as described by Leonard in *The Favorite Game*, also included "candle-butts from years of Sabbath evenings," "brass keys to locks which have been changed," "toothpicks they never used" and a "broken pair of scissors."

Memorial Prize; a cover line on the March 1956 edition of *The Forge* and, at the top of the pile, his first published volume of poetry, *Let Us Compare Mythologies*, Leonard enrolled as a graduate student at Columbia University and left Montreal for Manhattan.

Four

I Had Begun to Shout

Let Us Compare Mythologies was published in May 1956. The slim hardback, containing forty-four poems written by Leonard between the ages of fifteen and twenty, was the inaugural release of a new imprint that aimed to introduce the public to new young writers of merit. It was funded by McGill University and edited by Louis Dudek. Leonard himself designed the book, which was illustrated by Freda Guttman, his artist girlfriend and the muse for several poems. Her mysterious pen-and-ink drawings are Edenic at times and at others tortured; the image on the front cover is of a cowed, misshapen human, who looks to be under attack from doves or miniature angels. On the back, in the author's photograph, the twenty-one-year-old Leonard gazes unflinchingly at the camera. In spite of the sober expression, the stubble and those deep lines running from nose to mouth, he looks very young. In the poems, by contrast, he appears a much older man—not just the maturity and authority of his language and his command of poetic technique, but the "raging and weeping"[1] of the kind that suggests a man who has lived long, seen much and lost something very precious. Leonard dedicated the book to the memory of Nathan Cohen. His father's death is the subject of the poem "Rites":

> the family came to watch the eldest son,
> my father; and stood about his bed
> while he lay on a blood-sopped pillow
> his heart half-rotted
> and his throat dry with regret . . .
> but my uncles prophesied wildly
> promising life like frantic oracles;
> and they only stopped in the morning
> after he had died
> and I had begun to shout.

The themes and content of much of the poetry would feel perfectly familiar to those who would come to know Leonard as a singer-songwriter. There are poems—some of them titled, in Lorcan fashion, "Song" or "Ballad"—about religion, myth, sex, inhumanity, humor, love, murder, sacrifice, Nazis and Jesus on the cross. There are echoes of Joan of Arc and the Holocaust in "Lovers," where a man has erotic feelings for a woman who is being led to the flames. Several poems contain naked women and wounded men, the two conditions not unrelated. In "Letter," a poet armed with only his pen and his indifference claims victory over the femme fatale fellating him:

> I write this only to rob you
> that when one morning my head
> hangs dropping with the other generals
> from your house gate
> that all this was anticipated
> and so you will know that it meant nothing to me

The poems have a sense of timelessness, or of multilayered time. Ancient wrongs are juxtaposed with modern-day atrocities, and archaic language—courtly, biblical, Romantic—with contemporary irony. Leonard employs both the traditional poetic form and prose poetry. Like a twentieth-century troubadour, or a nineteenth-century Romantic, he places his own inner experiences and feelings at the center—often feelings of failure and despair. The epigraph comes from William Faulkner's novel *The Bear* and refers to a comment a young man makes during a conversation on the meaning of Keats's "Ode on a Grecian Urn": "He had to talk about something." As Leonard explained later, when a writer "has some urgency to speak," the subject matter of what he writes "becomes almost irrelevant."[2] Leonard had that urgency.

The original print run for *Let Us Compare Mythologies* was around four hundred copies. Ruth Wisse, Leonard's fellow student in Louis Dudek's class and editor of the *McGill Daily*, took on the role of head of Leonard's sales team and sold half that number on campus. The book received a handful of reviews in Canada, largely positive. *Queen's Quarterly* called it "a brilliant beginning."[3] The *Canadian Forum*'s critic Milton Wilson wrote, "He knows how to turn a phrase, his poems at their best have a clean, uncluttered line, and he writes 'about something.'"[4] *Fiddlehead*'s Allan Donaldson found Leonard's virtues "considerable" but had problems with what he described as Leonard's greatest weakness, "an overuse of images of sex and violence, so that at its worst his work becomes a sort of poetic *reductio ad absurdum* of the Folies Bergères and of Madame Tussaud's Chamber of Horror. It was, I believe, Mr. Harry Truman who remarked of the Folies Bergères that there was nothing duller than the protracted spectacle of a large number of bare breasts."[5] Leonard and Truman would have disagreed. The criticism appeared to be less about the quality of the work and more a reflection of the conservatism and puritanism of Canadian literature, against which Irving Layton had so loudly raged. Leonard's book contained a poem to Layton, titled "To I.P.L.," in which he described his friend affectionately as

> *. . . depraved*
> *hanging around street corners*
> *entertaining hags in public places.*

"I felt that what I wrote was beautiful and that beauty was the passport of all ideas," Leonard would say in 1991. "I thought that the objective, open-minded reader would understand that the juxtaposition of spirituality and sexuality justified itself entirely. I felt that it was that juxtaposition that created that particular beauty, that lyricism."[6] Later still, on the publication in 2006 of a fiftieth-anniversary facsimile edition, Leonard said, "There are some really good poems in that little book; it's been downhill ever since."[7] The coda might well be one of his familiar self-effacing tics—it is hard to argue that Leonard has not produced better work since. But there was something in this first book that Leonard would often, subsequently, seem to long for—the innocence, the confidence, the prolificacy and hunger of his youthful self.

Let Us Compare Mythologies won Leonard the McGill Literary Award. It also brought him attention from the Canadian media. The Canadian Broadcasting Company invited him to participate in a project titled *Six Montreal Poets*, a spoken-word album. The other five were Irving Layton, Louis Dudek, A. M. Klein, A. J. M. Smith and F. R. Scott, the leading members of the so-called Montreal Group— prestigious company for a new, young writer. The album, studio-recorded, was produced by Sam Gesser, a folklorist and impresario who founded and ran the Canadian division of the American label Folkways and promoted Pete Seeger's and the Weavers' first Montreal shows. Leonard made his first-ever appearance on record on side one, between Smith and Layton, reading eight poems from *Let*

Us Compare Mythologies: "For Wilf and His House," "Beside the Shepherd," "Poem," "Lovers," "The Sparrows," "Warning," "Les Vieux" and "Elegy." Listening to it today, Leonard's voice sounds high and forced, somewhat British. The last of these he blamed on "the influence in the [Canadian] universities" during that period. "That accent was meant to dignify the poem. The declamative style that the Beats introduced hadn't quite gotten there yet."[8]

It had, however, gotten to New York. In 1956, the same year that Leonard published *Let Us Compare Mythologies*, Allen Ginsberg, an American Jew and Columbia University graduate, published his visceral, personal poetry book *Howl*. In 1957, the same year that *Six Montreal Poets* was released in the U.S. on the Folkways label, Jack Kerouac, an American Catholic of Quebec ancestry who had gone to Columbia on a football scholarship, published his landmark autobiographical novel *On the Road*. These two books were sacred texts of the Beats, a literary movement dedicated to personal liberty, truth and self-expression and influenced by bebop jazz, Buddhism and experiments with drugs and sex. The Beats were hard-core. *Howl* had been banned for obscenity, before a celebrated court case put it back on the shelves, and Kerouac had conducted a private, backyard ceremony before sending out his first manuscript, in which he dug a hole, inserted his penis and mated with the earth. Though it was not quite the same as Leonard's interment of his first piece of writing in his father's bow tie, Leonard felt a kinship. In December 1957, when Kerouac made an appearance at the Village Vanguard in New York—a bohemian Greenwich Village speakeasy turned jazz club—Leonard was there. Kerouac, extremely drunk—he found drinking helped with his shyness—read to the accompaniment of jazz musicians. Leonard, who was also shy, and who claimed to have "never really liked poetry readings; I like to read poetry by myself,"[9] was impressed. If poems were to be delivered publicly, this was a fine way to do it.

Leonard liked the Beats. They did not return the sentiment. "I was writing very rhymed, polished verses and they were in open re-volt against that kind of form, which they associated with the op-pressive literary establishment. I felt close to those guys, and I later bumped into them here and there, although I can't describe myself remotely as part of that circle."[10] Neither did he have any desire to join it. "I thought that our little group in Montreal was wilder and freer and that we were on the right track, and we, in our provincial self-righteousness, felt that they were not on the right track and that they were getting some kind of free ride, that they weren't honoring the tradition as we felt we were."[11]

It is interesting that someone who in high school and university had seemed keen to sign up for, even lead, any number of groups should choose not to join this particular club at such a pivotal mo-ment for poetry. In the fifties, the Beats made poets the counter-culture spokesmen, the rock stars, if you like, of their generation. It's interesting too that although Leonard was younger than Ginsberg and Kerouac, they viewed him as part of the old guard. In the sixties, when rock stars would become the counterculture spokesmen and poets of their generation, Leonard would once again be considered old—if with better reason this time; he was in his thirties when he made his first album—and would feel himself to be an outsider.

Leonard did not appear at all troubled at his outsider status. In fact, a certain sense of isolation seems to have set in toward the end of his years at McGill and his first term at Columbia University, which seemed to coincide with Leonard's first bouts of serious depression. "What I mean by depression isn't just the blues, it's not just like a hangover from the weekend, the girl didn't show up or something like that," said Leonard, describing the paralyzing darkness and anx-iety he experienced. "It's a kind of mental violence which stops you from functioning properly from one moment to the next."[12] Leonard took to spending "a lot of time alone. Dying," he said. "Letting my-self slowly die."[13]

———————

Leonard's first address in New York was International House, at 500 Riverside Drive, where Columbia billeted its foreign students. It was on the Upper West Side, a stone's throw from the Hudson River. At nights Leonard would head downtown, much as he had done in Montreal, and seek out the city's netherworlds, of which New York had many. Greenwich Village was a particular draw. Leonard's days were not devoted to studying; at Columbia, as at McGill, Leonard was not much interested in academic study. He was less interested in reading than in writing himself—or writing about himself, as he did when one professor, knowing when he was beaten, allowed Leonard to submit a term paper on *Let Us Compare Mythologies*.

In his room, sitting at the table by the window from which he could watch the sunset turn the gray river gold, he wrote a number of poems and short stories. One story, "The Shaving Ritual,"[14] was inspired by a piece of advice his mother had given him. Whenever things got bad, she said, he should stop what he was doing and have a shave, and he would feel better. It was counsel he found himself taking often, as the episodes of depression increased.

Leonard had gone to New York to be a writer—a serious writer, but also a popular writer. Even at this early stage, when the Canadian literary world was starting to talk about him as Canada's best young poet, he wanted his work to be read and liked by more than just Canadian literati, the small group that Irving Layton used to refer to as the "Canuckie Schmuckies." Enrolling at Columbia had really been a cover, something to keep Leonard's family happy. Going to America to do postgraduate studies at a renowned university was an acceptable activity for a young man from a conservative, upper-middle-class Montreal Jewish background; going to America to become a writer, not so much. Mort Rosengarten explains, "It was not, and still is not, encouraged by that community. They don't want their children becoming artists. They're very hostile to it. They don't want to know about themselves. But Leonard got away with it."

How Leonard got away with it had a lot to do with having lost his father when he was nine years old. "I never had to come up against that powerful male influence that a young man meets as he grows older,"[15] he says. The powerful influence in his childhood was female, his mother, who was "a generous Chekhovian spirit, very accepting in her way. She was alarmed when she saw me running around Montreal with a guitar under my arm, but she was very kind in her observations. She would occasionally roll her eyes, but that was about as far as it went."[16] His uncles would step in now and then with "indications and suggestions and advice and lunches held, but very subtly. Considering the tales one hears of the tyrannies of family, mine was very gentle in that respect."[17] Nevertheless, the other big reason for going to New York was to get away from Montreal, to put space between himself and the life his upper-class Montreal Jewish background mapped out for him: from Westmount to McGill, then on to studying law or commerce, and finally taking his place in the family business.

Leonard was writing in New York, but he was also floundering. After the euphoria of his first publication and the attention it brought him in Canada, now he was in a place where no one knew who he was, and if they did, they wouldn't have cared. For New Yorkers, Canadian literature was a dot on the cultural map barely visible to the naked eye. As a means of making contact with fellow writers— and having some status among them—Leonard founded a literary magazine, *The Phoenix*, but it was short-lived. Leonard was lonely. He missed his old crowd in Montreal; he really did believe that they were special. "Each time we met we felt that it was a landmark in the history of thinking. There was a great deal of fellowship and drinking. Montreal is tiny, it's a French city and the number of people writing in English is small; it didn't have any prestige prizes at the time, not even any girls. But a few of us were on fire and we would write for each other or any girl that would listen."[18]

And then, in New York, Leonard met a girl. Her name was Georgianna Sherman; Leonard called her Anne, or Annie. A year and a half older than Leonard, she had already been married once, briefly, at a very young age and was now working as the program coordinator at International House. Sherman was tall and very attractive, with long, dark hair, soulful eyes and a modulated, aristocratic voice. She came from a patrician New England family; her grandmother was a Daughter of the American Revolution. "Irving and I had heard so much from Leonard about this Annie and how beautiful she was," says Aviva Layton, "that she almost became a legend in our minds before we met her. But she really was exquisite, a beautiful soul, from very, very good American blood. She was an extremely cultivated young woman—great cook, wrote poetry, played piano—and here was this little Montreal Jew, Leonard. She had never met anyone like him before and he'd never met anyone like her, and they just fell for each other." Leonard moved into Sherman's upper Manhattan apartment.

"Annie was very, very important in Leonard's life at that time," says Aviva. "It was when he was just starting out on the enterprise of being a writer and he had moved to New York—this at a time when Canadians weren't crossing the border and going to the U.S. to make their careers—and Annie was in the thick of things in New York. She introduced him to a lot of people. And Leonard began to see that there was a whole other world outside of the world of Montreal."

In the summer of 1957, Leonard took Annie to Quebec to show her off to the Laytons, who had rented a summer cottage in the Laurentians. "Leonard and Annie would follow us, then find a lake and pitch an ordinary little tent and that was where they would stay. They would read to one another—they'd brought along lots and lots of poetry—and Leonard would play his guitar. They would go to bed when the sun went to bed and get up in the morning with the sun. Sometimes they'd row across the lake to us and spend a couple of days in our cottage. Annie was Leonard's first great love." She was also a muse, inspiring the poem "For Anne," in *The Spice-Box of Earth*, and the character Shell, the lover, in *The Favorite Game*.

The relationship did not last. It was Leonard who left; it had started to head down another path Leonard was keen to avoid in his life, which was marriage. As he wrote in *The Favorite Game*, "Supposing he went along with her toward living intimacy, toward comforting, incessant married talk. Wasn't he abandoning something more austere and ideal, even though he laughed at it, something which could apply her beauty to streets, traffic, mountains, ignite the landscape—which he could master if he were alone?" In other words, he had work to do, man's work. However much a woman's love might ease the loneliness and darkness, still it disturbed him, "as generals get uneasy during a protracted peace." The breakup was painful for Annie. It was for Leonard too. Being the one to end it did not mean that he did not miss her terribly. Years later, as he sat at a wooden table in a white house on a hill on a Greek island, staring out at the solid blue sky, he would write her letters, asking her to come and join him there. When she declined, he wrote her poems.

With Annie gone
Whose eyes to compare
With the morning sun?

Not that I did compare,
But I do compare
Now that she's gone.

"FOR ANNE," *SELECTED POEMS 1958–1968*

Annie went on to marry Count Orsini, the owner of Orsini's, the famous New York restaurant. In 2004 she published a book, *An Imperfect Lover: Poems and Watercolors.* In the poem "How I Came to Build the Bomb," she describes falling in love with "a wandering Jew" and learning that for "a traveling man, love / was a burden he couldn't take on."[19]

Having spent one year in New York, Leonard moved back to Montreal and into 599 Belmont Avenue. So did his grandfather Rabbi Klonitzki-Kline. The old man was suffering from Alzheimer's disease; once again Masha became the caregiver. To a fly on the wall it might have looked much like the old days—Masha in the kitchen, making food; Leonard tapping away on a manual typewriter; the old man poring over the dictionary he was trying to write from memory, and all the while his memory was disintegrating.

Leonard was working on a novel titled *A Ballet of Lepers.* It opened with: "My grandfather came to live with me. There was nowhere else for him to go. What had happened to all his children? Death, decay, exile—I hardly know. My own parents died of pain."[20] It was a depressing way to begin a book, and Leonard acknowledged this: "But I must not be too gloomy at the beginning or you will leave me, and that, I suppose, is what I dread most." After putting the novel through several drafts, Leonard sent it out to publishers in Canada. For a while it looked as if Ace Books might take it, but in the end, along with all the other publishers, they turned it down. *A Ballet of Lepers* was not, as some have thought, an early version of *The Favorite Game.* In Leonard's view it was "probably a better novel. But it never saw the light."[21] Leonard filed the manuscript away.

The rejection did not stop Leonard from writing. He continued to take a notebook with him everywhere. His friend from McGill Arnold Steinberg recalls, "Of all the things about Leonard, the first thing that comes to mind was he was constantly, constantly writing—writing and sketching. One always sensed that there was an inner need—pushing out words and pictures, never ending, like a motor running." Phil Cohen, a Montreal jazz musician and music professor, remembers seeing Leonard sitting, writing at a table in the corner of a drugstore at the intersection of Sherbrooke and Côte-des-Neiges. "I'm guessing it was just a place where nobody knew him and he could sit and do what he wanted. A couple of times he looked up, and he looked like he was totally out of it—not drugged, just in a totally different world, he was so into what he was doing. From my experience of working with a lot of performers, there was this sense of almost desperation that I picked up from the look on his face that said, 'Don't disturb me.' I said to myself, 'This guy is very serious.'"

Leonard was finding it impossible to stay at his mother's house after having lived on his own, and with Annie. He found an apartment on Mountain Street, and in order to pay the rent (and since he no longer had the excuse of studying in New York), he agreed to take a job in one of the Cohen family firms. For a year Leonard worked at W. R. Cuthbert & Company, the brass foundry that his uncle Lawrence ran. A reference letter written by the foundry's personnel manager in December 1957 stated: "Leonard Cohen was employed by us for the period Dec 12th 1956 to Nov 29th 1957 in various capacities: Electro-cycle turret lathe operator, Brass die-casting machine operator, Time and motion study assistant. During the time of his employment, Mr Cohen was known to be honest, capable and industrious. We have no hesitation in recommending him for any sort of employment and would like to express our regret at his departure."[22]

Leonard, who did not share this regret, was looking for work in America. He applied to the U.S. Department of the Interior Bureau of Indian Affairs in Washington, DC, for a teaching position on a reservation. The bureau, oddly, had little use for a Jewish poet from Montreal with electro-cycle turret lathe skills. (It would be nine more

years before Leonard would display his Native American scholarship
in his second novel, *Beautiful Losers*.) So he moved on to another of
the family firms, the Freedman clothing company, run by his uncle
Horace. Leonard spent his days in the office, moving papers around,
or in the factory, hanging the finished suits and coats on racks. His
nights were spent in the clubs and bars of Montreal, which in the late
fifties could still boast the liveliest nightlife in Canada—so lively that
the military authorities had designated certain streets off-limits to
its personnel because of the number of brothels. Montreal then was
Canada's New York, the city that never slept; musicians who played
in its many nightclubs were expected to keep on playing until the last
drunk was carried out.

With the new decade, and Quebec's "Quiet Revolution," just two
years away, it was hard not to notice there was a change in the air.
"People of different backgrounds—linguistic, religious and the rest—
were beginning to come forward and take chances," says Phil Cohen.
Some of the clubs had started to feature more experimental musical
acts. Among them was a jazz pianist named Maury Kaye. A small
Montreal Jew whose goatee, thick black-framed glasses and unruly
hair made him look like a beatnik, Kaye had become well-known on
the Canadian jazz circuit as a big-band leader, a composer and a noted sideman who had played with Edith Piaf and Sammy Davis Jr. He
also had a small, less mainstream jazz band that played late-night gigs
at clubs like Dunn's Birdland on Saint Catherine Street, a jazz parlor
above a popular smoked-meats delicatessen, which was reached by
a flight of rickety stairs. One night in April 1958, at midnight, when
Kaye came onstage with his band, Leonard was with them.

Among the audience of around fifty people was Henry Zemel,
a math and physics student at McGill, who had no idea at that time
who Leonard was, although in the sixties they would become close
friends. "It was curious," remembers Zemel, "a little place with a
small audience and a little stage. Leonard sang and he read some po-

etry but, as I remember, he sang more than he read poetry." Recalls
Aviva Layton, who went to Leonard's first night with Irving to give
moral support, "I don't remember him reading poetry, I remember
him singing and playing the guitar. He perched himself on a high,
three-legged stool and he sang—his own songs. That magic that he
had, whatever it was, you could see it there at these performances."

*"Maury Kaye was a very gifted pianist and jazz arranger. He would
play something, and I would improvise. That was probably the first time
that I . . ."*

Performed onstage as a singer?

*"Well, I was invited to read poetry now and then, but I never really
enjoyed it, I was never terribly interested in that kind of expression. But I
liked singing, chanting my lyrics, to this jazz group. It felt a lot easier and
I liked the environment better. [Smiles] You could drink."*

*Was it new to you, improvising? You're better known for a more studied
approach.*

*"Well, I would sit with friends on the steps of the place we were living
in when we were at college on Peel Street and calypso was popular in a
tiny corner of Montreal—there was a tiny black population and there were
some calypso clubs there that we started going down to quite a lot—and I
would improvise calypso lyrics about the people who were passing in the
street, things like that."*

Along with the Beat-style improvisations he had witnessed in
Greenwich Village, Leonard had prepared some set pieces, among
them "The Gift," a new poem that had its premiere on his first night
at Dunn's.* "They called it Poetry to Jazz," remembers David Cohen,
Leonard's cousin. "It was a very fifties-ish thing. Leonard wrote poetry and a little blues stuff and I remember him reading this poem
very seriously: 'She knelt to kiss my manhood,' or something like
that. I was cracking up, and all the young girls were going, 'Ooh, isn't

---

* "The Gift" was later published in *The Spice-Box of Earth*.

he something else?' Did it make Leonard popular with women? As the old expression goes, it didn't hurt." Leonard also ad-libbed and made jokes. Irving Layton, always his biggest cheerleader, declared him a natural comic.

Ever since Mort left Montreal to study sculpture in London, Leonard had increasingly come to rely on Layton for friendship and support. Several times a week he would go to Irving and Aviva's place for supper. Often, after they had eaten, they would "crack a poem." Aviva explains, "We would choose a poem—Wallace Stevens, Robert Frost, anyone—and we'd go through it line by line, image by image. How did this poet put together those images? What does this poem really mean? How do we crack this poem? Honestly, it was worth more than a PhD from Columbia." Some evenings they would go to the cinema—Leonard and Irving "both adored trashy movies," Aviva says—"and then we would sit up till dawn talking about the movie, analyzing the symbolism, and try and trip each other up on how many symbols we'd seen." On the nights they stayed in, they would "wheel in this old black and white television set with the rabbit ears on top and, while eating lots of candy—Leonard would always bring over a huge slab of his favorite, which was dyed sugar made to look like bacon—they would talk about what they'd seen until the cows came home."

Although Layton was still married to Betty Sutherland, he and Aviva had been living together openly for some time. The arrangement worked as well as such things could, until Aviva took a job as a teacher in a private girls' school—an institution not known for its sympathies toward alternative lifestyles. Irving and Aviva needed to marry. But Irving did not want to divorce his wife. Instead he proposed a solution: he would buy a wedding ring for Aviva and they would have a mock marriage ceremony—Leonard would be best man—and she could change her name legally to Layton. A date was set, and the three met at a bistro near Leonard's apartment for lunch and champagne, "Irving wearing some awful bottle-green coat, [Aviva] in a white, seersucker secondhand dress with curtain bobbles on the bottom, and Leonard, of course, the only one dressed beautifully." They headed off together to a small jewelry boutique on Mountain Street to buy the ring. "While I'm looking at the wedding rings," says Aviva, "all of a sudden I notice that Irving is on the other side of the shop saying, 'I've come to buy a bracelet for my wife. She's an artist.' Leonard, who just understood what I was going through, said, 'Aviva, I'm going to buy you a wedding ring,' and he did. He slipped it on my finger and said, 'Now you're married.' And I thought, who the hell am I supposed to be married to? I'm telling you this story because that is so part of Leonard. I'm sure he can be absolutely impossible if anyone wants a marriage kind of relationship with him, but he was, and always has been, impeccable—thoughtful, courtly, generous, really the most honorable man."

———

For detectives seeking to put together a picture of Leonard's activities and state of mind, a file in one of the stack of boxes in his archives in Toronto might provide some interesting clues. Or muddy the water entirely. Alongside Leonard's unpublished novel *A Ballet of Lepers* are a guitar string, a driving license, a vaccination certificate, a chest X-ray form, a leaflet marking the declaration of independence in Cuba and a library card. Whatever crime it was, the evidence pointed to its having been committed by a troubadour planning an overseas journey, likely somewhere exotic. There is also a number of forms filled out by Leonard requesting arcane publications. Several of these are for books and articles on the benefits, problems, philosophy and technique of fasting. These include "Notes of Some English Accounts of Miraculous Fasts," by Hyder Rollins, from the *Journal of American Folklore* in 1921, and the intriguingly titled "Individual and Sex Differences Brought Out by Fasting," by Howard Marsh, from a 1916 issue of *Psychological Review*. Leonard also requested the books *Mental Disorders in Urban Areas* by Robert E. Faris and *Venereal Disease Information* by E. G. Lion. On thin yellowed paper is a typewritten essay titled "Male Association Patterns." In it the author, Lionel Tiger, from the University of British Columbia—one of Leonard's fellow counselors at summer camp—discussed male homosexuality and the desire for same-sex companionship, as displayed in "sports teams, fraternities, criminal organizations like the Cosa Nostra, drinking groups, teenage gangs, etc. The list is long," Tiger wrote, "but the common factor is male homogeneity and the communal sense of maleness which prevails."

Fasting was something Leonard would pursue with enthusiasm in the coming years; he appeared as ardent about losing weight as Masha was to put it on him. As to homosexuality, by all accounts this was merely an intellectual curiosity, a subject that had been thrust into the zeitgeist by the Beats. When the British journalist Gavin Martin asked Leonard in 1993 if he'd ever had a gay relationship, Leonard answered, "No." Asked if he regretted this, Leonard said, "No, because I have had intimate relationships with men all my life and I still do have. I've seen men as beautiful. I've felt sexual stirrings toward men so I don't think I've missed out."[23] His friendships with his male friends were, and remain, deep and durable.

The summer of 1958 found Leonard back again in the Laurentians and at summer camp—as a counselor this time, at Pripstein's Camp Mishmar, which opened its doors to children with learning difficulties. Leonard took with him his guitar and a camera. He went home with a roll of film that contained a series of pictures of women he met there. Nudes. Now that he no longer lacked the female company he had so long craved, he was making up for lost time. "Leonard's always had yearnings for sainthood, [but] at the same time there's certainly been a strong streak of hedonism in him, as there is in almost every poet and every artist," said Irving Layton. "It's because the artist is dedicated to pleasure and bringing pleasure to others particularly. And if he takes a little bit himself in giving pleasure to others, so much the better."[24]

―――――――

While Leonard was at college in New York and Mort at art school in London, they sublet their room in the boardinghouse on Stanley Street to friends. When Mort returned to Montreal, he converted the double parlor into a sculpture studio for himself, and he and Leonard talked about turning it into an art gallery. The two put in long hours fixing up the place and planning how it should be. They did not want the hushed formality and office hours of the other Montreal galleries, which "would all close at five o'clock," says Rosengarten, "so if people were working they weren't free to go." The Four Penny Art Gallery, as they named it, was open every night until nine or ten, later on weekends, "and much later," says Rosengarten, "if we had a vernissage." Opening parties would carry on long into the night. Leonard immortalized one of these evenings in his poem "Last Dance at the Four Penny." In the poem, the room on Stanley Street and all its associations—art, friendship, freedom and nonconformity—became a fortress against the savagery of the world outside its walls, in Montreal and beyond.

> Layton, my friend Lazarovitch,
> no Jew was ever lost
> while we two dance joyously
> in this French province.

The artists they exhibited were those whom the Montreal establishment ignored, among them Layton's wife, Betty Sutherland. "We had some of the best young active artists at any given time, and it was very hard to find their work because the galleries were all stuck with their own rigid history and ideas," says Rosengarten. "We sold poetry books, because no one else would sell them, and ceramics, because no one else would sell them either." The Four Penny, says Nancy Bacal, became "a gathering place, a haven for art and music and poetry. On warm evenings we would all go up to the roof and sing folk songs and protest songs; Morton would play his banjo and Leonard would play his guitar."

"The gallery," Rosengarten says, "was starting to work. Starting to get the attention of the critics. And then in the dead of winter there was a huge fire and the building burned down. Completely. And that was the end of it, because we didn't have insurance. We had a huge show on at that time and there were paintings from floor to ceiling, all gone. I had a little wax sculpture, which survived the fire, which was amazing. It was such a remarkably delicate thing and the only thing to survive." The Four Penny was dead and cremated.

And Masha was in the hospital. Leonard's mother had been admitted to a psychiatric ward at the Allan Memorial Institute, suffering with depression. The Allan, as locals called it, was housed in a grand mansion at the top of McTavish Street in Mount Royal. From its immaculately kept grounds, the view across Montreal was even better than from the park behind Leonard's family home. "Loonies," wrote Leonard, revisiting the incident in *The Favorite Game*, "have the best view in town."*

It's not surprising that Masha, a woman with a leaning toward melancholy, would be seriously depressed, after her infirm second husband had moved out of the house on Belmont Avenue and gone to live in Florida and then her infirm father had moved in. Nor was it strange that she should lean so heavily on her only son when he visited her—which he dutifully did—berating him for having more time

---

* The Allan would later gain notoriety for its participation in Project MK-ULTRA, a covert CIA research program into mind control from 1957 to 1964, using drugs, abuse and sensory deprivation.

for his shiksas than for his mother and, in the next breath, worrying that he wasn't taking care of himself or eating properly.

It is also no surprise that Leonard would feel frustrated, helpless and angry—a multipurpose frustration, helplessness and anger that seemed to take in his own condition as well as Masha's. He knew by now that he had inherited her depressive tendency, and he was not at his happiest himself. Every weekday, from seven in the morning, he worked in his dead father's clothing company at a job he loathed, while the gallery he had helped create with Mort had literally gone up in smoke. But while Leonard soldiered on, uncomplaining—as Mort says, echoing the sentiments of many of Leonard's friends, "He wasn't the kind of moany-groany depressed person; he has a great sense of humor, and depression didn't stop him from being funny"— the woman who had always supported him and indulged him could lie around all day in a place that looked to Leonard like a country club. There must have been fear too—not just at seeing his sole parent helpless but at the responsibility that came with that, and the vision of what might await him if he stayed in Montreal. The city he had escaped New York to come back to had become uncomfortable, even threatening.

An article that appeared in the Canadian magazine *Culture*, written by Louis Dudek, must have been the final blow. Leonard's former teacher, publisher and champion criticized his writing as "a rag-bag of classical mythology" and a "confusion of symbolic images." Layton leapt to Leonard's defense immediately, branding Dudek "stupid" and declaring Leonard "one of the purest lyrical talents this country has ever produced." But the damage was done; although Leonard remained friendly with Dudek, he could no longer feel safe in his position as Montreal's golden boy of poetry. It was time to move. For which he needed money. But he could not bear to stay at the Freedman Company, and he knew he could not make a living as a poet. Leonard quit his job and devoted his energies to applying for schol-

arships and grants. In between working on poems, short stories and
the occasional freelance review for the CBC, he and Layton sat together for hours on end, filling in applications and writing proposals.
Leonard requested money to travel to the ancient capitals—London,
Athens, Jerusalem, Rome—around which, he said, he would write a
novel.

In the spring of 1959, two letters arrived from the Canada Council
for the Arts: Leonard's and Irving's applications had been approved.
Leonard was granted $2,000. Immediately, he applied for a passport.
In December 1959, shortly after his return from a poetry reading at
the 92nd Street Y in New York with Irving Layton and F. R. Scott,
Leonard boarded a plane for London.

Five

A Man Who Speaks
with a Tongue of Gold

It was a cold gray morning and starting to rain when Leonard walked down Hampstead High Street, clutching a suitcase and an address. It was just before Christmas and the windows of the little shops were bright with decorations. Tired from the long journey, Leonard knocked at the door of the boardinghouse. But there was no room at the inn. The only thing they could offer was a humble cot in the living room. Leonard, who had always said he had "a very messianic childhood," accepted the accommodation and the landlady's terms: that he get up every morning before the rest of the household, tidy up the room, get in the coal, light a fire and deliver three pages a day of the novel he told her he'd come to London to write. Mrs. Pullman ran a tight ship. Leonard, with his liking for neatness and order, happily accepted his duties. He had a wash and a shave, then went out to buy a typewriter, a green Olivetti, on which to write his masterpiece. On the way, he stopped in at Burberry on Regent Street, a clothing store favored by the English upper-middle classes, and bought a blue raincoat. The dismal English weather failed to depress him. Everything was as it should be; he was a writer, in a country where, unlike Canada, there were writers stretching back forever: Shakespeare, Milton, Wordsworth, Keats. Keats's house, where he wrote "Ode to a Nightingale" and love letters to Fanny Brawne, was just ten minutes' walk from the boardinghouse. Leonard felt at home.

Despite its proximity to the center of London, Hampstead had the air of a village—a village that crawled with writers and thinkers. Among the permanent residents in Highgate Cemetery, which was also a short walk away, were Karl Marx, Christina Rossetti, George Eliot and Radclyffe Hall. Back when London was shrouded in toxic smog, Hampstead, high on a hill, with eight hundred acres of heath land, drew consumptive poets and sensitive artists with its cleaner air. Mort had been the first among Leonard's crowd to stay there, renting a room from Jake and Stella Pullman while he was at art school in London. Next was Nancy Bacal, who had gone to London to study classical theater at the London Academy of Music and Dramatic Art, and stayed on to become a radio and television journalist. Nancy, like Leonard, had been given the "starter bed" and a hot-water bottle in the living room until Mort moved out and Mrs. Pullman, judging her worthy, allowed her to take over his room. Which is where she was when Leonard showed up in December 1959.

Bacal, a writer and teacher of writing, cannot remember a time when she did not know Leonard. Like him, she was born and raised in Westmount. They lived on the same street and went to the same Hebrew school and high school; her father was Leonard's pediatrician. "It was a very strong community, inbred in many ways, but in no way was he the usual person you'd find in the Westmount crowd. He was reading and writing poetry when people were more interested in who they were going to date for their Sunday school graduation. He pushed the borders from a very early age." What made it more curious was that Leonard was not openly rebellious; as Arnold Steinberg noted, he seemed conventional, respectful of his teachers, the least likely to rebel.

"Here you have the contradiction," says Bacal. "Leonard was embedded in religion, deeply connected with the shul through his grandfather, who was president of the synagogue, and because of his respect for the elders; I remember Leonard used to recount how his grandfather could put a pin through the Torah and be able to recite every word on each page it touched, and that impressed me enormously. But he was always prepared to ask the hard questions, break down the conventions, find his own way. Leonard was never a man to assault or attack or say bad things about anything or anyone. He was more interested in what was true or right." She recalls the endless talks she and Leonard would have in their youth about their community, "what was comfortable, where it left us wanting, where we felt people weren't penetrating to the truth." Their conversation had taken a break when Bacal left for London, but when Leonard moved into the Pullmans' house, it picked up where it left off.

Stella Pullman, unlike most residents of Hampstead, was working-class—"salt of the earth, very pragmatic, down-to-earth English" is Bacal's description. "She worked at an Irish dentist in the East End of London; took the tube there every day. Everyone who lived in the house used to schlep down there once a year and have their fillings done. She was very supportive—Leonard still credits her with being responsible for him finishing the book because she gave him a deadline, which made it happen—but she was not what you'd call impressed by him, or by any of us. 'Everyone has a book in them,' she'd say, 'so get on with it. I don't want you just hanging around.' She'd been through the war; she had no time for all that nonsense. Leonard was very comfortable there because there was no artifice about it. He and Stella got along very, very well. Stella liked him a lot—but secretly; she never wanted anyone to get, as she would say, 'too full of themselves.'" Leonard kept to his part of the agreement and wrote the required three pages a day of the novel he had begun to refer to as *Beauty at Close Quarters*. In March 1960, three months after his arrival, he had completed a first draft.

Late at night, after closing time at the King William IV pub, their local, Nancy and Leonard would explore London together. "To be in London in those times was a revelation. It was another culture, a kind of no-man's-land between World War II and the Beatles. It was dark, there wasn't much money and it was something we'd never experienced, London working class—and don't forget we'd started with Pete Seeger and all those workingman songs. We'd start out at one or two in the morning and wander way out to the East End and hang out with guys in caps with Cockney accents. We'd visit the night people in rough little places, having tea. We both loved the street life, street food, street activity, street manners and rituals"—the places and things Leonard had been drawn to in Montreal. "If you want to find Leonard," says Bacal, "go to some little coffee bar or hole in the wall. Once he finds a place, that's where he'll go, every night. He wasn't interested in what was 'happening'; he was interested in finding out what lay underneath it."

Through her broadcast work Bacal became familiar with London's West Indian community and started to frequent a cellar club on Wardour Street in Soho, the Flamingo. On Friday nights, after hours, it transformed into a club-within-a-club called the All-Nighter. It began at midnight, although anybody who was anybody knew it did not get going until two A.M. "It was, theoretically, a very dodgy place but it was actually magical," said Bacal. "There was so much weed in the air it was like walking into a painting of smoke." She and Harold Pascal, another of the Montreal set who was living in London, would go there most Friday nights. The music was good—calypso and white R & B—jazz acts like Zoot Money and Georgie Fame and the Blue Flames—and the crowd was fascinating. Quite unusually for the time, it was 50 percent black—Afro-Caribbeans and a handful of African-American GIs; the white half was made up of mobsters, hookers and hipsters.

On the first night Leonard went with Nancy to the club, there was a knife fight. "Somebody called the law. Everyone was stoned and dancing," she recalls, and then the police arrived. "I don't know if you've ever been to any of these sleazy joints, but you don't want to be there when they turn on the lights. Suddenly all the faces were white. The incident didn't last long, but we were all pretty shook up. I was worried about Leonard, but he was cool." Leonard loved the place. After a subsequent visit, Leonard wrote to his sister, Esther, saying, "It's the first time I've really enjoyed dancing. I sometimes even forget I belong to an inferior race. The Twist is the greatest ritual since circumcision—and there you can choose between the genius of two cultures. Myself I prefer the Twist."[1]

With the first draft of his novel finished, Leonard turned his attention to his second volume of poems. He had gathered the poems for *The Spice-Box of Earth* the year before and, at Irving Layton's recommendation, had given it to the Canadian publisher McClelland & Stewart. Literally. Driving to Toronto with a friend, Leonard handed his manuscript to Jack McClelland in person. McClelland had taken over his father's company in 1946 at the age of twenty-four and was, according to the writer Margaret Atwood, "a pioneer in Canadian publishing, at a time when many Canadians did not believe they had a literature, or if they did have one, it wasn't very good or interesting."[2] So impressed was McClelland by Leonard that he accepted his book on the spot.

Poets are not especially known for their salesman skills, but Leonard worked his book like a pro. He even instructed the publisher how it should be packaged and marketed. Instead of the usual slim hardback that poetry tended to come in—which was nice for pressing flowers in but expensive to print and therefore to buy—his should be a cheap colorful paperback, said Leonard, and he offered to design it. "I want an audience," he wrote in a letter to McClelland. "I am not interested in the Academy." He wanted to make his work accessible to "inner-directed adolescents, lovers in all degrees of anguish, disappointed Platonists, pornography-peepers, hair-handed monks and Popists, French-Canadian intellectuals, unpublished writers, curious musicians etc., all that holy following of my Art."[3] In all, a pretty astute, and remarkably enduring, inventory of his fan base.

Leonard was sent a list of revisions and edits and given a tentative publication date of March 1960, but the date passed.

In the same month, Leonard was in the East End of London, walking to the tube station from the dental surgery where Mrs. Pullman worked, where he had just had a wisdom tooth pulled. It was raining—Leonard would say "it rained almost every day in London," which sounds about right—but, that day, it rained even more heavily than usual, that cold, sideways, winter rain in which England specializes. He took shelter in a nearby building, which turned out to be a branch of the Bank of Greece. Leonard could not fail to notice that the teller wore a pair of sunglasses and had a tan. The man told Leonard that he was Greek and had recently been home; the weather, he said, was lovely there at this time of year.

There was nothing to keep Leonard in London. He had no project to complete or promote, which left him not only free but also vulnerable to the depression that the short, dark days of a London winter are so good at inducing. On his application for the Canada Council grant, Leonard had said he would go to all the old capitals—Athens, Jerusalem and Rome, as well as London. On Hampstead High Street he stopped in at a travel agent's and bought tickets to Israel and Greece.

———————

Survival, in discussions of the mystery and motivations of Leonard Cohen, has tended to be left in the corner clutching an empty dance card while writers head for the more alluring sex, God and depression and haul them around the dance floor. There is no argument that between them these three have been a driving force in his life and work. But what served Leonard best was his survival instinct. Leonard had an instinct for self-protection that not all writers—or lovers, or depressives, or spiritual seekers, or any of those creative types that nature or nurture made raw and sensitive—possess. Leonard was a lover, but when it comes to survival he was also a fighter.

When Leonard's father died, what the nine-year-old boy wanted to keep of his was a knife and a service revolver; when Leonard was fourteen, the first story of his ever published (in his high school yearbook) bore the title "Kill or be Killed." Yes, young boys like guns and gangsters, and small Jewish boys who grow up during World War II have even more layers to add to the general chromosomal bias, but Leonard definitely has a fighting spirit. Asked who his hero was, he rattled off the names of spiritual leaders and poets—Roshi, Ramesh Balsekar, Lorca, Yeats—adding the caveat, "I admire many men and women but it's the designation 'hero' that I have difficulty with, because that implies some kind of reverence that is somewhat alien to my nature." But the following day Leonard sent an e-mail, having thought about the question. His message said, without qualification this time:

> *i forgot*
> *my hero is muhammad ali*
> *as they say about the Timex in their ads*
> *takes a lickin'*
> *keeps on tickin'*[4]

Leonard still is a fighter. Some years after this correspondence, when Leonard, in his seventies, discovered that his former manager had bled his retirement account dry, he dusted off his suit, put on his hat and set off around the world to win his fortune back. But the gods conspired to give him an instinct for flight as well as fight. When it came to survival, Leonard would often turn to the first of the two for, as he put it, "the health of my soul."[5]

Leonard was not entirely joking when he spoke about having had a "messianic" childhood. From an early age he had a strong sense that he was going to do something special and an expectation that he would "grow into manhood leading other men."[6] He had also known from an early age that he would be a writer—a serious writer. Of all the trades a sensitive and depressive man could follow, few are more hazardous than being a serious writer. Acting? Actors are on the front line, yes, but most of the damage occurs during auditions. Once they land a role, they have a mask to hide behind. But writing is about uncovering. "Not I, but the poet discovered the unconscious," said Freud, through what an analyst's analyst would recognize as the gritted teeth of envy. It's about allowing the mind to be as noisy and chaotic as it wants and leaping into the dark depths of this pandemonium in the hope of surfacing with something ordered and beautiful. The life of a serious writer requires long periods of solitary confinement; the life of a writer as serious, meticulous, self-critical and liable to depression as Leonard means solitary confinement in one's own personal Turkish prison, cornered by black dogs.

During childhood he had the comfort and kindness of women for protection. In his youth he had come to depend on having a community of like-minded, mostly (but not exclusively) male friends. He had no problem with leaving one place and moving to another—he traveled light and wasted little time on sentimentality. But wherever he lived, he liked to surround himself with a clan of fellow-thinkers: people who could hold a conversation, could hold a drink and knew how to hold their silence when he needed to be left alone to write. Athens couldn't provide that. But an acquaintance in London, Jacob Rothschild (the future fourth Baron Rothschild, young scion of a celebrated Jewish banking family), whom he had met at a party, had talked about a small Greek island named Hydra. Rothschild's mother, Barbara Hutchinson, was about to be remarried to a celebrated Greek painter named Nikos Hadjikyriakos-Ghikas, who had a mansion there. Rothschild suggested that Leonard go and visit them. The island's small population included a colony of artists and writers from around the globe. Henry Miller had lived there at the start of World War II and written in *The Colossus of Maroussi* about its "wild and naked perfection."

After leaving London, Leonard stopped first in Jerusalem. It was his first time in Israel. By day he toured the ancient sites and at night he sat in the Café Kasit, the haunt of "everybody that thought they were a writer."[7] Here he met the Israeli poet Natan Zach, who invited him to stay at his house. After a few days, Leonard took a plane to Athens. He stayed in the city one day, during which he saw the Acropolis. In the evening he took a cab to Piraeus and checked into a hotel down by the docks. Early the next morning, Leonard boarded a ferry to Hydra. In 1960, before they started using hydrofoils, it was a five-hour journey. But there was a bar on board. Leonard took his drink up on deck and sat in the sun, staring out at the rumpled blue sheet of sea, the smooth blue blanket of sky, as the ferry chugged slowly past the islands scattered like a broken necklace across the Aegean.

As soon as he set eyes on Hydra, in the distance, before the ferry even entered the port, Leonard liked it. Everything about it looked right: the natural, horseshoe-shaped harbor, the whitewashed buildings on the steep hills surrounding it. When he took off his sunglasses and squinted into the sun, the island looked like a Greek amphitheater, its houses like white-clad elders sitting upright in the tiers. The doors of the houses all faced down to the port, which was the stage on which a very ordinary drama unfolded: boats bobbing lazily on the water, cats sleeping on the rocks, young men unloading the day's catch of fish and sponges, old men tanned like leather sitting outside the bars arguing and talking. When Leonard walked through the town, he noticed that there were no cars. Instead there were donkeys, with a basket hung on either side, lumbering up and down the steep cobblestone streets between the port and the Monastery of the Prophet Elijah. It might have been an illustration from a children's Bible.

The place appeared to have been organized according to some ancient ideal of harmony, symmetry and simplicity. The island had just one real town, which was named, simply, Hydra Town. Its inhabitants had come to a tacit decision that just two basic colors would suffice—blue (the sea and the sky) and white (the houses, the sails and the seagulls circling over the fishing boats). "I really did feel I'd come home," Leonard said later. "I felt the village life was familiar, although I'd had no experience with village life."[8] What might have also given Hydra its feeling of familiarity was that it was the nearest thing Leonard had experienced to the utopia he and Mort used to discuss as boys in urban Montreal. It was sunny and warm and it was populated by writers, artists and thinkers from around the world.

The village chiefs of the expat community were George Johnston and Charmian Clift. Johnston, forty-eight years old, was a handsome Australian journalist who had been a war correspondent during World War II. Charmian, thirty-seven, also a journalist, was his attractive second wife. Both had written books and wanted to devote themselves to writing full-time. Since they had two children (a third arrived later), this necessitated finding a place to live where life was cheap but congenial. In 1954 they discovered Hydra. The couple were great self-mythologizers and natural leaders. They held court at Katsikas, a grocery store on the waterfront whose back room, with perfect Hydran simplicity, doubled as a small café and bar. The handful of tables outside overlooking the water made the ideal spot for the expats to gather and wait for the ferry, which arrived at noon,

bringing the mail—all of them seemed to be waiting for a check—
and a new batch of people, to watch, to talk to, or to take to bed.
On a small island with few telephones and little electricity, therefore
no television, the ferry provided their news and entertainment, and
their contact with the outside world.

Leonard met George and Charmian almost as soon as he arrived.
He was not the first young man they had seen walking from the port,
carrying a suitcase and a guitar, but they took to him immediately,
and he to them. Like Irving and Aviva Layton, George and Charmian
were colorful, charismatic and antibourgeois. They had also been doing for years what Leonard had wanted to do, which was live as a
writer without the necessity of taking regular work. They had very
little money but on Hydra they could get by on it, even with three
children to provide for, and the life they were living was by no means
impoverished. They lunched on sardines fresh off the boat, washed
down with retsina—which old man Katsikas let them put on a tab—
and seemed to glow in the warmth and sun. Leonard accepted their
invitation to stay the night. The next day they helped him rent one
of the many empty houses on the hill and donated a bed, a chair and
table and some pots and pans.

Although he had been brought up with so much, Leonard was
happy with very little. He thrived in the Mediterranean climate. Every morning he would rise with the sun, just as the local workmen
did, and start his work. After a few hours' writing he would walk
down the narrow, winding streets, a towel flung over one shoulder, to
swim in the sea. While the sun dried his hair, he walked to the market to buy fresh fruit and vegetables and climbed back up the hill.
It was cool inside the old house. He would sit writing at George and
Charmian's wooden table until it was too dark to see by the kerosene
lamps and candles. At night he walked back again to the port, where
there was always someone to talk to.

The ritual, routine and sparsity of this life satisfied him immensely.

It felt monastic somehow, except this was a monk with benefits; the Hydra arts colony had beaten the hippies to free love by half a decade. Leonard was also a monk who observed the Sabbath. On Friday nights he would light the candles and on Saturday, instead of working, he would put on his white suit and go down to the port to have coffee.

One afternoon, toward the end of the long, hot summer, a letter arrived by ferry for Leonard. It told him that his grandmother had died, leaving him $1,500. He already knew what he would do with it. On September 27, 1960, days after his twenty-sixth birthday, Leonard bought a house on Hydra. It was plain and white, three stories high, two hundred years old, one of a cluster of buildings on the saddle between Hydra Town and the next little village, Kamini. It was a quiet spot, if not entirely private—if he leaned out of the window he could almost touch the house across the alley, and he shared his garden wall with the neighbor next door. The house had no electricity, nor even plumbing—a cistern filled in spring when the rains came, and when that ran out he had to wait for the old man who came past his house every few days with a donkey weighted on both sides with containers of water. But the house had thick white walls that kept heat out in summer, a fireplace for the winter and a large terrace where Leonard smoked, birds sang and cats skulked in the hope that one might fall from its perch. A priest came and blessed the house, holding a burning candle above the front door and making a black cross in soot. An elderly neighbor, Kiria Sophia, came in early every morning to wash the dishes, sweep the floors, do his laundry, look after him. Leonard's new home gave him the pure pleasure of a child.

"One of the things I wanted to mention and which a lot of people haven't caught," says Steve Sanfield, a longtime close friend of Leonard, "is really how important those Greece years and the Greek sensibility were to Leonard and his development and the things he carries with him. Leonard likes Greek music and Greek food, he speaks Greek pretty well for a foreigner, and there's no rushing with Leonard, it's, 'Well, let's have a cup of coffee and we'll talk about it.' He and I both carry *komboloi*—Greek worry beads; only Greek men do that. The beads have nothing to do with religion at all—in fact one of the Ancient Greek meanings of the word is 'wisdom beads,' indicating that men once used them to meditate and contemplate."

Sanfield's friendship with Leonard began fifty years ago. He is the "Steve" described in Leonard's poem "I See You on a Greek Mattress" (from the 1966 book *Parasites of Heaven*), sitting in Leonard's house on Hydra, smoking hash and throwing the I Ching, and the "great haiku master" named in Leonard's poem "Other Writers" (from the 2006 collection *Book of Longing*). He is also the man who would introduce Leonard to his Zen master, Roshi Joshu Sasaki. In 1961, when Sanfield boarded a ferry in Athens and, on a whim, alighted at Hydra, he was "a young poet seeking adventure." Like Leonard, he "fell in love" with the place. The people he met in the bar at the port told him, "Wait until you meet Leonard Cohen, you're both young Jewish poets, you'll like him." He did.

Sanfield's memories of Hydra are of light, sun, camaraderie, the voluptuous simplicity of life and the special energy that emanated from its community of artists and seekers. It was a small community, around fifty in number, although people would come and go. The mainstays, the Johnstons, he says, "were vital in all of our lives. They fought a lot, they sought revenge on each other a lot with their sexuality, and things got very complicated, but they were really the center of foreign life in the port." Among the other residents were Anthony Kingsmill, a British painter, raconteur, and bon vivant, to whom Leonard became close; Gordon Merrick, a former Broadway actor and reporter whose first novel, *The Strumpet Wind*, about a gay American spy, was published in 1947; Dr. Sheldon Cholst, an American poet, artist, radical and psychiatrist who set his flag somewhere between Timothy Leary and R. D. Laing; and a young Swedish author named Göran Tunström, who was writing his first novel and was the model for the character Lorenzo in Axel Jensen's 1961 novel *Joacim* (although many still believe Lorenzo was based on Leonard).

"A lot of people came through in those early years," says Sanfield, "like Allen Ginsberg and Gregory Corso"—the latter of whom was living on the neighboring island, coaching a softball team. Leonard met Ginsberg on a trip to Athens. Leonard was drinking a coffee in Saint Agnes Square when he spotted the poet at another table. "I went up to him, asked him if he was indeed Allen Ginsberg, and he came over and sat down with me and then he came and stayed in my house on Hydra, and we became friends. He introduced me to Corso," said Leonard, "and my association with the Beats became a little more intimate."[9]

Hydra in the early sixties was, according to Sanfield, "a golden age of artists. We weren't beatniks, and the hippies hadn't been invented yet, and we thought of ourselves as kind of international bohemians or travelers, because people came together from all over the world with an artistic intent. There was an atmosphere there that was very exciting and I think touched everyone who was there. There were revolutions going on in literature, and there was the sexual revolution, which we thought we'd won and we probably lost, and a number of us—George Lialios, Leonard and myself—began to examine different spiritual paths like Tibetan Buddhism and the I Ching."

George Lialios was a significant figure in Leonard's life on the island. Nine years older than Leonard, with a thick black mustache, bushy beard and bright, piercing eyes, he owned a seventeen-room mansion at the top of the hill. "He was a remarkable man and a mysterious man," says Sanfield, by various people's accounts a philosopher, a musician, a semiaristocrat and an intellectual. Lialios himself says that he was "from Patras, born in Munich, both parents Greek, the family returned to Athens from Germany in 1935. Studied law, did three years' military service during the so-called civil war, then followed studies of music and composition in Vienna, 1951–1960. An inclination toward philosophy is correct." His Greek father had been a composer and a diplomat who was in Germany during World War II. George was fluent in Greek as well as in German and English. Leonard spent many evenings on Hydra with Lialios, mostly at Leonard's house. Sometimes they would have deep conversations. Often they did not talk at all. They would sit together in silence in Leonard's barely furnished, white-walled room, much as Leonard would with Roshi in years to come.

Another expat islander who played a part in Leonard's life was Axel Jensen. A lean, intense Norwegian writer in his late twenties, he had already published three novels, one of which was made into a movie. The house where Jensen lived with his wife, Marianne, and their young child, also named Axel, was at the top of Leonard's hill. Sanfield stayed in the Jensens' house when he first arrived on Hydra; the family had rented it out while they were away. Its living room was carved out of the rock of the hillside. There were copies of the I Ching and *The Tibetan Book of the Dead* on the bookshelves.

When Marianne came back to the island, her husband was not with her. "She was the most beautiful woman I'd ever known," says Sanfield. "I was stunned by her beauty and so was everyone else." Leonard included. "She just glowed," said Sanfield, "this Scandinavian goddess with this little blond-haired boy, and Leonard was this dark Jewish guy. The contrast was striking."

Leonard had fallen in love with Hydra from the moment he saw it. It was a place, he said, where "everything you saw was beautiful, every corner, every lamp, everything you touched, everything." The same thing happened when he first saw Marianne. "Marianne," he wrote in a letter to Irving Layton, "is perfect."[10]

———

"It must be very hard to be famous. Everybody wants a bit of you," Marianne Ihlen says with a sigh. There were muses before Marianne in Leonard's poetry and song and there have been muses since, but if there were a contest, the winner, certainly the people's choice, would be Marianne. Only two of Leonard's nonmusician lovers have had their photographs on his album sleeves and Marianne was the first. On the back of the naked, intimate *Songs from a Room*, Leonard's second album, there she sat, in a plain white room, at his simple wooden writing table, her fingers brushing his typewriter, her head turned to smile shyly at the camera and wearing nothing but a small white towel. For many of the young people seeing that picture for the first time in 1969—a troubled year, particularly for young people—it captured a moment and a need and longing that has gnawed at them ever since.

Marianne at seventy-five years old has a kind, round face, deeply etched with lines. Like Leonard, she does not enjoy talking about herself but is too considerate to say no; one might imagine that is how she ended up with a Norwegian-language book about her life with Leonard, after agreeing to do an interview for a radio documentary.* She is as modest and apologetic about her English, which is very good, as she once was about her looks. Despite having been a model, she could never understand why Leonard would say she was the most beautiful woman he'd ever met. Fifty-three years before, "twenty-two, blond, young, naïve and in love," to the chagrin of her traditional Oslo family she had run off with Jensen, traveled around Europe, bought an old Volkswagen in Germany and driven it to Athens. An old woman invited them to stay and let them leave their car in her overgrown garden while they took a trip around the islands. On the ferry they met a fat, handsome Greek named Papas who lived in California, where he had a candy and cookie company that bore his name. They told him they were looking for an island. "He told us to get off at the first stop; it was Hydra."

---

* *So Long, Marianne: Ei Kjaerleikshistorie* by Kari Hesthamar.

It was mid-December, cold and raining hard. There was one café open at the port and they ran for it. It was neon-lit inside and warmed by a stove in the middle of the room. As they sat shivering beside it, a Greek man who spoke a little English came over. He told them of another foreign couple living on the island—George Johnston and Charmian Clift—and offered to take them to their house. And so it all began. Axel and Marianne rented a small house—no electricity, outside toilet—and stayed, Axel writing, Marianne taking care of him. When the season changed, Hydra came alive with visitors, and the two poor, young, beautiful Norwegians found themselves invited to cocktail parties in the mansions of the rich; Marianne recalls, "One of the first people that we met was Aristotle Onassis." During their time on Hydra, people of every kind drifted by. "There were couples, writers, famous people, homosexuals, people with lots of money who didn't have to work, young people on their way to India and coming from India, people running away from something or searching for something." And there was Leonard.

Much had happened in Marianne's life in the three years between her arrival on Hydra and Leonard's. She and Axel had broken up, made up, then married. With the advance for his third novel, they bought an old white house on top of the hill at the end of the Road to the Wells. When the rains came, the street became a river that rushed like rapids over the cobblestones down to the sea. Her life with Axel was turbulent. The locals talked about Axel's heavy drinking, how when he was drunk he would climb up the statue in the middle of the port and dive from the top, headfirst. Marianne, they said, was a hippie and an idealist. She was also pregnant. She went back to Oslo to give birth. When she returned to Hydra with their first child, a boy they named for her husband, she found Axel packing, getting ready to leave with an American woman he told Marianne he had fallen in love with. In the midst of all this, Leonard showed up.

She was shopping at Katsikas's when a man in the doorway said, "Will you come and join us? We're sitting outside." She could not see who it was—he had the sun behind him—but it was a voice, she says, that "somehow leaves no doubt what he means. It was direct and calm, honest and serious, but at the same time a fantastic sense of humor." She came out to find the man sitting at a table with George and Charmian, waiting for the boat with the mail. He was dressed in khaki trousers and a faded green shirt, "army colors," and the cheap brown sneakers they sold in Greece. "He looked like a gentleman, old-fashioned—but we were both old-fashioned," says Marianne. When she looked at his eyes, she knew she "had met someone very special. My grandmother, who I grew up with during the war, said to me, 'You are going to meet a man who speaks with a tongue of gold, Marianne.' At that moment she was right."

They did not become lovers immediately. "Though I loved him from the moment we met, it was a beautiful, slow movie." They started meeting in the daytime, Leonard, Marianne and little Axel, to go to the beach. Then they would walk back to Leonard's house, which was much closer than her own, for lunch and a nap. While Marianne and the baby slept, Leonard would sit watching them, their bodies sunburned, their hair white as bone. Sometimes he would read her his poems. In October, Marianne told Leonard that she was going back to Oslo; her divorce proceedings were under way. Leonard told her he would go with her. The three took the ferry to Athens and picked up her car, and Leonard drove them from Athens to Oslo, more than two thousand miles. They stopped off in Paris for a few days en route. Marianne remembers feeling like she was cracking up. Leonard, in turn, recalled "a feeling I think I've tried to re-create hundreds of times, unsuccessfully; just that feeling of being grown up, with somebody beautiful that you're happy to be beside, and all the world is in front of you, where your body is suntanned and you're going to get on a boat."[11]

From Oslo, Leonard flew to Montreal. If he was to stay on his Greek island, cheap as it was, he needed more money. From his rented apartment on Mountain Street he wrote to Marianne telling her of all his schemes. He had applied for another grant from the Canada Council and was confident of getting it. He was also "working very hard," he said, on some TV scripts with Irving Layton. "Our collaboration is perfect. We want to turn the medium into a real art form. If we begin selling them, and I think we will, there will be a lot of money. And once we make our contacts," he wrote, "we can write the plays anywhere." They'd talked about writing years ago, Leonard and Layton, when they sat on the couch with Aviva, watching TV, improvising their own dialogue and scribbling it down on yellow legal pads. Layton was in much the same bind as Leonard, having been fired from his teaching job for one revolutionary comment too far, so they were pursuing the project with particular enthusiasm. "Irving and I think that with three months of intense work we can make enough to last us at least a year. That gives us nine months for pure poetry," Leonard wrote. As for his second book of poetry, *The Spice-Box of Earth*, that would be published in the spring; the publicity might help them sell the screenplays. There would be a book tour too, he said, and he wanted Marianne to come with him. "Mahalia Jackson is on the record player, I'm right there with her, flying with you in that glory, pulling away the shrouds from the sun, making music out of everything." Man, he wrote a mean letter. The telegram he sent was shorter but equally effective: "Have a flat. All I need is my woman and her child." Marianne packed two suitcases and flew with little Axel to Montreal.[12]

Six

Enough of Fallen Heroes

———

It was not easy for Marianne in Montreal. But then, it had not been too easy anywhere for Marianne after one Axel arrived and the other Axel left. Marianne loved Leonard and loved Montreal and got along well with his mother, whom she describes as "a beautiful, strong woman, who was sweet to me and the child." But she knew no one in Montreal and had nothing to do, besides look after her son. Leonard on the other hand seemed to know everyone and had plenty to do. He and Irving Layton had completed two TV plays, *Enough of Fallen Heroes* and *Lights on the Black Water* (later retitled *Light on Dark Water*), which they submitted along with a play Leonard had written alone, titled *Trade*. They waited expectantly for the dollars and praise they were convinced would arrive by return of post. Nothing came.

Beauty at Close Quarters, the novel Leonard had written in London, fared little better. The editors at McClelland & Stewart, as Leonard reported in a letter he sent the writer and critic Desmond Pacey, judged it "disgusting," "tedious" and "a protracted love-affair with himself."[1] Jack McClelland appeared to be confused as to what his golden-boy poet had sent him; was it an autobiography? Leonard answered that everything in the book had happened in real life bar one incident (the death of the boy at the summer camp in part 2), but that the protagonist, Lawrence Breavman, wasn't Leonard. He and Breavman "did a lot of the same things," he wrote, "but we reacted differently to them and so we became different men."[2] McClelland rejected the novel but remained enthusiastic about Leonard's second volume of poetry. *The Spice-Box of Earth* had been scheduled for publication in the spring of 1961. On March 30, the galleys were at the publisher's, ready for Leonard to look at. Only Leonard wasn't in Canada, he was in Miami, boarding a plane to Havana.

It is no great surprise that Leonard should have wanted to see Cuba. Lorca, his favorite poet, had spent three months there when the country was America's playground, calling it "a paradise" and extolling its virtues and vices.[3] The recent revolution had made it even more irresistible to Leonard, with his interest in socialism, war and utopias. What was puzzling about the trip was the timing. Leonard had gone to Montreal to make money, not spend it; after a two-year wait his second book was at last coming out, with its attendant publicity; and he was leaving behind the woman who had only recently, at his behest, moved continents to be with him. It was a dangerous time to visit too. Relations between America and Cuba had been tense since Castro's forces ousted the U.S.-friendly Batista government. When Leonard checked into his room in the Hotel Siboney in Havana, Castro and President Kennedy were in a face-off. There was talk of war. But this only added to the attraction.

So, you went there looking for a war?

"Yes, I did. Just because of the sense of cowardice that drives people to contradict their own deepest understanding of their own natures, they put themselves in dangerous situations."

As a test?

"A kind of test, and hoping for some kind of contradiction about your own deepest conviction."

Sounds like a male thing.

"Yeah. A stupid male treat."

In Havana Leonard dressed as a revolutionary soldier: baggy, mud-green trousers; khaki shirt; beret. In tribute to Che Guevara, he grew a beard. It was an incongruous look. In one of four poems Leonard wrote in Cuba, he described himself, with some justification, as the sole tourist in Havana ("The Only Tourist in Havana Turns His Thoughts Homeward" in *Flowers for Hitler*). In the song he wrote twelve years later about his Cuban experiences, "Field Commander Cohen," he described himself, with no justification whatever, as

our most important spy
wounded in the line of duty
parachuting acid into diplomatic cocktail parties.

He also began work on a new novel, to which he gave the title *The Famous Havana Diary.*

Two years into the new regime, the city was already fraying at the edges. There were broken windows in the modern offices of downtown Havana and cracks in the concrete through which weeds grew. The grand colonial houses where millionaires once lived were now home to peasants whose goats chewed lazily at brown stubble recognizable only to professional botanists as having once been lawn. But despite Castro's having overturned the moneylenders' tables, closed the casinos, rounded up the hookers and sent them off for retraining, there was still a nightlife in Havana and plenty of women to be found. Leonard found them. He drank into the early hours of the morning at La Bodeguita del Medio, one of Hemingway's favorite bars, and, following his routine in Montreal, New York and London, wandered the alleys of the old town, a notebook in one pocket, a hunting knife in the other.

Leonard spoke in an interview a year later of his "deep interest in violence." "I was very interested in what it really meant for a man to

carry arms and kill other men," he said, "and how attracted I was exactly to that process. That's getting close to the truth. The real truth
is I wanted to kill or be killed."[4] There was not much violence or killing to be had, but he did succeed in getting arrested by a small troop
of armed Cuban soldiers on a day trip to the seaside town of Varadero.
Dressed in his army fatigues, he was taken for part of an American
invasion force. After finally persuading them of his Canadian-ness,
his socialist credentials and his support for Cuban independence, he
posed smiling with two of his captors for a photograph, which they
gave him as a souvenir.

Like a good tourist, Leonard wrote postcards. In the card he sent
Jack McClelland, he joked about how good it would be for publicity
if he should be killed in Cuba. He sent three cards to Irving Layton,
including one with a picture of Munch's *The Scream* and a quip about
another man who had fled from a woman, screaming. If this was a
reference to himself and Marianne it was a curious one, since it was
he who had asked her to come to Montreal, and their relationship was
not over. But if Leonard sometimes appeared to court domesticity, he
also ran from it. It was so much more exquisite to long for somebody
than to have her there beside him.

On April 15 a group of eight Cubans exiled in the U.S. led bomber
raids on three Cuban airfields. A couple of days later, late at night,
writing at the table beside the window in the room of his Havana hotel, Leonard was surprised by a knock at the door. In the corridor was
a man wearing a dark suit. He told Leonard that his "presence was
urgently requested at the Canadian embassy."[5] Leonard, still in his
military khakis, accompanied the official; finally, Field Commander
Cohen was being called to action.

At the embassy, Leonard was led into the vice consul's office. The
vice consul did not seem impressed to see him. He told Leonard,
"Your mother's very worried about you."[6] Having heard the reports
of the bomb attacks and talk of war, Masha got on the phone to a

cousin, a Canadian senator, and urged him to call the embassy in Cuba and have them track Leonard down and send him home. Of all the reasons for this summons that had gone through Leonard's mind on the drive to the embassy, this was not one of them. At twenty-six years old he was long past the age of having his mother tug at his leash. At the same time he was rather on the old side for swashbuckling and dressing up. It was understandable that Masha would be concerned; war held little romance for her, since she had witnessed one and nursed one wounded veteran, Leonard's father. But Leonard chose to stay.

He was in Havana on the day of the Bay of Pigs invasion, April 17, 1961. From his hotel room he could hear antiaircraft fire and see troops running through the streets. He did not leave the city until April 26. Although he admired the revolutionaries and had seen many happy Cubans, he had also seen the long lines of people waiting anxiously outside police headquarters, trying to get news of relatives who had been rounded up by Castro's forces and imprisoned, artists and writers among them. Nothing was straightforward; "I felt that I was defending the island against an American invasion and planning that invasion at the same time," he said. "I was behind everything. I couldn't see the megalomania that made up my perspective at that time."[7] He admitted that he had "no faith" in his political opinions and that "they changed often," saying, "I was never really passionate about my opinions even back then." He was attracted to Communist ideas, but in much the same way as he was "attracted to the messianic ideas in the Bible," he said: "the belief in a human brotherhood, in a compassionate society, in people who lived for something more than their own guilt." He had gone to Cuba feeling "that the whole world was functioning for the benefit of [his] personal observation and education."[8] Having observed, it was time to leave.

José Martí Airport swarmed with foreign nationals trying to get a seat on one of the few planes out of Havana. Leonard joined one long queue after another, finally procuring a ticket. When he stood in the last line at the departure gate, he heard his name called. He was wanted at the security desk. Officials had gone through his bag and found the photograph in which he posed with the revolutionary soldiers. With his black hair and sun-darkened skin, perhaps they thought he might have been a Cuban trying to escape. Leonard was taken to a back room and left in the charge of a teenage guard with a rifle. Leonard tried, unsuccessfully, to engage the young man in conversation. He told him he was Canadian and pleaded his case, but the boy just looked bored—the kind of boredom that might possibly be alleviated by shooting somebody. So Leonard sat quietly and stared out of the window at the plane he was supposed to be on. All of a sudden a tussle broke out on the runway. Armed guards rushed out onto the tarmac, including Leonard's, who in his enthusiasm failed to lock the door behind him. Leonard slipped out. Walking as calmly as he could, he headed for the departure gate and, unchallenged, went outside and up the steps into the plane.

———

Back in Canada, and back in civilian clothes, Leonard spent barely a week in Montreal before taking off again, this time for Toronto. He and Irving Layton had been invited to read at the Canadian Conference of the Arts on May 4. A clean-shaven Leonard read from *The Spice-Box of Earth*. Three weeks later, at 599 Belmont Avenue, the book was launched with a party over which Masha presided—a peace offering to her from Leonard, perhaps, for the Cuban escapade.

This was not the budget paperback Leonard had originally proposed to Jack McClelland but an elegant hardback, containing eighty-eight poems. Six of them dated back to Leonard's Columbia University days and had had their first printing in his literary magazine, *The Phoenix*. The book was dedicated jointly to the memory of his maternal grandfather, Rabbi Kline, and his paternal grandmother,

Mrs. Lyon Cohen. On the dust jacket were comments from the literary critic H. N. Frye and the poet Douglas Lochhead, the first commenting that "his outstanding poetic quality, so far, is a gift for macabre ballad reminding one of Auden, but thoroughly original, in which the chronicles of tabloids are celebrated in the limpid rhythms of folksong," and the second describing Leonard's poetry as "strong, intense and masculine," with "a brawling spirit and energy." There was also a paragraph about Leonard that appeared to have been written by Leonard himself in the third person. It painted a romantic picture of the author, mentioning his trip to Cuba and the year he spent writing on a Greek island. He quoted himself saying, in his familiar partly humorous, partly truthful fashion, "I shouldn't be in Canada at all. I belong beside the Mediterranean. My ancestors made a terrible mistake. But I have to keep coming back to Montreal to renew my neurotic affiliations."[9] Clearly though, his roots were more important to him than that. He ended with an unexpected attack on the modern buildings that were taking over his favorite streets in Montreal. This might well have been ironic; Leonard knew his old neighborhood had more serious things to worry about, now that its grand residences had become the target of militant French separatists and mailbox bombs. But Leonard was genuinely fond of the old Victorian houses, and if, for now at least, he seemed to have soured on change, it was understandable so soon after his experience in Havana, where he saw for himself that life post-revolution was no less desperate than it had been before.

The position Leonard occupied on the conservative-modernist scale was an ambiguous one. A CBC TV presenter, curious to know where he thought he stood as a writer, asked Leonard if he considered himself a "modern poet." His answer was deflective. "I always describe myself as a writer rather than a poet, and the fact that the lines I write don't come to the end of the page doesn't qualify me as a poet. I think the term 'poet' is a very exalted term and should be applied to a man at the end of his work. When you look back over the body of his work and he has written poetry," Leonard said, "then let the verdict be that he's a poet."

The Spice-Box of Earth is the work of a major poet, profound, confident and beautifully written. The title makes reference to the ornate wooden box of fragrant spices used in the Jewish ceremony marking the end of the Sabbath and the beginning of the secular week, but this spice box is of earth. The poems dance back and forth across the border between the holy and the worldly, the elevated and the carnal. The opening poem, "A Kite Is a Victim," presents the poet as a man with some control over the heightened world but whose creative work is also subject to strictures and restraints, just as the kite, though it appears to fly freely, is tethered like a fish on a line. The poet makes a contract in the poem with both God and nature and keeps it throughout the book, which abounds in orchards, parks, rivers, flowers, fish, birds, insects. The killing of a man ("If It Were Spring") is romanticized through images from nature; "Beneath My Hands" likens Marianne's small breasts to upturned, fallen sparrows. In "Credo," the grasshoppers that rise from the spot where a man and his lover have just had sex leads to thoughts on biblical plagues. Sex and spirituality share a bed in several poems. In "Celebration," the orgasm from oral sex is likened to the gods falling when Samson pulled down their temples.

There are poems about lovers (Georgianna Sherman was the muse for "I Long to Hold Some Lady" and "For Anne," the latter singled out for praise by critics) and about angels, Solomon's adulterous wives and a sex doll made for an ancient king ("The Girl Toy"). Irving Layton, Marc Chagall and A. M. Klein are the subjects of other poems; Leonard's father and uncles appear in "Priests 1957." The masterful prose poem that ends the book, "Lines from My Grandfather's Journal," is one of three about Leonard's late grandfather. Rabbi Kline was a scholar and mystic, a holy man, a man of conviction; Leonard considered him the ideal Jew, someone who did not struggle with ambiguities as Leonard did. From Leonard's description of himself in "The Genius" ("For you / I will be a banker Jew . . . / For you / I will be a Broadway Jew," etc.) he was less sure what kind of Jew he was himself. And yet, in "Lines from My Grandfather's Journal," there are passages that might apply to Leonard as much as to his grandfather: "It is strange that even now prayer is my natural language. . . . The black, the loss of sun: it will always frighten me. It will always lead me to experiment. . . . O break down these walls with music. . . . Desolation means no angels to wrestle. . . . Let me never speak casually."

As in *Let Us Compare Mythologies*, there are poems that are called "songs." When Leonard became a songwriter, some of their content would be taken up in actual songs. Fans of his music will recognize King David and the bathing woman seen from the roof in "Before the Story" in the song "Hallelujah," the "turning into gold" in "Cuckold's Song" in the song "A Bunch of Lonesome Heroes," and the poem "As the Mist Leaves No Scar" as the song "True Love Leaves No Traces."

Critical reaction to *The Spice-Box of Earth* was for the most part very positive. Louis Dudek, who two years earlier had taken Leonard to task in print, applauded the volume unconditionally. Robert Weaver wrote in the *Toronto Daily Star* that Leonard was "probably the best young poet in English Canada right now."[10] Arnold Edinborough, reviewing for the *Canadian Churchman*, concurred, stating that Leonard had taken Irving Layton's crown as Canada's leading poet. Stephen Scobie would later describe the book in *The Canadian Encyclopedia* as the one that established Leonard's reputation as a lyric poet. There were a few barbs; David Bromige, in *Canadian Literature*, had problems with "the ornateness of the language" and felt that Leonard should "write less about love, and think about it longer," but concluded that "the afflictions mentioned here are curable, and once

Cohen has freed his sensibility from 'the thick glove of words' he will be able to sing as few of his contemporaries can."[11] The first edition of the book sold out in three months.

Looking back, it is curious to see how this mature, important book sat between two incongruously immature incidents. Just prior to publication there had been his adventure in Havana. Postpublication there was a stranger and even riskier episode, involving a junkie Beat novelist, a rescue mission and an opium overdose. Alexander Trocchi was a tall, charismatic Scotsman of Italian descent, nine years Leonard's senior. In the fifties he had moved into a cheap hotel in Paris, where he founded the literary magazine *Merlin*, published Sartre and Neruda, wrote pornographic novels and espoused his own Beat-meets-early-hippie interpretation of Situationism. An enthusiast for drugs, he turned his heroin addiction into Dadaist performance art; Trocchi, as Leonard would describe him in verse, was a "public junkie."

Trocchi moved to New York in 1956, the same year that Leonard went there to attend Columbia University, and took a job working on a tugboat on the Hudson River. He spent his nights, as Leonard did, in Greenwich Village, before taking over a corner of Alphabet City and founding the "Amphetamine University." "Trocchi and a bunch of his friends painted bits of driftwood, mainly, in psychedelic colors, really bright. With all this high-intensity speed going on, they were painting away in the most minute little detail," says the British author and sixties counterculture figure Barry Miles. "Allen Ginsberg took Norman Mailer there because it was just amazing to see." In this drab, run-down part of the Lower East Side, it looked like somebody had bombed a rainbow. Trocchi named these artworks "futiques"— antiques of the future. It's easy to see why Leonard was drawn to Trocchi.

In the spring of 1961, still a cheerleader for heroin, Trocchi gave some to a sixteen-year-old girl. "He wasn't a dealer; he had this absurd, fairly sick thing that he just loved turning people on to smack," explains Miles, "but it was a capital offense in New York." Trocchi was arrested. Facing the possibility of the electric chair, or at least a very long prison term, he went on the run. Nancy Bacal, whom Leonard introduced to Trocchi when she was making a program for CBC about drug use in London, says, "Alex was a strange, brilliant, one-of-a-kind person. Leonard was extremely fond of him." Evidently so. Leonard arranged to meet Trocchi at the Canadian border, then took him to Montreal and put him up in his apartment. The Scotsman did not like to visit empty-handed; he brought some opium with him and set to cooking it up on Leonard's stove. When he was done, he handed Leonard the pan with the leftovers. Apparently he left a little too much. When they set off on foot to find a place to eat, Leonard collapsed as they crossed Saint Catherine Street. He had gone blind. Trocchi dragged him out of the way of the passing cars. They sat together on the curb until Leonard came round. He seemed none the worse for wear. For the next four days Leonard played host to Trocchi until someone—some say George Plimpton, others Norman Mailer—came up with false papers for Trocchi to travel by ship from Montreal to Scotland. Alighting in Aberdeen, Trocchi made his way to London, where he registered as a heroin addict with the National Health Service and obtained his drug legally.

In his poem "Alexander Trocchi, Public Junkie, Priez Pour Nous," which would appear in Leonard's third book of poetry, *Flowers for Hitler*, Leonard wrote of the outlaw he helped rescue,

> *Who is purer*
> *more simple than you? . . .*
> *I'm apt to loaf*
> *in a coma of newspapers . . .*
> *I abandon plans for bloodshed in Canada. . . .*
> *You are at work*

in the bathrooms of the city
changing the Law . . .
Your purity drives me to work.
I must get back to lust and microscopes

———————

The Spice-Box of Earth, despite its excellence and acclaim, failed to win the Governor General's Literary Award for poetry. According to Irving Layton, this hurt Leonard; whatever else might not work out the way he might like, Leonard could at least rely on being the darling of the Canadian poetry world. Then the Canada Council came through like the cavalry with a grant of $1,000. In August 1961, Leonard was back in Greece, writing.

"It was a good place to work," says Mort Rosengarten, who stayed with Leonard on Hydra for two months. "It was very special—no electricity, no telephone, no water. It was beautiful and, back then, very inexpensive, so it was the best place for him to be to write. We had a nice routine. We would go to sleep about three in the morning but we'd get up very early, six A.M., and work till noon. I started drawing—in fact the first time I really started drawing was there; I'd studied sculpture but I'd never drawn or painted—and he also got me a bag of plaster so I made some sculptures. At noon we would go down to the beach and swim, then come back, have lunch at the port, and then we would go up to the house, have a siesta for a couple of hours and then start happy hour. It was very good—a lot of fun and very productive. Leonard worked his ass off. But I couldn't—I'm sure neither of us could—maintain that schedule."

Leonard had the assistance, or at least the companionship, of a variety of drugs. He had a particular liking for Maxiton, generically dexamphetamine, a stimulant known outside of pharmaceutical circles as speed. He also had a fondness for its sweet counterpoint Mandrax, a hypnotic sedative, part happy pill, part aphrodisiac, very popular in the UK. They were as handsome a pair of pharmaceuticals as a hardworking writer could wish to meet; better yet, in Europe they could still be bought over the counter. Providing backup was a three-part harmony of hashish, opium and acid (the last of these three still legal at that time in Europe and most of North America).

Mandrax I get, but speed? Your songs don't sound like they come from a man on amphetamines.

"Well, my processes, mental and physical, are so slow that speed brought me up to the normal tempo."

And acid and the psychedelics?

"Oh, I looked into it quite thoroughly."

As in studied or dropped a few?

"Of course. A lot more than a few. Fortunately it upset my system, acid—I credit my poor stomach for preventing me from entering into any serious addiction, although I kept on taking it because the PR for it was so prevalent. I took trip after trip, sitting on my terrace in Greece, waiting to see God, but generally I ended up with a very bad hangover. I have a lot of acid stories, as everyone does. At the side of my house there was a kind of garbage heap that during the spring would sprout thousands of daisies, and I was convinced that I had a special communion with the daisies. It seems they would turn their little yellow faces to me whenever I started singing or addressing them in a tender way. They would all turn toward me and smile."

Is there a Leonard Cohen acid song or poem?

"My novel Beautiful Loser *had a bit of acid in it, and a lot of speed."*

"Did he tell you about the writing on the wall?" asks Marianne. "It was in gold paint and it said, 'I change, I am the same, I change, I am the same, I change, I am the same, I change, I am the same.' I think it was beautiful." Steve Sanfield remembers that they "smoked a lot of hashish and began to use LSD and psychotropic drugs more as a spiritual path than recreational." There was a variety of paths to follow. Hydra, says Richard Vick, a British poet and musician who lived on the island, "always had the odd shaman who came and went and would be the feature of the winter, who would be into the tarot or sandbox play or something." The I Ching and *The Tibetan Book of the Dead* were popular. George Lialios was also investigating Buddhism and Jung.

Leonard continued to fast, as he had in Montreal. The discipline of a week of fasting appealed to him, as did the spiritual element of purging and purification and the altered mental state that it produced. Fasting focused his mind for writing, but there was vanity in it also; it kept his body thin and his face gaunt and serious (although the amphetamines helped with that too). There seemed to be a deep need in Leonard for self-abnegation, self-control and hunger. In *Beautiful Losers* he would write, "Please make me empty, if I'm empty then I can receive, if I can receive it means it comes from somewhere outside of me, if it comes from outside of me I'm not alone. I cannot bear this loneliness. . . . Please let me be hungry. . . . Tomorrow I begin my fast." The hunger he wrote of appeared to be all-encompassing. In the *Spice-Box of Earth* poem "It Swings Jocko," a bebop song to his prick, he wrote,

> *I want to be hungry,*
> *hungry for food,*
> *for love, for flesh.*

Leonard abstained from eating meat, but he was less restrained when it came to his appetite "for the company of women and the sexual expression of friendship."[12] Sit in a taverna by the harbor in Hydra long enough and you could compile quite a catalog of who slept with whom and marvel at the complexity of it all and that so little blood was spilled. You might hear a tale of a woman, an expat, so distressed when Leonard left on the ferry that she threw herself into the sea after it, even though she could not swim; the man who dived in and rescued her, they say, became her new partner. "Everyone was in everyone else's bed," says Richard Vick. Leonard too, although compared to other islanders he was, according to Vick, "very discreet as a whole." Vick recalls one evening in a bar in Kamini where he was drinking with his then-girlfriend and her female friend. Leonard and Marianne showed up. During the course of the evening it came out that both of the women with Vick knew Leonard intimately. The women, says Vick, told Leonard genially, "You know, Leonard, we were never in love with you." Leonard replied equally genially, "Well, me too." "Those were innocent times," remarks Vick, but they could be difficult for Marianne. "Yes, he was a ladies' man," says Marianne. "I could feel my jealousy arousing. Everybody wanted a bit of my man. But he chose to live with me. I had nothing to worry about." It did not stop her worrying, but she was not one to complain, and she loved him.

In March 1962, two years after he had left London for Hydra, Leonard made the return journey and moved back into Mrs. Pullman's boardinghouse in Hampstead. He had found a London publisher—Secker & Warburg—for the novel he had begun writing there. At the publishers' urging, he was in London to revise it. For someone who described the writing process as being "scraped" and "torn from his heart," the cutting and revising of a manuscript he thought finished was torturous. He wrote to Irving Layton about wielding "a big scalpel" and how he had "torn apart orchestras to arrive at my straight melodic line."[13] The operation was performed with the aid of amphetamines and the pain eased by Mandrax and hashish. But still, it was difficult going back over something he'd been happy with, like being locked in a room with an old love he had once considered beautiful but could now see only her flaws. He wrote to friends about his dark dreams, his panic and depression. The flat gray sky over London did not help. The King William IV pub was not the Bodeguita del Medio, and Hampstead wasn't Hydra. He wrote a letter to

Marianne telling her how much he longed for her. In his novel he wrote how "he needed to be by himself so he could miss her, to get perspective."

As he had during his last stay in London, Leonard spent time with Nancy Bacal, who had since moved out of the Pullmans' house. Through Bacal, he came to know an Afro-Caribbean man from Trinidad named Michael X. Like Trocchi, Michael X was a complex, charismatic and troubled man. "Leonard was fascinated with Michael," says Nancy Bacal. "Everyone was. He was an intriguing man, all things to all people. He was a poet and rabble-rouser and a charmer and a bullshitter and a lovely, joyous, marvelous man and a potentially dangerous man. And so Leonard was drawn to him, as I was obviously." Before Nancy and Michael X became lovers in 1962, Michael de Freitas, as he was then named, had been a hustler whose résumé included working as an enforcer for Peter Rachman, a London slum landlord so notoriously iron-fisted that his last name has entered the lexicon.* Over time, Michael de Freitas had amassed his own little empire of music clubs and hookers. But Michael X, the man Bacal lived with, was a civil rights activist, an articulate man and a bridge between London's black underground and the white proto-hippie community. Together, Michael and Nancy founded the London Black Power Movement. They "churned out pamphlets on Xerox machines aimed to change the world for the better." On this and subsequent trips to London, Leonard got to know Michael "very well." He, Nancy, Michael and Robert Hershorn, when he was in London, would spend evenings in Indian restaurants, deep in discussions about art and politics.

"Michael said to me he was completely against arming the blacks in America," Leonard told a journalist in 1974. "He said it was crazy,

---

* Rachman also made the newspapers as the owner of the house that served as the place of business of Christine Keeler and Mandy Rice Davies, the call girls who almost brought down the British government in 1963 in the Profumo Affair.

they would never be able to resist that machine. They own the bullets and the armaments factories and the guns. So you give the blacks a few guns and have them against armies? He was even against knives. He said we should use our teeth, something everybody has. That was his view of the thing. It was a different kind of subversion. The subversion of real life to implant black fear."[14] Leonard recalled going to Michael's house and complimenting him on a drink he'd given him. "God, how do you make this?" Leonard asked. Michael replied, "You don't expect me to tell you. If you know the secrets of our food, you know the secrets of our race and the secrets of our strength."

As Bacal says, "These were very outrageous times. It was as if everything was and wasn't political. You never knew how far it would go or how dangerous it would get or how effective it would be or if it was just another flower [power] episode. Michael was one of these people who might say something as a joke but you never really knew what was truth and what wasn't—which made him fascinating, because we don't really know in life what is truth and what is fabrication or a dream. He just lived like that, openly. It was very lively."*

Rather too lively as it turned out. In 1967, when things started getting too dark, Bacal left Michael. That same year, her former partner became the first black person to be imprisoned under Britain's Race Relations Act—a statute originally passed to protect immigrants from racism—after calling for the shooting of any black woman seen with a white man; Bacal is white. On his release from prison, now using the name Michael Abdul Malik, he founded a Black Power commune run from a storefront in North London, supported and funded by wealthy, often celebrated white people. John Lennon and Yoko Ono donated a bag of their hair to auction. Lennon also paid Michael's bail when he was arrested for murder. The killing took place in Trinidad, Michael's home country, where he

---

* Bacal is in the process of writing a memoir of this period, *A Different Story.*

had returned to start another revolutionary commune. Two of the commune's members, one the daughter of a British politician, were found hacked to death, reportedly for disobeying Michael's orders to attack a police station.

In London Michael X had told Leonard—perhaps in jest, perhaps not—that he planned to take over the government of Trinidad. When he did, he said, he would appoint Leonard minister of tourism. An odd office, you might think, to choose for Leonard; he might have made a better minister of arts. "I thought it was rather odd too," said Bacal, "but for some reason Leonard thought it was marvelous." In some ways Michael X had him nailed; from Michael's point of view, as a black man in London involved in revolutionary politics, Leonard was a tourist, just as he had been in Havana. "I remember them shaking hands on it," said Bacal. "Leonard was very, very pleased and happy, and that was the end of that story." The end of De Freitas/X/ Malik's story came in 1975, when he was hanged for murder. The Trinidad government ignored pleas for clemency from people in the U.S., UK and Canada, many of them celebrities. They included Angela Davis, Dick Gregory, Judy Collins and Leonard Cohen.

In London in 1962, Leonard continued to turn out pages for Stella Pullman. He stayed in London for as long as he could stand to—four months, which was four weeks more than he managed the first time. He did not quite finish the revisions to his novel, but he was making great inroads into a new book of poetry. By the summer he was back in his house on Hydra, playing host to his mother. Masha still fretted that her boy wasn't looking after himself, but this time, rather than send in the consulate, she decided to go there and check on him herself. Marianne and little Axel moved in with a friend for the duration of her visit. Although Masha knew Marianne in Montreal and was aware that she was living with Leonard, there was a strong sense that she would not have been comfortable being under the same roof with her son and his Scandinavian, non-Jewish girlfriend.

Forsaken by one woman who loved him—if only temporarily and with his collusion—and engulfed by another, Leonard was unable to write. Masha stayed with him for a month. When she left, Leonard returned gratefully, joyfully, to his life with Marianne, little Axel and his Olivetti, and finished the novel he had variously retitled *The Mist Leaves No Scar, No Flesh So Perfect, Fields of Hair, The Perfect Jukebox* and, finally, *The Favorite Game.*

Seven

Please Find Me,
I Am Almost 30

———

"A biography is considered complete," Virginia Woolf wrote in *Orlando*, "if it merely accounts for six or seven selves, whereas a person may well have as many thousand." True, if not words to warm the heart of a biographer. Autobiographers have it easy; they can stand in front of the mirror and wear any mask they fancy. *The Favorite Game* is a sort of autobiography, though more accurately it's a sort of biography. A sort of biography of Leonard Cohen written, and at the same time ghostwritten, by Leonard Cohen. It recounts Leonard's life from childhood to early manhood through an alter ego named Lawrence Breavman, who looks like Leonard and has (name changes aside) the same family, friends, lovers and accumulation of experiences, to which he may or may not have reacted in the exact same way as Leonard did. Or as Leonard believed, or might like to think he did, autobiography, even sort of autobiography, can be one of the most fictional of genres. First novels often have a good deal of autobiography, but to complicate matters further, *The Favorite Game* was not technically Leonard's first novel. Before that there was the unpublished *Ballet of Lepers*, the unfinished *Famous Havana Diary*, and all those unpublished or unfinished, to some degree, autobiographical short stories, stacked up like mirror-lined Leonard Cohen Russian dolls reflecting, and deflecting, ad infinitum.

It is a beautifully written book and very funny in a dark, wry, incisive, exuberant, erotic, self-aware, playful, Cohenesque kind of way. It opens with scars: scars of beauty (his lover's pierced ear), scars of war (his father's battle wound), the scar from a fight with a boyhood friend over aesthetics (the correct style for a snowman's clothes). And it ends with a scar, the indelible memory of a game he played as a child and the mark a body leaves in the snow. In between, our self-inflated yet self-mocking, scarred hero chronologically contends with his father's death, Jewish summer camp, the synagogue, sexual longing, getting laid, and becoming a writer—"blackening pages," possibly the debut of Leonard's much-used line to describe his work. Although it irked Leonard that some reviewers dealt with the book as if it were autobiography, not a work of art, and though the contents of the novel might not stand up in court, it still provides useful evidence on Leonard's life for a biographer tired of digging in the trenches, who fancies a few hours in a comfy chair in the ivory tower.

The unconventional form in which Leonard arranges his "life" resembles a film more than a novel—more specifically an art-house coming-of-age film and a buddy movie, in which Breavman/Leonard and Krantz/Mort play the "two Talmudists delighting in their dialectic, which was a disguise for love." Each chapter of his account of how his life led to his becoming the writer of this story is presented as a separate scene, which he scripts, directs, stars in, and at the same time observes from the back row, smiling, while perfectly executing the popcorn-box trick on the girl in the next seat.

The Favorite Game was published in September 1963 in the UK by Secker & Warburg, and in the U.S. the following year by Viking. Reviews on both sides of the Atlantic were positive. The U.S. *Saturday Review* described it as "interior-picaresque, extraordinarily rich in language, sensibility and humour." The *Guardian* newspaper in the UK called it "a song of a book, a lyrical and exploratory bit of semiautobiography." It even made it into Britain's esteemed *Times Literary Supplement*, earning a short yet favorable critique in an "Other New Novels" roundup. The Canadian writer Michael Ondaatje praised its "tightly edited, elliptical poetic style"[1] and pointed out connections with James Joyce's *Portrait of an Artist*. (There were indeed several, and Leonard did study Joyce at McGill University with Louis Dudek.) Some years later, writer T. F. Rigelhof made comparisons with Hungarian-Canadian writer Stephen Vizinczey's *In Praise of Older Women*, likewise "poignant, hilarious and erotically-charged." Both novels, Rigelhof wrote, "were too brave and unbridled for Jack McClelland."[2] McClelland might have been slow to warm to a book that would become a cult classic, but he was by no means conservative in his tastes. According to the writer and editor Dennis Lee, who later worked for him, McClelland was a flamboyant man, "a real wild man, who kept pace with some of the wilder writers he was publishing." If he had an issue with Leonard's book, it was less likely to be its sexual content than that it was not poetry, and he had signed Leonard, personally and at first sight, as a poet. McClelland did eventually publish *The Favorite Game*, seven years behind the British. Until that time, Leonard's first novel was available in Canada only on import.

Still, life continued to lead Leonard back to Montreal, as it would for periods in the early and midsixties. "We didn't have any money so he went to Montreal. He left because he had to," said Marianne, who mostly stayed behind on Hydra, "not because he wanted to. He had to make money." The checks that arrived for him on the ferry rarely amounted to more than $20 at a time. Marianne helped out where she could. She sold her house at the top of the hill, took modeling assignments, and, when the annual dividend arrived from a small inheritance she had, she paid the tab that they had run up at Katsika's. Leonard and Marianne did not spend much on themselves, but there was the child to feed and clothe. They simply did not have enough. So, in order to keep the dream alive of living as a writer on an island for another year, Leonard hustled for money in Montreal. It became an increasingly tiring enterprise. It did not help when, in 1964, George Johnston and Charmian Clift, the first to show Leonard the possibility of leading such a life, decided to leave Hydra and move back to Australia. Johnston's latest book, *My Brother Jack*, was a bestseller—something that all the expat writers were hoping for to solve their financial problems.* But Johnston, in his fifties now, was suffering from tuberculosis. He wanted to go home for medical treatment and to capitalize on his success.

Leonard, no youngster himself by the standards of the sixties with his thirtieth birthday approaching, soldiered on, applying for grants and taking the odd job. He looked into the possibility of selling movie rights to *The Favorite Game*, but there were no takers until 2003, when the Canadian filmmaker Bernar Hébert made a film of it, curiously turning it into more of a conventional narrative on-screen than it was in the novel. Leonard also approached a Montreal book dealer with his archive of manuscripts, this time with more success. In 1964 the director of the Thomas Fisher Rare Book Library at the University of Toronto, Marian Brown, purchased the first of its collection of the Cohen papers.

It would be wrong though to picture Leonard plodding woefully through his hometown, black cloud above his head, begging bowl in hand. Although he often felt the need to escape from Montreal, he loved the place. Montreal for Leonard was much like Dublin was to

---

* Leonard was responsible for the title, according to Aviva Layton. "George said, 'I just don't know what to call it.' Leonard said, 'What's it about?' He said, 'My brother Jack,' Leonard said, 'There you are.'"

Joyce. He immersed himself in the city, luxuriating in the company of friends. Lovers also. Leonard was devoted to women, and they returned the sentiment in numbers that increased with his renown. As Leonard saw it, he had slaved for years trying to write "the perfect sonnet to attract the girl,"[3] then he had looked up from his "blackened pages" to find that women were making themselves sexually available. It had happened on Hydra, and now it was happening in Montreal. "It was terrific," he said. "It was a moment where everybody was giving to the other person what they wanted. The women knew that's what the men wanted."[4] Asked whether having so much of what he wanted devalued it for him, he said, "Nobody gets the right amount in terms of what they think their appetite deserves. But it lasted just a few moments, and then it was back to the old horror story. . . . I'll give you this if you give me that. You know, sealing the deal: what do I get, what do you get. It's a contract."[5] Leonard did not like contracts. He did not have one with McClelland; it was a handshake, a gentleman's agreement. It was not a question of loyalty for Leonard but of having freedom, control and an escape hatch.

Leonard had rented a furnished duplex in the west of Montreal, an old stagecoach house. Once again Marianne flew out to join him. The house was within walking distance of McGill University, and on warm days Leonard would go there and sit in the spot in front of the Arts Building where the grass curved down like a bowl and where people played guitar and sang. It was here that Erica Pomerance first saw him. Like most McGill art students, she knew who Leonard was and counted herself among the "circle of admirers" that surrounded him on the grass on the campus or in "the continental hipness of Le Bistro. If you were looking for Leonard," says Pomerance, "Le Bistro was the first place you would go."

Le Bistro looked like someone had smuggled it in from Paris, with its zinc-topped horseshoe bar, blackboard menu and long mirror along one wall. On another wall, Leonard had scribbled a poem:

MARITA
PLEASE FIND ME
I AM ALMOST 30

"MARITA," SELECTED POEMS 1956–1968

He had written it in response to having had his advances spurned by Marita La Fleche, a Montreal boutique owner, who told him to come back when he had grown up. Le Bistro was the meeting place of choice for both French- and English-speaking artists and intelligentsia, who would sit there, talking, long into the night, drinking red wine and smoking French cigarettes. On any given night you might see Leonard, Irving Layton, Mort Rosengarten, Derek May, Robert Hershorn, the sculptor Armand Vaillancourt and Pierre Trudeau, the socialist writer and law professor who would go on to become prime minister of Canada and whose beige Humphrey Bogart raincoat became as famous as Leonard's blue one.

Another regular haunt was the 5th Dimension, a coffee bar and folk club on Bleury Street. Leonard was with Hershorn the night he first met Pomerance there. Leonard remarked to Hershorn that she reminded him of Freda Guttman, his old girlfriend at McGill, and introduced himself. Pomerance says, "He was a ladies' man, an extremely magnetic personality, someone with a special aura, even before he burst on the music scene. I was eighteen and very impressed by these people. They were very sophisticated and very much into their own style in the way they dressed—black, very simple—and in what they talked about, art and literature mostly, not so much politics. They just seemed to have a handle on life. They were so sure of themselves and where they were going, and at the same time not too focused on any specific thing except creativity and art. As a younger girl I guess they were my ideal, particularly Leonard and Derek May. Leonard seemed to be the epitome of cool."

For a while, Leonard courted her. "He didn't seduce you in the typical way; he was very obtuse, very laid back. You felt drawn to him on some sort of spiritual level." He took her to the house on Belmont Avenue, where his mother still kept his bedroom. "There were photographs of his dad and of him as a boy. We smoked hash and he nearly seduced me in that room. But I was still a virgin, and I remember thinking that even though he was hard to resist I didn't want to make love for the very first time with someone who was living with another woman." She was referring to Marianne.

Leonard introduced the young woman to his mother. "A very attractive woman, very strong face, strong features, with steely gray hair and dressed like a high-class Westmount Jewish woman who had means," recalls Pomerance, herself a Montreal Jew. "She was halfway in the old world and halfway in the new. She ruled the roost; she was what you would call now a domineering mother. My feeling was that she was thirsty. She wanted to be let into Leonard's life and his successes." Leonard, though, "was like quicksilver, a free spirit who looked like he was doing just what he wanted and you couldn't tie him down anywhere. I think she would have liked to have had more of a piece of the pie in terms of having more time with him, but Leonard would come and go. When he'd enough of her he escaped, but he always remained close to her."

After dispensing with her virginity elsewhere, Pomerance "did not remain resistant forever" to Leonard's charms. "He took me to all the haunts where he took most of his paramours, like the Hotel de France, which was this seedy hotel which he loved, on Saint Laurent Street on the corner of Saint Catherine, and we went for walks in the mountains. At one point he took me to his house," she says, referring to where Leonard was living with Marianne. "That's where I heard him play guitar for the first time. We sat around and smoked a bit, because Leonard was into pot and hash, and we'd jam." Pomerance played guitar and sang. "I remember Leonard liking a western style of music."

Leonard also introduced her to Marianne. "She seemed so cool and beautiful and calm," says Pomerance. "Everything I wasn't was this woman. I think they must have had an understanding. He probably brought other women there he was having casual relationships with, and then when you were there it was obvious Marianne was his common-law wife, his muse, the queen, and that she had a tremendous amount of respect and they seemed to be on an equal footing. She was very nice and warm and very accepting—you didn't feel that she was jealous or anything—but I think that she probably put up with a lot to remain with him, because he was moody and he had his own rules and needed his freedom. I remember one day, it was his birthday, we went back to his room in his mother's house and he was lying down on his bed, and he had this yellow rose on his chest and he was just being very, very passive and Buddha-like, inviolable and untouchable, in some remote area.

"You could only get so much of him that he was willing to give at the moment. He was somebody who was not trying to fill up the spaces of silence with idle chatter; everything he did had to have meaning and importance. But on the other hand you got the feeling from him that time was seamless, that he didn't run on the same time or rhythm as other people. He didn't run after journalists, getting himself publicized; his magnetism is such that it's like a boat creating a wake and people are drawn to him and his ideas. For me what he emanated was model of creativity and freedom to explore and express."*

Throughout everything Leonard was writing, typing pages, filling notebooks. He was working on a new volume of poetry to follow up the successful *Spice-Box of Earth*, to which he had given the title *Opium and Hitler*. He sent the manuscript to Jack McClelland. His

---

* In 1968 Pomerance released her experimental debut album titled *You Used to Think*, which contained her song "To Leonard from Hospital." She went on to become a documentary filmmaker.

publisher objected to the title and, judging by the long correspondence between them, seemed not entirely convinced by the content. Michael Ondaatje, who, like Leonard, was published by Jack McClelland, wrote that McClelland was "uncertain of Cohen's being a genius, yet rather delighted at its possibility, and so constantly presenting him to the public as one."[6]

This would have been a comfortable position for someone of Leonard's sensibilities, able to float contentedly on a sea of praise while all the time shrugging modestly. But Jack McClelland could be far more critical in his letters to Leonard than he was when he talked about him to other people. He told Leonard he would publish his book anyway, "because you are Leonard Cohen"[7]—which was in many ways the inverse of a famous incident that would occur twenty years later, when the head of Leonard's U.S. record company, having heard Leonard's seventh album, would tell him, "Leonard, we know you're great, but we don't know if you're any good,"[8] and refused to release it.

Leonard's reply to McClelland contained none of his usual humor and mock braggadocio; it was angry, honest and sure of itself. He knew his book to be "a masterpiece," he wrote. "There has never been a book like this, prose or poetry, written in Canada." Yes he could write another *Spice-Box* and make everyone happy, himself included, since he had nothing against flattering reviews. But he had moved on. "I've never written easily: most of the time I detest the process. So try and understand that I've never enjoyed the luxury of being able to choose between the kinds of books I wanted to write, or poems, or women I wanted to love, or lives to lead."[9]

Leonard also argued to keep the title. It would appeal, he wrote, to "the diseased adolescents who compose my public."[10] But when it came down to it, Leonard was a practical man. He agreed to many of the revisions McClelland called for, saying, "I'll carve a little here and there, as long as I don't touch the bone."[11] He ended up sending

McClelland fifty new poems. He also gave the book a new name, *Flowers for Hitler*, and removed the dedication, which McClelland had disliked:

> *With scorn, love, nausea, and above all,*
> *a paralysing sense of community*
> *this book is dedicated*
> *to the teachers, doctors, leaders of my parents' time:*
> *THE DACHAU GENERATION*

This bitter moniker had been taken from the poem Leonard wrote to Alexander Trocchi, his "public junkie" friend. In it, Leonard made excuses for his own inability to take such a committed stance:

> *I tend to get distracted . . .*
> *by Uncle's disapproval*
> *of my treachery*
> *to the men's clothing industry.*
> *I find myself . . .*
> *taking advice*
> *from the Dachau generation . . .*

Leonard had already felt his uncles' disapproval of *The Favorite Game;* they had been not well pleased, he said, with his description of them as having betrayed their priestly name of Cohen and pledged themselves only to financial success. (Nor for that matter had his uncles approved of his having written about Masha's stay in a mental hospital.)

The book was now dedicated not to the Dachau generation but to Marianne. He also wrote "A Note on the Title," which, like the original dedication, was arranged in the form of a poem:

*A
while ago
this book would
have been called
SUNSHINE FOR NAPOLEON
and earlier still it
would have been
called
WALLS FOR GENGHIS KHAN*

In turn, McClelland agreed to some of Leonard's requests, in particular that the original design for the front cover be scrapped—Leonard's face, superimposed on a woman's naked body. "Nobody is going to buy a book the cover of which is a female body with my face for tits," Leonard wrote in September 1964 in a long, heated letter to McClelland. "The picture is simply offensive. It is dirty in the worst sense. It hasn't the sincerity of a stag movie or the imagination of a filthy postcard or the energy of real surrealist humor." He told McClelland that he would not be returning to Canada to promote the book. "I'd really be ashamed to stand beside a stack of them at a cocktail party. . . . So why don't we forget about the whole thing? You never liked the book very much."[12]

Flowers for Hitler was published in the autumn of 1964. The dust jacket, which bore a different design, contained an excerpt from one of Leonard's letters to McClelland. "This book," it read, "moves me from the world of the golden-boy poet into the dung pile of the front-line writer. I didn't plan it this way. I loved the tender notices *Spice-Box* got but they embarrassed me a little. *Hitler* won't get the same hospitality from the papers. My sounds are too new, therefore people will say: this is derivative, this is slight, his power has failed. Well, I say that there has never been a book like this, prose or poetry, written in Canada. All I ask is that you put it in the hands of my generation and it will be recognized."[13]

Thematically, *Flowers for Hitler* "was not entirely new for Leonard; there had been sex, violence, murder and the Holocaust in his first two books of poems, as well as songs to lovers and celebrations of teachers and friends. What was different was its style. It was much less formal and its language freer and more contemporary, which made the darkness and torture it described seem more personal—self-torture, the darkness within—and the love it expressed, for Marianne, for Irving Layton, more heartfelt. As an epigraph Leonard chose the words of Primo Levi, a concentration camp survivor: "Take care not to suffer in your own homes what is inflicted on us here." A warning not so much that history can repeat itself but that history is not something frozen in some other place and time; it's the nature of humanity.

In a 1967 interview in the University of British Columbia student paper the *Ubyssey*, Leonard explained, "[Levi is] saying, what point is there to a political solution if, in the homes, these tortures and mutilations continue? That's what *Flowers for Hitler* is all about. It's taking the mythology of the concentration camps and bringing it into the living room and saying, 'This is what we do to each other.' We outlaw genocide and concentration camps and gas and that, but if a man leaves his wife or they are cruel to each other, then that cruelty is going to find a manifestation if he has a political capacity; and he has. There's no point in refusing to acknowledge the wrathful deities. That's like putting pants on the legs of pianos like the Victorians did. The fact is that we all succumb to lustful thoughts, to evil thoughts, to thoughts of torture."[14]

His interviewer, literary professor Sandra Djwa, asked Leonard if he wasn't mining the same seams as William Burroughs, Günter Grass and Jean-Paul Sartre in *Nausea*. He answered, "The only thing that differs in those writers and myself is that I hold out the idea of ecstasy as the solution. If only people get high, they can face the evil part. If a man feels in his heart it's only going to be a mundane confrontation with feelings, and he has to recite to himself Norman

Vincent Peale slogans, 'Be better, be good,' he hasn't had a taste of that madness. He's never soared, he's never let go of the silver thread and he doesn't know what it feels to be like a god. For him, all the stories about holiness and the temple of the body are meaningless. . . . The thing about Sartre is that he's never lost his mind. . . . The thing that people are interested in doing now is blowing their heads off and that's why the writing of schizophrenics like myself will be important."[15]

It was a curious answer. It appeared to be equal parts megalomania and madness, anti–New Age yet Newer Age, though with an Old Age patina. Or quite possibly he was high. Leonard clearly considered *Flowers for Hitler* an important book; in 1968 he would choose around half its content for his anthology *Selected Poems*. If Leonard truly believed, though, that *Flowers for Hitler* would prove too provocative for the literati and strip him of his "golden-boy poet" status, he would have been disappointed with the favorable reaction it received. It prompted the critic Milton Wilson to write in the *Toronto Quarterly* that Leonard was "potentially the most important writer that Canadian poetry has produced since 1950," adding, "not merely the most talented, but also, I would guess, the most professionally committed to making the most of his talent."[16] (Somewhat prophetic, since one of its poems, "New Step," would be staged as a theatrical ballet on CBC TV in 1972, and another poem, "Queen Victoria and Me," would become a song on his 1973 album *Live Songs*.)

Flowers for Hitler did little to heal relations between Leonard and the Montreal Jewish establishment, nor presumably with his uncles. In December 1963 at a symposium held in the city on the future of Judaism in Canada, Leonard had given an address titled "Loneliness and History," in which he castigated the Montreal Jewish community for abandoning the spiritual for the material. As he wrote in *The Favorite Game*, the men, like his uncles, who occupied the front pews at the synagogue were pledged only to their businesses; religious observance was an empty masquerade. "They did not believe their blood was consecrated. . . . They did not seem to realize how fragile the ceremony was. They participated in it blindly, as if it would last forever. . . . Their nobility was insecure because it rested on inheritance and not moment-to-moment creation in the face of annihilation."

Businessmen, Leonard told the assembly in the Montreal Jewish Public Library, had taken over and made a corporation of the religious community. Jews were "afraid to be lonely" and sought security in finance, neglecting their scholars and sages, their artists and prophets. "Jews must survive in their loneliness as witnesses," he told them. "Jews are the witness to monotheism and that is what they must continue to declare." Now that A. M. Klein, the great Canadian Jewish poet, a friend of Layton's and much admired by Leonard, had fallen silent—mental illness, attempted suicide and hospitalization had led Klein to stop writing—it remained to young Jewish writers and artists, Leonard said, to take on the responsibility of being the lonely witnesses and prophets. His indictment made the front page of the *Canadian Jewish Chronicle* with the headline POET-NOVELIST SAYS JUDAISM BETRAYED. The controversy was now national. Two months later, during an appearance at the University of British Columbia Jewish Community Center in Vancouver—part of a reading tour of Western Canada, which also included a Dunn's Birdland–style performance in Manitoba where Leonard was accompanied by jazz guitarist Lenny Breau and his band—Leonard was unapologetic. He seemed energized, manic almost, as he talked about his work. He announced that he planned to retreat from the world and consecrate himself to writing a liturgy and confessional that would take the form of a new novel.

Back in Montreal, the snow was falling thicker than ever. The cold of a Montreal winter was brutal. It mugged you. Leonard headed for his favorite sanctuary, Le Bistro. It was there, on a glacial night, that Leonard met Suzanne.

———————

Suzanne Verdal has long black hair and wears long flowing skirts and ballet slippers. For years she has lived a gypsy life in a wooden caravan, with cats and planters of geraniums. It was built for her in the nineties and is towed by an old truck but otherwise seems straight out of a fairy tale. It is parked in Santa Monica, California, where Suzanne works as a masseuse and is writing her autobiography, by hand.

In the early sixties, when she and Leonard first met, Suzanne was a demure seventeen-year-old, "just out of an Ontario boarding school, with a future dream of bohemian heaven." She frequented the art galleries and the café scene, "making notes and observing the people; there was always some young artist passing through, to partake of long discussions on art or political issues." Suzanne wrote poetry, but her talent was as a dancer. She worked two jobs to pay for dance classes, and late at night, she would go to Le Vieux Moulin, one of the nightclubs Leonard and his friends frequented, where jazz was played into the early hours and Montrealers drank and danced their way through the glacial winter. One night, on the dance floor she met Armand Vaillancourt, a strikingly handsome man—long haired, bearded and fifteen years her senior. Vaillancourt, a friend of Leonard, was a Quebecois sculptor of some renown; he had a public sculpture on Durocher Street. Suzanne and Vaillancourt became dancing partners, then lovers, and then the parents of a baby girl. They lived in Vaillancourt's studio, an "uninsulated wooden shack" on Bleury Street.

The first time Suzanne met Leonard was at Le Bistro. She had seen him there on several occasions, sometimes sitting with Marianne at a small table under the long mirror on the wall. Suzanne could not recall what they talked about, but "more than conversation was our eye contact. It was the most intimate of touches and completely visceral. We were simultaneously witnessing the magical scenes unfolding at the time and, truly, it felt we were genuinely on each other's wavelength."

Suzanne had signed her first professional dance contract at the age of eighteen and, after spending a summer studying with Martha Graham in New York, had started her own modern dance company in Montreal, "experimenting with music such as John Cage and Edgar Varèse." They performed at the Beaux-Arts; at L'Association Espagnole, where flamenco was played long into the night; and also on television. She began to make a name as an avant-garde dancer and choreographer. Erica Pomerance says, "Suzanne was cool and creative and one of the beautiful people, an icon to dance like Leonard was to the poetry and artistic set. She would combine classical, modern and ethnic dance styles and she had a style about her that was the epitome of bohemianism, very New Age. She would design these sort of Gypsy clothes that she wore," sewn together from silks, brocades and old drapery she found in the Salvation Army store on Notre-Dame Street.

When her relationship with Vaillancourt ended, Suzanne would go for long walks along the harbor by the Saint Lawrence River. "I loved the huge ships that docked there and the taste of faraway travel," she says. "I related to the sounds of the slow-moving freight trains— hauntingly poetic and somehow soothing. I admired the centuries-old architecture and the grain elevators." She decided to rent a cheap apartment in one of its large, dilapidated buildings, becoming the first in their circle, she says, "to colonize Old Montreal." Today the area is fashionable; the half-abandoned rooming house from the 1850s where she lived with her child became a hotel charging $300 a night for a room. In the midsixties the only other occupants were "an elderly couple and an old British lady and her cat." The building reeked of old pipe tobacco and the floors were all crooked, but they were of fine old burnished wood, and there were stained-glass windows. Suzanne found the place "absolutely beautiful, inspirational."

There were few restaurants or cafés nearby, so her friends would come to the house. Suzanne would serve them "jasmine tea or Constant Comment and little mandarin oranges and lychee nuts from Chinatown," which was a short walk away. Among her visitors was Philippe Gingras, a poet friend "who wrote a beautiful homage to me way before Leonard did, in French, in a tome called *Quebec Underground*. When Philippe came I would light a candle to invoke the Spirit of Poetry—I called the flame Anastasia, don't ask me why." She performed the ceremony for Leonard. "I'm quite sure that Leonard observed that little ritual every time we sat and had tea together; that was a rarefied moment, a spiritual moment, because I would invite the Spirit of Poetry and quality conversation." They would walk through Old Montreal together, silently, "the click of his boots and the sound of [her] shoes almost like a synchronicity" as they went down to the river, past Notre-Dame-de-Bon-Secours, where the sailors went to be blessed before going to sea and where the Virgin, wearing a halo of stars, reached out to them across the harbor.

"We were definitely on the same wavelength," Suzanne says. "We could almost hear each other think at times and that was such a delight to us. I sensed a deep, philosophical side to Leonard that he seemed to see in me as well, and he got a kick out of it in that I was a sort of fledgling in a way, just emerging as a young artist." Leonard, though younger than Vaillancourt, was ten years older than Suzanne. On one visit, Leonard stayed overnight. "We didn't sleep together, although Leonard was a very seductive man. I didn't want to mar or contaminate that purity of my esteem for our relationship and for him and for myself."

In August 1967, Suzanne left Montreal for San Francisco. It was around this time, she says, that she learned from a mutual friend that Leonard had written a poem about her, titled "Suzanne." Not long afterward, when somebody played her a record of Judy Collins singing its words, she discovered it was also a song. The first time she heard it, she says she felt "cut to the core" and like someone was holding a magnifying glass to her life. When Suzanne returned to Montreal she was famous—not as a dancer, choreographer or designer but as the muse for a Leonard Cohen song that everyone seemed to be talking about.

Suzanne had been a muse for other men besides Leonard, but for nothing as iconic and ubiquitous as "Suzanne." It is possible that her view might have been more positive had "Suzanne" remained a poem, something more acceptably bohemian, or, since it had entered the world of commerce, if some of the financial benefits had come her way, since her own career had not taken off as conspicuously and successfully as Leonard's had done with this song that bore her name. Also, the song as Suzanne saw it concerned an intimacy, and in reality there was only distance. Leonard had moved on.

In a 2006 CBC television documentary on Suzanne Verdal, the professor of literature Edward Palumbo was asked if the muse is expendable. "I think in the case of Suzanne it appears she really is, or was", was his answer. "On the other hand, the muse is bigger than the poet, at least in the mythology. The muse is the source of what there is, the inspiration. Does the muse have a claim on anything more than that role?" His conclusion was that she did not.[17]

It was Jung's belief that the muse *was* the poet, or his anima anyway, his unconscious image of the Feminine. It was himself that Leonard saw in the mirror Suzanne held. Allan Showalter, a psychiatrist,* explains, "The key task of a muse is to allow the artist to see his own feminine aspect that is otherwise invisible to him and to be a screen that fits the artist's projections. What completes the artist isn't the intrinsic qualities of the romantic interest but the artist's own feminine archetype. So, to the extent that the artist's projections dominate or replace the muse's own qualities, the muse's soul is dissipated."

The relationship between artist and muse is invariably one-sided:

---

* Showalter is known in Leonard Cohen circles as the webmaster of 1heckofa guy.com.

photographers "steal" their subjects' souls; novelists shamelessly make characters out of family and friends. Leonard the poet transformed the physical Suzanne into the metaphysical "Suzanne" and made her an angel. Leonard the magician sawed her down the middle, then put the two parts back together—the carnal and the spiritual—and made her more perfect than before. Leonard the composer made a hallowed melody of her, both implausibly intimate and ineffably spacious. "Suzanne" is a weightless, mysterious song. The great songs, the ones that keep drawing us back again and again, are mysteries. We go to them not for familiarity and solace—although there is solace in "Suzanne"—but for what is unknown, for something that's hidden in them that continues to haunt us and makes us seekers.

Leonard has spoken about the song and its muse often over the years; because it was his first, and, until "Hallelujah," best-known song, interviewers have kept asking him about them. In the liner notes for his 1975 *Greatest Hits* album, Leonard wrote, "Everything happened just as it was put down. She was the wife of a man I knew. Her hospitality was immaculate." To the filmmaker Harry Rasky in 1979 he elaborated: "An old friend of mine whose name was Suzanne invited me down to her place near the river. . . . The purity of the event was not compromised by any carnality. The song is almost a reportage. . . . But the song had been begun. It was as though she handed me the seed for the song." In a 1993 interview he generalized, "I find there's usually somebody in my life from whom I'm drawing enormous comfort and nourishment. . . . I always find there is someone in my life whom I can describe, without whom this wouldn't have happened."[18]

In 1994 he spoke about it at some length in a BBC radio interview. "The song was begun, and the chord pattern was developed, before a woman's name entered the song. And I knew it was a song about Montreal, it seemed to come out of that landscape that I loved very much in Montreal, which was the harbor, and the waterfront, and the sailors' church there, called Notre-Dame-de-Bon-Secours, which stood out over the river. . . . I knew that vision." Into that picture came "the wife of a friend of mine. They were a stunning couple around Montreal at the time, physically stunning—everyone was in love with Suzanne Vaillancourt, and every woman was in love with Armand Vaillancourt. But one would not allow oneself to think of toiling at the seduction of Armand Vaillancourt's wife. First of all he was a friend, and second of all as a couple they were inviolate. I bumped into her one evening, and she invited me down to her place near the river . . . She served me Constant Comment tea, which has little bits of oranges in it. And the boats were going by, and I touched her perfect body with my mind, because there was no other opportunity. There was no other way that you could touch her perfect body under those circumstances. So she provided the name in the song."[19] In recent years he described "Suzanne" as "a kind of doorway. I have to open it carefully, otherwise what's beyond is not accessible to me. It was never about a particular woman. It was about the beginning of a different life for me, my life wandering alone in Montreal."[20]

In a letter sent by Suzanne following our interview there was a footnote: "Leonard has stated publicly that he did not attempt to seduce me. He forgets that, much later, when he had achieved great fame, I had the opportunity to visit him in an East End hotel on rue Saint-Laurent. I was back from one of my travels and wanted to wish him well. He clearly expressed his desire to have physical intimacy but I declined. I had cherished the sanctity of our connection. I felt that if I had shared a sexual encounter with him it would shift that vibration that once had inspired us both. Ours was a soul connection as far as I was concerned."

"I read somewhere that we don't originate a thought, that thoughts arrive spontaneously, then fractions of a second later we take possession of them. In that sense nobody has an original thought. But original thoughts arise and we claim them."

So you didn't write "Suzanne" or "So Long, Marianne" or "Sisters of Mercy" about women you knew, they were outside thoughts that you claimed the copyright on?

"Einstein was modest enough to say that his theory of relativity came from outside. We'd like to think that we make these things up but actually the thing arises and we explain it as our own."

Are you still in contact with these women who have inspired your songs?

"Except for Suzanne Vaillancourt, who I just haven't bumped into in the past thirty years, I'm in contact with most of my friends, both men and women."

––––––––

Leonard's experiments with acid continued in Montreal. Says Aviva Layton, "The first-ever acid trip I ever went on was in 1964 in Leonard's apartment in Montreal. He gave me the acid on the end of his white handkerchief. It was from the very first batch from those professors from Harvard, Timothy Leary and Ram Dass. He sat with me for the entire day—which shows his generosity, because it's really boring to sit with somebody when they're on an acid trip." Three weeks later, at the Laytons' apartment, he did the same for Irving. "Irving resisted any drugs whatsoever, but Leonard persuaded him and I persuaded him, 'You've got to take acid.' Irving said, 'Acid will do nothing for me because I already live in an hallucinatory world.' Leonard gave him a little bit of blotting paper." For almost an hour they sat there, with Irving periodically interjecting, "See, nothing's happening." And then the drug kicked in. "Leonard saw Irving staring hard at the bookcases and Leonard said, 'What are you looking at?' Irving said, 'All the books are coming out one by one and bowing before me, every one of them.' We had tons and tons of books, a whole wall of them, each coming out and doing an obeisance in front of Irving, and then they all bowed in front of a painting of his mother." Irving never would admit that the drug had any effect on him. This, he told Leonard, was his "normal life."

In October '64, after receiving the Prix Litteraire du Quebec for *The Favorite Game,* Leonard and Irving Layton left with two other poets, Phyllis Gotlieb and Earle Birney, on a whirlwind reading tour of the university circuit—six schools and a library in one week. A filmmaker and sometime poet named Don Owen, an acquaintance of Leonard's, shot the performances for a purported National Film Board of Canada documentary—a project that was shelved when two of the poets proved less than engrossing on film. In the end, the footage would be employed in a documentary about just one of the poets. Right now that poet had gone to Greece; Leonard had a novel to write.

Leonard sat in his room in his house on the hill in Hydra, writing furiously. He was driven by an overpowering sense of urgency. He had the feeling, he said, of time running out. This was a strange sentiment for a thirty-year-old man, unless he were Jesus, or seriously ill, or thinking about suicide. "Around thirty or thirty-five is the traditional age for the suicide of the poet, did you know?" Leonard told Richard Goldstein of the *Village Voice* in 1967. "That's the age when you finally understand that the universe does not succumb to your command."[21]

It could be argued that the universe had done quite a good job of succumbing to Leonard. Within days of his thirtieth birthday he had been feted with a literary award and filmed on a poetry tour for a documentary, which would end up being entirely about him. He had good reviews and the respect of Canada's literati. He had a congregation of female admirers. He had won a grant that allowed him to live on a Greek island, where a beautiful woman kept house, put meals on his table and flowers on his desk, and allowed Leonard to do what he wanted to do, which was write his new novel, *Beautiful Losers.* "But when he worked," said Marianne, "sometimes it was torture to get it the way he wanted. Some of it came, *pouf!*, just like that, but he was a perfectionist, a man who demands much of himself."

Leonard went on to say that, in the process of writing *Beautiful Losers*, "I'd thought of myself as a loser. I was wiped out; I didn't like my life. I vowed I would just fill the pages with black or kill myself." He also said, "When you get wiped out . . . that's the moment, the REAL moment"—the true, ecstatic moment he had spoken of earlier, perhaps, which he said writers who hadn't been high or tasted madness could never know. Whether Leonard was high or mad during this period is debatable. He was unquestionably in an altered mental state while writing *Beautiful Losers*, smoking hash and taking acid and, above all, speed. A man can do a lot on amphetamine, and Leonard had given himself a great deal to do in his follow-up to *The Favorite Game*, with more mythologies to compare and another quest to undertake—or perhaps the same quest undertaken by another of his six or seven thousand selves.

Beautiful Losers is a prayer—at times a hysterically funny, filthy prayer—for the unity of the self, and a hymn to the loss of self through sainthood and transfiguration. Jesus might have nodded with fellow feeling; God might have finished it in six days instead of the nine months it took Leonard. It was "written in blood," Leonard said.[22] He was writing, at various points, ten, fifteen, twenty hours a day. He wrote on his terrace, in his basement room and "behind his house on a table set among the rocks, weeds and daisies."[23] He wrote with the Ray Charles album *The Genius Sings the Blues* for company, until the LP warped in the sun and then he turned on the radio, tuning it to the American Forces station, which mostly played country music. "It was a blazing hot summer. I never covered my head. What you have in your hands is more of a sunstroke than a book."[24] In a letter to Jack McClelland he talked his book up as "The Bhagavad-Gita of 1965"[25]; decades later, he talked it down in his foreword to the 2000 Chinese-language edition as an "odd collection of jazz-riffs, pop-art jokes, religious kitsch and muffled prayer." He told the press, "I think it's the best thing I've ever done."[26] It was all of the above.

When he finished typing the seven last words—"forever in your trip to the end"—Leonard went on a ten-day fast. He says, "I flipped out completely. It was my wildest trip. I hallucinated for a week. They took me to a hospital in Hydra." He was put on a protein drip. After they sent him home, he spent weeks in bed, hallucinating, he said, while Marianne took care of him. "I would like to say that it made me saintly," he said.[27]

It is tempting to suggest that Leonard was suffering manic-depression, a disorder thought to peak in men at the same age Leonard gave for poets committing suicide and whose indications include bouts of intense creative activity followed by paralysis, and a "messianic complex," a deep conviction of having something great or world-saving to do. On the other hand a similar effect might be achieved from taking large amounts of amphetamine, topped up with LSD, for long periods, working without a break and concluding all this with a ten-day fast. "Without a detailed set of observations by a witness on which to base a diagnosis," says Dr. Showalter, "I think the most one can claim would be that it is possible that Leonard Cohen's underlying diagnosis was bipolar disorder rather than major depressive disorder. But those symptoms could also result from a number of other disorders, including agitated psychotic state, intoxication, and various depressive and psychotic syndromes confounded by alcohol or drug abuse."

As Leonard told the story, one afternoon he looked up at the sky over Hydra and saw that it was "black with storks." The birds "alighted on all the churches and left in the morning." Leonard took this for a sign that he was better. "Then I decided to go to Nashville and become a songwriter."[28] Although he did not act on this decision immediately, music was certainly near the front of his consciousness during the writing of *Beautiful Losers*. One draft was subtitled *A Pop Novel*. Another included a section in which the narrative was set to guitar chords. In the published version, Leonard chose as an epigraph

"Somebody lift that bale," from the Kern-Hammerstein song "Ol'
Man River," in which a man tired of life and scared of death chooses
laughter over tears.

Leonard could not leave for Nashville at once because he was still
in time-limbo. He was coming down off speed and trying to adjust
to a place where time had already slowed down to a crawling pace,
a place where if you wanted to wash your face you might have to
wait for the water to come uphill on the back of a donkey. "Coming down is very bad," Leonard said. "It took me ten years to fully
recover. I had memory lapses. It was as if my insides were fried. I
couldn't get up anymore; I was in bed like a vegetable, incapable of
doing whatever for a long time."[29] He was exhausted. But he found
the wherewithal to send off copies of his manuscript to Viking in
New York and McClelland in Canada; the original was sold to the
Toronto University library that held his archive. He wrote a précis of
the book in which he spoke of a modern-day Montrealer "driven by
loneliness and despair" who "tries to heal himself by invoking the
name of Catherine Tekakwitha, an Iroquois girl whom the Jesuits
converted in the 17th century, and the first Indian maiden to take an
oath of Virginity."

"*Beautiful Losers*," he wrote, was "a love story, a psalm, a Black
Mass, a monument, a satire, a prayer, a shriek, a road map through the
wilderness, a joke, a tasteless affront, an hallucination, a bore, an irrelevant display of diseased virtuosity. In short," he concluded, it was
"a disagreeable religious epic of incomparable beauty."[30]

Eight

A Long Time Shaving

While Leonard was on Hydra, wasted and unglued, Marianne nursing him as Masha had nursed his father, in Canada two men were making a film that painted an entirely different picture. Its opening scene, shot in October 1964, showed a self-possessed young man who looked nothing like a speed freak, more like a well-bred, young Dustin Hoffman who still had a touch of baby fat. Standing onstage, entertaining a college audience with a story about visiting a friend in a Montreal mental hospital and being mistaken for an inmate, Leonard was droll, dry, self-deprecating and mannered, with the delivery and timing of a stand-up comic.

Ladies and Gentlemen . . . Mr. Leonard Cohen, which appeared in 1965, is a forty-four-minute, black-and-white documentary made up of footage shot by Don Owen on the previous year's four-poet university tour and new material shot by the National Film Board documentarian Donald Brittain. The latter depicts Leonard doing an assortment of cool-looking things in various cool-looking Montreal locations to a soundtrack of cool jazz. A voice-over describes him as "a singular talent with four books under his belt." (*Beautiful Losers* was finished but not yet published.) As affirmation of Leonard's celebrity in Canadian literature, this was several rungs up from the literary prizes and the *Six Montreal Poets* album.

It is a curious film, somewhere between a Leonard Cohen infomercial and a fly-on-the-wall study of Leonard at work and play. We observe him in Le Bistro and walking down the streets he used to roam as an adolescent, stopping to admire old movie posters outside a beautifully run-down cinema. We see him read a poem to a rapt audience of young women with teased hair and sixties makeup, then read the same poem to friends—Mort, Layton, Hershorn, May—only this time accompanying himself on guitar. We watch as he handles journalists and academics. We catch him unawares in his underpants in a cheap hotel room, which costs three dollars a night, we're told. We spy on him as he shaves, bathes, sleeps, expounds, ponders and sits writing at the small desk in his room, cigarette in one hand, pen in the other, while the streetlamp illuminates an overspilling ashtray and the lumps in the cheap wood-chip wallpaper.

Old home-movie footage underlines how much this contrasts with the life Leonard gave up for poetry: here's a cherubic little boy, standing by a car with the family's black chauffeur; here are his uncles, formally dressed in smart suits with boutonnieres; here are the grand houses of Westmount, whose residents, Leonard says, dream "of Jewish sex and bank careers." The path he chose, Leonard says, was "infinitely wide and without direction." His first concern when he wakes in the morning is "to discover if I am in a state of grace," which he defines as "the balance with which you ride the chaos around you." The film is full of the grand, ironic, playful and deflecting statements of the kind Leonard would come to employ in interviews throughout his career. Irving Layton was correct when he said on camera that Leonard's main concern really was "to preserve the self." Despite the appearance of vérité, much of the film is pure theater, as inscrutably and entertainingly fictionalized an account of Leonard's life as is *The Favorite Game.*

Being shown living in a run-down hotel in Montreal was better for the *poète maudit* image than the duplex Leonard rented near McGill, and it also guarded his privacy. Yet he was being truthful when he talked in the film about hotels being a "kind of a temple of refuge, a sanctuary of a temporary kind, so all the more delicious." Leonard would often seek out refuges and sanctuaries—spiritual, terrestrial and sexual—and show no inclination to want to linger too long in any. The hotel life might have been made for him. It was uncomplicated. The cheaper the hotel, the more uncomplicated it was: just the basics, no one bothering you, you're left alone to do what you want. And in a hotel, whatever you might do, the next morning your room will be cleaned, your sin expunged, leaving you free to start over or move on.

"Whenever I come into a hotel room," Leonard told the camera, "there is a moment after the door is shut and the lights you haven't turned on illumine a very comfortable, anonymous, subtly hostile environment, and you know that you've found the little place in the grass and the hounds are going to go by for three more hours and you're going to drink, light a cigarette and take a long time shaving." A good solution, as his mother advised him, when things got tough. Released on the cusp of Leonard's move into a music career, *Ladies and Gentlemen . . . Mr. Leonard Cohen* appears in retrospect less a portrait of a serious literary figure than of a pop/rock celebrity in training.

"Find a little saint and fuck her over and over in some pleasant part of heaven, get right into her plastic altar, dwell in her silver medal, fuck her until she tinkles like a souvenir music box . . . find one of these quaint impossible cunts and fuck her for your life, coming all over the sky, fuck her on the moon with a steel hourglass up your hole."

Beautiful Losers was published in the spring of 1966. There had been no book in Canada like it—nothing by Leonard Cohen like it either, even if some of its motifs (love, loneliness, friendship, God, ecstasy, the atrocities of modern life) might have had a familiar feel. The protagonist, whom we know only as "I," is an anthropologist, "an old scholar, wild with unspecific grief," who has fallen in love with a dead, young seventeenth-century Indian whose picture he happened upon while studying a near-extinct Native Canadian tribe. Catherine Tekakwitha, or "Kateri," is a martyr and a saint, the first Iroquois to take an oath of virginity, and an outsider, unable to live in the world she inhabited. "I" is an outsider too, and lonely, so lonely; despite its frenzied humor and bombast, this is one of the loneliest of Leonard's books.

I's wife, Edith, had committed suicide by sitting at the bottom of an elevator shaft, waiting quietly to be crushed. "F.," the protagonist's best friend, guru, masturbation buddy and sometimes lover (and Edith's lover too), is a madman, savant, Canadian separatist politician and, possibly, saint, who is in the hospital dying from syphilis, a martyr to Montreal but even more so to his cock. However, it's possible that F. is I, that all the characters might be the same person. There's a peyote quality to the book, its characters shape-shifting and dissolving. Sometimes they appear to be gods, but there's a comic earthiness too. *Beautiful Losers* is a prayer for both union and emptiness, and a quest for sexual and spiritual fulfillment. It's a satire on life in the sixties. It's also a treatise on the history of Canada: before the Jesuits came to the country, Catherine would have frolicked happily in the long grass with the boys of her tribe, at one with nature, the gods and man. Canada too had fallen from grace, with the vacuity of urban life and the "two solitudes," the schism between its English and French populations. Maybe it would set things right if he could go back in time and fuck this young saint, or if he could fuck like his old, sainted friend/teacher, or if he himself could be a modern saint, a celluloid Buddha.

Beautiful Losers is "a redemptive novel, an exercise to redeem the soul," Leonard said in a 1967 interview. "In that book I tried to wrestle with all the deities that are extant now—the idea of saintliness, purity, pop, McLuhanism, evil, the irrational—all the gods we set up for ourselves."[1] In a CBC television interview he said, "I was writing a liturgy, but using all the techniques of the modern novel. So there's this huge prayer using the conventional techniques of pornographic suspense, of humor, of plot, of character development and conventional intrigue."[2] He said he "was not interested in guarding anything," and he didn't. *Beautiful Losers* is excessive, manic, free—not tidied up into perfectly edited scenes like *The Favorite Game*. It mixes high and low art, poetry and Hollywood, lyrical beauty and the language of comic books. *The Favorite Game* had been considered a groundbreaking book; *Beautiful Losers* was truly groundbreaking. The *Globe and Mail* described it as "verbal masturbation"; the *Toronto Daily Star* called it "the most revolting book ever written in Canada," but also the "Canadian book of the year."

Leonard was most unhappy at how the book was received on publication and at how badly it sold in Canada—an understandable reaction given how intense the experience of writing the book had been. Word reached Jack McClelland that Leonard blamed his publisher, complaining about the book's price, its design, its poor distribution and lack of advertising. McClelland was angry. He felt that he had gone out on a limb to publish the book. When he had first read Leonard's manuscript in May 1965, McClelland found it "appalling, shocking, revolting, sick," but also "wild and incredible and marvellously well written." "I'm not going to pretend that I dig it, because I don't," he wrote to Leonard. "I'm sure it will end up in the courts, but that might be worth trying. You are a nice chap, Leonard, and it's lovely knowing you. All I have to decide now is whether I love you enough to spend the rest of my days in jail for you."[3] He had proven that he did, and now a year later, Leonard was "bitching because *Beautiful Losers* is not available in all stores. . . . Just what in hell did you expect?

You may be naïve but you are certainly not stupid. Booksellers have a perfect right to decide what they will sell and what they will not sell. Many stores have decided that they don't want to take the risk of handling this book." McClelland reminded Leonard that they had thrown a big promotional party for the book, whose value was "almost totally lost because you didn't think it suited your image or were unwilling to put yourself out. . . . I am beginning to think," McClelland concluded, "that the National Film Board did you no favor."[4] What McClelland was implying was that *Ladies and Gentlemen . . . Mr. Leonard Cohen* had gone to Leonard's head.

Beautiful Losers did not enjoy huge sales in the U.S. either (although one copy would be bought by a young Lou Reed), despite the review in the *Boston Globe* that declared, "James Joyce is not dead. He is living in Montreal." In 1970 the book was given its UK publication by Jonathan Cape. The publisher, Tom Maschler, was "amazed by *Beautiful Losers*." "I thought it quite wonderful," he says, "an original and important novel." The *Times Literary Supplement* ran a review whose length reflected Leonard's celebrity as a recording artist by that time:[*] "*Beautiful Losers* is an abstraction of all searches for a lost innocence. . . . [It] suffers badly from uncharacterised characters, cosmic desperations, unresolved even in the throes of frantic sex, the compulsively-listed paraphernalia of the environment and the iconographic employment of all the modern communications phenomena the author can manage to drag in. It's a novel that features wanking in a moving car, a masturbation machine that goes over to its own power supply, Brigitte Bardot and (you guessed) the Rolling Stones. It's a novel that's got everything, and that is exactly its trouble: with everything for a subject it has no subject and rounds itself out with

---

* The critic, Nicolas Walter, was clearly no fan of Leonard's music: "The impact on a young student of a song like 'Dress Rehearsal Rag' must be overwhelming," he wrote, "but in fact the song is merely an abstraction of all currently fashionable moods of doom, and in any case, overwhelming art is the kind you grow out of."

rhetoric like a bad poem trying to talk itself into shape. There is talent here, but no sense of limit."[5]

Leonard, said Irving Layton, "is one of the few writers who has voluntarily immersed himself in the destructive element, not once but many times, then walked back from the abyss with dignity to tell us what he saw, to put a frame around the wind. I see Leonard as the white mouse they put down into a submarine to see if the air is foul— he is the white mouse of civilisation who tests its foulness."[6]

The gospels diverge on exactly when and where Leonard decided to become a singer-songwriter. According to the journalist and socialite Barbara Amiel, it was in the summer of 1965, in Toronto, in a suite at the King Edward Hotel. Leonard was composing tunes on a harmonica and singing his poems to a female friend while elsewhere in the suite a naked couple were "getting it on." Leonard took this as a positive response. He announced, "I think I'm going to record myself singing my poems." His companion winced and said, "Please don't"[7]—though she was a touch too late, since Leonard had been filmed singing and playing guitar in *Ladies and Gentlemen . . . Mr. Leonard Cohen*. The song he performed was called "Chant"— he would later describe it as the first song he ever wrote.[8] It had a somewhat "Teachers"-like melody, over which Leonard chanted the words:

> *Hold me hard light, soft light hold me*
> *Moonlight in your mountains fold me*
> *Hold me hard light, soft light hold me*

Ira B. Nadel dated it to some six months later in his Cohen biography, at a poetry event presided over by F. R. Scott and attended by Irving Layton, Louis Dudek, Ralph Gustafson, A. J. M. Smith and Al Purdy. "Leonard played his guitar, sang, and raved about Dylan," and since no one in the room had ever heard of Dylan, Scott took off for a record shop, returning with *Bringing It All Back Home* and *Highway 61 Revisited*. He put the albums on, Nadel wrote, "to the chagrin of everyone" besides Leonard, who listened "intently, solemnly" and announced to the room "that *he* would become the Canadian Dylan."[9] But by Leonard's own account—in 1967 in the *Village Voice* and to any number of music journalists since, this biographer included—his intention was to write country songs, not to be a folk-rock singer-songwriter. He was more comfortable with country, given his history of being in the Buckskin Boys, than he was with folk or rock, genres with which he felt out of touch. Leonard himself dated his decision to a few weeks after the completion of *Beautiful Losers*, following a ten-day fast and a period in the wilderness.

Marianne Ihlen says that Leonard was talking about making records as far back as the early sixties. "We were sitting in one of these diners in Montreal where there are two leather couches and a table in the middle and on the wall was one of those little jukeboxes. Leonard said, 'Marianne, my dream is to have one of my songs in one of these boxes.' It was a long process. Leonard always had a guitar with him. If he sat at a table playing, suddenly there were twenty-five people standing around the table, so you could call it a performance, even though what he was doing was playing for us. You could hear in his voice that something was happening."

In the midsixties, Leonard's Montreal filmmaker friend Henry Zemel, who had heard him sing at Dunn's Birdland in 1958, recorded Leonard playing guitar and singing on an old Uher reel-to-reel at Zemel's house on Sherbrooke Street. The room had exceptional acoustics, Zemel says, and Leonard, Mort, Derek May and various musicians, including local folk band the Stormy Clovers, would come over to jam. The music on Zemel's tape sounds neither country nor folk. It is mostly instrumental, a mysterious mix of John Cage, Eastern music, flamenco and ancient field recordings, but one can hear

Leonard—accompanied by Zemel, improvising on tom-tom and Chinese flute—seeming to be working out his signature guitar sound. The last piece on Zemel's tape is an unknown and untitled song written by Leonard, on which he sings/intones, as if it were a dirge, the words "I can't wait." During this period Leonard also composed instrumental music for a short, experimental film made by his friend Derek May, titled *Angel*, in 1966. Leonard made an appearance in the film, conversing in a park with a woman with a dog who took it in turns to wear wings. His music was performed on the soundtrack by the Stormy Clovers.

So it happened by degrees, sometimes in public, more often in private, alone or with friends. In February 1966 in New York, appearing at the 92nd Street Y for a reading, Leonard closed by singing "The Stranger Song"—a little slower, his voice strained and plaintive, and with a handful of different words, but otherwise much as it would appear two years later on his first album. In 1968 Leonard told the *Montreal Gazette*, "I just see the singing as an extension of a voice I've been using ever since I can remember. This is just one aspect of its sound." In 1969 he told the *New York Times*, "There is no difference between a poem and a song. Some were songs first and some were poems first and some were situations. All of my writing has guitars behind it, even the novels."

But everybody, including Leonard, agrees on why he decided to be a singer-songwriter: economics.

"Well, I always played the guitar and sang. I'd been living in Greece for a number of years and it was a very good way of living, I could live in Greece for eleven hundred dollars a year, but I couldn't pay my grocery bill, so I would come back to Canada, get various jobs, get that money together plus the boat fare, come back to Greece and live for as long as that money lasted. I couldn't make a living as an author. My books weren't selling, they were receiving very good reviews, but my second novel Beautiful Losers *sold about three thousand copies worldwide. The only economic alternative*

was, I guess, going into teaching or university or getting a job in a bank, like the great Canadian poet Raymond Souster. But I always played the guitar and sang, so it was an economic solution to the problem of making a living and being a writer."

Hydra was cheap, and Leonard had a $750-a-year inheritance, but living there had proven impossible on a writer's income. *Beautiful Losers*, despite the controversy and attention, did not sell in significant numbers until Leonard became a recording artist and it was reissued in paperback. He published a fourth volume of poetry in 1966, which made no impact on his bank balance. The poems in *Parasites of Heaven*—some dating back to the late fifties—were also about love, loneliness and despair, but more conventional in structure than those of *Flowers for Hitler* and more personal, more like songs. Michael Ondaatje noted that while the poems in *Flowers for Hitler* "had a cast of thousands, these have a cast of one or two [and] the objects of his descriptions are not intense public tortures but private pain and quietness."[10] He could well have been describing a sensitive sixties singer-songwriter. And *Parasites of Heaven*, while it was generally treated by literary critics as an insubstantial work, was significant for fans of Leonard's music, as it included a number of his future songs: "Suzanne," "Master Song," "Teachers," "Avalanche" and "Fingerprints."

In the summer of 1966 CBC offered Leonard a position cohosting a new television show. His job would entail interviewing guests, making short films and commentating. Leonard accepted enthusiastically; he had often spoken about looking for an audience beyond the ivory tower—"I think the time is over when poets should sit on marble stairs with black capes"[11]—and this seemed a golden opportunity. He told the *Toronto Daily Star* that his intention was "to get close to the viewers, get them to participate in the show, even send in home movies"[12]—an interactive approach that was unusual in the middle sixties. But the TV show came to nothing. The producer Andrew Simon was reported as saying that Leonard changed his mind: "There was no fight. It was a personal-emotional thing. Leonard felt that God hadn't put him here to be a TV star." In the same article, though, Leonard said that he had no problem with the idea of a poet being on television: "I've always felt very different from other poets I've met. I've always felt that somehow they've made a decision against life. Most of them have closed a lot of doors. I never felt too much at home with those kind of people. I always felt more at home with musicians. I like to write songs and sing and that kind of stuff."[13]

All the signs were pointing to music. In 1966 Leonard borrowed some money from his friend Robert Hershorn and set off for Nashville.

Why Nashville and country music? There was a lot more interesting music going on and places to be in 1966.

"I listened to the Armed Forces Radio that came out of Athens and it had a lot of good country music on it. I had a few records there—Ray Charles, Edith Piaf, Nina Simone, Charlie and Inez Foxx, Sylvie Vartan; she did a Nashville record, in French; I don't know if you ever heard it, it's a great record—and I listened to those and to the radio. But I didn't know what was going on in America. Elvis Presley was the only guy that I was listening to, and the Shirelles, and the very early murmurings of Motown. I thought I would head down to Nashville and maybe get work down there. On the way down I stopped off in New York, and that's where I bumped into the so-called folk-song renaissance, which included Joan Baez and Dylan and Phil Ochs, Judy Collins, Joni Mitchell. This was the first time I'd heard their songs. I thought: I'd been writing those little songs for a while, just playing them for my friends, so I thought I'd try my hand at that and try presenting them to some kind of commercial institution who might be able to use them."

———

Stepping from the train at Pennsylvania Station, dressed in his blue raincoat, Leonard walked along Thirty-fourth Street to the Penn

Terminal Hotel, suitcase and guitar in hand. A New York noir movie of a hotel, it was cheap and it looked it: dark brown brick, dark narrow corridors, an elevator just big enough for a man and a corpse. The window in his oddly shaped room had been screwed into a position that was neither open nor closed; the radiator hissed like a steam train, to which the dripping tap in the brown-streaked washbasin added a slow, perpetual accompaniment. It was a terrible room, Leonard concluded with no real animosity—he would think that whenever he stayed at the Penn Terminal, which was fairly often, even when he could afford somewhere better. His clothes hung loosely on his 116-pound postamphetamine frame. When he looked at his reflection in the mirror he saw a man who looked like he had lived on a mountain for several years. Leonard had a shave and then he headed out. He had a woman to meet.

Robert Hershorn had told Leonard about Mary Martin. She had moved from her native Toronto to New York in 1962, finding her way to Greenwich Village. She had worked her way up from a hostess job at the Bitter End folk club to executive assistant to Albert Grossman, Bob Dylan's manager, then director of A & R at Warner Bros. and, in 1966, the head of her own artist management company. In the male-dominated music business of the early sixties—what few women there were were mostly behind a microphone: Joan Baez, Judy Henske, Carolyn Hester, Judy Collins—Martin was an exception. She had a track record of helping Canadian musicians: she had been instrumental in getting the Hawks, later known as the Band, the job as Dylan's backing band, and she also managed Leonard's acquaintances the Stormy Clovers. "A very enterprising and very sensitive woman," said Leonard, "and very supportive."[14] Leonard liked supportive women. He talked to Martin about his novels and his poetry and told her he had written a couple of things that he thought might be a song. Impressed with what she had heard, she told him she'd see what she could do. Then she called her friend Judy Collins.

Collins, then twenty-seven years old, was an aristocrat of the Greenwich Village scene: cool, elegant, with long straight hair and such remarkable blue eyes that Stephen Stills wrote a song about them.* She had begun as a classical pianist from Seattle, first performing with a symphony orchestra when she was thirteen, and then she discovered folk music. It led her to New York in 1961, where she moved into a two-dollar-a-night hotel, and barely had time to unpack before Jac Holzman, who owned and ran Elektra Records, saw her play at the Village Gate and offered her a record deal. Her first album, *A Maid of Constant Sorrow*—traditional folk—was released the same year. Holzman had previously tried without success to sign Joan Baez, who was the reigning queen of traditional folk and protest songs. He had been looking for his own Baez ever since, but it did not take him long to see that he had a quite different artist in Collins, who was musically much more experimental. This made her a more valuable commodity in the midsixties, at a time when traditional folk began its move into folk-rock.

When Leonard arrived in Manhattan in the summer of 1966, Collins was working on her sixth, and until then most innovative, album, *In My Life*. As well as the Beatles song of the title, she covered songs by Dylan, Donovan, Randy Newman, even Brecht and Weill. But Holzman, though he liked where she was heading, still thought there was something missing. "I told her, 'It doesn't fly yet, we need more songs,'" says Holzman. "Judy said, 'Where the hell am I going to get more songs?' I said, 'Put it out there that you're looking.' So she did, somewhat downheartedly. Then about ten days later I get a call from Judy saying, 'I've met the most wonderful writer.'"

Telling the story of the first time she met Leonard, Judy Collins laughs out loud. Two businessmen sitting at the next table in the

---

* "Suite: Judy Blue Eyes" was recorded with David Crosby and Graham Nash in 1969.

hushed hotel in Beverly Hills look up from their expense-account lunches to stare at this magnificent seventy-one-year-old with a long mane of pure white hair and dressed in a sharp rockabilly jacket.

It was early evening, she remembers, in early fall. She opened her door and there stood "a small man in a dark suit, good-looking, shy." He said Mary Martin had sent him and he had come to sing her his songs. "All the singers with new songs would come to me," she said, "because I had the record contract and I could get them out, and because I didn't write my own songs—not until 1967, and I only wrote them because Leonard said to me, 'Why aren't you writing your own songs?'" Mary Martin "would always talk about Leonard," Collins recalls. "It was 'Leonard this,' 'Leonard that.' She kept saying, 'Oh you've got to help him, you've got to hear the songs.' I liked and respected Mary so I said, 'Well what does he do?' She said, 'He writes poetry and he has written a novel, and he's written something he thinks is a song, and he wants to come down here and see you.' Most of the people in the Village would literally grab you on the street, throw you down on the floor and sing you the song before you'd even said hello. So I said, 'By all means, let him come.'

"He came to my house, we had some wine, and then we went to Tony's [a neighborhood Italian restaurant] for food, and then he left—no songs! We were having a conversation, you see, about things that mattered, and of course music matters, but not when you can have a really good conversation with someone. We talked about life, living in New York, Ibiza—Leonard had just come back from Ibiza and so had my lover Michael. And we talked about literature. By then I'd read of some of his poetry, and also *Beautiful Losers*. Michael was a writer also—he wrote a movie called *Scandal*, which is about the Profumo Affair—so we had a lot to talk about. When Leonard left I think I said, 'I've heard about these famous songs. Why don't you come back tomorrow?'"

Leonard returned the next day with his guitar. This time he sat in her living room and sang three songs: "Suzanne," "Dress Rehearsal Rag" and "The Stranger Song." Collins was "bowled over," she said, "particularly by 'Dress Rehearsal Rag.' Talk about dark: a song about suicide. I attempted suicide myself at fourteen, before I found folk music, so of course I loved it. We were desperately looking for something unusual for my album and when I heard 'Dress Rehearsal Rag,' that was it. 'The Stranger Song' I thought the least accessible of the three songs he sang—nowadays I love it and would do it in a second, but I was not there yet. Then Michael said, 'You have to do that "Suzanne" one too.' I thought about it and said, 'Yes, it has to be "Dress Rehearsal Rag" and "Suzanne" as well.'"

In accounts of the story elsewhere, Judy did not hear anything that day that she could use but told Leonard to keep in touch if he wrote any new songs, which reportedly he did, playing "Suzanne" to her over the phone from his mother's house in Montreal in December 1966. "Bullshit," says Collins. "We talked about my recording 'Dress Rehearsal Rag' right away and 'Suzanne' the next day." The evidence is in Collins's favor given that *In My Life*, which contained her covers of "Dress Rehearsal Rag" and "Suzanne," was released in November 1966. Jac Holzman confirms that Collins recorded the songs almost as soon as she heard them. "They were great," says Holzman, "the quality of the songs, the simple complexity, the internal rhymes—the lyrics are magical in their completeness. You finish listening to a song of Leonard's and you know he's said everything he had to say, he didn't let that song go until he's finished with it. Those two songs were the glue we needed to hold it all together." With the other songs ready to go and the photo for the front sleeve in place, it was a simple case of correcting the titles and credits before the record was in the stores and starting its climb into the Top 50.

"Suzanne" had its first airing on the New York radio station WBAI. "Judy Collins had a regular program," says disc jockey Bob

Fass. "It would be on for an hour, and she would sing herself and play records and have other musicians on; it was very popular. I was the engineer. Judy would give me her records a little in advance so I could play them on my program. She played me 'Suzanne' and I said, 'Judy, did you write that?' She said, 'No, Leonard Cohen.' 'Who's Leonard Cohen?' 'He's a Canadian poet.' Funny, after Judy Collins mentioned him, a young woman appeared at my door on Greenwich Avenue, climbed the steps and said, 'I'm here to talk about Leonard Cohen,' and we had some very pleasant hours together. I think she was a friend of his—I felt like I was being checked out. And I never saw her again. One of those mysteries."

Collins was so supportive of Leonard and sang his praises so generously that many assumed they were lovers. "We weren't," says Collins. "He's the kind of dangerous man that I would have gotten involved with and gotten into a lot of trouble with. He was charming and very intriguing, very deep, but I never had those feelings about him. I loved his songs and that was plenty. That was enough trouble." Collins laughs. "But his songs—there was nothing like them around. Nobody, including Dylan. Leonard was an unskilled, untrained musician, but because of his intelligence and sheer stubbornness, I suppose, he taught himself the guitar and he came up with songs which were very unusual—the melodic structure is not something that you would normally find and there are unexpected changes and twists and turns in every piece he does. They're brilliant, articulate, literary and utterly beyond. That's what hooked me. And the fact that a Jew from Canada can take the Bible to pieces and give the Catholics a run for their money on every story they ever thought they knew."

Leonard did continue to send Collins songs. "He was writing new songs all the time. By that time I was in so over my head with his material that I was ready to record anything he sent me. And as you know, I practically did—anything, everything. I think there was a Leonard song on practically every album after that"—three on her 1967 album and first Top 5 hit, *Wildflowers*: "Sisters of Mercy," "Priests" and "Hey, That's No Way to Say Goodbye," this last song composed to the sound of a radiator and dripping tap in a thin-walled hotel room on Thirty-fourth Street. It arose "from an over-used bed in the Penn Terminal Hotel in 1966," Leonard wrote in the liner notes to his 1975 *Greatest Hits* album. "The room is too hot. I can't open the windows. I am in the midst of a bitter quarrel with a blonde woman. The song is half-written in pencil but it protects us as we maneuver, each of us, for unconditional victory. I am in the wrong room. I am with the wrong woman."[15] This was not Marianne—though, when she saw the lyrics in his notebook, Leonard said she did ask whom it was about. Marianne was on Hydra. In the maelstrom of his life in New York, Hydra felt a million miles away.

Less than two months after arriving in Manhattan, Leonard had a manager and two songs on a major artist's album. He had discovered, to his joy, that he could write songs "on the run,"[16] that writing did not have to be the life-and-death ordeal it had been with *Beautiful Losers*. He had found that he could live in real life as he had on film: in a cheap hotel, unfettered and within arm's reach of an exit. Leonard put his plan to go to Nashville on hold. Instead, he packed his case and moved into the Henry Hudson Hotel on West Fifty-seventh Street. It was not, in the midsixties, the glamorous boutique hotel it is today; it was more like a low-rent version of the Chelsea Hotel, with the look and smell of a Victorian hospital for down-and-outs. If someone were taking a register of junkies, hustlers, drifters and penniless artists, many of its residents would have raised their hands.

Leonard's room, with its flowery curtain and threadbare counterpane, was barely twice the size of its single bed. But the window closed, at least, and there was a swimming pool in the hotel, as well as hashish and several young women willing to keep him warm at night. There was a tall Swedish woman who studied yoga and turned tricks; a pretty young writer, barely twenty years old, who was fighting a narcotics charge, with a little financial support from Leonard; and the lovely homeless artist whom Leonard invited in off the street and who, he found, shared his fascination with Saint Catherine Teka-kwitha. Saint Catherine's image was embossed on a door of Saint Patrick's Cathedral on Fifth Avenue between Fiftieth and Fifty-first Streets. Leonard would go there and climb the stone steps, a pilgrim, and lay a flower at her feet.

———————

Although it might not have won an arm-wrestling contest with Green-wich Village, the Montreal folk music scene was thriving. Penny Lang, a singer and guitar player, had been playing the city's coffee-houses since 1963. "If you liked folk music you didn't have to search for it, it seemed like it was everywhere. There were seven or eight coffeehouses but a lot of music happened spontaneously, in parks and other places. It felt very vibrant, as if a side of the city woke up which had been sleeping for a long time." Lang did not hear of Leonard ("I didn't read poetry") until 1966, when the Stormy Clovers started playing "Suzanne." "Then the song sort of passed down to the other singers around town and I learned it, and came up with a sort of dif-ferent version. He's an exquisite writer, there was no one who writes as he does. And that's really all I knew about Leonard Cohen."

It was December and Leonard, back once again in Canada, was thinking hard about this music career into which he had made his first inroads. He wrote a letter to Marianne telling her that he knew what he must be, "a singer, a man who owns nothing. . . . I know now what I must train myself for."[17] He phoned Penny Lang. "It was the first time I'd ever spoken to him and he just called and said, 'Would you consider teaching me some guitar'?" says Lang. "But I was in very bad shape—I'm bipolar—and I said, 'No, I'm very depressed,' and that was the end of that. Later I realized that if anyone would have understood the word 'depression' at the time, it probably would have been Leonard." Lang would make her own way to New York a few months later, where a talent scout from Warner Bros. heard her play "Suzanne" at Gerde's in Greenwich Village and offered her a deal if she would record it with a rock band. "When 'rock band' came into the picture I said no." Lang did say yes to giving guitar lessons to Janis Joplin. Janis wanted to be able to accompany herself onstage when singing her version of Kris Kristofferson's "Me and Bobby McGee." "But it never happened, because Janis died." Leonard did not ask again. He practiced alone, playing in front of a full-length mirror to an audience of one, the only one whose opinion really mattered.

What was with the mirror?

"Through some version of narcissism, I always used to play in front of a mirror—I guess it was to figure out the best way to look while playing guitar, or maybe it was just where the chair was and the mirror in the room I happened to be living in. But I was very comfortable looking at myself playing."

The more he played, the more songs would come. It was as if his relatively minimal skills as a guitar player added a simplicity to the proceedings. "I was always interested by minimalism, even if we didn't use that term. I liked simple things, simple poetry, more than the decorative."[18] In the same way that the poetry he wrote had an implied melody, his melodies had an implied poetry. "I generally find the song arises out of the guitar playing, just fooling around on the guitar. Just trying different sequences of chords, really, just like playing guitar every day and singing until I make myself cry, then I stop. I don't weep copiously, I just feel a little catch in my throat or something like that. Then I know that I am in contact with something that is just a little deeper than where I started when I picked the guitar up."[19]

Leonard's letter to Marianne closed with the words, "Darling, I hope we can repair the painful spaces where uncertainties have led us. I hope you can lead yourself out of despair and I hope I can help you."[20] The mailman arrived with a package for Leonard from New York: Judy Collins's new album. Carrying it carefully, by the edges, to the turntable, he placed the needle on track four. The snow was thick outside; in a few days baby Jesus would be reborn. Leonard, alone in his room in West Montreal, listened to Judy sing "Suzanne." When it was done playing he lifted the needle and put it back at the start of the track, over, and over, and over.

Nine

How to Court a Lady

———

The ad in the *Village Voice* read "Andy Warhol Presents Nico Singing to the Sounds of the Velvet Underground." It was February 1967 and Leonard, back in New York again, turned up the collar on his raincoat and walked through the East Village to the Dom. The cavernous room in a row of Victorian town houses on Saint Mark's Place had been a German immigrant community hall, a Polish restaurant and a music venue before Warhol had taken over the lease a year earlier and transformed it into an avant-garde circus-discotheque. It was the stage for his Exploding Plastic Inevitable performance art shows, offering experimental films (Warhol's and Paul Morrissey's), dancers (beauties and freaks from Warhol's Factory studio, like the socialite-turned-Warhol-film-star Edie Sedgwick and poet-photographer Gerard Malanga) and music. The house band was the Velvet Underground, whom Warhol managed. At his decree, their singer and songwriter Lou Reed, a short, young, Jewish New Yorker, shared the spotlight with a tall, blond German in her late twenties. Nico, said Lou Reed, "set some kind of standard for incredible-looking people."

Leonard happened upon Nico by chance. One night, during his last stay in New York, he had wandered into a nightclub and there she was, an ice queen, posed like Dietrich at the end of the bar. She had a chiseled face, porcelain skin, piercing eyes and a pretty-boy guitar player, who was her sole accompanist as she sang her songs in a strange, deep monotone. "I was completely taken," Leonard said. "I had been through the blonde trip; I had lived with a blonde girl and I had felt for a long time that I was living in a Nazi poster. This was a kind of repetition."[1] (Since he was presumably referring to Marianne, it might also have some bearing on why Marianne had to move out during Leonard's mother's visit.)

The woman who would become Leonard's next muse was born Christa Päffgen in Cologne in 1938, four years after Leonard was born and five years after Hitler came to power. She was a fashion model in Berlin and an actress who studied alongside Marilyn Monroe at Lee Strasberg's Method school in New York, and won a small role in Fellini's *La Dolce Vita* (1960) and a large one in Jacques Poitrenaud's *Strip-Tease* (1963). The first time she went into a recording studio was in Paris, with Serge Gainsbourg, to sing the title song for *Strip-Tease*, which he wrote. Her somber, death's-head voice was not to Gainsbourg's taste and a version by Juliette Gréco was used in its place.* Nico's second attempt at recording was more successful—in London this time, in 1965, with an equally celebrated producer, guitarist Jimmy Page. Her cover of Canadian folksinger Gordon Lightfoot's song "I'm Not Sayin'" was released as a single on Immediate Records, a label owned by Andrew Loog Oldham, the manager of the Rolling Stones; the Stones' guitar player Brian Jones was Nico's lover.

A liaison with Bob Dylan brought Nico back to New York. While Dylan was babysitting her son, Ari—the result of her brief affair with

---

* Nico's version was released posthumously on the compilation album *Le cinéma de Serge Gainsbourg* (2001).

the French movie star Alain Delon—Dylan wrote the song "I'll Keep It with Mine," which he gave to Nico. When his manager Albert Grossman sent her a plane ticket to New York, she assumed it was because Grossman wanted to manage her as a singer. He did not. But through the Dylan/Grossman connection she met Warhol, and Warhol thought her perfect. He put her in his films—most famously *Chelsea Girls,* in which Ari, then four years old, also appeared—and he put her in the Velvet Underground. Her bored, narcotic, gothic voice was featured on both sides of the band's first single, "All Tomorrow's Parties"/"I'll Be Your Mirror," which was released in October 1966, around the same time that Leonard was playing Judy Collins his songs. Leonard took to following Nico around New York, his unwitting tourist guide leading him from one haunt of the hip and demimonde to another.

"I remember walking into a club called Max's Kansas City that I'd heard was the place where everybody went—I didn't know anybody in New York—and I remember lingering by the bar, I was never good at that kind of hard work that's involved with socializing, and a young man came over to me and said, "You're Leonard Cohen, you wrote Beautiful Losers," *which nobody had read, it only sold a few copies in America. And it was Lou Reed. He brought me over to a table full of luminaries—Andy Warhol, Nico. I was suddenly sitting at this table with the great spirits of the time. [Laughs]"*

But you were more interested in talking to Nico. How did it go?

"I was among the multitudes that wanted Nico. A mysterious woman. I tried to talk to her, I introduced myself, but she wasn't interested."

Says Lou Reed, *"Beautiful Losers* is an incredible book, an amazing book, and on top of everything else, incredibly funny and very tricky. I remember later Leonard said to me he started writing songs after hearing 'I'll Be Your Mirror.' Who knows."[2] Leonard took a liking to Reed, at least in some part because Nico liked him.

You would imagine that Leonard and Warhol might get along, two men who believed in making their life their work, and their work their life. But, as with the Beats, Leonard claimed not to fit in. They made him feel provincial. According to Danny Fields, though, "There was no club that Leonard wasn't part of. We loved him, Nico loved him, I loved him, he was loved. His reputation then was fierce—and he was sexy. He didn't have to do very much except not vomit on the table." Fields was Elektra Records's New York A & R man, a close friend of Nico, who knew the midsixties Manhattan scene like the back of his hand. It was something else with Leonard, a kind of shyness, or a taste for being an outsider, or both, that turned the once-clubby youth into a man who really did not want to join any club, whether they wanted him or not.

Nico told Leonard she liked younger men and did not make an exception. Her young man du jour, her guitar player, was a fresh-faced singer-songwriter from Southern California, barely eighteen years old, named Jackson Browne. A surfer boy crossed with an angel, his natural good looks appeared unnatural alongside the cadaverous Warhol and his black-clad entourage. Browne had gone to New York on an adventure: some friends were driving cross-country and needed someone to split the bill; Browne grabbed his acoustic guitar and his mother's gas station credit card. When they rolled into Manhattan, Browne, looking up through the back window, saw "all these huge Nico posters everywhere, really beautiful, just amazing."[3] They were advertising her solo shows. Opening the show was Tim Buckley, a singer-songwriter Browne knew from the Orange County coffeehouse circuit. Buckley told him Nico was looking for a full-time electric guitarist and, since he "had his own thing going," he didn't want to do it. Browne borrowed an electric guitar.

Nico opened the door to her apartment. She looked him up and down with her famous stare. Liking what she saw, she invited him in. She sang the boy her songs, and he assured her he could play them. She asked him if he had any songs and he did, quite a lot of them;

although he did not yet have a record deal, Browne had a publishing contract. The first of his songs he played Nico was "These Days," an exquisite, pensive ballad he wrote when he was sixteen years old, after his second acid trip. Says Browne, "She said, 'I vill do zis song'—everybody did a Nico impersonation, she's fun to imitate."[4] She chose two more of Browne's songs and appointed him her new accompanist and lover, both effective immediately.

"Nico lived in this apartment with her little son who was about four years old. She had a roommate, a really big guy named Ronnie who wore big fur coats and had a lot of money and I don't know what he did, but I think that maybe he was a club owner or restaurateur or something. He was a very nice guy and amazingly he didn't seem to have any interest in her at all except as a friend; I thought, 'Wow, that's incredible.'" Browne laughs. "I remember Leonard used to come over to her house. I knew he had just become kind of very celebrated for 'Suzanne,' which Judy Collins covered, and he had this really great book he had written, *Beautiful Losers,* which he seemed to be embarrassed by for some reason, who knows. He used to also come to the club where we played. He'd just sit there at the front table and write and look at her."[5]

The picture he paints is somewhat reminiscent of *Death in Venice*—a solemn, love-struck old writer (at thirty-two years old, Leonard would have appeared quite old to the teenage Browne) mooning over a dangerous, unattainable beauty. Browne simply assumed that Leonard was "writing her a song," and in a way he was, although he was hoping for more than a cover. "She'd been given a song by Bob Dylan, one by Tim Hardin; she was gathering these great songs to interpret and they were songs that no one had ever heard of—sort of what Judy Collins was doing at the time, so if anybody cares to make the connection between Judy Collins and Nico, there it is."[6]

Leonard befriended the pair of them. "He would read us the poems he wrote while he watched her, very dreamy, and they were amazing poems," says Browne. On a few occasions he would go with the two of them to the Dom, before Browne broke up with Nico. "I was into her," Browne says, "and it took me a while to realize I was a fling. So I quit, but even though we weren't lovers anymore I was working for her and seeing her every night. Then things got weird. There was somebody calling and harassing her, a stalker, and she accused me of making the calls and she kind of flipped." Browne flew back to California—just in time for the Summer of Love. "Nico was crazy and mysterious," says Browne. "She wouldn't tell anyone where she was from—I don't think she wanted to be thought of as German—and she had this ice-queen countenance. But she also had this really girlish smile, and when she laughed she was like a little kid, and she spent almost all her time with her son. There was this side of Nico that I don't think many people know. I really dug her."[7]

So did Leonard. Although he never won her, he was "madly in love with her."[8] Exclaims Danny Fields,* "She didn't with Leonard? She did it with Lou [Reed], God knows! And Nico *worshipped* Leonard. She would call him up: 'Ohh, Lennhaarrrdt'—that's the way she said his name, in that Germanic voice. 'Vat do you think, Lennhaarrrdt?' 'Would Lennhaarrrdt like my songs?' Nico was eager to ally herself with creative people. Leonard was *very* important to her. She certainly was a girl of conflicted emotions." Though she was consistent in her taste in men. After Jackson Browne, Nico moved on to Jim Morrison and Jimi Hendrix, both in their early twenties.

"I bumped into Jim Morrison a couple of times but I did not know him well. And Hendrix—we actually jammed together one night in New York. I forget the name of the club, but I was there and he was there and he knew my song 'Suzanne,' so we kind of jammed on it."

---

* Fields was responsible for signing, among others, Iggy Pop, the MC5 and the Ramones. Iggy, whom Nico did not turn down, would go on to write an almost Leonard Cohenesque song to her titled "Nazi Girlfriend"; its opening lines were "I want to fuck her on the floor / Among my books of ancient lore."

You and Hendrix jammed on "Suzanne"? What did he do with it?

"He was very gentle. He didn't distort his guitar. It was just a lovely thing. I did bump into him again. I remember I was walking up Twenty-third Street, which is the street the Chelsea Hotel was on, and I was with Joni Mitchell, a very beautiful woman, and a big limousine pulled up and Jimi Hendrix was in the backseat, and he was chatting up Joni from the inside of the limo."

It didn't matter to him that she was with another man, specifically you?

"Well, you know, he was a very elegant man so it wasn't impolite."

Did Joni go off with him and leave you?

"No, she didn't. But Nico did. I went with Nico to hear Jim Morrison—I think he was playing for the first time in New York at a club—and Hendrix showed up and he was glorious, very beautiful, and I'd come with Nico and when it was time to go I said, 'Let's go,' and she said, 'I'm going to stay. You go.' [Laughs]"

Some years later, Leonard and Nico bumped into each other in the Spanish restaurant and bar El Quijote. When the bar closed, they wound up in Leonard's room in the Chelsea Hotel next door. It was one of the smaller guest rooms—Leonard was only passing through—and so they sat together on the bed, side by side, continuing the conversation they had begun downstairs. At one point, feeling encouraged, Leonard put a hand on her arm. Nico swung round and hit him so hard he levitated. "There are stories of her flare-ups and physical brutality," says Fields. "Her other brutality, the passive brutality, was just making you wonder what she was thinking, so much that people fell in love with her. Maybe it was a love punch, 'I don't vont to fall in love viz you'—*pow!* Maybe she wanted him to be a caveman conqueror, because men were so afraid of her. Nico loved Leonard. We all did."

But in 1967, feeling he "had no skill" and that he "had forgotten how to court a lady,"[9] Leonard went back alone to his hotel room. His thoughts full of Nico, he wrote "The Jewels in Your Shoulder" and

"Take This Longing," then titled "The Bells," both of which he later played and taught to Nico. She was the both "the tallest and blondest girl" in the song "Memories" and the muse for "Joan of Arc" ("This song was written for a German girl I used to know. She's a great singer, I love her songs. I recently read an interview where she was asked about me and my work. And she said I was 'completely unnecessary,'"[10] he told a Paris audience in 1974). She also inspired "One of Us Cannot Be Wrong." After one of the occasions on which Nico spurned him, Leonard went back to his room "and indulged [himself] in the black magic of candles"—the green candles he bought at a magic and voodoo shop—"and," he says, "I married these two wax candles, and I married the smoke of two cones of sandalwood and I did many bizarre and occult practices that resulted in nothing at all, except an enduring friendship."[11]

Leonard now lived in the Chelsea Hotel. An imposing redbrick Victorian at 222 West Twenty-third Street in what once was New York's theater district, it had four hundred rooms, a great many of which were occupied by artists, writers and bohemians. Mark Twain had stayed there; Arthur Miller lived there for six years, praising it as a place with "no vacuum cleaners, no rules, no shame." Dylan Thomas died there in his room and Sid Vicious killed his girlfriend Nancy Spungen in his. The hotel was the setting for Andy Warhol's film *The Chelsea Girls*.

The Chelsea was popular with Beat poets and equally popular with their successors, rock musicians—among them Bob Dylan, Jimi Hendrix, Janis Joplin and Patti Smith, who lived there with her photographer lover Robert Mapplethorpe. Smith described the hotel as "a doll's house in the Twilight Zone."[12] (Leonard had met Patti Smith the year before and taken her to dinner with Irving and Aviva Layton. "She was just a young kid then," says Aviva, "a skinny little waif, no breasts, and wearing rags, not feathers; I think she may have been living on the street—and Leonard told us, 'She's a genius, absolutely brilliant, she's going to be a real force.'")

The walls of the lobby of the Chelsea jostled with paintings, which had been given or hocked to Stanley Bard, the hotel manager, in lieu of rent. A door from the lobby led to the Spanish restaurant and bar next door, El Quijote. The slowest elevator in American hostelry crept up the twelve floors, opening out onto corridors painted yellow and a warren of rooms of various shapes, sizes and luxury. Leonard's, on the fourth floor, was lit by an overhead bulb and had a small black-and-white television, a hot plate and a washbasin where the water ran rust-brown until you counted to ten. More than half the hotel was taken up with long-term residents. Some gave the impression that they lived there for the sole purpose of getting an upgrade to a bigger, better room. It was "a big boho fraternity house," says the writer and journalist Thelma Blitz, and Leonard, the former fraternity house president, "felt entirely at home."

He had everything he needed in this latest version of home, including the succor of women. From the age of nine, when his father died, Leonard had been nurtured by women. During his infancy in the music business, those women were Mary Martin and Judy Collins. *In My Life* had been Collins's biggest-selling album to date, spending thirty-four weeks on the U.S. charts and getting a good deal of attention and radio play. "It was really the edge of the 'pop success' era," said Collins, "so it was partly that and the kind of promotion I was getting from Elektra." With "Suzanne" being such a powerful song and Collins such an evangelical cheerleader for its writer, Leonard was getting attention too, including from John Hammond, the leading A & R man at America's foremost record company, Columbia.

Hammond was a New York aristocrat—his mother was a Vanderbilt, his grandfather a Civil War general. His upbringing was extremely privileged, but, like Leonard, he chose a different path. Hammond aligned himself with the civil rights movement and became a jazz critic, a record producer and an A & R man with a remarkable résumé. Among the many greats Hammond signed and/or produced were Billie Holiday, Pete Seeger, Count Basie, Aretha Franklin and

Bob Dylan. "John Hammond was a genius," said Collins. "With Dylan he was able to see beyond his boring Woody Guthrie blues and signed him up for a three-record deal before 'Blowing in the Wind' ever happened. He was always carefully watching what was going on, and listening. He listened to what I was doing—he tried to sign me to Columbia, but I'd promised my hand to Elektra the week before—and that's where he heard Leonard, because there was nowhere else to hear him at that point." Mary Martin, meanwhile, was calling Hammond, talking Leonard up, sending him copies of Leonard's books and persuading him to go to CBC's New York office for a private screening of *Ladies and Gentlemen . . . Mr. Leonard Cohen.* She had Leonard record a demo tape of his songs, in her bathroom, sitting in the empty bathtub and singing into a borrowed Uher tape recorder. A copy was made for Garth Hudson, the keyboard player with the Band, to do the lead sheets of each of the songs, for publishing purposes. Another copy was delivered to Hammond personally at his office, Martin and her lawyer colleague E. Judith Berger having changed into their tiniest miniskirts.

Leonard received a phone call from Hammond inviting him to lunch at a nearby restaurant. Afterward, Hammond asked if he might come back to the Chelsea with Leonard and hear him play his songs in his room. Perched on the edge of the bed, beneath the overhead light, Leonard sang to him for an hour: songs including "Suzanne," "The Stranger Song," "Master Song," "Hey, That's No Way to Say Goodbye," "The Jewels in Your Shoulder," and a song he told Hammond he had just written that day, "Your Father Has Fallen." Hammond sat in the only chair, eyes closed, stone quiet. When Leonard finally stopped playing, Hammond opened his eyes and smiled. "You've got it," he said. Leonard, not entirely sure what it was he had, thanked him and showed him out. Back at Columbia Records, Hammond announced that he planned to sign Leonard. Not for the last time, this did not meet with universal enthusiasm at the label. The acting chief executive, Bill Gallagher, said, "A thirty-two-year-old poet? Are you crazy?"[13] He had a point; in 1967 rock was the new poetry, and the rock world did not trust a man over thirty. But Hammond persisted. Larry Cohen, former vice president of Columbia/Epic, who had the office next door to his, recalls Hammond telling him that "out of all the artists he had ever signed that Leonard was the most intelligent. That's saying something coming from John. If you knew John, he was not given to extraordinary platitudes. He thought very highly of Leonard Cohen."

On February 22, still unsigned, Leonard made his official live debut as a singer in New York. It was a benefit concert for WBAI, held in the Village Theatre on Sixth Street at Second Avenue, with an impressive lineup that included Pete Seeger, Tom Paxton and Judy Collins. It had been Bob Fass's suggestion that Collins bring him onstage and introduce him as a new artist, much as Joan Baez had once done with Dylan. Collins jumped at the idea but Leonard said no. "He said, 'I can't sing and I certainly can't perform,'" remembers Collins. "I said, 'Of course you can.' But Leonard never dreamed of being a performer. I said, 'Why don't you just come and sing "Suzanne"? Everyone will know the song so it'll be comfortable for you.' Finally he consented."

"Judy told me, 'I don't think he wants to,'" says Bob Fass, "then she called back again and said, 'He's changed his mind, he's going to come,' so we advertised him. On the night, Judy came onstage and sang a song, then called for Leonard to come out. And he came out, and he had trouble tuning his guitar and she finally gave him hers. He began to sing, but maybe it was in the wrong key or something or he couldn't hear, and his voice broke. He said, 'I can't go on,' and he left the stage. I thought, 'That's really too bad,' and went on with the show." Much later in the show, Collins told him Leonard would like to come back on. "And he did. I said, 'This man has balls.'" Says Collins, "Leonard was very, very nervous, shaking like a leaf. He hadn't sung in public like this before, only in these little clubs in New York where he read his poetry, and he started singing 'Suzanne' and about halfway through the song he stopped and walked off the stage. But everybody just adored him. So I went back and told him, 'You've got to come back and finish the song.' He said, 'I can't,' and I said, 'I'll come out and do it with you.' So I went onstage with him and we finished the song up together—and that was Leonard's debut."

In a letter to Marianne dated February 23, 1967, Leonard wrote, "Darling. I sang in New York for the first time last night, at a huge benefit concert. Every singer you've ever heard of was there performing. Judy Collins introduced me to the audience, over 3000 people." He described hitting a chord and finding his guitar "completely out of tune, tried to retune it, couldn't get more than a croak out of my throat." He managed to sing just four lines of "Suzanne," he said, his voice "unbelievably flat, then I broke off and said simply, 'Sorry, I just can't make it,' and walked off the stage, my fingers like rubber bands, the people baffled and my career in music dying among the coughs of the people backstage." He described to Marianne how he had stood and watched numbly from the wings while Collins played some more songs, and how he had finally come back on and managed to get through "Stranger Song," even though his voice and guitar continued to break down. "I finished somehow and I thought I'll just commit suicide. Nobody really knew what to do or say. I think that someone took my hand and led me off. Everybody backstage was very sorry for me and they couldn't believe how happy I was, how relieved I was that it had all come to nothing, that I had never been so free."*

Marianne says, "I was sitting in my mother's house in Oslo with little Axel at the time and something very strange happened. Suddenly my son stood up and said, 'Cohne died, Marianne'—he called

---

* Other accounts place Leonard's first appearance with Collins on April 30 at the Town Hall at a benefit concert for the National Committee for a Sane Nuclear Policy (SANE); the date on Leonard's letter belies that, as does an ad listing the participants in the SANE benefit.

Leonard 'Cohne' in those days—and, as Leonard told the story himself, he 'died' that night on the stage." Leonard's letter closed by saying that he would be back in Hydra in a month or two to start working on another book. "I hope you're feeling good, little friend of my life," he closed the letter. "Axel's card was beautiful, hug him from me. Goodnight darling. Leonard."[14]

Leonard was still talking about writing a book when he wrote to Marianne in April, three days after performing to a sold-out crowd at an arts festival at the State University of New York in Buffalo. He had been offered a forty-date tour of American colleges in the fall, he said, and, prior to that, the Newport Folk Festival and Expo 67 in Montreal, and he was "very anxious" to write a book before it started. But "it" had already started. A second recording artist, Buffy Sainte-Marie, was covering two of his songs, and Nico was planning to sing "The Jewels in Your Shoulder" on her debut solo album—all women. Yet he wrote to Marianne that he was "dead to lust, tired of ambition, a lazy student of my own pain." He told her that he had "given up plans for sainthood, revolution, redemptive visions, music mastery." What he wanted, he said, was to be with Marianne on Hydra.[15] Days later he wrote to Marianne again, this time describing the thin green candle he kept burning in his room that was "dedicated to St Jude Thaddeus, Patron Saint of Impossible Causes."[16] He made no mention of Nico in the letter. But clearly Nico was not the only lost cause on Leonard's mind.

John Hammond had not given up on Leonard. When Columbia Records appointed a new head, Clive Davis, Hammond persuaded him to give the go-ahead to sign Leonard. A contract dated April 26, 1967, naming Mary Martin Management Inc. as representative and Bob Johnston as producer, was delivered to Martin's Bleecker Street office. It offered four one-year options and an advance of $2,000, which would be paid within thirty days of his completing the recording of two sides of an LP. Leonard took out his pen and signed. He was a recording artist.

————

Columbia Studio E was on the sixth floor of the old lead-lined CBS Radio building on East Fifty-second Street. Stepping out of the elevator on May 19, 1967, his first day of recording, Leonard's eye was caught by a large canvas sign that read THE ARTHUR GODFREY SHOW. Godfrey, a popular radio personality, broadcast his daily program from a room next to the recording studio. Godfrey was known for his cheery persona; he even had his own line of plastic ukuleles and played one regularly on his shows. But the warmth did not spread to the freaks and long-haired musicians with whom he was obliged to share the floor.

Leonard, carrying a briefcase and a guitar, looking more like a college professor than a musician, pushed through the heavy door and into a room about thirty feet square with a nineteen-foot-high ceiling. Sitting on a couch in the control room, dressed in a suit and reading a newspaper, was John Hammond. Bob Johnston, the staff producer named on the contract, had been taken off the project. "I told Leonard I wanted to do it so bad," says Johnston, "and Leonard wanted me to do it, but they told me absolutely not because I had too many artists already—Dylan, Johnny Cash, Simon and Garfunkel." Six months earlier, the last of these had been in Studio E with Johnston recording their hit album *Parsley, Sage, Rosemary and Thyme*. John Hammond had decided to take over Leonard's album himself and brought along a small handful of session musicians.

In that first three-hour session, they recorded five takes of "Suzanne," six of "Stranger Song"—with guitar and organ, guitar and bass, and just guitar—and six of "Hey, That's No Way to Say Goodbye," five described as "rock versions" with the band and one "simple version," performed solo. Hammond, behind the glass, would call enthusiastically over the talk-back, "Watch out, Dylan!" Hammond "never said anything negative," said Leonard. "There were just degrees of his affirmation. Everything you did was 'good' but some things were 'very good.'" Over time Leonard came to learn that "if it was just 'good,' you knew you had to do another take."[17] At the second session he recorded four takes of "So Long, Marianne."

There was a lot of time in which to learn. Leonard often said that *Songs of Leonard Cohen* was a hard album to make, and job sheets found in Columbia's archives—handwritten cards that logged the dates, times and content of each recording session—back this up. Leonard recorded the album from May 19 until November 9, with two different producers in three different studios. For the fourth and fifth sessions in June, the operation shifted to Studio B, a penthouse in the old Columbia building on Seventh Avenue, where the elevators had operators who wore gray uniforms with brass buttons and piping. It was a smaller room at least, with a drab functional appearance that Leonard tried to alleviate with candles and incense. It made him no less uncomfortable.

"It's never come easily. I've never been particularly confident about the process and I was never able to exactly get what I wanted. I always had that sense, if I can just finish the damn thing! And you keep notching your standards down, degree by degree, until finally you say, 'I've finished, never mind.' Not, 'Is it going to be beautiful, is it going to be perfect, is it going to be immortal?' 'Can I finish?' became the urgent question."

As it was your first time, did you simply let Hammond get on with doing it the way he wanted to, or did you have any particular requirements?

"I asked them for a full-length mirror. That was my only requirement. And he had some very good ideas about how it should be done. He brought in a bass player whose name is on the tip of my tongue, a really fine bass player, and we just laid down a lot of the songs, just the two of us together. And he was a very sensitive player. I think those were the core tracks of at least half the songs on that record, just the guitar and bass."

Leonard knew how he wanted to sound, or at least how he did not want to, but as an untrained musician he lacked the language to explain it. He could not play as well as the session musicians, so he found them intimidating. "I didn't really know how to sing with a band, with really good, professional musicians that were really cooking, and I would tend to listen to the musicians rather than concentrate on what I was doing, because they were doing it so much more proficiently than I was."[18] Hammond, smartly, let the band go and had Leonard work with a single accompanist: Willie Ruff, a sophisticated, intuitive bass player who had played with Dizzy Gillespie, Count Basie and Louis Armstrong. Ruff did not care that Leonard could not read music or charts. "He supported the guitar playing so well. He could always anticipate my next move, he understood the song so thoroughly," said Leonard. "He was one of those rare musicians that play selflessly, and for pure and complete support. I couldn't have laid down those tracks without him."[19]

The location changed once again, this time to Studio C, a converted Greek-Armenian Orthodox church on Thirtieth Street where Miles Davis recorded *Kind of Blue*. By this point, Leonard was cutting his sixteenth take of "Suzanne" as well as a song titled "Come On, Marianne." "I thought it always was 'Come on, Marianne, it's time that we began to laugh and cry,'" says Marianne, "but—unless I'm dreaming—there was a group in California, maybe the Beach Boys, who had similar words in a song. When he wrote it, for me it was like, 'Come on, if we can just keep this boat afloat.' And then we found out that we could not."

Leonard had begun writing the song the year before, in Montreal, and finished it in the Chelsea Hotel, but he was still vacillating in the studio over these two words in the title and chorus that gave the song very different meanings. "I didn't think I was saying good-bye," said Leonard, "but I guess I was." He did not write it as a farewell song; it was almost as if the song made the decision for him. "There's a certain kind of writer that says hello to people in their songs and there's a certain kind of writer that says good-bye to people—and you know

I'm more a writer of elegies, at least in that particular phase," he said in 1979. "I think for many writers the work has a prophetic quality, I don't mean in a cosmic or religious sense but just in terms of one's own life; you are generally writing about events that haven't taken place yet."[20] It was an interesting statement. The first half of it suggests that saying good-bye is a songwriting conceit, something that suited his taste and style; as to the second part, he was surely not so superstitious as to believe that the songs dictated his actions as they took form. When Leonard wrote a song, though, he did go deep, and it appears that what he found there was an urge to leave.

In July, Leonard took a monthlong break from the studio; it felt like he'd been released from jail. So much had happened while he was in New York, wrapped up in his new music career. There had been a coup d'état in Greece, which was now ruled by a military junta, and in Israel there had been the Six-Day War. His friend Irving Layton had gone to the Israeli consulate to offer his services in the army. They were declined.[21] Leonard's duties, and the reason for the break, were a series of concerts he had to perform.

The first, on July 16, was at the famous Newport Folk Festival, for which once again he had Judy Collins to thank. Collins was on the festival's board of directors and, two years after Bob Dylan had been booed for going electric, was still fighting the traditionalists to acknowledge the new direction folk music, including hers, was taking, Collins wanted to stage a singer-songwriter workshop, and finally she got her way. Topping her list of participants were Leonard and another newcomer, an unsigned singer-songwriter named Joni Mitchell.

Says Collins, "I came to know Joni through Al Kooper," a rock musician friend who had played with Dylan in his historic Newport electric set. "He called me up, it was three in the morning, and he was hanging out with this girl who had told him she was a singer and writer, and he went home with her because he thought he could get laid, but he found out when he got to her house that she really *could* sing and write. He put her on the phone and had her sing me 'Both Sides Now,' which of course I had to record."

"Judy," says Danny Fields, "was a fountain of discovery. Leonard first turned up in my consciousness, as with many other people, with the song 'Suzanne' on Judy's 1966 album *In My Life*. After closing time at the Scene, a club where Hendrix and Tiny Tim became famous, a bunch of us who thought ourselves the cool rock 'n' roll crowd would go back to the owner Steve Paul's little house on Eighteenth Street and listen to that album. Then in early 1967 I started working at Elektra and Judy was one of my artists, and then came Leonard. But when I really met him was at Newport. I'd gone to the festival as representative of my record company and, like everybody, stayed at the Viking Hotel. It was beautiful and peaceful and I didn't have to drive so I took LSD. I was with Judy and Leonard and they said, 'Let's go back to Leonard's room.'"

Fields remembers "sitting on the floor, contemplating the carpet, while they sat on the two beds with their guitars. Leonard was teaching Judy 'Hey, That's No Way to Say Goodbye,' and that was the audio track to the universe and the eight dimensions of existence in the shag rug. When I woke up it was just predawn, they were still sitting on the two beds with the guitars, and Judy said, 'Oh, I think Danny looks as though he could use some fresh air, Leonard, let's take him for a walk,' and we went walking around the bay, where up on the cliffs the great robber baron palaces of Newport are, as the sun rose. It was wonderful. And when I flew back to New York, the next night Judy was doing the Central Park concert"—the Rheingold Festival—"and she brought Leonard up onstage with her to perform 'Suzanne.'"

The *New York Times* review of Leonard at Newport described him as an "extremely effective singer, building a hypnotic, spellbinding effect." Still, as he had been at the WBAI benefit, Leonard was terrified. "He told me he was *terribly* nervous," recalls Aviva Layton, who was in the audience in Central Park. "It was the middle of summer, the place was packed with people and the sun was setting, and Judy Collins said, 'I want to introduce to you a singer-songwriter, his name is Leonard Cohen.' Leonard came out with his guitar strapped on— and some people groaned, because they'd come to see Judy Collins, not this unknown Leonard Cohen. So he had to win over the crowd. He was facing thousands of people, standing packed like sardines, and he just said, very quietly, 'Tonight my guitar is full of tears and feathers.' And then he played 'Suzanne,' and that was it. Incredible." Leonard celebrated having made it through the performance, privately, in his Chelsea Hotel room. With him was his new inamorata, a woman he had met at Newport, a twenty-three-year-old, willowy blond singer-songwriter with a voice every bit as unique as Nico's.

Joni Mitchell, like Leonard, was from the East Coast of Canada. But their versions of Eastern Canada were vastly different—Leonard's urban and cosmopolitan, Joni's vast prairie skies. Joni, the daughter of a Canadian Air Force officer, had been raised in a small town in Saskatchewan. She was a talented painter, and when, as a child, she contracted polio (in the same epidemic in which her fellow small-town East Canadian Neil Young also contracted it), during her long, lonely convalescence she also discovered a talent for music. She taught herself to play the ukulele, then guitar, excelling at the latter and inventing her own sophisticated tunings and style. In 1964 Joni quit art school to be a folksinger, moving to Toronto and the coffee-houses around which the folk scene revolved. In February 1965 she gave birth to a daughter, the result of an affair with a photographer. A few weeks later she married folksinger Chuck Mitchell and gave the baby up for adoption. The marriage did not last. Joni left, taking his name with her, and moved into Greenwich Village, where she was living alone in a small hotel room when she met Leonard.

It was an intense romance. At the outset Joni played student to

Leonard's teacher. She asked him for a list of books she should read. "I remember thinking when I heard his songs for the first time that I was not worldly," she said. "My work seemed very young and naive in comparison."[22] Leonard gave her some suggestions, including Lorca, Camus and the I Ching. But he was quickly aware that Joni needed little help with anything, particularly her songwriting. They each wrote a (very different) song called "Winter Lady"—Joni's appears to have been written first—and Joni wrote two love songs referencing Leonard's song "Suzanne": "Wizard of Is," with an almost-identical melody and near-quoted lines ("You think that you may love him," she wrote of the man who speaks "in riddles") and "Chelsea Morning," set in a room with candles, incense and oranges, where the sun pours in "like butterscotch" instead of honey.

Leonard took Joni to Montreal. They stayed in his childhood home on Belmont Avenue. In her song "Rainy Night House" she described the "holy man" sitting up all night, watching her as she slept on his mother's bed. They painted each other's portraits. Leonard's was the face Joni drew on a map of Canada in her song "A Case of You," in which a man declares himself to be as "constant as a northern star." When it turned out he wasn't, Joni wrote about that too, in "That Song About the Midway" and in "The Gallery," in which a man who describes himself as a saint, and complains of her description of him as heartless, pleads with her to take him to her bed.

For the first time the tables were turned: Leonard was the muse for a woman. Not just any woman but one whom David Crosby—who also had an intense and short-lived love affair with Joni Mitchell in 1968—calls "the greatest singer-songwriter of our generation." Within a year Leonard and Joni's affair was over. Leonard told journalist Mark Ellen, "I remember we were spending some time together in Los Angeles years ago and someone said to me, 'How do you like living with Beethoven?'" How did Leonard like living with Beethoven? "I didn't like it," Leonard said, laughing, "because who would? She's prodigiously gifted. Great painter too."[23] As David Crosby says, "It was very easy to love her, but turbulent. Loving Joni is a little like falling into a cement mixer."

In later years Mitchell seemed keen to distance herself from Leonard artistically. "I briefly liked Leonard Cohen, though once I read Camus and Lorca I started to realize that he had taken a lot of lines from those books, which was disappointing to me," she said in 2005 of the man she had once described as "a mirror to my work," someone who "showed me how to plumb the depths of my experience." She would go on to describe him as "in many ways a boudoir poet"[24]—a grander term than "the Bard of the Bedsit," one of the nicknames the UK music press would later give him, but reductive nonetheless. Any close inspection of Mitchell's songs pre- and post-Leonard would seem to indicate that he had some effect on her work. Over the decades, Leonard and Joni have remained friends.

On July 22, 1967, Leonard was in Montreal, performing at Expo 67, the world's fair. It was an important concert. Canada, conscious of the eyes of the world on it, was treating the expo as a celebration of Canadian independence and, in the case of Quebec, harmony. As the Canadian journalist Robert Fulford wrote, its success marked "the end of Little Canada, a country afraid of its own future, frightened of great plans. Despite the spectre of French-Canadian separatism that haunted Canada through the early and middle 1960s, Expo seemed to suggest that we were now entering a new and happier period in our history."[25] Leonard, *"poète, chansonnier, écrivain,"* as he was described on the bill, would perform at the Youth Pavilion (being two months off thirty-three did not exclude him). It was one of the smaller marquees, set up like a nightclub with chairs and tables, and it was sold out.

Leonard had been nervous playing in Central Park, but this hometown performance terrified him. His family was there—his mother was in the front row—as were many of his friends. Erica Pomerance was there, along with "a flock of Leonard Cohen aficionados who were half friends, half admirers, basically fans of his poetry." Leonard had littered the small stage with candles. He told the audience to come forward and fetch a candle for their table so that he could sing. "He was tentative and earnest, very unpolished," says Montreal music critic Juan Rodriguez. Nancy Bacal concurs. "He was horrified, just frozen. He told me, looking out at these people, how could he just become this other person? How could he become this performer when they knew him, they'd known him all his life? It was just too hard for him."

There was one more summer festival for Leonard to play—the Mariposa Folk Festival, at Innis Lake, near Toronto—before going back to New York to continue work on his album. There were two more sessions with Hammond in August and then another three-week break, during which Leonard flew to L.A. Director John Boorman was talking about making a movie based on the song "Suzanne" and having Leonard score it. No one had ever paid his way across the continent before. There were even matchboxes with his name on them waiting for him in his room at the Landmark Hotel. Lighting a cigarette, Leonard sat at the desk and wrote a song called "Nine Years Old," which would become "The Story of Isaac." Nothing came of the film. At various times Leonard has said that he "couldn't relate" to the idea or that it was dropped when it was discovered he did not own the rights to the song. The rights to "Suzanne," "Master Song" and "Dress Rehearsal Rag," he said, had been "pilfered in New York City."[26] Leonard, assisted by his manager, had set up his own publishing company, Stranger Music. An arranger, producer and music publisher named Jeff Chase whom Mary Martin thought might prove helpful was brought in, and somewhere in the process Leonard appeared to have somehow signed over the songs to him.

Said Leonard, "My mother, who I always thought was kind of naive—she was Russian, her English was imperfect—said to me, 'Leonard, you be careful of those people down there. They're not

like us.' And of course, I didn't say anything to disrespect, she was
my mother, but in my mind I thought, 'Mother, you know, I'm not a
child.' I was 32, I'd been around the block a few times. But she was
right. She was right."*[27]

On September 8, in Studio B, Leonard recorded four more songs
with Hammond. It would prove to be their last session together.
Several reasons have been posited for Hammond's dropping out.
Leonard always said that Hammond became ill, and certainly he
had health problems: when he signed Leonard to Columbia it was
shortly after he had taken time off following a heart attack, and in
subsequent years he would suffer several more. Another reason given
was the illness of Hammond's wife. In his autobiography, Hammond
said nothing about illness and implied that there were musical differences. Leonard, he wrote, "got the jitters" at Hammond's simple
production approach and "could not conceive of his voice being commercial enough to sell records. Simplicity was his greatest asset and
we told him so. It was not what he wanted to hear. . . . I was overruled
and another producer brought in."[28]

Hammond's recollections about signing Leonard admittedly include several errors, but Larry Cohen, his associate at Columbia,
backs up what Hammond said about his production style. "John's
MO, having known him for years, was not to change people or their
sound, other than what they normally were, and what he did was bring
out the best in people doing what they did. He didn't give Dylan any
directions—Dylan came in with the things that he wanted to do and
that's why John signed him and he let him do what he did."

Leonard himself said something once that suggested he wanted
something more than just simple voice and guitar. "I was trying to
find—I wanted a kind of 'found sound' background to a lot of my
tunes. What I wanted running through 'The Stranger Song' was

---

* Chase and Cohen came to a settlement in 1987.

the sound of a tire on a wet pavement, a kind of harmonic hum. [Hammond] was almost ready to let me take a recording device into a car. He let me do the next best thing. I got in touch with mad scientists around New York who had devices that would create sounds. Unfortunately, he got sick in the middle of this operation."[29] Whatever the explanation, after four arduous months of work on his debut album, nothing came of it. Leonard was back to square one.

Ten

The Dust of a Long Sleepless Night

So much had happened in the year since Leonard played Judy Collins his songs that the world itself seemed to be on speed. But some things had not happened—primarily, Leonard's album. It seemed to Leonard that this inability to make a record was a problem peculiar to him. Judy Collins had just finished her seventh LP, *Wildflowers*, which contained three more songs that Leonard had written but that he had not yet recorded himself. There was a second cover of "Suzanne" in the singles charts too, sung by Noel Harrison, an English actor, the same age as Leonard. It must have felt to Leonard that he had lost the rights to his song in more ways than one, and since "Suzanne" was by consensus his signature song, that he was losing himself as well. When the recording sessions stopped, Leonard behaved like a lost man. For a week he stayed shut in his hotel room, smoking a great deal of hashish. He had felt lost in New York once before, when he was attending Columbia University, and on that occasion he had left after a year and gone back home to Montreal and his friends. But with Columbia Records there was unfinished business, and so he stayed, turning to the nearest thing he had in New York to an artists' community: the Warhol set and the denizens of the Chelsea Hotel.

Occasionally the two would overlap. Edie Sedgwick, a gamine blond beauty and the most famous of Warhol's socialite starlets, had moved into the Chelsea, having accidentally burned down the apartment her mother bought for her. Edie had crawled along the floor and escaped with only a burned hand. Her new home at the Chelsea was on the fourth floor, down the hall from Leonard's room. Her friend Danny Fields, who was visiting Leonard, inquired if he had ever met Edie. Leonard said he had not. "Would you like to?" Fields asked. "She's a magical person that everyone falls in love with." Leonard said he would. Fields ran off to Edie's room. He found her there with Brigid Berlin, another of Warhol's renegade socialites. Plump and homely, Brigid might not have been blessed with looks but undeniably had personality—when Fields first set eyes on her, Brigid was climbing out of a yellow cab wearing nothing but a sarong around her waist, with a toy doctor's kit dangling between her naked breasts, and carrying the big fake doctor's bag that she took with her everywhere. It was filled with vials of "something she'd concocted like a mad scientist," its ingredients mostly liquid amphetamine and vitamin B. "She'd run around with a syringe, screaming, 'I'm going to get you!' and she did, injecting you in the butt right through your pants." It earned her the name Brigid Polk, as in "poke." Warhol gave her a starring role in *The Chelsea Girls*, alongside Edie and Nico.

When Fields walked into the room, he found the two women "pasting sequins one at a time in a coloring book," an activity pursued after the age of seven only if a person is on speed. "Brigid had fallen asleep on a tube of Ready Glue and she was stuck to the floor; she tried to turn around and gave up and was just lying there. There was the remnants of a fire in the fireplace and there were candles in candlesticks that she'd bought at the voodoo store where everybody went to get spells and unguents," Leonard included. "I said, 'Edie, Leonard Cohen the famous poet and songwriter is here and he'd like to meet you.' She said, 'Oh, bring him over, I'll just get made up.' When Edie put on makeup it could take three hours, literally. So I said, 'He's a simple guy, and anyway you look beautiful, I'm going to go get him.'"

Fields returned with Leonard. On entering the room, Leonard's eyes were immediately drawn to Edie's candles. He headed straight for them and stood there, staring. "The first thing Leonard said to her was, 'I'm wondering about these candles. Did you put them here in this order?' 'Order? Please! It's just candles.' And he said, 'No, it's a very unfortunate order that you've placed them in. It means bad luck or misfortune.' Edie giggled, and that was it, I left them alone with these candles. But wait. They caught fire soon afterward and the room was burned completely black. Edie got out a second time by crawling across the floor, and when she reached for the door handle, once again she burned her hand."

Brigid Polk was an artist. Among her best-known works was her series of "tit paintings," made by dipping her breasts in paint and pressing them onto paper. She also had a "Cock Book," a blank-paged book in which she asked people (women as well as men) to do a drawing of their penis. Among the participants were the painter Jean-Michel Basquiat, the actress Jane Fonda, and Leonard. Leonard, declining to illustrate his privates, wrote on a page, "Let me be the shy one in your book." He was involved and yet not involved—which described his general dealings with the Warhol set. They were more to his taste than the hippie scene on the West Coast that had begun to infiltrate New York: "There seemed to be something flabby about the hippie movement. They pulled flowers out of public gardens. They put them in guns, but they also left their campsites in a mess. No self-discipline," he said.[1] In addition, Warhol's Pop Art was an interesting study for Leonard as he made the shift from literature to pop music, from ivory tower to commercial art, and the models and starlets who surrounded Warhol were an interesting diversion and occasional indulgence. He was accidentally captured on film in the company of Warhol starlet Ivy Nicholson in *B.O.N.Y. (Boys of New York)*, made by a Texas film buff named Gregory Barrios, under Warhol's patronage. But in truth, Leonard was just passing through.*

He missed Marianne and Hydra. He took to eating alone in a Greek restaurant, drinking retsina, ordering from the menu in Greek, playing Greek records on the jukebox. He sent Marianne a long, tender poem he had written to her. It began,

> *This is for you*
> *it is the book I meant to read to you*
> *when we were old*
> *Now I am a shadow*
> *I am as restless as an empire*
> *You are the woman*
> *who released me.*

It ended,

> *I long for the boundaries*
> *of my wandering*
> *and I move*
> *with the energy of your prayer*
> *for you are kneeling*
> *like a bouquet*
> *in a cave of bone*

---

* This was Leonard's second movie appearance that year. He was filmed performing "The Stranger Song" in Canadian director Don Owen's *The Ernie Game*.

behind my forehead
and I move towards a love
you have dreamed for me.[2]

At Leonard's bidding, Marianne flew over to New York with little
Axel. Leonard set about introducing Marianne to his life in the city,
taking her, she says, to all the "funny little coffeehouses he loved."
She would go and shop at the Puerto Rican magic store that Leonard
and Edie frequented, buying candles and perfumed oils that made
beautiful patterns on the water in Leonard's rust-stained hotel bathtub. They lunched at El Quijote, where Leonard introduced her to
Buffy Sainte-Marie, whom Marianne liked. He also introduced her
to Andy Warhol and to his fellow hotel residents, many of whom she
found bizarre. It was "a strange scene," said Marianne. She couldn't
help but contrast the dark, detached hedonism of his life in New York
with their life on Hydra, when they were "barefoot, poor and in love."
But it also became evident that Leonard really did not want her to
live with him. While Leonard stayed on at the Chelsea, Marianne
moved with Axel, who was now nine years old, into an apartment
on Clinton Street, which she shared with Carol Zemel—the wife of
Leonard's friend Henry Zemel—who was studying at Columbia.

During the daytime, while Axel was at school and Carol Zemel
was at the university, Marianne would make little handicrafts, kit-
tens made out of wool and steel. At night, while Carol kept an eye
on the child, she sold them on the street outside clubs. It was not
the best of neighborhoods, and Leonard asked her to stop, telling
her that he worried about her, but she continued. The only time she
encountered any trouble was when she was robbed of her earnings at
knifepoint after leaving a cinema where she had gone alone to watch
a Warhol film. Leonard and Marianne still saw each other; he took
her to a Janis Joplin concert and introduced her to Joplin backstage.
But the time he spent with Marianne grew less and less. She knew

he was seeing other women. Things brightened for Marianne when Steve Sanfield, their friend from Hydra, showed up in New York on a mission to raise funds for Roshi's new Zen center, giving her someone else to talk to and see. She tried her best to make it work, staying for a year, but ultimately she was not happy in New York. When the school year was over, she went back to Europe.

Leonard packed his bags and moved out of the Chelsea, and back into the Henry Hudson Hotel, the dive on West Fifty-seventh Street. "It was a forbidding place, a hole and a holdout," says Danny Fields. "I thought maybe the Chelsea got a little too happy for him and he needed someplace more suitably grim and desolate."

Four weeks after Leonard's album had been put on hold, it was once again back on. Columbia had appointed a new producer. John Simon was twenty-six years old, "just another junior producer among many at Columbia Records—that is, until I made a lot of money for them with 'Red Rubber Ball.'" The song, cowritten by Paul Simon (no relation) and recorded by the Cyrkle, whom John Simon produced, was such a big hit that even Leonard was aware of it. ("I loved it," said Leonard, "still do.") As a result John Simon earned "an office with a window and some decent artists to produce," first Simon & Garfunkel, then Leonard Cohen.

John Simon knew nothing about Leonard or the album's troubled history. "Leonard told me that he'd been living in the Chelsea Hotel waiting for John Hammond to schedule a session, and, just as a recording date was approaching, John called him to put off the date for a month. Leonard, as I remember it, asked for a different producer because he was tired of waiting. As far as I know, Hammond was not ill. I visited with John in his office and he had nothing but praise for Leonard."

Simon started reading Leonard's poetry and, in order to get better acquainted, invited him to stay with him at his parents' empty house in Connecticut, where they could discuss the album in peace.

"I think Leonard saw a familiar milieu in that house; both our families were middle-class, intellectual Jews. I went to bed and when I woke up in the morning, I found Leonard poring through my father's books. He said he had stayed up all night." Simon listened to the "acoustic, demo-y" recordings that Leonard had done with Hammond, and they set a date to start work, October 11, 1967. This time, when Leonard arrived at Studio B for the first session, there were no musicians waiting for him, just his young producer and the two union-mandated engineers. ("Producers could only talk," says Simon. "Unless you were in the union, you were strictly forbidden from touching any equipment, mics, mixing board, etc.")

Leonard "appeared confident," says Simon, "and he was singing great—nice quality, great pitch." There was no full-length mirror this time; Leonard simply sat, played and sang. There were eleven sessions with Simon over the space of two months in Studios B and E. Steve Sanfield was still in town, so Leonard invited him along. "He laid down all of his songs, one after the other, and I was blown away by them," Sanfield remembers. "The producer seemed blown away too. He said, 'We're going to make a great album.'"

Sanfield was staying with a friend who lived in New York, Morton Breier, the author of *Masks, Mandalas and Meditation*. They had made plans to meet with a group of young Hasidic students—despite his deep involvement with Zen Buddhism, Sanfield had not lost interest in Judaism. Neither had Leonard, who accepted the invitation to go with them. On their way they happened upon a chanting circle—a group of Hare Krishnas, led by Swami Bhaktivedanta, who was on his first visit to the U.S. Allen Ginsberg was there, chanting with them. Leonard told Sanfield he wanted to stay and to go on without him. Sanfield, having found the meeting with the Hasidim unfulfilling, came back just as the chanting circle was breaking up. Leonard had not moved from where he had left him. "What do you think?" Sanfield asked him. Leonard answered, "Nice song."

Leonard was similarly unresponsive when Sanfield talked to him about his own teacher, Roshi Sasaki, and the effect he had had on his life. But that night Leonard came to Breier's apartment to see Sanfield and told him, "I need to tell you a story." Late into the night, says Sanfield, "he told me a long version of the tale of Sabbatai Sevi, the false Messiah. I said, 'Why did you tell me that?' He said, 'Well, I just thought you should hear it.' I think it was because I was talking in such superlative praise of my Roshi." Leonard was suspicious of holy men. "They know how to do it," he would explain three decades later, when he was living in Roshi's monastery. "They know how to get at people around them, that's what their gig is." The reason he understood was, as he said, "because *I* was able to do it in my own small way. I was a very good hypnotist when I was very young."[3]

It was four in the morning when Leonard and Sanfield left to get breakfast, "and who should come walking down the street," says Sanfield, "but Bhaktivedanta, in his robes." When the guru came close, Leonard asked him, "How does that tune go again?" Bhaktivedanta stopped and sang them "Hare Krishna," "and we picked it up, and continued walking down the streets, singing it ourselves."

Leonard was still finding it a struggle in the recording studio, but by the fourth late-night session with Simon he had succeeded in doing three final takes: "You Know Who I Am," "Winter Lady," and, after nineteen failed attempts at recording it, "Suzanne." Three weeks and four sessions later, Leonard nailed "So Long, Marianne," a song he had recorded more than a dozen times with two producers and with two different titles. In total, since May 1967 Leonard had recorded twenty-five original compositions with John Hammond and John Simon. Ten of these songs made it onto Leonard's debut album. Four would be revisited on his second and third albums, and two would appear as bonus tracks on the *Songs of Leonard Cohen* reissue in 2003 ("Store Room" and "Blessed Is the Memory").

The other nine songs Leonard recorded—almost enough for a

whole other album—were "The Jewels in Your Shoulder," "Just Two People" (a.k.a. "Anyone Can See"), "In the Middle of the Night," "The Sun Is My Son," "Beach of Idios," "Nobody Calls You But Me," "Love Is the Item," "Nancy, Where Have You Been Sleeping" and "Splinters." As of this writing, all of these songs appear to be unreleased. Leonard played "Jewels in Your Shoulder" at his performance in April 1967 at the university in Buffalo, New York, and somewhere in circulation there's a very rare acetate of early demos that includes "Love Is the Item." The rest remain on the shelf.

When Leonard had finished recording his vocals and guitar, John Simon took over. He came up with string arrangements and added backing vocals, the principal backing singer—uncredited on the album—being Nancy Priddy, Simon's then girlfriend. Simon also overdubbed other instruments onto Leonard's track. "What I welcomed, to satisfy my own creative impulse, was Leonard's allowing me some room with his arrangements," says Simon. "To this day, I'm real happy with the arrangements I did using women's voices instead of instruments." However, when Leonard heard what his producer had done, he was not happy. If he had indeed thought that Hammond's production was too raw, Simon's was not raw enough.

What exactly didn't you like about it?

"John Simon wrote some delightful arrangements like the one to 'Sisters of Mercy,' still based around my guitar playing. I wanted women's voices and he came up with some nice choirs of women. We did have a falling out over 'Suzanne'—he wanted a heavy piano syncopated, and maybe drums. That was my first requirement, that I didn't want drums on any of my songs, so that was a bone of contention. Also he was ready to substitute this heavy chordal structure under the song to give it forward movement and I didn't like that, I wanted it to be based on just my picking, and he felt it lacked bottom. And then where we had another falling out was 'So Long, Marianne,' in which there were certain tricky conventions of the time where a song would sometimes just stop and start again later, and I thought that

interrupted the song. But I do think he's a really fine producer and he did bring the project to completion. As my friend Leon Wieseltier said, 'It has the delicious quality of doneness.' "

Particularly delicious by that stage, I would imagine.

"Well, when John Hammond got sick it kind of threw me for a loop and I felt that I'd lost contact with the songs. I actually went to a hypnotist in New York—I wanted her to return me to the original impulse of the songs. It was a desperate measure but I thought I'd give it a shot. And it didn't work, I couldn't go under. [Laughs] The whole episode had a comic quality that I could not escape."

The disagreements continued until Simon finally threw up his hands. "He said, 'You mix it. I'm going on vacation,'" said Leonard, "and I did."[4] Leonard worked with the studio engineer, Warren Vincent. When Vincent asked Leonard what the trouble was, he answered that he disliked the arrangements: the orchestration on "Suzanne" was too big, and "Hey, That's No Way to Say Goodbye" sounded too soft. "I'm not that kind of guy," Leonard told him. "I don't believe that tenderness has to be weakness." Vincent said, "We'll see what we can do." "Well, if we can't," said Leonard, "I'll commit suicide."[5]

It happened that Nico was performing in New York that week at Steve Paul's the Scene, a cellar nightclub that was part cave and part labyrinth and was popular with both the rock crowd and high society. The series of shows was to promote Nico's solo debut *Chelsea Girl*, an album that included songs by Jackson Browne and Bob Dylan but ultimately nothing by Leonard. The house band at the Scene was a young West Coast psychedelic folk rock group called the Kaleidoscope; David Lindley, Chris Darrow, Solomon Feldthouse and Chester Crill were musical virtuosos who played a variety of stringed instruments of various ethnicities. It was their first East Coast tour and they were supposed to have been playing a series of shows at the Café Au Go Go, but, after the first night, the owner told them not to come back, that no one liked long-haired California hippies in New

York. Steve Paul took pity on them and offered them a three-week residency at his club.

"The Scene," says Chris Darrow, "was the heavy club in town at that time, and everybody who was anybody showed up the first night we played: Andy Warhol and all his people, Frank Zappa with the Mothers of Invention, the Cyrkle; Tiny Tim was the emcee. That was the night we met Leonard Cohen. He came up to me after our first set. In that light he looked like the palest human being I had ever met. He was wearing a black leather jacket and he was carrying a black briefcase—I remember this so particularly because he was out of place in terms of what a musician in 1967 looked like. My dad was a college professor and Leonard looked like a college professor—a real academic vibe. He appeared very confident, like he belonged there. He just walked right up to me and said, 'I'm doing an album for Columbia Records and I think you guys are really great. Would you be interested in playing on my album?'"

After the last set of the night, they met in the Greek hamburger joint above the club. Conversation turned to Greece and how much Leonard liked living there. As Chester Crill recalled, one thing Leonard said he liked about Greece was that he could get Ritalin there—a stimulant widely used for both narcolepsy and hyperactivity—without a prescription. Crill told Leonard that he had stopped taking acid since some of the manufacturers starting cutting it with Ritalin. "Leonard said, 'Oh, I really loved that.' He said it was very good for focus."

The following afternoon Leonard, carrying a briefcase and a guitar, met with the band at the Albert Hotel, where they shared a room. Sitting on a bed, the only place not taken up with one or another of their instruments, Leonard sang them his songs. "I didn't really know what to make of them," says Crill. "It sounded like it was probably an attempt at folk music, but kind of in the pop genre, but then the songs were a little unusual for pop, not your typical A-B, A-B." David Lindley says, "I liked them. I thought it was kind of an unusual approach, but in those days people did a lot of things that were unusual—every kind of approach. A lot of the words to the songs were great, and he had a real understated way of delivering them. And he really seemed to like us, so it was good." They agreed to come to the studio and play on his album. "I thought, 'Nothing's going to come of this,'" says Crill, "'but we're starving to death and we'll get enough money to eat and do our gigs in Boston then go home.' It really saved our asses."

The Kaleidoscope showed up at Studio E laden with stringed instruments, including harp guitar, bass, violin, mandolin and some of Feldtman's Middle Eastern assortment. Crill and Darrow found themselves sharing the elevator with Arthur Godfrey. "I remember listening to his radio show on the cab ride back with the guys and he was saying, 'I had to share the elevator with a bunch of those filthy hippies,'" recalls Crill. In the candlelit studio, Leonard was deep in discussion with the man behind the control desk, who was saying, "'We've spent all the money, it's already the most expensive album we've ever been associated with,' blah, blah, blah. Then they would play a track for us and the producer would come on the talk-back and say, 'We only have one track open so we can't put two instruments in here,' and a ten-minute argument would begin. Leonard, poor guy, would be, 'We don't want the glockenspiel'—because on every one of these tracks it sounded like there was two orchestras and a carousel. It was like a fruitcake, it was so full of stuff. Making the room for us to play on anything took more time than actually having us play, because of the old technology. And to go from a guy who was sitting in your room, just playing a guitar and singing a song in a nice quiet voice, to the Entrance of the Gladiators—Jesus! His songs weren't the kind that needed all that orchestration and women's voices to get them across. It sounded like Tiny Tim's first album. I felt really sorry for the guy."

In the studio, Leonard sang the songs as he had originally played them, before the overdubs. "He went through a lot of songs," says Chris Darrow, "basically trying to figure out if anybody had any ideas. I remember him playing the guitar and having a hard time myself trying to figure out what the groove was, because he had this sort of amorphous guitar style that was very circular. I think one of the problems that he was having was that he wanted something very specific and he understood what it was that he wanted, but I think he was having a hard time at that time either getting producers or other musicians to understand. I never remember him being disparaging about anybody else or anything, but it being his first record and him not being really known as a musician I think there were things he was having a hard time communicating."

There was no rehearsal. The band improvised, and Leonard told them when he liked something and if he wanted them to add another instrument. The latter would prompt a voice from the control room, over the talk-back, telling Leonard that he could only have one. When Leonard protested, Crill recalls, "he was told, 'We can't change it; we're locked into this.' It was horrible for him. It wasn't for us, because every minute we were getting more money for getting out of New York."

The Kaleidoscope did three Leonard Cohen sessions in all, two long and one short, playing on "So Long, Marianne," "Teachers," "Sisters of Mercy," "Winter Lady" and "The Stranger Song." They were not in the album credits, but neither were any of the other musicians; as Lindley points out, at that time "it was like dancing bears or performing seals"; you just did the job and moved on. John Simon too had moved on; he was now producing the band Blood, Sweat and Tears and, he said, pretty sure that he was not in the studio when Leonard and the Kaleidoscope played. Simon felt that he had done all he could for Leonard, and if Leonard wanted to change what he'd done, yes, he was disappointed—"But," he said, "it was *his* album. Plus he was older than I, so I was conditioned to back off graciously."

Talking to Simon more than forty years later, he still rhapsodizes about the album. "'Suzanne': fucking gorgeous, I love this track; the strings and the girls together with the rich vocal and guitar make a lush blanket of sound. 'Hey, That's No Way to Say Goodbye' is another of my favorites—this and 'Suzanne' both have a guitar line in thirds with the vocal. I like the girls' parts a lot—they're mine—and I love the instrument that sounds like a Brazilian *berimbau* or a low-pitched Jew's harp, which must be the Kaleidoscope. The mandolin on 'Sisters of Mercy' is probably the Kaleidoscope—talk about elaborate. 'So Long, Marianne': I heard somewhere that Leonard specified there be no drums on his album; well, there are drums on this. Incidentally, stereo was so new and strange to me—or to whomever mixed this; who knows at this point?—that I placed the bass and drums fully to one side of the stereo, a no-no. 'The Stranger Song' made me think about his lyrics. Although Bob Dylan paved the way for the lyricists who followed him, in that he got an audience to accept lyrics that were more thoughtful, less banal than the average pop lyric, Leonard's seem to show more finesse. His scansion is stricter, his rhymes truer, as a rule. Whereas Dylan's language had a connection to 'the people,' in the tradition of Woody Guthrie, blues and folk, Leonard's lyrics reveal a more educated, exposed, literate poet. But Leonard was not just a poet who strummed a little. What a marvel the speed of his finger-picking pattern is. I like the humor in the lyrics of 'One of Us Cannot Be Wrong,' they have an undercurrent of ardent young lust, but they're so funny at the same time. As for the questionable taste of the ending with the recorder, the whistle and Leonard screeching way up high, what can I say? We were young."

Said Leonard, "I always think of something Irving Layton said about the requirements for a young poet, and I think it goes for a young singer, too, or a beginning singer: 'The two qualities most important for a young poet are arrogance and inexperience.' It's only some very strong self-image that can keep you going in a world that conspires to silence everyone."[6]

Songs of Leonard Cohen was shipped on December 26, 1967, in the winter of the Summer of Love.* Leonard was thirty-three years old—by sixties standards antediluvian. He made no attempt to disguise his age in the photograph on the album's front sleeve, a head-shot, taken in a New York subway station photo booth. Sepia-toned and with a funereal black border, it showed a solemn man in a dark jacket and white shirt, unmistakably a grown-up; it might well have been the photo of a dead Spanish poet. Viewed alongside the head-shot on the back of *Let Us Compare Mythologies*, in which Leonard looked more buttoned-up, less defiant, it appeared that Leonard's bottomless eyes had seen too much in the eleven years between his first book and first LP. The back cover was taken up with a colorful drawing of a woman in flames—a Mexican saint picture Leonard found at the store where he bought his candles and spells. It was quite unlike any other album sleeve of its time.

Then, Leonard's album was like nothing of its time—or of any time, really. Its songs sounded both fresh and ancient, sung with the authority of a man used to being listened to, which he was. Their images and themes—war and betrayal, longing and despair, sexual and spiritual yearning, familiar to readers of his poetry—were in keeping with the rock music zeitgeist, but the words in which they were expressed were dense, serious and enigmatic. There is a hypnotic quality to the album—the cumulative effect of the pace and inflection, the circular guitar, Leonard's unhurried, authoritative voice—through which the songs are absorbed and trusted as much as understood.

There are characters in the songs as cryptic as those in Bob Dylan's, like the man with the sadism of a Nazi and the golden body of a god with whom the singer shares a lover in "Master Song." Dylan,

---

* Because of the holidays, the release date is generally considered January 1968.

in fact, was the name that came up most often in the reviews of *Songs of Leonard Cohen*, particularly in discussions of the lyrics. "One of Us Cannot Be Wrong," Leonard's wryly humorous song, inspired by Nico, about a man battered but unbroken by lust, shared a small patch of common ground with Dylan's "Leopard-Skin Pill-Box Hat." But the poetry of Leonard's lyrics was more honed and controlled, steeped in literary and rhetorical technique. In liturgy also.

"Suzanne," the opening song, appears to be a love song, but it is a most mysterious love song, in which the woman inspires a vision of Jesus, first walking on the water, then forsaken by his father, on the Cross. "So Long, Marianne," likewise, begins as a romance, until we learn that the woman who protects him from loneliness also distracts him from his prayers, thereby robbing him of divine protection. The two women in "Sisters of Mercy," since they are not his lovers, are portrayed as nuns. (Leonard wrote the song during a blizzard in Edmonton, Canada, after encountering two young girl backpackers in a doorway. He offered them his hotel bed and, when they fell straight to sleep, watched them from an armchair, writing, and played them the song the next morning when they woke.) Yet, however pure and holy, a sense of romantic possibility remains for a man who in *The Favorite Game* described the woman making up the hotel bed in which they had just made love as having "the hands of a nun." There are many lovers in these songs, but also teachers, masters and saviors. In the song titled "Teachers," the initiate is offered a variety to choose from, including a madman and a holy man who talks in riddles.

Perhaps the most cryptic track on the album is "The Stranger Song," a masterful, multilayered song about exile and moving on. It was born, Leonard said, "out of a thousand hotel rooms, ten thousand railway stations."[7] The Stranger might be the Jew, exiled by ancestry, perpetually on the run from his murderers and God; the troubadour, rootless by necessity; or the writer, whom domesticity would sap of his will to create. Here love is once again presented as something dangerous. We have Joseph, the good husband and Jew, searching for a place where his wife can give birth to a child who is not his, and whose existence will come to cause more problems for his people. In the "holy game of poker," it is of no use to sit around and wait in hope for a good hand of cards. The only way to win is to cheat, or to show no emotion, or to make sure to sit close to the exit door.

If Leonard had recorded just this one compelling album and disappeared, as Anthony DeCurtis, the American music critic, wrote in his liner notes to the 2003 reissue, "his stature as one of the most gifted songwriters of our time will still be secure." On its original release, the U.S. press was considerably more lukewarm. Arthur Schmidt in *Rolling Stone* wrote, "I don't think I could ever tolerate all of it. There are three brilliant songs, one good one, three qualified bummers, and three are the flaming shits. . . . Whether the man is a poet or not (and he is a brilliant poet) he is not necessarily a songwriter."[8] The *New York Times*'s Donal Henahan damned it with faint praise: "Mr. Cohen is a fair poet and a fair novelist, and now he has come through with a fair recording of his own songs." Leonard sounded "like a sad man cashing in on self-pity and adolescent loneliness," he wrote, placing him "somewhere between Schopenhauer and Bob Dylan" on the "alienation scale."[9]

In the UK the album was received positively. Tony Palmer praised it in the *Observer* newspaper.* *Melody Maker* critic Karl Dallas wrote, "I predict that the talk about him will become deafening. His songs are pretty complex things. No one could accuse him of underestimating his audiences."[10] The album failed to enter the charts in Canada. In America it scraped into the lower reaches of the Top 100, while in the UK it made it to No. 13 on the charts—a division of devotion that would continue throughout much of Leonard's musical career.

In interviews he gave in 1968 to promote the album, Leonard appeared to be feeling his way through this new pop music world he

---

* The same Tony Palmer would shoot the 1974 Leonard documentary *Bird on a Wire.*

had entered. He complained to the UK press that New York did not understand him: "[They] kept putting me in an intellectual bag, but that's not where I'm at. I never thought of myself as a Poet with a capital 'P,' I just want to make songs for people because I reckon that they can understand things that I understand. I want to write the sort of songs you hear on the car radio. I don't want to achieve any sort of virtuosity. I want to write lyrics that no one notices but they find themselves singing over a few days later without remembering where they heard them."[11] But despite his protestations that he wanted to be considered a popular artist, he had turned down "$15,000 worth of concerts," he said, "because I didn't want to do them," adding that "the presence of money in the whole enterprise has been having a sinister magical effect on me." Although money had been a big motivation for the shift from literature to the music business, he told *Melody Maker*, he was already thinking of giving music up. "Right now I feel like I did when I finished my novel [*Beautiful Losers*]. At the end of the book I knew I wouldn't write another because I'd put everything I had into that one."[12]

He talked about going back to Greece. But for now he stayed on the promotional treadmill and continued to try on masks to see how they fit. He described himself in *The Beat* as an anarchist "unable to throw the bomb."[13] He told the *New York Times*, "When I see a woman transformed by the orgasm we have together, then I know we've met. I really am for the matriarchy." He was also for the Cross: "The crucifixion will again be understood as a universal symbol, not just an experiment in sadism or masochism or arrogance."[14] In a 1968 *Playboy* article he said, "I had some things in common with the Beatniks and even more things with the hippies. The next thing may be even closer to where I am."[15] The headline of the *Playboy* article summed it up quite perfectly: RENAISSANCE MENSCH. The photo, shot on Hydra, made the melancholy Canadian New Yorker look curiously like a silent movie actor playing a Florida real estate salesman: wide-brimmed hat, thin mustache and villainous smile.

Leonard's U.S. record label changed its original advertisement for the album, which included a quote from the *Boston Globe* review, "James Joyce is not dead . . . ," to one with a quote from *Playboy:* "I've been on the outlaw scene since I was 15." They added a rather incongruous photo of a smiling, bestubbled Leonard, dressed in striped pajamas, lying alongside his somber self-portrait on the album sleeve. As part of a more sensible promotional campaign in the UK, CBS released in early 1968 a low-priced sampler album titled *The Rock Machine Turns You On.* Among tracks from Dylan, Simon & Garfunkel, Spirit, Tim Rose and Taj Mahal was Leonard, singing "Sisters of Mercy."

Leonard, meanwhile, was in a dreary room at the Henry Hudson, talking to a journalist from the *Montreal Gazette,* assuring him that his next album—the album that only weeks ago he was unsure he was going to make—would be a country and western record. As he had planned to do in the first place, he said, he was going to Tennessee.

Eleven

The Tao of Cowboy

He could ride a horse, he knew how to shoot a rifle and, for a man who claimed to have not a sentimental bone in his body, he could sing a Hank Williams song to break your heart. Out of all the thirtysome-thing urban sophisticates in New York City, the likeliest to survive being dropped from the sky into rural Tennessee was Leonard. But New York was not quite done with him yet. His American publisher, Viking, hitching a ride on the album's publicity campaign, issued a second edition of *Beautiful Losers* and was gearing up for the June 1968 release of a new poetry book, *Selected Poems 1956–1968.** The first of Leonard's poetry books to be published in the U.S. offered twenty new poems, including the one he once scrawled to Marita on Le Bistro's wall, along with a selection from earlier volumes. Many were handpicked by Marianne and the emphasis was on his lyrical and personal poems of love and loss. Although their love affair was all but over, eroded by time and distances and Leonard's ways in matters of domesticity and survival, there were still ties that bound.

---

* The UK edition appeared in 1969.

If there were good reasons not to leave New York, there were none to stay in the Henry Hudson Hotel. Leonard checked back into the Chelsea. Not many days passed before he noticed a woman who seemed to share his timetable, wandering the hotel at three in the morning looking for a drink and company. Janis Joplin had moved into the Chelsea while recording her second album with Big Brother & the Holding Company, which John Simon was producing. One night, as Leonard was on the way back to the hotel from the Bronco Burger and Janis from Studio E, they found themselves sharing the elevator, and then an unmade bed. In later years, after Leonard immortalized Janis's blow job in song—first in "Chelsea Hotel #1," which he sang live but never released, then "Chelsea Hotel #2," recorded on 1974's *New Skin for the Old Ceremony*—he polished the encounter into a stage anecdote. "She wasn't looking for me, she was looking for Kris Kristofferson; I wasn't looking for her, I was looking for Brigitte Bardot; but we fell into each other's arms through some process of elimination."[1] His words had the dark humor of both loneliness and honesty. Leonard's later refinements to the anecdote were less black, more stand-up comedy. He said he asked her who she was looking for and when she told him he quipped, "My dear lady, you're in luck, I am Kris Kristofferson."[2] Either way, she made an exception.

Interestingly, the anecdotes followed a similar pattern to the songs. "Chelsea Hotel #1" was the more open and emotional of the two:

> *A great surprise, lying with you baby*
> *Making your sweet little sound. . .*
> *See all your tickets*
> *Torn on the ground*
> *All of your clothes and*
> *No piece to cover you*
> *Shining your eyes in*
> *My darkest corner.*

The second was more guarded and unsentimental:

> *I can't keep track of each fallen robin. . . .*
> *I don't think of you that often*

making the encounter sound humdrum—particularly when compared with the extravagance in his poem "Celebration," where the
orgasm from oral sex felled the protagonist "like those gods on the
roof that Samson pulled down." Leonard expressed regret on several
occasions later at having named Joplin as the fellatrix and muse of the
song. "She would not have minded," he said. "My mother would have
minded."[3] Quite possibly, but really it was Leonard who minded—
not just this rare lack of good manners, but having revealed so much
of the mystery, shown how the trick was done. Janis was a one-night
stand and, it's safe to say, not the only woman in the Chelsea to have
given him head, yet something about her, or about what happened to
her—less than three years later, at the age of twenty-seven, in a hotel
room in Los Angeles, Janis Joplin OD'd and died—seemed to have
gotten under Leonard's skin.

———————

David Crosby was in Miami, in the brief hiatus between being fired
by the Byrds and cofounding Crosby, Stills & Nash, when he first set
eyes on Joni Mitchell. She was singing alone in a coffeehouse and
Crosby was "smitten." He brought her back with him to Los Angeles
and she moved in with him. Crosby set about finding his new love
a record deal and appointed himself her album producer. "She was
magnificent and magical, and though I wasn't really a producer, I just
knew that somebody needed to keep the world from trying to translate what she did into a normal bass, drums and keyboards format,
because that would have been a fucking disaster." Despite his good
intentions, making an album with Joni "really wasn't fun"—working

with Beethoven was no easier than living with Beethoven. When it was done, and the blood washed from the walls, Joni surprised Crosby by suggesting that he produce her friend Leonard Cohen's second album.

Crosby knew nothing about Leonard, other than "Suzanne," Judy Collins's version; he thought it "one of the prettiest songs" he'd heard. But Joni was persuasive. Crosby booked two sessions, on May 17 and 18, at Columbia's Los Angeles studio, a large room in which he had previously worked with the Byrds, and Leonard, who appeared to have no objection to the plans Joni had made for him, flew to L.A. "I don't remember him saying anything about what he really wanted to have happen," says Crosby, "he just put himself in my hands. Poor fellow." On the first day, they recorded one song, "Lady Midnight." On the second they recorded two, "Bird on the Wire" and "Nothing to One."

"It really was not a happy experience," says Crosby. "It's an embarrassing story for me and a bitter pill to swallow because I could produce him now in a minute, but then I had no idea how to record him. I listened to him sing, and I'm a melodic singer, so I didn't know what to do with a voice like Leonard's. The only other singer vaguely like Leonard was Bob Dylan, and I couldn't have recorded Dylan either. When the Byrds tried to record Dylan songs, we changed them completely, gave them a beat, put harmonies to them, translated them completely from their original form. It was quite obvious that Leonard was one of the best poets and lyricists alive, so I imagined that the way to go about it was to take him in the direction that Dylan had gone and speak the lyrics more than sing them. It did not make him happy."

The Crosby-produced "Nothing to One" has Crosby singing harmony, while his production of "Bird on the Wire" has something of a solo, coffeehouse Byrds feel: folk rock with a touch of rhythmic pop. These two recordings were eventually unearthed as bonus tracks on the 2007 reissue of *Songs from a Room*. The Cohen-Crosby version of "Lady Midnight" remains in the vaults. "I've wondered over the years," says Crosby of the experience, "if Leonard forgave me. God knows he deserved somebody a bit smarter and more experienced than I was. But Bob Johnston knew *exactly* what he was doing."

Leonard ran into Bob Johnston in L.A. Normally Los Angeles is not a place to run into people, since they're all in cars inching along endless boulevards to some important meeting or other, but Johnston made a point of being the exception to the rule. Johnston, as Bob Dylan wrote of the man who produced many of his finest albums, was "unreal."[4] Like God, Johnston was everywhere, he had fire in his eyes, and heaven help you if you questioned his ways, particularly if you worked for a record company. Johnston was—still is at age eighty, at the time of writing this book—a maverick, a wiry, bearded redhead with a thick Texas accent and music in his blood. His great-grandfather was a classical pianist, his grandmother a songwriter, his mother won a songwriting Grammy at the age of ninety-two, and his wife, Joy Byers, had written songs that Elvis Presley covered. Johnston wrote songs too, but he was best known at that time as the producer of many of the era's greatest and most influential artists. Just four and a half months into 1968 he had recorded Bob Dylan's *John Wesley Harding*, Simon and Garfunkel's *Bookends*, Marty Robbins's *By the Time I Get to Phoenix*, Flatt & Scruggs's *The Story of Bonnie and Clyde* and Johnny Cash's *At Folsom Prison*, some of these albums still waiting their turn to come out, like buses in a depot. But having been thwarted the first time, he was still determined to produce a Leonard Cohen album.

"I had no plans to make another record," Leonard said. "I didn't think it was necessary. Then one day I met Bob Johnston and I liked the way he talked and how he understood my first album, exactly what was good and what was bad about it."[5] Johnston says, "Leonard said, 'Let's get together,' and I said, 'Fuck yeah.' I had just rented a farm, two thousand acres, Boudleaux Bryant's place"—Bryant and his wife, Felice, were successful Nashville songwriters, with hits that included "Love Hurts" and "All I Have to Do Is Dream"—"and I told Leonard about it. He said, 'Someday I'll have a farm like this and I'll write a couple of albums.' I said, 'Here, do it now,' and I gave him the key, and he moved in for two years."

But first Leonard went to Hydra. His affiliations with his second home were the opposite of his "neurotic affiliations" with Montreal. He wanted to sit in his shirtsleeves in the sun and smoke a cigarette and watch life crawl slowly by; he wanted to return to the simple life in the house on the hill with Marianne and her child. He was pleased to discover that the military junta had not had much tangible effect on the place. At first, when the new Greek government announced bans on long hair, miniskirts and a number of musicians and artists, the expats would gather in the tavernas at night, lock the doors, pull the shutters closed and play the outlawed music. But really the colonels hadn't noticed Hydra, or if they had, they did not much care. Still, there were some changes on the island that Leonard could not ignore. For one, George Johnston and Charmian Clift were no longer sitting at a table in the sun outside Katsikas, waiting for the ferry to arrive with its news and its newcomers. For another, at night the houses on the hills were lit up with electric lights.

It had been three years since Leonard had woken to find his house newly tethered to the twentieth century. Says Marianne, "Leonard got out of bed after a week of feeling lousy—he had been for a trip around the islands with Irving Layton and had some kind of flu. He came to his studio and he looked out and discovered that during the night they had put up all the new electric wires and they crossed in front of his window. He was sitting in this rocking chair that I brought from my little house. I brought him a cup of hot chocolate, and I took the guitar down which was hanging on the wall and it was totally out of tune. While we're sitting there, birds are landing on the wire like notes on a music sheet. I heard '*Like a bird—on the wire . . .*' So beautiful. But it took him three years before he felt the song was finished."

Finishing their relationship also took a long time. Leonard would say in 1970 (when introducing the song "So Long, Marianne" at a concert), "I lived with her for about eight years, about six months of the year, then the other six months I was stuck somewhere else. Then I found I was living with her four months of the year and then two months of the year and then about the eighth year I was living with her a couple of weeks of the year, and I thought it was time to write this particular song for her." But soon after starting the song he stopped singing and added, "I still live with her a couple of days of the year."[6]

All that Marianne will say about the end of the affair is, "To me he was still the same, he was a gentleman, and he had that stoic thing about him and that smile he will try to hide behind—'Am I serious now or is all this a joke?' We were in love and then the time was up. We were always friends, and he still is my dearest friend and I will always love him. I feel very lucky to have met Leonard at that time in my life. He taught me so much, and I hope I gave him a line or two."

From Hydra Leonard went to London, where that summer he made two appearances on the BBC: the radio show *Top Gear*, hosted by John Peel (the revered and influential British DJ was an early Leonard Cohen enthusiast) and a television concert in which he performed almost all the songs from his first album, along with three songs that would appear on later albums, and an improvised, self-deprecating, stoned-sounding sing-along titled "There's No Reason Why You Should Remember Me." Both shows were very well received. By now *Songs of Leonard Cohen* was in the Top 20 in the UK. He was to all intents and purposes a pop/rock star. There was some attention from the U.S. too. That summer, Leonard was featured in two different articles in the *New York Times:* one was an examination of the new singer-songwriter movement in pop; the other, illustrated with photographs of Leonard and Dylan, debated whether pop lyrics should be considered "poetry."

That Leonard's latest book of poetry, *Selected Poems*, was proving popular in America only muddied the waters. The dust-jacket blurb made an appeal to the pop/rock market by mentioning Leonard's album and the covers of his songs by Judy Collins, Buffy Sainte-Marie and Noel Harrison. It also appealed to the literary underground by recalling the outrage that greeted his novel *Beautiful Losers*, to critics and academics by calling him "a contemporary *Minnesinger*" (a singer-poet in the German chivalric tradition), and to sensitive souls with its description of him as "eclectic, searching, deeply personal."[7]

But the literati, particularly in Canada, did not take warmly to his move into the popular field. It made him a "personality," which brought with it the danger, as Michael Ondaatje wrote, that "our interest in Cohen makes the final judgement, not the quality of the writing."[8] Cohen and Dylan, Ondaatje said, were "public artists" who relied heavily "on their ability to be cynical about their egos or pop sainthood while at the same time continuing to build it up. They can con the media men who are their loudspeakers, yet keep their integrity and appear sincere to their audiences." It was a reasonable argument, although the media was often well aware of this game and interpreted Leonard as a work of fiction in action, where academics interpreted the words on the page. Leonard's words, thanks to the publicity and sales of his first album, had now started to sell in previously unimaginable quantities. Rock album numbers, not poetry book numbers. *Selected Poems* would sell two hundred thousand copies.

After his short promotional trip to London, Leonard returned to New York and the Chelsea. He checked into room 100 (which Sid Vicious and Nancy Spungen would later make notorious) and propped his guitar in the corner and put his typewriter on the desk. On the bedside table he put the books he was reading: Gore Vidal's *Myra Breckinridge* (a book that, like *Beautiful Losers*, had been deemed pornographic by several critics) and *Tales of the Hasidim: Later Masters* by

Martin Buber, stories about rabbis searching for enlightenment. As to this particular descendant of Aaron, he had started attending the Church of Scientology.

Scientology was a new religion, founded a decade and a half earlier by an American science fiction novelist named L. Ron Hubbard. It had some of the trappings of the old religions, like its eight-pointed cross and its sacred books. The first such book, *Dianetics*, an imaginative hodgepodge of, among other things, Eastern mysticism and Freud, read like an early self-help book and, like one, sold in enormous quantities. It claimed to heal the unconscious mind and, along with it, man's physical and psychological problems, resulting in liberation from pain and trauma, universal brotherhood, the end to war and oneness with the universe. Scientology, unsurprisingly, did good business in America in 1968, when there was no shortage of traumatized young people looking for some kind of answer. It was a year of turbulence and paranoia—the assassinations of Martin Luther King and Robert Kennedy, riots in the ghettos, protests in the universities, young Americans still being sent to Vietnam and coming home in caskets—and neither the drugs nor the old orthodoxies were working.

Hubbard's religion, in keeping with the times, had a slogan, "Scientology works," and spread the word through young adherents approaching other young people on the street. It also reflected its founder's origins in science fiction, coming with extraterrestrials, strange contraptions and its own language. Man's strongest urge, Hubbard wrote, was survival, but this survival was under attack by engrams, cellular memories of physical and mental pain that chain him to his past. The way to remove these charges was by auditing— revisiting past traumas under supervision with an auditor, a Scientology counselor, while wired to an e-meter, a device that resembled a couple of small tin cans and a dial. After a course of successful auditing, you go clear and are ready to take the next step toward becoming an Operating Thetan and living in a pain-free present. Leonard thought Scientology, for all its snake oil, had "very good data."[9] He signed up for auditing.

————

At night the Chelsea Hotel came to life. People who rarely left their rooms by daylight emerged and came together, often in Harry Smith's room. Smith was an extraordinary man, a forty-five-year-old in the body of an eccentric old man: wild white hair, scraggly beard, towering forehead and oversized spectacles that magnified his bright, intelligent eyes. He lived with his pet birds in a dark, tiny, room with no bathroom on the eighth floor. It was crammed with curios: magic wands, Seminole Indian clothes, painted Ukrainian eggs, a collection of paper airplanes, esoteric books and weird old American records. In music circles Smith was renowned for his *Anthology of American Folk Music*, three double albums he compiled from his collection of old, raw folk, blues and gospel. The albums were an enormous influence on Dylan and the sixties folk revival. Smith was not only a musicologist but an anthropologist, an expert on Native America and shamanism, an experimental filmmaker, a raconteur and a mystic, who claimed to have learned the art of alchemy at around the same age Leonard was studying hypnotism. Little surprise that Leonard was drawn to him. Along with other assorted Chelsea residents and writers and music celebrities who were passing through, he would sit at Smith's feet and listen to his labyrinthine monologue.

"We saw Harry as a national monument and sardonic guru from whom even Leonard had something to learn," says Terese Coe, the author of the play *Harry Smith at the Chelsea*. "That's why Leonard was there. Harry could be expounding upon any number of intellectual, historical and artistic themes, he might be showing his paintings, talking about his recent misadventures in filmmaking, bewailing his financial disasters, insulting present guests in elliptical terms, playing Brecht-Weill or Woody or Arlo Guthrie—I never heard him play any Leonard Cohen songs. As far as anyone could tell, we were hanging out with a sage who was also at times an antihero, an amusement where anything could happen, but nothing truly decadent ever did in my experience. We were rather well behaved."

Leonard, noticeably more formally dressed than the others in the room, sat quietly, Coe recalls, and rarely said a word. She was a young poet and journalist for an underground newspaper when she met Leonard in Smith's room. She became the muse for two poems in *The Energy of Slaves* (1972): "It Takes a Long Time to See You Terez" and "Terez and Deanne." Says Coe, "I was a passing fancy and he made a fancy pass with provocative lines." She recognized him as "an incurable romantic. In that 'love and peace' era, many were caught in that conundrum. He wasn't one to speak about his philosophy of love in person. He kept his private life and friendships close to the vest. The answers are in his songs, and they are many and mercurial."

There were a number of regulars at Harry Smith's evenings. Peggy Biderman worked at the Museum of Modern Art and had a teenage daughter, Ann (now a successful TV screenwriter), whom Leonard saw for a while. Claude Pelieu and Mary Beach were collage artists who edited a magazine and translated Burroughs and Ginsberg into French. Stanley Amos ran an art gallery from his Chelsea room, complete with vernissages, and would come to Harry's room and read the tarot. Sandy Daley was a photographer, cinematographer and friend of Warhol and of Leonard. In 1970 Daley shot an underground film in her room, on the tenth floor, which was painted and decorated all in white. The film was called *Robert Having His Nipple Pierced*, the Robert being Mapplethorpe. The narrator of the film, Mapplethorpe's partner Patti Smith, was another close friend of Harry Smith. There was also Liberty, a beautiful blond poet and model, with whom Leonard had an affair. Liberty had sat for Salvador Dalí and was a muse for Richard Brautigan and Jerome Charyn, but she was also active in feminist politics, having left her Republican politician husband for the Yippies and the counterculture. After the gatherings everyone, Harry included, would meet up in El Quijote, at the large table at the back of the bar. Leonard would often discreetly pick up the tab for the whole crowd and leave before they discovered it had been paid. Being generous with money was one of the few things Leonard seemed to like about this new level of success.

September 21, 1968. The sun cast long shadows, three-quarters of the year had now passed and Leonard was still in New York. It was the eve of the most solemn day in the Jewish calendar, and Leonard's thirty-fourth birthday. To celebrate, he went by himself to a very crowded place, the Paradox, a macrobiotic restaurant in an East Village basement run by Scientologists. It was a hippie hangout, a place where a person could come to trip out and no one would bother them. If they had no money, they could work in the kitchen for food. Thelma Blitz, a young woman who worked as an ad agency copywriter, sat at one of the long, communal tables and looked up from her dinner to see the man sitting opposite looking deeply into her eyes.

"I didn't know him. He didn't look like a lot of the other people. He had short hair—everyone else there had long hair—and he looked kind of straight; he was dressed conservatively, not like a businessman, more like a college professor." And a lot like Dustin Hoffman, Blitz told him. "Leonard said, 'People often tell me that.'" They talked about all sorts of things—poetry, metaphysics, vegetarianism—with Leonard cordially taking the contrary position to everything she said. "It was a great debate. I didn't know until I read biographies of him that he was president of his debating club in college." They argued all night, until the Paradox closed and Leonard asked if she would like to walk with him. They strolled along Saint Mark's Place, where the freaks congregated. Leonard stopped to talk to a young man who was taking a large tortoise for a walk. "He asked him, 'What do you feed that thing?' and the young man said, 'Hamburger meat, speed and smack.'"

As they walked, Leonard told her that they were going to the Chelsea Hotel. "I didn't know what the Chelsea Hotel was so I said, 'What's there?' and he said, 'Nico.' I only had a vague idea then of Nico and Andy Warhol but he had a wistfulness in his voice when he said 'Nico,' which makes me think that was why he was there." At the hotel, Leonard went straight to the mail desk at the back of the lobby and gave them his name. "Which is how I found out who he was," says Blitz. "I freaked out a little bit, because I realized this man is important—his first album was in the window of the Saint Mark's bookstore—but I didn't recognize him, he didn't look anything like the picture on the cover. But instead of trying to floor me with his accomplishments, like the usual fellow who picks you up, he wouldn't even tell me who he was. He said, with a tinge of self-irony, downplaying his achievements, 'Well, I have some following in Canada.'"

He told Thelma that it was his birthday and they toasted it in El Quijote with a plate of celery and olives in place of alcohol. Then they went to Leonard's room on the first floor. "He took out a guitar and sang two songs to me that I didn't recognize until the second album came out, 'Bird on the Wire' and 'The Partisan Song' [*sic*]. When he sang, I saw this remoteness, and I noted in my journal that his mask of grief and remoteness deepened as he sang. He kept spacing out, coming back and forth, something like the nictitating membrane of a frog came over his eyes and he would seem not to be there. I thought, 'Am I boring him?' I told him I was sick of being an advertising writer, and he suggested starvation and several good books. He talked about teachers and masters and conquering pain, saying things like, 'The more we conquer pain, the more pain we incur on a higher level'—which sounds like the line from [the song] 'Avalanche,' '*You who wish to conquer pain.*' But there was a lot of pain at that time among the people who made up the counterculture: the pain of hating your culture, hating the system, being completely at odds with everything. Everybody was into something."

Leonard did not talk much to Blitz about Scientology, except "to say that it worked." She remembered his talking to her about money, saying that "he had a hundred thousand dollars and he didn't know what to do with it—buy land in Nova Scotia? I remember him looking kind of agonized as he talked about money." They spent the night together. The following morning, when Leonard walked her to the bus—she was off to spend the Jewish New Year with her family—he told her to call him when she got back. When she did, the operator at the Chelsea said he had checked out. He had gone to Tennessee.

———————

Two years behind schedule, and three days before his first session for *Songs from a Room*, Leonard was finally in Nashville. His friend from Montreal Henry Zemel flew out with him. There at the gate to meet them was large man with long hair, a bandanna and a mustache. He was part hippie, bigger part good ol' boy. Since Bob Johnston was, as always, busy in the studio, he sent Charlie Daniels to pick them up. In 1968 Daniels wasn't the Opry-inducted, hard-core country star with the big beard and Stetson, but a songwriter and session musician—fiddle, guitar, bass and mandolin. Johnston first met Daniels in 1959 when he produced the Jaguars, the rock 'n' roll band Daniels fronted. They spent years playing the circuit, getting nowhere. One night Daniels called Johnston and asked if he could get him out of jail—it was advance planning; Daniels was about to get into a fistfight with a club owner. Johnston hollered down the phone that he should "get the fuck out to Nashville," and he did. Johnston had kept him busy ever since, playing on albums by Johnny Cash, Marty Robbins, Bob Dylan, and now Leonard Cohen.

For a city, Nashville felt like a suburb. On the drive from the hotel Leonard saw more men in suits than cowboy hats and more churches than bars. The town's biggest businesses were insurance and Bible publishing; Music Row was all dinky buildings and tidy lawns. But Nashville was the second-biggest music city in America behind New York, home of the Grand Ole Opry and a magnet to songwriters, Tin Pan Alley with twang. It was—like Leonard used to say on Hydra— where the money was. Nashville was chock-full of songwriters— most, like Leonard, hailing from anywhere but Nashville—and it was full of ghosts, of men who'd left wives and families in the mountains to sell their songs and wound up drinking away what little cash and dignity they had left. After checking into their hotel, Leonard and Zemel set off on foot, mapping out the city: the YMCA for a morning swim, the greasiest hole-in-the-wall diners and the dingiest, smoki- est heartbreak bars.

On September 26, 1968, the pair arrived at Nashville's Columbia Studio A for the first session. Leonard was carrying a guitar and Ze- mel a lion tamer's whip. Looking around the room, Leonard took a deep breath: he would need a lot of candles to light up this place. It was enormous, large enough for a symphony orchestra with space left over for a football game. Bob Johnston was behind the glass, play- ing cheerleader, smiling and animated. But starting his second album couldn't help but bring back for Leonard unhappy memories of his first. Having his friend there helped. Zemel would crack the whip and keep him on task, which bemused the musicians almost as much as the Jew's harp he played on half the cuts. "I'm ready," Leonard said, a brave man facing the firing squad. "What do you want me to do?"

The first question Johnston would always ask the artists he worked with was, "What do *you* want to do?" This was quite a concept at a time when recording artists were more used to being told what to do. Johnston had a reputation for going into battle with record company executives to get what his artists wanted. But Johnston was smart enough to know that this question would not help Leonard. Instead he said, "Play a song." Leonard took out his guitar and started to sing.

As he did, Johnston stood up and announced, "Okay, we're going out to have a hamburger and a couple of beers." Leonard said, "Well, I was ready to do the song." Johnston said, "You can do it when you come back." They left to go to Crystal Burger. While they were gone, the engineer, Neil Wilburn, set up the mics the way Johnston liked them. Wilburn had worked with Johnston when he recorded Johnny Cash's prison albums and helped him get that deep, dark, jail-cell voice. For Leonard's album they used three microphones on his vocal, putting them through old echo plates for reverb.

"When we got back," says Johnston, "Leonard said, 'What'll I do?' I said again, 'Just play a song,' and he did." It was "The Partisan." "Then I played it back to him. His voice sounded like a goddamn mountain. When he heard it he said, 'Is that what I'm supposed to sound like?' I said, 'You're goddamn right.'" On that first day, starting at six in the evening and stopping at one in the morning, Johnston taped Leonard singing ten songs. Five would appear on *Songs from a Room;* one would be put aside for the third album, *Songs of Love and Hate;* and four have never as yet been released: "Baby I've Seen You," "Your Private Name," "Breakdown" and "Just Two People" (Leonard had also tried recording this last song with John Hammond for his debut).

For the same reason that Nashville teemed with songwriters, it also crawled with top-notch musicians. Johnston told Leonard he could have the cream of session men on his album, "but he said no, I want friends of yours, so they'll be friendly." Johnston put together a small team of outsiders, men who could play country music but weren't part of the mainstream "Nashvegas" system. As well as Charlie Daniels, there was Ron Cornelius on guitar, Charlie McCoy on bass and Elkin "Bubba" Fowler, a guitarist and banjo-playing preacher who had been half of a toga-wearing psychedelic pop duo called the Avant-Garde. There was no drummer—Johnston was of a mind with Leonard on this—and Johnston himself played keyboards.

Ron Cornelius, to whom Johnston had given the role of bandleader, played with a young, hippie, country rock/electric folk band from Northern California called West. They had come to Nashville in 1967 to work with Johnston on their debut album and returned in 1968 to have Johnston produce their second. West's members prided themselves on not taking outside gigs, but things weren't going well with the band's career when Johnston persuaded him to play on Leonard's album. When Johnston played him Leonard's songs, "I went, you've got to be kidding me," says Cornelius. "I was used to guitars, bass, drums, piano and loud, rock-out, amplified playing. I thought, 'Man, this is really weird stuff.' But then, I guess like anyone who becomes a Leonard Cohen fan, as soon as you get ankle-deep in the lyrics, you're 'Well, I don't care if I've never played anything like this in my life. This is very, very deep stuff.'"

The artist's cards for *Songs from a Room* are not as tidy or detailed as those for *Songs of Leonard Cohen;* Johnston did not have the time or inclination for paperwork. "Bob didn't fill out anything," says Cornelius, laughing. "He just rolled the tape and went to the airport." Johnston would rush off to New York in the morning, work with Simon & Garfunkel, fly back in the afternoon, record Dino Valenti, maybe slot in a session with Dylan or Cash or Dylan and Cash together, grab a beer and some burgers and an hour's nap in his red Eldorado and then work five or six hours with Leonard. The artist's cards list just ten studio sessions with Leonard—four in September, one in early October and, after a month's break, five in November—plus a few more sessions without him for Johnston to do overdubs.

Life in Nashville fell into as much of a routine as something revolving around the workaholic Johnston's schedule would allow: a morning swim at the Y, lunch at Bob and Joy Johnston's place on a workday, then in the evening, Studio A. While the engineers set up the room they would hang out in the basement, which Johnston had converted into a Ping-Pong room. It doubled as a vocals room, as did

the broom closet, if there was a particular sound Johnston was going for. When the session was over Leonard and Zemel would go for
bacon and eggs at their favorite diner—"Bright fluorescent lights, a
blond floozy waitress and a short-order cook with tattoos who looked
like he was on parole," says Zemel—and then a bar, where, unsurprisingly, they proved a success with several of Nashville's womenfolk.

Charlie Daniels recalls the recording as "very relaxed. All the candles were going and everything was so quiet. There were no charts—
we changed things constantly—and nobody in the control room saying you need to do this or that. One of Bob Johnston's great strengths
as a producer was that he stayed out of an artist's way and let the artist
be who he was. He did it with every artist he produced, but it was
very evident with people like Dylan and especially with Leonard
Cohen. With Dylan it was a little different environment, because we
used drums and electric instruments and it was more of a band concept. I remember one time, when Dylan wanted me to take a solo,
Charlie McCoy said, 'Well how much do you want him to play?' and
Dylan said 'All he can'—that was his attitude: 'Well, I'm doing what
I do, you do what *you* do.' But Leonard is a very unique individual.
The thing about Leonard is it's the lyrics, it's the melody and it's
the way he tunes his guitar—I've never seen anybody that had that
softness of touch that could play a gut-string guitar with the strings
tuned down like that, almost flabby. He has a very unique kind of
music, very fragile, that could very easily be bruised or destroyed by
somebody being heavy-handed.

"Leonard would stand there with his guitar and sing a song and
we would try and create something around it that would complement
it. If there was a place that we felt needed enhancing, in one way or
another that's what we tried to do. The main thing was being part of
it but unobtrusive, very transparent, nothing that would distract from
his lyric and melody. You could put something in there that would
mess it up real quick. I learned a lot of things by working with Leon-

ard that I probably wouldn't have known otherwise, that sometimes less is more. Because when you've got a studio full of musicians, everybody's going to want to play something, but with these songs it's more about what you leave out. And Bob was very good at keeping it together and letting you know when it fit or [saying] 'I think we need to go in a different direction on that.'"

Cornelius remembers, "It became a team. I'm sure that Leonard, when he first looked at Charlie Daniels and me, went, 'Oh brother, what have I got myself into here.' But then he saw that we got it, that we understood, musically, what he was doing and were in awe of him as a songwriter, and this was a project we thought about all day long, every day, until the album was over. And Bob Johnston is a very rare breed. He was born with a gift which I've never run into anywhere else, that he could make a stranger want to play or sing, right here tonight, better than they've ever sung or played in their life. Not by saying, 'Here's what I want you to play'; he just had a way of drawing out of a musician or a singer the best in them." Leonard would look up at the glass and see him swaying, sometimes dancing, lost in one of his songs. When he'd finished singing, Johnston would say, "Man! That is a fantastic song. We've got to have that on the album. My God, you've got to do that again," at the same time boosting Leonard's confidence and getting him to do another take he could capture live.

One song whose recording did not come easily was "Bird on the Wire." Leonard tried it over and over, in countless different ways, but every time he listened back, he thought it sounded dishonest somehow. Finally he told Johnston he was done, and the musicians were sent home. "Bob said, okay, let's forget it," said Leonard. "I went back to my hotel to think matters over, but got more and more depressed."[10] He was determined to get this song right. It was as if the song, as well as being a letter to Marianne, were personal treatise of sorts, a "My Way," but without the braggadocio (Leonard was never a big fan of Sinatra; he did have a fondness for Dean Martin, though). "In a way the history of that song on the record is my whole history," Leonard said. "I'd never sung the song true, never. I'd always had a kind of phony Nashville introduction that I was playing the song to, following a thousand models."[11]

Four days before his last recording session on November 25, 1968, Leonard asked everyone to leave except Zemel, McCoy and Johnston. "I just knew that at that moment something was going to take place. I just did the voice before I started the guitar and I heard myself sing that first phrase, '*Like a bird*,' and I knew the song was going to be true and new. I listened to myself singing, and it was a surprise. Then I heard the replay and I knew it was right."[12]

Another song Leonard was not entirely convinced by was "The Partisan," the song he had first learned to play at Camp Sunshine, from *The People's Song Book*, when he was fifteen years old. Johnston says, "He played it for me and it was beautiful, but Leonard wasn't happy with it. He was pacing up and down saying it would be great with some French voices. I said, 'I'll see you in a couple of days.' He said, 'Aren't we recording?' I said, 'Not right now.' The next day I flew to Paris and found three girl singers and an accordion player through some people I knew, and they came in and they did that, overdubbing Leonard's recording. I came back without saying anything to Leonard and I played it. He said 'They're good, they really sound French.' I said, 'That's because they are.'" Johnston laughs. "He was so mad at me for not taking him to France with me."

―――――――

Hank Williams called country music "the white man's blues." By that definition you might say that, with *Songs from a Room*, Leonard succeeded in making his country album. The songs, like the raw, old country, folk and blues on Harry Smith's *Anthology*, are about God, death, love, loss, sin, redemption and soldiering on, and the sound is spare, much less ornamented than *Songs of Leonard Cohen*. "A lot of my friends who were musical purists had castigated me for the lushness and overproduction of my first record," said Leonard, "and I think that got to me somewhere and I was determined to do a very simple album. It's very stark."[13] But, aside from the jaunty "Tonight Will Be Fine" and "Bird on the Wire"—a song that Johnny Cash would cover many years later and whose sing-along melody Kris Kristofferson once compared with Lefty Frizzell's "Mom and Dad's Waltz"—these were not "Nashville" songs; you could not imagine singing them on a back porch or in a bar. Despite the chirping-cricket sound of the Jew's harp, its overall feel is less of wide, open rural America than small, plain, European or New York City rooms.

The album teems with killers: religious fanatics, revolutionaries and suicides. In the beautiful and mournful "Seems So Long Ago, Nancy," Leonard sings about a young woman he knew in Montreal, a judge's daughter, who shot herself when her illegitimate baby was taken away. In the haunting "Story of Isaac" Leonard takes the same biblical story Dylan referenced on "Highway 61 Revisited"—God commanding Abraham to sacrifice his son—and transforms it into a protest about violence and atrocities both ancient and modern, public and personal. The song has a novelist's eye for detail, the potency and elegy of his early poetry and also a touch of autobiography in the protagonist being a nine-year-old boy, Leonard's age when his father died. "The Butcher," raw acoustic blues, uses the Passover Haggadah to similar ancient/contemporary effect.

The reviews in the U.S. were not good. *Rolling Stone*'s Alec Dubro wrote, "In 'Story of Isaac,' he is matter of fact to the point of being dull. When he's not being matter of fact, but rather obscure, as he is in 'A Bunch of Lonesome Heroes,' he's just irritating. Other singer-poets are obscure, but generally the feeling comes through that an attempt is being made to reach to a heart of meaning. But Cohen sings with such lack of energy that it's pretty easy to conclude that if he's not going to get worked up about it, why should we."[14] The *New York Times*'s William Kloman was kinder, remarking that "as a story-teller Cohen is superb, even when he tacks self-effacing morals onto the end of his tales," but he disliked the album's more understated production and concluded, "Cohen's new songs are short on beauty."[15]

Released in April 1969, *Songs from a Room* performed better than its predecessor. It made it to No. 12 in Canada and No. 63 on the U.S. charts. In the UK, though it soared to No. 2, it was kept from the top position by a budget-priced compilation of hit singles titled *20 Dynamic Hits*, by artists from Deep Purple to Cilla Black. Reviewers across Europe all seemed to appreciate this new, unadorned production style. It was right that Leonard came to us naked, with very little baggage besides these strangely comforting songs that seemed to be written from a life led in the long dark hours before dawn, by someone whose word you could trust.

"I think that element of trust is critical. Certainly I think what draws anyone to a book or a poem or a song is that you trust the guy, the woman."

You too? Is that what draws you to others' work?

"I never put it that way but yes, I think that's so, I go for that feeling of trust. When I listen to somebody like George Jones, he's working with the best studio musicians in Nashville and it's an absolutely impeccable production, sometimes over the top, but it doesn't matter, you trust the voice."

———

Some thirty-five miles south of Nashville—the last half dozen of them down a winding dirt road from the outskirts of Franklin, the nearest town—was 5435 Big East Fork Road. The Bryants' two thousand acres encompassed forests, a creek, horses, herds of thoroughbred cattle, wild peafowl, chickens, four barns and a cabin. Stepping down from his new jeep, Leonard surveyed his new kingdom. He had sung in "Stories of the Street" about finding a farm—it was a common sentiment in the late sixties, going back to the land, since urban life had become increasingly dystopic—and here it was, his for two years for $75 a month. The cabin, in contrast to the rest of the place, was tiny. The front door opened straight into a living room, with a small kitchen at the back, two tiny bedrooms and a bathroom at the side. The back door opened onto the creek. It was plainly decorated and modestly furnished, a rural Tennessee version of his house on Hydra, only more isolated.

His nearest neighbor lived almost half a mile away, in a small tar-paper-roofed house raised up on cement blocks; out back there was an illegal still. Willie York was a toothless moonshiner who, along with his brother, had served eleven and a half years for the killing of a sheriff in 1944. The country singer Johnny Seay immortalized York in a song—"Willie's Drunk and Nellie's Dyin'," Nellie being his wife—which led to *Life* magazine descending on Big East Fork Road for the story. Leonard, who had had his own experience with *Life* when they came to Hydra to profile its expat artists, took a shine to York. Often at night he'd walk across the fields with a bottle of whiskey and visit.

Leonard bought pistols and a rifle at the army surplus store and a horse from a friend of York's, Ray "Kid" Marley, a champion rodeo rider from Texas who moved to Tennessee and trained horses. "Kid was truly one of a kind," says Ron Cornelius. "He was a big, big guy, a mountain of a man, who used to run with us [the band West] quite a bit when we were in town and stayed drunk all the time." Leonard said, "I thought I could ride—we used to ride at summer camp—but the horse Kid Marley sold me changed my idea of whether I could ride or not. I guess he saw this city slicker and it was a kind of practical joke of his to sell me this horse that I could rarely catch to saddle him up. This horse was mean." Leonard would later immortalize the horse in the song "Ballad of the Absent Mare,"* and would have done

---

* *Recent Songs*, 1979.

the same for Marley and York in "Chelsea Hotel," had the original version not been usurped by "Chelsea Hotel #2," which had quite different words.

"I was pretty much a bust as a cowboy. [Laughs] But I did have a rifle. During the winter there, there were these icicles that formed on this slate cliff a few hundred yards from my cabin, and I'd stand in the doorway and shoot icicles for a lot of the time so I got quite good."

Were you living alone in the cabin?

"I was living alone for much of the time but Suzanne would come down from time to time."

You liked it better on your own.

"Yeah, I've always liked that."

It is strange to think how different Leonard's life was now from nine months ago in New York. In Tennessee Leonard was Nature Boy. When Ron Cornelius took Bill Donovan—a close friend of Cornelius from San Francisco, who would become Leonard's and the band's tour manager—to the cabin to meet Leonard, "Leonard opened the door and he's stark naked," Donovan remembers. "He says, 'Welcome, friends, come in,' like it's nothing." Leonard offered them tea and declined a joint, "and he walked round the whole time naked," entirely unself-conscious and making friendly conversation.

"I thought," Leonard said, "I was living the life down there." In a poem written in the cabin and published in *The Energy of Slaves*, "I Try to Keep in Touch Wherever I Am," he wrote,

> *The sun comes in the skylight*
> *My work calls to me*
> *sweet as the sound of the creek*

Twelve

O Make Me a Mask

———

The sixties had no intention of slipping out quietly. The last year of the decade witnessed the first man walk on the moon, while on Earth, in America, there was the Woodstock festival, the gathering of the hippie tribes, and also Charles Manson and Altamont, the death of the hippie dream. For Leonard too, 1969 would be a momentous year. It was the year in which he met the woman who would make him a father and the man who would make him a monk.

Joshu Sasaki Roshi is a short, round Japanese man, a Zen master of the Rinzai school—hard-core Buddhism—born on the first day of April 1907. In 1962, when Roshi was fifty-five, just a kid with a crazy dream, he left Japan for Los Angeles to establish the first Rinzai center in the U.S. Leonard first heard of Roshi through his friend Steve Sanfield, who studied with him and had lived for three years in the garage of his small, rented house in Gardena, an inexpensive Los Angeles suburb. Sanfield had fallen in love with another student's wife and Roshi had asked them to leave. Several months later, when the couple were expecting a child, Roshi told them to come back and he would marry them at the newly opened Zen Center on Cimarron Street. Sanfield wrote to Leonard in Nashville, asking him to be best man. There was no reply, but when he and his partner arrived for the wedding, Leonard was there, waiting.

Leonard appeared fascinated by the ceremony, particularly the Ten Vows of Buddhism, and how Roshi ignored the one about not indulging in drugs and alcohol by drinking an impressive amount of sake. Leonard and Roshi barely exchanged a word that day, which was fine with Leonard. Since becoming a music celebrity, Leonard seemed to have acquired a large number of "friends" he barely knew who wanted to talk to him. In his view, the ancient Japanese way, where men would meet and "bow to each other for as much as half an hour speaking words of greeting, gradually moving closer together, understanding the necessity of entering another's consciousness carefully,"[1] was a good one.

Some weeks later Leonard made another unannounced appearance, this time in Ottawa at a celebration thrown by Jack McClelland for the winners of the coveted Governor General's Award for literature. Leonard had won for *Selected Poems 1956–1968* but sent a telegram, declining to accept the award. This was most unusual. Only one other winner in the past had refused the honor and its $2,500 purse—a French separatist, who was making a political protest. Even more unusual, though, was turning down the prize and showing up at the party.

Mordecai Richler cornered Leonard and demanded to know his reasons; Leonard replied that he did not know what they were himself. In his telegram to the committee Leonard had written, "Much in me strives for this honour, but the poems themselves forbid it absolutely." Whether he meant that he had written books more deserving of the award than this anthology or that his poems had had it with being judged by anyone but himself is open to debate. Certainly since he had become a recording artist his work was receiving far more attention from far more critics. It had also brought a large increase in income, which meant that Leonard no longer depended on awards to help to pay the bills. However, to Canada's literary world, such behavior would have seemed nothing more than an expatriate pop celebrity rejecting his old country and his former life.

From Ottawa, Leonard traveled to Montreal, where he went to his old workplace, his uncle Horace's factory, to visit his cousin David. Over lunch in the factory cafeteria, David told Leonard, "You're famous, you're a big star." "I didn't mean it sarcastically," he recalls, "and he didn't take it that way. He just said, 'You get into Columbia's publicity mill and you cannot help but become very well-known. I'm no child, and I've seen it destroy a lot of young people who go from nothing to stardom. I've been through the mill. You can't escape it. Once you become an artist with them, that's it.'" When Leonard left Montreal for Nashville, once again he stopped off first in New York. After checking into the Chelsea Hotel, he went to the Scientology Center. There he met a woman.

———————

"It was early spring in 1969. We both seemed to have signed up for a Scientology class the same day. He was getting into the elevator at the Scientology Center as I was coming out of it and our eyes locked. Some days later we both took seats near each other. Although I had another person I was living with, I left that relationship immediately for Leonard and moved into the Chelsea with him." Suzanne Elrod was a dark-haired beauty from Miami, Florida—some people in Montreal said she bore a resemblance to the Suzanne of Leonard's song. She was nineteen years old.

Leonard, at thirty-four, was fifteen years older than her—almost the same age difference as there was between his mother and father—but considerably younger than the wealthy man Suzanne was living with at the upscale Plaza Hotel. Suzanne declines to talk about her family background, which was secular Jewish. She had come to New York not for study or adventure or escape but as "a very young, naïve girl only armed with the typical romantic fantasies of my generation, wanting a family of my own. I had a river of love to give and found Leonard," she said. "I knew he was destined to be the father of my children and the love of my life, no matter what happened." When she told the man she lived with that she was leaving, he insisted on meeting "the poor poet" who had usurped him and organized a dinner for the three of them. Then, "he locked himself in one of the suites for hours and listened to the music and read the books he had his chauffeur go out and buy of Leonard's. He came out and said he at least felt I was leaving him for someone worthwhile."

Their life together in Leonard's room in the Chelsea was by Suzanne's account reclusive, with little partying or socializing. Leonard seemed as smitten with this headstrong, sexual young woman as she was with him. But he also appeared to have one eye on the door. In his passport was a folded sheet of motel notepaper containing a list of names and numbers of people all over the world,[2] among them Viva, one of Warhol's stars; folksinger Dave Van Ronk; folk rocker Julie Felix; Judy Collins; Marianne; and a "Jane" who lived at 41 West Street. Also on the list were the composer-conductor Leonard Bernstein and the Italian film director Franco Zeffirelli. In June 1969, not long after meeting Suzanne, Leonard joined Bernstein and Zeffirelli in Italy, where Zeffirelli was making a film on the life of Saint Francis. He took the two Leonards to Saint Francis's tomb and discussed the possibility of collaborating on the score. Nothing came of it, unfortunately; when *Brother Sun, Sister Moon* premiered in 1972, it featured a soundtrack by Donovan.

From Italy, Leonard went to Greece. Suzanne flew over and stayed with him in his little white house on Hydra. "My first impression was that the rooms were so small and run-down," Suzanne recalls. Over time she "changed many things, rebuilt the downstairs room and garden," but she says, "I kept the authenticity of the house, as that's what Leonard and I loved about it. I was very respectful of the spirit of the house. I liked it elegant, sparse and white, in all its Greek peasant simplicity."

While they were on the island, news came of the suicide of Charmian Clift. On July 8, on the eve of the publication of her husband's new novel, *Clean Straw for Nothing*, Clift took an overdose of barbiturates. (George Johnston would die a year later from tuberculosis.) Leonard mourned with the rest of the island, but on Hydra, as in New York, he and Suzanne kept mostly to themselves.

When he returned to his cabin in Tennessee, Leonard took Suzanne with him. He introduced her to Willie York and Kid Marley. The rodeo rider "would come by, uninvited and often drunk, to tell sometimes hilarious, sometimes insipid stories while he spat on the floor and dug his cowboy boot heels, spurs and all, into the wood floors, and slapped his hand on his knee saying, 'But ain't we having fun!' Sometimes he was fascinating," says Suzanne, "and we laughed and kept him drunk. Sometimes we got rid of him as fast as we could, politely, without being shot. They all had rifles in their back windows of their trucks. Did I mention the many Confederate flags that were still up down there 'in the holler'? It was an interesting place to visit and understand, but we lived there quietly, and briefly, thank goodness, as we lived everywhere else."

Leonard also took Suzanne to Montreal to meet his mother. For a short while, they stayed at Leonard's childhood home on Belmont Avenue, while he set about finding them a place of their own. Masha, said Suzanne in 1980, "was his most dreamy spiritual influence. The only thing that bothered me was that she always called me Marianne."[3] Leonard bought a cheap little cottage near the Parc du Portugal, off the Main, a neighborhood mostly populated by Portuguese and Greek immigrant families but that still retained the old Jewish delis with oilcloth-covered tables. The couple had barely moved in before they left for New York once again. In the city, Leonard revisited some of his old haunts—including the Gaslight, where he caught a show by Loudon Wainwright III—but this time with Suzanne. But Leonard no longer attended the Scientology Center. Disenchantment had set in, as well as anger that the organization had begun to exploit his name. Leonard had "gone clear"; he had a certificate confirming him as a "Senior Dianetic, Grade IV Release."[4] "I participated in all those investigations that engaged the imagination of my generation at that time," said Leonard. "I even danced and sang with the Hare Krishnas—no robe, I didn't join them, but I was trying everything."[5]

The dawn of the new decade found Leonard and Suzanne in their little house in Montreal until Suzanne could no longer take the cold and flew to Miami. Leonard in turn returned to Nashville. Bob Johnston was talking about a third album. And Columbia Records was talking even more loudly about a European tour.

———————

Leonard had never really toured but he knew he did not like touring. Traveling wasn't the problem; "I tossed myself around like a cork," he said, "for most of my life."[6] But it was a different matter if someone else did the tossing, telling him where he had to be and when. Leonard's uncles would have been pleased to confirm his distaste for clock-punching, while his habit of becoming president of many of the clubs he joined might give some indication that Leonard did not much like following rules, unless they were his own. He also had a problem with stage fright—"I felt that the risks of humiliation were too wide"[7]—and had to psych himself up to perform. But mostly he was afraid for his songs. They had come to him in private, from somewhere pure and honest, and he had worked long and hard to make them sincere representations of the moment. He wanted to protect them, not parade and pimp them to paying strangers in an artificial intimacy. "My idea was to be able to make records only," he told Danny Fields. He said he had hoped his songs "would make their way through the world" on albums, audio equivalents of poetry books, without his having to get onstage and perform them.

Leonard called Bob Johnston. He told his producer that he would not tour unless Johnston agreed to manage him and play keyboards in his band. It was a good ruse. Johnston would have been the first to admit that he was not a musician, and the likelihood of Columbia letting the head of its Nashville division simply take off and go on tour would have seemed slim. Except that Johnston had just left Columbia to go independent. Celebrating with a trip around Europe, all expenses paid by his former employers, struck Johnston as a fine idea. As for management, he told Leonard that he would play in his band and look after him on the road, and not charge a dime for doing so, but that he would do better to talk to Marty Machat, the lawyer-manager who handled Johnston's business affairs. Machat had been the right-hand man of Allen Klein, who managed the Beatles and the Rolling Stones. Leonard and Johnston shook on it, and Johnston appointed Bill Donovan as tour manager and summoned the band for rehearsals—Cornelius, Daniels, Fowler and backing singers Susan Mussmano and Corlynn Hanney. Leonard, in turn, phoned Mort Rosengarten in Montreal and asked him to come to Tennessee.

"Leonard asked me to make a mask for him," says Rosengarten. "A theatrical mask. He said he wanted to wear it while he was performing. So I went out to his little place, down the dirt road, in the middle of nowhere." There was nowhere to buy materials, but they found a hobby shop in Franklin that sold "these little packages for model kits." "I bought them all," he says, "and Leonard came back from Nashville with a bag of plaster." While Leonard was in Nashville, rehearsing, Mort stayed in the cabin and worked on the mask. "With Leonard gone there was no one around except for this old guy who made moonshine and Kid Marley, who dressed like a cowboy and never went anywhere without his horse, which was in a trailer at the back of his pickup truck. One night he turned up at the cabin, drunk, and we were waiting for Leonard to come back, but then he decided to go back into town and get more booze. So I went with him and the horse came with us too, in the trailer."

The mask he made for Leonard to perform in was actually a mask of Leonard himself: a live death mask made from a plaster cast of his face, expressionless, with gaps for his mouth and eyes. Leonard clearly had enough self-regard that he did not want to operate behind someone else's face. The mask of himself would give him a thicker skin to cover his sensitivity and help protect his songs from contamination, but it also would make it obvious that the public Leonard was a performance and that he was well aware of the masquerade. As he wrote on the bathroom mirror in *Ladies and Gentlemen . . . Mr. Leonard Cohen*, *"caveat emptor"*—"Let the man watching me know," he said, "that this is not entirely devoid of the con." Leonard also knew his Dylan Thomas ("O make me a mask and a wall to shut from your spies / Of the sharp, enamelled eyes and the spectacled claws") and his Nietzsche ("Such a hidden nature, which instinctively employs speech for silence and concealment . . . desires and insists that a mask of himself shall occupy his place").

Rosengarten says, "Leonard felt it was helpful in deciding his persona onstage. A mask is neutral, it's the person that wears it that gives it life, the way you move your head and your eyes and all that stuff. It becomes very powerful." In the end Leonard decided not to wear the mask. He held on to it for decades though. Mort eventually had it cast for him in aluminum.

"Oh man," says Bob Johnston. "There was never anything like that tour." It began with nine shows in eight European cities in two weeks and was fuelled by LSD and Mandrax. Leonard, dressed in a khaki safari suit and wielding Henry Zemel's whip, was a quixotic General Patton leading his ragtag army. Or, at the Hamburg concert, more like cannon fodder. It was May 4, 1970, the day of the Kent

State massacre in the U.S., and, as some kind of convoluted anti-authority peace gesture, Leonard decided to start the second half of the show by clicking his heels twice and giving the Nazi salute. He had come back onstage to lighted matches and a long standing ovation, but the mood changed instantly.

The large crowd "went nuts," says Johnston, "cursing and throwing shit. One guy came running down the aisle with a gun. He was five feet from the stage when security wrestled him to the floor. Charlie Daniels turned to me and said, 'I'm out of here.' I said, 'Don't move, if they're going to kill someone it's Leonard.' But the crowd quieted when Leonard took up his guitar. He said, 'Are you finished, are you all through?' and they applauded as he started playing. But it was an old Yiddish song. And he started dancing on one leg across the stage like Jews do, singing 'Ai-eee, ai-eee,' and they started cursing and throwing things again. Then he started one of his own songs and we all joined in, and it calmed down. Leonard was always pulling stunts like that, and getting away with it." The next morning at the hotel, though, Daniels told them he was quitting. "I've had it," he said, "I've got a wife and kid and you guys don't. I can't get shot out here over Leonard Cohen." It took the whole band to talk him into staying.

In London, Leonard gave a poetry reading at the ICA and played two nights at the Royal Albert Hall, which sold out the moment the concerts were announced; his first album had recently gone gold in the UK and the second was high on the charts. The *Guardian* reported, "The fashionably hippy audience cheered hysterically. But I hope they understood what Cohen is all about." If they didn't, the reviewer Robin Denselow explained that Leonard's songs reflected a "peculiarly Canadian wasteland" and that their message, with the poetry peeled off, was "self-obsession, cynicism, non-communication; it is two strangers frantically making love in a shadowy hotel bedroom."[8]

Leonard called Nico, who was also in London, but she turned

him down once again. He made the acquaintance of several women who were more generous with their affection. He bought a book for Suzanne titled *The Language of Flowers*, which he inscribed to her, writing that she was "a fragrant breath amid the foul storms of life."[9] Leonard took Cornelius, Johnston and Donovan to meet a friend in London who—he told them—had the best acid anywhere. "It was called Desert Dust and it was like LSD-plus," says Cornelius. "You had to take a needle—a pin was too big—and touch your tongue with this brown dust, and with as much as you could pick up on the end of that needle you were *gone*, sixteen hours, no reentry." Ample supplies were purchased and consumed; it would get to where the tour manager made them all hold hands at the airport as they walked to the plane so that he would not lose anyone—"a big conga line," Donovan says, "with everybody just singing along."

On the plane to Vienna the stewardess informed them that they had heard that there were around three hundred fans waiting for them at the airport. "Leonard said, 'Oh, they love me in Vienna,'" says Johnston, "but when we landed and he went out and waved to the crowd, they were all hollering, 'Where's Bubba?' Turned out Bubba Fowler had a big hit in Vienna but didn't know it." But the audiences across Europe loved Leonard, even when he provoked them—which could have been why he provoked them, although his pharmaceutical intake might have had something to do with it too. Much as Leonard claimed not to like performing, his feelings toward his audiences were of affection and gratitude. At the Amsterdam concert, he invited the entire crowd back to his hotel, which resulted in police action. At the Paris Olympia he invited the audience to come onstage, and once again the police were called.

It was his first real tour and he was still finding his way as a stage performer, but for a first tour it was quite remarkable. The band left France for New York in July, just as the Royal Winnipeg Ballet were getting ready to premiere *The Shining People of Leonard Cohen* in Paris.

Choreographed by a McGill University graduate named Brian Macdonald, who had met Leonard in 1964, it featured an electronic score and the reading of several of Leonard's poems, among them the erotic "When I Uncovered Your Body" and "Celebration."

In the U.S. Leonard was booked to play at the Forest Hills folk festival. To leave the grand opera houses and music halls of Europe for a show at a tennis stadium put a dent in Leonard's mood, which seemed to linger. Bob Dylan, who was also at the festival, had chosen that day to meet Leonard. Dylan was not in the best of humor either, having been barred from going to Leonard's dressing room by an official, who must have been the only man at a folk festival to fail to recognize him. The official called Johnston over: "This guy says he's Bob Dylan and he says he knows you." Johnston deadpanned, "I've never seen the son of a bitch in my life. But okay, let him in." "Man, that wasn't funny," said Dylan.

Leonard was backstage with Ron Cornelius, who was restringing his guitar. Johnston put his head around the door saying, "Bob Dylan's here."

"So?" said Leonard.

"He wants to meet you," said Johnston.

"Let him in, I guess," said Leonard. Dylan came into the room and for a while he and Leonard just stood there, saying nothing. Dylan broke the silence. "How're you doing here?" he said.

"Well you've got to be somewhere," Leonard answered.

"It was the strangest conversation," says Cornelius, who knew Dylan and had worked with him in the past. "They were talking between the sentences, if you know what I mean. You could see they were communicating, however it really had nothing to do with the words coming out of their mouth. It was one of the weirdest atmospheres I've ever been in in my life—just a tiny bit hostile. But that also goes along with the fact that we'd been playing in places where Leonard was number one and Dylan was number two—Leonard

could sell out the Albert Hall in thirty-two minutes—and then we
came to the U.S. and Bob Dylan is number one and nobody's ever
heard of Leonard." However strange the encounter, Leonard and
Dylan each left considering the other a friend. But Cornelius was
correct about Leonard's lack of status in the U.S. A review of the
show in *Billboard* described him as "nervous" and "lifeless." Wrote
Nancy Erlich, "He works hard to achieve that bloodless vocal, that
dull, humorless quality of a voice speaking after death. And the voice
does not offer comfort or wisdom; it expresses total defeat. His art is
oppressive."[10]

Leonard and the band still had two festivals left to play in Europe, so they flew straight back. The first festival was in the South
of France, in the Provençal countryside six miles outside Aix. Their
hotel was an old country lodge on the outskirts of the city. The hotel
had stables and the band had the afternoon to themselves; they hired
horses and rode through a landscape that looked like a Cézanne
painting, singing cowboy songs. Unbeknownst to them, the three-
day festival, whose bill included French bands and international
acts—Mungo Jerry and Johnny Winter among them—had turned
into a mini French Woodstock. More people had shown up than the
organizers planned for, and many refused to pay fifty-five francs for
a ticket and broke down fencing to get in. The local prefecture, concerned about the "hordes of destructive hippies in search of uproar
and scandal" who were setting up makeshift camps in the meadow,
dancing with the Hare Krishnas and basking stoned and naked in the
sun, issued a ban on the festival and sent in the CRS—the French
riot police. The show went on, by all accounts without any problems,
apart from the demands from the more vociferous festivalgoers that
the festival be free and the concerns of the organizers that they might
not make enough to pay the acts.

Driving along the tree-lined road to the festival site, Leonard and
the band found it completely blocked with parked and abandoned

cars. There were still some miles to go—too far to walk, and they
had instruments—and there was nowhere to call for help. Which was
when Bob Johnston thought of the horses. Back at the inn, after negotiating terms through a translator, they set off again on horseback,
taking the back route along narrow mountain roads, on a warm, starlit
night, toward the distant lights.

"About halfway there," says Johnston, "Leonard said, 'We can't
play the concert. We've run out of wine.' We were in the backwoods
out there. I said, 'Leonard, don't worry.' Then about a mile down the
road in the middle of nowhere we saw a bar called Texas." The good
Lord had blessed and guided them to an unlikely Wild West theme
bar. There was even a hitching post. They dismounted. In the bar,
they hatched a plan to make their festival entrance by riding their
horses onto the stage. It was the kind of decision that a large intake
of wine mixed with the leadership style of Bob Johnston and the bravado the European tour had engendered might produce. When they
rode into the backstage area, they headed toward the ramps and up
onto the stage. "The stage was swinging up and down," says Johnston. "The French festival guys were all waving and screaming that it
was going to collapse." This seemed a genuine possibility. The white
stallion that Leonard was riding seemed to believe it and refused to
move. In the end it was persuaded. "I gave it a kick on the ass," said
Johnston, "and Leonard rode it up there into the middle of the stage,
where it reared up, and Leonard saluted the audience."

At that moment, Leonard was the consummate showman, appearing to be in full control of both the spontaneity and the artifice. The
only problem was that his grand entrance was greeted with hisses and
boos. Hecklers began to shout insults: that Leonard was a diva, making such a grandiose entrance; that he was a capitalist and the tickets
were so expensive because of his exorbitant fee; that he was a fas-
cist sympathizer, having a house in Greece yet refusing to speak out
against the military government. Leonard, as was his tendency, tried

to engage "the Maoists"—as he called his detractors—in a debate in between songs. Their response was to throw bottles. At one point Leonard thought he heard gunshots, but it was only a stage light smashing. Still, whatever might happen, Leonard was not afraid. He was no longer Field Commander Cohen, he was Conquest, the white Horseman of the Apocalypse. He told the hecklers that if they wanted a fight they should come onstage: he and his men were ready to take them on. By the end of their performance, Leonard's band had an official name: the Army. Their next campaign would be to take a small island four miles off the coast of southern England, which had been invaded by six hundred thousand young people—ten times more than attended the Aix festival. But before landing in the Isle of Wight, Leonard went to a mental hospital.

———————

On August 28, two days before he was due to play the Isle of Wight Festival, a sedan pulled up outside the Henderson Hospital in Sutton, on the southern edge of London. Looking up, Leonard saw an old, imposing building with a tower with narrow windows. It had the look of an institution you might check into and never leave. Leonard went inside. Bill Donovan was there, telling him everything was set up for him in the tower. "Oh boy," said Leonard to Bob Johnston as the medical director of the hospital led them in, "I hope they like 'So Long, Marianne.'"

"Leonard said, 'I want to play mental asylums,'" says Johnston. And just like he'd done when Johnny Cash told him he wanted to play prisons, Johnston said, "Okay," and "booked a bunch of them." Despite appearances, the Henderson (closed now, due to funding cuts) was a pioneering hospital with an innovative approach to the treatment of personality disorders. It called itself a therapeutic community and the patients residents. "It was all talking therapy," says former charge nurse Ian Milne. "No medication, no 'zombies.'" Most of the patients were Leonard's age or younger, and so were the staff; to outsiders they would have been barely distinguishable. Both were at the morning Community Meeting where the medical director announced that he'd had a call saying, "Some guy wants to come and sing to us and run through his program for the Isle of Wight. His name's Leonard Cohen." Every mouth dropped; for once the talking stopped.

Ron Cornelius remembers the first time Leonard told the band of his intention to play at mental hospitals. "We were at the Mayfair Hotel and he said, 'We're going to enjoy this tour. We're going to see these cities and spend two or three days in them sometimes. And when we're not playing, I want to go and play mental institutions.' I went, 'What? I'm not going in a nuthouse to play. Yes, count me in for the Albert Hall, but count me out for the nuthouse.' Well they talked and talked and talked until Leonard finally said, 'Ron, just come one time.' After seeing what that music did for those people I ended up enjoying many of those, and we played a lot of them, all over Europe, Canada, even in America."

Leonard did not say why he wanted to play to mental patients and the band didn't ask, but Johnston recalls Leonard telling him once that "he had to go to the loony bin one time, when he wrote *Beautiful Losers* or something." As Johnston remembers it, Leonard said he had taken a lot of acid, gone out on a little boat and stared at the sun too long. He told journalist Steve Turner in 1974 that he was drawn to mental hospitals through "the feeling that the experience of a lot of people in mental hospitals would especially qualify them to be a receptive audience for my work. In a sense, when someone consents to go into a mental hospital or is committed he has already acknowledged a tremendous defeat. To put it another way, he has already made a choice. And it was my feeling that the elements of this choice, and the elements of this defeat, corresponded with certain elements that produced my songs, and that there would be an empathy between the people who had this experience and the experience as documented in my songs."[11]

So, fellow-feeling had something to do with it; in a 1969 interview he said, "I always loved the people the world used to call mad. I used to hang out and talk to those old men, or with the junkies. I was only 13 or 14, I never understood why I was down there except that I felt at home with those people." There was also something of "there but for fortune," given his own history and that of his mother. On a practical level, it was also a good place "to tighten the band up," says Donovan, "and blow their minds." Leonard did it at his own expense and without fanfare. Although there were two big Johnny Cash prison albums, there was no Leonard Cohen *At Henderson Hospital*. But a tape of the concert exists, and it's good. Milne, who was also an amateur sound recordist, captured it on his four-track stereo Stella reel-to-reel.

The concert started around seven P.M. in the high-ceilinged tower attic. There was a small stage, so crammed with the band and their regular concert equipment that Leonard had to play at floor level. He stood beneath one of the tall, narrow windows that gave the room the feel of a chapel. Around fifty residents made their way into one of a half dozen rows of folding chairs while the band did a quick sound check—"Arms of Regina," an unreleased song, sounding here like a midtempo country ballad with heart-tugging harmonies. To the audience Leonard said, "There was a fellow I spoke to last night, a doctor. I told him I was coming out here. He said, 'They are a tough bunch of young nuts.'" While playing the opening bars of "Bird on the Wire," Leonard stopped. "I feel like talking. Someone warned me downstairs that all you do here is talk. That's psychotic, it's contagious." Apparently so. Leonard spoke a lot during the eighty-minute concert, in between the eleven songs and one poem, and often more freely than at regular shows. He talked of how his affair with Marianne slowly faded and died and told the stories behind some of his songs: "You Know Who I Am" had "something to do with some three hundred acid trips I took" and "One of Us Cannot Be Wrong" "was written coming off amphetamine." "Tonight Will Be Fine" was played like a country hoedown, upbeat and raucous, and with extra verses. There were signs of "Tennesseefication" too in "Suzanne," where the lonely wooden tower became "lonesome." Here and there Leonard tried out different lyrics; in "Bird on the Wire," *I have saved all my ribbons for thee* was changed to the quite different "*I have broken all my sorrows on thee.*" There was no recognition or response from the audience when he added, "It was written in the Chelsea Hotel in New York City, a place where you never leave the elevator alone," but "Chelsea Hotel #2" and the Janis stories were still some years off.

There appeared to be quite a few Leonard Cohen fans in the audience. One called out a request for "Famous Blue Raincoat," "a song," he said, "that I didn't know anybody knew about, that we have only sung in concerts. It's a song that I wrote in New York when I was living on the east side of the East Side, and it's about sharing women, sharing men, and the idea of that if you hold on to somebody . . ." Leonard let the conclusion drift away. During the songs, the audience was silent, entranced. When the band stopped, the applause was loud and rapturous. "I really wanted to say that this is the audience that we've been looking for," said Leonard, who sounded moved and happy. "I've never felt so good playing before people." People who were mentally damaged seemed to make Leonard and his songs feel at home. They performed other mental hospital concerts later that year, "and those shows were one of the best things about the whole tour, every one of them," said Donovan, "just the way the audience locked in on what Leonard was doing and how he just interacted with them."

In early November 1970 they would play at the Napa State mental hospital, a colossal nineteenth-century Gothic pile set on 190 acres in California wine country. The band had a temporary new backing

singer in California, Michelle Phillips of the Mamas and the Papas.*
A few days earlier, on Halloween, Phillips had married the actor Dennis Hopper. Leonard, whom Hopper considered a friend, was at the ceremony. "So we dragged Hopper up to the hospital too," says Bill Donovan. "On the way he took some acid." It started to kick in just as the limo pulled into the grounds. As they started unloading, they could see the staff bringing the audience into the building in which they were to perform. Many of the patients were in wheelchairs; others lurched slowly on foot. The hospital housed many severely damaged and highly medicated patients; it also had a separate wing for the criminally insane. "When Hopper saw this," Donovan says, "he freaked out, like it was *The Night of the Living Dead* or something. Hopper ran back into the limo and locked the door and wouldn't come out." Leonard, performing for the patients, sang and played and talked a little, then jumped down among them with his guitar, "and anyone who could move followed him around the room and back and forward and over the stage."

In Montreal, when the band performed at a hospital there, a young woman patient told Leonard she was not crazy, and that her father had put her there because she had taken drugs. She begged him to help her get out. There was something in her story that brought to mind Nancy, the judge's daughter about whom Leonard wrote "Seems So Long Ago, Nancy." They formulated an escape plan. It did not succeed—fortunately, it seems, since they discovered that she did have a serious mental illness. "There are things that happened that would take your breath away," says Ron Cornelius. "At one show eight or nine people in wheelchairs all decided that at six o'clock exactly they would all shit their pants. They were marched out with their dirty gowns and they were all crying, because the mu-

---

* She sang at two official dates, the Berkeley Community Center and the Hollywood Bowl.

sic was doing something for them that they had never had. One kid
stood up with a triangle missing from his skull—you could see the
brain beating—and he started screaming at Leonard in the middle
of a song, to where we actually ground to a halt. The kid said, 'Okay,
okay, big-time poet, big-time artist, you come in here, you've got the
band with you, you've got the pretty girls with you, you're singing all
these pretty words and everything, well what I want to know, buddy,
is what do you think about me?' And Leonard just left the stage and
before you knew it he had the guy in his arms, hugging him."

———————

On their way to the Isle of Wight, Leonard studied the music magazine that Johnston handed him. It was opened to a full-page ad for
his album, which pictured Leonard, dressed in a black polo-neck
sweater, gazing off to the left, as if trying to ignore what his record
company had written at the back of his head. It said, "Do you ever
get the feeling that you want to disengage yourself from life? To withdraw into some kind of solitary contemplation just to think about
everything for a while? Everything. You. Her. It. Them. Well that's
how a poet feels, because he's no different from everyone else. What
makes a poet different is that he takes time to put it all down on
paper. Beautifully. And what makes Leonard Cohen a very different
poet is that he turns his poetry into songs. He did it for *Songs of Leonard Cohen*. Then came *Songs from a Room*, the second Leonard Cohen
album for the growing number of people who have identified with
him. And what he feels. But don't have that rare poetic vision. There
could be millions of Leonard Cohens in the world. You may even,"
it ended, "be him yourself." If Mort had only mass-produced those
Leonard masks, they could have made a fortune. A slow, stoned smile
grew across Leonard's face, for which much of the credit went to his
drug of choice on this part of the tour. The Army had taken to calling
him Captain Mandrax.

The Isle of Wight, a four-mile ferry ride from England's south coast, is a placid little island, encircled by yachts and popular with retired naval officers and genteel holidaymakers. For five days in the summer of 1970, it was invaded by hundreds of thousands—six times the island's population—of young music lovers, hippies and militants. From the hill above the festival site in the west, on Afton Down, you could see dust rising from corrugated fences that had been trampled and the smoke rising from trucks and concession stands set on fire. Nicknamed Devastation Hill—for obvious reasons to anyone who was there—it had been taken over by ticketless squatters, some of whom were responsible for the disturbance. Off in the distance, crammed in front of the stage, were thousands of exhausted festivalgoers, who had spent days watching a bill that rivaled Woodstock. The artists who played that year included the Who, the Doors, Miles Davis, Donovan and Ten Years After. Leonard had the slot before last on the fifth and final day, after Jimi Hendrix and Joan Baez and before Richie Havens.

Tension had been rising at the festival for days. The promoters had expected a hundred and fifty thousand people but half a million more turned up, many with no intention of paying. Even after the promoters were forced to declare it a free festival, ill will remained. During a set by Kris Kristofferson, bottles were thrown and he was booed offstage. "They were booing everybody," says Kristofferson. "Except Leonard Cohen." As the day progressed, things only got worse. Baez offered to go on before Hendrix to try to calm things down; she said, "I knew that my music was a little more difficult to burn fires to."[12] During Hendrix's set, someone in the crowd threw a flare that set fire to the top of the stage. Flames shot up while Hendrix played on. Leonard and Johnston stood nearby and watched.

"Leonard wasn't worried," says Johnston. "Hendrix didn't care and neither did we. Leonard was always completely oblivious to anything like that. The only thing that upset him was when they told him that they didn't have a piano or an organ—I don't know, someone had set them on fire and pushed them off the stage—so I couldn't play with him. Leonard said, 'I'll be in the trailer taking a nap; come and get me when you've found a piano and an organ.'" He took some Mandrax. It was around two in the morning when they woke Leonard and brought him onstage, in his safari suit, his chin stubbled, hair long, eyes very stoned. As the Army took their places, he stood staring out into the pitch-black night.

Jeff Dexter, a well-known British DJ of that period who was onstage playing records between sets, made the introduction. He saw immediately that Leonard and the band "were totally Mandraxed; they were in such a state I could have fucked them all and they wouldn't have known it." He was worried for their safety. So was Murray Lerner, the American documentary filmmaker who was shooting the festival. "I thought, 'This is going to be a disaster,' and that what happened to Kristofferson would happen to him," says Lerner. "But he looked so calm." Johnston says, "He was calm, because of the Mandrax. That's what saved that show and saved the festival. It was the middle of the night, all those people had been sitting out there in the rain, after they'd set fire to Hendrix's stage, and nobody had slept for days"—all the ingredients for turning nasty. "But then Leonard, with the Mandrax in him, started out singing, very slowly—so slowly it took him ten minutes to sing it—'Like . . . a . . . bird.' And everybody in that audience was exactly with him. It was the most amazing thing I've ever heard." Charlie Daniels says, "If Leonard was in a zone with Mandrax, it certainly didn't cause any bad musical decisions. Crowds can be kind of funny and it was getting late and he just seemed to feel the mood. He just kind of laid it down, eased it down."

Before he sang, Leonard talked to the hundreds of thousands of people he could not see as if they were sitting together in a small, dark room. He told them—slowly, calmly—a story that sounded like a parable, worked like hypnotism, and at the same time tested the temperature of the crowd. He described how his father would take him to the circus as a child. Leonard didn't much like circuses, but he enjoyed it when a man stood up and asked everyone to light a match so they could locate each other. "Can I ask each of you to light a match," said Cohen, "so I can see where you all are?" There were few at the beginning, but as the show went on he could see flames flickering through the misty rain.

"He mesmerized them," says Lerner. "And I got mesmerized also." For the lovers in the audience, Leonard sang "Suzanne," saying, "Maybe this is good music to make love to," and for the fighters he sang "The Partisan," dedicating it to "Joan Baez and the work she is doing." Says Johnston, "It was magical. From the first moment to the last. I've never seen anything like it. He was just remarkable." Thirty-nine years later the spellbinding performance was released, along with Lerner's footage, on the CD/DVD *Leonard Cohen: Live at the Isle of Wight 1970*.

————

A month after the festival, Leonard, Johnston and the Army were back in Nashville's Columbia Studio A, recording Leonard's third album, *Songs of Love and Hate*. Work began on September 22, 1970, four days after Jimi Hendrix died at the age of twenty-seven in London, and continued daily until the twenty-sixth, eight days before Janis Joplin died at the same age in a Los Angeles hotel. The break from recording was to play a handful of U.S. and Canadian shows in November and December. The first was an anti–Vietnam War concert at a university in Madison, Wisconsin; a homemade bomb had gone off there that summer and Leonard was offered protection by the White Panthers, which he declined. He began the show with a song he had learned at Socialist summer camp, "Solidarity," and dedicated "Joan of Arc," a song written to Nico, to the memory of another muse, Janis.

When they reached Montreal on December 10 for the last show of

1970, the city was under martial law following the kidnappings of a journalist and the British trade commissioner in Leonard's old neighborhood, Westmount. Canada's prime minister Pierre Trudeau—Leonard's old friend from Le Bistro, he of the famous beige raincoat to Leonard's famous blue one—was on CBC television, angrily telling the reporter, "There's a lot of bleeding hearts around who don't like to see people with helmets and guns. All I can say is go on and bleed." Meet the new decade, same as the old decade. In their little house in the immigrant quarter, Leonard and Suzanne watched the snow steadily fall and settle on the street, silently, whitewashing everything.

Thirteen

The Veins Stand Out
Like Highways

He smiled like a holy fool from the photo in the bottom corner of the album sleeve, which had been shot on tour—eyes ecstatic, face unshaven, his head dissolving into the black background. On the back cover, in place of song titles there was, written in white on black like a message on a madhouse chalkboard,

THEY LOCKED UP A MAN
WHO WANTED TO RULE THE WORLD
THE FOOLS
THEY LOCKED UP THE WRONG MAN

Critics had called *Songs from a Room* bleak; it wasn't, it was stark. *Songs of Love and Hate* was bleak: songs of pain and self-disgust of endless variation, including a hunchback, an immolation, a cuckold, a suicide, an abortion, broken limbs, a broken sky and a washed-up writer—"Last Year's Man"—who felt unable to move his hand and write the world back into being. Leonard was depressed and wasted. He'd had it. He had been backstage and he knew how they hid the rabbits in the hat. Those reviewers who had seen through the con and called his voice "weak and pitiful" and his songs "self-indulgent" had been right. There had been no victories. The medals were a sham. Almost four years had passed since he had written to Marianne describing his excruciating first stage appearance with Judy Collins and the freedom and beauty he felt from his "total failure." But now, living in the Tennessee cabin with Suzanne and contemplating a third album he did not want to make, didn't believe that he could make, but that his record contract required that he make, Leonard felt only "a deep, paralyzing anguish."[1]

Love, lust, the Bible Belt and the company of men, musicians, whom he trusted and admired might appear to an outsider to be the ideal Leonard Cohen setup. Then, they might have said the same thing about his life with Marianne in the little house on Hydra. Leonard's depression begged to differ. Says Suzanne, "Of course, it can feel like a dark room with no doors. It's a common experience of many people, especially with a creative nature, and the more spiritual the person, the closer to the tendency resembling what the church called *acedia*"—a sin that encompassed apathy in the practice of virtue and the loss of grace. "Maybe the biggest struggle—what permits the work to shine or lets you shine through the work—is the undressing, being only truly who you are, [and] tailoring the pathos, quieting the daily pettiness and ending the second-guessing, just in action"—knuckling down and getting on with it.

Leonard's contract with Columbia stipulated two more albums from him. He asked Bob Johnston if they could give the record company two live albums, since they'd recorded most of the shows on the last tour. Johnston said they might be able to get away with one live album, but not until they'd given the label a new studio album. So Leonard knuckled down and got on with it. He took a room in a hotel in Nashville, he swam in the pool at the Y twice a day and for five days straight he went to the studio. The recording was relatively painless at first; there was an easy familiarity with the road-honed band, the engineers and the studio. Charlie Daniels says, "We'd gotten used to each other and had much more of an idea of where we were going and what to do with his songs." And there were only eight songs, almost all of which Leonard had previously attempted to record on his first two albums and/or had performed with the band onstage. The version of "Sing Another Song, Boys" that appears on the album was in fact recorded live at the festival outside Aix.

After five days in Studio A, the band went their way and Leonard and Johnston took the master tape to London to do overdubs: Leonard's spoken-word part on "Joan of Arc," the children's choir on "Last Year's Man" and the string arrangements by Paul Buckmaster, a classical cellist and experimental rock bassist who had arranged Elton John's first two albums. They gave him "a free hand," Buckmaster said, but "Cohen's music is almost unarrangeable." His contribution was to add "little areas of emotional texture and color."[2]

Cornelius remembers, "It started out the way we recorded *Songs from a Room* but then it grew as things got deeper. 'Famous Blue Raincoat' kind of matured right before your eyes, and also 'Avalanche.' It's so easy to get too much going on, and yet at the same time without enough horsepower behind it that song would have never had the energy that it has. But it kind of grew into a monster." Cornelius and Leonard agreed there was something not quite right about the album. Leonard flew him to London. "For a while," says Cornelius, "with Bob [Johnston] and I, it was flat-out almost fistfights over things going in the record—fighting over wanting it to be the best for Leonard. There was tons of stuff that Buckmaster wrote that Leonard and I would finally just end up putting great big red X's

through, because it would actually have been too much; but if you
listen closely there's a heck of a lot on there."

"It was an odd sort of record," said Leonard.[3] There's barely a
trace of Tennessee in it at all, except at a push the skewed back-
porch rhythm of "Diamonds in the Mine," a snarling, screaming sing-
along about the nothingness of it all. The album contains some of
Leonard's blackest songs and also some of his most beautiful. The
resigned eroticism of "Joan of Arc" and the serene bittersweetness of
"Famous Blue Raincoat"—another of Leonard's triangle songs, this
a letter written to a rival or friend or both in the dark hours before
dawn—sound almost unbearably lovely alongside the dark, disturbing "Sing Another Song, Boys," "Dress Rehearsal Rag" (of which
Leonard said, "I didn't write that song, I suffered it"[4]), and "Avalanche," the intense, compelling song with which the album opens.
It is sung in the character of a hunchback, a grotesque creature with
a mountain of gold lusting over women—a Nazi caricature of a Jew.
Or from the depths of hell by a tormented man who longs for connection with the Divine. Or by a man who already has the woman but
does not want her or the domesticity she offers. And/or it is sung by
God—a gentle, New Testament Jesus, with the crumbs of the Last
Supper on the table and a wound in his side, who turns out to be
as hard and demanding as an Old Testament Jehovah. In these six
verses, sung in a minor key, untempered by women's voices, there are
layers upon layers, a whole house of mirrors, but the constants are a
sense of loneliness and longing, depression and despair.

Songs of Love and Hate, along with the first two albums *Songs of
Leonard Cohen* and *Songs from a Room,* make up a kind of trilogy
wherein killers march alongside suicides, martyrs with soldiers, and
gurus with Old Testamentarians, and men who long for love and their
lovers march in opposite directions. As in Leonard's books of poetry,
there are recurring themes and motifs, lessons learned and unlearned,
joy becoming love becoming pain. Joan of Arc, whose picture was on

the back sleeve of Leonard's first record, is the subject of a song in his third. Marianne Ihlen, pictured on the back of his second album, was the subject of a song on the first. "Dress Rehearsal Rag," a song written for the first album and recorded for the second, finally made it onto the third, three years after its appearance on the Judy Collins album that effectively launched Leonard's musical career.

When *Songs of Love and Hate* was released in March 1971, an imaginary whistle blew and the U.S. and UK ran to opposite ends of the playground. In Britain the album was a Top 5 hit. In America, despite a promotional campaign, it was an abject failure, not even making it into the Top 100. Canada did not take to it as warmly as to his last album, but Dalhousie University in Halifax was moved to award Leonard an honorary doctorate in the month that it came out. The citation read: "For many young people on both sides of the Atlantic, Leonard Cohen has become a symbol of their own anguish, alienation and uncertainty." It echoed the Columbia Records ad about there being millions of Leonard Cohens out there, disengaging themselves from life. "People were saying I was 'depressing a generation,'" said Leonard, "and 'they should give away razor blades with Leonard Cohen albums because it's music to slit your wrists by.'"[5] The UK press had taken to calling him "Laughing Len."

Spring in Montreal is a wonder. That after such prolonged abuse it still has the will to follow winter seems always little short of a miracle. The sun, no longer slacking on the job, got on with melting the snow. Tables and chairs sprouted outside cafés, where survivors, peeled of their winter armor, sat marveling at the flowers. The darkness had passed, for now. Leonard and Suzanne were installed in their little cottage near the Parc du Portugal. Suzanne had adopted "three adorable but constantly quacking ducklings, until Leonard said, 'It's me or the ducks, Suzanne.'" Leonard was trying to write. "He was always writing," says Suzanne, "even when he thought he wasn't. Continuously." Suzanne was writing too, a pornographic novel. "It was an innocent ruse, catnip for a blank page, not only to amuse Leonard, but to get him to continue [to try] to write another novel again. I believed—and still do—that he had another novel waiting to be born, that I wished he would consecrate himself to. So I started this book—pornographic, I suppose, for 1969/70, but in today's market it would be just another modern sardonic/romantic novel—pretending I was having the writer's block, not him. I asked him if I wrote a paragraph if he would write one, to push me along, and he did, and that's how it began, playfully," each writing a page and reading it to the other. "I never imagined I'd actually finish it, but I did"—it took Suzanne around two years. They sent it off to some publishing houses. "We laughed as the rejection letters came in, because along with the regrets they asked to meet me anyway."

Leonard completed his novel too, although not until the midseventies. It was accepted by his publisher, but at the proof stage, Leonard withdrew it. One friend to whom Leonard spoke of the book had the impression it was an autobiography, in which Leonard discussed the nature of fame and the sexuality of celebrity—what people expected of him and what they offered him now that they had not offered him before he became a music star. Another friend gathered that it was fiction, largely autobiographical, and that he had written so frankly about his family that he had second thoughts about making it public—curious when Leonard wrote about his family with such candor in *The Favorite Game*. A 1976 interview with *Melody Maker*[6] appears to confirm the latter. He had written about his family, Leonard said, but he felt "that it wasn't honest enough. In other words, it would hurt them but it didn't have the good side. So I took it back at the last moment. But I feel good because it's written. Maybe there'd be an appropriate time for it some time. But not for a while," and not by the time of this book's publication.

In the summer a new film appeared in theaters featuring a soundtrack by Leonard Cohen. Robert Altman's *McCabe and Mrs. Miller* was a Western of sorts, starring Warren Beatty and Julie Christie as a gambler and prostitute who team up to run a bordello. Altman was a great fan of *Songs of Leonard Cohen*—he played it so often he wore more than one copy out, adding considerably to its U.S. sales. Altman called Leonard to ask if he might use it in his film; Leonard agreed, although given his experiences with directors he was not holding his breath. Then Altman called the production company, Warner Bros., to see if they could procure rights from Columbia. At the time the music department of Warner Bros.'s films division was run by Joe Boyd, an American who had made his name in Britain in the sixties, producing or launching the careers of artists such as Pink Floyd, Nick Drake and the Incredible String Band. Altman invited Boyd to a screening.

"The lights went down and onto the screen comes Beatty," says Boyd, "walking down a hill to the arpeggio guitar intro of 'The Stranger Song.' And then a couple of scenes with Julie Christie and Leonard Cohen's guitar and voice. I thought, 'Huh? That's a little wacky'; I didn't have any great feeling of 'Oh my god, Leonard Cohen's music, incredible.' But when the film finished and the lights came up, everyone else in the room—crew, editors—turned to Robert and said, 'Oh my God, Bob, that's *so* unbelievable, you're such a genius.'" So Boyd phoned Columbia Records. He ended up talking to Bob Johnston and asked him if he knew how they could get hold of the guitar tracks without the vocals. Although Johnston had not recorded that album, he knew that they could not have the guitar tracks, because the performances were recorded live in the studio, "the voice singing at the same time as the guitar was played." But they did find some instrumental passages that the Kaleidoscope had done without Leonard's vocals, which did not make it onto the album. Watching the movie in a cinema, Chris Darrow almost jumped out of his seat when he recognized the instrumentation they had improvised to "Sisters of Mercy," "Winter Lady" and "The Stranger Song." Chester Crill had much the same reaction. "When I heard it I said, '*That's* the way the album was supposed to be mixed, stripped down, with the instruments actually responding to Leonard's vocal.'"

That same year "Sisters of Mercy" would also feature five more of Leonard's songs in the Rainer Werner Fassbinder film *Warnung vor einer Heiligen Nutte—Beware of a Holy Whore*. (Fassbinder, an early fan, would go on to employ Leonard's songs in several films.) Another German film, Werner Herzog's *Fata Morgana*, used "Suzanne," "So Long, Marianne" and "Hey, That's No Way to Say Goodbye." Others of Leonard's songs were also keeping busy. Tim Hardin covered "Bird on a Wire" (one of several cover versions to substitute an "a" for Leonard's "the"), and the ever-faithful Judy Collins included two more Cohen songs on her new album *Living*, "Famous Blue Raincoat" and "Joan of Arc." A live recording from the Isle of Wight of "Tonight Will Be Fine" turned up on a triple album, a compilation titled *The First Great Rock Festivals of the Seventies: Isle of Wight/Atlanta Pop Festival*, released in the summer of '71. Delighted that so many of his songs were making a living without his having to perform them, Leonard settled down to his writing. He was working on the final edits of a new book of poetry, as well as on what he described to Danny Fields as "a new big chunk of prose." It was called *The Woman Being Born*—a title that was also given to an early draft of Leonard's book *Death of a Lady's Man*.

Leonard had been in Montreal with Suzanne for six months now. It had begun to feel like a very long time. He took a trip to London in August, with the excuse that he was finding a UK publisher for an anthology of Irving Layton's poems that Leonard wanted to release. The following month, accompanied by a very attractive English girlfriend, an artist, he flew to Switzerland. He was there to meet his friend Henry Zemel, who was making a documentary film about Immanuel Velikovsky, the Russian psychoanalyst and catastrophist.

Leonard had first read about Velikovsky in *Reader's Digest*; the maga-zine had been a particular favorite of his father. In later years Leon-ard explored Velikovsky's writings on the sexuality of the gods and his theories that evolution, religion and myth were a response to real catastrophes of celestial origin—comets and colliding planets causing the biblical floods and plagues as well as a collective post-traumatic amnesia in mankind.

Having been dismissed as a kook by the science community, Ve-likovsky had agreed to take a teaching position at the University of the New World—a utopian educational experiment founded in Swit-zerland by the American political and behavioral scientist Alfred de Grazia, a former writer of psychological warfare manuals for the CIA. His fellow professors were to include William Burroughs and Ornette Coleman. When would-be student Brian Cullman, a writer and musi-cian from New York, showed up in September 1971, "there was noth-ing, no campus, no buildings, just fifteen or twenty mostly rich kids who were using this as a way to avoid the draft and avoid college." Billeted in a resort hotel, they were given a small list of classes, in-cluding one on sexuality, which essentially consisted of "a sexy older woman with glasses and a lot of cleavage directing the students in sex games."

Then Velikovsky arrived, with Leonard and Zemel, and started giving lectures. Leonard attended them. He wanted, he told Cull-man, to ask the professor about the sexuality that generated the first life on Earth. "I was really excited to meet Leonard," says Cullman, "but most people there, even the university kids, couldn't care less. One evening I sat around in the hotel lobby with Leonard and Henry, and Leonard had a guitar and played 'Bird on the Wire' and songs from *Songs of Love and Hate*. There were some very beautiful French girls in the lobby who had no idea who he was, and there was this long period of Henry talking Leonard up, Leonard talking himself down, then trying to talk himself back up again: 'Well have you heard of Charles Aznavour?' 'No.' 'Have you heard of Bob Dylan?' 'Yes.' 'Well,

I'm sort of this, sort of that,' and they weren't vaguely interested. He was putting on a show about not being concerned about the French girls, but clearly wounded that they had no idea who he was."

Leonard made an appearance in Zemel's film, near the end, asking Velikovsky questions. What effect would man's collective amnesia have on the future, what rituals might repeat the trauma and when would the next catastrophe happen? It would not stop happening, Velikovsky answered, while man continued to live "in a role that he created himself, in his arrogance, in his violence, in his misunderstanding of what happened in the past." The film, *Bonds of the Past*, was broadcast by CBC in February 1972—a month after the publication of Leonard's newest volume of poetry.

"I've just written a book called *The Energy of Slaves* and in there I say that I'm in pain," Leonard told journalist Paul Saltzman. "I don't say it in those words because I don't like those words, they don't represent the real situation. It took eighty poems to represent the situation of where I am right now. It's carefully worked on, you know. It's taken many years to write . . . and it's there . . . between hard covers. It's careful and controlled and it's what we call art."[7] The "real situation" appeared to be as savage and lost as it was on *Songs of Love and Hate*. He wrote,

> *I have no talent left*
> *I can't write a poem any more*
> *You can call me Len or Lennie now*
> *Like you always wanted*[8]

and elsewhere,

> *The poems don't love us anymore*
> *they don't want to love us . . .*
> *Do not summon us, they say*
> *We can't help you any longer*[9]

He was "one of the slaves," he wrote; "You are employers." Everybody wanted something from him that he no longer had the energy to give—the record company, his audience, and "all the flabby liars of the Aquarian age."[10] Even the women who had always been there for him, even though he was not always there for them, had started to become hard work.

> *You are almost always with someone else*
> *I'm going to burn down your house*
> *and fuck you in the ass . . .*
> *Why don't you come over to my table*
> *with no pants on*
> *I'm sick of surprising you*[11]

He was a celebrity now and women were his reward:

> *The 15 year old girls*
> *I wanted when I was 15*
> *I have them now . . .*
> *I advise you all*
> *to become rich and famous*[12]

THE ENERGY OF SLAVES

The review in the *Times Literary Supplement* sneered, "Teenyboppers of all ages will have the book on their shelves between the Bhagavad Gita and the unopened copy of the Cantos."[13] Other critics were not much kinder. Stephen Scobie, who was often Leonard's champion, described it as "blatantly bad . . . deliberately ugly, offensive, bitter, anti-romantic."[14] The last four words are hard to argue with, but Leonard was deliberately no longer writing for beauty, he said, but truth. He had been brutally honest in *Songs of Love and Hate* bar the one untruth in the song "Last Year's Man," in which he wrote

that he was unable to write. Clearly he had found the clarity to finish
the album.

The Energy of Slaves has a similar brutal honesty. Revisiting it today, it almost reads like punk poetry. The poem "How We Used to
Approach the Book of Changes: 1966" strips all of Leonard's darkness down to a prayer, one he would return to in the turbulent coming year:

> *Good father, since I am broken down, no leader*
> *of the borning world, no saint for those in pain,*
> *no singer, no musician, no master of anything, no*
> *friend to my friends, no lover to those who love me*
> *only my greed remains to me, biting into every*
> *minute that has not come with my insane triumph*
> *show me the way now . . .*
> *. . . and let me be for a moment in*
> *this miserable and bewildering wretchedness, a happy*
> *animal.*

Columbia Records tugged on Leonard's chain. They needed him
to play the places where people were buying his record: seventeen
cities across Europe and two in Israel, all within the space of a month.
It was nearly two years since his last tour—he must have thought he'd
got away with never doing another—and he didn't have a band; the
Army had been decommissioned more than a year before. Charlie
Daniels was making a second album of his own and Bubba Fowler
had left his wife and kids and run off with Susan Mussmano, one of
the backing singers. The pair, who had become lovers on Leonard's
1970 tour, had no place to go, so Bob Johnston let them live on his
boat—a cabin cruiser that had belonged to the country great Hank
Snow, before Johnston bought it and paid another country great,
though poor and unknown at the time, Kris Kristofferson, to work

on it. Says Bill Donovan, "Leonard and I went out there a couple of times and saw them; and then they pulled out of the harbor, said they were going to take it out to the gulf, and we never heard or saw them again."*

Bill Donovan signed on for the second tour, as did Ron Cornelius and Bob Johnston, who put a new band together. Fowler and Daniels were replaced by two Californians, David O'Connor, a flamenco guitarist, and Peter Marshall, a jazz bassist, who was living at that time in Vienna. Johnston was still looking for backing singers as the three weeks of rehearsals began. "There was a redheaded girl who was gorgeous; she said, 'You'll be making the biggest mistake in the world if you don't take me with you,' and I said, 'I know it, I haven't heard anybody better yet.' Then the next day this girl came in—a horse face, big glasses and ragged from a trip from L.A." She told him she had sung in the musical *Hair* and made regular appearances on television in the Smothers Brothers' show. Johnston listened to her sing. "She was incredible—and she knew every song Leonard did. Though I hated to turn down the redheaded girl I told the horse-faced girl, 'You're going.'" Her name was Jennifer Warnes. The second female vocalist was another Los Angeleno, Donna Washburn, the daughter of the president of the 7-Up soft drinks company; her musical résumé included singing with Dillard & Clark and Joe Cocker.

Leonard was focusing all his efforts on holding it together and getting in shape for the campaign: yoga, swimming twice a day, fasting. He had a habit of fasting once a week, usually on a Friday if a tour did not get in the way. Brian Cullman recalls that when he and

---

* Susan Mussmano changed her name to Aileen Fowler, the one under which she is credited on the 1970 recordings on the *Live Songs* album. She and Fowler, who adopted the new name Elkin Thomas, finally left the boat for a farm in the North Texas prairies. They still live there, when not touring together as folk duo Aileen and Elkin Thomas. Leonard's second backing singer, Corlynn Hanney, went on to make spiritual albums.

Leonard talked in Switzerland, Leonard spoke more about fasting than he did poetry. "But even his fasting was elegant; while fasting, he would drink white grape juice with lemon and seltzer." Fasting was important to Leonard and had been ever since he began the task of chiseling away the softness that his old family photographs showed a tendency toward. He needed to keep the edges sharp.

Suzanne flew out to Nashville to join Leonard. She was there when Paul Saltzman interviewed Leonard in their hotel room. He noted how Leonard sat there quietly while Suzanne caressed his foot. Suzanne appeared to dote on Leonard, telling him at one point, "You've taught me most everything I know." They looked "so fine together," the journalist wrote, "warm and calm and loving."[15] Marty Machat was also working on ways to ease the pain of touring for him: they would take a filmmaker on the road with them, who would shoot and record every show. That way, once this tour was over, if anyone wanted to see Leonard in concert, here he was, on film.

The man Machat had in mind for the job was Tony Palmer, a young Londoner, who had made films on Frank Zappa, Gustav Mahler and the band Cream, all of which had won acclaim. Palmer was also a music critic with the *Observer*—"the first person," Palmer claims, "to review Leonard's first LP, and extremely favorably." Machat flew him to New York to meet Leonard. "We talked for three hours, Leonard was extremely self-effacing, humble, almost apologetic—he kept asking, did I think the songs were any good?—and he expressed a certain amount of dissatisfaction with the existing recordings, going back to the first album and 'Suzanne.' I asked him why and he said that they didn't really express the emotion that he'd felt when writing the songs; but probably, it was more complicated than that." He told Palmer "he didn't like filming, and gave [Palmer] all the reasons why he thought it was a bad idea," but added, "This will probably be the only tour I will make ever in my life. I'd like a proper record of what happens." "Then it was just a discussion about how I would do it," Palmer recalls. He signed a contract that gave him $35,000—"a low budget," says Palmer, since it had to cover a four-man crew, their travel expenses and their equipment; he paid himself £2,000—but it also gave him free range to shoot what he wanted, be it a butt-naked Leonard in a sauna, Leonard weeping onstage or Leonard taking acid before the show. Machat, Palmer says, told him he was putting up the money for the film himself, "so that Leonard doesn't have to worry about it."

"The impression one had was that he was very much a father figure for Leonard, his protective shield, who nursed him and looked after him. It was the same in the day-to-day life on the road: he was very solicitous, he'd always go and check out Leonard's room in the hotel first to see if it was okay and that Leonard felt comfortable. Leonard never wanted a grand suite on the top floor of the Ritz but he wanted the shower to be working." Leonard had told Johnston that on this tour, unlike the last, where their hotels were among the grandest in Europe, they were going to stay "in little rooms with a little bed and a table." He did not get his way. But that seemed to be happening a lot lately. When Leonard left with the band for Dublin, where the tour began on Saint Patrick's Day 1972, Suzanne was pregnant.

It was an extraordinary tour, all of it recorded by Palmer's camera, both the incandescent performances and the shambles, when the sound equipment, and on occasion Leonard, broke down. Palmer shot backstage too, and offstage, filming Leonard being interviewed by various European journalists asking much the same questions in different accents. Leonard would answer them patiently, sometimes candidly, more often evasively, or an inseparable mixture of the two. When asked by one reporter if he was a practicing Jew, he said, "I'm always practicing." He told a German journalist, "I can't say my childhood was in any way inconvenienced by [World War II but] I did have a sense of empathy for my race."

The Berlin concert was in the hall where Goebbels made his speech announcing total war. Leonard, echoing the Nazi salute on his last tour, decided to give the same speech. There were some boos and catcalls from the crowd, but mostly they loved him. The connection between Leonard and the audience at many of the concerts, as the film footage shows, was palpable, very physical. In Hamburg, Leonard jumped into the crowd and kissed a young woman—a deep, long kiss. "It just went on and on and on," Cornelius recalls. "It ended up with Leonard on the floor, and you wondered if they were going to start taking their clothes off now." Backstage Leonard told Palmer, "I've disgraced myself." The next night, in Frankfurt, he invited the audience onstage, and while the band played on, the fans pulled Leonard to the floor and lay on top of him. "There were people all over him, writhing like a pile of worms," says Cornelius. "He just lost it; he just got so sexually involved with the crowd that he took it to a new level."

A procession of women offered themselves. One woman, a beautiful actress, came backstage with her husband and, while her husband watched and Palmer kept filming, hit on Leonard. He turned her down. "There were numerous ladies he took a shine to," says Palmer. "I had thought at one point he was feeling very close to Jennifer [Warnes]. If they were they were very discreet, but we certainly filmed them looking very happy together." The camera also caught Leonard in crisis, debating with himself—and with his band, the fans, the media and Palmer—about performance and celebrity and their corruptive nature, the damage that they do to an artist. "One feels a sense of importance in one's heart that is absolutely fatal to the writing of poetry," he told an interviewer. "You can't feel important and write well."

He spoke of his humiliation at "not having delivered the goods," meaning the songs; it was always the songs. When Palmer remonstrated that "the audience was absolutely transfixed," Leonard said,

"There's no point in them being transfixed if I am not conveying my songs to them properly." At the Manchester concert, Leonard tried to explain to the audience that he was striving for more than "just the observance of a few 'museum' songs." He elaborated, "I wrote the songs to myself and to women several years ago and it is a curious thing to be trapped in that original effort, because here I wanted to tell one person one thing and now I am in a situation where I must repeat them like some parrot chained to his stand, night after night." He also called himself a "broken-down nightingale." At several shows he offered to give everyone their money back. Offstage, he recited his prayer-poem from *The Energy of Slaves* to the cameraman: "*Let me be for a moment in this miserable and bewildering wretchedness a happy animal.*"

———————

On the plane journey from Paris to Israel, Leonard was quiet. "He liked to sit near the front of an aeroplane, usually with me," says Palmer, "and, because he hated aeroplane food, he always had his little bowl of inexpensive caviar and lemons and a slice of brown bread. He was contemplative." He was looking forward to playing Israel. He was terrified of playing Israel. The day before he had played to doting crowds and he had gone on a date with Brigitte Bardot—he had invited Bill Donovan to come to lunch with them and meet her, but Donovan had to leave for Israel before the rest of them to make sure everything was set up for the shows.

Their first show, at the Yad Eliyahu Arena, was on the same day that Leonard and the band flew into Tel Aviv. Airport security was slow and grim, guns everywhere, but they arrived at the venue in good time. When they came out onstage though, the floor was completely empty. The audience was packed into the stands around the edges, like they were there to see an invisible basketball game. Security had been told to keep everyone off the floor, which had been newly varnished. When Leonard, disturbed by the distance between them, invited the audience to come down, they were set upon by armed guards in orange boiler suits. "They freaked out and started clubbing everybody, beating kids up," Donovan remembers. "Leonard jumped off the stage into the crowd and a guy ran up onstage and grabbed Ron's guitar and I knocked the guy offstage and then somebody hit me from behind and knocked me out. It ended up as sort of a riot." Peter Marshall says, "I was hiding behind my string bass and there was some guy raising a chair, like it was a movie, and he's going to hit me in the face, but somebody grabbed the chair from behind."

The band reconvened backstage. Jennifer Warnes said she was scared. Leonard wondered aloud, "Maybe I pushed it too hard." Then he led everyone back onstage. "I know you're trying to do your job, but you don't have to do it with your fists," he told the guards, then dedicated a song to them. He urged the audience to sit down and enjoy the concert. "Eventually," says Marshall, "he got everybody to calm down and he completed that show." As soon as it was done, they dashed out of the hall and into the tour bus—an Israeli street bus they had hired for the stay. As they drove toward Jerusalem, "the whole band drinking wine, playing music, having a grand old time," Marshall recalls, "there was this one Israeli soldier hitchhiking way out in the country. We pulled up. This guy thinks he's just getting on a regular bus and there's this gigantic party. We took his rifle and gave him whatever was going around"—pot, acid—"and the look on his face, I can still see it. Those guys had a tough life at that time."

The Binyanei Ha'uma hall in Jerusalem was small and new, with excellent acoustics. The audience were where they ought to be, sitting downstairs near the stage. In the dressing room, Bob Johnston handed around the LSD du tour, Desert Dust. "Think that stuff still works?" asked Leonard. "We'll be in serious trouble if it works—or it doesn't work." Standing at the microphone, looking out at the attentive, adoring crowd, he appeared even more affected than usual.

The connection he shared with them was more than just emotional; it encompassed their shared Jewish history and blood. Leonard's eyes were stoned and bright. He looked both energized and enervated, a tightrope walker who might fall any moment or be taken up out of his body into the sky. The songs sounded beautiful as he sang, and the band seemed to be wired into his nervous system. But Leonard felt that it was not good enough, that he was letting down this precious audience and these precious songs. He tried to explain this to them, but his explanation kept getting more and more complex.

"They become meditations for me and sometimes, you know, I just don't get high on it, I feel that I am cheating you, so I'll try it again, okay? If it doesn't work I'll stop. There's no reason why we should mutilate a song to save face. If it doesn't get any better we'll just end the concert and I'll refund your money. Some nights one is raised off the ground and some nights you just can't get off the ground and there's no point lying about it, and tonight we just haven't been getting off the ground. It says in the Kabbalah that if you can't get off the ground you should stay on the ground. It says in the Kabbalah that unless Adam and Eve face each other, God does not sit on his throne, and somehow the male and female part of me refuse to encounter one another tonight and God does not sit on his throne and this is a terrible thing to happen in Jerusalem. So listen, we're going to leave the stage now and try to profoundly meditate in the dressing room to try to get ourselves back into shape and if we can manage," Leonard said, "we'll be back."[16]

Backstage, Leonard was having a meltdown. He announced, "I'm splitting." He said he would give the fans their money back. But the fans didn't want their money back, they told him, the tickets weren't expensive, and some people had come two hundred miles for this show. Someone came to the dressing room door and told him that the audience was still out there, waiting, and that they wanted to sing Leonard a song. At first Leonard misunderstood. But then he heard them. They were singing him "Hevenu Shalom Aleichem," "We Bring You Peace." Marshall took Leonard aside. "We have to take care of business and finish the show or we might not get out of here in one piece." Leonard said, "I think what I need is a shave." That's what his mother had told him to do when things got bad. There was a mirror and a basin in the dressing room and someone fetched him a razor. Slowly, serenely, while the crowd clapped and sang in the auditorium, Leonard shaved. When he was done, he smiled. They went back onstage. As Leonard sang "So Long, Marianne," immersing himself in the song he'd written to a woman in a moment in a less complicated time, changing her description from "*pretty one*" to "*beautiful one*," tears began to stream down his face.

Backstage, when the show was over, everyone was crying. It was the last night of the tour; they were going home. Leonard picked up his guitar and started to sing "Bird on the Wire" in the style of a country song. Bob Johnston sang a verse and turned it into a gospel blues, and then the whole band joined in, making instruments with their voices, humming softly in the background, as sweet and comforting as a lullaby.

————————

Adam Cohen was born in Montreal on September 18, 1972—"not an *enfant du hasard*," said Suzanne, but "planned." If Leonard had planned on becoming a father, he did not behave that way. When Steve Sanfield showed up at the house with his wife and son to congratulate his friend on his first child, Suzanne was there, "very solemn," and Leonard was in New York. He was at the Chelsea, having what might have been a somber, one-man bachelor party. The hotel would have been the perfect setting, the Chelsea scene having become as fractured and dark at times as Leonard's state of mind.

"There were a lot of factions, a lot of drugs and trauma, a lot of rough stuff going on, a shooting," says Liberty, the model turned poet and feminist writer who lived in the Chelsea Hotel and who was Leonard's lover at one time. "I had a room with high ceilings, a fireplace and a wrought-iron balcony, but my next-door neighbors were cocaine dealers and pimps." If Leonard had gone back there to remind himself of a time when he was free and unencumbered, he did not strike Liberty as "someone [who was] reaching for freedom. . . . In some ways he seemed to carry the vestiges of a privileged middle-class background," particularly in the context of the early seventies and the Chelsea circle. She remembers him as "sweet and gentle" but "constrained." Liberty says, "I felt he hadn't yet gone through the looking glass, had not entered his own 'house of mystery,' or hadn't stayed there long enough—though, of course, Leonard survived. Many of the wild ones did not."

Even if Leonard were not wild, he clearly felt trapped. At the same time, his upbringing, his patriarchal roots, his sense of duty ensured that he could not shrug off fatherhood. He returned home, but reluctantly and impossibly weary. He was depressed. It was hard work, trying to find a way to keep going and not be pulled off course. Sanfield and his wife returned to the house for dinner. It was a "very uncomfortable" evening. Once they had eaten, says Sanfield, "Leonard said, 'Let's go,' and we got up and went to a couple of clubs. I was thinking, 'This guy just had a child; what are you doing, man?' Leonard said, 'It's tough, this life. It's just tough.'"

Later that year, when Sanfield was back in California, Leonard called him. "He said, 'Would you bring me to your teacher? He's been on my mind for a long time.'" Sanfield asked Leonard where he was. Montreal, he said; he was going to go to Tennessee and pick up his jeep and drive cross-country. It was more than two thousand miles from Tennessee to the Santa Barbara mountains and took several days. The mountain road was thick with snow when Leonard arrived at Sanfield's house. When they left together for L.A., the jeep got stuck on a back road and they had to hike through deep snow to find a pickup to pull them out. They stopped on the way in Fresno, where they took in an afternoon movie, then set off again for the Zen Center in L.A. "I brought Leonard to Roshi and we sat down and had tea," said Sanfield. "It was mostly silent. Then Roshi said, 'You bring friend to Mount Baldy.' So a couple of days later Leonard and I drove up there in his jeep, and Roshi said to Leonard, 'Okay, you stay here.'"

He stayed, but for barely a week. It was winter, it was Mount Baldy, it was a Buddhist boot camp, grim, with all these broken young people trudging through snow in walking meditation at three o'clock in the morning. Leonard came down from the frozen mountain and flew with Suzanne to Acapulco and the sun.

Fourteen

A Shield Against the Enemy

March 15, 1973: "Thank you for the knife and the good belt. I used them to scratch and choke her a little. While she suffers I have a chance to breathe the free air and look under the flab for my body." March 17: "Listening to gypsy violins, my jeep rusting in Tennessee, married as usual to the wrong woman. She loves the way I make love to her." March 19: "Lie down, there's no one watching you . . . the show is over."[1]

Leonard had given up the Tennessee cabin. He left his jeep in Bob Johnston's drive and went back to Montreal and Suzanne. He bought the house next door to his cottage—they were a matching pair, with a shared dividing wall—and designated the ground floor a sculpture studio for Mort and the upstairs his writing room. A place to escape to when domesticity became too much. To all appearances, a man not cut out for domesticity was making a real effort to make his domestic situation work. What Leonard was writing, though, did not give much cause for optimism.

In April, Columbia released Leonard's fourth album, *Live Songs*.

Although it failed to make even the UK charts, it was a contender for the most somber live album ever. The album contains nine songs recorded on the 1970 and 1972 tours and one that Leonard recorded alone, in the cabin, on a tape recorder borrowed from Johnston. It opens with "Minute Prologue," a despairing rumination on "dissension" and "pain," improvised over a slow solo guitar, and closes with the doleful cabin recording of "Queen Victoria," a poem from *Flowers for Hitler* ("*my love, she gone with other boys*") to which he had given minimal musical adornment. In between, alongside naked and emotional performances of songs from his first two albums, are "Please Don't Pass Me By (A Disgrace)," a thirteen-minute revival meeting sing-along with a Holocaust reference ("*I sing this for the Jews and the gypsies and the smoke that they made*"), "Passing Thru," performed as a weary country hymn, and "Improvisation," a mournful riff on the instrumental intro to "You Know Who I Am." The bleached-out photograph of Leonard on the front sleeve was taken by Suzanne. He is thin and blank faced, ashen, his hair shorn, his white-clad body fading like a ghost into the backdrop of white bathroom tiles.

The liner notes came from a letter to Leonard from a young British writer and artist named Daphne Richardson, with whom he had a correspondence. Richardson had first written to him about an experimental book she was working on, which included collages of Bob Dylan and Leonard Cohen poems. She asked for permission to use them, which (unlike Dylan) Leonard gave. Some time later Richardson, who had been in and out of mental hospitals, wrote to Leonard from a hospital, sending him a book she had written while she was there. Leonard had found it "shattering. A testimony of pain I've never read anything like."[2] When he was next in London, they arranged to meet; he found a "very attractive girl in her thirties" and a talented artist. He asked Richardson if she would like to illustrate *The Energy of Slaves*. During a period when he failed to check his mail, a pile of letters from her had accrued. She wrote, with growing desperation, that she had been readmitted to the hospital and had insisted on leaving because she had work to do on Leonard's book. They did not believe her, she said, and strapped her down. Leonard tried to get in contact, but he says, "I was just too late." She had killed herself three days before. Leonard was mentioned in her suicide note. He published her letter on the album sleeve, he said, because she had always wanted to be published and no one would do so.[3]

In February 1973, Leonard was back again in London, this time to meet with Tony Palmer and Marty Machat and see *Bird on a Wire*, Palmer's film of the previous year's tour. As he watched himself, there were tears in Leonard's eyes. "He wept for a good 50 percent of the film," Palmer says. "He kept saying, 'This is too true, this is too true,' repeating it like a mantra." Machat liked the film; "I'm very happy about this," he told Palmer. So did the BBC, who bought it on the spot, effectively covering 75 percent of what the film had cost to make. A week later, Machat called Palmer. There was a problem. Leonard thought the film "too confrontational." A meeting was set up during which, according to Palmer, a film editor named Humphrey Dixon, who had worked as his editing assistant on the film, stepped up and said that he could rescue it. "Go ahead," said Palmer, and the long, expensive business of remaking *Bird on a Wire* began. "I've read that, according to Leonard's testimony, a further half a million dollars was spent," Palmer says. "Marty looked at me somewhat wryly and said, 'Don't worry, it's not my money this time.'"

In an interview Leonard gave *Melody Maker*'s Roy Hollingworth while in London, he described the film as "totally unacceptable" and said that he was paying from his own pocket just to get it finished. When it was done, he said, he would "get out of the scene." Asked what he meant by that, Leonard answered, "Well, I'm leaving. I want to return to another rhythm. Somehow I haven't organised my life within rock very well. Somehow *it*—the rock life—became important rather than the thing that produced the song. I don't find myself leading a life that has many good moments in it. So I've decided to screw it, and go. Maybe the other life won't have many good moments either, but I know this one, and I don't want it." Throughout the interview, various people from Leonard's UK record company fussed about him. They had brought him a gold disc for UK sales of *Songs of Love and Hate*, which he had put on the floor, with no great regard for its well-being. By the end of the interview it was covered with trash, including an upturned coffee cup. "I've found myself not writing at all," he said, lighting another Turkish cigarette from the butt of the one he had just finished. "I feel that I'm no longer learning. I began to feel I was doing some of the songs a disservice. So I have to get into something else."[4]

Leonard hired Henry Zemel to work on *Bird on a Wire* with Dixon as coeditor; he needed someone he trusted to watch his back. Zemel, watching the footage from the tour, could see his friend's struggle with celebrity and how hard he worked at trying to maintain the sincerity of his engagement with both the audiences and his songs. He knew that Leonard felt that celebrity had taken a toll on his work. "He very much saw himself as a lyric poet," says Zemel, and "a lyric poet has a certain kind of innocence and naïveté and an uncompromising relationship with the world and with what they're doing. When something cracks that vision and idea of what the world could be and what they're devoted to making it be, can they ever put the pieces back together again? The quality of the work, the voice, is never the same."

Marianne was back on Hydra, in the house where she and Leonard had lived, when one day Suzanne appeared at the door. She had a baby in her arms who was crying loudly. She told Marianne, over her son's sobs, that she had been staying at a hotel and wanted to know when Marianne was moving out. Marianne packed her things and left. "That was a sad scene," says Marianne quietly. When Leonard heard about this he offered to buy Marianne a house—she had sold her own back in their impecunious days—or, if she wanted to stay, he would buy another house for Suzanne. "He was always very generous," says

Marianne, who declined his offer. It was time to return to Norway. When Leonard joined Suzanne and Adam in the little white house on the hill, it is hard to imagine that, as he tried to find his old rhythm, his thoughts did not turn now and then to life there with another woman and child in more innocent, nurturing times.

He resumed his old routine of a morning swim in the harbor. Afterward "he just hung around on the port, sitting on rocks and staring at people, for hours," says Terry Oldfield, a young composer and musician who had moved to Hydra in the early seventies; for a while he gave flute lessons to Marianne's son. Leonard was one of the first people Oldfield met on the island. Leonard, who struck Oldfield as being "in a very lucid state of mind," told him that he had recently been staying in a monastery.

On Hydra Leonard painted and also worked on the book of prose he had begun in Montreal, its title since changed from "The Woman Being Born" to "My Life in Art." Meanwhile, several of his old poems and songs were strutting the boards without him, sometimes in curious guises. "The New Step," from *Flowers for Hitler*, had been turned into a one-act ballet-drama of the same name, which was aired on CBC television, and an assortment of his lyrics and poems on the subject of women made up Gene Lesser's off-Broadway musical *Sisters of Mercy*. What Leonard was writing about women—or one particular woman—in "My Life in Art" was not pretty. "Fuck this marriage [and] your dead bed night after night."* He needed, he wrote, to "study the hatred I have for her and how it is transmuted into desire by solitude and distance."[5] He voiced the sentiment less savagely in a new song:

> *I live here with a woman and a child*
> *The situation makes me kind of nervous*

---

* These words would later appear in the prose poem "Death to This Book" in *Death of a Lady's Man* (1978).

The title he gave the song, which was in great part about his domestic situation, was "There Is a War."

———————

On October 6, 1973, Egypt and Syria launched the attack on Israel that began the Yom Kippur War. The next day Leonard left Suzanne and Adam on Hydra and flew from Athens to Tel Aviv. His plan was to enlist in the Israeli Army: "I will go and stop Egypt's bullet. Trumpets and a curtain of razor blades," he wrote.[6] His motives, as these words might suggest, were complex: commitment to the cause certainly ("I've never disguised the fact that I'm Jewish and in any crisis in Israel I would be there," Leonard said in 1974. "I am committed to the survival of the Jewish people"[7]), but also bravado, narcissism and, near the top of the list, desperation to get away. "Women," he said, "only let you out of the house for two reasons: to make money or to fight a war,"[8] and in his present state of mind dying for a noble cause—any cause—was better than this life he was living as an indentured artist and a caged man.

Suzanne says, "I felt proud about Leonard's heroic actions and acts of generosity but fear about something happening—there was much hostility at that time—which turned into a fear of loss and dread of the worst. Knowing his mind couldn't be changed, I remember putting a blue ribbon inside his breast pocket without telling him, so that—in my mind—he'd be safe. And I was truly praying those first days." Leonard, on the other hand, sitting on the plane, heading for what he called his "myth home," felt free. He was "thin again and loose."[9] Shortly after arriving in Tel Aviv, Leonard met Oshik Levi, an Israeli singer. Levi was putting together a small team of performers to entertain the troops—Matti Caspi, Mordechai "Pupik" Arnon, Ilana Rovina—to which he was pleased to add Leonard. This was not what Leonard had in mind. He protested that his songs were sad and not known for their morale-boosting qualities. But Levi was per-

suasive and there had been no better offer from the Israeli Army. For
the next few weeks Leonard traveled by truck, tank and jeep to outposts, encampments, aircraft hangars, field hospitals, anywhere they
saw soldiers, and performed for them up to eight times a day. The
soldiers would gather closely around—sometimes barely a dozen of
them—and, if it was night and too dark to see, they would shine their
flashlights on him as he played.

"Every unit we came to, he would ask what is the position of this
or that soldier, and each and every time he wanted to join the forces
and be one of them," Levi told the newspaper *Maariv*. "I used to
tease him: 'Make up your mind, do you want to be a pilot, or an artillery man, or a naval commando diver? Each day you get excited by
something else.'" The musicians would camp with the soldiers and
talk to them all night long. "He was a modest person, with the soul
of a philosopher, wondering about the meaning of human life," said
Levi. "He had many talks with Arnon about philosophy, astrology
and the Bible. He used to talk often about the essence of Judaism,
and about his Hebrew name, Eliezer."[10]

In the notebook Leonard always carried with him, he made notes
of what he had seen in Israel—the beauty of the desert, the kinship
of the soldiers, the dead and wounded, who had made him weep. As
he had in Cuba, he also wrote fantasies of glorious escapades, such
as stealing a gun and killing the officer who bugged him "with relentless requests to sing 'Suzanne.'"[11] He wrote a song in Israel—
miraculously quickly—called "Lover Lover Lover." Caspi remembered Leonard improvising it in front of the soldiers during their
second performance.

> *May the spirit of this song*
> *May it rise up pure and free*
> *May it be a shield for you*
> *A shield against the enemy*

On his 1974 tour Leonard would introduce it as a song "written in the Sinai desert for soldiers of both sides."[12] That same year, when describing his experience to *ZigZag* magazine, he said, "War is wonderful. They'll never stamp it out. It's one of the few times people can act their best. It's so economical in terms of gesture and motion, every single gesture is precise, every effort is at its maximum. Nobody goofs off. There are opportunities to feel things that you simply cannot feel in modern city life"[13]—all of these, and the last in particular, having been things that had long exercised him.

From Israel he flew directly to Ethiopia, a country that was also on the brink of war. He appeared to be courting danger, tempting fate. Instead of attempting to take up arms, this time he took a room in the Imperial Hotel in Asmara. While the rain poured down outside, freed up, Leonard wrote. "I had my guitar with me and it was then I felt the songs emerging—at last, the conclusions that I had been carrying in manuscript form for the last four or five years, from hotel room to hotel room."[14] He refined "Lover Lover Lover," changing its opening line from "*I saw my brothers fighting in the desert*" to

I asked my father . . . "Change my name."
The one I'm using now it's covered up
With fear and filth and cowardice and shame

In Ethiopia he also finally "broke the code" of "Take This Longing"—a song he had written years ago to Nico and that Buffy Sainte-Marie had recorded as "The Bells"—in order "to get a version for" himself.[15] He made final edits to the lyrics of "Chelsea Hotel #2," a second version of the song that described his sexual encounter in New York with Janis Joplin. Leonard and Ron Cornelius had written the music together on his last tour, on a transatlantic flight from Nashville to Ireland. "It was back when you could sit in the back of the plane and smoke," Cornelius remembers, "and for the best part of this eight-and-a-half-hour flight Leonard and I sat there smoking and worked on that song. When we finally landed in Shannon, it was complete." Leonard told Billy Donovan, the tour manager, that it was the first song he had ever cowritten. The other song that came together in Ethiopia was "Field Commander Cohen," an ironic account of his imagined heroic military exploits. But in reality, in traveling to these combat zones, Leonard was avoiding the war that awaited him at home with Suzanne.

He was weary, though, and ready to make peace. He had seen too much blood and death and hatred in Israel. He felt he should go back and tend this little garden whose seed he had planted and see if somehow he could make a success of family life. But first he went to the monastery to sit in retreat with Roshi. When he finally went home to Suzanne and Adam at the end of the year, peace reigned in the cottage in Montreal, long enough for Suzanne to become pregnant with their second child.

In July 1974 the new version of the concert film *Bird on a Wire* opened in London. It did not stay in circulation long. The BBC by this time had given up on broadcasting it. It was shown on German TV, but effectively it disappeared (bar the odd bootleg copy) for almost four decades. Leonard flew to London for the premiere. He seemed "very cheerful" to the journalist from *ZigZag* for whom he played three of his new songs—even while recounting that he'd had to give up his writing room, now that there was a new baby on the way, and he was obliged to go to the garden shed to write. This was quite a change in mood from his last visit to London, when his interviews suggested that he planned to quit the music business. "I don't want to give you the impression that I was very sick and have just come through it, that's not true," said Leonard. What had happened was that "two months ago I had a golden week, my guitar sounded good, a lot of unfinished songs suggested conclusions."[16]

Leonard had renewed his contract with Columbia Records. He

had spent most of the past month in a New York studio working on a new record called *New Skin for the Old Ceremony*. Drawing a line under his first four albums, on this one he was trying for a different sound, using all new musicians and a new, young producer. John Lissauer was fifteen years younger than Leonard and not long out of Yale music school, where he had studied classical music and jazz. They met by chance in Montreal, at the Nelson Hotel, where Lissauer performed in a band with Lewis Furey, whose first album Lissauer had just produced. Leonard was in the audience; he had known Furey since 1966, when Furey was a sixteen-year-old violin player and fledgling poet. He had asked Leonard to look at his poetry, which Leonard did, giving him homework—read Irving Layton; write a sonnet—and becoming his mentor.

After the show, Furey introduced Lissauer to Leonard. This impressed Lissauer's girlfriend, who was a big Leonard Cohen fan, rather more than it did Lissauer, who "wasn't really into the folk singer-songwriter thing." Leonard told Lissauer, "I like what you're doing; would you like to talk about recording?" Lissauer said, "Sure." He heard nothing more for some time until, out of the blue, Leonard called and told him he was at the Royalton Hotel in New York and ready to start work.

Lissauer lived in a large loft space in a four-floor walk-up on Eighteenth Street—it had been a Mafia after-hours club in the fifties— that was strewn with "every instrument known to man." Lissauer told Leonard to come over. He should ring the downstairs bell, then stand under the window, and Lissauer would throw down the front-door key. Some hours later, as Lissauer sat at the piano, playing quietly, listening for the doorbell, in walked Leonard, a large grin on his face. At the front door he had run into a pizza deliveryman with an order for Lissauer's neighbor. When she threw down her key, Leonard caught it, paid for the pizza and said he would take it up with him. "She was the biggest Leonard Cohen freak, so you can imagine, opening the door and having her pizza delivered by her idol. She screamed," says Lissauer. "It was nuts." He was beginning to get the idea that Leonard was popular with women.

Marty Machat, who had never heard of Lissauer, was not convinced by Leonard's choice of producer. He called John Hammond, Leonard's A & R man and first producer, who booked an afternoon session at Columbia Studio E. On June 14, 1974, Leonard and Lissauer arrived, accompanied by four musicians. Under the watchful eye of Leonard's doubting manager and Columbia's most celebrated executive, they recorded demos of "Lover Lover Lover," "There Is a War" and "Why Don't You Try." "I'd put together an Ethiopian, Middle Eastern kind of thing," says Lissauer. "Leonard had never had rhythm like this on any of his songs and it worked great." Hammond gave his endorsement: it was going to work, he told Leonard, he didn't need him there. Machat gave his more grudging assent. "I sensed that Marty didn't like me and I wasn't used to this because I'm easygoing and work hard and I get along with everybody. Maybe it was a possessive thing; Leonard was *his* guy and he was looking to me for stuff. Marty was obsessed with Leonard. Leonard was the only artist he cared about because he thought that by associating with Leonard he got some class and some humanity. I don't think he ever cheated Leonard—and it's legendary what a bad guy he was with other artists. But he did the right thing by Leonard. Whatever it was, it was not a comfortable situation."

Lissauer asked that the studio be closed to everyone—managers, record company, girlfriends—except Leonard, the musicians and himself. Sometimes Machat would come by to listen to the rough mixes, but for the most part Lissauer's request was granted. So too was his decision to record not in one of the Columbia studios but in a small, intimate studio called Sound Ideas. "It was much more comfortable, the engineers were younger and hipper and not in lab coats, looking things up in reference manuals." The team included a female

engineer—a rarity in the early seventies—named Leanne Ungar;
this album marked the beginning of one of Leonard's most enduring
musical associations. "The atmosphere in the studio was really fun
and really light" and the recording process "very experimental," Ungar says. "We tried lots of different instruments and different things."

Generally these ideas were Lissauer's. He would take home a
simple guitar-vocal demo of the song and "fool with it," Lissauer
remembers, "and then come back and say to Leonard, 'How about
we do it this way?' I wanted to take him out of the folk world. I
wanted the record to take the listener places, give them a little vi-
sual, cinematic trip. 'This is poetry,' I said to him. 'When you do a
straight-ahead singer-songwriter album like the last two, it becomes
easy to stop listening to the poetry and they're just songs.' I felt that
I was illustrating the poetry with these little touches here and there,
these unusual combinations of instruments." Onto Leonard's basic
guitar and vocal recording he added strings and brass from the New
York Philharmonic; woodwinds and piano, which Lissauer played;
a viola played by Lewis Furey and a Jew's harp played by Leonard. There were also banjo, mandolin, guitar, bass and—unusually
for a Leonard Cohen album—drums, played respectively by Jeff
Layton, John Miller, Roy Markowitz and Barry Lazarowitz. Singer-
songwriter Janis Ian, who happened to drop by the studio, sang
some backing vocals.

On this occasion Leonard, according to Lissauer, showed "no
insecurities about his singing. He felt he wasn't a 'singer' singer,
that he didn't have that pop tenor thing, but he knew that he carried musical attention and that he could communicate a story. We
never talked about pitch; what we talked about was, 'Have you
kept your line?' In other words, has the narrative stayed intact?
Do we believe this verse? That's all-important with Leonard. He
never hides behind vocal tricks; that's what you do when you don't
have anything to say. Sometimes he would say, 'Let me do that

again and see if I can get my energy up, see if I can find that line,'
and use his finger to point the way. But for the most part, his vocals
were effortless."

A quite different approach was taken to "Leaving Green Sleeves,"
the song that closed the album. Leonard's interpretation of the
sixteenth-century English folk ballad was a live-in-the-studio recording with the band, "the product," Lissauer says, "of *ng ka pay*"—a
sweet Korean liqueur with 70 percent alcohol content. Reportedly
good for rheumatism, it was a favorite of Roshi, who was in the recording studio drinking with Leonard. An exception to the closed-
studio rule had been made for him. Lissauer had found a place in
Chinatown where *ng ka pay* could be bought, "and once in a while
we would do a run and pick up a bottle. Hence some of the, shall we
say, exotic vocals. On 'Leaving Green Sleeves,' we almost had to hold
Leonard up to sing; he was *ng ka pay*'ed out of his mind."

While Leonard sang, his hands held up in front of him as if he
were reading an invisible book, Roshi sat on the couch in his *tabi*
socks, saying nothing. Lissauer remembers he was "just beaming and
emanating good vibes."

What was Roshi doing in the studio?

"He was nodding off most of the time; he was already an old man."

I meant, why was he there at all?

*"We had been traveling to Trappist monasteries—at that time there
was a rapprochement between Catholicism and Zen under the tutelage of
Thomas Merton, who was a Trappist monk who wrote beautiful books—
and I would go with Roshi and he would lead these weeks of meditation
at various monasteries. We happened to be in New York at the time I was
recording. So he came to the studio."*

*Since everyone, even Zen masters, secretly want to be music critics, what
did Roshi say about the songs and your performance?*

*"The next morning when we were having breakfast I asked him what he
thought and he said that I should sing 'more sad.' "*

A lot of Leonard Cohen fans would have bought him a drink and employed him as your musical director. What was your reaction?

"I thought, 'Not more sad, but you've got to go deeper.' "

To all appearances you were sad enough during that period. Because of your domestic situation?

"I don't think that was the case at all. Of course when this kind of condition prevails, it's almost impossible to sustain friendships."

When you're so busy torturing yourself?

"You don't have time for anybody else. It's time-consuming. And, although I think everyone lives their life as an emergency, the emergency is acute when you're just trying to figure out how to get from moment to moment and you don't know why, and there are no operative circumstances that seem to explain. Of course the circumstances become disagreeable because of the relationships that you can't sustain, but I don't think it's the other way round."

Did becoming a father make any difference to your depression, distracting it or shifting the focus in some way?

"It didn't happen in my case, although it's true that having kids gets you off center stage; you can't really feel exactly the same way about yourself ever after. But it didn't seem to mitigate that gloomy condition. I don't know what the problem was, still don't. I wish I did. But that was a component of my life and was the engine of most of my investigation into the various things I looked into: women, song, religion."

In August Leonard was back home in Montreal, doing an interview with an Israeli-Canadian writer and broadcaster named Malka Marom for the CBC program *The Entertainers*. The interview took place in his garden shed—his new writing room—which was illuminated by candles. Marom recalls, "He was very whimsical. Soon after I set up the recording equipment, Leonard's hand went right underneath my skirt. I said, 'What are you doing?' and he said, 'This is the real dialogue,' or something to that effect. I said, 'Well, aside from this physical thing, is there any other dialogue?' He said, 'It can only be expressed in poetry.' So I asked the most mundane things just to see how far the poetry would go, like 'When do you get up in the morning? What do you have for breakfast? Are you happily married?' and he answered everything with poems that he had not published."

She also asked him his views on marriage and monogamy, given the imminent arrival of his second child with Suzanne. "I think marrying is for very, very high-minded people," he said. "It is a discipline of extreme severity. To really turn your back on all the other possibilities and all the other experiences of love, of passion, of ecstasy, and to determine to find it within one embrace is a high and righteous notion. Marriage today is the monastery; the monastery today is freedom." He told Marom that he had arrived "at a more realistic vision" of himself. There was no "high purpose" in his activities. "I'm just going," he said, "so that I don't have to keep still."

In September, barely a month after the release of his new album, Suzanne gave birth to Leonard's second child, a girl. Leonard named his daughter Lorca, for the Spanish poet.

————————

New Skin for the Old Ceremony was the first of Leonard's five albums not to include the word "songs" in the title, nor to have a picture of him on the sleeve.* Instead there was a drawing of a winged, naked couple copulating above the clouds. It was a woodcut from *Rosarium philosophorum*—the sixteenth-century alchemical text that had so fascinated Carl Jung—depicting the *coniunctio spirituum*, the holy union of the male-female principle. But the union described in these songs seems decidedly unholy. Their lyrics are caustic, mordant and black—blackly humorous at times but no less dark and brutal for that. The love he sings about is as violent as the war about which he also sings. His woman is *"the whore and the beast of Babylon."* Leonard, her poor beleaguered lover and servicer, is in various songs pierced,

————————

* Except in the U.S., where a "modesty sleeve" with a photo covered the censored illustration.

hung, lashed, captive and—with a knee in the balls and a fist in the face—sentenced to death.

He was not without self-pity, this *"grateful faithful woman's singing millionaire . . . Working for the Yankee dollar."* His only power was in his contempt and in the brilliant cutting edge of his words. Even in his version of that most courtly of songs "Greensleeves," when he sees his woman *"naked in the early dawn,"* he hopes she will be *"someone new."* In "A Singer Must Die" he sings a scathing *"goodnight"* to his *"night after night, after night, after night, after night, after night."* "Why Don't You Try" is more vitriolic still:

> *You know this life is filled with many sweet companions,*
> *many satisfying one-night stands.*
> *Do you want to be the ditch around a tower?*

This barb is perfectly cruel in its encompassment of sex and captivity. Although his muse is not mentioned by name, never before had Leonard treated one quite so discourteously. The songs, aware of this, plead their case before courtrooms, his ancestors and his God.

What makes this album so different from its predecessors is that its dark poetry—every bit as dark as on *Songs of Love and Hate*—is often clad in sophisticated, unexpected musical arrangements, ranging from Afro-percussive to Brecht-Weill, to modern chamber music. Said Leonard, "It's good. I'm not ashamed of it and I'm ready to stand by it. Rather than think of it as a masterpiece, I prefer to look at it as a little gem."[17] The critical response was also generally favorable. In the UK, *Melody Maker* found it "more spirited than the past four,"[18] while *NME* described it as "an agreeable blend of vintage Cohen and some new textures. Armageddon has been postponed if only temporarily."[19] In the U.S., *Rolling Stone* took the middle ground, saying it was "not one of his best" but that it had some songs "which will not easily be forgotten by his admirers."[20]

Leonard's first photo session at four months old. *Leonard Cohen personal collection*

Nathan Cohen, Leonard's father (*top left, then clockwise*); Herbert Vineberg; Leo Livingstone; Horace Cohen, Leonard's uncle; and Joseph Leavitt: as the original caption read, "Five Montreal officers photographed in Brighton, England, in the fall of 1918 while on leave to observe Yom Kippur."

Left: Leonard and Esther Cohen, Belmont Avenue, Westmount. *Leonard Cohen personal collection*

Leonard, Esther and
their mother, Masha
Cohen, Murray Hill
Park.

Below: Leonard and
Masha, Montreal.
*Leonard Cohen personal
collection*

**LEONARD NORMAN
COHEN**
"We cannot conquer fear yet
we can yield to it in such
a manner as to be greater
than it."
"Quin" says: "Sir, can I
make an announcement?" Pet
Avers.: The coke machine, Pas-
time: Leading sing-songs at in-
termissions. Ambition: World
famous orator. Prob. Dest.: Mc-
Gill Cheerleader. Prototype: The
little man who is always there.
Hobby: Photography.
Activities: Students' Council
President, Menorah Club, Art
Club, Vox Ducum, Current Events
Club, Y.M.H.A., Cheerleade.

Above: Leonard
Norman Cohen, Students'
Council President and
cheerleader, Westmount
High School yearbook,
1951. *Steve Brewer personal
collection*

Leonard and Robert
Hershorn. *Leonard
Cohen personal collection*

Above: Leonard and
Mort Rosengarten.
*Leonard Cohen personal
collection*

The Buckskin Boys.
From the top:
Terry Davis, Mike
Doddman and
Leonard Cohen, 1952.
*Sue Sullivan personal
collection*

On the beach near New York, 1958. *Left to right:* Leonard, Harry Parnass, Masha Cohen and Georgianna "Anne" Sherman.

Left to right: Aviva Layton, Irving Layton, Anne Sherman and Leonard in the Laurentians, Quebec. *Leonard Cohen personal collection*

Leonard and Saint Kateri, New York City. *Leonard Cohen personal collection*

At Mrs. Pullman's boardinghouse, Hampstead, London, 1960. *Leonard Cohen personal collection*

Irving Layton on the terrace of Leonard's house, Hydra, early 1960s. *Aviva Layton personal collection*

Leonard and Marianne, Hydra. *Aviva Layton personal collection*

Marianne and Irving Layton, Hydra. *Aviva Layton personal collection*

With revolutionary
soldiers, Cuba, 1961.
*Leonard Cohen personal
collection*

Backstage at a Joni
Mitchell concert,
Wisconsin, 1969.
Photo by Joel Bernstein

The difference a year
makes. Backstage on
the Leonard Cohen
tour, 1970. *Photo by Joel
Bernstein*

With his Zen master, Joshu Sasaki Roshi. *Leonard Cohen personal collection*

Leonard and Willie York, Big East Fork Road, Tennessee, circa 1969. *Leonard Cohen personal collection*

Leonard and Suzanne. *Photo by Danny Fields*

Leonard and Suzanne, Miami, 1973. *Suzanne Elrod personal collection*

On a tour bus, smoking and writing "Song of Bernadette" with Jennifer Warnes, Europe, 1979. *Photo by Roscoe Beck*

Onstage with Roscoe Beck, Sharon Robinson and the band, 1980. *Roscoe Beck personal collection*

Dominique Issermann, photographed by Leonard. *Photo by Leonard Cohen*

Leonard and Nancy
Bacal. *Leonard Cohen
personal collection*

With backing singer
Perla Batalla, 1993.
*Photo by Julie Christensen,
Perla Batalla personal
collection*

With Adam Cohen in
the hospital, Toronto,
1990. *Suzanne Elrod
personal collection*

Leonard and Rebecca
De Mornay backstage on
The Future tour.
Photo by Perla Batalla

Leonard and the
girls (*from left to
right*): Rebecca
De Mornay, Lorca
Cohen and Perla
Batalla. *Perla Batalla
personal collection*

With backing singer
Julie Christensen,
1993. *Photo by Perla
Batalla, Julie
Christensen personal
collection*

Above: In Venice (*left to right*): Steve Zirkel, Dominique Issermann, Leonard Cohen, Tom McMorran, Julie Christensen. *Julie Christensen personal collection*

Leonard's cabin home on Mount Baldy. *Photo by Sylvie Simmons*

This broken hill: the view from the cabin window. *Photo by Sylvie Simmons*

With Hal Willner.
Photo by Perla Batalla

Below: With Anjani
in Leonard's living
room, Los Angeles,
2006. *Anjani Thomas
personal collection*

Above: Chelsea Hotel
commemoration. *Photo by
Linda Straub*

At the Albert Hall, 2008. *Photo by Eija Arjatsalo*

Leonard and the band, Helsinki, 2008. *Photo by Jarkko Arjatsalo*

Soundcheck, 2009 tour. *Photo by Eija Arjatsalo*

Poster boy, Venice, 2009. *Photo by Eija Arjatsalo*

The two most enduring songs on *New Skin* were quite different from one another. "Chelsea Hotel #2" was one of the album's most straightforward, singer-songwriter productions. "Who by Fire" had been directly inspired by a Hebrew prayer sung on the Day of Atonement when the Book of Life was opened and the names read aloud of who will die and how. Leonard said he had first heard it in the synagogue when he was five years old, "standing beside my uncles in their black suits."[21] His own liturgy ended with a question that his elders had never answered and whose answer Leonard still sought: what unseen force controls these things and who the hell is in charge?

New Skin for the Old Ceremony had not been a great commercial success outside of Germany and the UK, where it was certified silver. In the U.S. and Canada it completely bypassed the charts. But there was an album, ergo there had to be a tour. In September 1974—the month of Lorca's birth, Adam's second birthday and their father's fortieth—Leonard embarked on his biggest tour to date. Two months of concerts had been booked in Europe, including a performance at a CBS Records conference in Eastbourne, England, followed by two weeks in New York and L.A. in November and December. The first two months of 1975 were also taken up with concerts, bringing him back and forth between Canada, the U.S. and the UK.

As Bob Johnston had done in the past, Leonard's new producer put together his touring band—a small group of the multi-instrumentalists and singers who had played on the album: John Miller, Jeff Layton, Emily Bindiger and Erin Dickins. Also like Johnston, Lissauer joined him on the road, playing keyboards. It was "very different to his last tour with the country boys," says Lissauer. "We had a lot of artistic detail." Leonard's new band was very young. "We were all kids. I was twenty-two and I had never played a concert before such a big audience, and I've never been on tour with a guy who's revered like he was. In Europe Leonard was bigger than Dylan—all the shows were sold out—and he had the most sincere, devoted, almost nuts following. Serious poetry lovers don't get violent but, boy, there was some suicide watches going on, on occasion. There were people who Leonard meant life or death to. I'd see girls in the front row"—women outnumbered men three to one in the audiences, by Lissauer's count—"openly weep for Leonard and they would send back letters and packages. And invitations. We would see people after the show—somebody intriguing or good-looking would get backstage—and they'd say things like, 'I was suicidal and I put on one of your records and you saved me.'"

The *Guardian* review of the Manchester show described Leonard as having "the inspired and fragile air of a consumptive. He cut a lonely and sensitive-looking figure centre-stage, wrapped around his guitar, plucking away with an ill mustered resolve at what passed for a melody line. Cohen generated an atmosphere of vulnerability and regret, an odd sensation in pop. None of his songs showed a sense of humor, none was bright and breezy. But the whole thing had a gloomy warmth."[22]

The tour, particularly when compared with the last two, unfolded largely without incident, apart from the bus breaking down on the way to the Edinburgh show (they divided into pairs and hitchhiked to the venue) and the showdown between Marty Machat and Herbert von Karajan in Berlin when the famed conductor, still rehearsing the Berlin Philharmonic, refused to let them in to do their sound check. "Marty's ego and von Karajan's ego—that was quite something," Lissauer recalls. Among the more memorable performances was the Fête de l'Humanité in Paris. "Half a million people and all these little communist factions had come together for a festival, and they'd given us big limousines to take us there," Lissauer says. "We dressed down for the occasion in fatigues and had them drop us off half a mile from the site, where we got into a bunch of beat-up little Renaults to drive up there, because we didn't want to be seen showing up [in the limos] because a lot of the people there were very fired up. There was a lot of very passionate political talk and fatigues and berets and Gauloises. Leonard hung out with them and fit right in."

When the band arrived in New York for the November shows, Suzanne was there to meet Leonard. He took her along with him to his interview with Danny Fields.* He told Fields he had given up smoking, while elegantly eulogizing the beauty of the cigarette. He was no longer drinking either and tried to give Fields the bottle of vodka that had been given to him by Harry Smith. Fields asked him if his children were being raised as Jews. Leonard answered, "Unless I change my name, I will definitely raise them Jewish." Meaning yes. The pleas in the song "Lover Lover Lover" to his father/Father to change his name were rhetorical. "I never liked the idea of people changing their names. It's nice to know where you come from."[23]

In an interview around the same time with Larry "Ratso" Sloman, for *Rolling Stone*, Leonard complained, "I think I'm getting old. My nails are crumbling under the assault of the guitar strings. My throat is going. How many years more do I have of this?" But, far from giving up, he said he wanted to keep going "forever." Every man, he said, "should try to become an elder."[24]

In Los Angeles, a residency had been set up for Leonard at the Troubadour, the famous West Hollywood folk club where Tom Waits was discovered on an open mic night and where Joni Mitchell made her L.A. debut. "He did two shows a night, five nights, all sold out," says Paul Body, the Troubadour doorman. "I was the ticket-taker, so I remember Phil Spector coming in on the Sunday with Lenny Bruce's daughter, Kitty. Dylan also showed up one night. There were quite a few different celebrities—and tons of beautiful women. The only guy I've seen who drew better-looking women than Leonard Cohen was probably Charles Bukowski. These women were all dressed up

---

* The interview was intended for Andy Warhol's *Interview* magazine but at the last minute the editor decided Leonard "wasn't chic enough." It ran in *Soho Weekly* in December 1974.

in seventies style and hanging on Leonard's every word, during the show and afterwards." Leonard wore a gray suit—"He reminded me of the French actor Jean Gabin," says Body—and the band were all dressed in black. "The manager of the Troubadour, Robert Marchese, told me, 'You'd better check the bathroom for razor blades, because this stuff is real depressing.'"

Between sets, journalist Harvey Kubernik asked Leonard about the new album. "For a while I didn't think there was going to be another album. I pretty much felt that I was washed up as a songwriter because it wasn't coming any more," Leonard said. "Now I've entered into another phase, which is very new to me. That is, I began to collaborate with John on songs, which is something that I never expected, or intended, to do with anyone. It wasn't a matter of improvement, it was a matter of sharing the conception, with another man." His previous album, *Live Songs,* he said, represented "a very confused and directionless time. The thing I liked about it is that it documents this phase very clearly. I'm very interested in documentation."[25] Leonard was going to visit Dylan at his house in Malibu, he said, mentioning that Dylan had called him one of his favorite poets. Leonard also went to an Allen Ginsberg performance in Los Angeles and to dinner with Joni Mitchell. Kubernik, who accompanied Leonard, recalls a smiling Mitchell telling him off the cuff, "I'm only a groupie for Picasso and Leonard."

Aside from the New York and L.A. concerts, Leonard's U.S. tour earned a lukewarm reception at best. In a couple of places, tickets barely sold. "He was almost unknown," Lissauer says. "Leonard didn't really want to play the States, he didn't feel they understood him, and because they weren't putting out he wasn't putting out, so he had a nonaudience. This was distracting for me, as a record producer; I wanted to see him be big in the States. But on the Canadian tour he was mobbed, and some of those shows were really fabulous. We recorded a bunch of them."

While on the road, Leonard was already planning a new studio album. This time he wanted a full collaboration with Lissauer. "Leonard really liked my melodies, so we decided to write together. It was going really well, we wrote some really strong songs and worked on them on the road"—"Came So Far for Beauty," "Guerrero," "I Guess It's Time," "Beauty Salon" and "Traitor Song." They also worked on new and different versions of "Diamonds in the Mine," "Lover Lover Lover" and "There Is a War." When the tour was over, the two of them went to New York and straight to work on the album Leonard called *Songs for Rebecca*.

Leonard once again moved into the Royalton Hotel. Lissauer would meet him there and Leonard would give him some lyrics, which they discussed, before Lissauer took them home and started coming up with melodies. "Then we would get together at my loft," Lissauer remembers, "and work at the grand piano. Leonard didn't bring his guitar because my chord changes weren't, I think, the kind he naturally gravitated to. I mean, I was trying to write for him in a style that was comfortable—not just write a pop song and have him sing it—but I also lifted the melodies and structures a little out of his zone, which was mostly simple chords, no extended chords or inversions, that kind of thing. Also, he tended not to want to sing leaps, he liked to sing notes close together, almost speak-sing like a French *chanteur*. But I think he was tired of writing the same kinds of songs and wanted to break out of it, and he trusted me enough." Lissauer made demos of the songs so that they could evaluate what they had. Leonard seemed happy with where it was going. Then he decided to leave for Greece.

On Hydra the songs were put to one side. Leonard went back to working on "My Life in Art." "It was pretty bad ten years ago, before the world knew me, but now it's a lot worse," he wrote; he was going to have to "overthrow [his] life with fresh love."[26] There were a number of liaisons. He continued to live with Suzanne, but what he wrote about her was vituperative. Suzanne, by her own account, did not take this personally: "Living with a writer, you feel that it's all a white page, that it's all a rehearsal, that the author has the right to pause, erase, repeat, vary and repeat again. So I let him. Leonard found solace, purpose and comfort in the deconstruction and complaint of daily woes. I wanted to be a good audience and company, not just the reactive wife, although the last was inevitable at times of course."

When Leonard returned to America in the fall, it was to spend more time with Roshi. In an unpublished piece with the pessimistic title "The End of My Life in Art," he wrote: "I saw Roshi early this morning. His room was warm and fragrant. . . . Destroy particular self and absolute appears. He spoke to me gently. I waited for the rebuke. It didn't come. I waited because there is a rebuke in every other voice but his. He rang his bell. I bowed and left. I visited him again after several disagreeable hours in the mirror. . . . I was so hungry for his seriousness after the moronic frivolity and despair of hours in the mirror."[27] Leonard was also hungry for hunger. This domestic life had caused him to put on weight and what he needed was to be empty. As he wrote in *Beautiful Losers*, "If I'm empty then I can receive, if I can receive it means it comes from somewhere outside of me, if it comes from outside of me I'm not alone. I cannot bear this loneliness . . ."—a loneliness deeper than anything that the ongoing presence of a woman and children could relieve.

Lissauer flew to L.A. to meet Leonard and they resumed work on *Songs for Rebecca*. "We took a couple of rooms at the Chateau Marmont with an outdoor patio and rented an electric piano. We worked on these songs and got them happening and I taught him some chords for a couple of the songs so he could play his guitar. And then he and Marty said, 'Let's go back out on tour.'" A week of concerts had been booked in the U.S. Leonard's American record label was releasing a *Best Of* album, presumably having figured that *New Skin for the Old Ceremony*, which failed to even make it into the U.S. Top 200, was a dead horse no longer worth flogging. The compilation album was released under the title *Greatest Hits* on the other side of the Atlantic, where Leonard actually had hits—*New Skin* had made it to No. 24 on the UK charts. Leonard picked the songs for the compilation himself and wrote the liner notes.

For this tour Lissauer put a new band together, which this time included a drummer. They set off on the road in November, taking with them the new cowritten songs, adding them to the regular set. "Leonard was thrilled, I was thrilled, even Marty seemed to be happier than expected given that he didn't want Leonard to collaborate with me in the first place," Lissauer says. After the last concert, Leonard and Lissauer went into the studio—first Sound Ideas in New York, then A & M in Los Angeles. They recorded all the new collaboratively written songs and their new version of "Diamonds in the Mine." "And then the faucet shut off. Leonard disappeared. Marty wouldn't take my calls, I said, 'What the hell's going on?' It just evaporated. Without a word from anyone."

It was December 1975 and Leonard had gone home to Montreal. It turned out that Bob Dylan was also in Montreal, on his Rolling Thunder tour—a traveling rock revue whose guests included Joni Mitchell, Joan Baez, Roger McGuinn, Ronee Blakley, Bobby Neuwirth, Ramblin' Jack Elliott and Allen Ginsberg. Dylan was keen to add Leonard to the lineup. Ratso Sloman, who was traveling with the tour as a reporter,* remembers, "Bob was incredibly intent on getting Leonard to come. He was obviously a fan of Leonard's work, and vice versa. Dylan was proud of what he was doing on Rolling Thunder because those performances were intense and enthralling, and Montreal was Leonard's town, so it meant a lot to him for Leonard to be there. Bob was hounding me—'Make sure he comes'—and he dispatched me to Leonard's house."

When the car pulled up outside a "crazy little bungalow" off Saint Dominique Street, Sloman double-checked the address. It did not

---

* His account of the tour became the 1978 book *On the Road with Bob Dylan*.

give the appearance of a celebrity's house. When Suzanne let him in, Sloman ducked instinctively, the beamed ceiling was so low. The floor sloped and the walls were crammed with shelves filled with books, framed pictures and dusty tchotchkes. It looked like a fairy-tale grandmother's gingerbread house. Leonard was inside with a bunch of his friends, who were all playing music, Mort Rosengarten playing spoons to Leonard's harmonica. Suzanne took Sloman upstairs to see the children. "They looked so sweet, these little angels in their cribs in this ramshackle little room, and Suzanne was so patient. It looked like a very tranquil domestic scene."

It was hard work persuading Leonard to leave the house and come with him to the Forum. When he finally succeeded, Leonard insisted on taking his friends and his harmonica along with him. Everyone piled into the car and sang old French folk songs along the way. When they pulled up at the venue, Dylan came right out to greet Leonard. He told him that if he wanted to come up and play a couple of songs, it would be fine by him. Ronee Blakley, Bobby Neuwirth, and Ramblin' Jack came over too, as well as Dylan's wife Sara and Joni Mitchell. Leonard addressed Mitchell as "my little Joni," and the two appeared very relaxed around each other. Joni joined Sara in asking Leonard to sing something in the revue, but Leonard declined. "It's too obvious," he said. Leonard, Sloman surmised, was "a bit of a control freak, in the sense of controlling his own music, of presenting the songs and the context. He doesn't strike me as someone who jams with the band, unless it's his friends, at home." Although Leonard did not participate, Dylan dedicated a song to him—"a song about marriage," "Isis," whose lyrics included the sentiment "What drives me to you is what drives me insane." "This is for Leonard," said Dylan, "if he is still here."

Leonard was still trying to make his relationship with Suzanne work. He bought a small apartment building across the road from the Montreal cottages in order to have more space. A nanny had moved into his writing room in the cottage, and since it was too cold to use the shed, he worked in the kitchen. "I loved hearing him in the background playing the guitar, quietly singing or writing," says Suzanne. "When he wanted to enjoy the children he did. I never put pressure on him or made it an obligation, there was no domestic tyranny, but he was a loving, solid, dutiful father. He sung them lullabies and the normal tender gestures."

Come the spring, Leonard left once again on another European tour. This one was considerably longer, with more than fifty dates, starting in Berlin in April 1976 and ending in July in London. John Miller replaced Lissauer as musical director, the rest of the band consisting of Sid McGinnis, Fred Thaylor and Luther Rix. Leonard's new backing singers were Cheryl Barnes (who three years later would appear in the film of the musical *Hair*) and a nineteen-year-old Laura Branigan (who three years later would sign to Atlantic and become a successful solo pop artist). The set list this time included some new—or, technically, old—songs: "Store Room" was an outtake from Leonard's first album, "Everybody's Child" was an unreleased track from the second album, and "Die Gedanken Sind Frei," a German folk song about freedom of thought, had been written in the nineteenth century. A live review in *Melody Maker* noted how cheerful Leonard appeared onstage. "Gone is the doom and gloom, [he's] at his funkiest and wittiest."

After the final concert Leonard went to Hydra. Suzanne and the children were there and Irving and Aviva Layton were visiting. Leonard was eager to show Irving what he had been writing. "They always read to each other what they'd written," says Aviva. Irving was as effusive as ever about his friend's work. "The only time I ever heard Irving even mildly criticize Leonard was when Leonard went through a very religious, sort of mystical, semi-Judaic, semi-Christian stage and that was very much not Irving's sensibility. But that was all; Leonard loved Irving's poetry and Irving loved his."

When the Laytons left, Leonard spent hours with Anthony Kingsmill, the painter who lived on Hydra. Richard Vick remembers Kingsmill as "an incredibly witty and quite wise little man, as well as something of a drinker, [who] had quite a strong influence on Leonard. I remember an occasion at one of the places at the port where people would gather at dawn, after having gone around the bars during the night. Leonard was there, strumming a few chords, and Anthony, who was in his cups, got very frenetic and said, 'And who do you think *you're* fooling, Leonard?'" Leonard appeared to ponder the question deeply. He continued pondering after he left Hydra for the U.S.

Leonard rented a house in Brentwood, on the west side of Los Angeles, just off Sunset Boulevard. His reason for living in L.A. was that Roshi lived there, and Leonard was spending a great deal of time with Roshi, at the Zen Center in Los Angeles and on Mount Baldy, often acting as his chauffeur and driving him between the two. Roshi told Leonard that he should move to Mount Baldy with Suzanne and the children—there were family quarters at the monastery as well as individual monks' cabins—and stay there and study. It was tempting—at least it was to Leonard. Suzanne had accompanied him on one retreat but found that "sitting all through the night was an austerity [she] couldn't share." Leonard was also spending a lot of time in L.A. with a record producer with whom he was cowriting songs—not John Lissauer but Phil Spector. These days Spector is an inmate of a California state prison, serving nineteen years to life for second-degree murder, but at that time Spector lived in a mansion in Beverly Hills.

"So," says John Lissauer, "the famous missing album. I have the rough mixes but the master tapes just disappeared. Marty culled the two-inch tapes from both studios. He never returned my calls and Leonard didn't return my calls. Maybe he was embarrassed. I didn't find out what happened for twenty-five years. I heard this from a couple of different sources. Marty managed Phil Spector and Spector had not delivered on this big Warner Bros. deal; they got a huge advance, two million dollars, and Marty took his rather hefty percentage, but Phil didn't produce any albums. So Warner Bros. go to Marty, 'He comes up with an album or we get our money back.' So Marty said, 'I know what to do. Screw this Lissauer project, I'll put Phil and Leonard together.'" Which is what he did.

Fifteen

I Love You, Leonard

Phil Spector was thirty-six years old, five years younger than Leonard, a small, fastidious man with bright eyes and a receding hairline and chin. In matters of dress Spector favored bespoke suits and ruffled shirts, or sometimes a cape and wig. Between them they reflected his status as "the first Tycoon of Teen" (as Tom Wolfe dubbed him) and, for many years, the Emperor of Pop. Spector had been nineteen years old when he wrote and recorded his first No. 1 in 1958, a song called "To Know Him Is to Love Him," its title taken from the words on his father's tombstone. In 1960 Spector became a record producer, then the head of his own record label. During the first half of the sixties he turned out more than two dozen hits.

There had been record producers before Phil Spector but there was nobody like him. Other producers worked behind the scenes; Spector was up front, flamboyant, eccentric and more famous than many of the acts whom he recorded. His records were "Phil Spector" records, the artists and musicians merely bricks in his celebrated "Wall of Sound"—the name that was given to Spector's epic production style. It required battalions of musicians all playing at the same time—horns bleeding into drums bleeding into strings bleeding into guitars—magnified through tape echo. With this technique Spector transformed pop ballads and R & B songs, like "Be My Baby," "Da Doo Ron Ron" and "Unchained Melody" into dense, clamorous, delirious minisymphonies that captured in two and a half exquisite minutes the joy and pain of teenage love.

Leonard was not a teenager. It is quite possible he never was a teenager. Leonard's songs, like his poetry, were a grown-up's songs. His lyrics were sophisticated and his melodies uncluttered, which gave his words room to breathe and resonate. His delivery was plain and his taste in production, as in most everything else, was subtle and understated. Other than finding themselves the last two left at a key party, it is hard to picture Leonard Cohen and Phil Spector ever ending up as musical bedfellows. But by the grace of Marty Machat they did. Machat's logic was simple. He had a client—Spector—who was one of the best-known names in American pop, but who had hit a rough patch and was about to lose them a lot of money if he didn't give Warner Bros. an album soon. And he had another client—Leonard—who was revered almost everywhere but America, who was cowriting songs with a producer far less celebrated than Spector—Lissauer—and whose last album with Leonard did nothing to get him onto the U.S. charts. Spector had seen Leonard play at the Troubadour and told Machat he had been "entranced." Leonard had confessed to being a fan of Spector's early records, considering them "so expressive I wouldn't mind being his Bernie Taupin."[1] So why not put them together and have Leonard do the lyrics and Spector the music? It would solve the Spector problem, and perhaps even Leonard's problem too.

As it turned out, Leonard and Spector had more in common than one might think, besides both being East Coast Jews who shared a manager. Spector and Leonard had both lost their fathers when they were nine years old—Spector's committed suicide—and had very close relationships with their mothers. Each deeply loved the sound of women's singing voices—Spector, who often wrote for women, had put together several sixties girl groups. Both were very serious about and protective of their work. They were also both subject to black moods and, in 1976, when they began working together, were in disintegrating relationships and drinking heavily. So began the extraordinary story of *Death of a Ladies' Man*.

Spector lived in a twenty-room mansion, a Spanish–Beverly Hills movie star hacienda built in the early twenties. There was a fountain in the front, a swimming pool in the back and, all around, lush gardens. The property was ringed with a barbed fence hung with "Keep Out" signs. Should someone choose to ignore the warning, there were armed guards. When Leonard first walked up its front steps, Suzanne beside him, the maid who answered the door led them past an antique suit of armor and walls hung with old oil paintings and framed photographs—Lenny Bruce, Muhammad Ali, Martin Luther King, John Lennon, Spector's heroes and friends—to the living room. Like the rest of the house, it was cold and dimly lit; there was more light coming from the aquarium and the jukebox than from the grand chandelier overhead.

Spector had invited the couple to dinner. It was a small gathering and Spector turned out to be a charming host—smart, funny and convivial. But as the night wore into morning and the empty bottles piled up, Spector became increasingly animated. One by one the guests took their leave; only Leonard and Suzanne remained. When they finally got up to go, Spector shouted to his staff to lock the doors. "He wouldn't let us out of his house," Suzanne says. Leonard suggested that if they were going to stay all night, they might find something more interesting to do than shout at the servants. By the next day, when the door was unlocked and Leonard and Suzanne were allowed to go home, Leonard and Spector had worked up a new arrangement of country singer Patti Page's "I Went to Your Wedding" and had made the first forays into cowriting songs.

Over the coming weeks, Leonard was a regular visitor to the mansion. Spector was a night owl, so it would be afternoon before Leonard would drive the short distance from his rented house in Brentwood. Leonard was dressed for work, wearing a suit and carrying a briefcase. He looked, Dan Kessel recalls, "like a suave, continental Dustin Hoffman." The maid would take Leonard to the living room, where the thick velvet curtains were firmly drawn against the bright California sun and an air conditioner blasted icy air, and leave him there alone, giving his eyes time to adjust to the round-the-clock twilight. A few minutes later Spector would make his entrance, flanked by Dan and David Kessel. The Kessel brothers had known Spector since childhood; their father, the jazz guitarist Barney Kessel, was a close friend of Spector who had played on a number of his hit records. His sons, who were also guitar players, had in turn appeared on several Spector records, including John Lennon's *Rock 'n' Roll* album, which Spector produced.

An antique silver cart was rolled in, laden with drinks and food. While the Kessel brothers retired to the adjoining room, Spector's office, Leonard and Phil hung out for a while and chatted before getting to work. Sometimes they would pick a song to listen to from Spector's jukebox, which was stacked with obscure R & B and rock 'n' roll as well as old hit singles: Elvis, Dion, Dylan, Sun-era Johnny Cash, Frankie Laine. Then they would start work on the songwriting, sitting together at the piano on the long mahogany bench. The Kessel brothers would listen in on the studio monitors in the office, giving an opinion when Spector asked for it and, when their services were required, coming in and playing guitar. The rest of the time they shot pool.

"All day and into the night, every day, they would work for a while, break for a while, work for a while, break for a while," says David Kessel. "Suggestions went back and forth between them. Leonard had notes with him and Phil would say, 'Well okay, that story line goes on this kind of a music track,' or Phil would have the music track and Leonard would go, 'Hey, man, that kind of brings to mind this for me.' Many times during breaks I sat outside with Leonard by the fountain and he would go, 'Wow, this is different.' 'This is interesting.' 'This should be quite something.' 'I've never done this like this.' He would use us as sounding boards: could we give him any insights as to where this was headed or what he could expect? All Phil said about it was, 'This is cool, it's going to be interesting; I want to see how it comes out and hopefully it'll come out pretty good.'" Dan Kessel remembers, "Leonard was notoriously slow and deliberate; Phil got straight on it and got it done. Even so, or maybe because of that, they complemented each other as songwriters. There was plenty of laughter." When Doc Pomus, the blues singer-songwriter, Spector's friend, came by the house one day to visit Spector, they were "like two drunks," he said, "staggering around."[2]

Among the papers Leonard carried in his briefcase were lyrics of some of the songs he had worked on with John Lissauer for *Songs for Rebecca*—"Guerrero" and "Beauty Salon," given different melodies and arrangements, would become "Iodine" and "Don't Go Home with Your Hard-On." Leonard also brought along an unfinished song called "Paper-Thin Hotel," which he had begun writing on the *New Skin* tour. The song "Memories," though, was written at the piano in Spector's mansion. Introducing it at a concert in Tel Aviv in 1980, Leonard called it a "vulgar ditty that I wrote some time ago with another Jew in Hollywood, in which I have placed my most irrelevant and banal adolescent recollections."[3] Leonard's lyrics recalled, in an almost Spectorian fashion, his high school days and the near-terminal case of sexual longing with which he was plagued. At times it also evokes his failed seduction of Nico:

I pinned an Iron Cross to my lapel
I walked up to the tallest
and the blondest girl
I said . . . Won't you let me see
Your naked body

In less than a month, they had around a dozen songs ready to go. In January and February 1977—plus one last session in June—they recorded nine of them: the eight songs that made it onto the final album plus one that didn't, another of the *Songs for Rebecca* songs, "I Guess It's Time." Recording began in Gold Star, a small, dark studio in the shabby heart of Hollywood. Spector's favorite place to record, its old tube equipment gave the studio its rich, expansive sound, as well as a distinctive smell of burning dust when the tubes in the mixing board started heating up. "It also had a famous echo chamber," says Hal Blaine, "like a cement casket running the length of the studio; an amazing sound. We did so many hits with Phil at Gold Star." Blaine, a drummer, was a linchpin of the loose group of top-notch, versatile L.A. studio musicians nicknamed the Wrecking Crew. Spector would always hire them when he needed a band; *Death of a Ladies' Man*, says Blaine, "was just another job. We never knew what we were going to do until we got there and did it."

On January 24, 1977, Leonard arrived at Gold Star for the first session dressed in pale slacks and a dark blue blazer, "looking," as David Kessel recalls, "like he was entertaining a date on the Riviera." Walking into the studio, Leonard was taken aback. The room was crammed with people, instruments and microphone stands. There was barely space to move. He counted forty musicians, including two drummers, assorted percussionists, half a dozen guitarists, a horn section, a handful of female backing singers and a flock of keyboard players. "It blew his mind," says David Kessel. "He was kind of disoriented, like, 'Whoa. Okay. Is this how he normally does it? What

are we doing here? Can you help me figure it out?' This was a different thing for him." Spector, who was up in the control room and
even more sharply dressed than Leonard, in an expensive black suit,
green shirt and Cuban-heeled boots, called over the studio monitor,
"Anybody laid-back in this room, get the fuck out of here."[4] On the
console was a bottle of Manischewitz Concord grape wine. Spector
picked it up, poured it into a Tweetie Pie glass and sucked it through
a plastic straw.

There was another face in the room Leonard recognized: Ronee
Blakley, the vivacious folksinger he had met in Montreal on Dylan's
Rolling Thunder tour. Blakley, who had recently become famous for
her portrayal of a fragile country star in Robert Altman's 1975 film
Nashville, was a friend of Spector. "I wasn't his girlfriend," says Blakley, "but I went around with him a little bit. Phil has a very, very
dear, sweet side to him." Spector had asked her to come and sing
duets with Leonard on "Iodine"—the first track they recorded—a
song about failure, loss and the wounds of love, which had been given
a beguiling Nino Tempo arrangement. She also sang with him on the
album's bittersweet opening track, "True Love Leaves No Traces,"
which was based on the poem "As the Mist Leaves No Scar" from
Leonard's 1961 book *The Spice-Box of Earth*, and "Memories," a ram-
bunctious burlesque number whose lyrics make wry reference to the
kind of teen-angst pop in which Spector specialized and whose chorus was made for drunks in midnight choirs to sing along with.

It seemed to be the first time Leonard had heard anything about
duets, but he raised no objection. "He was an elegant man, soft-
spoken and thoughtful and kind," Blakley says. "He was not mean,
not sharp, never 'I'm intelligent and I have a way with language and
I know how to make a remark that may sound fine but has a cruel
edge to it.'" There were no rehearsals or charts; they simply sang
the song through together once or twice and Blakley made up her
part. She remembers that "it wasn't that easy." As Hal Blaine points

out, Leonard's "weren't regular rock 'n' roll songs. These were songs written by a poet for a rock 'n' roll record and kind of off the wall. Leonard was in a whole other world." The other problem was that Leonard seemed insecure about his singing. Says Blakley, "He really believed that he doesn't have a great voice, although it's amazing—so sensitive and vulnerable. It trembles at times, but at the same time it almost rumbles, it has that biblical quality. I think it's a voice that female voices work with especially well."

The sun was starting to come up by the time the first recording session ended. The Kessels checked that the tapes had been correctly cataloged and oversaw the loading of them onto a dolly, which was wheeled out to Spector's car after every session under armed guard— Spector's bodyguard George. "Phil always took his tapes home," says Dan Kessel. "He didn't single Leonard out, that's just the way Phil conducted his business. Studios don't protect your tapes with the same stringency you do." George was a retired U.S. federal marshal. Like Spector, he wore a gun in his shoulder holster. The difference, says Dan Kessel, was that "the bodyguard's gun was always loaded. Phil's never was." Leonard joked about getting his own armed bodyguard and having a shoot-out on Sunset Boulevard. He asked Malka Marom, who was visiting him in L.A., to come to the studio with him. He told her that Spector was afraid of her because he thought she was an Israeli soldier. Marom agreed to go to the studio. She found the atmosphere "very scary—because Phil Spector was sitting there with bottles of Manischewitz wine and a gun on the table. I said to Leonard, 'Why are you recording with this madman?' He said, 'Because he's really very good at what he does.'"

Harvey Kubernik, who had been given the job of food runner— Spector or Marty Machat, who would come by the studio with his girlfriend Avril, would dispatch him to Canter's deli to bring back chopped liver and corned beef sandwiches—had witnessed Spector in the studio before. Compared with other albums, he recalls, Spector's sessions with Leonard were "not too chaotic." But for Leonard, says David Kessel, "it was a bit of a whirlwind."

It was late on the second night of recording when Bob Dylan showed up at the studio. "He comes in through the back door," says David Kessel, "and he's got each arm around a different woman. In his right hand, around the woman, he's got a bottle of whiskey and he's drinking the whiskey straight." Allen Ginsberg followed close behind with his lover, the poet Peter Orlovsky. Seeing them, Spector jumped up and hailed them over the monitor. There were so many Jews in the room they could have a bar mitzvah, he joked. Work stopped while Spector came down to socialize. There was much hugging and drinking, then, as happened to anyone who came into Spector's studio, the visitors were put to work.

Leonard was recording "Don't Go Home with Your Hard-On," a boisterous commentary on domestic bliss. Dylan, who was in the process of being divorced by his wife, Sara, seemed to have no problem entering into the spirit of the song. Ginsberg said later that "Spector was in a total tizzy, ordering everybody around, including Dylan: 'Get over there! Stay off the microphone!'"[5] Dan Kessel remembers, "He was very animated. He was behind the console, then with us in the studio, back and forth, interacting with everyone and conducting us." Says Blaine, "It was like he was conducting the philharmonic, and it went on for hours. But that's the way we worked with Phil; he wasn't trying to run us into the ground, he was looking for that feeling. That magic."

The session had turned into a boozy party. By daylight, when most of the revelers had gone, Spector and Leonard listened to the tape through the big studio speakers, the volume up, the music ferocious. "This," said Spector, sipping at his Manischewitz, "is *punk rock*, motherfucker!" Leonard poured himself a glass of Cuervo Gold. "Everybody will now know," said Leonard, "that inside this serene, Buddha-like exterior beats an adolescent heart."[6]

At Dan Kessel's suggestion, the next session was moved to Whitney Studios in Glendale. A new building in a more sedate neighborhood, with all new, state-of-the-art equipment, it was owned by the Church of Latter-Day Saints; Frank Zappa and Captain Beefheart had recorded there. "One night," says Dan Kessel, "Phil was monitoring at supersonic levels—Leonard had to put his hands up over his ears—and suddenly one of the two huge playback speakers completely blew out, rattling the three-paned soundproof glass window separating the studio room from the control booth. The roar of the Wall of Sound at high volume can do that." While the speaker was being fixed, the recording moved again, this time to Devonshire Sound Studio in the San Fernando Valley.

Leonard could not say precisely when he lost control of the album, but he knew that he had. "It definitely wasn't hippie or mellow, but Leonard was very together, very dignified and professional," says David Kessel. "Then it got a little freaky for him." The "entire enterprise," as Leonard described it, was as "an ordeal." Spector, as painstaking at getting the instruments and sound right as Leonard was with his endless rewriting, would often make him wait until two, three, even four in the morning to sing, at which point Leonard was exhausted and his nerves were shot. "It was just one of those periods where my chops were impaired and I wasn't in the right kind of condition to resist Phil's very strong influence on the record and eventual takeover of the record," Leonard said.[7] In the early hours of morning, after watching Spector's car drive away, taking the tapes of the day's recording to his mansion, Leonard drove back to his rented house in a foreign city, to a family on the verge of breaking up.

"I'd lost control of my family, of my work and my life, and it was a very, very dark period," Leonard said. "I was flipped out at the time and [Spector] certainly was flipped out." Where Leonard's darkness manifested as "withdrawal and melancholy," with Spector it was "megalomania and insanity, and the kind of devotion to armaments that was really intolerable. People were armed to the teeth, all his friends, his bodyguards, and everybody was drunk or intoxicated on other items, so you were slipping over bullets, and you were biting into revolvers in your hamburger. There were guns everywhere. Phil was beyond control." During one session, at four o'clock in the morning, as Leonard was finally getting to sing, Spector came down from the control room. In his left hand was a half-empty bottle of Manischewitz and in his right hand a gun. Spector wrapped an arm around Leonard's shoulder in a comradely manner. Then he pushed the nuzzle of the gun into Leonard's neck. "Leonard, I love you," he said, cocking the trigger. "I hope you do, Phil," Leonard replied.[8]

"Bullets all over the floor is an exaggeration," David Kessel says, and in all likelihood that is true; the more media interviews a person does, the more an incident gets polished and hyperbolized. "There weren't bullets on the studio floor," Kessel continues. "He's probably talking about Phil's house. By the way, there are a lot of Americans who have firearms for whatever purpose, and the Constitution says you can have that." Dan Kessel says, "Leonard seemed intrigued with the whole Spector milieu and often made witty comments and observations about us, but I never got the feeling he was uneasy about the guns or anything else. On the contrary, in his own low-key way, he seemed to enjoy himself during the production."

Stan Ross, the assistant engineer and co-owner of Gold Star, took an opposite view. "My main memory of that whole episode was that Phil and Leonard were both very unhappy with what was coming off and I think rightly so."[9] Devra Robitaille, Spector's assistant and, until recently, girlfriend, who played synthesizer on the album, agreed with Ross. She told Spector biographer Mick Brown that Leonard and Spector "didn't see eye to eye at all. There were a lot of creative differences. It was always very tense, very uncomfortable." And unpredictable. Spector "could be in a great mood or he could be a raving lunatic. A lot of it was the drinking. Someone would say something, or he'd just get in a mood and stalk off. Everybody would be hanging around and then tempers would start to build and it's five o'clock in the morning and everyone's exhausted. . . . There were a couple of times when he would pass out drunk and Larry [Levine] and I would have to haul him back into his chair and revive him, and sometimes he'd somehow rally and that would be the brilliant take, the moment of genius."[10] Even Levine, Spector's longtime engineer and friend, had to say that Phil was "not at his best" and Leonard "deserved better than he got."[11]

The fiddle player who had a gun pulled on him during the recording was Bobby Bruce. It was late, and he was doing a solo on "Fingerprints," a countrified song about a man in love losing his identity, and Spector, Dan Kessel remembers, "wanted Bobby to do it again with a certain feeling. 'Do it this way, Bobby. No, more like that.'" The atmosphere in the studio was tense and, in an attempt to lighten it, Bobby started affecting an effeminate manner: "Why of course, Phillip, I'm just mayonnaise in your hands," says Don Kessel. "Ordinarily Phil might have laughed but he wasn't in a lighthearted mood." Spector pulled out his gun. Levine stepped in to try to calm things down, but Spector refused to put away the gun. The engineer had to threaten to turn off the equipment and go home if he did not. "He finally realized I was serious and put the gun away," said Levine. "I loved Phil. I knew that wasn't the real Phil."[12] Bruce quietly shut his fiddle in its case and quit.

For the recording of the album's title track at Whitney Studios, Leonard brought along his own protection: Roshi. Dan Kessel remembers, "Leonard's Zen master was nice and friendly and spoke quietly. He was wearing proper monk's garb." Says Ronee Blakley, "He was the kind of man you wanted to be around, funny, kind and disciplined—special. Leonard was also serving as Roshi's driver. It was—I hope I'm not saying this wrong—a lesson in humility. He was learning to serve." Leonard had tried to persuade Ronee to go to

Mount Baldy and sit with Roshi. "He told me," she says, "that it had saved his life."

The session started as usual at seven thirty P.M. but by three thirty A.M. they had still not played "Death of a Ladies' Man" all the way through; Spector had the musicians play no more than six bars at a time. At four A.M., Spector stood at the window of the control room and clapped his hands, and Leonard began singing his nine-minute meditation on love, marriage, emasculation and the emptiness left behind when *"the great affair is over."* The enormous studio room had a cathedral pipe organ in it, which Spector told Dan Kessel to play. Kessel had never played one before. "I turned on the power switch, sat down and quickly experimented with the stops till I got the hugest sound I could find." Then Spector "began leading us like a symphony orchestra conductor and Leonard came in at the perfect moment and started singing his heart out, while forty musicians came in together with sensitive attention to every breath of Leonard's vocal. Miraculously, without a chart and with no rehearsal, we all managed to glide in together for a smooth landing. We were all exhilarated when we wrapped," says Dan Kessel, "and no one more so than Leonard."

Four months after the last Whitney session in February, during which "Fingerprints" and "I Guess It's Time" were recorded, there was one session in June, back in Gold Star, for "Paper-Thin Hotel." The song, with the familiar Leonard Cohen themes of separation, cuckolding and surrender, had been given a bittersweet, romantic arrangement with choirs, pianos and pedal steel. And that was it. Spector took home the tapes under armed guard, as he always did, and went to work mixing them in a secret location.

No one appeared to have told Leonard that the album was finished. He believed that the exhausted parts he sang in the early hours of the morning were rough vocals that he would have the chance to redo. They were not. When Leonard listened to the playback of the finished album, he flinched. What he heard coming out of the large speakers was a spent man, a punch-drunk singer, lost in the tracks. "I thought he had taken the guts out of the record and I sent him a telegram to that effect," Leonard said.[13] He asked Spector if they might go back into the studio so that he could sing his parts again, but Spector demurred. "In the final moment," Leonard said, "Phil couldn't resist annihilating me. I don't think he can tolerate any other shadows in his darkness."[14]

Leonard told the *New York Times* that he liked nothing about the album. "The music in some places is very powerful but, by and large, I think it's too loud, too aggressive. The arrangements got in my way. I wasn't able to convey the meaning of the songs"[15]—songs that feature some of Leonard's most powerful lyrics about desperate, suffocating, true, faithless, tender, but more often murderous, love. Yet, however he felt about *Death of a Ladies' Man*, it would be hard to deny that Spector had captured Leonard's own sense of annihilation during that period of his life. Leonard *was* lost and spent, and there *was* nothing left. Suzanne had left him. Leonard's mother was in the process of leaving too.

Masha was in the late stages of leukemia. Leonard had been flying back and forth to Montreal, jet-lagged and heavyhearted. While all this was going on, he was also making the final edits to a new book, titled *Death of a Lady's Man*. Marty Machat, meanwhile, had recruited his son Steven, just out of law school, to persuade Warner Bros. to release the record. Mo Ostin, the head of the label, wanted nothing to do with it. Neither, for that matter, did Leonard's label, Columbia.

"That record," says Steven Machat, "was two drunks being no different than any other boys, making an album about picking up girls and getting laid. It was the most honest album Leonard Cohen has ever made." Steven Machat succeeded in winning over a Warner Bros. product manager, and from there he "got the deal done for [his] father." He made it clear that he did not do it for Leonard, for whom he has no great affection, although there may have been some satisfaction in knowing that Leonard "didn't want the album to see daylight." In his book *Gods, Gangsters and Honor* Steven Machat wrote that Leonard told him, "This album is junk. It's your father's masturbation. I love Marty, he's my brother. But I never want to see that man Spector again. He is the worst human being I have ever met."

"At home Phil was delightful—except for the air-conditioning and the fact that he wouldn't let you leave. When it was just the two of us it was a very agreeable time. You know Phil, he has something endearing about him; it's impossible not to be fond of him. It was only when there was a large audience that a kind of performance that he's famous for would arise."

What changed when you went in the studio?

"He got into a kind of Wagnerian mood. There were lots of guns in the studio and lots of liquor. It was a somewhat dangerous atmosphere. There were a lot of guns around. He liked guns. I liked guns too but I generally don't carry one."

Were the guns being fired?

"No firing, but it's hard to ignore a .45 lying on the console. The more people in the room, the wilder Phil would get. I couldn't help but admire the extravagance of his performance. But my personal life was chaotic, I wasn't in good shape at the time mentally, and I couldn't really hold my own in there."

Death of a Ladies' Man was released in November 1977, credited in large letters, front and back, to "Spector & Cohen." It was not surprising that Spector should have given himself equal billing, but for the producer to put his name ahead of the artist's was a curious outcome for an album that Leonard told Harvey Kubernik was "the most autobiographical album of [his] career."[16] Its gatefold sleeve opens out to a panoramic, sepia-tinged photograph shot in a restaurant in L.A., where Leonard sits at a table, flanked by Suzanne and her woman friend, looking like a deer in the headlights, the expression on his face some unidentifiable place between stoned and stunned. The moment the picture captures could hardly be more different from the only other Leonard Cohen album sleeve with a photo of one of his nonmusician lovers—*Songs from a Room*, where Marianne, dressed only in a towel, sits at his writing table in their house on Hydra, smiling shyly.

Critics seemed unsure what to make of the album; it was such a departure from what one had come to expect from Leonard. Yet the reviews were not particularly savage. In the U.S., in fact, they were quite positive, particularly in comparison with those for Leonard's earlier albums. The *New York Times* wrote, "This record may be one of the most bizarre, slowly satisfying hybrids pop music has ever produced."[17] Robert Hilburn of the *Los Angeles Times* was "convinced it's *the* album of '77. Everything is done with an ear for intensity and nerve-edged emotion." Paul Nelson wrote in *Rolling Stone*, "It's either greatly flawed or great *and* flawed, and I'm betting on the latter," noting that in spite of their differences ("the world's most flamboyant extrovert producing the world's most fatalistic introvert") Spector and Cohen had a lot in common, such as both being members of "that select club of lone-wolf poets," and each painfully aware of "what fame and longing are."[18]

In the UK, the music paper *Sounds* compared the album with Dylan's *Desire* and the title track with John Lennon's "Imagine" and John Cale's "Hedda Gabler," while adding, "Diehard acolytes need not worry; it still sounds like [Cohen] but with a much wider appeal."[19] It did turn out to be a durable album. Many who disliked it intensely for its incongruous bombast would warm to it in later years. Leonard also became less negative toward it in time, although, with the exception of "Memories," he would rarely play songs from it in concert. The album did nothing to help Leonard's standing in the U.S.; it did not enter the charts. But had he wanted proof of how much he was loved overseas, it made it to No. 35 in the UK.

With Suzanne gone, Leonard moved out of the house in Brentwood and back to Montreal. He wanted to be close to his mother for whatever time she might have left. When she was taken into the hospital, Leonard visited her every day and sat by her bed. One time Mort Rosengarten came with him and they smuggled in a bottle of alcohol so that they could all raise a glass together, like the old days. He phoned Suzanne and told her Masha was dying. "The last phone call convinced me to come home immediately," Suzanne says. She flew to Montreal with the children. In February 1978, Leonard's mother died. Shortly before her death, someone broke into the house on Belmont Avenue; the one thing that was stolen was Leonard's father's gun.

You ask me how I write. This is how I write. I get rid of the lizard. I eschew the philosopher's stone. I bury my girlfriend. I remove my personality from the line so that I am permitted to use the first person as often as I wish without offending my appetite for modesty. Then I resign. I do errands for my mother, or someone like her. I eat too much. I blame those closest to me for ruining my talent. Then you come to me. The joyous news is mine.

"I BURY MY GIRLFRIEND," *DEATH OF A LADY'S MAN*

Death of a Lady's Man, Leonard's new book, which he dedicated "to Masha Cohen, the memory of my mother," was published in the autumn of 1978. Although the title was almost identical to that of his new album, there was a small but telling difference. Here it referred to one woman in particular. The illustration on the front and back cover—the *coniunctio spirituum*, symbol of the union of the male and female principle—was the same as on the sleeve of his album before last, *New Skin for the Old Ceremony*. "I thought I'd confuse the public as much as I was confused myself," Leonard said.[20] Its ninety-six poems and prose poems had been written largely over a period of ten years—the span of Leonard's "marriage" to Suzanne—in a number of places, including Hydra, Mount Baldy, Montreal, the Tennessee cabin and Los Angeles. Some of them had been reworked from the novel Leonard had withdrawn from publication, which at various junctures had been titled "The Woman Being Born," "My Life in Art" and "Final Revision of My Life in Art."

At the core of *Death of a Lady's Man* is the story of a marriage and the capacity of this particular union—whose rise and fall are digested in the poem "Death of a Lady's Man," much as they were in the album's title song "Death of a Ladies' Man"—to both heal and wound. The discussion extends beyond man-woman union to a man's relationship with God and the world, and a writer's relationship with his words, but in all cases war and peace, victory and defeat, seem to be separated by a paper-thin wall. Leonard's intention had been to publish the book before the album's release. He had submitted the manuscript in 1976, but at the last minute he withdrew it. He wanted to write a series of companion pieces to its contents to—as he put it—"confront the book," go back through it page by page, and write his reaction to what he read.

Leonard's commentaries appear on the facing page of eighty-three of the poems. The device gives *Death of a Lady's Man* the appearance of a school textbook, crib notes to *Death of a Ladies' Man* or a Leonard Cohen I Ching. The commentaries take on a variety of forms. In some Leonard offers critiques of his poems—at various times serious, playful, critical, laudatory, ironic, enlightening and obfuscating. Some commentaries are prose poems in themselves. On several occasions the poems appear to be in an ongoing debate with their companion piece. Some commentaries, adding a further layer, are made not in the voice of the author but of a character in the poem. In others, like a professor teaching a course on the writings of Leonard Cohen, he tells us what meaning we should take from the poems, referring the student to the unpublished "My Life in Art," "Final Revision of My Life in Art" and "the Nashville Notebooks of 1969," which of course the reader is unable to consult. His commentary to a poem titled "My Life in Art" offers a Buddhist teaching: "Destroy particular self and absolute appears." The commentary on "Death to this Book"—the book is full of deaths and births—makes a close study of the poem's angry, brutal rant and declares, "It will become clear that I am the stylist of my era and the only honest man in town." The last poem in the book, just five lines long, is "Final Examination":

> *I am almost 90*
> *Everyone I know has died off*
> *except Leonard*
> *He can still be seen*
> *hobbling with his love*

The commentary questions the accuracy of this ending to the story and, after raising more questions than it answers, concludes with a declaration of union: "Long live the marriage of men and women. Long live the one heart."

Death of a Lady's Man is a remarkable book, as tightly structured as Leonard's first novel, *The Favorite Game*, and as complex, puzzling and ambiguous as his second, *Beautiful Losers*. It is a mirror, a hall of mirrors, and smoke and mirrors, all of its many layers bleeding into each other like, well, a Phil Spector production. It was not Leonard's most popular book of poems but, particularly when coupled with *Death of a Ladies' Man*, it is one of his most wide ranging and fully realized. Leonard thought the book "good" and "funny" and felt "very warm" toward it, but it was "very coldly received in all circles. It got no respect." Hardly anyone reviewed it, he said, and when they did they "dismissed it uniformly . . . And that was it. That was the end of the book."[21]

A month after Masha's death, Leonard was back in L.A. with Suzanne and the children. Suzanne never could stand the Montreal cold. They were renting a new place in the Hollywood Hills. Then, when spring arrived, Suzanne "abruptly left." "I loved him one day and said good-bye that evening," Suzanne says. "It was the story of 'the mouse that roared' and shocked both of us." Although they were never legally married, in 1979 Leonard and Suzanne divorced. Steven Machat took care of the arrangements. "They both came in and they told me everything they owned and they told me the deal that they'd made and I drew up the deal. What I was told," says Machat, "was he honored every single clause in it."

Sixteen

A Sacred Kind of Conversation

_____

In November 1978, in Montreal, Leonard was in a studio, recording. He worked by himself, no musicians, no producer. It felt good to be alone. It felt bad to be alone. It was Leonard's first summer in a decade without Suzanne. Suzanne was in Leonard's house on Hydra with her lover. Leonard was in his house in Montreal with Adam and Lorca. Barbara Amiel was there, interviewing Leonard for *Maclean's* magazine, when the telephone rang. It was Suzanne, calling long-distance from the police station on Hydra. After locals had complained about "commotions" at the house, she and her boyfriend had been arrested for possession of drugs. The combination of the Kama Sutra woodcuts she had hung on the walls and the absence of the beloved patriarch had, it seemed, proven too much for the locals to bear. Leonard told Amiel that he had warned Suzanne that her new decor would offend the cleaning lady. The case against Suzanne and her friend was dropped, but at the cost of several thousand dollars to

Leonard. "These days," he told Amiel, "I work to support my wife, my children and my responsibilities."[1]

When Suzanne returned to Montreal, she took the children and moved with them to France, renting a house in Roussillon, in the Vaucluse. If Leonard wanted to see them—and he did; after his initial misgivings about fatherhood he had taken to it seriously, and his friends say he was grief-stricken at being separated from them—there were negotiations to be made. Leonard had chosen not to tour with *Death of a Ladies' Man*, saying, "I didn't really feel I could be behind it."[2] Aside from its having been such a volatile and enervating experience, the large-scale, sometimes brawling, songs that resulted would have to be seriously de-Spectorized for him to sing them onstage. Not touring also gave Leonard more time to negotiate this new, long-distance family life, which would involve spending even more time on transatlantic flights. Leonard chose, somewhat curiously, to move back to Los Angeles, making the journey to France considerably longer than from Montreal. He bought, along with two fellow students of Roshi, another cheap house in an inexpensive neighborhood. The duplex was a short drive from the Cimarron Zen Center. Every morning at the same time, Leonard would go to the Zen Center to meditate. From there he would go to the gym, before returning to his sparsely furnished part of the house to write. His life without Suzanne and the children was, it seemed, more structured, not less.

Leonard's old friend Nancy Bacal was also living in Los Angeles. When Leonard showed up at the door of her home in the Hollywood Hills, she had recently suffered a terrible loss; her fiancé had been killed in a motorcycle accident. Bacal was "devastated," she remembers. "I could barely breathe. Leonard looked at me, smiled his sweet wry smile and said quietly, 'Welcome to life.'" He urged her to come with him to Mount Baldy and sit with Roshi, saying, "It's perfect for you. It's for the truly lost." That Leonard clearly considered himself among that congregation was evidenced by the central role that Roshi and his austere form of Zen Buddhism played in his life at this time. When Leonard was not at the Zen Center in L.A., you might find him in the monastery on Mount Baldy—a "hospital for the broken-hearted," as he called it[3]—or accompanying Roshi to various monasteries of other religious denominations around the U.S.

Leonard also became a contributing editor of a new Buddhist magazine called *Zero*, which had been founded a year earlier and was named for Roshi's fondness for mathematical terms—zero, to Roshi, was the place where all the pluses and minuses equated in God, the absence of self, and true love. Steve Sanfield had been one of its first editors. Each issue contained some words from Roshi, interviews with artists such as Joni Mitchell and John Cage, articles by scholars and poems by, among others, Allen Ginsberg, John Ashbery and Leonard Cohen.

In spite of his deep involvement with Buddhism, Leonard insisted to anyone who asked that he remained a Jew. "I have a perfectly good religion," he said, and pointed out that Roshi had never made any attempt to give him a new one.[4] When Bob Dylan went public with his conversion to Christianity in 1979 "it seriously rocked [Leonard's] world," said Jennifer Warnes, who was staying at that time at Leonard's house. He would "wander around the house, wringing his hands saying, 'I don't get it. I just don't get this. Why would he go for Jesus at a late time like this? I don't get the Jesus part.'"[5]

In the summer of 1979 Leonard began work on a new album to which he had given the working title *The Smokey Life*. Still smarting from his experience with Phil Spector, he planned to produce, or at least coproduce, it himself. He had been thinking about working with John Lissauer again, but Lissauer was in New York and Roshi was in L.A. and Leonard did not feel ready to leave him. Joni Mitchell, with whom Leonard had remained friends, suggested that he work with her longtime engineer-producer, Henry Lewy. Since Leonard had ignored her last recommendation—that he not work with Phil

Spector—at his peril, he agreed. Leonard met Lewy, a soft-spoken man in his fifties, and liked him immediately. Lewy was born in Germany and had been in his teens when World War II broke out and his family had bribed their way out of the country. His background was as a radio man and a studio engineer, which made him more interested than the average record producer in simply getting things done, rather than having them done his way.

Leonard played Lewy the new songs he had recorded in Montreal, including "Misty Blue," a cover of a country-soul song from the sixties written by Bob Montgomery, and "The Smokey Life," which Leonard had recorded in some form with both Lissauer and Spector (with the latter under the title "I Guess It's Time"). Lewy liked what he heard and suggested they book a studio and make some demos—very informal, just the two of them. The place Lewy chose was Kitchen Sync, a small eight-track studio in East Hollywood that was popular with L.A. punk bands. Harvey Kubernik, who was in Kitchen Sync recording *Voices of the Angels*, an album of punk artists reading poetry, "was startled," he says, to see Leonard, "a guy who's been in the biggest studios in the world," recording there. "This was Bukowski land, the only place where you'd get hit on by a hooker and she'd say, 'I've got change for a fifty,'" says Kubernik. When he asked Leonard what he was doing there. Leonard answered, "My friend Henry Lewy and I are doing some exploratory navigation."

As work on Leonard's album continued, Lewy suggested they bring in a bass player. The man he had in mind was Roscoe Beck. Beck was a member of a young jazz-rock band based in Austin, Texas, named Passenger. They had come to L.A. because Joni Mitchell was looking for a backing band for her tour and Lewy had put their name forward. The tour failed to materialize. Lewy called Beck and booked a session. Beck says, "I went to the studio, met Leonard, shook his hand, and we sat down one-on-one to record. He showed me, on guitar, the two songs we did that day, 'The Smokey Life' and

'Misty Blue,' and Henry pushed 'record' on the tape machine and that was that." Leonard, dressed in a dark gray suit, a tie and black cowboy boots, "had a very gentlemanly manner about him and a lot of charisma," Beck remembers. "I was really struck by that. I had the immediate feeling that it was the beginning of something." Noting how pleased Leonard had been with the session, Lewy said, "He has a whole band, you know." Leonard said, "Well, great, next time bring them all."

The album, retitled *Recent Songs*, was recorded at A & M, a major studio situated on Charlie Chaplin's old lot in Hollywood. There were no guns, no bodyguards, not even any alcohol in the studio that anyone can recall. Lewy "created an extremely hospitable atmosphere where things could just happen," Leonard said. "He had that great quality that Bob Johnston had: he had a lot of faith in the singer, as he did with Joni. And he just let it happen."[6] Mitchell was actually at A & M herself, working in a studio down the hall on her album *Mingus*, which Lewy was producing at the same time as he was making Leonard's. Sometimes she would drop by Leonard's sessions. It was all very easygoing. "Henry's spirit was just lovely," says Beck, "and 'lovely' was a word he used a lot. You would finish a take and Henry would hit the talk-back and say, 'That was just lovely.' I don't recall ever hearing a negative word out of Henry's mouth."

After laying down the tracks with Passenger—augmented on "Our Lady of Solitude" by Garth Hudson, the keyboard player with the Band—Leonard brought in Jennifer Warnes as his main backing vocalist. He also hired John Bilezikjian and Raffi Hakopian to play oud and violin solos on "The Window," "The Guests," "The Traitor" and "The Gypsy's Wife." Another thing in Lewy's favor was that, since he was not a musician—he was an engineer—he worked best with artists who had their own strong vision of what they wanted to do. "The musical ideas were specifically mine," said Leonard. "I'd always wanted to combine those Middle Eastern or Eastern European sounds with the rhythmic possibilities of a five- or six-piece jazz band or rock 'n' roll rhythm section."[7]

In his album credits, Leonard thanked his mother for reminding him, "shortly before she died, of the kind of music she liked." When he had played her his last album, *Death of a Ladies' Man*, she had asked why he didn't make songs like the ones they used to sing together around the house, many of these being old Russian and Jewish songs, whose sentimental melodies were often played on the violin. So Leonard did. He found the classical violinist Bilezikjian through a mutual acquaintance, Stuart Brotman.* When Bilezikjian came to the studio, he also brought with him his oud. Leonard was so taken with his improvisations on it that he had him switch instruments, hiring Bilezikjian's friend and fellow Armenian Hakopian to play the violin.

That the album would include a mariachi band was a spontaneous idea of Leonard's. He and the band had taken to enjoying a post-session burrito and margarita at El Compadre, a Mexican restaurant favored by rock musicians, on Sunset Boulevard, nearby. Mariachi bands would often perform there into the early hours, and Leonard approached one of them and asked if they would be willing to come to the studio and play on his record. The band, who seemed to have no idea who Leonard was, performed on "Ballad of the Absent Mare," a song inspired in equal parts by the horse Leonard had bought from Kid Marley in Tennessee and Roshi's teachings on the Ten Bulls, illustrated poems depicting the stages along the path to enlightenment. They also played on "Un Canadien Errant" ("The Wandering Canadian"), a patriotic folk song from the 1840s, about a rebel from Quebec, banished to America and longing for home. Being sung in English by a Canadian Jew who had wandered to California of his own volition, accompanied by a Mexican band living in L.A.,

---

* Brotman, coincidentally, had joined the band the Kaleidoscope shortly after their appearance on Leonard's debut album.

brought new layers to the song's theme of exile. And Leonard, newly orphaned and divorced, did appear, despite his self-proclaimed lack of sentimentality and nostalgia, to be longing for home—or some sort of home. The nearest he had was with Roshi, to whom he wrote in the album credits, "I owe my thanks."

Leonard also thanked his late friend Robert Hershorn for introducing him to the Persian poets and mystics Attar and Rumi, "whose imagery influenced several songs, especially 'The Guests' and 'The Window,' even if the imagery in 'The Window'—spears, thorns, angels, saints, *"the New Jerusalem glowing,"* the *"tangle of matter and ghost"* and *"the word being made into flesh"*—appears largely Christian.* The image of the window had long been important in Leonard's poetry and song, as a place of light and observation, as a mirror and as a boundary between different realities, between the internal and external. Leonard, talking about this song, described it as "a kind of prayer to bring the two parts of the soul together."[8]

Recent Songs teems with feasts, thorns, roses, smoke and sainthood, songs about light and darkness, and about loss and being lost. "The Gypsy's Wife" directly addresses the loss of Suzanne. Its sensual melody is paired with dark, accusatory lyrics that are biblical in tone. Leonard said it was one of the quickest songs he had ever written. After Suzanne left him, he was in a woman's apartment in Los Angeles, and the woman had a guitar, which he picked up and played while she got ready to go out. "And that is exactly what I was thinking," he said, "'Where, where is my gypsy wife tonight?' In a sense it was written for . . . the wife that was wandering away, but in another way it's just a song about the way men and women have lost one another."[9] It does seem a touch disproportionate that a man who had referred to himself in song as "some kind of gypsy boy"[10] and

---

* In the version of "The Window" published in *Stranger Music,* Leonard's 1993 collection of poetry and songs, Leonard changed the "New Jerusalem" line to the nondenominational "the code of solitude broken."

who clearly did not want for female company should be so apocalyptically stern in song about the judgment that awaited whomsoever might come between a man and his wife. But the pain of losing his family was still acute.

Recent Songs also featured three songs from the abandoned *Songs for Rebecca* album: "Came So Far for Beauty," "The Traitor" and the jazzy "The Smokey Life." The first gave John Lissauer credit as its cowriter and coproducer. "It was exactly as I recorded the demo," Lissauer says—Lissauer playing piano, John Miller on bass. "They didn't do anything to it." Lissauer received no credit on the other two songs, although he says that they too were very much as he and Leonard had done them together.

"I was so brokenhearted by this whole thing," says Lissauer. "I was doing dozens of other albums and Leonard wasn't selling a ton, so I wasn't losing big dollars or anything, I just was disappointed by how I was treated. I've always said, it's not Leonard, it's Marty [Machat]." There appeared to be no other *Rebecca* songs among the outtakes, which included "Misty Blue," "The Faith," "Billy Sunday" (an unreleased song Leonard would sing on several dates of the 1979–80 tour) and "Do I Have to Dance All Night," a dance song recorded at a 1976 concert in Paris and released as a single (backed with "The Butcher") in Europe.

Recent Songs was released in September 1979, two years after *Death of a Ladies' Man*—a quicker follow-up than fans had come to expect from Leonard. It was dedicated to Irving Layton, Leonard's "friend and inspiration, the incomparable master of the inner language." The portrait of Leonard that took up the entire front cover was based on a photo shot by his friend and onetime lover Hazel Field; the illustrated version made him look less haggard and more Dustin Hoffmanesque than in the photograph. After the incongruous rage and bombast of *Death of a Ladies' Man*, its largely acoustic style and graceful arrangements, along with the romantic gypsy-folk flavor of the violin and the Near East exoticism of the oud, were greeted by critics as a return to form. The *New York Times* placed it among its top ten albums of the year. *Rolling Stone* wrote, "There's not a cut on *Recent Songs* without something to offer."[11] Larry "Ratso" Sloman, reviewing for *High Times*, predicted it would be "Cohen's biggest LP" and said it was "sure to go silver, if not gold."[12]

But John Lissauer was correct; the album did not sell many copies. Despite the warm critical response, it barely sold at all in the U.S. and failed to make the charts in Canada. In the UK it reached No. 53—but this was the lowest position yet for a Leonard Cohen studio album; even the widely unpopular *Death of a Ladies' Man* had made it to No 35. *NME*, echoing the generally middling reviews it received in Britain, described it as "Cohen's most accomplished album in musical terms," but took it to task for its "detached, almost impersonal air" and lyrics that "tend towards a rather fey obscurity."[13] But Leonard was pleased with *Recent Songs*. "I like that album," he would say more than twenty years later. "I think I like it the best."[14]

The *Recent Songs* tour began in Sweden, in October 1979. Leonard's band for the fifty-one-date European tour was Passenger—Roscoe Beck, Steve Meador, Bill Ginn, Mitch Watkins and Paul Ostermeyer—plus John Bilezikjian and Raffi Hakopian. "It was world music before the term existed," says Beck. "Leonard and I have talked about what a unique group it was for its day." Leonard was also accompanied by two of his finest female backing vocalists, Jennifer Warnes, who had toured with him at the beginning of the decade, and a newcomer named Sharon Robinson.

Robinson had been singing and dancing in Las Vegas in the Ann-Margret revue when Warnes, who had taken on the task of finding a second backing singer, called out of the blue, asking if she would like to audition for Leonard Cohen's European tour. Robinson was not familiar with Leonard's work, but Europe sounded good. "Jennifer vetted me beforehand at her house on her own, then she brought me to audition for Leonard." Sharon remembers, "The whole band was there. I was a little nervous, but Leonard, sitting on the couch, seemed to exude a really bright kind of energy and a real warmth and friendliness that I really appreciated. I felt at home right away."

Helping make Leonard feel at home was Roshi. He traveled with the band on the tour bus, dressed in his robes, reading quietly through his big square spectacles as Europe rolled by on the other side of the glass. "He came to the concerts and he was there backstage," Beck recalls. "It's very odd, his presence was at once large and yet almost invisible at times. Not a lot of words were spoken, and he seemed to disappear into the wall of the greenroom. He is really a Zen master!" It was in tribute, perhaps, that when Leonard sang "Bird on the Wire" he changed the "worm on a hook" into "a monk bending over a book." On the long drives between cities, Leonard and the band would sing "Pauper Sum Ego" ("I Am a Poor Man"), a monastic chant in Latin in the round. During the long bus rides, Leonard and Jennifer Warnes cowrote a song about a saint called "Song of Bernadette." Sometimes Bilezikjian would go to the back of the bus when the rest of the band were in their bunks, sleeping, and play his oud and violin, "softly so I wouldn't wake anyone up." But when everyone was up, he remembers, "all of us would sing Leonard's songs. They became like our anthem. We'd come up with a vocal arrangement, singing as if we had our instruments. I think Leonard was touched by that. I saw a big smile on his face." As on their 1972 tour, they had a filmmaker with them on the road. Harry Rasky, a Canadian, was making a documentary on Leonard for CBC. Their number increased again when Henry Lewy flew out to join them for the UK tour—a hectic eleven shows in twelve days—recording the concerts with the aim of making a live album. Despite Leonard's sounding less improvisational and significantly more cheerful on this tour than he had on his last live album, 1973's *Live Songs*, Columbia chose not to release the album recorded on the 1979 tour—at least not until two decades later, when it finally appeared in 2000 under the title *Field*

Commander Cohen.* The tour came to an end in Brighton in December, sixteen days before the end of the seventies. After two months off (two weeks of which Leonard spent in a monastery)—it resumed in the eighties with a successful tour of Australia.

When the band members flew back to their respective homes, according to Jennifer Warnes, they did not know what to do with themselves. "[There were] two or three divorces right after the tour, and I think they were simply because the mates couldn't understand what had happened. There had been severe altering of personalities. Roscoe started wearing Armani suits. It was a mess. We'd call each other and say, 'What do we do now?' The aperture of the heart had been broken open."[15] Beck and Warnes were now a couple, having become romantically involved halfway across Europe. Like the rest of the band, they wanted nothing more than to take the tour across America. "We couldn't mount enough interest to put one together," says Beck. Curiously though, at around this time an interview with Leonard appeared in the U.S. celebrity weekly magazine *People*.

Readers more used to stories about movie stars and the Betty Ford Center read how a Canadian singer-songwriter who could not sell records in America recovered from his "brief periods of collapse" in Roshi's "center for meditation and manual labor." Leonard explained, "When I go there, it's like scraping off the rust. . . . I'm not living with anybody the rest of the time. Nobody can live with me. I have almost no personal life." As this last statement was a concept alien to *People*, they also interviewed his former partner. Suzanne was quoted as saying of Leonard, "I believed in him. He had moved people in the right direction, toward gentleness. But then I became very alone—the proof of the poetry just wasn't there." The article reported Suzanne's claim that Leonard had not kept to their child-support agreement. Leonard in turn complained about Suzanne's "Miami consumer hab-

---

* The original photo of Leonard on which the *Recent Songs* portrait was based was used on its front cover.

its," adding, "My only luxuries are airplane tickets to go anywhere at any time. All I need is a table, chair and bed."[16]

Harry Rasky's documentary *Song of Leonard Cohen*, which was broadcast in Canada in 1980, made a far more dignified setting for Leonard. The film opens with Leonard sitting in the window—that most symbolic of places for him—in his apartment in Montreal. The apartment looks sparse and uncluttered—much more like Leonard's home in L.A. and his house on Hydra than the nearby cottage crammed with knickknacks and books where he had lived with Suzanne and their children. This has white walls, bare; painted floorboards; an old wooden table, and a small claw-footed bathtub. Leonard also appears to be surrounded by friends and supporters. Hazel Field, who lives in the neighboring apartment, is seen clambering over the balcony, all long limbs and ironed hair, carrying a cup of coffee for Leonard, and Irving Layton drops by, bringing a young, blond companion with him. The two sit spellbound when Leonard plays them his song "The Window" on a boom box.

"Leonard was a genius from the first moment I saw him," Layton states, adding, "[His songs have] the quality of mystery, of doom, of menace, of sadness, the dramatic quality that you find in the Scottish ballads, the English ballads" from the twelfth and thirteenth centuries. Asked by Rasky if he found Leonard's songs sad or joyful he answers, "Both. What I like particularly in Leonard's songs is what I call the depressive manic quality. If you notice, in some of his most telling and moving songs, he always begins on a note of pain, of anguish, of sadness, and then somehow or other works himself up into a state of exaltation, of euphoria, as though he had released himself from the devil, melancholy, pain."[17] Then, Jews, Layton says, "have always had the gift of anxiety and pain and solitude."[18] The Wandering Canadian tells Rasky that "he is tired of moving around" and would like to "stay in one place for a while." The problem is that "there always seemed good reasons to move.[19]

On October 24, 1980, Leonard was back in Europe for five more weeks of concerts. Jennifer Warnes chose not to join him this time, leaving Sharon Robinson as his sole backing singer. By this time Leonard and Sharon had become close. In Israel, where the tour ended, they started writing a song together, called "Summertime." Sharon, says Leonard, "had this melody that I hadn't written a lyric for but I really loved." In the lobby of their Tel Aviv hotel there was a baby grand piano, so she played it to Leonard, who liked it. "Right on the spot," she says, "he started looking for the appropriate lyric." Although Leonard did not record the song himself, their first cowrite would be covered by both Diana Ross and Roberta Flack.

The tour ended with two dates in Tel Aviv. Sharon remembers Leonard taking the band on a trip to the Dead Sea and also to visit a kibbutz. When it was over, Leonard flew to New York. In his room at the Algonquin Hotel, he prepared to celebrate Hanukkah with Adam and Lorca. He had brought candles and a prayer book with him, and also a notebook. When Hanukkah was over and the children gone, he opened it to the page where he had started to write a powerful and beautiful hymn of surrender, titled "If It Be Your Will."

––––––––

And so the curtain came down and Leonard stepped out quietly through the backstage door. It seemed as good a time as any to make an exit from the music business. The tour was over and, though the concerts had been good, his album had not sold well. The world had other things to occupy it; Leonard did not think he would be missed.

Had you lost interest, or simply run out of steam?

"I don't know, I suppose it reflected a certain insecurity about what I was doing. I kind of lost the handle of it, I thought. Although in retrospect, even in examining the work of other writers, that's a very common and almost routine assessment of one's work at different periods. Often one's best work is at the time considered inadequate or incompetent. I certainly struggled with those notions, and not just as a writer— but, as any man

or woman locates a large component of their self-respect in their work, it's always an issue."

Did you have any plans for how you would spend this time away?

"My children were living in the South of France and I spent a lot of time visiting them there and going back and forth. The pieces in 'Book of Mercy' were coming and I was writing the album that ended up being called Various Positions. *At a certain point my work was so slow and it became such an ordeal that I was discarding much of what I did, so I think it was legitimate for me to say that my life and my work was in disarray."*

The next four years were spent out of the public eye. If you were looking for Leonard you might find him in the monastery on Mount Baldy, in his apartment in Montreal, in his house on Hydra or in France, in a trailer at the bottom of a path leading to the house where Suzanne and the children lived. Leonard flew to France often.

Adam Cohen, speaking some three decades later, described it as "admirable, the way in which he managed to keep in touch with us, despite the . . . domestic unrest, shall we say, the post-divorce antagonisms."[20] Things between Leonard and Suzanne remained contentious, although in Suzanne's opinion, "We worked it out—over many years with many highs and lows—better than most that I've ever met and heard of since. The voyeurs and gossipers will only want to exaggerate the difficult times and the ill-willed will be suspicious of the best."

The house that Suzanne found and Leonard purchased was on a seventeenth-century farm in Bonnieux that had been owned and run by monks. The surrounding countryside was littered with old, rural churches. Sometimes Suzanne took the children there, "although," she says, "I didn't whisper sweet nothings in the children's ears about Jesus walking in the Garden." She was aware that Leonard "would have liked me to educate them with at least the knowledge of the Jewish tradition in some way," but there were no synagogues in the area, she says. Later, when she and the children lived in Manhattan,

she "looked into it in earnest, but the rabbi I spoke to just didn't
make it accessible to me and I gave up. And to do it without Leonard didn't make sense to me." Leonard took on the children's Jewish
education himself. "I told them the stories, I told them the prayers,
I showed them how to light the candles, I gave them the A to Z of
the important holidays," he says, and he celebrated the holidays with
them.

When he was on Hydra Leonard fell gratefully into his old rhythm
of swimming, writing and socializing at the bar by the harbor. He
heard from Anthony Kingsmill about a concerto that Terry Oldfield,
one of the younger expat residents, was working on, and asked Oldfield if he could hear it. Having heard it, he offered to go to Athens
with Oldfield and have it recorded. "A very generous guy," says Oldfield. "I was somebody trying to make it with music and really trying
hard at it, and I think he identified a bit with that. Maybe it took him
back to his early days on the island when he was writing." Leonard
invited Oldfield to his house and showed him the room where he
wrote. "It was in the basement, very dark, and looked like a kind of
womb, and it had a little electronic keyboard he played around with,
one of those battery-operated Casios. And this was the room where
he wrote a lot of his best stuff. He said, 'This room has been very
kind to me.'"

———————

In early 1982 Leonard's friend Lewis Furey came to Hydra for a
month with his wife, Carol Laure. With them was a friend of theirs, a
French photographer named Dominique Issermann. Furey, who had
made two records as a singer, was, like Leonard, "not that thrilled
with the music industry and the idea of making records." He says, "I
was more interested in theatrical song, song cycles that told a story."
One reason for his visit was that he had the idea for a musical, a rock
opera, and was hoping that Leonard would write the song lyrics.

At the time, Leonard was "working experimentally, for my own instruction, on the form of the Spenserian sonnet," he said, "which is a very complex metrical and rhyme form—just to keep my chops up in meter and rhyme." When Furey asked if he wanted to write lyrics for his rock opera, his answer was "Not particularly." But Furey was persuasive, and when the conversation turned to their releasing it on video disc—a new format the size of a record album, one not destined to survive—Leonard was intrigued. "He gave me some very elementary plot outlines," said Leonard, "and I wrote lyrics to them as an exercise."[21]

Over the next four weeks Leonard came up with "at least four or five complete lyrics," Furey recalls, "very technical and all perfectly structured," like sonnets. Furey began writing music to them. The project, which they titled *Night Magic*, was "very much a Faust story," says Furey, "only the Mephistopheles character is three teenage angels who appear at the window, and the price you have to pay is suffering joy, redemption and decay." Leonard and Furey worked on the musical on and off over the next year and a half—mostly in Paris, where Furey and his wife lived and where Suzanne was planning to move with Adam and Lorca. Dominique Issermann also lived in Paris. Leonard had begun an enduring relationship with the beautiful photographer on Hydra.

While Furey set about getting funding, Leonard started work on a short musical film for CBC television called *I Am a Hotel*, whose plot revolved around characters in an imaginary hotel. Leonard made an appearance in the film as a long-term resident of the hotel, smoking a cigarette and watching as the various characters' stories played out—with no dialogue—to five of his songs. These were "The Guests," the song that had been the inspiration for the project; "Memories"; "The Gypsy's Wife"; "Chelsea Hotel #2"; and "Suzanne." It was broadcast in 1983 and won an award at the Rose d'Or, the Montreux television festival. Leonard, meanwhile, was meeting with McClelland & Stewart about the new book he was writing, which he first titled *The Name*, then *The Shield*, and finally *Book of Mercy*.

Dennis Lee, whom McClelland had quite recently hired to head the poetry department, is a poet and essayist, author of a 1977 book called *Savage Fields: An Essay in Literature and Cosmology*—a joint study of Leonard's novel *Beautiful Losers* and Michael Ondaatje's *The Collected Works of Billy the Kid*. Says Lee, "For ten or twelve months, Leonard and I lived in each other's back pockets and got to know each other very intensely within this one very narrow sphere of the new book he was working on." Leonard described this new book as "a book of prayer . . . a sacred kind of conversation." It was "a secret book for me," he said, "meant for people like myself who could use it at a particular time."[22] He wrote it, he said, because he found himself "unable to speak in any other way. I felt I had been gagged and silenced for a long, long time, a number of years. It was with the greatest difficulty that I could communicate with anybody, even for the simplest thing. And when I was able to speak it was in these terms, an address to the source of mercy."[23]

In utter defeat I came to you and you received me with a sweetness I had not dared to remember. Tonight I come to you again, soiled by strategies and trapped in the loneliness of my tiny domain. Establish your law in this walled place.

"6," BOOK OF MERCY

"The content, the prayerful quality of what he was doing had in some ways always been there," says Lee, "but he really took off his gloves and went into it more directly and explicitly than he had before. I was very conscious that he was breaking new ground for himself." Lee remembers that the first draft he saw of *Book of Mercy* "was much sketchier than what you read in the book now. A number of the very best pieces were written later in the process. I remember we were working away in Toronto and partway through he took off for a month or two to France—he told me that he was very much on his own when he wasn't with his kids—and he told me when he got back that, while he was there, he kept hearing my voice in his head saying what I'd said before he left: 'I think there's still more.' There was no prima donna 'I'm Leonard Cohen, you shouldn't be making any suggestions.' He was the most charming and thoroughbred human being, and really focused on trying to get the book right, despite the other stuff going on in his life. In the evenings there was nothing to do but hone in on the manuscript, probing for more material. He came back with some things that really knocked my socks off."

On Leonard's last trip to Toronto before the book's publication, the main discussion between the two of them was the title. "One question Leonard had was: was there a danger of putting a title out that might sound pretentious or guilty of religiosity, that would invite suspicion from a reader even before reading it? But in the end, for Leonard it came down to a question of whether it should be called *The Book of Mercy* or just *Book of Mercy*, and we decided the 'the' should be omitted so that it didn't sound like this was the *definitive* book of mercy, or a book in the Bible. It's a more modest title. Maybe he doesn't like to appear to be making a larger claim than he wants to." (Perhaps for the same reasons, Leonard often dispensed with the definite article in titles of his albums and songs.) After their work was done on *Book of Mercy*, Leonard and Lee went to the set of *Fraggle Rock*, a children's television series made in Toronto by Jim Henson. Leonard wanted to meet the man who invented the Muppets. Says Lee, "He got a real kick out of watching him shoot the show."

Book of Mercy, Leonard's tenth book, was published in April 1984. Its front cover was illustrated with a symbol designed by Leonard that he called "the emblem of the Order of the Unified Heart." It took the form of a hexagram, the Star of David, made up of two interlinked hearts, or as Leonard described it, "a version of the yin and yang, or any of those symbols that incorporate the polarities and try and reconcile the differences." The book was dedicated to his "teacher." What Leonard had learned from studying with Roshi had also brought him a deeper understanding of the Talmud, the Torah, the Kabbalah and the Jewish prayer book. He said he had reacquainted himself with his Jewish studies after having "wrecked [his] knees"[24] and finding himself unable to sit for long periods in *zazen*—seated meditation. "I had decided to do what I had never done which was to observe the [Jewish] calendar in a very diligent way, to lay *tefillin* every day and to study the Talmud. *Book of Mercy* came out of that investigation."[25] Although there are Christian and Buddhist, as well as secular, references in the book, Leonard's aim in writing it was, he said, "to affirm the traditions I had inherited" and to "express my gratitude for having been exposed to that tradition."[26]

The book is made up of fifty short, numbered prose pieces, one for each year of Leonard's life. In them, he talks, pleads, confesses and prays—to himself, to his friend, to his teacher and to his woman, but mostly to his God—for deliverance and mercy. The pieces are written with the rhythm, tonality and implied music of psalms, and in "the charged speech that I heard in the synagogue, where everything was important." Leonard said, "I always feel that the world was created through words, through speech in our tradition, and I've always seen the enormous light in charged speech, and that's what I've tried to get to."[27] When one finds oneself "unable to function," he said, the only option is "to address the absolute source of things. . . . The only thing you can do is prayer."[28]

The review in Canada's *Globe and Mail* described *Book of Mercy* as "an eloquent victory of the human spirit in combat with itself." The Canadian Author's Association gave it the CAA Award for Poetry. Rabbi Mordecai Finley (whom Leonard would come to know later) remembers that one day, after synagogue, he said to Leonard, "So many of your poems have the feel of Jewish liturgy. Did you consciously write something liturgical?" Finley continues, "He said, 'That's what I thought I was always writing, liturgy,' meaning, something out of the heart so that, in recitation, you're brought to a deeper place. His poetry had a liturgical feel, rhythmic; it almost bypasses the brain and enters straight into us. We have a liturgical tradition in Judaism where great Jewish poets wrote poetry and then they incorporated it into the prayer book—they didn't try to write prayers—and I think Leonard is actually the greatest liturgist alive today. I read his poems aloud at high holidays, from *Book of Mercy*. I think *Book of Mercy* should be in our prayer book."

Seventeen

The Hallelujah of the Orgasm

Psalms were meant to be sung. As soon as Leonard was back in Los Angeles, he called Henry Lewy. The two went into the studio to make an album of Leonard reading *Book of Mercy*, accompanied by a string quartet. The record was not released. Instead Leonard flew back to New York and called John Lissauer, to make another album whose content was different from, but in its own way a mirror to, *Book of Mercy*.

Leonard said that during the writing of *Book of Mercy*, "the public almost evaporated"[1]; he had written these prayers for himself. He also said that he had no intention of becoming "known as a writer of prayers."[2] Once the book was completed, the public had come sharply back into focus. One big reason for this was that Leonard was running out of money. If Leonard lived like a celebrity, if he'd had a yacht or a cocaine habit, it might be easier to understand. But though he did not spend much money on himself, he still had expenses: Suzanne, the children, Roshi's monastery and various friends whom he supported financially in one way or another. The majority of Leonard's income came from his songs, not his books, and five years had passed since his last album.

John Lissauer was "a little surprised" when he picked up the phone and Leonard was on the line, saying he was in New York and ready to record again—an understandable reaction given that Leonard had walked out on the last album and had gone on to rewrite or record the songs with two other producers. Upset as he had been, Lissauer—like Ron Cornelius, who had been uncredited for many years as the co-writer of "Chelsea Hotel #2"—blamed Marty Machat. "It was just one of those things, a lesson to watch out for managers, or for managers who were obsessed. Leonard knew that Marty was Marty, but Marty had taken such good care of him, so Leonard was in a little bit of Machat denial. He and I have joked about it since and he has admitted what Marty was really like, but at the time it was an unbroachable subject." Lissauer did not mention the aborted *Songs for Rebecca*. "What was the point of making Leonard uncomfortable? It would have put the kibosh on this, and I was happy that he was calling."

In his room at the Royalton, "Leonard had this shit-eating grin on his face—and Leonard, when he's grinning like a little boy, is something you never forget. He had this little crap Casio synthesizer which he'd bought on Forty-seventh and Broadway at one of those camera shops for tourists, where you push your finger down on a key and it'll play a dinky rhythm track. And then he sang me 'Dance Me to the End of Love.'" Leonard played Lissauer several songs in various stages of completion, and only one of them on guitar. On the others he was accompanied by the jaunty parping of the Casio. Lissauer came to the conclusion that Leonard had reached a point in his songwriting where he had "run out of ideas as a guitar player. There were certain things he could do with his guitar playing, but this dopey Casio did things that he couldn't on his guitar and made it possible for him to approach songwriting in a different way." Writing songs was certainly proving torturously difficult for Leonard again. But this cheesy little two-octave keyboard that Leonard seemed so fond of gave him a whole new set of rhythms to work with, and he found he was able to come up with things he could never have created with six strings and what he called his "one chop."

This time Marty Machat made no objection to Leonard's working with Lissauer. His only stipulation was that the budget be kept as low as possible. The impression Lissauer got from Machat was that Leonard had been spending "a ton of money unwisely and hadn't been touring." Lissauer called Quad Recording and negotiated a good deal by block-booking four or five days of studio time. Quad was on Broadway and Forty-ninth, thirteen floors above the Metropole, an upscale strip club "where a guy would stand outside with fliers under a big rotating disco ball." Lissauer put a small band together: his friend Sid McGinnis, who played guitar in the David Letterman show band; Richard Crooks, a drummer who had played with Dr. John; and Ron Getman and John Crowder, two Tulsans who would later front a successful country group, the Tractors. Lissauer himself played keyboards and Synclavier.

"Instead of basing it around Leonard and his guitar and over-dubbing things, we went in and started doing tracks as a band and tried to make a little performance out of it," says Lissauer, "which is something I don't think he'd done in quite a while. I brought in my Synclavier, a very early prototype, a phenomenally big thing, four rolling cases and computers and floppy discs, that cost around thirty-five thousand dollars. Leonard's Casio would have been ninety-nine dollars, if that much, but I couldn't get Leonard to drop his Casio." It did not even have an audio output and needed to be miked. "I tried everything, we tried recording it with real drums, but he liked the sound of the Casio, and in a way it was very charming. So we added stuff to it so that it wasn't quite so embarrassing."

Leonard had "always been interested in electronic machines and keyboards," he said. "In fact, for my first record I interviewed one or two people who were doing experimental work in electronic instruments. I tried to get a sound, a drone, that would go behind 'The Stranger Song'—I never managed to get the right kind I was looking for—but the technology had reached a sophistication by this time where I could use my little toys in the actual recording."[3] The first song to feature Leonard playing his Casio was the new album's opening track, "Dance Me to the End of Love." The seed of the song was something Leonard had read about an orchestra of inmates in a concentration camp, who were forced by the Nazis to play as their fellow prisoners were marched off to the gas chambers. As a testimonial to Leonard's way with words and a romantic melody, it would go on to become a popular song at weddings.*

Leonard named his seventh studio album *Various Positions*, a title suggestive of a Cohen Kama Sutra. But his aim with the album was to explore "how things really operate, the mechanics of feeling, how the heart manifests itself, what love is. I think people recognize that the spirit is a component of love," he said, "it's not all desire, there's something else. Love is there to help your loneliness, prayer is to end your sense of separation with the source of things."[4] The songs take a variety of positions. Different characters in different songs offer different instructions: his dead mother sends him back into the world in "Night Comes On"; the commanding officer sends him back to the battleground in "The Captain." Sometimes similar characters reappear in different songs in different contexts—"Heart with No Companion" has a mother with no son and a captain with no ship. "Hunter's Lullaby," sung in the persona of a wronged woman, the

---

* In 1995 it would also provide the title and words to an eponymous book of art and poetry, whose introduction describes "a deliriously romantic song by Leonard Cohen that is brilliantly visualized through the sensual paintings of Henri Matisse." None of the paintings depicted the Holocaust.

deserted wife and mother of his children, has echoes of Leonard's commentaries in *Death of a Lady's Man*.

The song "Hallelujah" contains a multiplicity of positions. It is a song about the reasons for songwriting (to attract women; to please God) and about the mechanics of songwriting (*"it goes like this, the fourth, the fifth . . ."*), about the power of the word and of the Word, about wanting sex, about having sex and about the war of the sexes. It is also a song about "total surrender [and] total affirmation." As Leonard explained it, "This world is full of conflicts and . . . things that cannot be reconciled, but there are moments when we can transcend the dualistic system and reconcile and embrace the whole mess. . . . Regardless of what the impossibility of the situation is, there is a moment when you open your mouth and you throw open your arms . . . and you just say 'Hallelujah! Blessed is the name.'"[5]

"Hallelujah" took Leonard five years to write. When Larry "Ratso" Sloman interviewed him in 1984, Leonard showed him a pile of notebooks, "book after book filled with verses for the song he then called 'The Other Hallelujah.'" Leonard kept around eighty of them and discarded many more. Even after the final edit, Leonard kept two different endings for "Hallelujah." One of them was downbeat:

> *It's not somebody who's seen the light*
> *It's a cold and it's a broken hallelujah*

The other had an almost "My Way" bravado:

> *Even though it all went wrong*
> *I'll stand before the Lord of Song*
> *With nothing on my tongue but*
> *Hallelujah*

Bob Dylan said he preferred the second version, which was the one Leonard finally used on the album, although he would return to the darker ending at various concerts. Leonard and Dylan had met up when they both found themselves in Paris and sat in a café, trading lyrics back and forth. Dylan showed Leonard his new song "I and I." Leonard asked how long it took him to write, and Dylan said fifteen minutes. Leonard showed Dylan "Hallelujah." Impressed, Dylan asked how long it took Leonard to write it. "A couple of years," said Leonard, too embarrassed to give the true answer. Sloman, who was a friend and admirer of both Leonard and Dylan, says, "I always had this kind of debate in my own head over who's the better songwriter. Bob had those amazing feats of imagination that I don't think anybody could ever come close to, these lines coming out of nowhere—'I wrote it in fifteen minutes in the back of a cab'—which would literally knock you over. But I think that as a formal, structural writer Leonard is the superior writer."

"Hallelujah" was the one song Leonard had played to Lissauer in his hotel room on which he did not use the Casio. "He played me some verses on the guitar in his six-eighths style," Lissauer remembers. "Kind of *chung-chiggie, chung, chung, chung-chung-chung chung,* you know, with chords that didn't really go anywhere. That song was one of the first things I started working with. I took it home and started to work on the chords to make it more gospel and give it a lift. We went in the studio right away, and I sat down at the grand piano and played and sang it for him in a big, grand, gospel way. Leonard said, 'That's fabulous.' So that's the version we did. His original version was really quite different."

Lissauer brought the band in. "I didn't want to make a power ballad out of it, so I told the drummer not to play with sticks but use brushes, nothing loud. I wanted it to be really exposed in the beginning, like the voice of God." Then Lissauer added a choir. "Not a big gospel choir but regular people, people singing 'hallelujah' like they would in church, people who weren't really singers, like the guys in the band, so that it had a feel of sincerity and it wasn't 'We Are the World.'" Among the women singers were Erin Dickins, Crissie Faith, Merle Miller and

Lani Groves (one of Stevie Wonder's backing vocalists) and a jazz singer and keyboard player making her first appearance with Leonard, Anjani Thomas. Leonard's own voice echoed as if he were singing in a cathedral. "I remember being begged by Leonard for reverb," says Leanne Ungar. "Leonard always liked reverb." There is certainly plenty of it on *Various Positions,* on which Leonard's already deepened voice sounds cavernous. When they finished recording "Hallelujah," Lissauer played it back, and everybody, he says, was stunned. "We were like, 'Whoa, this is a standard. This is an important song.'"

Dylan had told Leonard that he thought Leonard's songs were becoming "like prayers," and none more so that the album's closing song, "If It Be Your Will." It was, Leonard said, "an old prayer that it came to me to rewrite."[6] The first draft was written in the Algonquin Hotel in New York in December 1980, shortly after Hanukkah was over and his children had gone back to their mother. It is a song about surrendering, resigning completely to the will of another, whether it be to *"speak no more and my voice be still"* or *"sing to you from this broken hill."* It is a prayer for conciliation and unity, its last verse beseeching, *"draw us near / And bind us tight / All your children here."* And, like *Book of Mercy,* it is a prayer for mercy:

> *Let your mercy spill*
> *On all these burning hearts in hell*
> *If it be your will*
> *to make us well*

It is an intensely moving song, intimate and fragile, and sung in a voice that had deepened with age. Lissauer noted that it had dropped four semitones since he and Leonard had last worked together. "It was a heavenly recording," Lissauer says. "Jennifer Warnes came in and sang with him. Just one take." Leonard was very pleased with it. Asked in an interview in 1994 which song he wished he had written, Leonard answered, "'If It Be Your Will.' And I wrote it."[7]

The whole album, according to Lissauer, had been easy to record. "The boys in the band weren't drinking or getting high, nor was Leonard, and Leanne Ungar is very straight; I was probably doing some coke at the time at two in the morning because I was working so much and staying up longer than my body could do on its own, but it was very straight-ahead." Yet it had taken a long time, "about seven months, because Leonard would keep leaving for a couple of months." This time, unlike on *Songs for Rebecca*, Leonard would come back, and they would work on one or two more songs. One reason Leonard would leave was to write. "He was still shy a song or two for an album," says Lissauer, "and he was working at that as we went along."

Things might have been going well in the studio, but in his room at the Royalton Hotel, Leonard was tearing his hair out. "I found myself in my underwear, crawling along the carpet, unable to nail a verse, and knowing that I had a recording session and knowing that I could get by with what I had, but that I'm not going to be able to do it."[8] Part of the problem was perfectionism; it was not that Leonard literally could not write but that what he wrote was not good enough. "I had to resurrect not just my career," he said, "but myself and my confidence as a writer and singer."[9] Among the songs attempted and abandoned for the album were "Nylon and Silk"—so called, says Lissauer, "because he was playing a nylon guitar and I was playing some silky synthesizer sounds. I don't think he ever had any lyrics to it"— and also "Anthem," a very different early version of the song that would finally appear two albums later on *The Future*. Due to a technical problem, the intro to "Anthem" was accidentally erased by a technician. "I'd thought of a few different ways to fix it," says Leanne Ungar, "but Leonard decided that meant the song was not ready to be recorded yet."

When Leonard and Lissauer heard the final mixes of the album, they were both excited. Leonard was happy with the modern sound, the subtle arrangements and the smooth, high-tech production.

"There were some exquisite moments on it," says Lissauer, "'Hallelu-jah,' 'If It Be Your Will.' I was like, 'This is special. This is *it*. This will be the record that's going to do it for Leonard in the States.'" Leonard and Marty Machat took the tape to Columbia and played it to Walter Yetnikoff, the head of the music division. He did not like it. Leonard remembers, "Walter Yetnikoff said, 'Leonard, we know you're great, we just don't know if you're any good.'" They neglected to inform him that they had decided against releasing his new album in the U.S.

How did you learn that Various Positions *would not get an American release?*

"I happened to pick up a catalog of their recent releases and I just looked through it to see a picture of my record in the pamphlet. I couldn't locate it, so I thought there must be a typographical error. They didn't have to tell me why. From their point of view, the market was so limited that it didn't justify the distribution machinery that would have to go into operation."

Had you resigned yourself by that time to not having an audience in the U.S.?

"I thought they were making a mistake. I thought that there was *an audience in the United States and Canada. What I didn't understand at that time—because I thought that if they had bothered to promote it, the work would have sold more widely—but what I understand now, very thoroughly, is that the dollar they spend on promoting me can much more profitably be spent on promoting another singer, so I completely understand their strategy and I have no quarrel with it. I don't think I suffered any sense of remorse or bitterness. Most of the energy was devoted to trying to find some little label that would put it out."*

"When Leonard told me he'd had that meeting with Yetnikoff and he wouldn't release the album," says Ratso Sloman, "I was so infuriated that I literally started hounding Yetnikoff. I would go to all these Columbia events, like Dylan's, and go up to him and say, 'The nerve of you not releasing Leonard's album, shame on you.'" He wrote in a 1985 article for *Heavy Metal* magazine that Columbia had sent "Leonard's new kid straight to the showers. Aborted in the USA, as 'the Boss' would say. But, as Dylan told me a few months ago in the studio as he was finishing up his newest Columbia LP, 'Somebody'll put out Leonard's record here. They have to.'" As for John Lissauer, he was devastated, he says, "because I knew how good the whole album was. So I said, 'Okay, I've had it with the music industry, they're a bunch of idiots,' and I quit." He says he was never paid for producing the album.

In retrospect *Various Positions* can be viewed as a stepping-stone between the timelessness and guitar-ballad style of Leonard's earlier albums and the slick electronics and almost anthemic sound of those that followed. The minor-key melody of "Dance Me to the End of Love" has a familiar Old European romance and gravity but also the modernity and jarring novelty of the tinny Casio. Where once there might have been dark, Old Testament lyrics, sung by Leonard alone, there are the transcendent prayer "If It Be Your Will," sung serenely with Jennifer Warnes, and the hymn "Hallelujah," sung with a choir of voices and a synthesizer.

The album was released worldwide, excluding America, in January 1985. Unusually, it was largely ignored by the UK music press. *NME* noted the "sad gaiety" that hung over much of it, "the maidenly correctness" of Jennifer Warnes's harmonies and the album's overall resemblance to "a French movie soundtrack, or even Scott Walker in his Brel period. . . . If the title proposes another thesis of sexual sneering, the songs are complex but peaceful reports from a wearied heart."[10] *Sounds* magazine reviewed its first and only single, "Dance Me to the End of Love," describing its chorus as "inspiration copulating with commerciality" and predicting a hit.[11] It flopped. The album did not fare much better. In the UK it made it to No. 52, one of Leonard's lowest chart positions. With the exception of Norway and Sweden, Leonard's first album in five years did remarkably little across Europe, although it did make the lower half of the Top 100 in Canada.

The *Various Positions* tour began on January 31, 1985, in Germany—a lengthy tour with seventy-seven concerts. Leonard, who had turned fifty a few months earlier, had no desire to go back on the road but dutifully dusted down his suit. John Lissauer could not go with him as his new wife was expecting their first child, but he put a band together for him: John Crowder, Ron Getman and Richard Crooks, who had played on the album, and Mitch Watkins, a veteran of Leonard's 1979–80 tours. All it lacked was a keyboard player and backing singers. "I thought of Anjani," says Lissauer, "killing two birds with one stone."

Anjani Thomas, then in her early twenties, was a singer and piano player who had played in a jazz trio in her native Hawaii. She had recently moved to New York, and Lissauer was one of the first people in the music business she met. He had hired her to sing a background vocal on "Hallelujah" after the main recording was finished, and two months later invited her to audition for Leonard's tour. "So I went to John's loft on Thirteenth Street," Anjani remembers. "I got there first, then Leonard arrived. I remember John opening the door and I looked down—I was very shy then; I'd just moved to the big city from a little island in Hawaii, and I really knew nothing about Leonard or his work and stature. I saw his black shoes first. As my eyes traveled up I saw the black pants and the black belt and the black shirt and the black jacket, the black bolo tie, and I thought, 'Wow.' Where I come from the men wear aloha shirts and shorts. I'd never seen anyone so present in black like that before. He was very nice, shook my hand, and I played him a song and he said, 'Well great, now I know you can sing and play. You've got the job.'"

The European leg of the tour included, for the first time, Poland—the People's Republic of Poland was not well-known for welcoming Western pop musicians. The four dates had been a last-minute addition resulting from the efforts of an independent promoter who was a Leonard Cohen fan. Leonard's name was known in Poland largely through Maciej Zembaty, a comedian, writer and popular radio personality who had been translating and singing Leonard's songs—more than sixty of them—since the early seventies, and who had been imprisoned in 1981 for organizing a festival of songs banned by the regime. Zembaty's Polish version of Leonard's adaptation of "The Partisan" had become an unofficial anthem of the Solidarity movement. The concerts were instant sellouts (the first show was delayed by two hours while police at the front door confiscated thousands of forged tickets) and the fans so spirited that Anjani was given her own bodyguard, a man previously assigned to protect the pope.

Leonard, with his Lithuanian ancestry, appeared touched by his visit to Poland. He talked onstage about the "thousands of synagogues and Jewish communities which were wiped out in a few months" during the war. But when word reached him that Lech Walesa, the leader of Solidarity, had requested that Leonard appear onstage with him, he declined, perhaps out of concern for the promoter who had fought hard to get him there, or likely his usual disinclination to take political sides. During that Warsaw concert Leonard also said, "I don't know which side everybody's on anymore, and I don't really care. There is a moment when we have to transcend the side we're on and understand that we are creatures of a higher order. It doesn't mean that I don't wish you courage in your struggle. There are on both sides of this struggle men of goodwill. That is important to remember—some struggling for freedom, some struggling for safety. In solemn testimony of that unbroken faith which binds a generation one to another, I sing this song." It was "If It Be Your Will."

Anjani was the sole woman on the tour (there was no second female vocalist; John Crowder, Ron Getman and Mitch Watkins also sang harmonies) and also the youngest member of the band. Neither of these things was a new experience for her, but a tour of this size was. "A couple of times on that tour I'd run into Leonard at the hotel sauna, and we spoke about spiritual matters, and that was a bit of a relief, you know, connecting with a kindred soul on the path."

Anjani had started meditating when she was sixteen years old, after a couple of her friends died from drug overdoses. "I knew that if I stayed in music and kept on doing drugs that that could very well be a possibility for me. I had to go in another direction completely, so I went off on a spiritual trek. I was young enough to believe that if you put in the time, you'll become enlightened. It didn't happen, but it certainly made my life miserable on the way. I also saw that Leonard was having a tough go of it on a certain level—because everyone on that spiritual journey is having a tough go of it, for the most part."

Before leaving for the tour, Leonard had told Ratso Sloman, "Look, nobody enters a Zen meditation hall to affirm his health. You enter because you have a doubt and because you want to study how the mind arises, so they make you sit still for seven days, and finally you get so bored and fatigued with your mind that you might be lucky enough to let it drop for a second. As soon as that mind is at rest, the Mysteries manifest as reality. It ain't no mystery." Leonard also told Sloman that this was the first time in his life that he'd had to work, to support his kids, but that it was the thought of his kids that kept him going. "Other than that," Leonard said, "it's bleak, it's bleak."

When the European tour ended on March 24, they flew back to the U.S. to play a handful of East Coast concerts. At the Boston show, at a safe distance from Poland, Leonard dedicated "The Partisan" to the Solidarity movement. Crossing the border to Canada for a whirlwind tour, Leonard learned while he was there that *Night Magic*, his musical film collaboration with Lewis Furey, had won a Genie Award for Best Original Song, "Angel Eyes."[*] The tour continued in Australia, then returned to America, the West Coast this time, for shows in San Francisco and Los Angeles. Then it was back to Europe again for fifteen more shows, plus one in Jerusalem.

---

* The soundtrack was released as a double album in France in 1985, where the film was also an official selection at the Cannes Film Festival.

It was the midsummer of 1985 when Leonard was finally home in L.A. In his still-barely-furnished half of the duplex, he unpacked his case, opened a bottle of wine and heated up a TV dinner.

———————

Various Positions was finally released in America in January 1986, on the tiny Passport label. It did not trouble the U.S. charts. But the Lord works in mysterious ways, and particularly so in the miraculous story of "Hallelujah." John Lissauer had told the record label that he thought it should be a single; "I thought it the best single I'd ever made for a serious artist. But they said, 'What *is* this? We don't even know what it is.' 'Well, it's kind of an anthemic thing,' I said." They told him, "It will never get off the ground." Some twenty-five years after its first appearance on *Various Positions*, "Hallelujah" would become, as *Maclean's* magazine described it, "the closest thing pop music has to a sacred text."

In recent years a number of essays and lengthy articles, as well as an hour-long BBC documentary, have appeared across the world on the subject of this one Leonard Cohen song. At the time of the writing of this book, "Hallelujah" has been covered by a remarkable assortment of artists, more than three hundred of them. Some interpretations favored one ending of the song over another. John Cale went so far as to ask Leonard for all the verses he had written so that he could compile his own version; Leonard offered him fifteen. "Subsequent covers tinkered here and there with the words to the point where the song became protean, a set of possibilities rather than a fixed text," wrote Bryan Appleyard in the *Sunday Times*. "But only two possibilities predominated: either this was a wistful, ultimately feelgood song or it was an icy, bitter commentary on the futility of human relations."[12] He forgot to mention a third category, "the hallelujah of the orgasm," as Jeff Buckley described it onstage, although arguably this might fit into the first possibility. But Appleyard was right; "Hallelujah" would become a kind of all-purpose, ecumenical/secular hymn for the new millennium. As k. d. lang remarked, "It just has so much fodder, so much density, it can be deep, simple, mean a lot of things to different people, there's so much in it."[13] Also, as with many of Leonard's songs, the melody's spaciousness was generous to people who chose to cover it.

Among them were Bob Dylan, Neil Diamond, Willie Nelson, Bono, Hawaiian ukulele master Jake Shimabukuro and San Franciscan a capella group Conspiracy of Beards. Rufus Wainwright sang it on the soundtrack album to the animated film *Shrek*.* Justin Timberlake and Matt Morris from *The Mickey Mouse Club* sang it in the *Hope for Haiti* telethon. Jeff Buckley's transcendent version, recorded on his 1994 album *Grace*, was used on the soundtracks of numerous American television series, including *ER*, *Scrubs*, *The OC*, *The West Wing* and *Ugly Betty*. "Hallelujah" was sung in the finale of *American Idol*, where the judge Simon Cowell declared it (specifically the Buckley rendition; fans of the song take distinct sides) one of his favorite songs of all time. In similar fashion, it made the finale—it's a song made for finales—of the UK TV talent show *The X Factor*, where the big, gospel version by the young winner Alexandra Burke became the fastest-selling Internet download in European history.

Burke's version topped the UK singles chart over the Christmas of 2008, prompting protest action from outraged Jeff Buckley fans that resulted in the late singer's "Hallelujah" taking over the No. 1 position and pushing Burke down to No. 2. In the aftershock, Leonard's original version rose to No. 36—a trinity of "Hallelujahs" in one chart at the same time. Leonard's version also resurfaced the following year in the movie *The Watchmen*, providing the background music to a sex scene between two superheroes. For most who knew the song, it brought a wry smile to the face. But one exasperated journal-

---

* John Cale's version was used during the movie itself, having previously appeared in the more sympathetic setting of *Basquiat* (1996).

ist called for a moratorium on the use of "Hallelujah" on film and TV soundtracks. "I kind of feel the same way," said Leonard in a CBC TV interview. "I think it's a good song, but too many people sing it." He couldn't help mentioning that there was also "a mild sense of revenge that arose in [his] heart" when he recalled that his American record label had refused to release it. "They didn't think it was good enough."[14]

––––––

Jennifer Warnes, who had signed to Arista as a solo artist, had been talking to Clive Davis, the head of the record label, about the new album she wanted to make. On Leonard's 1979 tour, on which Warnes and Roscoe Beck became a couple, they had the idea of making an album of her singing only Leonard Cohen songs, which Beck would produce. "I could hear it before it became a reality," remembers Beck. "I specifically recall watching Leonard and Jennifer doing their duet on 'Joan of Arc' every night, and visualizing it with Jennifer singing the lead." Davis, who had been the head of Columbia Records when Leonard was signed by John Hammond, seemed to hold much the same view of the marketability of Leonard's songs in America as had Walter Yetnikoff, the man who succeeded him in the job. Davis turned her down. But Warnes saw it as "a record that had to be made"—not just for herself, but for Leonard. "Leonard had years of mixed reviews and I think he had lost faith."[15] Warnes, on the other hand, had enjoyed considerable commercial success with her duets with Joe Cocker ("Up Where We Belong") and Bill Medley ("[I've Had] The Time of My Life"). Says Beck, "We would have given our dying breath to finish that record." Finally, they found a small independent label that was willing to release it and started work.

Around forty musicians appeared on Warnes's *Famous Blue Raincoat*. They included David Lindley, who had played on Leonard's first album; Sharon Robinson, who sang with Warnes on the 1979 tour; guitarist Stevie Ray Vaughan; R & B singer Bobby King; and

composer, arranger and keyboard player Van Dyke Parks. As the recording progressed, Beck would call Leonard and update him on how
it was going. He told Leonard they had recorded the Cohen-Warnes
cowritten "Song of Bernadette" and asked if he might have any more
new songs they could hear. "He played me his working copy of 'First
We Take Manhattan' over the phone. I taped it and we came up with
our own arrangement, a bluesier version. As soon as I heard it I knew I
wanted Stevie Ray Vaughan to play on it." Beck knew the celebrated
young blues rock guitarist from Austin, where Passenger was based:
"Stevie and I were friends from the age of twenty; he used to sit in
with Passenger quite often and I used to sit in with his band. He was
in L.A. for the Grammy Awards, so I tracked him down to play on the
song." Vaughan was performing at the Greek Theatre; Beck invited
Leonard and Jennifer to go with him. "They had never seen him live.
Jennifer was amazed, as was Leonard. I remember him commenting,
'Now that's what I've been trying to get my guitar players to do for
years: make the guitar talk.'"

Beck played Jennifer Warnes's record for Leonard, and Leonard
listened in silence. Impressed, Leonard began to take a much closer
interest in the album. He sang a duet with Warnes on "Joan of Arc."
He also gave her another of his new, unreleased songs, "Ain't No
Cure for Love," whose title he had come up with after reading about
L.A.'s AIDS crisis.

Famous Blue Raincoat was released in 1987. It featured nine
songs,* including a few that Judy Collins had previously covered
("Bird on the Wire," "Joan of Arc," "Famous Blue Raincoat") and
a few that Warnes—like Collins in the past—would release before
Leonard had recorded his own versions. It was to some degree a tribute album, but really it was a Jennifer Warnes album whose songs all
happened to have the same writer. Her impeccable vocal brought
out the lyricism of Leonard's songs. By removing the factor that

---

* There were four more on the 2007 twentieth-anniversary reissue.

some people seemed to have problems with—Leonard's voice—
they sounded smoother, more melodious, and with Beck's polished
production, more contemporary. "She transformed grappa into
Chardonnay," said the review in *Saturday Night*. "A perfect elixir for
mid-Eighties audiences."[16]

Warnes's album sold three quarters of a million copies in the U.S.
It went gold in Canada and spawned a single, "Ain't No Cure for
Love," that was a hit in both the adult-contemporary and the country music charts. The artwork on the inner sleeve was a drawing
that Leonard had made: a hand—Leonard's—holding out a torch to
Warnes, with the caption "Jenny sings Lenny." He was happy and
grateful to pass the torch on to her. With *Famous Blue Raincoat*, he
had finally succeeded in hiding his own voice and giving his songs
entirely over to the female voice.

Leonard was writing songs for his own new album. Once again it
was a slow and painful process. Over a glass of brandy, he complained
to Roshi how difficult it was and asked him what he ought to do. Roshi answered, "You look up at the moon, you open your mouth and
you sing." So Leonard sang, recording as he went along over a span of
a year and a half, running up studio bills in three different countries
as he bounced back and forth between his lives in Paris, Montreal
and L.A., leaving a paper trail of abandoned words as he went. He
was happy to hear, as he had been before, that the songs he had managed to write in the past were getting on without him. Aside from
Jennifer Warnes, Nick Cave had covered "Avalanche" on his first album with the Bad Seeds. Leonard's children were telling him that he
had become something of a cult figure among younger musicians: Ian
McCulloch and Suzanne Vega were singing his praises in interviews,
and the British band Sisters of Mercy, having taken their name from
one of his songs, had nicknamed their drum machine Doktor Avalanche. Leonard also learned that there was another musical based on
his work being made in New York, called *Sincerely, L. Cohen*, its title
taken from the closing words of "Famous Blue Raincoat."

It was intriguing, this resurgence of a song that Leonard had always had problems with—that he had "never been satisfied with, never really nailed the lyric, always felt there was something about the song that was unclear."[17] His mother had liked the melody though. "I remember playing the tune for her, in her kitchen, and her perking up her ears while she was doing something else and saying, 'That's a nice tune.'"[18] And the song had held up and served him well, just like the old Burberry raincoat that inspired it. It seemed a lifetime ago that he had bought the coat in London, when he was a twenty-five-year-old writing his first novel and sleeping on a cot in a cold Hampstead boardinghouse. A girl Leonard had pursued during his first London winter had told him that it made him look like a spider—which might, he thought, be why she refused to go to Greece with him. "It hung more heroically when I took out the lining," he wrote in his liner notes to *Greatest Hits* (1975), "and achieved glory when the frayed sleeves were repaired with a little leather. Things were clear. I knew how to dress in those days." The coat was stolen from the loft where Marianne had lived when she visited New York, while he was recording his first album. Leonard said, "I wasn't wearing it very much toward the end."

In September 1986, while in Paris visiting Dominique Issermann, Leonard recorded a new song called "Take This Waltz." The lyrics were Leonard's English adaptation (assisted by a Spanish-speaking Costa Rican girlfriend) of a poem by Federico Garcia Lorca. It was for a compilation album, *Poetas en Nueva York*, that would mark the fiftieth anniversary of Lorca's death. It had been hard work—it took a hundred and fifty hours, Leonard said—but it was more than a translation, it was a poem in itself, and one that seemed to reflect Leonard as much as Lorca. For example, Leonard rendered Lorca's macabre image of a forest of dried pigeons as "a tree where doves go to die." After recording the song, Leonard flew to Granada to attend a gala in Lorca's honor. Then he flew back to the U.S. to take a role in the TV detective series *Miami Vice.* Over the years the program had invited an eclectic list of guest stars, such as Frank Zappa and James Brown, to make cameo appearances. Leonard's character, the French head of Interpol, was on screen for barely a minute, murmuring in a dark, French manner into a telephone, but it had the effect that Leonard desired when he took it on: it impressed his now-teenage offspring.

Leonard's relationship with Dominique, though, was going the way of all flesh. In 1987, back in Paris again, he wrote in a poem, titled "My Honor":*

> *My honor is in bad shape*
> *I'm crawling at a woman's feet*
> *She doesn't give an inch.*
> *I look good for fifty-two*
> *but fifty-two is fifty-two*
> *I'm not even a Zen master. . . .*

He was nothing more than

> *that asshole in a blue summer suit*
> *who couldn't take it any longer*

"Then I broke down," said Leonard, "and went to a monastery. . . . I thought, I don't have to do a record any more, I'll be a monk."[19]

Leonard had gone to the monastery to be nowhere and to be no one. He had gone to sit in this austere place for hour upon hour with no goal. It said in the literature that if he were able to sit goal-less for long enough, all the versions of himself would arise and, having aris-

---

* Published in the book *You Do Not Have to Love Me,* 1996, with lithographs by Josette Trépanier.

en, decide there was nothing to stick around for and take off, leaving only perfect peace. He had gone to be with Roshi, whom he loved, and who both cared deeply and deeply didn't care who Leonard was. Leonard had gone to work hard, to bang nails, to fix and mend things, at least physically. Roshi knew how much Leonard liked austerity, solitariness and work. He instructed him to go and find a tennis court, and play.

Eighteen

The Places Where
I Used to Play

Iggy Pop has a story about Leonard Cohen. Iggy was in Los Angeles, recording an album, when one night Leonard phoned. "Leonard said, 'Come over, I've got a personal ad from a girl who says she wants a lover who will combine the raw energy of Iggy Pop with the elegant wit of Leonard Cohen. I think we should reply to her as a team.'" Iggy said, "'Leonard, I can't, I'm married, you're going to have to do this yourself.' I guess he did," says Iggy. "I don't know if he got laid."

Iggy Pop was curious as to the outcome of a reply you sent a woman seeking love through a personal ad.

"[Smiles] As I remember it, I bumped into Iggy at a session being produced by Don Was, a friend of mine, and I showed him the clipping that someone had sent me from a San Francisco newspaper. We decided to reply, and to certify its authenticity, Don took a Polaroid of Iggy and myself sitting together in my kitchen. We spoke to the young woman—at least I spoke to her—on the telephone. But there was no personal involvement."

Leonard surely felt an empathy with this woman who named herself "Fearless" and whose ideals, when it came to romantic partners,
seemed almost as formidable as his own. If nothing else, answering
the ad with Iggy was an exercise in making the impossible possible—
if only for a moment, and for someone other than himself. Leonard
had been living with impossibilities for some time, one of them being the idea that he might ever finish another album. For more than
three years he had been writing, unwriting and rewriting songs, then,
having finally deemed something ready to record, after listening to
himself singing it, he would decide that it did not sound honest and
needed to be rewritten yet again. Leonard had been serious when he
spoke about never wanting to make another album, and the thought
of giving it up and going to a monastery was certainly a possibility.
However arduous that existence might be, it had nothing on the hard
labor that songwriting had become.

Various Positions, the album he had hoped would resurrect his
career and his confidence as a songwriter and help take care of his
financial responsibilities, had done none of these things. It took "a
great deal of will to keep your work straight," he told Mat Snow in the
Guardian, but "with all the will in the world you can't keep your life
straight. Because you're too much of an asshole. . . . As you get older,
you get very interested in your work, because that's where you can
refine your character, that's where you can order your world. You're
stuck with the consequences of your actions, but in your work you
can go back."[1] He had left behind him, he said, a "shipwreck of ten
or fifteen years of broken families and hotel rooms for some kind of
shining idea that my voice was important, that I had a meaning in the
cosmos. . . . Well, after enough lonely nights you don't care whether
you have a meaning in the cosmos or not."[2]

But still he worked. He lived alone and he recorded alone—no
musicians, no producer, just an engineer—slowly and painstakingly,
at a glacial pace. Leonard was spending long periods in Montreal,

so several of his new songs were recorded there, in Studio Tempo. Anjani Thomas—who by coincidence was also living in Montreal at that time; her boyfriend, Ian Terry, was the studio's head engineer— added backing vocals to some of them. "It really was a solo affair," said Leonard, "because I had the conception very clearly in mind, I knew exactly the way I wanted it to sound, and I was using a lot of synthesised instruments."[3] But by 1987, Leonard had reached a point where he could use an outside pair of ears. Having been impressed by his work on *Famous Blue Raincoat*, he called Roscoe Beck and asked him to book a studio in L.A.

Beck remembers the first time he heard the song "First We Take Manhattan," which Leonard had given Jennifer Warnes for her album. What stood out was its "harmonic sophistication. It was no longer just folk songs on guitar. Now that Leonard was writing on keyboards, he was writing from a different perspective." Leonard had become used to playing his new songs alone and was keen to retain as much of that spare, unembellished feel as possible on the album. "He wasn't sure at first whether we were going to hire a band," Beck says. "I think it was a mutual decision not to and to record them as they were, just as he was playing them on his keyboard." Leonard had upgraded from his ninety-nine-dollar Casio to a Technics keyboard, but it was still a primitive synthesizer with no individual outputs, making it a challenge to record. The engineers, technicians, keyboard players and track performers listed in the credits far outnumber the conventional musicians. There were drum machines, synthesized strings and push-button cha-cha rhythms, as well as some of the most singular keyboard playing to have ever made it onto a major-label album, such as the proudly plinked one-finger solo on "Tower of Song." Toward the end they brought in "a few last people to sweeten it," says Beck, including Sneaky Pete Kleinow on pedal steel on "I Can't Forget," John Bilezikjian on oud on "Everybody Knows," and Raffi Hakopian on violin on "Take This Waltz," the song Leonard had recorded in

Paris for Lorca's fiftieth-anniversary album. Jennifer Warnes came in to sing on several tracks, including the catchy, retro-pop "*dee-do dum-dum*"s in "Tower of Song."

Eight songs had been completed, but an album that was eight songs and forty minutes long looked a good deal more undersized on compact disc than it would have done on a vinyl LP. So Leonard tried for a ninth. He recorded a new version of "Anthem" with Beck, and strings and overdubs were added before Leonard once again pulled the song. They also recorded an early, very different version of "Waiting for the Miracle." This Leonard liked. He called Beck to say how happy he was with it. Three weeks later, he called again to say that he had rewritten the lyrics and wanted to redo the vocal. In the studio, Beck discovered he had also rewritten the melody, "and it didn't match up with the track [they'd] cut." They kept working at the song, long into the night. "We cut several vocals until he got very tired. Finally he said, 'I'm done, comp it'" (meaning, make a master vocal out of the best bits of his various vocal takes). Leonard found a place to lie down and sleep while Beck worked. "Just as I had it together, Leonard woke up, walked into the control room and said, 'Well, let's hear it.' I played it for him and he said, 'I hate it.' He left and that was that."

The song went through several more changes before it was finished. At one point Leonard gave it to Sharon Robinson—although they had not worked together since the 1980 tour, they had remained close friends—who came back with "a completely different version," says Beck, "that I played guitar on. I really liked Sharon's version, but that didn't end up being the final version either" (which was the one that would appear on his 1992 album *The Future*). Another Cohen-Robinson cowrite made it onto this album. On a visit to her house, he had handed her a sheet of verses—a litany of world-weary wisdom and cynicism—and asked her if she could write a melody. She did, and it became the song "Everybody Knows."

What struck Beck most strongly when working with Leonard on the album was the change in his voice. "I thought, 'Wow, Leonard has found a whole new place to sing from.' The baritone element in his voice was always there—on the song 'Avalanche,' for instance, he's singing deep in his chest—but here he was really making use of it and his singing voice was becoming more narrative." His delivery was laconic, almost recitative, like an old French *chansonnier* who had mistakenly stumbled into a disco. It was urbane and unhurried; as one UK critic would put it, Leonard lingered on every word "like a kerb crawler."[4] His voice was as deep and dry, sly and beguiling, as his songs. His new album had everything. It was polished and mannered but very human, it was brutally honest but very accessible and its songs covered all the angles: sex, sophistication, love, longing and humor—particularly humor.

> *I was born like this*
> *I had no choice*
> *I was born with the gift*
> *of a golden voice*

"TOWER OF SONG," *I'M YOUR MAN*

The humor had always been there, but many had failed to see it—it was dark and ironic and generally aimed at himself. But the gags were never as overt as on this album.

I'm Your Man was released in February 1988 in the UK and Europe and two months later in the U.S. and Canada. The title track presents the prophet as lounge lizard, falling to his knees, howling at the sky, trying to figure out what it is that women want and ready to give it to them in whatever form they might require. While "Ain't No Cure for Love," a sing-along about love, sex and God, was inspired by reports of the AIDS crisis, it was imbued with Leonard's own take on love: that it is a lethal wound that a man can no more avoid than Jesus could the Cross. "I Can't Forget," which started life as a song about the exodus of the Jews from Egypt, has Leonard moving on once again but unable now to remember his motive, having spent so long living in the myth of himself. "Everybody Knows" is an infectious paean to pessimism. "First We Take Manhattan" is very likely the only Eurodisco song to reference the war between the sexes and the Holocaust. "Tower of Song" is about the hard, solitary, captive life of a writer (going so far as to evoke a concentration camp in the line "They're moving us tomorrow to that tower down the track") but substitutes self-mockery for the usual self-indulgence of this type of song: he was still "crazy for love" but now he ached "in the places where [he] used to play" and in spite of all his hard work, none of it was of any significance to women, to God or even to pop-music posterity; his writing room was still a hundred floors below Hank Williams."

The photo on the front sleeve shows Leonard dressed in a smart pin-striped suit, wearing big French-film-star sunglasses, his hair slicked back, his face as unsmiling and impenetrable as that of a Mafia don. In his hand, where a gun might be, or a microphone, is a half-eaten banana. It was shot at the former Ford Motor Company assembly plant in Wilmington, California, a gigantic windowed room with a vast steel-girdered indoor parking lot that is often used as a movie location. Jennifer Warnes was there shooting the video for her version of "First We Take Manhattan," in which Leonard had agreed to appear. Sharon Weisz, the publicist for Warnes's record label, was on the set, shooting stills, when the steel doors of the truck-sized elevator opened and Leonard stepped out with the banana. "I pivoted and took one picture of him," says Weisz, "and forgot about it. When I got back the proof sheet and saw it, I thought it was really funny and had a print made and sent it to him. A few weeks later he called and said, 'What would you think if I put it on the cover of my album?' I didn't even know he was making an album. I asked him what he was calling it, and he said *I'm Your Man*, and I started laughing uncontrollably." Although the pose was a lucky accident, Leonard could not fail to recognize how perfectly it summed up the heroics and absurdity that went into the album's creation.

I'm Your Man rebranded Leonard, not least among younger fans, from dark, tortured poet to officially cool. Although it sounded different from Leonard's early albums, it had that feeling of instant familiarity, rightness and durability that makes for a classic. It was preceded in January 1988 by a single, "First We Take Manhattan"— one of the two songs on the album already familiar to many listeners thanks to the success of Jennifer Warnes's album. *Famous Blue Raincoat* had definitely helped pave the way for Leonard's eighth album (in America in particular) and *I'm Your Man* sped along it, propelled by its more upbeat songs and contemporary sound. The album was a success—Leonard's biggest since the early seventies and biggest in America since his debut. It made No. 1 in several European countries, went platinum in Norway, gold in Canada and silver in the UK, where it sold three hundred thousand copies before it was released in the U.S. It even sold well in America. Leonard waggishly attributed this to the payola he sent the marketing department of Columbia in New York.

It was a scheme he hatched up with Sharon Weisz, whom he had asked to do publicity for the album. "He had kind of an odd relationship with the record label, since they had refused to put out his previous record, *Various Positions,* and he was very cynical about it," says Weisz. "So I was trying to figure out how he was going to work with these people and how receptive they were going to be to a new record by him." They did not appear overenthused, judging by the poor turnout of people from Columbia Records at a party in his honor in New York, where the international division presented him with a Crystal Globe award for sales of more than five million albums outside the U.S. "From that point on, it sort of became the two of us against the world," says Weisz. She came up with a list of names of the various Columbia promotion reps across the U.S., and Leonard sent each of them a hand-signed letter.

"Good morning," Leonard typed on a plain, gray sheet of paper, dated April 1, 1988. "I don't quite know how this is done so please bear with me. I have a new record, I'M YOUR MAN, coming out next week. It is already a hit in Europe and I'm on my way there now for a major concert tour. I know I can count on your support for this new record in the U.S., and if you can make a couple of phone calls on my behalf, I would really appreciate it. I've enclosed a couple of bucks to cover the calls. Thank you in advance for your help," the letter concluded. "Regards, Leonard Cohen. PS. There's more where this came from." ("We went back and forth on whether the dollar bills should be brand-new or really old," Weisz remembers, "and we settled for the kind that looked really mangy.")

I'm Your Man was lauded by critics on both sides of the Atlantic. John Rockwell in the *New York Times* called it "a masterpiece"; Mark Cooper wrote in UK rock magazine *Q* that it was Leonard's best album since the midseventies. Leonard had perfected "the art of being Leonard Cohen . . . the usual gorgeous melodies and an ageing poet taking himself very seriously, until he twinkles."[5] "All the major critics of the era reviewed it," says Weisz, "and the reviews were extraordinary." Those who seemed to think that Leonard had gone away hailed it as a comeback.

On February 7 Leonard left for Europe on a promotional tour to do interviews. There was great anticipation for the concert tour, which was due to begin in April. Leonard went back to Los Angeles to prepare for it, but there was a serious problem. His manager was dying. Marty Machat was gravely ill with lung cancer, and although it was clear to almost everyone else that his condition was terminal, Machat was convinced he was going to pull through. In early March, with only weeks to go before the tour began, Leonard was getting anxious. A large sum of money had been paid into Machat & Machat's attorney account as a tour advance, and Leonard needed access to it. He called Marty. Avril, Marty's lover, picked up the phone.

Says Steven Machat, "Dad was very quiet, very shy, Leonard was very quiet, very dark, and in the middle of their relationship was Avril." Machat dismisses his father's romantic partner as "a woman who Dad gave money to, to do Leonard's PR" and someone whom he "kept around because he thought Leonard Cohen wanted her around." Steven Machat did not like Leonard either. "I never liked him from the moment go; he never looks you in the eyes, ever. He plays victim." But Marty Machat, he says, loved Leonard and would have done more for him than for anyone. Since this presumably included his son, it might not have helped relations between Steven and Leonard. "My dad would get on the phone with Leonard. My dad didn't give a fuck about anyone, he wanted the money, but Leonard he would sit there with, he'd listen to Leonard. If Leonard got sick, my dad would be upset—'Oh, Leonard's got a cold.' It was interesting. When Leonard went to Israel making believe he was going to fight in the war, all of a sudden my dad rediscovered that he was of Jewish blood."

Steven knew that his father did not have long to live. In his mind he saw vultures circling and among them he included Leonard. But Leonard, on the eve of a major tour for what was potentially the most commercial album of his career, was doing his best to take care of business. Steven Machat says that Leonard turned to him for help and that, for his father's sake, he agreed. Perhaps he did, although the evidence seems to indicate that Leonard turned to lawyers for advice and to women for help. With Marty's blessing, Avril went with Leonard to the bank to withdraw the money he needed. Kelley Lynch, Marty's secretary and assistant, stepped up and offered to take care of administrative matters for the tour. When Marty Machat died on March 19, 1988, aged sixty-seven, Lynch took various files on Leonard from the offices of Machat & Machat that the lawyers said could be taken legally, including documents relating to the publishing company that Marty Machat had set up for Leonard. Lynch took the files to L.A., where she set up shop and began making herself as indispensable to Leonard as Marty had once been. At one point Leonard and Kelley became lovers. Eventually she became his manager.

Meanwhile, Roscoe Beck had been putting together Leonard's touring band. Leonard had asked him to come along as his musical director, but Beck was scheduled to produce albums by Eric Johnson and Ute Lemper. So Leonard went on the road with a band made up of Steve Meador and John Bilezikjian, both of whom had played on Leonard's 1979–80 tour; Steve Zirkel (bass); Bob Metzger (guitar and pedal steel); Bob Furgo; Tom McMorran (both keyboards); and two new backing singers, Julie Christensen and Perla Batalla.

They were quite a pair—Julie a striking, statuesque blonde who, for half of the eighties, had sung with her then husband Chris D. in an edgy L.A. punk-roots band called the Divine Horsemen, and Perla a petite, sparkling brunette of South American ancestry, with her own band and a background in jazz and rock. Both were stylish and mischievous, and accomplished singers who had sung together in the past. Christensen was the first of the two to be hired. Beck had known her from Austin, where she sang jazz and occasionally played gigs with Passenger. Christensen can remember seeing Passenger when they returned from Leonard's 1979–80 tour and noticing how "they all came back changed; everyone had some kind of aura around them of having become citizens of the world." So there was no hesitation when Beck invited her to audition for Leonard's 1988 tour. Henry Lewy, overseeing the rehearsals with Beck, was impressed with not just her singing but her knowledge of Leonard's songs; she had sung them at the piano with her mother since she was a young girl. "I didn't have to audition for Leonard," says Christensen, "but he wanted to meet me, because being on the road is like this marriage that's going on." Over lunch, Leonard told her, "This is going to be a very difficult tour; we'll be playing four or five nights a week in different cities." Christensen laughed and told him, "'Leonard, I had just got done doing CBGB's and the Mab and these places where I had to pee by the side of the road and change in awful restrooms.' I was like, 'Come on, let's roll up our sleeves and go.'" Leonard was charmed.

When Beck called Perla to audition, having not grown up playing Leonard Cohen songs, she went straight to the record store and bought as many cassettes of his as she could find. This being America, there were not many. But Roscoe told her not to prepare anything, "because," she says, "99 percent of this was Leonard's feelings about me as a person. Which made me nervous. I remember walking in, dressed in white from head to toe, and Leonard was there completely in black. We just looked at each other and laughed and that was it." Again, Leonard was charmed. "But the true magic happened when Julie and I started singing. We read each other's minds musically; we'd never say which part we'd take, our voices were constantly mixing. Together we were a real force as a backup singing pair, and it showed onstage." The day they left for Europe, Perla's mother and father came to the airport to see her off. "It was my first time out of the country. My dad was really an old-fashioned kind of guy, very ill, but an elegant man, who dressed in a suit—he was like Leonard in that way—and it was a big deal to him that I was leaving for Europe. He asked Leonard to take care of me and they shook hands and Leonard promised him he would."

The tour—fifty-nine concerts in three months—began on April 5, 1988, in Germany. "There was a good feeling among all the people on that tour," Julie says. "Leonard just had this way of being really like the camp counselor. We would do this thing on that tour where, if we were jet-lagged and wide-awake in the middle of the night, we would hang a hanger on the door to indicate that we were awake and it was okay to come in, and there were several times when I would go to Leonard's room and just have snacks and chat." Perla remembers Leonard seeming "very happy, and very playful. A lot of people don't know that side of him, but Leonard was one of the funniest people I've ever met, so hilarious at times you just want to crack up." When she and Julie came up with a spontaneous vaudeville routine onstage, Leonard happily played along with them. During the Spanish leg of the tour, Leonard had Perla translate for the audience what he said between songs, which, depending on his mood and his red wine intake, could be long, complex and mortifying—and terrifying for a woman who had been raised speaking English. "Every night we were on the edge of our seats to see where he was going to go," Perla says. "It was so much fun, and as risky as live theater sometimes."

In Europe, Leonard was often mobbed by fans. "Women would follow us around," Julie says, "and men for that matter, and go, 'Where is Leonard staying?'" In Sweden they had to fight their way through a crowd of teenage girls to get on the ferry to Denmark. Perla says, "If Leonard was in the street or in a café people would come up to him; there was no privacy whatsoever. But he was very happy. We'd take long walks through the streets together and he was in his element, I think, delighted with his success." In the UK, the BBC made a documentary about him, *Songs from the Life of Leonard Cohen*, and Buckingham Palace sent him an invitation to appear at the Prince's Trust concert, alongside Eric Clapton, Elton John, Dire Straits, the Bee Gees and Peter Gabriel. Julie remembers, "Peter Gabriel came up to Leonard with a couple of albums for Leonard to sign. He was like a little disciple: 'Can you sign this one? And this one's for my son.'" Prince Charles, whose charity the concert benefited, was also a Leonard Cohen fan. "The orchestration is fantastic and the words, the lyrics and everything," the prince said in a British television interview. "He's a remarkable man and he has this incredibly laid-back, gravelly voice."[6] In Iceland, Leonard was received by the president of the country.

On the eve of Independence Day they flew back to the U.S. By now Leonard had become used to the difference between the European and American tour experience. But the Carnegie Hall concert on July 6 could not have gone much better. The show was sold out and the media had come in droves. "I remember thinking that if they dropped a bomb on the place, American rock music criticism would be over," says Sharon Weisz, "because of the number of journalists who had requested tickets to this show." The *New York Post* reviewer Ira Mayer wrote, "If ever there is an award for emotional laureate of the pop world, Leonard Cohen will be the uncontested winner. He gave vent—magnificently—to all the doubts, fears, longings, memories and regrets that comprise love in the twentieth century."

Following two West Coast shows, in Berkeley and L.A., there was a three-month break before the North American tour resumed in October. At Halloween, in Texas, they performed in a TV studio for *Austin City Limits*, a popular long-running concert program that airs on PBS. On November 16 the tour ended, as it had begun, in New York, where the *New York Times* named *I'm Your Man* its album of the year. Leonard stayed on in New York. Adam and Lorca were living there now and Hanukkah was just a couple of weeks away. Leonard rented a room in a hotel in one of Manhattan's less fashionable neighborhoods and began preparing for the holiday.

––––––––

The eighties had not been easy on many of the recording artists who had come up in the sixties. They tended to flounder in a decade when style took the place of substance, yuppies replaced hippies, shiny CDs made vinyl LPs obsolete and the drugs of choice were designed to boost egos, not to expand consciousness. Although Leonard had had a tough time of it during the first half of the eighties, by the end of the decade he had adapted far more successfully than most of his near-contemporaries. He had the style, the beats, the synthesiz-

ers and the videos—two excellent videos made by Dominique Issermann, to whom *I'm Your Man* had been dedicated. (Written around
a picture of a man and woman ballroom dancing were the words "All
these songs are for you, D.I.")

I'm Your Man had outsold all of his earlier albums. "In terms of my
so-called career," Leonard said, "it certainly was a rebirth. But it was
hard to consider it a rebirth on a personal level. It was made under
the usual dismal and morbid conditions."[7] Suzanne was suing him
over money, and his romantic relationship with Dominique was unraveling. This was a dance whose complicated steps Leonard knew
well: the intimacy and the distance, the separations and reconcilia-
tions, running on the spot and, when the music stopped, good-bye.
Romance would often be replaced by an enduring friendship; Leonard appears to have remained good friends with many of his former
lovers, remarkably few of whom seem to bear him any ill will. But
the more immediate result of the end of a long love affair would be a
rush of freedom, which gave way to depression, from which Leonard
might emerge with a poem or a song.

Leonard has claimed in several interviews—and confirmed it in
the closing verse of "Chelsea Hotel #2"—that he is not a sentimental or a nostalgic man, that he does not look back. Religion would
validate this as a healthy position: when Lot's wife looked back at
Sodom she was turned into a pillar of salt. As a writer, although he
tended to look inside himself or at his immediate environs, Leonard also looked back at lovers from whom he had parted. In *The
Favorite Game,* Leonard's fictional alter ego writes to the girl he
loved in fond anticipation of their separation: "Dearest Shell, if you
let me I'd always keep you 400 miles away and write you pretty poems and letters. . . . I'm afraid to live any place but in expectation."
As a writer Leonard seemed to thrive on this paradox of distance
and intimacy. As a man, it was more complicated. Often it seemed
to make him wretched, and, as a wretch, he turned to God. But as

Roshi told him, "You can't live in God's world. There are no restaurants or toilets."[8]

Back in L.A., with little to keep Leonard occupied, his depression reappeared. It came "in cycles," he said[9]—sometimes even when things were going well, which would make him feel ashamed. "One might think that success helps you fix up your personal problems," he said, "but it doesn't work that way."[10] When things were not going well, though, depression could send him into a serious tailspin.

"I never knew where it was coming from and I tried everything to shake it, but nothing worked."

What did you try?

"Well, I tried all that stuff, all the antidepressants before Prozac, like Demerol, desipramine, the MAO inhibitors."

Valium? The morphines?

"No, not morphine. That would have been deadly. But I tried everything right up to Zoloft and Wellbutrin. I tried everything they had. Most of it made me feel worse than when I started."

So, you're an expert in all things pharmaceutical when it comes to depression?

"I think I am. But nothing worked."

Leonard told the actress Anjelica Huston, "When I was on Prozac my relationship with the landscape improved. I actually stopped thinking about myself for a minute or two." He stopped taking it because, he said, "it didn't seem to have any effect whatsoever on my melancholy, my dark vision," and because "what it does is completely annihilate the sexual drive."[11] He had friends who had recommended psychotherapy, but, he said, "I never deeply believed. I had no conviction that this model was workable. And having observed a number of friends who for many years had undergone this treatment, it began to be clear that it wasn't terribly effective for these people, so I was never convinced in the value it would have for me."[12] It might be that Leonard felt that, as a former debating society president and a man of words, he could run rings around anyone trying to administer the talking cure. There were also his dignity and an almost British stiff upper lip to contend with. Leonard was not the kind of man to give someone else the responsibility of removing the suffering from him. Amphetamines helped, if he didn't use them too much for too long— though now that he was in his fifties he was finding them hard to take at all. Drinking was also helpful, as was sex—Leonard had become something of an expert at self-medication. But what seemed to work best of all was a disciplined routine. The long hours of meditation and study Leonard had put in with Roshi had not cured him of depression but had helped him view the situation from a more useful perspective. He had come to recognize that his depression "had to do with an isolation of"[13] himself—an isolation he had tried to address through his various spiritual pursuits. The hard part was making it work in the world of restaurants and toilets.

————————

For the first time in a long while, the world was treating him well, as regards his work. The success of *I'm Your Man* had pushed Leonard's *Best Of* album back again onto the UK charts, and his American label had been inspired to give a belated release to his slighted last album, *Various Positions*. In Canada his poetry was being celebrated in an exhibition at the Library and Archives. Both Leonard and his music appeared in a Canadian television program called *A Moving Picture*, a dance fantasy that featured the National Ballet of Canada. In February 1989 Leonard was in New York, where he was invited to perform on the U.S. TV show *Night Music*, cohosted by David Sanborn and Jools Holland. One of its young producers was Hal Willner.

"Like they say about the Kennedy assassination," Willner says, "you remember the first time you heard Leonard Cohen. It was on WDAS in Philadelphia, I was very young, and 'Suzanne' came on the radio, and there was nothing like it. Hearing Leonard, I think even more than Dylan, I was able to see music as poetry. When I moved to New York, I had a little internship job at Warner Bros., around the time they were doing *Death of a Ladies' Man*, and I remember seeing what a controversial figure he was within the industry. They either got it or they didn't, there was nobody who was in the middle. That record had a very big effect on me, and Doc Pomus loved that record too; we used to listen to it all the time." Willner considered *I'm Your Man* a "masterpiece." He had gone to see Leonard's last show in New York at the Beacon Theatre and thought it "one of the most perfect concerts I've ever seen. Since he was doing TV for the album, I jumped at having him on the show."

Willner had become known for curating albums and performances that featured eclectic ensembles of musicians and singers performing material written by another artist. As Willner put it, he was "trying to combine things that are sort of fantasy." He took the same approach to Leonard's appearance on *Night Music*. "Leonard said he wanted to do 'Tower of Song,' but I had a fantasy in my head of doing 'Who by Fire' with Leonard and Sonny Rollins, who was another guest on the show. Usually when people jam they go with up-tempo things; that song had a spiritual aspect, but I knew that people would relate." When he mentioned his idea to Leonard, "there was this silence. Then he said—tentatively—'Will he do that?'" At the rehearsal, Leonard appeared wary. Sonny Rollins was watching him closely as if trying to read him. Leonard looked behind him: Julie and Perla were there, watching his back, and they smiled. Leonard started singing "Who by Fire." Then, Willner recalls, "Sonny Rollins, who was sitting there staring at Leonard the whole time, picked up his horn and started wailing in a different kind of understanding of the song." After the rehearsal, says Julie, Rollins—"this saxophone colossus, this master"—came up to her and asked, quietly, "Do you think Mr. Cohen likes what I'm doing?"

Back in Los Angeles, a heat wave had set in. Leonard was upstairs in his duplex, in the corner of the living room, playing his Technics synthesizer—something he spent much of his time doing when he was not needed elsewhere. He was happy enough in his cell with its bare floorboards and its plain white walls, no pictures or distractions. The windows were open, letting in the sweltering heat. He had thought about installing air-conditioning but would not get around to it until the next decade. He was interrupted by the phone ringing. It was a young woman friend, Sean Dixon, who sounded distressed and wanted Leonard to come over. They had met when Leonard was working at Rock Steady Studios on *I'm Your Man;* Dixon was the receptionist. One day Leonard had gone to the studio with Leanne Ungar to pick up the master tapes, since they planned to mix them in another studio. When they arrived, Dixon was there on her own, nursing a stray dog she had just found in the street. Leonard decided on the spot that they would stay and mix at Rock Steady. "Every day," Dixon remembers, "I would come in with this little lost dog which was very depressed. And we would just sit there when Leonard wasn't working and hold this little dog, while he talked and thought about what he wanted to do."

Dixon was actually phoning Leonard about a cat. Her roommate had gone back to Texas, leaving her with Hank, a long-haired cat of indeterminate age, which was now very sick. The vets could not figure out what was wrong with it. The enema and IV fluids they had given him on the previous two visits had not helped. Hank had crawled under the Murphy bed in her small apartment. Dixon thought he was dying. The next morning she went to take him back to the vet, but her car was gone; it had been stolen. She says, "I pleaded with Leonard, 'Can't you please just come and look at him? I don't know what to do.'"

Leonard drove over and Dixon pulled the cat out from under the bed. "He looked horrible, he was covered with all this medicine he had spit up and he hadn't groomed in days. But right away Leonard said, 'Oh, I don't think this is a dying animal.' He said, 'I'm going to chant to him.' I thought, 'Oh my God, Leonard is such a freak,' but he was, 'No, really, it vibrates all the internal organs, it's a really good thing.' I was desperate so I said, 'Okay, fine, you do whatever you want to do.' So he put Hank on the bed.

"There was a chair at the end of the bed, right up against the bed, and Leonard sat and leaned over, put his mouth right up against Hank's forehead, and he just chanted like they chant at the monastery, '*Ooooooooooooooooooom*,' very, very deeply, way lower than he sings, like a rumble. He did that for ten minutes—and he's allergic to cats so his nose was running and his eyes were running and he was getting stuffed up, but he just kept doing it. And Hank just sat there, didn't try to get away or scratch him or anything. Then finally Leonard stopped and said, 'That's it, darling, that'll fix him up,' with total confidence." He gave her $1,000, insisting that she use it to get another car, and left. Hank slunk back under the bed. "But in the middle of the night I heard him get up and wander into the kitchen and I heard a lot of strangled sounds coming from the cat box. The next thing I heard in the morning was Hank crunching away on his food. I couldn't believe he was eating, he hadn't eaten in days. Then I looked at the cat box, expecting to see something really horrible, but the weird thing was there wasn't anything—the miracle of the cat box. And the cat was fine. Apart from the odd hairball he was never sick again."

Dixon witnessed another demonstration of Leonard's skills at his house, when his kitchen was invaded by ants. "They were all over the counter and I was looking for something to spray them with, and he said, 'No. I'll get them to go. Watch.' He leaned over, pointed his finger and admonished them: 'You get out of my kitchen this instant, all of you, right now, get going!' He did that for a few minutes and, I swear, the ants all left and didn't come back. A cat whisperer and an ant whisperer."

Two miracles. Enough to qualify Leonard for sainthood. He had also, miraculously, found another love and muse—a beautiful blond actress, smart, successful and almost thirty years younger than him. "I don't think anyone masters the heart," said Leonard. "It continues to cook like a shish kebab, bubbling and sizzling in everyone's breast."[14] Or it does on the flames in the ovens in the tower of song.

Nineteen

Jeremiah in Tin Pan Alley

———

"Interestingly, he thinks we first met when I was five or six years old," says Rebecca De Mornay. Leonard would have been in his early thirties. It was in the late sixties, in England, when Rebecca attended a boarding school named Summerhill. A friend of Leonard had a child there and Leonard had gone to give a little concert. Summerhill was an early experiment in progressive education, a school with no rules; Leonard remembered seeing a female teacher walking about the place, topless. He also remembered seeing Rebecca. "I said, 'How could you remember me from then?' He said, 'It was something about your light.' Amazing, but Leonard would remember light, and he doesn't tend to make things up."

Rebecca was born in California and raised there until her father, the conservative talk-show host Wally George, left her bohemian mother. From then, she spent her childhood on the move, from Austria to Australia and several points in between. Rebecca's mother had been a Leonard Cohen fan and would play her his records when she was small. "I remember going to sleep listening to his music, almost as a lullaby—'Suzanne,' 'The Stranger Song,' 'One of Us Cannot Be Wrong.'" When Rebecca started playing the guitar, his were some of the first songs she learned, and when she decided to become a singer-songwriter in her midteens, his songs were an influence. In her late teens, Rebecca turned to acting and moved back to California, where she started her successful movie career at the age of twenty-two in Francis Ford Coppola's *One from the Heart*.

The first time Leonard and Rebecca met as adults was in the mideighties, at a party thrown by film director Robert Altman, another Leonard Cohen fan. Rebecca, having recognized Leonard from across the room, remembers that she went over to him "and sat down and proceeded to talk to him, which is actually very unlike me with someone I don't know. I just had this feeling I could and should talk to him. I don't know what I said, but he seemed a little skeptical. I remember a great reticence on his part—I couldn't tell if he was shy or wary of me. There's that saying, 'Trust the art, not the artist,' which is almost always true, but when I met Leonard, the person was as interesting, if not more so, than the art."

Their paths crossed again in 1987 in Los Angeles at a Roy Orbison concert that was being recorded for a PBS TV special, *A Black and White Night*. Among Orbison's guests were Bruce Springsteen, Tom Waits, Jackson Browne and Jennifer Warnes. Leonard was in the audience. So, separately, was Rebecca. "I saw Leonard and again I went up to him: 'Hey, remember we met?' And again there was the skeptical look. It was funny, as if he anticipated that making a connection with me might wind up some kind of arduous enterprise. Which maybe it did." Rebecca laughs. "I said, 'You know, I'd really like to get together and talk.' He simply said, 'All right,' and it sounded like a reluctant surrender."

So they got together and talked, and continued to do so. "We had this friendship at first that lasted two or three years. Strictly a friendship; I had a boyfriend," says Rebecca. They talked about art and work, in particular Leonard's. "I ask a lot of questions if some-body interests me and he enjoyed talking to me about his process." Slowly, imperceptibly, it became a courtship. "It started to become this meaningful relationship to me; we started talking about our real lives, our secret lives. Then at some point after all this talking, I'm not sure exactly how it happened, but it turned this corner and we were just suddenly madly, passionately in love. He gave me a very beautiful ring. Unbelievably, in a way, we were to be married."

There was a proposal—"*Ah, baby, let's get married, we've been alone too long*"—in the song "Waiting for the Miracle." A very Leonard Co-hen proposal admittedly: resigned, cheerfully pessimistic and with references to nakedness and war. Leonard and Rebecca discussed moving in together, but for now it suited them to keep their sepa-rate homes. Rebecca lived with her cats in a house in the hills, two miles north of Leonard's, and Leonard shared his with his daughter, Lorca. She had taken a job working for a distress help line. He could hear her at night through the bare floorboards, downstairs, talking to would-be suicides on the phone. Of his relationship with Rebecca, Leonard said, "I find the whole thing very workable." Although he felt it "incautious to declare yourself a happy man," even he had to admit that he "couldn't complain."[1]

Those who have read this far and are not punching the air or say-ing "at long last" might be thinking this a curious development. Not that Leonard had a beautiful girlfriend, or even that he was happy, but that he was taking a wife. An old Eastern European adage says that a man should pray once before going to sea, twice before going to war and three times before getting married, but when it came to the last of the three, Leonard never seemed to stop praying. But marriage to Rebecca De Mornay really did appear to be workable. Movie stars are used to early starts, so they are unfazed by someone who sets his alarm for four thirty every morning to go to the Zen Center. Their work requires them to leave home for lengthy periods, so they are less likely to be bothered if you do the same. They are committed to their work. They have their own income. They are accustomed to being around people who are distracted or self-involved. To have got where they are in their business, they have to be fiercely tenacious. And, if they are Rebecca De Mornay, they are young, strikingly beautiful, very sexy and love music, and Leonard's music in particular. So, if Leonard should forget to pray for the angels, perhaps it might not be quite so perilous now that the miracle appeared to have come.

"In the midst of all this," says Rebecca, "I was doing what turned out to be so far the biggest movie of my career and he was trying to get his record *The Future* together, which also turned out to be his biggest American success. We had a very creative, inspiring impact on each other, smoking up a storm of cigarettes, drinking cauldrons of coffee—just together, living, working." Rebecca had won the starring role in *The Hand That Rocks the Cradle*, in which she plays a disturbed young woman pretending to be a nanny. The film was shot in Tacoma, a suburb of Seattle. Leonard went with her, "which very few men would feel comfortable doing," Rebecca points out. This was Leonard's first significant relationship with a woman more celebrated and successful than himself, but it appeared not to trouble him in the least. "He stayed with me at a house I rented there, and actually spent time in my trailer, happily songwriting while I was shooting, playing his synthesizer. The last track on *The Future* is called 'Tacoma Trailer,' and that was the trailer."

It is a nice image, Leonard noodling contentedly on his keyboard while Rebecca goes off to play a psychotic nanny, and playing a song to her when she comes home from work. "Tacoma Trailer" is an instrumental, but it came quickly. Rebecca was doing a good job as a muse. And Leonard needed one. Writing songs had become no less arduous. There had rarely been a time when it was easy, but sometime around 1982 something had changed in him—he couldn't say exactly what—and it had become much worse. It appeared to be some kind of acute perfectionism related to a craving for complete authenticity. He could write a "perfectly reasonable" song, he said, even "a good song," but when he listened to it sung he could hear "that the guy was putting you on."[2]

Leonard speculated that the problem might have to do with a sense of mortality, "that this whole enterprise is limited, that there was an end in sight."[3] As deadlines do, it focused him, but instead of moving things along, it kept him in the same place, going deeper, trying to find "the kind of truth that I can recognize, the kind of balance of truth and lies, light and dark."[4] He would work on the same song over and over, diligently and devotedly, for years, forever if need be, trying to make it work. Ever since he was a young poet, he had felt intensely passionate about writing, he said, and the feeling "of being in this *for keeps*."[5] When it came to his romantic relationships, he did not appear to have given that kind of dedication to staying in one place, with one person, "for keeps," and doing whatever it took to make it work. The problem with romantic relationships, though, was that they tended to get in the way of the isolation and space, the distance and longing, that his writing required. In 1993, Leonard wrote an advice page (sadly just a one-off) for the American men's magazine *Details*. He answered the question "What is the one thing men ought to know about women?" with "Women are deeply involved in a pattern of thought centered around the notion of commitment."[6] Yet he seemed at last ready to commit to Rebecca. He told journalists that his and Rebecca's was "an exclusive and highly conventional relationship,"[7] and said, "There is a formal arrangement between us, yes."[8]

The success of *I'm Your Man* had resulted in anticipation for a new album. That did nothing to speed up the process. Nor did the fact that more than half the songs Leonard was working on had been around in some unfinished form or other for a long time. He was writing the sixtieth verse for one such song, "Democracy," when he was interrupted by the phone. His son, Adam, had been in a serious car accident in Guadeloupe, where he had been working as a roadie for a calypso band. He was badly injured: fractured neck and pelvis, nine broken ribs and a collapsed lung. The eighteen-year-old was air-ambulanced, unconscious, to a hospital in Toronto. Leonard flew up to meet him as he was taken into intensive care. During the four months Adam spent in the hospital, Leonard stayed there, keeping vigil. He would sit in the room quietly, watching his son, who remained in a coma. Sometimes he would read aloud to him from the Bible. When Adam finally regained consciousness, his first words to his father were, "Dad, can you read something else?"[9] Suzanne says, "Leonard wanted to stay there by his bedside—for months—and did practically nothing else, dropped everything else to be there. Finally, if I had forgotten why I loved him even for a moment with what might have been a heart full of resentments, after Guadeloupe, to see how he was so solidly there for our children, I remembered."

Adam made a complete recovery. During the process, father and son became very tight. Leonard, having put all thoughts of work aside while he focused on Adam, had once again begun to think that, if he never got around to finishing another album, it was not the end of the world. As had happened in the past, his songs seemed to be doing all right without his direct involvement. One of them, "Bird on a Wire" was at No. 1 on the U.S. charts, a soulful version by the Neville Brothers, taken from the soundtrack of a romantic comedy of the same name. Another contemporary movie, *Pump Up the Volume*, used his song "Everybody Knows"—two versions of it, in fact, Leonard's original and a cover by Concrete Blonde. As it happened, the soundtrack of the latter also featured a hip young rock band called the Pixies, whose front man would, inadvertently, be the impetus for a Leonard Cohen tribute album.

The French rock magazine *Les Inrockuptibles* had thought up the idea of making an album of Leonard Cohen covers by artists from the more interesting end of the rock spectrum after an interview with the Pixies' Black Francis, during which he raved about *I'm Your Man*. Francis had not been a fan of Leonard's music until 1990, when, on a particularly grim European tour with his band, he happened upon a cassette of *I'm Your Man* in a French highway service station. The tape remained unopened in his bag until the bus reached Spain and the band had a few days off. "The plan," says Francis, "had been for us to all go to a beach town with nightclubs. But the band wasn't in a happy space and I really wanted to get away from everybody—in particular Kim, the bass player." He asked the tour manager to take him somewhere quiet, where he could be alone. He was dropped at a large, empty tourist hotel farther down the coast. Checking in, he saw to his chagrin that Kim Deal had had the same idea. "The hotel assumed we were the best of friends and, although there were eight hundred rooms in this hotel and no one in it, they put us right next to each other. We were both too exhausted to resist and just accepted our fate."

Francis stayed locked in his room and did not come out. He had brought with him the two new cassettes he had bought on the road, one being *I'm Your Man*. "It was summer, bright and sunny, but I had all the curtains drawn and it was very dark and black in my little room, and I played *I'm Your Man* on my boom box. It was all I listened to for three days straight, over and over. I was in the right kind of emotional state—kind of lonely, frustrated, bored, a whole combination, and alone in this empty place, this hotel at the end of the universe—and I got it. The voice, those little Casio keyboards, that kind of lush but spacious artificial landscape that frames his work on that record, just brought everything about him right to a head: everything that's sexy about him was extra sexy, anything funny about him extra funny, anything heavy was extra heavy. I was a fan."

Nick Cave was a Leonard Cohen fan too, but of longer standing. He had first heard Leonard's music in his teens, in a small country town in Australia, when a girlfriend made him sit with her in her room

and listen to *Songs of Love and Hate*. Many were the men introduced
in such fashion to Leonard's early albums. "I'd never heard anything
like it," says Cave. "It remains one of the seminal albums that completely changed the kind of music I would make. It was really the
first record that showed a way where it was possible to take some of
the kind of dark, self-lacerating visions we found in much of the European poetry and literature we were reading in those days and apply
them to a kind of rock sound. When the Bad Seeds put out our first
record we did a version of 'Avalanche' as the first track—even more
lugubrious than his—as a kind of attempt to set the tone." When
seven years later *Les Inrockuptibles* asked Cave and the Bad Seeds to
appear on the album, he declined; he despised tribute albums and
"could not think of anything worse. Then what happened was we
went to the pub and spent the afternoon there, and came back into
the studio rather intoxicated, and just started to play 'Tower of Song.'
We played it for about three hours nonstop, kind of segueing through
all the different kinds of musical styles in history, just playing around,
and then we forgot about it. Someone found it and did an edit on it,
and it sounded good, or it at least like there was a sense of humor
behind it. That was one fucked-up version of that song." It wound up
on the tribute album.

I'm Your Fan was released in November 1991, with eighteen
Leonard Cohen songs covered by, among others, the Pixies ("I
Can't Forget"), R.E.M. ("First We Take Manhattan"), James ("So
Long, Marianne"), Lloyd Cole ("Chelsea Hotel") and Ian McCulloch ("Hey, That's No Way to Say Goodbye"). John Cale, the oldest
of the contributors, gave "Hallelujah" its first cover by any artist of
substance—*NME* described his version as "a thing of wondrous, savage beauty." Leonard was "tickled pink" by the whole album. It did
not bother him so much, he said, if his books were left to gather dust
on shelves, "but the song really has an urgency, and if it isn't sung, it's
nowhere."[10] Everybody, he said, could use some encouragement, and

if you hung around long enough it was bound to happen, and Leonard's time had come. The same year, Leonard was inducted into the Juno Hall of Fame in Canada. In his acceptance speech he quipped, "If I had been given this attention when I was twenty-six it would have turned my head. At thirty-six it might have confirmed my flight on a rather morbid spiritual path. At forty-six it would have rubbed my nose in my failing powers and have prompted a plotting of a getaway and an alibi. But at fifty-six, hell, I'm just hitting my stride and it doesn't hurt at all."[11] Which was fortunate, since his countrymen gave him an even higher honor in October, making Leonard an Officer of the Order of Canada.

Perhaps to help balance the scales, Leonard agreed to Hal Willner's request to appear on a tribute album to Charles Mingus, *Weird Nightmare*. "I went over to his house in L.A. one night with a bunch of Mingus's poetry," Willner says, "and he picked out one stanza that he loved in a poem called 'The Chill of Death.' I had a little DAT recorder and he sat at his desk and repeated the poem over and over again into the microphone for half an hour. While he was doing so, someone made a phone call, and he picked up the phone, still reading the poem. They said, 'Leonard, what are you doing?' 'I am a man reading "The Chill of Death." ' That's on the record too."

In March 1992, Rebecca attended the Oscars ceremony. Her escort, the immaculately dressed man who walked down the red carpet beside her, was Leonard. Cameras buzzed like mosquitoes, and photos of Rebecca and Leonard made it into a number of tabloids. "There was an English magazine that printed pictures of us and said 'Beauty and the Beast,'" says Rebecca. How mean of them to call her a beast. It brought to mind the headlines that greeted Serge Gainsbourg when he was photographed with his famous lovers Bardot, Gréco and Birkin. The difference was that Leonard, unlike Gainsbourg, had always gone out of his way in the past to avoid such attention. "The Academy Awards *was* probably the least likely place to sight Leonard Cohen," Rebecca says. "I asked him to go with me, because they asked me, and I was with him at the time, and he just went, 'Okay.' He didn't do the regular guy thing of having some reaction or anti-reaction to it, he just accepted it. It wasn't something he was looking forward to, but it wasn't something that he was going to say no to and leave me standing there without him. I think Leonard, like I am, is really in the moment with the individual he's with, as opposed to the image of what the person is supposed to be. There was just the reality of us as two people, irrespective of me being an actress, Leonard being a famous songwriter."

Leonard, as well as working at home, was writing songs at Rebecca's house on her synthesizer. Two of those songs in particular stuck in her mind. One was "A Thousand Kisses Deep," which Leonard kept writing over and over, "like a painter who paints over his original painting that you loved, and paints a whole new painting on top of it, and then he paints a whole new one on top of that, and ten years later it exists on a record* and doesn't have a single note or word that's the same as anything I heard when he first played that song." The other was "Anthem." "He got stuck on this one song. He was at my synthesizer and played it again—I'd heard it for years by now—and I suddenly said, 'Just like that, *those* words, *that's* the song.' Again he looked at me kind of skeptical; I guess I just must provoke that response in him. He said, 'You know what? You produce this song. I think you really know what this song has to be, I think you ought to produce it with me.' So he sort of launched me into this position, which I was extremely flattered by, and surprised. But I really did feel that I knew the song—in fact I just played it before I spoke to you for this interview and it still makes me cry. It has the impact of 'Auld

---

* *Ten New Songs*, 2001.

Lang Syne,' it's just immortal, it's the final statement on the subject, it's the searing authenticity that he has in his voice when you talk to him, the presence that he is in person. He is so fully present, with compassion for the underdog, as well as genuine compassion and understanding for the enemy—which is very hard to do and hard-won.

"However," Rebecca says, "within this stance it's extremely hard to be Leonard Cohen. He's on his own solo voyage, and he's lying on a bed of cactus perpetually, but somehow finding windows into infinity everywhere: '*Every heart to love will come, but like a refugee. . .; Forget your perfect offering / There is a crack in everything / That's how the light gets in.*' It's definitive. Such a unique way to describe the wisdom of compassion. I heard from a friend of mine who was in one of the established rehab places that they quoted this line in their pamphlets on recovery. He has taught me so much; he's humble but also fierce. He has this subtext of 'Let's get down to the truth here. Let's not kid ourselves.'" Early on in their relationship, Rebecca was "whining about the various pain I had, my childhood, and this and that. And Leonard is the best listener, but at a certain point he said, 'I understand, it must have been really terrible for you, Rebecca, having had to grow up poor and black.'" Rebecca laughed. "It wasn't in any way mean-spirited, there was no judgment from him; there never is. Leonard developed the tenacity and character to sit still within suffering—even though in earlier years, like many people, he tried every form of escape, be it drugs, sex, music, fame, money, all the usual things—but, early in his life compared to most people, he was brave enough to sit in the suffering, and write out of it, and live out of it, and not try to escape from it."

April 1, 1992, was Roshi's eighty-fifth birthday. Shortly after the Academy Awards, Leonard threw a grand party of his own. A hundred people gathered in one of the big hotels on Sunset Boulevard. There was a band, fronted by Perla Batalla, and Leonard asked them to end the evening by singing "Auld Lang Syne," Roshi's favorite song. By the time they got to it, the old man had nodded off in his chair. Leonard smiled. "It was a great sign if he's asleep," he said. Guests left with a book that Leonard had organized and published, with help from Kelley Lynch, celebrating the old man's life. Leonard had it bound in gold, like an Oscar.

———————

Leonard was in the studio, working on his new album *The Future*, when the L.A. riots broke out on April 29, 1992. Four white police officers had been acquitted of the beating of a black motorist—an incident that had been caught on video by an onlooker and was frequently aired on television—and South Central L.A., a predominantly African-American neighborhood, erupted. Cars and buildings were set on fire and stores attacked and looted. A white man was dragged from his truck by a mob and severely beaten. As the violence spread, the dinner-party conversation in affluent white neighborhoods turned to buying guns. By the fourth day, the government sent in the marines. There had been fifty-three deaths, hundreds of buildings destroyed and around four thousand fires. Leonard could see them burning from his window. There was a layer of soot on his front lawn. His home was not far from South Central. The Zen Center was closer still. He had become used to hearing gunshots on his way to the *zendo* in the early hours of morning and to stepping over syringes to get through the gate. Now from his car he could see boarded-up stores and the charred remains of a gas station. It was "truly an apocalyptic landscape and a very appropriate landscape for my work."[12] He had started writing the song "The Future"—then titled "If You Could See What's Coming Next"—in 1989, when the Berlin Wall toppled, and just as he had predicted, it was all coming down.

"I said to him, 'Why do you even want to live in Los Angeles?'" says Rebecca De Mornay. "'You have a place in beautiful Montreal, and Hydra, and you've lived in New York and Paris. Why here?'

Leonard said something like, 'This is the place. It's like a metaphor of the decline. The whole system is coming apart, I can feel it. The future is grim, and Los Angeles is at the center of it. It has the decay, and some sort of wild hope too, like weeds growing through the asphalt. I want to write from this place, from what's really going on.' So I was like, 'Wow, okay, we're living in the decay, you at the bottom and me at the top of this one street. Great.' And from within that he wrote 'The Future'—and it was very different Leonard Cohen writing from what I'd ever seen him do." Leonard renamed his new album—which he had had previously titled *Be for Real*, then *Busted*—after this apocalyptic song.

The Future was recorded with a large revolving cast of musicians and engineers whose numbers rivaled Phil Spector's on *Death of a Ladies' Man*. The credits list almost thirty female singers, including Jennifer Warnes, Anjani Thomas, Julie Christensen, Perla Batalla, Peggy Blue, Edna Wright, Jean Johnson and a gospel choir. There were string players and synthesizer programmers, an R & B horn section and various country music instruments—mandolin, pedal steel—as well as the usual rock instruments and an "ice rink organ." Perla Batalla, Rebecca De Mornay, Jennifer Warnes and David Campbell are credited as arrangers and Rebecca, Leanne Ungar, Bill Ginn, Yoav Goren and Steve Lindsey as coproducers of various tracks, but on the label it is described as "A Record by Leonard Cohen."

"It was a difficult birth," remembers Leanne Ungar, the album's chief engineer. "It was done kind of a song at a time and each song had its own specific method. A lot of the songs Leonard started at home with Yoav Goren, who was specifically working with him to program synthesizers on several songs to help him get the sounds he wanted. At the time, I was also working in another studio on another project, with Steve Lindsey, doing some overdubs and mixing for [R & B band] the Temptations. I mentioned that to Leonard and he said, 'Oh, I want to do some Motown-flavor tracks,' and he asked if I would introduce him to Steve." Leonard described Lindsey as "a man of great musical sensibilities. He's produced Aaron Neville, among others, and Ray Charles. He put together 'Be for Real' "—Leonard's cover on *The Future* of a soul ballad by Frederick Knight—"which I couldn't have done without him."[13]

Lindsey also played a key role in the album's second cover song, the Irving Berlin standard "Always." It was a favorite of Leonard's late mother. Leonard said, "He assembled those very fine musicians and organized the wonderful evening when we produced about an hour's worth of 'Always.' Basically, I prepared my drink that I invented in the city of Needles, California, during a heat wave in 1976, the Red Needle—tequila and cranberry juice with fresh fruit and lemon and lime—for myself and for everybody else who wanted communion. The session became fairly animated, and we played for a long, long time."[14] Everyone was "bombed," said Lindsey, and it sounds like it. "After doing multiple takes, we finally got the take we thought was really great. Leonard went in to do the vocals. He cut out during the solo, but when the solo was over he never came back. I found him lying on the floor in Capitol Studios' bathroom. He wanted me to get the janitor so he could thank him for cleaning up after him."[15] Said Leonard, "Several musicians told me it was the happiest time they ever spent in a recording studio."[16] Kelley Lynch, Leonard's manager, was also there for the recording. Leanne Ungar remembers seeing "sparks flying a little bit between Steve and Kelley." The two would go on to have a relationship that produced a son.

Ungar was "thrilled" to see the return, after almost ten years, of Leonard's song "Anthem." Although it was not she who had accidentally erased the version Leonard did for *Various Positions*, she says, "As the engineer of the project I always felt somehow responsible." The new version was significantly different. "Closing Time" also went through several changes. "When it first came into the studio it was this absolutely gorgeous slow, slow song with slowed-down synthesized strings," says Ungar. "I was in love with it. And Leonard came in and said, 'We're going to have to scrap the whole thing and start over.' I was, 'No, you can't!" But he came in the next day with his fast version of it, and went on not only to have a huge hit with it in Canada but the Male Vocalist of the Year award." In his acceptance speech at the 1992 Juno Awards ceremony, Leonard deadpanned, "It's only in a country like this that I could win a best vocalist award."

Rebecca, who went to Canada with Leonard for the ceremony, would also frequently drop by the recording studio while the album was being made. She was there for the recording of "Waiting for the Miracle," the song that contained Leonard's marriage proposal, and for "Anthem," for which Leonard gave her a coproduction credit. This was not a lover's indulgence, he said. "I generally designate the producer as the person without whom that particular track wouldn't exist. Rebecca happens to have an impeccable musical ear, a very highly developed musical sense. I had played many versions of 'Anthem' to her—fully completed versions with choruses and overdubs, and none of them seemed to nail it—and while I was revising it for the hundredth time, at a certain point she stopped me and said, 'That's the one.' It was quite late at night, but we managed to find a studio, and she lent me her Technics synthesizer and we produced the session that night, the basic track and the basic vocal. So her contribution was not insignificant."[17] The mixing of the album "took forever," says Ungar, but finally it was done. Four years after *I'm Your Man*, *The Future* was ready to go.

The Future was released in November 1992. Instead of a picture of Leonard on the cover, there was a simply drawn, quasiheraldic design of a hummingbird, a blue heart and a pair of unlocked handcuffs. They might have symbolized beauty, bravery, freedom, loss of freedom, S & M or all of the above; with Leonard one never knew. He dedicated the album to his fiancée with three verses from Genesis 24: "And before I had done speaking in mine heart, behold,

Rebecca came forth with her pitcher on her shoulder, and she went down unto the well and drew water. And I said unto her, let me drink I pray thee. . . ."

Almost an hour in length, *The Future* was Leonard's longest album to date, containing nine songs, seven of them originals, one of those a cowrite and another an instrumental. Following the line begun by its predecessor, it is accessible and contemporary sounding, the songs catchy, the tempos often upbeat and the melodies sung in a deep, gruff, yet seductive voice somewhere between a prophet of doom with a black sense of humor and Barry White. The title track, which opens the album, sets gleeful pessimism to a synth-pop dance groove. *"I've seen the future, baby: / it is murder,"* Leonard prophesizes—going one step farther than Prince, whose own song called "The Future" says, "I've seen the future and boy it's rough"—and name-checking Stalin, the devil, Charles Manson and Christ. Leonard catalogs the sins of the West—crack, abortion, anal sex, Hiroshima and, worse than all of these, bad poets—and takes a bow as *"the little Jew who wrote the Bible."* ("I don't exactly know where that line comes from," said Leonard, but "I knew it was a good line when it came."[18]) It is his rap moment, his "Hoochie Coochie Man." "It's humorous, there's irony, there's all kinds of distances from the event that make the song possible. It's art. It's a good dance track. . . . It's even got hope. But the place where the song comes from is a life-threatening situation. That's why you're shattered at the end of it."[19]

In the lyrics of the stirring "Democracy," Leonard seems at his most sociopolitically direct. There are no Abrahams, Isaacs and butchers here:

> *It's coming . . . from those nights in Tiananmen Square . . .*
> *from the fires of the homeless,*
> *from the ashes of the gay . . .*
> *I love the country but I can't stand the scene*

And I'm neither left or right
I'm just staying home tonight,
getting lost in that hopeless little screen.

In interviews at the time Leonard referred to democracy as "the greatest religion the West has produced," adding, "[as] Chesterton said about religion, it's a great idea, too bad nobody's tried it."[20]

There are moments of calm amid the chaos and apocalypse: "Light as the Breeze," on the healing power of cunnilingus, and "Always"—though the latter's schmaltz is given an ironic edge by its over-the-top barroom performance, and the former's sweetness is tempered by a sense that the comfort of sex and love is fleeting, little more than a Band-Aid to get you back into the ring for another round. Leonard sings in the album's masterpiece, "Anthem":

Ah the wars they will
be fought again
The holy dove
She will be caught again
bought and sold
and bought again
the dove is never free

And yet it also has hope.

Forget your perfect offering
There is a crack in everything
That's how the light gets in.

"The light," Leonard explained, "is the capacity to reconcile your experience, your sorrow, with every day that dawns. It is that under-standing, which is beyond significance or meaning, that allows you to live a life and embrace the disasters and sorrows and joys that are our common lot. But it's only with the recognition that there is a crack in everything. I think all other visions are doomed to irretrievable gloom."[21] Leonard had spoken in the past of wanting a balance of dark and light and dark, and truth and lies, in his songs, and on *The Future* he achieved it.

Reviews of the album were resoundingly positive. The album was a commercial success, doing particularly well in English-speaking countries. It made the Top 40 in the UK, went double platinum in Canada and sold almost a quarter of a million copies in the U.S. Three of its songs, "The Future," "Anthem" and "Waiting for the Miracle," were included on the soundtrack to Oliver Stone's 1994 movie *Natural Born Killers*. Leonard, meanwhile, was on the promotional treadmill, doing more interviews than he had in years, saying much the same things about America, the apocalypse and, very occasionally, his relationship with Rebecca, to scores of journalists. To the bemusement of the Toronto press, Rebecca—who happened to be in Toronto to make a movie with Sidney Lumet—joined Leonard in his interviews. When the journalist from *Maclean's* noted that she looked "demure and a little out of her element," he might have been describing Leonard at the Oscars.[22] Rebecca, taking over Dominique Issermann's previous role, directed the video for *The Future*'s first single, "Closing Time." Perla Batalla, who appeared in the video alongside a pregnant Julie Christensen, remembers Rebecca turning up on the set at the end of a day's shooting with Lumet "and she would bring bottles of Cristal, which we would drink out of Styrofoam cups." To loosen Leonard up even more, Rebecca feigned a striptease and flirted with him from behind the camera.

Leonard agreed to interview Rebecca for *Interview*, the upscale celebrity gossip magazine, founded by Andy Warhol, that had once refused to run Danny Fields's Leonard Cohen story because Leonard was not a big enough star. Their interview was a mixture of insight and flirtation, and repartee of the kind that showed either that Leonard had met his match or that Rebecca had acquired something of his style. Rebecca began it by saying that the best thing about being interviewed by Leonard Cohen was that she would not be asked "what the exact nature of [her] relationship is with Leonard Cohen." Naturally that was Leonard's first question. He asked Rebecca if she viewed acting as "a form of healing." She answered, "If you have wounds that are bleeding I don't think acting will ever get them to stop. But I find acting is a form of illumination." When he asked her what roles she would like to play, she said, "Joan of Arc." Like the softest TV talk-show interviewer, or ironist, or older man in love with a beautiful young woman, Leonard asked her, "How do you maintain your pure and rosy complexion?" Did he want a beauty tip, she asked? He said, "Yes." Rebecca said, "To be more beautiful, Leonard, you have to be happier."[23]

———————

With the album done, Leonard returned to a long-unfinished book project: the anthology of his poems and song lyrics he had been working on since the mid to late eighties. Sorting through stacks of material, trying every method he could conceive of to arrange his work, he had compiled three different books—one small, one medium, one large—and abandoned all three. His publishers were getting impatient; Leonard's celebrity was at an all-time high, and it had been nine years since his last book and twenty-five since his last anthology, *Selected Poems 1956–1968*. Marianne had helped him choose the poems for that. Leonard asked his friend Nancy Bacal if she would help.

"He had been sitting with a huge pile of poems and lyrics for months, years," says Bacal. "It was a life's work, overwhelming, impossible for him to get to. So we took a very esoteric route. We wanted only to use the poems that were more current and sparse, more elliptical than the younger man's voice. We put together a book of those, which took quite some doing, and we were really quite pleased." One day while they were working on it, Rebecca came in. He showed her what they had done. Noticing that none of her favorite poems were there, Rebecca came up with her own list, which, like Marianne's, included his more romantic poems. "We kind of looked at each other, bewildered," Bacal remembers, "and I could feel him begin reconsidering, 'Well, maybe they should be there.' So it changed. And once the doors of possibility opened there was the chaos, and it was hard to make decisions. I remember the agony he was in. He faxed changes till the last minute. I'm sure the editors at the publishing company were going mad. At the very end I drifted away; it was far too confusing for my brain to handle."

Stranger Music: Selected Poems and Songs, dedicated to Adam and Lorca, was published in March 1993. A substantial book—some four hundred pages—its selections are arranged chronologically, concluding with eleven previously unpublished "uncollected poems" from the eighties. Although not the authoritative collection it was presented as being, it is a fairly comprehensive cross-section of his work, but with some curious choices and omissions. There are excerpts from his second novel, *Beautiful Losers,* for example, but not his first, *The Favorite Game,* and he chooses the well-known song versions of "Suzanne," "Master Song" and "Avalanche," for example, over their less familiar poetic versions. Leonard also took the opportunity to make textual changes, sometimes quite drastic, to several of the pieces. But with a new generation of music fans curious about his literary background, and with so many of the books containing the original poems out of print, *Stranger Music* sold very well.

———————

The tour for *The Future* was due to begin on April 22, 1993, in Scandinavia. Leonard had with him an eight-piece band—Bob Metzger, Steve Meador, Bill Ginn, Bob Furgo, Paul Ostermayer, Jorge Calderon, Julie Christensen and Perla Batalla. All bar one, Calderon, were old companions of the road, and several had been with him on his successful, enjoyable *I'm Your Man* tour. Spirits were high. During the last week of rehearsals Leonard's U.S. label, marking his new status in America, had arranged for them to play a private concert in their L.A. rehearsal studio, the Complex, which was syndicated to a hundred radio stations across the country as *The Columbia Records Radio Hour Presents: Leonard Cohen Live!* In recent weeks, Leonard had also appeared in two U.S. TV shows, *In Concert* and *David Letterman.* Tickets to his sixteen U.S. concerts—which were intermingled with twenty-one dates in Canada—were selling well.

The European tour schedule included several sports arenas, stadiums and two rock festivals. As was invariably the case in Europe, the crowds were good and the critics generally favorable. A review of the Royal Albert Hall concerts in the *Independent* remarked on Leonard's new sense of showmanship and the large number of screaming women of mature years in the audience. Leanne Ungar, who accompanied her now-husband Bob Metzger on the road, recorded the shows. (Eight songs from these concerts, along with five from the 1988 tour, would make up Leonard's first live album in eleven years, *Cohen Live,* released in 1994.) Along the way, Leonard appeared on the UK TV show *Later . . . with Jools Holland,* and on TV shows in Spain and France. He recorded a duet with Elton John, for Elton's *Duets* album, choosing to sing a Ray Charles song that he knew by heart, having heard it so often on Hydra, "Born to Lose." At the concert in Vienna, Rebecca showed up with an enormous cake. It had a hummingbird as its centerpiece and the iced inscription "R. loves L. Loves R. Loves L." Whenever her schedule allowed, Rebecca traveled with Leonard and the band on the tour bus for three or four days at a time, in Europe and in the U.S.

The U.S. tour also brought positive reviews, with *Rolling Stone* describing him as a contemporary Brecht and the *New York Times* describing the audience reaction as "almost reverent, waiting for every phrase."[24] In Canada, Leonard narrated a two-part Canadian TV series on *The Tibetan Book of the Dead*, a book he had first encountered in Marianne's old house on Hydra. In the last poem in *Stranger Music*, "Days of Kindness," written on Hydra in 1985, he had been thinking about

> *Marianne and the child*
> *The days of kindness*
> *It rises in my spine*
> *and it manifests as tears*
> *I pray that a loving memory*
> *exists for them too*
> *the precious ones I overthrew*
> *for an education in the world.*

Unsentimental as he said he was, something seemed to be drawing Leonard back to the past. Perhaps it was his current preoccupation with not just *The Future*, but the future. He had spoken about having a sense of mortality in terms of his work, of the end being in sight; he had also committed to spending this future with one woman. And still he had so much work left to do.

The attention and the adulation, although he was grateful for it, were beginning to get to him. Just as he thought that Canada had at last run out of laurels to bestow—in the past two years he had been inducted into the Canadian Music Hall of Fame; made an officer of the Order of Canada; won two separate Junos for Songwriter of the Year, two for Best Video and one for Best Male Vocalist; and even been awarded an honorary degree by his old university, McGill— Leonard learned he had won the Governor General's Award for Lifetime Artistic Achievement. It is the kind of award that makes a man feel old and finished—even a man whose last album and book were bestsellers and who was last seen with a beautiful young blond fiancée on his arm.

In November 1993 Leonard flew to Ottawa, accompanied by Julie and Perla; there was to be a tribute gala performance at which the two women were to sing "Anthem," backed by an orchestra and a gospel choir.

At the presentation ceremony in Rideau Hall, Leonard, his hair shorn almost to a stubble, said, "I feel like a soldier." From the stage he could see his old comrade-in-arms Pierre Trudeau in the audience. "You may get decorated for a successful campaign or a particular action that appears heroic but probably is just in the line of duty," he continued. "You can't let these honors deeply alter the way you fight."[25] His acceptance speech was a perfect Cohenesque mix of modesty, honesty and statement of intent. Irving Layton, as ever, rose to the occasion, declaring, "He makes you think of a Jeremiah in Tin Pan Alley. He wants to be bare-knuckled and smash whatever remaining illusions people have about the time in which they're living and what they can expect."[26] Leonard also seemed compelled to smash his own.

Work was under way in Canada on another tribute to Leonard, a book titled *Take This Waltz*, with contributions from writers and personalities such as Louis Dudek, Allen Ginsberg, Judy Collins and Kris Kristofferson, scheduled for release in September 1994 to celebrate Leonard's sixtieth birthday. Leonard, meanwhile, had flown back to L.A. He unpacked his suitcase, packed a knapsack and climbed in his car and drove away from the city and from a future with a beautiful young actress. He was returning to the place where he had moved quietly, with no announcement, a few months before, not long after the last date of the *Future* tour. A small, bare hut on a mountain, where he had chosen to live as the servant and companion of an old Japanese monk.

Twenty

From This Broken Hill

―――――

The day was hot and dry but a sliver of snow still clung to the mountaintop like a broken fingernail on a worn sweater.

Leonard, dressed in a long black robe and sandals, walked briskly along the winding path, eyes cast down, hands folded in front of him. There were other black-clad figures on the path and they marched in formation, silent but for the sound of stones crunching underfoot. "People have romantic ideas about monasteries," Leonard said. Mount Baldy Zen Center was decidedly unromantic, an abandoned Boy Scouts camp sixty-five hundred feet up in the San Gabriel mountains, fifty-five miles east of L.A., where the pine trees were as thin as the atmosphere.

Leonard's new home looked like the archaeological remains of a small, civilized community cruelly reduced to rubble—a scattering of simple wood cabins, a small statue of Buddha, the stone circle where the scouts once had their campfire sing-alongs—that some kindly souls with primitive tools had done their best to fix up. It did not even offer the romance of seclusion, being just off the road that linked the university town of Claremont below with the ski slopes above. On the other side of the road was an inn, whose sign, offering cocktails, food and lodging, only served to remind the monks of the pleasures of the flesh. On Saturday nights, laughter and music would waft on the cold night air through the monks' thin wood cabin walls. In winter the Zen Center was shrouded in deep snow. On summer days there were swarms of gnats. The place seemed full of things that bite—rattlesnakes, even the occasional bear, which the monks would chase off by throwing rocks, as compassionately as possible of course.

There are a lot of rocks on Mount Baldy. The slopes are heaped with large boulders, sharp edged and ash gray. They give the appearance of having stopped midtumble, as if a vote had been taken midavalanche and they had unanimously chosen not to continue. The paths that circle the property and link the residences with the common buildings—meditation hall, refectory, outhouses and showers (no hot running water until the late nineties)—are bordered with medium-sized stones and surfaced with small crumbly ones. The place looks like a rock pile, a hard-labor camp.

It was, Leonard admits, "a rigorous and disciplined existence."[1] During *sesshin*—weeklong periods of intense Buddhist study—a three A.M. wake-up call gave the residents ten minutes to dress and trudge through the pitch-darkness (and in winter shovel through the snow) to the kitchen/dining hall, where tea was served in a formal manner and drunk in silence. Fifteen minutes later a gong signaled that it was time to file silently into the meditation hall and take their allotted place on the wooden benches around the walls, facing center. An hour of chanted meditation—"very long chants, all one note"[2]—was followed by the first of six daily periods of *zazen*, an hour or more of seated meditation, legs crossed in full lotus, back rigid, eyes pointed at the floor. Monks carrying sticks patrolled the room on the lookout for anyone who appeared to be nodding back to sleep, whom they would return to consciousness by giving them a sharp rap on the shoulder. After the meditation came more meditation, *kinhin*, walking meditation, outdoors, whatever the weather—and this high up the mountain the climate was extreme; sometimes there were hailstones the size of limes. Then came the first of several daily *sanzen*, individual meetings with Roshi for instruction and *koan* (riddle) practice.

There were short breaks for meals at six forty-five A.M., noon and five forty-five P.M. for dinner, during which everybody filed into the dining room, took their allotted plastic bowl set, wrapped in a napkin, from the shelf, and sat at one of the seven long tables, where they would eat in silence. After lunch came shower breaks and work duties; after dinner there was *gyodo*—simultaneous walking and chanting meditation—and more *zazen* and *sanzen* until nine, ten, maybe eleven at night, depending on how long Roshi decided it should continue. But however late the day might run, the next morning at three A.M. promptly, the whole process would start again.

The daily schedule when there were no *sesshin* was somewhat less relentless, beginning at five A.M. and ending at nine P.M. and allowing for some private time between study and work duties. Nevertheless, for a man in his early sixties, for a musical icon whose last album was the biggest seller of his career, for a sophisticate, a man of the world, a ladies' man, none of this life Leonard had chosen was anything but extraordinary. The first rule of celebrity is that celebrities are to be served; but here was Leonard, chopping wood, banging nails, fixing toilets, doing whatever the monk charged with doling out and supervising work duties assigned him to do. Kigen, who held that position when Leonard first moved into the monastery, says he had "no idea at all that Leonard was a celebrity. I didn't know Leonard from beans." Leonard was perfectly happy with this. When Kigen told Leonard to rake out the bamboo and, having checked his work, told him to go back and do it again, that he'd missed some, Leonard did as he was instructed without protest.

Leonard lived in a wood cabin in the center of the monastery, close to the path. A doormat on his front step read WELCOME. A brave cluster of yellow wildflowers had forced their way through the stones to bloom beside his front door. Leonard had always been partial to small, plain dwellings and this answered the description perfectly. A white-walled room about nine feet square—between the size of a U.S. and a Canadian prison cell—held a narrow, metal-framed single bed and a chest of drawers. There was a menorah on the dresser and a tiny mirror on the wall. Its one small window was covered by a thin white curtain and a fly screen, which at nighttime was layered with dust-brown moths, attracted by the light. Leonard's cabin also had an additional room the size of a walk-in closet, in which were a desk, an old Macintosh computer, some books, a bottle of liquor or two and a Technics synthesizer. There was no TV, radio or stereo; if Leonard wanted to listen to a CD he would have to do so in his jeep, which was parked near the Zen Center entrance. His main luxuries were having his own toilet and a coffee machine. Roshi had granted Leonard special dispensation to get up earlier than the others and enjoy a solitary cigarette and coffee—sipped from a mug decorated with the album sleeve design of *The Future*—before joining the other residents in their daily tasks and observances.

Leonard's main job was working directly with Roshi, mostly as his chauffeur and cook. In the monastic tradition, the monks subsisted on lentils, lima beans, rice, split peas and pasta—there was a row of large garbage cans in the kitchen filled with them—and on food donations, which came once a week. These last made for all manner of curiosities, like the sweet wafer biscuits that appeared to have time-traveled from a 1940s English afternoon tea tray, which fortuitously arrived on the same day as a separate consignment of Indian tea marked for export to Russia. Leonard became expert at rustling up soups. At the age of sixty-one, he would earn a certificate from San Bernardino County that qualified him to take work as a chef,

waiter or busboy.* Sometimes he would ask himself what he was doing living like this, in this "land of broken hearts,"[3] as he called it, but
he knew the answer. There was nowhere else he could be.

Leonard had been coming to Mount Baldy for *sesshin* and retreats
for more than twenty years; he was familiar with everything about
the place. He knew what he was in for—this was no celebrity-friendly
Zen-lite retreat, of which California had no shortage. Rinzai monks,
Leonard liked to boast, were "the Marines of the spiritual world"[4]
with a regimen "designed to overthrow a twenty-year-old."[5] Why he
should have chosen to sign up full-time at the age of sixty, when he
was too old for the regimen and old enough to know better, is a question that has a three-part answer: Rebecca, the record business and
Roshi.

Shortly before he left L.A. for the monastic life, Leonard ran into
Roscoe Beck. He told his former musical director, "I've had it with
this music racket." He was getting out. Strange timing, one might
think. *The Future* was no *Various Positions;* it had been one of Leonard's most successful albums. But the tour that followed the album's
release had been a dislocating and debilitating experience. He hated
it and he was drinking heavily. So heavily that Roshi, a man by no
means averse to alcohol, expressed his concern.

Leonard's relationship with touring had always been complicated.
From the outset he viewed it at best as a necessary evil, foisted upon
him by his record contract, and he approached it under sufferance,
usually with the aid of alcohol, or in the early days, other palliatives.
Stage fright was a part of it, a shy man's fear of humiliating himself. Though the attention and the stage had not appeared to trouble
him as a young poetry reader, his insecurities as a singer and a musician made his fear of failure more acute. His first-ever major concert

---

* The test, taken after studying a DVD course on safe handling of food, required correct answers to forty out of fifty multiple-choice questions. Leonard's
exact score is unknown.

appearance—when Judy Collins had brought him out in 1967 at a benefit in New York—had been a "total failure."[6] Over the next few years, as he became more used to performing, the fear had mutated into a kind of public projection of his perfectionism, "that to take up people's time with anything but excellence is really too much to think about."[7] He was never able to take a concert he did casually, he said—which is believable, since Leonard had never shown any great ability at doing "casual" in any aspect of his life. If a show did not go well, "you feel you've betrayed yourself," he said,[8] which in turn evolved into a fear of betraying his art, by making it work like a prostitute night after night.

But Leonard also wanted people to hear his songs and buy his records. Given his general lack of radio attention and the geographical distance between him and his main fan base, which was not in the U.S. or even Canada, this meant going on the road and playing them. And as time passed, sometimes he would actually quite enjoy it, so long as everything ran smoothly and nothing felt out of his control. He had felt "entirely at home" on the *I'm Your Man* tour. Those who knew him well remarked how relaxed he seemed; he had even stopped drinking by the intermission. In 1993, when it came time to go out with *The Future*, Leonard rehired several crew members from the 1988 tour as well as five of its musicians for the eight-piece band he took on the road. Julie Christensen, who was on both tours, says, "I think Leonard really depends on the people around him to sustain the magic. He knows he can't do it all alone." But this time the magic didn't work.

Perla Batalla, who was also on both tours, describes the *Future* tour as "very, very drama laden." Though it might not have appeared so dramatic to an outsider, to someone as sensitive and conflicted about touring as Leonard, it was. The scheduling was more onerous than usual, with a great deal of travel and little time to catch one's breath. The North American leg, which followed almost directly on

from the twenty-six European concerts, had been particularly exacting: thirty-seven shows in under two months, with meet-and-greets
arranged backstage after almost every show—Leonard's second album in succession to be well received in the U.S. seemed to have
sent his once-indifferent U.S. record label into overdrive. (The *I'm
Your Man* tour, by comparison, had twenty-five dates separated by a
fifteen-week summer break.) The routing, which doubled back and
forth across the border, was also stressful, while the tour bus, which
suffered from defective shock absorbers, was hell on Canada's curvy
mountain roads and did nothing to help with bonhomie. Spirits were
already at an all-time low. Leonard's keyboard player Bill Ginn had
an addiction problem, which other members of the band were trying
and failing to help him with. That Perla Batalla had married since the
last tour and Julie Christensen had a young baby she had had to leave
behind only compounded the feeling that this was not the carefree
tour experience it had been five years before. Leonard had more than
once expressed anxiety that he was pulling families apart.

Leonard's fiancée, Rebecca De Mornay, had shown up at various
points in Europe and North America and on occasion traveled on
the bus with them for three or four days at a time. She could see that
touring was "very rough on him. It's a terrific conflict of taking someone who really likes to spend his time in one room that he could probably not leave for three days at a time, and to suddenly thrust himself
onto a stage with thousands of people listening." Rebecca appeared
well liked by everyone, but however good her intention she was a distraction, sometimes good, sometimes not. His energy seemed to shift
when she was there, affecting band rapport, which some of the musicians believed could be felt sometimes onstage. Offstage, there were
times when Leonard seemed elated at having Rebecca there. But
other times, later on the tour, raised voices could be heard behind the
closed dressing room door. By the midsummer of 1993, when the tour
was finally over, Leonard and Rebecca's engagement was too.

One of the most public of Leonard's relationships ended privately and quietly. Neither of them spoke about it to the press. Later Leonard would say, "She kind of got wise to me. Finally she saw I was a guy who just couldn't come across. In the sense of being a husband and having more children and the rest."[9] Rebecca disagrees. "I think the real truth is that Leonard in fact did come across more than he ever had with anyone. I think that's why there's no hard feelings, because we both know we each gave it our all."

Leonard did not tell Rebecca that he was leaving for the monastery. "But," says Rebecca, "all those things are just details. The real thing is we really impacted each other's lives in incredibly positive ways. One of many things Leonard said in the course of our relationship that was very wise was, 'Look, here's what I know: marriage is the hardest spiritual practice in the world.' I said, 'What are you talking about?' He said, 'People wonder how anybody can sit on Mount Baldy for hours on end, weeks, months, even, but it's nothing compared to marriage. If you're really there, really present, for marriage, it's self-reflection, twenty-four/seven. In other words, who you are is reflected back to you in the mirror of your marriage partner, daily, minute by minute, hour by hour. Who can take that?' He's very self-aware."

Leonard, says Rebecca, "was searching all of his life to figure out what is it, where is it, or maybe just, how do I get the hell out of here? Having all these relationships with women and not really committing; having this elongated history with Roshi and Zen meditation and yet always running away from it also, and having this long relationship to his career, and yet feeling like it's the last thing he wants to be doing. I have a feeling that a lot of things came to a head for him within the context, or the time frame, of our relationship; I think we each crystallized something for each other once and for all. And after we broke up, he committed to the other thing that he'd been unwilling to commit to: he became a monk, which he'd never done, and which, by the way, has given me a fearsome reputation: 'God, after you men run off and become monks; what do you do to them?'"

With Rebecca gone from his life, and having taken his leave of the music business, there was no reason for Leonard to remain in L.A. The reason Leonard himself gave for going to the monastery was "for love"[10]—not so much love of Buddhism and the idea of living as a monk, but love of Roshi, the old man with whom he could sit in silence on this broken hill. As Leonard described it, "Something like this you can only do for love. If Roshi had been a professor of physics at Heidelberg University, I would have learned German and gone to Heidelberg to study physics. I think that one approaches a master in many various conditions. If you want a master, he becomes your master; some people want a disciplinarian, so there's a strict regime available for such people. I was more interested in friendship, so he manifested as a friend. When I finished my tour in 1993 I was approaching the age of sixty; Roshi was approaching ninety. My old teacher was getting older and I hadn't spent enough time with him, and my kids were grown and I thought it was an appropriate moment to intensify my friendship and my association with the community."[11]

Leonard had gone there ostensibly to be of service to Roshi, but the arrangement worked for him and Roshi both. He had also been drawn to the monastery, he understood a few years later, by "the sense of something unfinished, something that would keep me alive."[12] He likened the Zen Center to a mountain hospital and he and his fellow residents to "people who have been traumatized, hurt, destroyed, maimed by daily life," sitting in the waiting room, all waiting to see this small, rotund Japanese doctor. Whatever its hardships and deprivations might be, the monastic life had its own voluptuous luxury for a man with an appetite for discipline, who was harsher on himself than any punishing regime an old monk with a bagful of koans could devise. The emptiness and silence, the lack of distractions, the sense of order counteracted the confusion of words and anxieties in his head. Here Leonard was no one special. He was a cog in the machine, everyone and everything interconnected, simply one of a small and constantly changing community who all dressed alike, shared chores and ate together at the same time from identical plastic bowls. Leonard had no problem with that in the least. Right now he had very little interest in being "Leonard Cohen." What he was looking for was a kind of emptiness—something he had sought in many different ways throughout his adult life, be it through fasting, sex or Scientology auditing. It was "this emptiness" that had first attracted him to Roshi's monastery. "It's a place where it's very difficult to hold fast to one's ideas. There is this sort of charitable void that I found here in a very pure form."[13] At Mount Baldy Zen Center he had no decisions to make, he was told what to do and when and how to do it, but—unlike a record company contract or a marriage—there was an escape clause. Leonard could leave if he wanted to.

On a few occasions he did. Hanging his robes on the peg, he would drive down the mountain, past the signs that warned against throwing snowballs, and join the freeway traffic heading northwest to L.A. He was going back not for some decadent lost weekend, but to be alone. A small monastery on a mountain might sound like an isolated existence, but it did not appear that way to Leonard: "There's very little private space and private time. There's a saying in the monastery, the monks are like pebbles in a bag; one is always working shoulder to shoulder, so it has the same quality as life anywhere, the same sensations of love, hate, jealousy, rejection, admiration. It's ordinary life under a microscope."[14] Leonard's first stop was McDonald's, to buy a Filet-O-Fish; he would wash it down later with a glass of good French wine. But after a day or two at home watching television—*The Jerry Springer Show* was a favorite—having been reminded of how his life would be were he not in the monastery, Leonard drove back up the mountain and slipped back into his robes.

The days ran into one another, divided into segments of near-constant, mostly regulated activity. "You don't sleep for very long and you work many hours a day and sit in the meditation hall for many hours a day, but once you get the hang of it," Leonard said, "you go into ninth gear and kind of float through it all."[15]

This level of acceptance did not come immediately. He and Kigen, being considerably older than many of the people who came to Mount Baldy for the *sesshin*, would commiserate with each other over the severity of the place. "The landscape is austere and that altitude very challenging. Leonard said it was designed for people with a ton of energy," says Kigen. "But what a lot of the practice is about is being able to go with confidence to a place that normally you would become very insecure about, and realizing that you *can* make your home there, that you can actually live and thrive and find peace in those extreme places." Leonard felt more at peace for longer stretches of time than he cared to remember. "They just work you to death so that you forget about yourself," Leonard said, "and forgetting about yourself is another kind of refreshment. There is a strict sense of order, but I like that sort of thing. Once you overcome your natural resistance to being told what to do, if you can overcome that, then you begin to relax into the schedule and the simplicity of your day. You just think about your sleep, your work, the next meal, and that whole component of improvisation that tyrannizes much of our lives begins to dissolve."[16]

It is a popular belief that an artist or writer needs an element of disorder, misery and improvisation in order to create. As Leonard himself said, "It's true that God himself, as it relates in Genesis, uses chaos and desolation to create the order of the universe, so chaos and desolation could be understood as the DNA of all creativity."[17] But the highly structured existence, in conjunction with his desire to forget who he was and overcome his ego, appeared to free up Leonard's creativity. That last might appear paradoxical, when the urge to create would seem to come from an expression of the artist's ego. But the removal of internal distractions—anxiety, expectations— from his Zen practice was as important as the lack of external distractions in these plain, orderly surroundings. In the precious, circumscribed hours between duties, Leonard was busy writing, drawing and composing music on his synthesizer—delicate, poignant music he described as "a lot like French movie music from the fifties."[18] Some of this poetry and artwork would appear in *Book of Longing*, but that would be a decade in the future. Working in the back room of his little cabin, Leonard gave no thought to publishing a book or releasing an album. He worked for the sake of the work, with as little attachment to its outcome as a man who had not yet attained *satori* (enlightenment) could muster.

Busy as Leonard's life was on Mount Baldy, time seemed to stand still. Although the world outside went on without him, Leonard showed little interest in the details, letting it slip off the reel like an old film he had no real desire to see again. Months went by, then years, marked only by the changes in season and the periodic earlier alarm calls that signaled the start of another rigorous *sesshin*. During the many long hours Leonard sat in *zazen*, his mind would wander from the pain in his knees to the songs he was writing in his head, or even to sexual fantasies. "When you're sitting for long hours in the meditation hall you run through all your numbers. It takes a while to exhaust those things and maybe they're never fully exhausted, but after a while you get tired of running your own Top 40 scenarios about the girl you want or lost or the one you need to recover."[19] Though they were fewer in number than monks, there were nuns on Mount Baldy. They had their own quarters, and liaisons with the male residents were not encouraged. Of course, they went on. "The situation offers up certain erotic possibilities," Leonard said. "It's a lot easier than cruising the terrace cafés of Paris. For a young person with energy—since there's not much free time—it's a very promising environment." When he was younger, Leonard "had several brief, intense liaisons" at Mount Baldy,[20] but he was no longer "terribly active in that realm."[21]

He was not entirely devoid of female companionship. Chris Dar-row, whose band the Kaleidoscope played on Leonard's debut album, lived in Claremont, at the base of Mount Baldy, and was surprised to spot Leonard sitting in the sun on the patio of the local Greek restau-rant, Yanni's, drinking a Greek coffee, in the company of a beautiful nun. Were it not for the black robes and shaved heads, it might have been Hydra. Darrow went up to their table. "Hi, Leonard, remember me?" They had not seen each other since the *Songs of Leonard Cohen* session in 1967. "Sure," said Leonard. "You saved my record."

While Leonard showed no interest in making a new album, in September 1995, after he had been living in the monastery for two years, another tribute album was released. *Tower of Song* differed from *I'm Your Fan* in a number of ways. The first tribute had been an inde-pendent album, a labor of love compiled by a French rock magazine, on which predominantly young, edgier rock artists covered Leon-ard's songs. *Tower of Song*, by contrast, was a major-label album set in motion by Kelley Lynch, produced by her romantic partner Steve Lindsey, and featuring more mainstream, big-name acts. At Lynch's urging, Leonard had taken a few days away from the monastery to assist her in contacting some of the musicians on the wish list. He tackled the uncomfortable task with humor, sending a message to Phil Collins that asked, "Would Beethoven decline an invitation from Mozart?" No, Collins replied, "unless Beethoven was on a world tour at the time."

Among the lineup on *Tower of Song* were Collins's former Gen-esis bandmate Peter Gabriel as well as Elton John, Don Henley, Wil-lie Nelson, Billy Joel, Tori Amos, Suzanne Vega and Aaron Neville. Sting and the Chieftains teamed up to perform a Celtic "Sisters of Mercy," while Bono took a break from U2 to record an ambient Beat poetry-gospel version of "Hallelujah."

"Nobody," the author Tom Robbins wrote in the album's liner notes, "can sing the word 'naked' as nakedly as Cohen." This was probably not the best endorsement for an album of Leonard Cohen songs not sung by Leonard Cohen. But Leonard, who had also been persuaded to do a few interviews to help promote the album, told the press he was very pleased with it. "Except for being written, this is the best thing that has happened to these songs and I am deeply grateful to these eminent artists, who could so easily have done without this project, for their kindness and solidarity."[22] Reviewers, however, were not kind. As a sales ploy, the record company sent free copies to bars and cafés (and this long before Starbucks became a music-marketing machine) that had what they referred to as the "Leonard Cohen vibe." Presumably what they had in mind were sophisticated, elegant establishments. Certainly not a small wooden cabin on a rock-strewn hill, which Leonard returned to as swiftly as etiquette allowed and which he showed no inclination to leave.

On August 9, 1996, three years into his life in the monastery, Leonard was ordained a Zen Buddhist monk. Steve Sanfield, the friend through whom Leonard first became acquainted with Roshi, drove up for the ceremony and Esther, Leonard's sister, flew in from New York. Leonard, dressed in robes, his head shaved, turned to Sanfield and whispered wryly, "You got me into this, can you get me out of it?" Leonard had agreed to the ordination not as a step toward sainthood, nor as a step away from the religion he was born to. As he wrote in his 1997 poem "Not a Jew,"

Anyone who says
I'm not a Jew
is not a Jew
I'm very sorry
but this is final
So says:
Eliezar, son of Nissan,
priest of Israel;
a.k.a.
Nightingale of the Sinai.

Yom Kippur 1973;
a.k.a.
Jikan the Unconvincing
Zen monk,
a.k.a.
*Leonard Cohen . . .**

He had agreed to ordination to "observe protocol."[23] Roshi had told him it was time for him to become a monk, and so that is what he did. Leonard had also recently taken on responsibilities for which official status might be deemed appropriate: Roshi had asked him to preside over his funeral. The old man, now approaching his ninetieth birthday, instructed Leonard that he wanted a traditional, open-pyre cremation. If Leonard would like to, Roshi said, he could keep one of his bones.

At the ordination ceremony, Leonard was given a new name: Jikan. "Roshi doesn't speak English very well so you don't really know what he means by the names he gives you," Leonard said. "He prefers it that way because he doesn't want people to indulge themselves in the poetic quality of these traditional monks' names. I have asked him what Jikan meant many times, at the appropriate moment over a drink, and he says 'ordinary silence' or 'normal silence' or 'the silence between two thoughts.'"[24] Dangerously poetic. And deliciously ironic for a singer and a man of words.

In all, the silence of the monastic life seemed to suit Leonard. There were occasional visitors, however. Adam Cohen, who had just signed a record deal with Columbia, came and discussed with his father the lyrics for the songs he was working on for his first album. Leonard gave his son a song that he had been "working on for years" and knew he'd "never get around to doing,"[25] "Lullaby in Blue." Sharon Robinson, who knew the Zen Center, having been there her-

---

* Leonard published a six-line edit of "Not a Jew" in *Book of Longing* (2006).

self on retreat, drove up and, over a bottle of wine, listened as he played for her on his synthesizer the latest of his countless versions of "A Thousand Kisses Deep." Among the uninvited guests, in Kigen's words, was "a beautiful young lady who came up one evening and was wearing rags and feathers, literally. 'Where's Leonard? I'm here for Leonard.'" But really there were remarkably few celebrity-seekers; Kigen says he could count them on one hand.

Two separate, small film crews also made their way up the mountain, one from France, the other from Sweden. The result was two insightful TV documentaries, Armelle Brusq's *Leonard Cohen: Portrait: Spring 96* and Agreta Wirberg's *Stina Möter Leonard Cohen*. The French film showed Leonard working in the monastery kitchen, sitting in the meditation hall, reading the chants through a large pair of tinted spectacles and marching outside with the other monks. He assured Brusq that his life wasn't one of isolation. Real life was far more solitary, he said. When a tour ended, he would return to the "tyrannical solitude" of home, where he might spend days alone, speaking to no one, doing nothing.

The Swedish presenter, Stina Dabrowski, questioned Leonard about love, and he answered like a man who'd had the time and space to think about it. "I had wonderful love but I did not give back wonderful love," he said. "I was unable to reply to their love. Because I was obsessed with some fictional sense of separation, I couldn't touch the thing that was offered me, and it was offered me everywhere." Nonetheless, at times when the world started feeling bright again, he would forget now and then that he lived "in this sixty-three-year-old body" and he would think about finding a young girl, marrying her, buying a house and getting a real job, maybe working in a bookstore. "I could do that now. I know how to do it now," he said. When he was asked the inevitable question about coming back to music he answered no, saying, "I can't interrupt these studies. It's too important for me to interrupt . . . for the health of my soul." Quoting the Jewish sage Hillel the Elder, "If I'm not for myself, who will be for

me? And if not now, when? But if I'm only for myself, who am I?"
Leonard asked his fans to please forgive him. He was trying to learn
some things, he said, that would result in "songs that are deeper and
better."[26]

In the absence of Leonard or any word of a new album from him, in
1997 Columbia Records released a compilation, *More Best Of* (1997).
Twenty-two years had passed since the first *Best Of* album—or *Greatest Hits*, as it was called in the UK and Europe, where Leonard actually had hits—and Leonard had felt "no great urgency" for another.
But it was the thirtieth anniversary of his having signed to Columbia;
he said, "Although I myself feel very little nostalgia, I went along
with it."[27] Leonard was asked to choose the songs, which he did—
enough songs to fill a double album. In the end the label decided on
a single album, which they wanted to focus on his more recent material. They also asked Leonard if he had any new songs he might give
them. Leonard had actually finished a jaunty and self-deprecating
number titled "Never Any Good." Another new song was a short,
computerized piece called "The Great Event," its melody a backward *Moonlight Sonata*, its vocal a synthesized version of Leonard's
own real voice.

Leonard had been working in the monastery on experimental
music. One idea he had come up with, but had been unable to realize on his elderly computer and synthesizer, was to create a vocal
that sounded "like some broken-down speaker that was left after the
destruction of the cosmos, just filled with some kind of absurd hope
for regeneration"[28]—the next step from "The Future," as interpreted
by a Zen monk. Around this time, Mount Baldy for the first time had
connected to the Internet—a slow, dial-up connection through the
monastery's one and only phone, but Leonard was online.

Jarkko Arjatsalo, an accountant living in Finland, was surprised
to receive a message from a monk in California, asking if he would
call him. Leonard had heard about the Leonard Cohen Files, a web-

site devoted to his work that Arjatsalo and his teenage son Rauli had created in 1995. If Arjatsalo could create a website, Leonard thought, perhaps he could answer his technical questions (this being pre-Google, and the connection being so painfully sluggish). "Leonard was looking for software that could imitate his voice—not a perfect copy, something that was obviously mechanized though recognizably him," Arjatsalo remembers. Through his website's global network he found a scientist at the University of California at Berkeley who came up with a solution. It was the start of a close association and friendship between Leonard and the man he dubbed "the general secretary of the party." LeonardCohenFiles.com would become known as Leonard's digital archive and the communications hub for the international fan community.

Leonard asked if he might add some material of his own to the website. He submitted early versions of lyrics for songs, including "Suzanne," and drafts of new songs and poems. He wanted to "make the process clear, or at least throw some light on the mysterious activity of writing," he wrote. He also sent copies of his artwork, which ranged from drawings on napkins to digital art. Leonard particularly enjoyed creating art on a computer. He just liked computers. "They say that the Torah was written with black fire on white fire. I get that feeling from the computer, the bright black against the bright background. It gives it a certain theatrical dignity to see it on the screen."[29] His interest in Macs started early on, thanks in part to the Apple company giving away free computers to select Canadian writers—among them Leonard, Irving Layton and Margaret Atwood—and sending tutors to their homes to show them how to use them.

Leonard said in an interview with *Billboard* in 1998 that he had been "posting a lot of original material on the Finnish site." He said, "I don't know what the ramifications are. Speaking as a writer toward the end of his life, where most of my work is out there, I've collected royalties on it, I've been able to live and maybe even provide for a respectable retirement. I'd be happy to publish everything on the Internet at this stage of the game."[30] His record company did not share his sentiments. When he included the website addresses of the Leonard Cohen Files and other related sites on the back sleeve of *More Best Of*, they told him to take them off, talking about "permissions" and "compliance." But Leonard insisted and the URLs remained in place.

Leonard had taken to the Internet wholeheartedly—and this some considerable time before the decline of the recording industry and the expansion of the Web made it a necessity for artists. For someone who had essentially cut himself off from the world, it allowed him to communicate with the world on his own terms. He could keep in touch with his fans around the globe without having to get out of his robes and onto a plane. He could keep his work in the public eye without having to go through an intermediary, like the record company. He was already living, to some degree, a virtual existence up there in that remote spot a long way above the ground and a longer way from heaven; in the Internet he'd found a perfectly Cohenesque way of being both not there and never more fully present.

Leonard logged off for the night. There was a good bottle of cognac on the table that he'd picked up on his last grocery run to Claremont. Tucking it underneath his arm, he crunched up the hill in his flip-flops to Roshi's cabin.

Autumn 1998. Leonard had been living in the monastery for five years. He was as thin as the air; his long black robes hung loosely on his body. During countless hours of meditation, he had had out-of-body experiences and moments when "the sky opens up and you get the word." There had been periods during his life on Mount Baldy when Leonard felt contentment and when everything seemed to make sense. This was not one of them. Pulling himself out of his bed in the middle of the night, putting the water on for coffee, fingers waxy from the cold, what Leonard felt was despair. In the meditation hall, where he sat listening to Roshi's familiar voice deliver the *teisho* from the lectern-throne at the front of the room, he realized that he no longer had any idea what Roshi was saying. "I used to be able to understand, but my mind had become so concerned with dissolving the pain that my critical faculties had become really impaired."[31] The anguish did not abate; it deepened. His doctor prescribed antidepressants, telling him they would put a floor on how low he could go. But "the floor opened up," Leonard said, "and I fell right through it."[32]

One day Leonard was taking Roshi to the airport—Roshi was flying to New Mexico to lead one of his periodic *sesshins* at his second monastery in Jemez Springs—and he needed to go back to Mount Baldy for something. Driving up the mountain's switchback roads, Leonard was suddenly seized by a panic so crippling that he had to pull over. He reached into the backseat for his knapsack and pulled out the shaving kit in which he kept his antidepressants. His heart pounding, he took out the pills, then threw them out of the car. "I said, 'If I'm going to go down, I'm going to go down with my eyes open.' There's something obscene about taking this stuff and going down. And then I went back to Mount Baldy," Leonard said, "and I *really* went down."[33]

He was unable to find his way back up. The winter months felt crueler than ever; Roshi's *teisho* sounded like gibberish. After five and a half years in the monastery and in the deepest pit of depression, Leonard felt that he had "come to the end of the road."[34] On a cold early January night in 1999, Leonard walked up the hill to Roshi's cabin. It was black and starless; there was snow in the air. Roshi, shrunken with age, peered over the reading glasses whose magnification made his eyes look profoundly deep. The two sat together in stillness, as they had so often done. Leonard broke the silence. "Roshi," he said, "I've got to go. I'm going to go down the mountain."

Roshi said, "How long?" Leonard said, "I don't know." The old man looked at him. "Okay," Roshi said. "You go."

Leonard's note of apology to Roshi for his desertion read: "I'm sorry that I cannot help you now because I met this woman. . . . Jikan the useless monk bows his head." The words were accompanied by a drawing of a female Hindu temple dancer.* Less than a week after leaving Mount Baldy, Leonard was in India. Leonard had left Roshi to be with not a woman but a man.

Ramesh S. Balsekar was eighty-one years old, a strip of a lad compared with Roshi. He had studied at the London School of Economics and had been the president of a leading bank in India until, in the late seventies, he became a devotee of Nisargadatta Maharaj, a master of the Advaita (meaning non-dual) school of Hindu philosophy. Ramesh now received students of his own in his apartment in South Mumbai. Among them, just days after having left Roshi's monastery, and "in a state of acute depression and deep distress," was Leonard.[35]

Leonard had first encountered Ramesh's teachings while living on Mount Baldy. A few years earlier, someone at the monastery had given him a book called *Consciousness Speaks*, a question-and-answer session with Balsekar, published in 1992. At the foundation of Ramesh's teaching is that there is one supreme Source, Brahman, which created everything and is also everything it created. Since there is only this one single consciousness, then there is no "I" or "me," no individual doer of any action, no individual thinker of any thoughts, no experiencer of any experiences. Once the sense of self drops away, once a person deeply understands that he has no free will, no control over what he does nor over what is done to him, when he takes no personal pride in his achievements or personal affront at what might befall him, then that person becomes one with that single consciousness or Source. When Leonard read the book that first time, he liked

---

* Later published in *Book of Longing*, 2006.

it but could not say that he understood it. He put it aside, and during "those last dark days"[36] at the monastery he found himself drawn back to it. This time when he read it, it seemed to make more sense. He even found that by applying Ramesh's teachings to Roshi's *teisho*, he could once again understand Roshi. But it was a purely intellectual understanding that did nothing to ease the intensity of his mental torment. Leonard drove to the Bodhi bookstore to look for more books by Balsekar and decided to go to India to hear him in person. He booked a flight to Mumbai.

The years Leonard had spent in the monastery had done nothing to dull his talent at sniffing out a nondescript hotel room. Kemps Corner was a two-star hotel in the south of Mumbai in a busy, built-up neighborhood. A small place—just thirty-five rooms—it was not more than a couple of hundred yards from the beach, though closer still to a highway overpass. The building was old but not elegant. There was a jaunty striped awning over the entrance door that led into a miniature, dimly lit lobby. Leonard took a small single room at the back of the building, where there was less street noise. There was a narrow bed, one side pushed up against the white-painted wall; an armchair; a wooden desk beneath a wood-framed mirror; a tiny TV; and a white-tiled bathroom.

In Mumbai Leonard once again kept to a fairly strict schedule. Every morning a little after eight he would leave the hotel, dressed in Western clothes—loose black shirt tucked into light-colored linen trousers, Leonard's formal take on casual—and walk to the *satsang*, which was a mile away. He always took the same route, which led him through the congestion of people and traffic, beggars and eternal car horns, and onto Warden (now Bhulabhai Desai) Road, the main road that ran beside the beach and the Arabian Sea. The buildings he passed—the Breach Candy Club and Gardens, the U.S. consulate— grew increasingly privileged the closer he came to North Gamadia Road, the small, quiet lane where Ramesh lived on the top floor of a five-story art deco apartment building, Sindula House. This part of town was considerably more upmarket than Leonard's, its residents a mix of old money, successful writers, well-known actors and retired bank presidents like Balsekar.

The apartment was well appointed though not luxurious. It had four rooms, the largest of which, the living room, was used for the *satsang*. It could accommodate around forty people sitting on the floor. Leaving his shoes outside the door, Leonard sought out an inconspicuous spot in a back corner and sat there, cross-legged, eyes cast down. At nine A.M. Ramesh, a small, trim man, his hair white, like his clothes, entered from the next-door room and took his chair at the front. Following a short formal reading, the question-and-answer session began, which Ramesh would start by inquiring of someone—usually a newcomer—what had brought them to India and what their background was.

"Most of the attendees were foreigners—a lot of them from Israel—with maybe three or four Indians in a group of thirty-five or forty," says Ratnesh Mathur, an Indian banker who became friendly with Leonard during Leonard's first trip to Mumbai. Mathur had not heard of Ramesh until Leonard spoke about him and invited him to a *satsang* (the first of around forty *satsang*s Mathur would attend over the next four years) since Ramesh was relatively unknown as a spiritual leader among his countrymen. "Ramesh alienated himself from the cults," Mathur says, "he didn't target the Indian mass media. He was not a big publicity seeker and he was clearly living on a pension so there was no financial motive. His articulation was in English, his mannerisms were Western, his message was rather erudite and intellectual, and his style was not part of the Ramana Maharshi legacy." Ramana was a popular guru and some of his followers had cast aspersions on Ramesh as a spiritual leader. "Really, he lived like a retired banker—he liked his occasional golf and whiskey—except that one or two hours a day he would leave it open to have people come to his home. People came mostly by word of mouth. It was a very respectable crowd, not the traditional hippie crowd," although some seekers had come to Ramesh after visiting the Osho commune in Pune, two hours from Mumbai. (Its leader, Bhagwan Shree Rajneesh, had established an alternative living community in Oregon in the early eighties, before controversy and scandal, and the guru's deportation, led to its closure.)

Ramesh was a straight-talker. He dealt with his *satsang* audience much as you might imagine he would his employees at the bank, imparting information and instructions in a direct, no-nonsense manner. Mathur says, "Ramesh easily lost patience with folks who spoke too much and tried to involve him in some esoteric argument. He would remind them that he charged no entrance fee"—if someone wished to make a donation they could do so later—"and then show them to the exit door." When he spotted someone in the room who had been coming repeatedly for too long he would single them out and say, according to Mathur, "'Don't you have anything better to do? My main message to you is that God is everywhere, so you can't just focus on religion, you don't keep meditating your way to God.' Basically he said, 'Get a life.'" Ramesh never said this to Leonard, though, whom he had also seen privately and with whom he became friendly. "He was always very polite and nice about Leonard."

After approximately two hours Ramesh would look at his watch, which indicated that the questions and answers had come to an end. When Ramesh left the room, a *bhajan* singer, Mrs. Murthy, came in to lead the gathering in the singing of the traditional Hindu songs. A paper was passed around the room with the words written in both the original Sanskrit and the Roman alphabet. "But Leonard didn't need that," Mathur remembers. "He knew every word." When the singing stopped, everyone filed out past the table where Mrs. Murthy's husband sold copies of Ramesh's books and of the audiotapes made of every *satsang*. The tapes dating from Leonard's earliest months of attendance—when he had asked Ramesh questions, rather than sit quietly, as he would do later, concentrating on what he was saying— proved a popular sales item once word started to spread about Leonard's studying with Ramesh. Mathur started noticing that some attendees seemed to be seeking Leonard more than Ramesh. No one bothered Leonard during the *satsang*, but people would come up and talk to him by the table or on his way out of the building.

"He was normally very polite," says Mathur. "He would talk to them. Occasionally if he found someone interesting, he would take them to a small tea stall," an unassuming little spot some fifty yards away, the kind of place Leonard consistently found and frequented in whichever city he happened to be living. The workers in the tea shop all recognized him, greeting him with a smile and a respectful exchange of *namaste*. They did not know him as a celebrity but as a Westerner with short silver hair, a friendly man who came in regularly and always treated them well. "He told me most people didn't recognize him on the street when he walked and he loved that about being here." Leonard, Mathur observed, "deliberately avoided spending time with the Mumbai rich and famous." People always came to him with invitations, Mathur included, to which Leonard would politely make his excuses, "but he told me once about going to some taxi driver's slum home. I remember being surprised to see how he developed these bonds with folks who knew nothing of him as a famous singer-songwriter. Perhaps the folks who spent the most time with him in India are the cleaners of Kemps hotel and the workers at the tea stall."

After tea Leonard left for the other regular item on his schedule, his midday swim. There were YMCAs with pools in Mumbai but nothing convenient, so Leonard joined the Breach Candy Club, an exclusive, private club on the seafront on Warden Road, which had a lap pool as well as an enormous outdoor pool, built in the shape of

India.* The rest of the day was usually spent alone in his hotel room, meditating, sketching, writing and reading books written or recommended by Ramesh. Mathur had offered Leonard some books on related topics but he declined them politely; he did not want distractions. Early evening he would take himself off to a restaurant for a vegetarian meal, then return to his room, light some incense, put on a CD of Indian music and meditate and read some more. He had little interest in sightseeing, but he paid a visit to the Keneseth Eliyahoo Synagogue, which served a small Jewish community. Not far from the synagogue was a large, bustling record store, Rhythm House. He asked if they had any Leonard Cohen albums. They did. He could find them, he was told, under "Easy Listening."

Leonard flew home back to L.A. in the spring. There he put the finishing touches to a song he was writing for an event in tribute to the late Canadian poet and intellectual Frank "F. R." Scott, whom Leonard had known from his McGill University days. The song "Villanelle for our Time" was a Scott poem of the same name that Leonard had set to music. Working on the song, Leonard realized it needed a woman's voice. He called Anjani Thomas, one of his former backing singers, and asked if she would come over. They completed the recording in a single afternoon.

Then Leonard drove to Mount Baldy. It had been almost four months since he had seen Roshi and he wanted to pay his respects. As they had done so many times, they sat with a cognac in the old man's cabin, the world outside swollen up in darkness, moths pressed against the fly screen on the window like dried flowers in a poetry book. They talked little but when they did it was not about Leonard studying another discipline with a different master. Nor did Leonard discuss with Roshi what he had learned from Ramesh. "Roshi doesn't discuss," not even his own teachings, Leonard said. "He's not

---

* Salman Rushdie, who grew up in the area, describes the pool in his book *Midnight's Children.*

interested in perspective or talking. You either get it or you don't. He doesn't give you any astounding truths that we come to expect from spiritual teachers, because he's a mechanic—he's not talking about the philosophy of locomotion, he's talking about repairing the motor. He's mostly talking to a broken motor. Roshi is direct transmission."[37]

Leonard did not stay in the monastery long. In June he came back down from the mountain. His close friend Nancy Bacal, who met with him in L.A., observed that "he was like a kid when he came back from Baldy; suddenly he could come and go as he pleased, do whatever he wanted. It took him a moment or two to figure that out, but when he did, it was a delight to see him so happy and so joyous. Baldy was wonderful for him. Now it was time to take the next step."

For the first time in years, Leonard went back to Hydra. He packed the notebooks he had filled during his long stay in the monastery, and, in his old study, in the white house on the hill, he went to work on poems and songs in various states of completion. He also returned to Montreal and visited his old friend Irving Layton, now eighty-seven years old, suffering from Alzheimer's and living in a nursing home. Leonard had been rereading a good deal of Layton's poetry lately and was thinking about setting some of it to music, as he had done with F. R. Scott's.

Leonard also returned to Mumbai, once again taking his old room at the Hotel Kemps Corner. In 1999 the room was his home for almost five months. He spent his last birthday of the millennium there. When Mathur met with Leonard that day, he could not fail to notice how happy Leonard seemed. Leonard celebrated after *satsang* with a birthday lunch. "There was one girl who had come along with us, a girl who had come to Ramesh's sessions and was clearly enamored of Leonard. He had picked up a flower in the hotel vase and put it in the lapel of his jacket, and he smoked a cigarette or two that day, although I think he had given them up at the time. He said that he was very happy to be here, and this happiness was evident all the way through. It was on his face and in everything he was saying, which was all very, very positive."

Something had happened to Leonard in India. Something, as he told Sharon Robinson, "just lifted" the veil of depression through which he had always seen the world. Over the space of several visits Leonard would make to Mumbai over the next few years, returning to his room at the Hotel Kemps Corner and making his daily walk to *satsang*—altogether, he spent more than a year studying with Ramesh—"by imperceptible degrees this background of anguish that had been with me my whole life began to dissolve. I said to myself, 'This must be what it's like to be relatively sane.' You get up in the morning and it's not like: Oh God, another day. How am I going to get through it? What am I going to do? Is there a drug? Is there a woman? Is there a religion? Is there a something to get me out of this? The background now is very peaceful."[38] His depression had gone.

Leonard was unable to articulate precisely what it was that had cured his depression. He thought he had read somewhere "that the brain cells associated with anxiety can die as you get older,"[39] although the general intelligence is that depression worsens with age. Perhaps this was *satori*—enlightenment—though if it was, it had come with "no great flash, no fireworks."[40] Why it had come with Ramesh and Core Hinduism rather than Roshi and Zen Buddhism he could not say. Despite the differences in their teaching methods and approaches—Roshi's strict, rigorous regimen and his repetitive *teisho,* delivered on the in-breath and the out-breath and addressed not to the intellect but to the meditative condition; Ramesh's direct, straight-talking question-answer approach and his instruction that his followers should live however they choose—there was a great deal of consistency in their doctrines: overcoming the ego, nonattachment, universal consciousness, *tendrel,* the interrelatedness of all things. Most likely it was a combination of the two and had simply happened on Ramesh's watch. Ramesh implied as much. "You got this very quickly," he told Leonard, adding that his thirty years with Roshi did not hurt.[41] Still, as Leonard's mother had always used to say to him, "Don't look a gift horse in the mouth," so Leonard didn't. What was left in the deep, dark hole left after the anguish had gone was "a deep sense of gratitude, to what or who I don't know. I focused it on my teachers and friends."[42]

———————

The year was drawing to a close. Back in Los Angeles, Leonard once again ran into his musician friend Roscoe Beck. The last time they had seen each other had been more than five years before, just as Leonard was leaving to go live with Roshi. Beck reminded Leonard of what he'd said on that occasion, that he'd "had it with the music racket." Leonard smiled. "Ah," he said, "now I've had it with the religious racket. I'm ready to take up music again."

Of course he hadn't really had it with religion. Religion, as Leonard has said on any number of occasions, was his "favorite hobby." He still studied with Ramesh, he still meditated at the Zen Center in L.A. and he continued to read the Jewish scriptures and light the Sabbath candles at dusk every Friday. But what he had said about taking up music again was true. Leonard picked up the phone and called Sharon Robinson and Leanne Ungar, asking them to come over. It was time to record his first album of the new millennium.

Twenty-one

Love and Theft

Women. You couldn't move for them. After the largely male life of the monastery, it was a novelty and a delight. A comfort too; Leonard had not lived in such a female world since he was a nine-year-old boy in Montreal. In the apartment downstairs was his daughter Lorca. Upstairs, in the room above the garage, Sharon Robinson and Leanne Ungar were working in the studio they had put together for Leonard to make his album at home. Sharon and Leanne would arrive at noon to find him in the kitchen, preparing them lunch. Kelley Lynch, Leonard's manager, would often show up at around the same time and eat with them.

Cooking was one of the habits Leonard had brought home with him from the monastery. Another was getting up at four A.M., having a quiet coffee and a cigarette, then starting his day's work. Although he had quit smoking, he had taken it up again during a visit to India; a wise man had said to him, when he refused the offer of a cigarette, "What is life for? Smoke." While the world still slept, Leonard recorded in the aerie above the garage, until the birds began their dawn chorus in the grapefruit trees and the sound of the neighbors starting up their cars bled through the unsoundproofed walls. His computer screen lighting up the darkness, he would murmur softly into an old microphone linked to Pro Tools recording software, the harrowed young man playing a Spanish guitar to a sad-eyed girl in a bedroom seeming a lifetime away.

Leonard was happy. He was fully aware of the novelty of such a circumstance, but it was something he tried not to think about too much; he did not want to risk thinking himself back into his old familiar state of unhappiness. Nor did he wish to tempt fate, acknowledging, "God may take it away."[1] The depression and anxiety had been so much a part of him for such a long time that on occasion they seemed hard to separate from the depth and seriousness of his work. They had certainly been the drive behind the great majority of his pursuits in his adult life—"the engine," as Leonard expressed it, "of most of my investigation into the various things I looked into, whatever it was: wine, woman, song, religion."[2] Women and drugs, as well as mantras and fasting and all the various regimes of physical and spiritual self-discipline he had pursued, had had their pleasures, but they were also palliatives, medication, attempts to "beat the devil, try to get on top of it,"[3] or help ease the pain. Now the pain had gone. Sometimes, as he went about his work, he surprised himself with the ease with which he adapted to this new lightness of being and peace of mind.

There was also a new woman in Leonard's life. Readers will not find this surprising, although Leonard seemed to. He thought he'd had it with the romance racket, thinking perhaps that it might have vanished along with the depression and anguish. "I think one becomes more circumspect about everything as one gets older. I mean, you become more foolish and more wise at the same time as you get older," he said. In his midsixties, he had been reminded that the heart could not be mastered: "I think one is vulnerable at any moment to those emotions."[4] His first new love since leaving the monastery was, like his last love before he entered it, a talented beauty twenty-five years his junior: a singer and keyboard player from Hawaii who performed under her first name, Anjani.

Anjani Thomas had been in and out of Leonard's musical life since 1984, when John Lissauer, the producer of *Various Positions*, hired her to sing on "Hallelujah" and tour with Leonard. Although Leonard was not immune to office romances, there had been nothing between them on the 1985 tour, nor when Anjani sang on *I'm Your Man* or *The Future*—on the latter singing on "Waiting for the Miracle," the song containing Leonard's marriage proposal to Rebecca.

In the period between those two albums, Anjani had moved to Los Angeles and married an entertainment lawyer, Robert Kory. Around the same time that Leonard parted with Rebecca and the music industry and left L.A., Anjani's life took something of a similar turn; her marriage was over and her music career seemed to be heading the same way. But while Leonard chose to become closer with his spiritual teacher, Anjani had become disillusioned with hers, the Maharishi Mahesh Yogi, whose Transcendental Meditation practice she had followed for years. Making a clean break from everything, she moved to Austin, Texas, where she bought a little house and took a job as a saleswoman in a jewelry store. She was living in a city full of clubs and musicians but refused to even listen to music on her car radio on the way to work. "I was burned out," she says. "I didn't want anything to do with it." Four or five years later, while she was visiting her family in Hawaii, Anjani opened the closet in her old bedroom and saw her guitar. She took it out and started writing songs—"Two records' worth of material," she says. "I was thirty-nine at the time and I said to myself, 'I'm going to be forty. If I don't do this record I'll regret it the rest of my life.'" She sold the house and moved back to L.A. around the same time Leonard returned from Mount Baldy. Sometime later, when their paths crossed again, she played him one of the songs she had written, "Kyrie,"* which he liked and encouraged her to record. The two became musical coconspirators and lovers; later they would become musical collaborators. But for now Anjani worked on her album and Leonard worked on his.

Leonard had left the monastery with around two hundred and fifty songs and poems in various states of completion. An idea of what he might do with them came to him while he was at a classical concert in Los Angeles in late 1999. The performer was his godson, whose mother is Sharon Robinson. Leonard took Sharon aside during the intermission and said, "I've got some verses and things and I'd like for you to work on a record with me."[5] Not simply a song or two, as they had done in the past, but a whole album. Her job would be to write the melodies. It turned out to be a good deal more; *Ten New Songs*—at Leonard's insistence—was as much Sharon's album as it was his.

One might have imagined that Leonard's first album since his return to the music business would be all about Leonard—down from the mountain in a blaze of glory, imparting his wisdom on tablets of stone. It is not that Leonard had no melodies; he did. He either preferred Sharon's melodies, or he preferred collaborating; perhaps one after-effect of his studies with Roshi and Ramesh was to put ego aside and be inclusive. What's more interesting is how very female this album was. Women had always played a part in Leonard's songs, but mostly as backing singers and muses. Here he handed almost everything over to the women. Apart from an appearance on one song by Leanne's guitarist husband, Bob Metzger, and a string arrangement on another by David Campbell, Leanne Ungar engineered and mixed, and Sharon produced, arranged, played the instruments and wrote the melodies. In this supportive environment, all Leonard had to do was to sing the words over which he had labored so long.

---

* It would appear on her second album, *The Sacred Names* (2001).

"Sharon, I would say, was the person who has had the most success writing with Leonard," Leanne says. "She doesn't seem to have experienced some of the difficulties other people have had. Sharon understands a lot about what Leonard likes to sing, what he's capable of singing, then writes melodies that fit his sensibility; she comes up with the most beautiful music for him. And sometimes Sharon understands his lyrics in that he'll give her a poem he's written and she'll pick out the phrases she thinks will make a chorus and construct the song based on that. I know there's a lot of back-and-forth between Leonard and Sharon."

Leonard and Sharon did not discuss the album; they did not even refer to what they were working on as "an album." It was important "to keep it open," Sharon remembers. "'Well, we might be doing an album but maybe not, I don't know.'" Leonard was loath to introduce the expectations of other people into the exercise, particularly those of the music business. Instead they simply got together and worked at a song—"one song at a time, no pressure"—as if that was something they always did when they met up. "The first day, we sat quietly, listening to the music of an Indonesian singer that involved chants and ethnic rhythms. I think, in hindsight, that it helped set the tone for the workdays to come, which had a certain serene quality to them."

Working in Leonard's home and not in a studio also helped maintain the illusion of two close friends just hanging out and playing some music. The room above the garage, which Leonard nicknamed Small Mercies Studio, was, unlike regular studios, very bright, its windows looking out onto a small garden of grapefruit trees, jasmine and morning glories. He had furnished the room with a couple of art deco pieces from his mother's house in Montreal, and the sun streamed in on the curved-armed sofa where he and Sharon would sit, talking. They talked about the old soul and R & B records that both of them loved and whose sound influenced several of Robinson's melodies—

Sam Cooke, Otis Redding. Sometimes Leonard would have come up with a rhythm he liked, or a few changes, which he would play for her on the keyboard. Other times, when he handed her a set of lyrics, he might mention that he wrote them with a specific musical style in mind—"That Don't Make It Junk" was a country song, for example. Mostly though, he was interested in seeing where Sharon would go with it. She would take the lyrics home and work on them alone in her home studio, save the melodies she had come up with onto a hard drive, then give it to Leanne, who transferred it onto Leonard's computer, which she had set up so that he could simply push a button and continue to work on the song on his own in the early hours of the morning. Leonard enjoyed this way of working—relaxed, collaborative, but also alone.

His relationship with Anjani appeared to follow a very similar pattern: they were a couple but they were also, as Leonard termed it, "impossibly solitudinous people" and did not live together. "I like to wake up alone," said Leonard, "and she likes to be alone."[6] Anjani had moved into a house within walking distance of Leonard's duplex. Leanne, who had worked with Leonard for many years, couldn't help but notice how much happier and more secure he seemed. "I think he had found a kind of domestic peace. Or maybe it's because we worked at his house and, instead of being in this impersonal room and ordering out, we were sitting in his kitchen and he was cooking. It had a kind of intimacy that I think you can hear in the vocals." There was no deadline, no meter running in a studio. A song might go back and forth between Leonard and Sharon numerous times before it was finished and the next one begun. There were also breaks between recording, three or four weeks at a time, while Leonard wrote or rewrote lyrics.

During these absences, Leanne was busy going through tapes from Leonard's 1979 *Recent Songs* tour. Henry Lewy, his producer, had recorded all the UK concerts. The tapes had been gathering dust for decades, but Leonard had not forgotten them and was curious to see if they deserved resuscitating. In February 2000, an album of twelve of these songs was released with the title *Field Commander Cohen*. Leonard's first album of the new millennium presents a polished performance with the jazz group Passenger, the violin and oud players Raffi Hakopian and John Bilezikjian, and backing singers Jennifer Warnes and Sharon Robinson, who was at that time a newcomer to Leonard and was now his songwriting partner.

During a longer break, Leonard returned to Mumbai. Reinstalling himself at the Hotel Kemps Corner, he slipped back into his old schedule, taking his daily walk along Warden Road to *satsang* with the sea breeze in his hair, then on to the Breach Candy Club for a swim. The city was a riot of color and noise, but nothing disturbed Leonard's sense of peace. So comfortable did Leonard appear with his life in Mumbai that Lorca, curious as to what kept her father there so long, flew out and stayed with him for a week or two. At Leonard's suggestion she spent some of the time hunting through Mumbai's markets for old furniture to ship back to the antiques store she now ran in L.A.

In Canada, meanwhile, where new ways of honoring Leonard were still, miraculously, being found, Stephen Scobie organized an event in Montreal in May 2000 titled *Some Kind of Record: Poems in Tribute to Leonard Cohen*. Leonard, as seemed to have become an unspoken policy, declined to attend. A cartoon in a Montreal newspaper showed a woman of a certain age, hippily dressed, with an acoustic guitar, sitting forlorn on a park bench while a policeman tells her, "C'mon now, lady, everyone else has gone home. Leonard Cohen isn't coming." Leonard did go to Montreal not too long afterward, but on private business, to visit Pierre Trudeau, who was terminally ill. Leonard returned in September, at the request of Trudeau's children, to be a pallbearer at Trudeau's funeral.

While he was in his old hometown, Leonard took the opportunity to go see Irving Layton in the nursing home. When Leonard entered his room, the eighty-eight-year-old poet, who was suffering from Alzheimer's, stared at Leonard with a blank, bewildered face. Leonard said, "It's Leonard." Irving replied, "Leonard who?" Leonard's face fell. Layton laughed uproariously. He knew who it was. The moment the nurse left the room, they had an illicit smoke, Leonard lighting his old friend's pipe because Layton's big boxer's hands shook too much to do it himself.

———————

September 2001. It was still monsoon season in Mumbai, but the rains had started to ease up. Having finished work on his new album, Leonard had returned to India and Ramesh. One day, as he walked into the lobby of the Hotel Kemps Corner, the desk clerk offered his sincere condolences. This was how Leonard first heard of the 9/11 terrorist attack on New York. Not long after, Leonard's phone rang; a journalist from the *New York Observer* wanted his reaction to what had happened, since Leonard after all had predicted apocalypse in his last album *The Future*. Leonard was reluctant to give an opinion— "In the Jewish tradition one is cautioned against trying to comfort the comfortless in the midst of their bereavement." But, when pressed, he offered something he told the reporter he had learned from his Hindu studies: "It's impossible for us to discern the pattern of events and the unfolding of a world which is not entirely of our making."[7]

In October 2001, *Ten New Songs*, Leonard's new album, was released. The photo on the front sleeve, which Leonard took on his computer's built-in camera, pictured Leonard and Sharon, side by side. "The album," Leonard said, "could be described as a duet." She had expected, and sometimes urged, him to replace her vocals and remove the synthesizers on which she composed her melodies, "but as the sound unfolded," said Leonard, "I began to insist that she keep her voice on there and that we use these synthesizer sounds, because the songs seemed to insist that the original treatments were appropriate. Also I like the way Sharon sings."[8]

Leonard's voice on the album—so different from the voice on *Field Commander Cohen*—is a soft, dry baritone that unfurls like smoke over the translucent, skeletal, yet soulful-sounding digital keyboard tracks. The instruments make no attempt to disguise that they are not "real," giving a lo-fi charm not normally associated with synthesizers. The intimacy in Leonard's voice reflects how he recorded his vocal parts, murmuring quietly while his neighbors slept, and there's a meditative quality to how the songs seem to flow gracefully and solemnly in and out of one another. Leonard's own description of the album was "serene."

The lyrics are about wounded dawns and light, America and Babylon, about praying to God and just getting on with it. The words of "Love Itself"—which Leonard dedicated to his friend, the writer and critic Leon Wieseltier—are an account of Roshi's *teisho* on love, while "By the Rivers Dark" ("*By the rivers of Babylon we sat and wept*") is loosely based on Psalm 137, which laments the destruction of the temple and exile of the Jews. The dreamlike "Alexandra Leaving," which Leonard had been writing since 1985, was inspired by a poem by Constantine P. Cavafy, "The God Forsakes Antony." The dazzling "A Thousand Kisses Deep" has multiple layers of meaning, among them holding, letting go, creating and surrendering to the Creator. This song too had been through numerous incarnations, melodically and lyrically. Rebecca De Mornay remembers hearing various versions of it in the early nineties; in 1995 Leonard told the *New York Times* that he wanted it to feel like "an old folk song."[9] Its companion piece "Boogie Street" is, at first glance, about Leonard accepting who he is and what he has to do, even if he does not know why, and leaving the monastic life for the music business. It opens with a prayer and a kiss before moving on to the unreality of real life, the impermanence of romantic love and the permanence of desire. "Boogie Street," said Leonard, "is that place that we all live, whether you're in a monastery or down in the city."[10] It is also a real place, in Singapore. Leonard had been there once.

"During the day it's a place of bazaars and shops and booths with a lot of bootleg records. Since I didn't see any on display, I asked one of the vendors if he had any Leonard Cohen records. He went back to where he kept his inventory and came out with an entire box of my catalog—much more thorough than most of the stores that I'd been to, and a dollar apiece. Very reasonably priced, I thought. At night, Boogie Street transformed into this alarming and beautiful sexual marketplace, where there were male and female prostitutes, transvestites, extremely attractive people offering to satisfy all the fantasies of their numerous customers."

An all-service paradise, then.

"As my old teacher used to say, 'We can visit paradise but we can't live there because there are no restaurants or toilets in paradise.' There are moments, as I say in that song, when 'You kiss my lips, and then it's done, I'm back on Boogie Street'—*in the midst of an embrace with your beloved you melt into the kiss, you dissolve in the intimacy, [it's like] you take a drink of cold water when you're thirsty; without that refreshment you would probably die of boredom in a week or two. But you can't live there. Immediately, you're plunged back into the traffic jam."*

Leonard dedicated the album to Roshi.

The critics, bar a very few dissenters, were full of praise. They welcomed Leonard back, told him how much his voice, his profundity and his sly humor had been missed—even if the new album did not have all the cool, playful one-liners of *I'm Your Man*—and that *Ten New Songs* was worth the long wait. He was asked in interviews if he planned to tour behind it. Leonard demurred, saying he doubted he could still fill seats. It was a typically Cohenesque answer, modest and self-deprecating. Perhaps there was an element of insecurity after so much time had passed since his last tour, but what it really came down to was that he did not want to tour. There was clearly an audience for him in Europe, where *Ten New Songs* was a hit—Top 30 in the UK, No. 1 in Poland and Norway and gold in seven other countries. In America, reverting to Leonard's pre–*I'm Your Man* pattern, it sold poorly, failing to make the Top 100. In Canada, though, it went platinum and brought him four more Juno awards: Best Album, Best Artist, Best Songwriter and Best Video (this last one for the smooth soul single "In My Secret Life").

Leonard's fellow countrymen now seemed unable to stop with the honors and homages. The Canadian consulate commissioned a tribute concert to Leonard in New York as part of its Canada Day celebrations, hiring Hal Willner to put it together. Willner was renowned for the concept ensemble projects he produced—Nino Rota, Thelonious Monk, Kurt Weill. The last time Willner had seen Leonard was pre-monastery, on the *Future* tour. Willner had gone to the New York show with Allen Ginsberg and remembers, "You could tell there was something going on; the vibe wasn't as much fun as on the *I'm Your Man* tour. I went back with Allen to say hello, and Leonard had ducked out even then."

Willner called Kelley Lynch to make sure that Leonard had no objection to the Brooklyn concert. He was fine with it, she said, as long as he did not have to do anything, so Willner got going. Among the first people he called was Julie Christensen, looking for a contact for an artist he wanted to ask to perform. Julie told him, "If you're doing Leonard stuff, you should have Perla and me come sing backup." He thought it an interesting idea and called Perla Batalla, who told him that the date conflicted with another gig. "Then I got off the phone with Hal and I just started to cry," Perla remembers. "I can't *not* be involved." She called back and told Willner she would cancel the other show on the condition that she could sing "Bird on the Wire" and duet with Julie on "Anthem." Hal said, "'Anthem' is not in the show." He changed his mind later when Leonard, over a coffee with Perla and Hal, agreed that it might make a good addition to the set list. This would be Leonard's only involvement.

More than half the singers Willner invited to perform were women. There were Laurie Anderson, Linda Thompson, Kate and Anna McGarrigle, Kate's daughter Martha Wainwright, Perla, Julie and Rennie Sparks, of the duo the Handsome Family. "It just seemed to make sense," Willner says. "We weren't trying to imitate him, and Leonard loved women—a true, true love. They're great songs for women to sing, the way he has of taking emotion into words." Nick Cave, one of the five male singers on the bill (along with Kate McGarrigle's son Rufus Wainwright; Linda Thompson's son Teddy Thompson; Marc Anthony Thompson, no relation; and Brett Sparks, the other half of the Handsome Family), found it "really moving to hear a lot of women singing Leonard's songs. They made wonderful sense of his stuff—I think more effectively in a lot of ways than the male singers. What I hadn't always realized was that these were extraordinary songs on any level and that, although I love his voice—which is incredibly affecting and has a tone that's totally unique, something like Miles Davis's trumpet—it doesn't need Leonard's voice to carry these songs. They're just really good songs—and there's a lot of them. I'd always had a particular love for the early stuff, particularly *Songs of Love and Hate* because it's punk rock, raw as can be. But he just got deeper, more humane."

Willner decided who would sing what. "I put a show together, like a script, a play, so it's more about the cast with this material we all love than a 'tribute show.' And you don't want everyone coming out and doing their favorite song and moving on. That way you don't get a real balance of the material. I wanted to have some of the more obscure things, like 'Tacoma Trailer' and 'Don't Go Home with Your Hard-On,' from *Death of a Ladies' Man*." Willner had a particular fondness for the latter.

In February 2003, Phil Spector was arrested for the murder of Lana Clarkson, an actress and nightclub hostess he met at the House of Blues and had taken back to his mansion. Shortly after the arrest, two detectives from the homicide bureau paid Leonard a visit. They had been poring through old press clippings of stories about the eccentric producer and his guns—and there were many, involving famous names like John Lennon, Stevie Wonder, Michelle Phillips and the Ramones, as well as Leonard. "Apparently the detectives had come across some old interviews I did in 1978 or 1979 in which I spoke of the difficulties of recording *Death of a Ladies' Man:* the brandishing of guns, armed bodyguards, drunkenness and Phil's famous megalomania." Leonard told the detectives, "Even though Phil put his arm around my shoulder and pressed an automatic into my neck, except for the real possibility of an accident I never at any moment thought that Phil meant to do me harm. I never felt seriously threatened." It was "basically just a good rock 'n' roll story," he told them, that had become exaggerated over the years.

They asked him when he had last seen Spector. "Over twenty years ago," he said. "They were very surprised. They said they were under the impression we were close friends. I said no. Hearing this, they thanked me for their time, finished their coffees and left. It was clear that I was not to be considered a valuable witness. I was never approached again by anyone concerned with the case, [and] needless to say, I did not testify before a grand jury."[11]

On June 28, 2003, Hal Willner's *Came So Far for Beauty: An Evening of Songs by Leonard Cohen Under the Stars* took place in Prospect Park in Brooklyn. The stage was draped with a large maple-leaf flag and a female representative of the Canadian consulate came out during the intermission and lauded Leonard as "the sexiest man alive." The concert was a success and quickly led to offers for Willner to stage it overseas. Since it had been more than a decade since Leonard last played a concert—a situation he showed no inclination to change— this tribute concert not only helped satisfy the demand from fans to see his music performed live, it also helped to keep his songs as Willner said, "out there."

Leonard's record label was also doing its part in this enterprise. Two different, career-encompassing, double-album retrospectives were released in 2002 and 2003: *The Essential Leonard Cohen* and *An Introduction to Leonard Cohen* (the latter in the UK as part of the "*MOJO* Presents" series). There was a new, fortieth-anniversary edition of *The Favorite Game* as well, to tie in with the premiere of Bernar Hébert's film. As for Leonard, he was working on his first collection of poems since 1984, titled *Book of Longing*. Much of the material—artwork as well as poetry—he was sorting through and editing had been created when he lived in the monastery. In the Swedish documentary shot on Mount Baldy, Leonard, describing himself as "a writer who failed his promise," points to a pile of notebooks and adds, "I may redeem myself."[12]

In October 2003 Leonard was made a companion of the Order of Canada—one of the two highest civilian honors his country could bestow. Leonard sent his thanks and got back to work—not on his book but, remarkably, a new album.

———

Dear Heather, Leonard's eleventh studio album, was released in October 2004, two weeks after Leonard's seventieth birthday and three years after *Ten New Songs*. In Leonard Cohen terms, this was surprisingly fast; his fans and his record label had become used to four-, five-, even nine-year gaps between album releases. Since Leonard had come down from the mountain he had been working nonstop, but this was nothing new; Leonard was always working. He simply chose not to release the majority of the material he had worked on. This apparent new urgency appeared to have nothing to do with the sense of mortality he had talked about more than ten years before. If anything, at seventy Leonard appeared to be in better condition, mentally, physically and emotionally, than he had been at sixty. Thoughts of being "old" did not seem to trouble him. In fact he played on the word in the original title for the album, which had been *Old Ideas*. It was a reference to his intention to bring together various odds and ends on this album: songs he'd written in tribute to the work of other poets, recordings of him reciting his own work, little musical sketches and half-finished ideas. Some of these ideas were old—"The Faith," for example, a song based on an old Quebec folk ballad that he had recorded with Henry Lewy in 1979–80 and shelved; "Tennessee Waltz," a live recording from 1985 of the weepy country standard, for which Leonard took the liberty of writing an even darker, sadder closing verse—but the majority dated from August 2003, when he began recording the album. Leonard was persuaded to substitute *Old Ideas* with *Dear Heather* only when it was pointed out that his fans might mistake it for yet another retrospective album.

If *Ten New Songs* was Leonard's most collaborative album (*Death of a Ladies' Man* had been written with Spector as equal, but Leonard had no say in the recording, and the Cohen-Lissauer project *Songs for Rebecca* was never released), *Dear Heather* is his most experimental. Its thirteen songs, recorded once again in his home studio, make up a sort of scrapbook, a collage of word, image and sound. The CD liner-note booklet, in which the lyrics appear side by side with Leonard's sketches, might have been a pocket-sized companion for *Book of Longing*, on which he worked at the same time. His idea, Leanne Ungar remembers, had been "to put together some melodies that the songs evoked and to actually do some poetry readings"—reminiscent, perhaps, of the shows he had performed in the late fifties with Maury Kaye.

The opening song, "Go No More A-Roving," is (in the manner of "Villanelle") a poem by Lord Byron set to music by Leonard. The accompanying drawings in the booklet are of Irving Layton, to whom the song is dedicated—wide hangdog face, crushed poor-boy cap—

and the entirely Cohenesque image of a guitar by an open door. "To a Teacher" also concerns a poet who was important to Leonard, A. M. Klein, who was silenced in his later years by mental illness. This time the poem set to music is Leonard's, from his 1961 collection *The Spice-Box of Earth*:

> *Let me cry Help beside you, Teacher*
> *I have entered under this dark roof*
> *As fearlessly as an honoured son*
> *Enters his father's house*

For an avowed nonsentimentalist like Leonard, there seems to be a good deal of looking back in these songs, from absent friends to the unnamed women he thanks in the delightful "Because Of," for having been inspired to take off their clothes by *"a few songs / Wherein I spoke of their mystery."*

The sense of collage is also evident in the music, which is diverse in style: folk, beatnik jazz, waltzes and some of the French-sounding music Leonard had talked about having written on his synthesizer on Mount Baldy. The title track takes lyrics not much longer than a haiku and repeats them, deconstructs them, then folds them over the keyboards and trumpet like aural origami. "On That Day," a ballad written about the 9/11 terrorist attacks, has the sentimentality and straight-talking of a Randy Newman song. There is no lack of synthesizers, but there are real instruments too, including a Jew's harp, which Leonard plays on "Nightingale," a collaboration with Anjani, and "On That Day." On two of the collaborations with Sharon Robinson, "There for You" and "The Letters," Leonard's voice is almost a whisper; most of the singing is left for the women to do. On "Morning Glory," sung by its muse, Anjani, Leonard sounds like a ghost of himself, hovering around the beauty of her multitracked voice. On some songs Leonard lets the women sing alone; on others he speaks his words over their voices, murmuring softly, deeply and close to the microphone, like Serge Gainsbourg, or "bassing in" once in a while like a Jewish-Buddhist A. P. Carter. Although there was a very strong female presence on his previous album, on *Dear Heather* the women are given even greater prominence.

Anjani says, "That record was a turning point, for both of us." Leonard had initially called her in to sing harmony on "Undertow," then decided that he wanted to scrap the melody and use the harmony as the lead. The song was about a bereaved, lost woman; what he liked about the harmony part was that it did not get to the root note except at the very end of the song, which gave it a tension that mirrored her emotional distress. He left Anjani and Leanne Ungar to record it while he went back to the house and made some phone calls. "I went through it a couple of times," Anjani remembers, "and we ended up with this track that I thought was gorgeous, the best thing I've ever done, and Leanne loved it." When Leonard came back, she said, "Wait until you hear this." "Leanne ran the playback," says Anjani, "and he does what he always does when he listens to music, which is stare off into space, no expression—I don't care if you're playing a salsa tune, he won't move, he just sits there motionless. At the end of it he said, 'That's beautiful. Now sing it but don't sing it.'" Anjani looked at him quizzically. "He said, 'This is not an anthem. It's the song of a broken woman, so *be* the woman on the deserted beach with nothing left.' I remember feeling outraged that he didn't like the superb performance that I'd just belted out, and then I thought, 'What am I supposed to do?' and I got really nervous and kind of shaky, like every tool I had just went out the window; I really truly had nothing left. And when I sang, this really tentative, broken thing came out. At the end of it he said, 'That's it. Now you've got it,' and that's when he said he had never heard me in that way before. He later described it as 'Her voice dropped from her throat to her heart.'"

What also distinguishes *Dear Heather* from earlier albums is the gentle modesty with which it deals with the Big Subjects, like love, death, life, faith and madness. As Leon Wieseltier noted in his album review, it "revels in its own lack of monumentality."[13] There was simplicity instead of grandiosity in his song mourning the 9/11 terrorist attacks, "On That Day," while in the title track whimsy replaced the more common anguish about women and lust. "The longing persists," Wieseltier concluded, "but the slavery is over. And the evidence of inner freedom is everywhere in *Dear Heather*. It is a window upon the heart of an uncommonly interesting and uncommonly mortal man."[14]

Leonard was for the most part straightforward and unambiguous in his lyrics (although it's perfectly possible that he had attained such Zen mastery that the lack of ambivalence was actually a refined ambiguity). Whatever it is, it's a beautiful, muted, beguiling album. On its front cover is a sketch by Leonard of Anjani; on the back is a photo by Anjani of Leonard, bestubbled, crushed-capped and clutching a coffee cup. Leonard dedicated the album to the memory of Jack McClelland, his longtime Canadian publisher, who died in June 2004, the year of its release. Leonard declined to tour behind the album— not even a promotional tour, as he had done for *Ten New Songs*. As soon as he had finished it, he had left for Montreal, where he spent the summer, happily sitting in the Parc du Portugal with the other old men, watching the world go by.

The album seemed content to sell itself without Leonard's help. It made the charts just about everywhere in Europe, reaching No. 34 in the UK and going gold in Canada, Poland, Demark, Ireland, Norway and the Czech Republic. In the U.S., oddly, it made it into the Top 20 of the World Music chart, while failing yet again to make *Billboard*'s Top 100. In the absence of any word from Leonard, many journalists appeared to view the album as the Last Word of Leonard, a prelude to retirement. But, as Leonard wrote to Jarkko Arjatsalo at the Leonard Cohen Files in the summer of 2004, he saw it as closing a circle in his work before moving on to the next record, which he was "deep into," he wrote, "six or seven songs already sketched out, and, g-d willing, it will be done over the next year. Also the B of L [*Book of Longing*], or something resembling it, seems to be about to step out under a new name and form."[15] Leonard clearly had no plans for retirement. Which was fortunate, since a strange and unexpected set of circumstances dictated that he could not have retired if he had wanted to.

In October 2004, the telephone rang in Leonard's Montreal apartment. It was his daughter, Lorca, calling from L.A. She had just had an enigmatic conversation with the boyfriend of an employee of Kelley Lynch, who had come into her shop. He told her that Leonard needed to take a look at his bank accounts, and quickly. It was as puzzling to Leonard as it had been to Lorca. Kelley took care of Leonard's business affairs—good, reliable Kelley, not simply his manager but a close friend, almost part of the family; he even employed Kelley's parents. Leonard, who took little interest in such things, had given Lynch broad power of attorney over his finances. He trusted her enough to have named her in his living will as the person responsible in an extreme medical circumstance for giving the order as to whether he should live or die. Lynch had been there almost continuously during the making of *Dear Heather* and they had been in regular contact since the album was completed, just as they always were, and Kelley had said nothing about any financial problems. But Lorca was uneasy, so Leonard agreed to fly back to L.A. He went straightaway to his bank—he had been there so infrequently he could barely remember the address—and they pulled up his accounts. Apparently, it was true; just a few days earlier Leonard had paid an American Express bill of Kelley's for $75,000. As the clerk scrolled through his earlier statements, it became clear that this was not an isolated incident. Almost all of Leonard's money was gone.

Back at the house, Leonard lit a cigarette. He dialed Kelley's office number. Her voice on the phone was bright and friendly. Leonard told her that he had removed her name as a signatory on his accounts, and he fired her. Kelley. Of all the women in his life to do him wrong. Leonard knew that Lynch—like Marty Machat, his previous manager and Lynch's previous employer—had her faults, but like Machat she knew Leonard's business and had taken care of it. In 1998 Leonard had told *Billboard* (in a special feature celebrating Leonard's thirtieth year as an artist), that in matters of business he had been "taken many, many times," but then "I found Kelley and set my house in order and I've been making a living ever since . . . almost exclusively because of Kelley. Kelley, bless her heart, organized me and my son."[16]

Kelley, also like Marty Machat, loved Leonard—or had given every appearance of loving him for years. They had been lovers some fourteen years earlier, but it was "a casual sexual arrangement," Leonard said; he "never spent the night, and it had been mutually enjoyed and terminated"[17] giving no appearance of having damaged their close friendship. To have had almost all the money he had made stolen out from under him was difficult to take in, but also remarkably easy. It was the oldest story in showbiz. Hadn't his mother warned him about it when he left for New York in the sixties with his guitar? "You be careful of those people down there," she had told him. "They're not like us." To which Leonard responded with an indulgent smile before going on to unwittingly sign away the rights to several songs. But losing a few songs was a drop in the ocean compared to the epic financial impropriety this would turn out to be. That it appeared to have dated back to the time when Leonard left the material world to live in a monastery added more than a touch of irony. That it continued after Leonard came down from the mountain proved only what many already know, or at least suspect: musicians and monks tend to have few skills in matters of finance. Leonard had been happy to let his manager Kelley take care of the business and money, but now Kelley was gone, and so was the money, leaving Leonard with a monumental mess to take care of, and no manager or money with which to do it. If not quite a koan, it was a hell of a conundrum, and a debilitating distraction. "It's enough to put a dent in one's mood," Leonard told his friends. He repeated the same understatement to the media once the lawsuits began and the story went public. And what a strange story it would turn out to be, one with a tangled plot whose cast of characters included a SWAT team, financiers, a tough-talking parrot, Tibetan Buddhists and Leonard's lover Anjani's ex-husband.

Twenty-two

Taxes, Children, Lost Pussy

———

Death by a thousand paper cuts. To have been redeemed from depression in his old age only to have to spend it in an eternity of legal and financial paperwork was a cosmic joke so black as to test even Leonard's famous gallows humor. His temptation had been to simply let the whole thing go. He had been broke before, he did not need much to live on and he had a roof—roofs, in fact—over his head. If, on balance, he would have preferred having money in the bank to not having it—and when he did have it, he tended to spend it on other people and on Roshi's monasteries, in his own personal version of his ancestors' philanthropy and synagogue-building—there was very little evidence in his lifestyle or his career, apart from the initial move into songwriting, that money was anywhere near the top of Leonard's motivations.

When he had unknowingly signed away the rights to "Suzanne" in the sixties, his response had reportedly been sanguine; it was appropriate somehow, he had said, that he did not own a song that he felt had become beyond ownership. Admittedly that is what he told the press; in private he might well have expressed a different view, since it is unlikely that a man in his thirties, renowned in the Canadian literary world and unused to being treated dishonorably, would feel anything but incensed at having been duped of his first known—and for years best-known—and most successful song. But what Leonard said both publicly and privately about the business with Kelley Lynch suggested that it meant less to Leonard to lose his fortune than his songs. Though as the story continued to unfold, it appeared he might have lost them too.

Leonard's relative calm in the face of financial disaster might have reflected his long, hard Zen training with Roshi, or the perspectives he learned from his studies with Ramesh, but his survival instinct may have also played a part; to risk becoming too engaged might have invited the return of his anxiety and depression. Leonard had wanted to walk away from the whole thing, but the lawyers said he couldn't. They told him that lot of the missing money had been in retirement accounts and charitable trust funds, which left Leonard liable for large tax bills on the sums withdrawn and no money with which to pay them. It was no good telling the IRS that he had not been the one who had made the withdrawals; they needed proof. Which was why Leonard was sitting at his desk with Anjani and Lorca, in the house he had been forced to mortgage in order to pay his legal bills, grimly going through stacks of financial statements and e-mails. It was a complicated business. Since Kelley Lynch, with his blessing, had dealt with his finances on his behalf, he knew few details himself about the various accounts, trusts and companies set up in his name. His lawyers had spent the past month trying to make sense of it and still Leonard seemed to be getting nowhere except deeper in debt.

Then something occurred to Lorca. Wasn't Anjani's ex-husband a music industry lawyer? Perhaps he might have some ideas. Robert Kory was indeed a lawyer. He had worked with the Beach Boys for ten years, although he had since sworn off the music business in favor of a practice in entertainment and technology finance. "But when Leonard Cohen shows up at your office," Kory says, "what are you going to do? Close the door?" He had opened it to see his ex-wife standing hand in hand with a man whose poetry books he had read as a student at Yale. "Hello," Leonard said. "I may have lost a few million dollars."

Kory agreed to help. Deferring his fees, he set about "trying to get a basic understanding of Leonard's affairs, to understand the history, understand what money he had and what happened to it, the magnitude of the loss, and figure out legally what they had done." Quite a challenge, since Kelley Lynch had the records. "I started making contacts in a very delicate way with bankers and with Leonard's accountant, who was also Kelley's accountant, and lawyers that represented Leonard in the sale of his music publishing and his future record royalties." Three months later, after Kory's then litigation associate and now partner Michelle Rice had conducted a comprehensive review of the available documents, along with bank records that had been subpoenaed, Kory and Rice explained to Leonard that a case could probably be made that between ten and thirteen million dollars had been improperly taken. "That stunned him," says Kory. "It stunned me."

Rice's analysis suggested it possibly dated as far back as 1996, the year Leonard was ordained as a monk. Around that time, Lynch, with the aid of Leonard's other financial advisers, made the first of two separate sales of Leonard's music publishing to Sony/ATV—127 songs. In Kory's opinion there had been no need for Leonard to sell his songs because he had money in the bank and income from royalties. Much of the proceeds from the sale, less Lynch's 15 percent commission, had been deposited in Leonard's bank account, over which Lynch had control, and some had been deposited in charitable trusts. To manage the investments, Lynch had brought in a friend, a Tibetan Buddhist financier named Neal Greenberg, who was the head of a securities company in Colorado. Greenberg had studied since the early seventies under the late Chögyam Trungpa Rinpoche. Lynch herself was a longtime student and friend of Trungpa, as was Doug Penick, the father of the older of her two sons, Rutger. (Penick had been involved in the 1994 Canadian documentary *The Tibetan Book of the Dead*, for which Leonard provided the narration.) Greenberg in turn brought in a lawyer and tax professor from Kentucky named Richard Westin. In 2001, Kelley, Greenberg and Westin orchestrated the sale of Leonard's future record royalties to Sony/ATV for $8 million. After various cuts, Leonard apparently netted $4.7 million, according to documents later filed in Los Angeles Superior Court. The money from this second sale of Leonard's intellectual property went into a company account, which had been set up with the intention of paying Leonard a pension when he retired and to provide an inheritance for his children. What went wrong, according to Rice's analysis and what was alleged in later litigation, was that the plan only worked if Leonard's children owned 99 percent of the company and Leonard 1 percent. At the last minute, Rice alleged, they gave Kelley 99 percent ownership instead of his children, and Leonard had no idea about the last-minute change in the documents.

Since Leonard had expressed a strong desire to avoid the ordeal of litigation, Kory, after consulting with the former L.A. district attorney Ira Reiner, wrote to Lynch, Greenberg and Westin. Greenberg's response was to file a preemptive lawsuit which accused Leonard and Kory of attempted extortion. Westin agreed to go into mediation, and a confidential settlement was reached. Lynch's lawyers insisted at first that their client had been given the authority to do what she did, though later they advised her to mediate. At that point, Lynch fired them. She made a phone call to Kory herself and asked him to meet her for lunch. This surprised Kory, but he accepted, and they agreed on a place.

At that meeting, Kory held out the possibility of a reasonable settlement if Kelley would disclose what had happened to all the money. The alternative, he said, would be serious litigation and ultimately the destruction of her life as she knew it. Her response, Kory said, was "Hell will freeze over before you find out what happened to the money. It was my money."

So in August 2005 the first of the lawsuits began. That same month, somewhat ironically, a short film titled *This Beggar's Description*, in which Leonard made an appearance, premiered on Canadian TV. It was a documentary about a schizophrenic Montreal poet named Philip Tétrault. Leonard had been his longtime supporter and friend. We see Leonard sitting on a park bench in Montreal with Tétrault, chatting about frostbite and Kris Kristofferson, while the soundtrack plays Leonard Cohen songs Leonard no longer owned.

Back in Los Angeles, the letters and lawsuits, accusations and counteraccusations continued, becoming ever more convoluted and bizarre. A particularly sorry and surreal episode occurred at Lynch's home in Mandeville Canyon. Looking out of her front window, she could see police officers cordoning off the road. Several police cars pulled up on her lawn. As Lynch described it, twenty-five armed men jumped out—a SWAT team—and aimed weapons at her house. The police had been called about an alleged hostage-taking. They were told there were guns in the house. Lynch, who had kept the younger of her two sons, Ray Charles Lindsey, home from school because he felt unwell, assumed that he must be the alleged hostage and that the call had been made by the boy's father, her estranged partner Steve Lindsey—the producer and musician Lynch had met when he worked on Leonard's album *The Future*. The boy was at that moment with his half brother, Rutger; Lynch had asked her older son to take Ray out of the house and down the road to where the actress Cloris Leachman, apparently, was waiting for them in her car.

Lynch came out of the front door, dressed in a bikini and holding a dog on a leash. As she walked toward the policemen, she said, several trained their guns on her and the dog while other officers ran into the house. When they entered, they were greeted by a voice screeching, "I see dead people! I see dead people!"—it was Lou, Lynch's gray African parrot. Lynch ran to the swimming pool and jumped in. She was removed by officers, handcuffed and taken away in a squad car, still in her wet bathing suit.

By Lynch's account, the police took her on a long drive, interrogating her en route about her friendship with Phil Spector (who had been freed on $1 million bail while awaiting trial for murder). The journey ended at a hospital across town, where Lynch was taken to the psychiatric ward. She claimed that she was involuntarily drugged and held in the hospital for twenty-four hours, and that during this time Steve Lindsey filed for and subsequently won custody of their son. Lynch believed that Leonard and Kory were behind the whole episode, as well as several other strange things she claimed had happened to her following the hostage incident, such as being rear-ended by a Mercedes and threatened by a mysterious man.[1]

Lynch's subsequent accounts, related in thousands upon thousands of words she posted on the Internet, involved long, elaborate conspiracies, in which Phil Spector's murder trial seemed to feature frequently and in which Lynch claimed to be a scapegoat in a scheme devised to hide Leonard's lavish spending and tax fraud. Rather than fight Leonard in court, Kelley did so in cyberspace. Wherever Leonard was mentioned online and there was a space for comments, she left them, and not in brief. She sent innumerable lengthy e-mails to Leonard and his friends, family, musicians, associates and former girlfriends, as well as to the police, the district attorney, the media, the Buddhist community and the IRS.

Leonard, who had been obliged to stay in L.A. while the litigation continued, kept his head down and tried to work. For such a private man, having his confidential affairs made so distastefully public was a real test of his Buddhist nature. It was hard to work under these conditions, but at the same time, focusing on work kept his mind off it. There was also the matter of having to try to make some money; at this point in the game, Leonard had no idea how things might turn out. Thanks in good part to this urgency, in the space of a few months Leonard had written and recorded almost an entire new album—not the album on which he had started work immediately after *Dear Heather*, but a collaboration with Anjani, titled *Blue Alert*.

Leonard also finally completed *Book of Longing*—which his friends had started calling *Book of Prolonging*, Leonard having spent so long working on it. The one thing that was missing was some artwork, which had been in one of the thirty boxes of sketchbooks, notebooks, journals and personal papers that Leonard had left in Lynch's office for safekeeping. Lynch, with her source of income cut off, had given up the office, so presumably they were in her house. Lynch wasn't saying. With her house now heading toward foreclosure, there had been reports that she had been looking into selling Leonard's archives.

Leonard, who had become close to Rice, called her about the pending foreclosure. Although she and Kory had engaged another law firm by then to assist in the litigation, Rice felt the situation was too pressing to wait for the slow resolution of the lawsuits. She employed a writ of possession, a rarely used self-help legal procedure in which someone can make a claim that another person has his or her property and refuses to give it back. Lynch had ignored Leonard's lawsuit, including requests for discovery, and he was frustrated by her ability to avoid any accountability, even in litigation. But once a court issues the writ, Rice explained, the person who filed it can take it to the sheriff's office and ask for officers to go with him to where his property is being held and take it back.

On a rainy October morning at nine A.M., Rice and her paralegal showed up, unannounced, at Lynch's house in Mandeville Canyon with two armed sheriffs in riot gear, to search the house and garage and take possession of Leonard's documents per the court order. The sheriffs emerged with one box after another. The process took nearly two days and required a moving truck, but they recovered a treasure trove: "precious notebooks, the history of 'Hallelujah' and how it got written, letters from Joni Mitchell, Dylan, Allen Ginsberg and all the drawings," Rice says. There were tears in Leonard's eyes as he opened the boxes and found what he thought had been lost. Among them was the sketchbook containing Leonard's drawing of a bird that would become the cover design of *Book of Longing*.

In December 2005, Lynch lost her home. For a while, she slept on the beach in Santa Monica, before setting off in a van across the U.S. In May 2006 a superior court judge granted a default judgment against Lynch for $7,341,345. Once again, she ignored it, and anyway, to all appearances she was penniless. Rice also prevailed in the lawsuits against Greenberg, insofar as she obtained dismissal of all Greenberg's claims against Leonard and Kory, and obtained an order that awarded Leonard the last $150,000 under Greenberg's control, even though Greenberg claimed these funds were owed to him for his legal fees. Through the various legal proceedings, Leonard had recovered some of his lost money, though nothing like all of it. Lynch, who continued her ceaseless assault of blogs and e-mails full of accusations and invective, also began to make threatening phone calls—to Leonard, to Kory and to friends and associates from various places across the U.S. State by state, Rice led an effort to obtain a series of restraining orders against Lynch. And so the ugly business dragged on.

Came So Far for Beauty, Hal Willner's Leonard Cohen tribute concert, had taken on a life of its own. Staged in New York in 2003 and commissioned as a one-off by the Canadian consulate, it had been adopted by other countries—"We kept getting asked to do it," says Willner—and had become something of an annual international event. First it went to England, as part of the 2004 Brighton Festival, surviving the transatlantic crossing with its spirit and almost the entire cast intact. Two more performers were added to the lineup, Beth Orton and Jarvis Cocker, and, to keep it fresh, some new songs.

Says Nick Cave, "Hal told you what songs he wanted you to do; you didn't get a choice. Nobody knows what's going on or gets time to rehearse, so it's done on a wing and a prayer, which was one of the great things about it." Between them the cast, each channeling their own inner Leonard Cohen, conjured up his humor ("I'm Your Man"), piety ("If It Be Your Will"), melancholy ("Seems So Long Ago, Nancy") and libidinous machismo ("Don't Go Home with Your Hard-On"). Willner says, "It became a team, all these artists who would never be in the same room, collaborating, watching each other at the side of the stage and cheering each other along."

"Those concerts started to become a parallel universe to all of our lives," says Rufus Wainwright. "We would meet up again in all these locations and it took on this mystical aura, like some exotic family get-together." Wainwright was already something of an extended Cohen family member. He and Leonard's daughter, Lorca, who had met in their teens in Montreal, had become close friends. When he moved to Los Angeles they became roommates, living in Lorca's half of Leonard's duplex. The first time Lorca took Rufus upstairs to meet her father, "I walked in and Leonard was in his underwear—boxers, nothing too risqué, and a T-shirt, kind of a Billy Wilder morning outfit—and he was chewing a boiled hot dog into tiny little bits and spitting it out and putting it on a toothpick and feeding this little bird that he'd rescued from the front yard that had fallen from a nest. He was very nice and he made me noodles and we talked for a while. We didn't necessarily connect—it was sort of right before the crash and he was going through some stuff, and I'm a pretty brash character, very extroverted, and he's very introverted, and I would be trying to tap-dance all the time around his soft-shoe. That's what struck me the most: how shy he is and how unassuming. But I think we've figured each other out since."

In 2005, the cast reconvened in Australia, for the Sydney Festival. Among them was a newcomer, Antony Hegarty, a New York singer with an otherworldly voice. "Before we met Antony," Julie Christensen remembers, "Hal was saying, 'Wait until you see this guy, he sounds like a cross between Janis Joplin and Tiny Tim.' We kind of wondered what this would be like." A big, cobwebby sweater draped over his rotund body like a worn tarp on a Volkswagen Beetle, Antony sang a soulful version of "If It Be Your Will" that earned a standing ovation. "I'm an Australian," says Cave, "I know what Australian audiences are like, and it was incredible to me to see their response to this guy." Says Rufus Wainwright, "It was boiling hot, an insane summer day; we were playing the Opera House and I almost felt like we'd gone to the Krypton palace to summon Superman, and we did this amazing show. Thank God, it got filmed."

Hal Willner had met Australian filmmaker Lian Lunson at a party in Los Angeles. After saying how much he had enjoyed her documentary on Willie Nelson, which had been broadcast on a public television station, he complained "that it was a shame these Leonard shows aren't going to be on film. So she did it." The only way she could do something with the footage, she told him afterward, was if she could interview Leonard on camera. With some persuasion, Leonard agreed. Lunson also filmed him in a New York nightclub playing a secret performance with U2. They sang just one song together— "Tower of Song," the title track of the 1995 Leonard Cohen tribute album on which Bono did his beatnik-soul version of "Hallelujah"— and there was no audience, but for a man who since 1993 had been content to let other people sing his songs onstage, it was not insignificant. Lunson's film, titled *Leonard Cohen: I'm Your Man*, was first screened in September 2005 at the Toronto International Film Festival. That same month, Leonard was awarded a plaque on the Canadian Folk Music Walk of Fame. Leonard, as had become his custom, sent his thanks and his apologies and stayed home in L.A.

Leonard flew to Montreal in January 2006 for a very different kind of ceremony. Irving Layton, at the age of ninety-three, was dead. At the funeral, his big white coffin was wheeled out to the strains of Beethoven's "Ode to Joy," while around seven hundred people, including ex-wives, former students, family, friends and media, looked on. Leonard, dressed in a thick overcoat with a fur collar and a crushed cap, slipped into the chapel quietly, taking a seat at the back, where he tapped his toe to the music. In his eulogy Leonard said, "What happened between Irving and me is between us and doesn't bear repeating. But what does bear repeating, and will be repeated, are his words." He read Layton's poem "The Graveyard," which ended with the lines "There is no pain in the graveyard, or the voice / whispering in the tombstones / 'Rejoice, rejoice.'" Layton was "our greatest poet, our greatest champion of poetry," Leonard said. "Alzheimer's could not silence him, and neither will death." When Leonard tried to slip out just as quietly, he was requisitioned as a pallbearer. Layton, Leonard thought to himself, smiling, would have heartily approved of the whole event.

It felt good to be back in Montreal, even in midwinter, and even for an occasion such as this. Leonard was going stir-crazy in L.A. For some time he had been thinking—as he often did—about moving back to Montreal, and Anjani seemed to agree that it was a fine idea. Leonard had recently hired a Canadian manager, Sam Feldman, whose clients included Joni Mitchell and Diana Krall. When, five months after his last Canadian award, Leonard was inducted into the Canadian Songwriters Hall of Fame in February, at Feldman's urging, since there were a new album and a new book both scheduled for release in May, Leonard agreed to attend.

"I'm not really drawn to these kind of events," Leonard said. "It's a very tricky occasion, being honoured. In one sense, it feels like an obituary and you don't really feel [that] about yourself."[2] The gala featured yet more tributes from artists performing Leonard's songs onstage—Rufus Wainwright once again; Willie Nelson, dressed for the occasion in a suit; and k. d. lang, whose rendition of "Hallelujah" moved Leonard to tears. There were more tears when Adrienne Clarkson, the former governor general, presented the award. "One of the reasons one avoids these things is because they summon some really deep emotional responses," Leonard told the *National Post*. "This happens to an artist or a writer very rarely, where you have in front of you the unconditional acceptance of your work."[3] In his acceptance speech he said, "We shuffle behind our songs into the Hall of Fame."[4] Leonard, Clarkson said in her speech, "changed all of our lives with the complexity of his sadness, the breadth of his love. . . . He gets inside your brain, your heart, your lungs. You remember him, you feel him, you breathe him. He is our connection to the meaning of ecstasy, our access to another world we suspected existed but which he puts into song." She thanked the millions of her fellow countrymen who failed to buy his early poetry books and novels, "because without that he might not have turned to songwriting."

In the various interviews he gave in Canada, Leonard appeared upbeat and lighthearted, even on the unavoidable question of his ex-manager and his missing money. There was no vitriol or attacks, just some self-reprobation for not reading his bank statements and that line about its being enough to put a dent in his mood, to which he added "Fortunately it hasn't."[5] Among these interviews was one with *CARP* magazine, the publication of the association for Canadian retirees. At Leonard's apartment journalist Christine Langlois found the septuagenarian who could not afford to retire sitting in a sunbeam at the kitchen table with Anjani, smiling and eating bagels. Surprised at such a picture of domestic bliss, she asked how it squared with his reputation. "Everything changes as you get older," Leonard said. "I never met a woman until I was sixty-five. Instead, I saw all kinds of miracles in front of me." In the past, he had always viewed women through his own "urgent needs and desires," he said, and "what they could do for me." But in his midsixties—which roughly coincided with Leonard leaving the monastery and his depression starting to lift—"that started to dissolve and [he] began to see the woman standing there." Anjani, laughing, pointed out, "I was the one standing there when that idea occurred to him." By this point she and Leonard had been together seven years. Leonard was quoted as saying that "old age" was the "best thing that ever happened to me." Despite the business with Kelley Lynch, he felt light and peaceful. "The state of mind I find myself in is so very different than most of my life that I am deeply grateful."[6]

———————

Book of Longing, Leonard's first new volume of poetry in twenty-two years, was published in May 2006 and dedicated to Irving Layton. Like *Dear Heather,* it is something of a scrapbook: a 230-page miscellany of poems, prose pieces and artwork. There are as many drawings as there are poems—among them sketches of Roshi and Leonard's fellow monks; of Irving Layton and Pierre Trudeau; of women, more often than not undressed; and several self-portraits, in which his expression ranges from hangdog to glum, and which are accompanied by wise, comic, morbid and/or mordant marginalia:

> *I never found the girl*
> *I never got rich*
> *Follow me*

or elsewhere,

taxes,
children
lost pussy
war
constipation
the living poet
in his harness
of beauty
offers the day back to g–d.

(Throughout the book, Leonard, in the respectful Jewish tradition, uses "g-d" in place of "God," and also hyphens in place of sexual expletives.)

The literary content is wide-ranging, from formal to pop cultural, from long, lyrical ballads to short, whimsical doggerel, prose pieces to songs, or poems that became songs—the quite different words of both the poem "Thousand Kisses Deep" and the song "A Thousand Kisses Deep" set side by side on opposing pages. Many of the poems—particularly those written on cold, dark nights or in snatched moments in a mountain monastery—are about death: anticipated, contemplated, mourned and recalled. "Who Do You Really Remember" catalogs various deaths—his dog, his uncles and aunts, his friends—that occurred between his father's death, when Leonard was nine, and his mother's, when he was forty-three. The prose poem "Robert Appears Again" describes a conversation with the ghost of a dead friend, conducted while Leonard was on the twenty-year-old speed he'd found in the pocket of an old suit. In "I Miss My Mother," Leonard wishes he could take Masha to India, buy her jewelry and tell her that she was

right about everything
Including my foolish guitar

And where it got me . . .
She'd pat my little head
And bless my dirty song

Often on Friday nights, when he lit the candles to mark the Sabbath and Adam, Lorca and Anjani came over for dinner, Leonard would imagine that his mother was there too and her reaction to "seeing how I've finally stabilised my life."[7]

But it is the *Book of Longing,* not the book of the dead, and these losses are only one of the "various forms of longing: religious, sexual, just expressions of loneliness," that Leonard addresses.[8] He berates himself for his failings as a Buddhist monk, from his inability to understand his teacher ("Roshi") to the "enormous hard-on" he has under the robes when he dresses for the morning meditation ("Early Morning at Mount Baldy"). In the abbreviated, six-line version of his poem "Not a Jew" he asserts that he remains unswervingly Jewish. In "One of My Letters" he signs off not with "L. Cohen" but with his Jewish and his Buddhist names, Jikan Eliezer.

He addresses the decline of his powers with age and his failures as an artist ("My Time") and as a ladies' man ("Never Once"). In the honest and erotic "The Mist of Pornography," he discusses his relationship with Rebecca De Mornay and why it had to end. In "Titles" he writes,

I had the title Poet
and maybe I was one
for a while
Also the title Singer
was kindly accorded me
even though
I could barely carry a tune . . .
My reputation
as a Ladies' Man was a joke

It caused me to laugh bitterly
through the ten thousand nights
I spent alone.

But despite these protestations, in "Other Writers," having extolled the virtues of his poet friend Steve Sanfield and of Roshi, he brags, "I prefer my stuff to theirs," and describes a sexual encounter with a young woman in the front seat of his jeep. Irving Layton, Leonard recalls in "Layton's Question," would always ask him: "Are you sure you're doing the wrong thing?" Layton would have been proud.

––––––––––

"As a person of Jewish ancestry," Leonard said in an interview with the Buddhist magazine *Tricycle*, "I find it deeply satisfying that the description of God's creative activity as it appears in the Kabbalah is remarkably parallel to that of my teacher Joshu Sasaki Roshi, contemporary Japanese Zen master."[9] Leonard and Anjani had begun to regularly attend a synagogue in Los Angeles led by Rabbi Mordecai Finley.

Finley, a martial artist, former military man and professor of liturgy, Jewish mysticism and spirituality at the Academy for Jewish Religion in California, founded the Ohr Torah congregation in 1993. Leonard and Anjani first encountered Finley at the wedding of Joni Mitchell's producer Larry Klein. "The rabbi gave an inspiring, extemporaneous speech about love and how to stay together as a married couple," says Anjani. "I looked at Leonard and said, 'I want to hear more from him.'" There was a moment's hesitation, then Leonard said, "I'm going to go with you.'" Finley remembers that he had talked about marriage "as an opportunity to be of service to another human being, an opportunity for the deepest human transformation, because you're so deep in the presence of another human being. Which takes work, it takes mindfulness, it takes commitment, it takes discipline. It probably resonated with Leonard's understanding of spirituality. A while later he just started showing up at the synagogue." He would often see Leonard sitting there, his back straight, his eyes cast down, as if in seated meditation in Roshi's monastery, but with Anjani by his side. It seemed to the rabbi that Leonard was taking in the mood and the energy as much as the meaning of the words.

In his first conversation with Leonard, the rabbi had asked him, "You're a Buddhist priest, how does that square with Judaism?" It was the same question Leonard had been asked by the press when he was ordained a monk; he had answered it in his poem "Not a Jew."

Leonard answered Finley that it did not have to square; Buddhism was nontheistic and Roshi was a great man with a great mind. "Leonard made it very clear to me that it had nothing to do with his religion, nor his beliefs. As we got to know each other better, I was delighted to see that he is a very learned Jew. He's deeply well-read, very committed to understanding Kabbalah and—in a very similar way that I do—is using the Kabbalah not so much as a theology but as spiritual psychology and a way to mythically represent the Divine. If you understand that human consciousness is basically symbolic, then one has to find some kind of symbol system that most closely articulates one's understanding of all the levels of reality."

Finley, being nearer to Anjani's age than Leonard's, and an American, did not grow up with any great awareness of Leonard and his work. He started to investigate; everything he read felt "like a prayer. He always operates in the metaphysical realm; even anything that he writes about on the material realm has the metaphysical echoing into it, an echo of the cosmic even in the most mundane of things." On one occasion, Leonard showed him the book his grandfather Rabbi Klonitzki-Kline had written. "It's a very fine volume, a substantial, learned book. It's tragic that it has not been translated and put out in wide circulation." They opened the book—which was written in Hebrew—and talked about various passages in it, and Finley was impressed by Leonard's scholarship. "He grew up in an ambience of deep, serious, Jewish study. He was up-to-date, he knew who the great Jewish thinkers were and understood their arguments. There are obscure parts of Kabbalah that we actually differed on and sometimes we would be talking about one thing and come back to that thing, 'Here we are again.' He could be a great teacher of Judaism. If that were his thing, to be a rabbi, he had it in his power to have been one of the greatest of our generation.

"By the way," Finley adds, "modern students of Kabbalah are very interested in Leonard's work, because they see Leonard as not a professor of Kabbalah, not a theologian, but someone who really understands Kabbalah from within, [and his poetry as] the best poetry on the Kabbalah they've ever read. He gets the inner ethos of brokenness and healing and the tragedy of the human condition, in that we're not particularly well suited for this life but you still have to find your way through."

———

On May 13, 2006, in Toronto, Leonard gave the closest thing to a public musical performance in more than a decade. It was at a bookstore, where he was signing copies of *Book of Longing*. Three thousand fans showed up—the book was already on its way to the top of the bestseller list—and the police had to close off the street. On a small stage, Anjani, Ron Sexsmith and Barenaked Ladies provided the entertainment. Leonard had not planned to sing, but during her set Anjani asked him to join her and would brook no refusal. After duetting with her on "Never Got to Love You," Leonard went on to sing solo "So Long, Marianne" and "Hey, That's No Way to Say Goodbye." The response was rapturous.

Blue Alert, the album Leonard and Anjani had worked on together, was released, as was *Book of Longing*, in May 2006. Like *Ten New Songs* it was a full collaboration—Leonard's words, Anjani's music.

But unlike *Ten New Songs* it was not a duet album, it was an Anjani album. Her picture adorned the front cover. Underneath her name, in much smaller letters, was written "Produced by Leonard Cohen." It was as if this man who so loved women, who so often wrote songs about women (or, as he had often claimed, wrote to attract women), who believed, as he said, that women "inhabited this charged landscape that poetry seemed to arise from, and that it seemed to be the natural language of women,"[10] had finally achieved with this album what perhaps he had been working toward since his debut, which he had experienced once with Jennifer Warnes's *Famous Blue Raincoat* and which, on the albums he had made since leaving the monastery, he had come ever closer to achieving: to hand his songs over to the female voice to sing.

It was a first for Leonard to make an album whose muse was not only his current romantic partner but his cowriter. The fact that it would be Anjani's album, not his, seemed to speed up the writing process. Anjani had found the words for what would become the title song on Leonard's desk—it was a new poem he had written for *Book of Longing.* She asked if she could try to make a song from it and when he consented, and told her he liked what she did with it, she moved on to another one. She took an old poem, "As the Mist Leaves No Scar," from *The Spice-Box of Earth*—a volume published when Anjani was two years old—and set it to music, unaware that Phil Spector had already done so with "True Loves Leaves No Traces" on *Death of a Ladies' Man.* Anjani's melody for the song, which she titled "The Mist," was very different though, with the feel of an old folk song. The ballad "Never Got to Love You," a noir short story of love, regret and moving on, was put together from unused verses for the song "Closing Time." Sometimes, as she went through Leonard's notebooks, Anjani would find small scraps of lyrics that she liked, and she would tell him, "Just finish the song." "Thanks for the Dance" started out as a few lines in one of Leonard's journals: *"Thanks for the dance, I hear that we're married, one-two-three, one-two-three, one.*" "I said, 'Finish that; I could really sing *that* song,' which is like telling Leonard to write 'Hallelujah' in a couple of weeks. But he enjoyed the task, because it was very freeing—he didn't have to sing it, he was writing it for me now, and the standards of what he would write for himself didn't apply, so it came quite easily. It also happened for 'No One After You.' It was funny because I said, 'Okay, it's almost there, it's almost good,' and then I remember there was one night when I was going in the studio the next day and I said, 'You've got one hour to come up with that last line.' He said, 'Okay, well give me some chocolate.' So he's nibbling at a bar of chocolate and he's wandering back and forth until he shouted, 'I'm a regular cliché.' I thought, 'Thank you, you *can* write under pressure.'"

The recording process was not so easy. "There were some moments when it really wasn't pretty," Anjani remembers. "I was crushed, especially early on. Don't get me wrong, he's wonderfully gracious, he's generous, he's everything that he appears to be, but nobody's perfect, myself included, and we both definitely have strong ideas. On *Blue Alert* I really started to get independent about what I wanted to do. In 2004, when we were making songs for his record *Dear Heather*, a friend of mine had died and I was really sad about it, and Leonard walked into the room and said, 'Here, maybe this will make you feel better,' and it was the lyric to 'Nightingale,'" a song that appeared on both *Dear Heather* and *Blue Alert*. "But the sections were reversed. It started off, '*Fare thee well, my nightingale.*' When I was reading it, the melody came into my head and I immediately thought, 'This should go here and that should go there.' It was like a puzzle I was solving. I took it home and I didn't change the words but I rewrote the structure and I recorded it and I played it for him. And I could see his eyes open wide, because I'd actually fucked with his song. It didn't even occur to me that he might react that way. He kept listening intently and afterward he said, 'Well of course it starts with "*I built my house.*"'" At some point, though, it became clear that they needed a referee. Leonard called John Lissauer, his old producer, and the man who had first brought Anjani into Leonard's life.

Lissauer describes what he witnessed in the studio as "a tug-of-war." As he saw it, when Leonard had worked with Sharon Robinson on *Ten New Songs*, it had been Leonard's record, but although *Blue Alert* was Anjani's album, "Leonard was still expecting it to be Leonard's record. Leonard would want one thing and Anjani would want another, and I was sort of in the middle of that because I knew them both and I was trying to answer to both of them." When he listened to the demos, Lissauer thought the songs beautiful but was not impressed with all the synthesizers and drum machines they played them on. "I said, 'Let me at least get some organic instruments and add some colors here and there.'" Taking six songs away with him, Lissauer added instrumental touches, much as he had done on Leonard's albums *New Skin for the Old Ceremony* and *Various Positions*. He thought they sounded "lovely," as did Leonard and Anjani, "but they were bickering quite a bit, like they were trying to get custody. And—this was the most bizarre thing—their trade-off was 'I'll throw that thing of John's out but you have to . . . ,' and one by one, in order to settle their arguments and to spite each other, they threw out the improvements and wore away all the colors and stripped it back down to the demo sound." All that remained of his work, Lissauer says, "was the baritone saxophone solo on 'Blue Alert' and the waltz song 'Thanks for the Dance' that we did together."

The album was ultimately recorded on neutral territory, with engineer and coproducer Ed Sanders in his analog studio in L.A. Sanders had worked with Anjani on her last album, *The Sacred Names*, and, ever since she introduced him to Leonard during the making of *Dear Heather*, he had also been working as Leonard's administrative assistant. No one had been killed in the making of the album, although Lissauer, as often seemed to happen, was left a little bruised by the experience. Still, it did not prevent him from describing *Blue Alert* as "one of the great albums of the decade." It is certainly fascinating to hear the erotic desires of an old man and lyrics about memories, fatigue and valedictions expressed in the voice of a young woman and couched in elegant folk-jazz melodies. In the liner-note booklet, Leonard is photographed sitting alongside the youthful, beautiful Anjani, his face out of focus, fading, as if he were in the process of becoming a ghost.

———————

In October 2006, *Came So Far for Beauty* took its final bow in Ireland as part of the Dublin Theatre Festival. The lineup included many of the previous participants and others including Lou Reed, Mary Margaret O'Hara and Anjani, the last of these three at Leonard's request. Willner was happy to oblige. Anjani broke with the tradition of singing whatever Willner allotted and performed two songs from *Blue Alert*. Lou Reed also selected his own songs—two from *Songs of Leonard Cohen*, the album that Leonard was in New York recording when Reed met him for the first time. Willner asked Reed if he would also sing "Joan of Arc" as a duet with Julie Christensen. "First of all I don't do *la-las*," said Reed, but he agreed. Nick Cave, who this time had been given two songs from *Songs of Love and Hate*, his favorite, remembers Reed's treatment of "The Stranger Song" as "extraordinary, so irreverent. It was a Lou song that happened to sound like Leonard Cohen had written it before Lou."

That autumn, Lian Lunson's film *Leonard Cohen: I'm Your Man* started to do the rounds of independent U.S. cinemas. Leonard slipped into a movie theater in L.A. to watch it with Anjani. It is a curious film, part concert movie, part biographical interview. Selected stage performances from the tribute concerts and testimonies from participants—"This is our Shelley," says Bono, "this is our Byron"—are interspersed with artily shot black-and-white footage of Lunson's conversation with Leonard. As the filmmaker and her subject tread gently through the touchstones of Leonard's past—his father's death, the Montreal poetry scene, the stories behind "Suzanne," the Chelsea Hotel, Phil Spector and the monastery—Leonard offers up old, familiar lines as if they have just occurred to him: "I started writing poetry trying to get girls interested in my mind"; "The less I was of who I was, the better I felt." For his newer fans, those who came to his songs through the famous cover versions that kept turning up on film and TV and in Willner's tribute concerts, it was an intriguing introduction. If Leonard, wise, dapper and self-deprecating, said nothing that his old fans did not already know, they were still happy to hear him, and especially see him, saying it, since few outside of Canada had seen him in years. And the scene in which he sings "Tower of Song," backed by a doting U2, showed he still had the chops. A soundtrack album was released, with sixteen Leonard Cohen covers recorded live at the Sydney and Brighton concerts. "Tower of Song" made it on, but one song that did not was the rousing "Don't Go Home with Your Hard-On." Phil Spector, Leonard's cowriter, refused to give his permission.

Leonard Cohen: I'm Your Man certainly helped pique and revive interest in Leonard. But another effect of the film was to prompt the question, why was everyone except Leonard singing his songs? A Canadian journalist asked Leonard directly if he ever intended to go back on the road. Leonard answered that it was "becoming more and more attractive to me as we drink," but he failed to mention that he rarely drank much anymore. In *Book of Longing* he had captioned one of his drawings with the verse

the road
  is too long

the sky
   is too vast
the wandering
   heart
is homeless
at last

But as the year drew to a close, Leonard showed no inclination to be anywhere other than home.

Twenty-three

The Future of Rock 'n' Roll

On the table were a slab of beef tongue and bottle of good cognac. Leonard knew what Roshi liked. He poured a large glass for Roshi and a small one for himself and they sat with their drinks in easy silence, Leonard and the old man who had named him Jikan but usually called him Kone (not quite "koan," but close). In a few weeks' time Roshi would be one hundred years old, and yet here he still was, the constant in Leonard's life, the good friend, the wise father figure who disciplined and indulged him and never left, not even when Leonard had left him. Life, aside from "the pesky little problem of losing everything I had,"[1] was treating Leonard kindly in his old age. He had Roshi, he had Anjani and he had a grandson, Cassius Lyon Cohen—two good names, Leonard's boxing hero and his grandfather—Adam's son, born in February 2007.

Leonard wore his own seventy-two years lightly. Still, he had noticed some changes, like losing his capacity for alcohol for one, as well as his taste for tobacco. When he quit smoking, Leonard had promised himself he could start again when he reached seventy-five. He blamed his abstinence from cigarettes for the loss of the two lowest notes in his vocal range, even if in truth they had only ever been audible to certain mammals and devoted female fans. His voice now was deeper than it had ever been. It was like old leather, soft and worn, a little cracked in places but for the most part supple, and hung suspended somewhere between word and song. Since Leonard's return from the monastery, it seemed to have been leaning more toward the word. Of course there was always music in the word, but when it came down to actual melodies, Leonard seemed as content to leave them to others to write as he had been to let others sing his songs.

Another project was about to come to fruition, which featured his words set to music that Leonard neither wrote nor sang. Unlike *Blue Alert*, this was a stage production, with music by Philip Glass— among the most distinguished, influential and prolific composers in postmodern American music. Almost a quarter of a century earlier, between writing his avant-garde opera *Einstein on the Beach* and scoring the Martin Scorsese film *Kundun*, Glass had taken a poem of Leonard's from *The Spice-Box of Earth*, "There Are Some Men," and turned it into an a capella hymn, which was performed as part of *Three Songs for Chorus a Cappella*, a work commissioned for the celebration of the 350th anniversary of Quebec. At that time, he and Leonard had never met. But having been introduced backstage at a concert somewhere along the way, they had talked about spending some time together and eventually, fifteen years later, they did, in L.A. They spent the day together, Glass recalls, "talking about music and poetry," by the end of the day, they had agreed to work together on something, though neither knew what or when.

Glass had collaborated over the years on diverse projects with orchestras, rock musicians and filmmakers, but he particularly enjoyed working with poets. One of his favorite collaborators was Allen Ginsberg, with whom he worked for ten years, until Ginsberg's death in 1997. Not long after, Glass tried to get in touch with Leonard again, but he says, "I discovered he had gone into the monastery." It would be several more years before Leonard e-mailed to say, "I'm out of the monastery, so we can go back to that project." Glass, who "was missing having that in-depth relationship with a poet that was *alive*," was delighted. "I kind of went from Allen Ginsberg to Leonard Cohen—a pretty good transition, don't you think?"

When Glass visited Leonard at his L.A. home, Leonard was still working on *Book of Longing*. He handed the composer a stack of loose pages, poems and illustrations, in no particular order. Sitting at the wooden table, Glass leafed through them, relishing the randomness. He started formulating categories into which he divided the contents: ballads, "the long poems I thought would be the pillars of the work"; rhymes and limericks, "the little ones"; dharma poems, "spiritual meditations"; love/erotic poems; and personal poems, about Leonard. He picked five or six from each category to write music for. Among them were some that Leonard had already recorded as songs. Tentatively, Glass asked Leonard if he would like to be involved in the music. "I was terrified that he might say yes, but he said, 'You write the music.'"

Glass composed a series of song cycles to be performed by four voices and a small ensemble made up of strings, oboe, horn, percussion and keyboards. To retain the sense of randomness he had felt and to give the theater audience a sense of "flipping through a book of poetry," he included in each song cycle a poem from each of his five categories. He also wanted to hear how the poems sounded in their author's voice, so he asked Leonard if he would record himself reading a few. Leonard recorded the entire book and sent that. "When I heard the quality of this reading," Glass says, "I thought I would put his voice into the piece itself. I said, 'Though you may not be there to perform it, may I use your voice?' He said, 'Yes.'" Leonard also gave Glass use of his artwork as a backdrop. When the composition was finished—ninety minutes, twenty-two poems—he played it for Leonard, who sat and listened quietly. "He said almost nothing. There was one vocal part that he felt was a little bit high and I eventually brought it down an octave, but that was the only thing, and it did work better."

The world premiere for *Book of Longing: A Song Cycle Based on the Poetry and Images of Leonard Cohen* was set for June 1, 2007, in Toronto, coinciding with the opening there of *Leonard Cohen: Drawn to Words*, a traveling exhibition of Leonard's drawings and sketches. Glass flew to Canada to conduct the final rehearsals. To his surprise Leonard flew there too and spent a week working with him and the cast. As with *Blue Alert*, Leonard was not without opinions on how his words ought to be sung. Glass remembers, "He met the singers and said, 'Well here I am, you can ask me anything you like.' They talked for hours. He had powerful insights into the approach to singing that worked with his words. He began talking about the 'voice' that they should employ in singing the work—I don't mean the *kind* of voice, I mean the aesthetic. At one point he said, 'You start by singing and make it simpler and simpler and simpler and where you reach the point where you're actually speaking, then you're finished.' He didn't actually literally mean they would be speaking, I believe he meant it would be *as if* you were speaking, that the affectations of singing were absent. And they followed that advice and they simplified their vocal style until it became almost like speech." Leonard had said much the same thing to Anjani.

Leonard stayed and joined Glass in a public discussion of the work. When he was asked whether he considered what Glass had done to be classical or musical theater, Leonard's answer, "Glassical," was wry but accurate. Although originally labeled minimalist for their haunting, repetitive rhythms and motifs, Glass's musical compositions were also earthy and erotic and drew on any number of different musical styles, all of them evident in this work. The *Toronto Star*'s reviewer's description was "a confusing work of considerable importance."[2]

Following three successful nights in Toronto, the show left on a small tour, and in December 2007 the album *Book of Longing: A Song Cycle Based on the Poetry and Images of Leonard Cohen* was released, making it to No. 17 on the U.S. classical music charts. Over the next two years, the production would be staged in a number of U.S. and European cities and at a festival in New Zealand. In 2009 it returned to America for a five-night stand in Claremont, the university town at the bottom of Mount Baldy. The theater in which it was staged faced the mountain. A college building nearby hosted an exhibition of Leonard's art. Both events had been arranged by Robert Faggen, a writer and professor of literature at Claremont Graduate University who had a cabin on Mount Baldy, a short walk from the monastery. He and Leonard had become good friends since their first encounter in Wolfe's Market—the store at the bottom of Mount Baldy where Leonard would go to buy treats for Roshi. On the occasion of their meeting, Leonard was standing in the deli aisle, dressed in his monk's robes, meditating on the merits of buying some potato salad.

Faggen took Glass, who flew out for the Claremont shows, to the monastery to meet Roshi. Glass, like Leonard a Jew of Lithuanian-Russian descent, also shared his deep involvement with Buddhism; he had himself been on long retreats (where, in his case, he was given special dispensation to take his piano) and had been a contributing editor to the Buddhist magazine *Tricycle*. At Mount Baldy Zen Center, Glass sat for a *teisho* with Roshi. Although the old teacher declined to come down from the mountain to go to the concert, the audience included a number of monks.

There were now three productions featuring Leonard's work without Leonard making the rounds: *Book of Longing: A Song Cycle*, *Came So Far for Beauty*, and *Leonard Cohen: Drawn to Words*. It was an invisible kind of visibility that suited Leonard just fine. "If you hang in there long enough, you begin to be surrounded by a certain gentleness and invisibility," he once told an interviewer. "This invisibility is promising, because it will probably become deeper and deeper. And with invisibility—and I am not talking about the opposite of celebrity, I mean something like The Shadow, who can move from one room to another unobserved—comes a beautiful calm."[3]

With age had come a greater degree of serenity than Leonard had ever felt in his adult life. With age too had come homages and awards without end. He had to stop counting how many tribute albums there were—more than fifty by this point, from twenty different countries. A couple had caught his eye. One, because it was recorded by his first and most stalwart champion, was *Democracy: Judy Collins Sings Leonard Cohen*—from 2004, the year Leonard turned seventy—on which Collins had gathered all her interpretations of his songs under one roof. Another that had delighted Leonard was *Top Tunes Artist Vol. 19 TT-110*, an instrumental album of his songs (packaged with an album of Enya songs) made specifically for karaoke bars. "At last," Leonard said, "somewhere to go in the evening,"[4] though in reality he was still happiest at home, "an old man in a suit . . . delicately talking about his work to somebody."[5] Then Sony decided to reissue *Blue Alert*.

On its original release the previous year, Anjani's album had reached No. 18 in the U.S. jazz charts but had had little impact anywhere else. For the new edition the record label added a DVD of videos and a documentary by Lian Lunson on the making of the album. The label also put together a short tour. In March 2007, shortly before Roshi's one hundredth birthday, Leonard flew with Anjani to Europe. The first three shows, in London, Oslo and Warsaw, were invitation-only events, media mostly, and Leonard Cohen fans who had won tickets through radio and website contests. Journalists who wanted to interview Leonard—and there were many—were told that they would have to talk to him and Anjani as a pair. As far as Leonard was concerned, the tour and the album were Anjani's, not his.

To a UK newspaper, Leonard described his work with Anjani as more than mere collaboration, "an expression of some kind of deep mutuality, some kind of marriage of purpose."[6] Picking up on the "marriage" aspect, the host of a Norwegian television talk show asked Leonard to talk about their "love story." Leonard's answer—that he "found it's best not to name a relationship"—demonstrated that he had lost none of his skills at deflection. However, Anjani did appear to be wearing an engagement ring. In an interview with the Buddhist magazine *Shambhala Sun* Leonard elaborated, "The woman is saying, 'What is our relationship? Are we engaged?' . . . and my disposition is, 'Do we really have to have this discussion, because it's not as good as our relationship?' But as you get older, you want to accommodate, and say, 'Yeah, we're living together. This is for real. I'm not looking for anyone else. You're the woman in my life.' Whatever terms that takes: a ring, an arrangement, a commitment, or from one's behavior, by the way you act."[7]

During the *Blue Alert* tour Leonard had restricted his role to making the introduction, then taking a seat in the audience to watch the show. But one night, partway through a concert in a nightclub in London, Anjani invited Leonard to come up and sing with her, an invitation he accepted, shyly. His appearance was greeted by rapturous applause. When the tour arrived in the U.S., Leonard would show up on occasion and duet with Anjani on the song "Whither Thou Goest." As word of this spread, the small venues where Anjani had been booked to play started to attract large crowds—people who were hoping to see Leonard. The question was, did Leonard want to see them?

Leonard had never much enjoyed touring, however good the concerts might have been. He toured simply because if you were in the music business that was what you did. You made an album and when it was done you went on the road to check in with your fan base and sell it. This ritual was of particular importance to an artist like Leonard, whose records were not all over the radio. It had been almost fifteen years since Leonard had last toured, with *The Future*, and it had been such a disagreeable experience that it was one factor in Leonard's decision to leave the music business and go live in the monastery. Since his return to the music business, none of his albums had sold a fraction as well as *The Future*, so there seemed even less point in going out on tour.

But the music business had changed drastically during Leonard's absence. As the Internet grew and people increasingly wanted music for free, or at best to buy it online one song at a time, even big-name, established artists were no longer selling albums in the large numbers they had before. Musicians were starting to look for new ways to sell their music and themselves, coming up with all manner of solutions. Joni Mitchell, for example, had signed a deal with the coffee shop chain Starbucks, which played her CD as background music and sold it alongside lattes and croissants. Joni had been on Leonard's mind lately; Herbie Hancock had asked him to appear on a tribute album, *River: The Joni Letters* (2007); Leonard recited "The Jungle Line."

Major artists were increasingly making their money from touring, charging considerably higher ticket prices than under the old system, when concerts existed to promote album sales. Although Leonard refused to consider himself a major artist, he also knew that the tributes, the collaborations, the signed limited editions of his artwork and even the lawsuits had done little to refill his empty retirement account. Of all the options available to him for making a living, the only one that appeared even remotely feasible was going back on the road. But Leonard was almost seventy-three years old, and it had been so long since he had last toured, it seemed to him, that to expect that he would still have an audience would be like making a sandcastle and going back a decade and a half later and expecting it to be there waiting for him.

Still, he thought, it was not going to be any easier when he was seventy-five or eighty. And due to the combined publicity from the film and the tribute concerts, Anjani's album, Glass's production and the media interest in his financial problems, Leonard was as much in the public consciousness as he was likely to ever be again. Tentatively and ambivalently—very ambivalently—Leonard began to consider the idea of a tour. Since he had no manager to look into setting one up, having parted company with Sam Feldman some time ago, Leonard asked Robert Kory if he would do it.

As it happened, Leonard was not the only one considering the possibility. Steven Machat had heard from Leonard's old European promoter, asking if he would help him talk Leonard into touring. Machat knew Leonard had financial problems; he had first read about the business with Kelley Lynch in the *New York Times*, and though he was not entirely sympathetic—he had not forgotten that Lynch, who had once been his father Marty Machat's assistant, had, as he saw it, purloined Leonard's files, with Leonard's support, as his father lay dying—he was curious. He put in a call to Leonard, as he had promised the promoter he would. Leonard invited him to his house for lunch. Standing at the stove in his small kitchen, cooking, Leonard conceded to his guest that he might indeed have to tour, since he had no money. "I said to Leonard, man to man, why would any human being allow someone else to have the access to his fortune for five years? But Leonard is an extremely fearful man," Machat says. "Kelley Lynch played that to the hilt."

If Leonard was going to tour, it certainly would make sense to start in Europe, where he had his most loyal following. Robert Kory had thought as much and had already put in a call to AEG Live, a London-based promoter. He asked what they knew about Leonard Cohen and the response was "Not much, but there's a man in the company who is a big fan." That man was Rob Hallett. Hallett had an impressive record in the business. In the eighties he had been Duran Duran's worldwide promoter, and he had been behind Prince's recent sold-out twenty-one-night stand at the twenty-three-thousand-capacity O2 Arena in London. Kory called Hallett, who flew to L.A. to meet with him and Leonard and make his pitch. "I've got every album you've ever made," Hallett told Leonard. "I've read every novel, every poem, I bore all my friends regularly with quotations from your songs, and I've lived my life by a couplet from a poem that you wrote in 1958, 'He refused to be held like a drunk / under the cold tap of fact.'"

Leonard listened soberly. The more he heard, the more he saw the potential for humiliation. "He wasn't sure he could do it," says Hallett, "and he wasn't sure if anyone cared. I said, 'I'm a cynical old bastard and I don't want to see anything, but I want to see Leonard Cohen, so there must be others.' I was convinced there were hundreds of thousands of people out there who wanted to see him. His biggest concern was that he didn't want to embarrass himself. But also, he didn't have any money left. So I said, 'I'll tell you what, do some rehearsals, do as long as you want, audition as long as you want, and I'll pick up the tab and pay for everything. If at the end of it you say, "Thanks, but this isn't working for me, I can't go out there and perform," I'll go, "Well, we tried," and you won't owe me anything.'" It was an offer Leonard couldn't refuse. There were no strings and it had an escape clause, two of his favorite things. "That sounds like a reasonable deal," Leonard said. They shook hands on it. Kory began putting together a touring plan, while Hallett set about convincing the industry that Leonard Cohen concerts would be a going concern.

When Sharon Robinson opened her door one day soon after, she saw Leonard on her doorstep with a worried look on his face. "Darling," he said, "I think I'm going to have to go on tour again." He didn't want to do it, he said, but all the signs were pointing that way. He did not ask Sharon to come on the road with him. Nor did he ask Anjani. He thought—because the tour for *The Future* had soured him on working with old friends, perhaps, or because he did not want to let old friends down or let them see him fail—that he should take all new people with him, musicians he'd never worked with before. The one exception was Roscoe Beck, whom he asked to be his musical director.

"Leonard was very apprehensive about the entire enterprise," Beck remembers. "He didn't even want to talk on the phone about it. He flew down to Austin to talk to me in person. He said, 'I'm thinking about touring again. Would you help me put the band together and would you go?' I said, 'Yes, of course, I had already promised myself if I ever heard from you again I would go.'" (Beck had put together Leonard's *I'm Your Man* touring band but had been unable to join himself.) "Leonard said, 'Look, I don't know if I'm really going to do this. I hope you won't hold it against me if I decide to back out.' He really wasn't sure he could go through with it. He said, 'I'm 92.7 percent sure'—the numbers would change all the time—'I'm 82 percent sure, I'm 93 percent sure.' He said, 'I have the option of backing out at any time if I don't like the way it's developing, and if I do go I'm only committed to do six weeks. But if the whole thing doesn't happen would you forgive me?' I said, 'Of course.'"

Leonard had begun to feel less concerned about the actual touring—as long as his vocal cords didn't give out, he felt confident he could keep up the pace—than about the band. It had been so long since he'd played with one, he had no idea what kind of band he wanted. He was used to working at home with Anjani and Sharon, but an old man with two women and two synthesizers would not really cut it onstage. In January 2008, Beck started making calls and holding auditions. The first person Beck hired was actually someone Leonard knew well—Bob Metzger, Leanne Ungar's husband, who had played on the *I'm Your Man* tour and on the album *Ten New Songs*—though the next two recruits were new to Leonard, Neil Larsen, a keyboard player whose résumé ranged from Kenny Loggins to Miles Davis, and Javier Mas, a Spanish bandurria, laud and twelve-string-guitar player. Mas had been the musical director of a Leonard Cohen tribute concert in Barcelona, in which Leonard's son, Adam; Jackson Browne; and Anjani had performed. Leonard had seen a DVD of the concert and Mas had impressed him.

Beck was also trying to work out exactly what kind of show Leonard had in mind. Over the years, as Leonard's voice became increasingly deeper and his musical approach more refined, the bands and the volume level had changed accordingly. It appeared to Beck that this band he was putting together was "more like a chamber group." Six weeks into rehearsals they still had no drummer. Eventually they hired Mexican-born Rafael Gayol, another newcomer to Leonard; Beck had worked with Gayol in Austin. At one point Leonard decided he wanted a violin player, and a female violinist joined the band. Then Leonard realized he did not need a violin, and she was let go, and once again Leonard began to doubt himself—to regret, as he put it, "that I had started the whole process."[8] Instead, Beck brought in a multi-instrumentalist, Dino Soldo, to play saxophone, woodwind and keyboards.

All that remained to find were the backing singers. Beck asked Jennifer Warnes, but she declined. Anjani had dropped by for some of the early rehearsals, but no mention was made of her joining the tour. Says Beck, "I just wasn't sure what was going to happen in that regard because of the personal relationship between Anjani and Leonard." Anjani herself attributes it to "a difference of opinion" in their approach to the concerts. "I had in mind a revolutionary approach to Leonard's music; I wanted to showcase it in ways that hadn't been done before, with arrangements that were innovative and unexpected. The other approach was to re-create the past tours. In the end he went with what he felt comfortable with, and I understand the decision." Beck called Sharon Robinson, who expressed interest. But Leonard wanted two backing singers, and the search went on.

It was March 2008; the tour, if there was going to be one, was just two months away. Leonard meanwhile was in New York, being inducted into the Rock and Roll Hall of Fame—the American hall of fame, the big one, the greatest honor the once-dismissive U.S. music industry could bestow on him. Lou Reed was there to introduce

Leonard and present his award. In an odd little ceremony-within-a-ceremony Reed, dressed in a black leather suit and fuchsia shirt and carrying a stack of typewritten notes and a copy of *Book of Longing*, gave a reading instead of an introduction. Now and then he paused to interject his own comments like an enthusiastic college professor: "He just gets better. . . . We're so lucky to be alive at the same time Leonard Cohen is."[9]

Leonard, silver haired and dignified in his tuxedo and black bow tie, came out onstage, bowed deeply to Reed and thanked him for reminding him that he had written a few decent lines. This was "such an unlikely event," Leonard said, and it was not just modesty; he meant it. It brought to mind, he said, "the prophetic statement by Jon Landau in the early 1970s: 'I have seen the future of rock 'n' roll, and it is not Leonard Cohen.'"[10] Leonard was making a joke; what Landau, the head of the Hall of Fame's nominating committee, had actually said back in the days when he was a journalist for *Rolling Stone* was that he had seen the future of rock 'n' roll, and it was Bruce Springsteen. But *Rolling Stone* magazine had certainly dismissed Leonard's early albums, describing *Songs from a Room* as "depressed and depressing"[11] and *Songs of Love and Hate* as "unlikely to make you want to shake your little body."[12] As Lou Reed had, Leonard gave a recital in place of a speech—a solemn reading of the first five verses of "Tower of Song." He declined to follow the Hall of Fame tradition of performing with the other inductees; he was not ready to perform yet. But he was getting there. Leonard left the stage to Damien Rice to sing "Hallelujah," a song that at that time was No. 1 on the iTunes chart—the late Jeff Buckley's version. That it had been propelled back into the national consciousness had nothing to do with Leonard's finally taking his official place among the popular music pantheon, but through the sheer number of online discussions that followed Jason Castro's performance of "Hallelujah" on *American Idol*.

Back in Los Angeles, Beck was pulling out his hair. None of the women singers he had auditioned had worked out. He asked Sharon Robinson if she could think of someone—anyone. Sharon mentioned Charley and Hattie Webb. The Webb Sisters were in their early twenties. Born in England two years apart, they had sung and played as a duo since their teens, Charley on guitar, Hattie on harp. They had come to L.A. to work on an album and, during the process, their record label asked them to write some songs for a children's album they planned to release. Sharon, who had a publishing deal with the same company, was also brought in on that project. All three women remember how well their voices blended when they sang together.

Since that time, the Webbs had lost their record deal and were on the point of giving up and going home to the UK when Sharon called, telling them that Leonard was looking for a singer. They replied that they did not know many Leonard Cohen songs; although they had grown up on their parents' record collection of sixties and seventies singer-songwriters, their hairdresser father had banned Leonard's albums from their home because a colleague at the salon played nothing but Leonard Cohen albums all day long. They also told Sharon what she already knew: that they came as a pair and would not separate.

The whole band was in the rehearsal studio at SIR when the Webb Sisters arrived. Beck played a recording of "Dance Me to the End of Love" and told the three women to work out some parts. After singing them, the Webbs took their harp and guitar out of their cases and played two of their own songs, "Baroque Thoughts" and "Everything Changes." When Beck had first checked the sisters' Myspace page, he thought they looked too young, but the moment he heard them sing, this changed to, "Here are our singers." When they left, he called Leonard in New York. "I said, 'I've got good news and bad news. The good news is I think I've found our singers.' Leonard said, 'Great.' 'The bad news is now there's three.' We arranged for the sisters to come back when Leonard returned from New York, and it was a no-brainer. We knew we had our vocalists, and at last, our band."

Rehearsals resumed in earnest; there were less than six weeks left to go. "It was an interesting way of rehearsing," Charley remembers. "There wasn't a strong direction, Roscoe wasn't turning around and bossing anybody, and Leonard wasn't." "I felt that they were both allowing everyone to come to the song," says Hattie. "We would rehearse a few songs and then people would stop for tea and sandwiches, and while we were pottering Leonard would go back up just with his guitar, and play 'The Stranger Song' or 'Avalanche.' I felt he was just getting his bearings at this new time and in this environment." At the end of the week the sisters were dispatched to England to pick up work visas. They stayed the weekend, then flew straight back again for the next rehearsal on Monday.

In these last few weeks of rehearsal, Beck began noticing a change in Leonard's attitude to the tour. "The band really started taking shape and Leonard was able to conduct the rehearsals, fine-tune the band to his specifications and get exactly what he was looking for musically." He was also working on his showmanship, "falling to his knees even in rehearsal. It wasn't just an effect for the audience, it's for the band in a way, because if he goes down on one knee and cups his microphone, he's giving us a signal which we will interpret as, 'Play softer.' It's becoming more intimate."

Rob Hallett was getting anxious. Leonard had been rehearsing for at least four months now and all he had was bills. "About a million dollars later, I started panicking. Then Leonard said, 'Okay, come and see the rehearsals.'" They set up a sofa just for Hallett in front of the instrument-and-equipment-laden rehearsal-room stage. "I was blown away," says Hallett. "It was sublime." The show was ready to go. "And then Leonard insisted that before doing anything serious he wanted to do all these shows in the wilds of Canada—tiny places; he named some towns I'd never heard of." As the tour began to look like a reality, Leonard had asked Kory to set up what he called a "pre-tour tour," eighteen small, low-key warm-up shows in the Maritimes, away from the eye of the world. The kind of places where it was less likely there would be people waiting to see him fall. He also asked Kory if he would be his manager.

The very first concert took place on May 11, 2008, in Fredericton, New Brunswick. "The joke at the time," Hallett remembers, "was, 'First we take Fredericton, then we take Berlin.'" Leonard, the band and crew, and Kory and Hallett arrived several days early so that they could rehearse some more in the theater, five, six hours a day. The show couldn't have been better prepared. The tiny playhouse theater—just 709 seats—sold out in minutes; they could have sold it out ten times over, Hallett thought to himself, if Leonard had not insisted on such a small venue and Kory had not done his best to keep the show quiet.

Standing in the wings on opening night, his double-breasted suit hanging on his slight frame, Leonard still couldn't have sworn on the Scriptures that he was 100 percent sure about this tour. "He was nervous," says Hallett. "You wouldn't have known it on the outside, but he was incredibly nervous." If Leonard's mother had been there she would have advised him to have a shave. A few stiff drinks and a smoke would have helped as well, but this was going to be Leonard's first tour without alcohol and cigarettes. He took a deep breath; one lesson he had learned from his years at the monastery was to "stop whining."[13] Taking off his hat, he bowed his head and mumbled a little prayer. The house lights went down. Straightening his spine and pushing his fedora back firmly on his head, Leonard stepped out onto the stage.

Twenty-four

Here I Stand, I'm Your Man

The applause was deafening. It bounced off the walls of the small theater and resounded in Leonard's ears. The whole room was on its feet. A minute ticked by, then another. Leonard had not sung a word and no one had played a note, but still they applauded. Leonard smiled shyly. He took off his hat and held it over his heart, in a gesture of humility, but also as armor. The response was gratifying—whatever they told him, he had never been entirely confident as to what the reception might be—but also worrying, having such expectations to fulfill. Though in reality there were no expectations. It was the opening night. The audience had as much of an idea of what to expect of Leonard as he had of them. For all they knew—which was not very much, because, at Leonard's insistence, the whole thing had been kept as low-key as possible—it might be some broke and broken old man with a nylon-string guitar, singing them through their memories, accompanied by a female vocalist or two if he could afford them. Everyone had read about Leonard's money troubles and how they had forced the old monk back on the boards with his begging bowl.

But here he stood in the spotlight in his sharp suit, fedora and shiny shoes, looking like a Rat Pack rabbi, God's chosen mobster. He was flanked by three women singers and a six-piece band, many of whom also wore suits and hats, like they were playing in a casino in Las Vegas. The band started up. Leonard pulled his fedora down low on his forehead, and cradling the microphone like it was an offering, he began to sing, *"Dance me to your beauty with a burning violin,"* his voice a little rough at the edges, but deep and strong, *"Dance me through the panic till I'm gathered safely in"* ("Dance Me to the End of Love"). On this small, crowded stage, shoehorned with musicians and instruments and equipment, the women so close to him that if he felt the need he could reach out and hold on to them so he would not fall, Leonard sang as if he had come to this place alone to tell all these people in the seats, individually, a secret. He sang as if he had brought nothing with him onto the stage but this life of songs.

He told the audience, as he would go on to tell hundreds more, that the last time he had done this he was "sixty years old, just a kid with a crazy dream." He admitted to being nervous but chatted and joked with the audience, commiserating with them over the town's recent floods and paying tribute to its local poets—among them Fred Cogswell, who, more than half a century earlier, had published a review of Leonard's first book in his magazine *Fiddlehead*. The songs Leonard had selected for the show ranged across his career, while bypassing his darkest and most brutal material. (An exception was made for "The Future," although its "anal sex" was changed to something less anatomically specific.) While Roscoe Beck was putting the band together, Leonard had been going back through songs he had not listened to in years in search of those he felt he could still "live in."[1] It surprised him he had found so many—and that he remembered the words. That his choices leaned toward the more stirring, later songs than the naked early ones was perhaps in part an old man's delicacy, but more likely because they worked better with a large band, and Leonard needed a large band to drown out the noise of doubt. Equally important was that those early songs were largely solo guitar based. As relatively easy as it had been to reenter his songs, he found it much harder playing the guitar; it had been so long since he had played it that it needed to be restrung. He had to practice long and hard, he said, "to get [his] chop back," the one on "Suzanne," one of the few songs he played without adornment. Mostly, on the occasions when he did play an instrument, it was his synthesizer, acknowledging with a humble bow the applause for his mock-solemn, one-finger solos. But more often Leonard just sang, sometimes like a supplicant, his head bowed low over the microphone cupped in his hands, other times like a showman, the microphone cord draped casually over his arm, falling to his knees, working the crowd with meticulously choreographed moves—an intricate dance between self-awareness, irony and emotional honesty that he pulled off gracefully and well.

His band was smooth, elegant, note-perfect, its sound brush-stroked, its volume turned way down. "We called ourselves the world's quietest band," says Beck, "or at least the quietest with electric instruments. The focus was finely tuned to Leonard's voice and to making sure that the audience heard every word." But Leonard also gave the musicians solo spots. Stepping away from the light, he would watch them, rapt, his hat over his heart, marveling along with the audience when Javier Mas played the laud or twelve-string or Sharon sang him into "Boogie Street," as if he too was hearing this excellence for the first time and was humbled by it. They played for almost three hours that night, with a short intermission—and no one played three-hour shows, certainly not a man in his seventies who had not sung more than a handful of songs in succession on a stage in a decade and a half. Leonard's son, Adam, had tried to persuade him to keep it to an hour and a half, but Leonard was having none of it. And, remarkably, he seemed to be enjoying it. It was not simply relief that the rehearsals had paid off, the band worked and people were thrilled to see him. It was something deeper. There was some necessary rite that was being performed here, some gift being exchanged and something important being shared.

"I saw people in front of the stage, shaking and crying," remembers Charley Webb, "not just one person and not children. You don't often see adults cry, and with such violence." Says Hattie Webb, "The audience reaction from that first night was, 'This is hugely momentous.' It was for us too." With the first show behind them, everybody relaxed, even Leonard, as they headed in the bus to the next tiny Canadian venue. These shows had been booked at Leonard's insistence. His response to the tour schedule his manager had shown him was, "What have you gotten me into?"[2] "He set out a series of conditions," says Robert Kory. "I said, 'Leonard, this is a no-compromise tour, we will do it exactly the way you want to do it or we won't do it.' Every element of the tour articulated his vision, from three months of rehearsals to the warm-up dates."

There were eighteen of these dates in Eastern Canada. "You pick up a rock," says Rob Hallett, "and there's a town under it. One place I remember had a sign with those clip-on letters, advertising a local brass band on Monday, Leonard Cohen Tuesday and on Wednesday an Elvis Presley impersonator." At another of the concerts, two young women rushed the stage, prompting Leonard to comment wryly, or wistfully, or both, as security gently led them off, "If only I were two years younger." Kory also instituted a policy of no one being allowed backstage who did not need to be there, meaning no meet-and-greets, nor even visits from celebrity friends, before or after shows. This tour, Kory declared, would be "fueled on silence and deep rest and providing the level of support that helps him to do these performances night after night." This was quite a change from Leonard

Cohen tours in the past, which had been fueled by cigarettes and alcohol or the drug du jour. (By the end of his last tour, with *The Future*, Leonard had been smoking two packs a day and drinking three bottles of Château Latour before every show.)

The official starting date of the tour was June 6 in Toronto, where Leonard had sold out four nights at the three-thousand-seater Sony Centre. This time Leonard skipped onstage—literally skipped, like a little child—the very picture of gaiety and delight. Although the Toronto crowd had a better idea than Fredericton of what to expect, they had not anticipated this. "It was a surprise to me too," says Roscoe Beck, laughing. Leonard had also taken to dancing a light-footed shuffle during the song "The Future" whenever it reached the words "white man dancing." The set list had also lengthened. Among the four additional songs were "A Thousand Kisses Deep," whose words Leonard recited as a poem over Neil Larsen's hushed keyboard playing, and "If It Be Your Will," which was sung by the Webb Sisters, accompanying themselves on harp and guitar. The room was so completely silent during the performances of the songs that you could hear the hairs stand up on people's arms. But when the music ended, there were standing ovations—so many that the *Toronto Star* reviewer described the concert as "a love-in."[3]

This time the international press was welcomed to the concerts. The critic from *Rolling Stone*, having confessed to trepidation at the prospect of a comeback show by a man "older than Jerry Lee Lewis" trying to make enough money to retire on, called it "stunning."[4] Leonard told *Maclean's* magazine that he had decided—100 percent now—that the tour would go on. "As the Irish say, with the help of God and two policemen, [it] may last a year and a half, or two."[5] Four days after their last Toronto show, Leonard and the band were in Ireland, playing three consecutive nights in Dublin. There was a day off for travel, then four more concerts in a row in Manchester, followed by an appearance at the Montreal International Jazz Festival and, immediately afterward, another transatlantic flight back to Britain to play at the Glastonbury Festival. This was a punishing schedule by anyone's standards, let alone a man in his midseventies. Leonard had known what he was taking on and held up without complaint. Still, he was not looking forward to Glastonbury.

Michael Eavis was. The dairy farmer who founded the UK's biggest and best-loved rock festival had been trying to get Leonard to agree to play there, he said, "for almost forty years."[6] The Webb Sisters were so looking forward to it that they showed up two days early and melted into the crowd. When Leonard and the band arrived on the day of their performance, they were stunned at what they saw. Only seven weeks after having played to seven hundred people in Fredericton, they would be playing to a hundred thousand. "It was so . . . ," says Sharon Robinson, searching for a word to describe the magnitude of it and settling for "huge. And very exciting." Leonard did not share the excitement. He had never much enjoyed festivals, however successful his performances had been. It was not his crowd, one never knew who one was playing to, he could not spend a couple of hours sound-checking, and they had been instructed to shorten their usual set by almost half, which drastically altered its rhythm. None of these would please a perfectionist, a creature of habit or a man who needed to feel in control, in particular when it came to performing. Leonard peered out at the audience from the side of the stage. It was still daylight. A blanket of people stretched back from the stage as far as he could see. Those at the front all seemed to be youngsters. He slipped farther back into the wings and bowed his head. He might have appeared to be praying, but he was singing— "Pauper Ego Sum" ("I Am a Poor Man"), the Latin song-in-the-round he used to sing with his band on the tour bus half a lifetime ago. The Webb Sisters and Sharon, who were beside him, took up the song, and the rest of the band joined in. They were still singing it when they came out onstage, to be met with a roar of applause.

"There will never be anything better than Leonard Cohen's performance that night, for me," said Michael Eavis. The sun was starting to set when Leonard started singing "Hallelujah," and "people were just lifting off the ground."[7] Some of the young people singing along appeared to be wondering what this cool-looking old guy was doing up there singing a Jeff Buckley/Rufus Wainwright/*American Idol/X-Factor* song, while at the same time marveling at what a great job he did of it. The response from the audience was ecstatic, and reviewers agreed with Eavis, calling Leonard's performance the highlight of the festival. Leonard and the band did not have a chance to read the reports in the next morning's newspapers before they were on their way to Scandinavia for a whirlwind tour of Europe—at one point playing three-hour concerts in three different countries on three consecutive days. Everywhere they played, they were buoyed by this massive wave of love from the audience.

In July, still only two months into the tour, and back once again in England, Leonard headlined his first big arena show. The twenty thousand tickets to London's O2 Arena, a large, round, permanent marquee by the river Thames, sold out quickly. The vast stage had been strewn with Turkish rugs, to make it appear more homey, but it still looked like Leonard was playing inside a gigantic, sterile, skewered contraceptive cap. "It's wonderful," Leonard deadpanned, "to be gathered here on the other side of intimacy." The *London Evening Standard* reviewer described an audience "overpowered by a magnificent performance," and the closing song, "Whither Thou Goest," as "the most final of farewells."[8] Except the tour showed no sign of stopping anytime soon.

There were more concerts scheduled in the same arena in November. Meanwhile Leonard was on another lap around Europe, including a headlining appearance at the UK's Big Chill Festival and a tour of Eastern Europe. Sharon Robinson remembers everyone feeling like they were "on this ever-expanding, growing magic carpet, where it's, 'Okay, they love us in Northeast Canada, great,' but then we'd get the same thing again and again in bigger places. It was a kind of a curious, gradual acceptance of being involved in something very special." Leonard himself said, "I'm being sent like a postcard from place to place." Given his statements in the past on such a circumstance, it was not insignificant that he should add, "It's really wonderful."[9]

The bookings kept coming; Leonard was playing to the biggest and most age-diverse audiences of his career, and every show was a sellout. Following a six-week break for the holidays, during which Leonard spent Hanukkah with Adam and Lorca, and "Hallelujah" spent Christmas dominating the UK charts (three different versions, including one by Leonard), the tour resumed in January 2009 in New Zealand and Australia. Again Leonard triumphed. But he had always done well in these countries, just as he had in the UK, where even his bleakest albums made the Top 10, and in Europe, where he was feted for the very things that had turned the North American music industry off: his dark humor, old-world romance, existential gloom and poetry. North America was the next stop—his largest U.S. tour to date, interspersed with shows in Canada. Most of the American shows were in smaller venues, theaters, but he had also been booked to play at the Coachella festival and the Red Rocks Amphitheatre. Sensibly, Leonard started the tour on familiar ground, in New York City, with a show at the Beacon Theatre whose audience was crammed with media and hard-core fans alerted through the fan sites.

Rolling Stone reported a scene of "absolute chaos" outside the theater, "with hordes of people desperately looking for tickets. The few scalpers were getting upwards of five hundred dollars a seat";[10] *Billboard* said seven hundred.[11] In honor of the place he had once called home, Leonard added "Chelsea Hotel #2" (which he had been practicing in his room, privately, surprising the band by picking up his guitar and launching into it onstage). The show was now more than three hours long. "Fortunately there are curfews in most places," Robert Kory says, "or he would sing more." Both the critics and the audience were fulsome with praise—a response that would continue through the rest of the tour, with its sold-out shows, scalpers and standing ovations. It seemed as if suddenly everyone, everywhere, was talking about Leonard, asking themselves and each other, was he always this good, this wise, this droll, this cool.

Following the first leg of the U.S. tour, Leonard and the band flew back to Europe for forty more shows, some in new locations such as Serbia, Turkey and Monaco, but many in places they had already played but could still sell. There were ten dates booked in Spain, all in large venues, all sold out, and the majority in September, the month in which Leonard would turn seventy-five years old. During the September 18 concert in a cycling arena in Valencia, while singing "Bird on the Wire," Leonard collapsed. His bandmates, shocked, rushed over to him. His small limp body was carried gently off the stage, as fans near the front held up their mobile phone cameras to capture what looked like Leonard Cohen having sung himself out of the world, and having chosen the country of his beloved Lorca in which to do it. Farther back in the crowd, there was confusion. After some time Javier Mas came back onstage and explained in Spanish that Leonard was okay, he had regained consciousness and was on his way to the hospital, but the show was over and they would get their money back. The doctors diagnosed food poisoning. Several members of the band had apparently also been affected, but none of them was a gaunt seventy-five-year-old front man. Two days later, Leonard was back on the bus. Looking frail but unbroken, he celebrated his seventy-fifth birthday playing a three-hour performance in a packed sports arena in Barcelona.

In Montreal, his birthday was marked with a book launch. *Leonard Cohen You're Our Man: 75 Poets Reflect on the Poetry of Leonard Cohen*— the most celebrated of these poets being Margaret Atwood—was a fund-raising project by Jack Locke, founder of the Foundation for Public Poetry, to establish a Leonard Cohen Poet-in-Residence program at Leonard's old school, Westmount High. In New York, it was celebrated with the unveiling of a plaque on the wall by the entrance to the Chelsea Hotel. This project, spearheaded by Dick Straub, was funded by donations from Leonard Cohen fans across the world, and the ceremony was attended by Leonard's former producer John Lissauer, his writer friend Larry "Ratso" Sloman, and Esther, Leonard's ever-loyal sister. The plaque put Leonard in good company—Dylan Thomas, Arthur Miller, Brendan Behan, Thomas Wolfe—though none of these great writers' plaques could boast a quotation that alluded, as Leonard's did, to a world-famous blow job performed within the hotel's walls.

Three days after his birthday, Leonard was in Israel, playing his first concert in that country in more than twenty years. Ramat Gan Stadium, near Tel Aviv, held fifty thousand people and had sold out. Proceeds from what was billed as "A Concert for Reconciliation, Tolerance and Peace" were to go to Israeli and Palestinian organizations and charities promoting peace. "Leonard decided that if he was going to play there, he wanted the money to stay there," Robert Kory says. Still, there was controversy. When the show was announced, there were letters in the press and protests on the Internet by those urging a cultural boycott of Israel. In Montreal, a small demonstration was held outside one of Leonard's favorite Jewish delis. Leonard responded by adding a smaller show the next night in Ramallah, on the West Bank. But the organizers, the Palestinian Prisoners Club, pulled out, as did Amnesty International, who were to distribute the proceeds; both felt under pressure, that the event had become too politicized. So Leonard founded his own charity to allocate the almost two million dollars that the Tel Aviv concert made.

It was a warm summer night; the air shimmered with the glow sticks that the crowd held aloft like thin green candles. There were screens displaying translations of the songs Leonard sang through the three-and-a-half-hour show, the words in Hebrew of "Who by

Fire" reading like a page from the prayer book. Leonard dedicated "Hallelujah" to all of the families who had lost children in the conflict and expressed his admiration for those who in spite of this had resisted "the inclination of the heart to despair, revenge and hatred." When he told the audience, "We don't know when we'll pass this way again," they seemed visibly moved. Coming from a man of Leonard's age, his words had that sense of valediction that reviewers had also noted in his last album and his last volume of poems. When the last song was sung, Leonard raised his hands to the sky. Speaking in Hebrew, the descendant of Aaron gave the crowd the "Birkat Kohanim," the "Priestly Blessing."

Back in the U.S., with a few days off before the next leg of the tour, Leonard learned that Ramesh Balsekar was dead. His teacher died at the age of ninety-two on September 27, 2009, in the Mumbai apartment where Leonard had so often gone for *satsang*. Although his concert schedule had prevented him from spending much time with Ramesh, they had kept in touch by e-mail. "Just before he passed away," Ratnesh Mathur remembers, "I had a conversation with Ramesh, who mentioned that he was in correspondence with Leonard and said that it was good to see that he was performing again." The tour resumed in mid-October—fifteen more dates, including a return visit to New York to play Madison Square Garden.

It was getting to where past and present seemed to constantly bump into each other. While Leonard was writing and trying out new songs onstage (the first of them being "Lullaby") his record label re-released two old compilation albums from different periods—*Greatest Hits*, also known as *The Best of Leonard Cohen* (1975), and *The Essential Leonard Cohen* (2002)—as well as his first three studio albums from the late sixties and early seventies. *Songs of Leonard Cohen* came with two old songs released for the first time: "Store Room" and "Blessed Is the Memory," which were recorded during the 1967 sessions and shelved.* The reissued *Songs from a Room* also had two additional songs, the previously unheard versions of "Bird on the Wire" (titled "Like a Bird") and "You Know Who I Am" (titled "Nothing to One") that Leonard recorded with David Crosby before making the album with Bob Johnston. As its sole bonus track, *Songs of Love and Hate* had one of the many early outtakes of "Dress Rehearsal Rag." Still, it was one too many for Leonard, who disliked these additions and had not given his blessing for their inclusion. Feeling they ruined the integrity of the original album, he put a stop to the label's doing it again.

One remarkable temporal overlap was the release within weeks of each other of two new live CDs and DVDs. *Live in London* was recorded in 2008 at Leonard's first triumphant London O2 Arena show. *Live at the Isle of Wight 1970* contained recently unearthed recordings and footage of a 1970 performance. Watched side by side, these two UK concerts from each end of Leonard's touring career make for fascinating viewing. The 1970 show, outdoors, before a crowd of six hundred thousand in the early hours of a rainy morning, has Leonard—bestubbled, stoned and dressed in a safari suit—playing guitar backed by his small band, the Army; it is a spontaneous, edgy and seductive performance, with an intimacy that seems unfeasible in such a vast, inhospitable space. Four decades later, playing indoors in an arena, Leonard—silver haired, sober and in a smart suit—plays synthesizer with a nine-piece band; the show is as planned and rehearsed as a military operation, yet it is still magnificent, and once again Leonard makes a cavernous, anonymous space as small and intimate as a bedroom.

It was a reflection of Leonard's growing confidence onstage that he premiered more new material on the 2009 U.S. tour, "Feels So Good" and "The Darkness." The set list, remarkably, had continued to expand, now featuring more than thirty songs. Even "So Long,

---

* A *Songs of Leonard Cohen* tribute album by the rock musician Beck and friends, including Devendra Banhart, was also released in September 2009.

Marianne" came with an additional verse. Leonard's showmanship had also become more polished—the skipping on- and offstage, the falling to his knees, the playful dance during "The Future," to which the Webb Sisters had long ago added synchronized cartwheels. In November 2009, at the last show of the year in San Jose, California— which many in the audience took to be his last show, period—in "I'm Your Man" Leonard added the wearing of "an old man's mask" to the full services he offered the women gazing up at him from the metal folding chairs of the soulless Silicon Valley arena. During the extended encores, some of these women threw flimsy garments onto the stage in a mock Tom Jones tribute.

A year and a half had gone by since that first small show in Fredericton; Leonard had celebrated his seventy-fourth and seventy-fifth birthdays on the road. His 2008 tour had been named by business magazines as one of the year's most successful, and the rock press had designated the 2009 tour the best of the year. Between them, these two years of concerts had grossed well over $50 million. Not all of it went into Leonard's pocket—a band, crew and tour that size was an enormous expense—but as the promoter Rob Hallett put it, "I think it's safe to assume the garden's rosy again." Leonard had earned back all he had lost and more. He could stop now, hang up his guitar and never set foot onstage again. But it had gone beyond a moneymaking exercise a long time ago. Leonard wanted, perhaps even needed, this tour, and—remarkably, in a business and at a time where attention spans were not long—people continued to want to see him. A 2010 tour was scheduled, due to start in Europe in May, followed by another trip across Australia and shows in Cambodia and Hawaii, before ending in a victory lap of North America.

But for now Leonard had three and a half months to himself. Very much to himself; Leonard was once again a single man. Whether it had been the distances put between them by two years of touring or that the age difference between a fifty-year-old and a seventy-five-year-old seemed more daunting than that between a forty-year-old and a sixty-five-year-old, Leonard and Anjani were too discreet to say. "Relationships are not stagnant, they change and grow," says Anjani, who remains Leonard's close friend and collaborator. "Rather than me explaining it to you or him explaining it, I should send you something he wrote, called 'I'm Always Thinking of a Song for Anjani to Sing.' All there is to know about our relationship is in that poem. I told him I cried when I read it. And he answered, "I cried too."

I'm always thinking of a song
For Anjani to sing
It will be about our lives together
It will be very light or very deep
But nothing in between
I will write the words
And she will write the melody
I won't be able to sing it
Because it will climb too high
She will sing it beautifully
And I'll correct her singing
And she'll correct my writing
Until it is better than beautiful
Then we'll listen to it
Not often
Not always together
But now and then
For the rest of our lives[12]

It felt good to be back in Montreal, trudging through the December snow with Mort to the deli on the Main for bagels and beef tongue— Mort's old favorite before it was Roshi's—and listening to his oldest friend complain about the new coffee bars and boutiques that had sprung up in their old neighborhood. "He and I have been here longer than most of the people around here," says Rosengarten. "We're the old fogies. He seems to be spending more time here now." Leonard, as he often did, thought about staying in Montreal. It had changed a little, in ways other than Mort had mentioned—people would recognize him and approach him on the street or in restaurants in a way that they had not done in the past. Being Canadian, most were very polite about it, and Leonard had also come up with some evasive tactics, such as going for dinner in the afternoons when no one was there. One person in particular, who had come up to him in the park and introduced herself—a beautiful young singer named NEeMA—became his protégée; Leonard coproduced her album *Watching You Think* and drew a portrait of her for the front sleeve.

But once again Leonard was drawn back to Los Angeles. His children and his grandchild were there, and Roshi. In his 103rd year now, Roshi still presided over the Zen Center, and Leonard still went there to meditate when he was in town. Earlier in the year, when the tour came through L.A., Leonard had taken several members of the band to one of Roshi's early-morning teachings. When he had finished, Roshi gave Leonard a bottle of *ng ka pay* to open, and at eight in the morning, they all sat around enjoying a glass of the old man's favorite liqueur. It was one of the few times Leonard took a drink. Though on the road he was happy to mix drinks for the band, he made chocolate whey protein shakes for himself. He meditated in his dressing room, in the hour and a half of quiet time he liked to take between the sound check and the show. He meditated on airplanes too, back straight, eyes cast down, hands cupped in his lap, thankful that, if he fell asleep—which in truth he did, more than once—there was no one wandering the aisle with a stick, ready to prod him back to consciousness.

Ten years had passed since Leonard's life as a monk and yet, in this equally (perhaps from Leonard's perspective, more) unexpected incarnation as the hardest-working man in show business, there were many parallels, one of which was the strange quality of timelessness that time had taken on. His life was a blur of busy-ness, with one day, one year even, barely distinguishable from the one before. The new decade began with "Hallelujah" at the top of the iTunes download charts in 2010—the version Justin Timberlake and Matt Morris sang on the *Hope for Haiti* telethon—and the first of a new slew of awards. In January Leonard was presented with a Grammy Award for Lifetime Achievement. "I never thought I'd get a Grammy Award," Leonard said in his acceptance speech. "In fact, I was always touched by the modesty of their interest as to my work." (The only recording of his the Academy apparently deemed worthy was his recitation of his ex-lover's lyrics on Herbie Hancock's Grammy-winning Joni Mitchell tribute album.) But America was doing its best to make up for lost time. At a party thrown by the Canadian consulate in L.A. in honor of its Grammy-nominated countrymen, Leonard made a speech in honor of his native land. "My great-grandfather Lazarus Cohen came to Canada in 1869, to the county of Glengarry, a little town in Maberly. Because of the great hospitality that was accorded my ancestor who came here over a hundred and forty years ago, I want to thank this country, Canada, for allowing us to live and work and flourish in a place that was different from all other places in the world."

Leonard had been off the road for less than two months, but he was counting the days until spring, when the tour was due to resume. Then, while doing a Pilates exercise, he threw out his back—a spinal compression injury, the doctors told him, that would take four to six months of physical therapy to fix. Leonard insisted he was fine. His friends say he was not, that he was in great pain and could barely move. The tour was postponed. Since he was stuck in one place, Leonard thought he might as well do something. He began recording a new album.

In June Leonard flew to New York for another American award ceremony—induction into the Songwriters Hall of Fame. He was dressed in an identical tuxedo to the one he wore to the Rock and Roll Hall of Fame two years earlier but looked several years younger. As before, he quoted one of his songs in his acceptance speech— "Hallelujah" this time—and k. d. lang, as she had in Canada, serenaded him with the song. Judy Collins was there too and sang him "Suzanne." "A sublime experience," said Leonard, staying just long enough to have his photograph taken with an arm around Taylor Swift and to tell *Rolling Stone* that his new album, "God willing, will be finished next spring."[13]

The 2010 tour began in Croatia on July 25, followed by thirty-four European and Eastern European concerts and one in Russia. The eight-month break appeared to have no ill effect on the performances. The shows were long, the band a well-oiled machine, and Leonard, despite his back injury, still skipped on and off, fell to his knees and held his hat over his heart while his musicians soloed or sang or cartwheeled. His voice sounded softer and rougher at the edges now, a little cracked, but no matter, that was how the light got in.

A few of the critics, particularly those who had seen multiple shows, made mention of how it had become a kind of smooth-jazz traveling theater, with the same production, the same choreography, night after night. In the beginning, this kind of military precision and discipline, leaving nothing to chance, knowing what was going to happen and when, was the only way that someone so anxious about performing was going to be able to do it after so long away. "You never know what's going to happen when you step on the stage, whether you're going to be the person you want to be, or if the audience is going to be hospitable," as Leonard told Jian Ghomeshi, who interviewed him for CBC. "Even when you've brought the show to a certain degree of excellence," he said, "there are so many unknowns and so many mysteries."[14] But as his anxiety subsided somewhat over time, there were subtle changes to the blueprint, with Leonard frequently adding or replacing a song, sometimes during the show. For the 2010 tour they devised a communication system, whereby Leonard would whisper a song title to Beck, and by pressing a foot pedal, Beck would convey it quietly to the rest of the band and crew. Among the songs added to the set list was "Avalanche," one of the dark songs Leonard had eschewed in the earlier shows, and another new song, "Born in Chains," which Leonard recited, then sang, in an almost Tom Waits growl:

> *I was taken out of Egypt*
> *I was bound to a burden*
> *but the burden it was raised*
> *Oh Lord I can no longer keep this secret*
> *Blessed is the Name*
> *the Name be praised.*

September 2010 saw the release of a second live CD/DVD from the tour, the first having given Leonard a top 10 hit in twelve countries. *Songs from the Road*, like its predecessor, was produced by Ed Sanders, who had been recording the entire tour from the first concert in 2008. The gatefold sleeve opens up onto photos of Leonard with his hand wrapped variously around a glass of whiskey, a wineglass and a microphone. In another he stands silhouetted in a doorway, the bright sky behind him. Aside from the fedora, one imagines this must have been how Leonard had first appeared to Marianne on Hydra when he asked her to join him. Leonard no longer went to Hydra. He still had his little white house on the hill, but his son and daughter used it mostly. Marianne, ever loyal, had come to the show in Oslo, though she did not go backstage. "Because I know he is working, I try not to impose," she says, "but I believe he somehow knows I am there." At other stations on the way there were other muses—Joni, Dominique, Rebecca.

This new live release, as it had the year before, coincided with the appearance of something else from the past: a DVD of *Bird on a Wire*, Tony Palmer's long-lost documentary of Leonard's 1972 European tour, which Leonard had rejected as too confrontational and had had remade. Steven Machat had somehow managed to get hold of two hundred reels of film footage that Palmer had long thought lost. Using the soundtrack as a guide, Palmer painstakingly pieced his original movie back together. Even if the film was not to Leonard's taste, it is a remarkable account of the intense, often improvised, sometimes chaotic concerts in Europe and Israel, a tour beset by equipment problems and riots, journalists wanting to interview him, women wanting sex with him and Leonard trying desperately to deal with fame, trying to retain the purity of his vision as a poet and stay true to himself and his songs. "Although I didn't think this at the time," says Henry Zemel, the friend Leonard had hired to help reedit the film, "you could see his life to a large extent as an effort to recapture a purity."

The 2010 tour was heading toward the finish line. In its closing weeks there were concerts as far apart as Slovakia, New Zealand and Canada, before Leonard worked his way back down the west coast of America toward home. The last two dates of the tour, December 10 and 11, were to be held in, of all places, a Las Vegas casino. The soaring, fake Corinthian-capitaled billboard outside Caesars Palace displayed an image of a small, white-haired Leonard, clutching his fedora, beneath a large gold sign reading JERRY SEINFELD.

There was a rodeo in town when Leonard arrived and, farther along the Strip, the American Country Music Awards. Sin City was teeming with Stetsons and men as big as beef cattle. There was a photo of a country singer on the backstage pass for Leonard's show too—Hank Williams, part of a collage Leonard had made of his heroes, who included Ray Charles and Edith Piaf; the poets Lorca, Yeats and Irving Layton; Leonard's parents; Saint Kateri Tekakwitha; Ramesh; and Roshi. Standing on the stage of the Colosseum theater, Leonard looked around him. "So strange a place, so unmagical, and with such great effort to achieve the unmagical," he told the audience with a lopsided smile, "you've really got to love." He looked old and frail, thinner than three years ago when the tour began, and he was thin enough then. He also looked unstoppable. "We seem to have come to the end of a chapter," he said. When it began, he "was seventy-three, just a kid with a crazy dream." As he reworked his old joke, there was emotion in his voice. He assured the audience that he and the band would give them "everything we've got." At the end of the first half of the four-hour set, a woman ran onstage while Leonard was on his knees and held on to him like a crucifix. During the intermission, a group of fans gathered at the front and sang a song Leonard was filmed singing in *Bird on a Wire*, "Passing Thru." When Leonard came back out onstage, he joined in the singing.

The band struck up "Tower of Song." Leonard stood to one side, watching as the women sang the *"da doo dum dum"*'s. He refused to come in, making them sing their part over and over again, with a big smile on his face like a child, or like a voyeur, or somebody who really had just seen the light. "Listening to you," he said, "all the unimaginable mysteries are unraveled. I understand it now; it is a matter of your generosity. It has taken three years, I have found the answer to the riddle. It was so simple I should have known from the beginning. Here it is, the answer: *da doo dum dum dum, da doo dum dum*." He had spent a lifetime trying to get to the bottom of the big, timeless subjects, going back over them again and again, digging deeper, trying to come up with some answer, or at least some beauty, or at the very least a gag. It had been hard work. Leonard had no problem with hard work.

These past three years on the road, with their three-hour shows and two-hour sound checks, sometimes barely a day off in between, had been more than rigorous, but much as Leonard had said of Roshi's monastery, "once you get the hang of it, you go into ninth gear and kind of float through it all." Leonard was floating. The parameters of this life, like his life on the mountain, had paradoxically given him a kind of freedom. The falling to his knees and the bowing—to the musicians who did him the honor of delivering his words, and to the audience who did him the honor of accepting them—satisfied a sense of rite that was rooted deep in him. More than one reviewer had likened Leonard's concerts, the quiet, the jubilation, the sense of grace, the reverence for the beauty of the word, to religious gatherings. One or two went so far as to compare them to papal visits, but most alluded to some nondenominational yet authentically pure spiritual fellowship of the faithful. Leonard could joke onstage—and he did, frequently, as he settled into these tours—but at the same time he was intensely serious about his work. Always had been. It was evident when he was a nine-year-old boy, burying the first words he had written, to his dead father—words never revealed—in a secret ceremony. It was there too when he moved to the U.S. and took his first steps into pop music, and dissolved all boundaries between word and song, and between the song and the truth, and the truth and himself, his heart and its aching.

All the heavy labor, the crawling across carpets, the highs, the depths to which he had plummeted and all the women and deities, loving and wrathful, he had examined and worshipped, loved and abandoned, but never really lost, had been in the service of this. And here he was, seventy-six years old, still shipshape, still sharp at the edges, a workingman, ladies' man, wise old monk, showman and trouper, once again offering up himself and his songs:

"Here I stand, I'm your man."

Twenty-five

A Manual for Living with Defeat

So the stage was dismantled one last time, the rabbit was put back in the hat, the equipment was loaded on the truck and everyone, Leonard included, was sent home. There were tears and emotional farewells; it had been quite a ride. As to the financial transgressions that had forced Leonard back on the road, there is an interesting footnote, and one that might indicate that the laws of karma might be more efficient than the courts of law.

In 2008, as the tour was about to begin, the U.S. Securities and Exchange Commission brought its own case against Neal Greenberg, the financier whom Kelley Lynch engaged to manage Leonard's investment accounts, charging him with fraud and breach of fiduciary duty related to more than a hundred clients. Says Robert Kory, "According to the reports, his clients apparently lost a great deal of their money, tens of millions. The irony is that if Kelley had not taken the money, [leading to the] discovery earlier, which then prompted Leonard to re-examine what he was doing in his life and to go on tour, Leonard might well have lost all that money anyway, because it was invested with Neal Greenberg. And he would have lost it at a time when [because of the market crash] it would have been impossible for me to persuade promoters to finance Leonard's tour."

The tour not only restored Leonard's lost funds, it improved on them considerably. But it also brought Leonard something more important: vindication as an artist. Even in parts of the world where he had spent almost his entire career undervalued, he had been playing to packed crowds in enormous venues, received universally with acclaim and love. If this were a Bible and not a biography, Kelley would have the Judas role, since it was her betrayal that set in motion the course of events that led to this remarkable resurrection. Lynch, after losing her house in Mandeville Canyon, continued to move around America, blogging, e-mailing and leaving offensive and threatening messages on answering machines as she went.* Greenberg, prohibited from working in investment as a result of the Securities and Exchange Commission case, moved to Leonard's hometown, Montreal, where he was last reported working as a Buddhist teacher.

Back in his Los Angeles duplex, Leonard hung up his stage suit and put on a pin-striped suit, the old-fashioned kind with wide lapels

---

* Lynch was living in Berkeley, California, when on March 1, 2012, shortly before this book went to press, Michelle Rice led a team effort with private investigators and the LAPD Threat Management Unit to have her arrested. Lynch was charged with violating a permanent protective order that forbade her from contacting Leonard, which she had ignored repeatedly. After her arrest, she was transferred to a detention facility in L.A. County to await trial. On April 13, the jury found her guilty on all charges. On April 18, she was sentenced to eighteen months in prison and five years' probation. "It gives me no pleasure to see my onetime friend shackled to a chair in a court of law, her considerable gifts bent to the services of darkness, deceit and revenge," said Leonard in his statement to the court. "It is my prayer that Ms. Lynch will take refuge in the wisdom of her religion, that a spirit of understanding will convert her heart from hatred to remorse."

that you find in thrift shops, as Leonard did. Along with the white-stubbled five o'clock shadow and the rakish tilt of the fedora he wore indoors, he looked less like a showman with connections than a private detective, retired, but should his services be required, still ready for the game. At home, Leonard was dressed for work. As soon as the tour ended, he picked up where he had left off on the album begun in 2007 and put on hold by the ever-expanding tour. Eager to finish it, he could not blame the urgency on his finances this time, so he rationalized it as being in "the homeward stretch"[1] and the sense that time was running out. From a seventy-six-year-old this sounds plausible, although Leonard had said much the same thing when he was fifty-six.[2] In truth, Leonard was in excellent shape—better shape, in many ways, than he had been twenty years earlier. Besides the food-poisoning incident and the exercise injury, he had breezed through the previous three years and the three-hour shows. More than anything, it appeared that he was so keen to complete this new album because he wanted an excuse to tour again.

After his initial reservations, Leonard had come to love this life on the road, the small, closed community of supportive fellow travelers and the almost military regime. Being in service and being of service both held enormous appeal for a poet who had so often seemed born to be a soldier or a monk. It is possible too that the rush of such an intense, heightened existence had become addictive—Leonard, after all, had for many years been inordinately fond of amphetamines. Having given up his last two vices, cigarettes and alcohol, for the tour, he was probably in no mood to quit cold turkey. But the most important thing about the tour, for a man of Leonard's age and temperament, was the feeling of full employment: of doing what he had spent a lifetime training to do and doing it successfully and well. There had been times before the tour—and even farther back, times before his financial troubles—when he felt to some degree like he was treading water or even withdrawing. He had felt, he said, as he imagined Ronald Reagan had felt "in his declining years"—remembering that once upon a time, he'd "had a good role, he'd played the President in a movie, and I felt, somewhat, that I 'had been' a singer."[3] Although Leonard had never stopped writing and drawing, and likely never would, the desire to engage in the business of making his work public had become less and less urgent. Touring, he said, "really reestablished me as being a worker in the world. And that was a very satisfactory feeling."[4] Through his own hard work, Leonard had won back his lost retirement fund. Now that he had it, he did not want to retire.

———

In Leonard's half of the duplex, the living room, which doubled as a dining room, had been temporarily requisitioned as an informal music room, with two full-sized synthesizers squeezed between the three-piece suite, large dinner table, small marble-topped table and potted bamboo plant. Leonard went to one of the synthesizers and pressed the power switch.

"There's one song that I've been working on for many, many years— decades. I've got the melody and it's a guitar tune, a really good tune, and I have tried year after year to find the right words. The song bothers me so much that I've actually started a journal chronicling my failures to address this obsessive concern with this melody. I would really like to have it on the next record, but I felt that for the past two or three records. Maybe four. It's a song I'd really like to complete. So, these are hard nuts to crack."

And when you do crack them after all these years, sometimes is there nothing in there but dust?

"My father kept a bottle of champagne downstairs in a cabinet in the cellar. He died when I was quite young, but as soon as I got the keys to the cabinet, which my mother finally gave me when I was a little older, when we broke out this bottle that my mother had been keeping since maybe their wedding, it was undrinkable. So you have to develop a perspective about

the whole thing. I mean it's not the siege of Stalingrad. In the great scheme of things it's not terribly important, but it bothers me a lot."

The puzzle of the song?

"Yeah, the puzzle of the song. You know that. I'd like to finish my work; still in the back of my mind is: 'What is the groove for that song?' I've got the words and the tune but I don't know the groove or the arrangement, and that's going on in my mind as we speak; that's what I'm thinking about."

He pressed a button that struck up an electronic rhythm track, and over it he played a melody.

"I'm in this key."

The music floated along serenely, hypnotically, until Leonard hit an unexpected chord. He stopped short, like he had hit a wall. His face had a quizzical expression that seemed to say, "Where the hell do I go now?"

"So, that's what my work is right now and that's what I think about. My mind is not given to philosophy, it's given to a kind of prayer, a kind of work. But mostly it's about that problem of getting back to the key I started off in."

In reality the problem seemed mostly about Leonard's pitilessness toward his songs when it came to judging them done. He already had enough material for an album. Prior to the tour he had amassed a small stack of songs, which included "The Captain," "Puppets" and "Different Sides," a cowrite with Sharon Robinson. There was "Lullaby," an early version of the song he premiered on tour; "Treaty," a song he had been tinkering with for at least fifteen years; and the even older "Born in Chains," which he began writing in 1988, the year he released *I'm Your Man*, and which he described when trying it out onstage as having been based "on some general appetite for prayer."[5] Leonard had also been trying his hand at writing blues songs. "I've always loved the blues and I've always loved the musical construction of the blues," he said, but he had never felt he had the right to sing the blues. "Somehow the right was granted me, I don't know by what authority, and a number of songs came to me in that way now that I have permission to sing the blues."[6] Two of these songs, "Feels So Good" and "The Darkness," also made their way onto the tour's expanding set list. Since his return from Las Vegas, he had been working with Anjani on new versions for his album of three songs they cowrote for her album *Blue Alert*—"Crazy to Love You," "Thanks for the Dance" and "Whither Thou Goest"—as well as on a song they wrote together in 2001 called "The Street." Anjani, who continued to live around the corner, came by often; they were still close. The second synthesizer was for her.

His life was busy and full, but he missed touring. On tour, "you know exactly what to do during the day and you don't have to improvise—as you do here, especially now, in the midst of composing. There's always something to draw you away."[7] Some distractions were less galling than others. Less than two months after the last date of the tour, the household had a new member, Viva Katherine Wainwright Cohen. Lorca, who still lived downstairs, gave birth to her first child—Leonard's second grandchild and first granddaughter—in February 2011. The tiny girl was the progeny of two Canadian musical dynasties, her father being Rufus Wainwright, the singer, Lorca's close friend and, in the period when he shared Lorca's apartment, Leonard's downstairs neighbor. When fans of Rufus referred to Lorca as a "surrogate mother" online, the whole family, including Leonard, stepped up to correct them. The baby would be raised by Lorca, Rufus and "Daddy #2," as Wainwright referred to his fiancé Jörn Weisbrodt. Leonard doted on the baby. When Lorca came upstairs with Viva or Adam came by with Cassius, Leonard would happily spend all day playing with them. Smiling, he said, "I feel I'm off the evolutionary hook. I've done my bit." This, he said, was the legacy that mattered. "As to my own work, inhabiting the great scheme of things and knowing you're going to leave pretty soon, you know that whatever you're doing is tiny as hell, but on the other hand it's your work, so you treat it with respect."[8]

On April 1, as he donned his monk's robes to visit Roshi, who was celebrating his 104th birthday, Leonard learned that he had won the prestigious Glenn Gould Prize. The award, given to a living artist for a lifetime contribution to the arts, came with a $50,000 purse. Previous winners had included Pierre Boulez and Oscar Peterson. The chairman, Paul Hoffert, told a press conference in Toronto that Leonard Cohen had been the unanimous choice of all seven members of the international jury, which included the filmmaker Atom Egoyan (whose 1994 film *Exotica* featured "Everybody Knows" on its soundtrack) and actor and writer Stephen Fry (who deadpanned, "I thought we agreed on Justin Bieber"). Hoffert praised Leonard's poetry and song for transcending boundaries and cultures and "touching our common humanity. His unique voice is nonetheless the common voice of people around the globe telling our stories, expressing our emotions, reaching deeply into our psyches."[9]

Leonard had met Glenn Gould in the early sixties, when *Esquire* sent him to interview the celebrated Canadian pianist. The piece was never published. Leonard had been so enraptured by what Gould said that he stopped taking notes, believing it "indelibly imprinted in [his] mind." When he got home, he "could not remember a single thing" Gould said to him.[10] Leonard did not mention this mishap in his letter to the award committee, in which he thanked them for "a great honor, sweetened by [his] love of the work of Glenn Gould." Leonard continued to work on his album, which now had a title— the same title his last studio album had, before he was persuaded to change it to *Dear Heather—Old Ideas*.

Adam Cohen was also working on a new album, his fourth, which, at his father's suggestion, he had titled *Like a Man*. The album, Adam said, was an homage to his father, "a fusion of elegance and humour, of eloquence and effortless casualness" and "the consummate gentleman."[11] Adam had written some of its songs more than a decade earlier but had shelved them because he felt that they bore too much of his father's influence. His sister, Lorca, did not appear to share

Adam's need to distance herself from their father and his work. She had joined Leonard at several points on the tour, making videos and shooting photos for his CD sleeves; in April 2011, she staged a series of short films by artists and experimental filmmakers, inspired by *New Skin for the Old Ceremony*, the album Leonard released the year she was born. But finally, a year away from turning forty, Adam felt ready to "come out" as Leonard Cohen's son. "Despite my efforts to carve out a different identity," he said, "really I belong to a long line of people who have embraced their father's business."[12]

Delighted with his son's album, Leonard was also taken with the album's producer, Patrick Leonard, a piano player, composer and songwriter who had a long history of working with Madonna, with whom he cowrote "La Isla Bonita" and "Like a Prayer." Adam introduced them, and Leonard and Leonard started to meet for coffee. Before long they were writing together. "Pat saw the lyric for 'Going Home' and he said, "This could be a really good song.' I said, 'I don't think so.' He said, 'Can I have a shot at it?' I said, 'Sure.' He came back with the music—I don't know if it was the next hour or the next day, but it was very fast. He was working quickly and I was working quickly, and, very quickly, we wrote several more songs."[13]

Leonard revealed the existence of his new album in the late summer of 2011, at almost the same time that his U.S. record label was preparing to release yet another career retrospective, *The Very Best of Leonard Cohen*, a single CD whose songs were selected by Leonard. The compilation was put on hold, but not the far more copious retrospective CD box set, *Leonard Cohen: The Complete Columbia Albums Collection*, which contained all of Leonard's albums, studio and live, from *Songs of Leonard Cohen* in 1967 to *Songs from the Road* in 2010.

The imminent arrival of another album did rather spoil the title, but in fairness, his record company was not alone in taking the end of Leonard's triumphant tour for the end of his career as a recording artist. Leonard himself appeared to be leaning that way at the beginning of 2010 when, in his acceptance speech for the Lifetime Achievement Grammy Award, he referred to making his way toward "the finishing line." He was more likely talking in veiled terms about death, which he did often enough, than about the last dates of the tour. But in September 2011, as he celebrated his seventy-seventh birthday, sharing his cake with Roshi, even Leonard had to admit that he was "in good form."

In October, Leonard was in Oviedo, Spain, to receive his second major honor of the year. The Prince of Asturias Award for Letters came with a fifty-thousand-euro purse and a Joan Miró sculpture. It had not gone unnoticed that this was an award for literature; past laureates, who included Günter Grass and Arthur Miller, were not known for their songs. But as the statement from the jury read— mirroring in many ways what the Glenn Gould Prize jury had said— Leonard had been chosen for "a body of literary work in which poetry and music are fused in an oeuvre of immutable merit." It was another vindication. Although it often seemed to fall on the deaf ears of academics and literary critics, this is what Leonard had been saying all along.

Leonard had always been good with an acceptance speech, but at the Prince of Asturias ceremony he excelled himself. His address to the distinguished audience, among whose number were the Spanish royal family and Federico Garcia Lorca's niece, was at once personal and a polished piece of prose (despite his claim of having sat up all night in his hotel room, scribbling notes, none of which he consulted). It was also a performance—as accomplished, practiced, dignified, humble, intimate, graceful and grateful a performance as any of the concerts on his last tour. It opened with the usual expression of gratitude and followed with his habitual self-deprecation, protesting how uncomfortable he felt being honored for his poetry when "poetry comes from a place that no one commands, no one conquers, so I feel somewhat like a charlatan." As if to underline the "charlatan" claim, he tossed in a line he had used countless times in countless interviews: "If I knew where the good songs came from, I would go there more often." His unease had led him, he said, to seek out the old Spanish guitar he had bought some forty years ago. He took it out of its case and held it to his face, inhaling "the fragrance of the cedar, as fresh as the day that I acquired the guitar." "A voice seemed to say to me, you are an old man, and you have not said thank you, you have not brought your gratitude back to the soil from which this fragrance arose . . . [and] the soul of this land that has given me so much."

Leonard talked about the tragic young Spaniard he had encountered in his teens, playing a guitar in Murray Hill Park, at the back of his family home on Belmont Avenue. Girls had gathered around to listen, and Leonard listened too. When he stopped playing, Leonard urged him to teach him how to play like that. Over the course of three lessons, he taught Leonard the "six chords" and the flamenco guitar pattern Leonard called "the basis of all my songs and all my music."

Leonard spoke even more eloquently about the impact on his life of another Spanish man. When he had begun playing guitar, he said, he was also writing poems. He had been copying the styles of the English poets he had studied at school, but he "hungered for a voice." He said, "It was only when I read—even in translation—the works of Lorca that I understood that there was a voice." Leonard said that he did not copy that voice—"I wouldn't dare"—but he listened closely to what it said. It gave him permission "to locate a self, a self that is not fixed, a self that struggles for its own existence." It also told him "never to lament casually, and, if one is to express the great inevitable defeat that awaits us all, it must be done within the strict confines of dignity and beauty."

The ceremony was followed by a tribute concert. It began with a short video Leonard's daughter had made. There were filmed interviews with Leonard's band. A member of the prize jury, Andrés

Amorós, recited Spanish translations of Leonard's poetry and lyrics, accompanied by the Webb Sisters. Laura Garcia Lorca thanked Leonard for being "the best ambassador" her late uncle could have had. Musicians, including the flamenco singer Duquende, the Irish singer-songwriter Glen Hansard and Leonard's comrade of the road Javier Mas, performed his songs. Leonard was a veteran of tributes. He had sat through more heartfelt covers of his songs these past ten years than he could count. Yet there were tears in his eyes. During the closing song, "So Long, Marianne"—just as he had when he sang the same song in Jerusalem on the last night of a tour almost forty years before—he let them run freely down his face.

———

At the long wooden desk in his small study, Leonard searched through numerous icons on the oversized computer monitor. Now and then he stopped and clicked on one; it usually turned out to be a photograph of one of his grandchildren. He was looking for a liner-note booklet. Unable to locate the digital version, he got out of the typing chair to look for the mock-up. He found it on the bookshelf, where it was keeping company with three volumes of the Zohar, Bukowski's *The Pleasures of the Damned*, Braque's *Lithographie*, a small row of Leonard Cohen books, *The Language of Truth*, a book on the Greek poets and an Allen Ginsberg bobblehead.

Leonard returned with the *Old Ideas* booklet, whose pages were stuck together with glue, like a child's arts and crafts project. On the cover is a photograph of Leonard, sitting, reading, on a garden chair downstairs on the small front lawn. The shadow of the woman who shot the picture (Leonard's assistant) takes up as much space as Leonard himself. He is dressed formally in a black suit, black fedora, black shoes, black socks and black sunglasses, but his black tie is awry and the top of his white shirt is undone. Inside the booklet, along with the words of the songs, are earlier versions of the lyrics, reproduced from pages of Leonard's pocket-sized notebooks and illustrated with his artwork. There is a self-portrait—crushed cap, grim face. There is a naked woman with long black hair, posing next to a skull.

Leonard clicked on a file on the computer screen and leaned back in the chair. The album began to play. Leonard straightened his spine a little and lowered his eyes; he might have been meditating. Now and again, his lips barely moving, he silently mouthed the words. By the middle of the third song his eyes had closed, and remained closed for the rest of the album. Which meant that he did not notice when his computer went into screen-saver mode and a parade of news flashes started a stately procession across the monitor—Republican party candidates, the UK phone-hacking scandal, the controversy over the sale of emergency contraceptives—adding random and sometimes oddly apposite captions to the music.

The album had gone through a number of changes since Leonard had resumed work on it at the beginning of the year. Of the new songs he introduced on tour, only two are included: "Darkness," still largely recognizable as the song he played onstage, and "Lullaby," with drastically rewritten lyrics. Leonard's cowrite with Sharon Robinson "Different Sides" is here, but his cowrite with Anjani "The Street" is not. There is just one of the three reworked *Blue Alert* songs, "Crazy to Love You," which has some minor lyrical changes but, far more significantly, is now a guitar, not a piano, song. After a long stretch of contentment with his synthesizer, Leonard found himself returning to the guitar, playing it on four of the tracks. His guitar on "Crazy to Love You" takes the listener back to his earliest albums, in particular to *Songs from a Room*. There are keyboards on the album too, and violins, horns, drums, banjo and archilaud, and Jennifer Warnes, Dana Glover, Sharon Robinson and the Webb Sisters on backing vocals. The credits name as producers Leonard Cohen, Ed Sanders, Anjani, Dino Soldo and Patrick Leonard, who cowrote four songs.

When the tenth and final song ended, Leonard opened his eyes.

This was the first time he had heard the album since they mixed it almost two months ago. He had been listening, intently, "for any false steps, or if there's anything that could have been done another way, or if somehow the reverie were interrupted." If it were, he said, he would have taken it back into the studio and worked on it some more. Smiling, he said, "I didn't find any traitorous elements. I had not misjudged its readiness."[14]

Old Ideas was released on January 31, 2012. The accompanying press release described Leonard as "a spiritual guy with a poetical streak" and the album as his "most overtly spiritual." But though the first single, "Show Me the Place," does have churchlike qualities— the slow piano, the deep, solemn voice intoning, "*Show me the place / Where you want your slave to go . . . For my head is bending low*"—anyone in the least familiar with a Leonard Cohen album would recognize that the words might as easily be addressed to a naked woman as to an Old Testament God. (The first press release was quickly replaced with one from which the unfortunate phraseology was deleted. Perhaps by way of compensation, the record label erected a giant billboard of the album sleeve in New York's Times Square.)

Leonard's flair for fusing the erotic and the spiritual remains unparalleled on his twelfth studio album. Even in "Amen," where, in perfectly biblical fashion, "*the filth of the butcher*" is "*washed in the blood of the lamb*," the angels at Leonard's door are "*panting and scratching*," and the "*lord*" to whom "*vengeance belongs*" has a lowercase "l." It would probably be a safe bet that the lines "*Dreamed about you baby / You were wearing half your dress*," in "Anyhow," are not directed at Jehovah. And though "The Darkness" might arguably be about depression, disease or the darkness of the grave, the words "*You said: Just drink it up . . . You were young and it was summer / I just had to take a dive*" seem just as unarguably about cunnilingus.

The album has levity as well as gravity. It skips and it cartwheels, falls to its knees, bows its head in prayer, hat over its heart, and flirts with the women in the front row. The protagonist of the album's opening song "Going Home"—God, presumably, or some kind of higher power concerned with giving Leonard orders and pulling his strings—is less than pleased with this lighthearted attitude to the job he wants Leonard to do. Which is throw off his burden, go home behind the curtain, sing himself off this earthly stage and on to a better place, like an old man ought, like an old icon certainly should, like Bob Dylan did in "Beyond the Horizon," and Glen Campbell with *Ghost on the Canvas*, and Johnny Cash on almost all of his late-life recordings. But Leonard Cohen, this so-called "*sage*," this "*man of vision*," is nothing more than a "*lazy bastard living in a suit*" who wants to write about the same things he has been banging on at forever: "*a love song, an anthem of forgiving, a manual for living with defeat*"; the same old ideas that were on his first album, *Songs of Leonard Cohen*, and that have been on every Leonard Cohen album since. Something as insignificant as old age was not going to change that. And, anyway, Leonard always was old. He was old on his first album—thirty-three, a decade older than the other singer-songwriters making their debuts. He did not need age to give him authority; he already had it. Instead, the passing of the years appeared to have given him a lightness—the same lightness we saw on the last tour, when he skipped out from behind the curtain and onto the stage, night after night.

As Greg Kot noted in his *Chicago Tribune* review, "*Old Ideas* is not another of the dreaded winter-of-my-years albums that have become a cottage industry in recent decades. [Cohen is] still feisty after all these years, his entanglements with love and aging documented with wicked wit and an attitude that is anything but sentimental."[15] Kitty Empire wrote in the *Observer*, "*Old Ideas* is not all about death, betrayal and God, juicy as these are. As the title suggests, it is more of the stuff that has made Cohen indispensable for six decades: desire, regret, suffering, love, hope, and hamming it up."[16] The reviews were almost universally positive, although some critics focused more

on the "ultimate defeat" than on Leonard's "manual for living"—
Rolling Stone saw him "staring down the eternal with unblinking
honesty"[17]—and treated the album as if it were a last farewell, a bone
of the saint that was still just a little warm. "It is difficult, albeit a little
ill-mannered, not to regard *Old Ideas* as possibly Leonard Cohen's
final recorded testament," wrote Andy Gill in the *Independent*. "But
if it is to be his last communiqué, at least the old smoothie's going
down swinging."[18]

For now, the old smoothie packed his good suit and left for a short
promotional tour—New York, Paris, London. There were countless
requests for interviews, which he turned down, having appeared to
have entirely lost interest in the interview process. Perhaps he had
never had much interest in the first place, but he had been happy
(or courteous enough, or curious enough) to participate in the game
and proffer exquisitely structured, perfectly worded bons mots.
Instead he held a few press conferences—theatrical affairs, with a
handpicked media audience. He played his album, then invited a few
questions. A master of deflection, with great charm he parried almost
every one. He recycled old lines and gags into new column inch upon
column inch in major publications. "How is it for you to listen to your
own records?" asked Jarvis Cocker, the Britpop star who moderat-
ed the London event. "I wasn't listening," Leonard replied. Cocker
asked him how he felt about his latest award. PEN New England,
an American literary association whose jury included Bono, Elvis
Costello, Rosanne Cash and Salman Rushdie, had named Leonard
Cohen and Chuck Berry as joint winners of their inaugural prize for
Song Lyrics of Literary Excellence. Leonard replied, "The thing I
liked about this award was that I'm sharing it with Chuck Berry. 'Roll
over Beethoven and tell Tchaikovsky the news': I'd like to write a
line like that."[19]

At the press conference in Paris (which Leonard's old lover Dominique Issermann attended), when someone asked him about death

he answered, in a perfect imitation of solemnity, "I have come to the conclusion, reluctantly, that I am going to die." As to the follow-up question, of what he would like to be in his next life, Leonard the Jew answered, "I don't really understand that process called reincarnation," while Leonard the Buddhist monk said without hesitation, "I would like to come back as my daughter's dog."[20]

———————

Back in Los Angeles, Lorca's dog was at the vet's and Leonard was heading back from the doctor's. He had just taken Roshi for his checkup. Leonard had returned, at least part-time, to his old job of driving Roshi around, running errands and taking him food; Roshi had become quite fond of Leonard's chicken soup. Roshi, weeks away from his 105th birthday, was still working; Leonard had recently gone to the *sesshin* he led in New Mexico. It was as tough as it had ever been. Tougher, in fact. "Roshi has ratcheted up his schedule a few degrees," Leonard said, the smile on his face indicating that he was not displeased with this adjustment. "He's at the top of his game; it's like he's digging in. All the monks feel it and they're making the most of him." With customary modesty, Leonard shrugged off any mention that much the same might be said about him, despite having followed the most successful tour of his career with what was starting to look like his most successful album. *Old Ideas* debuted in the Top 5 of the charts in twenty-six countries, reaching the No. 1 spot in seventeen of them, including the UK and Canada, and topping *Billboard's* folk chart in the U.S.

Leonard had been asked at the press conferences whether he was going to tour. He answered ambiguously that he planned to tour but that he had no touring plans. Meanwhile, negotiations were under way for another very lengthy tour, which Leonard remained very keen to do. But it was complicated. Given Roshi's age, Leonard was loath to commit to spending lengthy periods a long way away from him. He did not say so because it would have been ungracious, and he knew what the old man's reaction would have been. Back when they sat drinking cognac in Roshi's cabin on Mount Baldy, Roshi, then in his midnineties, would apologize to Leonard for not having died; Leonard had moved to the Zen Center when Roshi was eighty-seven, wanting to spend time with the old man while he still could. Instead, Leonard reasoned that, rather than go back on the road and enjoy himself, he should follow Roshi's lead and ratchet up his schedule, and dig in and do his work, saying, "One does have a sense that this is not going to last forever, that one's health is going to become more of a consideration at a certain point, so I would like to bring as many things to completion as possible."[21] Leonard had begun a new album.

Epilogue

It is beautiful winter's day in Los Angeles. Leonard suggests we make the most of it and sit outside. Since the sun is losing the battle against the nip in the air, he urges me to wrap up and invites me to borrow a hat. There are four on the hall stand: two crushed caps and two fedoras besides the one he has on his head. He is dressed almost exactly as he was in the *Old Ideas* sleeve photo, except that his tie is straight and the top of his shirt is buttoned. On his wrist he wears a cheap metal bracelet, the kind they sell in Mexican stores: twelve tiny cameos of Jesus, Mary and the saints strung together with elastic. He is slight as a jockey and lean as a runner, and has more than a touch of Fred Astaire. That slight stoop he'd had since he was a young man, as if deep inside he felt himself much taller than he was, appears to have vanished, along with whatever else had been weighing him down.

The brightest, most sheltered spot is the balcony, which is off his bedroom. It is a small balcony, just big enough for two chairs, a little table and a plant in a terra-cotta pot. It overlooks a small neat garden with two grapefruit trees, one sun lounger, and two dogs—Lorca's—that are padding idly about the lawn. Beyond them is the garage-turned-studio where Leonard is working on his new album. He is already four or five songs into it. It's remarkable, I say, that little more than a year ago he was still on the last leg of the tour. "Was it really just a year ago?" he asks. His face has one of those smiles little boys make when they're caught doing something they shouldn't, but of which they are secretly rather proud. "I don't know if it's a function of the imminent departure, or just a habit of work, or having very few distractions now. Before the tour, I was very busy with trying to sort out my economic and my legal life, and once the tour started I got back into the mode that I'm very familiar with, and which I like, which is working and writing. And I would like to finish my work. You don't feel like wasting too much time at a certain point."

Time speeds up, they say, the closer it gets to the end of the reel. "It is odd," Leonard says. "There are metaphysicians who tell me that time actually has collapsed. Although I don't understand the mechanism and I think they may be putting me on, it certainly feels that way." Is there one piece of work that he is dying to finish, I ask, before noticing the morbid choice of word. "Oh, please," Leonard says, smiling, "do get morbid. There's that [nameless] song I'd like to complete that bothers me a lot, and I would really like to have it on the next record. But I've felt that for the past two or three records, maybe four." He doesn't think too much about the future, he says, other than looking forward to the promise he made himself to take up smoking again on his eightieth birthday. He thinks, or hopes, he will be touring when he's eighty and is looking forward to the prospect of sneaking outside the bus for a quiet cigarette. One thing he does know is that he has "no sense of or appetite for retirement."

A leaf-blower starts up in a garden down the street. It almost drowns out Leonard's voice, which is already soft—softer still when he is asked to talk about himself. There were times as I tried to retrace his life, I tell him, when he wore me out with all his worrying and hard work—times when I wanted to say to him, "For heaven's sake, what are you doing? What is it that you want?" "Right, right," he says, nodding sympathetically. "But this conversation for me is part of another world because I'm not in it anymore. I have little or no interest in any of these matters. I never talk about them to myself." He is not, he says, much of a self-examiner. "I suppose it's violating some Socratic imperative to know thyself, if that's who it was, but I've always found that examination extremely tedious. Sometimes elements of my life arise and an invitation to experience something that is not mundane arises, but in terms of a deliberate investigation of my life to untangle it or sort it out or understand it, those occasions rarely if ever arise. I don't find it compelling at all."

What is going through his mind right now is a song. "One of my mother's favorite records was 'The Donkey Serenade.' Have you heard the song?" He sings, *"There's a song in the air, yet the fair senorita, doesn't seem to care, for the song in the air."* "My mother seemed to love that song," he says. "I think she was learning a dance step to go with it. The dance teacher would come to the house—it's very touching—and she did this step. I saw the diagram once. It looked like a square." Leonard gets up out of the chair. In a neat little square of sunlight, against the backdrop of a solid blue sky, quietly humming the melody, he dances alone the dance of "The Donkey Serenade."

———

*Coming to the
end of the
book
but not
quite yet
maybe when
we reach
the bottom*[1]

Author's Note

———

The sun was starting to set, so we moved indoors to the kitchen, where Leonard set about plying me solicitously with food and drink: tea, cognac, wine, a hot dog, perhaps some scrambled eggs? We finally shook on lattes, which he served in two of the coffee mugs his record company made some twenty years before to promote his album *The Future*. While we sat drinking at the small kitchen table, which was pushed up against the wall, by an open window through which a cool breeze blew, he asked how things were going with the book—a book, I should add, that he did not ask me to write and did not ask to read, neither of which appeared to inhibit his support. He was just making conversation, really. I gathered his only interest in the book was that it wouldn't be a hagiography and that its author shouldn't starve to death, at least not on his watch. "Think about this seriously before you answer," he said in that solemn voice. "Would you like a scoop of ice cream in your coffee?"

To write a biography, particularly of a someone still living, is to immerse yourself in that person's life to a degree that would probably get you locked up in any decent society. Without the tolerance, trust, candor, generosity and good humor of Leonard Cohen, this book would not be what it is. The same can be said for his manager, Robert Kory. I am deeply grateful to them both. I also owe a great debt to the more than one hundred people—friends, family, associates, musicians, muses, writers, record producers, publishers, lovers, rabbis and monks—who kindly granted me interviews. Their names—some well known, others people who were speaking to a biographer for the first time—can be found at the head of every chapter to which their stories and insights contribute.

Several went way beyond the call of duty and offered, along with ongoing encouragement, access to their personal archives, letters, diaries, address books and photographs. Special thanks to Marianne Ihlen, Aviva Layton, Rebecca De Mornay, Suzanne Elrod, Julie Christensen, Perla Batalla, Anjani Thomas, Judy Collins, Steve Sanfield, Roscoe Beck, Bob Johnston, Chris Darrow, Dan Kessel and Steve Sanfield; to Thelma Blitz for her diaries and contacts; to Ron Cornelius for copies of the journals and short stories he wrote while touring with Leonard; to Ian Milne for playing me the rare reel-to-reel recording he made of one of Leonard's mental hospital concerts; and to Henry Zemel for the CD he made for me from an even earlier reel-to-reel recording of Leonard and his friend playing music in the midsixties.

Biographies also have a lot in common with detective stories, the lack of corpse aside. An enormous amount of time is spent on footwork, knocking on doors, looking for fresh information, double- and triple-checking that information, establishing motives and checking alibis. Since Leonard moved around so much—geographically, spiritually, in all sorts of ways—it made for an enviable air-mile balance, but also presented challenges. I was extremely lucky to have found so many people around the world who were ready and able to help. In Montreal, my thanks to Rabbi Shuchat and Penni Kolb at Shaar Hashomayim; Honora Shaughnessy at the McGill Alumni Association; Leonard's cousin, the late David Cohen; Mort Rosengarten; Arnold Steinberg; Erica Pomerance; Penny Lang; Suzanne Verdal; Phil Cohen; Jack Locke; Janet Davis; Dean Davis; Sue Sullivan; Rona Feldman; Melvin Heft; Malka Marom; Gavin Ross; and journalist

Juan Rodriguez, who generously handed over his Leonard Cohen newspaper archive. In Toronto: Greig Dymond, who unearthed a mighty stash of Leonard Cohen interviews from the CBC archives; Steve Brewer, president of the Westmount High Alumni, for his copy of the school's 1951 yearbook (Leonard's graduation year); Dennis Lee; and at Thomas Fisher Rare Book Library Jennifer Toews and the late Richard Landon, who were an enormous help in negotiating a path through the mountain of file boxes that constitute the University of Toronto's Leonard Cohen archives.

In California I am very grateful to writer-producer Harvey Kubernik, who generously offered memories, contacts and old interviews; to photographer Joel Bernstein, who shared his stories and pictures; to Robert Faggen, who took time away from writing his Ken Kesey biography to lead me (via a shooting gallery, where he showed me how to use a handgun) to the monastery on Mount Baldy; to Andy Lesko, Arlett Vereecke and Colleen Browne, who between them kept me sane; and to my interviewees Ronee Blakely, David Crosby, Hal Blaine, Rufus Wainwright, Jackson Browne, Rabbi Mordecai Finley, monks Daijo and Kigen, Jac Holzman, Sharon Robinson, Sharon Weisz, Larry Cohen, Paul Body, Sean Dixon, Peter Marshall, Chris Darrow, Chester Crill, David Kessel and David Lindley. (Biographers always lament the ones who got away, and I was sad not to have added Joni Mitchell, Jennifer Warnes and Phil Spector to this list. I tried.)

In New York I had the excellent company and assistance of Randy Haecker at Sony Legacy; Tom Tierney, director of the Sony Music Archives Library—their artist's cards from Columbia Studio gave invaluable clues to the recording of Leonard's first seven albums; Danny Fields; Dick and Linda Straub; my East Coast interviewees John Simon, John Lissauer, Hal Willner, Bob Fass, Terese Coe, Liberty, Larry Cohen, Harry "Ratso" Sloman and Philip Glass; and my manager, rock and longtime friend Steven Saporta. In Nashville, I was grateful for the help of John Lomax III, Charlie Daniels, Kris

Kristofferson and Christian Oliver, and in various other U.S. cities not yet mentioned, of interviewees Leanne Ungar, Black Francis, John Bilezikjian and Murray Lerner.

In the UK and Europe I was blessed with the assistance of Helen Donlon, friend, researcher and book editor, who tracked down the people whose interviews helped me fill the gaps in Leonard's early days on Hydra, and in London and New York: Barry Miles, Richard Vick, Terry Oldfield, Jeff Baxter, Ben Olins, Don Wreford and George and Angelika Lialios. Thanks also to Kevin Howlett at the BBC, Richard Wootton, Kari Hesthamar, and to Tony Palmer, Joe Boyd, Tom Maschler, Rob Hallett, Ratnesh Mathur and Charley and Hattie Webb for the interviews.

They say you can judge a man's character by the company he keeps, and the same might apply to a musician's fans. I've been around a lot of fans in my many years writing about musicians, but there are few as erudite and informed as Leonard's or as generous with their expertise. A round of applause for my unofficial international team of Cohenologists, who were always there to answer the stickiest questions and pull rare acetates out of hats: Jarkko Arjatsalo, founder and overseer of LeonardCohenFiles.com—Leonard calls him "the General Secretary of the party"—to whose website Leonard contributes; Allan Showalter, psychiatrist, wit and webmaster of 1heckofaguy.com, a site Leonard is known to frequent; Tom Sakic of LeonardCohenCroatia.com; Marie Mazur of Speaking Cohen; writer John Etherington; Hebrew scholar Doron B. Cohen; and Jim Devlin, author of three books on Leonard Cohen, though that did not stop him from helping me with mine.

I was also helped by a great many music journalists, who from start to finish stepped up at all the right moments with clippings, alcohol, commiseration and words of advice. A couple volunteered, without me being forced to use my new shotgun skills, to read and critique the entire book in draft form. Another leapt in to help with an eleventh-hour subedit. Yes I'm biased, I love music journalists, and I fully intend to go back to being one soon (in tandem, of course, with my illustrious career as a ukulele-playing singer-songwriter, performing to crowds that on a good day you can count on two hands). I would like to salute, for their various services rendered, Phil Sutcliffe, Johnny Black, Fred Dellar, Peter Silverton, Joe Nick Patoski, Lucy O'Brien, Paul Trynka, Rob O'Connor, Jonathan Cott, Fred de Vries and Phil Alexander and all at the world's best music magazine, *MOJO*, reserving a very special thanks to Brian Cullman, Michael Simmons and Neil Spencer.

Thanks to my agent, Sarah Lazin; her assistant, Manuela Jessel; and the unflappable Julian Alexander in the UK. My book has three different English-language publishers—Ecco in the U.S., McClelland & Stewart in Canada and Jonathan Cape in the UK—and it could not have found better homes. I count myself extremely fortunate to have as my publisher and lead editor Dan Franklin at Jonathan Cape in London. I'm deeply grateful to Dan and to his assistant, Steven Messer, for their care and support and all their hard work. My sincere thanks and appreciation also to Daniel Halpern and Libby Edelson at Ecco and Ellen Seligman at McClelland—and a hearty round of applause to all the tireless copyeditors and proofreaders.

Most of all, thank you, Leonard Cohen, for being so considerate as to choose the second I hit puberty to release your first album, for continuing to move and enlighten me with your music and words ever since, for permitting me to out you as a ukulele player, and for living a remarkable life that has run me ragged these past few years. What can I say; it was a swell party. Now if you'll excuse me, I've got to go empty the ashtrays and take the bottles out. I hear you're heading back on the road any day now. Good. We need you out there. Hope to see you somewhere along the way.

Sylvie Simmons
San Francisco, 2012

Notes

Unless otherwise stated, all extracted quotes in the form of a Q & A are taken from the author's interviews of Leonard Cohen. These interviews are indicated in the sources by the initials SS and the date of the interview.

Prologue

SS, 2001.

One: Born in a Suit

Author interviews with: Leonard Cohen, David Cohen, Mort Rosengarten, Arnold Steinberg, Rabbi Wilfred Shuchat

Books and documents: Miriam Chapin, *Quebec Now*, Ryverson Press, 1955. L. S. Dorman and C. L. Rawlins, *Prophet of the Heart*, Omnibus, 1990. Leonard Cohen, *The Favorite Game*, Secker & Warburg UK, 1963 (Viking U.S., 1964). Leonard Cohen Archive, Thomas Fisher Rare Book Library, University of Toronto, Canada ("Archive"). Ira B. Nadel, *Various Positions*, Bloomsbury, 1996. Harry Rasky, *The Song of Leonard Cohen: Portrait of a Poet, a Friendship and a Film*, Souvenir Press, 2001.

Chapter heading: Leonard Cohen to SS, 2001.

1. SS, 2001.

2. Rasky, 2001.

3. Ibid.

4. Christian Fevret, *Les Inrockuptibles*, August 21, 1991, reproduced in *Throat Culture*, 1992, trans. Sophie Miller.

5. Ibid.

6. William Ruhlmann, "The Stranger Music of Leonard Cohen," *Goldmine*, February 19, 1993.

7. SS, 2001.

8. SS, 2011.

9. Chapin, 1955.

10. Fevret, 1991.

11. Archive (undated, likely late 1950s).

12. Dorman and Rawlins, 1990.

13. Pamela Andriotakis and Richard Oulahan, *People*, January 14, 1980.

14. Fevret, 1991.

15. Arthur Kurzweil, "A Conversation with Leonard Cohen," *Jewish Book Club*, 1994.

16. Fevret, 1991.

17. Archive (undated, likely late 1950s).

Two: House of Women

Author interviews with: Leonard Cohen, Mort Rosengarten, David Cohen, Steve Brewer, Rona Feldman, Phil Cohen, Nancy Bacal

Books and documents: Anonymous, *25 Lessons in Hypnotism: How to Become an Expert Operator*, undated, Archive. Miriam Chapin, *Quebec Now*, 1955, Ryverson Press. Leonard Cohen, *The Favorite Game*, Secker & Warburg UK, 1963 (Viking U.S., 1964). Leonard Cohen, "The Juke-Box Heart: Excerpt from a Journal," unpublished, undated, Archive. Ira B. Nadel, *Various Positions: A Life of Leonard Cohen*, Bloomsbury, 1996. Mordecai Richler, *Home Sweet Home: My Canadian Album*, Chatto & Windus, 1984. Mordecai Richler, *Oh Canada! Oh Quebec!*, Penguin Books Canada, 1992. Summer camp reports, Archive. *Vox Ducum*, Westmount High School Yearbook, issues 1950 and 1951.

Chapter heading: SS.

1. Anonymous, *25 Lessons in Hypnotism*, Archive.

2. Cohen, 1963.

3. Brian D. Johnson, *Maclean's*, December 7, 1992.

4. Richler, 1992.

5. Archive.

6. Cohen to Bruce Headlam, *Saturday Night*, December 1997.

7. Archive.

8. Cohen, 1963.

9. Archive.

10. Federico Garcia Lorca, "Gacela of the Morning Market," *Divan Del Tamarit*, 1936, published in *The Selected Poems of Federico Garcia Lorca*, ed. F. G. Lorca and Donald M. Allen, New Directions Publishing, 1955, 2005 edition, trans. Stephen Spender and J. L. Gili.

11. Marco Adria, *Aurora*, July 1990.

12. Arthur Kurzweil, "A Conversation with Leonard Cohen," *Jewish Book Club*, 1994.

13. Christian Fevret, *Les Inrockuptibles*, August 21, 1991, reproduced in *Throat Culture*, 1992, trans. Sophie Miller.

14. Cohen, Prince of Asturias Award speech, October 21, 2011.

15. Fevret, 1991.

16. SS, 2011.

17. SS, 2001.

18. Ibid.

19. Cohen, Asturias Award speech.

20. Cohen, 1963.

Three: Twenty Thousand Verses

Author interviews with: Leonard Cohen, Mort Rosengarten, Nancy Bacal, Arnold Steinberg, David Cohen, Steve Brewer, Dean Davis, Janet Davis, Melvin Heft, Rabbi Wilfred Shuchat, Aviva Layton

Books, films, publications and documents: *CIV/n*, 5, 1954, and 6, 1955. *The Forge*, March 1955 and March 1956. Irving Layton, *The Love Poems of Irving Layton: With Reverence and Delight*, 1984. Leonard Cohen Archive, Thomas Fisher Rare Book Library, University of Toronto, Canada ("Archive"). Lian Lunson, *Leonard Cohen: I'm Your Man*, Lionsgate, 2006. Hugh MacLennan, *Two Solitudes*, 1945. McGill University alumnus archives. McGill University Rare Books Library. Ira B. Nadel, *Various Positions: A Life of Leonard Cohen*, Bloomsbury, 1996. Harry Rasky, *The Song of Leonard Cohen*, documentary film, 1980. *Vox Ducum*, Westmount High School yearbook, 1951. Ruth Wisse, "My Life Without Leonard Cohen," *Commentary*, October 1995.

Chapter heading: Mort Rosengarten to SS, 2009.

1. *Vox Ducum*, 1951.

2. Archive.

3. Christian Fevret, *Les Inrockuptibles*, August 21, 1991, reproduced in *Throat Culture*, 1992, trans. Sophie Miller.

4. Rasky, 1980.

5. Wisse, 1995.

6. Fevret, 1991.

7. Ibid.

8. Cohen, speech given at Irving Layton's funeral, January 2006.

9. Cohen in Lian Lunson, 2006.

10. Fevret, 1991.

11. Rasky, 1980.

12. Ibid.

Four: I Had Begun to Shout

Author interviews with: Leonard Cohen, Aviva Layton, Mort Rosengarten, Arnold Steinberg, Phil Cohen, Henry Zemel, David Cohen

Books, documents and publications: Leonard Cohen, *A Ballet of Lepers*, Archive. Leonard Cohen, *The Favorite Game*, Secker & Warburg, 1963 (Viking U.S., 1964). Leonard Cohen, *Let Us Compare Mythologies*, 1956. Leonard Cohen, *The Spice-Box of Earth*, 1961. L. S. Dorman and C. L. Rawlins, *Prophet of the Heart*, Omnibus, 1990. Letters, Archive. Ira B. Nadel, *Various Positions*, Bloomsbury, 1996. Georgianna Orsini, *An Imperfect Lover: Poems and Watercolors*, Cavankerry, 2002.

Chapter heading: Leonard Cohen, "Rites," in Cohen, 1956.

1. Cohen, from "For Wilf and His House," in Cohen, 1956.

2. Dorman and Rawlins, 1990, p. 79.

3. Cited anonymously in ibid., p. 80.

4. Milton Wilson, review of *Let Us Compare Mythologies*, in *Canadian Forum* 36, March 1957.

5. Allan Donaldson, review of *Let Us Compare Mythologies*, *Fiddlehead* 30, November 1956.

6. Christian Fevret, *Les Inrockuptibles*, August 21, 1991, reproduced in *Throat Culture*, 1992, trans. Sophie Miller.

7. *Let Us Compare Mythologies*, McClelland & Stewart, 2006 edition.

8. SS, 2001.

9. Ibid.

10. Ibid.

11. Ibid.

12. "Synergie, Jean-Luc Esse and Leonard Cohen," radio program, France-Inter, October 1977, trans. Nick Halliwell.

13. Fevret, 1991.

14. Archive, file 5.

15. SS, 2001.

16. Ibid.

17. Ibid.

18. Fevret, 1991.

19. Orsini, 2004.

20. Archive, boxes 1 and 3.

21. William Ruhlmann, *Goldmine*, February 19, 1993.

22. Archive.

23. Gavin Martin, *NME*, January 1993.

24. Irving Layton, interviewed by Ian Pearson, *Saturday Night*, March 1993.

Five: A Man Who Speaks with a Tongue of Gold

Author interviews with: Leonard Cohen, Nancy Bacal, Mort Rosengarten, Steve Sanfield, George Lialios, Angelika Lialios, Marianne Ihlen

Book: Kari Hesthamar, *So Long, Marianne: Ei Kjaerleikshistorie*, Spartacus, 2008.

Chapter heading: Marianne Ihlen to SS, 2010.

1. Ira B. Nadel, *Various Positions*, Bloomsbury, 1996, p. 110.

2. Jack McClelland, *Imagining Canadian Literature: The Selected Letters of Jack McClelland*, ed. Sam Solecki, Key Porter Books, 1998.

3. Cohen, letter to McClelland & Stewart associate editor Claire Pratt, July 21, 1959, in Archive.

4. SS, 2001, for the article "Heroes' Heroes," in *MOJO*, March 2002.

5. SS, 2001.

6. Richard Goldstein, *Village Voice*, December 28, 1967, reproduced in *Goldstein's Greatest Hits: A Book Mostly About Rock 'n' Roll*, AbeBooks, 1970.

7. SS, 2011.

8. Arthur Kurzweil, "A Conversation with Leonard Cohen," *Jewish Book Club*, 1994.

9. SS, 2001.

10. Cohen, letter to Layton, April 21, 1963, in Archive.

11. Cohen, Kari Hesthamar, Norwegian radio interview, 2005.

12. Cohen, letter to Marianne Ihlen, December 24, 1960.

Six: Enough of Fallen Heroes

Author interviews with: Leonard Cohen, Steve Sanfield, Marianne Ihlen, Aviva Layton, Nancy Bacal, Richard Vick, George Lialios, Barry Miles

Books, films and documents: Donald Brittain and Don Owen, *Ladies and Gentlemen . . . Mr. Leonard Cohen*, documentary film, 1965. *The Canadian Encyclopedia* (online). Leonard Cohen, *Beautiful Losers*, 1966. Leonard Cohen, *Flowers for Hitler*, 1964. Leonard Cohen, *The Spice-Box of Earth*, 1961. Leonard Cohen Archive, Thomas Fisher Rare Book Library, University of Toronto, Canada ("Archive"). Ira B. Nadel, *Various Positions*, Bloomsbury, 1996.

Chapter heading: Leonard Cohen and Irving Layton, *Enough of Fallen Heroes*, unpublished work for TV, 1961.

1. Cohen, letter to Desmond Pacey, February 23, 1961, Archive.

2. Cohen, letter to Jack McClelland, October 12, 1960, Archive.

3. Lorca, letter to his parents, April 5, 1930, cited in Nadel, 1996.

4. Brittain and Owen, 1965.

5. Interview in Nadel, 1994.

6. Ibid.

7. Christian Fevret, *Les Inrockuptibles*, August 21, 1991, reproduced in *Throat Culture*, 1992, trans. Sophie Miller.

8. Ibid.

9. Cohen, *Spice-Box of Earth*, first edition, dust jacket.

10. Robert Weaver, *Toronto Daily Star*, June 10, 1961.

11. David Bromige, *Canadian Literature*, Autumn 1961.

12. Cohen, radio interview with Kari Hesthamar, 2005.

13. Cohen, letter to Layton, October 15, 1962, Archive.

14. Robin Pike, *ZigZag*, October 1974.

Seven: Please Find Me, I Am Almost 30

Author interviews with: Leonard Cohen, Erica Pomerance, Suzanne Verdal, Marianne Ihlen, Aviva Layton, Dennis Lee, Allan Showalter, Mort Rosengarten

Books and publications: Leonard Cohen, *The Favorite Game*, Secker & Warburg, 1963 (Viking U.S., 1964). Leonard Cohen, *Flowers for Hitler*, 1964. Ira B. Nadel, *Various Positions*, Bloomsbury, 1996. Michael Ondaatje, *Leonard Cohen*, McClelland & Stewart, 1970. Jack McClelland, *Imagining Canadian Literature: The Selected Letters of Jack McClelland*, ed. Sam Solecki, Key Porter Books, 1998. T. F. Rigelhof, *This Is Our Writing*, Porcupine's Quill, 1998.

Chapter heading: Leonard Cohen, "Marita," in *Selected Poems 1956–1968*.

1. Ondaatje, 1970.

2. Rigelhof, 1998.

3. Danny Fields, *Soho Weekly News*, December 1974.

4. Sarah Hampson, *Globe and Mail*, May 25, 2007.

5. Ibid.

6. Ondaatje, 1970.

7. Cohen, letter to McClelland, August 1963, Archive.

8. Cohen, quoting a 1984 conversation with Walter Yetnikoff, to SS, 2001.

9. Cohen, letter to McClelland, July 1963, Archive.

10. Cohen, letter to McClelland, March 1964, Archive.

11. Cohen, letter to McClelland, September 9, 1963, published in McClelland, 1998.

12. Cohen, letter to McClelland, September 2, 1964, published in McClelland, 1998.

13. Cohen, letter to McClelland, September 9, 1963, published in McClelland, 1998.

14. Sandra Djwa, *Ubyssey*, February 3, 1967.

15. Ibid.

16. Milton Wilson, *Toronto Quarterly*, July 1965.

17. Paul Kennedy, *The Story of Suzanne*, CBC TV Canada, 2006.

18. Ian Pearson, *Saturday Night*, March 1993.

19. Interview with Kevin Howlett, *Leonard Cohen: Tower of Song*, BBC Radio One, August 7, 1994.

20. Brian D. Johnson, *Maclean's*, June 11, 2008.

21. Richard Goldstein, *Village Voice*, December 28, 1967.

22. Susan Lumsden, "Leonard Cohen Wants the Unconditional Leadership of the World," September 12, 1970, reproduced in Michael Gnarowski, *Leonard Cohen: The Artist and His Critics*, McGraw-Hill Ryerson, 1976.

23. Cohen, letter to editor at Yilin Press, China, regarding the foreword to a Chinese edition of *Beautiful Losers*, February 2000, Archive.

24. Ibid.

25. Cohen, letter to McClelland, March 20, 1965, Archive.

26. Lumsden, "Leonard Cohen Wants."

27. Jon Ruddy, *Maclean's*, October 1, 1966.

28. Goldstein, *Village Voice*.

29. Christian Fevret, *Les Inrockuptibles*, August 21, 1991, reproduced in *Throat Culture*, 1992, trans. Sophie Miller.

30. Cohen, letter to McClelland, August 1965, Archive.

Eight: A Long Time Shaving

Author interviews with: Leonard Cohen, Judy Collins, Bob Fass, Jac Holzman, Marianne Ihlen, Penny Lang, Tom Maschler, Henry Zemel

Books and films: Donald Brittain and Don Owen, *Ladies and Gentlemen . . . Mr. Leonard Cohen*, National Film Board of Canada, 1965. Leonard Cohen, *Beautiful Losers*, 1966. Leonard Cohen, *Parasites of Heaven*, 1966. Kari Hesthamar, *So Long, Marianne: Ei Kjaerleikshistorie*, Spartacus, 2008. Jack McClelland, *Imagining Canadian Literature: The Selected Letters of Jack McClelland*, ed. Sam Solecki, Key Porter Books, 1998. Ira B. Nadel, *Various Positions*, Bloomsbury, 1996. Michael Ondaatje, *Leonard Cohen*, McClelland & Stewart, 1970. Harry Rasky, *Song of Leonard Cohen*, documentary film, 1980.

Chapter heading: Leonard Cohen, in Brittain and Owen, 1965.

1. Sandra Djwa, *Ubyssey*, February 3, 1967.

2. Interview for CBC with Phyllis Webb, cited in Ondaatje, 1970.

3. Jack McClelland, letter to Cohen, June 1965, reprinted in McClelland, 1988.

4. Jack McClelland, letter to Cohen, May 1966, reprinted in McClelland, 1988.

5. Nicolas Walter, *Times Literary Supplement*, April 23, 1970.

6. Irving Layton, in *Chatelaine*, September 1983.

7. Barbara Amiel, *Maclean's*, September 18, 1978.

8. Paul Zollo, *Songwriters on Songwriting*, 1992, revised edition, Da Capo, 2003.

9. Nadel, 1996.

10. Ondaatje, 1970.

11. Cohen, interview with Adrienne Clarkson, *Take 30*, CBC TV, 1966.

12. Robert Fulford, *Toronto Daily Star*, 1966.

13. Jon Ruddy, *Maclean's*, October 1, 1966.

14. Interview on *The John Hammond Years*, BBC, September 20, 1986.

15. Leonard Cohen, *The Best of Leonard Cohen* liner notes, 1975.

16. Zollo, 2003.

17. Cohen, letter to Marianne Ihlen, December 4, 1966, reprinted in Hesthamar, 2008.

18. Christian Fevret, *Les Inrockuptibles*, August 21, 1991, reproduced in *Throat Culture*, 1992, trans. Sophie Miller.

19. Harry Rasky, *The Song of Leonard Cohen: Portrait of a Poet, a Friendship and a Film*, Souvenir Press, 2001.

20. Cohen, letter to Marianne Ihlen, December 1966, published in Hesthamar, 2008.

Nine: How to Court a Lady

Author interviews with: Leonard Cohen, Judy Collins, David Crosby, Danny Fields, Lou Reed, Jackson Browne, Bob Johnston, John Simon, Jac Holzman, Aviva Layton, Thelma Blitz, Larry Cohen, Bob Fass, Marianne Ihlen, Juan Rodriguez, Joel Bernstein, Nancy Bacal, Erica Pomerance

Books, films and documents: Artist's cards, Columbia Records Archive. Patti Smith, *Just Kids*, Ecco, 2010. John Hammond and Irving Townsend, *On Record*, Ridge Press/Penguin US & UK, 1981. Kari Hesthamar, *So Long, Marianne: Ei Kjaerleikshistorie*, Spartacus, 2008. Mary Martin televised interview, Louise Scruggs Memorial Forum, Country Music Hall of Fame, November 17, 2009.

Chapter title: Leonard Cohen, at Henderson Hospital Concert, UK, August 1970.

1. Leonard Cohen, Henderson Hospital concert, UK, August 1970, taped by Ian Milne.

2. Reed, interview with the author, 2005.

3. Browne, interview with the author, 2008.

4. Ibid.

5. Ibid.

6. Ibid.

7. Ibid.

8. John Walsh, *MOJO*, September 1994.

9. Prologue to live performance of "Joan of Arc," Paris, October 20, 1974, leonardcohen-prologues.com.

10. Ibid.

11. Prologue at Henderson Hospital concert, UK, August 1970.

12. Smith, 2010.

13. Hammond and Townsend, 1981.

14. Cohen, letter to Marianne Ihlen, February 23, 1967, Ihlen private collection.

15. Cohen, letter to Marianne, April 9, 1967, Ihlen private collection.

16. Ibid.

17. Cohen, letter to Marianne, April 12, 1967, Ihlen private collection.

18. John Hammond and Leonard Cohen, BBC radio interview, September 20, 1986.

19. Ibid.

20. Harry Rasky, *The Song of Leonard Cohen: Portrait of a Poet, a Friendship and a Film*, Souvenir Press, 2001.

21. Layton, interview with the author.

22. Robert Enright, *Border Crossings* 7, February 2001.

23. Mark Ellen, *Word*, July 2007.

24. Enright, *Border Crossings*, 2001.

25. Robert Fulford, *This Was Expo*, McMaster Libraries, 1968.

26. Leonard Cohen, liner notes to *Greatest Hits/The Best of Leonard Cohen*, 1975.

27. Simon Houpt, *Globe and Mail*, February 27, 2009.

28. Hammond and Townsend, 1981.

29. Susan Nunziata, *Billboard*, November 28, 1998.

Ten: The Dust of a Long Sleepless Night

Author interviews with: Leonard Cohen, John Simon, Marianne Ihlen, Danny Fields, Steve Sanfield, David Lindley, Chris Darrow, Chester Crill

Books, documents and films: Artist's cards, Columbia Records Archive. Armelle Brusq, *Mount Baldy, Spring '96*, documentary film, 1997. Kari Hesthamar, *So Long, Marianne: Ei Kjaerleikshistorie*, Spartacus, 2008.

Chapter heading: Leonard Cohen, "One of Us Cannot Be Wrong," *Songs of Leonard Cohen*, 1968.

1. SS, 2001.

2. Leonard Cohen, "This is for you," later published in *Stranger Music: Selected Poems and Songs*, 1993.

3. Brusq, 1997.

4. SS, 2001.

5. Paul Grescoe, *Montreal Gazette*, February 10, 1968.

6. John Hammond and Leonard Cohen, BBC radio interview, September 20, 1986.

7. Prologue at concert in Antwerp, April 1988, leonardcohen-prologues.com.

8. Arthur Schmidt, *Rolling Stone*, September 2, 1971.

9. Donal Henahan, *New York Times*, January 29, 1968.

10. Karl Dallas, *Melody Maker*, February 17, 1968.

11. Ibid.

12. Ibid.

13. Jacoba Atlas, *Beat*, March 9, 1968.

14. William Kloman, *New York Times*, January 28, 1968.

15. *Playboy*, November 1968.

Eleven: The Tao of Cowboy

Author interviews with: Leonard Cohen, David Crosby, Bob Johnston, Marianne Ihlen, Terese Coe, Liberty, Thelma Blitz, Danny Fields, Kris Kristofferson, Steve Sanfield, Richard Vick, Terry Oldfield, Henry Zemel, Bill Donovan, Ron Cornelius, Charlie Daniels

Books, films and documents: Artist's cards, Columbia Records Archive. Leonard Cohen, *Selected Poems 1956–1968*, Jonathan Cape, 1969. Bob Dylan, *Chronicles: Volume One*, Simon & Schuster, 2004. Lian Lunson, *Leonard Cohen: I'm Your Man*, documentary film, Lionsgate, 2005. Michael Ondaatje, *Leonard Cohen*, McClelland & Stewart, 1970.

Chapter heading: SS.

1. Prologue at concert in Paris, June 6, 1976, leonardcohen-prologues.com.

2. Prologue at concert in Nuremberg, May 10, 1988, leonardcohen-prologues.com.

3. Lunson, 2005.

4. Dylan, 2004.

5. Rainer Blome, trans. Nick Townsend, *Sounds*, 1969.

6. Prologue at Henderson Hospital concert, UK, August 1970.

7. Leonard Cohen, *Selected Poems 1956–1968*, dust jacket of U.S. first edition, Viking, 1968.

8. Ondaatje, 1970.

9. SS, 2001.

10. Blome, 1969.

11. Michael Harris, *Duel*, Winter 1969.

12. Ibid.

13. SS, 2001.

14. Alec Dubro, *Rolling Stone*, May 17, 1969.

15. William Kloman, *New York Times*, April 27, 1969.

Twelve: O Make Me a Mask

Author interviews with: Leonard Cohen, Suzanne Elrod, David Cohen, Steve Sanfield, Danny Fields, Bob Johnston, Charlie Daniels, Ron Cornelius, Mort Rosengarten, Bill Donovan, Ian Milne, Kris Kristofferson, Jeff Dexter, Murray Lerner

Film and documents: Artist's cards, Columbia Records Archive. Murray Lerner, *Leonard Cohen: Live at the Isle of Wight 1970*, CD and documentary film, Columbia Legacy, 2009.

Chapter heading: Dylan Thomas, "O Make Me a Mask," 1938.

1. Paul Saltzman, "Famous Last Words from Leonard Cohen," *Maclean's*, June 1972.

2. Archive.

3. Pamela Andriotakis and Richard Oulahan, *People*, January 14, 1980.

4. Archive.

5. SS, 2001.

6. Gavin Martin, *NME*, October 19, 1991.

7. Harvey Kubernik, *Melody Maker*, March 1, 1975.

8. Robin Denselow, *Guardian*, May 11, 1970.

9. Archive.

10. Nancy Erlich, *Billboard*, August 8, 1970.

11. Steve Turner, *NME*, June 29, 1974.

12. Lerner, 2009.

Thirteen: The Veins Stand Out Like Highways

Author interviews with: Leonard Cohen, Suzanne Elrod, Charlie Daniels, Ron Cornelius, Joe Boyd, Chris Darrow, Chester Crill, David Lindley, Henry Zemel, Brian Cullman, Bob Johnston, Bill Donovan, Peter Marshall, Steven Machat, Liberty, Steve Sanfield, Tony Palmer

Books, films and documents: Artist's cards, Columbia Records Archive. Leonard Cohen, *The Energy of Slaves*, McClelland & Stewart, 1972. Tony Palmer, *Bird on a Wire*, documentary film, 1974. Henry Zemel, *Bonds of the Past*, documentary film, 1972.

Chapter heading: Leonard Cohen, "Dress Rehearsal Rag," *Songs of Love and Hate*, Columbia, 1971.

1. SS, 2001.

2. Roy Shipston, *Disc & Music Echo*, November 14, 1970.

3. John Walsh, *MOJO*, September 1994.

4. Martin Walker, *Guardian*, November 8, 1972.

5. SS, 2001.

6. Karl Dallas, *Melody Maker*, May 22, 1976.

7. Paul Saltzman, "Famous Last Words from Leonard Cohen," *Maclean's*, June 1972.

8. Leonard Cohen, "I have no talent left," *The Energy of Slaves*, June 1972.

9. Cohen, "The poems don't love us anymore," Ibid.

10. Cohen, "How we loved you," Ibid.

11. Cohen, "You are almost always with someone else," Ibid.

12. Cohen, "The 15-year-old girls," Ibid.

13. *Times Literary Supplement*, January 5, 1973.

14. Stephen Scobie, *Leonard Cohen*, Douglas & McIntyre, 1978.

15. Saltzman, 1972.

16. Palmer, 1974.

Fourteen: A Shield Against the Enemy

Author interviews with: Leonard Cohen, John Lissauer, Lewis Furey, Mort Rosengarten, Bob Johnston, Suzanne Elrod, Tony Palmer, Henry Zemel, Marianne Ihlen, Terry Oldfield, Leanne Ungar, Malka Marom, Danny Fields, Harvey Kubernik, Paul Body, Richard Vick, Aviva Layton, Larry "Ratso" Sloman

Book, films and documents: Artist's cards, Columbia Records Archive. L. S. Dorman and C. L. Rawlins, *Leonard Cohen: Prophet of the Heart*, 1990. Ira B. Nadel, *Various Positions*, Bloomsbury, 1996. Tony Palmer, *Bird on a Wire*, documentary film, 1974. Larry "Ratso" Sloman, *On the Road with Bob Dylan*, 1978; reprinted by Three Rivers Press, 2002.

Chapter heading: Leonard Cohen, "Lover Lover Lover," *New Skin for the Old Ceremony*, Columbia, 1974.

1. Archive, "The Woman Being Born/My Life in Art," 1973.

2. Robin Pike, *ZigZag*, October 1974.

3. Ibid.

4. Roy Hollingworth, *Melody Maker*, February 24, 1973.

5. Leonard Cohen, "My Life in Art," unpublished manuscript, Archive.

6. Ibid.

7. Pike, *ZigZag*, 1974.

8. Gavin Martin, *NME*, October 19, 1991.

9. Leonard Cohen, "The Final Revision of My Life in Art," unpublished manuscript, cited in Nadel, 1996.

10. Article marking the twentieth anniversary of the war, *Maariv*, 1993, trans. Doron B. Cohen.

11. Cohen, "The Final Revision."

12. Leonard Cohen, prologue to live performance of "Lover Lover Lover," Frankfurt, Germany, October 6, 1974, leonardcohen-prologues.com.

13. Pike, *ZigZag*, 1974.

14. Harvey Kubernik, *Melody Maker*, March 1, 1975.

15. Leonard Cohen, liner notes to *Greatest Hits/The Best of Leonard Cohen*, 1975.

16. Michael Wale, *ZigZag*, August 1974.

17. Kubernik, *Melody Maker*, 1975.

18. Cited in Dorman and Rawlins, 1990.

19. Clipping from *NME*, 1974 (author and date unknown).

20. Paul Nelson, *Rolling Stone*, February 26, 1975.

21. Prologue at concert in Melbourne, Australia, March 1980, leonardcohen-prologues.com.

22. Barry Coleman, *Guardian*, September 13, 1974.

23. Harry Rasky, *The Song of Leonard Cohen* (documentary film), 1980.

24. Larry Sloman, *Rolling Stone*, November 1974.

25. Kubernik, *Melody Maker*, 1975.

26. Archive, "My Life in Art."

27. Leonard Cohen, "The End of My Life in Art," unpublished essay, Archive.

Fifteen: I Love You, Leonard

Author interviews with: Leonard Cohen, Dan Kessel, David Kessel, Harvey Kubernik, Suzanne Elrod, Hal Blaine, John Lissauer, Steven Machat, Malka Marom, Ronee Blakley

Books, films and documents: Artist's cards, Columbia Records Archive. Leonard Cohen, *Death of a Lady's Man*, 1978. Mick Brown, *Tearing Down the Wall of Sound: The Rise and Fall of Phil Spector*, Knopf, 2007. *Leonard Cohen Under Review 1934–1977*, documentary film, Chrome Dreams, 2007. Steven Machat, *Gods, Gangsters and Honour*, Beautiful Books, 2010. Richard Williams, *Phil Spector: Out of His Head*, 1972; Omnibus reprint, 2003.

Chapter heading: Phil Spector, quoted by Leonard Cohen to Kevin Howlett, *Leonard Cohen: Tower of Song*, BBC Radio One, August 7, 1994.

1. Cohen, interview with Harvey Kubernik, 1977, later published in *LA Phonograph*, January 1978.

2. Brown, 2007.

3. Leonard Cohen, prologue to live performance of "Memories," Tel Aviv, 1980, leonardcohen-prologues.com.

4. Cohen, interview with Harvey Kubernik, 1977.

5. Ginsberg in *Record Collector*, February 1995.

6. Cohen, interview with Harvey Kubernik, 1977.

7. SS, 2001.

8. Kevin Howlett, *Leonard Cohen: Tower of Song*, BBC Radio One, August 7, 1994.

9. *Leonard Cohen Under Review*, 2007.

10. Brown, 2007

11. *Leonard Cohen Under Review*, 2007.

12. Brown, 2007.

13. Stephen Holden, *Rolling Stone*, January 26, 1978.

14. Ibid.

15. Janet Maslin, *New York Times*, November 6, 1977.

16. Cohen, interview with Harvey Kubernik, 1977.

17. Maslin, *New York Times*, 1977.

18. Paul Nelson, *Rolling Stone,* February 9, 1978.

19. Sandy Robertson, *Sounds,* November 26, 1977.

20. SS, 2001.

21. William Ruhlmann, *Goldmine,* February 19, 1993.

Sixteen: A Sacred Kind of Conversation

Author interviews with: Leonard Cohen, Suzanne Elrod, Rabbi Mordecai Finley, Nancy Bacal, Steve Sanfield, John Lissauer, Lewis Furey, Roscoe Beck, Harvey Kubernik, John Bilezikjian, Terry Oldfield, Dennis Lee, Sharon Robinson

Books and films: Leonard Cohen, *Book of Mercy,* 1984. Harry Rasky, *Song of Leonard Cohen,* documentary film, 1980. Harry Rasky, *The Song of Leonard Cohen: Portrait of a Poet, a Friendship and a Film,* Souvenir Press, 2001. Howard Sounes, *Down the Highway: The Life of Bob Dylan,* Grove, 2001.

Chapter heading: Leonard Cohen to Robert Sward, 1984.

1. Barbara Amiel, *Maclean's,* September 1978.

2. Columbia Records press release, 1979.

3. Nick Paton Walsh, *Observer,* October 14, 2001.

4. SS, 2001.

5. Sounes, 2001.

6. SS, 2001.

7. Ibid.

8. ZDF TV, Germany, October 31, 1979.

9. Rasky, 1980.

10. Cohen, "So Long, Marianne," *Songs from a Room,* Columbia, 1969.

11. Debra Cohen, *Rolling Stone,* February 21, 1980.

12. Larry "Ratso" Sloman, *High Times,* February 1980.

13. *NME,* 1979.

14. SS, 2001.

15. Brad Buchholz, *Austin American-Statesman,* March 31, 1979.

16. Pamela Andriotakis and Richard Oulahan, *People,* January 14, 1980.

17. Rasky, *Song of Leonard Cohen* film.

18. Ibid.

19. Ibid.

20. Nick Duerden, *Guardian,* October 7, 2011.

21. SS, 2001.

22. Robert Sward, "Leonard Cohen as Interviewed by Robert Sward," 1984.

23. *NME*, March 2, 1985.

24. Bruce Headlam, *Saturday Night*, December 1997.

25. Ibid.

26. Christian Fevret, *Les Inrockuptibles*, August 21, 1991, reproduced in *Throat Culture*, 1992, trans. Sophie Miller.

27. Sward, "Leonard Cohen."

28. Peter Gzowski, *Leonard Cohen at 50*, CBC, 1984.

Seventeen: The Hallelujah of the Orgasm

Author interviews with: Leonard Cohen, John Lissauer, Leanne Ungar, Larry "Ratso" Sloman, Anjani Thomas, David Lindley, Roscoe Beck

Chapter heading: Jeff Buckley, in *OOR*, 1994.

1. Robert Sward, "Leonard Cohen as Interviewed by Robert Sward," 1984.

2. SS, 2001.

3. Ibid.

4. Nigel Williamson, *Uncut*, October 12, 1997.

5. Cohen to John McKenna, RTÉ, May 9, 1988.

6. Paul Zollo, *Songwriters on Songwriting*, 1992, revised edition, Da Capo, 2003.

7. *Q*, September 1994.

8. Zollo, 1992.

9. Williamson, *Uncut*.

10. Richard Cook, *NME*, February 9, 1985.

11. *Sounds*, January 26, 1985.

12. Brian Appleyard, *Sunday Times*, January 9, 2005.

13. *Word*, July 2007.

14. Cohen, interview with Jian Ghomeshi, CBC TV, 2009.

15. Warnes, interview with Kevin Howlett, BBC Radio One, August 7, 1994.

16. Ian Pearson, *Saturday Night*, March 1993.

17. Cohen, interview with Kevin Howlett, BBC Radio One, August 7, 1994.

18. Ibid.

19. Marc Rowland, *Musician*, July 1988.

Eighteen: The Places Where I Used to Play

Author interviews with: Leonard Cohen, Iggy Pop, Roscoe Beck, Sharon Robinson, Sharon Weisz, Perla Batalla, Steven Machat, Sean Dixon, Julie Christensen, Hal Willner

Chapter heading: Leonard Cohen, "Tower of Song," *I'm Your Man*, Columbia, 1988.

1. Mat Snow, *Guardian*, February 1988.

2. Mark Rowland, *Musician*, July 1988.

3. SS, 2001.

4. Mark Cooper, *Q*, March 1988.

5. Ibid.

6. Prince Charles, interviewed on *Ant & Dec*, ITV1, May 20, 2006.

7. SS, 2001.

8. Ibid.

9. Ibid.

10. Christian Fevret, *Les Inrockuptibles*, August 21, 1991, reproduced in *Throat Culture*, 1992, trans. Sophie Miller.

11. Anjelica Houston, *Interview*, November 1995.

12. SS, 2001.

13. Elena Pita, *El Mundo*, September 26, 2001.

14. SS, 2001.

Nineteen: Jeremiah in Tin Pan Alley

Author interviews with: Leonard Cohen, Rebecca De Mornay, Anjani Thomas, Black Francis, Nick Cave, Hal Willner, Julie Christensen, Perla Batalla, Nancy Bacal, Leanne Ungar, Suzanne Elrod

Book: Leonard Cohen, *Stranger Music*, McClelland & Stewart, 1993.

Chapter heading: Irving Layton to Ian Pearson, *Saturday Night*, March 1993.

1. Brendan Kelly, *Financial Post*, December 12, 1992.

2. Paul Zollo, *Songwriters on Songwriting*, 1992.

3. Ibid.

4. Ibid.

5. Ibid.

6. *Details*, July 1993.

7. Brian D. Johnson, *Maclean's*, December 7, 1992.

8. Alan Jackson, *Observer*, November 22, 1992.

9. Agreta Wirberg and Stina Dabrowski, *Stina Möter Leonard Cohen*, TV documentary, 1997.

10. Barbara Gowdy, November 19, 1992, reprinted in *One on One: The Imprint Interviews*, ed. Leanna Crouch, Somerville House, 1994.

11. Cohen, Juno Canadian Music Hall of Fame induction speech, March 3, 1991.

12. SS, 2001.

13. Ibid.

14. Ibid.

15. *Billboard*, November 28, 1998.

16. Gowdy in *One on One*.

17. SS, 2001.

18. Gavin Martin, *NME*, January 9, 1993.

19. Anthony De Curtis, *Rolling Stone*, January 1993.

20. Gowdy in *One on One*.

21. Ibid.

22. Johnson, *Maclean's*.

23. Leonard Cohen and Rebecca De Mornay, *Interview*, June 1993.

24. Jon Pareles, *New York Times*, June 16, 1993.

25. Cohen, induction speech, Governor General's Award, Canada, 1993.

26. Ian Pearson, *Saturday Night*, March 1993.

Twenty: From This Broken Hill

Author interviews with: Leonard Cohen, Kigen, Robert Faggen, Roscoe Beck, Rebecca De Mornay, Daijo, Sharon Robinson, Steve Sanfield, Jarkko Arjatsalo, Perla Batalla, Julie Christensen, Ratnesh Mathur, Chris Darrow, Nancy Bacal, Leanne Ungar, Anjani Thomas

Books and films: Armelle Brusq, *Leonard Cohen: Portrait: Spring 96*, documentary film, 1997. Leonard Cohen, *Book of Longing*, Ecco, 2006. Agreta Wirberg and Stina Dabrowski, *Stina Möter Leonard Cohen*, TV documentary, 1997.

Chapter heading: Leonard Cohen, "If It Be Your Will," *Various Positions*, Columbia, 1985.

1. SS, 2001.

2. Ibid.

3. Gilles Tordjman, *Les Inrockuptibles*, interview with the author, October 15, 1995.

4. Robert Hilburn, *Los Angeles Times*, September 24, 1995.

5. SS, 2001.

6. Cohen, letter to Marianne Ihlen, February 1967.

7. Billy Walker, *Sounds*, October 23, 1971.

8. Wirberg and Dabrowski, 1997.

9. Pico Iyer, *Buzz*, April 1995.

10. SS, 2001.

11. Ibid.

12. Wirberg and Dabrowski, 1997.

13. Gilles Tordjman, *Les Inrockuptibles*, March 15, 1995.

14. SS, 2001.

15. Ibid.

16. Ibid.

17. Ibid.

18. Ibid.

19. Bruce Headlam, *Saturday Night*, December 1997.

20. Tordjman, *Les Inrockuptibles*, 1995.

21. Neva Chonin, *Rolling Stone*, December 11, 1997.

22. *NME*, September 1995.

23. SS, 2001.

24. Ibid.

25. Ibid.

26. Wirberg and Dabrowski, 1997.

27. SS, 1997.

28. Ibid.

29. Paul Zollo, *Songwriters on Songwriting*, 1992.

30. Susan Nunziata, *Billboard*, November 28, 1998.

31. SS, 2011.

32. Ibid.

33. Ibid.

34. Ibid.

35. Ibid.

36. Ibid.

37. Ibid.

38. Ibid.

39. SS, 2001.

40. SS, 2011.

41. Ibid.

42. Ibid.

Twenty-one: Love and Theft

Author interviews with: Leonard Cohen, Robert Kory, Rufus Wainwright, Nick Cave, Hal Willner, Anjani Thomas, Leanne Ungar, Sharon Robinson, Ratnesh Mathur, Julie Christensen, Perla Batalla, Robert Faggen, Richard Landon

Books and films: Armelle Brusq, *Leonard Cohen: Portrait: Spring 96,* documentary film, 1997. Leonard Cohen, *Book of Longing,* Ecco, 2006. Agreta Wirberg and Stina Dabrowski, *Stina Möter Leonard Cohen,* TV documentary, 1997.

Chapter heading: Leonard Cohen, "To a Teacher," *The Spice-Box of Earth,* 1961.

1. Christian Langlois, *CARP,* June 2006.

2. SS, 2001.

3. Ibid.

4. Ibid.

5. Robinson, interview with the author, 2009.

6. Sarah Hampson, *Shambhala Sun,* November 2007.

7. Frank DiGiacomo, *New York Observer,* February 22, 2002.

8. SS, 2001.

9. Jon Pareles, *New York Times,* October 1995.

10. SS, 2001.

11. SS, 2011.

12. Wirberg and Dabrowski, 1997.

13. Leon Wieseltier, *Arts & Opinion* vol. 4, no. 2, 2005.

14. Ibid.

15. Cohen, e-mail to Jarkko Arjatsalo, June 2004.

16. Susan Nunziata, *Billboard,* November 28, 1998.

17. Katherine Macklem, Charlie Gillis and Brian D. Johnson, *Maclean's*, August 22, 2005.

Twenty-two: Taxes, Children, Lost Pussy

Author interviews with: Leonard Cohen, Robert Kory, Anjani Thomas, Hal Willner, Nick Cave, Rufus Wainwright, Julie Christensen, Perla Batalla, John Lissauer, Rabbi Mordecai Finley

Chapter heading: Leonard Cohen, self-portrait in *Book of Longing*, 2006.

1. Ann Diamond, "Whatever Happened to Kelley Lynch," riverdeepbook .blogspot.com, July 3, 2008.

2. J. Kelly Nestruck, *National Post*, February 7, 2006.

3. Ibid.

4. Cohen, speech at induction into the Canadian Songwriters Hall of Fame, February 5, 2006.

5. Angela Pacienza, *Toronto Canadian Press*, February 4, 2006.

6. Christine Langlois, *CARP*, June 2006.

7. Ibid.

8. Phoebe Hoban, *New York*, May 14, 2006.

9. Sean Murphy, *Tricycle: The Buddhist Review*, August 2007.

10. Biba Kopf, *NME*, March 1987.

Twenty-three: The Future of Rock 'n' Roll

Author interviews with: Leonard Cohen, Philip Glass, Robert Faggen, Hal Willner, Anjani Thomas, Robert Kory, Steven Machat, Rob Hallett, Sharon Robinson, Roscoe Beck, Charley Webb, Hattie Webb

Chapter heading: John Landau, *Rolling Stone*, 1974.

1. SS, 2011.

2. Greg Quill, *Toronto Star*, June 3, 2007.

3. Mireille Silcott, *Saturday Night*, 2001.

4. Leonard Cohen Files, April 29, 2002.

5. Mireille Silcott, *Saturday Night*, 2001.

6. Neil McCormick, *Telegraph*, May 26, 2007.

7. Sarah Hampson, *Shambhala Sun*, November 2007.

8. SS, 2011.

9. Lou Reed, Rock and Roll Hall of Fame speech introducing Cohen, March 10, 2008.

10. Cohen, Rock and Roll Hall of Fame induction speech, March 10, 2008.

11. Alec Dubro, *Rolling Stone*, May 17, 1969.

12. Arthur Schmidt, *Rolling Stone*, September 2, 1971.

13. Geoff Boucher, *Los Angeles Times*, February 27, 2009.

Twenty-four: Here I Stand, I'm Your Man

Author interviews with: Leonard Cohen, Sharon Robinson, Tony Palmer, Robert Kory, Rob Hallett, Anjani Thomas, Hal Willner, Roscoe Beck, Charley Webb, Hattie Webb, Henry Zemel

Chapter heading: Leonard Cohen, "I'm Your Man," *I'm Your Man*, Columbia, 1988.

1. SS, 2011.

2. Ibid.

3. Ben Rayner, *Toronto Star*, June 7, 2008.

4. Andy Greene, *Rolling Stone*, June 9, 2008.

5. Brian D. Johnson, *Maclean's*, June 11, 2008.

6. Johnny Black, *Audience*, September 2008.

7. Ibid.

8. John Aizlewood, *London Evening Standard*, July 18, 2008.

9. Johnson, *Maclean's*.

10. Andy Greene, *Rolling Stone*, February 20, 2009.

11. Lavinia Jones Wright, *Billboard*, February 20, 2009.

12. Leonard Cohen, "Now and Then."

13. Patrick Doyle, *Rolling Stone*, June 18, 2010.

14. Cohen, interview with Jian Ghomeshi, CBC TV, April 16, 2009.

Twenty-five: A Manual for Living with Defeat

Author interviews with: Leonard Cohen, Robert Kory

Chapter heading: Leonard Cohen, "Going Home," *Old Ideas*, Sony, 2012.

1. Simon Houpt, *Globe and Mail*, February 27, 2009.

2. Paul Zollo, *Songwriters on Songwriting*, 1992, revised edition, Da Capo, 2003.

3. Cohen to Jarvis Cocker, *Guardian*, January 19, 2012.

4. SS, 2011.

5. Cohen onstage, Las Vegas, December 11, 2010.

6. Cohen, press conference, Paris, January 16, 2012.

7. SS, 2011.

8. Ibid.

9. James Adams, *Globe and Mail*, April 1, 2011.

10. SS, 2011.

11. Adam Cohen, interviewed by Rebecca Ecker, *Maclean's*, October 6, 2011.

12. Ibid.

13. SS, 2011.

14. Ibid.

15. Greg Kot, *Chicago Tribune*, January 24, 2012.

16. Kitty Empire, *Observer*, January 21, 2012.

17. Jon Dolan, *Rolling Stone*, December 7, 2011.

18. Andy Gill, *Independent*, January 20, 2012.

19. Cohen to Jarvis Cocker, press conference, London, January 2012.

20. Cohen, press conference, Paris, January 16, 2012.

21. SS, 2011.

Epilogue

Author interview with: Leonard Cohen

1. Leonard Cohen, calligraphy, liner note artwork, *Old Ideas*, 2012.

Permissions

Index

REBELLION
IN THE BACKLANDS

Translated from

OS SERTÕES *by* EUCLIDES DA CUNHA

WITH INTRODUCTION AND NOTES BY

SAMUEL PUTNAM

UNIVERSITY OF CHICAGO PRESS

CHICAGO · ILLINOIS

Translated by permission from edition published by
Livraria Francisco Alves, Rio de Janeiro, Brazil

UNIVERSITY OF CHICAGO PRESS · CHICAGO 37

Agent: CAMBRIDGE UNIVERSITY PRESS · LONDON

✿ ✿ ✿

"BRAZIL'S GREATEST BOOK": A TRANS-LATOR'S INTRODUCTION

THERE can be no doubt that Euclides da Cunha's *Os Sertões*[1] is a work that is unique not only in Brazilian but in world literature as well. In no other instance, probably, has there been such unanimity on the part of critics of all shades of opinion in acclaiming a book as the greatest and most distinctive which a people has produced, the most deeply expressive of that people's spirit. On this the native and the foreign critic are in agreement. *"Nosso livro supremo*—our finest book," says Agrippino Grieco, in his study of "The Evolution of Brazilian Prose," and he adds that it is "the work which best reflects our land and our people."[2] Stefan Zweig, Brazil's tragic guest, saw in *Os Sertões* a "great national epic . . . . created purely by chance," one giving "a complete psychological picture of the Brazilian soil, the people, and the country, such as has never been achieved with equal insight and psychological comprehension. Comparable in world literature, perhaps, to *The Seven Pillars of Wisdom*, in which Lawrence describes the struggle in the desert, this great epic, little known in other countries, is destined to outlive countless books that are famous today by its dramatic magnificence, its spectacular wealth of spiritual wisdom, and the wonderful humanitarian touch which is characteristic of the whole work. Although Brazilian literature today has made enormous progress with the number of its writers and poets and its linguistic subtlety, no other book has reached such supremacy."[3]

"The Bible of Brazilian nationality," as it has been termed,[4] *Os Sertões* has "enriched Brazil with a book laden with seed, filled with perspectives for our triumph in the world of culture."[5] It is commonly looked upon as marking, in the year 1902, Brazil's intellectual coming-of-age. The site

---

[1] The title literally means "The Backlands." *Sertões* (pronounced "sair-toh'-ensh") is the plural of *sertão* (pronounced "sair-town"). The latter is a term, meaning the interior of the country or the hinterland, which is applied in particular to the backland regions of the Northeast, centering in the province of Baía. The author's name is pronounced "ŏŏ-kleé-des dah coón-yah."

[2] *Evolução da prosa brasileira* (Rio de Janeiro: Ariel, Editorial Ltda., 1933). On Euclides da Cunha and *Os Sertões* see pp. 281–86.

[3] *Brazil, Land of the Future* (New York: Viking Press, 1942), pp. 159–60.

[4] See an article by Olimpio de Souza Andrade, " 'Os Sertões' numa frase de Nabuco," *Planalto*, Vol. I, No. 14 (December 1, 1941).

[5] Grieco, *op. cit.*, p. 282.

where it was composed has now become a national shrine, and the volume itself, heralding the "rediscovery of Brazil," is indubitably a historical landmark. Revealing "the profound instability of our existence," as one literary historian puts it,[6] it was at the same time, in the author's own words, essentially based upon "the bold and inspiring conjecture that we are destined to national unity."[7]

Both book and author, it is true, remained more or less of an enigma to their age. As one Spanish-American critic has observed, Cunha was in reality taking arms against an era.[8] Skeptical, sincere, bitter, uncompromising, "almost brutal,"[9] displaying at times an "anomalous pessimism,"[10] particularly on the question of race, and endowed with an anguish-ridden personality that has in it more than a little of the pathologic,[11] this "son of the soil, madly in love with it,"[12] nonetheless emerges, alongside the nineteenth-century novelist, Machado de Assis, as one of the two outstanding figures in all Brazilian letters. As Zweig remarks, these are "the two really representative personalities" with whom Brazil enters "the arena of world literature."

In the case of so exceptional a writer and a work so truly amazing as *Os Sertões*, it is perhaps not surprising that Euclides da Cunha's admirers should range far afield in quest of comparisons. Thus, this "Beethoven of our prose,"[13] this *"genio americano,"* or "Latin-American genius," as the venerable Monteiro Lobato describes him, has been likened to authors as diverse as Dickens, Carlyle, and the prophet Ezekiel![14] As a reporter he has been compared to Kipling recording the exploits of Lord Roberts in the desert;[15] and a reporter of a most unusual kind he assuredly was, one who, writing amid the tumult of events and the emotional stress of the moment, succeeded in turning a journalistic account of a military campaign into an epic treatise on the geology, the geography, the climatology,

---

[6] Bezerra de Freitas, *História da literatura brasileira* (Porto Alegre: Livraria do Glôbo, 1939), pp. 251–52.

[7] See "Author's Notes," Note V, p. 481.

[8] Braulio Sánchez-Saez, "Euclides da Cunha, constructor de nacionalidad," *Agonía* (Buenos Aires), No. 4, October–December, 1939, pp. 50–56.

[9] The phrase is that of the French historian of Portuguese literature, M. Georges Le Gentil (see *La Littérature portugaise* [Paris: Librairie Armand Collin, 1935], p. 191).

[10] Andrade, *op. cit.*

[11] See Gilberto Freyre, *Actualidade de Euclides da Cunha* (Rio de Janeiro: Edição da Casa do Estudante do Brasil, 1941).

[12] See the biobibliographical sketch in the *Revista brasileira de geografia*, April, 1940, reprinted in separate form in *Vultos de geografia do Brasil*, November, 1940, p. 13.

[13] Bezerra de Freitas.   [14] *Ibid.*   [15] Agrippino Grieco.

the flora, the fauna, and the human life of the Brazilian backlands. *Os Sertões* is all this and a great deal more. Among other things, it is the definitive early-century statement of the national-racial question in Brazil, a problem that is a vital one today; and to his countrymen of the present its author remains "the representative genius *par excellence* of our land, of our people, and of our pure and lofty aspirations to heroism, beauty, and truth."[16]

Above all, however, it is a thrilling, vividly told tale, a "great document, which, though not a novel, reads like fiction."[17] Dealing with "one of the most virile episodes in our history," the incredibly heroic resistance of the backland natives at the siege of Canudos in 1896–97, it is a tale that should hold a special interest for this war-torn age of ours. Here is a campaign in which it required three months for a federal army of some six thousand men to advance one hundred yards against a handful of backwoodsmen! Here is guerrilla warfare in its pristine form, with the "scorched earth" and all the other accompaniments. And here, finally, after a months-long, house-to-house battle that recalls the contemporary epic of Stalingrad, are one old man, two other full-grown men, and a boy holding out against that same army until the last of them falls back dead in the grave which they themselves have dug!

"A cry of protest" the author calls his work, and it is indeed that. A protest against what he regards as a "crime" and an "act of madness" on the part of a newly formed republican government. For him, this "most brutal conflict of our age" was the "corpus delicti on the aberrations of a people," the "major scandal in our history." A clash between "two societies," between two cultures, that of the seaboard and that of the *sertão*, the Canudos Expedition appeared as a "deplorable stumbling-block to national unity." His book, accordingly, as he tells us,[18] is not so much a defense of the *sertanejo*, or man of the backlands, as it is an attack on the barbarity of the "civilized" toward those whose stage of social evolution was that of semibarbarians. In this connection we North Americans well may think of our own Indian wars of the early days.[19] The author's chapter on "Man" has been seen by Agrippino Grieco as "a precious lesson in things, given by a free man to the slaves of power, by a sociologist without a chair to the governors of the nation." Cunha, the same writer goes on to

[16] From a manuscript, "Noticia sobre Euclides da Cunha," by Afrânio Peixoto.

[17] See the paper by Carleton Beals, "Latin American Literature," in *The Writer in a Changing World* (New York: Equinox Press, 1937), p. 97.

[18] See p. 479 of the present translation ("Author's Notes," Note I).

[19] Cf. Washington Irving's story, "Philip of Pokanoket," *The Sketch Book* (New York: G. P Putnam's Sons, 1895), II, 168–96.

say, "told the truth in the land of lies and was original in the land of plagiarism." This honesty, set off by his originality and his boldness of attack, is perhaps his most prominent trait, the one on which all his commentators are agreed.

Whether or not his primary purpose was to defend the *sertanejo*, the author of *Os Sertões* certainly exhibits a passionate love of the mestizo backwoodsman and his way of life. The latter's customs, occupations, diversions, joys, and sorrows are all depicted with an affectionate wealth of detail. The "roundups," the merrymakings, the religious observances and superstitions of the region, are minutely chronicled, and the result is an authentic and unexcelled picture of the *vaqueiro*, or North Brazilian cowboy. Indeed, a Portuguese critic, none too friendly to Brazil, has said that this portion of the book contains the sixty-one finest pages ever written in the language.[20] The description of the devastating backland droughts holds the tragedy of a people struggling with a blind fate as represented by the relentless forces of nature. How deeply Euclides da Cunha felt for this folk, how close to them he was, may be seen from any one of a number of vignettes that he gives us, each a small masterpiece in its kind: the cowboy's dead child and the *festa* that marks its funeral; the cattle dying of thirst and starvation on the edge of the pool where they were accustomed to drink; the *vaqueiro* and his lifelong vegetable friends, the umbú tree, the joaz tree, and the others; the homeward-bound herd and the herdsman's home-going song, the *aboiado;* the stampede; and then the hours of ease and relaxation, swaying in the hammock, sipping the savory *umbusada;*[21] the festive gatherings and the "headstrong" *aguardente;*[22] the poetic tourneys, or "challenges." It is the life of a race, the mestizo race of the backlands, that lives for us here.

Those who are strangers to Brazil hardly will be in a position to realize that the picture which the author paints for us is by no means an anachronistic one from the point of view of the present. As the country's latest sociological historian, Senhor Caio Prado Junior says, the contemporary Brazilian who visits the backlands may be a witness to his nation's past.[23]

[20] The critic Bruno (José Pereira de Sampaio), cited by Agrippino Grieco.

[21] Drink made from the umbú tree (see p. 37).

[22] Brandy, the *aguardiente* of the Spanish-speaking countries (see p. 102, n. 91).

[23] Caio Prado Junior, *Formação do Brasil contemporâneo (Colonia)* (São Paulo: Livraria Martins, 1942), pp. 7–8: "Whoever traverses Brazil today is frequently surprised to come upon aspects [of our life] which he had imagined existed only in history books; and, if he studies them a little, he will see that they are not merely anachronistic reminiscences but represent deep underlying facts. . . . . A professor from abroad once upon a time remarked to me that he envied Brazilian historians who were thus able personally to witness the most stirring scenes of their past."

The "angry land"[24] still lives on and is still a national problem of the first importance, one which the airplane may eventually do much to solve.[25] Euclides da Cunha, meanwhile, is the greatest of those literary trail-blazers who, in the later 1890's, toward the end of the first decade of republican life, made their way into the *sertão*, to bring back its poetry, its tragedy, its myths, and the psychology of its inhabitants.[26] His fellow-explorers, however, were interested chiefly in the picturesque features of the locale, its Indian heritage of animistic beliefs and superstitions, its haunting, morbid, hallucinatory, dreamlike aspects. Cunha was the first to reveal its basic social life and implications; for he was not of those who believed that the hinterland, with all its backwardness, benightedness, and fratricidal religious mania, had been decreed of heaven for all time. A military engineer by profession, or, in the words of Gilberto Freyre, "a social engineer animated by a political ideal," he was at once reporter and scientist, man of letters and sociologist. To this day he is regarded as one of Brazil's greatest geographers. To quote a biobibliographical notice in the *Revista brasileira de geografia*,[27] "if there is one dominant aspect of the work of Euclides da Cunha, it is, certainly, the geographic. . . . . He wrote and made geography," and *Os Sertões* is "perhaps the most notable essay in human geography which a portion of our native soil has ever inspired in a writer." According to the well-known, present-day scientist, Roquette Pinto, Euclides was essentially an ecologist, being concerned with the relations between organisms and their environment. As a social scientist he is a forerunner of the brilliant group today which is represented by Gilberto Freyre, Arthur Ramos, Edison Carneiro, and others, even though these men frequently would disagree with his findings.

In literature, likewise, he was a pathfinder, being one of the two principal fountainheads of the modern Brazilian novel, the other being Machado de Assis. In the one case (Machado de Assis), the stress is on form; in the other, on content. *Os Sertões* may be said to have posed the problem which faces the twentieth-century novelist in Brazil: that of how to achieve an artistic synthesis of the rich social content which his country

[24] The phrase is Waldo Frank's (see his *South American Journey* [New York: Duell, Sloan & Pearce, 1943], pp. 311–19, 50, and 339). Frank calls *Os Sertões* "the greatest book in Brazil's literature," "Brazil's greatest book," etc.

[25] On this see Alice Rogers Hager, *Frontier by Air* (*Brazil Takes the Sky Road*) (New York: Macmillan Co., 1942).

[26] Cunha's immediate predecessors in this field were Coelho Netto, whose *Sertão* was published in 1897, the year of the Canudos Expedition, and Afonso Arinos, whose *Pelo sertão* ("Through the *Sertão*") appeared the following year (1898). The former felt much the same attraction for the region that a surrealist might today. The latter was especially interested in the psychology of the mestizo.

[27] See n. 12 above.

affords him. Because he grappled with this problem so valiantly and solved it in so extraordinary and individual a fashion, the author continues to be a symbol and an inspiration to creative writers. It is surely not without significance that there has grown up in this same general region, the Northeast, a school of novelists—Jorge Amado, Graciliano Ramos, José Lins do Rêgo, to mention but a few—who are at this moment bringing new life to Brazilian letters, and whose influence on the national literary scene has been so profound as to constitute something very like an "invasion."[28]

It is not surprising, therefore, if *Os Sertões* is rapidly taking its place as a great South American classic. Even though there are those who assert that it is untranslatable or should be read only in the original,[29] there can be no doubt that the recent Spanish-language rendering by Señor Benjamín de Garay of Argentina[30] is a valuable contribution to the cause of cultural understanding in this hemisphere; and it is hoped that an English-language translation may serve the same end, by bringing to readers who may have enjoyed a book like R. B. Cunningham-Graham's *A Brazilian Mystic*[31] the work which provided its inspiration.

In making the acquaintance of Euclides da Cunha, the North American has an experience awaiting him which is comparable in quality to that of the European of the last century listening for the first time to Walt Whitman's "barbaric yawp." The comparison is a particularly valid one on the side of form and style. Just as Whitman had to shape a new form, just as he had to forge a new vocabulary and a new style for a content that was quite new and which could not be run through the time-honored molds, so Cunha, in portraying the newly discovered, or "rediscovered," life of the Brazilian backlands, was compelled to hew out a literary implement that was suited to his needs. To his fellow-countrymen of the time, reared in a culture that was classic and prevailingly Gallic in character— to a Joaquim Nabuco,[32] for example—his "yawp" sounded quite as bar-

[28] For this "invasion" by writers of the Northeast see the review of José Lins do Rêgo's novel, *Usina*, by Rodrigo M. F. de Andrade, "Usina e a invasão dos nortistas," *Boletim de Ariel*, V, No. 11 (August, 1936), 286–87; see also the *Hand Book of Latin American Studies*, 1936, p. 340, and *ibid.*, 1937, p. 410.

[29] See the article cited, by Braulio Sánchez-Saez, n. 8 above.

[30] *Los Sertones*, trans. Benjamín de Garay (Buenos Aires: Imprenta Mercatali, 1938).

[31] R. B. Cunningham-Graham, *A Brazilian Mystic* (New York, 1925). An account of the career of Antonio Conselheiro.

[32] Consult Nabuco's treatise on his own cultural "formation," *Minha formação*, uniform edition of the *Obras* (São Paulo: Companhia Editora Nacional, 1934), where the author refers to the "*construção francesa do meu espírito*—the French mold (or structure) of my thinking." From early colonial times the French influence has been a strong, and frequently the dominant, one with Brazilian intellectuals, and it still persists today.

baric as did that of Whitman to an Emerson. It was Nabuco, the great abolitionist intellectual, who said of Cunha that the latter wrote *"com cipó*—with a liana stalk."[33] This expression as applied to the author of *Os Sertões* has since become a famous one and is proudly quoted by Cunha admirers as the highest tribute that could be paid him; for the liana to a Brazilian is the symbol of the inhospitable *sertão*. Of himself Euclides said that his was "the rude pen of a *caboclo*," that is, of an aborigine.[34] His palette, he tells us, is composed of "hues taken from the earth, from the black mud of the pits, with vermilion from the coagulated blood of the *jagunços*,[35] and the sepia of bandit affrays in the hinterland."[36] He does, in truth, paint the backlands, their suns and rains, their mountains, rivers, flora, with a barbaric brush, and this in a work which, starting out to be reportage, ends by being a blend of science, poetry, and color. It is easy to understand why this should have appeared as a "barbarous art" to another refined spirit of the age, José Verissimo, the historian of Brazilian literature. The colors at times are laid on with an exuberance that is truly tropical, accompanied by a certain primitive naïveté that puts one in mind of the Mexican canvases of a Douanier Rousseau. The style is then lush and sensuous in the extreme, marked by a verbal pomp that is almost purple-hued as "the adjective reigns with the splendor of a satrap."[37] This, however, is only in the author's more Amazonian moments, as they might be described. At other times—the greater part of the time— his prose is not tropical, but rugged, rugged as the *sertão* itself; it is nervous, dramatically intense, sculpturesque as the backland hills, and is characterized by a definite, brusque avoidance of lyricism and emphasis to the point of appearing overwrought and painful.[38] Here is the "liana stock." "But this liana ensnares the reader, obliging him to remain and view the flowers and trunks of this magnificent wood."[39]

In his passion for landscape, the depth and warmth of human feeling that he puts into the description of a *paysage*, whether it be the stricken

[33] Souza Andrade, *op. cit.*

[34] *Ibid.* The statement was made by Cunha in a letter to his intimate friend, Francisco Escobar.

[35] Term which comes to be synonymous with *sertanejo;* originally, a backlands "ruffian" (see p. 148).

[36] From Cunha's Amazon book, *A Margem da história*, cited by Bezerra de Freitas.

[37] Grieco, *op. cit.*, p. 285.

[38] See Gilberto Freyre's Preface to the collection of newspaper articles on Canudos by Cunha, recently given posthumous publication: *Canudos: Diário de uma expedição* ("Documentos brasileiros," Vol. XVI [Rio de Janeiro: José Olympio, 1939]).

[39] Grieco, *op. cit.*, p. 286.

hinterland flora in the time of drought or a geological formation, Cunha
has been compared to a poet-naturalist like Darwin; and he might also
in this respect—in capturing the emotional drama of inanimate nature—
be compared to a novelist like Thomas Hardy. He resembles Hardy, further, in the Latinizing tendency of his vocabulary, a quality that becomes
a defect of which he is conscious, and which got him into trouble with his
critics upon occasion.[40]

If in respect to form—originality and rugged strength and the shaping
of form to a novel subject matter—Cunha may justly be compared with
the North American Whitman, what then is to be said of his content? Does
he, here too, merit a comparison with the "poet of American democracy"?
This question cannot be answered by a mere abstract consideration of his
work. *Os Sertões* cannot be properly understood without an understanding of its author and the age in which he lived. The dramatic life and the
strange, tortured personality of Euclides da Cunha must be set against
the background of his time.

It was in the year 1866, at the close of our own Civil War era, that the
future historian of the Canudos Expedition was born. He was, accordingly, twenty-two years of age when slavery was abolished in Brazil in 1888
and twenty-three when Dom Pedro II and the Empire were overthrown
and the Republic was established in 1889. He lived, thus, in an era of
deep-going social change that was manifest in the realm of politics. He
grew up with a liberty-craving generation, a generation which intellectual-
ly had been nourished on Victor Hugo, Benjamin Constant, and Castro
Alves, "poet of the slaves." Racial freedom, the achievement of political
democracy, and, once the Republic had been set up, the forging of a true
Brazilian nationalism, a unified Brazil—these were the vital problems of
the age, and they were so intertwined as to be in reality inseparable.
Thanks to an abolitionist movement which represented one of the greatest, most edifying moral impulses on the part of an entire people that history has to show, the freeing of the slaves had been peacefully accomplished; but this act, accompanied by echoes of the French Revolution
and the Rights of Man,[41] dealt a deathblow to the imperial throne, which
tumbled in a year. There came then a period of revolutionary stress and,
to a degree, of democratic disillusionment, under the military dictator-

---

[40] See "Author's Notes," Note VIII, p. 483, where Cunha defends himself against the
charge of word coinages taken from the French (in reality, Latinisms).

[41] The connection was brought out clearly when, in 1883, five years before abolition was
achieved, Joaquim Nabuco exclaimed: "Slavery has now endured in Brazil almost a century
after the French Revolution taught the world to know and to love liberty."

ships of Deodoro Fonseca and Floriano Peixoto, as the newborn Republic struggled for its life. In 1893–94 came the counterrevolutionary[42] revolt of the fleet, with civil war in Rio de Janeiro harbor, provoked by Floriano's hard-fisted rule; and then, finally, in the autumn of 1894, civil government was restored in the person of President Moraes Barros.

Such was the turbulent era in which Euclides came to maturity. A transitional epoch, with forces at work that were so dubious and events so disheartening as almost to shake the faith of those who, like Cunha, had fought most staunchly for the Republic. In the politics of the day, spoils and gangsterism—in the provinces, an open banditry—prevailed; and, moreover, with a campaign like that of Canudos against the backland natives, one that was to lead to the seizure of Indian lands and the extension of landlord monopoly, it seemed as if republican Brazil were imitating the imperialist behavior of older democracies.[43] In the meantime, lost in the heart of the *sertão*, was that backlands race, constituting a third of the population of the country but forgotten by the rest of the nation for three whole centuries.[44]

The social-political currents which were to give direction to his life and work were already flowing, visibly and strongly, when, on January 20, 1866, Euclides da Cunha was born, at Santa Rita do Rio Negro, in the old province of Rio de Janeiro.[45] His father, Manuel Rodrigues Pimenta da Cunha, who came from the province of Baía, where the Canudos backlands are, "belonged to the romantic generation of Castro Alves."[46] Fond of literature and a great reader, the elder Cunha also wrote verses and gave his son a careful education. The death of his mother, D. Eudoxia Moreira da Cunha, when he was three years old is believed by some to have left a morbid imprint upon the lad's character. Certain it is that, from an early age, he was shifted about among relatives and boarding-schools, in Baía and in Rio, his formal education having been begun when he was five. What we would call his liberal arts course was completed at

[42] There is some disagreement among historians as to the precise political complexion of the revolt, which was brought to an end through the intervention of the United States Navy (see Samuel Flagg Bemis, *A Diplomatic History of the United States* [New York: Henry Holt, 1936], pp. 758–59). Bemis takes the view that it was, simply, promonarchist.

[43] On this see Beals, *op. cit.*; see also his *America South* (Philadelphia: J. B. Lippincott Co., 1937), pp. 247–48. Cunha himself does not mention this phase of the matter.

[44] See pp. 161, 405–6, and 408 of the present translation.

[45] In connection with this brief summary of Cunha's life, use has been made of Afrânio Peixoto's "Noticia" (n. 16 above), as well as of the standard sources (see the bibliography following this Introduction).

[46] Peixoto, *op. cit.*

the Colégio Aquino, in the capital, where he had a number of distinguished teachers, among them the republican leader and ideologist, Benjamin Constant. It was here, in company with his schoolmates, that he helped to found a youthful publication known as "The Democrat" (*O Democrata*), in the columns of which his first work appeared in the form of lyric poems.[47]

The picture that we get of the young Euclides of this period shows him as quiet and reserved, with few friends, fond of solitude and of reading. In the matter of his literary tastes, he would seem to have been especially fond of the poets, Castro Alves and Gonçalves Diaz among his country-men and Hugo among the bards of republican France. With the other young men of his day he must have read Aluizio de Azevedo's *O Mulato* ("The Mulatto"), Joaquim Nabuco's classic treatise, *O Abolicionismo*, and other works of similar social import.[48] Science, however, the positivistic science of the latter part of the nineteenth century, must have constituted a major portion of his mental diet; for his trend was in a scientific direc-tion, as is evidenced by his choice of profession, that of military engineer. A Spencerian positivism, in philosophy and in science, was in the very air that was breathed by the Brazilian intellectual of the eighties and the nineties, and Cunha's work is impregnated with it—with its virtues and its errors, its scientific half-truths and untruths, as in the field of an-thropology, for example. It was positivism which, through Constant and others, provided the philosophic impetus for the republican revolution in Brazil.[49] Euclides, like his fellows, drank all this in; and from Europe came such imported fare as Buckle, Bryce, Taine, Renan, Ratzel, Gum-plowicz, and Gobineau.[50] He was also to be influenced in his thinking by the North American geologist and physiographer, Orville A. Derby,[51] and by certain Brazilians as well.[52] This led to a rigid biologic determinism,

[47] Eighty-four of these poems were gathered in a notebook volume under the title of "On-das" ("Waves").

[48] Aluizio de Azevedo, *O Mulato* (3d ed.; Rio de Janeiro, 1889). Nabuco's *Abolicionismo* was published in London in 1883.

[49] On the positivist influence in the Brazilian republican revolution see Pedro Calmon, *História social do Brasil*, Vol. III: *A Época republicana* (São Paulo: Companhia Editora Na-cional, 1939).

[50] Gobineau is commonly given as one of Cunha's sources, but he is not mentioned in the present work. His influence, however, was strong in nineteenth-century Brazil, owing to his visit to that country and to his friendship and correspondence with the Emperor, Dom Pe-dro II.

[51] Of Cornell University, member of the Morgan Expedition to the Amazon, 1870–71, under Professor Charles F. Hartt (see p. 16 and n. 19).

[52] E.g., Theodoro Sampaio and Arnaldo Pimenta da Cunha (see Freyre, *op. cit.*).

tending to become fatalism, such as is apparent in passages of the present work.[53] Yet through it all a large element of the poetic persisted. His "formation," as his compatriots would say, was at once poetic and scientific.

In 1884 he entered the Polytechnic School, and two years later the Military School. Here, on the eve of the revolution, republicanism was rife, as is revealed by the organ of the student literary society, the *Revista da familia militar*. Then, of a sudden, in 1888, something appeared to snap with Euclides, and in an outburst of insubordination he hurled down his sword in the presence of the minister of war, thus ending his career as a soldier for a time. After a period of confinement in the military hospital, he was released from the army and, going to São Paulo, became a journalist, an occupation to which he had been attracted from his early student days.

What is to account for his conduct at the Military School? To be sure, in his later writings, in the pages of *Os Sertões*, even after he had been reconciled with the authorities and was back in the army again, he was to show himself extremely antimilitaristic in spirit—an antimilitarist but not a pacifist. War, he assures us, is "a monstrous thing . . . . utterly illogical" and with "the stigmata of an original banditry behind it." The soldier is "the sinister ideal of the homunculus," and the author has only contempt for "those doctors of the art of killing who today in Europe are scandalously invading the domain of science, disturbing its calm with an insolent jingling of spurs as they formulate the laws of war and the equations of battle." The latter portion of the book is by way of being a tract against militarism. How much of this did Euclides feel at the time he threw down his sword? How much of it came as the result of later experience, at Canudos and elsewhere? One thing we know is that he was to fight for the Republic, for the revolution and against the counterrevolution. But always he gave evidence of abhorring violence; for he was essentially "animated by a profound respect for the human personality."[54]

Meanwhile, in São Paulo, under the pseudonym of "Proudhon," Euclides was, as we would say today, conducting a column, one which at first bore the rubric, "Social Questions," and later, "Words and Deeds." After a short time he returned to Rio to resume his studies at the Polytechnic, and he was in the capital when the Republic was proclaimed. Upon the pleas of his fellow-students and through the influence of Benjamin Con-

[53] See pp. 84 ff.

[54] *Ibid.*: "animado do culto da personalidade humana." As a contemporary critic, Almir de Andrade, has pointed out, the same may be said of Freyre himself.

stant, he was reinstated in the army and promoted to the rank of student lieutenant; and, following a course at the Escola Superior de Guerra, he was made a second lieutenant and then a first lieutenant. Under Floriano Peixoto, he put in a year of field work as an engineer and had barely returned to Rio de Janeiro when the revolt of 1893 broke out. Once again he was on the side of the government, constructing trenches and sanitary works, both sides, it is said, being equally grateful for the latter. He was a democrat at heart, no doubt of that, a progressive-minded man of his age, even though his skeptical temperament and the social-political conditions of the time, the "fantasy of universal suffrage," may have caused him now and then to doubt the practical workings of democracy in Brazil. In certain respects, as in his attitude toward the inhabitants of the backlands, he was in advance of his age. At other times he seems to have reacted instinctively, and not always with clarity, in obedience to a deeply imbedded impulse of his nature against violence. An instance of this occurred upon the suppression of the revolt, when, by protesting in letters to a newspaper against the death sentence which had been imposed upon the dynamiters of a republican journal, he once more found himself in the bad graces of the army.[55]

Removed from posts of responsibility for a time, he was set to building barracks in the provinces; and in 1896 he left the army and took up civil engineering, being given employment on the public works of the state of São Paulo. He was engaged in this occupation when the Canudos "rebellion" broke out, and, in the company of the São Paulo battalion, he was sent to "cover" the uprising for the newspaper known as the *Estado de São Paulo*.

The story of Canudos, of the fanatic Messiah, Antonio Conselheiro, and his backwoods followers and their one-year war—for a war it proved to be—against the military might of the Brazilian government, cannot and need not be told here. It is the theme of this book. It may merely be remarked that "disturbances" and uprisings of this sort have been all too common in modern Brazilian history. There was the sanguinary episode of Pedra Bonita; there was the "revolution" of Padre Cicero, in Joazeiro, in 1914.[56] This was the tragic page of his country's annals that Euclides da Cunha scanned as he watched the last heroic resistance of the *sertanejos* at Canudos, in October, 1897. What were his reactions to it all? They will be found clearly set forth in the concluding pages of his chapter on "Man."[57] As he saw it, it was not the backland fanatics who were

[55] He also protested against the treatment of prisoners by the republican soldiers, an attempt to suffocate some of them in a jail (Grieco).

[56] See pp. 113–14, 117, 284.   [57] See pp. 50–168.

at bottom to blame but rather their countrymen of a higher stage of civilization who had left them in a centuries-old darkness, failing to prepare them for sharing the higher responsibilities of democracy. If he saw the cause, he also saw a remedy, the only remedy: "This entire campaign would be a crime, a futile and a barbarous one, if we were not to take advantage of the paths opened by our artillery, by following up our cannon with a constant, stubborn, and persistent campaign of education, with the object of drawing these rude and backward fellow-countrymen of ours into the current of our times and our own national life." Here again is the dream, the inspiring vision, of national unity—"the mystic concept of national unity," some have called it.[58] And this, when all is said, is the basic thesis of *Os Sertões*.

But it may be objected, what of Cunha's views on the racial question? It is frequently stated, by Brazilians and non-Brazilians alike, that he is an exponent of the doctrine of superior and inferior races.[59] Phrased in this manner, without qualification, the statement is inexact and misleading. It is based upon a superficial reading of Cunha. It is true enough, as Gilberto Freyre observes, that he was guilty of "ethnocentric exaggerations," that he was pessimistic with regard to the social-economic capacity of mixed races; but Freyre goes on to point out that this was due to that "rigid biologic determinism" which has been mentioned, and which in Cunha's case was inspired by the sources upon which he too completely and trustingly relied.[60] It was due to his positivistic upbringing. The laws of heredity, for instance, have for him the fixity of a dogma.[61] He was, in brief, to quote Freyre once more, "the victim of scientific preconceptions with the appearance of anthropologic truths" such as were common at the turn of the century;[62] but he did not carry his racial theories to any mystical extreme. While he was passionately concerned with national unity, he was no narrow nationalist; and the author of *Casa grande e*

[58] Freyre, *op. cit.*: "a mística da unidade brasileira."

[59] Frank, *South American Journey*, p. 339: "Da Cunha wrote Brazil's greatest book, *Os Sertões*, on the premise of Brazilian race inferiority." The Brazilian sociologist, A. Austregesilo, classifies Cunha among the "devotees of Aryanism" (see his paper, "A Mestiçagem no Brasil como factor eugénico," in the collection *Novos estudos afro-brasileiros*, ed. Gilberto Freyre [Rio de Janeiro, 1937], pp. 325–33). It should be noted that "Aryanization" in Brazil refers to the progressive "whitening" of the racial stock through intermarriage.

[60] Particularly Sampaio, Pimenta da Cunha, and Orville Derby (see Freyre, *Actualidade de Euclides da Cunha*).

[61] His stress on atavism is, for example, to be noted; even the self-sacrificing heroism and fervor of the young republican army officers are for him a manifestation of an atavistic mysticism (see pp. 365–66). He stresses heredity over environment. "Environment does not form races," he says (p. 66). A reliance upon anthropometric measurements, even, is a "quasi-philosophic materialism." Etc.

[62] In a writer like Silvio Romero, for instance (see Freyre, *Actualidade de Euclides da Cunha*).

senzala[63] is rightly convinced that Cunha, had he lived today, would not have been a totalitarian.

The idea is indeed unthinkable. The whole trend of his thought, his temperament, and his work is against it. His essential humanity, his respect for the human personality, his abhorrence of violence and militaristic aggression are too deep and all-pervading. If he was inclined to agree with Gumplowicz—inclined to fear?—that "strong races" were destined to wipe out the weak, this does not mean that he felt this was justifiable on the part of the strong. *Os Sertões* is a document against that. Having come to the conclusion that there is no such thing as a Brazilian race, a Brazilian type, he has no sooner written his "irritating parenthesis" on the inferiority of mixed stocks[64] than he discovers a "strong race" in the mestizo cowboy of the backlands, while in the *sertanejo* at Canudos he finds "the very core of our nationality, the bedrock of our race."[65] In the end it becomes a matter not of inherent inferiority but of the *stage* of racial evolution; and "biological evolution demands the guaranty of social evolution. . . . . We are condemned to civilization."[66]

The Argentine critic and student of Brazilian literature, Braulio Sánchez-Saez, sums it up when he remarks that Cunha "believed with all the strength of his heart that a Negro, an Indian, were as much Brazilians as the president of the nation, himself."[67]

Five years after the fall of Canudos, Euclides da Cunha had completed his magnum opus; but he encountered considerable difficulty at first in finding a publisher. When the book eventually appeared, in December, 1902, it had a startling overnight success, both critical and commercial; and two months later a second edition was under way. The present translation is made from the sixteenth Brazilian edition. The year following the publication of *Os Sertões*, its author was elected to the Historical Institute and to the Brazilian Academy. Among the votes which he received for the Academy seat was that of Machado de Assis. The speech of reception was made by Silvio Romero.

Whatever else he may or may not have been, Cunha was a hard worker. He was no ivory-tower inmate but a practicing engineer, toiling at his

---

[63] Gilberto Freyre, *Casa grande e senzala* (2d ed.; Rio de Janeiro: J. G. de Oliveira, 1936). This work is soon to appear in English translation. If *Os Sertões* is the early-century statement of Brazil's racial-national question, *Casa grande e senzala* is the contemporary one, indicating the solution which Brazilians believe they have found or are finding. See the article by Dr. Lewis Hanke, "Gilberto Freyre, Social Historian," *Quarterly Journal of Inter-American Relations*, I, No. 3 (July, 1939), 24–44.

[64] See pp. 84 ff. [66] See p. 54.

[65] "See Author's Notes," Note V, p. 481. [67] *Op. cit.*

trade. From 1898 to 1902 he was engaged, simultaneously, in building a bridge and in writing his masterpiece, and the two were completed at one and the same time. Directing the work of construction by day, at night he labored on the curious, rough-hewn architecture of his prose. São José do Rio Pardo, where the bridge and the book were built, is today the Mecca of *"euclidianismo,"* the Cunha cult, and the wooden shack in which *Os Sertões* was composed is a venerated relic.[68]

The closing years of Euclides da Cunha's brief life, from 1902 on, were spent as a sanitary engineer, as a government surveyor of frontiers—in which sense it was he "made geography"—and as a professor of logic in the Pedro II Institute. In 1905 we find him touring the Amazon region for the federal government and writing verses in his leisure hours.[69] His life, however, was far from being a tranquil one, for he appears to have had the faculty of becoming involved in bitter quarrels and disagreeable incidents.[70] In 1907 his book, *Perú versus Bolivia*, a treatise on the boundary dispute between the two countries, was written in a month's time, which was considered something of a miracle in those days. The same year saw the publication of his collection of Brazilian and South American studies, *Contrastes e confrontos* ("Contrasts and Comparisons"), a work which is by way of being an expanded epilogue to *Os Sertões*. This year, also, he delivered his lecture on "Castro Alves and His Times." In 1908 he entered the competition in logic at the Pedro II Institute and was awarded second place, first place going to Brazil's best-known philosopher, Farias Brito. In connection with this competition, Euclides submitted two theses, one for the written examination on "Truth and Error" and one for the oral on "The Idea of Being." The following year, 1909, he was appointed to a chair in the institution and had given nineteen lectures when he was struck down by an assassin's bullet.

It was on the morning of August 15, 1909, at the Piedade Station in the Estrada Real of Santa Cruz, that Euclides da Cunha was shot and killed in the street, by an army officer. The slaying, according to the commonly accepted account as given by Cunha's recent biographer, Sr. Eloy Pontes, came as the result of a grim domestic tragedy which long had

---

[68] See the article by Francisco Venâncio Filho, "A barraquinha de Euclides da Cunha," *Revista do Serviço do Patrimônio Histórico e Artístico Nacional* (Rio de Janeiro), No. 2, 1938, pp. 241–54.

[69] Agrippino Grieco. Cunha was a member of the Mixed (Peruvian-Brazilian) Boundary Commission of the Alto Purús. His Amazon papers are collected in his book, *A Margem da história*, published the year of his death (1909).

[70] The one with Estanlislau Zeballos, for instance.

rendered the victim's life a tormented one.[71] At the time of his death the author of *Os Sertões* was at work upon another book dealing with the backlands, to which he planned to give the title of *Paraíso perdido*—"Paradise Lost."

So died the man who had described himself in a verse couplet as "this *caboclo*, this tame *jagunço*, mixture of Celt, of Tapuia,[72] and of Greek." "And, indeed," says Agrippino Grieco, "there was a little of all this in him. An intimate acquaintance tells us of his disdain for clothes, of his face with its prominent cheekbones, his glance now keen and darting and now far away and absorbed, and his hair which fell down over his forehead, all of which made him look altogether like an aborigine, causing him to appear as a stranger in the city, as one who at each moment was conscious of the attraction of the forest." And Silvio Romero, upon seeing him for the first time, declared that he was the perfect type of Cariry Indian.

Toward the end of his forty-three years, Euclides would seem to have mellowed somewhat, if we are to judge from a letter to a friend which is published for the first time in the Spanish edition of *Os Sertões:*[73]

> You ask me to send you a copy of *Os Sertões;* but I must tell you in advance that I do not do so spontaneously; for this barbarous book of my youth, this monstrous poem of brutality and force, is so strange to my present tranquil way of looking at life that it is sometimes all that I myself can do to understand it. In any case, it is the first-born of my spirit, and there are audacious critics who assert that it is my one and only book. Can this be true, I wonder? It is hard to admit that with it I reached a culminating point and that I am to spend all the rest of my life coming down from this height. After you have read it, tell me, my distinguished friend, if I am to be condemned to so unenviable a fate as this. Your opinion will be most highly prized, and I should like to have it as soon as possible.

However this may be, *Os Sertões* remains a towering peak of Brazilian literature.

SAMUEL PUTNAM

PHILADELPHIA
August 6, 1943

---

[71] See Eloy Pontes, *A vida dramática de Euclides da Cunha* (Rio de Janeiro: Livraria José Olympio, 1938). For a different view of the matter, to the effect that Cunha's assailant acted in self-defense, see the rather sensational article, "Euclides da Cunha não foi assassinado," by Francisco de Assis Barbosa, in the fortnightly review, *Diretrizes* (Rio de Janeiro), V, No. 72 (November 6, 1941), 2–4, 14–20.

[72] I.e., Indian.

[73] Addressed to Mariano de Védia, son of Agustín de Védia, author of *Martín García*, for the posthumous edition of which Cunha had written an article.

TABLE OF CONTENTS

BIBLIOGRAPHY OF THE WORKS OF
EUCLIDES DA CUNHA[1]

Os Sertões (*Campanha de Canudos*). First edition, Rio de Janeiro: Laemmert & Cia, December, 1902. One volume, with vii and 632 pages, 4 maps, and 4 engravings; list of errata and index. Second edition, with notes and index, June, 1903. Third edition, 1905. (The second and third editions are of 611 pages each.)

Os Sertões (*Campanha de Canudos*). Fourth edition, Rio de Janeiro: Francisco Alves, 1911. One volume, with 620 pages, 4 maps, 6 engravings, and notes.

Os Sertões (*Campanha de Canudos*). Fifth edition, Rio de Janeiro: Livraria Francisco Alves, 1914. One volume, with 620 pages, 4 maps, 6 engravings, and notes. This is the *ne varietur* edition, based upon the copy found among the author's papers with the notation: "Text to serve as the definitive edition." Intended for the fourth edition, this revised text was found too late; it accordingly serves as the basis of the fifth edition, which was prepared under the supervision of Afrânio Peixoto. Between this and the first edition there are more than fifteen hundred stylistic emendations. The Preface is lacking. The treasured copy with the emendations is in the possession of Dr. Belisario Tavora.

Os Sertões (*Campanha de Canudos*). Sixth edition, 1923. Seventh edition, 1924. Eighth edition, 1925. Ninth edition, 1926. Tenth edition, 1928. (In this edition the "Preliminary Note" once more appears.) Eleventh edition, 1929. All these editions were published by Francisco Alves, in Rio de Janeiro.

Os Sertões (*Campanha de Canudos*). Twelfth edition, Rio de Janeiro: Livraria Francisco Alves, 1933. This edition was carefully revised by Fernando Nery, who added the marginal subtitles.[2]

Os Sertões (*Campanha de Canudos*). Thirteenth edition, Rio de Janeiro: Livraria Francisco Alves, 1936. Fourteenth edition, 1939. Fifteenth edition, 1940. Sixteenth edition, 1942. The sixteenth edition, upon which the present translation is based, contains x and 646 pages (614 pages of text proper). It has the "Preliminary Note," the "Author's Notes" to the third edition, an index, the publisher's notices to the fifth and twelfth editions, a photograph of the author, facsimile pages of the third edition with the author's corrections, 4 maps, and 3 full-page illustrations in the body of the text.

Los Sertones (*Os Sertões*). "Biblioteca de autores brasileños," No. IV. Buenos Aires: Imprenta Mercatali, 1938. Two volumes. This is the Spanish translation by Benjamín de Garay, with a Foreword by Mariano de Védia.

Relatorio da Comissão Mista Brasileiro-Peruana do Reconhecimento do Rio Purús. First official edition, Rio de Janeiro: Imprensa Nacional, 1906. One volume, with 180 pages, 2 maps. Out of print. This is the report, prepared by Cunha, of the Mixed Brazilian-Peruvian Commisson for the surveying of national boundary lines in the Alto Purús region.

Castro Alves e seu tempo. First edition, Rio de Janeiro: Imprensa Nacional, 1907. One volume, with 44 pages. Lecture by Cunha on "Castro Alves and His Times," de-

---

[1] Condensed from a bibliography by Afrânio Peixoto.

[2] These subtitles are centered subheadings in the present translation.

livered at the Centro Onze de Agosto, in São Paulo. Second edition, Rio de Janeiro: Gremio Euclides da Cunha, 1917. One volume, with 36 pages, 2 portraits.

Perú versus Bolivia. First edition, Rio de Janeiro: Livraria Francisco Alves, 1907. One volume, with 201 pages. (Out of print.) Second edition, Rio de Janeiro: Livraria José Olimpio, 1939. One volume, with 194 pages. Preface by Oliveira Lima.

La Cuestión de límites entre Bolivia y el Perú. First edition, Buenos Aires: Compania Sul-americana de Billetes de Banco, 1908. One volume, with 151 pages, 1 map. Translation of the *Perú versus Bolivia*, made on the order of the Bolivian plenipotentiary, Elliodoro Villazon.

Contrastes e confrontos. First edition, Porto: Empresa Literaria Tipográfica, 1907. One volume, with 248 pages, a portrait of the author, and a "Supplementary Note" (preface) by José Pereira de Sampaio (Bruno). This volume of "Contrasts and Comparisons" contains chapters on "Heroes and Bandits," "The Iron Marshal," "The Kaiser," "German Arcadia," "The Life of Statues," "Anchieta," "The Diamond-hunters," "An Historical Comedy," "Plan for a Crusade" (III), "The Mission of Russia," "Across the Himalayas," "Conjectures," "Contrasts and Comparisons," "Inevitable Conflict," "Against the Rubber-planters," "Between Madeira and Javari," "South American Solidarity," "The American Ideal," "Vague Fears," "The Sphinx," "Desert-makers," "Among the Ruins," "Provisory Nativism," "An Old Problem," "Along a Highway," and "Civilization." A second edition, in the same year (1907), contains, in addition to the chapters listed, a Brazilian Academy discourse by Cunha. 342 pages. Third edition, 1913. One volume, with 342 pages, same chapters, preface by Bruno, Araripe Junior, and João Luso. Fourth and fifth editions, same publisher and same contents, no dates supplied by the bibliographer. Sixth edition, Rio de Janeiro: Livraria Chardeon (Lelo & Irmão), 1923.

Martín García. By Agustín de Védia. First edition, Buenos Aires: Imprenta y Casa Editorial Coni Hermanos, 1908. One volume, with 113 pages. Contains the Spanish translation of Cunha's essay on *Martín García* and other Uruguayan and Argentine works.

A Margem da história. First (posthumous) edition, Porto: Livraria Chardeon (Lelo & Irmão), 1909. One volume, with 390 pages and a portrait of the author. Contains the following essays: (Part I) "Land without a History" (Amazonia), "General Impressions," "Abandoned Rivers," "A Calumniated Climate," "The Rubber-planters," "Judas Ahasuerus" (excerpt), "Brazilians," "Transacreana"; (Part II) "Miscellaneous Studies," "South American Railway," "Martín García," "The Primacy of the Pacific"; (Part III) "Outline of Political History," "From Independence to the Republic"; (Part IV) "Undecipherable Stars." Second edition, 398 pages, no date supplied. Fourth edition, 1926.

Canudos (Diário de uma expedição). Rio de Janeiro: Livraria José Olimpio, 1939. One volume, with 186 pages and Introduction by Gilberto Freyre. Cunha's original newspaper articles on the Canudos Campaign.

A SELECTED LIST OF WORKS, PASSAGES, AND ARTICLES ON EUCLIDES DA CUNHA[3]

Andrade, Olimpio de Souza. *"Os Sertões* numa frase de Nabuco," *Planalto,* Vol. I, No. 14, December 1, 1941. (Deals with Joaquim Nabuco's famous saying that Cunha wrote *"com cipó*—with a liana stalk.")

Filho, Francisco Venâncio (ed.). *Euclides da Cunha e seus amigos (Correspondência, colligida, prefaciada e annotada por Francisco Venâncio Filho).* São Paulo: Editora

[3] Compiled by the translator.

Nacional, 1938. (This collection of the correspondence, in addition to the editor's notes, has an interesting Introduction giving the various opinions on Cunha.)

———. "A Barraquinha de Euclides da Cunha," *Revista do Serviço do Partimônio Histórico e Artístico Nacional* (Rio de Janeiro), No. 2, 1938, pp. 241–54. (An account of the "shack" in which *Os Sertões* was written.)

FREYRE, GILBERTO. *Actualidade de Euclides da Cunha*. Rio de Janeiro: Edição da Casa do Estudante do Brasil, 1941. (Deals particularly with Cunha's social-racial views and the sources of those views.)

GRIECO, AGRIPPINO. *Evolução da prosa brasileira*. Pp. 281–86. Rio de Janeiro: Ariel, Editora Ltda., 1933. (A literary "placement" of Cunha by one of Brazil's leading contemporary critics.)

PONTES, ELOY. *A Vida dramática de Euclides da Cunha*. Rio de Janeiro: Livraria José Olimpio, 1938. (The life of the author of *Os Sertões*.)

SÁNCHEZ-SAEZ, BRAULIO. "Euclides da Cunha: Constructor de nacionalidad," *Agonía* (Buenos Aires), No. 4, October–December, 1939, pp. 5–56. (View by a Spanish-American critic and student of Brazilian literature.)

Vultos da geografia do Brasil: Coletânea das ilustrações publicadas na "Revista Brasileira de Geografia," oferta do Instituto Brasileiro de Geografia e Estatística, etc., pp. 12–13. Rio de Janeiro, 1940. (Portrait and biobibliographical sketch of Cunha as a geographer.)

WORKS IN ENGLISH

CUNNINGHAM-GRAHAM, R. B. *A Brazilian Mystic*. New York: 1925. (The story of Antonio Conselheiro, based upon the account in *Os Sertões*.)

FRANK, WALDO. *South American Journey*. Pp. 311–19 (see also pp. 36, 50, 339). New York: Duell, Sloan & Pearce, 1943.

ZWEIG, STEFAN. *Brazil, Land of the Future*. Pp. 158–60. New York: Viking Press, 1942.

ACKNOWLEDGMENTS AND EDITORIAL NOTE

THE translator desires to acknowledge his indebtedness and express his thanks to a number of persons for their invaluable assistance in the preparation of the English-language version of *Os Sertões*. He wishes first of all to thank Dr. Lewis Hanke, assistant chief, Division of the American Republics, State Department; Dr. Robert C. Smith, assistant chief, Hispanic Foundation, Library of Congress; and Major Preston E. James, chief, Latin American Division, Office of Strategic Services, for their kindness in reading the manuscript and their numerous helpful suggestions. He is particularly indebted to Major James for much patient assistance with the troublesome geological passages in chapter i. The *Strategic Index of Latin America* at Yale University has been constantly helpful with regard to botanical, zoölogical, and topographical terms and special idioms. Among the members of this project who freely gave their help were Dr. Benjamin Paul, supervisor, Dr. Benjamin Keen, bibliographer, and Mr. Donald Farquahar, Mrs. Helen MacMillan, and Mr. Bernard Siegel. Dr. Paul Russell, associate botanist, Bureau of Plant Industry, United States Department of Agriculture, has graciously checked the botanical nomenclature; and thanks must be extended to Dr. Walter T. Swingle of the same bureau for his kind co-operation. Help on "Brazilian language" expressions has been given by Mr. Ben Brender, of Brooklyn, New York. Thanks for research assistance are due to Dr. Charmion Shelby and Dr. Alexander Marchant, Library of Congress; to Dr. Manoel Cardozo, Lima Library, Catholic University of America; to Dr. W. Rex Crawford, University of Pennsylvania; and to the translator's son, Hilary Whitehall Putnam. The general and final shaping of this version owes much to Mr. W. K. Jordan, editor, and Mr. John T. McNeill, acting editor, of the University of Chicago Press. And, finally, the translator wishes to thank his wife, Riva Putnam, for her constant encouragement and her assistance in the preparation of the manuscript.

In the spelling of Brazilian geographic names in this translation, the simplified orthography adopted by the Instituto Brasileiro de Geografia e Estatística has been followed.

Footnotes by the translator are in brackets; those by the author are without brackets. Cross-references outside of brackets are by the editor of the Brazilian edition.

The illustrations were selected especially for the American edition.

S. P.

PREFACE

BY

AFRÂNIO PEIXOTO
Member of the Brazilian Academy of Letters

EUCLIDES DA CUNHA was a military engineer, one who came up from the ranks; later, he reported a military campaign for a large daily; and, finally, he was a builder of bridges and a surveyor of frontiers. This is as much as to say that his training as a writer had a scientific basis, with mathematics and geography as the vigilant handmaidens of his mind. In place of that bookish erudition which is common with those who set out to win fame in literature, he had a knowledge of nature gained through his previous studies which was to make of him an outstanding figure in our national letters.

This is reflected not alone in the content of his works but in the very style in which his thought is clothed. That freshness of imagery and of concepts which came to him from his exact and experimental knowledge of science stood in contrast to the artificial flowers of rhetoric to be found in other writers. With it, he cast a spell upon his contemporaries, a spell that endures to this day, after forty years; for the new generations which have since come upon the scene have not yet succeeded in emancipating themselves from the moldy images of the literary huckster's stock-in-trade, and Euclides da Cunha's directness and exactness in the matter of language only serve to throw into relief the general obsolescence of our writers, old and new, all of whom belong to the past in their way of thinking and their mode of speech. Euclides remains fresh and original. To employ the American word, he is *different!*

Meanwhile, the time has come to appraise him, not merely with regard to the external aspects of his style, but with regard, as well, to the contexture of ideas and tendencies discoverable in his writings. Euclides is our number-one geographer and sociologist, one who, in place of viewing his native land with patriotic emphasis as "my country, right or wrong," has, rather, seen it and studied it, and has drawn his deductions as to what this land really is and, as a consequence, what manner of man it is that springs from such a soil—how the land may be changed and man thereby may become a different being from the one he is. Sociology here is made dependent upon a historical moment in which human intercom-

munication, through miscegenation, is incapable of altering the population of a land—a population that remains a direct expression of the soil.
The truth is that the more rudimentary a civilization, the more it depends upon the physical environment; and civilization itself may be defined as the process of removing man from territorial contingencies. The
prisoner of his native heath then becomes, through civilization, a man
who has made his escape into the world.

Starting from the premise of the land, Euclides sketches in for us the
rudimentary geography of the Brazilian backlands and the transitory,
changing sociology of the backlands peoples. His masters were certain
scholars, and it is a pleasure to state that they were North American
scholars. From Orville Adelbert Derby he learned applied geography, and
with John Caspar Bramer he delved into the mysteries of geology, having previously studied aboriginal archeology with Charles Frederick
Hartt. And there were Maury and Milnor Roberts—how many others?—
who were his able tutors, all of them. If as a reporter he was first of all
impressed by the human panorama, as a scholar he looked beyond the
apparent reality and from the earth proceeded to derive its people, explaining the human rebellion, half-religious, half-political, implicit in a
civil war, by the backwoodsman's lack of culture and the primitive character of life in the hinterland.

Out of all this came his great book, *Os Sertões*, in which the shortsighted
will find merely an account of a very ordinary military campaign in
Brazil's uncivilized backlands; those of keener vision, on the other hand,
looking beyond appearances, will find in it a scientific document dealing
with a phase of human civilization in which man was governed by the
earth and his destiny was determined by it. If it be true that natives
alone are in a position to judge of the freshness, and I should go so far as
to say the unexampled originality, of the style, yet even when translated
into another language, leaving aside the reportorial leitmotiv of the military campaign, the better and greater part of the book, the definitive, the
human part, remains, in the form of an always impressive document of
man's struggle with the earth—an earth that bestows upon him its own
direct imprint. In North America, where this sociological phase has long
since passed, and in Brazil, where it still is to be seen here and there in all
its virgin primitiveness, the geographer and the sociologist will ever welcome a work of science which is at the same time a work of art; for what
this particular geographer and sociologist is giving us here are the history
and the biography of our soil, nothing other than a slice of our Brazilian
life and the life of our backlands.

If the Book of Genesis may be said to be, in the symbolism that it holds for the faithful, a biography of earth, Euclides da Cunha's *Os Sertões* is a Genesis which in epic accents tells of the meeting of civilization and barbarism; it is a saga of the first flaming days of the earth and of man and of primal man's first direct contact with other men known as civilized, from other, supposedly cultured, lands that did not know how to bring civilization and, creating a slaughter-house of banditry, were able only to destroy. Like Genesis, *Os Sertões* has its moral.

Such is this book, worthy of appearing in a language that is broader, more universal in its appeal. It is a book that represents a moment in the history of humanity; and, thanks to its style, its art, and its science, that ephemeral moment is destined to be eternal.

RIO DE JANEIRO
1943

PRELIMINARY NOTE

WRITTEN in the rare intervals of leisure afforded by an active and tiring life, this book, which originally set out to be a history of the Canudos Campaign, subsequently lost its timeliness when, for reasons which need not be mentioned here, its publication was deferred. We have accordingly given it another form, the theme which was the dominant one in the beginning and which inspired the work being now little more than a variation on the general subject here treated.

It is our purpose to sketch in, however inadequately, for the gaze of future historians, the most significant present-day characteristics of the subraces to be found in the backlands of Brazil. We do this for the reason that the instability of the multiple factors and diverse combinations that go to make up this ethnic complex, together with the vicissitudes of history and the lamentable lack of mental enlightenment which prevails among them, is likely to render these races short-lived, destined soon to disappear before the growing exigencies of civilization and the intensive material competition offered by the stream of immigrants that is already beginning to invade our land with profound effect. The fearless *jagunço*, the ingenuous *tabaréo*, and the stolid *caipira*[1] are types that will soon be relegated to the realm of evanescent or extinct traditions.

The first effects of various ethnic crossings are, it may be, initially adapted to the formation of a great race; there is lacking, however, a state of rest and equilibrium, which the acquired velocity of the march of the peoples in this century no longer permits. Backward races today, tomorrow these types will be wholly extinguished. Civilization is destined to continue its advance in the backlands, impelled by that implacable "motive force of history" which Gumplowicz, better than Hobbes, with a stroke of genius, descried in the inevitable crushing of weak races by the strong.

The Canudos Campaign[2] has, therefore, the undeniable significance of a first assault in a struggle that may be a long one. Nor is there any reason to modify this assertion in view of the fact that it was we, the sons of

[1] [The meaning of these terms, applied to backland types, is made clear later. Consult the "Glossary of Terms"]

[2] [The newspaper articles which the author wrote in connection with this campaign, recently given posthumous publication, bear the subtitle, "Diary of an *Expedition*" (see *Canudos: Diário de uma expedição* [Rio de Janeiro, 1939]).]

the same soil, who staged this campaign; inasmuch as, being ethnological-
ly undefined, without uniform national traditions, living parasitically on
the brink of the Atlantic in accordance with those principles of civilization
which have been elaborated in Europe, and fitted out by German industry,
we played in this action the singular role of unconscious mercenaries.[3]
What is more, these extraordinary native sons, living in a prevalent dis-
unity upon a land that was in part unknown to them, are wholly separated
from us by a co-ordinate of history—time.

The campaign in question marked a backward step, an ebb in the direction of the past. It was in the integral sense of the word a crime and,
as such, to be denounced.

Hence, in so far as lies within our power, we propose to do justice to
that admirable saying of Taine concerning the honest narrator who looks
History in the face as she deserves: "... Il s'irrite contre les demi-vérités
qui sont des demi-faussetés, contre les auteurs qui n'altèrent ni une date,
ni une généalogie, mais dénaturent les sentiments et les moeurs, qui gar-
dent le dessin des événements et en changent la couleur, qui copient les
faits et défigurent l'âme: il veut sentir en barbare, parmi les barbares, et,
parmi les anciens, en ancien."

EUCLIDES DA CUNHA

São Paulo, 1901

[3] [See "Author's Notes," Note I, p. 479].

I

THE BACKLANDS

CHAPTER I

THE LAND

I

THE central plateau of Brazil descends, along the southern coast, in unbroken slopes, high and steep, overlooking the sea; it takes the form of hilly uplands level with the peaks of the coastal mountain ranges that extend from the Rio Grande to Minas. To the north, however, it gradually diminishes in altitude, dropping eastward to the shore in a series of natural terraces which deprive it of its primitive magnitude, throwing it back for a considerable distance in the direction of the interior.

Accordingly, one who traverses it to the north is aware of notable changes in landscape relief: first of all, the continuous, dominant row of mountains which form a prominently jutting girdle above the projecting shore line; then, on the segment of seashore between Rio de Janeiro and Espírito Santo, a stretch of rocky coast made up of disjointed mountain ranges, studded with peaks and corroded by mountain streams, indented with bays and broken up into islands and naked reefs, mute evidence as it were of the age-old conflict which here has been waged between the sea and the earth; after which, once the fifteenth parallel has been passed, comes an attenuation of all these characteristics—rounded ridges and tempered acclivities, with hills whose slopes form a blur on the far horizon; until, as one comes out on the coast of Baía, his gaze at last is freed from the ramparts of mountains which up to now have repelled and hemmed it in and may wander at will to the west, plunging into the heart of the broad-sweeping land that slowly emerges in a distant roll of highland plains.

This geographical facies sums up the morphogeny of the great continental mass and may be established by a closer analysis made along any short meridian following the basin of the São Francisco.

It is, in fact, evident that what we have here is three different geological formations, of ages hard to determine, one supplanting another or the three intermingling in discordant stratifications, the predominance of one or two or the combination of all three going to form the variable features of the earth's physiognomy. First, there are the powerful gneiss-granite

3

masses which, starting on the extreme south, curve around in a huge amphitheater, rearing those admirable landscapes which so enchant and at the same time prove such an illusion to the unaccustomed gaze of strangers. Beginning at a point where they overlook the sea, they proceed in successive chains, without lateral spurs, to the edge of the São Paulo littoral, constituting a broadened wall to support the sedimentary formations of the interior. The land here lords it over the ocean, dominating it from the top of the cliffs; and to climb these heights is like coming out to the edge of a majestic dais: one is ready to approve all the exaggerated descriptions—the Gongorism of a Rocha Pita,[1] the inspired extravagances of a Buckle[2]—which would make of this land a privileged region of the earth, one where Nature has fitted out her most prodigious workshop. And, indeed, from the threefold point of view—astronomic, topographic, and geologic—it is hard to imagine any so propitious to life as this.

When the mountains have been crossed, along the gleaming line of the tropic, there may be seen stretching away to the northwest extensive plains whose warp, consisting of horizontal layers of clayey sandstone, intercalated with juttings of limestone, or *dikes* of basic eruptive rocks, at once explains this unparalleled exuberance and these vast level-lying areas. The earth here exercises an irresistible attraction for man, hurling him into the very current of those rivers which, from the Iguassú to the Tieté, forming a most original hydrographic network, flow down from the coast through the interior, as if they had taken their rise in the sea, to carve a channel for their eternal energies in the depths of the opulent forest. They readily break through these strata in uniform beds, without depressed thalwegs, and give to the general lay of the land up to the far side of Paraná the form of broad, undulating, immeasurably large plains.

Meanwhile, to the east, Nature takes on a different aspect. Here, it is harshly stereographed in the rigid folds of gneiss formations; and the slope of the plateaus drops in the terrace of Mantiqueira, where the Paraíba flows, or breaks up into spurs which, after skirting the heights centering about Itatiaia, go on to carry the Alpine landscapes of the shoreland all the way to the heart of Minas. Upon entering this latter state, however, despite the tumultuous appearance of the mountain lands, one is aware of a general slow descent to the north. As on the high plains of São Paulo and Paraná, all the tributaries disclose this imperceptible slope by the

---

[1] [Sebastião da Rocha Pita, a seventeenth-century writer, imitator of the Spanish Góngora and author of a "History of Portuguese America" (*História da América portuguesa*).]

[2] [See Henry Thomas Buckle, *Introduction to the History of Civilization in England* (London: George Routledge & Sons, Ltd., 1872), chap. ii, "Influence Exercised by Physical Laws," pp. 59–61.]

tortuous character of their river beds, revealing the effort made to over-come the permanent antagonism of the mountains. The Rio Grande by the sheer force of its current breaks through the Canastra Range, and, along the meridian line, the deep erosion valleys of the Rio das Velhas and the São Francisco may be seen opening up. At the same time, beyond the elevations which run from Barbacena to Ouro Preto, the primitive forma-tions disappear, even in the major eminences, and are replaced by a com-plex series of rock-crystal formations with fertile veins running through them, in this the legendary land of gold.

The structural change gives rise to landscape pictures that are more imposing than those of the seaboard. The nature of the rocks, as revealed along the edges of the quartzite hills or in the heaped folds of quartz over-running the summits, exhibits all the characteristics to be met with, from the mountain mass that extends from Ouro Branco to Sabará, to the dia-mond zone which stretches away to the northeast, in rolling hills that rise to the level of the peaks of the Espinhaço Range; and this latter, notwith-standing the suggestive term employed by Eschwege,[3] hardly stands out among those tablelands which go to determine the dominant character of the landscape. It is from here that all those bubbling streams, from the Jequetinhonha to the Doce, descend to the east, falling in cascades or leaping over a succession of "crossings"[4]—streams that go to water the lower-lying terraces of the plateau along the base of the Aymorés Range. To the west, those waters destined for the catch basin of the São Francisco turn stagnant; and in this latter valley, after one has passed the interesting limestone formations of the Rio das Velhas, sprinkled with lakes and un-dermined with subterranean brooks and rivulets (where the caverns of the prehistoric man of Lund are to be found), one becomes aware of other marked transitions in the superficial contexture of the soil.

As a matter of fact, those former layers which we found superimposed on the granite rocks now fall away in turn, being overlaid with other, more recent ones, composed of dense strata of sandstone. A fresh geo-logical horizon appears, with novel and interesting features. Insufficiently studied up to now, the truth is, it is a more than usually significant one, particularly with regard to the distribution of the mountain chains. The

[3] [M. C. von Eschewege, German explorer who traveled in Brazil in the year 1811. For an account of his travels, translated from the German, see *Diário de uma viagem do Rio de Janeiro á Villa Rica, na capitania de Minas Geraes no anno de 1811* (São Paulo: Imprensa Official do Estado, 1936). The Portuguese rendering is by Lucia Furquim Nahmayer, librarian of the Instituto Histórico e Geográfico Brasileiro.]

[4] [*Travessões*: A *travessão* is "a river crossing, such as is provided by a sand-spit or series of stones" (*Strategic Index of Latin America*).]

ranges that are most prominent in the south disappear, being deeply buried under here by thick strata of later formation. The land, however, remains elevated, stretching out in broad-sweeping plains or rising in what seem to be mountains, with steep, barren sides, whose backs, nonetheless, extend in flat surfaces on a level with a horizon that is but faintly outlined by the tops of the distant saddlebacks which prolong the coast line. The tendency to a general flattening-out is thus verified. For in this coincidence of interior highlands with depressive Archaean formations, the mountainous region of Minas is seen to be a direct continuation of the extensive zone of northern plateaus.

The Grão Mogul Range, reaching out to the borders of Baía, is the first specimen of those magnificent cordillera-like uplands which have given careless geographers so much trouble; and the neighboring ranges, from O Cabral, the nearest one, to that of Mata da Corda, which stretches away toward Goiaz, are formed in the identical manner. The erosion furrows that cut them offer significant geological cross-sections. In a vertical plane proceeding upward from the base are to be viewed the same rocks which we found appearing in a line protracted along the surface: at the bottom, granite spurs tumbled into the bottom of the valleys in the form of scattered hillocks; halfway up the slopes, at an incline, the more recent folds of schist; and, at the top, overhanging these or flanking them in sharply dipping valleys, the dominant beds of sandstone, affording an admirable plastic medium for the most capricious designs of the meteorological agents. With no distinguishing row of summits, the major highlands are no more than extensive elevated plains, which end of a sudden in abrupt slopes, exhibiting the striking sculptural effects of torrential downpours on a permeable and easily dissected ground. Falling here for centuries, the mighty rains, flowing off at first to the sides in divergent lines of drainage, have little by little hollowed out these channels, carving for themselves beds which became canyons and steep-sided valleys, until the elevated plains came to be bordered with cliffs and precipices. And, depending upon the resistance of the materials in which the elements had to work, the results were various: here, they have strongly outlined upon the surface areas the last fragments of buried rock, disclosing them in the form of ridges which in height are scarcely reminiscent of the "Brazilian Himalayas" of the long ago, now crumbled in a constant ages-old disintegration; farther on, they have capriciously formed the incorrect lines of colossal *menhirs*[5] or have taken the shape of enormous circles, which, in the arrangement of their great blocks piled one upon another, call to mind

[5] [The word is in English.]

the dismantled walls of cyclopic coliseums, lying in ruins; or, again, the tops of the cliffs scattered here and there, which obliquely overhang the plains, remind one of irregular archways, the remains of the monstrous vault of the ancient cordillera, now fallen.

But these cliffs entirely disappear at various points. There is now to be seen a vast extent of plains. Climbing to them by the bordering steep slopes which give them the precise appearance of suspended "tablelands,"[6] one finds, some hundreds of feet above, extensive areas which, rounded to the view, extend for a seemingly indefinite distance, like seas. This is the exceedingly beautiful region of the Campos Gerais,[7] an expanse of undulating hills—an enormous stage where the rude company of vaqueiros, or cowboys, holds forth.

Let us cross this stage. Further along, from Monte Alto on, these natural formations break up; in a direction due north the sandstone continues to the sandy plateau of Assuaruá, until it reaches the limestone formations which give life to the landscapes along the edge of the great river,[8] extending to the line of hills broken by fissures which stand out so effectively in the fantastic outlines of Bom Jesus de Lapa;[9] while to the northeast, owing to the deep-going denudation of the slopes (for the Serra Geral continues to serve as a rampart against the trade winds, condensing them in diluvial showers), the ancient formations come to the surface and are once more visible. The mountains are disinterred.

The diamond region now appears, in Baía, a region wholly reminiscent of that of Minas, a reproduction, one might say, or, better, a prolongation, of the latter; for there is to be found here the same mineral formation, finally breaking through the sandstone beds, and rearing with the same disturbed Alpine contours along the slopes which spread out from the Tromba, or which, to the north, rise in the rock-crystal formations of the Huronian epoch to be found in the parallel Sincorá chains.

From this point onward, however, the axis of the Serra Geral becomes fragmentary and ill defined. It breaks up. The cordillera now bristles with counterforts and depressions, from which, to the east, the sources

[6] [The word *taboleiro* literally means a tea or coffee tray or a board with a brim (cf. the French *plateau*); topographically, it comes to mean a tableland.]

[7] ["The term *Campos Gerais* is used in a vague general sense for open country, which is not heavily forested. . . . . The term *gerais* and *Campos Gerais* are very vague terms and really can be used to distinguish only that country which is not heavily forested—in other words, 'open country' " (Major Preston E. James in a letter to the translator). Caio Prado Junior, in his *Formação do Brasil contemporâneo (Colonia)* (São Paulo: Livraria Martins, 1942), p. 199, n. 42, says: "Campos Gerais is a generic term, but in its special application becomes a place name, given to those *campos* which today form the Paraná plateau."]

[8] [The São Francisco.]   [9] [See pp. 176–77.]

of the Paraguassú leap forth, to tumble, foaming, over precipitous water-falls; and an irregular line of low hills, many in number, forms a confused crisscross over the entire breadth of the Campos. The topography of the region undergoes a transformation, reflective of the furious clash of the elements which has raged here for thousands of years, among these tumbled mountains; and the slope of the plateaus, until now a gradual one, begins to show considerable unevenness. This is revealed by the windings and twistings of the São Francisco to the east, indicative of the general change in landscape relief that is taking place. The region is here more depressed and rugged in appearance. Along the lower terraces there is a jumble of hills scattered at random. A final spur of the principal range, that of Itiuba, brings together a few indeterminate offshoots, fusing the northern expansions of Furna, Cocaes, and Sincorá. The land rises for a bit, then falls away in all directions, producing, on the north, the corredeira[10] which extends for two hundred and eighty miles to the backwaters of the Sobradinho; to the south, in scattered segments, this terrain extends beyond Monte Santo; and, to the east, it passes beneath the uplands of Geremoabo, to come out in the prodigious Paulo Affonso Falls.

The observer who has followed such an itinerary, leaving behind him a region where the broad sweep of the Campos forms a most beautiful contrast with the mountain summits, upon reaching this point stops short in surprise.

ENTRYWAY TO THE BACKLANDS

He now finds himself upon a terrace of the continental range to the north. On the one side, the São Francisco River forms a semicircle about it, embracing two quadrants; and, on the other side, likewise curving to the southeast, in a normal line to the original direction, is the sinuous course of the Itapicurú-assú. Following a median running almost parallel between these two streams, with the same significant drop to the coast, may be seen the outline of another river, the Vasa-Barris, the "Irapiranga" of the Tapuias, of which the initial Geremoabo segment is a cartographer's fantasy. The fact of the matter is, the stupendous drop with which the eroded slopes of the plateau fall to the sea, or to the Paulo Affonso backwater, afford no point of equilibrium for a normal hydrographic network; and the torrential rains, together with the chaotic drainage system, accordingly give to this corner of Baía an exceptionally wild appearance.

---

[10] [A *corredeira* is a river course with a succession of small waterfalls.]

"TERRA IGNOTA"

As one approaches it, one begins to understand why it is that, until
now, the data or exact details concerning this vast tract of territory,
which is almost equal to the land of Holland in extent (9°11′–10°20′ of
latitude and 4°–3° of longitude), have been so very scarce. Our best maps,
conveying but scant information, show here an expressive blank, a hiatus,
labeled *Terra Ignota*, a mere scrawl indicating a problematic river or an
idealized mountain range.

The truth is, crossing the Itapicurú on the southern side, the most advanced bands of settlers came to a halt in small hamlets—Massacará,
Cumbe, or Bom Conselho—in comparison with which the ruins of Monte
Santo take on the aspects of a city. Crossing the Itiúba Range to the southwest and following the course of tiny streams, they spread out among the
settlements on the banks or among the rare cattle ranches, being bound,
all of them, for an obscure wilderness outpost—Uauá. To the north and
east they stopped on the banks of the São Francisco, between Capim
Grosso and Santo Antonio da Gloria.

In this latter direction they did not make their way beyond the centuries-old town of Geremoabo, the extreme point of penetration in these
regions, which were always avoided by that wave of humanity which
swept up from the Baian coast land in search of the interior. For one reason or another, the stay here of these pioneers was a short one, and they
speedily departed without leaving any trace. None settled here. None
could settle here. This strange region, at a distance of less than a hundred
and sixty-five miles or so from the ancient metropolis,[11] was destined to be
absolutely forgotten throughout the four hundred years of our history.
For, while the roving bands of the south would pause on the edge of it,
and, after squinting up the sides of the Itiúba, would hasten on by way of
Pernambuco and Piauí to Maranhão, those from the east, repelled by the
insurmountable barrier of Paulo Affonso, would go on to seek in the Paraguassú and the rivers that lie to the south of it a more practicable line of
access. Meanwhile, the region in between remained inaccessible and unknown. Even those who went in the latter direction, keeping to the shorter route, could not but be forcibly struck by the strange aspect of the land
and its unexpected changes of appearance.

Leaving the seashore and proceeding due west, these adventurous explorers would have gone but a few miles before they found their enthusiasm
diminished or completely evaporated, once the mirage of opulent shore

[11] [Baía.]

line had been blotted out. From Camassary on, the ancient formations are overlaid with thin Tertiary patches, alternating with chalk basins covered over with the sandy terrain of Alagoinhas and barely creating a rift, to the east, in the limestone outcroppings of Inhambupe. The vegetation round about undergoes a change, copying these alternations with the precision of a draughtsman's tracing. The forests thin out and finally disappear completely, after having sent out a few scattered growths over the top of the highlands; and these latter, here and there, becoming all the time fewer in number, form islands or promontories in the barren plains of the Campos, where a characteristic flora—twining shrubs interspersed with reddish bromelias—is the only one to be found over broad areas, closely rivaling the vigorous vegetation which radiates from Pojuca over the fertile topsoil, or *massapé*, of the decomposed chalk layers.

From now on the sterile Tertiary formations reappear above the more ancient ones which, meanwhile, are dominant throughout the entire zone centering in Serrinha. The Lopes and Lagedo Hills stand forth like misshapen pyramids of smooth, rounded blocks; and those that succeed them, skirting on one side or the other the Saúde and Itiúba ranges, all the way to Villa Nova da Rainha and Joazeiro, display precisely the same contours, with cracked slopes through which appears the buried framework of the mountains. The observer has the impression that he is passing around the scarped margin of a plateau. In reality, he is treading a path that is three centuries old, the historic trail along which the rude inhabitants of the backlands advanced on their excursions into the interior. They did not alter it in the least, and civilization later has not changed it by laying down alongside the bandeirante's[12] trail the tracks of a modern railway.

This road, whose four-hundred-mile length from Baía to Joazeiro is intersected by innumerable bypaths to the west and south, from its middle portion onward fails to show the slightest appreciable variation to the east and north. Following it in the direction of Piauí, Pernambuco, Maranhão, and Pará, the settlers, in accordance with their various destinations, would split up in Serrinha; and, going on to Joazeiro or turning to the right, by way of the royal highway of Bom Conselho, which, since the seventeenth century, took them to Santo Antonio da Gloria and Pernambuco, they would in either case invariably skirt and contrive to avoid this desolate and sinister region, thereby sparing themselves the hardship of crossing it.

[12] [Member of one of the *bandeiras*, or armed bands, of the pioneer days in Brazil.]

As a result, these two lines of penetration, bounded by the São Francisco at distant points—Joazeiro and Santo Antonio da Gloria—came to be looked upon in those days as marking the confines of a desert.

EN ROUTE TO MONTE SANTO

In the meanwhile, one who ventures to cross this tract, setting out from Queimadas for the northeast, finds nothing to surprise him at first. Along its meandering course the Itapicurú nourishes a lively vegetation, and the rocky banks of the Jacuricy are bordered with small forests. The level, sandy ground permits a rapid and easy transit. At the sides of the road are smooth, rolling tablelands. The rock, taking the form of horizontal slabs, barely pierces the topsoil and the thin sand layer that covers it.

After this, however, there are places which become increasingly arid. Having crossed the narrow strip of savannas beyond the last-named river, one is, to employ the expressive phrase of the backwoodsmen, "in the wilds." Here are shrubs with scarcely any roots in the scant earth and with intertwining branches, with solitary cacti here and there standing stiff and silent, giving to the region the appearance of the edge of a desert. The physiognomy of the inhospitable hinterland now begins to emerge, slowly and impressively.

Climb any of these rolling elevations, and you will descry, or will be able to divine, in the distance, against the melancholy of an unrelieved horizon, the uniform parched gray, without the faintest variation in coloring, of the caatingas.[13]

In the middle distance is a less sterile countryside, and in places where the decomposition of the granite is taking place *in situ*, giving rise to a few clayey patches, the tufts of the urucuri palms[14]—a brief parenthesis in the general aridity—may be seen bordering the ipueiras, or, according to the beautiful native etymology, the "dead lakes." These ipueiras marked an obligatory port of call for the traveler. Together with the water pits and rock openings known as "cauldrons," they afforded the only relief in a journey filled with many hardships. True oases, they nonetheless frequently have a gloomy appearance, being situated in depressions between barren hills, with stripped and spectral-looking mandacarú trees[15] standing all around; or else they are etched against the dusty gray of a plain, sharply

[13] [Scrub-forest lands (see pp. 30 ff.; see also Preston E. James, *Latin America* [New York: Lathrop, Lee & Shepard, 1942], p. 440).]

[14] [The *Attalea excelsa*.]

[15] [A variety of fig tree (see p. 34 and n. 47).]

outlined by the greenish-black of the unicellular algae with which they are coated.

Some of these ipueiras show the trace of exertions put forth by the sons of the hinterland. On their borders, erected like floodgates between the slopes, are crude walls of barren rock. They put one in mind of the monuments of a primitive people buried in obscurity. The common patrimony of those who here have to struggle with the privations of a fierce climate, they date in general from a remote past. They afford us a picture of those who first braved the vicissitudes of an expedition into these parts. They still stand there, indestructible; for the backwoodsman, even though he might be a lonely wayfarer, never failed to lift a stone to stay the structure at its swaying points of junction.

Having passed these structures—an imperfect copy of the Roman dikes still to be seen in Tunisia—we are once more in the drought-stricken areas. Advancing swiftly, especially along those stretches marked by a succession of small knolls, of precisely the same form and arrangement, all of them, even the most rapid traveler has a sensation of immobility. The same uniform landscapes against the same unvarying horizon, which recedes as he advances. Rarely, as in the small settlement of Cansanção, is there a wide layer of fertile topsoil bordered with greenery.

The humblest of dwellings now make their appearance, some of them having been deserted by herdsmen, who, frightened off by the drought, have left for other parts, while others are in ruins; but all of them by their impoverished appearance merely serve to heighten the melancholy aspect of the landscape.

In the vicinity of "Quirinquinquá," however, the earth takes on a more varied aspect. This small farm is situated upon a high expanse of granite, while to the north is to be seen a region of a different kind—one dotted with valleys and highlands, with fugitive peaks fading in the distance. Monte Santo, with a profile the exact opposite of those rounded contours attributed to it by the illustrious Martius,[16] rises perpendicularly in the foreground, in the form of a great dike of white quartzite with bluish tones, standing out in relief against the gneiss-rock mass which constitutes the whole of its base. Dominating with its row of almost rectilinear peaks the level land which extends to the southeast, its enormous bulk, creased by the strata exposed in the Aeolian erosion, stands forth as a monumental rampart of mountain wall. It ends in a very high crest which protracts its expanse in the direction of thirteen degrees northeast to the emplacement

[16] [C. F. P. von Martius, the early-nineteenth-century German explorer and geographer (see p. 21, n. 27).]

of the town erected at its foot. It forms the focal point of a vast horizon. It is then to be observed that, having undergone an attenuation to the south and east, the predominant characteristics of the region continue to be manifest throughout the northern quadrants.

The farm site known as the "Cauldron," some twelve miles beyond, is on the border of this metamorphic elevation; and, upon climbing the latter and leaving it behind him, one finds himself at last in the heart of the drought-ridden hinterland.

FIRST IMPRESSIONS

It is an impressive bit of country. The structural conditions of the earth combine with a maximum of violence on the part of the external agents in the carving of stupendous sculptural reliefs. The torrential rainfalls characteristic of such a climate of alternating flood and drought, coming of a sudden after protracted dry periods and beating down upon these slopes, carrying away all the loose rock mantle, have left largely exposed the older geologic series of these last mountain spurs: all the crystalline varieties, and the rough quartzites, and the phyllades and calcites, alternating or interlacing with one another and reappearing crudely at every step, barely covered with a stunted flora, and forming pictures which give the landscape here its impinging and tormented aspect.

For what all this points to—the accumulation of alluvium in the depressions, the dismantling of the hills, the winding of the river beds of intermittent streams, the constriction of the defiles, and the almost convulsive appearance of a deciduous flora lost in a maze of undergrowth—is, in a manner of speaking, the martyrdom of the earth, brutally lashed by variable elements which run the gamut of climatic conditions. On the one hand, there is the extreme dryness of the air, which in summertime, through nocturnal radiation, leads to the instantaneous loss of absorbed heat by rocks exposed to the sun's rays, subjecting them to a sudden rise and fall of temperature; whence a play of dilations and contractions that is disjunctive in effect lays them open along the planes of least resistance. On the other hand, the rains, which unexpectedly come to end the burning cycle of drought, precipitate these prolonged reactions.

The forces that work upon the earth attack both its inner contexture and its surface, with no letup in the process of demolition, one following the other with unvarying cadence in the course of the only two seasons that the region knows. The scorching summers loosen the rocks and the torrential winter rains crumble them. The process ranges from a quiet chemical decomposition to the violent disintegration produced by the tempests. The two processes work together and complement each other; and, depending upon the preponderance of one or the combination of both, they modify the aspect of Nature. The same gneiss hillocks, capriciously rent into almost geometric planes, which resemble square blocks, and which may be seen rising at various points, giving one the illusion at times of suddenly finding himself amid the lonely and deserted ruins of a majestic castle—these later on are surrounded by large stones scattered about in disorder, standing none too securely upon their narrow bases and inclining at a perilously unstable angle, which makes of them oscillating loggans or great tumbled dolmens; and, still farther along, they disappear completely beneath heaps of stone blocks, conveying a perfect picture of those "seas of stone" which are so characteristic of very dry or very cold climates. On the edge of the tumultuous hills round about, remnants of the most ancient erosion levels, they take on outlines which recall old glacier paths, here scattered at random, with their thick layers of slabs and pebbles bespeaking identical violent forces at play. The splintered fragments, where the feldspar crystals still remain cemented to the quartz, offer fresh testimony to those physical and mechanical effects which, splitting the rocks into pieces without at the same time decomposing their formative elements, exceed the slow normal action of the chemical-meteorological agents.

There is thus to be had, at every step and at all points, a sharp impression of extreme ruggedness. Relieving this in part is the appearance of depressed fields, the seat of ancient lakes now extinguished in marshy ipueiras, marking the halting-places of the herdsmen. These, however, are cut up by great boxlike river beds which are dry most of the time, being filled with water only during the brief rainy seasons. Obstructed for the most part by thick layers of stone blocks, between which, save in the case of sudden swellings, thin streams of water may be seen trickling, they are an exact reproduction of the wadies that border the Sahara. Perpendicular to their banks, as a general rule, are the strata of a dark-blue talc schist in burnished folds that give off a metallic gleam in the light—and above them, covering extensive areas, the less resistant layers of vermilion-colored clay, rent by quartz veins irregularly intercepting the stratigraphic planes. These last formations, Silurian it may be, wholly overlie the others, as one travels to the northeast, and take on there contours that are more regular. They explain the origin of those smooth-topped tablelands which, covered with a resistant vegetation of mangaba trees, spread out all the way to Geremoabo.

To the north, however, these layers show a more marked declivity.

There comes now a succession of barren hills, with gliding slopes that fall
in gullies where periodic torrents gush to undermine them; and on their
tops are to be seen, aligned in rows or taking the form of detached plates,
the same quartzose veins, exposed by the decomposition of the crystallized
formations in which they are imbedded.

In the crude light of day here in the backlands, these exceedingly rugged
hills shed about them a most ardent glow, and they glitter, darkly and
dazzlingly.

The rapid erosion, on the other hand, breaks the continuity of these
strata, which, moreover, at other points, disappear beneath the limestone
layers. This, however, does not alter the general appearance of the landscape. The ruiniform aspect of the latter formations goes well with the
other features. In places where they lie stretched out along the ground
and wholly unprotected against the erosive acidity of the tempestuous
rains,[17] they become riddled and scarified with circular cavities and deep
flutings, irregular in form but countless in number, which skirt one another
in jagged-edged corners, with very hard, sharp splinters that make walking over them impossible.

Thus, whatever path one takes, he comes upon these slight but abrupt
elevations, between which the roads wind, when they do not follow for
many miles the empty river beds of dried-up streams. And, however inexpert the observer may be, upon leaving behind him the majestic perspectives which unfold to the south and exchanging them here for the
moving sight of Nature in torment, he cannot but have the persisting impression of treading the newly upraised bed of a sea long extinct, which
still preserves, stereotyped in its rigid folds, the agitation of the waves and
the stormy deeps.

A GEOLOGIST'S DREAM

This is, indeed, a thought that lays hold of one. It is one that well
accords with the fancies of a somewhat romantic naturalist[18] who imagined that here, a long time ago, in the Tertiary period, the waves and
swirling currents of an ocean were to be found. For, despite the scarcity
of data which would permit of one of those retrospective prophecies, to
employ Huxley's polished phrase, a "prophecy" capable of delineating the
situation which prevailed in this zone in remote ages, all the characteristics which we have summed up here nonetheless go to reinforce this
hazardous conjecture.

Other considerations which strengthen it are the remarkable denuda-

[17] [See "Author's Notes," Note II, pp. 479–80.]   [18] Em Liais.

tion of the earth; the noteworthy lineal disposition of the fractures which border the mountainsides in true surface-level curves; the acclivities of the tablelands, which terminate in perpendicular slopes reminiscent of *falaises;* and, up to a certain point, the remains of Pliocene fauna, which make of the "cauldrons" enormous ossuaries of mastodons, filled with disjointed vertebrae, as if life here had been of a sudden assaulted and extinguished by the turbulent energies of a cataclysm.

There is, moreover, the presumption based upon a situation known to have existed in the past, as set forth in positive data. The researches of Frederick Hartt[19] have in fact established, in the regions roundabout Paulo Affonso, the undeniable existence of Cretaceous basins; and, inasmuch as the fossils that define these are identical with those to be met with in Peru and Mexico and are contemporary with those which Agassiz discovered in Panama—all these facts taken together lead to the deduction that a vast Cretaceous ocean rolled its waves over the frontier lands of the two Americas, joining the Atlantic to the Pacific. It thus covered a great part of the northern states of Brazil, beating there against the upper terraces of the plateaus, where extensive sedimentary deposits point to a yet older period, the Middle Paleozoic. It was then that the highest peaks of our cordillera, standing out from the great emergent islands, became barely visible to the north, in the immense solitude of the waters.

The Andes did not yet exist, and the Amazon, a broad canal between the high plains of the Guianas and those of the continent, made islands of these regions. To the south, the mountain mass of Goiaz—the oldest in the world, according to Gerber's brilliant deduction—that of Minas, and a part of the São Paulo Plateau, where the volcano of Caldas glowed in full activity, constituted the nucleus of the future continent.

For there was slowly taking place a general process of elevation: to the north, the granite masses were rising, effecting a general conjunction of the lands in a slow rotation about an axis which Liais imagines to have lain between the highlands of Barbacena and Bolivia. Simultaneously, at the beginning of the Tertiary period, there occurred that prodigious event, the elevation of the Andes; new lands now made their appearance in the waters, and the Amazonian canal became transformed into the greatest of rivers; the scattered archipelagoes formed in clusters, joined by isthmuses; the major contours of the coast were rounded out; and America slowly became a whole.

Then the lands in the far north of Baía, represented by the quartzite

---

[19] [Professor Charles F. Hartt, director of the Morgan Expedition (1870–71) for geological exploration in the Amazon region.]

rocks of Monte Santo and the summits of Itiúba, scattered through the waters, began a continuous ascent, with an increase of visible bulk. But in the course of this slow rise, while the highest regions, only recently raised above sea-level, were sprinkled with lakes, the entire middle portion of this promontory remained immersed. An impetuous current, of which the present one along our coast is a degenerate form, held it in its grip. Beating against it for a long time, while the rest of the country to the south was already above water and had assumed its present form—beating against it, eroding it, pulverizing it, swirling away to the west and carrying off all the products of erosion, the mighty current continued working on this corner of Baía, until, in accordance with the general movement of the lands, the region had wholly emerged and had become the shapeless heap of mountainous ruins that it is today.

It was at this point that the flagrant antagonism of the desert climate with the geographical lay of the land began, upon a promontory where there is nothing to recall those depressions with no outlet which are characteristic of classic deserts. We may well believe that the region, in this incipient stage, was still preparing itself for life; the lichen was still attacking the rock and fertilizing the earth. And, struggling tenaciously against the asperities of the climate, a flora endowed with a resistance that is rare in these parts was weaving its warp of roots, thereby in part preventing the torrents from carrying off all the eroded materials—gradually accumulating these latter in the conquest of a devastated land whose contours it thus softened—but, with it all, failing to prevent the inclement suns and savage waters from wearing away the soil in the course of the long summers.

Hence the dolorous impression that overcomes us as we cross this unfamiliar portion of the hinterland—it is practically a desert—whether we confine our gaze to the barren folds of the mountain lands or let it wander, monotonously, over the broad sweep of arid plains.

II

FROM THE TOP OF MONTE SANTO

From the top of Monte Santo,[20] surveying the region that extends for a radius of more than thirty miles, one may note as on a bas-relief map the disposition of its mountain ranges. It may then be seen that these ranges, in place of extending eastward on a median line with the courses of the Vasa-Barris and the Itapicurú, which would thus provide a *divortium aquarum* for these streams, continue on to the north.

[20] [See pp. 114 ff., 170 ff.]

The Grande and the Athanasio ranges now come into view. Distinct at first, the one running northwest and the other north, they come together in the Acarú Mountains, where the intermittent springs of the Bendegó and its tributaries gush forth. Thus unified, they join the Caraíbas and the Lopes ranges and are once more absorbed, forming the masses of Cambaio, from which radiate the small Caxomongó[21] and Calumby chains and, to the northwest, the towering summits of Caypan. Displaying the same tendency, the Aracaty chain, striking out to the northwest along the tablelands of Geremoabo, proceeds discontinuously in this direction, and, after having been cut through by the Vasa-Barris in Cocorobó, bends to the west, where it divides into the Canabrava and Poço de Cima, which are prolongations of it. All finally trace an elliptical curve, closed on the south by a hill, that of Favella, about the broad, rolling highlands where the settlement of Canudos stands. From this point northward, they once more scatter out, sloping down to the high plains that border the São Francisco.

Thus, as one ascends to the north, to the uplands where the Parnaíba's bed lies carved, this slope of the plateaus appears to bend back upon itself, thereby disturbing the entire drainage area of the São Francisco below its confluence with the Patamoté, with a tracery of torrential little streams that have no names and that are not to be made out on even the most favorable map drawn to scale; they impose upon the Vasa-Barris a tortuous course from which it frees itself in Geremoabo, as it curves down to the coast.

The Vasa-Barris, a river that forms no junction with any other large stream, does not conform to the declivity of the land. The small tributaries that it has, the Bendegó and the Caraíbas, with intermittent waters flowing along rudely excavated beds, do not reflect the depressions of the soil. They lead a fugitive existence, dependent upon the rainy seasons. They are, rather, drainage canals, opened at random by the torrents or swift currents which, conforming to the topographical relief of the immediate region, are, not infrequently, out of harmony with the general lay of the land as determined by the mountains. They are rivers that serve no purpose. They are suddenly filled and overflow their banks, scooping out their beds once more and overcoming the obstacle presented by the general declivity; they roll along for a few days toward the principal stream and then dry up, returning to their original aspect of winding trenches filled with stones and rubbish.

The Vasa-Barris itself, possessing no sources, while its bed nourishes a

21 [See pp. 417, 419, 420.]

growth of grasses on which flocks pasture, would not have its present course if there were a perennial current to assure it of a more stable one through the sustained force that would thus be brought to bear. Its function as a geological agent is a revolutionary one. Most of the time "cut up," broken up into stagnant ganglia, or dried up like a long, winding, dusty road, when it does rise, "full-bellied," at flood time, capturing the savage waters that beat down upon the slopes, it becomes filled for a few weeks with an ugly-looking clayey stream and is then extinguished by draining off completely, by *emptying itself*, as its Portuguese name indicates,[22] a name that happily has been substituted for the one given to this river by the natives.[23] It is a wave that billows down from the slopes of Itiúba to multiply the energy of the stream through the narrow defiles, flowing along swiftly between its banks, when it is not hemmed in by mountains, until it reaches Geremoabo.

We have seen how the natural life in these parts is limited by the cruel climate, how it is crushed to earth—an inhospitable earth—in a region that lacks the opulent landscapes of the mountains and tablelands and the boundless perspectives of the plains, one that represents, rather, an astonishing jumble of such features as the following: plains which, from close up, are seen to be a series of hillocks indented with pits or caverns; other hills that, by contrast with the surrounding fields, appear to be of great height and are in reality but a few dozen yards above the ground; and tablelands which, as one crosses them, display the ugly and chaotic features of filled-in chasms. No more of those beautiful effects which are the result of slow denudations, the remodeling of slopes, the widening of horizons, and the immeasurably broad expanse of the Campos over the breadth of the cordilleras—all of which confers upon the landscapes in question the alluring grandeur of perspectives where earth and sky appear to fuse in a distant and amazing blend of color.

Meanwhile, an unlooked-for picture awaits the traveler who, upon crossing this region, has had the sensation of treading the ruins of an earthquake, and who now climbs the slopes that are nearest to Canudos.

FROM THE TOP OF FAVELLA

It was to the top of Favella[24] that this particular traveler climbed, letting his gaze wander to take in at one sweep the entire region round about.

[22] [I.e., Vasa-Barris.]

[23] *Irapiranga*, i.e., vermilion-colored honey (see Theodoro Sampaio, *O Tupi na geographia nacional*).

[24] [See pp. 255, 305–6.]

What he saw was nothing like the scenes he had previously contemplated. Here before him was the antithesis of all that. Here were the same features, the same plain down below with the same essential ruggedness, beneath its crude covering of stony bogs and stripped caatingas. . . . . But the combination of so many harsh and irregular lines—the roving cracks that show where the pits and caverns are, the furrows that mark the precipices—created for him perspectives that were entirely new; and he almost began to understand how the credulous woodsmen, gifted with a naïve imagination, should have come to believe that "this was heaven."[25]

The settlement down below is built upon the same uneven ground. But viewed from this point, with distance softening and leveling out the slopes, all the innumerable small jutting spurs projected along the lower level and extending uniformly in all directions give it the illusory appearance of a great rolling plain. Round about, the mountains form a majestic ellipse.[26]

To the northeast, the arched and simple outlines of the Canabrava; the near-by Poço de Cima is higher and steeper; to the east is Cocorobó, with its undulating defiles and scattered spurs; the rectilinear slopes of Calumby to the south; the peaks of Cambaio, running westward; and, to the north, the restless contours of Caypan—all meeting, joining, and bending gradually to form a huge closed curve.

Viewing these proud peaks from afar, practically on a horizon level, this observer had the pleasant impression of standing upon an elevated plateau, a desert extraordinary resting on the mountaintops. On the furrowed plain below, the small, wandering, serpentine streams were scarcely distinguishable.

One alone stood out, the Vasa-Barris. It was to be seen crossing the plain, winding and twisting. At one of its turns there could be descried a major depression, surrounded by hills. And filling this depression with a jumble of innumerable rooftops, an enormous pile of huts.

III

THE CLIMATE

From the brief indications given, it may be seen that the geological and physiographic features on which the processes of denudation have been at work in these parts have succeeded in modifying the characteristic re-

---

[25] [See p. 143, where this passage is rendered clearer.]

[26] See pp. 143, 444.

sults of those processes in such a manner as to make it impossible to say which factor is the predominant one.

If, on the one hand, the genetic conditions react strongly upon the others, the latter in turn help to aggravate those conditions, and a reciprocal influence continues throughout. From this perennial conflict, staged in an endless, vicious circle, there are derived the peculiar characteristics of the locale. It is not possible to grasp these characteristics in all their manifestations. Even the most ordinary firsthand observations are lacking, thanks to the proverbial indifference with which we treat such matters in this country, with the comfortable inertia of well-fed beggars.

No scientific pioneer has as yet endured the discomforts of this corner of the hinterland for a sufficiently long time to enable him to make a definitive study of it. Von Martius came this way, with the prime objective of observing the meteorite which fell on the banks of the Bendegó and which was already, from 1810 on, known to European academies through the writings of F. Mornay and Wollaston. Making his way through this wild tract, the *desertus austral*, as he christened it, he paid little attention to the earth and the extravagant flora that covered it— *silva horrida*, in his alarmed Latin terminology. Those who preceded him and those who came after him, stung by the dog-day heat, made the same rapid tracks that he did in fleeing this region. As a consequence, this section of the backlands, always avoided, is to this day unknown and is likely to remain so for a long time to come.[27]

The result has been a set of vague conjectures. As for ourselves, we crossed this region at the beginning of a hot summer, and thus, being out of season as it were, saw it under its worst aspect. What we write here will have the disadvantage of an isolated impression, rendered all the more unfavorable by surroundings which, disturbed by the emotions of war, did not make for peace of mind. In addition, the data afforded by a single thermometer and a suspect aneroid, constituting the wretched scientific equipment with which we had to work, will fail to convey even a vague idea of a climate that varies with the slightest change in the earth's surface, showing pronounced variations within the confines of a given tract. The climate of Monte Santo, for example, which at first comparison is much superior to that of Queimadas, differs from the two places to the north of it without that intermediate continuity which we should have a

[27] [On Martius see J. B. von Spix and C. F. P. von Martius, *Travels in Brazil, 1817–1820* (London, 1924); the German original, *Reise in Brasilien*, was published at Munich in 1823–31. The Brazilian Historical and Geographical Institute, in commemoration of its centenary, published a Portuguese translation of this work: *Viagem pelo Brasil* . . . . (Rio de Janeiro, 1938).]

right to expect. The proximity of the mountainous masses gives it a stable climate, like that of a maritime region on the body of the continent. The thermometer shows only insignificant variations; a firmament where the air is always clear and wholly transparent; and prevailing winds, the southeast wind in winter and the northeast in summer, which alternate with a rigorous consistency that is rarely to be found. But it is insulated. Whatever direction the traveler takes in leaving it, he puts it behind him in a day's journey. If he goes northward, he meets with strongly marked changes. The temperature increases; the blue of the heavens is clouded over; the air is less pure; and the winds blow indiscriminately from all four corners of the compass, being sucked in by the expanse of open country that lies there.

At the same time the excesses of the climate are reflected by a thermometer whose abrupt oscillations, in the month of October, range from 95 in the shade at midday to mornings that are extremely cold. As summer comes on, this lack of balance is accentuated. Maximum and minimum temperatures are recorded at the same time of year; and at the height of the droughts, within the course of a few hours, there is an unnatural succession of scorching days and freezing nights. The barren earth, holding counterpoised the emissive and absorbent capacities of the materials that go to compose it, at once stores up the heat of the sun's rays and then, of a sudden, drains it off. It is sun-baked and turns freezing cold in twenty-four hours' time. The sun beats down upon it, and it absorbs the rays and multiplies them, reflecting and refracting them in a dazzling glow of light. Over the tops of the hills, down the furrowed slopes, the chips of broken silica appear to take fire and gleam vibrantly, like sparks; the quivering atmosphere near the ground is like that at the mouth of a furnace, its effervescence rendered visible in the expansion of heated air columns. The day, incomparably bright with the glow, blasts the silent landscape, and the leafless branches of a flora that has succumbed to the heat sink back into the bosom of a striken Nature, in the immobility and peace of a long-protracted spasm.

Night falls suddenly, without a twilight—darkness dropping from a peak of vermilion cloud fringe in the west—and all this heat is lost through a most intense process of radiation, as the mercury sinks alarmingly.

But there are certain harsh variations. Driven in from the northeast, dense, swelling clouds hover at nightfall over the parched sands. The sun disappears and the mercury remains stationary or, more likely, goes up. Night comes quickly. The earth, like a dark sun, begins radiating heat, and one has the uncomfortable feeling of invisible sparks; but all this heat is reflected back upon it by the clouds. The barometer drops as it does when a storm is coming, and one can scarcely breathe in the unnatural sultriness, with all the absorbed heat of the sun now concentrated in a single hour of the night.

By contrast, and understandably, this never happens in the paroxysmal seasons of summer drought, when there is an alternation of very hot days and frigid nights to add to the sufferings of the inhabitants.

Showing the same singular lack of balance to be found in those forces that work upon the earth, the winds that reach these parts are generally violent whirlwinds. And in those months in which it blows hardest, the northeaster leaves the signs of its passage everywhere.

These aerial disturbances, on the other hand, disappear for months at a time, and a heavy calm then prevails, with not a breath of air stirring in the luminous placidity of the blistering days. Imperceptible streams of heated vapor then rise, depriving the earth of what little moisture it has; and when this lasts for some time, saddening prelude to a drought, the atmosphere attains a most abnormal degree of aridity.

SINGULAR HYGROMETERS

Our observations were not made in accordance with rigorous classic procedure; if we were able to make them at all, this was owing to hygrometers of an unlooked-for and bizarre kind.

One time at the end of September, fleeing the monotony of a listless cannonading and the dull, heavy reverberations of rounds fired at intervals, we were wandering about the environs of Canudos, when, upon descending a slope, we came upon an irregular amphitheater, with a number of hills disposed in a circle around a single valley. Small shrubs, verdant icozeiros[28] growing in clusters, interspersed with brilliant-flowering palmatorias,[29] gave this place the exact appearance of some old abandoned garden. To one side a single tree, a tall quixabeira,[30] towered above the sparse vegetation.

The western sun was casting its long shadows over the plain, and in the shadow—arms flung out and face upturned to the heavens—a soldier was taking his ease. He had been taking his ease there—for three whole months.

He had died in the assault of July 18. The trampled gunstock, the sword belt and cap tossed to one side, and the uniform in shreds told that

[28] [A plant of the Caparidaceae family (*Capparis ico* Mart. and Eichl.) which grows in the scrub-forest region.]

[29] [This name is applied to any number of a species of plants belonging to the Cactaceae family and the genus *Opuntia* (*Opuntia vulgaris* Mill).]

[30] [Tree of the Sapotaceae family (*Bumelia sartorum* Mart.).]

he had succumbed in a hand-to-hand struggle with a powerful adversary. He had fallen, certainly, doubled over backward, as the result of a violent blow on his forehead, which was marked by a dark scar. And when they had come to bury the dead, days afterward, he had gone unnoticed. For this reason he had not shared the common trench of less than three-quarters of a yard in depth into which the comrades fallen in battle had been placed in a last reunion. The fate which had brought him so far from his abandoned fireside had made him at least one last concession: it had saved him from the mournful and repugnant promiscuity of a trench burial and had left him here as he was, three months ago—arms thrown wide and face turned heavenward—beneath the ardent suns, the bright moons, and the gleaming stars.

His body was intact. It had dried out a little, that was all; had undergone a mummification which had preserved the outlines of his physiognomy to such an extent as to give the precise illusion of a tired fighter taking a peaceful nap in the shade of that benevolent tree. Not even a worm —most vulgar of the tragic solvents of matter—had defiled his tissues. He had returned to life's melting-pot without any unseemly decomposition, through an imperceptible draining-off process. In brief, here was an apparatus that revealed, absolutely and in the most suggestive manner, the extreme aridity of the atmosphere.

The horses that had died on the same day looked like stuffed museum specimens. The neck appeared a little longer and thinner, the legs were withered, and the carcass was hard and shriveled.

At the storming of the Canudos encampment, one of these horses had stood out impressively, above all the others. This was the one ridden by the valiant Sublieutenant Wanderley,[31] who had fallen in death with his mount. Severely wounded and floundering, it had slid down the steep side of the hill and, halfway down, had become wedged in between the rocks. Struggling to regain its footing, it had planted its front feet firmly on a stone ledge. And there it had remained, like some fantastic animal, hanging perpendicularly over the hill and fairly prancing as it seemed, in a last forward bound of the steed and its paralyzed rider. There it was, still, with all the appearance of life, especially when a rude gust of wind from the northeast came to ruffle its long wavy mane.

When these gusts, subsiding suddenly, encountered the ascending columns of air in whirling eddies that resembled diminutive cyclones, one was conscious more than ever of the extreme aridity of this parched re-

[31] See pp. 329, 355, 365.

gion; each particle of sand suspended above the hard, chapped earth then became a calorific focus, diffusing the insensible combustion of the earth.

In addition to this, in the periods of prolonged calm, weird optical phenomena were to be observed. If from the top of Favella, the sun appeared to dart its rays down perpendicularly, while the stagnant atmosphere cast a motionless spell on surrounding nature, one had but to let his eyes wander to the desert lands in the distance, and the earth there was no longer to be made out at all. Troubled by the strata of unequally heated air, the observer's fascinated gaze seemed to be piercing a huge intangible prism, and he was no longer able to distinguish the base of the mountains, which appeared to be hanging in mid-air. Then, to the north of the Canabrava, on an enormous expanse of rugged plain, he became aware of an amazing undulation, a strange pulsation of distant waves, conveying the marvelous illusion that here was the bosom of a broad and variegated sea, where the diffused light fell and broke and rose again in dazzling scintillations.

IV

THE DROUGHTS

The Canudos region is an index to the physiography of the northern backlands. It sums them up, presenting their dominant aspects on a reduced scale. It is, in a manner of speaking, a central zone common to them all.

As a matter of fact, the peninsular bend which has its extremity in the Cape of São Roque serves as a point of convergence for the inner boundaries of six states—Sergipe, Alagôas, Pernambuco, Paraíba, Ceará, and Piauí—which either touch on it or lie but a few miles distant. It is, accordingly, natural that the climatic vicissitudes of these states should exhibit a common intensity, especially in the case of that acute manifestation expressed in a word which holds a maximum of terror for the natives in these parts—the word "drought."

We shall have to be excused from making an extended study of this subject. Feeling their way through a host of fugitive and complex factors, in an effort to find the underlying causes of the droughts, the most vigorous minds have met with failure, and we should be able to do no more than to put their failures into words. Nevertheless, we shall undertake to give a description of this inexorable fatality, based upon figures that do not lie.

The truth of the matter is, the drought cycles—for that is what they are, in the strictest sense of the term—follow a rhythm in the opening and closing of their periods that is so obvious as to lead one to think that there must be some natural law behind it all, one of which we are as yet in ignorance.[32] This was revealed for the first time by Senator Thomaz Pompeu, who drew up a table, in itself sufficiently eloquent, in which the appearances of the drought in the past century and the present one[33] display a singular parallelism, giving rise to the presumption that any slight discrepancies to be observed indicate nothing more than defects of observation or variations in the oral tradition which has handed down the results of such observation. In any event, a mere glance at this table shows a repeated coincidence which would seem to remove the element of chance.

Thus, to cite only the major instances, the droughts of 1710–11, 1723–27, 1736–37, 1744–45, and 1777–78 in the eighteenth century may be set alongside those of 1808–9, 1824–25, 1835–37, 1844–45, and 1877–79 in the present century. This coincidence, almost invariably reflected, as if it came from a tracing of one season laid upon another, is still further accentuated in the identity of the long periods of intermission, which in both cases halt the progression of the devastating phenomenon. Indeed, the major interregnum of the last century, one of thirty-two years (1745–77), corresponds to one in our own century that is exactly equal, and, what is especially noteworthy, one marked by an exact correspondence of dates (1845–77).

As we continue with a closer examination of the table, new data of a fixed and positive sort appear, with the rigorous consistency of unknown facts being brought to light. There is then to be observed a rhythm in the progress of the scourge that is rarely disturbed, being interrupted by intervals that vary little between nine and twelve years, and which follow one another in such a manner as to permit of safe predictions as to the time of the next irruption.

However, despite the extreme obviousness of these immediate results, the problem, which may be expressed in the simplest of arithmetical formulas, remains insoluble.

HYPOTHESES CONCERNING THE ORIGIN OF THE DROUGHTS

Anxious to find the cause of this alternation which so seldom varied, and fixing the length of the interval, somewhat arbitrarily, at eleven years, one naturalist, Baron de Capanema, had the idea of looking for its remote origin in extraterrestrial factors so characteristic for these inviolable peri-

---

[32] [For latest material on the droughts see James, *op. cit.*, pp. 393–96, 414–15, and 421.]

[33] [I.e., the eighteenth and nineteenth centuries.]

ods. And he found, in the regularity with which the spots in the solar photosphere are seen and then vanish, a complete analogy.

It is true that these dark nuclei, some of them larger than the earth, showing black within the gleaming compass of the faculae, and slowly evolved in accordance with the form of the sun's rotation, have a period between their maximum and minimum of intensity that may vary from nine to twelve years. And inasmuch as Herschel a long time ago, with inspired intuition, had discovered that they have an appreciable influence upon the proportion of heat emitted by the earth, there was derived an unimpeachable correlation, supported by geometric and physical data bearing upon a single effect. It remained to compare the minimum period of the sunspots, which are a shield to the great star's radiations, with the height of the drought season on the tortured planet in such a manner as to make it clear that the one period corresponded to the other. It was here, however, at the most interesting point, that the projected theory broke down: the dates of the summer paroxysm in the north rarely coincide with the minimum of sunspots.

But, when all is said, the failure of this attempted explanation points not so much to the futility of applying to the problem, in a hard-and-fast manner, a set of well-known circumstances as it does to the error of looking for one cause alone. For this question, marked by that complexity which is immanent in concrete facts, is one that has to do, rather, with secondary causes, nearer at hand and more forceful ones; and these causes, with continuous manifestations that range from the nature of the soil to the geographic lay of the land, will only be definitively systematized when an extensive series of observations shall permit us to say just which agents are the preponderant ones in the hinterland climate.

Be that as it may, the severe climate of the northern states is the work of fugitive and disorderly agents, operating in accordance with laws not yet understood, subject to local disturbances deriving from the nature of the land and to the widest range of reactions resulting from the geographic features. Hence, the air currents which unbalance it and cause it to vary so greatly.

A determining factor in good part, and possibly a preponderant one, is the northeastern monsoon, which is created by sucking in the air of the interior plateaus.[34] These plateaus, which extend in a vast expanse all the way to Mato Grosso, are, as is well known, the seat of great barometric depressions in the summertime. Attracted by these depressions, the lively

[34] [This is physically incorrect (see James, *op. cit.*).]

northeaster, in the months from December to March, upon blowing in to the north-lying coasts, is singularly favored by the very conformation of the earth, in its swift passage over the barren plains which, with their intense radiations, raise its point of saturation, diminishing the probability of rain and repelling it in such a manner as to permit it to carry intact, to the recesses of the continent and over the sources of the great rivers, all the moisture which it has absorbed in crossing the seas.

The fact is, slight variations aside, the orographic layout of the backlands—mountain ranges which, to the northeast, stand in a parallel line to the prevailing monsoon—facilitates the passage of this wind by canalizing it. It does not combat it with antagonistic slopes, walling it in, raising and cooling it, and condensing it in rains.

One of the causes of the droughts is thus seen to lie in the topography of the region. What the stricken lands to the north lack is a high mountain range which, running in a direction perpendicular to that of the wind, would "determine a dynamic cooling," to employ an expressive phrase.[35]

There is an impressive natural phenomenon which has a light to throw on this hypothesis, and that is the fact, long established in the experience of the sertanejos, that the droughts always appear between two fixed dates: December 12 and March 19. Beyond these limits there is not a single case of the droughts' being extinguished. If these limits are exceeded, the droughts are fatally prolonged throughout the course of the year, until the season opens once more. This being so, and bearing in mind that it is precisely during this interval that the extensive zone of equatorial calms, in its slow oscillation about the Equator, reaches the zenith in those states, until its border comes to touch the extremities of Baía, may we not look upon this phenomenon in the present instance as fulfilling the functions of an ideal mountain which, running from east to west and momentarily correcting the lamentable orographic plan, rises as a barrier to the monsoon, causing it to halt and the air currents to ascend and subsequently cool, to be immediately condensed in diluvian rains which then suddenly fall over the backlands?

This unraveling of conjectures has the sole value of indicating how many remote factors may have a bearing upon a question which holds a twofold interest for us: by reason of its higher scientific import and because of the more intimate meaning it has for the evolving destiny of an extensive portion of our country. The influence of the trade winds, which up to now has been needlessly stressed, is accordingly relegated to a secondary plane; and the hypothesis in question is in a manner strengthened

[35] [The author has, in English, "determine a *dynamic colding*."]

by the very intuition of the man of the hinterland, for whom a persisting northeast wind—the "drought wind," as he expressively terms it—means that he is in for a long, hard time of it, and one about which there is nothing to be done.

The beneficent seasons come on suddenly. After two or three years, as from 1877 to 1879, during which the barren plains are subjected to an intense scorching, the very intensity of this action generates an inevitable counteraction. The atmospheric pressure finally falls, everywhere and to a considerable degree; and the barrier created by the ascending currents of heated air, serving as a rampart against those currents blowing up from the coast, grows larger and is more clearly defined. Clashing one with the other and loosing violent hurricanes, these currents now rise and, shot through with lightning bolts, cloud over the entire sky in a few minutes, after which the clouds break in heavy downpours over the parched desert lands.

It is then that one fancies he can see the ascending columns of air which give rise to this phenomenon through their formidable collision with the northeast wind. According to the testimony of numerous witnesses, the first showers precipitated from a high altitude never reach the earth. Halfway down, they are evaporated between the layers of heated air which are coming up and so are driven back to the clouds, to be once more condensed, again precipitated, and to fall afresh in the form of rain. They do not so much as dampen the ground when they first reach it but very quickly return to space, being, as it were, vaporized, as if they had fallen on incandescent plates. Then they fall again, in a rapid and incessant permutation, until finally they come to form the first rivulets trickling away between the stones, the first torrents streaming down the slopes and flowing off in brooks, already swollen, along the gullies, to come to a head tumultuously in large rivers with powerful currents. These latter are muddy streams that follow a random course in accordance with the declivity of the land; and borne along on them are the boughs of uprooted trees, all rolling and crashing along on the same current, in the same chaos of dark and repulsive-looking waters.

Should this sudden assault be followed by regular rains, the backlands come to life and are transformed. Not infrequently, however, they find themselves caught in the grip of a cyclone. At other times the rapid drainage of the land and the accelerated evaporation render them desolate and arid. Laden with heated atmosphere, the winds double their hygrometric capacity and from day to day go on absorbing what little moisture the earth possesses—thereby reopening the unvarying cycle of droughts.

THE CAATINGAS

The traversing of the backland trails is then more exhausting than that of a barren steppe. In the latter case, the traveler at least has the relief of a broad horizon and free-sweeping plains.

The caatinga, on the other hand, stifles him; it cuts short his view, strikes him in the face, so to speak, and stuns him, enmeshes him in its spiny woof, and holds out no compensating attractions. It repulses him with its thorns and prickly leaves, its twigs sharp as lances; and it stretches out in front of him, for mile on mile, unchanging in its desolate aspect of leafless trees, of dried and twisted boughs, a turbulent maze of vegetation standing rigidly in space or spreading out sinuously along the ground, representing, as it would seem, the agonized struggles of a tortured, writhing flora.[36]

This flora is one that does not show even the reduced number of species common to desert regions—stunted mimosas or rugged euphorbia over a carpeting of withered grasses. It is not replete with distinct vegetable varieties; its trees, viewed in conjunction, appear to be all of one family, with few genera, being confined almost to one unvarying species, barely differing in size and all having the same conformation, the same appearance of moribund vegetable growths, practically without trunks and with branches that start at the ground. Through an explicable effect of adaptation to the cramped conditions of an unfavorable environment, those very growths which in the forests are so diversified are here all fashioned in the same mold. They undergo a transformation and by a process of slow metamorphosis tend to an extremely limited number of types, characterized by those attributes which offer the greatest capacity for resistance.

This is a hard-and-fast rule. The struggle for existence which in the forests takes the form of an irrepressible tendency toward the light, with distended and elastic creepers that flee the stifling shade and, climbing aloft, cling rather to the sun's rays than to the trunks of the centuries-old trees—all this is here reversed; all here is more mysterious, more original, and more stirring to the emotions. The sun is the enemy whom it is urgent to avoid, to elude, or to combat. And avoiding him means, in a manner of speaking, as we have already pointed out, the inhumation of the moribund flora, the burying of its stalks in the earth. But inasmuch as the earth is in turn hard and rough, drained dry by the slopes or rendered sterile by the suction of the strata, completing the work of the sun's rays, between these two unfavorable environmental factors—the overheated atmosphere and

[36] [For a definition and description of the *caatingas* see Richard Spruce, *Notes of a Botanist on the Amazon and Andes*, ed. Alfred Russel Wallace (London, 1908), I, 206-7.]

the inhospitable soil—the most robust growths take on a highly abnormal aspect, bearing the stigma, all of them, of the silent battle that is going on.

The leguminous plants, which grow high in other places, are here dwarfed. At the same time they increase the ambit of their foliage, thus broadening the surface of contact with the air, for the absorption of those few elements that are diffused in it. Their principal roots are atrophied as a result of beating against the impenetrable subsoil, and in their place is a wide expanse of secondary radicels, clustered in sap-swollen tubercles. The leaves are increased in number and, hard as chips, are stuck rigidly on the tip of the boughs, by way of reducing the amount of surface exposed to the sun. The fruits, stiff as cones sometimes, have a protective covering, and the dehiscence with which the pods open is perfect, as if manipulated by steel springs, an admirable arrangement for the propagation of the seeds, which are scattered profusely over the ground. And they all, without a single exception, in the form of the sweetest of perfumes,[37] possess a barrier which on cold nights is reared above them to prevent their suffering from sudden drops in temperature, charming and invisible tents to protect them. Thus does the tree apparel itself in reaction to a cruel climate.

The cautery of the droughts is adjusted on the backlands; the burning air is sterilized; the ground, parched and cleft, becomes petrified; the northeaster roars in the wilderness; and, like a lacerating haircloth, the caatinga extends over the earth its thorny branches. But the plants, all their functions now reduced, "weathering out the season," the life within them latent, feed on those reserves which they have stored up in the off seasons and contrive to ride out the ordeal, ready for a transfiguration in the glow of a coming spring.

Some of them, in a more favorable soil, owing to a most singular circumstance, are even more successful in eluding the inclemencies of their environment. Grouped in clusters or standing about isolated here and there are to be seen numerous weedy shrubs of little more than a yard in height, with thick and lustrous leaves, an exuberant and pleasing flora in the midst of the general desolation. They are the dwarf cashew-nut trees, the typical *Anacardia humilis* of the arid plains, the *cajuys* of the natives. These strange trees have roots which, when laid bare, are found to go down to a surprising depth. There is no uprooting them. The descending axis increases in size the further they are scraped, until one perceives it parting in dichotomous divisions which continue underground to meet in a single vigorous stalk down below.

[37] See Tyndall's brilliant induction.

These are not roots; they are boughs. And these tiny shrubs, scattered about or growing in clumps, covering at times large areas, are in reality one enormous tree that is wholly underground. Lashed by the dog-day heat, fustigated by the sun, gnawed by torrential rains, tortured by the winds, these trees would appear to have been knocked out completely in the struggle with the antagonistic elements and so have gone underground in this manner, have made themselves invisible, with only the tallest shoots of their majestic foliage showing aboveground.

Others, lacking this conformation, are equipped in another fashion. The waters that flee in the savage whirl of the torrents, or between the inclined schist layers, are retained for a long time in the spathes of the Bromeliaceae, thus bringing these plants back to life. At the height of summer, a macambira[38] stalk is for the thirsty woodsman a cup of water, crystalline and pure. The greenish thistles[39] with their tall, gorgeous flowers, the wild pineapples, and the silk grass,[40] growing in impenetrable thickets, all show the same form, one that is purposely adapted to these sterile regions. Their ensiform leaves, which, like those of the majority of plants in the backlands, are smooth and lustrous, facilitate the condensation of the scant vapor brought in by the winds, thus overcoming the greatest menace to vegetable life resulting from a broad field of evaporation on the leaves, which drains off and offsets the moisture absorbed by the radicels.

There are other plants equipped in a different manner, with another kind of protective apparatus, but one equally resistant. The Indian figs and cacti, native throughout the region, come under Saint-Hilaire's category of vegetable fountains. Classic types of desert flora, more resistant than the others, when whole trees blasted by lightning fall at their side, they remain unharmed and even flourish to a greater extent than they did before. Suited to cruel climates, they grow thin and etiolated in the milder ones; for the fiery environment of the desert appears to stimulate better the flow of sap in their tumid leaflike branches.

The *favellas*, nameless still to science—unknown to the learned, although the unlearned are well acquainted with them—a future genus *cauterium* of the Leguminosae, it may be, possess leaves which, consisting of cells elongated in the form of villosities,[41] are a remarkable means of

---

[38] [One of the Bromeliaceae, very common in the arid regions of the Northeast (*Bromelia laciniosa* Schult.).]

[39] [The *caroá* (see p. 91, n. 68).]

[40] [The Brazilian *gravatá* (*Bromelia fastuosa* Lindl.).]

[41] See "Author's Notes," Note III, p. 480.

condensation, absorption, and defense. On the one hand, their surfaces, cooling at night to a degree far below the temperature of the air, despite the aridity of the atmosphere, provoke brief precipitations of dew. On the other hand, whoever touches them touches an incandescent plate heated to an unnatural degree.

When, contrary to the cases mentioned, the species are not well equipped for a victorious reaction, arrangements which are, perhaps, still more interesting may then be observed. In this case, the plants unite in an intimate embrace, being transformed into social growths. Not being able to weather it out in isolation, they discipline themselves, become gregarious and regimented. To this group belong all the Caesalpinia and the *catingueiras*,[42] constituting in those places where they appear 60 per cent of the desert flora; and then there are the tableland evergreens[43] and the pipe reeds, shrubby, hollow-stemmed heliotropes, streaked with white and with flowers that grow in spiked clusters, the latter species being destined to give its name to the most legendary of villages.[44]

These are not to be found in Humboldt's table of Brazilian social plants,[45] and it is possible that the first named also grow, isolated, in other climates; but here they are distinctly social. Their roots, tightly interlaced beneath the ground, constitute a net to catch the waters and the crumbling earth, and, as a result of prolonged effort, they finally form the fertile soil from which they spring, overcoming, through the capillarity of their inextricable tissues, with their numerous meshes, the insatiable suction of the strata and the sands. And they do live. "Live" is the word— for there is, as a matter of fact, a higher significance to be discerned in the passivity exhibited by this evolved form of vegetable life.

THE JOAZ TREES

The joaz trees[46] show the same characteristics; they rarely lose their intensely green leaves, purposely modeled to cope with the vigorous action

[42] [Various plants that grow on the *caatingas*.]

[43] [The *alecrins dos taboleiros*. An *alecrim* may be either a tree or a bush, and there are a number of varieties. The bush (*Rosmarinus officinalis*) is fragrant. The trees are of the Caesalpiniaceae (*Holocalyx spp.*) (*Strategic Index of Latin America*).]

[44] [I.e., Canudos, from *canudo*, a tube formed from a reed; the pipe reeds are called *canudos de pito*.]

[45] [The allusion is to Friedrich Heinrich Alexander von Humboldt, German traveler and naturalist. He traveled in South America, Mexico, and the United States during the years 1797–1804 (see the work by Humboldt and A. Bonpland, *Personal Narrative of Travels to the Equinoctial Regions of America* [3 vols.; London: H. G. Bohn, 1852–53]).]

[46] [The *joazeiro*, of the Ramnaceae family, the tree which produces the joaz fruit.]

of the light. Scorching months and years go by, and the extremely rugged soil becomes utterly impoverished; but in those cruel seasons in which the heat of the sun's rays is aggravated by spontaneous combustions kindled by the powerful attrition of the dried and peeling branches in the high winds—even then, aliens to the march of the seasons, these trees, above life's widespread desolation all around them, have boughs that are always green and flowering and strew the desert with bright golden-hued blooms, which lie there in the gray of the stubble like festive, green-decked cases.

In certain seasons, however, the harshness of the elements increases to such a point that the joaz boughs are stripped. The bottoms of the fresh-water pits have long since been buried under; the hardened beds of the ipueiras, turned into enormous molds, show the ancient print of oxen; and throughout the entire backland region life comes to a standstill.

At such times, amid this still-life scene, only the cacti stand thin and silent, their circular stocks divided into uniform polyhedral columns with the impeccable symmetry of huge candelabra. And looming larger as the short-lived afternoon comes to these desert parts, with their large and gleaming vermilion-colored fruit standing out against the half-light of dusk, they convey the moving illusion of giant tapers stuck at random in the soil, scattered over the plains, and lighted. They are characteristic of the capricious flora here in the heart of summer.

The mandacarús (*Cereus jaramacarú*),[47] attaining a remarkable height, rarely appearing in groups but standing isolated above the chaotic mass of vegetation, are an attractive novelty at first. They serve as contrast, towering triumphantly while all about them the flora is depressed. One's gaze, disturbed by the painful contemplation of this maze of twisted boughs, grows tired and seeks relief in the straight and proper lines of their stocks. After a little while, however, they become an oppressive obsession, leaving on everything the imprint of an unnatural monotony, as they follow one another row on row, all uniform, identical, all of the same appearance, all equally distant, and distributed throughout the desert with a singular display of order.

The chique-chiques (*Cactus peruvianus*) are a variant of inferior proportions, with curved and creeping boughs teeming with thorns and covered with snow-white flowers. They seek out the hot and sterile sites. They are the classic vegetation of parched areas. They revel in the burning bed of sun-stricken granite blocks.

They have as inseparable companions, in this habitat which even the orchids avoid, the monkshoods, inelegant and monstrous melocacti, fluted

---

[47] [The *mandacarú* is a variety of fig tree.]

and ellipsoidal in form, with thorny buds that converge above in an apex formed by a single bright-red flower. They make their appearance in an inexplicable manner over the barren rock, really conveying, in their size, their conformation, and the manner of their dispersion, the singular impression of bloody, decapitated heads tossed here and there, without rhyme or reason, in a truly tragic disorder. An extremely narrow cleft in the rock permits them to insinuate their long capillary root until it reaches a spot down below where there may possibly exist a few drops of moisture that have not been evaporated.

The whole of this vast family, assuming all these varied aspects, gradually declines until we come to the humblest of them all in the thorny, creeping quipás,[48] spread over the earth like a harrowing matweed; and the sinuous rhipsalides,[49] twining like green vipers through the tree branches; along with those fragile epiphytic cacti of a pale sea-green hue, clinging by their tentacles to the stalks of the urucuri[50] palms, fleeing the unfriendly soil for the repose of their tufts.

Here and there are other varieties, among them the "devil's palms,"[51] diminutive-leafed opuntias, diabolically bristling with thorns, showing the vivid carmine of the cochineals that feed on them, and bordered with rutilant flowers; they form a bright spot that helps to break the mournful solemnity of the landscape.

There is little more to be distinguished by one who, on a clear day, strolls through these desert tracts, amid trees without either leaf or flower. All the flora, indeed, is jumbled in an indescribable and catastrophic confusion. For this is the *caatanduva*, the "ailing forest" in the native etymology, grievously fallen upon its terrible bed of thorns! Climb any elevation whatsoever and let your gaze wander, and it will encounter the same desolate scene: a shapeless mass of vegetation, the life drained from it, writhing in a painful spasm.

This is the *silva aestu aphylla*, the *silva horrida* of Von Martius, laying bare in the luminous bosom of tropical nature a desert vacuum. One now begins to appreciate the truth of Augustin de Saint-Hilaire's paradoxical statement: "There is here all the melancholy of winter, with a burning sun and the heat of summer!"[52]

---

[48] [The *Opuntia inanoena* Schum.]

[49] [Plants of the Cactaceae family, genus *Rhipsalis*.]

[50] [The *Attalea excelsa* Mart.]

[51] ["*Palmatorias do inferno.*" For *palmatoria* see p. 23, n. 29.]

[52] [Augustin François César Saint-Hilaire traveled widely in Brazil during the years 1816–22. His *Voyages dans l'intérieur du Brésil* was published in Paris in 1830. There is a Portuguese translation, with an Introduction, by Rubens Borba de Moraes, *Viagem á província de São Paulo* (São Paulo: Livraria Martins, 1940).]

The crude light of the long days flames over the motionless earth without bringing it the least animation. The quartz veins on the limestone hills scattered in disorderly fashion over the desert give off a gleam of *banquises;* and from the dried bough tips of the numbed trees hang whitish tillandsia, like melting snowflakes, giving to the picture the aspects of a glacial landscape, with a vegetation hibernating in the icy wastes.

THE TEMPEST

But at the end of any afternoon in March, swift-passing afternoons, without twilights, soon drowned in night, the stars may be seen for the first time, sparkling brilliantly.

Voluminous clouds wall off the far horizon, scalloping and embossing it with the imposing outlines of black-looming mountains. The clouds rise slowly and slowly puff out into great dark masses high above, while down below on the plains the winds are raging tumultuously, shaking and twisting the branches of the trees.

Clouded over in a few minutes' time, the sky is shot with sudden lightning flashes, one after another, which go to deepen the impression of black tempest. Mighty thunderclaps resound, and great rains begin to fall at intervals over the earth, turning then into a veritable cloudburst.

RESURRECTION OF THE FLORA

Upon returning from his stroll, the astonished traveler no longer sees the desert. Over the ground, carpeted with amaryllis, he beholds instead the triumphant resurgence of the tropical flora.

It is a complete change of scene. The rotund mulungús,[53] on the edge of the waterpits, which are now filled, display the purpling hue of their large vermilion-colored flowers, without waiting for leaves. The tall caraíbas[54] and baraúnas,[55] however, are leafing along the borders of the replenished streams. The stripped marizeiros[56] rustle audibly to the passage of the fragrant breezes. The quixabeiras, with their tiny leaves and fruits like onyx stones, take on a livelier appearance. Of a deeper green, the icoseiros grow thickly over the fields, beneath the festive swaying of the urucuri tufts. The flowering thickets of tableland evergreens with their fine,

[53] [Tree of the genus *Erythrina* (*Erythrina mulungú* Mart.), whose habitat ranges from Maranhão to Minus Gerais and Rio Grande do Sul.]

[54] [The *Simaruba versicolor var. angustifolia* Engl.]

[55] [The *baraúna* (also, *braúna*, *garaúna*, *arvore-preta-da-mata*, *Maria-preta-da-mata*) is a tree with very hard wood, of the Leguminosae family. It is used for shoring in mines, for railway ties, machinery parts, construction work, etc. (*Strategic Index of Latin America*).]

[56] [The *Cassia sp.*]

flexible stocks are in billowing motion, lending life to the landscape as they spread out over the plains or round out the slope of the hills. The umburanas[57] perfume the air, filtering it through their leafy boughs. And dominating the general revival, if not by their height, at least by the beauty of their appearance, the circular-spreading umbú trees[58] lift their numerous branches to a height of a couple of yards above the ground.

THE UMBÚ TREE

This is the sacred tree of the backlands. Faithful companion to the cowboy's swift, happy hours and long, bitter days, it affords the most apt example of the adaptation of the hinterland flora to its environment. It may be that once it grew taller and more vigorous, and that, as the result of an alternating succession of flame-belching summers and torrential winters, it has declined to its present stature and, in the course of its evolution, has undergone modifications that give it greater resistance, enabling it to defy the prolonged droughts by sustaining itself in the seasons of misery on the copious reserves of vital energy which it has stored up in its roots in more propitious times.

This energy it shares with man. This particular section of the backlands is so sterile that there is even a scarcity of those wax palms[59] which are so providentially distributed throughout the neighboring regions as far as Ceará; and, if it were not for the umbú tree, it would be uninhabited. The umbú is for the unfortunate woodsman who dwells here what the mauritia is to the denizens of the *llanos*.

It feeds him and assuages his thirst. It opens to him its friendly, caressing bosom, and its curved and interlacing boughs appear especially made for the fashioning of bamboo hammocks. And, when happy times arrive, it gives him fruit of an exquisite savor for the preparation of the traditional drink known as *umbusada*.

The cattle, even in times of plenty, love the acidulous juice of its leaves. It then elevates its posture, lifting the firm, rounded lines of its tuft in a perfect plane above the ground, at the height of the tallest oxen, like those ornamental plants which are commonly intrusted to the care of experienced gardeners. When plucked, these trees take on the appearance of large spherical segments. They dominate the backland flora in favorable seasons as the melancholy cacti do at the time of the summer spasm.

[57] [*Amburana cearensis* A. C. Sm.]

[58] [*Phytolacca dioica* L.]

[59] [The *carnaúba* (*Copernicia cerifera* Mart.) from the wax of which phonograph records are made.]

THE JUREMA

The juremas[60] are beloved of the caboclos[61]—their hashish, of which they are inordinately fond, supplying them gratis with an inestimable beverage that reinvigorates them after long walks, doing away with their fatigue in a few moments, like a magic potion. The juremas grow in hedges, impenetrable palisades disguised by a multitude of small leaves. There are, also, the marizeiros, mysterious trees which presage the return of rain and of the "green" season and the end of the "lean" days.[62] When, at the height of a drought, a few drops of water ooze along the withered bark of their trunks, they put forth leaves once more. The joaz trees may be bright in the copses, and the baraúnas with their clustering flowers, and the araticús[63] on the edge of the brooks. But, nonetheless, the umbús, adorned with their snow-white blossoms and budding leaves, of an elusive shade that ranges from a pale green to the vivid rose of the newest shoots, stand out as the brightest spot in the whole of this dazzling scene.

THE BACKLANDS ARE A PARADISE

The backlands are now a paradise.

At the same time the hardy fauna of the caatingas comes to life. From the damp lowlands the caitetús start.[64] Ruddy-legged boars go through the plantations in droves, with a loud crunching of jaws. Herds of swift rheas run over the high tablelands, spurring themselves on with their wings. The mournful-voiced seriemas[65] and the vibrant-toned sericoias[66] sing in the undergrowth along the brooksides, where the tapir comes to drink, pausing for a moment in his ugly canter, which is in an unvarying straight line across the caatingas, to the destruction of trees in his path.

[60] [Tree of the genus *Acacia* (*Acacia jurema* Mart.).]

[61] [The Indians; the word literally means "copper-colored."]

[62] *Verde e magrem*, names which the backwoodsmen give, respectively, to the rainy season and the season of drought.
[The "verdant" season and the "arid" would perhaps be a more literal rendering.]

[63] [*Araticú* (or *araticum*) is a term applied to various trees of the Anonaceae (custard-apple) family. It applies especially to the *Anonax* and *Rollinia* genera and to twelve others. A common English name, loosely applied, is "alligator-apple"; others are "bobwood," "corkwood," "monkey-apple," and "pond-apple" (*Strategic Index of Latin America*).]

[64] [The *caitetú* (author's spelling: *caititú*) is a forest pig (*Dicotyles torquatus*), smaller than the boar (*queixada*). Its flesh supplies excellent meat.]

[65] [A long-legged, crested cariamoid bird (*Cariama cristata*) of the plains of Brazil and Paraguay, sometimes domesticated (*Funk & Wagnalls' Standard Dictionary*).]

[66] [The *sericoia* (*sericora*) is a species of waterfowl (*Aramides cajanea cajanea*).]

Even the pumas, frightening the timid mocos[67] which seek shelter in their rock burrows, skip merrily about in the tall weeds before settling down in ambush for the coy stag or straying bullock.

HINTERLAND MORNINGS

There come then matchless mornings, as the radiating glow from the east once more tinges the erythrinas[68] with purple and wreathes with violet the bark of the umburanas, setting off to better advantage the multicolored festoons of the bignonias. The air is animated by the palpitation of swift, rustling wings. The notes of strange trumpets strike our ears. In a tumult of flight, this way and that, flocks of beautiful homeward-bound pigeons pass overhead, and one can hear the noisy, turbulent throngs of maritatacas.[69] Meanwhile, the happy countryman, forgetful of former woes, makes his way down the trails, driving a full-bellied herd and humming his favorite air.

And so the days go by. One, two, six fortunate months, blessed by the earth's abundance, elapse, until silently, imperceptibly, with an accursed rhythm, the leaves and flowers gradually begin to fall, and the drought once more descends on the dead boughs of the shorn trees.

V

A GEOGRAPHICAL CATEGORY THAT HEGEL DOES NOT MENTION

Let us now give a summary, by way of picking up the scattered threads.

Hegel[70] outlines three geographical categories as comprising the basic elements which, along with others, react upon man, creating ethnic differentiations: the steppes, or vast arid plains, with their stunted vegetation; the fertile valleys, abundantly irrigated; and the coastlands and islands.

The *llanos* of Venezuela; the savannas which broaden the valley of the Mississippi; the boundless pampas; and even the Atacama Desert, which lies spread out over the Andes—a huge terrace covered with shifting dunes —all strictly belong to the first category; for, in spite of long summers,

---

[67] [The Brazilian rock cavy (*Cavia rupestris*).]

[68] [A genus with more than 130 described species of trees, shrubs, and herbaceous plants, the best-known species being the coral bean. A number of Brazilian names are given to different species (*Strategic Index of Latin America*).]

[69] [The author has *maritaca;* the word also occurs as *maritacaca, jaritataca,* etc. A carnivorous animal of the Mustelidae family (skunks, weasels, and the like).]

[70] G. W. F. Hegel, *The Philosophy of History*, trans. J. Sibree (New York: P. F. Collier & Son, 1902), Introduction, pp. 144–48.

formidable air currents, and sudden inundations, they are not incompatible with life. But they do not bind man to the earth. Their rudimentary flora, of Gramineae and Cyperaceae, growing vigorously in rainy seasons, is an incentive to pastoral life, to a society of wandering herdsmen, constantly and swiftly on the move over these plains, constantly pitching and striking their tents, and dispersing at the first icy breath of winter.[71] But there is nothing attractive about them. They offer always the same overwhelming monotony of scene, varied only in the matter of coloring: an unruffled ocean, without waves and without shore.

Theirs is the centrifugal force of the desert; they repel, they disunite, they disperse. They are powerless to unite man in the nuptial bonds of the plowed furrow. They are an ethnic isolating factor, like mountain ranges and the sea, or like the Mongolian steppes, trampled by the turbulent Tartar tribes in their aimless wanderings.

As for our own northern backlands, which may at first sight appear to resemble these other regions, a place for them is lacking in the German thinker's scheme. Upon traversing them in summer, one would believe that they fell within the first subdivision, but in wintertime he would feel that they belonged essentially to the second. They are barbarously sterile, marvelously exuberant.

At the height of the droughts they are, positively, a desert, but, when the droughts are not prolonged to a point where they occasion a painful exodus, man may be seen struggling like the trees, with the aid of those reserve forces which he has stored up in the days of plenty; and in this fierce, unsung, terribly obscure combat, one enveloped in the solitude of the uplands, Nature does not abandon him wholly. Rather, she shelters him in those hours of desperation when he has drawn the last drop of water from the last of his pits.

When the rains come on, the earth, as we have seen, becomes transfigured, undergoes fantastic mutations, in contrast to the desolation that has gone before. The parched valleys now become rivers and the barren hills islands of green. The vegetation covers over the grottoes with flowers, concealing the harsh lines of the slopes and banks, turning the stone heaps into rounded hills, and softening the curve of the hillsides and their connecting valleys as they rise to meet the high tablelands. The temperature drops. With the disappearance of the sun's burning rays, the air loses its abnormal aridity. There are new tones to the landscape: the transparency of the atmosphere brings out its most delicate lines, in all their variations of form and color. The horizons expand, and the sky,

[71] [This would hardly seem to apply to the savannas of the Mississippi region.]

lacking the desert's heavy-laden blue, is at once higher and deeper in the presence of the new-unfolding life of earth. For this region is a fertile valley. It is one vast garden without an owner.

Then, all this comes to an end. The days of torture return; the atmosphere is asphyxiating; the soil is hard as rock; the flora is stripped bare; and on those occasions when summer meets summer without the intermittency of rain—the dreadful spasm of the drought. Nature here rejoices in a play of antitheses. And these antitheses accordingly call for a special division in the Hegelian scheme, the most interesting and significant of them all, one in between the overfertile valleys and the most arid of the steppes. Reserving for later pages a discussion of its importance as a factor in ethnic differentiation, let us see now what its role is in the economy of earth.

Nature does not normally create deserts. She combats and repels them. But inexplicable lacunae occur at times under those astronomical auspices which point to a maximum abundance of life. The Sahara is the classic type of desert and has become a generic term for the devastated region that stretches from the Atlantic to the Indian Ocean, making its way through Egypt and Syria, taking on there all the aspects of the enormous African depression, continuing to the very hot Arabian plateau of Nedjed and extending on to the sands of the *bejabans* in Persia. All this is so illogical that the majority of naturalists would look for the origin of this region in some tumultuous cataclysm, an irruption of the Atlantic, hurling its angry waters in an irresistible swirl of currents over the whole of northern Africa, leaving it desolate and bare.

This explanation of Humboldt's, put forth as barely more than a brilliant hypothesis, has, however, a deeper significance. As soon as there was no longer a preponderant central heat and the climates of the far north and the far south, starting from the uninhabitable polar regions, had been stabilized, life began progressing along the equinoctial line. This it was that served to determine the zones of superabundance, where the shrubs of other regions became trees and the climate, varying between two seasons only, gave rise to a uniformity favorable to the evolution of simple organisms, directly adapted to their environment. The astronomic fatality of the inclination of the ecliptic, which brought the earth under biological conditions inferior to those of other planets, is scarcely to be perceived in regions where a single mountain, from base to summit, affords a synthesis of all the climates of the world.

Meanwhile, passing through these zones and cutting across the ideal frontier of the hemispheres, is the thermal equator, which is most disturbed in its course, with sharp deflections. Starting from those exceptional points where life is impossible, it ranges from deserts to forests and flowering fields, from the Sahara, which pulls it up to the north, to India and its riches, after having skirted the southern tip of poverty-stricken Arabia; it crosses the Pacific in a long path—a rarefied necklace of barren, desert islands—to end, after a slow bend to the south, at the marvelous Amazon region.[72]

The fact of the matter is, the morphology of the earth violates the general climatic laws.[73] But, whenever geography does not wholly combat those laws, there is a reaction on the part of Nature. The earth may then be seen engaged in a silent struggle, the effects of which go back for historic cycles—a deeply stirring struggle for one who views it down the ages. Rendered torpid by the adverse agencies with which it has to contend, but holding on tenaciously, not to be coerced, it is transmuted like an organism, by intussusception, and remains indifferent to the riotous elements that lash it in the face.

Consequently, while certain large depressions, like that of Australia, for example, are condemned to an eternal sterility, at other points of the earth the deserts are annulled. The fiery temperature in itself ends by giving these regions a minimum atmospheric pressure, which attracts the rains; and while the shifting, wind-driven sands may for a long time deny roots to the humblest of plants, they are gradually immobilized when caught in the radicels of the Gramineae; the ingrate soil and the sterile rock fall beneath the imperceptible action of the lichens, which prepare the way for the more delicate Lecidea; and, in the end, the denuded plateaus, the *llanos* and the pampas with their sparse vegetation, the savannas, and the hardiest of the Central Asiatic steppes rise up in a crescendo, reflecting the successive stages of a marvelous transformation.

HOW A DESERT IS MADE

In spite of a lesser degree of sterility, the northern backlands judged by this natural criterion may be looked upon, possibly, as a unique point in a process of regressive evolution. We were imagining them in retrospect a moment ago, with fancy rebelling against the gravity of science, as we beheld them emerging in their geologically modern form from a vast Tertiary sea. Apart, however, from this absolutely untenable hypothesis, one

---

[72] [The text reads "a Hilae portentosa do Amazonas," *Hilae* being apparently an incorrect spelling for *hiléia* (old spelling, *hyléa*), the name given by Humboldt to the tropical rain forest of the Amazon.]

[73] See "Author's Notes," Note IV, p. 480.

thing is certain, and that is that a combination of circumstances has made it hard for them to have a constant environment such as would favor the growth of a hardier flora.

We have already sketched in a few of these circumstances; but there is one notable geologic agent that we have overlooked—man. The truth is, man has not infrequently exerted a brutal reaction upon the earth and, especially among us, has assumed, throughout the long course of our history, the role of a terrible maker-of-deserts.

All this began as the result of a disastrous native legacy. In the primitive agriculture of the aboriginal forest-dwellers the basic implement was fire. Having trimmed the trees with their sharp-edged *dgis*, fashioned out of diorite, they would make a pile of the dried boughs and then would strew them, crackling, over the tops of the tree trunks. They then would lay out, in the neighborhood of the burned stumps, an area that once was luxuriant forest, now in ashes, and would proceed to cultivate it. They would repeat this same process the following season, until this spot of earth had been completely exhausted and, being thenceforth untillable, had been abandoned as *caapuera*—"extinct forest," in the Tupi language. From then on it lay there hopelessly sterile, for the reason that, owing to a circumstance worthy of note, the vegetable families which subsequently sprang up on the burned-over patch were invariably types of scraggy shrubs wholly distinct from the vegetation of the primitive forest. The aborigine went on burning and clearing fresh plots, widening the circle of devastation with new *caapueras*, which he then, once again, left for others at other points—desert tracts whose stunted growth was ill adapted to cope with the external elements, and which, as they grew wider in extent, merely added to the rigors of a hostile climate. Interspersed with groves of red oak and buried in weeds, they took on the mournful aspect of the sinister *caatanduva*, which in appearance is something beyond the convulsive, wrath-stricken, whitening caatinga.

Came then the colonizer and copied the same procedure. He made matters worse by adopting, exclusively, in the heart of our country, beyond the narrow strip of canebrake along the coast, a full-fledged pastoral regime. From the beginning of the seventeenth century, in our abusively parceled backlands, huge tracts were opened up, common grazing lands without boundaries, stretching away across the uplands. And they were opened in the very same manner: by the free use of fire, without any segregated areas—fires which swept across the vast spaces, borne on the gusts of the northeast wind. In its work of devastation, the fire had an ally in the hardy backwoods pioneer, who, lusting for gain, had come in search of gold and the Indian. Lost in the depths of a stupendous flora, which shut off his view, and which cast menacing shadows on the hiding-places of the Tapuia[74] and the panther's dread retreat, he destroyed it by setting fire to it, in order to widen his horizon and obtain a glimpse of those mountains which, looming above the cleared fields, served as beacons in the onward march of the bandeiras.

He attacked the earth stoutly, disfiguring it with his surface explorations, rendering it sterile with his dredges, scarring it with the point of his pickax, precipitating the process of erosion by running through it streams of water from the wild torrents. And he left behind him, here, there, and everywhere, great melancholy and deserted *catas*, tracts forever sterile now, with the intense coloring of upturned clay, shedding a vermilion glow in the midst of the wilderness—tracts where not even the humblest of plants could thrive, and which bore the suggestive appearance of enormous dead cities, crumbled in ruins.

These barbarities are to be met with throughout the entire course of our history. As late as the middle of the present century,[75] according to the testimony of the oldest inhabitants of the settlements bordering the São Francisco, those explorers who, in 1830, set out from the left bank of that river, carrying with them their indispensable provisions of water in leather pouches, made use of the same sinister pathbreaker—fire—which at once opened up and illuminated the way for them, laying bare the earth ahead of them as they went; and for months afterward, of a night, the ruddy glow of conflagrations was visible in the western skies. One can imagine what the results of such a procedure would be when carried on uninterruptedly for centuries.

Those results were indeed foreseen by the colonial government, which, from 1713 on, issued a series of decrees designed to set limits to these abuses. At the end of the legendary drought of 1791–92, the "great drought," as it is still known to old woodsmen, one that immolated the entire north, from Baía to Ceará, the metropolitan administration, which appears to have attributed it to the practices that we have mentioned, forthwith issued a stern warning against cutting down the forests; but this was the only corrective measure taken.

The government, nevertheless, was preoccupied with this question for a long time. This is to be seen from the letters royal of March 17, 1796, appointing a judge-conservator for the forests; and those of the June 11, declaring that "we reprove the indiscreet and disorderly ambition of the inhabitants [of Baía and Pernambuco], who with iron and fire have de-

---

[74] [Brazilian Indian.]   [75] [The nineteenth century.]

stroyed precious forests . . . . which formerly did so abound, and which today are only to be found at considerable distances," etc.

Here are precious words, directly relevant to that region of which we have been able to give but a faint description; and there are others that equal them in eloquence.

Perusing the ancient logbooks of the northern *sertanistas*, those fearless *catingueiros*[76] who were fully a match for the bandeirantes of the south, one notes the constant sharp allusions to the repulsive appearance of the landscape, as they crossed the uplands in search of the "silver mines" of Belchior Moreya. They almost all skirted the Canudos region, making a stop at Monte Santo and another at Pico-arassá of the Tapuias. And we find them speaking of "the cold of the plains (certainly cold at night, due to the intense radiations from the unprotected soil), as we made our way through leagues of caatinga, with no water or hope of obtaining any, and with the roots of the umbú and the mandacarú serving our people in its stead,"[77] in their arduous pathbreaking expedition.

The evil is an old one. Working hand in hand with the meteorological elements, with the northeast wind, the suction of the air strata, the dog-days, the Aeolian erosion, the sudden tempests—collaborating with all of these, man became an unholy accomplice to the forces of demolition in this climate. If he did not create the climate, he transformed it, made it worse. He was an auxiliary to the work of soil erosion accomplished by the tempests, and to the ax of the *catingueiro;* he supplemented the effects of the parching suns.

He, it may be, made the desert. But he may still extinguish it by correcting the past. That the task is not an insuperable one is indicated by a historical comparison.

HOW THE DESERT IS EXTINGUISHED

Whoever to this day crosses the elevated plains of Tunisia, between Béja and Bizerte, on the edge of the Sahara, upon coming out from the valleys and following, normally, the capricious, winding course of the wadies, will come upon the remains of ancient Roman constructions. Old heaps of ruins composed of pebbles and crumbling rocks, partly covered with the detritus left by the rains of twenty centuries, these legacies of the great colonizers bespeak, at once, their active-functioning intelligence and the barbarous heedlessness of the Arabians who came after them. For

[76] [*Sertanista:* a pioneer of the *sertões*, or backlands; *catingueiro:* a pioneer who wrestled with the *caatinga.*]

[77] Letter of Pedro Barbosa Leal to the Conde de Sabugosa.

the Romans, after the task of destroying Carthage had been completed, had put their shoulders to the incomparably more serious one of overcoming the antagonism of Nature; and they have left here the most fascinating record of their historical expansion.

They saw definitely what was originally wrong with this region, whose sterility is due not so much to the scarcity of rainfall as to the very bad distribution of the water that falls, due to the topography of the region. They proceeded to correct this. They saw that the torrential rains which occur here, and which are very intense in certain seasons, giving rise to higher pluviometric readings than in other countries which are fertile lands of plenty, were, like those in the backlands of our own country, not merely useless but detrimental. These rains would fall upon the shelterless earth, uprooting a vegetation which had taken scant hold in the hardened soil; for a few weeks the brooks would overflow their banks, flooding the plains, and then would disappear, draining off along the slopes to the north and east, to empty into the Mediterranean, leaving the soil, after a brief period of revival, more barren and sterile that it was before. The desert to the south then seemed to advance, dominating the entire scene and sweeping before it all that was left which could not stand before the mighty breath of the simoon.

The Romans pushed the desert back. They dammed the torrents to restrain their powerful currents, and, as a result, the inhuman environment, tenaciously fought and thwarted, was compelled to yield at last, being completely overcome by a system of dikes. Avoiding the expedient of systematic irrigations, which would have been most difficult, they succeeded in compelling the waters to remain for a longer time upon the land. The ravines, turned into stagnant ponds, were divided into reservoirs surrounded by the walls which barred the valleys; and the wadies, now blocked, swelled up between the hills, holding for a long while those great masses of water which previously had been wasted; or else, when their banks overflowed, the water would run off in canals at the side, down to the nearest low places, where it would spread out in drainage trenches over the entire vicinity, thus saturating the soil. What is more, all these liquid surfaces, scattered about in large numbers in place of being brought together in a single—monumental and futile—Quixadá,[78] being exposed to evaporation could not but end by having an effect upon the climate, changing it for the better. In short, Tunisia, where once the proud sons of the Phoenicians steered their prows, but which had been reduced to a littoral populated by merchants and wandering Numidians, whose curved-top tents could be seen gleaming white in the sun, like stranded barks—Tunisia was trans-

[78] [See p. 49.]

figured and became once more the classic land of ancient agriculture. It was the granary of Italy, furnishing the Romans with nearly the whole of their supply of wheat.

The French today copy these processes in good part, but without the necessity of rearing monumental and costly walls. Those wadies which are most favorably situated they dam with barriers of earth and stone, resembling stockades; and on their banks, throughout the breadth of the neighboring highlands, they construct, for purposes of irrigation, a system of conduits flowing through the surrounding countryside. In this manner the wild waters are held back, rendered dead and stagnant, so that they do not acquire the accumulated force of violent inundations; and then, finally, through thousands of valves, they are distributed through the network of drains. Thus is this historic region, freed of the inert Moslem's apathy, transformed, to resume once more that aspect which it bore of old. France is saving what remains of the opulent heritage of Roman civilization, following its long decline down the centuries.

Now a mere glance at the hypsometric map of the northern backlands will show that use could here be made of an identical expedient, with equally certain results.

The idea is not a new one. It was brought forward long ago, in the course of the memorable sessions of the Polytechnic Institute of Rio, in 1877, by that fine mind, Councilor Beaurepaire Rohan, and was possibly suggested by the same analogy which we have been considering. The discussions which there took place, in which the greatest scientists of the day participated—from Capanema with his solid background of experience to André Rebouças[79] with his extraordinary mind—those discussions led to the doing of the one thing that was practicable, workable, truly useful. Various ideas were propounded on this occasion: cisterns of sumptuous masonry; myriads of artesian wells to be sunk in the highlands region; colossal depositories or huge storage tanks for accumulated reserves of water; vast dams forming artificial lakes; and, last of all, as if to bring out the utter confusion of engineering science before the enormity of the problem, stupendous alembics for the distillation of the waters of the Atlantic!

The most modest expedient of all, however, immediate result of a lesson taught by history and one prompted by the most elementary examples, came to supplant them all; for, in addition to being practical, it was obviously the most logical one.

[79] [André Rebouças was a famous Negro engineer who was fêted by the imperial court of Dom Pedro II. On one occasion, when a white lady had refused to be his partner, Princess Isabel, the heir apparent, danced with him.]

THE AGE-OLD MARTYRDOM OF EARTH

In reality, among those agents which have a determining influence upon the drought must be included, to an appreciable extent, the structure and conformation of the soil. Whatever may be the degree of intensity of the complex and more remote causes with which we have dealt, their influence is manifest when we consider that the absorbent and emissive capacity of the exposed surfaces, the inclination of the strata that cut through them, and the crudities of topographic relief all go to aggravate, at once, the intense heat of the summers and the intensive erosion produced by the torrents. Coming out of a prolonged hot period, only to have to endure sudden inundations, the earth, ill protected by a deciduous vegetation which is parched in the former and uprooted in the latter instance, is left a prey to the gradual invasion of the desert with all its characteristic features.

The great tempests which put out the silent conflagration of the droughts, despite the revival that they bring, in a manner prepare the region for worse vicissitudes. They denudate it rudely, leaving it all the time more exposed to the winters that are to come; they furrow it with harsh contours; they lash it and render it sterile; and, when they go, they leave it more barren than it was before it was scorched by the sun. And so the calendar goes round in a deplorable alternation, a vicious circle, one might say, of catastrophes.[80]

Accordingly, the only method to adopt is one that lies in correcting these natural defects. Putting to one side those factors that go to determine the droughts and which arise from the fatality of astronomic or geographic laws inaccessible to human intervention, they are the only ones that lend themselves to appreciable modifications. The process which we have indicated in brief historical retrospect by its very simplicity dispenses with superfluous technical details. France today is copying it without variations, reviving a type of construction invented by the ancients.

If certain of our valleys, intelligently selected at frequent intervals throughout the entire extent of the backlands territory, were to be walled in, three consequences would inevitably follow: (1) there would be a considerable attenuation of the drainage of the soil, with its lamentable effects; (2) fertile border regions for cultivation would be formed within the network of conduits; and (3) there would be created a state of equilibrium

---

[80] ".... worthy of note is the strong declivity toward the sea that exists in those areas of the region where its rivers flow..... When rain falls on the rocky tablelands with their rare vegetation, the waters stream off in furrows and trenches, producing veritable avalanches that destroy everything in their path" (J. Yoffily, *Notas sobre a Parahyba*).

against the instability of the climate, for the reason that the numerous small reservoirs, uniformly distributed and providing an expanded surface for evaporation, would naturally, in the course of time, come to have the moderating influence of an inland sea, a fact of extreme importance.

There is no need to have recourse to any other expedient. Cisterns, artesian wells, and lakes few or far between, like that of Quixadá, have but a slight local value. Their aim, in a general way, is to mitigate the final consequence of the drought—thirst. Whereas what has to be combatted and overcome in our northern backlands is—the desert.

The martyrdom of man is here reflective of a greater torture, more widespread, one embracing the general economy of Life.

It arises from the age-old martyrdom of Earth.

CHAPTER II

MAN

I

COMPLEXITY OF THE ETHNOLOGICAL PROBLEM IN BRAZIL

BOUND up with influences which, in varying degrees, are modified by three ethnic elements, the origin of the mixed races of Brazil is a problem which for a long time to come will defy the efforts of the best minds. It has as yet been barely outlined.

Meanwhile, in the domain of Brazilian anthropological investigations, are to be found names that loom large in the intellectual life of our country. The studies which have been made of the prehistoric native races are models of subtle observation and brilliant critical analysis; and thanks to them, and contrary to the way of thinking of those capricious builders of the Aleutian bridge, it would now appear to have been definitely established that the races of the Americas are autochthonous ones.

In the field of these notable studies, completed by the profound paleontological elaborations of Wilhelm Lund, there are other names and achievements that stand out: the name of Morton, for example; Frederick Hartt, with his inspired intuition; the entire work of scientific organization accomplished by a Meyer; the rare lucidity of a Trajano de Moura; and many other men whose writings go to reinforce those of Nott and Gordon. These researches, in a general but thoroughgoing manner, serve to define America as a center of creation wholly apart from the great Central Asiatic cradleland. There arises, autonomous among the races, the *Homo americanus*.

The primordial phase of the question was thus clarified. Whether they stem from the "man of Lagôa Santa" crossed with the pre-Columbian of the "Sambaquis,"[1] or whether, greatly modified by later cross-breeding, they sprang from some invading race from the north, from which it is supposed the Tupis came, who were so very numerous in the Era of Discovery—whatever their origin, our own forest-dwellers, with their striking anthropological characteristics, may be looked upon as vanishing types of the old autochthonous races of our land.

The preliminary question of the origin of the indigenous element hav-

[1] [Term applied to shell heaps on the site of prehistoric settlements.]

ing been cleared up in this manner, the investigations then centered upon a definition of the special psychology of the aborigines, and the results were embodied in certain assured conclusions. It is not our purpose here to go into all this. In addition to lacking the necessary competence, we should be digressing from the objective that we have set ourselves.

The two other formative elements of alien origin were not made the subject of similar investigations. The Bantu, or Kafir, Negro in his various manifestations has been up to now consistently neglected by us. Only in very recent times has a persistent investigator, Nina Rodrigues, subjected to painstaking analysis the Negro's interesting and original religious sentiments.[2] Nonetheless, whatever transplanted branch of the African race he may represent, the Negro has brought with him, certainly, the preponderant attributes of the *Homo afer*, son of those parched and barbarous regions where, more than anywhere else, natural selection is effected through an intensive exercise of force and ferocity.

As for the aristocratic factor of our own *gens*, the Portuguese stock, which links us with the vibrant intellect of the Celt, it in turn, despite the complicated melting-pot from which it emerges, is quite characteristic.

We are thus acquainted with the three essential elements and, albeit in an imperfect manner, with the physical environment which differentiates them—and, beyond that, we are familiar, in all their forms, with the adverse or favorable historical conditions which have reacted upon those elements. In considering, however, all the alternatives and all the intermediary phases of this admixture of anthropological types, of varying degrees of development as regards their physical and psychic attributes and under the influence of a changeable environment, with differing climates, producing discordant aspects and opposed conditions of life, it may be said that we shall have done little to advance our knowledge. We shall have written down all the variations of an intricate formula, representing a grave problem; but we shall not have brought to light the unknown factors.

It is obviously not sufficient in the present instance to align the Bantu Negro, the Guarany Indian, and the white man and apply to them Broca's anthropological law. That law is too abstract and inflexible. It does not tell us what the reagents are which may attenuate the influence of the more numerous or stronger race, or the causes which may obliterate or attenuate that influence, when, in place of the binary combination which

[2] [Rodrigues' classic work, first published in French, in Baía, in 1900, was *L'Animisme féti-chiste des nègres de Bahia*. The original Portuguese text was printed, with an introduction and notes, by Professor Arthur Ramos, under the title, *O Animosmo fetichista dos negros bahianos* (Rio de Janeiro, 1935). See also the same author's *Os Africanos no Brasil* (São Paulo, 1932).]

is presupposed, we have to deal with three diverse factors closely bound up with the vicissitudes of history and of climate. Broca's law is a rule that may serve to orient us in our search for the truth, nothing more. It is modified, as all laws are, by the pressure of objective data. But even if, through an extraordinary lack of mental discipline, someone were to attempt to apply it, wholly without regard to such data, it would not simplify the problem in the least.

This is easy to prove. Putting to one side the innumerable factors that disturb the equation, let us consider the three constituent elements of our race in themselves, with their characteristic capacities intact.

We see at once that, even under this favorable hypothesis, there does not result from these elements the single product immanent in binary combinations, in the form of an immediate fusion in which the constituent characteristics are juxtaposed or summed up, converging toward a union in an intermediary type. On the contrary, the inevitable ternary combination, in the simplest of cases, gives rise to three other, binary ones. The initial elements are not summed up and they are not united; they reproduce themselves, creating an equal number of subformations, their place being taken by these derivatives, without any reduction whatsoever, in a confused intermixture of races in which we may distinguish as the most characteristic products the mulatto, the mameluco or curiboca, and the cafuso.[3] The initial point of the investigation, if scarcely more confused than it was, is thus shifted by these reactions which express, not a reduction, but a reproduction. And the study of these subcategories takes the place of a study of the primary races, a task rendered all the more difficult when one stops to consider that these subformations comprise in their turn innumerable manifestations depending upon the varying admixture of blood.

The Brazilian, posed as an abstract type in process of formation, can arise only as the result of a more than ordinarily complex intermingling of races. Theoretically, he would be the *pardo* (brown-skinned) type,[4] toward which the successive cross-breedings of the mulatto, the curiboca, and the cafuso converge.

However, taking into account the historical conditions, differing in dif-

---

[3] Respectively: offspring of Negro and white; of white and Tupi (*cari-boc*, "coming from the white"); of Tupi and Negro. *Mameluco*, or better *mamaluco*, is employed as a generic term, embracing them all, though preferably applied to the second group. *Mamã-ruca*, "produced by mixture"; from *mamã*, "to mix," and *ruca*, "to draw out or produce."

[4] [On the categories employed in Brazilian vital statistics (in this instance, in the city of Baía) see Donald Pierson, *Negroes in Brazil: A Study of Race Contact at Bahia* (Chicago: University of Chicago Press, 1942), pp. 126–27. These categories are *branco* (white), *preto* (black), and *pardo* (brown-skinned, or mulatto).]

ferent regions; the climatic disparities, occasioning diverse reactions diversely borne by the constituent races; the greater or less degree of miscegenation in various parts of the country; and being further mindful of the intrusion—by arms in the colonial epoch, by immigration in our own day—of other peoples, another factor which was not and is not uniform, it may clearly be seen that the reality of such a type is highly doubtful, if indeed the supposition is not absurd.

Be this as it may, these brief remarks will serve to explain the divergence of view that prevails among our anthropologists. Shunning, generally, the laborious task of subjecting their researches to conditions so complex as these, they have given an inordinate amount of attention to the preponderance of ethnic capacities. Now, while we would not deny the weighty influence exerted by these factors, the stress upon them in this country was carried to the point of exaggeration, provoking an irruption of semiscientific nonsense in the form of extravagant, overdaring, and sterile fantasies. There has been something like an excess of subjectivism on the part of those of our writers who, in recent times, have dealt with things so serious with a volubility that was somewhat scandalous in view of the magnitude of the subject. They began by excluding, in large part, the objective data provided by environmental and historical circumstances and then proceeded to play upon the theme of the three races, intermingling them and fusing them according to their whims of the moment. And out of all this fanciful metachemistry there came some fictitious precipitates.

Some of them began by asserting, with an air of authority that was open to question, the secondary function of the physical environment, proclaiming first of all the almost total extinction of the aborigine and the declining influence of the African since the abolition of the slave traffic; they foresaw the final victory of the white man, who was stronger and more numerous, all this representing the general tendency of the mulatto, an ever more diluted form of Negro, and of the *caboclo*, in whom the characteristic features of the aborigine were being all the time more obliterated.

Others gave yet freer rein to their fancy. They stressed the aborigine's influence and erected fantasies which fell at the first mild shock of criticism—fantasies that were not devoid of rhyme and meter, inasmuch as these writers had invaded science to the rhythmic lilt of Gonçalves Dias' verses.[5]

Others, again, kept their feet on the ground. These latter exaggerated the

[5] [Well-known Brazilian poet of the last century (1823–64), noted for his love of nature, tinged with pantheism.]

African influence as being effectively capable, at many points, of reacting against the absorption of other types by the superior race. The mulatto now arose and was proclaimed to be the most characteristic of our ethnic subcategories.

In brief, the views put forward were many and multiform and more than a little dubious.

It is our belief that all this happened for the reason that the essential scope of the investigations had been reduced to the search for a single ethnic type, when, the truth is, there are many of them. We do not possess unity of race, and it is possible we shall never possess it.[6] We are predestined to form a historic race in the future, providing the autonomy of our national life endures long enough to permit it. In this respect we are inverting the natural order of events. Our biological evolution demands the guaranty of social evolution.

We are condemned to civilization. Either we shall progress or we shall perish. So much is certain, and our choice is clear.

This is scarcely suggested, it may be, by the heterogeneity of our ancestral elements, but they are reinforced by another element equally ponderable: a physical milieu that is wide and varied and, added to this, varied historical situations which in large part flow from that milieu. This is a subject which it will be necessary to consider for a few moments.

VARIABILITY OF THE PHYSICAL ENVIRONMENT

Contrary to the opinion of those who would assign to the hot countries an expanse of thirty degrees in latitude, Brazil is far from answering to such a description. From a twofold point of view, astronomic and geographic, these limits are exaggerated. In addition to the fact that it extends beyond the commonly accepted theoretical demarcation, our country is excluded from such a scheme by its natural features, of landscape relief, which mitigate or reinforce the action of the meteorological agents, creating equatorial climates in the high altitudes and temperate ones in the tropics. Its entire climatology, in any part, inscribed within the ample boundaries of the general cosmological laws, is likely to be subject to those particular natural causes which are nearest at hand. A climate is by way of being the physiological translation of a geographic condition. Defining it in this manner, we must conclude that Brazil, by its very formation, is not likely to have a uniform one.

This is demonstrated by the most recent results—the only ones to be trusted—of meteorological investigations. These show the country to be

[6] [See "Author's Notes," Note V, p. 481.]

divided into three clearly distinct zones: the definitely tropical zone, which extends through the northern states to southern Baía, with an average temperature of 88.8 degrees; the temperate zone, extending from São Paulo to Rio Grande, by way of Paraná and Santa Catarina, between the fifteenth and twentieth isotherms; and, as a transition, the subtropical zone, extending over the north central portions of certain states, from Minas to Paraná.

Here, obviously, are three distinct habitats. Even within their more or less definite limits, however, there are circumstances which diversify them. We shall indicate these in a few rapid strokes.

The disposition of the mountains in Brazil, great upheaved masses which follow the coast in a line perpendicular to the southeast, determines the primary distinctions over large tracts of territory which lie to the east, creating a significant climatological anomaly. The fact of the matter is, the climate here, entirely subordinated to geography, violates the general laws that ordinarily govern it. Starting from the tropics, on the side of Ecuador, its astronomical determination by latitudes yields to disturbing secondary causes, and it is, abnormally, defined by longitude.

This is a well-known fact. In the extensive strip of coast which runs from Baía to Paraíba more marked changes may be observed accompanying the parallel to the east then along the meridian northward. Those differences in climate and in natural features which in the latter direction are imperceptible stand out clearly in the former. All the way to the far northern regions, Nature exhibits the same unvarying exuberance in the great forests that border the coast; so that a stranger at a rapid glance would believe this to be a most fertile tract, of wide extent. On the other hand, beginning with the thirteenth parallel, the forests conceal a vast strip of sterile land, a barren tract, displaying all the inclemencies of a region in which the thermometric and hygrometric readings, marked by exaggerated extremes, vary in inverse ratio.

This is revealed by a brief journey to the west, starting from any point along the coast. The charm is broken, the beautiful illusion gone. Nature is here impoverished: no more great forests and mountaintops, but deserts and depressions, as the region is transformed into the parched and barbarous backlands with their intermittent streams and endless stretch of barren plains, forming a huge dais for the woebegone landscapes of the drought.

The contrast is most striking. A little more than a hundred miles distant are regions the exact opposite of this, with conditions of life that are equally different. It is as if one had found one's self suddenly in a desert.

And, certainly, those waves of humanity which, during the first two centuries of settlement, swept over the northern tracts on their way west to the interior must have encountered obstacles more serious than the roll of seas and mountains, when they came to cross the meager, bare-stripped caatingas. The failure of the Baians to penetrate to the interior of the country—and they, by the way, preceded the Paulistas[7]—is an eloquent case in point.

The same, however, is not true of the tropics to the south. Here, the geological warp of the earth, matrix of its interesting morphogeny, remains unalterable over large expanses of the interior, creating the same favorable conditions, the same flora, a climate greatly improved by altitude, and the same animated appearance as far as natural features are concerned.

The huge bulwark of the granite cordillera, standing perpendicular to the sea, along its inner slopes falls away gently in vast, rolling plains. It forms the abrupt, steeply inclined scarp of the plateaus.

Upon the plateaus, the landscape pictures are more ample and luxuriant, without the exaggerated overwhelming aspect of the mountains. The earth exhibits that "manageability of nature" of which Buckle speaks, while the climate, moderately warm, rivals in mildness the admirable one of southern Europe. It is not here, as in the north, exclusively governed by the southeast wind. Blowing down off the high plains of the interior, the northwest wind is the dominant factor, as throughout the whole of that extensive zone which ranges from the elevated lands of Minas and Rio to Paraná, by way of São Paulo.

We have done little more than sketch in these broad divisions, but enough has been said to show that there is an essential difference between the south and the north, two regions that are absolutely distinct as regards meteorological conditions, the lay of the land, and the varying transitions between the inland and the coast. Coming down to a closer analysis, we shall discover special aspects that are still more to the point. We shall avoid going into an extended explanation of the subject and shall confine ourselves to the most significant examples.

We have seen, in the preceding pages, that the southeast wind is the predominant regulator of the climate along the eastern seaboard but that it is replaced in the southern states by the northwest wind and in the far north by the northeaster. But these winds in their turn disappear in the heart of the plateaus before the southwest wind, which, like a mighty whiff

[7] [Inhabitants of the São Paulo region.]

of the *pampeiros*,[8] rushes down on Mato Grosso, occasioning thermo-metric variations that are out of all proportion, adding to the instability of the mainland climate, and subjecting the central regions to an extremely harsh set of conditions, differing from those that we have rapidly outlined above.

Indeed, it may be said that Nature in Mato Grosso lives up to Buckle's exaggerations.[9] It is quite exceptional, unique; there is nothing like it any-where. All the wild grandeur, all the inconceivable exuberance, along with a maximum of brutality on the part of the elements—qualities which the eminent thinker, in a hasty generalization, ascribed to Brazil as a whole—exist here in reality and are manifested in astounding landscapes. Beholding these landscapes, even with the cool eye of the naturalist who is not given to rhetorical descriptions, one realizes that this anomalous climate is one that affords the most significant example of the wide varia-tions of environment to be found in Brazil.

There is nothing like it, when it comes to a play of antitheses. The gen-eral aspect of the region is one of extreme benignity—the earth in love with life; fecund Nature in a triumphant apotheosis of bright, calm days; the soil blossoming with a fantastic vegetation—fertile, irrigated with rivers that spread out to the four corners of the compass. But this opulent placidity conceals, paradoxically, the germs of cataclysms, which, bursting forth always with an unalterable rhythm, in the summertime, heralded by the same infallible omens, here descend with the irresistible finality of a natural law. It is difficult to describe them, but we shall endeavor to give a sketch.

When the hot, moist squalls have blown for some days from the north-east, the atmosphere becomes motionless, stagnant—not a breath of air stirring. Then it is that "Nature, as it were, droops in an ecstasy of fear; not even the tops of the trees are swaying; the forests, frightfully still, ap-pear to be solid objects; the birds cower in their nests and sing no more."[10]

When, however, one looks up at the sky, there is not a cloud in sight! The limpid-arching blue is lighted still by a sun that is darkened, as if in eclipse. The atmospheric pressure, meanwhile, slowly but constantly drops, stifling all life as it does so. For moments, a dense cloud cumulus with copper-colored borders looms darkly on the southern horizon. Then

---

[8] [The *pamperos* of the Argentine pampas. "A cold, strong, dry southwest wind . . . . gen-erally advancing with a well-marked and very black cloud-front" (*Funk & Wagnalls' Standard Dictionary*).]

[9] [See pp. 52 and 144.]

[10] Dr. João Severiano da Fonseca, *Viagem ao Redor do Brasil*.

comes a breeze whose velocity rapidly increases, turning into a high wind. The temperature falls in a few minutes, and, a moment later, the earth is shaken by a violent hurricane. Lightning flashes; thunderbolts resound in a sky that is lowering now; and a torrential rain descends on the vast expanse of plains, wiping out in a single inundation the uncertain *divortium aquarum* that crosses them, uniting the sources of the rivers and embroiling their beds in a limitless overflow.

The assault is a sudden one. The cataclysm bursts precipitately in the vibrant spiral of a cyclone. Houses are unroofed; the aged carandá trees[11] are bent double, moan and split; the hills are islands; the plains deep in water.

An hour later the sun is shining triumphantly in the purest of skies! The restless birds are singing in the dripping foliage; the air is filled with gentle breezes—and man, leaving the shelter to which he had tremulously repaired, comes forth to view, amid the universal revival of Nature, the damage wrought by the storm. Trunks and boughs of trees rent by lightning and twisted by the winds; cottages in ruins, their roofs strewn over the ground; muddy rivers overflowing their banks with the last of the downpour; the grass of the fields beaten down, as if a herd of buffaloes had passed that way—sorry reminders, all, of the tempest and its fulminating onslaught.

Some days later the winds once more begin blowing up slowly from the east; the temperature begins to mount again; the barometer drops, little ·by little; and the feeling of general uneasiness constantly increases. This keeps up until the motionless air is caught in the formidable grip of the pampeiro, and the destructive tempest arrives, blowing in turbulent-whirling eddies, against the same lugubrious background, reviving the same old cycle, the same vicious circle of catastrophes.

And now, proceeding northward, we encounter, in contrast to such manifestations as these, the climate of Pará. Brazilians of other latitudes do not know a great deal about this climate, even through the pages of a Bates.[12] Mildly warm mornings, of about 73 degrees in temperature, coming unexpectedly after rainy nights; dawns that are a glowing revelation, bringing unlooked-for metamorphoses: trees which the evening before were bare now decked with flowers; marshy bogs changed into meadows. And then, again, complete transformations: silent forests, half-naked boughs with their parched or withered leaves; an air that is still and lifeless; branches shorn of their recently opened buds, whose dead, dried

[11] [*Copernicia australis* Becc., of the Palmaceae.]
[12] [H. W. Bates, *The Naturalist on the River Amazons* (London, 1892).]

petals fall upon an earth that lies motionless, enervated, in a heat of 95 degrees in the shade. "On the following morning, the sun rises without clouds, and in this manner is completed the cycle—spring, winter, and autumn on a single tropical day."[13]

The constancy of the climate is such that one is not aware of the passing of the seasons, which, all the while, as on a dial, follow one another in the hours of one day, although the average daily temperature throughout the entire year shows a variation of only one degree or a little more. Thus does life strike a balance, with a consistency that is not to be perturbed.

On the other hand, in the Upper Amazon region to the west, we come upon a new *habitat*, with different characteristics. And this, needless to say, imposes a painful process of acclimatization on the inhabitants of the bordering territories.

Here, at the height of the summer heat, when the last gusts of wind from the east are dying on the heavy-laden air, the thermometer comes to take the place of the hygrometer in the study of climate. The grievous round of human existence in these parts is dependent upon the emptying and filling of the great rivers. These streams rise in a most extraordinary manner. The Amazon, with a tremendous leap from its bed, in the course of a few days raises the water level to something like fifty-six feet. It expands in vast overflows, in a highly complicated network of pools and channels, *furos* and *paranamirins*[14] as they are called, forming an inland sea shot by strong currents, from which emerge the green-covered islanded *igapós*.[15]

The filling of the river brings a stoppage of life. Caught in the meshes of the *igarapés*,[16] man displays a rare stoicism, in the presence of a fatality which he is powerless to avert, and awaits the end of this paradoxical winter with its high temperatures. Summer is the ebb season. The inhabitants then resume their rudimentary activities, of the only sort compatible with a natural environment that displays so wide a range of manifestations, rendering impossible the exertion of any sustained effort.

[13] Daenert, *O Clima do Brasil.*

[14] [Cf. Richard Spruce, *Notes of a Botanist on the Amazon and Andes*, ed. Alfred Russel Wallace (London, 1908), I, 174. The form in Spruce is *paraná-mirí*. He alludes to the Paraná-mirí dos Ramos, the Furo de Uraria, and the Furo de Canomá.]

[15] [The *igapós* are bits of aquatic jungle, pools entirely grown over with vegetation. For a good description of the *igapó*, the *igarapé*, and the *paraná* (cf. the *paranamirim*, or *paraná-mirí*) see Rose and Bob Brown, *Amazing Amazon* (New York: Modern Age, 1942), pp. 24–25.]

[16] [The *igarapés* are canoe creeks, natural channels between two islands or between an island and the mainland.]

Such an environment encourages a frank parasitism. Man imbibes the milk of life by sucking on the tumid chalices of the siphonias.[17]

But in this singular yet typical climate there are other anomalies that make it worse. The alternation of rainy and dry seasons, coming like the systole and diastole of one of earth's major arteries, is not enough. There are other factors which render futile for the one not born in these parts any attempt at a real acclimatization. Many times in the season when the rivers are filling, in April or in May, in the course of a calm, clear day, the air will be suddenly chilled with cold squalls from the south. It is like an icy blast from the pole. The thermometer then drops suddenly, many degrees, and for a number of days an unnatural situation prevails.

The ambitious pack-peddlers who, spurred on by hope of gain, have ventured into these parts, and the Indians themselves, who are hardened to the climate by adaptation, now take shelter in their insubstantial huts, huddling around wood fires. All work and other activities once more cease. The great solitudes, now under water, are depopulated; the fish die of cold in the rivers; the birds in the silent forests either die or take flight; nests are empty, and even the wild beasts vanish from sight, seeking refuge in the deepest holes they can find. In brief, all this marvelous wealth of equatorial nature, fashioned by the brilliant tropical suns, now presents the cruelly desolate and mournful appearance of a region at the poles. It is the cold season, or the time of *friagem*.

However, we shall have to bring this hasty sketch to a close.

The northern backlands, as we have already seen, have in turn new climates to show, with yet other biological exigencies. Here, the same alternation of fair seasons and foul is, perhaps, more harshly reflected under other forms. Accordingly, if we stop to consider that these various climatic aspects do not represent exceptional cases but make their appearance, all of them, from the tempests of Mato Grosso to the cyclones of the northern drought area, with that periodicity which is immanent in inviolable natural laws, we shall then have to agree that the variability of our physical milieu is complete.

Whence the mistake made by those who, in studying our national physiology, fall into generalizations with regard to the particular effect of a tropical climate. It is undoubtedly true that such a climate tends to create a *sui generis* pathology throughout the whole of the northern coastal strip and a good part of the corresponding states, as far as Mato Grosso. The moisture-laden heat of the Amazon region, for example, is depressing and exhausting in effect. It forms stunted organisms, in which all activity

[17] [*Siphonia spp.*, genus of plants synonymous with *Hevea*.]

is subject to a permanent lack of balance between the impulsive energies of the strongly excited peripheral functions and the apathy of the central functions: marasmic intelligences, stupefied by the explosive force of the passions; feeble innervations, in contrast to the acuity of the senses, and ill compensated or repaired by a blood stream which has been impoverished by incomplete hematoses.

From this flow all the idiosyncracies of an exceptional physiology; lungs that are reduced in size, and which, in the obligatory elimination of carbon dioxide, are replaced by the liver, upon which falls life's heavy surcharge: organisms wasted by the persistent alternation of an impulsive exaltation and an enervating apathy, without the vibratility or energetic muscular tone of robust and full-blooded temperaments. Natural selection in such an environment is effected at the cost of grave compromises with the central functions of the brain, in a most prejudicial inverse progression between intellectual and physical development, assuring inevitably the victory of the expansive instincts and looking to the ideal of an adaptation which shall have as its sole consequences a maximum of organic energy and a minimum of moral fortitude. Acclimatization in such a case means a regressive evolution. The type wastes away in a constant decline, the effects of which are transmitted by heredity to the point of total extinction. Like the Englishman in Barbados, in Tasmania, or in Australia, the Portuguese in the Amazon region may flee miscegenation, but after a few generations his physical and moral characteristics will be profoundly altered, from his complexion, turned copper colored by the tropic suns and the incomplete elimination of carbon dioxide, to his temperament, which is weakened by having been deprived of its original qualities. The inferior race, the crude savage, dominates him; in league with the environment, he conquers him, crushes him, annihilates him, in formidable competition with malaria, hepatitis, debilitating fevers, the intense heat of summer, and the ague-breeding swamps.

This does not occur in a good part of central Brazil and throughout the southern regions. Even in the major part of the northern backlands the dry heat, largely counteracted by the strong air currents coming from the northeast and southeast, creates situations that are more encouraging, more beneficent and stimulating in their effect.

Returning to the south, to the territory which from northern Minas runs southeast to Rio Grande, we come upon conditions that are incomparably superior. An annual medium temperature ranging from 62 to 68 degrees, with a more harmonious and stable alternation of seasons, the summer rains being distributed over the autumn and spring in a manner favorable to cultivation. As winter comes on, the impression of a European climate is deepened: the frigid southwest wind brings drizzling rains and mist; the snow forms a lacework on the windowpanes; the brooks are frozen over; and the frost is white on the fields.

REFLECTION OF ENVIRONMENT IN HISTORY

Our history reflects in a noteworthy manner these environmental conditions. Considering the subject from a general point of view, leaving out of account for the moment the disturbing effect of nontypical details, we may behold diversified situations already taking shape in our colonial period. With the land under feudal rule, divided up among the fortunate proprietors on whom it had been bestowed, the settlement of the country was undertaken from north and south, with the same identical elements, and with the same show of indifference in either case on the part of a metropolis whose gaze was still turned to the last mirages of the "marvelous Indies"; and it was then that the radical separation between south and north began.

There is no need here for us to go into the decisive factors in the case of the two regions. They are two distinct histories, registering movements and tendencies opposed to each other. Two societies in process of formation, alienated by their rival destinies, one wholly indifferent to the mode of life of the other, and both all the while evolving under the influence of a single administration. In the south new tendencies were developing, a greater division of labor, more vigor in a stock that was hardier and more heterogeneous, more practical, and adventurous—a broad progressive movement, in short. And all this stood in contrast to the agitated, at times more brilliant, but always less productive life of the north: scattered and disunited captaincies, yoked to the same routine, amorphous and static, fulfilling the limited round of functions incumbent upon the pensioners of a distant court.

History here is more theatrical, less eloquent. There arise heroes, but they are great of stature only by contrast with the common run of men about them: brilliant, vibrant pages of history, but cut short, without definite objective, with the three formative races, wholly divorced from one another, playing their part in it all.

Even in the culminating period, that of the struggle with the Dutch, Henrique Dias' Negroes, Camarão's Indians, and Vieira's Lusitanians remained distinctly separate in their army tents.[18] If they were separated in

---

[18] [Allusion to the struggle between the Portuguese and the Dutch, in the Pernambuco region, 1644–54—a struggle led by João Fernandez Vieira, who is sometimes referred to as "the creator of Brazilian nationality."]

war, the distance between them grew in time of peace. The drama of Palmares,[19] the incursions of the Indians, the conflicts on the border of the backlands—all violated that truce which had been struck against the Batavian.

With the coastal region prisoned between the inaccessible backlands and the sea, there has been a tendency to hand down the old colonial alignment to our day, thanks to an obstinate and stupid centralization which has achieved the anomaly of dislocating in a new land the moral ambient of an old society. Fortunately, there was the impact of the impetuous wave from the south.

In the latter region, where acclimatization was a speedier process, in an environment that was less adverse, the newcomers soon attained an unwonted vigor. Out of the absorption of the aboriginal tribes came the mixed descendants of the backland conquests, the daring mamelucos. The Paulista—and this name, in its historic signification, takes in the sons of Rio de Janeiro, Minas, São Paulo, and regions south—now arose as an autonomous type, adventurous, rebellious, freedom-loving, the perfect model of a lord of the earth, freeing himself, rebel-like, from a distant rule, leaving behind him the sea and the galleons of the metropolis, casting in his lot with the hinterland, and carving out the unsung epic of the "Bandeiras."[20]

All this admirably reflects the influence of environmental conditions. There was no racial distinction whatsoever between the colonizers from the south and those from the north. In either case, there was a prevalence of those same elements which were the despair of Diogo Coelho: "Worse here in the land than pestilence. . . . ." But in the south the vital force of temperament remaining with those who had bested the unyielding ocean was not wasted by an enervating climate but found a fresh component in the very strength of earth, which changed it, and for the better. Man here felt himself strong and capable. With the theater of his great crimes shifted but a little, he might bring to bear upon the impervious backlands the same audacity which had hurled him into African circumnavigations.

In addition—and we must touch upon this point at the risk of scandalizing our puny historiographers—the mountains freed him from the preoccupation of having to defend a littoral where the bark of the covetous foreigner might put in. The Serra do Mar, towering perpendicularly above

[19] [The historic seventeenth-century runaway-slave colony, or *quilombo*.]

[20] [See p. 10 and n. 12.]

the Atlantic, like the curtain of a huge bastion, has played a notable role in our history. Against its cliffs the warrior passion of the Cavendishes and the Fentons beat in vain. On its heights, letting his gaze roam round about him over the plains, the newcomer felt secure. He felt himself on battlements that were not to be moved, which served at once as his protection against the foreign invader and against the cavalier from the metropolis. The mountains, arched like hoops of stone about a continent, were an isolating factor in both the ethnic and the historical sense of the word. They canceled out that irrepressible attraction to the seaboard which existed in the north, a seaboard reduced to a narrow strip of swamps and reefs, which held out nothing to excite man's covetousness; while there arose, superior to all fleets, intangible in the depts of the forests, the mysterious lure of the mines.

What is more, the special topographical relief of these mountains turns them into a condenser of the first order, in precipitating the evaporated moisture of the ocean. The rivers which flow down the slopes may be said in a manner of speaking to rise in the sea, rolling their waters in an opposite direction from the coast, carrying them to the interior, making straight for the backlands. They inevitably put the newcomer in mind of exploring expeditions. The earth attracts man, calls him to her fertile bosom, enchants him with her great beauty, and ends by snatching him, irresistibly, into the river currents.

The Tieté in its course is an eloquent case in point, giving direction to this conquest of the land. Whereas on the São Francisco, the Parnaíba, the Amazon, and all the other streams of the eastern seaboard, in proceeding up them to the interior, one has to battle the currents and the cataracts which fall from the terraces of the plateaus, the Tieté without the exertion of rowing carries the inhabitants of the region to the Rio Grande and thence to the Paraná and the Parnaíba. It was the means of penetration into Minas, into Goiaz, Santa Catarina, the Rio Grande do Sul, Mato Grosso, all Brazil. Following this line of least resistance, which at the same time affords the clearest outline of our colonial expansion, the bandeiras did not find, as in the north, a sterile earth and the intangible barrier of ugly deserts to slow their progress.

It is easy to show how this distinction of a physical nature sheds light on the anomalies and contrasts to be found in the course of events in the two parts of the country, above all in the acute period of colonial crisis in the seventeenth century. The Dutch rule at this time was centered in Pernambuco, but it affected the entire east coast from Baía to Maranhão; and in the struggle that ensued there were certain memorable encounters in which our three formative races joined forces against the common ene-my. The man of the south, on the other hand, held himself absolutely aloof from this movement and showed, by rebelling against the decrees from the metropolis, how completely divorced he was from his battling fellow-countrymen. He was in a way an enemy fully as dangerous as the Batavian. A strange race of mestizos, given to uprisings, swayed by other tendencies, guided by another star, setting off in other directions, these southerners resolutely trod underfoot all restraining bulls and letters patent. In stubborn reaction to the Jesuits, they entered into an open struggle with the Portuguese court. As for the Jesuit fathers, they, for-getting the Dutch, had recourse to Madrid through Ruy de Montoya, and to Rome through Dias Taño; which showed that they looked upon the southerner as being the more serious foe.

Indeed, while in Pernambuco Von Schoppe's troops were setting up the Nassau government, in São Paulo the groundwork was being laid for the somber drama of Guaira. And when the restoration in Portugal led to the defeat of the invader all along the line, bringing the exhausted combatants together once more, the men of the south made it still more plain that theirs was a separate destiny by taking advantage of this very fact to as-sert their full and free autonomy in the one-minute rule of Amador Bueno.

There is no greater contrast in all our history. It is one truly national in significance, but one of which there is barely a glimpse to be had in the spectacular courts of the governors in Baía, where the Society of Jesus held sway, with the privilege of the conquest of souls, a casuistic euphe-mism cloaking a monopoly of the native's good right arm.

In the middle of the seventeenth century the contrast becomes still more pronounced. The men of the south were spreading out over the in-terior, making their way as far as the extreme limits of Ecuador. Down to the middle of the eighteenth century, the settlers followed the confused trails of the bandeiras. Wave after wave of them came, with the untiring fatality of a natural law; and, indeed, they did represent a vast potential, these great warrior caravans, these human waves let loose on the four cor-ners of the compass, stamping over their country at every point, discover-ing it after the discovery, laying bare the gleaming bosom of its mines.

Leaving behind them the seaboard, which reflected the decadence of the metropolis, along with all the vices of a nationality in process of hope-less decomposition, these pioneers, making their way to the far lands of Pernambuco and the Amazon, gave the impression of being of another race, in their intrepid daring and their ability to withstand adversity. When the incursions of the savage threatened Baía, or Pernambuco, or

Paraíba, and the runaway-slave *quilombos*, last refuge of the rebellious African, were set up in the forest, the southerner, as the crude epic of Palmares tells us, thereupon arose as the classic hero vanquishing all perils, the chosen one for the undertaking of giant hecatombs.

The truth is, the northerner did not possess a physical environment which endowed him with an equal amount of energy. Had such been the case, the bandeiras from the east and those from the north would have come together and crushed the native, who would have disappeared without leaving any trace. But the northern colonist, to the west and south, found himself face to face with hostile Nature and speedily turned back to the coast; his was not the daring of those conquerors who feel themselves at home in a friendly land; his was not the self-assurance inspired by the very attractiveness of luxuriant and easily accessible regions. The explorations which were here begun in the second half of the sixteenth century, by Sebastião Tourinho on the River Doce, by Bastião Alvares on the São Francisco, and by Gabriel Soares in northern Baía, up to the headwaters of the Paraguassú, although they may have had the energetic stimulus of the Belchior Dias Silver Mines, are but a pallid imitation of the irruptions of the *Anhanguera*[21] or of a Paschoal de Araujo.

Caught between the coastal canebrakes and the backlands, between the sea and the desert, in a blockade that was rendered more formidable by the action of the climate, the northerner wholly lost that upstanding spirit of rebellion which resounds so eloquently throughout all the pages of southern history. Such a contrast, certainly, is not based on primordial racial factors.

Having thus outlined the environmental influence on our history, let us see now what its influence has been upon our ethnic formation.

ACTION OF ENVIRONMENT IN THE INITIAL PHASE
OF THE FORMATION OF RACES

Let us return to our point of departure. Agreed that environment does not form races, in our own special case, in various parts of the country, it produces an excessive variation in the degree of admixture of the three essential elements. Through the very diversity of the conditions of adaptation, it prepares the way for the appearance of different subraces. Moreover (and this today is an undeniable fact), external conditions gravely affect even well-established societies, which are dislocated by long-continuing migrations, even though these societies may be decked out with the

---

[21] [Large-scale *bandeirante* expedition.]

resources of a superior culture. If this is true in the case of thoroughly well-defined races in other climates, protected by a surrounding civilization which is like the blood plasm of these great collective organisms, what then shall we say of our own situation, which is very different in kind? In this case, it is evident, the juxtaposition of characteristics means an intimate transfusion of tendencies; and the corresponding long period of transformation is by way of being a period of debilitation so far as the capacities of the crossed races are concerned; all of which increases the relative importance of the influence of environment. Environment is then, as it were, better able to stamp its own characteristic features upon the human organism in process of fusion. Without venturing upon too daring a parallel, we may say that, for these complex biological reactions, it has more energetic agents than for the chemical reactions of matter. To heat and light, which exert their influence in both cases, there is added the lay of the land, the climatic manifestations, and that undeniable presence, that species of mysterious catalytic force, which is immanent in the various aspects of nature.

Among us, as we have seen, these latter elements are far from possessing that uniform intensity which is ascribed to them. As history shows, they have led to a diverse distribution of our ethnic strata, giving rise to dissimilar forms of racial admixture.

There is no such thing as a Brazilian anthropological type.

RACIAL FORMATION IN NORTHERN BRAZIL

Let us, nevertheless, continue, in this intricate labyrinth of races, to pursue the fugitive mirage of a subrace, possibly an ephemeral one. Not adept at discriminating between those of our races that are in process of formation, let us confine ourselves to our subject by outlining rapidly the historidal antecedents of the jagunço.[22]

As we have already seen, Brazilian racial formation in the north is very different from that in the south. Historic circumstances, deriving in large part from physical ones, gave rise to initial diversities in the intermingling of the races—diversities which have been handed down to our own day. The march of settlement from Maranhão to Baía reveals these differences.

THE FIRST SETTLERS

It was a slow process. The Portuguese did not approach the northern seaboard with that vital strength which comes from dense migrations,

[22] [This term as employed by the author is practically synonymous with *sertanejo*, or inhabitant of the backlands. For its original meaning see p. 148.]

great masses of invaders capable of preserving, even when uprooted from their native soil, all those qualities acquired in the course of a long historical apprenticeship. They were scattered, parceled out in small bands of condemned exiles or counterfeit colonists, lacking in the virile mien of conquerors. They still were dazzled by visions of the Orient. Brazil was the land of exile, a huge garrison for the intimidating of heretics and backsliders, all those victims of the somber *let-him-die-for-it* justice of those days. And so it was, in these early times, the reduced number of settlers stood in contrast to the vast expanse of the land and the size of the native population. The instructions given, in 1615, to Captain Fragoso de Albuquerque, concerning the regularizing with the Spanish ambassador in France of the truce agreement with La Revardière, are sufficiently clear in this respect. Here it is stated that "the lands of Brazil are not unpopulated, for the reason that there exist in them more than three thousand Portuguese."

This for the whole of Brazil—more than a hundred years after the discovery.

As Ayres de Casal tells us, "the population grew so slowly that at the time of the decease of Sr. D. Sebastião (1580), there was not a settlement outside the island of Itamaracá, the inhabitants of which locality numbered some two hundred, with three sugar plantations."

When, a few years later, Baía was a little better populated, the unfavorable disproportion between the European and the two other elements still continued, in perfect arithmetic progression. According to Fernão Cardim,[23] there were two thousand whites, four thousand Negroes, and six thousand Indians. It is obvious that the autochthonous element was for a long time the predominant one. In the first intermarriages, therefore, it must have had a large influence.

The newcomers who descended upon these regions were, moreover, of a type adapted to large-scale miscegenation. Men of war, without homes, given to the solitary life of camps, or else exiles and corrupt adventurers, they were all guided by the aphorism of Barleus: *ultra aequinoctialem non peccavi.*[24] Concubinage with the *caboclas*[25] degenerated into open de-

---

[23] [The sixteenth-century Jesuit missionary whose letters, containing an account of his travels in the Baía, Pernambuco, São Paulo, and Rio de Janeiro regions, are a rich source of information on folklore and ethnography. Among his works are *Do princípio e origem dos Indios do Brasil* and *Narrativa epistolar de uma viagem e missão jesuita*.]

[24] [Cf. Kipling's famous "east of Suez" couplet.]

[25] [The Indian women.]

bauchery, from which not even the clergy were free. Padre Nobrega[26] clearly establishes this fact, in his celebrated letter to the King (1549), in which, depicting with an ingenuous realism the laxity of manners, he declares that the interior of the country is full of the offspring of Christians, who increase and multiply in accordance with heathen custom. He thinks it would be better if orphans were sent out, or even *erring women, all of whom would find husbands, the land being so great and rich.* The first intensive mixture of races, between the European and the Indian, occurred, then, in these early times. "Soon," says Casal, "the Tupinquins, who are pagans of good disposition, were christened and married off to Europeans, there being innumerable natural whites in the country with the blood of the Tupinquins in their veins."

On the other hand, although they existed in large numbers within the bounds of the kingdom, the Africans in this first century played an inferior role. In many places there were few of them to be found. They were few, according to the trustworthy narrator just quoted, in Rio Grande do Norte, "where the Indians were long since reduced, despite their ferocity, and where their descendants through alliances with Europeans and Africans have augmented the classes of whites and brown-skins."

These excerpts are significant. Without any preconceived ideas on the subject, it may be asserted that the disappearance of the native in the north, as Varnhagen believes,[27] was due not so much to actual extermination as to repeated intermarriages.

We know, moreover, that the landed proprietors were anxious to make the most of such alliances in capturing the affections of the native. This attitude reflects the instincts of the metropolis, as is shown in the various royal charters from 1570 to 1758, in which, despite "a never interrupted train of hesitations and contradictions,"[28] there appeared a desire to mitigate the lust for gain on the part of the colonists, bent upon the enslavement of the savage. Some of these charters, that of 1680, for example, extend the royal protection to the point of decreeing that lands shall be granted the heathen, "even those uncultivated lands already given to others, inasmuch as those same Indians ought to have the preference, being the natural lords of the land."

[26] [The famous sixteenth-century Jesuit, Manoel de Nobrega, whose *Cartas do Brasil, 1549–1560* were published at Rio de Janeiro in 1886.]

[27] [Francisco Adolfo Varnhagen, Visconde de Porto Seguro (1816–78), one of Brazil's outstanding historians. Among his works is a *Historia geral do Brasil.* Varnhagen was noted for his antipathy to the Indian and his exaltation of the Portuguese element in Brazilian civilization; he was an ardent defender of the colonial regime.]

[28] João Francisco Lisboa.

THE JESUITS

In this persistent attempt at the assimilation of the native, an important part was played by the Society of Jesus, which, compelled in the south to submit to compromises, ruled supreme in the north. Putting aside any unworthy intentions, the Jesuits in this region performed an ennobling task. At the least, they were rivals of the colonist, who was bent on gain. In the stupid clash of perversity with barbarism, these eternal exiles found a function that was worthy of them. They did much. They were the only disciplined men of their day. Although the attempt to elevate the mental state of the aborigine to the abstractions of monotheism may have been a chimerical one, it had the effect of attracting him for a long time—down to the opportune intervention of Pombal[29]—into the stream of our history.

The record of the missions in the north, throughout the tract from Maranhão to Baía, reveals a slow effort at penetration into the heart of the backlands, from the slopes of Ibiapaba to those of Itiúba, completing in a manner the feverish activity of the bandeiras. If these latter, despite the disturbances which they brought with them, diffused widely over the newly discovered regions the blood of the three races, thereby occasioning a general miscegenation, the organized settlements, on the other hand, centers of the attractive force exerted by the apostolate, had the effect of unifying and integrating the native tribes, fusing their small communities into villages. Penetrating, as the result of a century-long effort, deep into the backlands, the missionaries were responsible for saving in part this factor in our racial picture. Some historians, distracted by the coming of the African on a large scale, an event which, beginning at the end of the sixteenth century, continued uninterruptedly down to our time (1850), have felt that the latter was the best ally of the Portuguese in the colonial epoch and, accordingly, attribute to him generally an exaggerated influence upon the formation of the inhabitant of the northern backlands. However, as far as any invasion by these conquered and unhappy beings is concerned, taking into account their extraordinary fecundity and their qualities of adaptation as tested by the burning suns of Africa, it is still debatable as to whether they exercised any profound influence on the back-country regions.

It is certain that the Afro-Lusitanian association is an old one, antedating even the discovery, since it goes back to the fifteenth century, to the *azenegues* and *jalofos* of Gil Eannes and Antão Gonçalves. In 1530

[29] [The Portuguese minister (1750–77), author of sweeping reforms, who decreed the Indians to be free men and provided for grants of land to them.]

there were more than ten thousand Negroes in the streets of Lisbon, and the same was true of other places. In Evora the Negroes were in a majority over the whites. The verses of a contemporary, Garcia de Rezende, are a document here:

Vemos no reyno metter,
Tantos captivos crescer,
Irem-se os naturaes,
Que, se assim fôr, serão mais
Elles que nós, a meu ver.[30]

THE ORIGIN OF THE MULATTO

Thus, the origin of the mulatto is to be looked for outside our own country. The first intermarrying with the African occurred in the metropolis. With us, naturally, the number of such marriages tended to increase. However, the dominated race found its capacities for development annulled by the social situation that prevailed. A powerful organism, given to an extreme humility, without the Indian's rebelliousness,[31] the Negro at once had the whole burden of colonial life placed on his shoulders. He was a beast of burden, condemned to labor unceasingly. Old ordinances, setting forth "how one may rid himself of slaves and beasts upon finding them sick or maimed," show the brutality of the age. Moreover, and the point is incontrovertible, the numerous slaves imported were concen-

[30] ["We see so many captives brought into the kingdom and their numbers so increasing that, if this keeps up, as I see it, they will become the natives and will outnumber us."]

[31] [It may be pointed out that present-day anthropologists and historians are not inclined to agree with this view. Arthur Ramos, for example, has this to say: "It has been repeatedly but erroneously asserted, by Brazilian historians and sociologists, that the Negro in Brazil . . . . was a passive element, resigned to a state of slavery. According to these historians, the African Negro, a humble, docile creature, permitted himself to be taken, and submitted without protest to slave labor. This is a view which is categorically refuted by a study of history and sociology. Such a study shows us, on the contrary, that the Negro was never this docile, submissive type, incapable of reacting to conditions. . . . . He was a good worker but a bad slave. Several centuries of slavery and slave revolts, not only in Brazil, but in other parts of the Americas as well, show us what his true reactions were. Those reactions ranged all the way from flight to suicide, from individual escape to great collective uprisings." Professor Ramos stresses the fact that if the Negro was enslaved in preference to the Indian, it was because he was "better adapted than the Indian to agricultural labor, by reason of his cultural background." Of Palmares, Ramos says: "The Republic of Palmares was a Negro state founded by slaves in Brazil, in the mid-seventeenth century. Situated in northeastern Brazil, in the heart of the present State of Alagôas, this extraordinary undertaking lasted from 1630 to 1697, or more than half a century." He quotes Rocha Pitta to the effect that Palmares was "a rustic republic, well ordered after its fashion" (see the article by Ramos, "O Espirito associativo do negro brasileiro," Revista do Arquivo Municipal [São Paulo], XLVII [May, 1938], 105–26). Cf. Henry Bamford Parkes, A History of Mexico (Boston: Houghton Mifflin Co., 1938), p. 95 n.: "Negroes had more physical strength—and also more aggressiveness—than Indians. . . . . In spite of their relatively small numbers the Spaniards were more afraid of Negro rebellions than of risings among the Indians." For a different view of Palmares cf. Pierson, Negroes in Brazil: A Study of Race Contact at Bahia, p. 50, n. 62; cf. also Rodrigues, Os Africanos no Brasil, pp. 111–43.]

trated on the seaboard. The great black border hemmed the coast from Baía to Maranhão but did not extend far into the interior. Even in open revolt, the humble Negro, become a dread *quilombola*[32] foregathering in *mocambos*,[33] appeared to avoid the heart of the country. Palmares, with its thirty thousand *mocambeiros*,[34] was, after all, only a few miles distant from the coast.

On the seaboard the fertility of the earth tended to retain there two of the three elements, while freeing the Indian. The extensive culture of sugar cane, imported from Madeira, led to the backlands' being forgotten. Already before the Dutch invasion, there were a hundred and sixty sugar plantations from Rio Grande do Norte to Baía.[35] And this exploitation, on an expanded scale, was later to increase in a rapid crescendo.

The African element, in any event, remained in the vast canebrakes of the coast, fettered to the earth and giving rise to a racial admixture quite different from the one taking place in the recesses of the captaincies. In the latter place the free Indian roamed, unadapted to toil and always rebellious or barely held in check in the settlements through the tenacity of the missionaries. Negro slavery, the result of the colonist's self-interest, left the padres less encumbered with manual labor than in the south and with more time for catechizing. As for the pioneers themselves, upon arriving at this last stage of their daring journey, they had all their combativeness extinguished. Some of them, like Domingos Sertão, brought an adventurous life to a close by seeking the profit to be made on the stock-breeding farms which had been opened on the great estates.

In this manner a thoroughgoing distinction arose between intermarriages in the backlands and those on the seaboard. As a consequence, with the white element the common denominator in both cases, the mulatto appeared as the principal result in the latter, and the curiboca in the former, instance.

II

ORIGIN OF THE JAGUNÇOS

There can be no doubt that there is a notable trace of originality in the formation of our backlands population, we shall not say of the North, but

[32] [Member of a *quilombo*, or runaway-slave colony, such as that of Palmares.]

[33] [Ramos (*op. cit.*, p. 117) says: "The center of political and social unity was the *quilombo*, a collection of small dwellings or *mocambos*, built within a fortified wooden enclosure. . . . . Within this enclosure the *mocambos* were situated, forming irregular streets." In modern Brazilian usage, *mocambo* means a hut or hovel in which the very poor live; on the social implications of the *mocambo* in this latter sense see João Duarte Filho, "O Mocambo," *Cultura política*, II, No. 15 (May, 1942), 17–25.]

[34] [The *mocambeiros* were those who lived in the *mocambos*.]

[35] Diogo Campos, *Razão do estado do Brasil*.

of subtropical Brazil. Let us try to sketch it in; and, in order not to stray too far from the subject, let us keep close to that theater in which the historic drama of Canudos was unfolded, by traversing rapidly the reaches of the São Francisco, that "great highway of Brazilian civilization," as one historian has put it.[36]

From the bird's-eye view given in the foregoing pages, we have seen that this river flows through regions that differ greatly in character. At its headwaters it spreads out, its expanded basin with its network of numerous tributaries taking in the half of Minas, in the zone of mountains and forests. Later, along its middle portion, it narrows, in the extremely beautiful region of the Campos Gerais.[37] Along its lower course, downstream from Joazeiro, where it is confined between slopes which render its bed uneven and which twist it about in the direction of the sea, it becomes poor in tributaries, almost all of them intermittent, and flows away hemmed in a single corredeira[38] of several hundred miles in length, extending to Paulo Affonso—and here it is that it cuts through the semidesert tract of caatingas.

In the threefold aspects of this river we have a diagram of the course of our history, one that reflects in parallel fashion its varying manifestations. It balances the influence of the Tieté. Whereas this latter river, with a course incomparably better suited to purposes of colonization, became the chosen pathway of pioneers seeking, above all, the enslavement and corruption of the savage, the São Francisco at its headwaters was essentially the center of the movement to the mines; in its lower course it was the scene of missionary activity; and, in its middle region, it became the classic land of the herdsman, representing the only mode of life compatible with existing social and economic conditions in the colony. Its banks were trod alike by the bandeirante, the Jesuit, and the vaqueiro.[39]

When, at some future date, a more copious supply of documents shall enable us to reconstruct the life of the colony from the seventeenth century to the end of the eighteenth, it is possible that the vaqueiro, wholly forgotten today, will stand out with that prominence which he deserves, by reason of his formative influence on the life of our people. Brave and fearless as the bandeirante, as resigned and tenacious as the Jesuit, he had the advantage of a supplementary attribute which both the others lacked—he had his roots fixed in the soil.

[36] João Ribeiro, *Historia do Brasil.*
[37] [See p. 7, n. 7.]
[38] [See p. 8, n. 10.]
[39] [The cowboy of the North (see pp. 77 ff.).]

As for the bandeiras,[40] there were two sides to their activity, which were at times distinct, at other times mingled in confusion. Sometimes they fell upon the land and sometimes upon man. Sometimes they went in search of gold and sometimes in search of slaves. But one thing they did do was to discover huge tracts of land—land which they did not cultivate and which, it might be, they left more of a desert than it was before, as they passed rapidly on through the villages and the *catas*.[41] Their history, at times as undecipherable as the deliberately obscure entries in their log-books, was a successive alternation and combination of these two stimuli, depending upon the personal temperament of the adventurers concerned or the greater or less degree of practicability of the enterprises planned. In the permanent oscillation between these two motives, their really useful function, which lay in discovering the unknown, appears as an obligatory incident, an inevitable consequence to which they gave no thought.

With the expedition of Glimmer (1601), the deceptive vision of the "Emerald Mountains" was no more—that vision which, from the middle of the sixteenth century, had lured to the slopes of the Espinhaço, one after another, unmindful of constant failures, such men as Bruzzo Spinosa, Sebastião Tourinho, Dias Adorno, and Martins Carvalho. The enchanted land idealized in the romantic imagination of a Gabriel Soares having vanished in the north, the greater part of the seventeenth century is dominated by the somber legends of slave-hunters, centering about the brutally heroic figure of Antonio Raposo. It was about this time that the mirage of the mysterious "Sabará-bussú" and the eternally inaccessible "Silver Mines" likewise vanished. These dreams were given new life by the indecisive explorations of Paes Leme, who, after they had lain untrod for the better part of a century, sought out the paths of Glimmer. They were kept alive by the golden nuggets of Arzão, who in 1693 followed in the very footsteps of Tourinho and Adorno. And then, at last, they were fully revived with Bartholomeu Bueno in Itaberaba and Miguel Garcia in Ribeirão do Carmo; the old passion for hinterland exploration lived again, and, radiating from the Ouro Preto district, and stronger than ever now, once more spread over the entire country.

It was during this brief period when, to all appearances, nothing of note was occurring on the seaboard beyond the struggle with the Batavian and, in the heart of the plateau country, the extraordinary surge of the

---

[40] [On the *bandeiras* see João Pandiá Calogeras, *A History of Brazil*, trans. and ed. Percy Alvin Martin (Chapel Hill: University of North Carolina Press, 1939), pp. 20 ff.]

[41] [Abandoned surface-mine clearings (see p. 44).]

bandeiras, that there began along the middle reaches of the São Francisco a process of settlement the results of which were only to become apparent later.

HISTORICAL FUNCTION OF THE SÃO FRANCISCO

It was a slow process. A determining factor in the beginning was the expeditions to the mines of Moreya, expeditions which, though their fame was scant, would seem to have extended all the way to the vicegerency of Lancastro, thus opening a path for successive swarms of settlers, to the highlands of Macaúbas, beyond Paramirim.[42] Deprived of direct routes in a normal line with the coast, which would have been shorter, but which were cut off by thick mountain walls and blocked by forests, explorers found access to the backlands by way of the São Francisco. Affording them two entrances, one at its source and the other at its mouth, and bringing the southerners to meet the men of the north, the great river from the beginning took on the aspect of an ethnic unifier, an extensive bond of union between two societies that were in ignorance of each other. Although coming from diverse points and with equally diverse backgrounds, the Paulistas of Domingos Sertão, the Baians of Garcia d'Avila, with the small armies of his Tabajara[43] allies, or even the Portuguese of Manoel Nunes Vianna, who set out from his "Fazenda do Escuro," in Carinhanha, to subdue the *emboabas*[44] on the Rio das Mortes—whoever they were, from wherever they hailed, the newcomers, upon reaching the heart of the backlands, seldom returned.

The land at once highly productive and readily accessible compensated them for the lost mirage of the longed-for mines. The original character of its geological structure created topographical conformations in which the highlands, the last spurs and counterforts of the maritime cordillera, were offset by vast tablelands. Its flora was complex and varied, interspersed with forests that were not so vast and impenetrable as those of the coast, along with the "charm" and "rustic beauty" of fields and plains that were suddenly lost, all of them, in the enormous glades of the caatingas. Its special hydrographic conformation, with tributaries running almost symmetrically east and west, linked it to the coast on the one side and, on the other side, to the center of the plateau region. All these were precious lures, attracting the scattered elements and leading to their fu-

[42] Letter of Pedro Barbosa Leal to the Conde de Sabugosa, 1725 (see F. A. Pereira da Costa, *Em prol da integridade do territorio de Pernambuco*, and Pedro Taques, *Nobilarchia Paulista*).

[43] [Indians of the state of Ceará, Serra da Ibiapaba.]

[44] [Nickname given by the descendants of the Paulistas near the mines, in colonial times, to the Portuguese who went to the backlands in search of gold and precious stones.]

sion. And, finally, there was the opportunity for a herdsman's life, the one that was naturally suited to this region of the Campos Gerais.

In this latter connection, in addition to the rare fecundity of the soil, there was not lacking an essential element, salt, which was to be found in the brackish lowlands of the "pits."[45]

Under these favorable conditions there was opened the extensive cattle-breeding zone, which already at the dawn of the eighteenth century extended from the northern sections of Minas to Goiaz, to Piauí, to the boundaries of Maranhão and Ceará on the northwest and the fertile highlands of Baía on the east. As it was populated, this region became a strong and autonomous one; but little was heard of it, since the chroniclers of the time paid small attention to it, and it accordingly remained utterly forgotten, not only by the distant metropolis, but by the governors and viceroys themselves. It did not produce taxes or revenues to interest a selfish-minded monarch. It represented, nonetheless, in contrast to the turbulence of the seaboard and the adventurous episode of the mines, "almost the only tranquil aspect of our culture."[46] Aside from the rare contingents of Pernambucan and Baian settlers, the majority of the well-to-do cattlemen who sprang up here came from the south, of the same enthusiastic and energetic stock from which the bandeiras sprang.

THE JAGUNÇOS: PROBABLE RELATIVES OF THE PAULISTAS

According to the information contained in the precious pages of Pedro Taques,[47] there were numerous families of São Paulo which, in continuous migrations, sought out these far corners of the land; and it is to be believed, if we accept the opinion of a perspicacious historian, that "the valley of the São Francisco, long since populated by the Paulistas and their descendants, from the eighteenth century became almost an exclusive colony of them."[48] It was, accordingly, natural that Bartholomeu Bueno, in discovering Goiaz, to his surprise should have come upon the obvious traces of predecessors, anonymous pioneers who had come there, certainly,

[45] "All the animals greedily seek out these places, not only the mammals, but the birds and reptiles as well. The cattle lick the ground, standing knee-deep in the pools; they drink the water with relish and eat the mud" (*Escragnolle Taunay*).

Alluding to sites on the slope of the Barra do Rio Grande, Ayres de Casal says: "There are various small lakes at a greater or less distance from the river, all with water that is more or less salty; and on their borders the sun's heat brings out the salt like hoar-frost. The water from these lakes (even the fresh-water ones) is filtered through a portion of the adjacent earth in pails of wood or leather with fine holes in them, and is then exposed to the weather on the tablelands, and in eight days it crystallizes, turning into salt as white as that from the sea. Nearly all this salt appears in the center of Minas Gerais" (*Chorographia Brazilica*, II, 169).

[46] João Ribeiro.

[47] *Nobiliarchia Paulista.*   [48] Dr. João Mendes de Almeida, *Notas genealogicas.*

from the east, after crossing the Paranan Range. And then, in 1697, the most notable of the cycle of gold rushes began, amid all the noise and stir created by the waves of immigrants who stamped up the eastern slopes of the Espinhaço Range, along the thalweg of the Rio das Velhas, the hardiest of all those immigrants, perhaps, and possibly the ones who preceded the others in the discovery of the Caethé mines—passing the others by from side to side, and advancing in a contrary direction, like a reflux emanating from the north—were the bands of "Baians," a term which, like that of "Paulista," was destined to become a generic one, being extended to take in all the northern settlers.[49]

THE VAQUEIRO

The truth is, there was already being formed in the middle valley of the great river a race of mestizos identical with those bold mamelucos who had sprung up in São Paulo. We shall not be indulging in too daring a hypothesis by asserting that this extraordinary type of Paulista, arising and decaying in the south, the completeness of his degeneration being shown by the fact that it occurred in the very region that gave him its name, was here reborn and, not having to face the perils of migrations and mixed marriages, was able to perserve intact, down to our own time, the virile and adventurous character of his ancestors. Here he remained utterly divorced from the rest of Brazil and the world, walled in on the east by the Serra Geral and shut off on the west by the broad sweep of the Campos Gerais, which stretch away toward Piauí, and which to this day the native believes to be boundless.

The milieu at once attracted and held him. The water gaps on one and the other side of the meridian did not invite to dispersion but rather facilitated the intermingling of the far sections of the country, binding them together in space and in time. Assuring in the interior a contiguity of the population which was in part lacking on the coast, this rude society, arising between the northeasterners struggling for the autonomy of their nascent fatherland and the southerners who were enlarging its area and who, at the same time, were supplying it with those fat herds which roamed the valley of the Rio das Velhas or which made their way down to the head-

[49] Professor Orville Derby says: "According to Antonil, the discoveries in the Caethé region antedated those of the Rio das Velhas and Sabará; and in this case, it is to be presumed that they were made by Ouro Preto miners—passing to the west of the headwaters of the Santa Barbara, or possibly by Baians coming from the north. The importance which certain Baians attached to the events of 1709, and Antonil's allusion to Captain Luiz do Couto, who with three brothers that were 'great miners' came from Baía to this region, tend to support this latter hypothesis," etc. (*Os primeiros descrobimentos de Ouro em Minas Geraes*). [Translated from the Portuguese version.]

waters of the Parnaíba—this society, misunderstood and forgotten, was the vigorous core of our national life.[50]

The first pioneers who were responsible for this creative effort, having overcome and supplanted the savage all along the line, proceeded now to capture and enslave him, making use of his capacities in the new industry which they were founding. The result was the inevitable intermarrying; and there appeared then a race of pure curibocas with almost no mixture of African blood, as is easily shown by the normal appearance of these inhabitants of the region. They sprang from the fierce embrace of victor and vanquished. They were created in a turbulent, adventurous society, settled upon a fertile land. By way of amplifying their ancestral attributes, they had a rude schooling in force and courage on those same broad-sweeping campos where even today the jaguar roars with impunity and the swift-footed rhea roams—or else on the mountainsides, crumbling from surface-mining operations, when the Baians later summoned these lusty-lunged cowboys from their roundups to work in the mines. It would take too long here to trace the evolution of their character. With something of the colonist's adventurous disposition, combined with the impulsiveness of the native, they were further subjected to the influence of their environment, which, by isolating them, helped them to preserve the attributes and habits of their forebears, only slightly modified by the exigencies of their new life.

Here they stand, then, with their characteristic garb, their ancient customs, their strange adherence to the most remote traditions, their religious sentiment carried to the point of fanaticism, their exaggerated point of honor, and their exceedingly beautiful folklore and folk poetry, three centuries old.

A strong and ancient race, with well-defined and immutable characteristics, even in the major crises of life—at which times the cowboy's leather garb becomes the jagunço's flexible armor—sprung from far-converging elements, yet different from all the rest of the population of the country, this stock is undeniably a significant example of the importance of those reactions induced by environment. Spreading out through the bordering or near-by regions of Goiaz, Piauí, Maranhão, Ceará, and Pernambuco, their character became marked by a high degree of originality, which was expressed even in the houses that they built. All the villages, towns, and cities that give life to this territory show a common origin and are quite distinct in appearance from those in the north and in the south. In the south their dwellings were erected in the neighborhood of the mines or on

[50] [See "Author's Notes," Note V, p. 481.]

the edge of the *catas;* while in the far north, starting from a protracted line between Itiúba and Ibiapaba, they were constructed in the locality of the ancient missionary villages; but in the region here under consideration they all of them sprang up from the old cattle ranches.

We may be excused from citing examples, of which there are many to be had. Whoever views the settlements along the São Francisco, from its source to its mouth, cannot fail to observe the three types of country that we have pointed out. Leaving the Alpine-like regions, with cities perched high on the mountainsides, reflecting the incomparable daring of the bandeiras, he will cross the great campos, a huge arena made to the measure of a rude, strong, and freedom-loving people, the vaqueiros; and then, finally, he will come to the unprepossessing district laid waste by drought and elected for the slow, laborious circuits of the missionaries.

There remains for us to describe, by way of rounding out these hasty comparisons, the Jesuit foundations in this tract of territory.

JESUIT FOUNDATIONS IN BAÍA

The truth of the matter is that the backland towns of the present day, wholly different in origin from those elsewhere, were formed from the old Indian villages which, in 1758, were wrested from the power of the padres as a result of the stern policy pursued by Pombal. Confining ourselves to those that still exist today, nearest to and round about the mud-walled Troy of the jagunços,[51] we may find even within this restricted area the best examples.

Indeed, throughout the whole of this tract, which abusive concessions had placed within the power of a single family, that of Garcia d'Avila (Casa da Torre), there are some very old settlements. From "Itapicurú-de-cima" to Geremoabo, and from there, following the São Francisco, to the backland regions of Rodellas and Cabrobó, the seventeenth-century missions proceeded at a slow pace, which was to continue until our own time.

They had no historian. It is difficult today to form a picture of this extraordinary undertaking from the few documents that exist and which are too scant to permit us to trace its continuity. Those that do exist, however, are an eloquent commentary on the special case here under consideration. They inform us, in a manner that leaves no room for doubt, that, while the Negro's days were spent amid the hurly-burly of the seaboard, the native was taking up a permanent abode in villages which were to become cities. The calculating solicitude of the Jesuit and the rare self-

[51] [See p. 143. The allusion is to Canudos.]

abnegation displayed by the Capuchins and Franciscans were responsible for incorporating the native tribes into our national life; and when, at the beginning of the eighteenth century, the Paulistas stormed into Pambú and Jacobina, they gazed with surprise at these parishes which already were growing up out of the collections of tribal huts. The former place, which is a little more than fifty miles up from Paulo Affonso, from 1682 was a part of the metropolitan administration. Its destinies were guided by a Capuchin, who settled all tribal dissensions and ruled most humbly over the peaceful Morubichabas. The latter village, likewise, was exclusively native and dated from the very old mission of Sahy.

As for Geremoabo, we find it already a borough in 1698, which permits us to ascribe to it an origin that is a good deal more remote. Here there was a slight admixture of the native element with the African, of the *canhembora* with the *quilombola*.[52] Incomparably more spirited than is the case today, the humble village not infrequently attracted the attention of João de Lancastro, governor-general of Brazil, principally when the rivalries of the Indian chieftains, equipped with perfectly legal letters patent from the captaincies, grew more acute. In the year 1702 the first of the Franciscan missions undertook to discipline these settlements, their efforts proving more efficacious than had the governor's threats. The tribes were reconciled, and the influx of captured Indians into the church was such that on a single day the vicar of Itapicurú baptized 3,700 catechumens.[53]

Near by was the mission of Massacará, also a very old one, where in 1687 the opulent Garcia d'Avila kept a company of his reginemt.[54] Farther south there were yet others: Natuba, quite an old village, built by the Jesuits; Inhambupe, which upon its elevation to the status of a parish created a prolonged controversy between the padres and the aforesaid distributor of lands; and, finally, Itapicurú (1639), founded by the Franciscans.

It was, however, in the north, from the beginning of the eighteenth century, that the work of settlement was carried on most intensely, with the same racial elements. In the second half of the seventeenth century the vanguard of the southern bandeiras made its appearance in the Rodellas region. Domingos Sertão's fazenda of Sobrado was then the center of the animated life of the backlands. The effect which this rude pioneer had

[52] *Quilombola*, fugitive Negro in the *quilombos*. *Canhembora* (*cânybora*), fugitive Indian. There is a striking likeness of form, meaning, and sound in these two words, the first of which sprang up in Africa, the second in Brazil, to describe a common misfortune which befell two races in origin so far apart.

[53] José Freire de Monteiro Mascarenhas, *Os Orizes conquistados*.

[54] Livro 3°, nat. gov. fl. 272.

upon the district has not been given the attention that it deserves. With a domain situated practically at the point of convergence of the northern captaincies, being near at once to Piauí, to Ceará, to Pernambuco, and to Baía, this rural *landlord*[55] made use of the restless, adventurous curibocas in the working of his half-hundred cattle ranches. Addicted to a crude variety of feudalism, which led him to transform his tributaries into vassals and the meek Tapuias into serfs, the bandeirante, once he had reached these parts and had attained his ideal of wealth and power, continued to fulfil his function of integrating the population in alliance with his humble but stubborn adversary, the priest. The northern metropolis, the fact is, unhesitatingly supported the efforts of the latter; for a long while since, the principle had been laid down of combatting the Indian with the Indian, each missionary village of catechumens being looked upon as a redoubt against the free-roaming and indomitable savage.

It was at the end of the seventeenth century that Lancastro with his catechized natives founded the settlement of Barra, against the depredations of the Acaroazes and Mocoazes; and from this point on, following the current of the São Francisco, there were to be found, one after another, the missionary villages of N. S. do Pilar, Sorobabé, Pambú, Aracapá, Pontal, Pajehú, etc. It is, then, evident that it was precisely in this section of the Baian backlands, the one with closest ties to the other northern states— along the entire border of the Canudos region—that there developed at the beginning of our history a strong colonization movement in which the aborigine played a leading role, intermingling with white man and Negro, with these latter elements never becoming so numerous as to destroy his undeniable influence.

Those foundations set up after the expulsion of the Jesuits follow the same model. From the end of the eighteenth century to our day, in Pombal, in Cumbe, in Bom Conselho and Monte Santo, etc., persevering missionaries, of whom Appollonio de Todi[56] is the outstanding exemplar, have continued the arduous labors of the apostolate.

What has happened is that this population stuck away in a corner of the backlands has remained there until now and has gone on reproducing itself without the admixture of foreign elements; it has been, as it were, insulated, and by reason of this very fact has been able to carry on the task of racial assimilation with a uniform and maximum intensity in a manner that would account for the appearance of a well-defined and well-rounded mestizo type.

Where on the seaboard there were a thousand and one complicating

[55] [The author uses the English word.]   [56] See pp. 114–15 and 198.

and disturbing factors, due to immigration and to war, while at other central points yet other impediments arose in the sweeping trail of the bandeiras, here, on the other hand, the indigenous population, in alliance with a few wandering *mocambeiros*,[57] white fugitives from justice or audacious adventurers, remained the dominant one.

CAUSES FAVORABLE TO THE FORMATION OF A MESTIZO RACE IN THE BACKLANDS, AS DISTINGUISHED FROM CROSS-BREEDING ON THE LITTORAL

Let us not play sophists with history. There were very powerful causes which led to the isolation and conservation of the autochthonous stock.

First of all, there were the great land grants, representing the most perduring aspect of our shamefaced feudalism. The possessors of the soil, the classic model being the heirs of Antonio Guedes de Britto, were jealous of their far-flung latifundia, which, with no boundary lines to demarcate them, made their owners the lords of the countryside, barely if at all tolerating the intervention of the metropolis itself. The erection of chapels or the establishment of parishes on their lands was always accompanied by controversies with the padres; and, although the latter won out in the end, they nevertheless, to a degree, came under the sway of these potentates, who made it difficult for new settlers or competitors to come in by turning their cattle ranches, which lay scattered around in the neighborhood of the newly formed church domains, into powerful centers of attraction for the mestizo race that inhabited the parishes.

That race accordingly developed without the influence of external elements. Devoting themselves to the herdsman's life, to which they were by nature well adapted, the curibocas or swarthy cafusos, immediate forebears of the present-day vaqueiros, being entirely cut off from the inhabitants of the south and the intensive colonization activities of the seaboard, proceeded to follow their own path of evolution, acquiring thereby a highly original physiognomy, like that of residents of another country. The royal charter of February 7, 1701, was a measure designed to increase this isolation. It prohibited, with severe penalties for infraction, any communication whatsoever between this part of the backlands and the south, the São Paulo mines. Not even commercial relations were tolerated, the simplest exchange of products being forbidden.

In addition to these factors there is, in view of the origin of the backwoodsman of the north, another that is to be taken into consideration: namely, the physical environment of the backlands, to be found through-

[57] [See p. 72 and nn. 33 and 34.]

out the whole vast expanse of territory which extends from the bed of the Vasa-Barris to that of the Parnaíba in the west.

We have seen something of the unusual physiognomy of this region: the aggressive flora; the merciless climate; the periodical droughts; the rugged, sterile soil of the barren mountain ranges, lying isolated amid the splendors of the majestic *araxa*[58] of the central plateaus; and the great forests that follow the curving border of the slopes. This unprepossessing region, for which the Tupi had a suggestive appellation, *pora-pora-eyma*[59] —a name that remains attached to one of the mountains (the Borborema) which wall it in on the east—was the asylum of the Tapuia. Beaten by the Portuguese, by the Negro, and by the Tupi combined, falling back in the face of superior numbers, the indomitable *Carirys* found their only protection on this rough neck of land, rent by tempests, indurated by the rigid structure of the rocks, parched by the suns, and breaking out in briar patches and caatingas. Here too it was, in these vast open wastes, with no sign of the longed-for mines in sight, that the impulse of the bandeiras finally spent itself. As for the mysterious *Tapuy-retama* region,[60] it appealed to the stoicism of the missionary, and its long and devious trails saw the slow, grievous, agonizing onward march of these apostles of the Church. The bandeiras, on the other hand, when they reached this district, speedily decamped, fleeing it for other parts: it may have been fashioned for the battles of the Faith, but to them it was overwhelming and depressing; and so they left it, and nothing could prevail upon them to return; they left it, and left the heathen in peace.

Hence the happy circumstance, as is revealed by observation, of the predominance of Tapuia terms in the geographic names of these places— terms that have resisted absorption by the Portuguese and Tupi languages, which have prevailed in other localities. Without going too far afield, let us take a glance at the lands round about Canudos by way of illustrating this matter of language which so well reflects the historic vicissitudes of a people.

Starting out from the São Francisco in a southerly direction, we find ourselves once more in an unfriendly region, beneath an inclement sky; and from here we go on to cross the elevated basin of the Vasa-Barris, before reaching those scattered and more depressed sections of the Baian plains which from the Paulo Affonso Falls, from Canudos and from Monte Santo, bring us to Itiúba, to Tombador, and to Assuruá. Here on this, the most ungrateful tract of our native territory, where once the persecuted rem-

[58] According to Couto de Magalhaes, this lovely word may be broken down into *ara*, day, and *echá*, to see at a distance. *Araxa*, a place where one first has a distant glimpse of the sun; by extension, the high plains of the interior.

[59] A sterile, unpopulated place.   [60] *Tapuy-retama*, region of the Tapuias.

nants of the Orizes, the Procas, and the Carirys[61] sought refuge, we find today, appearing once more as place names, barbarous words from the Tapuia tongue which neither Portuguese nor Tupi have been able to supplant; we discover on the map of the region, occurring with the frequency of topographical landmarks, names such as Pambú, Patamoté, Uáuá, Bendegó, Cumbe, Massacará, Cocorobó, Geremoabo, Tragagó, Canché, Chorrochó, Quincunca, Conchó, Centocé, Assuruá, Chique-Chique, Jequié, Sincorá, Caculé or Catolé, Orobó, Mocugé, and others equally strange and barbarous-sounding.[62]

It is natural that the great backlands populations, like the one which grew up in the middle basin of the São Francisco, should have been formed with a preponderant admixture of Tapuia blood. And there they remained in banishment, evolving in a closed circle for three centuries, down to our era —completely abandoned, wholly alien to our destinies, and preserving intact the traditions of the past. Accordingly, whoever today traverses these regions will observe a notable uniformity among the inhabitants: an appearance and stature that vary but slightly from a given model, conveying the impression of an unvarying anthropologic type, one which at first glance is seen to be distinct from the proteiform mestizo of the seaboard; for, where the latter shows all varieties of coloring and remains ill defined in type, depending upon the varying predominance of the formative factors, the man of the backlands appears to have been run through one common mold, with the individuals exhibiting almost identical physical characteristics: the same complexion, ranging from the bronze hue of the mameluco to the swarthy color of the cafuso; hair straight and sleek or slightly wavy; the same athletic build; and the same moral characteristics, the same superstitions, the same vices, and the same virtues.

This uniformity, in its various aspects, is most impressive. There is no doubt about it, the backwoodsman of the north represents an ethnic subcategory that has already been formed.[63]

AN IRRITATING PARENTHESIS

Here we must make a few parenthetical remarks.[64]

An intermingling of races highly diverse is, in the majority of cases, prejudicial. According to the conclusions of the evolutionist, even when

[61] [Native tribes.]

[62] Theodoro Sampaio, *Da Expansão da lingua tupi e do seu predominio na lingua nacional.*

[63] See "Author's Notes," Note V, p. 481.

[64] [On this passage see Gilberto Freyre, *Actualidade de Euclydes da Cunha; conferencia lida no Salão de Conferencias do Ministerio das Relações Exteriores do Brasil, no dia 29 de outubro de 1940* (Rio de Janeiro: Edição da Casa do Estudante do Brasil, 1941). Freyre discusses Cunha's "racial pessimism" or "racial fatalism," his "rigid biologic determinism," and his "ethnocentric exaggerations" and finds that he was "the victim of scientific preconceptions with the appearance of anthropologic truths" such as were common at the turn of the century, e.g., in a writer like Silvio Romero; in other words, these views, according to Freyre, were inspired by too great

the influence of a superior race has reacted upon the offspring, the latter shows vivid traces of the inferior one. Miscegenation carried to an extreme means retrogression. The Indo-European, the Negro, and the Brazilian-Guarany or the Tapuia represent evolutionary stages in confrontation; and miscegenation, in addition to obliterating the pre-eminent qualities of the higher race, serves to stimulate the revival of the primitive attributes of the lower; so that the mestizo—a hyphen between the races, a brief individual existence into which are compressed age-old forces—is almost always an unbalanced type. Fovel compares them in a general way to hysterics, but the nervous disequilibrium in such a case is incurable; there is no therapeutic for this clash of antagonistic tendencies on the part of races of a sudden brought together and fused in an isolated organism. It is not to be understood how, after they have diverged so extremely for long ages—ages compared to which history is but a moment—two or three peoples can suddenly come together and combine their diverse mental constitutions, thus annulling within a short space of time those distinctions which have resulted from a long, slow, laborious process of selection. As in algebraic sums, the qualities of the juxtaposed elements are not increased, subtracted from, or destroyed by the positive and negative signs that are present. The mestizo—mulatto, mameluco, or cafuso—rather than an intermediary type, is a degenerate one, lacking the physical energy of his savage ancestors and without the intellectual elevation of his ancestors on the other side. In contrast to the fecundity which he happens to possess, he shows extraordinary cases of moral hybridism: a brilliant mind at times, but unstable, restless, inconstant, flaring one moment and the next moment extinguished, victim of the fatality of biologic laws, weighted down to the lower plane of the less favored race. Impotent when it comes to forming any bonds of solidarity between the opposed forebears

---

a reliance on his sources. On racial attitudes (with particular reference to the Negro) in present-day Brazil cf. Pierson, *op. cit.*, pp. 207–33: "Racial Ideology and Racial Attitudes." According to Dr. Pierson, a number of prominent Brazilians of mixed descent would themselves be inclined to agree with Cunha. On the other hand, there is the opinion of Colonel Arthur Lobo da Silva, of the Health Service of the Brazilian Army, who, on the basis of actual investigations, concludes that "mixed blood" is physically superior to the parent stocks (*Anthropologia do Exercito Brasileiro* [Rio de Janeiro: Archivos do Museu Nacional, 1928], XXX, 281). A contemporary Brazilian sociologist who holds similar views is A. Austregesilo (see his paper, "A Mestiçagem no Brasil como factor eugenico," in Gilberto Freyre [ed.], *Novos Estudos Afro-Brasileiros*, [Rio de Janeiro, 1937]; see also Pierson, *op. cit.*, pp. 214–15). For a good general summary of the most recent views of accredited anthropologists, see Alain Locke and Bernhard J. Stern (eds.), *When Peoples Meet: A Study in Race and Culture Contacts* (New York: Progressive Education Association, 1942). See, in particular, the section on "Superiority Creeds and Race Thinking," pp. 420 ff. Cunha himself, it may be noted, pays tribute to the fine mind of the Negro engineer, André Rebouças (p. 47). Read also his moving description of the Negro captive going to his death at Canudos (pp. 440–41).]

from whom he sprang, he can reflect only their various dominant attributes in a permanent play of antitheses. And when, as not infrequently happens, he shows himself capable of broad generalizations and of grasping the most complex abstract relationships, all this mental vigor (saving those exceptional cases which merely go to prove the rule) will be found to rest upon a rudimentary morality in which is present the impulsive automatism of the lower races.

The fact is that in the marvelous competition of peoples, all of them evolving in a struggle that knows no truce, with selection capitalizing those attributes which heredity preserves, the mestizo is an intruder. He does not struggle; he does not represent an integration of forces; he is something that is dispersive and dissolvent, suddenly springing up without characteristics of his own and wavering between the opposing influences of a discordant ancestry. The tendency toward a regression to the primitive race is a mark of his instability. It is an instinctive tendency toward a situation of equilibrium. The very play of natural laws would appear to extinguish little by little the anomalous product which violates those laws, by sending it back to its own generative sources. The mulatto, then, has an irresistible contempt for the Negro and seeks with a most anxious tenacity such intermarriages as may extinguish in his progeny the stigma of the dark brow; the mameluco becomes the inexorable bandeirante and hurls himself fiercely on the conquered native villages.

This tendency is significant. In a manner of speaking, it picks up the thread of evolution which miscegenation has severed. The superior race becomes the remote objective toward which the depressed mestizos tend; and the latter, in seeking this objective, are merely obeying their own instinct of self-preservation and defense. The laws of the evolution of species are inviolable ones; yet, if all the subtlety of the missionaries was impotent when it came to winning the mind of the savage to the simplest conceptions of a superior mental state; if there is no force capable of causing the African, under the tutoring of the best masters, to approximate at least the intellectual average of the Indo-European—for every man is, above everything else, an integration of racial forces, and his brain is a heritage—if all this is true, how then account for the normality of an anthropologic type which suddenly makes its appearance, combining tendencies that are so opposed?

A STRONG RACE

Meanwhile, painstaking observation of the man of the north shows a distinct attenuation of this interplay of antagonistic tendencies and almost a fixation with regard to the physiological characteristics of the emergent type. This fact, which would appear to contradict what has just been said above, affords on the contrary the most striking counterproof of those assertions.

It is undeniably true that the abnormal aspect of mestizos who come from races that are very diverse is due in good part to the fact that the more elevated ethnic element brings with it a more elevated way of life, which renders the process of accommodation a difficult and painful one; and, when there falls upon them the intellectual and moral surcharge of a civilization, it is inevitable that they should be thrown off balance. The incoherent, uneven, and turbulent character of the mestizo may be looked upon as denoting an inner and intensive effort to eliminate those attributes that impede his way of life in an environment that is more advanced and complex. It reflects, within a small circle, that silent, formidable combat which is the very life-struggle of races, a deeply moving and everlasting struggle, one that has been described in Gumplowicz' brilliant axiom as the motive force of history. The great professor of Gratz does not consider it under the aspect with which we are dealing here. The truth is, however, that if the strong ethnic element "tends to subordinate to its destiny the weaker element with which it comes in contact," then it finds in miscegenation a disturbing factor. The irresistible expansion of its syngenetic circle, though eluded in this manner, nevertheless is merely retarded; it is not extinguished. The struggle is transformed and becomes one with much graver implications, ranging from the vulgar case of the frank extermination of the inferior race through war to its slow elimination, absorption, dilution in the form of intermarriage. And during the course of this process of reduction the mestizos that emerge—variable, of all shades of color and all the shadings of form and character, without a well-defined appearance, without vigor, and in most cases not viable—are nothing more, in the last analysis, then the inevitable casualties in an unseen conflict that endures down the ages. In this latter case the strong race does not destroy the weak by force of arms; it crushes it with civilization.

It was in this manner that our rude fellow-countrymen of the north were formed. The abandonment in which they were left by the rest of the country had a beneficent effect. It freed them from a highly painful adaptation to a superior social state and at the same time prevented their slipping backward through the aberrations and vices of a more advanced milieu. The fusion that took place occurred under circumstances more compatible with the inferior elements. The pre-eminent ethnic factor, while transmitting to them civilized tendencies, did not impose civilization upon them.

This is the basic and distinguishing fact with regard to miscegenation in the back-lying regions of the littoral. These are distinct formations, if not with respect to their ethnic elements, with respect to the conditions of environment. The contrast may be reduced to the simplest of parallels. The inhabitant of the backlands has in large degree taken from the savage the latter's intimacy with his physical surroundings, and this, instead of acting as a depressing influence, has enriched his potent organism. As a consequence, he reflects in character and costume only those attributes taken from other formative races which are most adaptable to his incipient phase of social life.

He is a retrograde, not a degenerate, type. The vicissitudes of history, by freeing him, in the most delicate period of his formation, from the disproportionate exigencies of a borrowed culture, have fitted him for the conquest of that culture some day.[65] His psychic evolution, however backward it may be, has therefore the guaranty of a strong, well-constituted physique. This crossed race, then, makes its appearance as an autonomous and, in a way, an original one, transfiguring within itself all the inherited attributes; so that, unfettered at last of a savage existence, it may attain to civilized life as a result of the very causes which prevent it from doing so at once. Such is the logical conclusion.

The situation here is the reverse of that to be observed in the cities of the seaboard, where an extravagant inversion prevails, highly complex functions being there imposed on feeble organisms, with the effect of compressing and atrophying them before they have attained their full development. In the backlands, on the other hand, the robust organic integrity of the mestizo remains unimpaired, inasmuch as, being immune to foreign admixtures, he is capable of evolving and differentiating himself in accommodation to new and loftier destinies; for the solid physical basis is there for the moral development that is to come.

Let us, however, have done with this digression, which is not too pleasing a one. Let us go on to consider in more direct fashion the original aspect presented by our backward fellow-countrymen. We shall do this unpretentiously and without method, taking pains to avoid those elegant neologisms of which ethnologists are so fond. We have neither the time nor the competence to become involved in those psychic-geometric fan-

[65] [See "Author's Notes," Note V, p. 481.]

tasies which today are exaggerated into what is practically a philosophic materialism; and so we shall not trouble with the facial angle or with tracing the *norma verticalis* of the jagunço.[66] Were we to encumber ourselves with the imaginary outlines of this species of psychic topography, which has been so much abused, we should not thereby make ourselves any more clearly understood; we should be a mere copyist.

Rather, we shall endeavor to reproduce intact all those true or illusory impressions which were ours when, upon accompanying a rapidly moving military expedition, we found ourselves suddenly, in making a tour of the backlands, brought face to face with these singular beings of whom so little is known, and who have been abandoned here for three whole centuries.

III

THE SERTANEJO

The sertanejo, or man of the backlands, is above all else a strong individual. He does not exhibit the debilitating rachitic tendencies of the neurasthenic mestizos of the seaboard.

His appearance, it is true, at first glance, would lead one to think that this was not the case. He does not have the flawless features, the graceful bearing, the correct build of the athlete. He is ugly, awkward, stooped. Hercules-Quasimodo reflects in his bearing the typical unprepossessing attributes of the weak. His unsteady, slightly swaying, sinuous gait conveys the impression of loose-jointedness. His normally downtrodden mien is aggravated by a dour look which gives him an air of depressing humility. On foot, when not walking, he is invariably to be found leaning against the first doorpost or wall that he encounters; while on horseback, if he reins in his mount to exchange a couple of words with an acquaintance, he braces himself on one stirrup and rests his weight against the saddle. When walking, even at a rapid pace, he does not go forward steadily in a straight line but reels swiftly, as if he were following the geometric outlines of the meandering backland trails. And if in the course of his walk he pauses for the most commonplace of reasons, to roll a *cigarro*, strike a light, or chat with a friend, he falls—"falls" is the word—into a squatting position and will remain for a long time in this unstable state of equilibrium, with the entire weight of his body suspended on his great-toes, as he sits there on his heels with a simplicity that is at once ridiculous and delightful.

[66] [As representative of the modern school of anthropology cf. Franz Boas, *The Mind of Primitive Man* (New York, 1939): "Differences between the white race and other races must not be interpreted to mean superiority of the former, inferiority of the latter, unless this relation can be proved by anatomical or physiological considerations."]

He is the man who is always tired. He displays this invincible sluggishness, this muscular atony, in everything that he does: in his slowness of speech, his forced gestures, his unsteady gait, the languorous cadence of his ditties—in brief, in his constant tendency to immobility and rest.

Yet all this apparent weariness is an illusion. Nothing is more surprising than to see the sertanejo's listlessness disappear all of a sudden. In this weakened organism complete transformations are effected in a few seconds. All that is needed is some incident that demands the release of slumbering energies. The fellow is transfigured. He straightens up, becomes a new man, with new lines in his posture and bearing; his head held high now, above his massive shoulders; his gaze straightforward and unflinching. Through an instantaneous discharge of nervous energy, he at once corrects all the faults that come from the habitual relaxation of his organs; and the awkward rustic unexpectedly assumes the dominating aspect of a powerful, copper-hued Titan, an amazingly different being, capable of extraordinary feats of strength and agility.

This contrast becomes evident upon the most superficial examination. It is one that is revealed at every moment, in all the smallest details of back-country life—marked always by an impressive alternation between the extremes of impulse and prolonged periods of apathy.

It is impossible to imagine a more inelegant, ungainly horseman: no carriage, legs glued to the belly of his mount, hunched forward and swaying to the gait of the unshod, mistreated backland ponies, which are sturdy animals and remarkably swift. In this gloomy, indolent posture the lazy cowboy will ride along, over the plains, behind his slow-paced herd, almost transforming his "nag" into the lulling hammock in which he spends two-thirds of his existence. But let some giddy steer up ahead stray into the tangled scrub of the caatinga, or let one of the herd at a distance become entrammeled in the foliage, and he is at once a different being and, digging his broad-roweled spurs into the flanks of his mount, he is off like a dart and plunges at top speed into the labyrinth of jurema thickets.

Let us watch him at this barbarous *steeple chase*.[67]

Nothing can stop him in his onward rush. Gullies, stone heaps, brush piles, thorny thickets, or riverbanks—nothing can halt his pursuit of the straying steer, for *wherever the cow goes, there the cowboy and his horse go too*. Glued to his horse's back, with his knees dug into its flanks until horse and rider appear to be one, he gives the bizarre impression of a crude sort of centaur: emerging unexpectedly into a clearing, plunging into the tall weeds, leaping ditches and swamps, taking the small hills in his stride,

[67] [The word is in English.]

crashing swiftly through the prickly briar patches, and galloping at full speed over the expanse of tablelands.

His robust constitution shows itself at such a moment to best advantage. It is as if the sturdy rider were lending vigor to the frail pony, sustaining it by his improvised reins of caroá fiber,[68] suspending it by his spurs, hurling it onward—springing quickly into the stirrups, legs drawn up, knees well forward and close to the horse's side—"hot on the trail" of the wayward steer; now bending agilely to avoid a bough that threatens to brush him from the saddle; now leaping off quickly like an acrobat, clinging to his horse's mane, to avert collision with a stump sighted at the last moment; then back in the saddle again at a bound—and all the time galloping, galloping, through all obstacles, balancing in his right hand, without ever losing it once, never once dropping it in the liana thickets, the long, iron-pointed, leather-headed goad which in itself, in any other hands, would constitute a serious obstacle to progress.

But once the fracas is over and the unruly steer restored to the herd, the cowboy once more lolls back in the saddle, once more an inert and unprepossessing individual, swaying to his pony's slow gait, with all the disheartening appearance of a languishing invalid.

DISPARATE TYPES: THE JAGUNÇO AND THE GAUCHO

The southern gaucho, upon meeting the vaqueiro at this moment, would look him over commiseratingly. The northern cowboy is his very antithesis. In the matter of bearing, gesture, mode of speech, character, and habits there is no comparing the two. The former, denizen of the boundless plains, who spends his days in galloping over the pampas, and who finds his environment friendly and fascinating, has, assuredly, a more chivalrous and attractive mien. He does not know the horrors of the drought and those cruel combats with the dry-parched earth. His life is not saddened by periodic scenes of devastation and misery, the grievous sight of a calcined and absolutely impoverished soil, drained dry by the burning suns of the Equator. In his hours of peace and happiness he is not preoccupied with a future which is always a threatening one, rendering his happiness short lived and fleeting. He awakes to life amid a glowing, animating wealth of Nature; and he goes through life adventurous, jovial, eloquent of speech, valiant, and swaggering; he looks upon labor as a diversion which affords him the sport of stampedes; lord of the distances is

[68] [Cf. Waldo Frank, *South American Journey* (New York: Sloan, Duell & Pearce, 1943), pp. 311–12: "*caruá*, the fiber of a sword-sharp cactus." Frank mentions this plant as typical of the *sertão*, or backlands, a region that breeds the *caruá* and "the toughest of all Brazilians, the *sertanejo*." *Caroá* is the more common spelling).]

he, as he rides the broad level-lying pasture lands, while at his shoulders, like a gaily fluttering pennant, is the inevitable scarf, or *pala*.

The clothes that he wears are holiday garb compared to the vaqueiro's rustic garments. His wide breeches are cut to facilitate his movements astride his hard-galloping or wildly rearing bronco[69] and are not torn by the ripping thorns of the caatingas. Nor is his jaunty poncho ever lost by being caught on the boughs of the crooked trees. Tearing like an unleashed whirlwind across the trails, clad in large russet-colored boots with glittering silver spurs, a bright-red silk scarf at his neck, on his head his broad sombrero with its flapping brim, a gleaming pistol and dagger in the girdle about his waist—so accoutered, he is a conquering hero, merry and bold. His horse, inseparable companion of his romantic life, is a near-luxurious object, with its complicated and spectacular trappings. A ragged gaucho on a well-appareled *pingo* is a fitting sight, in perfectly good form, and, without feeling the least out of place, may ride through the town in festive mood.

THE VAQUEIRO

The vaqueiro, on the other hand, grew up under conditions the opposite of these, amid a seldom varying alternation of good times and bad, of abundance and want; and over his head hung the year-round threat of the sun, bringing with it in the course of the seasons repeated periods of devastation and misfortune. It was amid such a succession of catastrophes that his youth was spent. He grew to manhood almost without ever having been a child; what should have been the merry hours of childhood were embittered by the specter of the backland droughts, and soon enough he had to face the tormented existence that awaited him. He was one damned to life. He understood well enough that he was engaged in a conflict that knew no truce, one that imperiously demanded of him the utilization of every last drop of his energies. And so he became strong, expert, resigned, and practical. He was fitting himself for the struggle.

His appearance at first sight makes one think, vaguely, of some ancient warrior weary of the fray. His clothes are a suit of armor. Clad in his tanned leather doublet, made of goatskin or cowhide, in a leather vest, and in skintight leggings of the same material that come up to his crotch and which are fitted with knee pads, and with his hands and feet protected by calfskin gloves and shinguards, he presents the crude aspect of some medieval knight who has strayed into modern times.

This armor of his, however, reddish-gray in hue, as if it were made of flexible bronze, does not give off any scintillations; it does not gleam when

[69] [*Bagual:* an unbroken horse, one that can be controlled only by the lasso.]

the sun's rays strike it. It is dead and dusty-looking, as befits a warrior who brings back no victories from the fight.

His homemade saddle is an imitation of the one used in the Rio Grande region but is shorter and hollowed out, without the luxurious trappings of the other. Its accessories consist of a weatherproof goatskin blanket covering the animal's haunches, of a breast covering, or pectorals, and of pads attached to the mount's knees. This equipment of man and beast is adapted to the environment. Without it, they would not be able to gallop through the caatingas and over the beds of jagged rock in safety.

Nothing, to tell the truth, is more monotonous and ugly than this highly original garb of one color only, the russet-gray of tanned leather, without the slightest variation, without so much as a strip or band of any other hue. Only at rare intervals, when a "shindig" is held to the strains of the guitar, and the backwoodsman relaxes from his long hours of toil, does he add a touch of novelty to his appearance in the form of a striking vest made of jungle cat[70] or puma skin with the spots turned out—or else he may stick a bright red bromelia in his leather cap. This, however, is no more than a passing incident and occurs but rarely.

Once the hours of merrymaking are over, the sertanejo loses his bold and frolicsome air. Not long before he had been letting himself go in the dance, the *sapateado,*[71] as the sharp clack of sandals on the ground mingled with the jingling of spurs and the tinkling of tambourine bells, to the vibrant rhythms, the "rip-snortings"[72] of the guitars; but now once more he falls back into his old habitual posture, loutish, awkward, gawky, exhibiting at the same time a strange lack of nervous energy and an extraordinary degree of fatigue.

Now, nothing is more easily to be explained than this permanent state of contrast between extreme manifestations of strength and agility and prolonged intervals of apathy. A perfect reflection of the physical forces at work about him, the man of the northern backlands has served an arduous apprenticeship in the school of adversity, and he has quickly learned to face his troubles squarely and to react to them promptly. He goes through life ambushed on all sides by sudden, incomprehensible surprises on the part of Nature, and he never knows a moment's respite. He is a combatant who all the year round is weakened and exhausted, and all the year round is strong and daring, preparing himself always for an en-

[70] [*Gato do matto:* name given to small wildcats of the jungle.]

[71] [From *sapata,* "a shoe"; the dance, as indicated, being marked by the clacking of shoes or sandals.]

[72] [*Rasgados:* from *rasgar,* "to rip," "to tear."]

counter in which he will not be the victor, but in which he will not let himself be vanquished; passing from a maximum of repose to a maximum of movement, from his comfortable, slothful hammock to the hard saddle, to dart, like a streak of lightning, along the narrow trails in search of his herds. His contradictory appearance, accordingly, is a reflection of Nature herself in this region—passive before the play of the elements and passing without perceptible transition from one season to another, from a major exuberance to the penury of the parched desert, beneath the refracted glow of blazing suns. He is as inconstant as Nature. And it is natural that he should be. To live is to adapt one's self. And she has fashioned him in her own likeness: barbarous, impetuous, abrupt.

THE GAUCHO

The gaúcho, valiant "cowpuncher"[73] that he is, is surely without an equal when it comes to any warlike undertaking. To the shrill and vibrant sound of trumpets, he will gallop across the pampas, the butt of his lance firmly couched in his stirrup; like a madman, he will plunge into the thick of the fight; with a shout of triumph, he is swallowed up from sight in the swirl of combat, where nothing is to be seen but the flashing of sword on sword; transforming his horse into a projectile, he will rout squadrons and trample his adversaries, or—he will fall in the struggle which he entered with so supreme a disregard for his life.

THE JAGUNÇO

The jagunço is less theatrically heroic; he is more tenacious; he holds out better; he is stronger and more dangerous, made of sterner stuff. He rarely assumes this romantic and vainglorious pose. Rather, he seeks out his adversary with the firm purpose of destroying him by whatever means he may. He is accustomed to prolonged and obscure conflicts, without any expansive display of enthusiasm. His life is one long arduously achieved conquest in the course of his daily task. He does not indulge in the slightest muscular contraction, the slightest expenditure of nervous energy, without being certain of the result. He coldly calculates his enemy. At dagger-play he does no feinting. In aiming the long rifle or the heavy *trabuco*,[74] he "sleeps upon the sights."

Should his missile fail to reach its mark and his enemy not fall, the gaucho, beaten or done in, is a very weak individual in the grip of a situation in which he is placed at a disadvantage or of the outcome of which he is uncertain. This is not the case with the jagunço. He bides his time.

[73] [*Pealador.*]

[74] [A species of catapult gun, for shooting rocks, horntips, etc. For a description see p. 145.]

He is a demon when it comes to leading his enemy on; and the latter has before him, from this hour forth, sighting him down his musket barrel, a man who hates him with an inextinguishable hatred and who lies hidden there in the shade of the thicket.

THE VAQUEIROS

These contrasting characteristics are prominent in normal times.

Thus, every sertanejo is a vaqueiro. Aside from the rudimentary agriculture of the bottom plantations on the edge of the rivers, for the growing of those cereals which are a prime necessity, cattle-breeding is in these parts the kind of labor that is least unsuited to the inhabitants and to the soil. On these backland ranches, however, one does not meet with the festive bustle of the southern *estancias*.

"Making the roundup" is for the gaucho a daily festival, of which the showy cavalcades on special occasions are little more than an elaboration. Within the narrow confines of the mango groves or out on the open plain, cowpunchers, foremen, and peons may be seen rounding up the herd, through the brooks and gullies, pursuing intractable steers, lassoing the wild pony, or felling the rearing bull with the boleador, as if they were playing a game of rings; their movements are executed with incredible swiftness, and they all gallop after one another, yelling lustily at the top of their lungs and creating a great tumult, as if having the best time in the world. In the course of their less strenuous labors, on the other hand, when they come to brand the cattle, treating their wounds, leading away those destined for the slaughter, separating the tame steers, and picking out the broncos condemned to the horsebreaker's spurs[75]—at times like these, the same fire that heats the branding iron provides the embers with which to prepare the roast, cooked with the skin on, for their rude feasts, or serves to boil the water for their strong and bitter-tasting Paraguayan tea, or *mate*. And so their days go by, well filled and varied.

UNCONSCIOUS SERVITUDE

The same thing does not happen in the north. Unlike the *estancieiro*, the *fazendeiro*[76] of the backlands lives on the seaboard, at a distance from his extensive properties, which he sometimes never sees. He is heir to an old historic vice. Like the landed proprietor of colonial days, he parasitically enjoys the revenues from vast domains without fixed boundaries, and

[75] [These spurs (*chilenas*) are wicked ones, their rowels sometimes having points that are several inches long.]

[76] [*Estancieiro*, proprietor of an *estancia; fazendeiro*, owner of a *fazenda;* the words *estancia* and *fazenda* both mean a country estate or ranch. The author is here making a distinction between the southern *estancia* and the *fazenda* of the northern regions.]

the cowboys are his submissive servants. As the result of a contract in accordance with which they receive a certain percentage of what is produced, the latter remain attached to the same plot of ground; they are born, they live and die, these beings whom no one ever hears of, lost to sight in the backland trails and their poverty-stricken huts; and they spend their entire lives in faithfully caring for herds that do not belong to them. Their real employer, an absentee one, well knows how loyal they are and does not oversee them; at best, he barely knows their names.

Clad, then, in their characteristic leathern garb, the sertanejos throw up their cottages, built of thatch and wooden stakes, on the very edge of the water pits, as rapidly as if they were pitching tents, and enter with resignation upon a servitude that holds out no attractions for them. The first thing that they do is to learn the *ABC*'s, all that there is to be known, of an art in which they end by becoming past masters—that of being able to distinguish the "irons" of their own and neighboring ranches. This is the term applied to all the various signs, markings, letters, capriciously wrought initials, and the like which are branded with fire on the animal's haunches, and which are supplemented by small notches cut in its ears. By this branding the ownership of the steer is established. He may break through boundaries and roam at will, but he bears an indelible imprint which will restore him to the *solta*[77] to which he belongs. For the cowboy is not content with knowing by heart the brands of his own ranch; he learns those of other ranches as well; and sometimes, by an extraordinary feat of memory, he comes to know, one by one, not only the animals that are in his charge but those of his neighbors also, along with their genealogy, characteristic habits, their names, ages, etc. Accordingly, should a strange animal, but one whose brand he knows, show up in his *logrador*, he will restore it promptly. Otherwise, he will keep the intruder and care for it as he does for the others, but he will not take it to the annual fair, nor will he use it for any labor, for it does not belong to him; he will let it die of old age.

When a cow gives birth to a calf, he brands the latter with the same private mark, displaying a perfection of artistry in doing so; and he will repeat the process with all its descendants. One out of every four calves he sets aside as his own; that is his pay. He has the same understanding with his boss, whom he does not know, that he has with his neighbor, and, without judges or witnesses, he adheres strictly to this unusual contract, which no one has worded or drawn up.

[77] An uninclosed pasture, sometimes at quite a distance from the farmhouse. When nearer at hand and situated in pleasant surroundings, they bear the special name of the herd (*logrador*).

It often happens that, after long years, he will succeed in deciphering the brand on a strayed bullock, and the fortunate owner will then receive, in place of the single animal that had wandered from his herd, and which he has long since forgotten, all the progeny for which it has been responsible. This seems fantastic, but it is nonetheless a well-known fact in the backlands. We mention it as a fascinating illustration of the probity of these backwoodsmen. The great landed proprietors, the owners of the herds, know it well. They all have the same partnership agreement with the vaqueiro, summed up in the single clause which gives him, in exchange for the care that he bestows upon the herd, one-fourth of the products of the ranch; and they are assured that he will never filch on the percentage.

The settlement of accounts is made at the end of winter and ordinarily takes place without the presence of the party who is chiefly interested. That is a formality that may be dispensed with. The vaqueiro will scrupulously separate the large majority of the new cattle (on which he puts the brand of the ranch) as belonging to the boss, while keeping for himself only the one out of every four that falls to him by lot. These he will brand with his own private mark, and will either keep or sell them. He writes to the boss,[78] giving him a minute account of everything that has happened on the place, going into the most trivial details; and then he will get on with his never interrupted task.

That task, although on occasion it can be tiring enough, is an extremely rudimentary one. There does not exist in the north a cattle-raising industry. The herds live and multiply in haphazard fashion. Branded in June, the new steeers proceed to lose themselves in the caatingas along with the rest. Here their ranks are thinned by intense epizootic infections, chief among them *rengue*, a form of lameness, and the disease known as the *mal triste*.[79] The cowboys are able to do little to halt the ravages of these affections, their activities being confined to riding the long, endless trails. Should the herd develop an epidemic of worms, they know a better specific than mercury: prayer. The cowboy does not need to see the suffering animal. It is enough for him to turn his face in its direction and say a prayer, tracing on the ground as he does so a maze of cabalistic lines. And, what is more amazing still, he will cure it by some such means as this.

Thus their days are spent, full of movement, but with little to show for

[78] In writing letters, he eschews the common formula, "Your humble servant," and naïvely substitutes for it "Your cowboy friend F." Occasionally, in conveying word of a disaster, a straying of the herd, for instance, his conciseness is startling: "Dear Boss. This is to let you know that your herd is *under control*. Only four steers lost their hides in the brush. The rest are still *alive and stamping*."

[79] [This term is applied sometimes to a leprous affection and sometimes (in southern Brazil) to a form of hydrophobia.]

it all. Rarely does any incident, some slight variation, come to break the monotony of their life.

Bound together by a spirit of solidarity, they unconditionally aid one another at every turn. Let a giddy steer flee the herd, and the vaqueiro will snatch up his *guiada*,[80] put spurs to his nag, and gallop after it in hot haste. If his efforts do not meet with success, he has recourse to his neighboring companions and asks them to "take the field," a phrase that is characteristic of these rustic knights; and his hard-riding, lusty-yelling friends by the dozen and the score will then follow him, scouring the countryside, riding over the slopes and searching the caatingas, until the beast, in the language of the cattlemen, has been "taken down a peg" and "turns up his nose" or else is thrown by main force when his horns are grasped in the cowboys' powerful hands.

THE COW-HUNT

This spirit of solidarity and mutual assistance is best evidenced in the cow-hunt (*vaquejada*), a labor that consists essentially in first rounding up and then separating the cattle of the various neighboring ranches which, mingled together, are in the habit of grazing on one huge common pasture ground, without any boundary walls or trenches by way of demarcation. It takes place from June to July.

Having selected a more or less central location, usually a bit of cleared and level bottom land, the one in charge of the roundup, the *rodeador*, proceeds to assemble all the cowpunchers in the vicinity. They all participate in the undertaking, and each is assigned his own particular share in the task. And then, scattering over the sandy ground, these leather-covered figures plunge into an athletic tussle with the surrounding caatingas.

The scene has all the fierce and terrifying movement that one associates with a band of Tartar horsemen. In a few minutes the sertanejos are lost from sight in the near-by brush, and for some while the spot is deserted.

Then suddenly, from one side, comes the noisy clatter of horses' hoofs over rocks, the sound of cracking branches, the clashing of interlocked horns; small clouds of dust go up in the air, and there bursts into the clearing a part of the herd, their horns padded with leather balls, followed by the cowboy standing tense in his stirrups and pulling up short.

He brings with him but a small part of the lot. Turning them over to his companions, who remain there "in their tracks," he returns at a fast

[80] Name given to the elongated, sharpened prong. [For a further description see p. 145.]

gallop to renew his search. In the meantime, farther down, others are to be seen and yet others, one after another, along the whole strip of scrub, and the entire roundup now becomes an animated and tumultuous affair, with steers locking horns or pawing the ground and horses rearing and prancing in a confused mêlée over the plains, which resound with the prolonged clamor of an earthquake. To the side, meanwhile, in the caatinga, the less fortunate vaqueiros are wrestling with the recalcitrant members of the herd. The bull running loose or the straying steer generally flees recapture. He plunges into the caatinga, and the cowboy follows him, keeps close on his trail to the end; he does not let him go but waits until the moment comes for decisive action; then he catches the fugitive with a sudden spring; slipping down in his saddle with his weight on a stirrup, he holds on to his horse's mane with one hand, while with the other hand he grasps the runaway bull's tail and, with a powerful side jerk, throws him heavily to the ground. He then slips the *peia*, or fetters, on him, or the leather blinkers, and brings him thus trammeled or blindfolded back to the foreman of the roundup.

Here he is greeted noisily by his companions. He tells them of his exploits, and they have identical ones to relate. This exchange of heroic impressions is accompanied by a great *ad hoc* display of adjectives, ranging in a crescendo from a harshly articulated *destalado* to a *temêro*,[81] uttered in a prolonged and husky tremolo.

At the end of the day there is one final task—that of counting and separating the heads of cattle that have been brought together. Each one then starts off for his own ranch, driving before him the cattle that belong to him. And over the deserted plains there now come the melancholy notes of the *aboiado*.[82]

But, even as this laborious task is brought to a close, there are other more important ones which have arisen.

HOMEWARD BOUND

Slowly the herd winds on, to the cadence of that mournful, lazy air. Hunched over his saddle in uncouth fashion, the cowboy dreams of calves to come and calculates the probable gain for himself, what the boss's share will be and what will be his own, in accordance with the terms of their contract. He then goes on to estimate the number which he will

[81] [Exclamations of admiration, evoked by a display of prowess.]

[82] "ABOIAR—To sing when driving cattle; a mournful air, with few variations, that serves to guide and pacify the herd, exerting over them a great and soothing influence, when they are going from one place to another" (Juvenal Galeno, *Lendas e canções*).

drive to the fair—and here he thinks of an aged steer that he has known for ten years; he has never driven this one to the fair, out of old friendship's sake. Then, there is that lame yearling with the sharp thorn in its side, which must be taken out. In front there, with the blinkers over his eyes and with his head defiantly up, barely held in line by the pressure of the others, is the unruly creature that he had to subdue by clamping the "petticoat" on him and throwing him, back there in the caatinga. And there, too, going along at a leisurely, self-assured gait, swinging his fine large neck, broad as a buffalo's, from left to right and keeping the others at a respectful distance, is the sturdy bull, envy of the countryside; his short, rigid horns, cracked and blunted and with the earth clinging to them, bring to mind formidable encounters with powerful rivals in the pasture lands. And there are many others, all down the line; the cowboy knows them all, can tell you a story about each of them, for these are the little details that go to make up his primitive, simple existence.

And so they continue on their way, slowly and orderly, to the rhythm of this melancholy tune, which appears to have a lulling effect upon them, like a cradlesong, with its monotonous refrain,[83]

> E cou mansão . . . .
> E cou . . . . cão . . . . ,

echoing nostalgically over the silent fields.

THE STAMPEDE

Of a sudden, however, a concerted shudder runs through the herd, over those hundreds of glossy backs. There is an instantaneous halt. Hundreds of pairs of horns then clash and lock, are tossed in the air writhing and twisting, are raised and lowered in lively confusion. The earth quivers with the beat of hoofs, and the herd *stampedes*.[84]

The herd breaks away, out of control. There is, sometimes, nothing to account for this occurrence, which is common enough, and which is the despair of cattlemen. The most trivial incident can precipitate it—the sudden low flight of a jacú[85] or the scurrying of a moco across the path. One of the cattle becomes frightened and the contagion, in the form of a quick discharge of nervous energy, runs through the entire herd. They all jerk in unison, in a terrifying manner, and these massive bodies, normally so phlegmatic and slow of movement, are hurled forward tumultuously, at

---

[83] [Cf. our western "hillbilly" song, "Get along, little dogie, get along."]

[84] [. . . . *a boiada estoura*. The author's footnote here reads:
"The verbs *estouar, arrancar*, or *arribar*, in connection with a herd of cattle, are synonyms, and perhaps more intensive ones, in the northern backlands, for the *disparadas* of the pampas."]

[85] [The *jacú* is a bird of the Cracidei family (*Ortalis squamata* Less.).]

one and the same time, and there is a vast confusion of padded horns as they mill about in dizzying fashion.

They are off now; there is no halting or overtaking them. The caatingas are trampled; trees are bent in two, their trunks shattered to splinters and kindling wood; the brooks suddenly overflow with a great surge of horns, and there is a torrent of hoofbeats on the shattered and crunching rocks; and over the tablelands comes the subdued roll of prolonged and distant thunder.

Age-old, laboriously cultivated plantations are destroyed in the course of a few moments; the smooth-bottomed ipueiras are transformed into rugged, upturned marshlands; dwellings are knocked down and trampled, or else the frightened inhabitants leave them and flee, to this side and that, anywhere to get out of the straight line in which the headlong "drove" is moving—thousands of bodies constituting one single, monstrous, shapeless, indescribable, fantastic animal mass, rushing onward in its mad career. And above all this tumult, skirting it or hurling himself impetuously into the path of destruction which this living avalanche leaves in its wake, making a stupendous circuit and taking all obstacles in his path, confronting all perils: sloughs, walls, hillocks, the horns of the maddened herd—couching his goad, reins loose on his mount's neck, feet loose in the stirrups, bending forward over the saddle, clinging to his horse's mane— the cowboy goes galloping!

His companions, who have heard the sound of the stampede from afar, have joined him by this time, and the toil and struggle of the afternoon are once more renewed: fresh exertions, a fresh onset to be made, more exploits to be performed, new risks and dangers to be met and overcome, until at last the unruly herd is retrieved, owing not so much to the efforts of the pursuing cattle-drivers as to the fact that it has little by little worn itself out and is now ready to stop from sheer exhaustion.

They get them on the homeward path once more, bound for the ranch; and then once again, over the deserted plains, there come the melancholy notes of the *aboiado*.

TRADITIONS

The cowboys return home, and there, lying in their bamboo hammocks, they go over all the escapades of the cow-hunt or their famous adventures at the fair, killing time in the full meaning of the term, quenching their thirst with the sweet-tasting *umbusada*, or lunching on that incomparable dish, gerimum with milk.[86]

If the season is propitious, and the bottom plantations are doing well,

[86] [For the *umbusada* see p. 37. The gerimum, or jurumum, is an edible gourd (*Concurbita maxima*).]

and the grazing grasses, the *panasco* and the *mimoso*, are growing in the broad pasture lands, and there is nothing to show that a drought is coming, they then take advantage of the leisure afforded them and indulge in some pleasurable idling. They will go to the towns, if there happen to be festivals there, cavalcades and Moorish mummeries, anachronistic divertisements which the backland settlements have preserved intact, in all their details, for three whole centuries. Among these is the exotic camisado,[87] as curious an example as any to be found of their adherence to the most remote traditions. A very old copy of ancient nocturnal sallies in the Peninsula, against the Moorish castles, and wholly forgotten now in the land of its birth, where the very name is an archaism, no longer in use, this diversion, a costly but an interesting one, is staged by the light of lanterns and grass torches, with long processions of men on foot, clad in white or in Mussulman garb, while others go on horseback, in weird animal disguises; they all file past rapidly, with skirmishes and mock encounters; and this, in his frolicsome moments, is the greatest delight the backwoodsman knows.

DANCES

Not all, however, can take part in such amusements as this. Being too short of resources to go far from the ranch, the others remain at home and indulge in traditional forms of merrymaking. Leather-clad as usual, they go through the steps of the noisy *sambas*[88] and *cateretés*, the unmarried ones, great improvisers in the poetic "challenges," doing the *choradinho* or the *baiano*,[89] their gleaming banjos under their arms, while the married couples do the "honors" of the occasion. In their festively decked huts they receive the guests with noisy greetings and hoarse shouts; and, since there is ordinarily not enough room for so many in the house, they go outdoors and set up a more commodious ballroom on the well-swept terrace, which is decorated with boughs, furnished with stumps, tree trunks, and a few stools, and lighted by the glow of the stars. They "take the edge off the day"[90] with large swigs of brandy, to which they give the name of *teimosa*, the "headstrong,"[91] and forthwith burst into loud and vigorous stamping.

[87] *Encamisada:* "A nocturnal assault in which troops put on flowing shirts (*camisões*) to disguise themselves" (C. Figueiredo, *Novo diccionario da lingua portuguesa*).

[88] [For an interesting note on the *samba* see Donald Pierson's *Negroes in Brazil: A Study of Race Contacts at Bahia*, pp. 249–50.]

[89] Dances common in the north.

[90] *Despontar o dia:* the first sip of any drink at the beginning of a party.

[91] The term *teimosa*, applied to rum, has a charming philosophy behind it. Nothing could be more expressive of the attraction which rum holds for these good people, and their desire, which they never succeed in realizing, to leave it alone.

An up-and-coming young buck[92] strikes up a lively air on the guitar,[93] the pretty caboclas begin making slow movements with their bodies,[94] and the "rough-and-ready" backwoods lad begins revolving in the dance.

THE POETIC CHALLENGES

In the intervals between the dances come the challenges, or *desafios*. A pair of adversaries, two homespun singers, start it off, and the rhymes leap forth and mate in quatrains which are sometimes very beautiful:[95]

> Nas horas de Deus, amen,
> Não é zombaria, não!
> Desafio o mundo inteiro
> P'ra cantar nesta funcção!

> In God's good time, amen!
> I am not jesting, no!
> I defy the entire world
> In singing at this show!

His adversary then retorts, picking up the last line of the stanza:

> P'ra cantar nesta funcção,
> Amigo, meu camarada,
> Acceita teu desafio
> O *fama* deste sertão!

> In singing at this show,
> My friend and comrade true,
> The one who accepts your challenge here
> Is the *fame* of this land, you know!

This is the beginning of the contest, which ends only when one of the bards becomes entangled in a difficult rhyme, falters, and starts strumming his banjo[96] nervously, to the accompaniment of an avalanche of laughter greeting his defeat. And so the night slips by rapidly in a general merry-making, until it "begins getting light around the edges," and the sericoias

[92] *Um cabra destalado: cabra* is a term commonly applied to the offspring of a mulatto and a Negro.
Destalado, brabo e corado ("rough and ready"), *bala e onça, destabocado*, and similar expressions are interchangeable, signifying a strong, capable individual.

[93] *Ralhar na viola:* to play noisily and with dexterity.

[94] *Serenar na dansa:* to dance very slowly, without making any noise with the feet.

[95] [On this passage see Luis da Camara Cascudo, *Vaqueiros e cantadores* (Porto Alegre: Livraria do Globo, 1939), pp. 125–26. On the *desafio* in general, a form that goes back to remote classical antiquity (Homer, Theocritus, Virgil, etc.) and which has come down through the medieval troubadours, see *ibid.*, pp. 125–80. Camara Cascudo gives examples of the music.]

[96] [For "banjo" the author employs the term *machete*. On this, Camara Cascudo (*ibid.*, p. 126) observes: "Euclydes gives the term 'machete' to the 'cavaquinho' and even to the smaller guitar. There is no trace of this term in the northeast, but it is found in the Portuguese *trovas*."]

start singing in the marshes, which is the signal for the breaking-up of this jolly gathering.

When the festivities are over, the cowboy goes back to his rude task or his lazy hammock. Occasionally, from year to year, he will leave his tranquil dwelling for remote regions. Crossing the São Francisco, he will lose himself in the enormous eastern Campos, those vast far-sweeping plains where the basins of the São Francisco and the Tocantins meet in the form of overflows, from which the rivers rise, indistinctly, to the east and to the west. From here he will go on into Goiaz or, taking a more northerly course, to the mountains of Piauí.

He goes to buy cattle. These faraway places, these obscure and poverty-stricken villages extending to Porto Nacional, then take on a passing animation with the pilgrimage of these "Baians." The latter are the autocrats of the fairs. Within their leather armor, they make a sprightly appearance for once, as they come riding their mettlesome horses and brandishing their cattle prongs; and they enter these hamlets with the bold and confident air of happy conquerors. Upon their return, when they do not become hopelessly lost in the dangerous "crossing" of the plains, with no landmarks to guide them, they take up once more their monotonous and primitive way of life.

THE DROUGHT

And then, of a sudden, there comes a tragic break in the monotony of their days. The drought is approaching.

Thanks to the singular rhythm with which the scourge comes on, the sertanejo is able to foresee and foretell it. He does not, however, take refuge in flight, by abandoning the region which is being little by little invaded by the glowing inferno that radiates from Ceará. Buckle has a striking passage in which he draws attention to the strange fact that man never learns to accustom himself to the natural calamities which surround him. There is no people more afraid of earthquakes than is your Peruvian; yet, in Peru, children in the cradle are rocked by the earth's tremors. The sertanejo, on the other hand, is an exception to the rule. The droughts do not frighten him; they serve merely to round out his tormented existence, framing it with tremendously dramatic episodes. And he confronts them stoically. Although this grievous ordeal has occurred times without number, as is borne out by traditions which he knows well, he is nonetheless sustained by the impossible hope of being able to hold out against it.

With the scant help afforded him by his own observations and those of his ancestors, in which common-sense directions are mingled with extravagant superstitions, he has studied this affliction as best he could, in order that he might understand it and be able to bear or to avert it. He equips himself for the struggle with an extraordinary calmness. Two or three months before the summer solstice, he props and strengthens the walls of the dams or cleans out the water pits. He looks after his fields and plows up in furrows the narrow strips of arable land on the river's edge, by way of preparing these diminutive plantations for the coming of the first rains.

Then he endeavors to make out what the future holds in store. Turning his eyes upward, he gazes for a long time in all directions, in an effort to discover the faintest hints which the landscape may have to offer him.

The symptoms of the drought are not long in appearing; they come in a series, one after another, inexorably, like those of some cyclic disease, some terrifying intermittent fever on the part of the earth. The brief period of October rains, the *chuvas do cajú*, goes by, with numerous showers that are quickly evaporated in the parched air, leaving no trace behind them. The caatingas are "mottled," here, there, and everywhere, speckled with grayish-brown clusters of withered trees, and the number of these splotches, which look like the ash heaps left by some smothered conflagration, without flames, all the time increases; the ground cracks; and the water-level in the pits slowly sinks. At the same time it is to be noted that, while the days are scorching-hot, even at dawn, the nights are constantly becoming colder. The atmosphere, with the avidity of a sponge, absorbs the sweat on the sertanejo's brow, while his leathern armor, no longer possessing the flexibility it once had, is stiff and hot on his shoulders, like a breastplate of bronze. And, as the afternoons, growing shorter every day, fade into evenings without twilights, he sorrowfully contemplates the first flocks of birds leaving the region and flying away to other climes.

This is a prelude to the trouble that is coming. And the situation is destined to grow more acute until December.

The vaqueiro takes his precautions and anxiously looks over his herds, making a tour of the far-lying pasture grounds, until he comes to those more fertile bottom lands, between the sterile uplands, where he turns his cattle out to feed. And he waits resignedly for the thirteenth day of this month; for on that day ancestral usage will enable him to sound the future and interrogate the designs of Providence.

This is the traditional experiment of Santa Luzia. On December 12, at nightfall, he sets out six lumps of salt in a row, where they will be exposed to the action of the dew; they represent, respectively, from left to right, the six coming months, from January to June. At daybreak the next morning, he observes them. If they are intact, it presages drought; if the first has dissolved somewhat, has been transformed into a soggy mass, he is certain of rain in January; if this happens to the second, it will rain in February; if it happens to the majority of the lumps, the winter will be a kindly disposed one.[97]

This experiment is a most interesting one. Despite the stigma of superstition which attaches to it, it has a positive basis and is acceptable when one stops to consider that from it may be gathered the greater or less amount of vaporized moisture in the air and, by deduction, the greater or less probability of barometric depressions capable of bringing rain.

Meanwhile, although this test is a traditional one, it leaves the sertanejo still uncertain. Nor does he invariably lose heart, even when the signs foretell the worst. He waits patiently for the spring equinox, to consult the elements again. He spends three whole months in anxious expectation, and then, on São José's Day, March 19, he has recourse to one last augury.

This day is for him an index to the following months. Within its span of a dozen hours, it will show all the climatic variations that are to come. If it rains during the day, the winter will be a rainy one. If, on the contrary, the blazing sun makes its way across an unclouded sky, it means that all hope for the earth is gone.[98] The drought is inevitable.

ISOLATION IN THE DESERT

He thereupon becomes another being. No longer is he the incorrigibly indolent and violently impulsive individual who spends his days in galloping over the cattle trails. He now transcends his primitive state. Resigned and tenacious, with that superior placidity which is characteristic of the strong, he looks the fatality, about which he knows he can do nothing, squarely in the face and prepares to meet it. The heroism of the backlands, the frightful tragedies which there take place, are a theme forever lost to us; they cannot be made to live again, nor can they be told in episodic form. They arise from a struggle which no one has described—the insurrection of the earth against man. At first, eyes turned heavenward,

---

[97] "It is related that, in Ceará, this experiment was performed in the presence of the naturalist, George Gardner. The scientist, who had made his own meteorological observations, and had arrived at a different result from that vouched for by the saint, exclaimed in his broken Portuguese: '*Non! Non! Luzia mentiu*' ('No! No! Luzia lies') . . . . " (Sylvio Romero, *A Poesia popular no Brasil*).

[Gardner is the author of *Travels in the Interior of Brazil, 1836–1841* (London, 1849).]

[98] [Compare our superstition with regard to Groundhog Day, February 2.]

the vaqueiro prays. His first reliance is his religious faith. With their miracle-working saints in their arms, with raised crosses, image-carrying litters borne aloft, and holy pennants fluttering, whole families may be seen—not merely the strong and healthy but the aged and infirm, the sick and the lame, as well—walking along with stones of the road on their heads and shoulders, as they transport the saints from one place to another. For long days the backland wastes echo to their mournful litanies, as the propitiatory processions slowly wend their way; and for long nights the plains are aglow with the tapers of the penitents as they wander here and there. But the skies remain sinister, devoid of clouds, and the sun blasts the earth, as the dreaded spasm of the drought comes on. The backwoodsman looks at his offspring. Sadly, he looks at his cattle, huddled down there in the marshy bottoms, or straying slowly at a distance, necks drooping, heads to the ground, bellowing plaintively as they "smell out the water." And without relaxing his faith, without doubting the Providence which crushes him, muttering the same customary prayers at the same hours, he prepares himself for the sacrifice. With hoe and spade he attacks the earth, seeking in the lower-lying strata the water which may have fled the surface. Sometimes he finds it; other times, after an enormous amount of exertion, he strikes a rock which renders useless all the labor he has expended. Yet again, and this is what happens most frequently, he lays bare a subterranean bed of water, only to see it disappear in a day or two, evaporated, or sucked back into the ground. He keeps after it, stubbornly, deepening his excavation in quest of the fleeing treasure, to reappear finally over the brim of the pit he has dug, like one coming back from the dead. But inasmuch as a rare frugality enables him to go for days on a few handfuls of passoca,[99] he is not so readily disheartened.

Here round about him is the caatinga, his own wild granary. He cuts up into bits the thirst-quenching mandacarús, or the greenish boughs of the joaz trees, which serve to nourish the lean and famishing members of his herd. He digs up the roots of the urucuris, scrapes them, bruises them, and then cooks them, making out of them a sinister bread which he calls *bró*, and which bloats the bellies of those who eat it in an illusory manner and gives to a starving person the sensation of being glutted. He fills the food containers with little coconuts. He excavates, also, the swollen roots of the umbú. These are to quench his children's thirst; for himself he reserves the astringent juice from the leaflike branches of the "chique-

[99] [*Passoca* consists of roasted Brazilian nuts ground up in a mortar with manioc flour, salt, and sugar.]

chique,"[100] which makes the one who drinks it hoarse or causes him to lose his voice entirely. In short, he labors excessively, making indefatigable use of every resource—a strong and affectionate being, looking out for himself, for his downcast progeny, and for the herds intrusted to his superhuman energy.

All his efforts, nevertheless, meet with frustration. He is put to it, in combating Nature with the desert. The seriemas[101] have fled to other *taboleiros* (tablelands),[102] and the parakeets have taken flight to the distant seashore, while he is left to contend with a cruel fauna. Myriads of bats now come to aggravate the "lean days," swooping down on the cattle and decimating them. In the patches of scorched weeds, the sound of innumerable rattlesnakes may be heard—the more intense the summer heat, the greater their number.

By night, the treacherous, thieving puma, which robs him of his calves and steers, comes up to the very threshold of his humble cottage. It is one more enemy with which he must cope. He attempts to frighten it off by running out into the yard with a lighted firebrand in his hand. If it does not beat a retreat, he attacks it. He does not, however, fire upon it, for he knows that, should he miss his aim, or should the bullet fail to finish off the beast, the puma, "coming in on top the puff," is invincible. The bout is a more exciting one than that. The weakened athlete, with a pitchfork in his left hand and his knife in his right, now irritates and challenges the intruder, provoking it to spring; he then wards it off in mid-air and dispatches it at a single blow.

Not always, though, does he dare risk such an exploit; for, to add to his other troubles, he suffers from a very strange malady—hemeralopia. This pseudo-blindness is due, paradoxically, to a reaction to the light; it is born of bright, hot days, gleaming skies, and the lively swaying of the currents of heated air above the barren earth. It is due to a plethora of sight. No sooner does the sun set in the west than the victim stops seeing; he is blind. Night swoops down upon him all of a sudden, before enveloping the earth. On the following morning, his extinguished vision is revived at the first ray of dawn, only to vanish once more, in the late afternoon, with a painful regularity.

With his sight, his energy comes back. He does not yet consider himself beaten. For quenching the thirst and satisfying the hunger of his young ones, there still remain the tender stocks of plants, the "truffles" of the wild bromelias, and with these barbarous messes he affords himself the illusion of satiety.

[100] [See p. 34.]   [101] [See p. 38, n. 65.]   [102] [See p. 7, n. 6.]

On foot now, for it tears his heart out so much as to look at his horse, he goes to the pastures, there to behold the ruins of his ranch: steers that look more like ghostly cattle, still alive, no one knows how, lying beneath the dead trees and barely able to raise their withered carcasses upon their thin legs, as they stagger about slowly and aimlessly; others that have been dead for days and are still intact, since, no matter how much they may peck, not even the vultures are able to pierce these sun-parched hides; cattle that are about to breathe their last, gathered about the clearing of clotted earth where their favorite drinking pool once stood; and, what grieves him more than anything else, those that are not yet wholly exhausted now come up to him and surround him confidently, bellowing piteously all the while, as if they were weeping.

Not even a cactus is left in the vicinity; the last green leaves of the joaz trees have long since been nibbled away.

However, there are still the impenetrable macambira thickets. They are a last resort. He proceeds to set fire to their dead and withered foliage, by way of stripping them of their thorns as speedily as possible; and, as the smoke comes puffing up and spreads out on the limpid air, there may be seen running up from all sides a sad-looking troop of sickly cattle, lean and famished, in search of one last meal.

Finally, all his resources are exhausted, and the situation remains unchanged. There is no likelihood whatsoever of rain. The marizeiros are the harbingers of rain, and their trunks are not oozing moisture. The northeast wind continues to blow intensely, roaring over the plains, rustling and howling in the noisy foliage of the caatingas; and the flashing sun in a cloudless sky pours down the irresistible heat of the dog days. Done in with all his adversities, the sertanejo at last gives up.

One day he sees going past his door the first lot of "quitters."[103] With deep forebodings he watches the wretched throng as they cross the village terrace and disappear in a cloud of dust, around the bend of the road. The next day there are more of them, and still more. It means that the region is being evacuated. He can hold out no longer but joins one of these bands, which leave their bones along the wayside as they go. He goes with them on this painful exodus to the coast, to the distant mountains—any place where life's primordial element is not denied to man. He reaches such a place. He is saved.

Months go by, and the scourge is at an end. Overcome by homesickness for the backlands, he returns. He comes back happy, reinvigorated, singing; forgetful of his misfortunes, he comes back in quest of the same

[103] [*Retirantes.*]

brief hours of unstable fortune, the same long days of anguish, of trials and tribulations long drawn out.

MESTIZO RELIGION

Isolated in this manner in a country that knows nothing of him, and engaged in an open warfare with an environment which would appear to have stamped upon his physical organism and his temperament its own extraordinary ruggedness, the sertanejo, either a nomad or with few roots in the soil, does not, to tell the truth, possess the organic capacity for attaining a loftier place in life. The restricted circle of his activities retards his psychic development. His religion is a monotheism which he does not understand, marred by an extravagant mysticism, with an incongruous admixture of the fetishism of the Indian and the African. He is the primitive individual, bold and strong, but at the same time credulous, readily permitting himself to be led astray by the most absurd superstitions. An analysis of these will reveal a fusion of distinct emotional states.

His religion is, like himself, mestizo in character. A résumé of the physical and physiological characteristics of the races from which he springs would likewise serve to summarize their moral qualities. It is an index to the life of the three peoples. And the sertanejo's religious beliefs reflect this violent juxtaposition of distinct tendencies. It is not necessary to describe them. The hair-raising legends of the waggish and wanton *caapora*, mounted on a peevish caitetú and crossing the plains on mysterious moon-lit nights; the diabolic *sacy*, a vermilion-colored bonnet on its head, assaulting the belated traveler on unlucky Good Friday eves; along with the werewolves and the night-wandering headless she-mules; all the temptations of the evil one, or Devil, that tragic bearer of celestial grievances, commissioned to the earth; the prayers addressed to São Campeiro, canonized *in partibus*, to whom candles are lighted on the plains[104] to obtain his help in recovering lost objects; the cabalistic conjurings for the curing of animals, for "bruising" and "selling" fevers; all the visions, all the fantastic apparitions, all the fanciful prophecies of the insane messiahs; and the pious pilgrimages and the missions and the penances—all these complex manifestations of an ill-defined religiosity are wholly explicable.

HISTORIC FACTORS IN MESTIZO RELIGION

It would not be too far amiss to describe them as a miscegenation of beliefs. Here they are, plain to be seen: the anthropomorphism of the savage, the animism of the African, and, what is more worthy of note, the

---

[104] [The name of this local saint, Campeiro, is derived from *campo*, a field or plain.]

emotional attitude of the superior race itself in the period of discovery and colonization. This last is a notable instance of historical atavism.

As we view the religious agitations of the hinterland, the singular evangelists and messiahs who at intervals make their appearance there, hair-shirt ascetics who are followed always by an imperious throng of fanatic, sorrowing, mad disciples, we instinctively recall the most critical phase in the spiritual life of Portugal, at the end of the sixteenth century, when, after having held for a moment or two the center of history's stage, this most interesting of all the peoples suddenly fell, entered upon a period of rapid decline which was ill disguised by the oriental splendor of Dom Manoel's court. The intensive settlement of Brazil took place under King John III, precisely at the height of this period of complete moral disequilibrium, when "all the terrors of the Middle Ages were crystallized in peninsular Catholicism."

The sertanejo is heir to a multitude of extravagant superstitions, which are no longer to be found along the seaboard, owing to the modifying influence of other creeds and other races, but which in the backlands have remained intact. This legacy was brought by those impressionable ones who flocked to our land after the miraculous dream of the Indies had been dispelled in the East. They came filled with a fierce mysticism, a religious fervor that vibrated to the brilliant glow of the inquisitorial fires which flared so intensely in the peninsula. They were part and parcel of the same people who in Lisbon, under the grievous obsession of miracles and assaulted by sudden hallucinations, had beheld above the royal palace prophetic caskets, mysterious tongues of flame, throngs of white-hooded Moors passing in procession, and paladin combats in the skies. They were the same people who, after Alcacer-Kebir, in the midst of a "national decline," as Oliveira Martins forcefully puts it, saw their only salvation, in the face of an imminent ruin, in a higher order of messianic hopes.

Indeed, as we view the backland disorders of today and the insane messiahs who provoke them, we are forcibly struck by their resemblance to the prophetic figures in the peninsula of former days—the King of "Penamacor," the King of "Ericeira," consecrated to martyrdom and wandering over the mountain slopes, infecting credulous multitudes with the same mad ideals, the same harassing dream.

This historical analogy is one that goes back for three centuries; but it is an exact one, complete and flawless. In the rustic society of the backlands time has stood still; this society has not been affected by the general evolutionary movement of the human race; it still breathes the moral atmosphere of those mad visionaries who pursued a Miguelhino or a Bandarra. Nor is there lacking, by way of rounding out the comparison, the political mysticism of *Sebastianism*. Extinct in Portugal, it persists unimpaired today, under a singularly impressive form, in our northern backcountry. But let us not run ahead of our story.

VARIABLE CHARACTER OF THE RELIGIOUS IMPULSE IN THE BACKLANDS

These atavistic stigmata with us found favoring climatic reactions that gave rise to a special psychology. The man of the backlands, as may be seen from the sketch we have given of him, more than any other, stands in a functional relation to the earth. He is a variable, dependent upon the play of the elements. Out of a consciousness of his own weakness in warding off those elements is born the strong and constant impulse to fall back upon the miraculous, representing the inferior mental state of the backward individual who feels himself the ward of divinity. In more favorable regions the necessity of such a tutelage as this would not be so keenly felt. Here, however, individual tendencies are, in a manner of speaking, bound up with external vicissitudes, and from the intermingling of the two—affording the contrast which we have already observed between an impulsive exaltation and an enervating apathy and inactivity—there results a fatalistic indifference toward the future and an accompanying religious exaltation. The teachings of the missionaries could not remain unaffected by the general tendencies of the age. And so it is not strange if, in troubled times, the lofty ideology of a Catholicism which is beyond the comprehension of these backwoodsmen breaks down, while the crude religious practices of the latter reveal all the stigmata of their undeveloped mentality.

The fact of the matter is that even in normal times their religion is a vague and varied one. Just as the Haussá Negroes, adapting to the liturgy the whole of the Jorubano ritual, afford the anomalous sight, but a common one in the Baian capital, of worshipers following the solemnities of the Mass in a manner to accord with their own fetishistic practices, so the sertanejos, unfortunate heirs to age-old vices, may be seen leaving the holy services for the pagan love-feasts of the African *candomblés*[105] or the Tupi *paracés*. It is not surprising, then, if in connection with this vague religiosity surprising anomalies are to be encountered.

It is a charming sight to see a backwoods family at nightfall kneeling before their rude altar or tawdry saint, by the dim light of oil lamps, praying for the souls of their loved ones who have died or seeking courage against the storms of this life. Their cult of the dead is most impressive. In remote localities, far from the towns, they bury them along the edge of

[105] [See the chapter on "The Candomblé" in Pierson's *Negroes in Brazil*, pp. 274–317.]

the road, in order that they may not be too lonely but may always have the benefit of the prayers of passers-by, and in order that these latter may be able to lay upon the angles of the cross some flower, some bough, some passing remembrance, but one that is ever renewed. And the cowboy, riding along at breakneck speed, will suddenly rein in his horse before this humble monument—a cross upon a few heaped stones—and, with bared head, he will then go slowly on his way, praying for the soul of one whom he perhaps has never seen, who may even have been an enemy of his.

The earth is an unbearable place of exile, and death a blessing always. The death of a child is a holiday. In the hut of the poor parents guitars twang joyfully amid the tears; the noisy, passionate samba is danced again, and the quatrains of the poetic challengers loudly resound; while at one side, between two tallow candles, wreathed in flowers, the dead infant is laid out, reflecting in its last smile, fixed in death, the supreme contentment of one who is going back to heaven and eternal bliss—which is the dominant preoccupation of these simple, primitive souls.

On the other hand, contrasting with these interesting aspects, their religion has certain repulsive manifestations, certain ugly aberrations, which corrupt and defile it.

"PEDRA BONITA"

The backland disturbances, from Maranhão to Baía, have not yet found their historian, and we shall not take that task upon ourselves. Instead, let us have a look at one incident among many, selected at random.

In the neighborhood of Pajehú, in Pernambuco, the last spurs of the granite formations of the coast heave and toss and assume capricious forms in the "Carved Mountains," the Serra Talhada, majestically dominating the entire region round about and converging in a great amphitheater that is reached by a narrow gorge between perpendicular walls. Here, like a gigantic pulpit, rises a solitary block of stone—the "Pedra Bonita," the Wondrous Rock.

In 1837 this site was a theater where scenes were staged that recall the sinister religious solemnities of the Ashantis.[106] A visionary mameluco or cafuso here gathered about him the entire population of the neighboring farms and, climbing up into the rock pulpit, proclaimed in a tone of conviction the near advent of the enchanted kingdom of Dom Sebastião. The rock having been shattered not by the blows of a mallet but by the miraculous blood of infants spilled upon it as a holocaust, the great king would then burst forth surrounded by his gleaming bodyguard and would visit

[106] The Ashantis are Negroes of the Gold Coast of Africa.

an inexorable punishment upon an ungrateful humanity, while heaping riches upon those who had contributed to his "disenchantment." A nervous shudder ran through the region.

This unbalanced individual had found a suitable setting for the spread of his insane teachings. Mothers with infants in their arms crowded around the monstrous altar and fought with one another to be the first to offer their young ones as a sacrifice. Blood gushed and spattered over the rock and stood about in pools—in such quantities, according to the newspapers of the time, that, when the lugubrious farce was at last ended, it was impossible for anyone to remain in the vicinity of this infected spot.

On the other hand, there are equally impressive occurrences to offset these aberrations. The backwoodsman's soul reacts inertly to the influences at work upon it, and, depending upon the nature of those influences, he may range from an extreme brutality to the height of devotion. We see him at this moment perverted by fanaticism. Let us view him now transfigured by faith.

MONTE SANTO

Monte Santo is a legendary site.[107] When, at the end of the seventeenth century, the discovery of the mines conferred upon the interior an attraction which the seaboard could not offer, those adventurous ones who descended upon the northern backlands, bound for the Jacobina Mountains, led on by the mirage of the silver mines, and following the enigmatic trail of Belchior Dias, would halt here for a long time. A solitary mountain—Mount Piquaraçá of the picturesque contours—commanding the horizon in all directions, served to guide them in their wavering course.

This peak, moreover, in itself held an irresistible attraction for them. As it happened, on one of its sides were engraved, in a gigantic handwriting formed by huge piles of rock, the mystifying letters—*A, L,* and *S*—flanked by a cross, which gave rise to the belief that here and not farther on, to the east or south, was the longed-for El Dorado. It was searched in vain, however, by those who sought to emulate the wily Muribeca,[108] and they in the end left for other parts, with their troops of friendly Potyguaras[109] and foreign-comers equipped with Biscayan muskets. The mountain then once more dropped from sight amid the plains which it overlooked.

At the end of the last century,[110] however, it was rediscovered by a mis-

107 See pp. 17 ff. and 198 ff.   109 [Or Potigoarras, an Indian tribe.]

108 See p. 199.   110 [The eighteenth century.]

sionary, Apollonio de Todi.[111] Coming from the mission of Massacará, the major apostle of the north was so impressed by the aspect of this mountain, "finding it like unto the Calvary of Jerusalem," that he resolved to erect a chapel here, one that should be at once the crudest and the most imposing temple of religious faith.

The priest describes at length the beginning and the progress of the work and the unstinted aid that was given him by the settlers of the immediate vicinity. He depicts the solemn ceremony when the temple was completed, the majestic procession slowly ascending the mountainside amid the gusts of a violent hurricane which, sweeping up from the plains, put out the torches; and, at the end, the penitential sermon, in which he exhorted the people that "on holy days they should visit the holy places, seeing that they lived in so great a forgetfulness of spiritual things."

"And then," he concludes, "without giving the matter any more thought, I told them that from this day forth they should not call this mountain Piquaraçá, but should give it rather the name of Monte Santo, Holy Mount."

In such a manner was this prodigious temple built, erected by Nature and by Faith, and higher than the loftiest of all the cathedrals of earth. The population of the backlands completed the missionary's undertaking.

Today, whoever climbs the long *via sacra*, some two miles in extent, along which at intervals are twenty-five stone chapels, housing the Stations of the Cross, will be able to form an idea of the constant, unremitting labor that was expended in the erection of this site. Supported by concealed walls, paved in some places while elsewhere the bed of living rock has been carved into steps, in other places sloping upward, this white quartzite roadway, where the litanies of Lenten processions resounded more than a century ago, and over which legions of penitents have passed, is a marvel of rude and bold engineering skill. At the beginning of the ascent it follows the line of maximum declivity along a slope of about twenty degrees. After the fourth or fifth chapel has been passed, it bends to the left and becomes less steep. Farther along, beyond the major chapel—a most interesting little church on a ledge of rock, overhanging the abyss below—it swerves back to the right, with the acclivity diminishing until the line of peaks is reached. Here it follows a small depression and then suddenly rises at a steep incline, making directly for the sharp-pointed summit, for the "Calvary" on top!

As the breathless observer makes this ascent, pausing at the stations, he encounters a crescendo of overpowering perspectives: first, the plains and

[111] See pp. 81 and 198–99.

tablelands, spreading out down below in vast level surfaces; then the far-off mountains clustering in the distance, in all four directions; and, finally, when he has reached the summit, the view of the mountaintops—the feeling of infinite space, the weird sensation of enormous height, which is increased by the sight of the little town at the foot of the mountain, of which he can perceive barely more than a choas of rooftops.

And when, during Holy Week, the families of the neighborhood come here, and believers pass over these same mountainsides where the restless and ambitious adventurers of old once roamed, it may be seen that Apollonio de Todi was more clever than Muribeca in deciphering the secret of those huge stone letters; for it was a marvelous El Dorado which he discovered, an opulent mine of the occult, here in the desert.

THE PRESENT-DAY MISSIONS

Unfortunately, the apostle had no successors. With rare exceptions, the modern missionary is a most prejudicial influence, serving to aggravate the state of emotional unbalance of the *tabareos*, or backland-dwellers. Lacking the spiritual stature of his predecessors, he produces a negative effect by destroying, obliterating, and perverting the good impulses which the early evangelists with their teachings had succeeded in implanting in these simple minds; his is not the talent and the art which was theirs, of transfiguring souls. His methods are the reverse of theirs; in place of counseling and consoling, he utters threats and maledictions; instead of praying, he blusters. He is brutal and treacherous. From the folds of his dark vestments, as from the shadow of an armed ambuscade, he leaps upon the unquestioning credulity of his listeners. When he mounts the pulpit of a country church, he does not hold up before the eyes of his congregation a picture of heaven and its delights; he portrays, instead, a cruel, flame-belching hell; his sermons are made up of gibberish and redundant phrases, accompanied by silly gestures and the grimaces of a clown. He is a ridiculous and a shocking figure, who enjoys the strange privilege of indulging in melodramatic buffooneries; but they are tragic words that fall from his lips. He does not depict for these simple backwoodsmen a better and nobler way of life—one with which he himself is unacquainted—but goes on bellowing against sin, describing in coarse language the scenes of future torment. Whole avalanches of penance are spewed upon the heads of his defenseless flock, as he rants and raves interminably, his dire forebodings being interspersed with his habitual pinches of snuff, as he opens now Pandora's box and now his snuff container.

And he succeeds in casting a spell on the credulous sertanejo; he hallucinates, depresses, and perverts him.

Let us take a single example, our last one. In 1850 the Cariry backlands were alarmed by the depredations of the "Serene Ones" who practiced large-scale robbery. This was the name given to bands of "penitents," hot-headed fanatics who, at night, at the desert crossways, congregated about mysterious crucifixes to practice the macabre rites of flagellants, torturing themselves with hairshirts, thorns, nettles, and other austere means of penance. One fine day these zealots suddenly sallied forth from the church of Crato and scattered out in disorderly fashion over the countryside— the women in mourning, the men apprehensive, the children in tears—as they went in fulfilment of punishments which had been rigorously imposed. Within the church, missionaries who had recently arrived had prophesied the nearing end of the world. God had said it—in bad Portuguese, bad Italian, and bad Latin—he was fed up with the sins of the earth.

And so these deluded ones went about, begging alms, weeping, praying, and living in a most demoralizing state of idleness; and, inasmuch as the public charity was not able to care for them all, they ended by—turning robbers. This was the last straw. The instigators of the crime were sent to take the blight of their teachings to other regions, while the strong arm of the law with some difficulty repressed the incipient banditry.[112]

IV

ANTONIO CONSELHEIRO, STRIKING EXAMPLE OF ATAVISM

It was natural that the deep-lying layers of our ethnic stratification should have cast up so extraordinary an anticlinal as Antonio Conselheiro.[113]

The metaphor is quite correct. Just as the geologist, by estimating the inclination and orientation of the truncated strata of very old formations, is enabled to reconstruct the outlines of a vanished mountain, so the historian, in taking the stature of this man, who in himself is of no worth, will find it of value solely in considering the psychology of the society which produced him. As an isolated case, this is one lost amid a multitude of commonplace neurotics; it could be included under the general category of progressive psychoses. Taken in connection with the social background,

---

[112] *Memoria sobre o estado da Bahia* (1893), an official publication, gives the details with regard to the founding of Monte Santo. On "Pedra Bonita" see the book by Araripe Junior, *O Reino encantado*, where this occurrence in all its deeply stirring aspects is put into the form of a brilliant novel.

[For a more modern treatment of the latter theme see the novel by José Lins do Rêgo, *Pedra Bonita* (Rio de Janeiro: Livrária José Olympio, 1938) (on the Lins do Rêgo work see *Hand Book of Latin American Studies*, p. 360, Item 4244, and p. 350).]

[113] Literally, "Anthony the Counselor." Conselheiro (pronounced "cohn-sel-yeh-ee'-roo") is a sobriquet.

on the other hand, it is sufficiently alarming. It is at once a diathesis and a synthesis. The various phases of this man's career do not, it may be, represent the successive stages of a serious ailment, but they most certainly afford us a condensed summary of a very grave social malady. As the upshot of it all, this unfortunate individual, a fit subject for medical attention, was impelled by a power stronger than himself to enter into conflict with a civilization and to go down in history when he should have gone to a hospital. For to the historian he is not an unbalanced character but rather appears as the integration of various social traits—vague, indecisive, not readily perceived when lost in the multitude, but well defined and forceful when thus summed up in a human personality.

All the naïve beliefs from a barbarous fetishism to the aberrations of Catholicism, all the impulsive tendencies of lower races given free outlet in the undisciplined life of the backlands, were condensed in his fierce and extravagant mysticism. He was at once an active and a passive element of that agitation which sprang up about him. A highly impressionable temperament led him merely to absorb the beliefs and superstitions of his environment, in which process his mind, tormented by adversity, was at first little more than the morbidly passive recipient; and, reflected by a consciousness that was in a state of delirium, these influences, greatly strengthened, in turn reacted upon the surroundings which had produced them.

In this particular case it is difficult to draw a dividing line between individual and collective tendencies. The life of this man at once becomes a synoptic chapter in the life of a society. In tracing the individual tendencies, we at the same time draw a rapid parallel for the social forces, and, in following out these two lines, we have a perfect example of the reciprocality of influences.

In surveying the scene about him, this false apostle, whose excessive subjectivism predisposed him to a revolt against the natural order of things, was in a manner observing the formula of his own madness. He was not a misunderstood being. The multitude acclaimed him as the natural representative of their highest aspirations. That was as far as it went with them; they were not concerned with his madness. As he continued to traverse a curve which would have led to the complete obscuration of reason, the milieu in its turn reacted upon him; it afforded him protection and corrected his aberrations to a degree, compelling him to establish some sort of unassailable logic even in his wildest imaginings, a certain show of order in his hallucinations, and a perduring consistency in everything he did. He manifested always a rare spirit of discipline in the control of his passions; and, as a consequence, the impressionable back-lands for long years could behold in his every word and deed the tranquillity, the moral elevation, and the sovereign resignation of an ancient apostle of the faith.

He was in reality a very sick man, to whom one could only apply Tanzi e Riva's concept of paranoia. In his ideational hallucinations the ethnic note was always prominent; one might say that it was the only one to be detected. He was a rare case of atavism. His morbid constitution led him to give a whimsical interpretation to objective conditions, thereby altering his relation to the external world; and this appeared as basically a retrogression to the mental state of the ancestral types of the species.

A CRUDE GNOSTIC

Without the necessity of medical intervention, an anthropologist would have found him to be normal, logically marking a certain level of human mentality, one that goes far back in time, a remote phase of evolution. What the medical man would describe as a characteristic case of systematic delirium, in the phase of persecution mania or delusions of grandeur, would be for the anthropologist the phenomenon of incompatibility with the higher exigencies of civilization—a clear case of atavism, with the revival of exceedingly remote psychic attributes. The most typical evidences of his strange mysticism, which to us was quite a natural thing, were already well known to our era under their everyday religious aspects. Even leaving aside the influence of lower races, we may find a comparatively recent example of it by a brief glance at the critical period of Portuguese life.

We might find examples on a still larger scale; but it is sufficient to go back to the early days of the Church, when a universal gnosticism was arising as the necessary form of transition from paganism to Christianity, in the last days of the Roman Empire, at a time when, just before the attack by the barbarians, Latin literature in the East had entered upon a sudden decline, its place being very unsatisfactorily taken by the sophists and petty-minded men of letters of Byzantium. As a matter of fact, the Phrygian Montanists, the infamous Adamites, the Ophiolaters, the two-faced Manichaeans, standing all of them in the middle ground between an emergent Christianity and ancient Buddhism, the disciples of Marcus, the abstinent Encratites, the Flagellants, and all the numerous sects into which the nascent religion was split up, with their hysterical doctors and hyperbolical exegeses—all these would be looked upon today as repugnant cases of insanity. Yet they were normal. They fitted in well with all the tendencies of an age in which the followers of an Alexander Abnoticus were rocking the Rome of Marcus Aurelius with their extravagances, their fantastic processions, their mysteries, and their tremendous holocausts of living lions, hurled into the Danube with imposing ceremonies presided over by the emperor-philosopher.

History repeats itself. Antonio Conselheiro was a crude gnostic. We shall see a little later just how exact this simile is.

A GREAT MAN GONE WRONG

"Indifferent paranoiac" is, possibly, an expression that is not wholly applicable to him. With an insane temperament marked by an obvious ideational retrogression, he was, certainly, a notable case of intellectual degenerescence; but this, in the milieu in which he lived, did not isolate him, did not lead to his being misunderstood and thrown off balance in such a manner as to render him outwardly retrograde and rebellious. On the contrary, all this strengthened him. He was the prophet, the emissary from heaven. He had, it was true, undergone a stupendous reincarnation, had been transfigured, but all the human contingencies involved had been strictly observed: he was a being capable of suffering and death, whose sole mission was to point out to sinners the way to salvation. And he remained satisfied with this role of heavenly delegate and did not go beyond it. He was a servant yoked to a harsh task; and we accordingly behold him year after year making his way through the savage backlands, dragging along his halting carcass, maddened by one fixed idea, yet somehow lucid-seeming in every act of his life, and giving the impression always of a firmness which nothing could shake, as he pursued his fixed objective with a finality that brooked no opposition.

His sickly consciousness oscillated about that ideal middle line which Maudsley regrets that he is unable to trace between good sense and insanity.[114] He remained there indefinitely on the wavering frontier of madness, in that mental zone where criminals and heroes, brilliant reformers and moral defectives, meet, and genius jostles degeneracy. That was all there was to it in his case. Held down by the vigorous discipline of a cultivated society, his neurasthenia would have exploded in the form of revolt, and his repressed mysticism would have burst the bounds of reason; but here, vibrating in sentimental unison with the environment, their effect was normalized, through the diffusion of his mystical teachings in the souls of those round about him.

[114] See p. 476.

A NATURAL REPRESENTATIVE OF THE MILIEU
INTO WHICH HE WAS BORN

The sociological factor, which favored this mystical psychosis in the individual, set bounds to it without restraining it unduly, and this led to a harmony which was the victim's salvation. A mind predisposed to open rebellion against the natural order was thus brought to yield to the only reaction that was open to it, by crystallizing in these favorable surroundings the prevalent errors and superstitions.

FAMILY ANTECEDENTS: THE MACIEIS

Antonio Conselheiro's biography is a compendium and résumé of social existence in the backlands. It throws light on the etiology of the disease of which he was the victim. Let us glance at it briefly, in passing.

The Macieis, in the regions between Quixeramobim and Tamboril, constituted a numerous family of strong, active, brave, and intelligent individuals who lived by cattle-herding and small-scale cattle-breeding. By a fatal law of the times they came to engage in a family feud and to take part in the great crimes of Ceará. Their rivals were the Araujos, a rich family related to others that were among the oldest in the northern section of the province. Both families lived in the same region, which had as its principal seat the town of Boa Viagem, situated about twenty-five miles from Quixeramobim. This was one of the bloodiest feuds that the Ceará backlands ever witnessed. In it two large groups of men participated, of varying degrees of fortune and official position, but fierce fighters all of them, and hardened in the practice of violence.

Thus does a conscientious narrator begin his brief account of Antonio Conselheiro's genealogy.[115]

The crimes referred to are little more than an episode among the never ending "rampages" that mark the turbulent life of these regions. They are but duplicates of a thousand others, which may serve as a commentary on the unbridled power that is enjoyed by the village authorities and the shameful manner in which they exploit the naturally fierce instincts of the sertanejo. This family feud is merely a variant on all the other interminable ones which spring up here, involving even the descendants of those who start them, with successive generations taking up the quarrels of their ancestors, all of which goes to create a physiological predisposition, with rancors and the passion for vengeance being passed on by heredity.

FEUD BETWEEN THE MACIEIS AND THE ARAUJOS

The feud between the Macieis and the numerous Araujos arose from a very minor incident, certain robberies which were asserted to have been committed by the former on the latter's estate. Everything pointed to the conclusion that the Macieis were the victims of an unfounded accusation; for they were "sturdy, likeable and likely-appearing fellows, truthful and

[115] Colonel João Brigido dos Santos.

obliging," who enjoyed an enviable reputation in all the neighborhood round about. Araujo da Costa, however, and his relative, Sylvestre Rodrigues Veras, were not inclined to look with favor on a poor family whose influence rivaled their own, without the justification of large herds and vast estates. Wealthy cattle-breeders, lords of life and death,[116] accustomed to taking justice into their own hands, they resolved to make an example of the alleged delinquents; and, inasmuch as the latter were brave to the point of temerity, the Araujos called in their pretorian guard of *capangas*[117] and, thus equipped, set out on the criminal expedition to Quixeramobim.

Not long afterward, however, contrary to the general expectation, they came draggling back in defeat. The Macieis, having rounded up all their clan of fearless, upstanding lads, had met the hired mob and had vigorously repelled them, riding roughshod over them and frightening them off. This happened in 1833.

Thus beaten and not being inclined to bear their disappointment and anger, these potentates, whose lordly imbecility had met with so rude a rebuff, thereupon had resort to more energetic measures. There were not lacking then, as there are not lacking today, criminals of renown whose courage was for hire; and the Araujos contrived to get hold of a couple of outstanding ones: José Joaquim de Menezes, a surly Pernambucan, celebrated for his bloody rivalry with the famous Mourões; and a terrible bandit by the name of Vicente Lopes, of Aracaty-assú. Having got their turbulent band together, along with Sylvester's sons and sons-in-law, they lost no time in embarking on their lawless enterprise.

As they approached the Macieis' home, however, the assassins, despite the fact that they were in the majority, grew alarmed at thought of the resistance they were bound to meet with and proposed that their victims surrender upon a promise that their lives would be spared. The Macieis, being certain that they would not be able to hold out for long, agreed to this and gave themselves up. The bandits' word proved to be worth just what one would expect it to be. Manacled and under guard, the captives were taken to the jail of Sobral, and there, on the first day's lap of their journey, they were slain. Among those who died on this occasion were the head of the family, Antonio Maciel, and a grandfather of Antonio Conselheiro.[118]

---

[116] ["Senhores de baraço e cutelo," a proverbial expression in Portuguese.]

[117] [*Capanga* sometimes means a backwoods Negro and sometimes a hired assassin.]

[118] Manoel Ximenes, speaking in his memoirs of these two unfortunate ones, observes that no one had ever had a word to say against them, not even their enemies, who had made accusations against their sons; he doubts that they had anything to do with the robberies in question.

One of Antonio's uncles, Miguel Carlos, managed to escape. Handcuffed and, what is more, with his legs bound beneath his horse's belly, how he managed to do it is a mystery; but we have it on the word of a faithful chronicler.[119] The Araujos, who had thus let slip their worst adversary, at once gave chase; well armed and mounted, they barbarously sought to ride him down, as if they had been on the trail of the fierce mountain lion. The fugitive, however, a master-woodsman, made his way to the home of a sister, and there for a time eluded the pursuing band, headed by Pedro Martins Veras. On the estate known as "Passagem," in the neighborhood of Quixeramobim, he hid himself away, exhausted, in an old abandoned shack overgrown with oiticica boughs.[120]

Here his pursuers soon caught up with him. It was nine o'clock in the morning. There was a tremendous fight, and a very uneven one. The brave sertanejo, although crippled and in pain from a dislocated ankle, boldly confronted the horde of assailants and stretched one of them out on the ground; this was a certain Theotonio, an audacious ruffian who had ventured in ahead of his companions. He fell directly across the doorsill, in such a manner that it was impossible to close the door. When Miguel Carlos' sister came up to drag the body away, she fell, pierced by a bullet. It was Pedro Veras himself who had fired the shot, and he paid for it by receiving a charge of lead, point-blank. Their leader dead, the attackers fell back for a moment, which gave the fugitive barely enough time to bar the door.

With this, the hut became a fort, and from minute to minute, through the chinks in the wall, came the burst of gunfire. Not daring to try to take the place by storm, and rendered all the more ferocious by their cowardice, the bandits proceeded to set fire to the leaves that covered it. The effect was instantaneous. Unable to breathe in his flaming shelter, Miguel Carlos resolved to abandon it. Dashing the contents of a jug of water on one end of the cabin, he succeeded in momentarily putting out the fire on that side, and, leaping over the dead body of his sister, with his rifle under his arm and his *parnahyba* (long knife) in his hand,[121] he hurled himself into the midst of his assailants and contrived to break through them and lose himself in the caatinga.

Some time afterward, one of the Araujos was about to be married to the daughter of a rich cattle-breeder of Tapayara; and on their wedding

---

[119] Manoel Ximenes, *Memorias.*

[120] [Oiticica is the name given to two trees, one of the Rosaceae family (*Licania rigida* Benth.), the other of the Moraceae family (*Clarisia nitida* Benth. Hook.).]

[121] [For a description of the *parnahyba* see p. 145.]

day, as they were approaching the church, he was killed by a bullet, to the great alarm of the guests and the despairing cries of the poor, unfortunate bride. The vengeance of the sertanejo never sleeps.

Miguel Carlos had another sister, Helena Maciel, who shared his deep and justifiable rancor and who was known as the "family Nemesis," according to the chronicler whom we have quoted. His own life was filled with perilous adventures, many of which were doubtless invented by the backwoodsmen's fertile imagination. One thing is certain: he succeeded in evading all the snares that were laid for him, while more than once the unwary informer who had sought him out in Quixeramobim fell beneath his knife. The narrative to which we have referred goes on to say:

It appears that Miguel Carlos had protectors there, who assured his safety. In any event, notwithstanding the fate which had befallen his companion, it was nothing unusual for him to be seen in the town.

One night, as he was standing in the doorway of Manoel Procopio de Freitas' shop, a certain individual came in to buy some brandy. Convinced that the man was a spy, Miguel Carlos was for killing him on the spot. He was restrained from doing so by the proprietor; and, accordingly, he followed the suspect and slew him with his knife, as the fellow was leaving the town along the Palha Creek.

One morning, finally, he left the home of Antonio Caetano de Oliveira, who was married to a relative of his, to go for a bath in the stream which runs in back of the house. The house itself is situated on the far side of the main square of the town, next the gully which leads to the little Cotovello Square. Behind the house at that time, as we have said, was the outlet of the Palha Creek, which flowed around the square in almost a perfect circle, forming in the winter a lovely girdle of standing water. Miguel and a large number of his companions were there and had already stripped, when they were surprised by a band of their enemies who had been squatting inside the dense underbrush in wait for them. Miguel Carlos' relatives and the others who were present, snatching up their clothes from the sand where they had dropped them, put them on as they ran and took to their heels. As for Miguel Carlos himself, clad only in his drawers, and with his knife in his hand, he made for the rear of a house which stood almost facing the creek, a house which, in the year 1845, was occupied by Manoel Francisco da Costa. The fugitive had succeeded in opening the wicker gate to the garden of this house; but, as he was in the act of closing it, he was struck by a bullet from behind. Others say that this happened as he was running through a hollow near a backwater pool which stood there. He had fallen, dagger in hand, and was already dying, when Manoel de Araujo, leader of the pursuing band and a brother of the bridegroom who had been slain, pinning him by one leg, finished him off with a dagger thrust. Even as he was dying, however, at the very moment of death, he responded with another thrust, in his adversary's jugular vein, and the two of them expired the same instant one on top the other! Helena Maciel, meanwhile, came running up furiously to the scene of the conflict, to kick her brother's slayer in the face. She was satisfied to lose her brother, she said, seeing that he had settled scores with their enemy!

The story goes that the assassins had spent the night in the house of Ignacio Mendes Guerreiro, of the Araujo family, the postmaster of the town. They had come under the pretext of taking the Macieis into custody, but their real purpose had been to kill them.

Helena was not downcast by all this. The Nemesis of the family, she proceeded to do away with an enemy as a sacrifice-offering to her brother's shade; for, as she herself confessed years later, it was she who instigated the brutal mauling of André Jacintho de Souza Pimentel, a lad belonging to an important family of the town and related to the Araujos, to whom she attributed the notices which the latter received in Boa Viagem of the comings and goings of Miguel Carlos. From this beating there resulted a cardiac lesion which caused the unfortunate youth to die in horrible anguish, as a result of his being blamed, and justly so, for this latest act of aggression on the part of the Araujos.

The fact of the matter is, the crime had been perpetrated, on Helena's orders, by soldiers of the line, belonging to a detachment commanded by Sublieutenant Francisco Gregorio Pinto, an insolent fellow of low origin and little education, whose enmity Pimentel had incurred; all of which for a long time led to the belief that this army officer of ill repute was the author of the crime.

Helena all the while kept silent.

This backlands feud claimed innumerable victims and decimated two whole families and their partisans, the last of the direct line of the Macieis being that Antonio Maciel,[122] brother of Miguel Carlos, who died in Boa Viagem.[123] The valor of Miguel Carlos became a legend, and both he and his relatives had the respect and esteem of their contemporaries, as bearing witness to the energy of a family which had produced so many strong individuals, capable of engaging in a feud with such powerful personages as those of Boa Viagem and Tamboril.[124]

There is no need to continue with the quotation.

A LIFE THAT PROMISED WELL

Nothing is known for a certainty as to the role which Vicente Mendes Maciel, father of Antonio Vicente Mendes Maciel (the *Conselheiro*, or Counselor)[125] played in this deplorable feud. His contemporaries depict him as "a short-tempered man, but of excellent character, a good deal of a visionary and inclined to be distrustful, but extremely capable—so capable that, although he was illiterate, he transacted much business at the great estates, keeping all accounts and measures perfectly in his head, without even having to write down the names of the debtors."

The son, under the discipline of a stern father of proverbial integrity, was given an education which in a manner isolated him from the turbulent life that his family led. Those persons still alive who knew him then picture him as a quiet, timid young man without that bounding enthusiasm which is commonly associated with early youth. He was reserved, averse to frivolity, and rarely left his father's place of business in Quixeramobim, where he was wholly and conscientiously devoted to the mysteries of the cash drawer, being content to let the glowing season of his

---

[122] [The singular form of the family name is *Maciel*, the plural, *Macieis*.]

[123] [Compare what is said on p. 122.]

[124] Colonel João Brigido, *Crimes celebres do Ceará, os Araujos e Macieis.*

[125] [*Conselheiro* is sometimes rendered as "Councilor," but the form Counselor seems preferable in view of the origin of the name (see p. 128).]

twenty years go by and vanish. In the meantime, he could not help hearing all the tales and legends that were told, interwoven with many exaggerations, as is the custom with backwoods story-tellers—tales in which his own flesh and blood were very often the protagonists, and in which they always exhibited the same rare but traditional courage. Any suggestive effect, however, which these stories might have had on the young lad was promptly corrected by the stern gravity of the elder Mendes Maciel, and they do not appear to have unduly excited his mind. It may be that all this was lying latent, ready to expand under more favorable conditions; but, in any case, following his father's death in 1855, twenty years after the tragic events which we have related, Antonio Maciel continued to lead the same quiet and highly respectable life.

Faced with the task of caring for three maiden sisters, he displayed an unusual self-abnegation. It was only after he had married them off that he set out to make a match for himself, one that was destined to be his undoing.

EARLY REVERSES

It is at this point that the drama of his life begins. A wife was for him merely an additional deadweight to the tremendous burden of his tarnished heredity, and marriage led to the unbalancing of a life which had begun promisingly enough. From 1858 on, everything that he does shows him to be a changed man. For one thing, he has lost his old sedentary habits. It may have been the incompatibility of genius or, what is more likely, his wife's bad disposition; but, whatever the cause, his existence was now an exceedingly unsettled one. Within the course of a few years, we find him living in various towns and cities and following various occupations.

Amid all this restlessness, nevertheless, there is to be perceived a character engaged in struggle, one that does not mean to let itself be defeated. Being left without any worldly fortune, Antonio Maciel, in this preparatory phase of his career, in spite of his unhappy home life, no sooner arrives at a new place of residence than he at once starts looking for employment, any means whatsoever of earning an honest livelihood. In 1859, removing to Sobral, he obtains a position as cashier, but does not remain there long. Going on to Campo Grande, he there finds work as scrivener to a justice of the peace; but again his stay is a brief one, and he is off for Ipú, where he becomes a court attaché.

In all this there is to be noted an evergrowing predilection for those occupations which are least laborious, requiring less and less of an expenditure of energy. Antonio Maciel is getting away from the discipline of his youth and displays a marked tendency toward those forms of activity which are more exciting and less productive; he is on the downward path which leads to open vagabondage. At the same time his troubles at home are robbing him of his old serenity.

This period of his life, nevertheless, shows him to be endowed still with worthy sentiments. Round about him permanent party strifes were going on, offering an adventurous career upon which, like so many others, he might have embarked, by allying himself with the first victor at the polls who came along; and he would have been welcome by reason of his family's traditional prestige. He always avoided this, however; and throughout the whole of his downward course there is to be glimpsed a man who is giving ground, it may be, but who does so slowly, struggling painfully to keep his footing, but with all the exhaustion of a weakened constitution.

DOWNFALL

Then of a sudden he meets with a violent mishap, and the inclined plane of his life at once comes to an end with a terrifying crash. At Ipú his wife left him, ran away with a police officer. This proved his complete undoing. Overcome with shame, the poor fellow sought to bury himself in the depths of the backlands, seeking out the most remote regions, where no one would even know his name and where he might find the shelter of complete obscurity. His course was to the south of Ceará. Upon passing through Páos Brancos, on the Crato Highway, he made an attack one night, with all the fury of a madman, upon a relative who had put him up. There was a brief investigation by the police, which was halted when the victim declared that his assailant had not been to blame. In this manner the latter was saved from going to prison. He then went on south, as fast as his legs could carry him, in the direction of Crato, and dropped out of sight.

Ten years passed by, and the unfortunate youth of Quixeramobim appeared to have been completely forgotten. Only once in a long while would someone recall his name and the scandal which had marked the close of his life in those parts—a scandal in which a certain local bigwig, a police sergeant, was *magna pars*, the Lovelace of the episode. Thanks to this somewhat ludicrous incident, the name of Antonio Maciel was barely kept alive on his native heath; but he might, to all intents and purposes, have been dead.

HOW A MONSTER IS FORMED

And so there appeared in Baía the somber anchorite with hair down to his shoulders, a long tangled beard, an emaciated face, and a piercing eye a monstrous being clad in a blue canvas garment and leaning on the classic staff which is used to stay the pilgrim's tottering steps.

What his life had been over so long a period of time, no one knows. An aged caboclo, captured in Canudos in the last days of the campaign, had something to tell me about this, but he was very vague and could give no exact dates or specific details. He had known Antonio Maciel in the backlands of Pernambuco, a year or two after the latter had left Crato. From what this witness told me, I gathered that, while still a youth, Antonio Maciel had made a vivid impression upon the imagination of the sertanejos. He had come there a vagabond, without any fixed destination, and he never referred to his past. His conversation was made up of short phrases and an occasional monosyllable. From one stop to the next he went, seemingly careless as to what direction he took, indifferent to danger, taking no thought of his life, eating little or nothing, and now and again sleeping out in the open, along the roadside, as if in fulfilment of a rude and prolonged penance.

It is not surprising, then, if to these simple folk he became a fantastic apparition, with something unprepossessing about him; nor is it strange if, when this singular old man of a little more than thirty years drew near the farmhouses of the *tropeiros*,[126] the festive guitars at once stopped strumming and the improvisations ceased. This was only natural. Filthy and battered in appearance, clad in his threadbare garment and silent as a ghost, he would spring up suddenly out of the plains, peopled by hobgoblins. Then he would pass on, bound for other places, leaving the superstitious backwoodsmen in a daze. And so it was, in the end, he came to dominate them without seeking to do so.

In the midst of a primitive society which, by its own ethnic qualities and through the malevolent influence of the holy missions, found it easier to comprehend life in the form of incomprehensible miracles, this man's mysterious way of living was bound to surround him with a more than ordinary amount of prestige, which merely served to aggravate his delirious temperament. All the legends and conjectures which sprang up about him were a propitious soil for the growth of his own hallucinations. His insanity therewith became externalized. The intense admiration and the absolute respect which were accorded him gradually led to his becoming the unconditional arbiter in all misunderstandings and disputes, the favored Counselor in all decisions.[127] The multitude thus spared him an agonizing quest in search of his own emotional state, all the effort, the anguish-

---

[126] [*Tropeiro:* one who drives a pack horse or a mule.]
[127] [See note on the name "Antonio Conselheiro," p. 125.]

laden questionings, the entire process of delirious introspection such as ordinarily accompanies the evolution of madness in sickly brains. The multitude created him, refashioning him in its own image. It broadened his life immeasurably by impelling him into those errors which were common two thousand years ago. The people needed someone to translate for them their own vague idealizations, someone to guide them in the mysterious paths of heaven.

And so the evangelist arose, a monstrous being, but an automaton. This man who swayed the masses was but a puppet. Passive as a shade, he moved them. When all is said, he was doing no more than to condense the obscurantism of three separate races. And he grew in stature until he was projected into History.

WANDERINGS AND MARTYRDOMS

From the backlands of Pernambuco he went on to those of Sergipe, appearing in the city of Itabaiana in 1874. He arrived there, as he did everywhere, unknown and under a cloud of suspicion, creating a startling impression by the extraordinary clothes that he wore—a blue tunic without a girdle, a hat with a broad turned-down brim, and sandals, while on his back he carried a leather bag containing paper, pen and ink, an *Abbreviated Mission* and the *Hours of Mary*.

He lived on alms but refused to take anything in excess of his daily needs. When it came to a place to lay his head, he sought out solitary spots. He would not accept any kind of bed whatsoever beyond a barren plank, and in default of that he would sleep on the hard ground.

He wandered about in this manner for a long time, until finally he appeared in the backlands north of Baía. His prestige, meanwhile, had been growing. He no longer went alone but was followed on his aimless way by the first of the faithful. He did not call them; they came to him of their own accord, happy at being permitted to share with him his days of trial and privation. These were, in general, individuals from the lowest social strata, those who, being averse to labor, were commonly looked down upon and viewed with suspicion; they were, in brief, a motley crew of human failures, accustomed to living in idleness and by their wits.

One of his followers then took it upon himself to build a temple, the only one which the diminutive and nascent sect possessed, in the form of a crude oratory, made of cedarwood and inclosing an image of Christ. On their stops along the road they would hang this upon the bough of a tree and then would kneel in prayer; and, bearing it triumphantly aloft, they would enter the towns and villages to a chorus of litanies.

It was in this manner, in the year 1876, that the "Counselor" made his appearance in the town of Itapicurú de Cima. His renown at this time was already very great, as is shown by an account which was published that very year, in the capital of the Empire:

There has appeared in the northern backlands an individual who goes by the name of Antonio Conselheiro, and who exerts a great influence over the minds of the lower classes, making use of his mysterious trappings and ascetic habits to impose upon their ignorance and simplicity. He lets his beard and hair grow long, wears a cotton tunic, and eats sparingly, being almost a mummy in aspect. Accompanied by a couple of women followers, he lives by reciting beads and litanies, by preaching, and by giving counsel to the multitudes that come to hear him when the local Church authorities permit it. Appealing to their religious sentiments, he draws them after him in throngs and moves them at his will. He gives evidence of being an intelligent man, but an uncultivated one.[128]

These statements, all of which are strictly true, published in a yearbook hundreds of miles away, are a good indication of the widespread fame which he had already attained.

LEGENDS

The town of Itapicurú, meanwhile, came near witnessing the end of his amazing career; for it was there, in this same year, amid the delirious ravings of his followers, that he was suddenly arrested. His imprisonment was due to a false accusation, to which his unusual mode of life and the family trouble he had previously had, appeared to lend credence: he was accused of having murdered his wife and his own mother. The story is a hair-raising one.

The mother, so the tale runs, had a violent dislike for her daughter-in-law and was bent upon doing away with her. With this object in view, she informed her son that he had been betrayed; and when the latter, taken by surprise, demanded proof of the assertion, she promised him that he should have it shortly. She then advised him to pretend that he was going away on a journey somewhere but, instead, to remain in the vicinity, so that he might with his own eyes see the seducer, the man who dishonored his wife, entering their home. This plan having been agreed upon, the poor fellow rode out a little over a mile from the town, and then, reining in, he stealthily turned back and returned by little frequented paths to a spot he had chosen, from which he might be able to observe what went on and be in a position to act promptly.

Here he remained for hours, until finally, late in the night, he did in fact see someone approaching his home. The stranger slipped up cautiously

[128] *Folhina Laemmert*, of the year 1877.

and was about to climb in one of the windows. The husband, however, did not give him time to do so but brought him down with a bullet. Then, at a bound, he rushed into the house and fired upon his faithless spouse, who lay sleeping. After which, he turned to see who the man was he had slain. He saw with horror that it was his own mother, who had disguised herself in this manner in order to carry out her diabolical plan. Terrified by what he had done, he took to his heels like a madman, abandoning everything, and fled to the backlands.

The popular imagination, as may be seen, was beginning to make a romance of his life, displaying in the process a tragic power of fantasy and a high degree of originality.

THE ASCETIC

However this may be, it is certain that, in 1876, the law laid hold of him just as his mental aberrations were taking final shape, just as he was becoming wholly immersed in the dream from which he was never more to awake. The ascetic sprang fully formed from the rude discipline imposed by fifteen years of penance, an apprenticeship in those martyrdoms which were so extolled by the ancient luminaries of the Church. His had been a harsh schooling indeed, in hunger, thirst, bodily weariness, repressed anguish, and deep-seated misery. There were no tortures unknown to him. His withered epidermis was as wrinkled as an old broken and trampled breastplate over his lifeless flesh. Pain itself had come to be his anesthetic; he bruised and macerated that flesh with hairshirts more cruel than any matweed; he dragged it over the stones of the road; he scorched it in the embers of the drought; he exposed it to the rigors of the cold night dew; in his brief moments of repose he put it to bed on the lacerating couch of the caatingas.

Many times he came near to death in his prolonged fastings, with a refinement of asceticism which would have astonished Tertullian, that somber propagandist of the doctrine of the gradual elimination of matter, "ridding himself of his blood, that heavy and importunate burden of the soul impatient to be gone."[129]

For one thus inured to suffering, prison was but a very minor incident. He accepted it with indifference and forbade the faithful to do anything in his defense. Instead, he gave himself up, and they removed him to the capital of Baía. There his strange appearance excited a universal curiosity: face lifeless and rigid as a mask, at once unseeing and unsmiling; eye-

[129] *De jejuniis.*

lids drooping over deep-sunken sockets; and then, his singular garb; his general aspect of a disinterred corpse, clad as he was in his flowing tunic suggestive of a black shroud; and, finally, his long, sleek, dusty-looking hair which fell to his shoulders, mingling there with his stiff, wiry beard, which came to his waist.

As he passed through the streets, he was greeted with the ovations and exorcisms ("by these signs") of frightened believers and terror-struck pious women.[130] The judges themselves were astounded as they interrogated him. They accused him of crimes committed years ago, at the place of his birth. Wrapped in a marble-like impassivity, he listened to their questions and their accusations without letting fall so much as a murmur from his lips. The guard that had brought him to prison, as was afterward learned, had mishandled him shamefully, and he had not voiced the least complaint but had remained tranquilly indifferent, with the bearing of a Stoic who is above it all. There was but one exception—and this curious detail we gleaned from a person whose word is not to be doubted: on the day that they set out for Ceará he begged the authorities to shield him from the curiosity of the public, which was the only thing that annoyed him.

When he had arrived at his former home, it was decided that the charges were unfounded, and he was set at liberty. That same year he reappeared in Baía, among his disciples who had been awaiting him all the while. Inasmuch as his return, so they say, coincided to a day with the date he had fixed at the time of his arrest, the whole thing took on the aspect of a miracle, and his influence was accordingly trebled.

He then wandered for some time among the backlands of Curaçá, his favorite place of abode being (in 1877) Chorrochó, a village of a few hundred inhabitants whose lively fair attracted to the place the majority of the settlers along this portion of the São Francisco. An impressive chapel to this day commemorates his stay there; but more venerated than this, perhaps, is the little tree at the entrance to the town which was for a long time the object of an extraordinary phytolatry.[131] It was in its shade that the pilgrim took his rest, and hence it was a sacred tree. Its shade likewise cured the sick, and its leaves were an unfailing panacea. The people were initiating the great series of miracles of which, quite possibly, the poor man did not dream.

---

[130] [*Beata:* properly, a woman designated by the Church as "blessed" but not in a religious order. In the case of the Counselor's followers, the *beatas* were women of a dissolute life who had reformed and were engaged in expiating their sins by penance (see p. 156).]

[131] [The author's word: *phytolatria*.]

From 1877 to 1887 he wandered through these backland regions in all directions, finally arriving on the seacoast, at Villa do Conde (1887). In all this area there was probably not a town or city in which he had not made his appearance. Alagoinhas, Inhambupe, Bom Conselho, Geremoabo, Cumbe, Mucambo, Massacará, Pombal, Monte Santo, Tucano, and other places had beheld him approaching, accompanied by his riffraff band of the faithful. And in nearly all these towns he left some mark of his passage: here the ruined walls of a cemetery had been rebuilt; there a church had been repaired; and farther on a chapel had been erected, with a display of fine artistry always.

His entrance into the towns, followed by a silent, contrite multitude bearing aloft images, crucifixes, and holy banners, was a solemn and impressive occasion. All normal occupations came to a standstill, as the population of the surrounding countryside bore down upon the town, where all the stir and movement of a fair prevailed; and for a number of days thereafter, casting the local authorities completely into eclipse, this humble, wandering penitent would give orders and have things all his own way, becoming in effect the only authority in the place.

In the public square they would erect leafy bowers, where, as evening fell, the worshipers would say their beads and intone litanies; and when there was a great concourse, they would throw up an improvised platform alongside the fair booth, in the middle of the square, in order that the prophet's words might be heard on every hand and believers be duly edified. He would then mount this platform and preach a sermon. Those persons still living who heard him preach tell us that his sermons were barbarous and terrifying, calculated to send chills down the spines of his listeners. They were made up of mutilated excerpts from the *Hours of Mary;* they were disconnected, abstruse; and at times, to make matters worse, he daringly had resort to Latin quotations. Couched in broken phrases, they were a hopelessly confused mixture of dogmatic counsels, the vulgar precepts of Christian morality, and weird prophecies.

It was a clownish performance, but dreadful. One has but to imagine a buffoon maddened with a vision of the Apocalypse.

Sparing of gestures, he would speak for a long time, eyes downcast, without looking his audience in the face as they stood there overwhelmed by this endless flow of jargon, the tiring lilt of nonsense. He was, however, it would appear, concerned with the effect produced by this or that outstanding phrase. He would enunciate it, then pause, raise his head, suddenly lift his eyelids, and one would then have a glimpse of his extremely black and sparkling eyes, his gaze—a dazzling flash. No one dared look at him then. His listeners would succumb, would drop their gaze in turn, fascinated by the strange power of hypnotism exerted over them by this awful form of insanity. And on such an occasion the poor unfortunate would achieve the one and only miracle he ever wrought: that of not appearing ridiculous.

In his sermons, in which he competed successfully with the wandering Capuchins of the missions, he promulgated a system of religious belief which was at once vague and incongruous. One who heard him might well have been led to make certain suggestive comparisons drawn from history. One might re-read those memorable pages[132] in which Renan, through the electrifying effect of his beautiful style, causes the mad cult leaders of the early centuries of our era to live for us again; and in the present instance he would note an integral revival of those long-vanished aberrations. One could not desire a more complete reproduction of the same system of dogma, the same images, the same hyperbolical formulas, the very same words almost. It is a splendid example of the identity of evolutionary stages among peoples. The retrograde type of the backlands reproduces the aspect presented by mystics of the past. Viewing him, one has the marvelous impression of a perspective down the centuries.

He is a being out of our time. He belongs wholly with those retarded types whom Fouillée happily compares to "coureurs sur le champ de la civilisation, de plus en plus en retard."

PRECEPTS OF A MONTANIST

He is a dissident of the exact mold of Themison. Rising up against the Roman Church and hurling rebukes at it, he makes use of the same argument that Themison does: she has lost the glory that was hers and is doing the will of Satan. He outlines a morality which is a line-for-line translation of that of Montanus: a chastity exaggerated to the point where woman is looked upon with horror, contending with the absolute license of a free love which means the practical extinction of marriage. The Phrygian, perhaps, like the man of Ceará, had in his mouth the bitter aftertaste of conjugal misfortunes. Both sternly forbade any decorative attire for young women; both raved against fancy garments; both especially insisted upon the lustful nature of headdresses; and—what is most strange—both threatened the same punishment for this sin: the demon would comb the tresses of the vain one with a comb of thorns. Beauty was the tempting face of Satan, and the Counselor accordingly displayed an invincible horror of it. Never again did he look at a woman. He even turned

---

[132] *Marc-Aurèle.*

his back when speaking to those aged pious women whose appearance would have been enough to tame a satyr.

PROPHECIES

As we continue to compare the absurd conceptions preached by this apostle to the sertanejos with those that were held in the past, the identity of the two sets of beliefs becomes more and more apparent. Like the Montanists, Antonio Conselheiro appeared at the time of earth's epilogue. The same extravagant millenarianism, the same dread of the Anti-Christ's appearing amid the universal wreckage of life. The nearing end of the world.

Let the faithful, then, abandon all their worldly possessions, anything that might defile them with the faintest trace of vanity. All fortunes stood on the brink of an imminent catastrophe, and it was useless and foolhardy to endeavor to preserve them. Let them give up all transient undertakings and make of their lives a stern purgatory. For the end was surely coming, and the great Judge of all.

He predicted the following misfortunes for various successive years:[133]

In 1896 a thousand flocks shall run from the seacoast to the backlands; and then the backlands will turn into seacoast and the seacoast into backlands.

In 1897 there will be much pasturage and few trails,[134] and one shepherd and one flock only.

In 1898 there will be many hats and few heads.

In 1899 the waters shall turn to blood, and the planet shall appear in the east with the sun's ray, the bough shall find itself on the earth, and the earth some place shall find itself in heaven.

There shall be a great rain of stars, and that will be the end of the world. In 1900 the lights shall be put out. God says in the Gospel: I have a flock which is out of this sheepfold, and the flock must be united that there may be one shepherd and one flock only!

As with the ancients, it was through the divine will that the Predestined was come to earth. It was Christ himself who foretold his coming when

at the ninth hour, as he was resting on the Mount of Olives, one of his disciples saith unto him: Lord! what signs wilt thou give us for the end of this time? And he replied: many signs, in the Moon, in the Sun, and in the Stars. There shall appear an Angel sent by my loving father, preaching sermons at the gates, making towns in the desert, building churches and chapels, and giving his counsels. . . . .

[133] These prophetic sayings were written down in numerous small notebooks which were found in Canudos. Those given here were copied on the spot from one of these notebooks, belonging to the secretary to the commander-in-chief of the expedition.

[134] ["muito pasto e pouco rasto": it is obvious that the preacher is at times inspired by the mere sound of words (echolalia). No attempt is made here to reproduce his bad Portuguese, misspellings, etc.]

And in the midst of these mad ravings, breaking through the teachings of the religious messiah, came those of the racial messiah, preaching insurrection against the republican form of government:

In truth I say unto you, when nation falls out with nation, Brazil with Brazil, England with England, Prussia with Prussia, then shall Dom Sebastião with all his army arise from the waves of the sea.

From the beginning of the world a spell was laid upon him and his army, and restitution shall be made in war.

And when the spell was laid upon him, then did he stick his sword in the rock, up to the hilt, saying, Farewell world!

For a thousand and many, for two thousand, thou shalt not come!

And on that day when he and his army shall arise, then shall he with the edge of the sword free all from the yoke of this Republic.

The end of this war shall take place in the Holy House of Rome, and blood shalt flow even in the great assembly. . . . .

A SECOND-CENTURY HERESIARCH IN THE MODERN WORLD

Prophecy in his mouth, as may be seen, was the same as it was in Phrygia, on its westward-bound course. Here was the same identical judgment of God, the same casting-down of the mighty, the same trampling of the profane world, the same millennium and its delights.

Is there not, to tell the truth, a trace of a higher Judaism in all this? There is no denying the fact. What is more, this return to an age of gold, favorite theme of apostles and sibylline prophets, this revival of age-old illusions, is no new thing but marks, rather, the permanent backflow of Christianity to its Jewish cradle. The figure of Montanus is to be met with throughout all history, being altered to a greater or less degree in accordance with the character of the various peoples, but with the same thunderings, the same rebellion against the ecclesiastical hierarchy, the same exploitation of the supernatural, the same heavenly longings, the same primitive dream which lay at the heart of the old religion before it had been deformed by the canonized sophists of the Councils. Like his correspondents of the past, Antonio Conselheiro was a pietist longing for the promised kingdom of God, which was always being put off, and which in the end was completely forgotten by the orthodox Church of the second century. His teachings were no more than an approach to a Catholicism which he did not thoroughly understand.

ATTEMPTS AT LEGAL ACTION

Pursuant to the mission to which he had devoted himself, after these homilies he would order penances which usually redounded to the benefit of the localities. They would rebuild places of worship that had fallen into disrepair; they would renovate abandoned cemeteries, erecting fine new structures. The stonemasons and carpenters would give their labor free of charge, the well-to-do would furnish gratis the necessary materials; the people carried the stones. For days on end, with pious zeal, these artisans would labor for the wages laid up for them in heaven.

And then, when the undertaking was finished, the Predestined would move on—whither? Wherever chance led him, taking the first path that he came to, into the backlands, over the rolling plains with their innumerable trails, without so much as a glance at those who followed him.

He did not have to contend with the antagonism of one who might have been a dangerous adversary, the priest. If we are to credit a reliable witness,[135] the padre generally permitted and encouraged these practices on the part of one who, without any usufruct for himself, promoted those rites which are a source of income for the clergy, such as baptisms, confessions, feasts, and novenas. The curates good-naturedly tolerated the excesses of this demoniac saint who at least helped increase their dwindled revenues. In 1882 the matter came to the attention of the archbishop of Baía, who sought to put a stop to this leniency, not to say ill-disguised protection, by means of a circular letter addressed to all pastors:

It having come to our knowledge that, in the central parishes of this archbishopric, there is a certain individual by the name of Antonio Conselheiro who goes about preaching to the people who come to hear him superstitious doctrines and an excessively rigid morality,[136] thereby disturbing consciences and weakening in no small degree the authority of the priests in these places, we ordain that your Reverence shall not consent to any such abuse in his parish, but shall let it be known to his parishioners that we absolutely forbid their congregating to hear such preachings. Seeing that in the Catholic Church the holy mission of indoctrinating the people belongs only to the ministers of religion, it follows that a layman, whoever he may be, and however well instructed and virtuous, does not have the authority to exercise that right.

In the meantime, let this serve to excite your Reverence's zeal in the exercise of the ministry of preaching, in order that your parishioners may be sufficiently well instructed not to permit themselves to be carried away by every wind of doctrine. . . . .[137]

[135] "When we were there [in Cumbe, in 1887], there was in the town a celebrated *Counselor,* a tawny-skinned fellow of low degree, with long black hair and beard, who went about clad in a blue-colored tunic, and who lived all alone in an unfurnished house, where the pious women flocked to see him, bringing presents of food that kept him alive. . . . . The people were accustomed to turn out in a body for the *Counselor*'s services; he had but to nod, and they would blindly do his bidding, even to the point of resisting any legal authority whatsoever; for which reason the curates permitted him with impunity to *pass himself off as a saint,* all the more readily for the reason that he took no money out of the parish, but on the contrary promoted baptisms, marriages, confessions, feasts, novenas, and all those rites from which the Church derives its enormous revenues" (Lieutenant Colonel Durval Vieira de Aguiar, *Descripções practicas da provincia da Bahia*).

[136] An excessively rigid morality!

[137] Circular letter of February 16, 1882, addressed to the Baian clergy by Archbishop D. Luiz.

The intervention of the Church was unavailing. Antonio Conselheiro continued without hindrance his aimless career as an apostle, continued to wander through the backland regions. As if desiring always to keep alive the memory of his former persecution, he would constantly return to Itapicurú; and the deputy of this place was finally compelled to call upon the constituted authorities, in the form of an official letter to the police in which, after a brief review of the agitator's antecedents, it is set forth that

he now makes his headquarters in this district and is at present engaged in building a chapel in the said town at the expense of the people. This work, it is true, is by way of being a public improvement, though by no means an indispensable one; but the good accomplished does not make up for the excesses and the sacrifices involved, and in view of the state of mind which prevails among the people, the fear of serious trouble to come is more than well founded.

In order that Your Honor may know who Antonio Conselheiro is, it will be sufficient to state that he goes accompanied by hundreds and hundreds of persons, who listen to his preachings and carry out his orders in preference to those of the curate of the parish. There are no limits to the fanaticism of this man and his followers; and without fear of error, being assured of the facts, I can tell you that they worship him as they would a God in the flesh.

On the days of sermons, beads and litanies, his congregation mounts to a thousand persons. In the building of this chapel, the cost of which in labor is nearly a hundred milreis, or ten times what it ought to be, this Antonio Conselheiro employs individuals from Ceará, to whom he accords a blind protection, tolerating and covering up the crimes which they commit; for all this money comes from the credulous and the ignorant, who not only do no labor for themselves, but who sell the few goods that they possess and even steal in order that not the slightest thing may be lacking which the Counselor requires. This is not to speak of the sums paid in for other works, at Chorrochó, in the Capim Grosso district.

The writer then draws attention to the latest instance of disorderliness on the part of the fanatics:

There having arisen a misunderstanding between Antonio Conselheiro and his group and the curate of Inhambupe, the former proceeded to draw up his forces as if for a pitched battle, and it is known that they were lying in wait for the curate, when he should go to the place known as Junco, in order that they might assassinate him. Those who pass that way are filled with fear at sight of these miscreants equipped with clubs, daggers, hunting knives, and blunderbusses; and woe to the one who is suspected of being hostile to Antonio Conselheiro.[138]

As may be imagined, this appeal, couched in terms so alarming, went unheeded. No measures were taken down to mid-year 1887, when the diocese of Baía once more intervened, the archbishop appealing to the presiding magistrate of the province for some action to restrain "the individual Antonio Vicente Maciel, who by preaching subversive doctrines does a great harm to religion and to the state, distracting the people from

---

[138] Official communication of November, 1886, addressed to the chief of police of Baía by the delegate of Itapicurú.

their obligations that they may follow him, and endeavoring to convince them that he is the Holy Ghost. . . . ."

Acting upon this information, the provincial magistrate had resort to the imperial minister, requesting the latter to find a place for the madman in the asylum for the insane at Rio. The minister in his reply put forward the notable plea that there were no vacancies in that institution, and the magistrate in turn informed the prelate of the admirable manner in which the government had disposed of the matter. Such was the beginning and end of the legal measures that were taken under the Empire.

MORE LEGENDS

Still without interference, the "Counselor" continued on his mission of arousing and perverting the popular imagination. It was at this time that the first legends about him became current. We shall not endeavor to exhume them all from the archives, but here are a few of them.

He it was who founded the settlement of Bom Jesus; and the astounded folk tell of him that on a certain occasion, as the lovely church that stands there was being built, and as a dozen workmen were doing their utmost to hoist a heavy beam, the Predestined stepped upon the plank and then ordered two of the men to lift the beam and himself, and those two succeeded in doing what all the others had not been able to do, quickly and without the slightest exertion.

Another time—and I had this from persons who had not been taken in by his fanaticism—he came to Monte Santo and announced that there would be a procession to the summit of the mountain, up to the last of the chapels, on the top. The ceremony began in the afternoon, the multitude spreading out slowly up the steep incline, intoning benedicites and pausing contritely at the stations. He preceded them—a grave and sinister figure—head bared, his long hair floating on the wind, and leaning on his inseparable staff. Night fell, the tapers of the penitents were lighted, and the procession along the line of peaks was like a luminous highway up the back of the mountain.

Upon reaching the Holy Cross, on the top, Antonio Conselheiro, panting for breath, seated himself upon the first step of the stairway of roughhewn stone, and sat there ecstatically contemplating the heavens, his gaze fixed on the stars.

The first wave of the faithful then began overflowing into the small chapel, while others remained without, kneeling on the hard rock. The contemplative mystic then arose, for weariness was something that he frowned upon. Making his way through the ranks of his respectful followers drawn up on either side, he in turn now entered the chapel, with lowered head, humble and downcast, gasping still. As he approached the great altar, however, his pallid face framed by his disorderly locks was upraised, and it was then that the multitude beheld a terrifying sight. Two bloody tears were slowly trickling down the immaculate face of the Blessed Virgin.

These and other legends are still current in the backlands. And this is quite natural. A species of great man gone wrong, Antonio Conselheiro in his sorrowing mysticism brought together all those errors and superstitions which go to form the coefficient of reduction of our nationality. He drew the people of the backlands after him, not because he dominated them, but because their aberrations dominated him. He was favored by his milieu, and at times, as we have seen, he had a realization of the utility of the absurd. He acted in obedience to the irresistible finality of old ancestral impulses and, in the grip of those impulses, displayed in everything he did the placidity of an incomparable evangelist. It was, indeed, this inexplicable placidity of his which deadened his neurasthenia.

One day, the curate of a certain backlands parish saw coming up to his door a man who was extremely thin and weary-looking: with long, disheveled hair down to his shoulders and a long beard falling over his bosom, the venerable figure of a pilgrim—not even the traditional crucifix was lacking, being suspended at the man's side between the chaplets of his girdle; cloak dusty and worn; leather water pouch, long staff, and all. The priest offered him something to eat, but he would accept no more than a crust of bread; he offered his visitor a bed, but the latter preferred a plank, upon which he stretched himself out, with no coverings, fully clothed, without even undoing his sandals.

The next day this most extraordinary guest, who had had little to say up to then, asked the padre if he would allow him to preach at the feast day which was to be celebrated in the church.

"My brother, you do not have orders, and the Church does not permit it."

"Then, let me make the *via sacra*."

"That I cannot do, either; I must do that myself," the curate once more replied.

The pilgrim thereupon stared at him fixedly for some time and then, without saying a word, took from under his tunic a kerchief and wiped the dust from his sandals. It was the classic, quiet, and inoffensive protest of the apostles.

HEGIRA TO THE BACKLANDS

As the feeling against him grew, however, his mind became embittered, and he who must be the unconditional master began to be irritated when he was crossed in his slightest whim.

Once at Natuba, the curate with whom he was not on good terms being absent, he appeared there and ordered the people to bring stones to repair the church. When the padre returned and beheld this invasion of his sacred domains, he was much upset by it and resolved to put an end to these disorderly carryings-on. Being a practical man, he decided to appeal to human selfishness. At Camara some days before, the property owners had been ordered to pave the walks in front of their houses; and so the priest now offered them for this purpose the stones which had been collected. The Counselor this time did not confine himself to shaking the dust from his sandals but, as he left town, paused at the edge of the city to utter his first malediction.

Some time afterward, at the request of this same curate, a certain political figure of the place summoned him to return. The church was falling in ruins, the forest was overrunning the cemetery, and the parish was poverty-stricken. If the necessary repairs were to be made, they must have someone who could handle the credulous backwoodsmen. The apostle condescended to accept the invitation but did so with certain discretionary stipulations and with a haughtiness that was foreign to the peaceful individual he once had been; for he remembered the affront he had received. His character was changing now, and for the worse.

For one thing, he looked upon the Republic with an evil eye and consistently preached rebellion against the new laws. From 1893 on he assumed an entirely new and combative attitude. This was due to an incident of no great moment in itself. The autonomy of the municipalities having been decreed, the chambers of the various localities in the interior of Baía had posted up on the traditional bulletin boards, taking the place of newspapers, the regulations governing the collection of taxes and the like. Antonio Conselheiro was in Bom Conselho at the time this novel procedure was instituted. He did not like the new taxes and planned an immediate retaliation. On a day of the fair he gathered the people and, amid seditious cries and noisy demonstrations, had them make a bonfire of the bulletin boards in the public square.[139] And, raising his voice above this "auto-da-fé," which the authorities out of weakness had failed to prevent, he began openly preaching insurrection against the laws of the coun-

[139] See p. 180.

try. Then, realizing the gravity of his offense, he left town, taking the Monte Santo Road, to the north.

This event had its repercussions in the capital, and a numerous detachment of police was sent out to take the rebel and dissolve these turbulent bands. The latter at this time did not exceed a couple of hundred persons in number. The police caught up with them at Massete,[140] a sterile and forsaken tract of land between Tucano and Cumbe, in the vicinity of the Ovó Mountains. The thirty well-armed troopers impetuously attacked the beggarly penitents, certain of being able to wipe them out at the first round; but they found themselves facing a band of fearless jagunços. The result was that they were utterly routed and took to their heels, their commanding officer himself being the first to set the example.

This diminutive battle, unfortunately, was later to be duplicated many times on a broader scale.

Having accomplished this exploit, the believers resumed their march, accompanying the prophet on his hegira; but they no longer sought out the towns as they had done before but instead made for the desert. Their routing of the police troop meant that a still more vigorous persecution was in store for them, and they felt certain that amid the wilds of nature they would be able to deal victoriously with their new enemies. The latter, as a matter of fact, lost no time in again setting out from Baía, to the number of eighty regular army men. They went no farther than Serrinha, however, where they turned back without venturing into the hinterland.

As for Antonio Conselheiro, he had no illusions regarding the inexplicable defeat which he had inflicted upon the police. Following a definite direction this time, he led his nondescript band, which from day to day was increased by dozens of proselytes, over the backland trails. He knew these regions well, having roamed them uninterruptedly for twenty years. He knew the isolated spots where the police would never be able to find him, and he was already marking out these hiding-places in preparation for the evil days ahead. He steered his course unswervingly due north.

The believers went with him. They made no inquiries as to where they were going. Over steep mountain slopes, sterile tablelands, barren plains, for days on end they marched, to the cadence of their litanies and in step with the prophet's slow and measured stride.

140 See p. 167.

V

CANUDOS: ANTECEDENTS

Canudos, an old cattle ranch on the banks of the Vasa-Barris, was in 1890 a backwoods hamlet of around five hundred mud-thatched wooden shanties. As far back as 1876 a number of priests, including the vicar of Cumbe, had paid a visit to the place, on a spiritual mission to the wholly unshepherded flock in this region; and we have the word of one of them that, at this time, clustered around the then still flourishing fazenda was an idle and suspect population "armed to the teeth . . . . whose sole occupation, almost, consisted in drinking brandy and smoking certain strange clay pipes with stems a yard long,"[141] made of natural tubes furnished by the solanaceae (*canudos de pita*, or pipe reeds), which grew in great abundance on the river's brink.

Even before the coming of the Counselor, then, this obscure hamlet, whose name is thus readily explained, like the majority of the unknown villages in our backlands, contained many of the germs of disorder and crime. At the time he arrived there, in 1893, it was definitely on the decline, its outbuildings abandoned, its dwellings vacant; while on a spur of Mount Favella, roof gone and only the outer walls left standing, was the old manor house, in ruins.

Its revival and subsequent rapid growth date from this year. This transient settlement of wandering woodsmen, clustered about the old church which was still in existence, was within a short space of time to be transformed and expanded into the mud-walled Troy of the jagunços.[142] It was to become a holy site, surrounded as it was by a protective ring of mountains, where the long arm of the accursed government never would reach. Its interesting topography in the eyes of these simple folk made it appear as the first broad step of the stairway to heaven.[143]

DIZZYING GROWTH

It is not surprising that, from all directions and coming from the most remote cities and towns, one band of settlers after another should have made its way to this place. As one chronicler[144] puts it:

Certain places in this district and others round about, as far away even as the state of Sergipe, became depopulated, so great was the influx of families to Canudos, the site selected by Antonio Conselheiro as the center of his operations. As a result, there was to be seen offered for sale at the fairs an extraordinary number of horses, cattle, goats, etc., as well as other things such as plots of ground, houses and the like, all to be had for

---

[141] Padre V. F. P., Vicar of Itú, Manuscript Communications, 1898.

[142] See p. 143.   [143] [Cf. p.20.]   [144] The Baron of Geremoabo.

next to nothing, the one burning desire being to sell and lay hold of a little money, and then go to share it with the Counselor.

And so it was that, in this manner, many homes were broken up. In-hambupe, Tucano, Cumbe, Itapicurú, Bom Conselho, Natuba, Massa-cará, Monte Santo, Geremoabo, Uauá and other near-by places, and En-tre-Rios, Mundo Novo, Jacobina, Itabaiana, and other remote localities, all furnished steady contingents. The few travelers who risked a journey in these regions would meet with band after band of the faithful, laden down with their few remaining worldly possessions, what little furniture they had, their hampers, and their portable altars, bound all of them for the city of the elect. Isolated groups at first, these pilgrims would meet with others at the crossroads, and they would all go on together until they finally arrived at Canudos.

The settlement, accordingly, grew in dizzying fashion, sprawling out over the hills. The dwellings which were thrown up being extremely rude ones, the homeless multitude was able to erect as many as a dozen a day; and, as this colossal weed patch[145] took shape, it appeared to reflect in its physical characteristics, as if by a stereographic process, the moral at-tributes of the social strata which had found refuge there. It was the ob-jectivization of a tremendous insanity. A living document whose implica-tions were not to be evaded, a piece of direct corpus delicti evidence on the aberrations of a populace. It was all done wholly at random, with the fer-vor of the mad.

ORIGINAL ASPECT

This monstrous *urbs*, this aggregation of clay huts, was a good indica-tion of the sinister *civitas* of the erring ones who built it. The new town arose within a few weeks, a city of ruins to begin with. It was born old. Viewed from afar, flung out over the hills and covering an enormous area, cut up into ravines and rugged-heaving slopes, it had the precise appear-ance of a city that has been rudely shaken and tumbled by an earth-quake.[146] There was no such thing as streets to be made out; merely a hopeless maze of extremely narrow alleyways barely separating the rows of chaotically jumbled, chance-built hovels, facing every corner of the com-pass and with roofs pointing in all directions, as if they had all been tossed together in one night by a horde of madmen.

Built of wooden stakes and divided into three tiny compartments, the houses were a gross parody of the ancient Roman dwelling: a narrow vestibule; an atrium, serving at once as kitchen, dining-room, and recep-tion room; and an alcove or bedroom at one side, a dark little hole-in-the-

---

[145] [*Tapera*. Literally, an abandoned estate.]   [146] See p. 255.

wall, with a low, narrow door that was barely visible. Covered with thick layers of clay, eight inches in depth, spread over a layer of boughs, these shacks resembled those of the ancient Gauls of Caesar's day. They represented a transitional phase between the primitive cave and a house. If our edifices in their evolutionary manifestations are to be taken as objectifying the human personality, then the clay-roofed hut of the jagunços, very like the *wigwam*[147] of the redskins, suggests a deplorable parallel: the same lack of comfort, the same repugnant destitution, reflecting in a manner not so much the poverty of man as that decrepitude which is due to race.

When one's eyes became used to the semidarkness of these narrow quarters, they would invariably descry certain odd pieces of crudely fashioned furniture: a rude bench, two or three footstools, an equal number of cedarwood boxes or hampers, a food container suspended from the ceiling,[148] and the hammocks. That was all the furniture there was. No beds and no tables. Hanging in the corners might be seen a few insignificant accessories: the *bogó*, or pouch, a sort of leather pail for carrying water; sets of wicker baskets;[149] and the *aiós*, hunting-bags made of caroá fiber. On the far side of this one room the visitor would see a rough-hewn altar, of the same homely appearance as the surrounding objects—atrociously carved saints and images, an objectivization of the mestizo religion with its pronounced traces of idolatry: proteiform and Africanized St. Anthonys with the gross appearance of fetishes, and Blessed Virgins ugly as Megaeras.

And, finally, there were their weapons, the same throwback to remote eras: the *jacaré*, or "alligator knife," with a broad, strong blade; the *parnahyba* of the bandits, long as a sword; the prong, or *guiada*, some three yards in length, without the gracefulness of a lance, more like the ancient pikes; the hollow cudgels, half-filled with lead, heavy as broadswords; the crossbows and the old-fashion muskets. The firearms ran the gamut from the slim barrel for fine shot to the "Braga regular" with the big bore, from the brutal *trabuco*, made after the manner of a portable culverin and capable of hurling flint stones and horntips, to the light rifle and the blunderbuss with the bell-shaped mouth.

That was all. That was all they had need of, these people. As Canudos sprang up, it took on an appearance midway between that of a warriors'

---

[147] [The English word is used.]

[148] [The *girão*, made of wooden stakes and resembling a hammock; the term is sometimes used for hammock or litter (as on pp. 223 and 373).]

[149] [*Cassuás (jacás de cipó)*. These were made of liana or ipecacuanha fiber.]

camp and that of an African kraal. The absence of streets, the squares which, apart from those where the churches stood, were no more than a common back yard to the jumbled hovels, turned it into one huge dwelling, rambling over the hills, one which, for a brief space of time, was destined to shelter Antonio Conselheiro's tumultuous *clan*.[150]

Without the revealing gleam of its whitewashed walls and calcined roofs, it was invisible at a certain distance, indistinguishable from the earth on which it stood. One could not see it until he came upon it suddenly, at a bend of the Vasa-Barris, which flowed around it on the southeast. It was framed in what was truly a still-life ("dead nature") setting: mournful landscapes; uniform, barren hills rolling away to the distant mountain ranges, without a patch of forest; strips of splintered talc-schist formations, with now and then a few bromelia clusters growing on them, or a slender, solitary cactus here and there. Mount Favella's bulk rose to the south, and at its base, opposite the square, a few quixabeira shoots growing wild in an untended garden; while halfway up the slope could be seen the lonely ruins of the old ranch house.

On one side, near at hand, is a dominating counterfort, Bald Pate Hill,[151] ending suddenly in a steep cliff above the river, which from here on, making a sharp bend around the side of the hill, girdles the town like a moat with its deep-hollowed bed. Here will be found ravines with perpendicular sides, with openings formed by intense erosions through which in winter roll the foaming seasonal streams incorrectly called rivers, such as the Mucuim, the Umburanas, and another which, as a result of subsequent events, was to bear the name Providencia (Providence).

These paths, joining other trails, served to connect the nascent settlement with the depths of the backland regions of Piauí, Ceará, Pernambuco, and Sergipe, and along them came one caravan after another of the faithful. They came from all directions, bringing with them all their worldly possessions; and, as they reached the last lap of their journey and caught sight of the humble belfry of the ancient chapel, they would drop to their knees in prayer on the hard ground. They had reached the end of their wanderings; they were now safe from the dreadful hecatomb foretold in the prophecies of the evangelist. They were treading at last the soil of the promised land—a sacred Canaan, which the Good Jesus had seen fit to isolate from the rest of the world by a girdle of mountains.

They arrived worn out by their long journey, but happy, and proceeded to camp out like vagabonds on the top of the hills. At night, bonfires were kindled before the resting-places of the dew-drenched pilgrims, and a

---

[150] [The author employs the English word.]   [151] See pp. 255–56.

gleaming band of light encircled the town, as voices rose in unison from among the newcomers and from the houses of the settlement, the plangent voices of a penitent multitude intoning their melodious benedicites.

At daybreak the next morning they would busy themselves with the task of building huts. These at first were clustered about the hollow where the original church stood; then they began building them slantingly along the short slopes which run down to the river's brink; and, after that, they spread out scatteringly over the rugged terrain beyond. Light structures, at some distance from the compact nucleus of huts, these dwellings appeared to have been erected in accordance with some preconceived plan of defense. They stood one above another at successive levels along the sides of the roads. They bordered the Geremoabo Road, being here built on either side of the Vasa-Barris, upstream, all the way to "Trabubú" and the Macambira River. They dotted the Rosario Highway, crossing the river here and skirting Favella. And they overran the innumerable hills in the direction of Uauá. Surrounded by impenetrable silk-grass thickets and bordering a moat that hemmed them in, each one of them was at once a home and a fort. Their arrangement was such that they formed irregular rows of bastions.

This city of the wilds from the beginning, as it grew, had the protection of a formidable circle of trenches excavated along all the slopes, affording a line of fire on a level with the ground and commanding the approaches in all directions. Concealed by a tangled growth of macambiras, or by stone heaps, these trenches were not visible at a distance. One who came in from the east, upon catching sight of the tiny huts scattered out like sentry boxes, would believe that he was approaching a ranch house and its outbuildings, inhabited by inoffensive cowboys; and he would be surprised when he suddenly came upon the compactly built hamlet—it was like falling into an ambuscade. One who came in from the south, on the other hand, by the Rosario or the Calumby roads, upon reaching the top of Favella or the steep slopes which descend to the Sargento River, would have an unobstructed view of the settlement down below, at a distance of three-quarters of a mile to the north, and would be able at a glance to appraise the defense conditions of the place.

These at first sight were deplorable. The village appeared to have been designed to receive the full impact of cannonading from above, with cannon balls, aided by the natural force of gravity, rolling impetuously down the steep slopes. The enemy, relieved of the necessity of an arduous assault, had but to pound the place with his artillery. He might lay effective siege to it with a single battery, commanding all the approaches.

The fact of the matter is, however, the tactical conditions were excellent, even though it required an uncouth Vauban to comprehend them.

Walled in on the south by the hill which, shot with ravines, ran down to the river's edge, it was protected on the west by a wall and a trench. Indeed, the Vasa-Barris, making a bend to the north here, with the outlying houses of the village on one side and the towering perpendicular cliffs on the other side, constitutes a deep canyon. Its sharp bend circumvallates the depression in which the settlement stands, closed in by hills on the east, and on the northwest by the highland slopes, which roll away to the far-lying counterforts of Cambaio and Caypan and the mountains to the south.

Canudos was a hamlet situated in a hole-in-the-ground. The square where the churches stood, on a level with the river, marked the lowest area of all. From here, following an axis to the north, the village gradually spread upward along a slight incline which formed the sloping wall of a long trench. In behind were the huts, entirely filling the hollow and scattering out over the eastern hillsides, a few of them, as we have seen, being sprinkled over the top of the hills, which were mined with trenches. The rebel community, it is obvious, was not taking refuge in any lofty eminence, in the direct line of fire of an attacking force. Instead, it was digging in. In this lovely region where the mountaintops merge with the high tablelands, they had selected precisely the spot which came the nearest to being one enormous moat.

REGIME OF THE "URBS"

The regime that was set up here was one modeled after the religious teachings of the extravagant apostle. With the population wholly under his sway, those conditions of life which accompany an inferior social status were here aggravated. Not being blood brothers, the inhabitants found a moral consanguinity which gave them the exact appearance of a *clan*,[152] with their chieftain's will as the supreme law, while justice lay in his irrevocable decisions. Canudos, indeed, was a stereotype of the dubious form of social organization that prevailed among the earliest barbarian tribes. The simple sertanejo, upon setting foot in the place, became another being, a stern and fearless fanatic. He absorbed the collective psychosis and even ended by adopting the name which up to then had been reserved for rowdies at the fair, bullies on election day, and the pillagers of cities—the name of *jagunço*.[153]

[152] [The English word again.]

[153] [Cf. p. 67, n. 22. The word is pronounced "zhah-goon'-soŏ."]

MULTIFARIOUS POPULATION

The population of Canudos was made up of the most disparate elements, from the fervent believer who had voluntarily given up all the conveniences of life elsewhere to the solitary bandit who arrived with his blunderbuss on his shoulder in search of a new field for his exploits; but, under the spell of the place, all these elements were welded into one uniform and homogeneous community, an unconscious brute mass, which, without organs and without specialized functions, continued to grow rather than evolve, through the mere mechanical juxtaposition of successive layers, in the manner of a human polyp. It is natural that such a community should have absorbed intact all the tendencies of the extraordinary individual whose protean appearance—that of a saint exiled on earth, that of a fetish in flesh and bone, and that of a limping bonze—was especially calculated to revive the degenerative stigmata of the three races. Accepting blindly all that he taught them, wholly immersed in their dreams of religion, living with the constant, sorrowing preoccupation of the life to come, they found their world within that protecting girdle of mountains and gave no thought to institutions such as might guarantee them a destiny of another sort here on earth. All this was meaningless to them. Canudos was their cosmos.

And even this was a brief and transient one, a mere stop along the way, a point of departure from which they would speedily set out, their last halt in the crossing of that desert which was the earth. The wandering jagunços were here pitching their tents for the last time, on that miraculous heaven-bound pilgrimage of theirs.

They asked nothing of this life; and, for that reason, property with them took on the exaggerated form of the tribal collectivism of the Bedouins. Personal property was limited to movable objects and their individual huts; there was an absolute community of land, pastures, flocks and herds, and the few cultivated products, the landlords receiving merely their quota, while the rest went to the "society." Newcomers turned over to the Counselor 90 per cent of what they brought with them, including those saints which were destined for the common sanctuary. They felt that they were blessed with the pittance that remained. It was enough and more than enough. The prophet taught them to fear the mortal sin of well-being, however short lived. The voluntary victims of poverty and suffering, they were fortunate in proportion to the privations which they endured. They were well clad when they went in rags. Carried far enough, this self-enforced destitution led to the loss of those high moral qualities which for so long had been instilled in them by the patriarchal life of the backlands. To Antonio Conselheiro—and in this respect, once again, he was merely copying the historic models of another day—strength of character was something like a higher form of vanity. It was almost an impiety. The endeavor to improve conditions on this earth in a manner implied that one was indifferent to the supernatural felicity that was soon to be; it implied a forgetfulness of the marvelous, longed-for *beyond*. His depressed moral sense was only capable of understanding the latter in contrast to sufferings endured. Of all the pages of the catechism that he spelled out, the one precept that stayed with him was: *Blessed are they that suffer*.

Extreme pain was an extreme unction. Harsh suffering meant a plenary absolution; it was the infallible antidote to the poison of the major vices.

As to whether men acted virtuously or otherwise, that was a meaningless question.[154] They might err, and he would put a good face on the matter; all he asked was that the impurities and dregs of an infamous life be finally purged, drop by drop, in the form of tears shed by the sinner. Upon hearing of a certain scandalous case in which the lust of a *débauché* had been responsible for the defiling of an unwary virgin, he gave utterance to a horribly cynical phrase which the sertanejos went about repeating, without grasping the turpitude of it: "She is fulfilling the destiny of all women; for all must pass beneath the tree of good and evil!" It is not to be wondered at, then, if promiscuity and an unbridled hetaeirism were the rule in Canudos. And the bastard offspring did not bear the indelible brand of their origin; their situation was by no means comparable to that of the unhappy *bantlings*[155] among the Germans, for their number was legion.

Their leader, if he did not encourage it, at least tolerated free love. In his daily "counsels" he did not deal with the subject of married life, indicating an ideal for these ingenuous households to follow. And this was logical enough. Seeing that the days of this world were numbered, it was a waste of time to preach vain precepts, when the imminent catastrophe might come at any moment to wipe out the most intimate relationships, to break up homes, and to confound all virtues and all abominations in the same swirling abyss. What he did urge was to prepare for this through privations and martyrdom. He preached prolonged fasts, the agonies of hunger, the slow exhaustion of life. He set the example in this respect by letting it be known to those closest to him that he contrived to get

[154] "Montanus ne prenait même pas la peine d'interdire un acte devenu absolument insignificant, du moment que l'humanité en était à son dernier soir. La porte se trouvait ainsi ouverte á la débauche" (Renan, *Marc-Aurèle*, p. 215).

[155] [The author has *bancklings*.]

through his days on a saucer of corn meal now and then. They tell of him that, being visited one day by a well-to-do believer of the neighborhood, he shared with his visitor his own scant repast; and the latter—a miracle which astounded the entire settlement—left the diminutive banquet full fed and gorged, as if he were returning from a sumptuous feast.

This stern regime had a twofold effect: on the one hand, by catering to their weaknesses, it keyed the sickly innervations of the believers to a higher pitch; and, on the other hand, it served to prepare them for the hardships of a siege, which may have been foreseen. Such, perhaps, was Antonio Conselheiro's secret intention; for in no other way can one understand why he should have permitted the presence in the settlement of individuals whose character was so opposed to his own humble and peaceful way of life.

Canudos was the refuge of renowned criminals. These heroes of the knife and gun came there to mingle with the credulous backwoodsmen and the deluded vaqueiros; and they were, to tell the truth, the ones who were most loyal to this singular leader; they were his chosen adjutants, who guaranteed his inviolable authority. They were likewise, by an understandable contrast, his best disciples; for this weird sect—a case of moral symbiosis, with the beautiful Christian ideal rising monstrously deformed by the aberrations of the fetishist—found its natural representatives in these truculent John the Baptists, capable of loading their homicidal blunderbusses with the beads of their rosaries.

BANDIT POLICE

Thanks to his own strong arms, Antonio Conselheiro dominated the settlement, correcting those who strayed from the beaten paths. In the jail which was there paradoxically established—the *poeira* ("dust-bin"), as the jagunços called it—could be seen daily those who had committed the slight offense of a few homicides, alongside those who had been guilty of the abominable crime of having failed to be present at prayers. Inexorable where small offenses were involved, absolutely unconcerned with the major crimes, justice, like everything else, was an antinomy in this *clan* policed by bandits. It had in view one particular delinquency, representing a complete inversion of the concept of crime. And stern justice, of its kind, was not infrequently meted out, with the severest of penalties for the slightest of misdemeanors.

The use of brandy, for example, was a serious offense, and woe to the incorrigible dipsomaniac who sought to evade the ban! The story goes that on one occasion certain pack-drivers from Joazeiro, who were unaware of the prohibition, came to Canudos with a few casks of the forbidden liquor. They were attracted by the prospect of inevitable gain, for were they not bringing the eternal accomplice to the woodsman's hours of ease? No sooner had they arrived in the public square, however, and deposited their precious burden than they found a disagreeable surprise awaiting them, when they saw their casks being hacked open with axes as the contraband contents, which here constituted a sacrilege, flowed away unutilized. They speedily left in disappointment, their hands empty of the profit they had hoped to make and smarting still from the many dozens of rude blows which had been rained upon them by these ungrateful customers.

This instance is a significant one. Well-grounded experience had taught the Counselor all the perils which come from the national hashish, and so he forbade it, not so much to prevent a vice as to forestall disorder. Outside the village, on the other hand, one could do as he liked, and turbulent bands would set out to roam the countryside. All kinds of disorders were permitted, provided only they served to augment the revenues of the community. In the year 1894 these incursions, led by ruffians of note, began to assume alarming proportions; there was such a crescendo of crimes and depredations as to attract the attention of the constituted authorities, giving rise to the usual heated and futile discussion in the state assembly of Baía.

DEPREDATIONS

For an extended radius round about Canudos, estates were laid waste, villages plundered, cities taken by storm! In Bom Conselho a bold horde, after having taken possession of the town hall, proceeded to put the place in a state of siege, dispersing the authorities from the district judge[156] down and, as a hilarious entr'acte in this scandalous bit of madness, torturing the marriage-license clerk, who was on tenterhooks to prevent the sarcastic religionists from shearing his head in the form of a huge crown, as a punishment for his having encroached upon the vicar's sacred domains. The hoodlums then returned to the village, laden with spoils, where no one took the least account of their disorderly doings.

Many times, so the backlands population is unanimous in stating, these expeditions had another motive. Some of the well-to-do among the faithful had political leanings, an election was coming on; and those great conquerors of the ballot box, who, like thousands of their kind throughout our land, would transform the fantasy of universal suffrage into the Hercules' club of our dignity, then had resort to the services of the Counselor.

[156] Dr. Arlindo Leoni (see p. 179).

Canudos thereupon became the provisional headquarters of the praetorian guard of gangsters, who would set out from there for certain definite points to reinforce by club and trigger the sovereign will of the people as expressed in the triumphant imbecility of the first petty chieftain who came along, by the tearing-up of records and by those periodical brawls appointed by law, under the name of "elections"—a euphemism which with us is the most striking instance to be found of the daring misuse of language. Our secondhand civilization, as always, was serving to regiment the banditry of the backlands.

These impulsive forays had their use; they were good training, a practical and indispensable exercise, serving to prepare those who took part in them for more valiant encounters. It may be that the Counselor realized all this. At any rate, he tolerated them. Inside the settlement, nonetheless, absolute order was preserved—we make use of this term from lack of any other, since our lexicons have no word to express a disciplined tumult.

Here, too, were those inoffensive ones—inoffensive out of weakness—who were his most worthy disciples: women, children, the aged and the infirm, and the sick who were good for no purpose. These lived parasitically off the generosity of the leader, who was their patron saint, and whom they greeted with the singing of certain stanzas which were current in the backlands twenty-odd years ago:

> Do ceu veio uma luz
>   Que Jesus-Christo mandou.
> Santo Antonio Apparecido
>   Dos castigos nos livrou!

> From heaven I see a light
>   Which Jesus Christ has sent.
> It is Saint Anthony in the flesh
>   To save us from punishment!

> Quem ouvir e não aprender,
>   Quem souber e não ensinar,
> No dia do Juizo
>   A sua alma penará!

> He who hears and does not learn,
>   He who knows and does not teach,
> Upon the Judgment Day shall find
>   His soul beyond Heaven's reach![157]

[157] Sylvio Romero, *A Poesia popular no Brasil.* Romero transcribed these stanzas in 1879, prefacing them with the following comment: "He was a missionary after his own fashion. With so very few resources, he succeeded in casting a fanatic spell over the towns and villages that he visited, where he was looked upon as Saint Anthony in the Flesh (*Santo Antonio Apparecido*)." And this as early as 1879!

These old quatrains which tradition has preserved for us served to remind the poor man of the early days of his tormented life, and it may be that they revived in him the last lingering traces of vanity, as he heard himself so flatteringly compared to the miracle-working saint par excellence.

In any event, it is certain that he threw open to these unfortunate ones the storehouses crammed with the gifts of the charitable and with the fruits of the common labor; for he realized that these beings, seemingly so useless, constituted the vigorous core of the community. They were the elect, happy in having nothing but rags on their backs, clad in the sackcloth of a penance which was their very life.[158] Stiff-jointed, dragging along on crutches, they felt themselves blessed, felt that they were making the most rapid progress possible along the path to eternal bliss.

THE TEMPLE

In addition, there awaited them at the end of their journey their final penitential work: the building of the temple. The antique chapel did not suffice. It was a small, unstable structure that barely rose above the level of thatched roofs around it. Its extremely modest appearance reflected the original purity of the ancient religion, whereas what was needed was a monstrous *arx* such as would embody in monumental fashion the spirit of this fighting sect.

And so they began erecting the new church. Before daybreak certain ones would set out to tend the crops, others to herd the goats or to embark on foraging expeditions to the near-by towns, while still others would scatter out over the neighborhood as pickets, keeping a close eye on each fresh arrival; and the rest of the population would then fall to at the holy task.

Facing the old church, the new temple stood at the far side of the square.[159] It was a huge, heavy, rectangular structure, its main walls being as thick as those of a fort; and for a long time it was to bear this anomalous appearance, until its two tall towers finally transfigured it with a crude and daring attempt at the Gothic style. The truth is, this admirable temple of the jagunços was possessed of that silent architectural eloquence of which Bossuet speaks.

[158] ["sambenitos de uma penitencia. . . . ." The allusion is to the *sacco beneditto*, which H. Michaelis (*A New Dictionary of the Portuguese and English Languages* [Leipzig, 1932]) defines as "a kind of linen garment of a yellow colour, with two crosses on it, and painted over with devils and flames, worn by persons condemned by the Inquisition to be burned, as they go to execution." This was the original connotation of the word.]

[159] See pp. 154–55.

It had to be as it was. Reared out of the extremity of human frailty, by the flabby muscles of the aged and the weak arms of women and children, it had to rise as an uncouth formidable mass midway between a sanctuary and a den, a fortress and a temple, bringing together in a common brotherhood, here on this spot where the sound of litanies was later to mingle with the whine of bullets, the utmost in piety and the bitterest of human hatreds.

It was the Counselor himself who designed the edifice. An old church architect, he outdid himself in this monument which was to mark the close of his career. There it stood facing the east, that stupendous disharmonious façade, without rule or proportion, with its gross friezes, its impossible volutes, its capering delirium of incorrect curves, its horrible ogives and embrasures, a brutish, shapeless hulk, something like an exhumed crypt, as if the builder had sought to objectivize in stone and cement the disorder of his own delirious mind. This was his first creation, and he spent days upon the high scaffoldings and bamboo framework. His people down below, busied with bringing up the necessary materials, were often astonished to see him walking unconcernedly along the bending, swaying planks, without the faintest tremor in his rigid sunburned face, like some wandering caryatid atop this monstrous structure which he was rearing.

There was no lack of workmen for the task. This colony camped out in the desert was constantly receiving aid and reinforcements. Half the population, roughly speaking, of Tucano and Itapicurú flocked to his assistance. From Alagoinhas, from Feira de Sant' Anna, from Santa Luzia they came. From Geremoabo, Bom Conselho, and Simão Dias came large supplies of livestock. And these newcomers were not in the least astonished at what they found awaiting them, for they looked upon all this as the obligatory test of the unshakable faith that was theirs.

ANTEROOM TO HEAVEN

The ingenuous backland legends had long ago taught them the fascinatingly treacherous nature of the paths that lead to Hell; and so Canudos, the unclean anteroom to Paradise, the impoverished peristyle of Heaven, must be just what it was—repugnant, frightening, horrible.

Meanwhile, many had come there cherishing strange expectations. "The corrupt leaders of the sect had persuaded the people that anyone who wanted to be saved must come to Canudos, since in other places everything was contaminated and damned by the Republic. Here, moreover, it was not necessary to work, for this was the promised land where flowed a river of milk with banks of corn meal and *cuscuz*."[160]

And so they came. They would cross the dry bed of the Vasa-Barris, or, when it was "big-bellied" with the muddied waters of the rainy season, they would make their way between the towering hillsides. Their blissful vision had vanished, it was true, but their lamentable mysticism still held them in its grip.

THEIR PRAYERS

As evening drew near, the bell would summon the faithful to worship. The people would cease their labors and would crowd beneath the leafy arbor or spread out over the *praça* as they dropped to their knees and a chorus of voices rose in the opening prayer. Night would come on suddenly, with little warning given by the brief and fugitive hinterland twilight. Bonfires were then kindled around the edge of the square, and their flickering glow served to frame a scene that was half-lost in shadows. In accordance with his ancient custom, or, better, his caprice, Antonio Conselheiro would have the throng separate, with the men on one side, the women on the other, in two distinct groups; but each of these enormous groups was in itself a weird assortment of contrasts.

BIZARRE GROUPINGS

Here were to be seen, infected with ancient sins for which a grievous penance must be done, the pious women[161]—rivaling the witches of the Church—clad in their black robes reminiscent of the funereal garment of the Inquisition.[162] Here, too, were the "old maids," a term which in the backlands has the unsavory meaning of shameful and dissolute creatures, loose women.[163] Here were the young girls and young women, the *moças donzellas* or *moças damas*, timid and circumspect. And here, finally, were the respectable mothers of families, all kneeling together in prayer. The wrinkled faces of old women, skinny old viragoes on whose lips prayer should have been a sacrilege; the austere countenances of simple-minded matrons; the naïve physiognomies of credulous maidens—all mingled in a strange confusion; all ages, all types, all shades of racial coloring.

---

[160] See the account given by Friar João Evangelista de Monte-Marciano.
[*Cuscuz:* a dish made of the finest flour. Cf. the Arabic word *couscous*, employed in French (it occurs in Rabelais, e.g., Book I, chap. xxxvii), Provençal *couscoussou*.]

[161] [Cf. p. 132 and n. 130.]

[162] [The *hollandilha*, made of coarse linen cloth.]

[163] [*Solteira*, a spinster; *solta*, a loose woman.]

Dyed and battered mops of hair; the straight, smooth hair of the caboclas; the outlandish topknots of the African women; the light-brown hair
of pure-blooded white women, all without a ribbon, a hairpin, a flower,
done up in the crudest fashion imaginable. Their ragged garments, of cotton or calico, loose-flowing and without style, offered not the slightest
hint of coquetry; a woolen shawl, a mantilla, or a colored scarf might have
relieved the monotony of their badly laundered clothing, which consisted
of little more than their tattered petticoats and chemises, the latter leaving exposed their breasts, covered with rosaries, holy medals, crucifixes,
charms, amulets, animal teeth, scapulars, or reliquaries containing "holy
writ." Such was the only garb permitted them by the evangelist in his
exacting asceticism.

Here and there, at a glance amid this rag heap, one might catch sight of
a very beautiful face, standing out impressively from the wretchedness
and gloom of the other wrinkled visages, and displaying the lines of that
deathless beauty which the Jewish type has immutably preserved down
the ages. The face of a madonna on a fury; deep, lovely eyes, black pupils
sparkling with a mystic madness; adorable brows glimpsed beneath the disheveled locks—all this was a cruel profanation, lost in this vagabond as-
semblage, from which there exuded at once the foul smell of unclean
bodies and the slow drone of benedicites, mournful as responsories.

Now and again, the bonfires dying down, barely smoldering beneath a
cloud of smoke, would suddenly flare at a puff of the night breeze, lighting
up the faces of the throng. At such times the closely huddled masculine
group stood out, affording the same identical contrasts: rude, strong cowboys, who like fallen heroes had exchanged their fine leathern armor for an
ugly canvas uniform; well-to-do cattle-breeders, happy at having abandoned their herds and stables; and, less numerous but more in evidence,
the vagabonds of every description, hardened criminals guilty of every offense. In the light from the dying embers, it is interesting to study their
various profiles. Some are already famous, renowned for their daring,
romantic exploits which the popular imagination has embroidered upon.
The armed lieutenants of this humble dictator, they occupy a place of
honor up in front; but at the moment there is in their bearing and gestures
not the slightest hint of the provocative boldness of the incorrigible ruffian. As they kneel there, hands folded across their bosoms, their ordinarily unfriendly, evil gaze is now a rapt and contemplative one.

There is José Venâncio,[164] the terror of Volta Grande; he forgets the
eighteen murders which he has committed and the specter of those judg-

[164] See p. 429.

ments by default, as he bends over contritely to touch his forehead to the ground. Alongside of him is the audacious Pajehú,[165] with his bronzed face and high cheekbones, his athletic but slightly stooping frame. Ecstatic, hands folded, he reminds one of a puma on a moonlit night as he sits there gazing skyward. Behind him is his adjutant and inseparable companion, Lalau, whose attitude is likewise a most humble one, as he kneels bent over his loaded *trabuco*.[166] There are Chiquinho and João da Motta, two brothers who are later to be put in charge of the pickets at the entrances to the village from the Cocorobó and Uauá roads. They give the impression of being a single individual as they say the beads of the same rosary with the air of staunch believers. There is Big Peter,[167] the ugly, broad-shouldered cafuso who with thirty picked men is to guard the Canabrava slopes. He is barely to be glimpsed there alongside a worthy rival in crime, Estevam, a burly, misshapen Negro with a body tattooed by bullet and dagger wounds, who, thanks to a miraculous invulnerability, has come off the victor in hundreds of conflicts. He is to be the guard of the Cambaio Road. There is "Shackle-Foot" Joaquim, another specimen of the grim warrior type, the one who is to stand guard at "Angico." He is now rubbing elbows with "Major" Sariema, of more refined appearance, a veteran without a definite assignment, fearless but restless, the very man for bold and sudden sallies. His direct opposite in appearance is "Crooked-Mouth" Raymundo of Itapicurú, a sort of gallows-bird mountebank with a face twisted in a cruel grimace, as if by some hideous traumatism. The agile-limbed "Kid Ostrich," who is to be intrusted with the command of the flying squadron of scouts, kneels next to a first-line chieftain, Norberto,[168] destined to hold the supreme command in the last days of Canudos. Finally, there is Quimquim de Coiqui, a self-abnegating religionist who is to win the first victory over the forces of the law; there is "Bold Anthony," tireless in winning proselytes; "Joe the Buck"; Fabricio de Cocobocó. . . . .

In the intervals of the "Kyrie eleison's," uttered with incredible faults of pronunciation, the rest of the faithful would from time to time cast hopeful and admiring glances at this group.

But there are others. Old Macambira,[169] who is little given to fighting, being, as the backwoodsmen expressively put it, too "softhearted," but who is the devil himself when it comes to laying an ambush, a sort of decrepit imam, but dangerous still—there he is, lying flat on the ground, alongside his son, Joaquim, a bold and dauntless lad, who later on is to

---

[165] See pp. 220–21, 301, 428–29, etc.   [167] See p. 429.   [169] Cf. p. 387.
[166] [See p. 145.]   [168] See p. 429.

give a fine example of heroism.[170] Aloof from the general credulity is the clever scout, Villa Nova,[171] who pretends to be doing figures in his head. And up in front of all is the commandant of the square, the "people's leader," the astute João Abbade;[172] he stands there letting his lordly gaze roam over the kneeling throng. Amid these tragic profiles there is the ridiculous figure of Pious Anthony,[173] a lean and seedy-looking mulatto, emaciated from fasting, who is very much in the Counselor's confidence; half-sacristan, half-soldier, a devotee of the blunderbuss, spying, watching, searching, shrewdly worming his way into the homes and ferreting out every nook of the village, he immediately reports all the latest happenings to the supreme leader, who rarely abandons the "Sanctuary." Sharing the same predilection, being in a manner Anthony's complement, is José Felix the "Chatterbox," the guardian of the churches and the Counselor's janitor and major-domo; he is in charge of the pious women, with their blue robes and hempen girdles, and he likewise has charge of the wardrobe and the scant repasts of the leader, and daily kindles the bonfires for evening prayers. And, last of all, there is that charming fellow, "Sturdy Manoel," who gazes over the throng with a noble indifference. He is the physician of the place, the quack doctor. Among all the shady characters assembled here, Nature has in him at least one worshiper, one who is alien to the disorder that prevails, and who spends his days endeavoring to fathom her secrets through the primitive drugs of the forest.

THE "KISSING" OF THE IMAGES

The prayers generally were long drawn out. Having run the gamut of litanies, said all the rosaries, and intoned all the rhyming benedicites, the faithful had a final obligatory ceremony awaiting them. This was the "kissing" of the images. It had been instituted by the Counselor himself by way of completing with this fetishistic rite the transformation of a Christianity which he could not understand.

Pious Anthony, the altar boy, would take a crucifix, gaze fixedly upon it with the moist eye of a fakir in a trance, press it to his bosom, and make a deep obeisance; then he would imprint upon it a prolonged kiss and, with a slow and worshipful gesture, pass it on to his nearest neighbor, who would go through the same bit of reverent mimicry without variations. Anthony would then raise aloft an image of the Blessed Virgin, and after that one of the Good Jesus, and the same acts would be repeated. Then came in succession all the saints, images, veronicas, and crosses, to

[170] See pp. 342, 387.

[171] See pp. 430, 438, 453.

[172] See pp. 168, 218–19.

[173] See pp. 430, 468 ff., 475.

be passed along from hand to hand, from mouth to mouth, from bosom to bosom, of the eager multitude. The dull smack of innumerable kisses could be heard and, rising in a crescendo above them, the indistinct drone of half-stammered exhortations, anguished *mea culpa*'s torn from panting bosoms, and the first stifled exclamations of the throng, repressed as yet in order not to disturb the solemnity of the occasion.

However, the mysticism of each individual gradually merged with the collective neurasthenia. From time to time the agitation would increase; it was as if this tumult were invading the assembly in accordance with the formulas of a pre-established program, as the sacred relics were passed around. Finally, the last of these were handed out by Pious Anthony, just as the first ones were reaching the back row of believers: and then it was that the intoxication and vertigo of these simple souls would reach a peak. Individual emotions now overflowed, finding themselves suddenly confounded with the general, irrepressible, and feverish contagion. It was as if the supernatural powers which a naïve animism had conferred upon these images had at last penetrated their consciousness, for they were writhing now in the throes of an irresistible hallucination. Exclamations burst from all sides, half-pious and half-angry, as the worshipers exhibited those impulsive movements which are associated with visionaries; and piercing cries rang out as many of them fell in a swoon. Clasping to their bosoms the images slavered with saliva, the deluded women would sink down in the violent contortions of hysteria, while the frightened children wailed in chorus. Laid hold of by the same aura of madness, the masculine group of fighters, amid the general uproar and the clash and jingle of their weapons, were quivering to the same terrifying rhythmic beat, one that marked the powerful explosion of a barbaric mysticism.

And then, of a sudden, the tumult would cease, and all would remain breathless, their eyes fixed on the far side of the arbor, next the open door of the "Sanctuary," where the weird figure of Antonio Conselheiro now stood framed. Coming forward to a small table, he would begin to preach.

WHY NOT PREACH AGAINST THE REPUBLIC?

He preached against the Republic, there is no denying that. This antagonism was an inevitable derivative of his mystic exacerbation, a variant of his religious delirium that was forced upon him. Yet he did not display the faintest trace of a political intuition; for your jagunço is quite as inapt at understanding the republican form of government as he is the constitutional monarchy. Both to him are abstractions, beyond the reach of his intelligence. He is instinctively opposed to both of them, since he is in that phase of evolution in which the only rule he can conceive is that of a priestly or a warrior chieftain.

We must insist upon this point: the war of Canudos marked an ebb, a backward flow, in our history.[174] What we had to face here was the un-looked-for resurrection, under arms, of an old society, a dead society, gal-vanized into life by a madman.[175] We were not acquainted with this soci-ety; it was not possible for us to have been acquainted with it. The ad-venturers of the seventeenth century, it is true, would encounter in it con-ditions with which they were familiar, just as the visionaries of the Middle Ages would be at home among the *demonopaths* of Varzenis or the Stun-dists[176] of Russia; for these epidemic psychoses make their appearance in all ages and in all places, as obvious anachronisms, inevitable contrasts in the uneven evolution of the peoples—contrasts which become especially evi-dent at a time when a broad movement is vigorously impelling the back-ward peoples toward a higher and civilized way of life. We then behold the exaggerated Perfectionists breaking through the triumphant indus-trialism of North America, or the somber *Stürmisch* sect, inexplicably in-spired by the genius of Klopstock, sharing the cradle of the German renascence.

With us, the phenomenon is perhaps still more readily to be explained. After having lived for four hundred years on a vast stretch of seaboard, where we enjoyed the reflections of civilized life, we suddenly came into an unlooked-for inheritance in the form of the Republic. Caught up in the sweep of modern ideas, we abruptly mounted the ladder, leaving be-hind us in their centuries-old semidarkness a third of our people in the heart of our country. Deluded by a civilization which came to us second hand; rejecting, blind copyists that we were, all that was best in the or-ganic codes of other nations, and shunning, in our revolutionary zeal, the slightest compromise with the exigencies of our own national interests, we merely succeeded in deepening the contrast between our mode of life and that of our rude native sons, who were more alien to us in this land of ours than were the immigrants who came from Europe. For it was not an ocean which separated us from them but three whole centuries.

And when, through our own undeniable lack of foresight, we permitted a nucleus of maniacs to form among them, we failed to see the deeper

[174] [Compare the conclusion of the author's Preliminary Note, p. 2.]

[175] See "Author's Notes," Note VI, p. 482.

[176] [An evangelical sect of southwest (Czarist) Russia, widespread among the peasantry. Ap-parently founded by German evangelical pastors, chiefly Lutheran, among the German settle-ments of that district (*Encyclopaedia of Religion and Ethics*, ed. James Hastings [New York: Scribner's, 1925], XI, 342–43).]

meaning of the event.[177] Instead, we looked at it from the narrow-minded point of view of partisan politics. In the presence of these monstrous aberrations, we had a revealing fit of consternation; and, with an intrepidity that was worthy of a better cause, we proceeded to put them down with bayonets, thereby causing history to repeat itself, as we made yet another inglorious incursion into these unfortunate regions, opening up once more the grass-grown trails of the bandeiras.[178]

In the backlands agitator, whose revolt was a phase of rebellion against the natural order of things, we beheld a serious adversary, a mighty foeman representing a regime which we had done away with, one who was capable of overthrowing our nascent institutions.

And Canudos was our Vendée.[179]

In the last days of the settlement, when it was permitted them to enter what was left of the huts, the conquerors found a grievous disappointment awaiting them. Their hard-won victory gave them the right to sack these ruined homes, and nothing was exempt from their insatiable curiosity; but it was one of the most unremunerative bits of pillaging that history has to record. In place of rich spoils, they found mutilated images and cocoanut-shell rosaries; but what most excited their covetousness was the scrawled documents, and especially the terrible verses which they discovered among the latter. Poor bedraggled sheets of paper on which the barbarous orthography paralleled the most naïve absurdities, while the irregular and unsightly handwriting seemed to be a photographic reproduction of the twisted way of thinking of these people; it appeared to sum up the psychology behind the conflict. These scraps of paper were worth everything in the world for the reason that they were worth precisely nothing. On them the sermons of Antonio Conselheiro were written down; and, as one read them over, one realized just how innocuous his preachings really were after all, reflecting simply the poor fellow's intellectual turmoil. Every line of them was vibrant with the same vague and incongruous religiosity, but there was very little of political significance to be found in any one of them, such as might have lent itself to the messianic tendencies revealed. If the rebel attacked the established order, it was because he believed that the promised kingdom of bliss was near at hand. He denounced the Republic as a mortal sin on the part of the people, the supreme heresy, heralding the ephemeral triumph of the Anti-Christ. And these rude poets had put his hallucinations into the form of colorless

---

[177] See "Author's Notes," Note VI, p. 482.

[178] [See pp. 66, 74 ff.]

[179] See p. 196. [The author at first thought of entitling the present work "Our Vendée."]

rhymes; for they lacked the strongly marked spontaneity of the backlands improvisers. Nevertheless, in these foolish verses they left us living
documents; and, as we read them, we could not but agree with Renan that
there is a rude and eloquent second Bible of the human race to be met with
in the stammerings of the people.

We will copy out a few of them.

> Sahiu D. Pedro segundo
>   Para o reyno de Lisboa
> Acabosse a monarquia
>   O Brasil ficou atôa!

> Dom Pedro the Second set forth,
>   For Lisbon he was bound,
> And so the monarchy came to an end
>   And Brazil was left aground.

The Republic was the essence of impiety:

> Garantidos pela lei
>   Aquelles malvados estão
> Nos temos a lei de Deus
>   Elles tem a lei do *cão!*

> Backed up by the law,
>   Those evil ones abound,
> We keep the law of God,
>   They keep the law of the *hound!*

> Bem desgracados são elles
>   Pra fazerem a eleição
> Abatendo a lei de Deus
>   Suspendendo a lei do *cão!*

> Oh, wretched ones are they,
>   When election comes around,
> It's down with the law of God
>   And up with the law of the *hound!*

> Casamento vão fazendo
>   Só para o povo illudir
> Vão casar o povo todo
>   No casamento civil!

> A mockery they make of marriage,
>   They'd have all true marriages cease
> And have us all get married
>   By a justice of the peace!

But this demoniac government is shortly to disappear:

> D. Sebastião já chegou
>   E traz muito regimento
> Acabando com o civil
>   E fazendo o casamento!

Dom Sebastian came
With a mighty regiment
And put an end to these marryings,
And we were all content.

O Anti-Christo nasceu
Para o Brasil governar
Mas ahi está o *Conselheiro*
Para delle nos livrar!

The Anti-Christ was born
That he might govern Brazil,
But here is our *Counselor*
To save us from this ill!

Visita nos vem fazer
Nosso rei D. Sebastião,
Coitado daquelle pobre
Que estiver na lei do *cão!*

Dom Sebastian our King
On a visit to us is bound,
And woe to that poor sinner then
Who is under the law of the *hound!*[180]

The *law of the hound*. . . . .

This was the most elevated apothegm that the sect knew. It summed up its program. It requires no commentary whatsoever.

They were really very weak creatures, these poor rebellious ones.

They should have met with another reaction on our part. They should have obliged us to enter upon a struggle of a different sort. Meanwhile, we were sending them the legislator Comblain,[181] and that one supreme incisive argument of the moralist—bullets.

But first an attempt was made that was at once nobler and more practical.

AN ABORTIVE MISSION

On a certain morning in May, 1895, there appeared on top a counterfort of Mount Favella a figure, flanked by two others that was strange to those parts. It was a Capuchin missionary. After surveying for a few moments the village sprawled beneath him, he slowly began descending the side of the hill. It was Daniel walking into the lions' den.

Let us accompany him.

Followed by Friar Caetano de São Leo and by the curate of Cumbe,

---

[180] We have preserved the originals of these stanzas, the orthography of which we have here altered somewhat.

[181] [Referring to the Comblain rifle.]

Friar João Evangelista de Monte-Marciano crossed the river and approached the first outlying huts. He made his way to the square, which was swarming with people, "near to a thousand men, armed with blunderbusses, shotguns, knives, etc.," and, as he did so, he must have had the impression of having been dropped down into the midst of a camp of Bedouins. Without any display of emotion, he went on to the space in front of the chapel, where a crowd of people huddled in the doorway. Followed by his apostolic companions, he came up by a winding alley; and, when those at the door beheld the newcomers, they were surprised and stood there "with a restless air, their gaze at once piercing and sinister, showing that they had bad consciences and harbored hostile intentions."

The priests continued until they reached the house of the aged curate of Cumbe (which had been closed for more than a year, owing to his prolonged absence, so great was his resentment at the disrespect that was shown him), and here they refreshed themselves as best they could from their tiresome journey. They were deeply moved by the sight of the poor unfortunates, armed to the teeth, whom they had just met in the square, and by the general aspect of this turbulent Thebaid; but there were yet more disagreeable impressions awaiting them. It was not long before there went past the door eight corpses which, without any religious ceremony whatsoever, were being borne to the cemetery in back of the old church: eight hammocks of caroá fiber, the puffing pallbearers who bent over them hurrying along with rapid step, anxious to dispose of their burdens, as if in this sinister city the dead were deserters from the cause of martyrdom and hence unworthy of the least attention.

In the meantime, news of their arrival had spread, but the Counselor made no move to go and meet these emissaries of the Church. Quite indifferent to it all, he went on directing the work of repairing the chapel. It was the padres who had to go in search of him.

Leaving the house, they once more followed the narrow, winding lane until they came out on the *praça*. Crossing the square, without meeting with a single catcall, they came to the place where the work was going on and where "a throng of men closed ranks alongside the door of the chapel," making a wide path for them. From the alarmed bystanders came a lively greeting, the salutation of peace: "Praised be Our Lord Jesus Christ," which called for the response: "May our blessed Lord be praised forever!"

They then entered the tiny temple and found themselves in the presence of Antonio Conselheiro, who received them affably enough, with his habitual placidity, as he addressed to them the same pacific greeting.

PORTRAIT OF THE COUNSELOR

"He was clad in a tunic of indigo-blue, head bared and staff in hand; his utterly unkempt hair fell to his shoulders; his beard was long and grizzly, with streaks of white; his deep-set eyes were seldom lifted to look anyone in the face; his countenance was of a pallor that was almost corpse-like; his air grave and penitent." From which, it may be seen, the new arrivals were strongly impressed.[182]

They were nonetheless encouraged by this all but cordial reception. Contrary to what they had expected, the Counselor appeared to be pleased by their visit. He dropped his habitual reserve, his stubborn silence, and proceeded to inform them of the progress of the work, inviting them to come and see for themselves. He courteously offered to act as their guide in showing them over the building. And so, they all went along, slowly following the old hermit, who must have been in his seventies, and who, leaning on his staff, walked with a lagging step, his frail body shaken from moment to moment by sudden fits of coughing.

They could not have asked for more favorable preliminaries to their mission.

This reception was half the victory, but the missionary by his lack of tact was to undo it all. Having reached the choir loft, where they were at some little distance from the crowd of the faithful who were following them, he deemed this to be the ideal moment for a decisive interpellation. His haste, however, merely served to defeat its own ends, and failure was inevitable.

Being practically alone, I seized upon the occasion to inform him that my mission was a wholly peaceable one, that I was greatly surprised to find armed men here, and that I could not but disapprove of all these families living here in idleness, lewdness, and under conditions so wretched that they led to eight or nine deaths a day. Accordingly, by the order and in the name of His Lordship the Archbishop, I proposed to give a holy mission and advise the people to disperse and to return to their homes and daily tasks, both for their own sakes and for the general welfare.

This intransigency, this thinly veiled threat, with the Friar dropping diplomatic niceties for the rigid points of dogma, would not, certainly, have met with the approval of St. George—the Great—who was not scandalized by the barbaric rites of the Saxons. It was, in brief, an imprudent act of defiance.

"Even as I was saying this, and before I had done speaking, the chapel and the choir loft filled with people, crying out with one voice: 'We want to go with our Counselor!' "

Disorder was imminent, but it was forestalled by the admirable placid-

[182] This follows the account (*Relatorio*) of Friar Monte-Marciano.

ity, the meekness—why not say Christian meekness?—of Antonio Conselheiro. But let the missionary himself tell the story:

> He made them keep quiet, and turning to me, said:
> "It is to protect myself that I keep these armed men with me; for your Reverence must know that the police attacked me and tried to kill me at the place called Masséte,[183] where the dead were piled up on one side and the other. In the days of the monarchy, I let myself be taken, for I recognized the government; but today I will not, because I do not recognize the Republic."

This explanation, respectfully and clearly stated, did not satisfy the Capuchin, who had the courage of a believer but not the fine tact of an apostle. Paraphrasing the *Prima-Petri*, the friar replied: "Sir, if you are a Catholic, you must remember that the Church condemns revolts and, accepting all forms of government, teaches that the constituted authorities rule the peoples in the name of God."

It was, almost without variation, the phrase that Paul used in the time of Nero.

"It is that way everywhere," the friar went on. "In France, which is one of the principal nations of Europe, there was a monarchy for many centuries, but for more than twenty years now there has been a republic; and all the people there, with the exception of the monarchists, obey the authorities and the laws of the government."

In thus rehashing these meaningless political considerations, himself ignorant of the real significance of the backland disorders, Friar Monte-Marciano shows us why it was his mission failed. The anomalous figure of the propagandist now becomes apparent, lacking only the rifle of the curate of Santa Cruz beneath the folds of his vestments.

"We here in Brazil, also, from the bishop down to the lowliest Catholic, recognize the present government; why will not you submit to it? Such thoughts are evil; that is a false doctrine which you hold!"

This final phrase rang out like an apostrophe. And from the multitude there came the prompt and arrogant response: "It is Your Reverence who holds a false doctrine, not our *Counselor!*"

By this time the tumult was nearing a climax; but the Counselor with a calm gesture restrained his followers, and, turning to the missionary, he said: "I will not disarm my people, but neither will I interfere with your holy mission."

The mission, accordingly, began under bad auspices. In spite of this, however, everything went smoothly and peaceably enough, down to the fourth day. There were about five thousand in the congregation, among whom the able-bodied men were especially prominent, "bearing blunder-

[183] See p. 142.

busses, shotguns, muskets, and large knives; from the cartridge boxes on their girdles to the round caps on their heads, they had the appearance of men who are about to go to war."

The Counselor also took part in the services, standing beside the altar, attentive and expressionless, like a stern inspector, "letting fall now and then a gesture of disapproval, which the majority of those in the congregation confirmed with sharp protests." These latter, moreover, so it would appear, preserved no sort of decorum whatsoever; and now and again some overwrought individual, violating the ancient privilege that is accorded to sacred oratory, would proceed to tear the sermon to tatters. Thus, when the preacher came to deal with fasting as a means of mortifying the flesh and bridling the passions through sobriety, without, however, calling for any prolonged self-mortification, but pointing out that "one often may fast by eating meat at dinner and taking in the morning only a cup of coffee"—when he reached this point, his sermon was irreverently and ironically interrupted: "Why! that's not fasting; that's stuffing your gut!"

On the fourth day, when the Capuchin came back to the dangerous subject of politics, things began to go from bad to worse. There was now much heated talk about "the preaching of this *Masonic, Protestant*, and *republican* padre," who was "an emissary of the government, in league with it, and who will lead the troops to come and take our Counselor by surprise and exterminate us all." The friar, however, was not intimidated by the nascent rebellion but faced it boldly, challengingly. He took the subject of homicide for his next sermon, and with no attempt to avoid the perils of his daring theme, speaking of rope as it were in the house of the gallows bird, he let himself go in imprudent allusions which we may be excused from repeating here.

The reaction was immediate. It was João Abbade who took the lead, his whistle sounding shrilly in the public square, calling all the faithful together. This happened on the twentieth day of May, the seventh day of the mission. When they had assembled, with a great hullabaloo of *vivas* to the Good Jesus and the Holy Spirit, they made for the house where the visitors were lodged, with the object of letting them know that, when it came to the matter of eternal salvation, the population of Canudos had no need of their ministrations.

This was the end of the mission. With the exception of "55 marriages of couples living in concubinage, 102 baptisms, and more than 400 confessions," the result was nil, or rather, negative.

A CURSE ON THE MUD-WALLED JERUSALEM

The missionary, "like the apostles at the gates of cities which had rejected them, shook the dust from his sandals," calling upon the tremendous *veredictum* of Divine Justice.

Accompanied by his companions in adversity, he availed himself of the safety of the narrow lanes and stole away. Climbing the roadway along the slopes of Favella, he paused for a moment on the summit and for one last time surveyed the settlement down below. Overcome by a wave of sadness, he was led to liken himself to "the Divine Master before Jerusalem."

But the friar uttered a curse. . . . .

II

THE REBELLION

CHAPTER III

THE CONFLICT BEGINS

I

PRELIMINARY OBSERVATIONS

AT THE time that it became urgently necessary to pacify the Canudos region the governor of Baía was very much occupied with other insurrections. The city of Lençóes had been boldly attacked by a mob of bandits, and their incursions were spreading to Lavras Diamantinas;[1] the town of Brito Mendes had fallen into the hands of another mob, while in Jequié all sorts of crimes were being committed.

BACKGROUND

The evil was an old one. That tract of land which, scalloped by the Sincorá Mountains, extends as far as the banks of the São Francisco, was, some while back, the extended theater of operations for the outlaws of the backlands. Rich in splendid mines, this region is cursed by its own opulence. Spurred on by the dream of dazzling wealth, restless adventurers were in the habit of seeking it out, a couple of hundred years ago, and, with their painstaking search of its mountainsides and riverheads, did more than merely devastate the land with the waste tracts (*catas*) left by their mining operations, their picks and dredges;[2] they bequeathed to their offspring and, by contagion, to the rude vaqueiros who followed them, the same turbulent and socially unprofitable way of life, which was given free rein here in this fertile district where for many years gold dust and diamonds in the rough were the current medium of exchange. As a consequence, without making any effort to get the most out of a soil on which they had no fixed abode, across which they were merely roaming in their search for "diggings," they continued to lead an idle and disorderly existence, one that reflected the adventurous temperament of their forebears, the original desert-makers.[3] And, when at last they had washed all the pebbles and had got to the bottom of their stock of furs, there was little else for them to do but turn bandits if they wished to go on living as they had been accustomed to live.

The jagunço, pillager of cities, thereupon took the place of the *garimpeiro*,[4] who pillaged the earth for diamonds. And the political chieftain re-

---

[1] ["Diamond Mines."]
[2] [Cf. p. 44.]
[3] [Cf. pp. 43 ff.]
[4] [A diamond-hunter.]

placed the *capangueiro,* or gang leader of old. This transition affords a fine example of environmental reaction. Let us, briefly, sum up its characteristic features.

We have seen how, amid the whirlwind movement of the bandeiras, on the one hand, and the leisurely course of the missions, on the other hand, there grew up here that race of brave and diligent mamelucos which so opportunely made its appearance in our colonial history as a conserva-

Courtesy of the Instituto Brasileiro de Geografia e Estatística

VIEW OF THE AMAZON

tive element, constituting the core of our nationality in process of birth and creating a state of equilibrium between the madness of the gold rushes and the romantic Utopias of the apostolate. This race, which represented, it may be, the only worth-while side of our activity in those days, from the beginning of the eighteenth century, when the mines from Rio de Contas to Jacobina began to be discovered, found itself confronted by dangerous forces which, if they did not succeed in corrupting its virile character, at least guided its destinies in a lamentable direction. The fact of the matter is, it underwent a transformation in contact with the gain-lusting sertanistas.[5] These latter came, at that time, from the east, frightening the

[5] [*Sertanista* is a term applied to the pioneer of the backland regions, or *sertões;* or it sometimes means a student of the life of the backlands; *sertanejo,* on the other hand, is a native or inhabitant of the *sertões.*]

savage with fire and sword and founding settlements which, unlike those already in existence, did not possess a cattle ranch as a nucleus but, instead, the ruins of the *malocas*, or native villages. They rode roughshod over the region, pausing for a long time before the barrier formed by the mountains which run from Caetité northward; but, when the exhausted mines called for such equipment as would make possible an intensive exploitation, they then began eyeing the virgin and opulent land which lay ahead of them, in the heart of the country, between the forests which extend from Macaúbas to Assuaruá.

They accordingly went on until they came to a fresh barrier, the São Francisco River, which they crossed. Before them as far as the eye could reach, carved out of the plains, lay that marvelous valley of the Rio das Eguas, so auriferous that the auditor of Jacobina, in a letter addressed to Queen Maria II (1794), asserted that "its mines are the richest thing that was ever discovered in Your Majesty's dominions." By this time they had reached the limits of Goiaz, but they did not go a step farther. The outcome of the whole thing was deplorable. Dotting the fields of the cattle-breeders there could be seen vermilion-colored heaps of upturned clay,[6] marking the site of the buried-under catas; while from the vaqueiro with his athletic build there sprang that fearless being, the jagunço. Our history, which has been so cursed with undisciplined heroes, acquired in him one of its most somber protagonists. It was an entire society which was here undergoing a metamorphosis; the old robust and peaceful peasant society was giving way to another, wandering and dissolute, restless and combative, an extraordinarily lazy one and given to misdemeanors.

Imagine the vaqueiro's titanic frame suddenly endowed with the tremendous nervous energy of the bandeirante, and you have the jagunço. He is a significant historic product. Born of a belated crossing of racial stocks which the physical environment has still further diversified, he sums up the essential attributes of both—in that twofold activity which oscillates between the laborious cow-hunt and the bandit's daring incursions. And the land, meanwhile, that incomparable land, which even in the grip of the drought, barren and impoverished, still sustains his herds in the brackish lowlands of the pits[7]—the land comes to his assistance, now as always, in the exigencies of his warrior's life; everywhere, it gives him gratis saltpeter for the making of gunpowder, while as for bullets, luxurious projectiles made of lead and silver, they are to be had in countless number in the silver-bearing lead ores of Assuaruá.[8]

[6] [Cf. p. 44.]   [7] [Cf. p. 76.]

[8] See Lieutenant Colonel Durval Vieira de Aguiar, *Descripções da Provincia da Bahia.*

It is natural that, since the beginning of the last century, the dramatic story of the São Francisco settlements should have begun to reflect an anomalous situation.[9] And, although it is true that in all the stirring episodes which go to make up that story the partisan rivalries and unpunished crimes of an intolerable political system, based upon local potentates, play a prominent role, yet these disorders, always breaking out as they do in the very places where the mining fever was formerly most intense, point to that remote origin which we have indicated.

Let us take an example. The entire valley of the Rio das Eguas and, to the north, that of the Rio Preto constitute the original home land of the bravest and most useless individuals that our country possesses.[10] From these points they are in the habit of setting out on adventurous expeditions, putting to rout the mock-bravery of the political bigwigs; but such expeditions invariaby end up with arson and the pillaging of towns and cities throughout the valley of the great river.[11] Making their way upstream, by 1879 they had already reached the mining town of Januaria, which they proceeded to take over; and they then returned to Carinhanha, their starting-point, laden with spoils. From this city in the north the history of their depredations all the time grows in volume until we come to Xique-Xique, which was legendary in the electoral campaigns under the Empire.

But all this cannot be told in the course of half-a-dozen pages. The most obscure of these settlements has its own especial and sinister tradition. There is one among them, alone, which stands out for a different reason, and that is Bom Jesus de Lapa. It is the Mecca of the sertanejos. Its decidedly original conformation;[12] its range of high peaks with their bell-like echoes; the capriciously formed grotto which they inclose, like the nave of a dimly lighted church, with the stalactites hanging like candelabra from the roof; the corridors running off to the sides, filled with ancient diluvian ossuaries; and, finally, the thrilling legend of the monk who lived there in the company of a jaguar—all this has rendered it the favored goal of pious pilgrims, who come here from the most distant places, from Sergipe, from Piauí, and from Goiaz. And, amid the offerings which lie in con-

---

[9] Caetano Pinto de Miranda Montenegro, coming from Cuiabá to Recife, in 1804, a distance of 1,675 miles, passed through Barra do Rio Grande; and in the account of his journey which he sent to the Viscount of Anadia, speaking of these places, he tells us that "in no part of the Portuguese dominions is there less security for human life."

[10] "Whoever along the São Francisco wishes to contract for the services of ruffians (*jagunços*), sends to this great breeding-ground for them. A rifle and ammunition is the price; the most of them come to terms readily enough, depending upon the employer's influence and the degree of impunity he has to offer" (Durval, *op. cit.*).

[11] [The São Francisco.]   [12] [Cf. p. 7.]

siderable number on the ground or hang from the walls, the visitor cannot fail to observe, among the images and the reliquaries, the depressing evidence of an unusual variety of religious sentiment in the form of knives and muskets.

The rifleman would enter here, head contritely bared, his leather cap in his hand, and his weapon in its bandoleer. He would fall on his knees, touch his forehead to the dank, sweating limestone, and pray. For a long time he would remain there, searching his conscience, beating his breast for old sins. Then he would devoutly fulfil the "promise" he had made at the time of his last fight, in case it came out in his favor; he would give the Good Jesus his famous *trabuco*, with a collection of notches made by his jackknife on its stock to show the number of men he had killed. He then would leave, filled with remorse but happy at the tribute he had paid. After which, he would go back once more to his banditry and resume his bold and carefree life.

Pilão Arcado, once a flourishing town, today deserted, in the last stage of a decline which began in 1856; Xique-Xique, where for decades liberals and conservatives fought it out; Macaúbas, Monte Alegre, and others, and all the ranches round about, their houses in ruins or riddled with bullets, bear evidence to this ancient regime of lawlessness. They are places where disorder has been normalized in the form of a disciplined banditry. That sounds paradoxical, but it is true.

The jagunços, the fact is, are a very orderly lot. Inordinately proud of their daring bandit role and fighting loyally for the chieftain who commands them, they limit their disorderly conduct to those diminutive battles in which they engage in true military, regimented fashion. As for the pillaging of the towns that they take, that is simply part of the spoils of war, and on this point all history will absolve them. Outside of this, cases of robbery are rare, this being something they look upon as beneath them, a blot on their escutcheon. The most helpless "partner"[13] on his way to the coast may go through these fields and forests unarmed and unharmed, his pouches bulging with diamonds and nuggets, and not a single one of them will be missing at the end of his journey. A stranger to the region, who is a stranger likewise to its partisan quarrels, may pass through with a similar immunity. It not infrequently happens that a peddler will come along, his beasts limping under the weight of their precious burden, and will draw up short in fright as he suddenly comes upon a band of jagunços camped out around a bend of the road. He soon loses his fear, however.

[13] [*Positivo:* see n. 27, p. 183, where the author gives the meaning of this term: "comrade," or, as the North American wild-westerner says, "partner."]

The chief rifleman comes up to him, gives him a friendly greeting, enters into conversation with him, laughing and jesting, and puts his terror to rout by this display of good humor. Then the jagunço will ask for his tribute—one *cigarro*. He lights it with a flourish and permits the peddler to pass on, life and fortune intact. There are numerous instances of this sort, revealing as they do a high sense of nobility on the part of these valiant but misguided beings.

Around twenty or twenty-five miles from Xique-Xique is the bandit capital, the settlement of Santo Ignacio, built among the mountains and to this day inaccessible to the police. The latter ordinarily merely step in to pacify those places where tumult prevails, intervening as neutrals between the opposing factions, like diplomats between powers. Armed justice parleys with the criminals, weighing the conditions put forward by one side and the other, discussing the matter, but avoiding all ultimatums. The upshot is that veritable peace treaties are signed, lending sanction to the unpunished reign of gangsterism. Thus the hereditary stigmata of the mestizo population are strengthened by the very leniency of the law. It is accordingly not surprising if these crimes have increased in number, with the bandits extending their sway over the entire valley of the São Francisco and overflowing to the north.

For the *cangaçeiro*[14] of Paraíba and Pernambuco is an identical product under a different name. He is distinguished from the jagunço by perhaps the slightest variation in weapons, the *parnahyba* of the long and rigid blade taking the place of the famous and traditional bell-mouth blunderbuss. These two social groups were for a long time isolated from each other. The cangaçeiros would make incursions to the south, the jagunços would make forays to the north, and they would confront each other without uniting forces, being separated by the steep barrier of Paulo Affonso. It was the insurrection in the Monte Santo district which united them; and the Canudos Campaign served to bring together, spontaneously, all these aberrant forces which were hidden away in the backlands.

II

IMMEDIATE CAUSES OF THE CONFLICT

The conflict in this case arose out of a trifling incident. Antonio Conselheiro had acquired in Joazeiro a certain quantity of lumber which the extremely impoverished caatingas of Canudos were unable to furnish him. He had contracted for it with one of the authorized representatives of

---

[14] Derived from *cangaço*, the outfit of weapons which the malefactors carried. The inhabitants of the backlands say: "The assassin was at the fair, under his *cangaço*."

that city,[15] but, when the time agreed upon for the delivery of the material, which was to be used in the completion of the new church, came around, there was no lumber in sight. Everything pointed to a deliberate affront, an open break.

The chief magistrate of Joazeiro,[16] the truth is, had an old account to settle with the backlands agitator, one that dated from the period when he was a judge at Bom Conselho and had been compelled to leave town hastily as the result of an attack by the Counselor's followers; and he was simply taking advantage of the present situation, which afforded him the chance he wanted for evening the score. He knew that his enemy would strike back at the slightest provocation. The latter, indeed, even before the contract was broken, had threatened to descend on the attractive little town in the São Francisco Valley and take by force the timber that he needed.

This happened in October, 1896. In the account which we give here, we shall confine ourselves strictly to the official documents.

Such was the situation,[17] when I received from Dr. Arlindo Leoni, justice of Joazeiro, an urgent telegram informing me of rumors which were current, and which were more or less well founded, to the effect that the flourishing city in question was to be assaulted within a few days by Antonio Conselheiro's followers. He requested my aid in assuring the safety of the population and in halting the exodus of the inhabitants, which had already begun. I replied that the government could not resort to force on the basis of mere rumors and recommended meanwhile that he station a guard along the roads for some distance in order to watch the movements of the bandits and that he advise me by telegram, whereupon the government would be notified to send immediately, by special train, such force as might be necessary for dispersing the marauders and safeguarding the city.

Inasmuch as the force of police stationed at the Capital had been depleted by reason of those matters to which I have already referred, I asked the commanding general of the district[18] for one hundred regular troops, which were to set out for Joazeiro the moment I received word from the justice of that place. A few days later the telegram came, informing me that Antonio Conselheiro's followers were a little more or less than a couple of days' journey from Joazeiro. I notified the general of this fact, who, in response to my request, sent by special train, and under the command of Lieutenant Pires Ferreira, the force which was in waiting, and which from then on was to act under orders from the judge of the district. This latter official, arriving at Joazeiro, joined with the local authorities in going out to meet the bandits, to prevent them from invading the city.

It would be hard to imagine a more trifling course of action for events of such gravity. The extract which we have quoted clearly shows that, dis-

---

[15] Colonel João Evangelista Pereira e Mello.   [16] See p. 152.

[17] Message of the governor of Baía (Dr. Luis Vianna) to the president of the Republic, 1897.

[18] [General Frederico Solon, Euclides da Cunha's father-in-law.]

daining to investigate the background of the affair, the governor of Baía failed to attribute to the occurrence the importance which it possessed.

At that time, some twenty-two years ago, or from 1874 on, Antonio Conselheiro was famous throughout the northern backlands and even in the cities along the coast, where word had come of the most interesting and semilegendary episodes of his romantic life, embroidered with many exaggerations; and, from day to day, his influence over the population increased. This was due to his fabulous wanderings for a quarter of a century through every remote corner of the region, where he had left behind him as he went enormous monuments to mark his passage. There were the towers of dozens of churches which he had built; he it was who had founded the settlement of Bom Jesus, now almost a city; from Chorrochó to Villa do Conde, from Itapicurú to Geremoabo, there was not a single town or obscure village in which he did not have his fervent disciples, and which did not owe to him the rebuilding of a cemetery, the possession of a place of worship, or the providential gift of a water dam.[19] For some time now he had audaciously been preaching insurrection against the government, against the new political order, and had been trampling with impunity on the edicts issued by the chambers of the cities that he visited, or, rather, on their ashes, after his followers had burned the bulletin boards.[20] In 1893 he had completely wiped out a detachment of police at Masséte[21] and had compelled another troop of eighty regular army soldiers, who had followed him as far as Serrinha, to turn back. In 1894, moreover, in the state assembly of Baía, the subject had occasioned a heated discussion.[22] One deputy had called the attention of the authorities to "that portion of the backlands which is being disturbed by the individual, Antonio Conselheiro"; but other representatives of the people, among them a priest, had held him up as a model of the most rigid Christian orthodoxy. In 1895 he had been responsible for the failure of the apostolic mission planned by the archbishop of Baía;[23] and, in the alarming account of this affair which had been written by Friar João Evangelista, the missionary had asserted that there were in Canudos—outside of the women and children, the aged and the infirm—no less than a thousand fearless and able-bodied men, "armed to the teeth." Finally, it was a known fact that he held undisputed sway over a wide area, rendering difficult of access the citadel where he had dug himself in. His followers were said to be absolutely devoted to him; and, in addition to the circle of the faithful

[19] [See pp. 136–37, 138, 141.]

[20] See pp. 141–42.

[21] See p. 142.

[22] [Cf. pp. 138–39.]

[23] [See pp. 164–69.]

who surrounded him, he had as obligatory accomplices everywhere those who feared him.

And to deal with such a situation as this, a force of a hundred soldiers was deemed sufficient.

General Frederico Solon, commander of the Third Military District, has this to say in his report:

At the end of this year [1896], in obedience to the order referred to above, I acted promptly upon the requisition personally made by the governor of the state, for a force of one hundred men from the garrison to go and combat the fanatics of the Canudos settlement, it being represented to me that such a number was more than sufficient. Relying upon the thorough knowledge which he must have of all that was going on in the interior of his state, I did not hesitate, but without delay sent him the valiant Lieutenant Manoel da Silva Pires Ferreira, of the Ninth Battalion of Infantry, who was to act under his orders and instructions. In carrying out those orders, the officer in question, on the seventh day of the said month, set out for Joazeiro, the terminal point of the railway, on the right bank of the São Francisco; he had with him 104 enlisted men of that Corps, with one small ambulance, and I afterward sent on a doctor[24] with a few additional supplies for the exercise of his profession. Most of these came from the state.

This handful of soldiers evoked surprise in Joazeiro, when the detachment reached there on the morning of November 7. The coming of the troops did not prevent the flight of a good part of the population but rather gave impetus to it. Knowing what the situation was, the inhabitants promptly saw that so small a contingent as this would have a purely negative effect, would merely constitute a greater attraction for the invading horde. They foresaw an inevitable defeat; and, while the undercover partisans of the Counselor—for he had a number of these in all the neighborhood round about[25]—were filled with jubilation, a few right-intentioned individuals begged the commander of the expedition to go no farther.

The difficulties which the troops encountered in procuring necessities for their march detained them until the twelfth day of the month, when they set out at nightfall; the news of their approach, meanwhile, had most assuredly reached Canudos.[26] They did not possess the indispensable equipment for a march of a hundred and twenty-five miles across a barren and unpopulated countryside; but, nevertheless, they went, with a couple of guides whom they had hired in Joazeiro to show them the way.

From the beginning, the commanding officer realized that it was not practicable to limit the day's march in such a manner as to spare his

[24] Dr. Antonio Alves dos Santos (see p. 188).

[25] [Cf. the "fifth column" of today.]

[26] A curious detail: the troops set out at nightfall, on the twelfth, in order to avoid a departure on the thirteenth, an unlucky day. And they were going to combat fanaticism!

troops. In the backlands, even prior to the midsummer season, it is impossible for fully equipped men, laden down with their knapsacks and canteens, to do any marching after ten o'clock in the morning. On the tablelands the day is blazing hot, with no shade in sight; the barren earth refracts and intensifies the sun's rays; owing to the exhausting effect of a very high temperature, all the vital functions are accelerated in an amazing fashion, and the result is a sudden collapse. On the other hand, it is

Courtesy of the Instituto Brasileiro de Geografia e Estatística

THE CAATINGA, OR SCRUB FOREST, TYPICAL OF THE CANUDOS REGION

rarely possible to plan the march in such a manner as to take advantage of the morning or the night hours, and the men are compelled to keep on going until they come to the dwellings of the vaqueiros with their water pits. In addition to all this, the region, as we have seen, is the least known of any in our land. Few there are who have ventured into the wilds of the Vasa-Barris Valley, which, starting at the eastern slopes that extend from Itiúba to Geremoabo, stretches out as an inhospitable, little-frequented tract with only a few tiny and scattered dwellings for many miles around. And the region near Baía is even more of a waste land by reason of the droughts.

By a contrast that is understandable in view of the disposition of the mountains, this expanse of wilderness is nevertheless surrounded by luxuriant landscapes: to the north, the beautiful Curaçá region and the extremely fertile fields which extend eastward as far as Santo Antonio da Gloria, beyond the right bank of the São Francisco; and, to the west, the highly productive tract which centers about Villa Nova da Rainha. These more favored regions, however, merely serve to frame the desert, through which the Vasa-Barris, which is almost always dry, wends its way like a long and torturous wadi. This part of the country is worse than the campos, and the wiliest of prospectors[27] will become "all tangled up"[28] here at times, without being able to tell one direction from another in this boundless expanse of plains, where the landscapes all have a uniform and unvaryingly melancholy appearance, with Nature in her most savage mood and a creeping flora to afford the only relief for the eye. Even the caatinga assumes a different aspect.[29] If one were to describe the backlands flora more accurately, taking into account the various changing aspects which it presents, calling for a diversified terminology, one would perhaps do better to refer to this region as the classic land of the *caatanduvas*,[30] which extend to the south and east all the way to the vicinity of Monte Santo.

The little expedition made its way into this region on the second day, when, after having bivouacked a few miles out of Joazeiro, it found itself under the necessity of marching twenty-five miles along a desert road, until it came to a diminutive ipueira, known as Ox Lake (Lagôa do Boi), where there were a few remnants of water. From here it continued on into the desert, with stops at Caraibinhas, Mary, Mucambo, Rancharia, and other isolated dwellings or fazendas. Some of these were abandoned, for the summer heat was presaging the drought. The few residents who had stayed behind, either with the object of avoiding the drought or because they were frightened by the fresh disturbances, had now made their way northward, driving their goats in front of them, for these are the only animals adapted to this soil and climate.

UAUÁ

The exhausted troops reached Uauá on the nineteenth day of the month, after a most arduous march. This settlement—consisting of two streets that meet in an irregular-shaped *praça*—is the most animated point in the entire section. Like the majority of those hamlets whose names are pompously inscribed on our maps, it was a sort of cross be-

---

[27] *Pombeiros: pombeiro—positivo* signify comrade (*camarada*). [See p. 177 and n. 13.]

[28] *Ficam varios:* "*ficar vario* is said of a traveler who loses his way on the trackless plains."

[29] See "Author's Notes," Note VII, p. 482.

[30] *Caatanduva, cahiva:* poor forest (*caa,* forest; *ahiva,* bad) (Beaurepaire-Rohan, *Diccionário de vocábulos brasileiros*).

tween an Indian camp and a village, consisting of an ugly-looking cluster of around a hundred ill-made houses and dilapidated shanties whose appearance was extremely mournful and depressing. This village is at the crossing of four highways—that of Geremoabo, which runs by way of Canudos, that of Monte Santo, that of Joazeiro, and that of Patamoté. These roads of a Saturday bring to its fair a large number of country folk who are without the means for a longer journey to more prosperous places. Hither they flock on feast days, as if to the capital of the "big lands,"[31] clad in their Sunday best or in brand-new leather garments, to gawk at the displays of the two or three shops and contemplate the sorry exhibit of industrial products in the fair booth, the tanned leathers, the caroá-fiber hammocks, and the like. The rest of the week, with one or the other shop open, the square deserted, Uauá takes on the appearance of an abandoned village; and it was on such a day as this, at a time when the population was within doors to avoid the midday heat, that the villagers were surprised by the sound of military trumpets. It was the troops approaching.

They entered the street from the highway that leads into it and stationed themselves in the square. This was an event. Torn between timidity and curiosity, the inhabitants eyed the soldiers—dust-covered, straggling in formation, their rifles with their gleaming bayonets on their shoulders—as if they had been gazing on a brilliant army. Having stacked arms, the troops were quartered for the night. A watch was to be kept on all sides, and sentinels were accordingly told off and posted along each of the four roads leading into the hamlet.

A warlike scene for the moment, this humble village was, however, no more than a wayside stop. After a brief rest, the expedition was to set out immediately for Canudos, at dawn of the following day, the twentieth. This it failed to do; for here, as everywhere else, there were all sorts of rumors, rendering it difficult to form a proper opinion as to what should be done. As a consequence, the whole of this day was wasted in futile inquiries, an immediate attack being finally resolved upon after a most harmful delay. At nightfall there occurred an incident which was only explained the following morning: almost the entire population stealthily fled the village. They left their houses and slipped away without being perceived, between the sentry outposts. In this sudden frightened exodus, whole families, including even the sick, took part, fleeing under cover of night to the open fields.

---

[31] *Terras grandes:* a vague phrase applied by the backwoodsmen to the unfamiliar seaboard. It takes in everything from Rio de Janeiro to Baía, Rome, and Jerusalem, which in their imagination are pictured as being near one another and very far from the backlands. It is all the rest of the world, the whole of civilization, which they fear and avoid.

This event was in fact a warning. Uauá, like the other places in the vicinity, was under the domination of Canudos. Antonio Conselheiro had consecrated followers there; and no sooner had the troops taken up their station in the square than these faithful ones set out for the threatened settlement, arriving there at dawn on the morning of the twentieth, giving the alarm.

This mass flight of the population showed that the emissaries had had time to return and warn the residents of the counterattack which the men of Canudos had resolved to make. They were simply leaving the field free to the combatants. The members of the expedition, on the other hand, attached no great importance to the occurrence but prepared to resume their march on the following day. Wholly unaware of the gravity of the situation, they slept peacefully in their quarters that night.

FIRST BATTLE

The enemy whom they had planned to take by surprise was, however, up and stirring. On the morning of the twenty-first the jagunços were sighted on the horizon.

A distant chorus of song could be heard, coming over the plains whose silence up to then had been unbroken, awakening far echoes in the desert waste. The warlike multitude was advancing on Uauá, marching along to the slow drone of "Kyrie eleison's," singing and praying. It resembled one of those penitential processions which the credulous backwoodsmen used to stage by way of propitiating Heaven when the long summers brought the scourge of the drought.

All this, however unusual it may seem, was quite typical. Eschewing the advantages of a night attack, the sertanejos came at daybreak and announced their coming from afar. They were waking the enemy for the fight. At first glance, they did not look like the warriors that they were. They came with the symbols of peace: the Banner of the Divine and, borne aloft in the hands of a sturdy religionist, a great wooden cross tall as a *cruzeiro*.[32] The fighting men, armed with old muskets, with the vaqueiro's pike, with scythes and long poles, were swallowed up in the throng of the faithful; the latter, unarmed, bore the portraits and images of their favorite saints and withered palms taken from the altars. Some of them, as if on a pious pilgrimage, carried stones of the road on their heads and were saying their cocoanut-bead rosaries as they marched. For them, the coming of the soldiers was the same as one of those natural plagues which visit the land ever so often. And so they went into battle

[32] [A large cross, built of stones, in a street or public place.]

praying, singing—as if seeking a decisive test for the faith that was in their souls.

There were many of them. Three thousand, according to later and exaggerated accounts. This was, perhaps, trebling the number. There was no order in their formation; and a small platoon of infantry distributed about in the surrounding caatingas would have been able to disperse them in a few minutes. At the settlement ahead of them, however, there were no defenders in sight. The latter were all asleep.

The advancing throng, all accounts indicate, had come up to the sentry outposts before the latter awoke. The sentries, starting up in surprise, fired a volley at random and then fled back precipitately to the square, where their rear guard was stationed, leaving in the hands of the enemy a comrade who had been slashed by a knife. Then it was that the alarm was sounded, as half-wakened soldiers came running down the streets and into the *praça*. Half-clad, they dashed through doorways and leaped out of windows, adjusting their clothing and their weapons the best way they could as they ran. They attempted no sort of formation but, under the command of a sergeant, scattered out like badly trained sharpshooters. The jagunços had already reached the square, close on the heels of the fleeing sentries, and a fierce hand-to-hand encounter now took place, a veritable free-for-all, clubs and gunstocks, knives and sabers clashing, amid the sound of musket and revolver shots, as the invaders bore down upon the ineffective line of defense, sweeping the soldiers back. With *viva*'s to the "Good Jesus" and the "Counselor," their taquara-cane[33] whistles sounding shrilly, the Banner of the Divine floating above them, as they flourished their saints and weapons in the air, the fanatics surged in behind the daring curiboca who, using his huge wooden cross as a battering-ram, cleared a path for them as they tumultuously overran the square.

All this happened in a moment's time; and, according to those who witnessed the action, this was the only thing in the way of a military maneuver which they were able to distinguish; from that time on they could not even tell friend from foe; all was confusion and disorder, like a fair at which a riot had broken out. In the majority of cases the soldiers, seeking cover of the houses and making loopholes in the walls through which to fire, did no more than defend themselves. The backwoodsmen, clustered around their sacred images in the *praça*, were now being shot down en masse. Large numbers of them fell; for, despite their numerical superiority, the battle was a one-sided affair. They were met with a fire of repeating-rifles and could only answer with one round of musketshot

[33] [The *taquara* (*taboca*) is a cane or reed with sharp, stout pricks that grows wild in Brazil.]

for every hundred from the Comblains. While the soldiers could pour a
steady rain of fire upon them, the jagunços, manipulating their ammunition pouches, had to go through the slow process of reloading their clumsy
weapons with gunpowder, gun wadding, and bullets; they had to plunge
the ramrod down the long barrel of their *trabucos*, slowly stuffing them
with the necessary ingredients as if they were filling up a mine, after
which they had to prime and cock and, at last, fire them, all of which
called for a heroic two minutes of immobility in the dizzying tumult of
the skirmish.

They accordingly, after some time, gave up the unequal struggle, and
fell upon the enemy with their knives unsheathed, their cattle prongs
couched, their gleaming scythes raised aloft. This dubious means of attack was to prove still more costly to them; their ranks were merely depleted, with no advantage to themselves, as they sought to dislodge their
sheltered adversary, who would suddenly fire upon them from a window,
flung open to the crack of bullets. At one of these windows a lieutenant,
tardily awakened and half-naked, fought for a long time, resting his rifle
on the ledge, aiming breast-high at his assailants and never missing a shot,
until he fell back dead on the bed where he had slept, and which he had
never had time to leave.

The conflict continued in this fashion, fiercely, for about four hours,
without any incidents worthy of note and without the faintest sign of any
tactical maneuver, every one fighting on his own account, as circumstances
demanded. In the garden of the house where he was billeted, the commanding officer did the one thing that could be done in all this disorder: he distributed cartridges by tossing them over the garden wall, snatching them
up greedily, by the handful, from cases opened with the blows of an ax.

Still rallying about the Banner of the Divine, bullet-riddled now like a
flag of war, the jagunços threaded their way through the streets, making
the circuit of the village and soon returning aimlessly to the square, with
loud *viva*'s and imprecations. Gradually, in the course of these senseless
rounds, they came to abandon the fray and scattered out over the neighboring countryside. It may be that they realized the futility of their efforts, or they may have thought to lure their antagonists out onto the
open plain. In any event, they little by little gave up the struggle, until
at last all that could be seen of them, dotting a distant point of the caatingas, was their Holy Banner which they were bearing back to Canudos.
The soldiers did not give them chase, for they were exhausted.

Uauá now presented a sorry picture indeed. Fires had broken out in a
number of places. On the blood-spattered floors, the balconies, and door-

sills of the houses, in the streets and in the square, the dead lay stretched out, while the wounded writhed in agony in the rays of the sun. Among these were dozens of sertanejos, a hundred and fifty of them according to the official report of the combat, an excessive figure it would seem in view of the ten killed—a lieutenant, a sergeant, six privates, and two guides— and the sixteen wounded among the expeditionary force. In spite of the fact that he still had seventy able-bodied men, the commanding officer gave up the idea of proceeding any farther. This assault had astonished him. He had witnessed at close-up the daring of these backwoodsmen and was frightened by the victory he had won, if such it could be called in view of its discouraging consequences. The physician who accompanied the troops went out of his head, driven insane by sight of the affray, and was accordingly of no use in treating the wounded, some of whom were serious cases.

It was, therefore, urgent that they retire before nightfall, or before another attack took place—the very idea causing these victors to tremble. They resolved to do so immediately, and, having given their dead comrades a rude burial at the Uauá chapel, they set out once more beneath the blazing sun. It was something very like a flight.

They made it to Joazeiro, by forced marches, in four days. Arriving there, the expeditionary band, their uniforms in shreds, wounded, crippled, exhausted, presented the very picture of defeat. Alarmed by this, the population prepared to flee. Locomotives with their fires going stood in readiness in the railway stations. All the able-bodied inhabitants who were fit for combat duty were pressed into service. Meanwhile, the telegraph lines carried to all parts of the country the news of this prelude to the backlands war.

III

PLANS FOR REPRISAL

The defeat of Uauá inevitably called for measures of reprisal on the part of the government. As it happened, however, there was a divergency of views between the commander of the federal forces in Baía and the governor of the state. The latter was inclined to be an optimist, looking upon the backland disturbances as mere disorders of a kind with which the police could easily cope; while the former regarded them as far more serious and as capable of leading to large-scale military operations.

The second expedition was thus organized without any definite plan or any definite responsibility for its conduct, in accordance with the conflicting instructions of two independent officials of equal rank. In the beginning it was composed of a hundred enlisted men and eight officers, with a hundred men and three officers from the state troops.

This force, on the twenty-fifth of November, set out for Queimadas, under the command of a major of the Ninth Battalion of Infantry, Febronio de Brito. At the same time, the commandant of the district called upon the federal governor for additional equipment, consisting of four Nordenfeldt machine guns, two Krupp field guns, and 250 more soldiers: 100 from the Twenty-sixth Battalion of Aracajú and 150 from the Thirty-third of Alagoas.

This request for extra equipment was justified; for alarming information was coming in, from day to day, with regard to the gravity of the situation. All exaggerations aside, two things were evident: the rebels were in large force and they had in their favor the wild nature of the region where they had sought shelter. This news, however, was gleaned through a number of contradictory versions, the confusion being heightened by dishonest political interests which did not appear on the surface, and concerning which we need not go into detail here. It may merely be stated that much time was lost in fussing over meaningless trifles, while all over Brazil the telegraph lines were humming with the news from the backlands, and while, at Queimadas, the commander of the fresh expedition was waiting expectantly with his 243 enlisted men. Short of resources and confronted with every sort of difficulty, wavering between all the conflicting reports that he received, now in despair, believing the whole undertaking to be a futile one, and now buoyed up with sudden hope of being able to achieve his objective, it was not until December that this officer with his troops set out for Monte Santo, while at the same time there was sent him from Baía a reinforcement of 100 men.

The assault was now to be carried out in accordance with a definite plan of campaign. The commandant of the district understood the situation and planned to attack the rebels at two points, with two columns converging upon a single objective, under the general command of the colonel of the Ninth Infantry, Pedro Nunes Tamarindo. This plan was one compatible with the exigencies of the conflict: namely, to establish first of all a wide circle around the insurgents, to fight them a few at a time, and, finally, to close in upon them in movements involving small, well-trained detachments. Freed of the slowness of movement which is incumbent upon large masses, these detachments would be able to adjust themselves better to the rugged terrain, and the chances of defeat would thereby be lessened. On the other hand, however original might be the backwoodsmen's mode of fighting—the bewildering strike-and-run warfare of invisible guerrillas—they would nonetheless be confined to this circle, and the battle would not be carried over onto such a plane as would permit the scattered groups to unite at any determined point. To attack them in this manner, by drawing them to different points, was surely to defeat them.

This was something which our native sons of a century ago had long since come to perceive; skilled in the vicissitudes of backland struggles, they had evolved a form of military organization that corresponded to the needs of the case[34]—what they had in view was the systematic formation of "irregular troops" which, unembarrassed by any hard-and-fast tactics and without any predetermined battle array, would be able to function readily within the depths of the forest and over the rugged lands as an auxiliary body of scouts to supplement the regular troops. Whence all the exploits which our history of the seventeenth and eighteenth centuries has to record; not to speak of the rebellions put down or the *quilombos*[35] broken up by these diminutive armies, led by their "forest captains," or all the fierce battles they fought which have not come down in history. Imitating the Africans' and the Indians' own mode of fighting, the pioneers were able to overcome them, thanks to a practice which is expressed in a paradoxical formula—divide and strengthen.

This is a formula which we ourselves should have followed under similar conditions. It was, without a doubt, a throwback to primitive warfare; but, if the brave and shrewd jagunço did not lead us to adopt it, then the exceptional character of the terrain which served as his protector certainly should have induced us to do so. How true this is we shall shortly see.

THE WAR OF THE CAATINGAS

Those doctors of the art of killing who today in Europe are scandalously invading the domain of science, disturbing its calm with an insolent jingling of spurs as they formulate the laws of war and the equations of battle, have well defined the role of forests as a tactical factor, both in offensive and in defensive action. And those wise old field marshals—warriors from whose hands the heroic francisca[36] has fallen, to be replaced by the pencil of the strategist—would certainly have laughed had anyone tried to tell them that our impoverished caatingas have a more clearly defined and important function in a military campaign than do the great virgin

[34] See the *Revista do Instituto Histórico e Geográphico Brasileiro*—the Royal Instructions of February 24, 1775, to the Captain General of Minas.

[35] [See p. 66.]

[36] ["A battle-ax used by the ancient Franks with a slightly curved, long, narrow head, and an outwardly curved edge, the head forming a slightly obtuse angle with the pole" (*Funk & Wagnalls' Standard Dictionary*).]

forests. For the former, notwithstanding their importance in the defense of a territory—bordering the frontiers as they do and serving to break the shock of invasion while hindering rapid mobilization and rendering impossible the transport of artillery—nevertheless become, in a manner of speaking, neutral in the course of the campaign. They may favor, indifferently, either of the belligerents, offering to each the same foliage for ambuscades and making equally difficult for both all those deploying and other maneuvers which strategy imposes upon the contending armies. They are variables in the formula of the dark problem of war, capable of representing the most opposite values.

With all this, the caatingas are an incorruptible ally of the sertanejo in revolt, and they do in a certain way enter into the conflict. They arm themselves for the combat, take the offensive. For the invader they are an impenetrable wilderness; but they have numerous paths by which they are accessible to the backwoodsman, who was born and grew up there. And so, the jagunço turns warrior-thug,[37] hard to lay hands on.

The caatingas do not so much hide him as extend him their protection. Upon catching sight of them in the summertime, a column of soldiers is not alarmed but continues to make its way, painfully, along the winding paths. Being able to see over the top of the leafless undergrowth, the men do not think of an enemy's being near. Reacting to the heat and with that relaxed air which is natural on long marches, they go along with a confused babble of conversation all down the line, punctuated by the clinking of their weapons and their jovial, half-repressed laughter. There is nothing, so it seems, that should alarm them. Certainly, should the enemy be so imprudent as to confront them here, they would make short work of him. These shoots of foliage could be slashed to bits by a few strokes of the sword, and it is not credible that this fine underbrush could impede the execution of prompt maneuvers. And so they go marching along, heroically unconcerned.

Suddenly, from the side, close at hand, a shot rings out.

The bullet whizzes past them, or perhaps one of their number lies stretched on the ground, dead. This is followed, after a while, by another, and another, whining over the heads of the troop. A hundred, two hundred, a thousand anxious eyes scan the foliage round about them, but can see nothing. This is the first surprise, and a shudder of fear runs from one end of the ranks to the other. The shots continue, not many of them, but there is no letup; they keep on coming at measured intervals, from the

---

[37] [The word in the original is *guerrilheiro-thug.*]

left, from the right, from in front of them, with the entire band now under a constant and a deadly fire.

It is then that a strange anxiety lays hold of even the bravest ones whose courage has many times been put to the test, in the presence of this antagonist who sees them, but whom they cannot see. A company of sharpshooters is quickly formed, being with difficulty separated from the main mass of the battalions caught in the narrow path. These men now spread out around the edge of the caatinga, whereupon a voice can be heard giving a command, and there is a resounding hail of bullets through the branches of the stunted undergrowth.

But constantly, always at long intervals, the missiles from those other sharpshooters, the invisible ones, keep humming, all up and down the line. The situation rapidly grows worse, calling for energetic action. Other combat units are now detached and are detailed along the entire stretch of road, ready to act at the first word of command. The commanding officer resolves to launch an assault on the hidden enemy but soon finds that he is assaulting a phantom foe. With their bayonets, his men impetuously beat down the undergrowth, amid a widening range of bullets. They go forward rapidly, and the enemy appears to fall back somewhat. And then it is, at this moment, that the caatinga shows what a formidable antagonist it can be. The details rush on to the points from where the gunfire had been heard and are brought up short by the yielding but impenetrable barrier of a jurema thicket. They become entangled in a liana bed, which trips them up, snatches their weapons from their hands, and will not let them pass; and so they are compelled to turn aside and make their way around it. There may now be seen what looks like a running flame, a row of bayonets along the dried brushwood. It glitters for a few moments in the rays of the sun, filtered down through the leafless boughs, and then is gone, to be seen, gleaming, here and there farther on, beating against the dense rows of chique-chiques,[38] bunched together in the close squares of an immovable phalanx, bristling with thorns.

In great bewilderment the soldiers make a wide detour. Spreading out, on the run, they plunge headlong into the labyrinth of boughs and branches. Tripped by the slipknot lassos of the creeping quipá vines, they fall, or else are brought to a standstill, their legs held motionless by the powerful tentacles. They struggle desperately, until their uniforms are in tatters, in the feline claws of the macambiras with their crooked thorns.

They stand there cursing impotently, in rage and disappointment, as

38 [See p. 34.]

they struggle furiously but without avail to free themselves. Finally, the tumult dies away as the men spread out more and more, firing at random, without aim, with an utter lack of discipline, their bullets likely as not hitting their own comrades. Reinforcements come up, and the anguished struggle with the underbrush is repeated all over again, on a yet larger scale, as the confusion and the disorder increase—and meanwhile, round about them, steadily, rhythmically, fall the deadly well-aimed missiles of the terrible enemy, safe in his hiding-place.

Of a sudden, the firing ceases. The enemy is gone, and no one has had so much as a glimpse of him. The detachments with their numbers depleted now return to the column after all this futile beating of the brush. It is as if they were coming back from a hand-to-hand encounter with savages; their weapons are lost or hopelessly battered; there are deep gashes on their hands and faces; they are limping, crippled, and it is all they can do to keep from crying out with the infernal pain inflicted upon them by the prickly leaves of the caatinga, the thorn wounds that they bear.

The troop is then reorganized and the march is resumed. Two abreast, it goes on down the paths, the blue uniforms of the soldiers with their vermilion stripes and the brightly gleaming, swaying bayonets giving a strong dash of color to the ashen-gray of the landscape. And so they march on until they are lost to sight in the distance.

Some minutes pass, and then, at the scene of the struggle, from the scattered thickets, five, ten, twenty men at the most rise up, and swiftly, silently, slip away among the parched shrubbery.

They meet on the highway and stand there for a moment or so gazing after the troop which is now barely visible on the horizon. And brandishing their muskets, still hot from firing, they hastily make for the trails that lead to their unknown dwellings.

As for the members of the expeditionary force, they will be more cautious after this. As they march along in silence, the soldiers cannot help thinking anxiously of this intangible enemy and are haunted by visions of sudden assaults. The commanding officer surrounds them with every possible precaution; detached companies skirt their flanks, and up ahead, a couple of hundred yards in advance of the column, is a squadron of picked men. Upon descending a rugged slope, however, they come to a ravine which has to be crossed. Fortunately, its sides have been swept clean by floods, leaving only a little grass stubble, a few slender cacti standing out here and there among the stone heaps and the dead and white-peeling boughs of the umbú trees, victims of the drought.

The advance guard goes down the side of the ravine, followed by the first of the battalions, slowly straggling after. One can see them now, down below, the entire vanguard of the column, following the twists and turns of the narrow valley, their weapons gleaming in the sun like some dark torrent shot with rays of light.

Then they suddenly haul up short with a convulsive shudder which they cannot control. A bullet has just whistled past them. This time the shots, fired at intervals as usual, appear to come from above and from a solitary marksman. Only discipline preserves order in the ranks now and restrains a panic which is on the verge of breaking out. As before, a detachment is told off and goes up the slope in the direction of the shots; but, owing to the bedlam of echoes, it is hard for the men to keep their bearings: and in this overheated atmosphere the sharpshooter's hiding-place is not revealed by the smoke from his weapon, owing to the absence of condensation; and so he continues firing, leisurely but with terrifying effect, assured meanwhile of his own safety.

At last the firing ceases, and it is in vain that the soldiers, roaming over the slopes, seek for their vanished assailants. They return exhausted, the bugles sound, and the band is on its way once more, with a few men less. And when the last of them are out of sight, beyond the roll of the hill, there rises up from among the stone heaps—like a sinister caryatid amid these cyclopic ruins—a hard and sunburned face, followed by the rude and leather-clad torso of an athlete. Running swiftly up the steep sides of the ravine, this dreadful hunter of armed men is gone in a few moments' time.

The troops continue on their way, completely demoralized. From now on, these hardened veterans are as timid as a child. A shiver runs up and down their spines at each bend of the road, at every dead leaf that crackles in the brush. The army has come to feel that its very strength is its weakness. Without any maneuverability, in a state of continual exhaustion, it must make its way through these desert regions under the constant threat of ambuscades and be slowly sacrificed to a dreaded enemy who does not stand and fight but flees. The conflict is an unequal one, and a military force is compelled to descend to a lower plane of combat; it has to contend not merely with man but with the earth itself; and, when the backlands are boiling in the dry summer heat, it is not difficult to foresee which side will have the victory. While the mighty Minotaur, helpless in spite of his steel armor and bayonet claws, feels his throat drying up with thirst and, at the first symptoms of hunger, turns back to the rear, fleeing the inhospitable and menacing desert, the aggressive flora of this region, on the other hand, takes the sertanejo to its friendly, caressing bosom.

Then it is—in these indeterminate seasons between the "green" and the "lean,"[39] when the last trickles of water are to be found in the mud of the marshlands and the last yellowed leaves on the boughs of the baraúnas, as the frightened stranger flees the imminent scourge of the drought— then it is the backwoodsman is blessed by knowing the ins and outs of every long and winding trail; for know them he does, knows by heart every nook and cranny of this enormous roofless home of his. It does not matter to him if the journey is long and the houses are few and far between, if the water in the wells is dried up, while the lowland coverts, where the weary cowboy is wont to take his noonday ease, are slowly thinning out. He is sustained by a sense of the long familiar. These trees are for him old companions. He knows them all. He and they were born and grew up together, like brothers; they have both had the same difficulties to face, have had to struggle with the same hardships, and have shared the same days of tranquillity. The umbú tree will quench his thirst[40] and give him the scant shade of its last-remaining leaves; the araticú,[41] the verdant urucuri, the shapely marizeiro, the quixabeira with its tiny fruit[42]—all will give him enough and more than enough to eat and drink. The palmatorias,[43] stripped of their numerous thorns by a process of rapid combustion,[44] the mandacarús,[45] carved up with a knife, or the leaves of the juás[46] will serve to keep his horse alive; the juás will also provide him with a covering for his improvised traveler's couch; the fibrous caroás afford him strong and supple ropes.[47] And if it should be necessary for him to continue his journey after nightfall, and in the darkness his eye is barely able to make out the bluish-phosphorescent glow of the cumanans,[48] hanging down like fantastic garlands from the tree boughs, then all he has to do is to light a green branch of the candombá[49] and wave it in front of him as he goes along the trail, thereby dazzling and frightening away the pumas with this gleaming torch.

Yes, Nature protects the sertanejo, renders him an indomitable Antaeus. And this is the bronzed Titan who causes armies to waver in their march.

[39] [See p. 38 and n. 62.]   [40] [See pp. 37–38.]

[41] [On the araticú (Annona spp.) see p. 38, n. 63.]

[42] [For urucuri see p. 11, n. 14; for marizeiro, p. 36, n. 56; for quixabeira, p. 23, n. 30.]

[43] [See p. 23, n. 29.]   [44] [Cf. p. 109.]   [45] [See p. 34, n. 47.]

[46] [Solanum balbisii Dun. The term juá is applied to a number of plants of the family Solanaceae, particularly, in Marajó, to the Solanum toxicarium Lam. (not poisonous, as the name might seem to indicate).]

[47] [The caroá fibers (see p. 91, n. 68) are used for the making of hunting-bags (see p. 101), bridles (see p. 91), hammocks (see p. 373), etc.]

[48] [Cumanan (cunanan), a shrub of the Euphorbiaceae family (Euphorbia phosphorea Mart.). For a description of this plant see pp. 300–301.]

[49] [The identification of this plant is in some doubt. It is, possibly, the Cunduma (Iriartea ventricola Mart.).]

IV

DOUBTFUL AUTONOMY

The campaign which was just beginning was to demonstrate all this. Here was the largest military force which had been seen throughout the whole of the north country, and that it should have to contend with such difficulties as these was something which might have been foretold. The measures planned by General Solon showed that he had indeed taken account of such contingencies in the course of this most unusual conflict, for which there was no Jomini to lay down the rules, inasmuch as conditions here ran counter to the commonly accepted precepts of the art of war.

Even though the comparison may not be wholly apt, Canudos was our Vendée.[50] The Chouan and his barren heaths are a fitting parallel to the jagunço and his caatingas. The same mysticism, born of the same political aspirations; the same daring with the same astuteness behind it; the same adverse terrain—all serve to recall that legendary corner of Brittany where the rebels, after having driven back an army that was destined to march over Europe, only yielded at last to the flying-squadrons of a commander whom no one had heard of, the "infernal columns" of General Turreau, less numerous than the main army, but swifter-moving, vying in this respect with the elusive Vendeans themselves, until finally the latter were penned up within a circle of sixteen entrenched camps.

This historical lessoning, however, went unheeded in the present instance, although it would have assured an inevitable victory in putting down this insignificant backlands uprising.

The governor of Baía asserted that "the steps taken will be more than sufficient to put down and stamp out the group of fanatics, and there is no necessity of reinforcing the federal troops for such a purpose, the measures adopted by the commandant of the district being largely preventive in character"; and he added that "Antonio Conselheiro's group is not so numerous a one, consisting of little more than five hundred men," etc.

The military commander was not in agreement with this view; he felt that the affair was by now beyond the bounds of ordinary police procedure, that it was no longer a matter of apprehending criminals "but of extirpating that tendency to moral decay which is to be observed in the settlement of Canudos, to the manifest impairment of authority and of our institutions." In addition, he felt that the federal forces should be sufficiently strong to prevent the contingency of "indecorous and prejudicial retreats." The governor of the state, however, acting within the elastic Article 6 of the Constitution of February 24, put an end to the controversy

[50] Cf. p. 162 and n. 179.

by raising the scarecrow of a threat to state sovereignty and by rejecting an intervention which implied an incompetence on his own part to preserve order in his dominions. He forgot that, in a document of record, he had confessed himself unable to put down the revolt and that, by the very act of calling upon the resources of the Union, he was, naturally, justifying the intervention which he wished to avoid.

It was rather late to be talking of sovereignty at a time when that sovereignty was being trampled by unpunished rioters. What was more, no one had any illusion as to the situation in the backlands. Over and above the deranged creature who was the moving spirit, there was a whole society of backward individuals to be dealt with. The moral environment of the region favored the contagion and spread of this particular form of neurasthenia, and this local disorder might well be the spark which would touch off a conflagration throughout the whole of the northern hinterland. In the light of all this, the intervention of the federal government merely gave expression to the deeper significance of the federative principles themselves: namely, the collaboration of the states in a matter which was of concern, not alone to Baía, but to the entire country.

And this, indeed, was what happened: the entire nation intervened. Yet over the troops which came from all parts of the nation, from the far north and from the far south, from Rio Grande to Amazonas, the banner of state sovereignty was always, somehow, intangibly and miraculously, being raised by the constitutional exegetes.

By way of better safeguarding that sovereignty, the commander of the military forces, whose conduct had been wholly in accordance with law, was removed from Baía. It was only after this was done that Major Febronio's expedition—which up to then had wavered between Monte Santo and Queimadas, reflecting in its countermarches all the vacillations of the government—was reinforced by the police troops and strictly subjected to the deliberations of the Baian authorities.

Meanwhile, time was being wasted—time of which the enemy availed himself in preparing for an energetic defense. Within a radius of seven miles round about Canudos, the countryside was laid waste. In all directions and along all the highways, in every place, the charred ashes of ranch buildings and farmhouses served to isolate the settlement within a huge circle of scorched earth.[51] The stage was now set for another stirring drama in our history.

---

[51] [A technique which has been employed in the Soviet Union and in China in the course of the present war. It is by no means a new one, having been made use of by Toussaint L'Ouverture in Haiti and doubtless long before that.]

CHAPTER IV

THE CROSSING OF MOUNT CAMBAIO

I

MONTE SANTO

O N THE twenty-ninth day of December the expeditionaries entered Monte Santo. The town of Friar Apollonio de Todi[1] was
from this day forth to be celebrated as the base of operations for
all the attacks on Canudos. It was the most advantageous point of that
region which lay in the general direction of the campaign; and, moreover,
it permitted of rapid communication with the seaboard by way of the
station of Queimadas.

In addition to such considerations as these, there were others. We have
see in previous pages the impressive manner in which this place came to be
built.[2] We should not go so far as to say, however, that in founding it the
stoic Anchieta of the north[3] was fully aware of all its favorable features.
The fact is, this town—erected at the foot of the one prominent peak in
these highlands—stands in isolated contrast to the barrenness of the surrounding country. The elevation of primitive rocks along its sides to the
north and east rises as a barrier to the regular winds which blow in from
the sea, serving as an admirable condenser for the scant moisture which
those winds still hold, thanks to the cooling effect of a sudden ascent along
the mountain wall; and this moisture is then deposited in the form of
fairly regular rains, thus creating a climate which is more endurable than
that of the sterile backlands only a few steps away, over which the winds,
now deprived of their humidity, continue to blow after they have crossed
the highlands. The result is, that while all around there is an expanse of
desolate plains, there is to be found, on the other hand, within the radius
of a few miles from Monte Santo, a region that is incomparably more fertile. Through it flow small streams that hold out well against the drought.
In the lowlands, at the foot of the hills, is a rudimentary forest growth, the
caatingas being here transformed into large and verdant thickets; and the
Rio de Cariacá with its tiny tributaries, which, like most of the others in

---

[1] See pp. 81 and 114–15. [2] See pp. 114–16.

[3] [Apollonio de Todi is here compared to one of Brazil's most famous missionaries, the sixteenth-century Anchieta. For an account of the latter's labors, by a poet-novelist of today, see
Jorge de Lima, *Anchieta* (Rio de Janeiro, 1934).]

the region, are intermittent streams, never runs wholly dry, no matter how intense or prolonged the drought; in such a case, it divides into a number of pools, reduced in size, with imperceptible rivulets slipping away between the rocks, which nonetheless make it possible for the neighboring inhabitants to withstand the scourge.

It is a natural thing that Monte Santo should for long have been a favored haven of calm for those who venture into these wild parts. This was not the first time that it had made its appearance in history. Centuries before the present ones, other expeditionaries, possibly more fearless and certainly more interesting, had passed this way with objectives of a different sort in view. But, whether it was the seventeenth-century bandeiras or the soldiers of the present day, this predestined site constituted but a wayside port-of-call, for a brief halt, and had but little part to play in events of greater moment. Its historic role is for all of that a significant one as far as the devastators of the backlands are concerned, differing so in their opposing instincts and with three centuries in between them, and yet, as we shall see, so very much alike in their hatreds and so similarly addicted to violent impulses.

It was here that the father of Roberto Dias, Belchior Moreya, made a halt on his bold journey "from the River Real to the Jacobina Mountains, by way of the Itapicurú River, upstream, on the way to the backlands of Massacará." After him came others, guided by the confused logbooks of previous travelers, in which, however, the mountain's ancient name—Piquaraçá[4]—is always to be found as denoting a beneficent region in the midst of these arid wilds.

For this reason it came to be the rallying-point for that first agitated movement which centered about the legendary "Silver Mines," and which ranged from the futile quest of Muribeca, who came thus far and no farther, "with little effect and little diligence," to the tenacious efforts of Pedro Barbosa Leal, who followed Moreya's trails, and who stopped here on the mountain for many days, where he found certain undecipherable signs which indicated that equally audacious predecessors had passed this way. As time went by, however, the mysterious mountain was lost from sight in the backlands, the mountain which many had imagined might be the longed-for El Dorado, until Apollonio de Todi, as we have seen, transformed it into a rude and majestic shrine.[5]

Today, anyone going along the road to Queimadas, over a soil blossoming with rocks and cacti, upon catching sight of the place, a few miles this side of "Quirinquinquá," will stop short; and, turning his dazzled gaze di-

4 [See p. 115.]   5 [See pp. 114–16.]

rectly to the east, will fancy, from all this shimmering, overheated air and bewitching play of sunlight, between a cloudless sky and the broad expanse of the plains below, that what he is beholding is one huge and stunning mirage. The mountain mass made of quartzite, a material which is so appropriate to Earth's monumental architectures, may be seen rising in the distance with its rectilinear line of peaks, its eastern sides falling perpendicularly like a rampart above the town, while along the bottom for a short distance runs a very low terrace, overshadowed by the majesty of the mountain that towers above. Along the top of this mountain is the most beautiful of Monte Santo's streets, extending from the public square all the way to the summit—the *via sacra* of the backlands, macadamized with gleaming quartzite, over which countless multitudes have passed in the course of a century of pilgrimages. Inspired by their own naïve religion, the backwoodsmen have here carved out thousands of winding, spiral steps along the acclivities, one after another, and have hewed out this white silica pathway of more than a mile in length, as if they had been building a road to heaven itself.

The illusion is a striking one at a distance. One can see the little white chapels that dot the road at intervals, as it starts off at a very steep incline, turning and twisting after that in accordance with the formation of the mountain, but going upward always; and these tiny chapels, built on precipices, structures constantly diminishing in size as one views them, little by little disappear and are lost in the serene blue of the heavens, all the way to the last one, on the very top.[6]

He who follows the Queimadas Road will have to cross a strip of desert partly covered by a miserable scrub foliage—trees with branches twisted as if in the contortions of a spasm, thistles clinging to the rocks like constricting tentacles, bromelias with their blood-red blooms—and he will hasten on with a feeling of dismay at this landscape which is emotionally so disturbing. Upon arriving at the town, he is by no means disappointed. The highway takes him all the way to the rectangular, sloping *praça* on a bit of ground guttered by torrents. In the center of the square is the never failing fair booth; at one side is the small church, and on the other side the one ornament which the town possesses, a tamarind tree, centuries old perhaps. Round about are low houses of great antiquity, and prominent among them is a single two-story one which is later to be the general headquarters of the troops.

This square affords a good picture of Monte Santo as a whole. A number of small streets end here, some of them running down the marshy

[6] [Cf. the description on pp. 115–16.]

slopes, some leading to the plain, while others end at the mountainside, with no outlet. As for the mountain itself, it loses something of its charm upon a nearer view, appears to diminish in height; it no longer has the regular outlines that it does at a distance. Covering its slopes is an incredibly hardy flora, rooted in the rock, blooming in the crevices of the strata, and barely contriving to keep alive, thanks to the effects of a marvelous sun. The chapels which looked so white from a distance now have a small and neglected appearance, the walls of masonry along the tortuous-winding

Courtesy of the Instituto Brasileiro de Geografia e Estatística

CATTLE-BREEDING RANCH IN SOUTHERN BRAZIL, HABITAT OF THE GAUCHO

roadway are crumbling in places, the steps are cracked, and the general impression is that of an enormous staircase in ruins. This gloomy town, in a state of absolute decay, reflects the abandonment and discouragements of a race which, unknown to history, is slowly dying within the walls of its mud huts. There is here none of the classic charm that is associated with back-country villages. The low houses, huddled one against another and built to meet the exigencies of the terrain, are all of the same form—low roofs over four mud walls—and are designed, all of them, in that ugly squat style of which the early colonizers were so fond. Some of them must be a hundred years old, but the majority of them are new and, copying line for line the hideous contours of the others, are in their turn born old.

Thus, it may be seen, Monte Santo rises gracelessly in the midst of a landscape which, like a parenthesis in that rude hinterland, is one full of natural charm; and the campaign which was about to begin was destined to aggravate its unpleasant features, transforming the obscure country town into a huge, low-stooped military barracks.

ANTICIPATED TRIUMPHS

It was here that the 543 regular army men were quartered, with 14 field officers and 3 surgeons—the whole of the *first regular expeditionary force* against Canudos. This was a heterogeneous outfit assembled from three battalions, the Ninth, the Twenty-sixth, and the Thirty-third, plus several dozen of police troops and a small division of artillery, with two $7\frac{1}{2}$ Krupp cannons and two Nordenfeldt machine guns. Less than a brigade and a little more than a full battalion.

Meanwhile, affected by the spirit of official optimism, the authorities of the place were giving the troops a triumphal reception before the battle. The humble village was transformed, decked out with flags and foliage set off by the bright-colored uniforms and glittering weapons of the soldiers in the street. It was better than a feast day; the best-attended mission, the liveliest fair, was never so animated as this. It was all a stupendous novelty. Coming in from their tiring journey, the vaqueiros were surprised to find the streets full of soldiers; and, after hitching their "nags" in the shade of the tamarind in the square, they would stand for a long time gazing at these "pieces"[7] of which they had "heard tell" so often, but which they had never seen—capable, so it was said, of blowing mountains to bits and of shaking the entire region with a single shot, more powerful than that of a thousand catapults.[8] And these Titans, hardened by the worst of climates, would shudder inside their leather armor as they viewed these portentous weapons of civilization. Many of them forthwith took to their saddles and, chilled with fear, rode out of town and made for the caatingas. Some rode northward at top speed, heading for Canudos, and no one paid any attention to them; amid the general merrymaking, Antonio Conselheiro's shrewd emissaries went unobserved, as they watched, spied, made inquiries, counted the number of soldiers, and thoroughly examined the entire expedition, only to slip away quickly as soon as their work was done and make for the holy village.

Others there were among these hidden sympathizers of the Counselor who remained there, viewing it all with a cruelly ironical eye, being certain that it was but the hilarious prologue to a tragic drama to come. The prophet could not be wrong; his victory was foreordained. He himself

---

[7] [Pieces of artillery.]

[8] [*Roqueira:* a cannon for shooting stones; catapult.]

had said it—the invaders would never so much as glimpse the towers of the sacrosanct churches. In the meantime, hidden altars were lighted; and the laughter of the soldiers, the clatter of their boots on the pavement, the vibrant notes of the bugles, and the enthusiastic *viva*'s in the street outside would filter through the walls and crannies of the houses and come to disturb the smothered prayers of the faithful on their knees.

At the banquet which was spread in the best house in town, meanwhile, there was a great display of oratory—that simple, moving kind of eloquence which is peculiar to the soldier, and whose expressiveness is in proportion to its crudeness—oratory made up of brief, jerky phrases, like a shrill command, with those magic words, "Fatherland," "Glory," "Liberty," uttered in every conceivable tone of voice, serving as the chief subject matter for the speaker's resounding periods. The rebels would be destroyed by fire and sword. Like the wheels of Shiva's chariot, those of the Krupp cannon, rolling over the broad plains, trundling over the mountains and the vast tablelands, would leave bloody furrows behind them. For an example must be made of these people; they must be taught a lesson. These ignorant and impenitent ones, these criminal degenerates, guilty of stupidly adhering to the most ancient traditions, stood in need of energetic corrective measures. They must be rescued from a barbarism which was a disgrace to our age, must at once be put upon the road to civilization, at the point of the sword.

An example would be made of them, such was the general conviction. The whole of a happy, unthinking, hasty-tempered population was agreed upon this point. And all this noisy, clattering merriment on the part of officers and men, all this festive celebration, was here taking place on the eve of battle, only a few paces distant from the backlands, bristling with ambuscades.

At a late hour in the afternoon noisy groups spilled into the *praça* and, making their way down the lanes, spread out over the town. Others, attracted by the prospect of a rare view, climbed the mountain by the winding path bordered with little white chapels. Exhausted by their exertions, they would pause for breath at the stations, where they would examine curiously the holy prints and images and the crude altars; after which, they would go on. On the "summit of the Holy Cross," lashed by the strong gusts of the northeast wind, they would come to a stop and look about them. There it lay—down there before them—the hinterland.

For a moment the more timid among them were overcome by an oppressive feeling; but it soon disappeared, and they tranquilly returned to the town, where the first lamps were being lighted, at nightfall.

Decidedly, the campaign was beginning under favorable auspices. Had not Monte Santo—already—bestowed upon them the laurels of victory?

II

FAILURE TO GRASP THE NATURE OF THE CAMPAIGN

All this was a misfortune. Under the influence of the warlike preparations, the fuss and show of the parade ground, the inhabitants of Monte Santo had given them the idea that victory was a certainty, and this spontaneous assumption had proved contagious for the troops, who based their hopes upon it. The defeat of the fanatics was assured in advance.

Now, in war, the preoccupation with defeat is an active, if a paradoxical, element. It is the best stimulus that there is to victory. The whole of military history is filled with strange contrasts; but, aside from this, war is in itself a monstrous thing, altogether illogical. In its present phase it is a matter of superior technical organization; but it is still corrupted by all the stigmata of the original banditry behind it. Superior to the rigorous thinking of the strategist, to all tactical precepts, to the feeling of safety that is given by death-dealing equipment, to the entire scope of a somber art which would express the bursting of a shrapnel in the cold formula of mathematics and subject to its inviolable parabolas the violent course of bullets and cannon balls—superior to it all is the brutality of primitive man, which remains intact; and this, when all is said, is still the *vis a tergo* of battles. The certainty of danger stimulates these impulses; the certainty of victory represses them.

This expedition, in everyone's opinion, was absolutely bound to conquer. A consciousness of danger would have led to a rapid mobilization and a surprise attack on the enemy. The certainty of success kept the troops marking time for a fortnight in Monte Santo.

Let us analyze the case. The commander of the expedition had left a good part of his munitions in Queimadas, in order not to delay the march any longer and thus give the enemy more time to strengthen his position. It was, thus, his intention to make a lightning attack. Discouraged by the difficulties that he met with, among which may be noted an almost complete absence of means of transport, he was of a mind to proceed at once to the rebel stronghold, even though he had little more in the way of ammunition than what his men were able to carry in their cartridge pouches. This, however, was not done; and, accordingly, his rapid departure from one place was offset by his fruitless delay in another. This would have been justified only if he had made use of the time to get his equipment together, especially by having the rest of his supply trains sent on from

Queimadas. The inconveniences of a long halt would thus have been compensated by the advantages gained. He would have gained in strength what he lost in speed, and for the overly adventurous plan of a direct attack, in an effort to take the enemy by storm, there would have been substituted a more leisurely scheme of operations, but a safer one. This he did not do. In fact, he did just the opposite. Following a prolonged inactivity at Monte Santo, the expedition set out less well equipped than it had been when it arrived two weeks before, abandoning (once again) a part of what was left of its already greatly reduced supplies.

In the meanwhile, contrary to the way of thinking of those who prophesied an easy victory, information was constantly arriving concerning the number of the fanatics and the resources which they had at their disposal; and amid this clash of opinions—between those who held that there were not more than five hundred of them at the most, and those who asserted that there were at least ten times as many, or around five thousand all told—it might have been possible to hit upon a reasonable figure. Furthermore, in all the cautiously whispered accusations and under-the-breath information, a reasonable basis was to be found for assuming that treason was afoot. There were, for one thing, certain influential local bigwigs whose former relations with the Counselor led to the strong presumption that they were underhandedly lending him aid, by furnishing him with supplies and keeping him informed of the slightest sign of an attack.

Moreover, it was known that the troops, even if the deliberations of their officers were surrounded with the utmost secrecy, would be preceded and accompanied on the march by the enemy's expert spies, many of whom, as was learned afterward, were within the town itself, rubbing elbows with the expeditionaries. Under such circumstances, with all the time that had been lost, it was inexcusable for the latter to be caught off guard. In Canudos the jagunços would be sure to know of the highway that had been chosen for the line of operations, and would know it sufficiently in advance to be able to fortify the most difficult stretches of that road; so that, with the affair at Uauá repeated all over again, a battle on the highway would be a necessary preliminary to the attack on the settlement. Hence, for the troops to leave their base of operations in the manner that they did was distinctly an error of professional judgment. As it was, the expedition started out for its objective as if it had been returning from a campaign. Abandoning still another part of its munitions, it went on, just as if, while it might have been underequipped at Queimadas and still more so at Monte Santo, it would nevertheless be able to provide itself with the necessary supplies—at Canudos. This is equivalent to saying that the expeditionaries disarmed themselves as they approached the enemy. They were going out to grapple as best they might with the unknown, having as their only protection that impulsive bravery of our people, which is in reality a weakness. Defeat was inevitable.

For these were not the only blunders; there were others that pointed to an utter ignorance of the art of war. This was revealed by the order of the day with regard to the organization of the attacking forces. Laconic as are most orders governing the distribution of detachments, it contained not the faintest indication as to the deployment, formation, or maneuvering of the combat units, in view of such contingencies as could readily have been foreseen. There was not a word about the certainty of attacks from ambush. Not a word, either, as to the distribution of the units in accordance with the special character of the enemy and the terrain. Limited to a few rudimentary principles of Prussian tactics, taken over and applied to our own forces, the commanding officer of the expedition, as if he were leading this little army corps through some unencumbered field in Belgium, proceeded to divide it into three columns, preparing it, as it seemed, to go into battle in the old formation of infantry and supporting detachments. These were all the instructions he had to give—nothing beyond a few ancient and rigid rules and classic maxims of warfare, which, as it happened, were not suited to the present instance.

Now, as Von der Goltz sees it, any military organization must reflect something of the national temperament. On the one hand, there are the hard-and-fast Prussian tactics, in which a mechanical precision of fire is everything; and, on the other hand, there are the nervous tactics of the Latin, with all the stress on a knightly and intrepid sword-play. As for ourselves, we have been used to a dangerous fencing with crafty warriors whose strength lies in their very weakness, in systematic flight, in a baffling strike-and-run attack, with the enemy making his escape by scattering out over a friendly terrain which serves as his protector. Under such circumstances the charges of troops or the discharge of weapons meant little. Against such antagonists and on such a terrain, any kind of battle line whatsoever was out of the question. It was not even possible to stage a battle in the strict technical sense of the term. This present conflict, or, to be more accurate, this man-hunt, this monstrous beating of the bush about the prey represented by Canudos,[9] was accordingly to be reduced to a matter of fierce attacks, watchful waiting, sudden skirmishes, engagements on the spur of the moment, from which it was absurd to assume that the principal phases of the classic battle would emerge, from the vio-

[9] Cf. pp. 215 and 414.

lent gunfire at the beginning to the delirious epilogue of the bayonet charge. In view of the kind of man the enemy was and the terrain on which it was fought, this war should have been in the decisive hands of a revolutionary strategist, an innovator. In this battle there were to arise tumultuously, in a simultaneous, interpenetrating admixture, all those situations which any military force may expect in the course of its operations, but which are ordinarily distinct—at ease, on the march, in battle. In this case the marching army had to be prepared to meet the enemy at every bend of the road; it had to be prepared to see him springing up suddenly within its own ranks; it had to take its ease while drawn up for battle.

In the face of conditions imperious as these, there was no deliberation on the part of the command. Having drawn up his three columns, the commanding officer merely took his place at the head of them. Against the subtle wits of the jagunços, he was pitting the unwieldy strength of his three solid phalanges—unarmed men bearing magnificent arms. Now, a military leader ought to be something of a psychologist. However mechanized a soldier may become through discipline, tending toward the sinister ideal of the *homunculus,* a bundle of bones covered by a bundle of muscles, unconscious energies on rigid levers, without nerves, without temperament, without a will of his own, reacting like an automaton to the bugle's call, he for all of that becomes another being when subjected to the emotions of war; and this march through the backlands was calculated to arouse those emotions at every instant. Following trails that are unfamiliar to him, surrounded by desert wilds, our Brazilian soldier, who is courageous enough when facing an enemy, becomes a coward, a prey to fears, when that enemy is a hidden one, who shows his presence without being seen as he lies in ambush. As a consequence, if an advance-guard skirmish ordinarily serves as a salutary warning to the troops behind, under these abnormal circumstances it becomes a peril. The frightened detachments almost invariably break ranks in sudden confusion and, by an instinctive reflex, tend to make for the rear.

These unavoidable contingencies ought all of them to have been foreseen. By way of lessening the effect of such skirmishes, the various units should have been spread out as much as possible, even though, in the first moment of the attack, it left them completely isolated. Such an arrangement would have given them more courage, through the certainty that those of their comrades who were not engaged in this particular encounter would come to their aid by attacking the enemy from the other side, which would greatly have aided morale; and, in addition to this, it would have averted the danger of a general panic and would have facilitated the handling of the men. Even though the command of the various engagements could not be vested in a single officer, the commanders of the small units being more effectively left to their own initiative, to act in accordance with the circumstances of the moment, this extensive subdivision of the troops was nonetheless imperative. What was to be done was to parody the normal mode of warfare of the enemy, with a formation running parallel to his, but subject to better discipline, and following the same open style of fighting. This was the only method capable of reducing the chances of defeat, the only one to counteract the effect of sudden ambuscades, by creating better conditions for dealing with them; it was, in short, the one method that would assure victory in the end, through the only means by which a victory could be won, namely, a series of partial attacks, one after another.

To sum up: the expeditionary force should have broken up from the time it set out on the march from its base of operations and, gradually closing in on the fanatics, should have come together again at Canudos. It did just the opposite of this. It set out in unified columns, in mass formation, by brigades, and blithely continued on its way. But it was to be broken up soon enough, suddenly—at Canudos.

ON THE MARCH TO CANUDOS

It was under these unfavorable conditions that they set out, on January 12, 1897, taking the Cambaio Road. This highway is at once the shortest and the most uneven route. It is deceptive at first, appearing to be a prolongation of the valley of the Cariacá, surrounded by fertile fields and shaded by large thickets which are a harbinger of the real forests to come. After one has gone along for a few miles, however, its unevenness becomes apparent; it is now a rocky trail, and the nearer one approaches the Acarú Mountains, the more impassible it grows. From here on it curves to the east, crossing the highlands by three successive slopes until one reaches the farm site of the "Lagem de Dentro," at an altitude of nearly a thousand feet above the valley.

Two days were wasted in reaching this point, for the artillery slowed the march. The Krupps lumbered up the incline with difficulty, while the sappers up ahead repaired the roadway, ridding it of stumps and rubbish and clearing winding paths to avoid the steeper declivities; and, although success or failure depended upon their mobility, the men found themselves trapped and paralyzed by the dragging movement of these huge masses of metal.

Having passed "Lagem de Dentro" and the divide between the banks of the Itapicurú and the Vasa-Barris, the road slopes downward. It now becomes all the more difficult by reason of those counterforts, where the seasonal tributaries of the Bendegó start.[10] The catch basin of the latter stream now comes in view, linking the fringes of the Acarú, Grande, and Athanasio ranges, which come together here in a huge curve. The expeditionary force then descended into this valley, which is deep as a pit, until it came to another farm, "Ipueiras," where it encamped. This was a foolhardy thing to do. Surrounded as it was by rocky ridges, the camp afforded a target for the enemy from all sides, should the latter appear suddenly on top the hills. Happily, the jagunços had not come as far as this; and the next morning, heading directly northward, the troops continued in the direction of "Penedo," having escaped from a very grave peril.

They had gone halfway now, and the roads were becoming worse, with innumerable trails that wound among the hills, now steeply rising and now descending in great open grottoes, without shade.

As far as "Mulungú," five miles beyond "Penedo," the sappers continued to clear the way for the cannons, the march still slowed to the lagging pace of the artillery division, whereas the one thing that was called for was the utmost haste. The landscape was now beginning to display telltale signs; the remains of bonfires along the road and farmhouses in ashes showed that the enemy had been there. In "Mulungú," at night, the enemy's presence became evident, and the entire camp was alarmed. Under cover of darkness the faces of spies had been glimpsed in the vicinity—it was no more than a glimpse, but the soldiers slept with their weapons on them. And at dawn of the seventeenth this expedition, now stuck in the mountains and still far from an objective which it should have reached in three days' marching, was subjected to yet another and terrible torture. Their provisions ran out, and the two remaining oxen had to be slaughtered to make a meal for the five-hundred-odd men. This in itself was as good as a battle lost, a defeat on the march, before they had fired a shot. To go on to Canudos, a few miles distant, was their only salvation. It was a battle for their very lives.

To add to their misfortunes, the pack-drivers whom they had hired in Monte Santo now slipped away during the night; while under the urgent pretext of going in search of munitions, the commissary of that town, who was with the expedition, left for parts unknown—and never came back.

There was one, however, who saved the day, and with it the tradition of backland loyalty. He was the guide, Domingos Jesuino, who conducted

[10] [Cf. p. 18.]

them to the "Rancho das Pedras" ahead, where they pitched camp. They were about five miles from Canudos now. Looking northward from the camp at night, an observer might have been able to make out in the distance certain shimmering lights here and there, now gleaming and now extinguished, intermittently, lights that were very high up, like stars in the mist. They showed where the enemy positions were. The next morning those positions were to become visible, and imposing ones they were.

III

MOUNT CAMBAIO

The rock masses of Mount Cambaio now rose up in front of them, capriciously formed, deeply cut by long, circular, trenchlike defiles, or rising in successive terraces which resemble the huge berms of some ruined bastion built by Titans.

The simile is quite exact. In this portion of the backlands these freakish aspects of the earth are common enough. This and none other is the explanation that lies behind those tales of "enchanted cities" in Baía; and in this case the backwoodsman's fantasy has led to serious investigations on the part of scholars, resulting in the publication of a number of studies which it would be out of place to mention here.[11]

Let it not be thought that these simple souls have been guilty of an imaginative exaggeration in this regard. The phenomena in question have exceeded the expectations of those same grave investigators who have pursued their researches on the spot, representing learned societies and institutes which were quite excited about the matter, finding it a most interesting subject for debate. Cool-headed observers who, traveling light of baggage, have crossed the valley of the Vasa-Barris, have stopped short in astonishment upon finding themselves face to face with "mountains made of stones laid naturally one upon another to form fortresses and inexpugnable redoubts, with such perfection that it appeared to be a work of art."[12]

At times this illusion is still further deepened. Vast necropolises then arise; for these hills, whose structure is revealed in sharp-pointed protuberances, heaps of stone blocks, and whimsically severed rocky ridges, do indeed appear to be great cities of the dead; and it is with trepidation that the backwoodsman gallops past them, without taking his spurs from his horse's flanks, imagining as he does that therein lies a silent, tragic population of "other-world souls."

[11] See Vol. X and other volumes of the *Revista do Instituto Histórico e Geográphico do Brasil*.
[12] Lieutenant Colonel Durval de Aguiar, *Descripções praticas*. . . . .

Of this type are the "little houses" which are to be seen in the vicinity of the Aracaty Range, near the highway which runs from Geremoabo to Bom Conselho; and there are others throughout the region, conferring upon these melancholy landscapes a singularly mysterious appearance.

BASTIONS "SINE CALCII LINIMENTI"[13]

Mount Cambaio is one of these rude monuments. Certainly, no one would discover in it the geometric lines of curtains or parapets or bulging redans surrounded by fosses. These barbarous redoubts were not so finished a piece of work as all that. They reflected the character of those who manned them. At a distance, with the rock ledges indistinct and the indentations made by the ravines smoothed over, the general appearance of the mountain would, indeed, give the observer the impression that here, running along the edges, mounting in successive terraces, and spreading out over the slopes, were the countermures of very old castles, which had seen assault after assault, and which had been dismantled, shaken to their very foundations, being reduced now to these heaps of stone clustered in enormous semicircles, to row on tow of plinths and towers and truncated pilasters, which, bulking large at a distance, took on the picturesque appearance of great fallen colonnades.

For Cambaio is a mountain in ruins. It rises as a shapeless mass, splitting under the periodic lash of sudden tempests and scorching suns, cleft and disjointed—in a slow and age-old disintegration.

The road to Canudos does not skirt the mountain; it runs directly up its side, along a steep path hemmed in by cliffs, to come out finally in a narrow, tunnel-like pass. And it was through this pass that the troops had to file.

At this hour of the morning the mountain was a dazzling sight. Beating down on the chips and splintered slabs, the sun's rays, intense and vibrant, were refracted over the heights, giving the illusion of feverish movement as they fell on the brightly gleaming weapons; it was as if a numerous force of men at a distance was preparing for battle. It was in vain, meanwhile, that binoculars roamed over the deserted mountainside. There was only the threatening aspect of the earth itself to betray the presence of the enemy. He was digging in as usual. Flat on the ground, crouching in the folds of the earth, squeezed into their dugouts—scattered, unmoving, waiting—fingers on the triggers of their guns, the sertanejos remained there, silently testing their rifle sights, eyes fixed on the distant column

[13] [I.e., without limestone veins or formations.]

down below as it marched along behind the scouts who were cautiously exploring the neighborhood.

They came on slowly until they had reached the first abrupt slopes half-way up the side, slowly and in straggling formation, handicapped by the heavy cannons, the soldiers panting and bent over as they took turns with the helpless mules in dragging them up the incline. And it was under these circumstances that the enemy surprised them. From their nooks and hiding-places, from thickets here and there, over the top of their rude breastworks, or lying flat on the sloping ground, the jagunços now made their presence known with a sudden burst of gunfire.

The entire expedition had been trapped all along the line, beneath the trenches of Mount Cambaio.

FIRST ENGAGEMENT

The opening of the engagement was accompanied by loud shouts, as the customary *viva*'s to the "Good Jesus" and "Our Counselor" mingled with scandalous oaths and obscene insults, among which one defiant phrase stood out which in the course of the campaign was invariably to resound, like an ironic refrain: "Come on, you government *weaklings!*"

The entire column wavered; the vanguard came to a halt and was about to fall back but was prevented from doing so by an imperious voice, that of Major Febronio. That officer, bursting through the alarmed ranks, brought some order into the fray and stiffened the resistance with a thundering response, and an admirable one it was in view of the disadvantageous conditions. Rapidly loaded, the cannons bombarded the backwoodsmen pell-mell; and the latter, upon beholding for the first time these mighty weapons, whose effect was tenfold, which could even pierce rocks, at once took to their heels in dismay. Taking advantage of this retreat, the hundred-odd men of the Thirty-third Infantry promptly launched an attack. Stumbling, slipping on the slabs, running around them or leaping over them, dashing ahead through the gullies, in any direction, the soldiers scrambled up the slopes; and, after that, the battle line for the attack was formed, an irregular, swaying one, stretching out from the Ninth Battalion on the right to the Sixteenth Battalion and the Baian police detachment on the left.

The fight in a few minutes became a general one; and, as was to have been foreseen, the lines broke in contact with the obstacles of the terrain.[14] It was a very disorderly advance. Separated from one another, dragging themselves up the cliffs by force of hand, their weapons clanging, their

[14] Cf. p. 308.

rifles in their bandoleers knocking against their teeth, the combatants came on tumultuously, without the least semblance of formation, battalions and companies mingled in confusion—human waves raging against the hills, a surge of bodies, accompanied by rifle fire, glints of steel, and deafening explosions, with the shrill notes of the bugle high above all, sounding the charge.

Down below, on the slope where the artillery was, the mules and their drivers, frightened by the rain of bullets, broke through the firing line, spilling hampers and luggage as they went, and galloped away or else went tumbling down the steep incline. Their example was followed by the rest of the drivers who, deaf to commands given them at the point of a revolver, insisted on fleeing, thereby adding to the tumult that prevailed.

On the heights, at a distance, along the back of the mountains the sertanejos now reappeared. There seemed to be two kinds of fighters in their ranks: those who ran swiftly up and down the roads, bobbing up and dropping out of sight from moment to moment, and those who remained stationed in their positions high up on the mountain. Taking advantage of these positions, they had an ingenious method of making up for the shortage of weapons and the time that it took to load the few they did possess. Forming groups of three or four about a single marksman, they sat in the bottom of the trench and, without being seen, passed the loaded weapons up to him. In this manner, if the marksman fell, one of the others was ready to take his place, and the attacking soldiers would see the same torso, apparently, rising up again immediately, before the smoke had cleared away, and once more aiming a musket at them. They would let him have another round, and once again they would see this fantastic marksman drop, only to rise miraculously, invulnerable and terrifying.

JOÃO GRANDE

This stratagem was discovered by those small attacking parties which made their way up to the highest positions. They arrived there one or two at a time. The elusiveness of the enemy and the nature of the terrain in themselves imposed upon the troops a tactical distribution of forces best adapted to the conditions; and this circumstance, together with the small range of the enemy's weapons, gave them a comparative immunity. The only obstacle in the way of the assault was the ruggedness of the ground. The effect of their fire was deadened by the cliffs. As for the jagunços, they did not wait to receive the brunt of it. Being certain of the inferiority of their rude equipment, they were merely bent, it seemed, upon leading their adversary to expend here the major portion of his munitions which had been destined for Canudos. What they did was to feign an open battle. There could be seen moving about among them a burly but active Negro, a short rifle in his hands. This was their leader, João Grande. He it was who designed their maneuvers, making use of all the wiles of a bandit long skilled in hinterland warfare; and it was his movements, his running leaps and primitive stratagems, that the backland rebels imitated. They could be seen now advancing, now falling back, now scattering out, and now forming in groups again, filing along in close formation or with ranks extremely thinned; crawling along on their hands and knees, tumbling over the slopes, running up, running down, attacking, fleeing, dropping dead in their tracks many of them, while others, badly wounded, rolled all the way down, into the midst of the soldiers, who received them with their rifle butts. At times, they entirely disappeared from sight.

The bullets continued to crack aimlessly against the rigid framework of the mountain. The more rapid advance detachments, meanwhile, overcoming the difficulties of the terrain, continued to make their way up the mountainside until they met with a sudden irruption of the enemy. Some of them then came to a halt, while others, seized with panic, even fell back, their disheartened officers making no attempt to inspire them with fresh courage. These officers have been spared in the official reports, where their names do not appear, but they were not spared the bitter comments of their comrades-in-arms. The greater part of the troops rallied and broke through the musket fire, falling upon the fanatics at close-up, decimating their ranks, striking terror into them, and sending them scurrying over the hills in all directions.

Finally, the crude rebel chieftain proceeded to draw his men up for what he believed would be the decisive hand-to-hand combat. With his gorilla-like features,[15] he could be seen striding boldly at the head of his suddenly congregated band. With a fine display of heroism, they now advanced upon the artillery but were stopped by the explosion of a case shot, which blew the nearest of their leaders to bits, while the rest fled back precipitately to their former positions, which were by now in the possession of the advance guard of the troops. Contingents of the latter, made up of men from all the corps, now leaped down into the last of the trenches to the right, losing as they did so the officer who had commanded them up to then, Wenceslau Leal.

The mountain had been taken after three hours of fighting. The victory, however, was due to blind courage coupled with the most utter lack of discipline in the matter of firing aim—and it is readily understandable

[15] [It is of interest to compare the North American gangster's term, "gorilla."]

why the order of the day which was later issued should have given chief credit to the men in the ranks. Upon the fleeing jagunços small groups of soldiers without any officers poured an aimless rifle fire, with all the fierceness, alacrity, and bluster of sportsmen on the last lap of a wild-boar hunt.

The jagunços fled and were pursued. In the meantime the artillery down below, drawn by hand, was being trundled up the slopes. The crossing of the mountain had been effected, and, aside from the expenditure of ammunition, at small loss—four dead and twenty-odd wounded. In exchange, the sertanejos left, by strict count, one hundred and fifteen corpses.

A TRAGIC EPISODE

This hecatomb was completed by a tragic episode. The tumultuous affray had a theatrical denouement. It happened as they reached the last spurs at the foot of the mountain.

There on the rugged slope, scarred with holes, was an enormous stone slab held between two others and slanting obliquely, with one end barely touching the ground, being supported by sheer attrition, all of which gave it the appearance of a tumbled dolmen. In front of this rude shelter was a countermure of living rock; and, inside it, a considerable number of sertanejos—some forty, according to one eyewitness[16]—had taken refuge, probably those who possessed the last remaining rounds of ammunition for the *trabucos*. The protecting earth had afforded them this one last stronghold, and they made use of it. They opened a scattering fire upon their pursuers, bringing them to a halt for a moment, as well as the artillery at a distance, which now prepared to bombard these foolhardy ones. It required but a single round. The grenade missed its mark slightly and struck instead one of the rocks on which the slab rested, shattering it, splitting it open from top to bottom. Deprived of its support, the stone fell heavily with a dull crash, upon the unfortunate ones beneath, burying them.

The march was resumed. As for the defenders of Mount Cambaio, they were evidencing a growing exhaustion as they neared Canudos, as was to be perceived from their diminishing musket fire, until at last no more was to be seen of them.

IV

ON THE "LITTLE TABLELANDS"

It was afternoon when the columns arrived at the "Little Tablelands," almost on the edge of the settlement, and, failing to utilize the advantage

[16] Dr. Albertazzi, surgeon of the expedition.

they had gained by pursuing the enemy, they halted here and pitched camp. Weakened by the engagement they had just fought and having had nothing to eat since the evening before, they were barely able to quench their thirst in the diminutive Lake Cipó.[17] Nevertheless, as a result of their accumulated fatigue, and possibly also under the illusion of having won a victory, they proceeded to take their ease, without noticing that the jagunços were keeping a counterround about them. The news of the attack had reached the settlement with the fugitives, and by way of absorbing the shock of the imminent invasion, a large number of combatants had set out from the village, taking up their positions unperceived in the caatingas and gradually drawing near the encampment.

Night now surrounded the sleeping troops, as a terrible enemy stood guard over them.

SECOND ENGAGEMENT

The next morning, however, there was still no sign of the foe, as the columns, forming quickly, prepared for a final assault upon the settlement, after a quarter of an hour's marching over a terrain which here is level and unencumbered.

Before they got under way, a slight contretemps occurred. A shrapnel shell became stuck in the bore of one of the cannons, and all efforts to dislodge it were unavailing. The best of expedients was then hit upon, that of firing the Krupp in the direction of Canudos. It would be a knock at the doors of the village, noisily announcing an importunate and dangerous visitor. And so the shot was fired. And at that moment the troops were themselves assaulted from all sides! The episode of Uauá was being repeated. Abandoning their defective firearms for poles, wagon bars,[18] scythes, pitchforks, long goads, and knives with broad blades, the sertanejos leaped to their feet with a cry, all at once, as if the firing of the cannon had been the signal agreed upon for the attack.

Fortunately, the expeditionaries, drawn up in marching order, had their weapons ready at hand, and they let the enemy have a sustained and running fire. But the jagunços did not fall back. Instead, they hurled themselves into the gaps between the platoons, and for the first time the soldiers had a chance to behold from close up the swarthy faces of their antagonists, the sullen faces of mountaineers.

The first victim was a corporal of the Ninth Regiment. He died killing his assailant; the jagunço who struck him down with his cowboy's cattle

---

[17] See pp. 218 and 418.

[18] [I.e., a bar fastened in the side of a cart or wagon to sustain the load (*fueiro*).]

prong[19] was himself transfixed on the soldier's bayonet, as the attackers surged forward like a wave over the two bodies. Leading them was a powerful mameluco with a bronzed, freckled face and the build of a gladiator, towering above the fray. This terrible warrior was not destined to go down in history; his very name has been forgotten—his name but not the proud cry which rang out above all the others, above all the din of battle, as he leaped upon the cannon to the right and threw his muscular arms about it, as if he were strangling a monster: "See, you swine, what it means to have courage!"

The men who manned the gun recoiled in terror, as the captured piece was rolled away by force of arm. Disaster was imminent. The commander of the expedition, who, everything goes to show, was the best soldier in the outfit, realized this. He valiantly encouraged his dumfounded men and, by way of setting them an example, dashed after the captors of the cannon. A brutal hand-to-hand struggle now took place—a struggle that was all but noiseless, without weapons, being limited to fist blows and the grappling of tangled bodies, accompanied by panting groans and the hoarse death rattles of those who were being strangled, the crash of violent falls.

The cannon was retaken and restored to its original position; but the situation did not improve. The jagunços could hardly be said to have been thrown back. They had, rather, fallen back in a movement which was not flight but a dangerous decoy; and they now circulated about in the scant underbrush, their faces fleetingly, indistinctly glimpsed for a moment, appearing and disappearing in those patches which were clear of boughs. Once more scattered and elusive, they hurled at the enemy crude and resounding projectiles—horntips, round pebbles, and the heads of nails—taken from their ancient arsenal of death, long since fallen into disuse.[20] They renewed the duel from a distance, pitting their flintlock muskets and their long-barreled *trabucos* against the death-dealing modern rifle. They were returning to their accustomed mode of warfare, which consisted in prolonging the action indefinitely. This was a more serious way of fighting than that represented by the violent attack they had just made. The struggle was now to become a cruelly monotonous one, marked by no events of outstanding importance but by a repetition of small incidents which were tiring in the extreme, until the enemy was completely exhausted and, with forces still relatively intact, should be finally overcome by the sheer weariness of diminutive victories and, like a hangman, grow tragi-

[19] [The *ferrão de vaqueiro;* for a description see p. 145.]

[20] The incidents of this day are taken from the trustworthy statement of Dr. Albertazzi.

cally disgusted with the act of killing, his fists battered and soft from all the blows he had struck, his men thrown away on dubious skirmishes with a vacuum. The situation was becoming decidedly hopeless.

The invaders had one despairing recourse left them: that of boldly shifting the field of combat and falling upon the settlement in a give-and-take attack, with these fearless warriors on their flanks, while perhaps up ahead, at the entrance of the village, there were reinforcements lying in wait to bar their passage. But in the course of the fighting along the mile and a quarter which lay between them and the settlement their munitions, which had been so prodigally wasted on Mount Cambaio, might well give out, and they would not be able to come within halfway of achieving their objective in an encounter without firearms—not with the weakened muscles of these famished troops, burdened with some seventy wounded comrades who were useless in a fight and whose presence merely added to the confusion. Moreover, an effective preliminary bombardment was out of the question, seeing that they had not more than twenty rounds of ammunition left for the artillery.

A retreat was now urgent and inevitable. Calling his staff together in the midst of the fight, the commanding officer outlined the situation to them and informed them that they must choose between the horns of a dilemma: they must either carry on the struggle to the point of sacrificing themselves completely or they must abandon it at once. The choice was for the latter, under the express condition that not a single weapon should be left behind, not a single wounded man or unburied body. Such a retreat, nonetheless, stood in contradiction to the direct results of the battle. As on the preceding day, the losses suffered by the enemy were out of all proportion to those inflicted on the troops. Of the latter, not more than four had been killed and thirty-odd wounded, whereas, while the exact number of their casualties was unknown, the ranks of the jagunços had been decimated. One of the surgeons[21] hastily counted more than three hundred corpses among them. The impure waters of Lake Cipó were stained with red, and the sun beating down upon its surface isolated it in sinister fashion against the dark grayish-brown of the parched earth, as a huge bloodstain.

JOÃO ABBADE'S LIGHTNING-STRUCK BRIGADE

A retreat was their salvation; but risking all by an attack upon the settlement would possibly have spelled victory.

[21] Dr. Everard Albertazzi.

Let us turn to the archives and, relying upon the testimony of supporting witnesses, have a look at one of the unusual incidents of this campaign. Some time after the engagement on the Little Tablelands, the inhabitants of Canudos, impressed by the intensity of the skirmishes, became alarmed; and so, foreseeing what the consequences would be, should the soldiers appear suddenly and fall upon the timid religionists, João Abbade[22] proceeded to assemble all the able-bodied men that were left, about six hundred of them, and started out to go to the aid of his comrades. When he was about halfway there, however, his column found itself unexpectedly under fire. What had happened was that the soldiers at the original scene of combat, firing upon the enemy there, did not prove to be good marksmen, and most of their shots went very high, over the heads of the combatants, carrying as far as the range of the weapons permitted. Now, all these spent bullets fell in the midst of João Abbade's troop, and the jagunços were bewildered at seeing their companions falling as if shot, although there was, apparently, no enemy in sight. The thin decorticated shrubbery all about did not afford any opportunity for an ambush, and the nearest hills, as they could see, were barren and deserted. Yet the bullets kept falling, incessantly, here, there, from in front of them, from the side, pouring down on the surprised brigade like a silent rain of lightning. A superstitious fear then cast its shadow over these energetic countenances, as they saw their companions dropping dead around them. In astonishment, they turned their gaze upward to the dazzling heavens, where the bullets were descending in invisible parabolas; and after that, there was no restraining them. They now rushed impetuously back to Canudos, creating terror with the news of what had happened to them.

There was no doubt about it: an enemy who had at his disposal such means of destruction as this would be there any moment, close on the heels of the last defenders. The Counselor's spell was broken. Crazed with fear, the naïve populace in a few moments lost the beliefs which had laid hold of them. Bands of fugitives carrying hastily scrambled bundles now fled at top speed, across the square and down the alleys, making for the caatingas; not even their most respected leaders were able to prevent their flight. Meanwhile the women, in great disarray, screaming, sobbing, clamoring, and creating an indescribable hubbub—but still under the Counselor's spell—waving their holy relics and praying, thronged about the door of the "Sanctuary," imploring the evangelist to come out and speak to them.

[22] See pp. 159, 168, 218–19, 241–42, 277, 372, 429.

THE COUNSELOR WORKS ANOTHER MIRACLE

But Antonio Conselheiro, who even in normal times avoided looking a woman in the face, at such junctures as this insisted upon a complete separation. Followed by a half-dozen of the faithful, he came out on the high scaffolding of the new church and then had the ladder withdrawn. Down below, the agitated group was praying, weeping, uttering imprecations. The disdainful apostle did not so much as glance at them, as he strode impassively along the swaying, creaking boards. Gazing out over the rebellious village, where the deserters of the faith were in haste to flee, he prepared himself for an inevitable martyrdom.

At this moment news came that the troops were leaving. It was a miracle. Disorder ended in a prodigy.

V

RETREAT

The retreat had, in fact, begun. With all hope of success gone, the only alternative for the ill-fated expedition was to remain there wavering between defeat and victory, fighting a battle which as a matter of fact had no victories to offer, as the vanquished continued to win at every step forward—an indomitable enemy treading his own soil and coming off the victor in every armed skirmish, at every turn of the road.

Major Febronio's retreat, the truth is, even though, by reason of the limited field of operations involved, it may not be comparable to other memorable events of a similar character, nevertheless, by reason of the circumstances surrounding it, is one of the most stirring episodes in our military history. The troops had fought there for two whole days without rations of any kind—two days with one night of alarms in between, a deceptive armistice. Their ranks were now encumbered with some seventy wounded, while a large number of others, severely crippled, were scarcely capable of bearing arms. The most able-bodied ones had to leave the firing line to drag the cannons or had to stagger along beneath stacks of rifles, or carry the wounded and dying on litters. At their rear, a rebellious mob; in front of them, a march of some sixty miles through a backlands desert, thick with ambuscades.

Upon perceiving what was afoot, the jagunços promptly gave pursuit. They were commanded now by an unusually fierce mestizo whose bravery was unexcelled, Pajehú by name.[23] A full-blooded cafuso, he was endowed with an impulsive temperament which combined the tendencies of the lower races from which he sprang. He was the full-blown type of primitive

[23] See pp. 158, 277, 301, 303, 308, 371, 372, 428.

fighter, fierce, fearless, and naïve, at once simple-minded and evil, brutal and infantile, valiant by instinct, a hero without being aware of the fact—in brief, a fine example of recessive atavism, with the retrograde form of a grim troglodyte, stalking upright here with the same intrepidity with which, ages ago, he had brandished a stone hatchet at the entrance to his cave.

It was this wily barbarian who now distributed his companions through the caatingas, along the side of the road over which the column would have to pass.

The troops were compelled to fight as they marched. Having fired a parting round, the assailants had begun filing along the paths that ran up the side of the mountain; and in the course of this movement, as serious a one as any that there is in war, the last remnants of military tactics were cast to the winds, with no heed being paid to the classic precept which stresses a staircase formation such as will permit the fighting units to relieve one another in repulsing the enemy. The fact is, the expedition had completely lost any semblance of discipline, officers and men being now faced with the same sacrifices. Meanwhile, the commanding officer, whose courage never failed him, sought out for himself the most dangerous posts, while captains and subalterns, shouldering rifles, mingled with the privates in firing with no word of command, and with a sergeant, in violation of all the rules of warfare, leading the van.

It was in such formation as this that they once more entered the defiles of Mount Cambaio. Here they were faced with the same perilous crossing that they had made before, along a path which now ran through narrow passes, and now, halfway up the mountainside, came out on a precipice overhanging a chasm. Between the cliffs the road would narrow, only to sprawl out aimlessly again along the slopes; and all the while, overlooking the entire route, were those enemy trenches high up on the mountain. The landscape, indeed, presented but one novelty: lying face downward or supine on the rocks, at the mouths of their dugouts or scattered over the slopes, were the bodies of the jagunços who had been slain the day before; and their surviving companions were now passing over them like an avenging horde of demons over a multitude of recumbent specters.

The enemy did not defy the last grenades by attacking the column in force; instead, he flanked it from above, leaving his formidable weapon—the earth—to bear the brunt of the struggle. And the earth did not fail him. The curiboca who had parted with his rifle or lost his cattle prong in the fray had but to glance about him—and the mountain was an arsenal. Lying all around or heaped in unsteady piles were huge blocks of stone, ready to be tumbled down the mountainside with great violence. He made good use of them. Transforming his faithful musket into a lever, he pried them loose, and these monoliths would then sway and fall, come crashing down, at first with uncertain direction, following the depressions in the terrain, but gaining momentum as they fell, following the line of maximum declivity, until they finally came bounding headlong, knocking against other rocks and reducing them to splinters, to descend like monstrous cannon balls on the heads of the terrified troops. Beneath this avalanche of stone, the men could only save themselves by huddling against the bends of the road halfway up the side. Weariness, to tell the truth, had done more than the enemy to defeat them. And, to top it all, a blazing sun, the crude light of a tropical day here in this barren, rocky region, appeared to have set the entire mountain on fire. In this dazzling light Nature all around them was motionless in the spasm of the summer heat. The very shots they fired scarcely broke the silence, for there were no echoes in this rarefied, irrespirable air; the dull sound of their cannon awoke no resonances. Yet here, amid this universal quiet, human brutality was at work; the boulders came tumbling down.

It was slow business making their way through the trenches; although the sertanejos, the truth of the matter is, could hardly be said to have attacked them. Leaping about gleefully like a lot of monkeys on the rampage, the backwoodsmen appeared to have transformed the battle into a sorry sport, that of heaving stones on the foe. Noisily and riotously they dashed here and there over the heights, while the troops down below continued on their way, the sorry actors in the epilogue of a drama that was very badly staged. All the excitement of the last two days, all the engagements and skirmishes, seemed now of a sudden to have ended in a sinister brawl. Harder to bear than gunfire were the ironic and irritating shouts, the long, shrill catcalls and bursts of laughter, as if they were being pursued by a gang of incorrigible hoodlums.

At length, after three hours of marching, they reached Bendegó de Baixo. The admirable location of this place stood them in good stead, the small plateau over which the highway flattened out affording a more efficacious means of defense. It was here that the last engagement occurred, at nightfall, in the dim twilight of the backlands. It was a brief but formidable one. The jagunços now made a last attack on the artillery, with the object of taking it from the troops. The machine guns, however, pouring down a fire upon them, drove them off, and having been thus routed by grapeshot, leaving a score of dead behind them, they disappeared in the direction of the lowlands, swallowed up in the night.

This was the last of the skirmishes, and it ended in a providential incident. Alarmed, it may be, by the bullets, a herd of wild goats invaded the camp, almost at the moment that the defeated sertanejos retreated. This was a fortunate diversion. The men, absolutely exhausted, now gave wild chase to the swift-footed animals, delirious with joy at the prospect of a banquet after two days of enforced fasting. And an hour later these unhappy heroes, ragged, filthy, repulsive-looking, could be seen squatting about their bonfires, tearing the half-cooked flesh as the flickering light from the coals glowed on their faces, like a band of famished cannibals at a barbarous repast.

The expedition went on to Monte Santo early the next day. There was not an able-bodied man among them. Even those who bore their wounded companions were limping at every step, their feet bleeding, slashed with thorns and gashed by the rocks. Wearing their broad-brimmed straw hats, their uniforms in shreds, some of them tragically ridiculous, their nudity barely concealed by their tattered capes, but with some attempt still at military formation, they entered the village like a band of "quitters," routed by the fierce suns and fleeing the desolation and misery of the droughts.[24]

The population received them in silence.

VI

PROCESSION OF THE LITTERS

On the afternoon of that very day the slopes of Mount Cambaio were again astir with life. This time, however, it was not the clash of armed combat but the sound of mournful litanies that was to be heard. Slowly, bound for Canudos, a long procession came down the mountain. These were not warriors, but believers, bearing on their shoulders, in rude litters made of round wooden stakes bound with liana stalks, the bodies of the martyrs for the faith. The entire day had been spent in the search for these bodies, a sorrowful task in which the entire population took part. They had explored every winding nook and crevice, every bit of tangled underbrush between the rocks, all the deep caverns and open clefts.

Many of the combatants, sliding down the mountainside, had fallen into caves and hollows; others, their clothes caught on the sharp-pointed rocks, had been left dangling over chasms; and accordingly, going down into the deepest holes and climbing to the top of the steep, rocky ridges, the jagunços had proceeded to collect the corpses of their unfortunate com-

[24] [See p. 109.]

rades. Night fell before their pious errand was completed. A few bodies only were missing—those that the troops had burned. The funeral procession then continued on its way to Canudos.

Very low on the horizon the sun was slowly setting, gilding the extremity of the far-lying plains with its rutilant glow; and its last rays, above the darkness which had already settled on the lowlands, now fell upon the mountain's back, illuminating it for a few moments. The fugitive gleams likewise illuminated the procession as it went along to the cadence of prayers. Imperceptibly, they glided upward as the shadows slowly mounted behind, until they reached the top, where the last beams sparkled on the lofty summits, glowing for an instant like enormous tapers, soon to be tremblingly extinguished in the dimness of twilight.

The first stars were shining, and gleaming now on the heights was Orion's resplendent cross, rising over the backlands.

CHAPTER V

THE MOREIRA CESAR EXPEDITION

I

THIS latest failure on the part of the forces of law and order, unforeseen by everyone, coincided with a critical period in our history. Still suffering from the lamentable consequences of a bloody civil war which had come to a close amid an uninterrupted series of seditions and revolts that had lasted since the first days of the new regime, Brazilian society in 1897 was one highly favorable to the work of revolutionary and disruptive elements. Whoever later shall undertake, in the light of significant documents, to weigh and define the interesting psychology of this era will have to bring out the inadaptability of the people to the higher legislation of the newly inaugurated political regime. It was as if that regime, by way of unduly speeding a process of slow evolution, had chiefly succeeded in diffusing over the country, which was still languishing from the wasting sickness of the monarchy, an intense spirit of disorder, thereby starting the Republic headlong on a downward path, with disasters appearing at rhythmic intervals, like the stages of some recurring malady.

The civil government set up in 1894 did not possess the essential basis of an organized public opinion. It found the nation divided into victors and vanquished; and it remained impotent when it came to correcting a situation which, without being openly revolutionary, was certainly not normal, and in dealing with which a resort to force and a reliance upon the tranquil influence of laws were alike unavailing. It was faced with a society which, proceeding by leaps and bounds from conditions of the utmost sloth to those of the most rigid discipline, from incessant conspiracies to states of siege, reflected the sharp contrast that prevailed between its lack of organization on the intellectual side and its high degree of political organization which the people were not capable of comprehending. And, inasmuch as it was not possible to substitute the slow process of evolution in elevating the intellectual to the level of the political, what inevitably happened was that the higher significance of the democratic principles became debased—turned into sophistries, inverted, annulled.

FLORIANO PEIXOTO

There was no way of halting this downward course. The preceding government, that of Marshal Floriano Peixoto,[1] owing to the circumstances that surrounded it, played a combative role, performed a work of demolition; but, as the indiscipline resulting from a series of seditious movements abated, the social instability grew and in a manner flagrantly contradicted and violated the pre-established program. Thus it was that, as a consequence of the suppression of a *coup d'état* in violation of constitutional guaranties, the procedure of suspending those guaranties was instituted; as a consequence of adhering tenaciously to the Constitution, the Constitution itself was set aside. With *legality* made the touchstone of all policy, that word came to be extended in such a way as to justify all crimes, was converted into the paradoxical formula of a lawless land; so that the unyielding iron marshal—involuntarily, it may be, for his highly original character is still an intricate enigma—may be said, in a manner of speaking, to have undone the work to which he had put his hand. In the overwhelming crises that confronted him, Floriano Peixoto made unconditional use of any means available and of any persons, no matter what their origin, who might be able to put them into effect; he acted wholly outside the bounds of national opinion, amid the passions and interests of a party which, with rare exceptions, was made up of all those ambitious mediocrities who, through a natural instinct of self-defense, sought to avoid the obligations laid upon them by a more civilized social environment. In the last days of his government he had the September rebellion to put down, one which summarized all the revolts and tumults of the preceding years; and, after this, the germs of more dangerous uprisings began slowly forming, rebellions latent as yet but ready to break out at any moment.

Floriano Peixoto destroyed, and by destroying created, rebels. He put down disorder with disorder. Upon retiring from office, he did not take with him all those who had stood by him in the most difficult hours of his government. There remained many restless ones, hardened in an intensive apprenticeship to crime, who were put out at being naturally relegated to the background. Their careers up to then had been easy ones, they were dizzy with success, and they found it hard to stop of a sudden like this; accordingly, they prepared to make the most of the present situation from within.

---

[1] [For the historical allusions here and in the following pages to events and circumstances which are difficult to summarize in a footnote, the reader may be referred to João Pandiá Calogeras, *A History of Brazil*, trans. and ed. Percy Alvin Martin (Chapel Hill: University of North Carolina Press, 1939), pp. 288–95; see also F. A. Kirkpatrick, *Latin America: A Brief History* (New York: Macmillan Co., 1939), pp. 301–3.]

What happened, then, was a common-enough instance of collective psychology. Taken by surprise, the majority of the population of the country was inert and absolutely neutral, becoming thereby a favorable vehicle for the propagation of those subversive forces which the individual citizen deplored. In accordance with an instinctive process which in the social sphere is reflective of the heritage of a remote biologic predisposition, as so well expressed in that "psychic mimicry" of which Scipio Sighele speaks, the conscientious but timid majority now took on, in part, the moral aspect of those bold mediocrities who were in the leadership. There then arose, on the public platform, in the press, and in the streets, individuals who in normal times would have been laughed into obscurity. Devoid of ideals, without any ennobling objectives, and confined in their thinking to a narrow circle of ideas in which a suspect enthusiasm for the Republic was mingled with an extemporaneous nativism[2] and with a grossly copied Jacobinism that was little in keeping with history, these agitators began living most shamefully through the exploitation of a corpse. The grave of Marshal Floriano Peixoto was transformed into an arch of alliance for the impenitent rebels, and the great man's name became the password of disorder.

The thinking majority of the country washed their hands of it all, making possible all sorts of excesses; and, in the midst of this general and criminal indifference, the disgruntled mediocrities succeeded in setting the characteristic tone for this era, which fortunately was a brief and transitory one. The dissensions that remained from the former regime were not enough for them, nor were they dismayed by a desperate economic situation. What they wanted was to increase the former and to render the latter insoluble; and, since the army, from the days of the abolitionist movement down to the proclamation of the Republic,[3] had illogically come to hold the balance of power in national affairs, they imprudently and at great pains set out to court and to capture it.

Now, of all the officers in the army, it was the colonel of infantry, Antonio Moreira Cesar, who appeared to have fallen heir to the mantle of the great subduer of revolts and to have inherited likewise his rare tenacity. Political fetishism called for idols in uniform, and he was the latest idol.

[2] [In Brazil, as in other Latin-American countries, *nativismo* (cf. *indigenismo, indianismo, americanismo*, etc.) refers sometimes, as here, to a political program based upon the wrongs and demands of the aboriginal population and sometimes to cultural forms based upon aboriginal art or with the aborigine as subject matter.]

[3] [Slavery was abolished in Brazil in 1888; the Republic was established in 1891.]

MOREIRA CESAR

Upon receiving news of the disaster, which greatly enhanced the gravity of the backlands conflict, the government could think of no one better qualified than Moreira Cesar to meet the pressing exigencies of the situation, and so he was appointed to the command of the fresh expedition of reprisal.

About the new appointee there had already grown up a legend of bravery. Having recently come from Santa Catarina, where he had played the leading role in the epilogue to the federalist Rio Grande campaign, he was possessed of an exceptional renown, being commonly greeted with acclamations and familiar nicknames in keeping with the unrestrained and unthinking fashion of the day; for this, it is to be remembered, was a period in which the most minor incidents of the civil war—a war that, by the revolt of the fleet, had been extended all the way from Rio de Janeiro Bay to the south—were still fresh in mind. Between the two extremes of Gumercindo Saraiva's intrepidity and Gomes Carneiro's self-abnegation, the opinion of the nation wavered, evidencing the most widely separated conceptions of victor and vanquished; and out of all this mental instability and confusion, all this inflamed and more than a little suspect display of emotion on the part of our people, the one thing that unmistakably emerged was a caricature of heroism, achieved through every tone of voice, every color of the palette, and under every varying aspect. The immortal heroes of a quarter of an hour, destined to the supreme honor of a statue in the public square, found themselves suddenly and unexpectedly shoved into history like the intruders that they were, without its being made quite plain whether they were saints or bandits, being overwhelmed as they were with panegyrics, on the one hand, and with insults, on the other hand, to the accompaniment of fervent dithyrambs, diabolical ironies, and irreverent invectives, as they came to take their places—from the blood pool of Inhanduhy, from the slaughter-house of Campo Osorio, from the memorable siege of Lapa, from the barricades of Pico do Diabo, or from the martial Platonism of Itararé. There were heaps of them. Legions of them. And they were all of them acclaimed, all of them roundly cursed out.

Among all these, however, Colonel Moreira Cesar was a figure apart. Enemies and admirers alike were equally taken aback when they saw him for the first time; for his personal appearance tended to detract from his fame. Low in stature, with a flabby chest over a pair of legs bowed like parentheses, he was organically ill adapted to the career he had chosen. He lacked the upright bearing and wholesome air which in a soldier constitute the physical basis of courage. Laced into his uniform, which he seldom left off, with his military cape over his narrow adolescent shoulders, he presented a still more unprepossessing appearance, his physical frailty being heightened by an inexpressive, morbid-looking countenance. There

Courtesy of the Instituto Brasileiro de Geografia e Estatística

BRAZILIAN VAQUEIRO, OR COWBOY, OF THE NORTHERN CATTLE COUNTRY

was nothing, absolutely nothing, to betray the man's surprising energy and the rare courage of which he had given proof, in this convalescent's face, without a single firm and distinctive feature—a pale face, elongated by the baldness in front above a bulging forehead, and with a pair of lifeless, mournful eyes. It was a face immobile as a waxen cast, showing that impenetrability which comes from nothing other than muscular atony.

Paroxysms of anger and the greatest bursts of energy would go unperceived there, owing to the lassitude of the tissues, which left it always fixed and rigid, impassive in appearance.

Those who saw him for the first time found it hard to believe that this mild-mannered, rather timid man, so cold in bearing and slow of gesture, could be the brilliant warrior or the heartless demon that they idealized. He did not possess the characteristics of either one or the other. Possibly the reason was that he happened to be both of them at the same time. Those who applauded him and those who railed against him thus found equal grounds to justify their opinions; for in this singular individuality there was a hostile clash of monstrous tendencies and superior qualities, both existing with the same degree of intensity. He was tenacious, patient, devoted, loyal, fearless, cruel, vindictive, ambitious: a proteiform soul confined in the frailest of bodies.

These attributes, however, were concealed by a cautious and deliberate air of reserve. One man alone had perceived them, or had succeeded in deciphering them, and that was Marshal Floriano Peixoto. There was an affinity between the two men, based upon identical inclinations. The Marshal accordingly made use of him just as Louis XI made use of Bayard, if the romantic bravery of the stainless knight may be compared to the cunning of a Fra Diavolo. Moreira Cesar was far from possessing the noble-mindedness of the former and was still further from the moral depravity of the latter. Nevertheless, it would not be an unpardonable exaggeration to look upon him as being a reduced mixture of the two. There was in him something of the great man fallen short, as if evolution in his case, engaged in the marvelous process of creating a being destined for greatness, had stopped when it came to the final selection of those rare qualities with which such a being should be endowed, and this precisely at the critical stage when it was to be decided whether he should be a great hero or a great criminal. The result was that he was an unbalanced individual. In his soul, the most utter devotion could turn to the bitterest hate, a sovereign calm into sudden rudeness, a knightly bravery into the most revolting barbarity.

His was the weird, uneven temperament of the confirmed epileptic, the nervous instability of a very sick man, hidden beneath a deceptive placidity. His serenity, however, was not infrequently broken by the impulsive movements characteristic of the malady; although it was not until later, when it came to take the form of violent disturbances, that the disease became fully manifest through the physical symptoms of those attacks. Were we able to trace his life, what we should behold is the continuous development of this illness, giving to the victim, as to other of his fellow-sufferers, an original and interesting turn of character, revealed by a series of acts which, so far as that is concerned, speak for themselves, and which, interspersed with ever shortening periods of calm, constitute the determining points of an inflexible curve, result of a biologic fatality which holds him in its grip.

The truth is, his comrades-in-arms were familiar with certain striking episodes that, from time to time, with an unaltering rhythm, came to interrupt an unusually promising military career. Space does not permit of our relating them here, not to speak of the danger of being taken in by false or exaggerated versions. All doubtful instances aside, however, marked as these always are by a preponderance of the element of violence—now the flogging of a military surgeon; and now an attack with a dagger, fortunately wrested from him in time, upon an Argentine official over a word which he had failed to understand—putting aside all these cases, we shall relate briefly only those that are most generally known.

It was in 1844 in Rio de Janeiro. A certain journalist,[4] or, better, a madman, thanks to the laxity of the laws governing such offenses, had created a scandal of long duration by the intolerable insults which he heaped upon the court of the former Empire; and after he had flung a number of his indecorous allusions at the army—insults which for the matter of that were the concern of all classes from the lowliest citizen to the monarch—certain officers were unfortunately led to resort to desperate measures and resolved to have recourse, the only recourse within their power, to the summary justice of lynch law.

This resolve was put into effect; and among the officers intrusted with the execution of the sentence, the young captain, Moreira Cesar, then a little over thirty years of age, was the one who played the most prominent part. His record up to then had been an exemplary one, and he had been cited from time to time for the manner in which he had carried out various commissions. On the present occasion—there in the open street, in broad daylight, in the presence of armed justice as represented by the entire police force—he proved to be at once the boldest and the most merciless of them all. The victim, having sought the protection of the law, was riding along in a carriage beside a high-ranking officer of the army itself, when Moreira Cesar stepped forward and plunged a dagger between his ribs.

This crime led to his being transferred to Mato Grosso, and it was not until after the proclamation of the Republic that he returned from the army's sweltering Siberia.

[4] Apulchro de Castro.

At this period he was still a captain, and, although he had never drawn a sword in battle, he assumed all the airs of a conqueror. The new regime was still a tottering one, and the government seemed to wish to have near it this firm prop—a man for dangerous crises and bold deeds. Whether in the barracks or the street, his boyish figure was greeted with sympathetic whispers and fawning praise. He was the man for the major crises of life; although, if the truth were told, he was merely a timid and inoffensive little bureaucrat upon whom encomiums had been heaped for the performance of tasks that were wholly pacific in character. Significantly enough, all that the records of the military profession had to show was an extremely uneven and turbulent career, in the course of which the dagger had not infrequently gleamed beside a sword that was still stainlessly virgin.

It was not until the latter years of his life that his sword was to leave its scabbard. In 1893, having been thrice promoted in two years and being then a colonel, when the revolt of the fleet broke out, he was appointed by Marshal Floriano Peixoto to go to Santa Catarina and stop the conflagration which was spreading again in the South and threatening the border states. He went, invested with discretionary powers; and at no other place in our land was the state of siege enforced so firmly or so ruthlessly as it was by Moreira Cesar's mailed fist.

The unpardonably wicked shootings which took place at this time are too well known for comment. The public opinion of the nation was so shocked that, when the revolt had been put down, the newly inaugurated civil government demanded an accounting of the principal responsible for them. The reply came promptly, in the form of a telegram. It was a simple "No," sharp, defiant, ending the matter—a direct blow at the imprudent curiosity of the constituted authorities, without any trimmings, with no beating around the bush, and without the saving grace of the briefest of explanations.

Months afterward he was summoned to Rio de Janeiro. He embarked with his battalion (the Seventh) on a merchant vessel, and while they were at sea, to the surprise of his own comrades, he arrested the commandant. Without the slightest basis for it, a suspicion of treason had laid hold of him, owing to a slight deviation in the ship's course which he looked upon as sinister. Such an act would be absolutely inexplicable were we not able to characterize it as a special manifestation of the psychic disorder with which he was afflicted.

But, for all of this, his prestige was not diminished. He made himself unconditional master of the battalion that he commanded, increasing its personnel to a number far in excess of the regulations; and, what is more, in open violation of the law, there were dozens of minors in the ranks who were incapable of bearing arms. His will was law, however, and he succeeded in organizing the best corps in the army; for, in his long intervals of lucidity, he exhibited the eminent and rare qualities of an outstanding military leader and intelligent disciplinarian, all of which was in contrast to the intermittent paroxysms of rage that assailed him.

Those spasms, marked by a crescendo over which he had no control, were occurring a good deal more often now and were more evident to those about him. Having been placed in command of the Canudos expedition, he indulged in a series of indiscreet acts which finally culminated in a catastrophe. Two of these acts stand out particularly, as instances of purely impulsive conduct. One was his sudden and capricious departure from Monte Santo, to the dismay of his own general staff, one day ahead of the official schedule. The other occurred three days later, when, again one day ahead of time, he launched an assault on the settlement, with a thousand men more or less who were utterly exhausted from their long march. These two incidents, an objective expression of his intermittent neurosis—two attacks occurring with a brief interval between—were in the nature of a revelation. All the strange things that he had done in the course of his incoherent life were now seen to be warning symptoms, which could point to but one unmistakable diagnosis.

Epilepsy, the truth is, feeds on the passions, and grows in volume with strong and sudden outbursts of emotion; but when it is still in the larval state, or is reflected in the form of mental disturbances that are barely perceptible, it then quietly undermines the human consciousness, finding a saving outlet in what appear to be the free manifestations of the latter. It may accordingly be said, without any exaggeration, that a crime or a rare burst of heroism is often but the mechanical equivalent of an attack. Should the homicide's arm be restrained or the hero stopped short as he is leading the glorious charge, the sick man may abruptly make his presence known by succumbing to an access of fury. Whence all those unlooked-for, incomprehensible, or brutal actions by which the victim instinctively seeks to elude his malady, often turning to crime as an alternative to madness. For a long time, only half-conscious of his state, while suffering a series of brief and transient fits of delirium which no one else perceives, and of which he himself sometimes is not aware, he feels his life constantly becoming more unstable and does all he can to struggle against his illness. His lucid intervals serve as a point of support for his wavering consciousness, as he seeks for a means of inhibition in a painful attempt to adjust himself to the normal conditions surrounding him. His inhibitions, meanwhile, gradually grow weaker, and his sickly intelligence finds it increasingly more difficult to adapt itself to external conditions and to bring facts into proper relation with one another—continually on the downward path now, it confuses, jumbles, inverts, and deforms them. The sick man then falls into a twilight state of mind, as someone has happily put it; his enfeebled brain as it were now condenses all his preceding delirious states, which may at any moment break out in violent actions, and which may lead him to crime or, by accident, to glory, as the potential of his madness.

There is nothing for society to do in such a case but to confer upon him a strait jacket or the royal purple; for collective passions are ruled by the same general law of relativity; and if a great man, thanks to the dazzling effect of genius, may impose himself upon a great people, so may dangerous fanatics exert an equally strong fascination for backward multitudes. Our society then was under the sway of the *"caput mortuum"* element; singular individualities flitted across the scene, and, among them, that of Colonel Moreira Cesar stands out in bold relief, the insignificance of his past merely serving to emphasize the ferocious energy which he displayed in his last days.

It is too early as yet to undertake to define the degree of elevation or depression of the social milieu that produced him. In the appraisal of facts such as these, time must be substituted for space in bringing the historic picture to a focus; the historian stands in need of perspective for the scene he views. Let us, accordingly, bring to a close this perilous essay of ours.

FIRST REGULAR EXPEDITION[5]

In obedience to orders, Colonel Moreira Cesar on the third of February set out for Baía, with his own Seventh Infantry Battalion intrusted to the command of Major Raphael Augusto da Cunha Mattos, a battery of the Second Regiment of Artillery commanded by Captain José Agostinho Salomão da Rocha,[6] and a squadron of the Ninth Cavalry under Captain Pedreira Franco. This was the nucleus of a brigade representing three branches of the service and assembled with that haste which the circumstances called for; it was reinforced by three other corps, incomplete all of them: the Sixteenth, which was stationed in São João d'El-Rei, and which now set out under Colonel Souza Menezes, with 28 officers and 290 men; around 140 men from the Thirty-third; and the Ninth Infantry of Colonel

5 [The Moreira Cesar expedition was the second regular one (cf. p. 202), the third one in all.]

6 See p. 202.

Pedro Nunes Tamarindo, together with a few contingents of the Baian state troops.

The commander of the expedition did not tarry in Baía but, gathering the forces that he had, started at once for Queimadas, where, barely five days after he had left the capital of the Republic, on February 8, the entire expedition was united—some 1,300 men, thoroughly equipped, with 15,-000,000 cartridges and 70 rounds of cannon shot. As may be seen, this force had been mobilized with miraculous rapidity, and things continued to move forward at the same swift pace. Leaving Queimadas, the "first base of operations," under the command of a lieutenant, and nominally garrisoned with 80 sick soldiers and 70 minors who could not support the weight of a knapsack, the major part of the troops set out for the "second base of operations," Monte Santo, where it arrived on the twentieth with everything in readiness for the attack.

Its arrival, however, was not under propitious circumstances. The day before, the commanding officer's illness had taken on the violent form of an epileptic convulsion. This had happened along the way, at the farm site known as, "Quirinquinquá," and had been of such a character as to lead the five surgeons of the sanitary corps to foresee a recurrence, with lamentable consequences. The principal officers, on the other hand, knowing as they well did the serious implications of such a diagnosis in view of that firmness and sense of responsibility which is demanded of a commander under stress of action, nevertheless cautiously and timidly avoided committing themselves in the slightest degree on the subject; and, so it was, Colonel Moreira Cesar was proceeding toward the objective of the campaign, a condemned man on the word of his own staff surgeons.

It is, therefore, natural that the operations should not have been carried out with that lucidity and concerted planning which are so essential and that, from the moment the expedition set out on the march, all those mistakes, all the inexplicable lack of foresight and neglect of rudimentary precepts that characterized its predecessor, should once more have been in evidence, despite the fact that these errors had already been corrected in the hard school of experience or at least had been made exceedingly plain by the disasters that had gone before. No measures were adopted to accord with the very special circumstances of the undertaking. Instead, all decisions were dominated by one fixed plan, such a plan as an energetic police officer might follow: that of hurling a thousand-and-some bayonets against Canudos in double-quick time.

The military engineers, Domingos Alves Leite and Alfredo do Nascimento of the headquarters general staff, who had been assigned to the

brigade, had exactly one week in which to reconnoiter a most difficult terrain with which they were utterly unfamiliar. In so short a time as that it
was not possible for them to select such strategic points as were indispensable for the strengthening of the line of operations. The haste with
which most military surveys have to be carried out was as nothing compared to the speed required of the engineers in this case, limited as they
were to fanciful triangulations, bases measured by the eye, diverging lines
measured by mountaintops, indistinctly glimpsed, and distances verified
by the hands on the pedometers attached to the boots of the hurried opera-
tives. They sought to get their bearings by making inquiries of the few
inhabitants of the places through which they passed, but this was difficult,
distances being calculated in a treacherous unit, the league, which the
backwoodsman's *amour propre* led him to exaggerate, accustomed as he
was to long journeys, while all directions were hopelessly confused; and
if the engineers' lines, as a consequence, showed an error of no more than
five degrees, this was attaining a maximum of nicety. As for information
regarding features of the terrain, the contexture of the soil, fresh-water
supplies, and the like, it was all highly unreliable, and the existence of the
features specified was problematical. They submitted the results of their
survey to the commanding officer, who approved them without further investigation.

In accordance with that survey, a new route was chosen. Running east
of the Cambaio Road and longer than the latter by twenty or twenty-
five miles, it was thought to have the advantage of avoiding the mountainous zone. Starting out from Monte Santo, the expedition made for the
settlement of Cumbe, in a direction due east by southeast, and, having
reached this point, it then turned and marched directly northward, skirting the fringes of the Aracaty Mountains, along a winding path which
gradually led north by northwest, and which, at the country place of
"Rosario," came out on the old Massacará Road. As the troops took this
latter road, it did not occur to their officers to transform it into a line of
operations by selecting two or three points which could easily be defended,
and which, even with very small garrisons, might serve to stiffen their resistance in case they met with defeat and had to fall back or had to stage a
full retreat.

CRITICAL OBSERVATIONS

No one gave so much as a passing thought to the possibility of a defeat.
Such scouting as had been done was merely a dispensable concession to the
hoary old precepts of military strategy; the keen-sighted eye of their guide,
Captain Jesuino, on the road ahead was enough for them.

Meanwhile, it was known that this road ran through long stretches of caatingas, necessitating the use of the pick in clearing a path; and it was further known, or should have been known, that a march of twenty-five miles in this midsummer season was out of the question unless each man carried a supply of water on his back, in the manner of the Roman legions in Tunisia. To avoid this inconvenience, they had brought along an artesian pump, just as if they had been perfectly familiar with the deep underlying strata of the earth, when they did not even know its surface, or as if they had in their ranks skilled rhabdomancers capable of indicating with their mysterious wands the exact spot where a stream of water might be found. We shall see what part all this had to play a little later on.

In the meantime they marched on, to face the unknown, by little-frequented paths; for in these parts all the cross-country trails come together in that stretch of the centuries-old highway which runs from Bom Conselho to Geremoabo—a winding road that, turning eastward to avoid the rugged tablelands to the north, slopes down imperceptibly toward the Vasa-Barris, coming out finally on the slight *divortium aquarum* between that river and the Itapicurú, a region marked by huge areas in which there is not the slightest trace of a stream of any kind, since the earth here absorbs even the most driving rains with the suction of a sponge.

Their line of march, as they should have known, was a long one and beset with obstacles: a minimum of sixty miles, which, in view of the uninhabited and desert character of the country, was the equivalent of a distance ten times as great. The natural thing under such circumstances would have been to guarantee at least their base of supplies, so that they would not be entirely cut off in the desert; yet at Monte Santo, with its very bad conditions of defense, overlooked by a towering mountain from which a half-dozen of the enemy could demolish the place with a round of artillery fire, they had left under the command of Colonel Menezes a wholly ineffective garrison of a few dozen men. As a result, the jagunços might easily have taken it while the rest of the troops were on their way to Canudos. They did not do so, but it was to have been presumed that they might do so; for, according to all the information which was being received, the sertanejos were making the most energetic preparations for the coming battle.

THE POPULATION OF CANUDOS GROWS

The news that was brought the troops was very definite in character. In three weeks' time Canudos had grown in extraordinary fashion. Word of the victory over the Febronio expedition—a victory that was made to appear a good deal more important than it was—had spread and was being embroidered with numerous romantic episodes. This ended the last hesitation on the part of those of the faithful who up to then had been afraid to join Antonio Conselheiro's phalanstery. As in the early days of the settlement, groups of pilgrims in quest of the legendary haven were now to be seen at any moment of the day, coming over the tops of the hills with all their earthly possessions. Many of them bore in hammocks their relatives who were ailing—dying ones who sighed for a last resting-place in this holy ground; the blind, the paralyzed, the leprous, looking for a miraculous and immediate cure at a mere gesture of the venerated miracle-worker. There were, as always, people of all sorts: small-scale cattle-breeders; credulous cowboys of athletic build, along with the various types of backlands vagabond; simple-minded mothers of families, sisters now to the most incorrigible and artful hussies. And invariably bringing up the rear of the processions, without joining in the litanies, walking along in solitude and aloof, as if contemptuous of it all, were the desperadoes, the bandits and professional assassins, now seeking a more extended theater of operations in which to display their impulsive bravery and satisfy their longing for adventure. In the course of the day, down the Calumby, Geremoabo, and Uauá roads, converging from all directions, would come pack-bearers laden with all sorts of provisions, sent directly to Canudos by the faithful who dwelt at a distance, in Villa Nova da Rainha, Alagoinhas, and all the other towns and villages. There was plenty for all, and enthusiasm ran high.

ATTITUDE OF THE JAGUNÇOS TOWARD THE NEW EXPEDITION

At daybreak in the settlement tasks were assigned to all, and there were plenty of hands—enough and more than enough—to carry them out. Sentry forces of twenty men each, under the command of trusted leaders, were stationed along all the roads, at the junction of the Cocorobó and Macambira highways, in the Umburanas lowlands, and on the top of Mount Favella, relieving those who had kept watch there during the night. Some of those who the day before had paid tribute and become members of the community now went out to work in the small plantations along the banks of the river on either side, while others became building laborers at the church. Others still—the more crafty and active ones— scattered out in the direction of Monte Santo, Cumbe, and Queimadas on delicate missions. Their task was to pick up what information they could concerning the new expedition, by talking with the faithful, who in these localities defied the vigilance of the authorities by acquiring contraband weapons, which, after all, was easy enough to do, and storing them away in hidden places. The function of the scouts was to keep an eye on all that was going on and to learn all they could through cautious inquiries.

And they all were happy as they set out for their various tasks. Small but noisy groups went down the roads, bearing weapons or implements of labor, and singing as they went. They had forgotten the previous massacres, and deep in the soul of many lay the hope that now at last, perhaps, they would be left alone to live out their simple, uneventful lives here in the backlands.

THE TRENCHES

Their leaders, however, had no illusions on this score. They were taking no chances but were bending all their efforts on the urgent task of defense; and throughout the long hot day the sertanejos could be seen, on the hilltops or along the edge of the roads, rolling, carrying, or piling up stones, digging up the earth with picks and hoes, and laboring incessantly. They were engaged in building trenches.

This method of hastily throwing up temporary fortifications was an ideal one. It consisted of making a circular or elliptical cavity in the earth in which the marksman could conceal himself and move about at will; around the edge of this cavity breastworks consisting of stones laid alongside one another were erected, with openings for the musket barrels. The work of building these epaulements was facilitated by the character of the talc-schist formations, which afforded stones of whatever shape and size might be desired. This goes to explain the extraordinary number of those holes in the ground which are to be seen in all directions round about Canudos, at regular intervals, and which look like the embrasures of a monster fortress without walls. Located in a cross-line of fire commanding the approaches, they were so distributed, especially in those long stretches where they took advantage of the dry bed of the creeks, as to render it extremely difficult for even the best and lightest of troops to effect a passage. And inasmuch as the defenders foresaw that their enemy, wishing to avoid such a passage, would turn aside and assault the border trenches, they constructed secondary ones on top the slopes, close at hand, and other more distant ones arranged in the very same manner, in order that the marksmen driven back from the front line might be able to make a stand here and continue the fight. Thus, whether he kept to the highway or abandoned it, the enemy would find himself trapped in a network of rifle fire.

In making these preparations, the rebels stood in need of no tutoring.

The earth itself was an admirable model: jagged saw-teeth spurs rising up like redoubts; rivers carving out their beds in the form of fosses and covered passageways; and on all sides the caatingas plaited into naturally formed tree fortifications. The jagunços would select the tallest shrubs and those with the greatest amount of foliage and would skilfully interweave the inner boughs without disturbing the outer branches in such a manner as to form, a couple of yards above the ground, a small hammock or platform capable of supporting comfortably one or two invisible sharpshooters, concealed in the leaves. These singular turrets represented an old ancestral custom, a stratagem long employed in ambush warfare with the fierce panther and his kind. These native *mutans*,[7] constructed in the manner described and scattered here and there, served to complete the line of trenches. Occasionally, the sertanejos would undertake fortifications of a more imposing sort. They would discover a hill with great round blocks of stone piled on its summit; they would clear out the spaces between the rocks, wide openings filled with a rank growth of thistles and bromelias, thus forming narrow windows concealed by a dense growth of silk grass; after this, they would clear the spaces within, until finally they were able to move about freely in a huge blockhouse overlooking the trails and highways and from which they might without risk to themselves command the most remote points.

WEAPONS

Their preparations, however, did not stop here. They also put their weapons in order. The village was now filled with the sounds of a strident orchestra, hammers clanging on anvils as they beat their crooked scythes into shape, as they sharpened and steeled their polished cattle prongs, as they tempered the broad blades of their "scraping-knives," long as swords, as they braced their bows (which were by way of being a compromise between the weapon of the savage and the ancient crossbow), and as they adjusted the locks of their antique muskets and double-barreled shotguns. From all these glowing forges there arose a great metallic din, the resounding clang of a busy arsenal.

GUNPOWDER

The supply of gunpowder acquired in the neighboring towns not being sufficient, they proceeded to manufacture their own. They had the charcoal; the saltpeter was to be found along the surface of the earth, farther north, near the São Francisco; and they had laid in a supply of brimstone some while before. They were accordingly able to turn out an accurately

---

[7] *Mutan:* a platform on which the hunter waits for his game.

compounded product which rivaled the brand commonly used by hunters.

BULLETS

There was no lack of bullets, or at least of projectiles; the broad mouths of the blunderbusses took everything: round pebbles, nailheads, horntips, broken glass, rock splinters, etc.

FIGHTING MEN

And, last of all, there was no lack of "famous" fighters whose amazing adventures were the talk of the entire region. Religious sentiment is all-embracing in character, and, along with the instinct to disorder, it had here brought together not Baians alone but individuals from all the border states. In addition to the jagunço of the São Francisco[8] and the cangaceiro[9] of the Carirys, there were all sorts of traditional "bad men,"[10] heroes of former backlands conflicts and petty uprisings barely to be distinguished from one another even in the names they bore—that of the "lizards," that of the "hampers," that of the "baskets," etc. A call to arms was being sent out over the countryside.

JOÃO ABBADE

From day to day, strange-appearing newcomers arrived at the settlement, men who were absolutely unknown to anyone there. They came "under the *cangaço*,"[11] their cartridge belts stuffed with bullets and their powder cases full; a double-barreled shotgun slung across their sashes, from which dangled the inevitable parnahyba;[12] and on a bandoleer, the bell-mouthed blunderbuss. They simply appeared, that was all, and made their way to the public square without anyone's asking who they were or from where they came, as if they had been old acquaintances. The wily João Abbade[13] received them there. He was their equal when it came to a turbulent past but was possessed of more astuteness and had, besides, the smattering of an education; he had been at one time a pupil in a public school in one of the provincial capitals of the North but had been forced to flee after he had murdered his sweetheart, which was the first crime he had committed. In any event, he was the man to hold these rowdies in check and discipline them. "Commander of the Street" was the title he bore, an inexplicable one in that labyrinth of alleyways; but, without

[8] [See p. 176, n. 10.]
[9] [See p. 178 and n. 14.]
[10] ["*Valentões*."]
[11] [See p. 178, n. 14.]
[12] [See p. 145.]
[13] See p. 219, n. 22.

leaving the settlement, he exerted an absolute sway over the entire country-side for twelve miles around, being kept informed of what was going on by his swift-moving scouts who were constantly on the watch. All gave him unconditional obedience. In the assignment of numerous tasks of various sorts, in the performance of which the religious-minded country-man rubbed elbows with the hardened criminal, there was to be observed a rare co-ordination of forces; and the most perfect uniformity of views prevailed, with one purpose only in view, that of repelling the imminent invasion.

Nevertheless, as some of the prisoners afterward revealed, when the campaign was over, all these warlike preparations came near being brought to a sudden halt by one piece of news that was received, and the rebel community was so astounded and dismayed that it was on the point of immediately breaking up. This occurred when the scouts who had been sent out to various points to see what progress the invader was making came back and reported, as a matter of certain knowledge, not only the number and equipment of the troops, but the renown attaching to the name of the new commander. The feverish activity of the jagunços stopped short. They were terror-stricken as they listened to the most exaggerated, the most extravagant and fanciful tales of the commanding officer's boldness and daring. He was the Anti-Christ, come to put the unhappy penitents to a last proof. They pictured him as the hero of many battles—fourteen, according to the account of one rude backlands poet, in a song which was later composed to celebrate the campaign. They could foresee the devastation of their homes, days of nameless torture, catastrophes of every sort. Canudos itself would be wiped out by fire, sword, and bullet. They had a gruesome name for him—"Head-chopper."

As was afterward learned, none of the expeditions was looked forward to with so much anxiety. There were even a few desertions, thinning the ranks, chiefly, of those who should have been the staunchest, namely, those dangerous adventurers who had come there, not under the stimulus of religion, but from their love of a fight and the desire to indulge their disorderly instincts. The scouts upon returning from the outlying points would report that some of their sinister companions were missing. The upshot of it was, however, that the community, by this epidemic of fear, was purged of the unbelieving and the timid. The great majority of the true believers stayed on, resigned to their fate.

PROCESSIONS

Uninfluenced though they might be by the dread-inspiring rumors, the people nonetheless turned, at this juncture, to the solace of their religious faith; and not infrequently after that, their steeled weapons at their side, the entire population of the settlement would turn out in long penitential processions across the fields. The stream of incoming pilgrims had suddenly ceased. The feverish preparations for war were likewise at a standstill. The sentries as they left for their posts at daybreak no longer sang loud hymns of rejoicing as they went down the trails but scurried along cautiously in the thickets, remaining there, silent and watchful, for long hours at a time.

PRAYERS

It was under these most distressing circumstances that the frail but numerous legion of the pious ones took the field to encourage the more apprehensive of the able-bodied fighting men. And at nightfall, to the glow of bonfires, the kneeling multitude would prolong their prayers beyond the appointed time, there in the arbor[14] strewn with aromatic boughs from the caatingas. At the far end of the arbor, next the door to the "Sanctuary," was a small pine table, covered with a snow-white cloth; and, when they had done saying their beads, a strange figure would come and approach this table. Clad in a long blue tunic without a girdle, which fell gracelessly over his emaciated limbs, with his back bent, his head down, his gaze lowered, Antonio Conselheiro would make his appearance. He would remain for a long time silent and motionless in the presence of this quiet, waiting multitude. Then slowly he would lift his wan face, suddenly illuminated by his flashing, piercing eyes, and he would pray.

Night then would fall, deep night, and the settlement ruled by this humblest of evangelists, who was yet so formidable, would go to its repose.

II

DEPARTURE FROM MONTE SANTO

February 22 was the date set for the departure of the troops; and, in accordance with military custom, on the afternoon of the preceding day they were drawn up in marching order for review and an inspection of arms and equipment. On the supposition that this was no more than a review, inasmuch as their marching orders, according to "schedule," were definitely

14 [See p. 160.]

for the following day, the various battalions lined up in squadron formation, extending from the public square of Monte Santo.

There they all were: the Seventh, with an equipment above normal, temporarily commanded by Major Raphael Augusto da Cunha Mattos; the Ninth, which for the third time in this conflict was going into battle, with an enrolment slightly below normal, under the command of Colonel Pedro Nunes Tamarindo; detachments of the Thirty-third and the Sixteenth, led by Captain Joaquim Quirino Villarim; a battery of four Krupp field guns of the Second Regiment, commanded by Captain José Salomão Agostinho da Rocha; a squadron of 50 men of the Ninth Cavalry under the command of Captain Pedreira Franco; certain contingents of Baian police; the sanitary corps under the command of Dr. Ferreira Nina; and an engineering commission. Not included were 70 men of the Sixteenth, who were remaining with Colonel Souza Menezes as a garrison for the town.

There were 1,281 men altogether, each with 220 cartridges in his belt and luggage, in addition to a reserve of 60,000 rounds in the general store.

The review took place; but, contrary to general expectation, in place of a command to stack arms and disband, the bugle sounded alongside the commander-in-chief, giving the signal, "Column, march!" And Colonel Moreira Cesar, leaving the point where he had been stationed, galloped over and took his place at the head of the column.

It was almost dark when they set out on the march to Canudos. The whole thing was unexpected, but there was not the faintest murmuring in the ranks; the surprise reflected on all the faces did not interfere with the rigorous execution of maneuvers. The drums beat, up ahead; the various detachments fell in, marching two abreast as they entered the narrow highway; the artillery got under way, and the supply trains rumbled along.

A quarter of an hour later the inhabitants of Monte Santo had their last glimpse, in the distance, around the far bend of the road, of the third expedition against Canudos.

FIRST MISTAKES

The vanguard arrived at Cumbe within three days, the rest of the troops being detained for a few hours—with their commanding officer laid up in a near-by ranch house with another attack of epilepsy.

Before daybreak of the twenty-sixth, having reached the farm known as the "Cajá Trees" ("Cajazeiras")[15] the evening before, six miles distant from Cumbe, they struck out directly northward for the "White Hills" ("Serra Branca") more than eight miles farther on. This region, on the edge of the tablelands which extend as far as Geremoabo, is very different from those which we have hastily described before. It is at once less rugged and more arid. The steep-sloping hills are now few in number, and in their place is a vast expanse of highland plains. However, while the land here may be less rugged, it presents other obstacles which are perhaps even more formidable. The flat and sandy soil, with no depressions which in summer may provide life-giving water, is absolutely sterile. The rains are few and far between and do little more than wet the ground, being immediately sucked in by the sands; and, as a result, the flora is a sparse one, with the caatingas being transformed into caatanduvas.

In midsummer, from November to March, the desolation is complete. Whoever then ventures into this region has the impression of being in an enormous plantation of parched and interweaving boughs where the spark of a match would touch off a sudden conflagration, if indeed a conflagration did not occur by spontaneous combustion, in this season of drought, with the strong northeast wind rubbing the branches together in the blazing noonday sun. This particular section of the backlands, where there are no towns, and where only an occasional traveler hastens through, along the highway from Geremoabo to Bom Conselho, lies within a huge irregular circle which has as its determining points the border towns of Cumbe on the south, Santo Antonio da Gloria on the north, Geremoabo on the east, and Monte Santo on the west; and throughout this entire tract a desert is in slow process of formation. Trees are scarce now, and the chief vegetation—practically the only vegetation in certain parts—consists of the withered, interlacing shrubs of the mangaba tree,[16] the only plant that can grow here, thanks to a protective sap which, after the scorching heat of the summer suns, enables it to put forth leaves and flowers when more favorable seasons come again.

THE NEW ROUTE

It was at the most unsuitable time of the year that the expedition entered these parts, for a forced march, with the thermometer soaring; and in this dry, exhausting heat there was nothing to do but keep on marching

[15] [The cajá is a Brazilian fruit resembling a yellow plum (Spondiaslutea L).]

[16] [The mangabeira (Hancornia speciosa) is the tree that bears the mangaba, a round, orange-colored fruit that is eaten when overripe. It yields a milky juice from which "Pernambuco rubber" is produced.]

until they came to the nearest place where they knew they would find a well, which would make it feasible for them to halt. They had a hard time of it indeed. The character of the soil made walking difficult, as the shifting sand slipped beneath their feet; and it was even more difficult for the wagon trains, as they sank up to their hubs. They would suddenly find their way barred with briar patches, which it was necessary to hack down with their knives. And all the while the intense dog-day heat was radiated by the burning sands. Small wonder, then, if by the time they arrived at "White Hills," in the afternoon, the men were exhausted. Exhausted and very thirsty. They had marched for eight hours without a halt beneath that summer sun. But here, by way of quenching the unnatural thirst which came from the almost total depletion of their veins by perspiration, they found in the depths of a cave a few quarts of water.

All this, as we have said, had been foreseen; and they now tried to sink the artesian well. This operation, however—with everyone impatiently awaiting results—proved unsuccessful. It could not be done. In place of a pile-driver, which would have helped sink the plummet, they had brought along an apparatus of just the opposite kind: a windlass. Faced by this singular mishap, there was nothing for them to do, despite the long march they had already made, but to set out at once for "Rosario," a farm fifteen miles distant. Weakened as they were, the troops started off again, late in the afternoon; and, when night fell and the gleaming stars came out, they were still struggling along, doing their best to make their way through the tangled briar patches.

It may be imagined what this march was like, of twenty or twenty-five miles without a halt. A thousand and some thirst-ridden men fairly staggering beneath the weight of their equipment, in the heart of the enemy's territory. The dull thud of marching feet, the creaking of wagons and gun carriages, the clink of weapons in the desert stillness, an island of sound in a sea of silence—and all the while, in the tall weeds, there was an imperceptible crackling of boughs.

Accompanying the troops, creeping along the edge of the bypaths, were the spies sent out by the jagunços. No one paid any heed to them, however. Exhausted from their day's march, the expeditionaries had forgotten all about fighting; all that they could think of was the nearest wells, for which they were making, trusting implicitly, meanwhile, to the judgment and loyalty of their guides.

But at last they came to a halt in the middle of the road. Bringing up the rear, in the distance, a few crippled stragglers could be seen, while even the most able-bodied were limping along. The halt was a brief one, and such rest as they were able to snatch was an illusion. The officers slept—those who did sleep—with their horses' reins fastened to their hands. And the next morning, as they resumed their march before daybreak, they realized that they were in the danger zone. The remains of bonfires all along the way, some of them with the embers still glowing; the remains of excellent meals which had consisted of roast turtle and quarters of kid; fresh tracks in the sand, winding away, with many twists and turnings, into the caatingas—all these signs showed that the sertanejos had been there, and had even spent the night there, cautiously, invisibly keeping watch on the invaders. When the latter reached "Old Wicket" ("Porteira Velha"), it looked as if they had actually come upon the enemy, and the vanguard broke ranks precipitately. There beside a bonfire was a two-barreled pistol and a cowboy's cattle prong.

They arrived at "Rosario" shortly before noon, just as a violent but passing shower was falling, a thing that is likely to happen in the backlands at this season of the year. This farm, one destined to achieve notoriety in the course of the campaign, resembled most of the others in the vicinity: one or two houses built of hollow tile without any floors, surrounded by fences made of logs or stakes, and with a clean-swept terrace and a few scrawny trees out in front, while some distance away was the water pit or pond which had served to determine the choice of locality.

It was here that the expedition pitched camp, in the enemy's own country; and it is not strange if now, for the first time, the men began to experience that feeling of apprehension which goes with war. There was an incident which occurred that illustrates this. On the first day of March, just as another passing shower was beating down on the shelterless troops, the sound of an alarm was heard. It must surely be the enemy, taking advantage of the fury of the elements to fall upon the invader, springing up suddenly to open fire during this downpour, as the thunder crashed in the skies overhead.

Running, sliding, falling over the wet and slippery ground, bumping into one another in the lashing rain, officers and men strove to do the impossible and fall in line, putting on their clothes and fastening their belts and shoulder straps as they ran; paying no attention to the conflicting commands that were shouted at them, they lined up any way they could in squads and companies, to the accompaniment of a great hullabaloo. Out of all this confusion in the ranks a solitary horseman suddenly emerged, to the vast astonishment of the soldiers, and galloped wildly down the road in the probable direction of the enemy, while the military engineer, Domingos Leite, did his best to keep up with him. It was Colonel

Moreira Cesar. Fortunately, the imaginary enemy whom he was riding forth to attack in this futile manner was none other than a band of escorts sent out by a friendly ranch-owner of the vicinity.[17] Aside from this incident, the day was an uneventful one. In the afternoon a convoy arrived from Monte Santo, bringing horses for the squadron which up to then had been impracticably mounted on mules. At sunup of the second, the battalions marched on toward "Angico," where they arrived at eleven o'clock in the morning, pitching camp in the large stable yard of this abandoned farm.

All this was contrary to the definite plan which had been drawn up, with the object of lessening the fatigue of forced marches. In accordance with that plan, after resting the entire balance of the day at "Vicar's Farm" ("Rancho de Vigario"), the troops were to set out for "Angico" on the third, marching only some five miles, and there they would rest again and spend the night. Striking camp on the fourth, they would go directly on to Canudos, a march of a little more than three and a half miles. Since they were in enemy territory, they were to take proper precautions in safeguarding the camp by stationing outposts and roving sentries.

Colonel Moreira Cesar, meanwhile, had interned himself in the nearest caatinga, where he had ordered his tent set up. Receiving his staff officers there, he let them know that he was absolutely certain of victory. Various expedients were then suggested to him for rendering the attack safer. One of these, put forward by the commanding officer of the Seventh, called for first altering the order of march which had been followed up to then; it was suggested that the single column be divided in two, one portion to form a strong vanguard for reconnoitering and the first assault, while the other would come into action as a reserve force. In this way, should the enemy prove to be too strong for them, it would be possible to stage an orderly retreat to Monte Santo, where their forces could be reorganized and augmented. Contrary to what everyone expected, the commander-in-chief of the expedition did not turn down this proposal; and at dawn on the third the troops marched, in accordance with a clearly thought-out plan.

ON THE MARCH TO "ANGICO"

In the meantime, on the march to "Angico," the same formation was observed as when they had set out from Cumbe: at the head of the column, a band of mounted scouts, with a brave and experienced guide,

[17] Colonel of the National Guard José Americo C. de Souza Velho, proprietor of the "Cahimbé" and "Olhos d'Agua" estates. He was the one who had advised the expedition to take this route.

Manoel Rosendo, the engineering commission, and a company of riflemen of the Seventh, led by Lieutenant Figueira; then came the right wing of the Seventh under Major Cunha Mattos, marching alongside and convoying the munitions train in the center; the First Division of the Second Regiment under the immediate command of Salomão da Rocha; the left wing of the Seventh, led by Captain Alberto Gavião Pereira Pinto; the Second Division of Artillery, commanded by First Lieutenant Pradel de Azambuja; the right wing of the Ninth, under the command of Colonel Tamarindo, separated from the left, which was led by Captain Felippe Simões, by the respective supply trains. Bringing up the rear were the sanitary corps, certain detachments of the Sixteenth, under Captain Quirino Villarim, the general supply train of the expedition, guarded by Baian police, and, at the very end, the cavalry. Colonel Cesar rode at the head of the column, with his company of riflemen and the right wing of the Seventh.

It was five o'clock in the morning when they began the march, and they were soon in the immediate vicinity of Canudos with its characteristic terrain: a hilly country, covered with a scraggly vegetation of thistles and Bromeliaceae; with numerous tortuous-winding streams running through it, and with the land becoming all the while more rugged and hostile, save for those patches where the recent rains had left an ephemeral garment of green veiling the stone heaps and the mouths of caves. The evening showers, as usual in summer, had passed without leaving any trace, the parched earth, which had absorbed and repelled the moisture, remaining rough and dry. Round about for as far as the eye could reach, over the rolling hills and the elevated plains, along the surrounding trails and on the eroded mountainsides—everywhere were the same hues, the same monotonous yet impressive landscape; all Nature was motionless, gripped in the throes of an enormous spasm, without a bloom on the naked boughs, no beat of wings on the quiet and unruffled air.

The marching column, stretched out in a line almost two miles long, was a dark and winding streak across this landscape. Ahead of them to the north the troops could see, close at hand now, the final circle of hills about Canudos, and they were not the least disturbed in mind at thus drawing near their military objective.

PSYCHOLOGY OF THE BRAZILIAN SOLDIER

They marched quietly, at their accustomed steady pace. All up and down the line could be heard a vague, subdued murmur of thousands of voices, suddenly punctuated here and there with bursts of jovial laughter.

In this singular alacrity with which they approached the enemy, our soldiers were displaying their most prominent attribute. Men of all shades of color and of diverse races, they appeared on such occasions as this, involving dangerous undertakings and calling forth strong emotions, to be governed by some law of collective psychology; it was the instincts of the primitive warrior that ruled their minds: the improvidence of the savage, his unawareness of peril, his indifference to life and rashness in the face of death. They went into battle as if bound for some rowdy merrymaking. Intolerable creatures in times of peace, when they grew soft and flabby and relaxed; nondescript on parade in the street, without any kind of presence or aplomb, slouched beneath their awkwardly handled rifles, they were different beings in time of war. War, indeed, was their best training-ground and the enemy their favorite drillmaster, one who within a few days made them over into disciplined and hardened soldiers, giving them in a short while, through long and wearing marches and actual combat, what they never possessed in the flag-bedecked capitals—erectness of bearing, firmness of step, precision of firing aim, swiftness in reloading. They never give in to circumstances but will march for days at a time over the most impossible of roads. In this they are inimitable. There is never the least grumbling to be heard from them, no matter what may happen; and none can equal them when it comes to going without food and living for days "on wind," as they say in their own picturesque jargon. After the most trying of experiences, these wan-faced heroes will still make light of misery and scoff at martyrdom.

In battle, to be sure, the Brazilian soldier is incapable of imitating the Prussian, by going in and coming out with a pedometer on his boot. He is disorderly, tumultuous, rowdy, a terrible but heroic blackguard, attacking the enemy whether by bullet or sword thrust with an ironic jest on his lips. For this very reason he is ill adapted to the great mass movements of classic campaigns. He is impeded by correct formations and bewildered by the mechanics of complex maneuvers. It is a torture to him to be obliged to fight in strict adherence to the rhythm of bugles; and, while he will readily enough obey orders in the execution of broad strategic plans, going along uncomplainingly under the most trying conditions, yet, when the enemy charges him at the point of the sword, he wants to fight in his own way. And he does fight then, without any hard feelings, noisily, blusteringly, rejoicing in the rain of bullets and the play of swords, taking foolhardy risks and holding his courage cheap. All the while, however, he has his eyes fixed on his commanding officers, and his very life appears to hang on the energy which they exhibit. Let them waver ever so little, and all his daring is gone; he is instantly downcast and falls prey to a discouragement which he is powerless to overcome.

On the present occasion everything pointed to a victory for the expeditionaries. With such a commander as theirs, defeat was out of the question. And so it was with a firm stride that they made their way to the front, impatient to come to grips with this stubborn enemy. What they would do to these backwoodsmen was something scandalous; they would give them a dressing-down. They were already picturing their anticipated exploits; the stories they would have to tell would scare the wits out of the timid ones back home, who believed all you told them; what tragicomic scenes there would be—up there in that monstrous weed patch,[18] when they charged it with their rifles. They went on making bizarre plans, premature ones, and they all began with the same naïve preliminary, "When I go back. . . . ."

At times one of them would come out with some extravagant idea, only to be greeted with a ripple of suppressed laughter as the babble of voices stopped for a moment.

What was more, the glow of this resplendent morning cheered them. Above them was the beautiful blue-arching sky of the backlands with its rainbow tints, shading gently, imperceptibly, from the deep blue of the zenith to the dazzling purple in the East. Besides, had not the enemy left the road clear for them up to now, failing to take advantage of the most favorable stretches to attack them? There was but one thing that worried them: what if they should find this nest of rebels empty when they arrived? This likely disappointment proved an alarming thought: the entire campaign transformed into a long forced march; and then, their inglorious return, without having fired a single cartridge.

III

"PITOMBAS"

It was in this admirable frame of mind that they reached "Pitombas."[19] The small, deep, winding stream which is found at this point now flows alongside the highway and now crosses it, finally leaving the road before reaching the farm to which it gives its name, making a long, bowed curve, almost a semicircle, with the highway as the chord.

FIRST ENGAGEMENT

It was along this stretch of road that the troops came; and, as they reached the middle of it, there were half-a-dozen shots. It was the enemy

---

[18] [Tapera.]   [19] [See p. 303. The pitomba is a well-known Brazilian fruit.]

at last. It was some scout who had been accompanying the expedition, or who, lying in wait for it there, had taken advantage of the favorable conformation of the terrain for a sudden attack from the side and then had safely fled, protected by the banks of the stream. His aim had been a sure one, and one of the subalterns of the rifle company, Lieutenant Poly, fell mortally wounded, and six or seven soldiers besides. The cannons of the Salamão Division were quickly loaded, and machine-gun bullets tore into the weedy undergrowth, the shrubbery bending as it does when swept by harsh winds. Before the echoes had died down, there came the sound of rhythmic rifle fire and, detaching itself from the column where it had formed part of the other rifles, the right wing of the Seventh now charged in the direction of the enemy, plunging into the weeds at top speed, slashing them down with their bayonets. It was a swift and glorious sally, but the enemy fled the encounter. Minutes passed, and the detachment returned to the line amid general acclamations, while the bugles gave the traditional signal of victory by playing the "trinities,"[20] their notes ringing out loud and vibrant. The commander-in-chief, in an impulsive manifestation of sincere joy, embraced the fortunate officer who had given this repulse to the enemy; he looked upon the engagement as an auspicious beginning. It was almost too bad, all this fine equipment, all these men, all this impressive setting for a campaign that was to be ended with the firing of half-a-dozen shots.

"THESE PEOPLE ARE UNARMED"

The weapons of the jagunços were ridiculous. As spoils, the soldiers came upon a "woodpecker" rifle under the riverbank; it was light in weight, with a very slender barrel. The rifle was loaded, and, taking it in his hand as he sat on his horse, Colonel Cesar discharged it in the air. As a weapon, it was insignificant, good for killing a bird.

"These people are unarmed," he observed tranquilly.

The march was then resumed at a more rapid pace, the surgeons and the wounded being left behind in "Pitombas," under the protection of the police contingent and the rest of the cavalry. The majority of the men were already disappearing in the distance, at a double-quick step. The spell of the enemy was broken. The riflemen in the vanguard and those who guarded the flanks were now beating the brush alongside the road and plunging deep into the caatingas in search of any spies that might be lurking there, bent on routing them from their likely hiding-places or overtaking the fugitives who were making for Canudos.

[20] ["Trindades": the word is applied to the tolling of a bell, the "Angelus," etc.]

This engagement was like an electric shock. The troops as they continued their rapid advance were animated by the irrepressible lust of battle; they were in that highly dangerous state of mental intoxication in which the soldier feels doubly strong, through the certainty of his own strength and the knowledge that he will be permitted an absolute license in the indulgence of his most brutal instincts.

PANIC AND BRAVERY

In a pursuing army there exists the same impulsive automatism as in one that flees. Panic and a foolish bravery, extreme terror and an extreme audacity, are in either case intermingled. There is the same dazed bewilderment as the men stumble forward headlong in the face of the most formidable obstacles, the same nervous tremor running through the ranks, the same painful anxiety which stimulates and hallucinates with equally forceful effect the individual who is fleeing death and the one who is out to kill. The explanation lies in the fact that an army is, first of all, a multitude, a "mass of heterogeneous elements in which one has but to strike a spark of passion, and there is a sudden metamorphosis, a kind of spontaneous generation, by virtue of which thousands of different individuals become a single animal, a nameless monster of the wilds, going forward to a given objective with an irresistible finality." Only the moral strength of a commander can prevent this deplorable transformation, by clearly and firmly imposing a directive which will bring order out of chaos. The great strategists have instinctively realized that the first victory to be won in war lies in overcoming this violent emotional contagion, this undependable state of feeling on the part of the troops, which with equal intensity will impel a man to face the gravest of perils or to take refuge in flight. A plan of war as drawn up with a compass on a map calls for passionless souls—killing machines—steadily functioning within lines that are preestablished.

Moreira Cesar's soldiers, however, were far from having attained this sinister ideal; and their commander, in place of repressing the nervous excitement in the ranks, made it all the worse by the example of neurasthenia which he himself set. An opportunity had occurred, meanwhile, for bringing the situation back to normal. They had reached "Angico," the point which had been determined upon as their last halt. Here, their schedule called for a night's rest, and on the morning of the following day, they were to strike camp and, after a two hours' march, fall upon Canudos. The impulsive inclinations of the troops, however, were still further increased by those of their commander, and they were obsessed with one desire: to come to grips with the enemy. The halt at "Angico," accordingly, lasted but a quarter of an hour, barely time enough to summon the staff officers for a consultation, which was held upon a small hill affording a view of the panting troops drawn up round about. Forgetful of the maxim that nothing can be accomplished with tired soldiers, the leader of the expedition then proposed that they go on and attack at once.

"My comrades! As you can see, I am a sick man. I have not eaten for days. But we are very near to Canudos now—let us go on and take it!"

This suggestion was adopted.

"We will have breakfast in Canudos!" he shouted and was met with a true soldierly ovation.

The march continued. It was eleven o'clock in the morning. The company of marksmen up ahead was scattering out through the thickets, from which now and then a distant shot could be heard, as the enemy fled with the one purpose, seemingly, of luring the troops on to the settlement, where, weakened and exhausted by their six hours' march, they would have to fight under unfavorable conditions—such was the sum of their clever strategy.

"QUICKSTEP!"

It was a mad impulse, depriving the men of their rest like this on the eve of battle; and, as a consequence, so long as it did not slow down the advance of the infantry, they had to be permitted to discard their knapsacks, canteens, ration kits, and all the equipment they carried, with the exception of their weapons and cartridges, to be picked up by the cavalry in the rear. This fact speaks for itself.

Advancing hastily in this manner, they reached the small plain on top the Umburanas Hills. Canudos must be very close, within range of their artillery. The troops came to a halt.

"A COUPLE OF VISITING CARDS FOR THE COUNSELOR"

The guide, Jesuino, upon being consulted, pointed out the direction in which the settlement lay; he was quite sure of it. Moreira Cesar thereupon called the Pradel Division into battle and, setting the aim at one and four-fifths miles, ordered two rounds fired in the direction indicated.

"There go a couple of visiting cards for the Counselor," he said, half-jestingly, with that superior sense of humor which a strong man possesses. The phrase ran down the ranks and was greeted with acclamations. A feverish attack was at once launched. The sun was beating straight down upon them as the battalions, overcoming the last difficulties of the terrain,

went into action beneath a heavy, stifling cloud of dust. They now suddenly had a view of Canudos. They were on top of Mount Favella.[21]

A VIEW OF CANUDOS

Here at last was that enormous weed patch which previous expeditions
had not succeeded in reaching. It came into view all at once, lying there
in a broadened depression of the rolling plain.[22] At first glimpse, before his
eye had become accustomed to this pile of huts and labyrinth of narrow
alleys, some of which came out on the wide square where the churches
stood, the observer had the precise impression of having unexpectedly
stumbled upon a large city. Forming a huge, deepened moat to the left,
at the foot of the highest hills, the Vasa-Barris half-circled the village and
then took a sharp turn directly to the east, as the first waters of the flood
season rolled slowly along. The compact cluster of huts about the square
gradually spread out, sprawling over the hills to the east and north, with
the last of the outlying houses taking on the appearance of scattered sentry boxes; and, meanwhile, there was not a single white wall or rubble-
strewn roof to break the monotony of this monstrous collection of five
thousand shacks dropped down in a furrow of the earth. The two churches
stood out sharply.[23] The new one, on the observer's left, was still unfinished, and its main walls, high and thick, could be seen covered with scaffoldings, with wooden joists, beams, and planks, while from this maze
there emerged the rigid outlines of the cranes with their swaying pulleys.
This structure towered above the others in the village and overlooked the
broad expanse of plains; it was large, rectangular, solidly built, its walls
consisting of great stone blocks laid one upon another with perfect skill,
which gave it the exact appearance of a formidable bastion. More humble
in aspect, built like the common run of back-country chapels, the old
church stood facing it. Still farther to the right, roughly circular in shape,
dotted with little rudely fashioned crosses, but without a single flower bed,
a single bloom, a single shrub, was the cemetery of leveled graves, a
mournful *tybicuera*.[24] Directly opposite the cemetery, on the other side of
the river, was a small plot whose level surface was in contrast to the barren
rolling hills around it; a few scattered trees stood here, a few rows of
bright-hued palmatorias, and half-a-dozen quixabeira stalks with their
verdant branches, all of which gave the place the aspect of a rustic garden.
A spur of Mount Favella comes down here, jutting out into the river,

---

[21] [See pp. 19 ff.]   [22] Cf. pp. 144, 346–47.   [23] See p. 154.

[24] "*Tibycoara*: a hole in the ground, a pit, a grave" (Theodoro Sampaio, *O Tupi na geographia nacional*).

where it ends abruptly in a cliff. These last foothills bear the appropriate name of "Bald Pates," owing to the denudation of their slopes. Halfway down the rounded hillsides one could see the ruins of a dwelling, the "Old Ranch House," and overhanging it a steep terrace, "Mount Mario."[25] And there on the top of the mountain were the troops.

ARRIVAL OF THE TROOPS

The vanguard of the Seventh was the first detachment to arrive, along with the artillery; they were engaged in repulsing a violent attack on the right while the rest of the infantry climbed the last slopes. They paid little attention to the settlement itself, meanwhile. The cannon were aligned in battle formation, as the first platoons came up, their ranks in confusion, the men panting; and a cannonading then began, with all the guns firing at once, without co-ordination. There was no missing a mark as big as this one. The effects of the initial rounds were visible at various points: huts were shattered, ripped apart and buried in débris by cannon balls exploding in their midst; the splintered roofs of clay and wood were sent hurtling through the air; the adobe walls were pulverized; the first fires were started.

The bombarded village was now enveloped in a dense cloud of dust and smoke which hid it completely from view. The rest of the troops could not be seen. The solemn thunder of the artillery rent the air, awakening a far, deep resonance throughout the breadth of the desert lands, as the deafening echoes came back from the mountainsides.

DISCONCERTING INCIDENT

But, as the minutes passed, there were to be heard, sounding clear above the roar of the cannons, the sudden silvery notes of a bell. It was the bell of the old church down below, summoning the faithful to battle.

The battle had not yet started. Aside from a light flank attack made by a few guerrillas upon the artillery, the sertanejos so far had put up no resistance. The troops spread out over the sloping summit without their maneuvers being disturbed by a single shot; and when the shooting did begin, it was a sustained but aimless running fire. Eight hundred rifles blazing, eight hundred rifles aimed in a rasant line down the drop of the hill.

As the smoke cleared away now and again, the settlement could be glimpsed. It was a beehive in commotion: innumerable groups here and

[25] [The author here refers to this elevation as a *socalco*, "terrace"; later (cf. p. 266 and elsewhere), he alludes to it as a *morro*, "hill."]

there, weaving in and out of the square, scattering down the paths along the riverbank, making for the church, dashing down the alleyways with weapons in their hands, climbing up onto the roofs.

A few, at the far end of the village, appeared to be in flight; they could be seen wandering along the edge of the caatingas and disappearing behind the hills. Others displayed an incredible nonchalance by crossing the square at a leisurely pace, oblivious to the tumult and the stubborn spatter of bullets from the mountain.

One whole company of the Seventh at this moment trained its fire for several minutes upon a jagunço who was coming along the Uauá Road, but the sertanejo did not so much as quicken his step; indeed, he even came to a dead stop at times. His impassive face could be seen in the distance as he raised his head to gaze at the troops for a few seconds and then went tranquilly on his way. This was an irritating challenge. In surprise, the soldiers nervously concentrated their fire upon this exceptional being, who had now become the bull's-eye for an army. At one moment he seated himself beside the road and appeared to be striking a light for his pipe. The soldiers laughed. Then he got to his feet and, still at the same leisurely pace, was gradually lost from sight among the outlying houses.

From the village not a shot was fired. The commotion in the square had died down. The last of the stragglers were now coming in, among them a number of women with children in their arms or dragging them by the hand, as they went on in the direction of the arbor, seeking the barrier afforded by the big walls of the new church.

IV

THE ORDER OF BATTLE

The bell had finally stopped ringing. The troops now began the descent along the gentler slopes, hundreds of bayonets gleaming in the sun. As he surveyed them, the commander-in-chief of the expedition remarked to the commanding officer of one of the companies in his own regiment, beside whom he happened to be standing: "We're going to take the town without firing another shot—at the point of the bayonet!"

It was one o'clock in the afternoon. When the descent had been made, a part of the infantry took up its position in the vale where the quixabeiras stood; on its right was the Seventh, lined up along the course of the Vasa-Barris; and, on its left, the Ninth and Sixteenth, badly placed on unsuitable ground. The artillery was in the center, upon the last spur of the hills, in an advanced position directly above the river, facing the new church and on a level with its cornices; it thus became the axis of a pincers designed to close in and grip the flanks of the settlement. This was the most rudimentary of battle lines, a simple parallel formation, adapted to those rare cases of battle in the open country where a superiority in the matter of numbers and of bravery renders more complex maneuvers unnecessary and permits of a simultaneous and equal action on the part of all the fighting units upon a uniform terrain.

CHARACTER OF THE TERRAIN; CRITICAL OBSERVATIONS

Such a line of assault was inconceivable here. Centering at the eminence where the cannons were, the various parts of the line were confronted with absolutely different topographical conditions. On the right was a small level area that rendered an attack easy, for the reason that the river at this point had an even bed and its banks were low. On the left the land was more rugged, falling away in rolling hillocks and, moreover, was separated from the village by a deep trench. The most hasty observation would accordingly indicate that, while conditions on the extreme left were wholly unfavorable for combatants running forward to an assault, they were, on the other hand, a tactical asset of the first order if a reserve force were to be promptly stationed there, either as a slight diversionary movement, or in order that it might opportunely intervene, depending upon how the engagement developed. Thus it may be seen that the general configuration of the terrain in itself dictated an oblique line, either a simple one, or reinforced on one of its wings, and, in place of a simultaneous attack, a partial attack on the right, firmly supported by the artillery, the effect of whose fire, at a range of a little more than a hundred yards from the enemy, would be terrific.

Furthermore, such an arrangement would not permit of any surprises; and in case the enemy should display unexpected powers of resistance, the reserve troops, being outside the mêlée, would be able to move about more freely in accordance with the contingencies that might arise and would be able to engage in decisive maneuvers, with definite objectives. Colonel Moreira Cesar, however, disdained to take these imperative considerations into account and insisted upon lining up all his forces at once. He appeared to be relying not so much upon the bravery of his men and the loyalty and competence of their officers as upon a doubtful supposition: the fright and terror of the fleeing sertanejos as they found themselves suddenly hemmed in by hundreds of bayonets. This supposition was clearly an unjustifiable one, revealing an ignorance of the rudimentary principles of his profession and a forgetfulness of what had happened to previous expeditions; and he now topped it off by planning an assault under the most disastrous of circumstances.

The fact of the matter is that, with the battalions attacking at once from two sides and bearing down upon a single objective, within a short space of time they would be facing each other and exchanging bullets intended for the jagunço. While the artillery at the beginning might bombard the churches and the center of the town, the scope of its action would gradually be limited as the troops advanced, until finally it would be obliged to fall silent just as the battle reached its decisive phase, from fear of firing upon the troops themselves as they mingled in hand-to-hand combat with the enemy in that labyrinth of huts.

It did not require the eagle eye of any master-strategist to foresee all this; it was revealed plainly enough in the first minutes of action.

"WEED-TRAP CITADEL"

The battle began heroically, with all the troops moving into action at once and with all the bugles blowing. The church bell was once more ringing, and an intense rifle fire had broken out from the walls and roofs of the dwellings nearest to the river, while the blunderbusses of the guerrillas massed within the new church produced the effect of a single explosion. With the advantage of a favorable terrain, the Seventh Battalion marched forward on the double-quick, amid a hail of lead and pebbles,[26] down to the river; and it was not long before, having climbed the opposite bank, the first of the soldiers were to be seen at the entrance to the *praça;* they were in small groups, without anything whatsoever to suggest a battle formation. Some of them fell at the river crossing, or tumbled into the stream to be swept away by the current, which was streaked with blood; but the majority continued to advance under heavy fire from the front and sides. On the extreme left, one wing of the Ninth, having overcome the obstacles in its path, had taken up a position at the rear of the new church, while the Sixteenth and the right wing of the Seventh attacked in the center. A pitched battle was now raging around the column which was advancing in so rash a manner; and from then on, there was not the simplest military movement or joint maneuver such as might have revealed the presence of a commander.

The battle was now breaking up into smaller skirmishes which were at once futile and dangerous, with much fine bravery ingloriously thrown away. This was inevitable. Canudos, less than a couple of yards from the square, became a hopeless maze of alleys, winding and crossing in all di-

[26] [Fired from the blunderbusses or *trabucos*.]

rections. With its mud-built huts, the town may have given the impression of fragility, but this was an illusion; it was in reality more formidable than a polygonal citadel or one protected by strong armored walls. Lying wide open to attackers, who might destroy it with their rifle butts, who might with a blow knock down the clay walls and roofs or send them flying in all directions, it yet possessed the lack of consistency and the treacherous flexibility of a huge net. It was easy to attack it, overcome it, conquer it, knock it down, send it hurtling—the difficult thing was to leave it. A complement to the dangerous tactics of the sertanejo, it was formidable for the very reason that it offered no resistance. There was not so much as a hard-surface tile to break the percussion of the grenades, which fell without exploding, piercing dozens of roofs at once. There was nothing to cause the smallest band of attackers to waver, from whatever side they might come, once they had crossed the river. Canudos invited attacks; it exerted an irresistible attraction for the enemy who would bombard it; but when the invaders, drunken with a feeling of victory, began separating and scattering out down the winding lanes, it then had a means of defense that was at once amazing and tremendously effective.[27]

In the somber story of cities taken by storm, this humble village must stand out as an extraordinary and a tragic instance. Intact, it was very weak indeed; reduced to a rubbish heap, it was redoubtable. Yielding in order to conquer, it suddenly appeared before the victor's astonished gaze as an inexpugnable pile of ruins. For while an army with its iron grip might shake it, crush it, rend it asunder, leaving it a shapeless mass of mud walls and wooden stakes, that same army would of a sudden find itself with its hands tied, trapped between the tottering partitions of timber and liana stalks, like a clumsy puma powerfully but vainly struggling to free itself from the meshes of a well-made snare. The jagunços were experienced hunters, and this it was, perhaps, which led them to create this "weed-trap citadel."[28]

Colonel Moreira Cesar's troops were now engaged in springing that trap upon themselves.

SKIRMISHES

At first, after they had crossed the river in spite of a few losses, the attack appeared easy enough. One detachment, led by valorous subalterns,

[27] [It is of interest to compare the house-to-house street fighting in World War II, particularly on the Russian front, Stalingrad being the classic example.]

[28] ["*Cidadella-mundéo*" is the author's phrase. A *mundéo* is a trap placed on the path which animals take to go to the river to drink. It is made of planks, not fixed on the ground, but held together by lianas, which cross the path. The animal trips on the lianas, and this pulls the planks down, crushing it (*Strategic Index of Latin America*).]

boldly assaulted the new church, but without any compensating effect, and with the further loss of two officers and several men. Others, making a detour about this nucleus of resistance, fell upon the outlying houses along the river. They took them and set fire to them, as the inhabitants fled for shelter elsewhere. The latter were pursued as they fled by the soldiers; and it was in the course of this tumultuous pursuit that the one very grave peril of this monstrous undertaking became apparent: the platoons began to break up. The men now dashed down the narrow lanes, two abreast, in great confusion.[29] There were hundreds of corners to be turned, one after another, from house to house, and the soldiers rounded them in disorderly fashion, some of them without making use of their weapons, while others fired at random, straight ahead. In this manner the entire outfit gradually became split up into small wandering detachments, and these in their turn broke up into bewildered groups with numbers diminishing all the while as the forces became more and more scattered, until finally they were reduced to isolated combatants here and there.

From a distance the spectacle was a weird one, with whole battalions being suddenly swallowed up among the huts, as in some dark cave, while over the clay roofs there hovered a dense cloud of smoke from the first of the conflagrations. All in all, the attack was anything but military in character. It was no longer a battle but a series of skirmishes at the corners of the lanes and in the doorways of the houses.

Here, however, the attack was a fierce one, for there were no obstacles in the way. A blow from a rifle butt would effect an entrance through doors or walls, shattering them to bits and opening a free passage from any side. Many of the houses were empty. In others, the intruders would unexpectedly find a musket barrel against their chests, or else they would drop, riddled with bullets at close range fired from chinks in the wall. Their nearest comrades would then run to their assistance, and there would be a brutal hand-to-hand struggle, until the soldiers who outnumbered the inmates had forced their way through the narrow doorway of the hut. On the inside, crouching in a dark corner, a lone remaining inmate would fire his last shot at them and flee. Or it might be that he would stand his ground and stubbornly defend his humble dwelling, fighting terribly—and alone—to avenge himself on the victorious ruffians, boldly having recourse to any weapons at hand, repelling them with knife and bullet, slashing at them with scythe or cattle prong, hurling the wretched household furniture at their heads, or, weak and gasping for breath, rush-

[29] See pp. 311, 357.

ing upon them in an effort to strangle the first on whom he could lay his brawny arms. The womenfolk, meanwhile, would burst into sobs and cower in the corner, until at last the bold warrior lay on the ground, pierced with a bayonet, clubbed by gunstocks, trampled under the soldiers' bootheels. Scenes such as these were many.

PLUNDER BEFORE VICTORY

Almost always, after capturing a house, the famished soldier was unable to resist the longing he felt to have breakfast—at last—in Canudos. Suspended from the ceiling were the food containers,[30] and these he would search. In them he would find sun-dried meats, clay cups[31] filled with passoca (the sertanejo's wartime flour),[32] and bags brimming with the savory fruit of the urucuri. In a corner would be pouches with the moisture standing on them, swollen with water crystalline and fresh. The temptation was too much for him. Rashly, he would fall to for a minute's repast, topping it off with a large drink of water. Sometimes, however, he had a dessert of a cruel and bitter sort—a volley of lead.

The jagunços, coming in the door, would fall upon him, and the struggle would be repeated with the roles reversed this time, until the imprudent warrior lay on the ground, slashed with a knife, clubbed, trampled by the sertanejo's coarse sandals.

IN THE LABYRINTH OF LANES

Many became hopelessly lost in the alleyways. Hot on the heels of the fleeing woodsman, they would find themselves suddenly, as they rounded a corner, surrounded by a band of enemies. In their astonishment, they barely had time to take a bad aim and fire, then turn and run, dashing into the houses where, frequently, others lay in wait, ready to leap upon them; or else, they would attack and disperse the enemy group—whereupon the same scenes would be repeated all over again. And all the time they were buoyed by the illusion of a victory attained with dizzying ease. Was it not evident enough from all this disorder, all this fear and hubbub, all this terror on the part of the wretched, ugly little town? Why, the inhabitants were as frightened as the animals in a stable when the fierce and famished jaguars attack.

What was more, there were no insuperable obstacles in the invaders' way. The bold heroes who put in an appearance now and then, by way of

[30] [See p. 145 and n. 148 and p. 368.]

[31] [The *cuyas* (author's spelling: *cuias*) used by the Brazilian natives.]

[32] [See p. 107 and n. 99.]

defending their homes, had womenfolk to think about, driven out by fire, sword, and bullet, fleeing in all directions as they shrieked and prayed, or that armed legion of crutches—trembling old men and women, the lame and the halt of every description, the sick, the weak, and the maimed.

The upshot of it all was that in the fury of the chase many lost their way in that labyrinth of lanes and, in attempting to rejoin their companions, wandered farther astray than ever, as they madly dashed around a thousand little corners, only to become completely lost in the end in this enormous and convulsive-appearing settlement.

DISQUIETING SITUATION

Stationed in front of his headquarters on the right bank of the river, the commander-in-chief of the expedition was observing the attack, without quite being able to come to a decision regarding it. All he could make out was his men disappearing from sight among the thousand and one holes and hiding-places of Canudos, followed by a great uproar in which curses and shrill cries mingled with the sound of rifle fire. All that he could see was small groups, detachments of soldiers without any formation and small bands of jagunços suddenly coming into view now and then in the open space of the square, only to disappear once more amid the smoke, in a confused hand-to-hand struggle.

That was all, but it was enough to alarm him; the situation was now a disquieting one. There was nothing to indicate that the sertanejos were giving up the struggle. The sharpshooters at the new church were standing their ground, and were able with practical impunity to fire in all directions; for the artillery had finally ceased, from fear of striking some of the soldiers with a stray ball. And now, above all the din of battle, the bell of the old church was steadily ringing out once more. Only about half the village was involved in the fray; the other half, on the right, where the Geremoabo Highway came in, was unaffected by it. Less compactly built, it was at the same time less open to assault. Spread out over a large elevated plain, it could be defended on a line of fire level with the enemy, obliging the latter to the dangerous expedient of trying to take it by storm. Consequently, after the other part of the village had been stormed and taken, it still remained intact, and this, perhaps, meant that an even greater amount of effort must be expended here.

The truth is, while there were not the winding lanes to contend with, as down below, these scattered houses nonetheless, by the nature of their distribution which was vaguely reminiscent of a chessboard, afforded an extraordinarily good opportunity for cross-fire, so that a single marksman might command all four points of the compass without leaving his own small square. When one took this portion of the town into consideration, the full gravity of the situation became apparent. Even assuming that they had met with success in the center of the village, the victorious but exhausted troops would have to engage in a futile attack on that slope, which was separated from the *praça* by a deep gully. Colonel Moreira Cesar's eye took this in at a glance. Accordingly, when the rear guard consisting of the police detachment and the squadron of cavalry came up, he ordered the police to proceed to the extreme right and attack this unscathed portion of the settlement as a complement to the action which was taking place on the left. The cavalry, meanwhile, was to attack in the center, in the vicinity of the churches.

A cavalry charge in Canudos! This, surely, was an eccentric procedure. The cavalry is the classic arm of the service for use on open plains; its strength lies in the shock of a charge, when the mounted force comes in suddenly after a spirited attack by the infantry. Here, however, its movements were restricted by the walls of the huts and it had to charge, one man at a time, down those narrow corridors.

The cavalry—their winded mounts swaying on their unsteady legs— set off at a half-gallop down to the river's edge, where bullets were spattering in the water. That was as far as they could go, for their frightened steeds balked there. By digging in their spurs and lashing the animals with the flat of their swords, the cavalryman barely succeeded in making it to the middle of the stream, where, rearing and bounding, taking the bit in their teeth and sprawling their riders from the saddle, the horses made a wild rush for the bank from which they had started. The police for their part, after crossing the river in a downstream direction, in water up to their knees, came to a halt when they beheld the deep and slippery bed of the gully which at this point runs from north to south, separating from the rest of the town the "suburb" which they were supposed to attack. The complementary movement was thus frustrated at the very start; and it was then that the commander-in-chief of the expedition left the place where he had been stationed, halfway up the "Bald Pates" slope, between the artillery and the plain where the quixabeiras stood.

"I am going to put a little mettle into those fellows," he said.

MOREIRA CESAR "HORS DE COMBAT"

He started off but was no more than halfway there when, letting go the reins, he lurched forward over the saddlebow. A bullet had struck him in the abdomen. His staff now gathered about him.

"It is nothing," he said, "a slight wound," endeavoring to allay the fears of his devoted comrades. He was, as a matter of fact, mortally wounded.

He did not descend from his horse but, supported by Lieutenant Avila, returned to the place where he had been stationed, when another bullet struck him. He was *hors de combat* now, and Colonel Tamarindo, who was at once notified of the disastrous event, was the one who should have replaced him. The latter, however, was so preccupied with saving his own battalion, on the other bank of the river, that he could not think of taking over the command. A simple, good-natured, jovial fellow, going on sixty and looking forward to retirement and a peaceful old age, he was by nature averse to showy exploits. What was more, he had been assigned to the expedition against his will; and, even had he possessed the ability to deal with the present crisis, there was no way of remedying matters.

In the meantime the police in their attack had adopted the tactics of their comrades in the other part of the town by knocking down houses and setting fire to them. Disorder prevailed everywhere, without the slightest sign of any military maneuvers, which indeed were inconceivable under the circumstances. This was not an assault; it was merely a rash battering of a monstrous barricade, which became all the more formidable every moment as it tumbled in ruins and went up in smoke, for the reason that beneath the litter in the streets, the fallen roofs and the smoking timbers, the lurking sertanejos were all the better able to slip away in safety, or else found hiding-places there that were more secure.

And then there came a major misfortune, an inevitable one, as night suddenly swooped down on the mêlée of combatants, exhausted from five hours of fighting.

THE TROOPS FALL BACK

Already, however, before night came, the troops had begun falling back. On the left bank of the river scattered groups, the first of the fleeing detachments, could now be seen running about in confusion, and they were soon joined by others; breaking ranks entirely, dashing out from the corners of the churches and from behind the huts along the riverbank, officers and men together, filthy-looking, singed, their uniforms ripped to pieces, took to their heels in whatever direction seemed most favorable, depending upon the rifle fire of the enemy, a crazed, shouting, terror-stricken, staggering, fleeing mob.

Beginning on the left wing, this impulse spread to the far right. Compelled to retreat to its original positions, the entire battle line, raked by enemy fire, fell back in a writhing mass to the river's edge down below.

Without anyone to give the word of command, it was every man for himself. As they came to the river, a few small groups would split off, still, to set fire to the nearest houses or to engage in brief skirmishes, while the others, wounded or with no weapons left, were only interested in crossing the stream. It was a veritable rout.

And then, of a sudden, having fallen back to their last positions, under the hypnotic spell of panic and amid an indescribable tumult, the men, deserting their platoons, leaped headlong into the level-flowing current of the river! Struggling with one another, trampling the wounded, brutally beating off the maimed and exhausted, pushing them under and stifling them, the first of the fugitives made their way to the right bank and started to scramble up it. Getting such a hold as they could on the scant grass, propping themselves on their weapons, grasping the legs of their fortunate comrades ahead of them who were already clambering over the top, they became once more on the other side of the river a clamoring, fleeing mass. All that could be seen was a swarm of human bodies up and down the river, accompanied by loud, discordant cries. It was as if, as the result of some downpour, the Vasa-Barris had suddenly risen and leaped from its bed, bubbling, foaming, raging.

THE "AVE MARIA"

At this moment the bell ringer in the tower of the old church broke in upon the confusion. Night was falling, and in the half-light of dying day there cane the melodious notes of the "Ave Maria."

Baring their heads, tossing their leather hats or bright blue caps to the ground, the jagunços let fly one parting shot, as they murmured their accustomed prayers.

V

ON MOUNT MARIO

Having crossed the river, the soldiers gathered about the artillery. They were now a panic-stricken mob, without any resemblance whatever to a military force; they were an army in an advanced state of decomposition, all that was left being a number of terrified and useless individuals whose one thought now was to avoid the enemy with whom they had previously been so anxious to come to grips. The hill where they were at present was much too close to that enemy, who might, possibly, attack them there under cover of darkness, and it was accordingly necessary to abandon it. Still without any kind of order, dragging the cannons after them, they accordingly made their way to Mount Mario, four hundred yards farther on. There they improvised an incorrect square formation, with their broken ranks, their officers, the ambulances with the wounded, and the artillery and supply trains. In the center of their "camp" were the ruins of the "Old Ranch House," and here their commander-in-chief lay dying. All that was left of the expedition now was this hodgepodge of men, animals, uniforms, and rifles, dumped in a fold of the mountains.

Night had come, one of those intensely bright nights which are common in the backlands, when every star—fixed, not twinkling—seems to radiate heat, as the cloudless horizons light up from moment to moment with the reflected lightning gleams of distant tempests.

The settlement was invisible now; or, rather, all that was visible was a few smoldering fires where the wood beneath the mud walls and roofs was still being consumed, or the pale glow of a lantern shimmering in the darkness here and there and moving slowly about, as if the bearer were engaged in a mournful search of some sort. These lights showed that the enemy was keeping watch, but the firing had ceased and there was not a sound to be heard. The brilliant starlight made it barely possible to discern the faint outlines of the church buildings, standing out from the rest; but the compact mass of huts, the hills round about, the distant mountains—all were lost in the night.

The disorder of the camp afforded a contrast to the peaceful surroundings. Huddled in between their comrades more than a hundred maimed and wounded men, tortured with pain and thirst, writhed in agony or crept about on their hands and knees, in grave peril of being trampled by the frightened, neighing horses of the supply train. It was out of the question to undertake to treat them here in the darkness, where the careless lighting of a match would have been an incredibly foolhardy act. In addition to this, there were not enough surgeons to go around, one of them—either dead, strayed, or captured—having disappeared that afternoon, never to return.[33]

COLONEL TAMARINDO

What was lacking, above all, was a commander possessed of the requisite firmness. The burdens laid upon him were too heavy for Colonel Tamarindo, who inwardly cursed the turn of fate which had forced him into this catastrophic position. He made no plans, and to an officer who anxiously inquired as to what he meant to do he replied with a wry humor by quoting a popular north-country refrain:

> E'tempo de muricy
> Cada um cuide de si . . . .

[33] Dr. Fortunato Raymundo de Oliveira.

"The time has come to die; every man for himself. . . . ." That was his only order of the day. Seated on a drum case, sucking on his pipe in pained but stoic discouragement, he gave a similar reply or muttered a few monosyllables to all who sought his counsel; he had entirely abdicated his function of bringing order out of this disheartened mob by performing the miracle of dividing them into fresh combat units.

There were, assuredly, men of valor among them, and their officers were ready to sacrifice themselves; but the old commander's intuition told him that, under such conditions, the numerical aggregate was not equal to the sum of individual energies, and he could not but take into account those circumstances which, in the case of crowds that are a prey to violent emotions, always tend to offset the most brilliant of personal qualities. He therefore remained impassive, aloof from the general anxiety, thus tacitly yielding his command to the men at large. On their own account the indefatigable officers took those precautions which were most urgent, by rectifying as best they could the alleged square formation in which men of all companies were mixed together at random, by organizing the ambulance train and arranging for litters, and by attempting to raise the spirits of the soldiers. Many of them were inspired by the thought that the next morning at daybreak they would renew the assault by descending full force and launching a violent attack on the fanatics, after the latter had been given a taste of a stronger bombardment than the one they had had the day before. With such an idea in mind, they put their heads together in laying plans that would retrieve, through daring acts of valor, the defeat they had suffered; for victory must be obtained, no matter what the cost. Within the four sides of this ill-formed square, so their thoughts ran, the destinies of the Republic were at stake. They simply must win; they were revolted and painfully humiliated by this grave yet ridiculous situation in which they found themselves, surrounded by modern cannon, with the best weapons made, seated on packing cases filled to the brim with cartridges—and penned in a corner by a horde of riotous backwoodsmen.

The majority, however, took a dispassionate view of the matter. They were under no illusions. They had but to picture to themselves the troops as they had arrived a few hours before, enthusiastic and confident of victory, and contrast that picture with the one before them; when they did this, it was clear to them that there was but one solution possible—a retreat.

PROPOSED RETREAT

There was no other recourse to be thought of; they must retreat and retreat at once.

It was eleven o'clock at night when the officers unanimously adopted this plan, and a captain of infantry was appointed to make known their resolution to Colonel Moreira Cesar. The latter was surprised and dismayed when he learned of it. He remained calm at first, as he spoke of military obligations that must be fulfilled, pointing out that they still possessed sufficient resources to make another attempt of some sort, more than two-thirds of the troops being fit for combat duty and the supply of ammunition being adequate. Then, as his anguish and indignation grew, he began casting aspersions on the riffraff who would soil his name forever; and, finally, he could restrain himself no longer but burst out: No! he would not give in to such unbelievable cowardice.

In spite of this, however, the officers adhered to the resolution which they had adopted.

MOREIRA CESAR'S PROTEST

This was all that was needed to complete the agony of the unfortunate hero. In deep disgust he gave his last word of command: let them put all this in writing, leaving space in the margin for him to enter his protest, along with his resignation. Even this grievous reprimand on the part of their twice-wounded superior failed to sway his able-bodied staff from their decision. It was true enough that they still had hundreds of soldiers, eight hundred, it might be; they likewise had two-thirds of their ammunition intact and were in a position overlooking the enemy.

But this very night the backlands conflict had begun to take on that mysterious aspect which it was to preserve until the end. The majority of the soldiers were mestizos, of the same racial stock as the backwoodsmen; and in their discouragement over the inexplicable defeat which they had suffered and the loss of their commander who had been reputed to be invincible, they readily fell victim to the power of suggestion and, seeing in it all an element of the marvelous and the supernatural, were filled with an unreasoning terror—a terror that was further increased by the extravagant stories that were going around.

The burly and brutal jagunço was now transformed into an intangible hobgoblin. Most of the combatants, even those who had been wounded in the recent engagement, had not so much as laid eyes on a single one of the enemy. Others, who had been members of the previous expedition, were dumfounded to behold, resurrected in the flesh as they believed, two or three of the rebel leaders who, they asserted with conviction, had died at Cambaio. And to all of them, even the most incredulous, there did begin to appear to be something abnormal about these ghostlike, all but invisible fighters with whom they had struggled so impotently, having had no more than a glimpse of a few of them here and there, dodging boldly in and out among the ruins and dashing unscathed through what was left of the blazing huts. Many of the soldiers were from the North, and they, upon hearing Antonio Conselheiro's name, were inclined to associate him with the heroes of childhood tales. The extravagant legend which had grown up about him, his miracles, his unrivaled exploits as a sorcerer, now appeared to them to have been overwhelmingly verified by this tremendous catastrophe.

Along toward midnight their apprehensions were greatly increased, when the drowsing sentinels who had been posted to guard the laxly organized camp suddenly awoke in terror, uttering cries of alarm. The silence of the night was broken by a strange sound coming up the mountainside. It was not, however, the dull tramp of an attacking party. It was something worse than that. The enemy down below, in that invisible town—was praying. This extraordinary occurrence, at this time of night—mournful litanies, with feminine in place of masculine voices predominating, welling up from the ruins of a battlefield—all this was formidable indeed. The effect was heightened by contrast. As the astounded soldiers whispered in fear, those sorrowful-sounding tag ends of "Kyrie's" seemed worse to them than forthright threats would have been. In this eloquent manner they were being told that there was no contending with an enemy who was thus transfigured by religious faith.

Retreat was now more of a necessity than ever; and at dawn the next day a disturbing piece of news rendered it most urgent. Colonel Moreira Cesar had died.

THE RETREAT

This was all that was needed to complete the feeling of general discouragement. The preparations for departure were made in great haste and amid an indescribable tumult. At the first break of day a contingent made up of men from all the corps set out as a vanguard, closely followed by the supply trains and the ambulances and litters bearing the wounded, on one of which lay the body of the ill-fated commander of the expedition. There was nothing in all this to indicate that a serious military operation was under way.

The retreat was in reality a flight. Advancing over the summit, in the direction of Mount Favella, and then descending the steep slopes on the other side by the road which runs there, the expeditionaries spread out over the hills in a long and scattering line, without any semblance of military formation. In thus turning their back on the enemy down below, who, though alert, was not troubling them as yet, they appeared to be trusting solely to the swiftness of their movements to get them out of their plight. There was no defensive-offensive alignment by successive stages such as is the characteristic procedure in military crises of this sort. All that they did was to rush down the roads at top speed, with no thought of order or direction. They were not falling back; they were taking to their heels. One division alone, with two Krupp guns, under the command of a valorous subaltern, and strengthened by an infantry detachment, stood its ground for some time on Mount Mario by way of holding off the inevitable pursuit.

THE DRAMA ENDS IN HISSES

When it did finally get under way, this self-sacrificing detachment was fiercely assaulted. The enemy now had the impetus that comes from taking the offensive and was further aware of the dread he inspired in the fleeing troops. To the accompaniment of loud and enthusiastic *viva*'s, he attacked violently from all sides, in a circling movement. Down below, the bell was ringing wildly, and there was a burst of rifle fire from the new church, as the entire population of Canudos thronged into the square or dashed over the hilltops to view the scene, conferring upon the tragic episode an irritatingly mocking note, as thousands of throats gave vent to a prolonged, shrill, deadly intentioned whistling.

Once again, the fearful drama of backlands warfare was ending in lugubrious hoots and hisses.

The evacuation of the camp was accomplished within a short space of time. The final division of artillery returned the enemy's fire for a few moments and then in turn slowly lumbered off down the slope, in full retreat.

It was afternoon; and, as far as the eye could reach, the expedition, sprawled along the roadways, was from place to place flanked by jagunços.

VI

BROKEN RANKS; FLIGHT

The ranks were now completely broken. Eight hundred men were engaged in flight, throwing their rifles away, dropping the litters on which the wounded were writhing, abandoning their equipment, undoing their belts that they might be able to run the faster—running, running, in any direction, without weapons, in small groups and wandering bands, running down the road and along the intersecting paths, making for the depths of the caatingas, terrified, out of their senses, leaderless.

Among the burdens deposited along the side of the road when the panic broke out was—mournful detail!—the body of the commander. There was no effort to protect his remains, not the slightest effort to repel the enemy whom they had not glimpsed, but who made his presence known by noisy shouts of defiance and by scattering shots at irregular intervals, like those of a hunter in the brush. At the first sound of those shots, the battalions melted away.

SALOMÃO DA ROCHA

The artillery alone, in the extreme rear, proceeded slowly, one might say solemnly, with ranks unbroken and at its accustomed pace, as if on parade. Now and then it would halt, to sweep the treacherous weeds along the wayside with cannon fire, and then would continue to roll along leisurely, immune to assault, terror-inspiring.

The rout of the troops stopped here, with these steel cannon, and with the soldiers who manned them, who, inspired by the moral influence of a brave commander, stood out from all their fellows by reason of the marvelous courage they displayed. The result was that, after a while, the pursuers tended to concentrate upon the artillery detachment; and, if the rest of the expedition was able to make its escape, it was thanks to this battery.[34] To come up against Salomão da Rocha's four Krupps was like coming up against a dam; the swelling, roaring, mounting wave of jagunços would break and recede.

The pursuers, meanwhile, kept up their sinister hooting, which represented an ugly mixture of ferocity and cowardice. And then an episode occurred which was epic in character.

Held at a distance at first, the attacking sertanejos gradually closed in upon the two divisions, which either fought them off while continuing their slow retreat, or else, lining up in battle formation, let them have a devastating round of cannon shot.

The grenades, exploding among the dried stubble, set the weed patches on fire, and there could then be heard the crackling of a conflagration whose flames were invisible in the bright, clear air of morning. At the same time, cries of pain and anger were heard as the sertanejos, blinded

34 See pp. 271, 380.

with the smoke, leaped forth from their hiding-places and came trooping out along the edge of the caatinga next the road, shouting, cursing, running, firing off their blunderbusses and their pistols, unable to understand this resistance on the part of a small band of indomitable heroes whom they were bent upon attacking with knives and spears.

Those same heroes, in the meantime, their numbers greatly reduced, were making slow progress. One by one, the soldiers of this stoic detachment fell. Wounded or frightened, the mules of the supply train whirled and veered, blocking the way and making it impossible to go on. Finally, the battery came to a halt. The cannons were stuck at a bend of the road and could not be moved.[35]

Colonel Tamarindo had come back to the rear and was bravely and tirelessly exerting himself to encourage the fugitives, thereby heroically, at this moment of utter catastrophe, making up for his previous weakness. As he came upon this stupendous scene of rout, he was moved to do what he could to aid these soldiers of his, who, after all, were the only ones to have reached Canudos; but his efforts were in vain. With this object in view, he had ordered the bugles to sound the command, "Column right, halt!" But the buglers might blow for all that was in them; it had no effect whatsoever, or, rather, it had the effect of accelerating the flight of the men. Amid all this confusion there was but one command which could be given with any possibility of its being carried out, and that was "Break ranks!"

Vainly, a few indignant officers thrust revolvers against the fugitives' chests; there was no restraining them. On, on, they ran, ran madly, running from their officers, running from the jagunços; and, when those who brought up the rear were shot down, they did not so much as turn their heads. Captain Villarim fought valiantly and almost alone, and, as he lay dying, there was not a one of his men to place an arm beneath him. The maimed and wounded were left to stagger along, dragging themselves over the ground and cursing out their more active comrades.

Over all this tumult the notes of the bugler went unheard, unheeded. At last the bugles ceased. There were no longer any troops to summon. The infantry had disappeared.

Along the side of the road were to be seen scattered pieces of equipment, knapsacks and rifles, belts and sabers, thrown away at random as useless objects. Entirely alone, without a single orderly, Colonel Tamarindo dashed down the road—deserted now—at a desperate gallop, as if he were bent on personally heading off the vanguard. As for the artillery,

[35] See pp. 297, 316.

it was wholly abandoned, finally, before reaching "Angico," and the jagunços at once fell upon it. This was the end. Captain Salomão now had about him barely half-a-dozen loyal men; the enemy closed in upon him and he fell, cut to pieces with the blows of a scythe, beside the cannon which he had never abandoned. The catastrophe was complete.

Not long after this, as he was galloping along the ravine to "Angico," Colonel Tamarindo was knocked from his horse by a bullet. He was still alive when the army engineer, Alfredo do Nascimento, reached his side. Lying beside the road, the old commander whispered his last order in his comrade's ear: "Get Cunha Mattos."[36]

That order was a difficult one to carry out.

AN OPEN-AIR ARSENAL

The third expedition was now done for, dispersed; it had vanished utterly. Most of the fugitives, avoiding the highroad, lost their way and wandered aimlessly, with no sense of direction, over the desert wastes; and many of them here—many of the wounded, especially—were left to breathe their last in absolute abandonment. Some, striking off from the main route, made for Cumbe or points more remote. The rest of them, one day or another, showed up at Monte Santo. Colonel Souza Menezes, commander of the garrison, was not expecting them and, upon learning of the disaster, galloped away at top speed to Queimadas, which had become a terminus of this human stampede.

In the meanwhile, the sertanejos were gathering up the spoils. Along the road and in near-by spots weapons and munitions lay strewn, together with pieces of the soldiers' uniforms, military capes and crimson-striped trousers, which, standing out against the gray of the caatingas, would have made their wearers too conspicuous as they fled. From which it may be seen that the major portion of the troops not only had thrown away their weapons but had stripped themselves of their clothing as well.

Thus it was that, midway between "Rosario" and Canudos, the jagunços came to assemble a helter-skelter open-air arsenal; they now had enough and more than enough in the way of arms to satisfy their needs. The Moreira Cesar expedition appeared to have achieved this one objective: that of supplying the enemy with all this equipment, making him a present of all these modern weapons and munitions.

A CRUEL DIVERSION

The jagunços took the four Krupps back to the settlement,[37] their front-line fighters now equipped with formidable Mannlichers and Com-

---

[36] [See pp. 234, 244.]   [37] See p. 456.

blains in place of the ancient, slow-loading muskets. As for the uniforms, belts, military bonnets, anything that had touched the bodies of the cursed soldiery, they would have defiled the epidermis of these consecrated warriors, and so the latter disposed of them in a manner that was both cruel and gruesome.

The successes they had thus far achieved had exacerbated, at one and the same time, their sense of mysticism and their inclinations to brutality. The prestige of the soldier was gone, and the sertanejos' rude and swaggering leaders proceeded to make the most of every incident and detail. The government's strength was now, in truth, the government's *weakness;* and this term ("government weakling") was one that was destined to be employed by them throughout the balance of the campaign.[38] They had seen this force arrive, impressive and terrifying, equipped with weapons compared to which their own crude firearms were mere children's toys; they had seen the troops fall upon the settlement, attack it, invade it, set fire to it, overrun it; and then they had beheld them falling back, had seen them in flight, a flight that became a wild stampede, as they tossed their arms and equipment along the roadside. It was, without doubt, a miracle. The aspect of events troubled their minds, and they could see but one possible interpretation of it all: they were obviously under the protection of Divinity itself and its superior powers. This conviction, strengthened by the brutal nature of the conflict, continued to grow, and resulted in a revival of all their barbarous instincts, to the deterioration of their character.

There was a strange occurrence which bore witness to this, a kind of sinister diversion reminiscent of the tragically perverted religious sense of the Ashantis,[39] which came as a sequel to the events narrated. Having concluded their search of the roads and trails, and having gathered up and brought in all the weapons and munitions of war that they found, the jagunços then collected all the corpses that were lying here and there, decapitated them, and burned the bodies; after which they lined the heads up along both sides of the highway, at regular intervals, with the faces turned toward the road. Above these, from the tallest shrubbery, they suspended the remains of the uniforms and equipment, the trousers and multicolored dolmans, the saddles, belts, red-striped kepis, the capes, blankets, canteens, and knapsacks.[40]

The barren, withered caatinga now blossomed forth with an extrava-

[38] [Cf. p. 212.]

[39] [See p. 113 and n. 106.]

[40] See pp. 303–4, 375.

gant-colored flora: the bright red of officers' stripes, the pale blue of dolmans, set off by the brilliant gleam of shoulder straps and swaying stirrups.

There is one painful detail which must be added to complete this cruel picture: at one side of the road, impaled on a dried angico bough,[41] loomed the body of Colonel Tamarindo.

It was a horrifying sight. Like a terribly macabre manikin, the drooping corpse, arms and legs swaying in the wind as it hung from the flexible, bending branch, in these desert regions took on the appearance of some demoniac vision. It remained there for a long time.

And when, three months later, a fresh expeditionary force set out for Canudos, this was the scene that greeted their eyes: rows of skulls bleaching along the roadside, with the shreds of one-time uniforms stuck up on the tree branches round about, while over at one side—mute protagonist of a formidable drama—was the dangling specter of the old colonel.

[41] [The *angico* is a gum-bearing tree.]

CHAPTER VI

THE FOURTH EXPEDITION

I

DISASTERS

THE rout of the Moreira Cesar expedition was a major disaster, and the news of it aroused the entire nation. This state of mind, however, was reflected in measures which hardly corresponded to the gravity of the situation, as a fourth expedition got under way.

To begin with, there was widespread alarm; and, in the second place, the public indulged in the wildest variety of conjectures in an effort to explain how it was that so numerous and well equipped a force with a commander of such renown should have met with so crushing a defeat. Out of all this mental confusion there came the idea, at first vaguely voiced by a few individuals here and there but gradually growing into a firm conviction, that the riotous backlanders were not alone in their rebellion against the government but that they represented, rather, the vanguard of unknown phalanxes that were likely to spring up suddenly, everywhere at once, and bear down upon the new regime. And inasmuch as there were to be found in the federal and state capitals, some years back, half-a-dozen platonic revolutionaries of a tame and dreamy sort who were engaged in a futile propaganda for the restoration of the monarchy, this circumstance was taken as the point of departure for a most unproductive line of reasoning.

CANUDOS—A DIATHESIS

For events of such import an explanation of some sort was indeed necessary, and so they proceeded to find one: the backland disturbances were but the forerunners of a vast conspiracy against our newly established institutions. Canudos was a Koblentz built of hovels, and behind the uncouth figure of the rebel chieftain, Pajehú,[1] lurked the noble profile of some Brunswick. The deposed Bragança dynasty had finally found a Monk in João Abbade; and Antonio Conselheiro—a Messiah of the village fair— held in his palsied hands the destinies of a people.

The Republic was in danger; the Republic must be saved: this was the one cry that arose above the general delirium.

[1] [See pp. 158 and 220–21.]

Are we perhaps exaggerating? One has but to glance through any newspaper of those days, and he will come upon such dogmatic opinions as the following:

The thing which at one stroke has undermined the prestige of constituted authority and impaired the renown, the traditions, and the strength of our fatherland has been that armed movement which, under the guise of religious fanaticism, has violently attacked our institutions. No one can longer be under any illusions as to the course of action upon which the imperialist sympathizers have entered; they are now up in arms.

And the writer concludes:

There is no one who at this moment does not realize that revolutionary monarchism is out to destroy the Republic, and, with it, Brazilian unity.[2]

Or here is another explanation:

The tragedy of the third of March, in which, along with Moreira Cesar, the illustrious Colonel Tamarindo and so many of our most brilliant army officers lost their lives, only goes to show how the Monarchist party, taking advantage of the public tolerance and thanks even to the public's involuntary support, has grown in power and boldness.[3]

Such statements as this were common:

It is a question of a conspiracy to restore the monarchy, and an imperialist army is being formed to that end. The peril is a grave one, and the remedy must be equal to it. So the monarchy is arming itself, is it? Let the President call to arms all good republicans.[4]

And so on and so forth. It was in this manner that the public opinion of the nation was expressing itself in the press. In the press and in the streets.

A few active citizens called a mass meeting in the capital of the Republic and, as an expression of their patriotic anxiety, adopted the following sharply worded resolution:

The people of Rio de Janeiro, in meeting assembled, being aware of the grievous reverses which our armed forces have met with in the backlands of Baía, where they were fallen upon by monarchist gangsters,[5] do hereby voice our support of the government and our approval of all the energetic measures which the civil authorities may take by way of avenging this insult to our army and to the fatherland, as we anxiously await the suppression of the revolt.

The same note was to be heard on all sides. Everywhere there was an obsession with the monarchist specter, transforming into legions—mysterious cohorts, marching silently in the darkness—those half-dozen reactionaries who were no more than headstrong visionaries.

[2] *Gazeta de noticias.*

[3] *O Paiz.*   [4] *O Estado de São Paulo.*

[5] [*"Caudilhagem monárchica"*: referring to *caudilhos*, leaders or chieftains (cf. the Spanish *caudillo*).]

The president of the Republic for once abandoned his accustomed serenity: "We know that, back of the Canudos fanatics, politics is at work. But we are ready for them; we have all that we need to win, by whatever means may be necessary, against whomsoever it may be necessary to fight."

MOBBING OF THE MONARCHIST JOURNALS

Finally, the mob took a hand. We give the newspaper account:

It was already late and the excitement of the people grew as their numbers increased. In their indignation, they happened to think of the monarchist journals, and, as if moved by a single impulse of revenge, they made their way to the editorial offices and printing plants of the *Gazeta da tarde*, *Liberdade*, and *Apóstolo*. The police came running up to prevent an assault on these properties, but they did not arrive in time, and the mob, with shouts of "Long live the Republic!" and with cheers for the memory of Floriano Peixoto, proceeded to invade the establishments in question, destroying and setting fire to everything.

They began burning and putting out of commission everything that they could lay their hands on, and all these objects, books, papers, pictures, furniture, utensils, signboards, partitions, etc., were tossed out into the street, whence they were taken to the São Francisco de Paula Square, where a huge bonfire was made of them, while others were similarly piled up and reduced to ash heaps, in the Rua do Ouvidor itself.[6]

RUA DO OUVIDOR AND THE CAATINGAS

At this point we must interrupt our rummaging among the debris. Once again, in connection with those events which we have set out to narrate, we shall avoid a detailed analysis of episodes which belong to a higher realm of history. The foregoing lines were written with one object in view, namely, to call attention in passing to a certain similarity between the scene in the Rua do Ouvidor and a disturbance in the caatingas, one equaling the other in savagery. Backlands lawlessness was precipitately making its entrance into history; and the Canudos revolt, when all is said, was little more than symptomatic of a malady which, by no means confined to a corner of Baía, was spreading to the capitals of the seaboard. The man of the backlands, that rude, leather-clad figure, had partners in crime who were, possibly, even more dangerous. Is it worth while to be more explicit?

Here, as in all places and in all ages, the portentous force of heredity, out of the most advanced environment, was producing—gloved though they might be and with a veneer of culture—thoroughgoing troglodytes. Civilization in general, in its normal course, contemns such beings; it dominates and manacles them, rendering them useless and gradually destroying them by driving them back to the darkness of a meaningless ex-

[6] *Jornal do Brasil.*

istence, from which they are rescued only now and again through the curiosity of some fanciful sociologist or the researches of some psychiatrist. But it invariably happens that a profound shock will bring them into conflict with the law, and they then arise and invade history and a scandal ensues. They are the reverse side of the historic medal, affording that light and shade which is indispensable for events of major relief. Beyond this, they possess no function, no significance, that is to be revealed by analysis. Viewing them, the keenest intelligence becomes inert, like a *flintglass*[7] lens which is excellent for refracting and amplifying bright objects, but which is of no use in the dark. But let us leave them and go on. Not, however, before we have stressed this one point: that to attribute the backlands crisis to a political conspiracy of any kind is to reveal a glaring ignorance of the natural conditions surrounding our race.

REFLECTIONS

The case, as we have already seen, is a good deal more complex and interesting than that. It involves a set of facts with which those somnambulists who go about immersed in the dream of imperialist restoration have nothing to do. An ignorance of such facts leads to disasters worse than the wiping-out of these three expeditions. It shows that we ourselves are but little in advance of our rude and backward fellow-countrymen. The latter, at least, were logical. Isolated in space and time, the jagunço, being an ethnic anachronism, could do only what he did do—that is, combat, and combat in a terrible fashion, the nation which, after having cast him off for three centuries almost, suddenly sought to raise him to our own state of enlightenment at the point of the bayonet, revealing to him the brilliancy of our civilization in the blinding flash of cannons.

It was natural that he should react to this. The surprising thing is the surprise occasioned by such a fact. Canudos was a miserable weed patch, not even shown on our maps, lost in the desert and as indecipherable as a page torn from the book of our numberless national traditions. The only comparison that one can think of here is that of geologic strata, which not infrequently are disturbed and inverted, with a modern formation beneath an ancient one; so the moral stratification of peoples likewise may show an inversion and confusion of layers, with undulating furrows and abrupt synclinals, breaking out in *faults*[8] in the form of ancient stages through which the race has long since passed. So viewed, Canudos was, above all else, a lesson and should have awakened a lively curiosity, that same curi-

---

[7] [The word is in English.]

[8] [The text has *flaults*.]

osity which the archeologist experiences as he comes upon the palafittes of a pile-built village alongside an industrial city in modern Switzerland.

With us, however, as a general rule, it awakened only rancors. We failed to grasp the larger significance of the event. This most unusual efflorescence of the past, revealing all the cracks and fissures in our evolution, afforded us a fine opportunity to study, correct, and do away with those faults; but we could not understand the eloquent lesson that it offered. In the first city of the land, patriots were satisfied with making an auto-da-fé of a few hostile journals; and then the government began to act. And to act meant—to assemble fresh battalions.

CONFLICTING ACCOUNTS

When the first news of the disaster was received, the entire country was thrown into a state of excitement for days. The report of the battle made by Major Cunha Mattos[9] was highly unsatisfactory, barely indicating the main phases of the action; it was marred, moreover, by strange errors and was hardly written with the degree of emotional eloquence that might have been expected under the circumstances. Those of us who read it had the impression that what had occurred was an immense slaughter, and later information tended to confirm this view. That information was very unreliable and contradictory in character and merely had the effect of increasing the excitement and curiosity of the public. The result was an endless amount of gossip and conjectures. In all this medley of abstruse opinions, it was impossible to form the slightest notion as to the causes of it all. Accounts with all the appearance of reality were greedily accepted, until others of a different sort were received, whereupon these latter became the true story of what had really happened; one tale would hold the public's attention for a day or an hour and then give way to other equally ephemeral versions. Rumors were timorously whispered in the homes, and scandalous lies noisily went the rounds in the street; and the consequence was that the people, constantly tormented by excruciating doubts, grew more and more apprehensive and alarmed. Nothing definite was known. It was not even known who had participated in the rout. With all the inconsistent hearsay reports, a single bit of news was soon distorted in the telling beyond all recognition.

HEROIC LIES

It was asserted, for example, that Colonel Tamarindo was not dead; he had valiantly made his escape with a handful of loyal comrades and was at

[9] [See p. 274.]

this moment on his way to Queimadas. Then this rumor was corrected: he had escaped, that was true, but was lying gravely wounded in Massacará, where he had arrived at the point of death. This was followed in turn by a lugubrious affirmative: the unfortunate officer was in fact dead. And so it went.

The most alarming ideas, meanwhile, were being spread: the backlanders were not "a lot of crazy fanatics"; they were a "well-drilled, well-disciplined army," admirably equipped with Mauser rifles; and, what was more, they had artillery which they knew how to use very well. Some of our men, including Captain Villarim, had been blown to bits by splinters from their grenades.

CORPORAL ROQUE

Out of all these uncertainties the truth now and then emerged in heroic guise. The tragic death of Salomão da Rocha tended to salve the national pride. In addition, there was the legend of Corporal Roque, not quite so thrilling a one, but one nonetheless which made a deep impression on the public mind. A humble private who in a rare burst of courage had become another being, his heroism served to mark the culminating point of the battle. He was Moreira Cesar's orderly; and, when the troops fled and his commander's body was left lying alongside the road, he alone had remained with it, loyal soldier that he was, guarding the venerated remains which had been abandoned by an army. On his knees beside his commanding officer's corpse, he had fought there until his last cartridge was gone, being finally struck down, giving his life for a dead man.

This marvelous scene, highly colored by the popular imagination, was in itself almost a compensation for the enormity of the defeat that had been suffered. Patriotic subscriptions were taken up; public tributes were planned under civic auspices in commemoration of the event; and, to a chorus of glowing newspaper articles and stirring odes, this obscure soldier was on his way to a place in history when—unfortunate enough not to have died—he cut short the immortality that was being thrust upon him by making his appearance in the flesh, along with the last remaining stragglers, in Queimadas.

This was not the only disappointment that the public met with as the situation became clarified. While, on the one hand, the catastrophe was greatly reduced, on the other hand, its full import became all the more manifest. The three-hundred-and-some dead of the official reports came to life. Barely three days after the battle a good part of the expedition had already arrived in Queimadas, at a distance of 125 miles from Canudos.

One week later it was ascertained that 74 officers were there. Two weeks later, on the nineteenth of March, 1,081 combatants were there—in safety.

We have seen how many there were in the beginning,[10] and we shall not here engage in any subtraction. The figures speak for themselves. Yet, with all their singularly negative significance, they did not dampen the fervor and enthusiasm of the public.

MASS LEVIES

The governors and congresses of the states and the municipal corporations continued to clamor loudly for vengeance. All the official pronouncements, couched in the same resounding phrases, were merely variations on a single, monotonous theme, whose burden was that the enemies of the Republic, armed by the monarchist leaders, must be crushed. Like the inhabitants of the federal capital, the people of the other cities held meetings, listened to speeches, and adopted resolutions supporting the government in whatever measures it might see fit to take by way of avenging the disgrace that had been inflicted upon the army and (the conjunction is equal to a hundred eloquent pages) the fatherland. A period of national mourning was declared, and formal action to this effect was registered in the minutes of the municipal councils of the most remote towns and villages. There were masses for the dead in all the churches; and, by way of lending religious sanction to it all, the archbishops sent out an order to both the secular and the regular clergy to include in these masses the prayer, "Pro pace." Able-bodied citizens were now everywhere volunteering their services, and a number of battalions were raised, among them the Tiradentes, the Benjamin Constant, the Académico, and the Frei Caneca, made up of hardened veterans who had been under fire at the time of the revolt of the fleet; and there were others still, with patriots of every stamp thronging to join their ranks: the Deodoro, the Silva Jardim, the Moreira Cesar battalions. Yet this did not suffice.

PLANS

At army headquarters a recruiting campaign was begun to fill the vacancies in the various corps, and the president of the Republic declared that, in case of necessity, he would call to the colors the members of the federal congress themselves, while the vice-president, in a burst of patriotic fervor, wrote to the Military Club, valorously offering to take up the sword of the avenger. There was a host of plans and rare, incomparable,

[10] [About 1,300 (see p. 235).]

genius-inspired ideas. Illustrious engineers offered the blueprints of a miraculous railway to be built from Villa Nova to Monte Santo, over the summit of Mount Itiúba, to be completed within thirty days, at the end of which time a shrill chorus of steaming locomotives would burst triumphantly upon the fierce backlands. For all this time, at Canudos, the fate of the Republic was at stake.

There was information to confirm this—information of an astonishing sort. Canudos was not a village of truculent bandits; there were men of rare valor there, and names were then mentioned, among them those of well-known army and navy officials, fugitives since the September revolt, whom the Counselor had summoned to his side.

THE TRAMP OF SAVAGE FEET

The fact was vouched for: one of the rebel leaders was an exceedingly clever Italian engineer, who, likely as not, was skilled in Abyssinian warfare. Extraordinary details were related. There were so many people in the rebel settlement that, when nearly seven hundred of them deserted, their absence was not even noticed until many days later. And still the reports kept coming, one after another, pitilessly, and each still further increased the wearisome burden of apprehension for minds that were already overwrought. Monte Santo, Cumbe, Massacará, possibly even Geremoabo, had already been taken by the jagunços. The invading hordes, after having sacked these towns, were now converging on the South; they had reorganized their forces in Tucano, and from that point, their ranks swollen by fresh contingents, they were now headed for the seaboard, marching on the capital of Baía itself.

Keyed as it was to so high a pitch, the populace imagined that it could hear the dull tramp of savage feet.

Moreira's Cesar's battalions were the legions of Varus. They were pursued in their flight by thundering multitudes. It was not merely the jagunços. In Joazeiro, in the state of Ceará, a sinister heresiarch, Padre Cicero,[11] was gathering fresh multitudes of schismatics for the Counselor. In Pernambuco a maniac, José Guedes, astonished the authorities who questioned him by displaying the high stoic fortitude of a prophet. In Minas a clever rascal, João Brandão, had routed the guards and made away with a pack train laden with rifles and was now hiding out somewhere deep in the São Francisco backlands. The aura of madness was also visible in the South, where the Monk of Paraná made his appearance in

---

[11] [A clerical visionary who later, in 1914, was responsible for a revolution in northern Brazil. See Irineu Pinheiro, *O Joazeiro do Padre Cicero e a revolução de 1914* (Rio de Janeiro, 1938).]

connection with this extravagant competition of history and the insane asylum.

All this was obviously the doings of a conspiracy which for long had been engaged in undermining our institutions. The monarchist reactionaries had finally taken the aggressive, and these were but the first skirmishes, extraordinarily successful so far, of a vanguard represented by the backwoods fanatics. The government must act, and act promptly.

II

MOBILIZATION OF THE TROOPS

The battalions from all the states were now mobilized: the Twelfth, Twenty-fifth, Thirtieth, Thirty-first, and Thirty-second from Rio Grande do Sul; the Twenty-seventh from Paraíba; the Thirty-fourth from Rio Grande do Norte; the Thirty-third and the Thirty-fifth from Piauí; the Fifth from Maranhão; the Fourth from Pará; the Twenty-sixth from Sergipe; the Fourteenth and the Fifth from Pernambuco; the Second from Ceará; the Fifth and a part of the Ninth Cavalry and a regiment of artillery from the federal capital; the Seventh, Ninth, and Sixteenth from Baía.

The commander of the Second Military District, General Arthur Oscar de Andrade Guimarães, having been offered the command of the new expedition, accepted it, after having previously set forth his view of the situation in a telegraphic statement: "All great ideas have their martyrs; and we are destined to a sacrifice which we shall not shun, in order that we may bequeath to future generations a Republic that is firmly established, honored, and respected."

It was the same theme everywhere: the Republic must be saved.

CONCENTRATION AT QUEIMADAS

The troops were assembling in Baía, arriving there in separate detachments and proceeding immediately to Queimadas. This arrangement not only was in keeping with the urgency of rapidly organizing a military force in the latter city—the provisional base of operations—but was rendered necessary by another equally serious consideration. In the minds of many of the new expeditionaries there was an exaggerated and quite unfounded suspicion respecting the monarchist sympathies of Baía, and they accordingly descended upon the town with the triumphant air of conquerors. This, they had made up their minds in advance, was but another Canudos, on a larger scale. The old and ancient-appearing capital high up on the mountainside, where for so many years the crews of Batavian and Norman "sea-sweepers" had put in, and which still preserved, in spite of time, the traditional aspect of the ocean metropolis of bygone days—a metropolis built for defense, with its crumbling old forts scattered over the heights

Courtesy of the Instituto Brasileiro de Geografia e Estatística

THE GAUCHO OF RIO GRANDE DO SUL

like a dismantled Acropolis, its cannon holes still looking out to sea, while its steep slopes overlooked the same line of mud-wall mountain trenches that Thomé de Souza[12] built—this ancient city with its maze of narrow

[12] [Thomé de Souza (or Tomás de Souza) was the Portuguese soldier appointed by King John III, in 1549, as governor of Brazil. He ruled the country from Baía, which became the capital for two centuries. On Fernão Cardim see p. 68 and n. 23; on Gabriel Soares see pp. 66, 74.]

streets through which today a Fernão Cardim or a Gabriel Soares could pass without being aware of any perceptible difference—this city was to them merely an amplification of the backlands weed patch. They were not moved by it; it irritated them. They were Cossacks in the streets of Warsaw. In public places the inhabitants were surprised to hear the rude comments that they made, as they swaggered about to the loud jingle of spurs and clink of swords; and, as this kept up from day to day, it led in the end to insults and disorderly acts.

We will cite here a single instance. The officers of one battalion, the Thirtieth, carried their devotion to the Republic to an iconoclastic extreme. In broad daylight they attempted to knock to pieces with a mallet a shield in the entryway to the custom-house on which the imperial arms were displayed, while their men, inspired by this edifying sight, were engaged in brawls and attacks on citizens.

THE FOURTH EXPEDITION IS ORGANIZED

Patriotic passion, the truth is, was verging on insanity. The press and the youth of the North finally protested; and what had more effect than any formal protests was the fact that popular unrest throughout the region had just about reached the point of explosion. Accordingly, as a preventive measure, the battalions upon arriving and detraining, promptly entrained again on the Central Railway and proceeded to Queimadas; and it was not long before all the detachments which were to march to Monte Santo had been assembled in the former village. The commanding general, in his order of the day for the fifth of April, was in a position to organize the expedition. We quote from that order:

Upon this date the forces under my command are definitively organized, as follows:

The Seventh, Fourteenth, and Thirtieth infantry battalions constituting the First Brigade, under the command of Colonel Joaquim Manoel de Medeiros; the Sixteenth, Twenty-fifth, and Twenty-seventh battalions of the same branch of the service constituting the Second Brigade, under the command of Colonel Ignacio Henrique Gouveia; the Fifth Regiment of field artillery, and the Fifth and Ninth infantry battalions forming the Third Brigade, under the command of Colonel Olympio da Silveira; the Twelfth, Thirty-first, and Thirty-third of the same branch of the service and a division of artillery constituting the Fourth Brigade, under the command of Colonel Carlos Maria da Silva Telles; the Thirty-fourth, Thirty-fifth, and Fortieth constituting the Fifth Brigade, commanded by Colonel Julião Augusto de Serra Martins; the Twenty-sixth and Thirty-second infantry and a division of artillery forming the Sixth Brigade, under the command of Colonel Donaciano de Araujo Pantoja.

The First, Second, and Third brigades form a column under the command of General João da Silva Barbosa; until the arrival of that general, the colonel commanding the First Brigade shall be the officer responsible for this column. The Fourth, Fifth, and Sixth brigades shall constitute a second column, commanded by General Claudio do Amaral Savaget.

CRITICAL OBSERVATIONS

Such was the makeup of the fourth expedition. The order of the day said nothing as to the plan of operations, perhaps for the reason that this plan had been a matter of common knowledge for some time and differed little from that of preceding expeditions. In place of a wide circle which, from various strategic points, should finally close in upon the settlement— and the sixteen army corps at their disposal favored such a plan as this —it was decided to attack the fanatics from two sides, one column, the first, proceeding by way of Monte Santo, while the second, after having reassembled in Aracajú, was to go on by way of Sergipe to Geremoabo; and from these towns they were to converge upon Canudos.

Surely, in view of what has been said in preceding pages, it is unnecessary for us to stress the significance of such a plan as this; former mistakes were here being repeated on a larger scale, with only one difference: in place of a single compact mass of soldiers there were now two which were destined to fall precipitately into the snares of backlands warfare. Even supposing, to look on the bright side of things, that this did not happen, it was easy to foresee that the carrying-out of such a plan would render the outcome of the campaign problematical. A mere glance at the map would have shown that the convergence of the two columns in the manner planned would not insure the crushing of the rebellion, even with the painful expedient of a pitched battle as the last resort.

The routes chosen, the Rosario and Geremoabo highways, which come together outside the town at a considerable distance from it, were not suited for a siege. The jagunços, attacked on one side, from the southeast, in case they were routed, still had open to them on the north and east the Cambaio and Uauá roads and that across the plain known as the Varzea[13] da Ema; they would then have the whole vast backland region of the São Francisco as an impenetrable asylum, to which they might flee and from which they might prepare a counterattack. However, to count upon this mass abandonment of the settlement showed an exaggerated optimism on the part of the besiegers. The sertanejos would resist, as they did resist, and, thus attacked from one side alone, would have, as proved to be the case, innumerable outlets on the other sides by which they might communicate with the surrounding region and keep themselves in supplies.

It should have been easy to foresee all this; and under the circumstances there was but one thing to be done, and that was to have a third column which, setting out from Joazeiro or Villa Nova and covering a distance equal to that traversed by the other columns, should meet with those

---

[13] [A *varzea* is a low plain bordering a stream. *Ema* is the rhea, or ostrich.]

columns, thus gradually cutting off the roads and establishing finally an effective blockade. No thought, however, was given to this additional division, which was so indispensable. There was not time for it. The disgrace inflicted upon the army and the fatherland must be avenged; the entire country was clamoring for it.

The thing to do was to march on and conquer. General Savaget accordingly set out early in April for Aracajú, as the commander-in-chief, in Queimadas, made ready for the attack.

DELAYS

The attack did not take place until two months later, at the end of June. Having come as far as an obscure railway station in the São Francisco Valley, soldiers and patriots impotently cooled their heels there, waiting for orders to proceed. All the great military stir of the month of March had been an illusion. We did not have an army, in the real sense of the term, which implies not merely so many thousands of men and rifles, but, what is of greater worth, an administrative, technical, and tactical command, embracing all branches of the service from the transport of vehicles to the higher strategy of campaigns—in brief, an organization par excellence for the planning of military operations.

As it was, everything was lacking. There was no organized supply service, and, as a consequence, in a provisional base of operations connected by railway line with the seacoast it was impossible to obtain rations. There was no transport service capable of handling nearly a hundred tons of munitions of war. And, finally, there were no soldiers; the bearers of arms that detrained here did not come from rifle ranges or drill grounds. The battalions, moreover, were incomplete, numbering less than companies, their equipment was in very bad shape, and the men lacked the most elementary notions of military tactics. It was necessary to fill out the battalions, to equip them, to clothe them, supply them with munitions, and train and instruct them.

Queimadas accordingly became a training station for recruits, and the days slipped by in a monotonous round of drills and exercises, with rifle practice on an improvised range set up in an open space in the nearest caatinga. It is not strange, therefore, if the martial enthusiasm which the men had felt in the beginning gradually cooled, as they grew soft in the insipid atmosphere of this inverted Capua, where, yawning and stagnating, hundreds of valiant fighters stood marking time in the presence of the enemy.

The transport facilities being insufficient, they had to proceed, a battalion at a time, to Monte Santo, where the same situation existed. They kept this up until the middle of June, going through the same exercises and leading the same precarious existence, with more than three thousand men under arms and ready for combat but unable to leave and living meanwhile—let us not overlook this most singular circumstance—on such resources as those with which an impoverished municipality, still laboring under the burden of previous expeditions, was able to provide them.

The one thing that was accomplished, with some difficulty, in all this time was the completion of the Queimadas telegraph line, under Lieutenant Colonel Siqueira de Menezes. Otherwise, it was so much time lost. Deprived of the most rudimentary resources, without even the wagons for transporting munitions, the commander-in-chief held no councils of war but simply remained there in the presence of his encamped forces, which were poorly supplied with food in the form of a few lean and famished oxen that they found wandering about among the dried weeds of the plains. The Quartermaster General's deputy[14] was not able to secure a regular supply service out of Queimadas such as might have kept the base of operations provided with at least enough reserves to sustain the troops for a week at a time. And so it was, when the month of July came around, as the second column was setting out by way of Sergipe for Geremoabo, there was not a single sack of flour in storage in Monte Santo, and penury and the threat of hunger thus condemned to immobility the division headed by the principal commander of the campaign.

This stagnation of effort took the heart out of the soldiers and alarmed the country. As a diversion, or as an excuse for getting rid of a thousand and some mouths to feed for a few days, with the column's resources as scant as they were at Monte Santo, two brigades were sent out on a futile reconnoitering expedition as far as Cumbe and Massacará. This was the only military maneuver that was carried out, and it did not even serve the purpose of allaying the impatience of the men.

One of these detachments—recently formed out of the Third Infantry, the Seventh Infantry (now detached from the First Brigade), and the Fifth and Ninth battalions of artillery to which had been added a rapid-fire battery—was under the command of an officer who was incomparable on the field of battle, but whose restless temperament unfitted him to cope with an apathetic situation of this sort. Along the road this detachment had seized upon a number of pack trains bound for the rebel settlement and, in place of returning to the base of operations, came near going on by way of the Rosario Highway to the village itself. By planning this rash

[14] Colonel Manuel Gonçalves Campello França (see pp. 296, 298).

and undisciplined action, Colonel Thompson Flores[15] was not only giving exaggerated expression to his own nervous disposition but was reflecting as well the morale and state of mind of his men; for all were ready to rebel against this marking of time that deadened the martial spirit with which they had embarked upon the campaign; and it was all the other officers could do to restrain their commander from putting his plan into execution.

While many were alarmed as they thought of how the sudden news of the taking of Canudos would be received by General Savaget, they could not but be aware of the effect of all this delay upon the public, which was anxious to see the affair settled; and they likewise were aware of how advantageous this three months' armistice was to an enemy already buoyed up by three victories in a row. This last was, after all, the prime consideration.

NO PLAN OF CAMPAIGN

General Arthur Oscar finally resolved to act, and in his order of the day for the nineteenth of June, announcing this decision, declared that he would "leave it to the impartial historian to justify such a delay as this." His order was not so laconic as most documents of the sort are. After having foretold an inevitable victory over the followers of Antonio Conselheiro, the "enemy of the Republic," he pointed out to the troops the perils which would await them once they entered the backlands, how "the enemy will attack us on our flanks and in our rear," in the midst of those "damnable forests," with their "obstructed roads, trenches, ambushes of every sort, and everything war has to offer that is most unpleasant."

While statements of this sort may have had an alarming effect, they were nonetheless true. In the report on its reconnoitering work, the engineering commission stressed the ruggedness of the terrain, whose topographical features made the success of the campaign dependent upon three conditions: forces well provisioned, so that they would not have to live off the impoverished countryside; a maximum of mobility; and a plastic formation, adapted to the terrain.

MORE CRITICAL REFLECTIONS

These were three essential, complementary conditions; yet not a single one of them was met. The troops left their base—on half-rations. On the march they were encumbered by a siege cannon weighing tons; and they advanced in brigade formation, with the battalions marching four abreast at intervals of only a few yards.

[15] See pp. 312 and 332.

The truth is, the obsession that this campaign could be conducted in the classic manner still persisted. This was shown in the instructions given days before to the commanders of the various corps. These were no more than a résumé of hoary precepts which any layman may find in the pages of Vial—reflecting a stubborn belief that the jagunços and their wily guerrilla bands could be fitted into a plan traced on a general's desk.

The commander-in-chief of the expedition was wholly concerned with the distribution of detachments; he was not at all concerned with the essential aspect of a campaign which, from the tactical point of view, consisted, when all was said, in making the best possible use of the terrain, along with a head-spinning mobility on the part of the troops deployed. Without any line of supplies and guided only by the slight amount of reconnoitering that had been done, or by such chance information as had been picked up from the officers of previous expeditions, his badly organized army was going out to meet a set of wholly unfamiliar conditions— and, incidentally, there were no practical directions given as to assuring the safety of the flanks and rear. On the other hand, there was a preoccupation with the traditional mixed order of battle, all the corps being supposed to fall out at the distance prescribed in the regulations, in such a manner that each brigade, maneuvering upon an open field, would be able geometrically—cordons of infantry, followed by supporting lines, reinforcements, and reserves—to act with that mechanical assurance that is demanded by the luminaries of the art of war.[16] Apropos of this, the commander cited Ther Brun. He had no desire to introduce any innovations. He could not imagine that the cool-headed strategist whose name he invoked, a genius who on this occasion would be no match for the subtleties of a backwoods captain,[17] might be willing to abandon these idealized precepts when brought face to face with the realities of a backlands war—a roving war, with no fixed rules or rigid plans to be upset by a thousand and one chance circumstances, by sudden assaults at the turn of the road and ambushes everywhere.

He was doing no more than to copy out instructions which were worthless, for the reason that they were too specific in character. He was trying to plot the unforeseen. A conflict which called merely for a daring commander and half-a-dozen bold and expert sergeants was being undertaken amid the tangled network of the old hierarchical structure—such and

[16] See pp. 206 ff.

[17] [*Capitão do mato* ("forest captain"). The phrase goes back to colonial days, when it was applied to the ruthless leaders of bands that set out to hunt down fugitive slaves, in the *quilombos*, in the depths of the forest. Cf. p. 190.]

such a number of solid battalions, to be trapped in the narrow, winding, hinterland paths by fierce adversaries who fought as they ran. And, to climax it all, they took with them a massive steel Witworth 32, weighing almost two tons![18] This tremendous weapon, designed for the reposeful environs of seaside fortresses, served only to block the road, to slow down the march, to interfere with the supply trains, and to clog and confuse any maneuvers that might be undertaken. It was, however, necessary to terrify the backlands with this monstrous steel scarecrow, even though other indispensable measures might be neglected.

Let us take an example. The columns set out from their base under conditions that are absolutely incredible—on half-rations. And on the line of march, as we shall shortly see, their formation was such as to afford them no protection against attack. In brief, they had neither the guaranty of an efficient vanguard nor scouts along their flanks who were capable of warding off ambuscades—the ones that they did have were worthless: the scouts had to march alongside the main body of the troops, and inside the caatingas this was impossible. Soldiers clad in cloth uniforms had to make their way through a tangled undergrowth of bromelias and briar patches, and the result was that they had ventured but a few steps before their clothing was torn to shreds. On the other hand, they might have been prepared for such a situation as this; it would have been sufficient to provide them with appropriate garb, for the costume of the vaqueiros should have been a lesson to them. The scouts should have gone through the caatingas clad in the leathern armor of the sertanejo—equipped with sturdy sandals, with shinguards and leggings against which the thorns of the chique-chiques would have no effect, with doublets and chest protectors, and with leather hats firmly fastened by chin straps;[19] so appareled, they would have been able to make their way with immunity through these thickets. One or two corps so clad and properly trained would have ended by imitating the astonishing movements of the jagunços, especially in view of the fact that there were in all the battalions men of the North who would not have been putting on this barbaric uniform for the first time in their lives.

After all, there would have been nothing so very unusual in all this. Bright-striped European dolmans and highly polished boots are a good deal more out of place among the brushwood of the caatingas. Moreover, our worthy countrymen of these backland regions have shown that their

[18] See p. 296.

[19] [Cf. the description of the *sertanejo*'s costume, pp. 92–93.]

bizarre attire, despite the crude material of which it is fashioned, is capable of enhancing the outlines of the human figure, conferring an appearance of athletic strength. It is the best kind of protector against the inclemencies of the weather: it lessens the heat of summer and moderates the cold of winter, rendering its wearer immune to sudden variations of temperature; in a word, it normalizes the physiological functions and tends to produce athletes. It is, further, adapted to the major vicissitudes of war. It does not tear or wear out; and, after a long battle, the exhausted warrior still has his uniform intact and may take his repose upon a bed of thorns. At the sound of the bugle, he is up at a bound and in the ranks, without so much as a wrinkle in this flexible armor of his. He can march through a violent downpour and not be dripping-wet. Ahead of him may be a pasture ground in flames, but he goes through it unscathed. In front of him there may appear a swift-running river; he fords it easily in his impermeable outfit.

To the minds of the strategists, however, this would have been an extravagant innovation. They feared to cover the soldier's skin with the tough hides of the jagunço. Everything about this expedition must be as correct as possible. Correct and very weak.

The first detachment to set out, on the fourteenth day of the month, was the engineering commission, escorted by a brigade. It was confronted with an arduous task, that of adapting the backland trails to the march of the troops, either by widening them, straightening them, leveling them, or covering them with a light bridgework, in such a manner that the altogether inappropriate artillery might be able to make its way down these tortuous paths, intercepted by pits and caverns and overlooked by the neighboring hills. This was to pave the way for the Krupp batteries, a few rapid-fire cannons, and the terrifying 32, which in itself required a firm and solid wheelwork roadway. That roadway was built and opened, thanks to the splendid efforts and rare tenacity of the engineering commission; it ran all the way to the top of Mount Favella, covering a distance of thirty-six miles.

THE ENGINEERING COMMISSION; SIQUEIRA DE MENEZES

The officer in charge of this notable undertaking was Colonel Siqueira de Menezes. No one at that time had a clearer understanding of the nature of the campaign or was better fitted for the task assigned him. With his solid theoretical background and keenly observant mind, he became the sole guide for these thousands of men groping their way through an unknown and barbarous region. He covered the ground thoroughly, in all directions, and almost alone, being accompanied only by adjutants. He knew all that there was to be known about the country. This indefatigable warrior, who had learned his trade outside the life of the barracks, and who did not know what fear meant, surprised even the rudest of backland fighters. He would roam over the broad, rolling highlands or lose himself in the ambush-filled desert, making observations, studying the lay of the land, and many times fighting the enemy as he went. Astride of limping mounts that were scarcely capable of even a mild canter, he would plunge into the hollows and gallop through them and up the steep hillsides on his perilous reconnoitering excursions; and you would find him on Caypan, on Calumby, on Cambaio, everywhere, more concerned with his notebook and his rapid *croquis* than he was with life itself.

This highly original landscape held an attraction for him. Its strange flora, its extremely rugged topographical outlines, its geognostic structure, which has not yet been studied—all this lay before him, all around him, a turbulent chapter in the history of Earth which no one as yet had read. Not infrequently, this fearless officer became the contemplative thinker. A piece of rock, the chalice of a flower, or a striking feature of the soil would free him from the preoccupations of war and lift him to the tranquil realm of science. He came to know and make friends with the cowboys of the vicinity and, in the end, with the jagunços themselves. He astonished them, this frail-looking individual with the Christlike face who was to be seen everywhere with his rifle in a sling and a pedometer on his boot; he defied their cunning and did not tremble when he found himself in the presence of an ambuscade, did not even stop reading the portable compass as the blunderbusses went off all around him.

The commander-in-chief for his part was quite well aware of this man's worth. Lieutenant Colonel Menezes was the eye of the expedition. Coming of a backlands family in the North, with close relatives among the fanatics of Canudos, this fair-haired, frail-looking jagunço, with the physical and moral polish conferred by modern culture, and endowed with a wit that matched his fearlessness, was the best guaranty of the army's safe-conduct. And he provided the expedition with a line of march which surprised even the sertanejos.

THE CALUMBY ROAD

Of the roads which led to Canudos, two had been taken by previous expeditions: the Cambaio and the Massacará highways. There remained the Calumby Road,[20] which was shorter and at many points less impracti-

[20] See pp. 416–19.

cable, without the lofty trenches that run alongside the former or the vast barren plains that border the latter; all of which led the sertanejos to believe that this would be the route chosen, and they proceeded to fortify it in such a manner that, had the expedition marched that way, it would have met with complete disaster long before reaching the settlement. The plan drawn up by the engineering commission avoided this by directing the route farther to the east, skirting the counterforts of the Aracaty.

THE MARCH ON CANUDOS

Along the route selected the brigades marched one at a time. The artillery, setting out from Monte Santo on the seventeenth, met with serious difficulties from the very first. When the light cannon, having covered a distance of six miles, were already at the Pequeno River, the cumbersome 32 was almost three miles behind. Along the slippery road, filled with quagmires, the twenty yoke of oxen which dragged the latter piece lumbered slowly along, guided by inexpert drivers, both animals and men being ill adapted to this wholly new mode of transport, with all sorts of obstacles arising every moment, at every step they took, in rounding the sharp bends of the road, in crossing the badly constructed bridges, in getting over the ruts where the heavy weapon bogged down.

Only on the afternoon of the nineteenth, after three days had been wasted in covering a distance of eight miles, did they finally succeed in getting the huge piece as far as "Caldeirão Grande," so that they might be able to organize the artillery brigade, which, along with the Second Infantry, formed the vanguard of Colonel Dantas Barretto's Twenty-fifth Battalion; and on the following morning this detachment proceeded to "Gitirana," a distance of five miles, at the same slow, obstructed pace.

On this same day the commander-in-chief set out from Monte Santo, along with the greater part of the column, formed by the First and Third brigades, with 1,933 men in all. The entire expedition, some three thousand men strong, thus being on the march, it advanced as far as Mount Aracaty, twenty-nine miles beyond Monte Santo, in the same manner, that is to say, with the large divisions proceeding one at a time, or sometimes concentrating and then spreading out, the light-equipped vanguard being constantly slowed down by the heavy pace of the artillery.

THE FIFTH BAIAN POLICE CORPS

At the rear of all the others came the general supply train under the immediate command of the Quartermaster General's deputy, Colonel Campello França, and guarded by 432 soldiers of the line and the Fifth

Corps of Baian Police—the only detachment in the entire expedition which was really prepared to cope with the conditions of the campaign. It was formed of sertanejos who had been recently recruited in the river regions of the São Francisco. It was neither an army battalion nor a battalion of police. These fierce and sturdy caboclos, a jovial, blustering crew, who later, in the anxious, wearisome days of the siege of Canudos, were to sing merry songs to the sound of their banjos even as the bullets flew—they in reality constituted a battalion of jagunços. Among the regular troops they stood out for their primitive type of bravery, which was at once of a rude and a romantic sort; there was something savage about it and at the same time heroic; it was at once chivalric and pitiless; in brief, it was the same kind of bravery which was displayed by those forest mestizos who fought with the bandeiras. What these men were exhibiting was the primitive temperament of a race which, in the isolation of the uplands, had been unaffected by outside influences, and which now of a sudden was making its appearance with its original characteristics intact. Here was an interesting admixture of illogical attributes, with a charming ingenuousness, a loyalty carried to the point of sacrifice, and a heroism that could readily become barbarism, all inextricably intermingled, as we shall see later on.

CHANGE OF FORMATION

The Fifth Corps and the supply train, being the last to set out from Monte Santo, at the rear of the expedition, were as a result completely isolated from the rest of the column when it became necessary to concentrate it, and the same was true of the remaining battalions. Despite the formation agreed upon, it was found impossible to effect an immediate concentration in the case of a battle. Being dependent upon the work of the sappers, the entire artillery train remained at times far distant from the rest of the column, like a huge encumbrance blocking the way between the advance guard and the rest of the convoy. As a consequence, had the jagunços from carefully chosen spots launched an attack on the rear of the line, the troops in front, falling back in order to come to the aid of their comrades, would have found the way blocked by the batteries stuck in the narrow paths.

CRITICAL OBSERVATIONS

All this is revealed by an examination of the detailed line of march as set down in the official record. While the main body of the column at daybreak of the twenty-first was setting out from Rio Pequeno, a little more than two miles beyond Monte Santo, arriving around nine o'clock in the morning at "Caldeirão Grande," after a march of five miles, the rear guard of the artillery was still at a considerable distance from this place, along with the 32-cannon, guarded by the Medeiros Brigade. At the same time the Gouveia Brigade, which was farther in advance, reached "Gitirana" that night, where the engineering commission was, along with General Arthur Oscar, who had arrived there at the head of a scouting force of twenty cavalrymen and members of the Ninth Infantry. When one reflects that the supply train, under the command of Colonel Campello França and guarded by the Fifth Police, was bringing up the rear, it may be seen that the troops were spread out over a distance of nearly ten miles, which was wholly in violation of the instructions given them.

At dawn of the twenty-second, while General Barbosa, who had remained the rest of the day at "Caldeirão," was striking camp and going on to "Gitirana," the commander-in-chief was setting out from that place with the First Brigade, the Ninth Battalion of the Third, the Twenty-fifth of the Second, the wing of cavalry under Major Carlos de Alencar, and the artillery, following the line of march agreed upon: in front the Fourteenth and Thirtieth battalions; in the center the cavalry and the artillery; followed by two other corps, the Ninth and the Twenty-fifth. While the commander-in-chief proceeded rapidly on this day, arriving in a short time with the advance guard at "Juá," four miles beyond "Gitirana," the artillery was held up at this latter place, waiting for the engineering commission to do the road work and the sapping; and, inasmuch as most of the troops were still coming along the Caldeirão Highway, these very frequently had to break up under conditions which would have been disadvantageous in case of an attack, for the reason that the men were not prepared for such large-scale maneuvers as this, which ought to have been planned in advance as an indispensable tactical requisite, in place of being forced upon them by circumstances.

The brigades finally came together that night, in "Juá," arriving there about six o'clock, the artillery being followed by the rest of the column made up of the Fifth, Seventh, Fifteenth, Sixteenth, and Twenty-second infantry corps, the only detachment missing being the supply train, which had been held up somewhere along the road. From this point the two generals set out for Aracaty, eight miles beyond, on the morning of the twenty-third, with Colonel Gouveia's battalions forming the advance guard. The artillery, however, under guard of Colonel Medeiros, did not get under way until midday, after the engineers supported by the Flores Brigade had made some exceedingly difficult repairs on the road.

If we go into such detail concerning this march, with regard even to minor incidents, it is for the reason that they reveal the exceptional conditions under which the expedition set out. After leaving "Juá," and reaching the old farmhouse of "Poço," which was wholly in ruins, there occurred an incident that indicates to what degree they knew the terrain over which they were advancing.

INCIDENTS

In place of continuing in a direction to the right to the farm known as "Sitio," belonging to a native of the region, Thomaz Villa-Nova, who was wholly devoted to our cause, the sappers took a side path to the left. After they had gone a considerable distance and had labored for a number of hours, Lieutenant Colonel Siqueira de Menezes realized the impossibility of putting the roads in condition with the speed which was necessary. "So great was the amount of earth to be removed from the thicket of this caatinga, so heavy the boulders to be lifted, not to speak of the unevenness of the terrain for the descent and mounting of vehicles." Abandoning, then, all the work that they had done, they went on to the Villa-Nova farm. Having learned a lesson by this experience, they fell to work upon a new path which, while it led them somewhat out of their way, was a good deal more viable. The artillery proceeded along this path late in the afternoon, passing by the "Pereiras" farm. They pitched camp at midnight at Lagôa da Lage, a little more than a mile this side of Aracaty, where the rest of the column had been for some time. There still remained the rear guard with the Third Brigade and the cumbersome 32, caught by nightfall on the steep bank of a stream, the Ribeirão dos Pereiras, which they were unable to cross in the darkness.

They were now entering the danger zone. That day, at Lagôa da Lage, a scouting party of the general command, led by a lieutenant, surprised some of the rebels engaged in dismantling a house which stood in that place.[21] There was a swift skirmish, and the sertanejos, greeted by a burst of rifle fire, fled without replying. One of them alone remained behind. He was upon the roof, and when he came down was at once surrounded. Despite the fact that he had been wounded, he grappled with his nearest adversary, a sergeant, and brought him down off his horse; snatching the soldier's rifle from his hand, he felled him with the butt of it. Then, backing himself up against the wall of the house, he whirled the weapon around his head like a windmill. Finally overcome by the entire troop, however, he lay upon the ground exhausted and done in, and they thereupon proceeded to kill him. This was their first exploit, and

[21] The house of Colonel José Americo.

a small enough one it was in view of the number of men which it took to accomplish it. There were to be others of the same sort.

On the twenty-fourth marching became more difficult. The column which set out from Aracaty at midday, for the reason that it had to wait for the stragglers of the evening before, having all its forces together now, headed for "Jueté," which was eight and a half miles distant—where once more it had to split up. The roads were growing worse, and in addition to the work of the sappers it was necessary to clear more than two miles with the pickax through a wild stretch of caatinga which well justified the local name given to the place.[22]

The military leader who was in charge of this notable work has left us an account of it:[23]

At Chique-Chique, Palmatoria, Rabo de Raposa, Mandacarús, Croás, Cabeça de Frade, Calumby, Cansanção, Favella, Quixaba, and even at highly respectable Macambira there was to be met with the much talked about and much feared cumanan,[24] a species of liana plant with the appearance of a shrub, looking exactly like the kind of cultivated plant with cylindrical leaves which is to be found in gardens. A few inches above the ground its stalk divides into many branches which grow in marvelous profusion, forming a huge chalice either suspended in the air by its own force or supported by plants that grow around it. It spreads out over the ground with its cylindrical leaves, with their eight flutings and an equal number of close-set gummy filaments, resembling an enormous polypus with millions of flexible and elastic antennae which not infrequently cover a wide surface, forming an impenetrable network over the sparse and scrawny vegetation of this region. The sharpest-pointed tool which the soldiers of our engineering contingent (the "Chinamen," in the slang of the fighting troops) and the police could muster, had extreme difficulty in penetrating this network of vegetation, which offered an unexpected resistance to all efforts to dislodge it and clear the way. Through this new kind of labyrinth the engineering commission in the course of a few hours had to open more than three miles of road, with the artillery close on their heels, impatient to advance. Despite the enormous and determined effort which was made by the republican patriots in accomplishing this most difficult of tasks, night came upon them before they had arrived at the species of clearing which to the natives of the region is known as Queimadas, where this treacherous vegetation suddenly disappeared from their path, as if it had taken fright and fled. Our soldiers, resigned to their task, labored on in the face of discouragement, weariness, and a desire to sleep. The officers in charge of this work, representing the aforesaid commission and the police, in addition to the commander, were Lieutenants Nascimento and Chrisanto and Sublieutenants Ponciano, Virgilio, and Melchiades, Captain Coriolano, and Lieutenant Domingos Ribeiro being further in the rear, engaged in other work. When darkness fell, the commission adopted the expedient of having great bonfires lighted from point to point in order that by their light these patriots might be enabled to continue their labors.

So it was that, amid general rejoicing and satisfaction, this last stretch of road was

[22] *Ju-eté:* great thorn; by extension of meaning: a large collection of thorns, a briar patch.

[23] Lieutenant Colonel Siqueira de Menezes, articles published in *O Paiz*, under the pseudonym "Hoche."

[24] [See p. 195.]

completed between eight and nine o'clock at night, up to that point where the cunanan is lost in a milder form of vegetation, at the clearing known as Queimadas, which we have already mentioned. The 32-cannon, being unable to overcome the obstacles that lay in its path in the darkness, remained in the shrubbery-grown trail until the following day, in charge of Dr. Domingos Leite, who with a crew of "Chinamen" had been engaged in bringing it up from the Pequeno River on the way to Canudos.

Shortly after nine o'clock the commission reassembled and pitched camp in the clearing, beneath a torrential downpour of rain which kept up until the following day, greatly to their discomfort and disgust. Here also were encamped the artillery brigade and the Sixteenth and the Twenty-fifth battalions of infantry, while the Twenty-seventh Battalion was left in charge of the 32-cannon, with its camp in the thicket. It was a splendid, nay more, a magnificent sight and one which made a vivid impression on all who beheld it, to see the artillery with its highly polished and gleaming metal surfaces proudly and imposingly, as if reveling in its superb strength, like a queen of the world, making its way by the fantastic light of those great fires kindled, one might say, by the genius of Liberty itself, which was thus pointing out to them the road of duty, of honor, and of glory.

Meanwhile General Oscar with his headquarters staff and a scouting detachment of cavalry had arrived at "Jueté," where they spent the night. At the same time General Barbosa with the First and Third brigades was making for the ranch known as "Rosario," three miles farther on. The commander-in-chief arrived there the following morning, and, later on, the rest of the division, whereupon it became necessary to slope the banks of the Rosario River in order that the artillery might cross.

A DARING SCOUT: PAJEHÚ

The enemy once again put in an appearance now, but a swift and fugitive one. It was merely a scouting party firing upon the troops and under the command of the jagunço leader, Pajehú.[25] The famous bandit was bent primarily upon a reconnoitering expedition; but as a matter of fact, as later events showed, he had a more definite objective in view, that of once more creating panic among the troops by this unseen rifle fire and leading them to quicken their pace as the previous expedition had done, so greatly to its detriment. The soldiers were subjected to a rapid running fire from the side, accompanying them as they made their way through the caatingas. The enemy would disappear and then spring up again farther on. He made a lively attack upon the vanguard, which on this occasion was the Ninth Infantry; then once again he sped on down the road. It was not possible to catch more than a glimpse of these attackers; having fired a few shots, they would promptly flee. One curiboca, a lad of twelve or fourteen years, was wounded and taken prisoner, but nothing was learned from him in the course of the questioning to which he was subjected.

[25] See pp. 220–21 and elsewhere.

AT "ROSARIO"

Without further incidents the troops camped on this farm. All the combatant forces were now reunited with the exception of the Third Brigade, which had gone on as far as "Baixas," four miles in advance. The commander-in-chief then sent a messenger to General Savaget to remind him of their previous understanding to meet on the twenty-seventh, in the neighborhood of Canudos.[26] On the twenty-sixth they struck camp, going on to "Vicar's Farm," eleven miles farther on, after a short halt in "Baixas."

They were now some fifty miles from Monte Santo, in the heart of the danger zone. The brief exchange of bullets the evening before was a forerunner of similar combats to come. Possibly having learned something from their reconnoitering, the jagunços were now preparing for more serious engagements. Here in a manner, as always, their lurking presence was to be deduced from the appearance of the earth itself, the conformation of the terrain, which from here on becomes more rugged, bristling with barren hills as far as "Baixas," where the Rosario Range rises with its steep, sparsely covered sides.

The troops now had to climb the countermure to the south which incloses Canudos. They made their way with extreme caution. The bugles no longer sounded. The battalions, quickly forming, marched on to the highlands, scaled them, and then spread out, on coming down through the ravine which separates the mountains from "Vicar's Farm." The entire column thereupon broke up into small divisions. As the advance guard was reaching the farmhouse at nightfall, the light artillery, having abandoned the cumbersome 32 to the engineers, was mounting the first foothills and slowly ascending the slope on the other side, in the wake of the sappers who were clearing the road for them. Night now fell upon the expeditionaries, and with it a torrential rain, under which conditions the enemy guerrillas, who knew the lay of the land from long acquaintance, might easily have fallen upon them. This they did not do; for, as we shall see, they had other and better positions prepared. They likewise left in peace the supply train, which was coming along at the rear by the Jueté Highway. The animals of this train had been unharnessed and the entire load of fifty-three carts and seven large ox-drawn wagons was parceled out and carried on the backs of the sturdy sertanejos of the Fifth Police Battalion.

Meanwhile, the night went by peaceably enough. The following day, the twenty-seventh, was the date fixed for the hazardous meeting of the

[26] See p. 329.

two columns, soon to be treading in triumph the ruins of the besieged settlement. Everything was set in motion for the final conflict; and amid all the extraordinary bustle, marked by great impatience and apprehension, and that vibrant enthusiasm which is customary on the eve of battle, no one so much as gave a thought to those of their comrades who had been left behind. The brigades got under way, wholly forgetful of the distant supply train, which was utterly unprotected, since the soldiers assigned to guard it either were bending under heavy burdens or else were busy helping out the few mules who drew the loads and hence were in no condition to engage in even the slightest skirmish. The brigades, nevertheless, went on. At the head of the column was that of Colonel Gouveia, with two pieces of ordnance; in the center, that of Colonel Olympio da Silveira and the cavalry; after which came the detachments led by Colonels Thompson Flores and Medeiros. On light pontoon bridges they crossed the small stream known as "Angico" and then slowly advanced, spreading out along a line six miles in length. The way was broken for the line of march by the Twenty-fifth Battalion, accompanied on its flanks by two quite useless platoons, which found great difficulty in cutting away the branches that impeded their progress.

ON THE WAY TO "PITOMBAS"

The consequence was that the jagunços staged a surprise attack before they had reached Angico, at noon that day. This was a skirmish of a more serious sort, even though it does not merit the name of "battle" which was later given it. Pajehú had assembled his scouts, who were scattered out all the way from here to Canudos, and they now fired upon the column from the side. The troops were upon a slope that was clear of shrubbery and thus, by reason of their elevation, afforded a good target for the sertanejos, who were barely to be glimpsed at the edge of the weeds down below. They nonetheless withstood the attack firmly, with but two casualties, one dead and one wounded. They then went on their way in good order, at their usual pace, until they came to that memorable site, the "Pitombas" farm,[27] where Moreira Cesar had met the fanatics for the first time. It was a place filled with memories that were anything but pleasant.

CRUEL REMINDERS

All the men were deeply stirred by the cruel reminders which they found here: the bleached shreds of uniforms swaying from the tips of withered

[27] See pp. 251, 252.

branches, and old saddles, and bits of military cloaks and capes scattered over the ground, along with fragments of bones.[28] At the left side of the road, on the bough of a tree—turned into a clothes rack from which hung a weather-beaten uniform—was the decapitated corpse of Colonel Tamarindo, the arms dangling, the skeleton hands clad in black gloves, while at the feet lay the colonel's cranium and his boots.

Upon leaving the side of the road and plunging into the weeds, the soldiers came upon the remains of other unfortunate ones: skeletons clad in tattered, filthy uniforms, lying supine here and there in tragic formation or parlously attached to flexible shrubs which, bending with the breeze, conferred upon them the weird movements of specters. All of which had been deliberately staged by the jagunços, who had removed nothing from the scene with the exception of weapons and ammunition. A soldier of the Twenty-fifth Battalion found in a handkerchief wrapped about the fleshless lower leg of one of these figures a packet of banknotes amounting to four contos de reis[29] which the enemy had disdained, along with other articles of value.

The frightened troops, however, had little time to take in the details of this scene, for the reason that the enemy was continuing his slantwise attack. Repelled in the previous encounter, after having been outflanked on the right by a company of the Twenty-Fifth led by Captain Trogyllio de Oliveira, the sertanejos had fallen back but kept up a running fire as they did so. The Twenty-fifth, followed by the Twenty-seventh under Major Henrique Severiano da Silva, gave chase to them, pursuing them as far as "Angico."

It was now midday and a battle was imminent. At various points, along the flanks and in front, scattered shots were to be heard; and the commander-in-chief accordingly took such precautions as were most suitable for repelling the adversary, who, everything indicated, was about to surround and attack them. A scouting detachment of cavalry led by Sublieutenant Marques da Rocha of the headquarters staff was sent out to beat the brush on the left, but with no results; and so the advance continued.

A couple of hours later, as they were crossing the brow of a hill, the attack suddenly broke out again and was met with a few rounds from the Krupp cannons. A cavalry sergeant with a few men plunged boldly into the caatinga, but once more found nothing. The troops meanwhile marched on, with the Twenty-fifth Battalion in front, preceded by a company of scouts and followed by the Twenty-seventh and the Sixteenth.

[28] See pp. 275, 375.   [29] [More than $2,000.]

These detachments replied to the enemy's scattered fire, thereby lending impetus to the assault.

Night was now coming on, and the advance guard was struggling up the last steep slopes of the Umburanas Road; they went up puffing but without swaying in their line of march, meanwhile fighting off more than one serious attack on their flanks. Then came the mountain. In the last stage of their ascent they found themselves upon a slightly inclined plain between two broad elevations with a few barren hills blocking the way ahead of them. They were on top of Mount Favella.

ON MOUNT FAVELLA

This legendary hill, at this point, is in reality a valley. Upon climbing it, one has the unexpected impression of coming out in the lowlands.[30] It is as if one were going downhill. The exhausted traveler is rudely disappointed after the laborious ascent that he has made. He finds his view hemmed in by all sorts of irregularities of the landscape. In place of a row of summits, he finds a "thalweg," which is really a prolongation of the Rosario Highway, in the form of an extensive furrow, a kind of huge trench a thousand feet long, walled off by a hillock at the far end.

Upon climbing the hillock, he has a view of the slopes on either side, gutted by deep ditches which carry off the water from the mountain torrents. On one side, to the right, the road may be seen descending very unevenly through a narrow passageway between tall, steep, almost vertical declivities which remind one of ancient tunnels. To the left is another depression, ending in the gentle slope of Mount Mario.[31] This runs north and south, and on the north is closed in by another hillock which hides the town from view; on the other side, it suddenly drops in a deep gully all the way to the bed of the Umburanas. In front, on a lower level, is the "Old Ranch House."[32] The small range of "Bald Pates"[33] then continues the descent all the way to the Vasa-Barris down below. And in all four directions—on the east, toward the valley of the Macambira, this side of the Cocorobó Range and the Geremoabo Highway which crosses it; to the north, spreading out over the vast undulating plain; to the west, in the direction of two small streams, the Umburanas and the Mucuim, near the end of the Cambaio Road—in all directions, on all sides, the sloping terrain presents the same appearance, that of a series of hillocks crowding one upon another in a confusion of summits and depressions. The picture afforded is that of a tempest-lashed mountain that is gradually crumbling,

---

30 See pp. 19 ff.

31 See pp. 256, 266, 271.

32 [See pp. 256, 267.]

33 [See pp. 146, 256, 264.]

with gorges which the torrential rains are constantly deepening from year to year, and with no vegetation to protect it from the burning heat of summer and the erosions of floods.

For Mount Favella, like the other hills and mountains in this portion of the backlands, does not have even the barbarous vegetation of the caatingas to cover it but is wholly barren and rugged-appearing. A few wasted shrubs without leaves, a rare cactus or two, and a bromelia here and there are the only plants to be found growing in the hard soil on its summit, in the crevices between the schist folds, which are visibly juxtaposed in stratigraphic planes, without the faintest covering in the form of a surface layer, revealing thus the interior structure of the earth at this point. However, even though it is barren of shrubbery, one who climbs the mount from the south has no view of the settlement to the north but, as we have seen, has to descend the gentle slope which leads down into the large fold of the mountain that is like a saddle between two parallel peaks.

FUSILLADE

Night was falling as the head of the column entered this depression, with a Krupp battery, followed by the rest of the Second Brigade and by the Third Brigade, the First Brigade and the bulk of the troops being still detained at the rear. They did not go far, however. The scattering fire which up to then had accompanied the expeditionaries now became a continuous crescendo as they completed the ascent, while those in front had to face a furious fusillade.

An engagement of a most unusual and bloody kind now began. The enemy was nowhere to be seen, being hidden away in holes and caves and safe within his trench shelters which mined the slopes on the side, as the first shades of night came to afford him an additional protection. The two companies of the Twenty-fifth Battalion withstood the attack valiantly. Breaking up into sharpshooting detachments, they came on, firing at random, as the two brigades in front opened ranks to permit the battery to pass. This battery, drawn by hand rather than by the exhausted and terrified mules that were harnessed to it, was now dragged forward violently between the ranks, at an accelerated pace and with a great clatter. Mounting the hillock at the far end of the depression, it took up battle position on the top. The national colors were then unfurled, and Canudos was greeted with a salvo of twenty-one rounds.

By the blinding light of the cannon fire, General Arthur Oscar, seated on one of the horses yoked to the battery, had his first glimpse of the mysterious backlands city down below and enjoyed the most fleeting of tri-

umphs on this eminence in the direct line of fire where he had so rashly exposed himself. For the situation was a desperate one. Attacked on all
sides, surrounded by an enemy intrenched above them, his troops were
confined within this narrow fold of the mountain which prevented maneuvers of any kind. Had all the troops been united, there was one solution possible, namely, to go on and complete the perilous crossing of the
mountain and join forces with General Savaget, who, after a march that
had been marked by intermittent skirmishes, had now made a halt two
miles farther on. The First Brigade, however, had not arrived; it had remained behind to guard the rapid-fire battery and the 32; and the supply
train was still farther back, at "Angico," five miles distant.

CRITICAL REMARKS

The plan of campaign which had been adopted resulted in the one outcome that was possible. In accordance with this initial plan, the expedition was compelled to operate as a unit. Being under a single command
and dependent upon a single supply train, it was unable to break up into
smaller units; yet precisely at the moment that it reached the scene of conflict, it had to break up, whether it wished to or not. In the light of all
this, that dubious form of attack represented by firing a salvo over Canudos was the most fruitless of victories. The commander-in-chief of the expedition nevertheless referred to it later as a brilliantly successful engagement, thanks to which the enemy was compelled to abandon to the troops
the position which the latter had stormed; whereas the fact is that later
events revealed an irrepressible desire on the part of the men to abandon
that position and a persistent attempt on the part of the jagunços to prevent them from doing so.

THE TRENCHES OF THE JAGUNÇOS

Here was a most unusual sort of trap, as anyone who later took a stroll
over the slopes of Mount Favella was able to see for himself. Those slopes
were mined. Every few paces there was a circular hole, its top being even
with the ground, and with a protecting breastwork of stone, showing
where a trench had been. There was a countless number of them, all affording a line of fire that was practically on a level with the earth, showing
that they had been deliberately arranged in anticipation of just such an
attempt as this to cross the mountain on the part of the troops.

This also went to explain the light character of the skirmishes along the
road, with the sertanejos, from "Angico" on, keeping up an ineffective
fire as they leaped and ran through the brush, with the obvious intention

of luring the expedition in a certain direction and preventing them from taking one of the numerous side paths which from there lead to the settlement. In this crafty plan of theirs they were successful. Goaded by an adversary who kept scattering out and fleeing as they advanced, the troops had imprudently, without any preliminary reconnoitering, entered a region with which they were wholly unfamiliar, being led on without knowing it by a wily and formidable scout, one with whom they had not reckoned—Pajehú.

And they fell into this trap with all the aplomb of conquerors. They speedily lost that aplomb, however, with their ranks thrown into writhing confusion, as, in reply to the thundering cannonade on one side, the entire range of slopes from top to bottom burst into running flame and a terrible, deadly rifle fire broke upon them from the hundreds of trenches, as if the very ground beneath their feet were exploding with shells.[34]

THE FUSILLADE CONTINUES

It was a mass slaughter.

The battalions, taken completely by surprise, became a terrified and panic-stricken mob, with hundreds stumbling about in every direction, trampling their fallen comrades, at once deafened and blinded by the cannonading and the rifle fire—in short, hopelessly trapped, without being able to go a step farther over a terrain that they knew nothing whatsoever about, and upon which night was already falling.[35] To try to repel the attack by storming the slopes was futile. The jagunço sharpshooters were safe in their positions, as they crouched or lay stretched out at the bottom of their trenches, with only their musket barrels protruding over the top. Putting aside the idea of attempting to dislodge them by a desperate bayonet charge up the slopes, and the alternative of going forward to meet, perhaps, an even worse assault, while leaving the rear guard behind, there was nothing for the troops to do but stand their ground firmly in this dangerous position and wait for morning to come.

ENCAMPMENT ON MOUNT FAVELLA

This solution, in reality the only one possible, appeared to be justified by the fact that the enemy's fire after an hour began diminishing and finally, to the surprise of the expeditionaries, ceased altogether. The brigades thereupon proceeded to pitch camp in battle formation. The Second took up an advanced position from right to center, with the First in its rear,

[34] See p. 361.   [35] Cf. p. 212.

while the artillery remained stationed on the hillock opposite with the rapid-fire battery on its right and the Witworth 32 in the center, guarded by the Thirtieth under Lieutenant Colonel Tupy Caldas. The general who had commanded this battalion as a colonel was personally responsible for its being assigned this dangerous post. "Relying upon the honor of the Thirtieth, I confidently intrusted it with the defense of the artillery."

The remainder of Major Barbedo's Fifth Regiment took up a position on the left, next to Major Carlos Alencar's wing of cavalry. Near the depression beneath the summit of Mount Mario, which was the weak point of their position as a whole, and upon which later events were to confer the name of "Death Valley," the battalions of Colonel Flores were crowded. In a gully which was less exposed to the enemy's fire, a field hospital was improvised, and to it they carried the fifty-five wounded and twenty dead (since there was no way of disposing of the latter), this bringing the total number of the day's casualties to seventy-five as the result of a little more than one hour's fighting.

A cordon of sentinels was thrown about the camp, as officers and men, stretched out on the ground in the most democratic promiscuity, took their rest in peace. This unlooked-for quiet on the part of the enemy gave them the illusion of victory; and, somewhat prematurely, the musicians of the Third Brigade struck up a triumphal air and kept on playing until an unseemly hour, exhausting their repertory. Meanwhile, a marvelous moon had risen in the sky and was shedding its rays on the sleeping battalions.

But this peace was deceptive. The sertanejos, the truth is, had achieved their crafty purpose. Having led the expedition to this point, they now had the unprotected rear guard at their mercy, along with the supply train containing both munitions of war and rations for the men. On the very same day they simultaneously attacked at two points, on Mount Favella and at "Angico"; and, although victorious in the former instance, the troops were now in the position of having to launch an attack on the settlement without munitions, that is to say, without the weapons of war.

CANUDOS

This circumstance, however, did not carry much weight with those who had thus precipitately approached the scene of operations. At dawn of the twenty-eighth, as they gathered on the eminence where the artillery was stationed, officers and men at last had a view of the "bandits' cave," to make use of the picturesque phrase employed by the commander-in-chief in his orders of the day.

Canudos was still growing in size, but it did not look much larger than before. There were the same red-clay roofs scattering out ever more and more over the tops of the hills round about the compact nucleus of huts at the sharp bend of the river. On the southwest and the northwest the river formed a moat about the town, while to the north and east the settlement was walled in by rolling hills, and, consequently, in the early morning light, it took on the exact appearance of a citadel which was going to be very difficult indeed to capture. It could readily be seen that for an army corps to fall upon that maze of gullies with which the rugged terrain was strewn would be like marching down the narrow lanes of a colossal armed field. It was impossible to descry any point at which it was wholly accessible. The Geremoabo Highway, two hundred yards distant, entering the village by the dry bed of the Vasa-Barris, ran between two rows of trenches which bordered it on either side, concealed by a continuous hedge of wild silk-grass. The "sacred" Massacará Road—the one taken by the Counselor in his peregrinations to the south—came down between the hills, along the banks of the Umburanas, and was equally impracticable. As for the Uauá and Varzea da Ema highways to the north, they were unobstructed; but to get to them would require a long and dangerous, roundabout march.

The new church, now almost completed, proudly reared its two tall towers over the cluster of low-roofed huts, completing the picture of an inexpugnable fortress. It commanded all the roads, the summits of all the hills, and the bottoms of all the valleys. The marksman perched on one of its heavy cornices had no re-entrant angle to contend with—indeed, all that was lacking to give it the appearance of a redoubt were merlons and embrasures.

The rugged, upheaved terrain which on the north sloped away from Mount Favella down to the river was, as we have seen, marked on the left by a broad depression leading to Mount Mario and the descending line of peaks in the direction of the "Old Ranch House." Here the Third Brigade, forming into columns, took up its position, with the artillery on the eminence to the right; after which came, respectively, the Second and the First brigades. Dawn found the troops in battle formation. In view of the tactical advantages of their position, it was felt that the battle must be begun and in large part sustained by the artillery, which, it was believed, with its cross-fire upon the village four thousand feet distant, would be able within a short time to achieve a complete victory. Accordingly, all hopes at this first moment were concentrated upon Colonel Olympio da Silveira's batteries. So great were their expectations in this regard that, shortly before the first round was fired at six o'clock in the morning, numbers of men from the other detachments gathered about the cannon in the role of spectators, anxious for a view of the terribly dramatic picture which was to follow: Canudos in flames beneath the "curtain of fire" laid down by the artillery, an entire population crushed beneath the ruins of five thousand tumbling huts. This was an illusion destined to be rudely dispelled.

The first shot was fired by the Krupp on the extreme right, and its effect was truly enough theatrical. All night long the jagunços had slept beside the troops on those slopes riddled with trenches; and now it was that they made their invisible presence felt and heard.

"RAIN OF BULLETS"

Later, in relating the event, the commander-in-chief of the expedition confessed that he was powerless to describe the tremendous "rain of bullets which descended from the hills and came up from the plains with a horrible whistling sound" that was dumfounding in effect. For his part, the commander of the First Column asserted, in his order of the day, that in the course of his five years in the Paraguayan war he had seen nothing to equal it. The truth of the matter is that the sertanejos were exhibiting an amazing firmness in their attack. Their fire was a sustained one, and the bullets came thick and fast, exploding along the sides of the hills as if from a single train of gunpowder. After falling upon the unprotected troops in the depression down below, they converged upon the artillery, decimating the ranks. Dozens of soldiers fell and half the officers. Those that were left of the force manning the guns nonetheless stood their ground; and in the midst of it all, striding up and down between the batteries, as unconcerned as if he were giving a lesson on a firing range was a brave old man whose serenity could not be perturbed—Colonel Olympio da Silveira. He saved the day; for, in such an emergency as this, to have abandoned the cannon would have spelled defeat.

CONFUSION AND DISORDER

All the troops were now seized with alarm. Instinctively, without any definite aim and with no orders to do so, three thousand rifles blazed away at one and the same time against the hillsides. All this happened in a few minutes' time, and within the course of those few minutes, in that narrow space where the expeditionaries were futilely floundering about, there was to be witnessed the most deplorable disorder.

No councils were held, no plans formed, but each acted on his own initiative. At random, without knowing what they were doing, without room for a charge or the simplest of maneuvers, the platoons thus engulfed fired in all directions, their weapons aimed high in order not to slay one another— fired at a sinister, intangible enemy who surrounded them, who was attacking them from all sides and yet was nowhere to be seen. In the midst of all this tumult the Third Brigade on the left flank, drawn up in battle formation, and with the Seventh Battalion leading the van, began to advance downward in the direction of the "Old Ranch House," the point from which the heaviest fire appeared to be coming. Four months previously the Seventh Battalion had come up this same road, fleeing in utter rout, with the corpse of Colonel Moreira Cesar left abandoned at one side.[36] It was now to do penance for this disgrace; and with it was another battalion, the Ninth, which had been its companion on that occasion. Major Cunha Mattos was in command of the advance guard.

These soldiers of the preceding expedition who had here met with defeat now had a rare opportunity for revenge; and they had a leader who in many respects resembled the unfortunate commander who had fallen here before. He was Colonel Thompson Flores,[37] a fighter of the first order. Although lacking in the essential attributes of a commander, especially in that serenity of mind which would have permitted him coolly to conceive and carry out maneuvers in the heat of battle, he was endowed with courage and to spare—a courage that was equal to any test—and with what amounted to a contempt for any antagonist however strong and bold he might be; all of which made of him an incomparable leader in the stress of action. This was shown in the rash attack which he now endeavored to launch. In doing so, he was acting wholly on his own judgment, in undisciplined fashion, with no orders from above and with the grim determination of leading his men in a single charge all the way to the village square where the churches stood—those same soldiers who had there been overcome and routed only four months ago. His brigade accordingly proceeded to attack, swept by the intrenched enemy's direct and telling fire. They had gone but a hundred yards or so from their original position when the vanguard broke up, every man for himself. Colonel Flores, who was riding at the head of the column, then dismounted in order personally to direct the line of fire. With an excess of bravery, he would not tear the stripes from his sleeves which made him a favored target for the jagunços; and, upon reassembling somewhat later, the advance guard found him lying dead of a wound in the breast.

[36] [See p. 272.]   [37] See pp. 291 and 332.

LOSSES

His place was taken by Major Cunha Mattos, who worthily carried on the movement which had been so rashly conceived; for, as it was, the Seventh Battalion was the only detachment which, on this terrain, was unable to fall back. His command, however, was brief. Having been shot from his horse by a well-aimed bullet, his place was taken by Major Carlos Frederico de Mesquita, who in turn was killed shortly afterward, the command of the brigade then going to Captain Pereira Pinto.

This engagement was a most disastrous one; within half an hour, 114 men and 9 officers of the Seventh Battalion had been either killed or wounded. The ranks of this detachment had been reduced by a third under the incessant fire. The same destruction was being effected at other points. Rapidly from minute to minute, with a steady and alarming rhythm, commanding officers were falling and their places being taken by those of lower grade. The Fourteenth Infantry, upon coming up to reinforce the line on the right flank, had gone but a few yards when it lost its commander, Major Pereira de Mello. His place having been taken by Captain Martiniano de Oliveira, it was not long before the latter was brought down with a bullet and carried to the rear. Captain Souza Campos was the next to assume command, and he had gone but a few paces when he was killed. The Fourteenth then went on under the command of a lieutenant.

The slaughter was general all along the line; and, to make matters worse, after two hours of fighting without any semblance of tactics, it was found that their munitions were exhausted. The artillery, with its ranks depleted, still stood its ground valiantly upon the eminence; but it now fired its last round and the cannons were silent. Half of the officers had been lost, among them a captain-commissary of the Fifth Regiment, Nestor Villar Barreto Coutinho. The headquarters staff was now receiving insistent demands for more munitions for the battalions.

Captain Costa e Silva, assistant to the Quartermaster General's deputy, was then dispatched to the rear to do what he could to hasten the supply train. This action was too late. A couple of adjutants who were sent after him came galloping back after having gone no more than half a mile. They had found it impossible to make their way through the fusillade which blocked their passage. This meant that the rear guard was now cut off; and, amid the tumult and the clash of arms, the uproar and confusion and the sound of bursting shells all about them, the troops on Mount Favella could hear the distant volleys of the Fifth Police, who were grappling with the jagunços five miles away.

The entire First Column was thus trapped. However strange the case may appear to be, these victors had no means of leaving the position which they had won. Their commander confessed as much: "The supply train being under attack and it being impossible for a single soldier to get through, as was shown by the attempts made, there was nothing to do but to send a cavalry detachment to General Claudio do Amaral Savaget with the object of procuring a supply of munitions from him; this, however, was contrary to my best judgment, for I knew that no detachment would be able to pass the enemy's line of fire on our left flank."[38] And so, attacked on the right flank, where the cavalry detachment was beaten back and had to return; attacked at the rear, where two intrepid auxiliary forces had been unable to break through; attacked on the left flank, where the Third Brigade was making a glorious and self-sacrificing stand; and, finally, attacked from in front, where the artillery, its ranks decimated and almost all its officers slain, had fallen silent—the expeditionaries were now completely in the hands of the enemy.

There remained one recourse of an extremely hazardous nature, the outcome of which was problematical, namely, to attempt to leave this sinister valley on the top of Mount Favella—a valley that was like one enormous trench—at the point of the bayonet and the sword. First, however, one last alternative was essayed. A messenger was furtively dispatched to creep through the caatingas in search of the Second Column, which was stationed about a mile to the north.

[38] Order of the Day 118.

CHAPTER VII

THE SAVAGET COLUMN

I

FROM ARACAJÚ TO CANUDOS

THE troops under General Claudio do Amaral Savaget, setting out from Aracajú, had come to a halt in the vicinity of Canudos after a march of 175 miles. They had made their way through the interior of Sergipe, a brigade at a time, as far as Geremoabo, where the organization of the column was completed on the eighth of June, after which, with its forces united, it had set out on the sixteenth for the scene of operations. With a fighting strength of 2,350 men, including the artillery with two light Krupps, it had gone along at a leisurely pace and in an order that was best adapted to the circumstances.

The general in question, without taking the whole authority upon himself in any martinet fashion, which would not have been productive of the best results, instead saw fit to share it, without any relaxation of military discipline, with his three immediate aides, Colonels Carlos Maria da Silva Telles, Julião Augusto da Serra Martins, and Donaciano de Araujo Pantoja, commanding the Fourth, Fifth, and Sixth brigades, respectively; and under the command of these officers an extraordinary march was staged all the way to the outlying houses of the settlement. There were no orders issued them in advance. There was no idea of employing in this rude theater of war the customary formations or of following preconceived plans. The campaign was understood as it should have been from the start, and it was realized that the formal theories laid down in the textbooks were wholly unsuited to this variety of backwoods warfare, where the range of tactics was limited, and where everything depended upon decisions of the moment.

For the first time the troops found themselves properly prepared to cope with the jagunço and his mode of fighting. Subdivided into autonomous, compact, but sufficiently mobile units, they were now capable of a maximum of rapidity in the execution of those movements and maneuvers which would protect them against surprise attacks and enable them to meet the one thing which was to be looked for in this novel and adventurous kind of warfare, with no fixed rules—the unexpected. The three brigades, active, flexible, yet stable in composition, had their own individual supply trains which did not hamper their movements. They were now able to spread out in the gymnastic manner of the guerrillas themselves and in accordance with the asperities of the terrain. The mass formation of the division had been broken up, and, in place of depending upon numbers, stress was rather laid upon the swiftness and vigor of such maneuvers as could be carried out within the most circumscribed area of combat, without those Pyrrhic elephants in the form of an artillery which, however imposing it might be, was useless under such conditions as these.

The Fourth Brigade now came up to the front, composed of the Twelfth and Thirty-first battalions under the command of Lieutenant Colonel Sucupira de Alencar Araripe and Major João Pacheco de Assis.

CARLOS TELLES

Colonel Carlos Telles was in command of this brigade—the most impressive military organization which our army has had to show in recent years. A perfect specimen of those extraordinary Rio Grande leaders—brave, jovial, and strong willed—he was, like them, fashioned in the mold of that soldier chieftain, Andrade Neves; he was at once bold and deliberate, fearless and prudent, rash and levelheaded in his bravery; and he did not disdain to fight alongside the man in the ranks, in the heat of battle, once he had coolly planned the operation in which they were engaged. The federalist campaign in the South had given him an enviable reputation. As a fighter, this tall and dominant figure, a giant in size, with a steady, unflinching gaze, had won his laurels in that heroic episode, the siege of Bagé, and the Canudos Campaign was destined to add to his renown. With the warlike intuition of the gaucho, he understood the conditions under which that campaign must be waged as few others did.

At the head of his brigade he set out alone for Simão Dias, where he arrived on the fourth of May; and, in the meantime, he had made of his detachment a small army corps thoroughly adapted to the exigencies of the conflict. He rendered it lighter and more flexible and trained his men; and, while it was not possible to transmit to the latter the practical knowledge acquired by soldiers in the stress of battle on the fields of Rio Grande, he did what he could, despite the difficulties of the terrain, to give them something of the same swiftness of movement, the same verve in charging the enemy. From among the companies of the Thirty-first he selected sixty trained horsemen, fallen "monarchs of the plains," who were ill adapted to the slow pace of the infantry platoons, and out of them he formed a squadron of lancers under the command of a sublieutenant. This was an innovation and appeared on the surface to be a mistake. The "cold and silent" weapon of Damiroff, made for clashes and cavalry charges on the steppes and pampas, at first sight appeared to be absolutely unsuited to this rugged, bramble-strewn soil. Later, however, the full significance of this step became apparent.

These improvised lancers were experienced riders, used to leaping the "bull pits" of the southern plains; and in the same manner they now took the pits and gullies of the northern backlands in their stride. And later, when the columns were reunited on the waste land of Mount Favella, the lance became for them the cowboy's goad in rounding up the stray cattle of the neighborhood, the only form of sustenance upon which the hunger-weakened troops could depend. As may be seen, the lancers thus fulfilled a double function. From the time General Savaget's division set out from Geremoabo for Canudos, they performed an invaluable service by keeping the line of march clear. Days before, a score of soldiers from this squadron had ridden down the road to the edge of the settlement, and as a result of their reconnoitering, the road was kept free as far as "Serra Vermelha," where the first foothills of the Cocorobó Range appear. Marching at the rate of five miles a day, the column passed, one after another, the small clearings known as "Passagem," "Canabrava," "Brejinho," "Mauary," "Canché," "Estrada Velha," and "Serra Vermelha," reaching the latter point on the twenty-fifth of June, in the certainty that they would encounter the enemy there. For the first time an expeditionary force in the backlands had not permitted itself to be taken by surprise.

COCOROBÓ

Cocorobó is the name given, not to a single hill, but to an innumerable cluster of hills. It brings to mind the remains of very ancient canyons, erosion valleys or ravines, formed by the Vasa-Barris in remote ages when the force of its waters was incomparably greater than it is today, due possibly to the overflow from a huge lake which covered the rugged plain of Canudos. The mass of waters that was then held in by the more massive hills that roll away from Favella to Caypan, to the southwest and the northwest, and which from Favella spread out to the northeast, being walled in by the highlands of "Poço de Cima" and "Canabrava," had no other course than to overflow to the east in narrow, trenchlike gutters.

A GEOLOGICAL RETROSPECT

The topographical configuration of this region invites to a geological retrospect. The highlands here are broken up into defiles and steep, jagged, saw-tooth acclivities, presenting the general appearance of a dike beaten into ruins by the floodwaters. These acclivities stand there as if carved out of the plain, and, in spite of their extremely irregular outlines, they enable one to reconstruct the original aspect of the land at this point. They are the fossil remains of a mountain. Showing the same Silurian layers which we have found elsewhere, the nucleus of the earth is here revealed at the ground-level to the degree in which the torrents have removed the more modern sedimentary formations. In the course of this process of exhumation, the primitive mountain emerges, exhibiting those bold hypsometric curves which indicate the potency of the elements which have beaten upon it for long ages. For, as in the case of Mount Favella, the resistant caatinga dies away at the foot of the mountain, leaving the sides barren. Those sides are sometimes strewn with boulders and at other times fall straight down like walls, with a few scrawny orchids clinging to the crevices; or they may rear in the form of reefs or abruptly jutting cliffs which rend and riddle their surfaces all the way to the summit, where they form a clustering row of peaks contrasting with the level-lying land round about, not merely in form but in essential structure as well.

Meanwhile, whoever makes the journey from Canudos to Geremoabo will come upon a unique passageway—the deep gap through which the eastward-flowing Vasa-Barris pursues its winding course. The river here becomes the real road; after one has followed its dry bed for a few yards, he has the sensation of having passed through a narrow wicket. The defile now comes to an end, the abrupt slopes along its sides rapidly disappear, and one finds himself in a huge arching amphitheater. The earth still continues rugged in appearance, and other hillocks form a point of focus in the center. The original passageway is bifurcated and on the right incloses the curving bed of the Vasa-Barris. These two gorges of varying breadth, narrowing at times to a width of about twenty yards, continue to follow a gradual curve determined by the two outlying mountain spurs and, after separating for a space, come together once more to form another single defile which leads out on the Geremoabo Highway. Before they meet, each of them along the sides is bordered by slopes, those of the hillocks in the center facing the larger encompassing slopes on the opposite side. These latter bristle with steep cliffs, scattered here and there at random or clustering in successive terraces like stairsteps, putting one in mind of the galleries of some monstrous coliseum.

The defile of Cocorobó will serve to give a faint idea of the ruggedness of the terrain in this region. At either of its funnel-like extremities it divides into two forking ravines which are, if anything, even less traversable. The road follows this dubious double bypath, which in the rainy season is filled on either side by the waters of the Vasa-Barris, with the hillocks in the center turned into islands—until, finally, when the two paths have met again, it comes out on the plain through which the Geremoabo Highway cuts, stretching away directly to the east.

On the other hand, one who comes from the opposite direction, that is, eastward from that town, encounters a similar bifurcation. In making his way across, he must take one or the other of two paths, to the right or to the left, until he comes to the single exit on the other side. However, once free of the devious-winding gorge, he does not, as on the other side, encounter a level plain; the soil here, though to a less degree, exhibits much the same ruggedness, with the Vasa-Barris meandering along, turning and twisting, between the rows of hills. The undulating road which skirts the river, or which follows its bed, is a very uneven one, filled with many impediments, and has to make a detour around the slopes and spurs of innumerable hills; it continues until it comes to the valley of a seasonal stream which bears the name of a backwoods chieftain who had a house there, "Macambira." From here it goes on, following one or the other bank of the river, all the way to Canudos, less than five miles farther on.

BEFORE THE ENEMY'S TRENCHES

The vanguard of the troops, marching in this direction, came to a halt some five hundred yards this side of the barrier, on the twenty-fifth of June, shortly before midday. The squadron of lancers had come upon the enemy. Galloping alongside the latter's crude trenches, they had had barely a glimpse of him. When the jagunços fired upon them, wounding two of their number, they returned at top speed to the Fifth Brigade at the head of the column, and one of that brigade's battalions, the Fortieth, under Major Nonato de Seixas, immediately broke up into small sharpshooting detachments, while the other two, the Thirty-fourth and Thirty-fifth, stationed themselves in reserve. Advised of the skirmish, General Savaget went forward with the Fourth Brigade and took up a position four hundred yards from the front, in order to wait for the Sixth, the artillery division, and the supply train, which were still some two miles to the rear. While this was taking place, the advance detachments, consisting of some eight hundred men under Colonel Serra Martins, launched a sustained attack, the scattering shots of the marksmen now mingling with the regular volleys of the supporting platoons, which had moved forward and were vigorously replying to the enemy's fire. The sertanejos met the attack valorously. "Daring and tenacious," says the report of the commanding officer, "they further had the advantage of excellent positions overlooking the entire extent of the plain and a good stretch of the road; and they did not yield one foot but on the contrary repelled our attack firmly and energetically, keeping up a stubborn fire upon our ranks which speedily began to tell as our men dropped, dead or wounded."

As may be seen, the episodes of Mount Cambaio and Mount Favella were being duplicated here.[1] In the identical setting, replete in all its details, the sertanejos were staging the same rude, sinister, monotonous drama of which they were the invisible protagonists. No matter how long or arduous their apprenticeship in the art of war, their system never varied, for the reason that, by its very excellence, it admitted of no corrections or additions. From those dismantled parapets, they could fire in safety on our men, who formed a perfect target there on the barren level plain down below. Their bullets were beginning to thin out the nearest ranks, killing first the sharpshooters, spraying the supporting detachments, and finally spreading out in high and distant trajectories to make furrows in the last rows of the rear guard, until the entire column was thus brought within their range.

With all of this, they did not waste their ammunition; they depended not upon quantity but upon the accuracy of their aim. It could be seen how miserly they were of their cartridges, counting them over one by one, in order that not a single one might be uselessly spent. And after a short while, as a result of their carefully calculated volleys, with eight hundred army rifles thundering away in reply, the havoc which they wrought began to assume alarming proportions.

The Fifth Brigade proved to be admirably disciplined, withstanding the enemy fire for two hours in the position which it had taken up on the banks of the Vasa-Barris, in the shelter of the few shrubs that grew there. In all this time our troops did not advance a single step. A mere glance sufficed to show the risks of a direct attack in view of those two gorges which opened in front of them; they would have had to thread their way through the defiles in small sections, which meant that, when the decisive moment came, the strength of numbers would have been lacking. On the other hand, there was no way of getting around these defiles by means of a detour. To the right and to the left were rows of hills with numerous counterforts, and to attempt to find some bypath through them would have necessitated a flanking movement, and possibly an extensive one, under the watchful eye of the enemy, all of which rendered highly problematical any conceivable advantage that was to be gained.

General Savaget took all these circumstances into account in estimating

[1] See pp. 212 ff. and 308 ff.

the highly critical situation which confronted his troops. So far as his eight magnificently armed battalions were concerned, the conflict was an unequal one. Their march thus far had been successful, their safety being assured by effective reconnoiterings which predetermined the day and place where they would meet the enemy; but for two whole hours now, his men, powerless to act, had been futilely sacrificed, beneath the rifle fire of a mob of backwoodsmen who attacked with impunity. It was a situation that called for concrete plans, formed on the spur of the moment, for an improvised strategy, quickly conceived and promptly executed. However, on the horns of that dilemma which has been explained, and in view of the positions held by the enemy, no one appeared capable of solving the problem. It seemed that the only thing to be done for the moment was to risk everything by standing firm under this savage fusillade. The advance guard was accordingly reinforced, and the artillery with one of the Krupps came forward and took up a position near the front lines.

A bombardment of the mountain now began. Fired from close up, the grenades and case shots beat against the mountain side or ricocheted, and the air was filled with a mixture of bullets, iron splinters, and the rough debris from the slopes which were being subjected to so strenuous a shelling. Bursting among the boulders, dislocating them, toppling them, sending them crashing down the slopes below like the sections of a wall that was caving in, the cannon balls appeared to have entirely unmasked the enemy positions. This, however, did not lead to any fruitful results but only served to stimulate the foe to a violent, indeed a stupendous and inexplicable, counterattack, greater and more intense than any that had gone before, from the ruins of his intrenched positions. It was all the attackers could do to withstand it. As it was, their ranks were depleted, and the two supporting battalions, now fully engaged in the action, proceeded to sacrifice themselves uselessly, with an ever growing number of losses. As for the rest of the column, extending over a line a mile and a quarter long from front to rear, it remained immobilized. This was something very like a defeat.

After three hours of fighting, the attackers had not gained one foot of ground. At a distance of five hundred yards from their adversaries, with thousands of eyes fixed upon those barren slopes, they had not caught a glimpse of a single man. There was no way of telling how many of them there were. The tallest of the hillocks, swelling out in a buttress-like spur over the plain, appeared to be deserted. A burning, dazzling sun was beating straight down upon them, and the slightest details of their physical structure could readily be made out; one could count, one by one, the great boulders scattered over them, swaying unsteadily on their narrow bases like loggans[2] that are ready to fall, or piled in imposing heaps; and in between them could be seen the scattered stalks of hardy bromelias, of caroás, and macambiras with their long, straight, bright-hued spathes, gleaming in the sun like swords. A few slim, desolate-looking cacti were also visible; and, in the distance, a confused cluster of peaks, with the same deserted appearance.

And out of all this desolation, this absolute and impressive solitude, there burst from along the slopes a "sustained and uninterrupted fusillade, as if an entire division of infantry had been stationed there!"[3]

AN EXCEPTIONAL BAYONET CHARGE

The jagunços may have been two hundred in number, or they may have been two thousand. Once again, the expeditionaries found themselves confronted with the enigma of this campaign, destined to remain forever indecipherable. Their passage having been cut off, it was necessary for them to make a radical decision of one sort or another: either they must fall back slowly, fighting as they withdrew, by way of getting out of range of the enemy's fire; or they must make a detour around this untraversable terrain by seeking another, more accessible path, in the course of a hazardous flanking movement which would result in an inevitable defeat; or, finally, they must storm the hills and take them. This last alternative was at once the simplest and the most heroic. It was suggested by Colonel Carlos Telles, and General Savaget adopted it. In an official document in which, greatly to his disgust, he admits that a formidable enemy had brought his troops to a halt, the general states that he could not think of permitting "two or three hundred bandits to hold up the march of the Second Column for so great a length of time." In the action little more than a third of his men were engaged, and this proved to be a saving factor, rendering practicable a bold maneuver which certainly could not have been carried out had all his battalions, massed for a concerted attack, endeavored from the very beginning to crowd their way through the two entrances of the mountain defile.

The plan was as follows: "The Fifth Brigade, which from the start had maintained its position among the caatingas, was to charge on the left flank and along the river bed, with the object of dislodging the enemy from the hillocks in the center and from the lateral slopes; and the Fourth Brigade on the right flank, after having deployed in battle formation at the point where the highroad comes out on the plain." Between these two

---

[2] [Cf. p. 14.]   [3] General Savaget's order of the day.

detachments, the squadron of lancers was to charge in the center. The Sixth Brigade was to take no part in the engagement but was to remain at the rear, as a reserve force and for the purpose of guarding the supply train.

Thus, the five battalions destined to take part in the attack were drawn up in perpendicular formation, being reinforced on one of the wings, the left, by successive columns of Colonel Serra Martins' advance troops, while four hundred yards farther back and to the right was the Telles Brigade, with the squadron of lancers on its left flank. This formation, viewed in projection against the surface level of the plain, took on the exact appearance of a huge hammer. And the charge up the slopes which was afterward carried out and which marked the climax of the engagement was as a matter of fact very like a percussion, a concerted blow struck by sixteen hundred bayonets against the mountainside.

The assailants advanced all at one time, the platoons in front charging up the hills and filing through the mouth of the passageway to the left, while the men of the Fourth Brigade in double-quick time, weapons suspended and without firing, swiftly covered the distance which separated them from the enemy. At their head was Colonel Carlos Telles. This distinguished officer—with the bearing of an Osorio and the knightly bravery of a Turenne—without so much as drawing his sword from its scabbard, a habit which he was to preserve throughout the campaign, now led his troops across the entire field under a hail of bullets.

At the foot of the highlands to the left was the right-hand mouth of the defile, through which the cavalry squadron now boldly galloped at breakneck speed. The Fourth Brigade, however, avoided the gap and instead charged up the slopes. The jagunços had not counted on a daring move of this kind, one which, despite the obstacles to an ascent, was aimed directly at the positions which they held. For the first time, they permitted themselves to be taken by surprise by an unlooked-for tactical maneuver which disarranged their plans. They had been stationed there to cut off the two narrow passageways, in the belief that they would thus be able to fall upon the entire column; but now they were obliged to abandon their positions and retire to other points. It was the Fourth Brigade, staging the most unusual of bayonet charges, up a steep mountainside filled with impediments, that was destined to decide the outcome of the engagement.

It was a magnificent charge. At first they came forward in perfectly correct military formation, as a gleaming row of bayonets hundreds of yards long swept up to the foot of the hills. Then they began to climb the slope. Swaying back and forth at various points, the line finally broke, became disjointed; and the sertanejos, aided as usual by the unevenness of the terrain, let them have the full force of their fire. With their lines broken at all points, the troops came on in platoon formation, spreading out and stumbling forward blindly up the rugged mountainside.

Colonel Telles, leading the right flank of the Thirty-first Infantry, on this occasion had his horse shot from under him by a bullet which pierced his saddle. Leaping on another mount, he brought the scattered units together, although he was scarcely able to distinguish any longer the two detachments which he commanded, as they were now intermingled. Encouraging his men, he led them valiantly in a charge on the nearest trenches. These they found to be empty, but at the bottom of each they discovered dozens of exploded cartridges which were still warm. In accordance with their customary tactics, the jagunços had slipped away, falling back and luring the enemy on, taking advantage of all the features of the terrain, shifting the field of combat, and imposing upon the troops all the exertions of a profitless pursuit. Within a short space of time, however, having taken the first positions, the Fourth Brigade could be seen scaling the slopes which form the wall of the gorge at this point. One could also see the dead and wounded falling, some of them all the way to the bottom of the gorge, to the point where the seventy men of the lancers' squadron and the artillery division had made their entrance into the defile. These two detachments were now caught between the strongly fortified trenches on either side of the river, at the point of bifurcation of the gorge, which resembles a floodgate. On the slopes to the left the Fifth Brigade had likewise lost its original formation and was fighting in the same tumultuous fashion.

The engagement had now become a formidable one indeed. Five battalions were floundering among the hills, with no perceptible advantage after four hours of fighting. Driven back by the enemy's heavy fire, they were constantly losing more and more men, and the wounded were to be seen staggering about, dropping to the ground, leaning on their rifles, or wandering aimlessly down the mountainside among the dead with which the slopes were strewn. Down below, in the narrow valley, the riderless horses of the lancers' squadron, neighing from fright, were galloping about in all directions; the men of this detachment were now engaged in boldly storming the strongly fortified river trenches.

THE CROSSING OF THE GORGE

In the enormous confusion which prevailed, certain platoons of the Thirty-first Infantry, with an incomparable display of bravery, finally succeeded in making their way up to the highest of the trenches on the right-hand slope. Thus cut off, the jagunços who manned these trenches at intervals along the row of summits were compelled to abandon them suddenly. This was not their usual cautious retreat; this was flight. The troops now had a glimpse of the enemy for the first time, as the sertanejos scattered out over the heights, running along with their muskets in hand, rolling and gliding down the slopes, and disappearing from sight. The soldiers gave chase, and the attack was renewed with fresh vigor all along the line; there was a concerted forward surge which spread as far as the extreme left wing. This spelled victory. Some minutes afterward, the two brigades, in great confusion and in double-quick time, thronged into the last and single passageway of the defile.

Although they had been thrown into disorder, the jagunços, after the first impulse to flight had spent itself, returned to the same inexplicable mode of resistance which they customarily practiced. Forsaking their positions and leaving the perilous gorge-crossing free, they now harassed the victors from afar with a scattering rifle fire at long intervals.

General Savaget was shot from his horse, along with an adjutant and a part of his staff, as the rear of the column was entering the defile on the right-hand side and just as the first triumphant shouts of the advance guard reached their ears. As always, the sertanejos were taking the edge off victory by unaccountably rising up again from the havoc of a lost battle. Beaten, they did not permit themselves to be crushed. Dislodged at all points, they found shelter elsewhere, at once conquered and menacing, fleeing and slaying as they fled, in the manner of the Parthians. They had, nonetheless, suffered a serious defeat, as is indicated by the name, "crack battalion," which was later bestowed upon the column that had inflicted it. For the battle of Cocorobó, while marked by wavering fortunes at the start, with the decision hanging in the balance for three hours of ineffectual firing, and with a dashing bayonet charge at the end, was as a matter of fact won by a bold action which, if not from the strictly military point of view, was at least justified by the special circumstances attendant upon it. The soldier from the Rio Grande was predominant in the ranks; and the fearless gaucho, however ill adapted he may be to enduring the hardships of a long-drawn-out war, is without an equal when it comes to bold and sudden sallies of this sort. In the South the shock troops are the infantry. Others may be better in the matter of discipline and precision on the firing line or in the execution of complex maneuvers; but in hand-to-hand fighting, with sword or bayonet, these dismounted centaurs attack the enemy in the same manner in which they would ride down the wild horses of the pampas. In the case of the present stupendous undertaking, fate smiled upon them, and they carried it through with the utmost brilliancy.

That afternoon, as the troops pitched camp beyond the gorge, they made a reckoning of the losses they had suffered. The casualties amounted to 178 men in all, 27 killed and the others wounded, including 2 officers killed and 10 wounded. The Sixth Brigade, which had not taken part in the engagement, was assigned the task of burying the dead; this detachment was encamped in the rear of the other two, which occupied an extensive tableland overlooking the highway.

"MACAMBIRA"

From this point on their march was a slow one and became one continuous battle. The entire day of the twenty-sixth was spent in traversing the short distance to the confluence of the Macambira, only a mile or so beyond Cocorobó.

General Savaget then informed his men that on the following day, the twenty-seventh, in accordance with the decision of the high command, they were to be at the outskirts of Canudos, where the six brigades were to be reunited for the purpose of an assault on the settlement. The village must be very near by now. Scattered over the hillsides, they could see the thatch-roofed huts arranged in that special manner which has already been described.[4] There they stood, among the pits and trenches concealed by bromelia stalks, like so many fortresses which were at the same time homes. The Second Column, in its advance on this day—the last lap of its long march—with the Sixth Brigade leading the van, followed by the Thirty-third Infantry, entered the "suburbs" of this enormous citadel; and it had gone barely a mile and a half, the bulk of the column being still in camp at the rear, when Colonel Pantoja's battalions, attacked from all sides, found themselves engaged in a pitched battle.

ANOTHER BAYONET CHARGE

The expedient which had proved so effective the evening before was thereupon promptly adopted. Forming in line with bayonets in position, the Twenty-sixth, Thirty-third, and Thirty-ninth battalions impetuously charged up the hillsides in great confusion. Round about them on every hand they could see other hills, countless others, all with the same rugged outlines, extending away for mile on mile.

And from all of those hills, from the huts with which their tops were

4 [See pp. 144, 145–46, 255–56.]

covered, there now came a deadly rifle fire, directed full upon them. The field of battle was an ample one indeed and well adapted to the wily enemy's mode of fighting. Having captured one of these elevations, our men would find that there were hundreds of others to be taken in their turn. To make a descent to the lowlands was to fall into a network of gullies. The attack was going to be an exhausting affair, up one hill and down another. A mile or so farther on they had an indistinct view of Canudos, which in its mournfully deserted appearance resembled a waste clearing left by surface miners.[5]

UNDER FIRE

The battle was now joined in the environs of the settlement, and a hotly contested one it was. After a short while the three vanguard battalions saw that they would not be able to withstand the attack. From the huts crammed with jagunços and from all the trenches scattered over the hills came a well-aimed fire that thinned their ranks. A company of the Thirty-ninth, at the beginning of the engagement, was literally pounded to pieces in attempting to storm one of these rude fortresses. Having suddenly come out on top the hill, the men found themselves on the edge of a wide trench which encircled the hut that stood there; and from the chinks in the wall of the hut as well as from the trench itself there now came a furious fusillade which mowed them down at close range. The detachment lost its commanding officer and immediately afterward two subalterns who had replaced him, one after the other. Led by a sergeant at the end, they finally conquered the position, but at great loss to themselves.

In view of this unlooked-for resistance, the one brigade alone being unable to cover the extensive field of operations, it was reinforced by two others. The Twelfth, Thirty-first, Thirty-fifth, and Fortieth battalions in succession were sent forward. This represented more than a thousand bayonets, or nearly the entire column, engaged in the conflict. The jagunços then fell back, fell back slowly, from hill to hill; dislodged at one point, they would spring up at another, obliging their attackers to be constantly running up and down the slopes. The obvious intention was to lure the troops on to the settlement, after they had been exhausted by this withering fire. The sertanejos were reverting to their unvarying tactics, and the field of battle began to flee beneath the feet of their assailants. The bayonet charges here lacked the brilliancy of those at Cocorobó, their effect being deadened by the extreme mobility of the enemy's retreat. Boldly charging up the hills, the platoons, when they reached the top, would find

5 [See p. 173.]

not a man in sight. On the heights, they were subjected to the enemy's
fire from the surrounding hills, and they would then dash down to seek
shelter in the lowlands—only to have to repeat the performance over and
over again: the same exhausting climb, to find themselves once more in a
dangerously exposed position.

The losses by now were heavy; in addition to a large number of privates,
more than one high-ranking officer had been killed or wounded. The commanding officer of the Twelfth Battalion, Lieutenant Colonel Tristão
Sucupira, was mortally wounded on his way to join the vanguard. The
commander of the Thirty-third, Lieutenant Colonel Virginio Napoleão
Ramos, was likewise wounded in action and carried to the rear, along with
Captain Joaquim de Aguiar, commissary of the same detachment. And
others, many others, sacrificed themselves in this bloody battle of "Macambira," so named from the adjacent farm. The terrain being unsuited
to any kind of tactical maneuvers which might have offset the enemy's
headlong, purposive flight, the only hope of success lay in an exhibition of
personal courage. Some of the officers, such as the captain adjutant of the
Thirty-second, though suffering from more than one serious wound, obstinately refused to quit the fight and remained deaf to the word of their
superiors ordering them back from the firing line. That line was now extended over two miles. The hills were aflame and thunderous with sound,
as the echoes died away over the lowlands in the direction of Canudos.

Night brought a halt to the fighting. The expedition was now within
three-fifths of a mile of the settlement, and the men could see the tall towers of the new church gleaming white in the falling dusk.

At last they had reached the end of their long march, which had started
from Geremoabo. The Second Column, however, had paid for it dearly.
Its losses on this one day alone amounted to 148 men, 40 killed, the others
wounded, including 6 officers killed and 8 wounded. Its total losses came
to 327, the price which had been exacted for crossing less than eight miles
of territory, from Cocorobó to the place where the column now was.

But everything pointed to a compensating victory. General Savaget's
troops had punctually fulfilled their pre-established schedule; and, a few
minutes after they had pitched camp, the silence of the hinterland night
was broken on their left by the sound of distant cannonading, echoing
among the counterforts of Mount Favella, as the advance guard of the
First Column at this time began shelling the settlement.

THE BOMBARDMENT

On the twenty-eighth, having quickly advanced and taken up a position on a small plateau a little more than a mile from the village, they be-

gan in their turn to bombard it, while the two battalions of the Carlos Telles Brigade went on farther to the front in a rapid reconnoitering movement. A detail of cavalry, led by a brave officer who was destined to meet a hero's death, Sublieutenant Wanderley,[6] explored the terrain on the left flank as far as Mount Favella, where at this hour—eight o'clock in the morning—an intense cannonading once more began.

With the headquarters staff only a few paces away, the Second Column was ready for the assault. It had reached this point after a march of 175 miles, ending in a three-day battle. Having mastered the unusual mode of fighting which was required of them here, the men were eager to come to grips with the enemy; they felt that the irresistible impetus which they had acquired through that initial charge at Cocorobó, and which had carried them uninterruptedly up to this point, well might sweep them triumphantly into the very heart of Canudos, into the center of the square where the churches stood. Despite the losses which they had sustained, they were filled with hope and a feeling of strength. The order of the day for the twenty-sixth, in which the commander informed them that they and their comrades of the First Column were very soon to attack the settlement is significant.

ORDER OF THE DAY AT "TRABUBÚ"

This order was issued at "Trabubú," as they were going through the defiles, and, laconic as it is, says much. The news of the coming attack, enthusiastically received by the soldiers, was set forth in a few courteous, unpretentious words:

In camp on the field of battle of Cocorobó, 26th of June, 1897.

My comrades. I have just received a telegram from our commander-in-chief, informing me that tomorrow we shall greet one another in Canudos.[7] Naturally, we cannot fail to accept this invitation which does us so much honor, and which is for us a cause of justifiable pride and a great joy.

This meeting so ardently desired was, however, fated to take place not in the village which was the objective of the campaign but outside it, with the enemy attacking from all sides.

AN UNEXPECTED EMISSARY

All eyes in the Second Column were fixed on Mount Favella, in the expectation of seeing the battalions of the First Column descend the northern slopes. What was their surprise, then, when there suddenly appeared in camp a sertanejo who notified them that he came by order of the com-

[6] See pp. 24, 353, and 356.

[7] See p. 302.

mander-in-chief[8] to inform them of the straits in which the other column
now found itself and imperatively to request their immediate aid. This
news was incredible; it looked at first like a trick on the part of the enemy.
The man was accordingly detained until a fresh emissary should arrive to
confirm it. This latter, an honorary sublieutenant who had been added to
the engineering commission,[9] was not long in putting in an appearance.
The commanding general of the expedition was urgently calling for assistance. Upon receiving this second message, along with information
which made matters clear, General Savaget, who at first had thought of
sending merely a brigade with a supply of munitions while the rest of his
column held the position they had won, now decided upon another course
and, turning to the left, proceeded with his entire force to the top of
Mount Favella, where they arrived around eleven o'clock, in time to
liberate the troops that were besieged there.

A PLAN OF CAMPAIGN CRUMBLES

The entire plan of campaign had now been upset, and it appeared that
all the effort expended on the marches from "Rosario" and Geremoabo
had been in vain.

Now that the columns had been reunited, it was possible to send a detachment to retrieve the supply train which had been held up at the rear
of the severed First Column. This task was intrusted to Colonel Serra
Martins, who promptly set out with the Fifth Brigade—a dangerous
movement in view of the two battles that were going on—and proceeded
to "Umburanas," where he was in time to prevent the rout of the Fifth
Police, being able to save a part of the contents of the 180 pack trains
which, scattered along the road, had been greatly damaged by the jagunços.

This fortunate move, however, did little to relieve the perilous plight of
the troops; the situation remained a critical one. There now began a series
of misfortunes of all sorts, enough to drive an army to despair.

II

SINGULAR VICTORY

The order of the day for the twenty-eighth of June described that day
as "a page of horrors, but one redolent with glory." But the fact of the
matter is that it was a day of defeat.

History is not to be taken in by the blustering of the vanquished. The
"victorious army," as the official reports glowingly put it—reports de-

[8] See p. 314.   [9] Henrique José Leite.

signed to cover up the failure with which our troops had met—had the exact appearance, that night, of a mob of fugitives. They were conquerors who dared not stir a foot beyond the position they had won.[10] The campaign had now reached a critical period. The high courage with which they had entered upon it had been squandered on futile skirmishes or doubtful victories which were equivalent to defeats, being a drain, at once, upon their spirits and upon their fighting strength. They now felt that they were bound together, if at all, by the mere external pressure of that enemy whom they had expected to trample underfoot so easily. Heroism was accordingly forced upon them, and bravery alternated with fear in a deadly compromise with terror. They were surrounded on all sides by the strangest kind of vanquished foe that they had ever heard of, a merciless one who had laid siege to them, a siege that would be lifted they knew not when—a foe who had made of himself an incorruptible morale officer, by cutting off all the avenues to desertion. However lacking in valor they may have been, our soldiers had no means of getting out of this exceedingly grave predicament in which cowards and heroes were of equal worth.

A WORD ON FEAR

Military history, which is so dramatic in texture and at times so embroidered over with strange antitheses, is filled with instances of the glorification of fear. The fury of the pursuing Persian resulted in exalting the heroic resignation of the "ten thousand"; the brutality of the Cossacks immortalized Marshal Ney.

We must now add to all this a stirring chapter, one which fits in perfectly with the others, even though the events with which it deals are on a lesser scale—for it was the ferocious tenacity of the jagunço that fashioned the halo for General Arthur Oscar's battered battalions. If those battalions stood their ground with ranks undiminished by desertion, it was for the reason that they were encircled by a stone wall of trenches; if they were intrepid, it was for the reason that retreat was impossible. They were heroes whether they wished to be or not, simply because they were stalled there, hemmed in by bullets in that hole in the ground.

LOSSES

There was nothing which in the least resembled a camp in these brigades huddled one upon another. They did not pitch tents, which would only have taken up more space in the narrow area to which they were confined. There was no attempt at an orderly division into fighting units.

[10] See p. 363.

This army of 5,000 soldiers, with more than 900 dead and wounded, a thousand-odd cavalry and draft horses, and hundreds of pack trains—an army without vanguard, rear guard, or flanks—was completely disorganized. The First Column had 524 men killed or wounded, which, with the 75 of the day before, brought their losses up to 599. The Second Column, which had now joined the First, had suffered the loss of 327 men. Altogether, the victims numbered 926. This is not to speak of the countless number of men who had been crippled, exhausted, weakened from hunger on the long march, or of those—including the vast majority—who, as a result of the recent slaughter, had been turned into cowards as they saw their companions who that morning had been enthusiastic and full of life now lying stretched out dead on the ground without the rites of burial.

Among the dead were: Thompson Flores,[11] ill-fated commander of the Seventh Infantry; Tristão de Alencar Sucupira, who arrived mortally wounded with the Second Column;[12] Nestor Villar, captain commissary of the Second Regiment, who met his death along with more than two-thirds of the officers commanding the artillery;[13] Gutierrez, an honorary officer who in private life was an artist and who had been attracted to the somber scene of battle for aesthetic reasons; Souza Campos, who for one minute was in command of the Fourteenth;[14] and others of all ranks and all detachments.

A long, deepened furrow carved out by torrents ran the length of this mountaintop ravine, and within this natural trench more than eight hundred wounded writhed in agony, adding their piercing screams to the general tumult. This fold in the earth, where a field hospital had been improvised,[15] was a physical image of what had happened to the expedition, which had been laid wide open from end to end. Viewing it, the strongest of heart grew faint. For, when all was said, there was nothing to compensate for such losses as these or to explain why a plan of campaign which had been so maturely formulated should thus seemingly have come to naught. Victorious and with their forces combined, the two columns were nonetheless immobilized and impotent in the face of this reality. The orders of the day with their resounding periods fell flat indeed on their ears. Here they were in the center of operations, yet they were unable to move a step forward or, what was worse, a step backward. They had lavishly expended more than a million bullets, they had driven the enemy back in all engagements, yet they still felt his presence around them, more menac-

[11] See pp. 291 and 312.
[12] [See pp. 316 and 328.]   [14] [See p. 313.]
[13] [See p. 313.]   [15] [See p. 309.]

ing than ever, it might be, cutting off their retreat after they had routed him in open battle.

Everything, the truth is, pointed to the fact that they were completely besieged. The Fifth Brigade, in its movement to the rear, lost 14 men; the Fifth Police lost 45. The march to the rear and back was made amid an incessant gunfire all along the trench-lined roads.

In the very heart of the enemy's territory, the expedition was now cut off, without the slightest strategic line of communication with its base in Monte Santo, unless the dangerous Rosario Road, which was filled with ambuscades, could be looked upon as such. They had their supply train now, but it was greatly reduced in size, more than half of its contents having been left in the hands of the sertanejos or rendered useless by them. The troops had thereby lost munitions which would have been of inestimable value in their present critical situation; and, what is more, they had made the enemy a present of from 400,000 to 500,000 cartridges, or enough to enable him to hold out indefinitely. They were, in other words, equipping their adversary. The preceding expedition had given the jagunços muskets, and the present one was now presenting them with the cartridges to put in those muskets. And, thus equipped, the "vanquished" fiercely renewed their attack on these foolish "victors" who were not able to reply in kind.

Night was falling, and the attack was still raging, without the slightest letup such as might have permitted our troops to bring some kind of order into their ranks. A brightly shining moon made the soldiers easy targets for the jagunços, and the latter with coolheaded calculation kept up a steady fire at long intervals, which showed that these daring backwoodsmen were still maintaining their watch. Breaking discipline now and then, some soldier or other would reply by firing at random into the air, while his comrades, overcome with fatigue and clutching their useless rifles, pillowed their heads on the packs that were scattered here and there over the hard ground.

A CHRONIC BATTLE BEGINS

The night of the twenty-eighth of June saw the beginning of a chronic battle. From that date until the end of the campaign, the troops were to live in a constant state of alarm. This was the beginning, also, of a deplorable series of misfortunes. At dawn of the twenty-ninth, it was found that there were insufficient rations for the men of the First Column, who as it was had been on reduced rations for a week past. The Second Column, although it was better stocked, did not have enough to guarantee its subsistence for three days after sharing with the other. The result was that, on this day, just as the conflict was entering its critical phase, they were compelled to lay hands on the last of their resources, by felling the oxen which up to then had drawn the heavy 32-cannon.

Meanwhile, they were confronted with a most difficult task: that of making an army out of this heap of men and baggage, by bringing order into the dissolved battalions and reconstituting the brigades, while caring for hundreds of wounded, burying the dead, and clearing the reduced area at their disposal of the luggage and pack trains with which it was cluttered on all sides. These indispensable tasks they carried out, but unmethodically and amid great confusion, with no firm will to guide them. The commanding officers and their subalterns showed a spontaneous desire, praiseworthy enough in itself, to collaborate on every hand, by suggesting an endless number of urgent things to be done; but as a result, after a short while, this jostling mass of human beings was moving about in all directions, at cross-purposes, as they hastily dug trenches and took up their positions at random in something that resembled military formation, or as they cleared the space of packs and corpses and led away the mules whose iron-shod hoofs were a constant menace to the wounded. The short of the matter is that their efforts, lacking co-ordination, proved of little avail.

They did not, however, entirely lose heart. Valor returned with the dawn; for, in spite of all the object-lessons they had had, they did not even yet sufficiently reckon with the fierce pertinacity of the sertanejos, and their minds were now filled with consoling thoughts of the vigorous bombardment which the artillery, taking advantage of its position on the heights above, would soon be inflicting upon the settlement. It was, surely, obvious that a village in the open country would not be able to withstand for many hours the cross-fire of nineteen modern cannon.

CANNONADE: THE JAGUNÇOS REPLY

The first cannon ball that was dropped on Canudos had the effect of a stone tossed into a beehive. Up to that moment, the camp on Mount Favella had been relatively calm, but, as on the evening before, it was now suddenly ablaze with rifle fire, and once again the soldiers realized that it was practically impossible to reply to this sweeping attack which came from a wide circle round about them. What was more, down in a fold of the earth as they were and firing upward without any definite target, their shots would have no effect and they would only be wasting what little ammunition they had. On the other hand, the effect of the cannonading was absolutely nil. The grenades, exploding inside the huts, merely tore holes in the walls and roofs and were practically deadened by the fragile clay partitions, bursting noisily but causing no wide destruction and many times falling intact without setting off their fuses.[16] For this reason, the favored target once more became the new church, towering above the low cluster of huts like an imposing rampart. It was here that the defenders were stationed, behind the cornices of the main walls, perched on the towers or at the ogival windows further down, or huddled at the ground-level along the foundation, pierced with narrow embrasure-like vents.

With the fire of the Witworth 32 directed upon them, one would have expected soon to see the walls crumbling; but on this particular occasion the artillery thundered away without hitting the church, the cannon balls whistling past the roof and falling into the cluster of huts. One alone fell into the churchyard, chipping the façade of the building. The other shots went wild. This very bad aim on the part of the giant gun was principally due to the haste with which it was fired. This huge weapon—the mastiff of the chase in the present instance—had become a foolish obsession, a monstrous fetish, and one tending to awaken primitive illusions. Breathlessly anxious and finding it hard to repress their disappointment when shots went astray, soldiers from all the other detachments crowded about it.[17] Finally, one of the onlookers, a surgeon by the name of Alfredo Gama, was unable any longer to repress his eagerness to have a hand in firing it. This resulted in his death. The gases escaping from the badly loaded cannon set fire to a keg of powder near by, which exploded, killing and burning to ashes Dr. Gama, Sublieutenant Odilon Coriolano, and a number of privates. This will serve to give an idea of how the battle was going.

It was to have been expected that this engagement would be a fruitless one, with the noisy but inoffensive bombardment being turned into a salute to the courage of the backwoodsmen.

Night fell, and nothing had been accomplished by this long-distance attack. At the same time the rifle fire all around made it plain to all that this was in truth a siege to which they were being subjected, even though the enemy's lines in the form of numerous trenches were spread out slackly, in an undefined radius, over the slopes of the hill. A brigade, a battalion, a company even, might sweep them from the clearings in between or might overcome them in a bayonet charge; but, the moment the troops were on the march again, they would be aware of this inexorable lurking foe who seemed to spring up from the ground, circulating around them, attacking them on the flanks, hampering their movements. The bold and

[16] [Cf. pp. 256–57.]   [17] [Cf. pp. 310–11.]

unvarying tactics of the jagunço were nowhere more clearly revealed than in this resistance which he offered even while retreating, as he sought out every means of shelter which the terrain afforded. This was the struggle of the sinuous boa[18] with the mighty bull. Coiled and captured, the former had but to uncoil its links; this permitted an unrestrained freedom of movement which proved exhausting to its adversary; after which it would seize its prey in those contractile coils, constrict him, then relax its hold and let him once more exhaust himself by pawing up the earth with his horns; and this process of attracting, retracting, leading on, would be continued until the victim had been completely drained of his strength.

There was here a certain inversion of roles. On the one hand were men equipped for war by all the resources of modern industry, materially strong and brutal, as from the mouths of their cannon they hurled tons of steel on the rebels; and, on the other hand, were these rude warriors who opposed to all this the masterly and unfathomable stratagems of the backwoodsman. The latter willingly gave their antagonist his meaningless victories, which served merely as a lure; but even as the "victor," after having paved with lead the soil of the caatingas, was unfurling his banners and awakening the desert echoes with his drumbeats, they, not possessing these refinements of civilization, kept time to the triumphal hymns with the whine of bullets from their shotguns.

The cannonading of the twenty-ninth of June did not stagger them. At dawn of the thirtieth, they attacked the entire camp. As always, it came as a sudden, instantaneous shock, and once more all the invariable features of a backlands skirmish were there. This meant another "victory." Attacking from all sides, the enemy was everywhere repelled, only to return hours later to be again repulsed. A brief interval elapsed, and there was another attack, another repulse—the whole carried out with an intermittent rhythm, like the ebb and flow of a wave beating monotonously against the sides of the mountain. The artillery, as it had done the day before, fired a few rounds upon the roofs down below; and, as on the preceding day, this was answered with a scattering fusillade, coming from the slopes of Favella and from the nearest hills, without any variation whatsoever, as the bullets all day long rained down upon the troops.

PRIVATIONS

Things were now becoming distinctly unbearable. This halt on Mount Favella was, above all, detrimental for the reason that, while their losses mounted daily and they were accomplishing nothing, it was having from

---

[18] [The *sucuri*, or anaconda (*Eunectes murinus*).]

day to day a demoralizing effect upon the expedition, tarnishing its reputation; and, now that their munitions were almost completely exhausted, it had become a wholly unnatural situation. To abandon their position involved a risk greater than that of an open battle; and some of the higher-ranking officers accordingly suggested, as the one urgent step to be taken, an immediate assault upon the settlement. To this there appeared to be no alternative.

However, be this as it may, on the thirtieth of June our forces were in good order; the artillery was in a position to continue its bombardment of Canudos for a few hours yet, after which it would be possible to launch an attack on the citadel. The commanding officers of the columns, brigades, and corps, as well as the subalterns and enlisted men, were all in favor of this course, their one burning desire being to reach the Vasa-Barris, which in their eyes stood for an abundance of all the things they lacked, here in this cramped position which was open to attack from all sides, and which was not big enough to accommodate two thousand, much less close on to six thousand men.[19]

The commander-in-chief, however, refused to adopt this plan, "believing that there would soon arrive from Monte Santo a supply of rations as the Quartermaster General's deputy had promised him; and only then, after three days of full rationing, would they attack the Counselor's defenses."

But this supply train did not exist. Sent out to meet it on the thirtieth, Colonel Medeiros' brigade, after having waited for it in vain at "Baixas" with the object of escorting it from there on into camp, continued on to Monte Santo, where likewise there was no trace of it. The army was already beginning to feel the first sharp pangs of hunger as this brigade left, and it now entered upon a period of indescribable sufferings.

RUNNING THE BLOCKADE: DANGEROUS HUNTING EXCURSIONS

They lived as best they could, from hand to mouth. On their own initiative, without the formality, which under the circumstances might be dispensed with, of any authorization whatsoever, the soldiers began making dangerous excursions through the neighborhood, either singly or in small groups, despoiling what few fields there were of millet or manihot, hunting the young goats which had been running half-wild since the war began, and rounding up the cattle. There was no way of stopping them from doing this, for it was their last resort. From July 2 on, the only food they had was flour and salt, nothing more, for the wounded. These hunting expeditions were, accordingly, in the nature of a necessity, despite the major risks involved; and those who took part in such extremely daring adventures proceeded to imitate the jagunço by donning the hides that he wore

[19] Colonel Dantas Barreto, *Ultima expedição a Canudos*.

and by following the same subtle methods which he employed, creeping along cautiously and taking shelter in every crease and furrow of the earth.

It would be impossible to narrate all the individual episodes which occurred during this dark and terrible phase of the campaign. The famished soldier, living off his cartridge box, now disappeared among the uplands, taking as many precautions as if he were going out to hunt lions, and was soon swallowed up in the wild-growing thickets. He had to break down the unyielding boughs, entwined with prickly silk-grass; and—eyes and ears alert to the slightest movement, the faintest sound—he would spend long hours in his exhausting search. At times his efforts were in vain, and he would come back to camp at night downcast in spirit and empty-handed. Others, still more unfortunate, were never seen again—lost in those desert wastes or slain in some fierce struggle which would remain forever unknown. For the jagunços finally began laying unexpected snares for these timid hunters, who, not being a match for the natives in subtlety, did not know how to avoid such pitfalls.

And so it was that, not infrequently, after many hours of futile effort, the famished hero would become aware of the sound of bells, indicating that the longed-for prey was near at hand; for it is the custom in the backlands to put bells on the female goats. Filled with hope, he would pluck up courage and his weariness would drop from him for a moment. Going forward now more cautiously than ever, in order not to frighten the fleet-footed game, he would leave the beaten paths through the thick of the weeds and would glide along in a roundabout way, following the notes of the bell as, sharp and clear, they broke the silence of the hills. He would keep on until the sound was very close, and, despite the grievous disappointment that he felt, he was happy to hear them again, at a distance, indistinct and unattainable amid the labyrinth of bypaths. For he was unable to imagine on certain occasions the risks that he might be running. In place of the coy game that he sought, in the depths of the caatinga, there lurked the wily jagunço, a sinister, treacherous being who in turn was hunting him. Flat on the ground with the lock of his musket on a level with his beard, the sertanejo was crawling very, very quietly through the weeds, and at each movement that he made the little bell hung about his own neck would tinkle; for, in place of the she-goat, it was the fierce goatherd who was stirring there; the game was hunting the hunter.[20] The latter, wholly lacking in experience, was usually dropped by a well-aimed

---

[20] [*A caça caçava o caçador.*]

bullet, without having had a chance to fire first at that face which he had no more than glimpsed at the last moment.

At other times a group of famished soldiers would sight a corral with a few oxen in it on the knob of a hill. This was a craftily arranged decoy, and the inclosure a gigantic hoax. In the presence of this unexpected find, however, with barely a glance about them, the men would bound forward and fall upon the oxen, to slay them with knife or gun . . . . and then, of a sudden, they would scatter in wild alarm as the bullets rained down upon them from all sides, fired from ambush.

In the camp, many times, the troops could hear the sound of heavy firing in the distance. Finally, these adventurous foraging parties were subjected to certain regulations. The orders issued the night before would detail those battalions which were to take part in the hunt on a given day. These were true armed sallies, but inglorious ones, an army advancing without banners and without trumpets through the desert wastes. Ahead of them lay the enemy's lines, scattered, invisible, treacherous. The foraging detachments would slip through the clearings and diligently, for a long while, would scour the countryside, where the advent of the dry season was already reflected in the withered foliage. In the course of their expedition, they would be fired upon half-a-dozen times, perhaps, by their incorporeal adversaries. In the end they would return discouraged and exhausted.

The lancers' squadron alone proved effective to a degree. It would daily gallop far and wide over the neighboring trails. Astride crippled mounts that broke into a limping canter when the spur was applied, the gauchos performed true cowboy exploits. Without thought of distance or the dangers to be met with, they roamed a region which was wholly unknown to them; and, having succeeded in capturing a few wild oxen, they would herd them every afternoon into a corral alongside the camp. They were, however, not free of molestation on these excursions. In addition to the labor of rounding up the skittish beasts, they had to see to it that the enemy, by a sudden attack, did not disperse them. In these swift and violent encounters, they had a double task, that of preventing the frightened cattle from stampeding and that of returning the hidden enemy's fire. They would be crossing the lowlands, when, unexpectedly, they would stumble upon an ambuscade; in which case, they would never once abandon their restless herd, but, riding round it and driving it forward, they would, at one and the same time, give a marvelous exhibition of courage and of horsemanship.

The cattle thus daily acquired—eight or ten head of them—were, however, quite insufficient to feed to that Minotaur with six thousand stomachs. Moreover, meat boiled without salt or other ingredient, in brackish water that was far from sanitary, or broiled on spits, was all but inedible; however hungry a man might be, he found it repugnant. The small plantations of millet, beans, and manihot, vegetables which at first had taken the edge off their wild beasts' diet, were soon exhausted, and it became necessary to look for other sources of supply.

Like the unfortunate "quitters,"[21] the soldiers now had resort to the providential plant,[22] by digging up the umbú trees for their swollen tubercles; they likewise sought out the fruit of the urucuri, carved up the soft stems of the mandacarús, or fed on cacti, which at one and the same time served to allay the pangs of hunger and of thirst. This recourse, however, did not suffice; for it was a dangerous one even for those who were experienced in the matter, and a number of the men died of poisoning from having eaten the wild manihot and other roots with which they were unfamiliar.

At last even their water gave out or became very hard to get. Along the brooksides in the Umburanas Valley, more than one thirsty soldier was brought down by an enemy bullet. Each day that passed augmented their distress. From July 7 on, they ceased distributing rations to the wounded, and these unfortunate ones, crippled, mutilated, fever-ridden, now had to depend on the uncertain charity of their comrades.

DISCOURAGEMENTS

As these misfortunes grew worse, they had to face others that were equally grave. The discipline of the troops was now relaxed, for the common soldier had reached the end of his patience and was no longer resigned to whatever might happen. There were certain surly murmurs of protest, but the officers, powerless to quiet the men, pretended to be deaf; there was nothing to be done about such complaints as these; they were as inevitable as a rumbling of the bowels when the stomach is empty.

In irritating contrast to the plight of the expeditionaries, the enemy, who had been defeated in all the engagements, appeared to be abundantly provisioned, to such an extent, indeed, that he scarcely found it necessary to make use of the supplies which he had captured. The Fifth Brigade on one occasion, on its way to "Baixas," found in the vicinity of that place, all the way along the road until just this side of "Angico," bundles of smoked meat and heaps of flour, coffee, and sugar, along with the ashes of bonfires where the jagunços had made a meal. This undoubtedly was but

[21] [See p. 109.]   [22] [See pp. 37–38.]

an evidence of that savage arrogance which the latter displayed in battle; for, after all, they did not possess so great an abundance as to justify such waste. The truth is, frugal and parsimonious in the extreme, these rude fighting men who in time of peace would go through the day with two or three handfuls of passoca[23] and a drink of water, had in time of war made abstinence a matter of discipline and had carried it to so high a point that they were capable of an extraordinary degree of physical endurance. Our own soldiers did not possess that capacity; it was not, in the nature of things, possible for them. At first they reacted well and even had a humorous epithet to apply to hunger. The dangerous foraging expeditions and the searching for odds and ends of food in the abandoned plantations served them as a distraction. No sooner was the alarm sounded than they would rush to the firing line, for, in spite of their enforced fasting, they had as yet lost none of their fighting spirit. But later they began to weaken. It was not merely physical exhaustion that laid hold of them but uncertainty with regard to the future. One of the brigades, the First, had gone out to look for the supply train, and nothing had been heard of it since. This added to their discouragement. Every day that went by without news of this detachment made them all the more dejected. Over and above all this, the insistent manner in which the enemy kept on attacking them had come to seem an unnatural thing. They were not given so much as an hour's respite. During the night, in the early morning, and all through the day there would be one sudden attack after another; and there was no telling when the attack would come; it was always at the moment when they were least expecting it. Sometimes it would be directed at the artillery; other times, at one of the flanks; and again—and this was the most serious case of all—the entire force would be brought under fire, with the bullets coming from every side. There would then be a blare of bugles, as the men fell in with very little sign of any tactical formation; and for some while they would fight on nervously, until their assailants had once more been repelled and the mountaintop was suddenly quiet again. But the enemy remained there always, only a few paces away, a sinister enemy, elbowing the "victors." The attack itself had ceased; but from minute to minute, with stubborn precision, a bullet would drop among the battalions. The direction of the shots constantly varied, until little by little all the ranks, from one side to the other, had come to experience them. The missiles came and went, tracing from point to point a large and terrifying circle. It was as if a single marksman, on top of some remote hillock, had taken upon himself the barbarous task of being the executioner of an

[23] [See p. 107 and n. 99.]

army. And that is precisely what he was. Brave men, still panting from an engagement in which they had fought without a trace of fear, would begin to tremble at last as they heard the whine of those bullets, those random shots fired at a huge target, and which, among the thousands there, were destined to find out their victims.

ASSAULT ON THE CAMP; THE "KILLER"

Thus the days went by, with quick and furious skirmishes alternating with long periods of calm, punctuated by bullets.

There were times now when the attacks did not cease as they usually did but, exhibiting an alarming crescendo, would engage the entire force, until they came to take on all the aspects of a battle. In the course of one of these attacks, that of the first of July, the sertanejos entered the camp and made their way to the center of the artillery post. The hatred they felt for those cannon, which day after day were demolishing their temples, had led them to conceive the incredible exploit of capturing or destroying the largest of them, the Witworth 32, the "Killer" as they called it. There were not many of them who embarked upon this undertaking, not more than eleven all told, led by Joaquim Macambira, son of the old chieftain of the same name.[24] This small group found themselves confronted with whole battalions. The bugle sounded and the men charged in closed ranks, as if they had been a legion. When it was over, all the jagunços save one lay stretched out on the ground; that one had miraculously made his escape by slipping through the ranks in the confusion that prevailed. The troops had the consolation of yet another victory, but it was not one of which they could be very proud; rather it served to increase their respect for the fearlessness of the enemy.

The ascendancy of the latter grew from day to day. The expeditionaries could see, close by, the trenches which ran around the camp and which were slowly closing in upon it; on their left, cutting off the approach by way of the "Old Ranch House"; on the right, threatening their corral and reducing more and more the small bit of pasture ground where their cavalry and draft horses were kept; in their rear, running along the Rosario Highway. The detachments sent out to take and demolish these trenches found no difficulty in doing so and would return with few losses or none at all; but, on the following day, they would have it all to do over again, for the trenches would have been reconstructed during the night and each time closer to the camp, more menacing.

Spending their days in this manner, they reserved their nights for bury-

24 See pp. 158 and 387.

ing the dead, which was not only a mournful but a perilous task. Not infrequently, one who bore the burden would himself fall and take his place among the corpses in the common grave which his own hands had helped to dig.

It is not strange, then, if a week after they had come to occupy the hill, discontent became rife, with a slackening of discipline all along the line. Even the artillery, having discovered the ineffectualness of its bombardment and faced with the necessity of sparing its ammunition, fired no more than two or three rounds, some days, at long intervals.

ATTITUDE OF THE COMMANDER-IN-CHIEF

They still waited for the return of the lost brigade, which was to prove their salvation. Had the enemy, as seemed not at all unlikely, succeeded in cutting off this detachment in the vicinity of "Rosario" or "Angico," then there was no hope left for the expedition. This was the general conviction. The troops were still able to put up a feeble sort of defense in their present position, but it was impossible to do so for more than a week longer. As it was, only the prestige of certain officers had prevented the army from going to pieces entirely; discipline had reached the breaking-point, but personal devotion to the commanders of certain brigades held the men in check.

General Arthur Oscar had stubbornly insisted upon remaining where they were. Under the illusion at first of a supply train that did not exist, he had later insisted upon the absolute impossibility of an evacuation. In taking this attitude, he was displaying his one most striking quality as a military leader, namely, his tendency to establish himself firmly in any position he had won, an attribute that stood in contrast to personal qualities of just the opposite kind. Restless of disposition and blusteringly frank, viewing the profession of arms as a knightly business, full of sound and fury, he was, indeed, all but a braggart when it came to relating his own astonishing exploits. He was incomparable in planning surprise attacks and at the most critical juncture would always find some explosive phrase, vigorously expressive of a hero's joviality and couched in a picturesque and incisive argot that struck an instant chord of response. Having exhibited always the unbridled impatience and the boldness of a strong nervous temperament, this same general now, in the midst of a campaign and amid an environment in which such outstanding qualities as these were imperatively demanded, became another being and, to the dismay of those who knew him, insisted upon one tactic only—that of immobility. He would listen to no reason on the subject; he simply held out.

Absolutely immobilized in the presence of the enemy, he did not even harass the latter with well-planned sallies or bayonet charges, but merely opposed him, obstinately, with the force of inertia. He did not fight the foe but sought to tire him out; he did not conquer him but strove to exhaust him. As chief of the expedition, he had his mind set on one thing only: the objective of the campaign. From the very beginning he was absorbed in the final phase of the conflict, and in this alone, without taking

Courtesy of the Instituto Brasileiro de Geografia e Estatística

SADDLE OXEN OF THE BRAZILIAN HERDSMEN

into consideration the intermediary circumstances; and in carrying out a most unusual form of attack, without supply bases or lines of operation, he did not take account of the possibility of failure or the eventual necessity of a withdrawal. He had one plan, and that was to go on to Canudos. Everything else was secondary. Come what might, with six thousand bayonets at his disposal, he would proceed to the banks of the Vasa-Barris and win the battle somehow. He would not retreat. He had changed a word in the old Roman's classic phrase: I came, I saw, I remained.

If on June 28 the mistake, so tardily corrected, of having abandoned the supply train was ample reason for his not proceeding with the attack, he should certainly have done so on the thirtieth, if we are to credit the statement of the ablest of his aides. But he did not do so. And this, despite the fact that the two columns were now reunited, while the settlement lay spread out down below within easy rifle range. He thus made a second mistake by taking up an untenable position, one from which he might never have extricated himself had it not been for the capricious turn of events that followed. He was not discouraged, however, but shared the common fate with a stoic resignation, stubbornly immovable.

"Don't weaken, my lads!" This was his favorite phrase, whipped out violently like a sword, cutting short the most discontented grumblings or the most disheartening conjectures. With the men it was different. They felt trapped, besieged as they were in this unbelievable manner by an ene- my whose elastic battle lines were immune to all charges, lines which were no sooner broken than they at once formed again at all points; exhausted from throwing this enemy back without ever being able to crush him, and feeling that their situation was growing more precarious, they were not inclined to hold out. In other words, they *were* weakening. Their discon- tent now took the form of bitter, rancorous mutterings and allusions to in- dividuals whom they imagined to be responsible for their present plight. The Quartermaster General's deputy was, then and afterward, the expia- tory victim of it all. He, the men grumbled, was the only one to blame. They did not stop to think that this illogical accusation was a reflection upon their commander-in-chief, who, if he was to be absolved in this in- stance, must of necessity be guilty of a graver fault in having failed to ex- ercise his supreme powers as head of the expedition. The fact is, on the other hand, that the officer in question, by virtue of the post which he continued to hold, had their full confidence.

Meanwhile, feverishly grasping the strategist's pencil by way of al- laying the general impatience, their commander continued to keep them there, futilely marking time on Mount Favella, as he added, subtracted, multiplied, and divided, making an equation of their hunger as he dis- cussed stupendous solutions having to do with imaginary supply trains, differentiating their transcendent misery, and constructing marvelous ab- stract formulas out of bags of flour and bundles of dried beef, dreaming still of those supply trains.

This was the only effort that he made. There was still no word of the First Brigade, and the battalions which were daily sent out as far as "Baixas" would return without having come upon a trace of its existence along the deserted highways. One of these, the Fifteenth, under the com- mand of Captain Gomes Carneiro, upon coming back from its useless search on July 10, brought with it an ox, a solitary ox, a lean and skinny animal weak from hunger, barely able to stand upon its withered legs—a mere mouthful of meat for six thousand empty stomachs.

ANOTHER VIEW OF CANUDOS

Worst of all, there was the overwhelming monotony. An unvarying succession of the same scenes in the same impoverished setting, with the same thing occurring in the same manner at the same hour of the clock. This gave the exhausted soldiers the impression, which they could not well define, that time had somehow come to a standstill.

At those rare moments in the course of the day when there was a letup in the jagunços' attack, some of the men would find distraction in viewing the intangible settlement. At such times they would creep along cautiously, one by one, with a considerable distance between them, until they came to some safely sheltered spot from which they could clearly see the jumble of huts down below.[25] Their gaze was troubled as they counted: one, two, three, four thousand, five thousand dwellings! Five thousand or more! Six thousand, it might be! Fifteen or twenty thousand souls burrowing in that Babylon of a weed patch. And invisible all of them. Here and there, at a rapid glance, they were barely able to make out a narrow lane or two branching off from the huge deserted square, after which they lost sight of them. That was all there was to be seen. And all this was set in a biblical landscape, against the infinite melancholy of the barren hills, where no trees grew. A river without water, winding about the town, was turned into a long and dusty highway. And in the distance, dominating the four corners of the compass, an undulating row of mountains, likewise deserted, and standing out sharply against the brightness of the horizon, like the giant frame of this strange picture.

The view was an impressive one, filled with connotations. It was as if certain earth-old dramas were being repeated here. There was something about the scene that put one in mind of some remote nook in Idumea, that legendary region south of the Dead Sea, lying sterile forever beneath the prophets' curse and as a result of the drought that comes from the burning plains of Yemen.

The settlement itself—"four square," like the cities in the Bible—completed the illusion. As night came on, there arose from the village waves of sound which, spreading afar across the desert wastes, awoke their sleeping solitudes, only to be lost in the dying echoes of the distant mountainsides. It was the "Ave Maria."

The cannon on Mount Favella bellowed once more, for they too had

[25] See pp. 144–46 and 255–56.

been awakened by those tranquil notes. That humble belfry became their target, as the shrapnel shells burst above and all around it. Yet slowly, slowly, at half-minute intervals, the notes continued, serene above the noise of the cannonading. The impassive sexton did not lose a second of that sacred interval; he did not miss a note. But once its religious duties had been fulfilled, even as the last stroke was echoing still, that same bell at once began ringing stridently, sounding the alarm. Huge licking tongues of flame could be seen about the cornices of the churches, and a train of fire was darting across the settlement. Over the square it ran and up the slopes of the hill, spreading rapidly. At that moment there came a loud and violent burst of rifle fire from the enemy on the mountaintop, causing the bombardment to cease; whereupon a numbing silence fell on both camps alike. And then the soldiers could hear, vaguely, mysteriously filtered through the thick walls of the half-ruined house of worship, the melancholy cadence of prayers.

SUPERSTITIOUS FEARS

This singular stoicism greatly impressed the men; indeed, it became an obsession with them. Inasmuch as they had, latent in their souls, the same superstitions and the same naïve religious impulses, they ended by wavering in the presence of this adversary who was thus allied with Providence. They imagined that he had extraordinary resources. The very bullets which the sertanejos used had amazing effects. They would burst in the air with a loud crackling sound, as if shattered into innumerable splinters. The troops thereupon came to believe the rumor, which was afterwards insistently spread, to the effect that the jagunços made use of explosive bullets. Everything pointed to this. They then came to accept the hypothesis that the shattering of the bullets was due to an unequal degree of expansion on the part of the metals of which they were composed, the lead inside expanding more rapidly than its steel covering; the exceptional character of the wounds inflicted was proof positive here. The bullet which entered the body, leaving behind it a small circular opening, would tear a wide gap as it came out through the mangled bones and tissues. Being unable to perceive the physical law which went to explain such facts as these, the men became convinced that the enemy, thus terrifyingly equipped, was indulging in refinements of savage cruelty.

HEROIC DESERTIONS

Then it was that the desertions began. Heroic desertions, all but incomprehensible, involving the greatest of risks under the incorruptible surveillance of the enemy. On July 9 twenty privates of the Thirty-third left their comrades and plunged into the desert; and daily, one by one, others followed their example, preferring a merciful bullet at the hands of the jagunço to this slow and agonizing death.

All minds were now filled with the one absorbing desire, become an obsession, to leave at last this sinister site on top of Mount Favella. The battalions that were sent out on excursions to various points were the object of envy to those that stayed behind. The latter envied the former the perils, the ambuscades, the skirmishes which they would encounter. There was at least the chance of booty and the consolation of being away from the misery of the camp, if only for a little while.

As in the lean days of those legendary sieges recorded in old chronicles, the commonest sort of articles now took on fantastic valuations. An umbú root or a bit of sugar scrapings was worth as much as the most sumptuous of dishes. As for a cheap *cigarro,* that was an epicure's dream.

There was talk at times of a retreat. This took the form of a rumor, timorously whispered by some despairing soul who had begun to waver, and who thus put the idea into the minds of his comrades; then it spread insidiously through the ranks of the battalions, where at first it occasioned violent protests and discussions, followed by a suspect and compromising silence. Retreat, however, was out of the question. A light brigade might with impunity make a sally through the immediate vicinity, engage in a few skirmishes, and return; the army was not in a position to do so. To make such an attempt, encumbered by the artillery, the ambulances, and the dead weight of a thousand-odd wounded men, would be to invite disaster. To stay where they were, in spite of everything, was their last and only recourse. But if the First Brigade should not return within a week, they would not be able to do even that. With the troops utterly exhausted as they were, the jagunços in one of their assaults would eventually succeed in breaking through their line of fire.

A GALVANIC SHOCK FOR THE WEAKENED EXPEDITION

On the afternoon of the eleventh of July a vaqueiro escorted by three cavalrymen unexpectedly made his appearance in the camp. He brought a message from Colonel Medeiros to the effect that the latter was on his way and was requesting the necessary forces for protecting the large supply train which he was bringing with him.

This was a galvanic shock for the weakened expedition. There is no way of describing it. The auspicious news gripped the troops as it ran from one end of the camp to the other. Downcast countenances were now transfigured, shoulders were thrown back, as the men dashed about feverishly in all directions, shouting, embracing one another, giving vent to noisy exclamations. Banners were unfurled, and the bugles sounded the reveille. All the detachments formed ranks. Hymns were struck up.

The rude leather-clad vaqueiro mounted on his sweating, puffing "nag" and grasping in his hand, lancelike, his long cattle prong, looked on in amazement at all this. His corpulent but athletic frame was in sharp contrast to the lean bodies in the surging throng about him. He was like a powerful gladiator among a multitude of turbulent bushmen.

The swelling torrent of acclamations rolled down to the field hospital, and the wounded and the dying ceased their groans—transformed now into *viva*'s.

A stiff northeaster ruffled the folds of the banners; and down below in the settlement the jagunços could hear the metallic notes of martial bands, intermingled with shouts of triumph from thousands of throats.

Night fell, and from the village there arose waves of sound which, spreading afar across the desert wastes, awoke their sleeping solitudes, only to be lost, little by little, in the dying echoes of the distant mountainsides. It was the "Ave Maria."

CHAPTER VIII

THE ASSAULT

I

PREPARATIONS

THE supply train reached the top of Mount Favella on the thirteenth of July, and on the following day the brigade commanders were called together to lay plans for the assault on the settlement. They met in General Savaget's tent, for that officer was still laid up with the wound he had received at Cocorobó. The date was a propitious one, a national holiday,[1] and a salvo of twenty-one rounds was fired that morning in observance of the occasion. The rude backwoodsmen, taken by surprise, leaped in bewilderment from their hammocks and wretched bunks, all because, a little more than a hundred years ago, a group of dreamers had spoken of the rights of man and had done battle for the marvelous utopia of human brotherhood.

The attack was now urgent. The commander of the First Brigade had returned to inform them that their supposed base of operations did not exist. He had found nothing there, and it was with great difficulty that he had been able to get together the supply train which he brought back with him. These supplies would be exhausted in a short while, and they would be in the same critical situation as before. A council of war was accordingly held. While opinions varied as to details, there was general agreement that there must be a huge mass attack on one flank only. The commanding officers of the Third, Fourth, and Fifth brigades expressed the belief that they should first abandon Mount Favella for a position closer up, from which they might launch the assault. The others, swayed by the vote of the three generals, took a contrary view; they favored leaving the field hospital and the artillery on Favella, along with two brigades to guard them.

This latter point of view, which, when all is said, differed little from the other, was the one that prevailed. They were here making another mistake, by once again pitting against the fleeing, elusive enemy the lumbering might of whole brigades. As may be seen, the majority of them still had no idea of doing what should have been done from the very beginning

---

[1] [The fourteenth of July, anniversary of the storming of the Bastille in the French Revolution.]

of the campaign: that is, splitting up the combat troops. The slightest observation of the theater of war should have shown that the one imperative plan, which they should have grasped intuitively, was to attack from two sides, by way of the Geremoabo Highway and on the extreme left, while leaving the artillery in its present position, to continue bombarding the center of the town. The theater of war, however, was something to which no one gave a thought. The plan adopted was a simpler one. The two columns which were to take part in the assault, after a flanking march of a mile and a quarter to the right of the camp, which, it was assumed, could be completed without molestation by the enemy, was then to take a slanting course to the left, down toward the Vasa-Barris. Here, turning once more to the left, it would attack the square where the churches stood, in full force. This maneuver, a wheeling one at the start, was thus to end in a direct-line assault. Supposing that it was successful, the jagunços, even in case they were utterly routed, would still have three directions open to them by which they might flee; they could retire in safety to the Caypan hills or some other point from which they would be able to resume their resistance. So much was certain and was to have been foreseen.

Recent happenings should have told them as much. Two weeks of cannonading and the arrival of a fresh supply of provisions on Mount Favella had not discouraged the sertanejos but had, rather, reinvigorated them. On July 15, as if they had been staging a bold parody on the latter event, whole bands of them, including women and children, were to be seen going along to the right of the camp, driving a numerous herd of cattle to the settlement. The Twenty-fifth Battalion, sent out to attack them, did not succeed in overtaking them. On that same day the now well-fed expeditionaries, elated with the hope of a coming victory, were forbidden any longer to roam at will about the camp, for the very good reason that to cross from one side to the other meant certain death. The sergeant adjutant of the Ninth and a number of privates were shot down in this manner. The pasture ground, only a couple of paces distant from the Second Column, was assaulted and several cavalry mounts and draft horses were captured, and the Thirtieth Infantry, which was immediately detailed to retrieve them, failed to do so. On the sixteenth the jagunços displayed the same defiant boldness toward their well-provisioned adversaries, by attacking all along the line. The engineering commission, having been sent out to do some slight reconnoitering in the vicinity, was compelled to fight its way, under the formidable escort of two battalions, the Seventh and the Fifth. All this showed that the enemy was prepared to put up a vigorous resistance; and, inasmuch as the extent of his resources was unknown,

the plan of attack should have observed the essential condition of not involving all the troops at once, such an expedient being, for one thing, unsuited to the zone of combat.

Viewed from the top of Mount Favella, the terrain seemed accessible
enough. Notwithstanding this, the rolling hills and gullies rendered impossible the rapid maneuvering of columns; and it was plain to be seen
that they would be forced to attack en masse, the only alternative, in view
of the special configuration of the terrain, being a loose and scattering formation. This in turn would be practicable only in case they abandoned all
idea of a bayonet charge up the hillsides by massed platoons and in case
there were to be a preliminary demonstration or energetic reconnoitering
on the part of a single brigade in loose formation, free of the crippling effect of compact ranks, which were quite useless under the circumstances.
This vanguard, fighting as it went and clearing the hills and slopes of
trenches, should have been followed in due order by the other detachments, which would have reinforced it at the most convenient points, until finally, advancing in the very footsteps of the retreating foe, the attacking forces should in the natural course of events have reached the settlement in concentrated strength.

What they were planning to do, however, was just the opposite of this.
The commander-in-chief was inclined to waver between two extremes.
His way of getting out of his state of paralysis was by a sudden leap from
absolute inertia to impulsive movement, by abandoning the vacillations
and inhibitions which had beset him on Mount Favella for a delirious obsession in which all he could think of was charging the enemy. This is the
predominant note of the battle orders which were issued on the sixteenth.
With all precautions which might have guaranteed the success of the engagement relegated to the background, those orders reveal an absorbing
preoccupation with violent attacks, five-thousand-and-some bayonets
rolling like a mighty river of steel and flame down the dry bed of the Vasa-
Barris.

"When the signal to charge has been given, no one is to think of avoiding the enemy's fire. You are to charge without wavering, with all the
strength that is in you. After each charge, each soldier will seek out his
company, each company its battalion, and so forth."

These instructions reflected the general inclinations of the troops.
Carefully planned and concrete battle maneuvers, adapted to the exceptional character of the terrain and the unusual kind of enemy they had to
fight, did not satisfy them. They were filled with rancor as a result of their
previous failures and must now have a crushing revenge; they must teach

those foolish bandits a lesson; they must make short work of them, by clubbing them back with rifle butts into that ditch they called Canudos. The order of the day for the seventeenth of July, setting the attack for the day following, the eighteenth, was received with delirious shouts of joy. Basing himself upon past exploits, the commander-in-chief, by a daring process of deduction, proceeded to turn a page of the future and to hold up before his men the mirage of victory.

Valiant officers and soldiers of the expeditionary forces in the interior of the state of Baía! From Cocorobó up to the present time, the enemy has not been able to hold out against your bravery. This is shown by the battles of Cocorobó, Trabubú, Macambira, Angico, two others on Mount Favella, and the two assaults which the enemy made on our artillery. On the morrow, we go to do battle in the citadel of Canudos. The Fatherland has its eyes upon you; all hope lies in your courage. The treacherous foe, who will not meet us face to face, who fights us without being seen, has nonetheless suffered considerable losses. He is demoralized, and, therefore, if. . . . .

Let us pause for a moment upon this significant "if." It was here that the order of the day, read to the plaudits of the soldiery on the seventeenth, should have been suspended until the evening of the eighteenth.

. . . . if your courage does not flag, if once again you show yourselves to be the bravest of the brave, Canudos will be in our hands tomorrow. We shall then take our ease, and the Fatherland will be grateful to you for the sacrifices that you have made.

Canudos was to fall on the following day. That was settled. The enemy himself appeared to be aware of this heroic resolve, for he ceased his irritating rifle fire. Fearful and very quiet now, he had taken refuge in the valley down below, vanquished on the eve of battle. The camp was left in peace at last, and the afternoon was vibrant with the melodic notes of the bugles, continuing until nightfall.

PLAN OF ASSAULT

The detailed plan of attack was now outlined. Some fifteen hundred men under General Savaget were to remain on Mount Favella, guarding the troops' position there; this detachment was made up of the Second and Seventh brigades of Colonels Ignacio Henrique de Gouveia and Antonino Nery, the latter a recently formed unit, along with the artillery, which was to support the assault with a sustained bombardment. The First Column, led by General Barbosa, was to march forward and give battle, closely followed by the wing of cavalry and a detachment with the two Krupp $7\frac{1}{2}$'s. The Second Column was to bring up the rear.

A total of 3,349 men, divided into five brigades, were thus being sent into action. The First Brigade, under the command of Colonel Joaquim Manoel de Medeiros, was composed of barely two battalions, the Fourteenth and the Thirtieth, commanded, respectively, by Captain João Antunes Leite and Lieutenant Colonel Antonio Tupy Ferreira Caldas. The Third Brigade, under command of Lieutenant Colonel Emydio Dantas Barreto, included the Fifth, Seventh, Ninth, and Twenty-fifth, led by Captains Antonio Nunes de Salles, Alberto Gavião Pereira Pinto, Carlos Augusto de Souza, and José Xavier dos Anjos. Colonel Carlos Maria da Silva Telles' Fourth Brigade consisted of the Twelfth and the Thirty-first battalions, commanded by Captains José Luiz Buchelle and José Lauriano da Costa. The commander of the Fifth Brigade, Colonel Julião Augusto da Serra Martins, had taken General Savaget's place as column commander, and this detachment was accordingly led by Major Nonato Seixas and was made up of the Thirty-fourth and Fortieth battalions of Major Olegario Sampaio and Captain J. Villar Coutinho. And, finally, there was the Sixth Brigade, commanded by Colonel Donanciano de Araujo Pantoja, composed of the Twenty-sixth and Thirty-second battalions, led by Captain M. Costa and Major Collatino Goes. The Fifth Baian Police, under the command of Regular Army Captain Salvador Pires de Carvalho Aragão, accompanied the Second Column as an autonomous detachment.

Lieutenant Colonel Siqueira de Menezes with a small contingent, while the bulk of the expedition was engaged in the attack, was to make a diversionary movement to the right, along the counterforts in the vicinity of the "Old Ranch House."

The list of commanding officers shows that there were some for whom the backlands of Canudos were a restricted field of combat, in view of past experience. There was Carlos Telles, hero of the siege of Bagé, beneath whose soldier's uniform there beat the stoutest of hearts. There was Tupy Caldas, nervous, restless, irascible, who had won an enviable reputation for courage in the deadly conflict with the southern federalists at Inhanduhy. There was Olympio da Silveira, commander of the artillery, with his statuesque bronzed countenance, set in immobile lines; he was that rare being, a modest man of arms, unconcerned with glory, yet fearless in the presence of the enemy; his life was spent amid the tumult of battles as he pursued his unwavering course, as if in obedience to some law of destiny. Among the lower-ranking officers were many young fellows, avid of renown, longing for dangers, a jolly, roistering crew who did not know what fear meant. There was Salvador Pires, commanding the Fifth Police, a detachment which he himself had organized and which was made up of sturdy back-country recruits from the settlements along the São Francisco. There was Wanderley, destined to die a hero's death in the last phase of a daring charge.[2] There was the intrepid gaucho, Vieira Pacheco, who commanded the lancers' squadron. There were Fructuoso Mendes and Duque Estrada, who could have torn down the walls of the new church stone by stone. There was Carlos de Alencar, who was left without a command when all the men in the cavalry wing which he led were shot and killed. And there were others.

They were all impatiently awaiting the battle, for this battle was one which was to mean a decisive victory. In accordance with old custom, the participants warned those who stayed behind on Mount Favella to be sure and have breakfast ready, for they would be tired and hungry when they returned.

THE ENGAGEMENT

The columns got under way well after dawn on the morning of the eighteenth. Countermarching to the right of the camp, they took a course directly east, down the slopes, toward the Geremoabo Highway. After some little while they turned to the left, still going downward but heading now straight for the banks of the Vasa-Barris. As they went along at their ordinary pace, they met with no traces of the enemy; it was as if the latter had been thrown off guard by this wheeling movement which they had executed. Their only annoyance at times was the two Krupps, groaning along over the uneven roadway. There were, it is true, a few slight obstacles in their path, but these were speedily overcome. Nothing was to be heard, meanwhile, but the continuous, dull, and menacing tread of marching feet.

The melancholy landscape was now coming to life. The birds had somewhile since abandoned this region where for nearly a month past the air had been thick with bullets. The morning was bright and without song, as little by little the desert tracts, wrapped in silence, came into view: the barren hillocks, the gently rolling highlands, the caatingas with their falling leaves, already "turning" in July, displaying large dark-gray splotches—a sign that the drought was slowly spreading. The rolling plain which stretches away indefinitely to the north, while to the northeast it extends as far as the foothills of the Canabrava Range and on the south to Mount Favella, to the west was to be seen swelling in a series of elevations gradually increasing in height until they merged with the distant peaks of Cambaio.[3] Cut up into scattered ganglions,[4] the Vasa-Barris winds through this plain. At one of its bends, after flowing directly west, it turns abruptly to the south and after a few hundred yards comes back to the

---

[2] [See pp. 24, 329, 365.]   [3] [See pp. 210-11.]   [4] [Cf. p. 19.]

east, thereby wholly altering the direction of its current and forming an imperfect peninsula with the settlement at its extremity. Thus, all the defenders had to do in order to protect their entire front from attack was to spread themselves out in such a manner as to link the two parallel branches of the river at the nearest point, along the chord of that huge semicircle formed by this natural moat; for the attack would come from a direction perpendicular to that chord. After having crossed the lowlands this side of "Trabubú," the assailants would then have to cross the dry bed of the Vasa-Barris and, making one last turn, to the left, would launch a frontal assault. Before they had executed this wheeling movement, however, the enemy had cut them off.

It was seven o'clock in the morning. The scouts were the first to receive the jagunços' fire, as they reached the left bank of the river. The terrain near by rose in a hillock, which, as they could see, was covered all the way to the top with rude stone trenches of irregular shape, presenting the appearance of crumbling walls. The settlement, fifteen hundred yards farther on, was now lost from sight in a more pronounced depression, and they barely had a glimpse, over the crest of the hills, of the two church towers. Two crosses, tall and threatening, stood out sharply in the sunlight of early morning.

The vanguard having been attacked, the soldiers of the Thirtieth Battalion returned the enemy's fire, without pausing, merely quickening their pace, while at the same time the bulk of the First Brigade and four battalions of the Third Brigade, marching in closed ranks, reached the river bed and crossed it. The entire First Column having come together, it now entered the arena of combat.

LINE OF BATTLE

Those slight obstacles in the way of the two Krupps had soon ended by slowing down the detachments at the rear. This to a degree relieved the inconvenient pressure of a mass of battalions, and General Barbosa felt that he might now attempt to draw up a line of battle; the First Brigade was to spread out in sharpshooter formation on the right; the Third Brigade in the same formation on the left; while the cavalry wing, galloping ahead at top speed, was to ride round the right flank and see to it that the enemy did not close in there.

CRITICAL REMARKS

But this general maneuver, as was to have been foreseen, was ill conceived. In addition to the fact that it had to be carried out under the eye of the enemy, the terrain was unsuited to it. The physical basis essential to such tactics was lacking here. The line as planned, with the brigades deploying over a distance of one and one-quarter miles, would be divided into vertical planes according to the maximum slope of the hills and the depth of the valleys; and, as the combat units detached themselves and exposed their flanks to the enemy in assuming new battle stations, they would all be forced into weak and unstable positions, and however transient such a situation was, it was impossible on the spur of the moment to make any calculations as to what the outcome might be. The plan was, therefore, impracticable.

Both impracticable and highly dangerous. This was clearly indicated by all the palpable, concrete conditions round about, from the rugged character of the terrain to the extraordinary vigor which was suddenly being displayed by the enemy, who from the first few minutes had attacked along the entire front with a deadly fire. The inadequacy of the plan was also shown the moment the action began. Breaking away from the loosely formed lines, rows of bayonets charged against the hills, stormed up their sides, and surmounted them with great difficulty; but all this without that firmness and velocity which were called for, if the maneuver was to be successfully executed. Not being able to carry it out in this essential manner, they proceeded to alter certain details which, insignificant in themselves perhaps, were giving rise to confusion in the ranks. Contrary to the original formation, the Third Brigade now began fighting on the right wing of the Thirtieth Battalion; the Ninth Battalion on the extreme left came down into the bed of the Vasa-Barris and began advancing under heavy fire from both sides; while the Twenty-fifth, the Fifth, and the right wing of the Seventh were somewhere in the center.

CONFUSION

It was impossible to establish a scattering formation while under fire on such a terrain. The detachments, the companies, the battalions, upon splitting off to the right, the only side that was suited to military alignments, found themselves in a labyrinth of winding gullies and within a short space of time were lost, floundering about with no sense of direction, without being able to see the rest of their comrades or even to hear the discordant notes of the bugles. Falling back at times in the confused belief that they were advancing along this twisting, turning line of march, they not infrequently had gone but a few paces when they unexpectedly would bump into other detachments, marching at double-quick time in the opposite direction.

The result was that they became hopelessly entangled. The very general who had led them into these narrow defiles was later, in his order of the day, to be at a loss for words in describing what took place here. Not being able to find in the opulent lexicon of our own tongue a legitimate term for the disorder that prevailed, he ventured to make use of a barbarous locution from the language of the gauchos, by saying that the troops *"entrelisavam-se"*—were "all balled up."

Accordingly, by the time the Second Column came up, half an hour later, their losses were already considerable. There were now two more brigades, one only, the Sixth, being held in reserve at the rear under the immediate command of General Oscar. Again, these detachments should have spread out to the right, in accordance with the one plan that was feasible under the circumstances; this would have intercepted the enemy along the entire front, preventing any flanking action on his part, and would further have facilitated the final concentrated assault. This was indicated by the field of battle itself, a broad sector whose radii converged on the church square. But, rudimentary as they were, these tactics were not adopted. As the auxiliary brigades came up under a terrific fusillade which threw their ranks into confusion, they were not able to form any kind of line whatsoever, by attaching themselves, as they should have done, to the brigades which had preceded them, reinforcing and strengthening the latter at the weak points and rounding out their movements—or they might have taken up positions on the extreme wings, expanding and amplifying the formation in such a manner as to confront these rude antagonists with a broad and powerful battle line of vibrant steel.

Colonel Carlos Telles, in his report of the battle—a document whose statements are not questioned—later made the flat assertion that he had noted upon his arrival that the troops taking part in the engagement did not have the proper formation. "Notwithstanding this, our one duty under the circumstances was to advance and charge."

They advanced and they charged.

It was now eight o'clock in the morning. A warm and beautiful backlands morning, one aglow, as always in this region, with the dazzling scintillations of the barren earth and its quartzite folds. And, had the troops succeeded, as planned, in adding to all this radiating brilliancy the metallic gleam of three thousand bayonets, the scene would indeed have been a singularly majestic one. As it was, it was funereal.

Ten mixed battalions now set out down the hillsides. Thronging through the lowlands, they climbed the opposite slopes. Having reached the top, they would go down the other side, with great clamor and confusion—only to have to repeat the performance over and over again; for the hills stretched away for an interminable distance on every hand, as these noisy, unleashed, turbulent waves of humanity came rolling up their sides, overflowing onto the small plains, foaming tumultuously down the declivities, to be halted as by a dam in the deep ravines below.

The invisible jagunços, meanwhile, kept up their devastating fire, now falling back, now concentrating on their assailant's flanks, at other times surrounding him entirely.

There was no saying what the outcome would be. The soldiers, it is certain, from then on began to gain ground valiantly, as they captured hill after hill. They would pause for a moment on the edge of a trench, and down below they would find a number of exploded cartridges, still warm, showing how recently the enemy had fled.[5] But, after a little while, they no longer knew the real direction of the attack which they were supposed to be making; and the enemy's fire, coming from first one direction and then another, seemed designed to confuse them. At one moment there would be a steady, well-sustained fire on their extreme right, where they had no cause to expect it. This would lead them to think that the sertanejos might be attacking in force there; and, if followed up energetically enough, this would inevitably bring the foe, triumphantly, into the very midst of their disordered ranks. Then they would perceive that this had been merely a slight demonstration, the enemy having let slip the opportunity for a concerted attack. This was discovered by the lancers' squadron in a bold reconnoitering movement. Galloping at top speed in the direction from which the firing came, down the slope of a hill, these troops suddenly found themselves confronted with about eighty jagunços. The latter were stationed in a corral, from which they had been firing upon our men from the side. They were dispersed, at the point of the lance and by the horses' hoofs, in a violent charge. The lancers galloped after them, pursuing them up a slope which was not so steep as the others, until, at the summit, they came out on an extensive plateau or tableland stretching away to the northeast. And then, unexpectedly, they had a view of the settlement, less than three hundred yards away.

In the meantime several platoons of infantry had come up in disorderly fashion. The situation was drawing to a climax. Along the edge of the outlying houses scattered over the opposite slope, some three hundred yards from the churches, was an area that was comparatively level and unencumbered and thus better suited to battle maneuvers. Heading for this point, the men arrived in small groups, without any kind of order,

[5] [Cf. pp. 324, 361.]

barely preserving their division by brigades, with the Fifth Brigade marching on the right, the Third and Fourth in the center, while the Sixth, which had been the last to come into action, was on the left, along the river.

It was the critical moment of the battle. On the height where they now were, the troops were completely exposed, especially their right and center, their position being overlooked by the churches and on a level with the upper part of the settlement, which rose along the slopes to the north. From this latter point all the way to the far end of the *praça* on the west— taking in the entire quadrant for a distance of not less than a mile and a quarter—there now came a tremendous blaze of converging rifle fire. The brigades, meanwhile, continued to advance but in a loose and unco-ordinated manner which was conducive neither to valor nor to firing aim; for they were without any kind of plan to guide them. And then, amid all the tumult which prevailed in the ranks, the men suddenly began running out of ammunition, for each soldier had brought with him only 150 cartridges in his pouch. It thereupon became necessary to halt whole battalions—in the midst of the battle and on an eminence swept by the enemy's fire—in order to smash open the munitions cases, obtain fresh cartridges, and distribute them.

In addition to this, in addition to the heavy fusillade which burst upon the troops from the settlement, where every wall was pierced with loopholes, the bold guerrillas now confronted their attackers at close range, keeping up a scattering fire that left great gaps in the latter's ranks. The comparatively small number of shots to be heard indicated that there were not many of these *franc-tireurs*, but they made up for it by the excellence of their aim and succeeded in bringing whole platoons to a stop. An episode occurred which illustrates this.

THE JAGUNÇOS' DUGOUTS

It was during the last stage of the attack. The attacking force was strengthened on this occasion by the Fourth Brigade, led by Colonel Carlos Telles,[6] who had lost nearly all his staff. They were engaged in crossing the last slope, when the farthermost detachments on this flank, taking a severe punishment, bore down in a swift movement to the right in an effort to repulse an adversary whom they could not see on that barren plain, although their eyes could take it all in at a glance. And so, on a mere chance, they attacked in the direction of an umbú tree that was still in leaf. It was the only tree in sight. The shots were being fired rapidly,

6 [See pp. 316–17.]

but one after another, as if they came from a single marksman. Falling on the detachments, they depleted the ranks, dropping the soldiers one by one with a deadly regularity. Many of the latter ended by hauling up short in amazement, being unable to conceive of such a fusillade on a clear and level stretch of ground like that, where there was not the slightest knoll behind which the inexorable foe might take shelter. Others, however, kept on running toward the solitary tree; and, when they were within a few paces of it, they finally saw on the edge of a circular pit a bronzed and hardened face peering over the rim. Leaping from the hole without letting go his weapon, the jagunço glided swiftly down the slope and disappeared in the maze of grottoes below. Three hundred and some voided cartridges in the trench showed that this fierce hunter of men had been lying there for a long time in that craftily placed ambuscade; and the earth all around was dotted with similar ones. In all of them were the same heaps of cartridge shells, showing that a sharpshooter had been there not so long ago. These were the deadly shells which had swept our lines, and which had made it seem that the ground was exploding under the very feet of the troops.[7] Dislodged from these hiding-places, the sertanejos fell back to others, which now in turn blazed with rifle fire, until they, too, had to be abandoned. Meantime, the troops were all the while bearing down on the settlement, whose outlying huts they finally reached around ten o'clock in the morning.

Drawn up to the east, they spread out over an extensive tableland, which lay more or less along a meridian line and which on the west sloped down gently to the church square beyond. Having reached this dominant position, they proceeded to occupy it by forming a winding, disjointed line which on the left extended to the Vasa-Barris. Some of the soldiers then took shelter in the captured huts, but the majority of them, led by officers who at this juncture showed themselves worthy of more glorious undertakings, kept on advancing under a heavy circling fire until they came to the foot of the old church. The Sixth Brigade and the Fifth Police, advancing along the dry channel of the river, completed the line of attack.

These were the last gains that the troops made. From there on they did not go a step farther. They had conquered a small suburb of this barbarous city but found themselves powerless to carry through the action to completion. Their losses were mounting, and the rear guard, hopelessly encumbered with dead and wounded, gave the impression of a rout; it was a moving sight to behold. And, with all this, the ranks now had to

[7] See p. 308.

open to permit the passage of the two Krupps, drawn by hand. Having taken their battle station, overlooking the churches, the cannon began a sustained bombardment; while on the top of Mount Favella, wreathed in smoke as in the gloom of a tempest, Colonel Olympio da Silveira's batteries thundered away. Under a merciless cross-fire from the artillery and the battalions along its entire eastern border, the settlement replied with a shower of bullets directed at the thin walls of the houses where the assailants had taken shelter, burying the latter in the ruins. From the new church on the river's edge came a withering fire on the Sixth Brigade. The Fifth Police, their ranks greatly thinned, finally came down into a narrow, winding grotto, which saved them from being slaughtered en masse. By midday the situation was grave indeed, the outcome extremely doubtful, with the battle which had been begun a little more than a mile away still continuing on the outskirts of the village, and with the enemy putting up a more stubborn resistance than ever.

At this critical point the commanders of the Third and Fourth brigades, which had advanced as far as the cemetery adjoining the old church, decided to send for General Oscar. The latter had to make his way to these detachments on foot, taking such shelter as he could along the walls of the small houses scattered over the slope; it was a brave thing to do. As he came up, he found that Colonel Carlos Telles, commander of the Fifth Brigade, and Captain Antonio Salles had both been seriously wounded, inside the very dwelling to which they had retired for safety. The conference, held there in that tiny hut, was a brief one. Round about, all was disorder: the whine of bullets; the sound of aimlessly running feet; the shrill notes of bugles; hastily shouted commands; cries of fear and anger; groans and imprecations. It was bedlam that had broken loose.

With the battalions completely disorganized, every man was now fighting for his own life. Small groups could be seen, brought together by chance and made up of men from all the corps, crowding in behind the walls of the mud huts, hiding around the corners, holding out as long as they could. Under such circumstances something like a natural selection of heroes occurred. With all hope gone, the animal instinct of self-preservation, as always happens in the somber epilogues of battles, put on the mantle of heroism—a brutal reflection of the primitive form of courage. Indifferent to the fate of their comrades, and with the battle reduced to that narrow bit of ground where their lives were at stake, these fighting units piled into the huts and followed the jagunços' example by piercing loopholes in the walls. Dodging round the corners and running down the lanes with the enemy only a couple of paces behind them, closing with the latter in what was practically a hand-to-hand encounter, they fought blindly and for themselves alone. Famished and suffering agonies of thirst, they would no sooner enter one of the small dwellings than they for the moment forgot there might be someone living there; for in the semi-darkness of the tiny windowless rooms they were not able to make out the presence of any human being. They would then grope their way about the place, in search of a jug of water or a hamper of flour.[8] And, as often as not, they would be struck down by a bullet fired from close up. Soldiers built like athletes, panting still from their exertions after four hours of fighting, would sometimes be killed by the womenfolk, many of whom were equal to their men. Old hags with wrinkled, ugly-looking faces, their eyes shooting sparks and their hair flowing wild, would grapple with the invaders in a delirium of fury. And even after they had been choked and all but strangled by the latter's powerful hands—after they had been dragged along the ground by the hair of their heads and trampled under heel by a soldier's boots—even then they did not weaken but died with the death rattle of wild beasts in their throats, spewing curses on their assailants, a painful and a tragic scene.

ANOTHER DISASTROUS VICTORY

In the midst of all this disastrous confusion the commander-in-chief made up his mind that he would hold the position won.[9] There was no other way out. Once again, at the end of a violent assault, the expedition found itself brought up short, stuck, in an insoluble situation. To advance and to retreat were alike impossible.[10]

As the afternoon came on, the troops took up their stationary position on the narrow border of the settlement—rather, on a fifth part of it, along the eastern side—on the long slope of a low hill that ran from north to south, a gentle declivity that fell away down to the village square. The houses here, less compactly huddled than elsewhere, were of recent date; for Canudos in its surprising growth had forsaken the depression in which it was born and was now making for the tops of the surrounding hills. It was one of these suburbs that our forces occupied. Properly speaking, they had not yet reached the citadel itself, which, with its highly original, barbarous, and menacing appearance, rose before them only a short distance away—without walls but, for all of that, inexpugnable, presenting the invader with thousands of entrances, thousands of gaps, opening into the inextricable network of winding alleys which composed the streets of the town.

8 See p. 262.   9 [Cf. pp. 343 ff.]   10 See p. 331.

However bold an attempt they might have made thus far, the expeditionaries were incapable of any further effort. The advance guard had definitely come to a halt and was consolidating its position. In the deep grotto which drained the flanks of Mount Favella, on the extreme left, the Fifth Police were intrenching themselves, their lines stretching to the right bank of the Vasa-Barris, where the Twenty-sixth Infantry was stationed. That detachment in turn, on the opposite bank, formed contact with the Fifth Brigade, next the cemetery. Then came, in succession, the Twenty-fifth, below the old church; the Seventh, parallel to the east side of the square; and, after the Twenty-fifth, the Fortieth and the Thirtieth, lost in the maze of huts to the north. From this point to the rear, the troops of the Twelfth, Thirty-first, and Thirty-eighth in loose formation curved away convexly from the main mass of huts, along the right flank of the camp, where general headquarters had been established on the opposite slope, under the protection of the Fourteenth, Thirty-second, Thirty-third, and Thirty-fourth battalions and the wing of cavalry.

The rest of the day and a good part of the night were spent in the construction of trenches, in fortifying the walls of the houses with planks or stones, and in picking out those points which were less exposed to rifle fire. The implacable enemy, meanwhile, kept an ever watchful eye on the expeditionaries, crowded together there on the side of the settlement. He had relaxed his fusillade, only to fall back on his old custom of fighting from ambush. Through every chink and cranny of every wall there now protruded a musket barrel with a searching eye behind it. Every step that a soldier took beyond the corner of a wall meant his death.

They were beginning to realize that they were in a worse situation than their previous one on Mount Favella. There they at least had had the hope of a victorious assault; they still despised the enemy, whom they had barely glimpsed at a distance, in his hiding-places. Now, not even that illusion remained. Here was the jagunço—indomitable, challenging them to hand-to-hand combat. The latter was not frightened by these professional men of arms whom the people of the "big country"[11] had sent out to attack him. Here they were, alongside of him, at a distance of a few paces, jostling him, finding shelter under the same mud roofs as he himself, and suddenly, within a few minutes' time, increasing the population of the sacred village by some three thousand souls. But for all of that, these newcomers had not succeeded in modifying the course of his primitive life. At nightfall the bell of the old church calmly sounded the "Ave Maria";

[11] [See p. 184 and n. 31.]

and then, from the ample depths of the other church, there came the melancholy drone of prayers.

It was as if all the stir and movement of the day were a commonplace incident, one that had been anticipated.

LOSSES

In the meantime the expedition was experiencing a violent crisis. It had lost around a thousand men, killed or wounded in this engagement, and these with previous losses had reduced its ranks considerably. Three brigade commanders, Carlos Telles, Serra Martins, and Antonino Nery (who had come up with the Seventh that afternoon), were *hors de combat;* and the number of casualties among the lower-ranking officers and privates was very large. Lieutenants and sublieutenants, with incredible fearlessness, had squandered their lives all along the line. The names and bold deeds of some of these were cited later: Cunha Lima, student of the Military School of Porto Alegre, who, wounded in the breast in a lancers' charge, expended the last breath that was in him in a daring attack, falling on the enemy like a human dart; Wanderley, who, galloping up the rugged slope of the last hill, was slain with his mount on top of a cliff; the two of them together rolling down until miraculously caught and pinned by the rocks, like some giant Titan and his steed;[12] and others, many others, who fell fighting bravely amid resounding *viva*'s to the Republic. These valiant ones had given to the conflict a singular imprint of ancient heroism, recalling the pathologic passion for self-sacrifice displayed by the mystical warriors of the Middle Ages. The parallel is perfect. In backward societies there are always to be found notable traces of atavism; and in our own country, in the turbulent days of the Republic, our young army men in particular had become imbued with a patriotic lyricism which wholly unbalanced them emotionally, inspiring them with illusions and the idealistic dreams of visionaries. The struggle for the Republic and against its imaginary enemies was a crusade. These modern Knights Templar, if they did not wear a coat of mail with the cross on their sword hilts, nonetheless fought with the same immovable faith as their prototypes of old. Those who fell in this manner, at the beginning of the assault on Canudos, without a single exception, wore above their hearts a medal bearing the likeness of Marshal Floriano Peixoto, whose memory they saluted in death. They were, in brief, displaying the same delirious enthusiasm, the same absolute self-dedication, and the same fanatic aberrations as did the ja-

---

[12] See pp. 24, 329, 355.

gunços when they shouted for the merciful and miracle-working Good Jesus as they went to their death in battle.

But this feverish enthusiasm, aside from the disastrous manifestations that have been described, proved to be the troops' salvation on the eighteenth of July.

When a fighting force whose morale depends exclusively upon discipline becomes disorganized in such a manner as this, it is lost. On the other hand, simple-minded soldiers, discouraged by reverses and the uncertainties that face them, will stand firm, hypnotized by an exhibition of personal courage on the part of their leaders or swayed by the prestige of officers who, mortally wounded, some of them barely able to lean upon a sword, come staggering down the line of fire—dying and death-defying. In a manner of speaking, in such an instance, they found themselves caught between the jagunços' fire and the intrepidity of their commanders.

ON THE FLANKS OF CANUDOS

The night of the eighteenth of July, contrary to general expectation, went by in relative calm. The sertanejos for their part were quiet. The commander-in-chief of the expedition was obsessed with the fear of a night attack, which there would have been no means of repelling. The fragile defense lines, even assuming the enemy did not break through at some point, could be outflanked, and, thus caught between two fires and unable to advance in the direction of the settlement, they would be easily destroyed. The situation, however, was resolved by the inertia of the adversary. On the following day a row of vermilion-hued streamers, made of blankets sewn together, were used to mark off a very small segment, a fifth of the enormous periphery of the town. This showed them what their situation was. On the east the bounds were indefinite. On this side the extreme right was a blank; and similarly on the left, along the slopes of Favella and on the edge of the Providencia arroyo, where the police corps was stationed, there was to be seen a large open space. In order to complete the circumference, they had need of a line which, running due north, would then curve to the west, skirting the river and following it in its bend to the south, and, scaling the major elevations on the first terrace of the Calumby and Cambaio ranges, would finally come back east along the "Bald Pates" spur. A circuit of four miles, approximately. The expedition, however, reduced to a little more than three thousand ablebodied men, hundreds of whom had been taken to guard Mount Favella, was not in a position to adjust itself to so ample a compass, even had the enemy permitted it. A temporary paralysis of operations was inevitable;

there was nothing to be done but to defend the positions which they held until the arrival of reinforcements should enable them to make a further effort.

A CRITICAL SITUATION

General Arthur Oscar took a calm view of the situation. Having asked for an auxiliary corps of five thousand men, he took precautions to guarantee the safety of his troops, which had wrested this singular victory from the jaws of defeat, a victory that once again left them in the torturing condition of not being able to risk a step forward or a step to the rear. Officially, the orders of the day decreed the beginning of a siege; but, as a matter of fact, as had happened ever since the twenty-seventh of June, it was the expedition itself which was being besieged. On their west was the settlement; on the south, their way was blocked by the heights of Favella, encumbered now with sick and wounded; while to the north and east there lay the impenetrable desert. To all appearances, the field of action had been augmented, there being now two distinct camps, which seemed to indicate a greater freedom of movement, beyond the constricting circle of the enemy's trenches. This illusion, however, was extinguished on the very day of the assault. The hillocks, which they had cleared with bayonet charges only a few hours before, were, they could see, already manned again. As for communications with Mount Favella, that was an exceedingly difficult matter. The wounded who tried to make it to the latter point were a second time shot down; and one surgeon, Dr. Tolentino, was gravely wounded on the afternoon of the battle, as he came down from the mountaintop along the banks of the river. How to cross the terrain which they had won was a serious problem for the victors. On the other hand, having invaded the outer edges of the settlement, they could do no more than to copy faithfully the tactics which they had observed on the part of the jagunços. Like the latter, they huddled into huts that were hot as bake ovens in the sultry heat of noontide, and there, forgetful of time, they would lie for long hours, their eyes glued to the chinks in the walls; for they had, unashamedly, fallen into the same mode of guerrilla-ambush fighting that the enemy practiced; their gaze roaming over the mass of huts, they would all fire at once—one hundred, two hundred, three hundred shots!—at any face or ragtag of a garment of which they might have caught an indistinct and fleeting glimpse from afar, amid that labyrinth of winding alleyways.

The last of the rations having been distributed—a liter of flour for every seven men and an ox to a battalion, all that remained of the supply train which had been their salvation a short while before—they now found that it was impossible or highly inconvenient to undertake to prepare their scant repast. A thread of smoke from the mud roof of a hut was a lure for bullets! At night a lighted match would touch off, seemingly, trains of gunpowder. The jagunços well knew that those fragile clay walls were no protection to the intruders who had sought shelter behind them. Colonel Antonino Nery was wounded as he was entering one of the huts, after he and his brigade had safely crossed the open, dangerous zone of combat. The troops accordingly proceeded to fortify the houses by strengthening their outer walls with inner ones of stone or covering them with planks. And then, their safety better assured, they would spend the greater part of the day lying at full length up under the thatched roof, above the food cages,[13] their eyes to the crevices, their fingers clenching the triggers of their rifles—terror-stricken victors lying in wait for the vanquished.

Above the general headquarters, with the commander-in-chief's tent in the center, the bullets whirred without doing any damage, being warded off by the re-entrant angle of the hill. Throughout the entire course of the night—a night that followed an exhausting day—the commander could hear above his head the whine of projectiles that came from the rifle duel being fought on the other side of the battlefield, between the enemy and our advanced lines. The commanding officers of those detachments, Lieutenant Colonels Tupy Caldas and Dantas Barreto, utterly fearless both of them, nevertheless felt that a disaster was imminent; for they realized that "one step to the rear at any point along the central line would have meant total perdition."[14] No one, indeed, made any effort to conceal this inescapable dread of nearing catastrophe. It was the unavoidable deduction from all that had gone before. It had to be. For many days their minds were preoccupied with this thought.

"An enemy accustomed to regulation fighting, who knew how to make the most of our tactical disadvantages, would certainly not have let slip this opportunity for revenge, which would have meant that we would be subjected to the most refined cruelty."

But the jagunço was not given to regulation fighting. He was not in any proper sense of the word an "enemy," which is an extemporized term, an exquisite euphemism, to take the place of "notorious bandit" as he was called in that form of martial literature known as orders of the day. The sertanejo was merely defending his invaded home, that was all. So long as those who threatened him remained at a distance, he simply surrounded them with snares to bring them to a halt; but, when they came battering

[13] [See p. 145 and n. 148 and p. 262.]

[14] Colonel Dantas Barreto, *Ultima expedição contra Canudos.*

at his gates and felling him with rifle butts, then he confronted them face to face with the only expedient that he knew: an unflinching resistance with the sole and worthy object of self-defense and in a spirit of noble revenge. Canudos could be taken only house by house. The entire expedition was destined to spend three months in crossing those hundred yards that separated them from the vault of the new church; and on the last day of this inconceivable resistance, for which there are few parallels in history, the last defenders—three or four nameless ones, three or four famished Titans, clad in rags—were to spend their last few remaining cartridges by firing on an army of six thousand men![15]

This formidable pertinacity was manifest from the eighteenth of July onward and was never once relaxed. The attack was over, but the battle continued, an interminable battle, monotonous and terrifying, exhibiting the same rhythm as the one on Mount Favella: a scattering fire from minute to minute, or a furious fusillade all along the line; sudden attacks, sudden skirmishes, lasting a quarter of an hour, quickly begun and quickly ended—even before the stirring notes of the bugle sounding the alarm had died upon the air. In these sudden assaults, interspersed with long hours of relative calm, there was always to be observed an inversion of roles.[16] The assailants were, strictly speaking, the assaulted. The enemy might be cornered, but he it was who determined the anxious moment for these engagements, which always came unexpectedly.

In the early hours of the morning, at times, breaking an armistice of some minutes which the soldiers in the van had made use of for snatching a bit of illusory repose, their heads nodding over their rifles—at such a time as this a large rocket would go up in the air with a harsh, whizzing sound, tearing a gap in the dark sky, and by its fugitive gleam they would see the cornices of the churches swarming with a black border of humanity. The battle would then continue in the darkness, to the intermittent glow of gunfire. At other times, contrary to expectation, it was at the break of dawn or in the middle of a bright, warm morning that the jagunços would boldly launch their attack.

NOTES FROM A DIARY

A minute diary of the conflict in these first days would bring out its abnormally barbaric character. We shall endeavor here to give the picture in a few broad strokes, down to the twenty-fourth of July, merely by way of making clear a situation which from that time forth did not change.[17]

[15] See p. 475.

[16] [Cf. p. 336.]   [17] See p. 399.

July 19.—The enemy begins firing at five o'clock in the morning. Keeps it up all day and part of the night. The commander of the First Column, in order to repel the enemy's attacks more vigorously, determines to bring up two more Krupp cannon which are at the rear, in order that they may be mounted at night. At 12:30 P.M., in his camp, inside the hut where he is resting in a hammock, the commander of the Seventh Brigade is wounded.[18] At 2:00 P.M., after the cannon on the right had been aimed and fired at one of the towers of the new church, Lieutenant Thomaz Braga was shot and killed. In the afternoon, with great difficulty, they bring down a few head of cattle from Mount Favella to feed the troops. Fired upon while crossing the Vasa-Barris, the herd breaks away; our men, however, round them up again with considerable effort, losing only a few. At the sound of taps the jagunços attack our lines and keep it up until 9:30 and sporadically thereafter. Result: a high-ranking officer wounded, one subaltern killed, and ten or a dozen casualties among the men.

July 20.—The camp is suddenly attacked as the bugles are sounding reveille for all the corps. Firing keeps up throughout the entire day. They have succeeded in mounting only one of the cannons which they brought down. Same number of casualties as the day before: one soldier killed.

July 21.—Peaceful dawn. Few attacks during the day. The cannons on Mount Favella keep up a bombardment until nightfall. Relatively calm day. Few casualties.

July 22.—Without waiting for the enemy to start firing, the artillery begins a cannonading at five o'clock in the morning, provoking a prompt and violent response from the sharpshooters perched on the walls of the churches. The last of the wounded are with great difficulty conveyed from the field of action to the camp on Mount Favella. Lieutenant Colonel Siqueira de Menezes makes a reconnoitering in the vicinity. Upon his return, he announces that the enemy is very strongly intrenched and that very few houses of Canudos, compared to the total number in the town, are in our possession. Only when night comes is it possible to distribute the scant rations to the soldiers in the front lines, this having been impossible during the day on account of the vigilance of the enemy. At 9:00 P.M. a violent assault on both flanks. Result: twenty-five casualties.

July 23.—Day dawns peacefully. Suddenly, an hour later, at six o'clock in the morning, following an unperceived flanking movement, the jagunços launch a violent attack on our rear. They are repelled by the Thirty-fourth Battalion and the police corps, leaving fifteen dead behind

---

[18] Colonel Antonino Nery (see p. 368.)

them, a cabocla[19] taken prisoner, and a bag of flour. Heavy firing at night. The three cannons fired only nine rounds, from lack of ammunition.

July 24.—Bombardment begins at sunrise. Contrary to custom, the settlement does not reply. The shrapnels from Mount Favella fall and explode in the town, as if the place were deserted. For a long time the cannons pound it without evoking any response. At 8:00 A.M., however, a few scattering shots are heard on the right, and then an assault is made upon the cannons on this flank. A hand-to-hand conflict ensues and spreads at an alarming rate. Dozens of bugles are to be heard up and down the line, and all the troops draw up in battle formation. The attack is aimed at cutting off the rear guard from the front line. A bold maneuver. Had they succeeded, the jagunços would have fallen upon general headquarters and would have placed the besiegers between two lines of fire. This was a plan of Pajehú;[20] for, having deposed the other leaders, he is now in command. The assault lasts half an hour. The enemy, having been repelled, returns a few minutes later, attacking with great fury on the right. Repelled again, though with difficulty, he falls back to the first of the houses not occupied by our troops and from there begins once more a heavy, constant fire. Among those who fell in this engagement were the commander of the Thirty-third, Antonio Nunes Salles, and many officers and men. At midday the action ceases.

A sudden silence falls on both camps. At 1:00 P.M. a fresh attack, more violent than ever. All the battalions form in line. It is like the movements of a battering-ram. The enemy is striking insistently at our lines on the right. The impetuous Pajehú now lies mortally wounded. On our side there are numerous casualties. Lieutenant Figueira of Taubaté was killed; and among the wounded are the commander of the Thirty-third, Captain Joaquim Pereira Lobo, and many officers. In order to distract the enemy's attention, the commander-in-chief determines to bring the detachments on the left flank, which are not yet under attack, into action. The entire body of the troops now fires on the settlement. A machine gun is hastily brought up to reinforce the right. The batteries thunder on Mount Favella.

The enemy is repulsed, Throughout the night there is a constant firing until dawn.

July 25.—On this day, as on others, the same incidents with little variation; this gives to the campaign a gloomy and monotonous character. The intrenchments which constitute the line of siege are constructed between

[19] [An Indian woman.]   [20] [See pp. 158, 220–21, 301 ff.]

skirmishes. Only at night can the insufficient rations be distributed to the famished soldiers, and only then, carrying their canteens and kettles, do the thirsty men dare risk the heroic journey of a few paces down to the pits of the Vasa-Barris in search of water. And so the days go by.

TRIUMPHS BY TELEGRAPH

These facts, by the time they reached the leaders of the Republic and the governors of the states, had been distorted utterly. From what has already been said, it may be inferred that this was inevitable. With the fighting men themselves, amid the contradictory course of events, unable to form any kind of judgment as to their own situation, it was natural that those who looked on from afar at this drama taking place in the recesses of the hinterland should have fallen back upon conjectures which were not merely unreliable but downright false. There was talk at first of victory. The crossing of Cocorobó showed that the army was speedily putting down the rebel uprising. In addition to this, such news as came to them from the field of action, not to speak of incisively worded telegrams from the commander-in-chief, indicated that it would all be over in two or three days.

When, however, a fortnight had elapsed, the inanity of such fancied triumphs became apparent. It was known that the jagunços had more than once broken through the circling line of bayonets. And so, while the expedition was exhausting itself on the desert wastes of Mount Favella and bleeding to death on the border of Canudos, the public opinion of the nation, finding expression in the press, was indulging in the most extravagant imaginings and was weighing and balancing against one another the most far-fetched hypotheses that had as yet found their way into print. The specter of the monarchist restoration once again loomed darkly on a political horizon that was lowering with storms; and despite the official orders of the day, which were in effect paeans of victory, the sertanejos once more appeared as the Chouans after Fontenay.[21] With history viewed through an inverted lens, the rude Pajehú emerged with the dominant mien of a Chatelineau, and João Abbade[22] as a Charette in a leather hat.

From July 18 on, the general anxiety increased. The news of the attack on this day, as that of previous ones, began as a hymn of victory but gradually died away, leaving tormenting doubts, until the people were all but convinced that the army had suffered another defeat. Meanwhile, from the zone of operations there still kept coming paradoxical and deplorably exaggerated telegrams. They were all of the same kind: "Bandits cor-

[21] [Cf. p. 196.] [22] See pp. 159, 218–19, 241–42.

nered! Victory certain! Within two days the citadel of Canudos will be in
our hands! Fanatics obviously beaten!"

But they were soon to learn the truth. From July 27 on, through the
seaboard region, bound for the capital of Baía, came the living proofs of
the catastrophe.

II

ALONG THE HIGHWAYS; THE WOUNDED

The removal of the sick and wounded to Monte Santo was now urgent.
The first groups of them accordingly set out, under the protection of in-
fantrymen as far as "Joá," on the extreme south of the danger zone.
Gushing from Mount Favella, the lamentable backwash of the campaign
then began flowing along the highways. Daily, whole bands of the disabled, all those who were of no use, left the camp on the hilltop, the weak-
est of them being carried in hammocks of caroá fiber or in rude wooden
ones made of rounded stakes such as are commonly used for storing food
beneath the ceiling;[23] others were painfully seated on limping horses unfit
for the road or else were crowded into lumbering coaches. The great majority went on foot. In a weakened condition as they were, exhausted from
all the privations they had suffered, yet resigned to their fate, they had almost no provisions to sustain them as they crossed this region laid waste
by war.

It was early summer, and the backlands were beginning to take on the
melancholy aspect of a desert. The sun-soaked trees were withering and
were shedding their leaves and flowers from day to day; and covering the
ground was the dark-gray stubble of the parched weeds, revealing the
latent presence of the drought with its unseen conflagration. The crude
bright light of the warm day was dazzling and implacable against a sky
that showed no appreciable change from dawn to dusk. Day would break
in a golden morning and, after having scorched the earth for hours, would
be at once extinguished in night. The water-level was falling in the pits,
and the intermittent brooks were running dry—in their pebble-strewn
beds were tiny trickles of water, all but imperceptible to the eye, as in the
African wadies. In brief, the superheated atmosphere and the dusty,
cracking earth indicated clearly enough that the desert was staging its
periodic invasion of this unfortunate region.[24] As for the temperature, it
showed enormous variations, with the flaming heat of the day being
followed by nights that were bitterly cold.

[23] [*Giráos de páos roliços.* On the *giráos*, or food cages, see p. 145 and n. 148.]

[24] [See pp. 104 ff.]

They were able to continue their march only in the early morning and late afternoon. As the sun reached the zenith, it was absolutely necessary to halt, for in this purest of atmospheres there was no protection against its rays, refracted with increased intensity by an earth with little or no vegetation. Those blinding rays were reflected not only from every fold in the earth's surface but from the mountaintops as well; and through the hot, unbreathable air it seemed as if sparks were flying from extensive conflagrations kindled over the tablelands. And so, from ten o'clock in the morning on, the caravans came to a halt in such places as they could find that were best suited to repose; they would pause on the edge of streams whose waters had collected in small stagnant pools here and there, where what little moisture that was left served to nourish the foliage of caraíbas and tall baraúnas; or they would stop at the cisterns, still filled with water, of abandoned farmhouses; or, if no place of this sort was available, they would draw up at the border of the ipueiras, sprinkled over the small plains and shadowed by the verdant boughs of icozeiros. There they would pitch camp; and that same day, at nightfall, only slightly rested, if at all, by their halt, they would be on their way again, going along without any kind of order, each one making such progress as his strength permitted.

Leaving Favella in a body, these bands would gradually break up, until finally they were scattered all along the road, in small groups or as solitary wayfarers. The strongest of them and those who were best mounted went forward rapidly, taking short cuts to Monte Santo and oblivious of their lagging comrades. Among those who were being sent back to the base of operations were a number of wounded officers; they were carried in hammocks by strapping soldiers. The great majority of the unfortunates, however, were unable to keep up the pace and dropped off along the wayside. Some of them, when their companions set out again following a halt, would quietly stay where they were, in the shade of the withered shrubbery, being wholly overcome with fatigue. Others, goaded by a thirst which the back-country pools had failed to satisfy, and driven by hunger, would change their direction and strike out on one of the numerous bypaths through the caatingas, seeking succor of that singular flora so rich in fruits and thorns; and, in so doing, they would lose their way, as they went about digging up the roots of the umbú, sucking on the swollen branches of the prickly thistle, and searching for any last remaining edibles that might be found on the leafless trees.

They had forgotten all about the enemy. The jagunço's ferocity was offset for them by the savage cruelty of earth.

After a few days' time, the tortuous Rosario trail was clogged with fugitives. This was the same road down which they had come a month before, fearless in the face of any encounter with the crafty enemy, their eyes dazzled by the glint of four thousand bayonets, their senses lulled to the jogging rhythm of battle charges. It had seemed to them then less rough and impassable—a winding road, with one bend after another, with gently gliding slopes and rising hillocks, a road which, circling the jutting cliffs, thrust itself firmly into the very heart of the mountains. They now gazed in astonishment upon that same road, which held so many memories.

Here in the neighborhood of "Umburanas" was the ruined hut from which the ambushed sertanejos had suddenly attacked the big supply train of the Arthur Oscar expedition. Beyond "Baixas," the roadside was still white with bones, deliberately placed there as a cruel stage-setting to commemorate the massacre of last March.[25] At the bend, just before they came to "Angico," was the point where Salomão da Rocha for some minutes had reared his steel barrage of artillery divisions against the roaring flood of humanity which had swept down on the Moreira Cesar column.[26] In the arroyo farther on was the perpendicular bank down which Colonel Tamarindo and his mount had fallen to their death. In the vicinity of Aracaty and "Jueté" was a row of cottages, their beams and rafters gutted by fire, their gardens and small plantations overrun with weeds, marking indelibly the path of previous expeditions.

Near "Vicar's Farm," with a refinement of macabre irony, the jagunços had covered the stunted and deciduous flora with another, fantastic one; from the twisted boughs of the angicos there hung the remnants of uniforms with their vermilion-colored stripes, tattered blue and white dolmans, the shreds of black and crimson socks, and the torn bits of red military cloaks—as if the dead foliage of the region were blossoming again, with sanguinary flowers.

On all sides, with no variation, was the same barbarous and lugubrious landscape. Hills buried under, the evanescent forms of mountains corroded by sudden and mighty downpours, revealing along their sides the inner structure of the earth in the form of rigid protuberances, or breaking up into stone heaps which hinted at the effects of violent cataclysms; barren, level-lying tracts of land now turned into huge plains or *lhanos;*[27] and everywhere, in the depths of the humid bottom lands, a scrawny, atrophied vegetation, scarcely able to withstand its environment and slowly dying amid a maze of tangled boughs—creeping along the ground and writhing in the air, floundering about in torture.

[25] [See pp. 275–76, 304–5.]   [26] See pp. 272–73.   [27] [Cf. the Spanish *llano.*]

Along various stretches of the road were poverty-stricken huts, their doors opening on the highway, their roofs still in place but their inmates gone; for they had been abandoned by vaqueiros frightened away by the war, or by fanatics who had migrated to Canudos. These dwellings were now tumultuously invaded, at the same time that other guests, taken by surprise, hurriedly left: coy and timid foxes, with flaming eyes and bristling backs, that leaped from windows or through the openings in the roof and bounded away to seek refuge in the weeds; and hundreds of bewildered bats that flew out of dark corners with a whir of wings.

The desolate abode then took on animation for a few hours. Hammocks were stretched in the tiny rooms, in the small living-room with its dirt floor, or outdoors under the trees on the lawn; the mules were tied to the crossed stakes that formed the fence of the deserted corral; and tattered overcoats, blankets, and old uniforms were spread out over the lawn. Small groups would wander about the place, curiously eying the neglected kitchen garden, now invaded by bright-hued flowers; and a murmur of voices that was almost festive would recall for a moment the happy, leisure hours which the backwoodsman spent here amid the peace of the backlands. Those who were more able-bodied would make their way down to the water pit a short distance away; and there, indifferent to their lagging comrades and forgetful of those to come after them, who for many weeks and months would be making the same obligatory halt, they would bathe themselves, wash down their sweating, dust-begrimed nags, and cleanse their wounds in water that was only refreshed from year to year by passing showers. They would come back with their canteens and kettles avariciously filled to the brim and overflowing.

Not infrequently, a few cattle—remnants of the great droves which had been turned loose as a result of the war—upon catching sight from afar of all this stir and bustle again on the premises to which they had grown accustomed, around the peaceful farmhouse where they had first felt the branding iron, would come up on the trot, bellowing joyfully, in search of their friend, the vaqueiro, who once more, to the lilt of well-known ballads or the melancholy refrain of the home-going song, the *aboiado*,[28] would take them to their favorite "runs," the rich *logradouros*, or pasture lands, and the cool, fresh pools and streams. And so they would come trotting up, stamping over the terrace.

The reception they met with was a cruel one indeed. With noisy shouts, the famished soldiers would surround them; rifles would be discharged, and there would be a great tumult as these men with their weakened

[28] [See pp. 99–100, 101.]

bodies came to life and began a wild chase, with the animals, stunned by it all, stampeding for the brush and their pursuers hot after them. After they had worn themselves out with running, their freshly opened wounds torn by thorns and their fever mounting, the men would finally succeed in killing one, two, or, at the most, three, firing so many shots, meanwhile, that it sounded like a pitched battle. And then, following such providential incidents as these, well fed for once and almost happy by contrast with their previous condition, they would await the dawn, which meant resuming their exodus.

At such times, in these brief periods of repose, an obsessing idea would lay hold of them, shattering their peace of mind—supposing the jagunços should attack them! Here they were, helpless, impoverished, ragged, repulsive-looking, one might say, livid with hunger, being swept across the desert like so many useless dead weights—they saw themselves as they were, and childish fears assailed them. That adversary, who had risked an encounter with veteran brigades, and who had carried his blind audacity to the point of trying to capture their cannon by hand, he would surely make short work of them, would slay them all in a few minutes. And so the night fell, dark with hidden menace. Brave men, used to the brutal life of the battlefield, would start up in fear at the slightest sound; and, in spite of their weariness, they would lie awake, cautiously tuning their ears to the vague and distant sounds of the sleeping plain. They were tortured all the while by cruel hallucinations. The bursting of pods in the caatingas, with a loud, sharp, cracking noise, was like the snapping of a trigger or the explosion of a fuse, creating the illusion of sudden shots from some nocturnal ambuscade; and in the distance they could see the phosphorescent garlands of the cumanans,[29] like the remains of bonfires around which, silently, expectantly, innumerable enemies kept watch.

The morning would free them from these fears. They then would leave those dread-inspiring surroundings. Some of them, however, would at times remain, calm and rigid in some corner—comrades whom death at last had freed of their sufferings. They did not bury them; there was not enough time for that. They would merely have broken their picks on the hard sandstone of the earth, which presented the consistency of solid rock. Among those who started, some after the first few steps would fall from exhaustion at the bend of the road. No one paid any attention to them; they simply dropped out of sight forever, completely forgotten and left to die absolutely alone. And die they did. For days, weeks, and months to come, those traveling along the road would see them sitting there in the

[29] See pp. 195, 300–301.

same posture, stretched out in the shade of a tree, flecked with gleams of light through the withered foliage, their right arms curved over their foreheads as if to protect their faces from the glare of the sun, which gave them the precise appearance of weary soldiers taking their ease. Their bodies did not decompose; the hot and arid atmosphere preserved them; they merely withered slightly, the skin shriveling; and there they would remain for a long time at the side of the road—dreadful-looking mummies clad in ragged uniforms.[30]

The truth is, however, they made little impression on those who saw them. Anyone who, in the heat of summer, ventures to cross the northern backlands, becomes accusomed to unusual scenes. Particularly as the cycle of the drought comes on, with its alternation of burning-hot days and all but frigid nights, the earth appears to strip itself of all humanity, with all life latent, merely immobilizing without decomposing the beings that live upon it. It thereby realizes to a high degree the physiological possibility of a virtual existence where no life seems to be, with all energies pent up, lulled to sleep simply, and ready to break out again of a sudden when favorable conditions return, giving rise to unforeseen and amazing resurrections.[31] Just as the parched and naked trees, upon the coming of the first rains, begin exuding sap and burst into flower without waiting for leaves, thus transforming the desert, within a few days, into a blooming meadow—so the birds that fall in death from the stagnant air, the hardy fauna of the caatingas which dies, and man who succumbs to the sun's deadly rays, all appear to lie there for a long while, without the worms troubling their tissues, waiting for the return of more beneficent seasons. Occasionally, one comes upon animals which look very much as if they were alive: pumas which have not been able to escape the incandescent circle of the drought by fleeing to other parts—there they lie, writhing, their claws dug into the ground, as if paralyzed in the midst of a leap—and, on the edge of the dried-up wells, their throats stretched out in search of a liquid that is not there, are skinny oxen, dead two or three months, no longer able to stand upon their withered legs, clustered now in motionless herds.

The first rains would quickly enough sweep away these sinister scarecrows. Decomposition would then be as swift as if they were being devoured by flames, the earth with its formidable suction avidly taking from them all those elements necessary for a triumphal renascence of the flora.[32]

The fugitives as they went along bestowed barely a glance on these funereal scenes. They were all of them obsessed with one thought alone,

---

[30] [Cf. pp. 23–24.] [31] [Cf. pp. 36 ff.] [32] [Cf. ibid.]

that of leaving behind them in the shortest possible time this brutal desert region of the backlands. Terror and a sense of their own wretchedness ended by overcoming the fatigue of the journey; it had a galvanic effect on them, desperately hurling them onward down that endless road, onward, onward.

There was no longer any trace of military formation in their ranks. For the most part, through a process of adaptation, they had come to adopt the garb of the sertanejos and were no longer to be distinguished by their faded uniforms hanging on them in shreds. Instead, they now wore true sandals on their feet, cotton shirts on their backs, with no caps or military bonnets but leather hats; all of which gave them the appearance of "quitters" with their families, thronging pell-mell to the coast, under the lash of the drought. This illusion was heightened by the presence among them of a few women, soldiers' mistresses, witchlike old camp followers with ghastly, wrinkled faces.

Distinguished officers, General Savaget, Colonels Telles and Nery, and others, returning sick or wounded from the front, upon passing through the midst of these bands were greeted with a painful indifference. The men did not salute them. These were less unfortunate comrades-in-arms, no more. They passed through and were quickly lost from sight in the distance, leaving clouds of dust behind them; but they were followed by sharp and menacing looks on the part of those who, scarcely able to conceal their feelings, envied them their fast-trotting horses.

After four days on the road, the more fortunate ones finally reached the point where the Rosario, Monte Santo, and Calumby highways come together, at the farmhouse known as "Joá," another mud hut on the slope of a hill shaded by tall joaz trees, with the highland plains stretching away in the distance. They now felt safe. One day more would bring them to "Caldeirão Grande,"[33] the best ranch in these parts, an almost lordly dwelling, built upon a broad hillock with a well-stored reservoir down below, fed by the dammed-up waters of a creek. Here within a radius of a few miles the landscape was transformed. Round about them now were small knolls bordered with a vegetation that was much livelier; and the wayfarers for a few hours were able to escape the saddening obsession of sterile plains and devastated mountains.[34]

They were now very near to the so-called "base of operations." The next day they set out for Monte Santo; and, after two hours on the road,

[33] [Literally, the "Big Cauldron"; on *caldeirão* as applied to a water pit or reservoir see p. 11.]

[34] [Cf. pp. 198–99.]

their spirits were revived by a glimpse of the small town, two and a half miles distant. It was a pleasant sight as it lay there amid the broad sweep of the tablelands—a cluster of little houses running up a gently inclined terrace to the foot of the steep-rising mountain. Perched on the summit up above, the chapel, gleaming white against the blue of the sky, appeared to be nodding them a friendly and affectionate welcome.

Their hopes, however, were short lived. Upon reaching Monte Santo, they found that they were still in the desert. This city of the dead, uninhabited, wholly unprovisioned, could give them shelter for little more than a day. The population had abandoned it, "ducking into the caatinga," in the woodman's expressive phrase, frightened off at once by the jagunço and by the soldiery. A small garrison was quartered in the humble village square and there spent its days in idleness, in a marking of time that was more unbearable than battles and forced marches. What was supposed to be a military hospital had been set up in a low, dark, but spacious dwelling; but this was a place that the sick and wounded dreaded; it merely added to their tortures. This village with its narrow, winding alleys, bearing sonorous names—"Moreira Cesar Street," "Captain Salomão Street"! —was merely an aggravation in a region where all nature was hostile; it was the desert within walls, lost in the maze of filthy little passageways, filled with detritus and with the offal of battalions that had camped there; it was more unpleasant than the desert itself, which at least was purified by suns and swept by cleansing winds.

Upon arriving in the town, the wayfarers, fleeing the unwelcome proximity of the bats which infested the abandoned houses, proceeded to camp out in the one square the village afforded, large and quadrangular in shape, where they disputed for the shade of the old tamarind tree that stood alongside the fair booth.[35] The next day they quickly left the place, every man for himself, striking out in the direction of Queimadas. This meant another long and exhausting journey across the desert; for Queimadas was forty miles away, six or eight more days of bitter hardship beneath the scorching sun, relieved only by the inevitable halts at the water pits: at Quirinquinquá, a couple of gloomy dwellings, surrounded by silent-standing mandacarú trees and built upon a broad ledge of exposed granite; at Cansanção, a tiny hamlet, a dozen houses with stagnant pools all around; at "Serra Branca," which put one in mind of a pack-drivers' ranch, festive in appearance, shaded by leafy urucuris; at the "Jacuricy"— in fact, at all the lakes and pools with their greenish, ugly-looking water.

[35] [See p. 200.]

DEPREDATIONS

The country along the roadside, which up to then had been populated, was now turned into a waste land, as these tumultuous bands stormed through it, leaving destruction in their wake, like the remnants of some caravan of limping savages. Anguish-ridden and rebellious, menacing groups of the sick and wounded, uttering cries and imprecations to make one's hair stand on end, would descend upon the huts along the highway, demanding an unconditional hospitality of the inmates. First, an angry request, not so much a threat as expressive of irritation. Then an open assault. The quiet, peaceful life which the backwoodsmen led in these humble dwellings, in contrast to their own tormented existence, goaded them on to such acts, inspiring in them an irresistible impulse to destruction which was hypnotic in character—leading them to batter down the doors with their rifle butts, as the terrified backlands family fled to the safety of the nearest weed patch.

CONFLAGRATIONS

Then—for it was necessary to find some stupidly dramatic diversion to distract them for a moment from their deep-seated agony—they would hurl lighted firebrands on the roofs thatched with sapé,[36] which would instantly go up in flames. The strong gusts of the northeaster would scatter the sparks over the dried and withered foliage of the caatinga; and, within a short space of time, swiftly kindled conflagrations which it was impossible to extinguish would spread for many miles around, lashed by the wind, spiraling upward in clouds of smoke and flame, as they rolled down the ravines, encircling and engulfing the slopes and hilltops with the glow of volcanic craters that had suddenly erupted.

Safe now from the enemy, the fugitives were only able to endure this last stage of their painful journey by resorting to misdemeanors of this sort, thereby broadening the circle of devastation wrought by the war, as they made for the coast. Spurred to evil by their wretchedness, they inspired at once both pity and hate—cruelly victimized and victimizing others in their turn. They reached Queimadas a few at a time, utterly exhausted, all but dying; and from there they took the train down to Baía.

FIRST DEFINITE TIDINGS

Their coming was awaited with great curiosity and anxiety. At last, the first victims of the conflict were returning, that conflict which had gripped the attention of the entire country. The arrival of these unfortu-

[36] [A fernlike Brazilian plant (polypody).]

nate heroes was viewed by a huge throng which filled the Calçada railway terminal, overflowing into the near-by streets all the way to Fort Jequitaia. The people had never thought to witness so dramatic a spectacle as this, and they experienced emotions which they had never felt before.

The wounded had arrived in a wretched state; and that repulsive backwash of the campaign which had been rolling along the hinterland trails now spread out through city streets, an ugly wave of rags and human carcasses. It was a heartbreaking procession. Officers and soldiers alike, leveled now in their misery, with all distinctions of rank gone, were clad in the same nondescript raiment: old socks strung together to form indifferent loincloths; tattered shirts; ragged dolmans on their shoulders; overcoats in shreds, draped over flabby chests—all this made a tragic picture indeed. As they hobbled along, dragging themselves on crutches, stumbling, falling, their hollow cheeks and drooping shoulders told their own story, the deeply moving story of this campaign, which now for the first time was to be seen for what it was, in these weak and mutilated bodies, gashed by bullets and by the thorns of the caatinga. And they kept on coming, hundreds of them every day: on the sixth of August, 26 officers and 216 men; on the eighth, 150; on the eleventh, 400; on the twelfth, 260; on the fourteenth, 270; on the eighteenth, 53; etc.

The population of the capital received them with deep emotion. As always happens, individual impressions were caught up in the collective reaction, which, with many persons experiencing the same feelings, thus became the exponent of individual sentiment; with all hearts beating as one, all were affected by the same contagion, the same suggestive images, and all individualities were merged in the ennobling anonymity of a pitying multitude, the like of which has seldom been seen in history. The vast city now became one huge home. On every hand, patriotic committees were organized to collect donations, which were numerous, constant, and spontaneous. In the Arsenal of War, in the Medical School, in the hospitals, and even in the religious houses infirmaries were set up; and in each one of these the mutilated heroes were placed under the patronage of some illustrious name: Esmarck, Claude Bernard, Duplay, or Pasteur never had a finer tribute from posterity. Without waiting for the government to act, the people constituted themselves the natural guardians of the patients, opening their homes to them, surrounding them with every attention, encouraging them, guiding their faltering steps in the street. On visiting days they invaded the hospitals in a body, silently—religiously. They would go up to the beds as if those were old friends that lay there. With the ones that were not too ill to converse, they would discuss the hardships which the troops had endured, the dangerous episodes that had occurred; and after such expositions as they then received—the terrible story as told by these sick and wounded men—they would leave feeling that they had at last a clear view of this, the most brutal conflict of our age.

Inexplicable as it may seem, however, this profound and general commiseration was accompanied by a spirit of the most intense enthusiasm. These martyrs were given the ovations due to conquerors. This would happen on the spur of the moment, without previous arrangement—a quick, spontaneous, emphatic demonstration which was over in a quarter of an hour, and which was purely due to the intermittent play of unrestrained impulse. The days now were filled with the movements of noisy crowds, storming in the streets and squares, shouting and laughing, weeping and wailing, which was their way of paying solemn tribute to the nation's heroes. The wounded were a painful revelation, certainly, but, in a manner, an inspiring one. In them was to be seen the energy of a race. These men who had come back lacerated by the jagunço's claws and by the thorns of the earth represented the strength of a people who had been put to trial—the trial by sword, the trial by fire, and the trial by hunger. Shaken by the cataclysm of war, the superficial layers of nationality had brought to light the deep-lying elements in these resigned and stoic Titans. Above all, there was another thought in the minds of all, unspoken but nonetheless dominant; and that was one of admiration for the daring of those rude backlanders who had thus been able to cut to pieces whole battalions.

It was all like a tonic for souls, and they took a deep, long draught of it. Vibrant with enthusiasm, they made pilgrimages to the Palma barracks, where Colonel Carlos Telles was lying wounded, and to Jequitaia, where General Savaget was convalescing; and, when the latter officer was able to venture a few steps in the street, the entire commercial life of the Lower Town at once came to a standstill, as a huge and spontaneous ovation broke out, with the entire population in a short while gathered about the heroic leader of the Second Column, who thus, merely by making his appearance in the street, had transformed a common workday into a national holiday.

LOSSES

These demonstrations were daily interrupted by irritating details. The full extent of the disaster was at length known, with arithmetic exactitude, and it was amazing. From June 25, the day on which the first shots were exchanged with the enemy, down to August 10, the expedition's losses had totaled 2,049. The official charts made this plain. The First Column had started with 1,171 men; the Second, with 878. The figures, respectively, were as follows:

First Column.—Artillery: 9 officers and 47 men wounded; 2 officers and 12 men killed; cavalry wing: 4 officers and 46 men wounded; 30 officers and 16 men killed; engineers: 1 officer and 3 men wounded; 1 private killed; police corps: 6 officers and 46 men wounded; 3 officers and 24 men killed; Fifth Battalion of Infantry: 4 officers and 66 men wounded; 1 officer and 25 men killed; Seventh Battalion: 8 officers and 95 men wounded; 5 officers and 52 men killed; Ninth Battalion: 6 officers and 59 men wounded; 2 officers and 22 men killed; Fourteenth Battalion: 8 officers and 119 men wounded; 5 officers and 42 men killed; Fifteenth Battalion: 5 officers and 30 men wounded; 10 privates killed; Sixteenth Battalion: 5 officers and 24 men wounded; 10 privates killed; Twenty-fifth Battalion: 9 officers and 134 men wounded; 3 officers and 55 men killed; Twenty-seventh Battalion: 6 officers and 45 men wounded; 24 privates killed; Thirtieth Battalion: 10 officers and 120 men wounded; 4 officers and 35 men killed.

Second Column.—One general killed; Artillery: 1 officer killed; Twelfth Battalion of Infantry: 6 officers and 126 men wounded; 1 officer and 50 men killed; Twenty-sixth Battalion: 6 officers and 36 men wounded; 2 officers and 22 men killed; Thirty-first Battalion: 7 officers and 99 men wounded; 4 officers and 48 men killed; Thirty-second Battalion: 6 officers and 62 men wounded; 4 officers and 31 men killed; Thirty-second Battalion:[37] 10 officers killed and 65 men wounded; 1 officer and 15 men killed; Thirty-fourth Battalion: 4 officers and 91 men wounded; 1 officer and 22 men killed; Fortieth Battalion: 9 officers and 75 men wounded; 2 officers and 30 men killed.

And still the casualties kept coming in, a daily average of eight. The enemy, on the other hand, appeared to have extraordinary resources at his disposal.

VARIOUS VERSIONS AND LEGENDS

Those resources, the truth is, were being grossly exaggerated by over-excited imaginations. The federal senate had also been affected by the wave of general commotion and had made a vehement demand for enlightenment with regard to a rumored shipment of arms to Buenos Aires, reported to be destined for the ports of Santos and Baía, everything pointing to the supposition that these were intended for the "Conselheiristas," or followers of the Counselor. An incident such as this, result of the widespread neurasthenia, came as a climax to all the imaginings on the subject which had been going the rounds and, accordingly, embroidered upon in the telling, took on the aspect of reality.

What the American Republics were thinking was shown by the news items that were being printed in their most serious organs of the press, and which, appearing to justify such a rumor as the one just mentioned, merely added to the general hysteria. The paper that perhaps carries most weight of any in South America,[38] after having related the curious

---

[37] [There is apparently a mistake here, two sets of figures being given for the Thirty-second. The text of the sixteenth Brazilian edition has been followed.]

[38] *La Nación* of Buenos Aires, issue of July 30.

events of the campaign, added certain details of a strange and dreadful portent:

It is a matter of two missives which, within two days' time, we have received from the "Buenos Aires Section of the International Union of the Friends of the Brazilian Empire," informing us, by order of the Executive Committee in New York City, that the said Union has a reserve force of not less than 15,000 men in the state of Baía alone, by way of reinforcing the army of the fanatics in case of necessity; and in addition to this, 100,000 in various northern states of Brazil, and another 67,000 at various points in the United States of North America, all of them ready to leave at a moment's notice for the shores of the former empire, and all of them well armed and well prepared for war. "We also have," the missives state, "arms of the most modern make, munitions, and an abundance of money."

The inscription and signature on these enigmatic communications, which are well written, with good penmanship and correct orthography, is in an ink which recalls the violaceous hue of the dead, the capitals being set off with vermilion-colored ink, the color of blood.

In the presence of this formidable array of men and arms, as pictured for us by the mysterious "friends of the Empire," we are at a loss whether to ascribe the communications in question to one of those terrible associations whose plans for destruction are forged in darkness or to certain gentlemen who may be given to mystifying their neighbors.

Meanwhile, whatever may be at the bottom of all this, we hereby announce and acknowledge receipt of the said missives.

All this was believed. Out there in that territory aflame with rebellion, the Fourth Expedition was cut off and on the brink of catastrophe. This was on good authority. From the municipality of Itapicurú alone, it was asserted, three thousand fanatics had set out for Canudos, led by a padre who, straying from orthodox principles, was going out to share the abstruse follies of the schismatic. Through Barroca thousands of armed ruffians had passed, all bound in the same direction. The names of these new rebel leaders were mentioned, clownish names, like those of Chouans: "Peter the Invisible," "Joe the Buck," "Bear's Noodle," and others of the same sort.

To aggravate these conjectures, there came news that was true enough. The sertanejos were scattering throughout the backlands in bold sallies. Led on by "Bold Anthony," they had attacked the territory of Mirandella; they had stormed, taken, and sacked the town of Sant' Anna do Brejo, and were here, there, and everywhere. The scope of the campaign was now enlarged, and it was evident that the jagunços were pursuing a definite line of tactics. In addition to the settlement, they had two new positions that were first rate from the point of view of defense, and which were well manned; these were the chaotic slopes of Caypan and the row of low hills about the river plain known as the Varzea da Ema. Surging out from Canudos, the insurrection was in this manner spreading along the

sides of an enormous triangle, capable of inclosing fifty thousand bayonets. The rebellion was growing.

The supply trains which set out from Monte Santo, even though reinforced not by battalions but by brigades, had an eventful march and were
constantly assaulted. When they reached Aracaty, it was indispensable to
send to Canudos for two or three battalions to come out and escort them
into camp. That sinister stretch of road between "Vicar's Farm" and
"Baixas" was enough to strike terror to the hearts of the bravest of veterans. This was the classic scene for the stampeding of herds and the dispersing of pack trains, by suddenly opening a heavy fire upon them, driving the platoons back in precipitate flight.

In the course of these successive encounters, deliberately staged with
the object of disturbing the line of march, our troops after a while began
to descry a new variety of jagunço, one who, motivated by other reasons,
was lending indirect aid to the enemy. They would catch sight of him
among the clearings where the branches were thin, darting swiftly here
and there in the headlong manner of guerrilla fighters; and then they
would see the gleam of buttons from a soldier's uniform, a flash of crim-
son-colored socks.

The famished deserter was attacking his former comrades. This was a
lamentable symptom, adding yet another trait to a campaign whose aspect was becoming all the time more grave as one trivial event after another added up to a dismaying sum.

The disabled soldiers, who were in constant contact with the people,
conversing with them daily, had set themselves up as the rude chroniclers
of events; and, however imaginative and naïve may have been the form
in which they narrated them, their tales were true in essence, even though
marred by exaggerations. Out of them, strange episodes were woven; and,
as a result, the jagunço now began to appear as a being apart, teratological
and monstrous, half-man and half-goblin; violating all biological laws by
displaying an inconceivable power of resistance; daringly attacking his adversary, yet himself unseen, intangible; slipping away invisibly through
the caatinga, like a cobra; gliding or tumbling down the sides of steep
cliffs like a specter; yet lighter than the musket that he bore; lean, dried
up, fantastic, melting into a sprite, weighing less than a child, his bronzed
skin stretched tautly over his bones, rough as the epidermis of a mummy.

The popular imagination from then on ran riot, in a drunken delirium
of stupendous happenings, woven out of fantasies. Some of these anecdotes were brief and to the point, affording a keen insight into the character of this indomitable hunter of armies.

"LONG LIVE THE GOOD JESUS!"

In one of the skirmishes following the assault on the settlement a young curiboca was taken prisoner, who to all the questions put to him automatically replied, with a proud indifference, "I don't know!"

Finally, he was asked how he wished to die.

"By shooting!"

"But it's going to be the knife," was the soldier's terrible answer.

And so it was. And, as the blade grated dully through the cartilages of his throat and the blood gushed forth, his last gurgling cry was: "Long live the Good Jesus!"

AN EPIC INCIDENT

Other of these tales took on epic proportions. On the first of July the eldest son of Joaquim Macambira,[39] a lad of eighteen, came up to the wily chieftain.

"Dad, I want to put the 'Killer'[40] out of commission!"

The crafty old warrior, a kind of rude, copper-colored imam,[41] gazed at him without any show of emotion.

"See the Counselor about it—and go ahead."

So, the bold lad set out with eleven picked companions. After making their way across the Vasa-Barris, which was "cut off" into pools,[42] they climbed the undulating slope of Mount Favella and glided through the denuded caatingas with the sinuous movement of cobras. It was midday, and the sun was beating down upon the earth, its vertical, ardent rays penetrating even to the bottom of the deepest grottoes, and casting no shadow anywhere.

In these parts, midday is a more silent and witching hour than is midnight itself. Shining through the layers of exposed rock, reflected by the barren plains, and refracted by the hard, parched ground, all the heat of earth flows back, tripled in intensity, into space, in mounting columns of incandescent and irrespirable air. An absolute quiet lies upon the enervated landscape, and not the faintest breeze is stirring. There is not a wingbeat on the air, whose transparency next the ground is disturbed by swift and bubbling waves of heat. The fauna of the caatingas, hidden away, is taking its noontide repose. The withered branches of the trees, stripped of their bark, hang motionless.

Unable to withstand the heat, the army on the mountaintop also was taking its ease. Sprawled at random here and there along the slopes, their bonnets down over their faces to shade them from the sun, the soldiers

---

[39] See pp. 58, 342.   [40] [See p. 342.]   [41] See p. 158.   [42] [Cf. p. 19.]

were sleeping, or were thinking of their distant firesides, as they snatched a few moments' respite by way of recuperating their strength for the exhausting battle soon to be resumed. Scattered over the hills opposite them was a multitude of tiny dwellings, huddled together in disorderly fashion, without streets or squares, a meaningless jumble of huts—this was Canudos, silent and deserted as some old abandoned farm site overrun with weeds.

The army was taking its ease.

Then, higher up where the artillery was stationed, there appeared above the creeping, tangled underbrush on the edge of the clearing a dozen faces with restless, roving, feline eyes darting swift glances all around. The faces of a dozen men lying hidden among the bromelia tufts. No one saw them; no one *could* see them, as they slowly rose, turning their backs with a sovereign indifference on the twenty peaceful battalions. There before them was the coveted prize. Like some fantastic animal ready for a sudden pounce, the Witworth 32 was poised on its solid base. Its truculent, bellowing mouth, which had hurled so many grenades on their holy churches, was turned toward "Bello Monte." The sun's rays, falling full on its gleaming black surface, caparisoned it with sparks, as the fanatics stood gazing at it for some little while. Then they sprang up from the edge of the clearing and fell upon it, assaulting it, grappling with it, attempting to strangle it. One of them carried a handspike, which he now raised in a quick, threatening gesture.

The blow fell, a resounding one, loud and harsh.

A cry of alarm then broke the silence that lay on every living thing, a cry that echoed down the gullies and ravines and over the hills and valleys, filling all space, as it seemed, with a thunderous reverberation, a cry of triumph and destruction that rocked the entire camp.

The detachments hastily formed ranks, and in a second's time the assailants found themselves surrounded by swords and rifles, as the blows fell and the bullets rained down upon them from every side. One alone made his escape—a wounded, battered creature—by running, leaping, tumbling through the ranks of the excited troops; under a hail of bullets, through a deadly ring of bayonets, he ran, plunging into the weeds, dashing through them at a headlong pace, down the steep mountainsides, hanging perilously over chasms, free at last.[43]

This and other incidents, representing a romantic exaggeration of the most trivial events, conferred upon the campaign an impressive legendary aspect which aroused the public of the old capital[44] and finally of the entire nation.

[43] [Cf. the account of this event given on p. 342.]　　　　[44] [Baía.]

III
MORE REINFORCEMENTS

More energetic action on the part of the government was now imperatively demanded. As a result of the latest catastrophes apprehension was
growing, along with the feeling that very little was known as to what was
actually taking place. As always, there was a clash of opinions. The majority believed that the rebels had strong support behind them. That was
evident. According to the orders of the day, couched in such heroic terms,
they had been defeated; but they still were in a position to flee to the backlands of the São Francisco region; instead of which, they insisted upon remaining there in the settlement, where all escape would be cut off once
the siege was rendered effective. It was really incomprehensible. From all
of this certain grave and logical corollaries were deduced. Aside from the
hypothesis of a superhuman degree of devotion such as would lead them
to die en masse beneath the ruins of their consecrated temples, they must
be possessed of formidable warlike qualities that baffled all the regulation
strategists. The number of those remaining in Canudos was said to have
diminished, but this, surely, was a trap to keep the army fighting there in
futile skirmishes while the enemy assembled strong forces at other points
for a final assault all along the line, with the besiegers thus caught between
two lines of fire.

There were, on the other hand, opinions that were more encouraging.
Colonel Carlos Telles, in a letter to the newspapers, stated clearly that the
number of jagunços had been reduced to two hundred able-bodied men,
possibly without any resources whatsoever, the fanatics being provisioned
and equipped with what they had taken from previous expeditions. However, this optimism on the part of one of the heroes of the conflict, an optimism which, to tell the truth, was exaggerated, had little effect on the
general incredulity. All the facts were against it, especially those daily irruptions of wounded men, which added to the ever growing feeling of alarm
all over the country.

THE GIRARD BRIGADE

But there were other disasters to come. In response to General Arthur
Oscar's first request for reinforcements, the government had promptly organized an auxiliary brigade which, unlike other bodies of its kind, was
not to be distinguished merely by a meaningless numeral but, in accordance with a laudable custom not current among us, by which a commander's renown is shed upon his command, was to have a name—the Girard
Brigade. It was commanded by General Miguel Maria Girard and was
made up of three units taken from the garrison of the federal capital: the

Twenty-second, commanded by Colonel Bento Thomaz Gonçalves; the Twenty-fourth, commanded by Lieutenant Colonel Raphael Tobias; and the Thirty-eighth, commanded by Colonel Philomeno José da Cunha. There were, in all, 1,042 men and 68 officers, perfectly equipped, with a magnificent supply of cartridges—850,000 of them—for the insatiable maw of backlands warfare.

However, through a combination of circumstances which it would take too long to relate here, in place of being an "auxiliary" force, this one turned out to be a liability. It set out from Rio de Janeiro under command of the leader whose name it bore and proceeded as far as Queimadas, which it reached on July 31. It set out from Queimadas on August 3 under the command of a colonel and marched to Monte Santo. It departed from Monte Santo for Canudos on August 10, commanded by a major.[45] Meanwhile, it had left behind in Baía a colonel and a number of other officers who were sick. In Queimadas it left a general, a lieutenant colonel, and still other officers—likewise sick. In Monte Santo it left a colonel and more officers, all of whom were sick.

STRANGE HEROISM

The brigade went to pieces along the road. From its ranks there now came requests for discharge that were more alarming than the annihilation of whole divisions. An exceptional kind of beri-beri had laid hold of the men, one that called not for the physician's skill but for the attention of astute psychologists. The simple truth of the matter is that fear on this occasion had its own great heroes, men so stupendously brave that they were willing to announce to the entire country that they were cowards.

It was as they left Queimadas for the backlands that these troops first encountered the throngs of wounded men returning from the front. General Savaget, Colonel Nery, Major Cunha Mattos, Captain Chacha Pereira, and other officers had passed through their encampment at "Contendas," and had been given an enthusiastic greeting, officers and men lining up alongside the road to salute. But, after that, their fervor began to die down. After a march of only three days, they were already beginning to suffer privations; for they had seen their supply of rations dwindling with each successive group of wounded that they encountered and with whom they had shared their provisions; and it was in a state of exhaustion and deep dejection that they finally arrived at Monte Santo.

[45] Henrique José de Magalhães.

EN ROUTE TO CANUDOS

The brigade took the road for Canudos, where it was anxiously being awaited, on the tenth of August, wholly deprived now of the resplendent hierarchy of officers with which it had started. It was now commanded by the commissary of the Twenty-fourth, Henrique de Magalhães, the battalions being under the command of Major Lydio Porto and Captains Affonso de Oliveira and Tito Escobar. Their march was a slow and arduous one. From Queimadas on, they encountered serious difficulties with regard to transport; their draft animals, old, worn-out mules, castaways that they had picked up in Baía, with drivers that had been impressed into service, went limping and stumbling down the road, holding up the troops and slowing their advance. In this fashion they arrived at Aracaty, where a supply train was turned over to them which they were to escort to Canudos.

In the meantime their ranks had been depleted by smallpox, with two or three cases daily being sent back to the hospital at Monte Santo. Others, crippled by the sudden transition from the paved streets of the capital to these rugged trails, straggled behind and were lost in the rear, where they mingled with the wounded who were bound in the opposite direction.

It was accordingly providential that, as they passed through "Jueté" on August 14, they should have made contact with the Fifteenth Battalion of Infantry, already hardened in backlands warfare, which had been sent out from Canudos to meet them. For on the following day, after they had left "Baixas," where they had halted the evening before to permit a large number of stragglers to catch up with them, they were violently attacked at "Vicar's Farm." From a trench along the side, overlooking the highway, the jagunços fell upon their right flank, firing on them all along the line. A sublieutenant of the Twenty-fourth, who was with the advance guard, and another of the Thirty-eighth, who was in the rear, were killed, along with a number of men in the ranks. Taken by surprise and terrified in the presence of these fierce warriors, some of the platoons were thrown into hopeless confusion, with the majority of the soldiers firing desperately at random. The bugles blew, and their loud and vibrant notes were intermingled with shouts of command. The frightened draft animals broke loose and fled, and the oxen stampeded, plunging into the caatinga.

The Fifteenth Battalion,[46] which was in the van, did its best to stay the wavering line, but the enemy was not repulsed, and the rear guard, upon passing this same point, was in its turn attacked. With regard to this de-

[46] Commanded by Captain Gomes Carneiro.

feat, for that is what it was, it will be sufficient to state that, of the 102 oxen which they were convoying, only 11 remained. At "Angico" the brigade was once more attacked, and, after making a nominal bayonet charge in which not a man was lost, it finally entered Canudos, where the hardened warriors, tyrannically disciplined by being under fire every day, greeted it with the nickname of "pretty brigade," a sobriquet which, thanks to its brave officers, it was later to shed, along with the name originally bestowed upon it.

IV

STILL MORE REINFORCEMENTS

By the time the news of this attack reached Baía, it had assumed the proportions of a battle lost, adding one more shock to the state of emotional unbalance that prevailed and half-a-dozen more rumors to the maze of conjectures. Then it was that the government began to act with the urgency demanded by the situation. Realizing the inefficacy of the reinforcements it had recently sent out, it began to form a new division by assembling the last of the battalions, scattered through the states, that were capable of a rapid mobilization. And, in order that it might have a first-hand view of the matter, it dispatched to the scene of operations one of its members, the Secretary of State for Affairs of War,[47] Marshal Carlos Machado de Bittencourt. The latter set out for Baía in August, as fresh fighting forces were being mustered in all corners of the country. The movement to take up arms now suddenly became general, assuming the form of mass levies.

From the far north and from the far south the troops kept coming, their numbers increased by the police corps of São Paulo, Pará, and Amazonas. The Paulista, reminiscent of the adventurous bandeirante of old, the bold horseman from Rio Grande, the curiboca from the northeast with whom few can compare in hardihood, all now were bearing down on the ancient metropolis;[48] men from the most diverse regions, of varying characters and temperaments, customs and ethnic tendencies, from the dark mestizo to the swarthy caboclo, marching alongside the white man, were united in the bonds of a common aspiration. And the former capital, nestling within its age-old bastions, greeted with a warm and glowing affection these wandering sons of hers—wandering for three whole centuries. Long dispersed, the various factors of our race, beautifully intermingled, were of a sudden returning to their point of departure. Baía decked herself out to receive them. Transfigured by the flux and reflux of the campaign—

---

[47] [Secretario de Estado dos Negocios da Guerra.]   [48] [Baía.]

martyrs arriving, fighters departing—she laid aside her habitual apathy and assumed once more the warlike appearance of bygone times. Her useless fortresses, which, like the middle-class houses that lined her streets, had fallen into decay, were now quickly put in repair and, when the trees that grew from their crevices had been felled, underwent a resurrection to the light of day, recalling the time when from those battlements the long bronze culverins had thundered.

It was in the old fortifications that the recently arrived contingents were quartered: the First Police Battalion of São Paulo, with 21 officers and 458 men, under the command of Lieutenant Colonel Joaquim Elesbão dos Reis; and the Twenty-ninth, Thirty-ninth, Thirty-seventh, Twenty-eighth, and Fourth battalions, commanded by Colonel João Cesar de Sampaio, Lieutenant Colonels José da Cruz, Firmino Lopes Rego, and Antonio Bernardo de Figueiredo, and Major Frederico Mara. These battalions had a strength, respectively, of 27 officers and 240 men; 40 officers and 250 men; 51 officers and 322 men; 11 officers, in addition to 36 sub-lieutenants who had been added, and 250 men; and 11 officers (all sub-lieutenants) and 219 men—this last battalion, the Fourth, had neither captains nor lieutenants. And, finally, there were two additional police corps: the police regiment of Pará, with a fighting strength of 640, commanded by Colonel José Sotero de Menezes; and another regiment from Amazonas, under the command of Lieutenant Colonel José Mariano, with 328 men.

These reinforcements, amounting to 2,914 men, with close to 300 officers, were divided into two brigades: one of the line, under command of Colonel Sampaio; and the police corps, which, with the exception of the São Paulo detachment, constituted a division under the command of Brigadier General Carlos Eugenio de Andrade Guimarães. The São Paulo police, commanded by Colonel Sotero, marched ahead of the other troops.

The entire month of August was spent in mobilizing these forces. They arrived in Baía a detachment at a time and, after being equipped, set out from there for Queimadas and thence to Monte Santo, where there was to be a concentration of all the troops early in September. The battalions of the line, in addition to being greatly understrength as the above figures will indicate, having been reduced to something like two companies each, had come without military equipment of any sort, even of the most rudimentary kind—if one excepts their ancient muskets and the old dappled-gray uniforms which they had worn in the recent federalist campaign in the South.

MARSHAL BITTENCOURT

Marshal Carlos Machado de Bittencourt, in whose hands the situation chiefly lay, then began displaying a notable degree of activity. He was, indeed, the man to confront the difficulties of the moment. Cold and phlegmatic in disposition, he was a bit of a skeptic in his quiet, inoffensive way. His thoroughly plebeian simplicity was not conducive to expansiveness and noble-minded impulses. To give him his due, he was capable—as he was later to show, by tragically ending his life—of running the gravest of risks, but coolly, with balanced mind, doing whatever lay within the inelastic bounds of his duty as he saw it. He was not a brave man; neither was he a coward. No one could conceive of his performing a feat of heroism. No one could picture him slowly and cunningly extricating himself from a dangerous situation. While he was not the perfect type of military man, he was nonetheless addicted to the typical automatism of those machines composed of muscles and nerves which are so constructed as to react mechanically to the irresistible pressure of laws.

All this, however, was due not so much to a thorough disciplinary education as it was to his own inert and passive temperament, moving comfortably like a cog in a wheel within the complex machinery of rules and regulations. Outside of this he was a nonentity. Written orders with him were a fetish. He did not interpret them and he did not criticize them; he carried them out. They might be good or very bad; absurd, extravagant, anachronistic, stupid, loathsome; or useful, fruitful, noble-minded, creditable—they were all the same to his proteiform mind. They were in writing; that was enough. For this reason it was that, every time there was a political upheaval, he cautiously withdrew into obscurity.

Marshal Floriano Peixoto, a profound judge of the men of his time, in those critical periods of his government when the personal character of followers or adversaries was a matter of moment would always, systematically, leave Bittencourt to one side. He did not summon him; he did not send him away; he did not lay hands on him; for the latter was equally unimportant as foe or partisan. Peixoto knew that this man, whose career had been so uniformly, so inflexibly dull and meaningless, would never make a move for or against the establishment of the states of siege.[49]

The Republic, for Bittencourt, was an unlooked-for accident, coming at the end of his life. He did not care for it in the least, as those who fought with him realized. For him it was an irritating novelty, not because it changed the destiny of a people, but because it altered a few ordinances

---

[49] [Referring to the states of siege which, in order to rule by decree, Peixoto declared in the stormy days of the young Republic.]

and a few decrees, a few formulas and hoary precepts which he knew by heart, which he had at his fingertips.

Upon his arrival in Baía, he put a damper on the enthusiasm of all who came into contact with him. Whoever approached him in search of encouragement, looking for some spark of happy intuition, some show of manliness in the face of the grave and deeply stirring situation which had brought him there, was surprised to encounter none but the most trivial ideas and long, rambling, incredibly boring discourses on the most frivolous of topics, interminable minutiae having to do with the distribution of rations and the remounting of cavalry—as if this world were one huge barracks and History merely a variation on a sergeant's records. He came to the city when the patriotic fervor of all classes was at its highest pitch, and in one way or another he cast a wet blanket on it. He might be greeted by noisy demonstrations, poets might read to him their flaming odes, his ears might be deafened on every hand by the explosive phrases of the orator and the shouts and hand-clapping of the multitude. He listened to it all with ill-concealed indifference. He did not know how to reply. His words were few, and it was hard for him to get them out; and, what is more, anything that was out of the ordinary course of life bewildered him and annoyed him. Those recently returned from the battle front, and who were in search of a transfer or a furlough, thinking to dispense with the formality of a doctor's certificate, might show him their shotgun wounds, their bloody gashes, their corpselike, fever-ridden faces; it made no impression on him—these were trivial matters, all in the day's work.

HEART-RENDING SCENE

On one occasion this lamentable lack of sensitivity made a deep impression on those about him. It was on a visit to one of the hospitals.

The scene in that big room was an impressive one. Imagine two long rows of white cots, and on those cots—in every conceivable attitude, lying rigid beneath the sheets drawn over them like shrouds; lying flat on their faces or huddled against the bolsters in mute paroxysms of pain; seated, or bent over, or writhing and groaning—four hundred wounded men! Heads bound in bloody bandages; arms gone or in slings; legs in splints, stiffly extended; thorn-pierced feet swollen out of shape; breasts marred by bulletholes and dagger slashes; every kind of injury, all the sufferings imaginable.

The committee which accompanied the minister—the state and military authorities, journalists, men of every walk in life—all entered that room in solemn silence, awed by the sight that met their eyes. Then the gloomy visit began. The Marshal went up to one cot after another, mechanically reading the chart that hung at the head of the bed, after which he would go on to the next.

But in one instance he had to pause for a moment, when there rose up from the covers in front of him the war-beaten face of an old corporal, a veteran of thirty-five years in the service. A face that had been battered by rifle butts all the way from the bogs of Paraguay to the caatingas of Canudos. The poor old fellow's wan face was wreathed in a hearty, good-humored smile. He had recognized the minister, whose orderly he had been in the good old days when, as a mere lad, he had accompanied him in battle, in the cantonment, and on long and wearisome forced marches. Highly excited, he told him all this, in a hoarse voice, tremulous with pain and joy, as the rude but sincere phrases gushed from his lips; his eyes gleaming feverishly, and forcing himself to sit erect, with his thin, trembling hands he bared his emaciated bosom, opening the cotton shirt he wore to reveal, on his collarbone, the scar of an ancient wound.

It was a touching scene. Those standing about drew a long, deep, painful breath, their eyes dimmed with tears—but Marshal Bittencourt went on, calmly, to continue his mechanical reading of the charts. All this, strong emotions or heart-rending scenes, was something not on the program. He was not to be distracted by it.

He was in all truth the man made for this emergency. The government could not have done better than it did, by placing in his hands the entire conduct of the campaign, without restrictions, leaving him to pursue his straight-line course amid the tumult of this crisis. In thus abdicating its own prerogatives, it made itself in the strict sense of the term the quartermaster general of a campaign the commander-in-chief of which was one of its own lower functionaries.

The fact of the matter is that the Marshal's sound common sense, protected by a cool head which kept him free of any emotional disturbances, enabled him to take in at a glance the real exigencies of the campaign, the least of which, as he realized, was the accumulation of a major number of fighting men for the conflict. Entering a region aflame with rebellion, the fresh troops would merely aggravate the condition of their comrades whom they were supposed to aid, if it meant that they were to share the same privations, with the same scant and penurious resources upon which to fall back. The thing that was necessary above everything else was to combat, not the jagunço, but the desert. It was indispensable to give the campaign the thing it had lacked up to now: a line and base of operations. It was ending where it should have begun. And this was the undertaking

which the minister carried through to success. In the course of his stay at
Baía he was confronted with numerous questions of detail—the equipment of arriving battalions, accommodations for the incessant throngs of
wounded returning from the front—but in his mind they were all subordinated to the prime objective and to the one and possibly the only serious
problem to be solved. Solve it he did in the end, by overcoming a host of
difficulties.

During the latter part of August there was finally, definitely, organized
a regular corps of supply trains, running continuously along the highways
at intervals of a few days and effectively linking the army in the field with
Monte Santo. This accomplishment foretold the nearing end of the conflict; for, from the beginning, the experience of previous expeditions had
shown that the causes of their failure, in good part, lay in the fact that
they had blindly shut themselves off in a sterile region, isolating themselves in the presence of the enemy while they engaged in a spectacular
police hunt without the faintest semblance of military strategy. Marshal
Bittencourt at least did this: he transformed a huge, unplanned conflict
into a regular campaign. Up to then there had been a prodigal but futile
display of bravery; but heroism and self-sacrifice had little to do with the
matter. The campaign had crystallized in a nominal siege, the outcome
of which was highly doubtful, with incessant fusillades that accomplished nothing while lives were being nobly but stupidly thrown away.
And this would keep up for an indefinite length of time, until that
sinister settlement ended by absorbing its attackers, one by one. Under
such conditions, merely to replace those who fell—eight or ten a day—
with others, was to keep turning around in a cruel and vicious circle.
Furthermore, a large number of assailants was a drawback. They might
surround the village and cut off all the exits, but, after a few days had
passed, they would find that they had, round about themselves, the
latent, intangible but formidable siege lines of another enemy—the
parched desert of the caatingas, with the growing, ineluctable pangs of
hunger rising up to confront them. Marshal Bittencourt foresaw all this.

PROSAIC COLLABORATORS

A higher strategist, concerned with the technical and broader aspects
of the question, would have drawn up stupendous tactical schemes which
would not have solved it. A brilliant fighter would have planned new and
impetuous attacks, with the object of putting down the rebellion in short
order; but he would have ended by wearing himself out with nothing to
show for it, as his troops marched here and there in double-quick time

through the caatingas. Marshal Bittencourt, indifferent to all this—unmoved by the impatience of the general public—organized supply trains and purchased mules.

For the truth is, this bloody and truly dramatic campaign was to be brought to a successful conclusion in one way, and one way only, and the solution was a singularly humorous one. A thousand domesticated burros in this emergency were worth ten thousand heroes. The backlands conflict, with all its train of bloody battles, had to be brought down to a deplorably prosaic and humble plane. Heroism could be dispensed with, military genius was disdained, the onslaught of brigades was excluded; and, in place of these, pack mules and their drivers were sought. This way of looking at things, which would make of History a malicious epigram, was incompatible with the overwrought patriotic lyricism of the day, but it was the only sensible view. It was none too flattering to have to have recourse to such collaborators as these in the working-out of our national destiny, but it was forced upon us. The most calumniated of animals was now master of the situation and was to plant his jagged hoofs squarely upon a crisis and crush it.

These beasts alone could give to the operations of the campaign that swiftness of movement which was demanded under the circumstances. The war, if necessary, could be prolonged for a couple of months, at a maximum; but three months—and there was no escaping the inevitable conclusion—would mean defeat, the loss of all that had been accomplished, and an enforced paralysis of effort. In November, in this zone, the rainy season would begin, and the consequences would be beyond remedy. The beds of the streams which up to now had been dry would then be foaming with muddy waters, and the Vasa-Barris, suddenly swollen, would be transformed into an enormous flood wave, overflowing its banks and spreading over the countryside; it would not be possible to cross it, and all communications would be cut off.

Afterward, when the torrential streams had rapidly subsided—for the vortex of waters, whirling toward the São Francisco and the sea, is drained off as quickly as it is formed—there would be complications still more serious in character. Under the burning heat of the days in this region, at this time of year, every brook, every seasonal pool, every "cauldron"[50] buried away among the rocks, every well, is an infernal laboratory, distilling and disseminating far and wide through the air the germs of swamp fever, with an infinite number of them ascending at every point where the

[50] [See pp. 11, 379.]

sun's rays strike, to fall upon the troops, those thousands of human organisms weakened by fatigue and hence in a morbidly receptive condition.
It was, accordingly, imperative to liquidate the war before the start of
this dangerous season, by so arranging matters that a real and effective
siege could be established such as would lead to immediate surrender. And
once they had conquered the enemy who *could* be conquered, they would
at once, without the loss of a moment's time, fall back before that eternal
and invincible enemy—the desolate and sterile earth. But, for this, it was
indispensable to guarantee the subsistence of the army, which, with its recent reinforcements, had been increased to around eight thousand men.
This was what had to be done, and the minister of war did it.

The consequence was that, by the time he set out for Queimadas early
in September, everything was in readiness to put a speedy end to the conflict; the brigades of the "Auxiliary Division" were awaiting him at their
concentration point in Monte Santo, and the first of the regular supply
trains, even though few in number as yet, now left for Canudos.

IN CANUDOS

They arrived in time to bring new hope to the expedition which up to
that date had spent more than forty days in dangerous and futile action,
hard up against the flanks of the settlement. We have already given brief
extracts from a diary of their days[51]—brief, because we wished to avoid a
tiresome repetition of episodes one of which was very like another: the
same sudden, instantaneous, and violent fusillades at irregular hours; the
same deceptive truces; the same shattering of apathy by battle alarms,
over and over again; the same strange and oppressive calm, broken by a
blaze of rifle fire. Daily engagements, at times deadly ones, thinning their
ranks and depriving them of their most capable officers; at other times
noisy and long drawn out, but, like those encounters between the mercenaries of the Middle Ages, innocuous in character, resulting in the expenditure of thousands of bullets but without a single wound, a single
scratch, on either side. And, finally, the hand-to-mouth existence that
they led, on third-rations when they had them, with an ox to a battalion
and a liter of flour to a squadron;[52] and, as during those terrible times on
Mount Favella, the daily forays in which whole detachments took part,
by way of rounding up the stray cattle of the vicinity.

The supply trains were few and far between, their schedule uncertain,
and by the time they arrived they would have left a part of their cargo

---

[51] See pp. 369 ff.   [52] [Cf. pp. 339-40, 391-92.]

behind them along the roads. The expeditionaries were once more confronted with the one real peril they had to face: hunger. Sheltered in the huts, or quartered in tents behind the hills, or huddled in their trenches, they had little to fear from the jagunço. Their dangers consisted exclusively in the enemy's sniping at those incautious ones who strayed from cover. The towers of the new church rose high above them like a couple of sinister *mutans*[53] overlooking the army, and no one escaped the marksmanship of those who manned those towers, and who never abandoned them, no matter how loud the cannon might roar. The crossing to Favella continued to be, for this reason, a dangerous one, it being necessary to station a guard along the riverbank at the point where the roadway runs in order to prevent any imprudent soldiers from taking this path. It was at this point that the troops sent as reinforcements received their baptism of fire: the Girard Brigade on the fifteenth of August, reduced now to 56 officers and 892 men; the São Paulo battalion, which arrived on the twenty-third with 21 officers and 424 men; and the Thirty-seventh Infantry, which preceded the "Auxiliary Division," and which numbered 16 officers and 205 men, under command of Lieutenant Colonal Firmino Lopes Rego. The enemy let them descend the last slopes in peace, lying in wait for them at the final stage, in the river bed down below, where they gave them a resounding and theatrical reception, consisting of a fusillade invariably interspersed with terribly ironic hoots and catcalls.

The truth is, the jagunços were not frightened by these fresh antagonists but remained unshaken in their attitude of calm defiance. They appeared to have set up a system of discipline and would send messages from one end of the village to the other, across the maze of huts, by firing their blunderbusses in a certain manner. They were, also, more orderly and assured in their bold attacks. They themselves received supply trains, which came in by the highways across the Varzea da Ema, without our troops' being able to capture these trains, for the reason that they feared to leave their positions unprotected or, a more serious consideration, dreaded falling into a trap; for over the hills to the north, and from there on to Canabrava and Cocorobó, circling the battalions at a distance, flying columns of jagunços roamed, swift-moving and invisible, but leaving behind them unmistakable signs of their presence. Not infrequently an inexperienced soldier, upon coming out on top of a hill, would be brought down by a bullet which came from outside the settlement, from those other intangible siege lines with which our troops were surrounded. The

53 [See p. 240, n. 7.]

cavalry and traction animals were often stampeded, in their pasture ground along both banks of the river, by the firing; and, one day in August, twenty of the artillery mules were captured by the enemy, in spite of the fact that the important task of guarding them had been intrusted to a veteran battalion, the Fifth of the line. These incidents showed an unusual vigor on the part of the rebels. Meanwhile, our forces gave the latter no respite. Since the nineteenth of July the three Krupps had been mounted on the slope, with the vanguard of the Twenty-fifth at the bottom; their position commanded the square, and they kept up a pounding fire day and night, starting conflagrations which were with difficulty extinguished and completely ruining the old church; the wooden framework of that structure could be seen jutting out through the roof, which had been in part destroyed, and it was incomprehensible how the fearless sexton could still make his way up into the belfry to sound the sacred notes of the "Ave Maria."

THE CHURCH BELL

As if this bombardment at close range were not enough, on the twenty-third of August the Witworth 32 was brought down from Mount Favella. That was the day on which General Barbosa was wounded as he was inspecting the center battery, next to the First Column's headquarters, and the arrival of the monstrous cannon afforded an opportunity for immediate revenge. This was had at dawn of the following morning, and it was indeed a terrible one. As the great piece thundered, the enormous shrapnel could be seen falling between the church walls with a loud crash, blowing the roof to bits and carrying away what was left of the belfry, while the old bell itself hurtled through the air, its clapper beating noisily, as if it were still sounding an alarm—that bell which so often, at twilight, had summoned the fighting jagunços to their prayers.

FUSILLADE

Aside from this incident, however, the engagement was a loss to our side; for a piece of apparatus had become stuck in the mouth of the cannon, silencing it forever. Eight soldiers dropped along the line of fire, as the enemy now began a heavy, truly stupendous, and incomparable fusillade, which lasted into the night and until dawn. It was resumed during the day, following a slight lull, and four of our men who fell, together with a half-dozen of the Twenty-sixth who had taken advantage of the tumult to desert, brought the day's losses to ten. It continued on the twenty-sixth, with four casualties in the ranks; on the twenty-seventh, with four killed; on the twenty-eighth, four casualties; on the twenty-ninth, one officer and four privates; and so on at the same rate, until our troops were completely exhausted.

These losses, along with those suffered in previous engagements, since the middle of August had made imperative a reorganization of the thinning ranks. With the number of brigades reduced from seven to five, and with more and more officers from the top down being killed or wounded, it was apparent that, despite the reinforcements which had arrived, the expedition was growing weaker.[54] Of the twenty battalions of infantry—

[54] "Headquarters of the Commander-in-Chief, Field of Battle at Canudos, August 17, 1897.—Order of the Day, No. 102.—Reorganization of the Forces Operating in the Interior of the State.

"On this date the following organization of my command was effected: Fourteenth Battalion of Infantry, under the command of Captain Antonio da Silva Paraguassú of the Thirty-second; the Twenty-second, under the command of Major Henrique José de Magalhães, of the same corps; the Thirty-eighth, under the command of Captain Affonso Pinto de Oliveira of the same corps; these infantry detachments constituting the First Brigade, under command of Colonel Joaquim Manoel de Medeiros of the Fourteenth; the Fifteenth, under the command of Captain José Xavier de Figueiredo Brito of the Thirty-eighth; the Sixteenth, under command of Captain Napoleão Felippe Aché of the Twenty-fourth; the Twenty-seventh, under command of Captain Tito Pedro Escobar of the Twenty-fourth; the Thirty-third, under command of Captain José Soares de Mello; these detachments constituting the Second Brigade, commanded by Colonel Ignacio Henrique de Gouveia of the Twenty-seventh; the Fifth, commanded by Captain Leopoldo Barros e Vasconcellos of the same corps; the Seventh, under command of Captain Alberto Gavião Pereira Pinto of the same corps; the Twenty-fifth, under the command of Major Henrique Severiano da Silva; the Thirty-fourth, commanded by Captain Pedro de Barros Falcão; these detachments constituting the Third Brigade, under the command of Lieutenant Colonel Emydio Dantas Barreto of the Twenty-fifth; the Fifth Regiment of Artillery, under command of Captain João Carlos Pereira Ibiapina of the same corps; battery of the Second Regiment, under the command of First Lieutenant Aphrodisio Borba of the Fifth Position Battalion; and a rapid-fire battery, commanded by Captain Antonio Affonso de Carvalho of the First Position Battalion; these detachments constituting the artillery brigade, under the command of Colonel Antonio Olympio da Silveira of the Fifth Regiment; the above brigades to remain a part of the First Column, commanded by Brigadier General João da Silva Barbosa; the Ninth Battalion of Infantry, under the command of Captain José Lauriano da Costa of the Thirty-first; the Twenty-sixth, under the command of Captain Francisco de Moura Costa of the Fortieth; the Thirty-second, under the command of Major Florismundo Collatino dos Reis Araujo Góes of the same corps; the Thirty-fifth, commanded by Captain Fortunato de Senna Dias; these detachments constituting the Fourth Brigade, under command of Colonel Donaciano de Araujo Pantoja of the Thirty-second; the Twelfth Infantry, commanded by Captain Joaquim Gomes da Silva of the Thirty-first; the Thirtieth, commanded by Captain Altino Dias Ribeiro; the Thirty-first, under the command of Major João Pacheco de Assis of the same corps; the Fortieth, under the command of Major Manoel Nonato Neves de Seixas; these detachments constituting the Fifth Brigade, under the command of Lieutenant Colonel Antonio Tupy Ferreira Caldas of the Thirtieth; these brigades to form the Second Column, temporarily under the command of Colonel Joaquim Manoel de Medeiros; while Major Aristides Rodrigues Vaz of the Sixteenth assumes temporary command of the First Brigade. The cavalry contingent, commanded by First Lieutenant João Baptista Pires de Almeida of the First Cavalry, is to form a part of the First Brigade and is to be at the disposition of the commander of that brigade, along with the engineering contingent and the Fifth Police Corps.—ARTHUR OSCAR DE ANDRADE GUIMARÃES, *Brigadier General*."

not including the Fifth Regiment of Artillery, the Fifth Baian Police, a rapid-fire battery, and a cavalry squadron—fifteen were now commanded by captains, while two of the brigades were under the command of lieutenant colonels; if the command of companies was not in the hands of sergeants, it was for the reason that, as it happened, there were fewer sergeants than sublieutenants.

The situation was soon to change, however, and Canudos was to have, in exact figures, thirty battalions, not counting other branches of the service.[55] The division which was to be their salvation was now on the road.

[55] The Fourth, Fifth, Seventh, Ninth, Twelfth, Fourteenth, Fifteenth, Sixteenth, Twenty-second, Twenty-third, Twenty-fourth, Twenty-fifth, Twenty-sixth, Twenty-seventh, Twenty-eighth, Twenty-ninth, Thirtieth, Thirty-first, Thirty-second, Thirty-third, Thirty-fourth, Thirty-fifth, Thirty-seventh, Thirty-eighth, Fortieth, all battalions of the line; the Fifth of Baía; one battalion from São Paulo; two from Pará; one from Amazonas; thirty all told. To be added are: the Fifth Regiment of Artillery; a battery of the Second Regiment of Artillery; a rapid-fire battery; a cavalry squadron; the Fourth Baian Police Corps; and the volunteer Moreira Cesar Battalion, in charge of the supply trains.

CHAPTER IX

NEW PHASE OF THE STRUGGLE

I

QUEIMADAS

QUEIMADAS, a settlement dating from the beginning of the century but now in full decline, had become a noisy armed camp. A collection of poverty-stricken huts awkwardly clustered about an irregular-shaped *praça*, deeply furrowed by torrential rains, it was in reality a clearing in the wilds, and the monotony of the surrounding plains and barren hills gave it a mournful air, the appearance of a deserted village fast falling in ruins and overrun by the wilderness.

There were, moreover, painful memories associated with the place. Here it was that all the previous expeditions had been assembled, on the bit of ground extending from the village square to the caatinga, whose parched, grayish-white leaves had given the place its name.[1] Repugnant heaps of rags and tatters, filthy multicolored shreds of old uniforms, old shoes and military boots, kepis and soldiers' bonnets, smashed canteens— all the odds and ends of a barracks were scattered over this extensive area, along with the remains of bonfires left by those who had pitched their tents here ever since the start of the Febronio expedition.[2] On this bit of offal-strewn ground ten thousand brawling men had bivouacked, with passions, anxieties, hopes, and discouragements beyond the power of description.

DEMONIAC PAGES

Having climbed a small knoll, one could see, cutting through the underbrush, a long, broad, rectilinear furrow of arable land, with a shooting target at the far end; this was the firing range where the Arthur Oscar Division was accustomed to practice. Near by, at one side, was the little, low chapel, like a walled tent, scrawled over with the coarse literature of soldiers, in their rude handwriting. All the battalions had collaborated on these pages, carving their impressions of the moment with the point of a saber or daubing them with chunks of coal on those holy walls. Demoniac pages, these, consisting of brief, incisive, hair-raising sentences, terri-

[1] [*Queimado*, burnt or parched; *queimar*, to burn; *queimada*, a conflagration.]
[2] [See pp. 189 ff.]

ble blasphemies, imprecations, exclamations, enthusiastic *viva*'s, sprawling all over the sides of the chapel, the black characters being interspersed with exclamation points as big as lances.[3]

It was here, along an imperceptible slope, that the Monte Santo Road began—that narrow, ill-famed trail down which three successive expeditions, filled with high hopes, had gone, while down that same road now, bound in the opposite direction, came bands of wretched fugitives. Having forded the shallow, stagnant waters of the Jacuricy, the trail bends and threads its way across the plains that lie beyond, flanked at the beginning by another road marked by the posts of the recently strung telegraph line.

A GEOGRAPHIC FICTION

The railway line runs along the other side. This mark of modern progress is, however, meaningless here and does not in the least alter the genuinely rustic character of the place. One alights from the train, walks a few hundred yards between rows of squat houses, and forthwith finds himself, at the edge of the village square—in the backlands.

For this is in reality the point where two societies meet, each one wholly alien to the other. The leather-clad vaqueiro will emerge from the caatinga, make his way into the ugly-looking settlement, and halt his nag beside the rails where natives of the seaboard pass, unaware of his existence.

BEYOND THE BOUNDS OF THE FATHERLAND

The new expeditionaries, upon reaching Queimadas, were aware of this violent transition. Here was an absolute and radical break between the coastal cities and the clay huts of the interior, one that so disturbed the rhythm of our evolutionary development and which was so deplorable a stumbling-block to national unity. They were in a strange country now, with other customs, other scenes, a different kind of people. Another language even, spoken with an original and picturesque drawl. They had, precisely, the feeling of going to war in another land. They felt that they were outside Brazil. A complete social separation expanded the geographic distance, giving rise to the nostalgic sensation of being very far from home. The mission which had brought them there merely served to deepen the antagonism. There was the enemy, out there to the east and to the north, hidden away in those endless highland plains; and far, far away, beyond the plains, a terrible drama was being unfolded.

It was, surely, a paradoxical kind of fatherland whose own sons had to

[3] See p. 411.

invade it, armed to the teeth, with martial tread, ripping out its very entrails with their Krupp cannon. And, all the while, they knew nothing whatever about it; they had never seen it before but viewed with amazement the arid earth, rugged and brutal, bristling with thorns, tumultuously littered with stone heaps and pulverized mountains, torn asunder with caverns and ravines, while all about were the parched and barren tablelands, great, rolling, steppe-like plains.

What they were being called upon to do now was what other troops had done—to stage an invasion of foreign territory. For it was all a geographic fiction. This other was the reality, plain for all to see from what had gone before. The soldiers felt this and were obsessed by the thought. Here were those unknown woodsmen sending back to them, day by day, mutilated and defeated, their comrades who, a few months previously, had gone down that same road, strong of body and proud in spirit. As a result, there was no heart left in them; they had not the courage to strike out, unconcerned with what might happen, into the depths of those mysterious and formidable backlands.

IN CANUDOS

Happily, upon their arrival at Queimadas, the effect of all this was counteracted to a degree by the receipt of encouraging news from the front. There had been no further disasters, and, in spite of the enemy's daily fusillades, our forces were still holding the positions they had won. The Girard Brigade and the São Paulo Battalion had reached Canudos in time to fill the gaps in the thinning ranks; and, meanwhile, the rebels were beginning to show the first signs of discouragement. They no longer rang the bell of the old church, by way of showing, vaingloriously, how unconcerned they were; for there was no bell to ring; and, in the intervals of firing, their melancholy litanies were no longer to be heard. They had ceased their attacks on our lines; and at night there was not a flicker of light, not a sound, as the settlement lay submerged in darkness.

The rumor then began going the rounds that the Counselor was being held prisoner by his own followers, who had revolted when he announced his intention of surrendering and giving himself up to martyrdom. Other details were cited, all of them pointing to a rapid dying-down of the conflagration.

PRISONERS

Indeed, the new combatants fancied that it had been extinguished even before they reached Canudos. Everything appeared to indicate as much. The first prisoners were at last being brought back, after all these months of fighting; and our men could not help noticing, without attempting to explain the fact, that there was not a full-grown man to be found among them.[4] These captives, escorted under heavy guard, were pitiful ones indeed: half-a-dozen women with infants wizened as fetuses at their bosoms, followed by older children, from six to ten years of age. The soldiers crowded around to stare at them curiously as they made their way through the town—a town swarming with uniforms of every branch of the service and of every rank.

It was a sorry spectacle as these ragged creatures, under the gaze of all those eyes—insatiable eyes that seemed to look straight through their tatters—came into the square, dragging their young ones by the hand. They were like animals at the fair, an amusing sight. Round about them could be heard comments of every sort, in every tone of voice, whispered comments, with lively interjections and expressions of astonishment. This wretched band was for the time being something to take one's mind off things; a pleasing diversion to lighten the long and tedious hours spent in camp. It excited the curiosity of all without touching their hearts.

THE CHILD IN THE KEPI

One of the children—a thin little mite, barely able to stand—wore on its head an old kepi which it had picked up along the road and which came down over its shoulders, covering a third or more of its emaciated bosom. This big, broad hat kept swaying grotesquely at every step the child took, and some of the spectators were so unfeeling as to laugh at the sight. Then the child raised its face and looked them in the eye. Their laughter died on their lips; for the little one's mouth was a gaping bullet wound, from side to side!

The women were for the most part repulsive-looking, with the hardened faces of old shrews and evil, squinting eyes. One of them, however, stood out from the rest. Suffering had chiseled her face without destroying its youth, and an Olympian beauty was to be descried in the firm, impeccable lines of that Judaic profile,[5] disturbed now by the protuberance of the cheekbones in a countenance which, pale and ravaged by hunger, was lighted by big black eyes filled with a deep and sovereign melancholy. She satisfied the curiosity of her listeners by relating a simple story. A tragedy in half-a-dozen words, a trivial enough one, in all truth, with the invariable epilogue of a bullet or a splinter from a grenade.

Having been placed in a hut on the ground-level next the square, the prisoners were surrounded by insistent groups and were compelled to sub-

[4] See pp. 437 ff.   [5] [Cf. p. 157.]

mit to interminable questionings. Finally, attention came to be centered on the children, in the belief that the truth might be learned from their ingenuousness and sincerity.

ANOTHER CHILD

One of these, however, a lad of less than nine years but with the shoulders of an embryonic athlete, amazed them all with his precocious swaggering and his craftiness. His answers were given between stout puffs on a *cigarro*, as he drew on it with the self-assured nonchalance of an old roué. He volunteered a stream of information, almost all of it false, revealing the astuteness of the consummate rogue. His interlocutors took it all in, religiously, for this was a child speaking; but, when a soldier entered with a Comblain rifle in his hand, the boy stopped his babbling and, to the astonishment of all, remarked in a tone of conviction that a *"comblé"* was no good. It was a "sissy" gun; it made a "damned big noise," but there was no force behind it. For himself he preferred a *"manulixe"*; that was a rifle that was a rifle. And so they handed him a Mannlicher, and he proceeded to work its lock as easily as if this had been some favorite childish plaything. They asked him if he had ever fired one of them at Canudos.

"What do you think?" he said. "Those soldiers down there are a bunch of old fogies! . . . . But when the young bucks get after 'em, they give 'em what-for, and they have to take it like a bull in a corner; the jig's up then; we take 'em down a peg or two."[6]

This lad was, of course, tremendously depraved; but he was a lesson to those who heard him, all the same. Here was a finished bandit, cast up by this backlands conflict, with a formidable legacy of errors resting upon his boyish shoulders. Nine years of life into which had been packed three centuries of barbarism. It was plain that the Canudos Campaign must have a higher objective than the stupid and inglorious one of merely wiping out a backlands settlement. There was a more serious enemy to be combatted, in a warfare of a slower and more worthy kind. This entire campaign would be a crime,[7] a futile and a barbarous one, if we were not to take advantage of the paths opened by the artillery, by following up our cannon with a constant, stubborn, and persistent campaign of education, with the object of drawing these rude and backward fellow-countrymen of ours into the current of our times and our own national life.

But, under the pressure of difficulties demanding an immediate and assured solution, there was no place for these distant visions of the future.

[6] ["A cabrada fechava o samba desautorisando as praças," etc. The lad speaks a backlands patois.]

[7] [Cf. the author's "Preliminary Note," p. 2.]

The minister of war, after stopping four days in Queimadas, where he removed the last obstacles to the mobilization of our forces, departed for Monte Santo.

EN ROUTE TO MONTE SANTO

Accompanied only by two headquarters staffs, his own and that of General Carlos Eugenio, Marshal Bittencourt had to make his way to the base of operations across a region clogged with wounded men. While his party may have been well mounted and well provisioned, they encountered along these well-traveled roadways as many difficulties as did those who came after them on foot along the rough backland trails. It took them three days to make the journey; and at every bend of the road they came upon some gloomy aspect of the war, the physical setting of which was becoming more accentuated every step of the way, as the earth grew increasingly rugged and became more calcined and sterile. The first farm at which they stopped, the one known as "Tanquinho" ("Little Cistern"), was a sample of what was in store for them. This was the best of its unnatural kind: half in ruins, with two abandoned houses hidden away behind the fine lacework boughs of the tableland evergreens, with slender, melancholy cacti running down to the roadway. The cistern which gave the farm its name was formed by a surface stratum of granite, providing a narrow strip of impermeable soil where stagnant water, freed from the avid suction of the surrounding sandstone, might collect and form a small lake. Along its edge, and the same was true of all the roadside pools, dozens of wounded men were resting, and it was here, also, that the waggoners of the supply train camped. There was lacking, however, the characteristic noise and bustle of a camp; all was mournful and silent, a saddening cluster of emaciated figures, lying motionless, as if paralyzed, in the utter stillness of complete exhaustion.

It was a deeply moving and a tragic sight, as night fell and the kindled bonfires cast their gleams on the dark water. Some of the men could be seen huddled around the fires, shivering with ague, while others hobbled slowly about, their huge misshapen shadows projected on the level surface of the lake. Thirsty officers who had gone down to the edge of the marsh for a drink would bump into specters barely able to stand on their feet as they strove to give the military salute; and these officers would come back depressed by the experience. From now on, it was to be the same scene many times repeated: along the roads, the same defeated "quitters"; and at the edge of the greenish-black, algae-covered swamps, the same wretched clusters of human beings.

A pleasing contrast to all this, adding a touch of health and strength to the picture, was afforded from time to time, when some quiet, inoffensive fellow would leave the caravan of wounded men and draw up along the wayside—some friendly vaqueiro whom they met at the bend of the road, an ally who had hired out to the transport service. Astride his leather-caparisoned steed, his broad-brimmed sombrero turned up jauntily above his swarthy, honest face, his long "alligator" knife in his belt and his harpoon-like cattle prong in his right hand, the backwoodsman would remain there, motionless, leaving room for the cavalcade to pass, with the proud, respectful bearing of the disciplined soldier. A staunch figure he was in his leather vest of vermilion-gray, which for him became a cuirass of bronze,[8] giving him the appearance of a robust warrior covered still with the dust of battles.

The Marshal's party went on and soon forgot this picture of the sturdy sertanejo, their attention being constantly attracted by the incessant bands of fugitives: soldiers going along slowly, leaning on their rifles; and officers carried in hammocks, their hats down over their eyes, deaf to the clattering hoofs of the passing cavalcade, immobile, rigid as corpses. Here and there were to be seen large dark splotches in the caatinga, the charred remains of conflagrations with the beams and ridgepoles of houses still showing, weaving a warp of ruins over the desert wastes as the terribly stupid background of this war.

At Cansanção they found relief from these cruel impressions. Here, for a couple of hours, they had a comforting sense of calm. This village was really a clan, belonging to one single family; and its chieftain, a patriarch of the old school, at once assembled his sons, grandsons, and great-grandsons for a rousing ovation to the Marshal. It was all done with a wholesome ingenuousness and alacrity that was pleasing in the extreme, the old "Monarch" even lifting the astonished minister down from his horse, taking him in his arms—those arms wearied from eighty years of toil.

This stop was a providential one. Cansanção was a parenthesis amid the general desolation. And this hardy old man who ruled the village was in his turn a revelation, with his assured and wholesome manner toward these men whom he had never seen before, as he introduced to them a white-haired son and grandsons whose hair was turning gray. The antithesis of the precocious young bandit of Queimadas, he was an embodiment of that miraculous robustness, that organic nobility and simplicity of soul, which is so characteristic of the backwoodsmen when they are not led astray by crime and fanaticism. This, to the Marshal's party, was an encouragement; and for this reason the tiny village of a dozen houses

[8] [Cf. pp. 92–93.]

crowded together along a street not many yards long is the only one which, in the history of this campaign, does not evoke painful memories. It was the one tranquil zone in all the hurly-burly. A small hospital had been set up there, in charge of two Franciscans, who cared for those wanderers bound for Queimadas who had not the strength to go any farther.

Upon leaving Cansanção, the Marshal and his companions went back to the hardships of the dusty trail—a hopelessly winding trail, with an infinite number of bends, branching off into many bypaths and bordered by ruined cottages, while down the road from time to time came one band after another of fugitives.

OUTRAGEOUS PALIMPSESTS

On every hand, after leaving "Contendas," on every white wall of every more presentable dwelling that made its appearance among the mud huts, the Marshal's party encountered a scrawled page of infernal protests.[9] Every wounded man on passing by had left there, daubed with lumps of coal, a reflection of his own bitterness of heart. They had all expressed themselves with the utmost license, taking refuge in a common anonymity. The army had here flattened its mailed fist to trace in enormous characters the plot of the drama. The result was a photographically exact reproduction of the outward aspect of the formidable conflict; that was the true significance of these monumental inscriptions with their crude handwriting, so glaringly expressive of their authors' feelings. Without any concern for form, with no deceptive fantasies, these rude chroniclers had left here, indelibly recorded, a concise but true account of the major scandal in our history. They had done it brutally, fiercely, in the form of incredible lampoons and pasquinades intermingled with the most revolting pornography and deep cries of despair, but without a sentence or a phrase anywhere that was worthy of a man. The dark wave of rancor rolling down the highway had covered the outer walls and then had entered the houses, daubing the inner walls all the way to the roof.

Upon going inside, the Marshal's party were repelled by the mute chorus of insults and profanity. Halting verses and equally halting rhymes gave voice to unbelievable obscenities accompanied by frightful drawings; it was as if the imprecations were being hurled back from the four corners of the room, with the turbulent letters on the wall doing a fantastic dance, the rigid exclamation points coming down violently, like the thrusts of a sword.[10] *Viva* this! and *Viva* that! Death to this! and Death to that! leaped from every side, coupling and defaming the most illustrious names,

9 See pp. 404-5.   10 See p. 405.

without rhyme or reason. Ferocious puns, bold and insulting allusions, the dismal humor of the barracks.

The undertaking, of a sudden, lost its heroic aspect; it was no longer a noble and a brilliant enterprise. Future historians will endeavor in vain to veil its true character with glowing descriptions; but, for every page they write, there will remain those outrageous and indestructible palimpsests.

IN MONTE SANTO

By the time they reached Monte Santo, the new troops felt little martial ardor. They were dejected. Their spirits were revived, however, as they entered the village which constituted the base of operations.

Within a few days' time Monte Santo had shed the shrunken, stagnant appearance that is common to backlands settlements where for a hundred years and more not a house has gone up. It was now a vastly larger place. The surrounding plains were white with tents, two thousand of them, forming a new quarter and one larger than the town itself in normal times, with long avenues which were plainly to be seen, the level-lying ground presenting no obstruction to the view. There were six groups of these tents, and, over them all, banners were floating in the breeze, and from them all, at almost every moment, came the vibrant, metallic notes of bugles and the beat of drums.

The town was now crowded with a multitude of new inhabitants from foreign parts, filling the square and overflowing down the narrow lanes, a heterogeneous assortment of men from all walks of life. There were officers of every rank and from all branches of the service; wagon-drivers, dust-begrimed from long journeys; soldiers bending under the weight of their equipment; the wounded and convalescent, limping along; women in tattered garments; busy tradesmen; groups of merry students; journalists eager for news, who went about asking questions incessantly—all this gave to the scene the appearance of a city *praça* on the day of a parade. Marshal Bittencourt at once put the town under strict martial law and lost no time in adopting such measures as accorded with the complex needs of the situation. The military hospital now became a reality, thoroughly well equipped and under the charge of skilled surgeons, aided by a number of students from the Faculty of Baía who had volunteered their services. A proper discipline was everywhere established; and, at last, the question which had originally brought the minister there—that of the transport service—was definitely settled. Almost daily, partial supply trains were leaving for and returning from Canudos.

The results of these efforts were immediately visible. They were apparent in the news coming from the battlefront, where everything pointed to a new spirit on the part of the besiegers, who were now engaging in decisive tactical maneuvers.

If this was so, it was owing to one individual, an individual seemingly so incapable of any enthusiasm, who even at the base of operations declined to lay aside his bourgeois' alpaca coat, clad in which he reviewed the brigades. It was due to the fact that this man, thanks to the high degree of devotion that he displayed—and this is said without any desire to offend the sensibilities of those who were engaging the enemy at close range—had made himself, in reality, the supreme commander in this conflict. At a distance of forty miles from the front, he was in fact directing that conflict, without any boasting, without any weighing and balancing of strategic plans, but by spending his days in the rude company of pack-drivers at Monte Santo; he could frequently be seen, amid a throng of them, rising to his feet impatiently, watch in hand, as he gave the signal for departure.

For each supply train that was sent was worth battalions. It was a battle won. It gave the fighting men fresh hope of victory and little by little was doing away with that stagnation which had paralyzed our siege lines. This was what one gathered from the latest reports.

IN CANUDOS

The month of September, the truth is, began auspiciously enough. Early in the month—on the fourth, to be exact—one of the jagunços' leading chieftains had been killed by a rifle bullet. He fell near the churches, and the haste with which the inhabitants of the settlement threw themselves on his corpse, to take it away, showed that he was a person of importance. On the sixth there was an event of greater significance, when, one after the other, the towers of the new church crashed to the ground. This happened after six consecutive hours of bombardment, and was entirely unexpected, being attributable to an unpleasant circumstance which had arisen. In dispatching munitions to the front, someone had made a mistake and, in place of grenades, had sent plain cannon balls for the Krupps, which were little suited for the purpose in hand, and it was accordingly decided to use them up by firing on the churches.

The surprising result was commemorated in a couple of enthusiastic orders of the day. The army at last had been freed of those high battlements from which the besieged had fired upon it with so deadly an effect; for the two towers had commanded our entire lines, reducing the effectiveness of our trenches. Ever since the eighteenth of July they had been manned by expert marksmen whose sharp eyes let nothing escape them, so that no one dared so much as show his face from behind the shelter of the huts. When the supply trains arrived, they had been greeted with a violent fusillade from the church towers, just as they reached the last lap of their journey and were crossing the river, before entering the gully which formed a covered passageway. It was from there that the newcomers, the auxiliary brigade, the São Paulo Battalion, and the Thirty-seventh Infantry, as we have seen, received the enemy's first savage salute.

ENTHUSIASTIC JEERS

And now, at last, those towers had fallen. It was an impressive sight to see them tumble, one after the other, carrying away with them large sections of the wall in the form of huge blocks and burying the bold sharpshooters in the ruins; the stones fell with a great crash into the village square, amid a cloud of pulverized mortar, as our entire army ceased firing and rent the air with triumphant cries. The commander of the First Column well described it in his order of the day: ". . . . our advance line and the supporting troops in the camp behind, on this occasion, breaking out with enthusiastic jeers directed at the jagunço rabble."[11]

That is a good description of the campaign itself. From beginning to end, one saddening hue and cry. "Enthusiastic jeers. . . . ."

However that may be, the enemy's spell was broken now. The enormous settlement had of a sudden shrunken in size. It seemed smaller and more squat than ever, appeared to be huddled more deeply than ever in the depression in which it was built, being deprived of those two tall and slender white towers which had been a landmark for herdsmen for miles around, and which, reaching up to the blue and mysteriously dissolving in

[11] "Headquarters of the Commander, First Column, Canudos, sixth of September, 1897, Order of the Day No. 13.

"For the information of the forces under my command, I publish the following:

"Having ordered the commanding officers of the artillery today to bombard the towers of the new church, the points from which the enemy had directed his most effective fire upon us, causing us many losses in killed and wounded and obstructing our own line of fire, I had the satisfaction, after six consecutive hours, of seeing those towers fall. This was due to the excellent aim of the battery directed by Second Lieutenants Manoel Felix de Menezes and Fructuoso Mendes and Sublieutenant H. Duque Estrada Macedo Soares, the first mentioned being on the sick list at the time. I desire especially to give credit to these brave officers who once more have shown their skill in directing the cannon under their command, and particularly Second Lieutenant Manoel Felix, who, though on the sick list, fulfilled his duties faithfully. I was gratified with the effect that all this produced on the army as a whole, which observed with great interest the result of the artillery's fire, our advance line and the supporting troops in the camp behind, on this occasion, breaking out with enthusiastic jeers directed at the jagunço rabble. The officer in question was the first to begin the bombardment and the last to fire on the tower to the right, Sublieutenant Duque Estrada being the last to fire on the one to the left, completing its demolition," etc.

it, or gleaming brightly on starlit nights, served to objectify the rude and credulous sertanejo's ingenuous mysticism, bringing nearer to the heavens his propitiatory prayers.

THE "SEVENTH OF SEPTEMBER TRENCH"

This event was an ill-omened one for the jagunços. The following day they suffered a major disaster. Intrenched for long at the "Old Ranch House," several dozen sertanejo warriors had been defying Colonel Olympio's cannon mounted on the rim of Mount Favella. Only a few paces from the artillery and the supporting contingents, the enemy had for more than two months prevented the expansion of our siege lines in this direction, in spite of the storm of bullets poured upon them in a direct line of fire. In a dominant situation as they were, above the bulk of our forces which were stationed on the edge of the village, they were able to sweep our thinning ranks, a fact which contributed greatly to the daily losses that we suffered. In brief, this position rivaled the church towers when it came to uncovering our most carefully planted breastworks and shelters. On September 7, however, at ten o'clock at night, the enemy was suddenly routed from it. Encouraged by the successes of the day before, and in obedience to an order from the commander of the First Column, Colonel Olympio descended the mountain with a force consisting of the Twenty-seventh under command of Captain Tito Escobar, a contingent of the Fourth Battery of the Second Regiment, another of the Fifth Regiment, and one machine gun. In the front and at the rear were former students of the military schools. The rest of his forces, Colonel Olympio deployed as sharpshooters along both flanks. Stealing silently down the slopes, this detachment fell like an avalanche upon the hill below. Taken by surprise, bowled over by the shock of three hundred bayonets charging from either side, with the machine gun in the middle firing at them point-blank, the jagunços were able to put up little resistance and were quickly dislodged from the stone trenches which they had constructed there, round about the ruins of the "Old Ranch House." The engagement lasted five minutes. Driven back and scattered, the fugitives were pursued by the vanguard all the way to "Bald Pates' Hill," where they plunged into the river bed down below and made their way across it, until they were lost from sight in Canudos. Our troops had suffered only two casualties.

Having captured this position, which occupied a broad stairstep on the slope of the hill between Mount Mario,[12] which had previously been occupied, and the Vasa-Barris, Colonel Olympio proceeded to pitch his tent

[12] [See p. 256 and n. 25; see also pp. 266, 271, 305, 309, 310.]

on the spot where, six months before, the leader of the third expedition had died. All the rest of the night was spent in building a strong redoubt, about a yard in height, out of stones taken from the enemy's trenches, along the entire outer edge of the terrace. The next day the "Seventh of September Trench" overlooked the settlement. The periphery of the siege had been increased by some fifteen hundred yards to the left, in a southerly direction, entirely cutting off the two eastern quadrants. On the afternoon of the same day it was expanded still farther, with a bend to the west, all the way down to the point where the Cambaio Road begins, near the confluence of the Mucuim, embracing the whole of the western sector.

THE CALUMBY ROAD

In the meantime a more serious military movement was being undertaken, the one truly strategic action of the campaign, it may be. It was conceived, planned, and carried out by Lieutenant Colonel Siqueira de Menezes. Relying upon information gathered from certain loyal vaqueiros, that officer had come to realize the advantages of another supply route, the Calumby Road,[13] one about which little was known. Running through the country that lay between the Rosario and Cambaio highways, in an almost straight line due north and south, it was shorter than either of those roads and made possible a rapid and easy communication with Monte Santo. He proposed to explore the route in question, although to do so involved the greatest risks.

The undertaking was carried out in three days' time. The lieutenant colonel left Canudos on the fourth day of September, at the head of 1,500 men, comprising the combined Twenty-second, Ninth, and Thirty-fourth battalions under the immediate command of Major Lydio Porto. The newly discovered road was duly traversed, the detachment returning on the seventh by way of the Cambaio trail, in a bold, swift movement the results of which were extraordinarily fortunate for the outcome of the war.

It was true enough, the new path, which was open to the transportation of troops and supplies and closed to the jagunços, whose favorite trail it had been in the past, in their excursions to the south, reduced the distance to Monte Santo by more than a day. Of all the roads, it was the one best adapted to resist invasion. Like the Rosario Highway, it forked off from "Joá," running to the left of that road in a due northerly direction. For many miles it skirted the interminably winding Caraíbas River, cutting across it at times, but keeping on always in the same direction, bordered

[13] See pp. 295–96.

here and there by small farms, until it came to another seasonal stream, the Caxomongó. From there on it became a highway of incomparable importance from the strategic point of view.

Running southeast were the Calumby Highlands, which for a considerable stretch bordered the road to the right, at a distance of three hundred yards. An army coming down the road would thus have to expose its flank to the enemy intrenched on the slopes. And, having passed this extremely dangerous point, it would find itself in an even more perilous situation; for, after climbing an extensive elevation, the road suddenly enters a short, narrow defile that is completely hidden from view by the tangled boughs of umburanas stalks which grow in the vicinity. Here was to be found a natural breastwork of siliceous marble only a little above the ground in height, a sort of rude countermure with a narrow, wicket-like fracture in the center. There were no trenches here. They could be dispensed with. Rifles leveled over the top of this rampart would be able to sweep the enemy's columns as they came along. And in case the enemy succeeded in going any farther, which was to presuppose a bit of rare good luck in the face of an adversary so well sheltered and raining bullets upon him, he would then to his surprise, after the first few steps he had taken, find himself trapped in a terrain that was all but impassable.

By a geological circumstance common enough in the northern backlands, the land continues to be as rugged as before, presenting the same sort of impediments. Thus, immediately beyond the defile, it slopes down to the "Varzea" farm, affording what is apparently an easy passage, but one which is in reality extremely difficult for troops under fire. A broad layer of limestone is spread out here in a notable state of atmospheric decomposition. Riddled with innumerable cavities separated from one another by sharp and lacerating edges, scarred with deep furrows and long, rigid chips that resemble knife blades, bristling with sharp-pointed spurs, its surface abruptly broken by wide burnished "cauldrons"—in short, as rugged as can be, at every point—the terrain here offers impressive evidence of the effects of energetic climatic agents which have been at work on it for centuries. Following prolonged periods of drought, tempestuous acid-like rains have corroded, perforated, and undermined it, and its turbulent, wasted appearance is but a reflection of the storms that have beaten upon it.

Treading this jagged terrain, the strongest-made boots would be ripped to shreds as their wearers unavoidably stumbled and fell in a highly dangerous manner. To give battle here was out of the question, where even peaceful travelers could only go forward, one at a time, along a side trail

that led to "Varzea" down below—a broad basin strewn with flint fragments and surrounded by dense caatingas. The consequence was that,
upon reaching this point, the invaders would be subjected to fire from all
sides. And, even assuming that they did succeed in advancing, after they
had gone a thousand yards beyond they would face an inevitable annihilation; for there the road disappears, dropping down into the deep and winding bed of the Sargento River, along the banks of which are to be seen the
large, gleaming, dark-blue folds of a superimposed talc-schist formation,
streaked with white quartz veins; in certain places these layers run hori-
zontally, from one bank to the other, almost, so that one has the feeling of
passing through an enormous ruined aqueduct, with the crumbling remains of its ancient vault still showing here and there. This extensive
ditch takes the place of the road for a distance of a mile. Like the others in
the neighborhood, it is not a river but a drain, filled from time to time with
floodwaters which here find a channel to the Vasa-Barris. Dotting the
banks on either side were to be seen the jagunços' trenches, a short distance apart, affording either a direct or slantwise cross-fire on the river-bed
road at every bend that it made.

The one thousand men of the Arthur Oscar column would never have
succeeded in effecting a passage here. They had taken the Rosario Road,
and that had been their salvation, while the expeditions that preceded
them had marched, in turn, by way of the Uauá, Cambaio, and Massacará trails, always varying the route chosen, which had led the sertanejos
to believe that this last expedition, following the usual practice, would
come by the Calumby path. Had it done so, not a soldier would have
reached Canudos,[14] and the result would have been a major disaster to
add to the defeats already experienced in this campaign; for our troops
would have gone along as chance guided them, in complete ignorance of
the formidable terrain and the grave difficulties that awaited them.

Now, however, the jagunços had abandoned these positions and had
withdrawn into the settlement. This movement, accordingly, on the part
of Lieutenant Colonel Siqueira de Menezes was an admirably conceived
and advantageous one. Having manned the principal points along the
way as far as "Joá," he then took the Calumby Road, which was lined
with empty trenches. Leaving a wing of the Twenty-second to occupy
these trenches, he went on to Lake Cipó,[15] where whitening bones served
as a reminder of the slaughter inflicted on the Febronio expedition. Here
he surprised a number of enemy scouts and captured from them thirteen

14 See p. 296.   15 See pp. 216, 218.

pack animals. From there he proceeded to the confluence of the Mucuim, where he took by surprise two enemy trenches that were still there.

The line of siege was widening. A quick and safe route had been opened for the mobilization of our forces. The main portion of this road, from the Sargento River to the "Sussuarana" farm, passing by way of "Varzea" and "Caxomongó," was now garrisoned by the Thirty-third, Sixteenth, and Twenty-eighth battalions of the Second Brigade and a wing of the São Paulo Battalion. Canudos was invested by a huge semicircle, extending from the extreme north to the "Old Ranch House" on the south, and from there eastward to the head of the Cambaio Road. There remained open to the jagunços, on the northeast sector, only the Uauá and Varzea da Ema trails. The nearing end of the campaign was to be foreseen.

II

MARCH OF THE AUXILIARY DIVISION

The new expeditionaries, coming along the recently opened road from Monte Santo, were possessed of a most unusual kind of fear: the haunting, besetting fear that they would not find a single jagunço left with whom to fight. They were certain they would find that everything had been settled, and they felt scandalously cheated by the course of events.

The first detachment to leave, on the thirteenth of September, was the brigade of northern police corps. This was due wholly to reasons of an administrative nature, but it rankled in the minds of those who composed the brigade of the line, which was to follow a few days later, under General Carlos Eugenio.

VAINGLORIOUS FEAR

So many of the rebels were falling every day, they had met with so many reverses, having been driven back from their best positions, and were so entangled in the meshes of the encircling siege lines that every passing hour appeared to these laggard heroes to diminish the probability of their being able to share in the victory celebration.[16] For this reason the northeast brigade advanced at a dizzying pace, stumbling over the roads from early dawn and only halting when the burning rays of the sun made it necessary for the exhausted soldiers to take a rest. The brigade of the line followed closely at the same swift pace, marching light of baggage and spurred on by the same foolish longing to measure its strength with the weakened enemy, if only in a skirmish. And so they strode on boldly—gal-

16 See p. 422.

lant, well fed, able-bodied—making all possible haste to the mud-hut citadel which for three months past had been swept by cannon fire, battered
by assaults, devastated by conflagrations, and which all the while was defended by a handful of men.

Upon reaching "Sussuarana" farm, fifteen miles from Canudos, they recovered their spirits, for they could now hear the dully echoing rumble of
the artillery; and in Caxomongó, when the wind was right, they could
even make out the steady crack of rifle fire.

CAXOMONGÓ

Amid all this warlike zeal there were certain unlooked-for incidents that
gave the men a start. The backlands conflict had not completely lost that
mysterious aspect which it was to preserve until the end. As they penetrated ever deeper and deeper into the hinterland, that region of great
barren highlands, as they passed the desolate little farms and the farmhouses in ruins—all in the open desert—the gluttonous warriors so eager
for battle could not repress a shudder of dread. I myself was the witness
of this on one occasion.

Colonel Sotero's brigade had arrived on the third day of its march, the
fifteenth of September, at the farm known as "Caxomongó," on the edge
of the danger zone. Anyone coming to this place from "Boa Esperança"
crosses an unencumbered plain bordered by picturesque highlands; or,
should he come by way of the "Sussuarana" ranch, he will follow the border of an ipueira well filled with water; but, once he arrives, he finds himself in the midst of a sterile and depressing landscape. The terrain is of
rough sandstone, vermilion in hue, its strata inclined at an exaggerated
angle of forty-five degrees. This it is that accounts for the rapid absorption of the rains that fall here, which gives to the tract the harsh imprint
of the caatinga. The farmhouse, a wretched one, stands on the bank of
the river, which is nothing more than a trench with perpendicular walls
three yards high; completely clogged with rocks of every size and shape
and wholly dry, the "river" disappears among the hills stripped bare of
foliage.

The troops arrived here at mid-morning. There were the two corps
from Pará, as well disciplined as the best of the line, and the one from
Amazonas; and all were clad in the characteristic uniform which had been
adopted from the time they left Baía, both officers and men wearing big
hats of carnaúba straw with turned-down brims, which gave them the appearance of a large band of woodsmen. Despite the early-morning hour,
they pitched camp; for they had found sufficient water in a neighboring

pit that was deep and dark as the mouth of a mine. This was their last halt. The next day they would be at the settlement. The lifeless landscape now took on a sudden animation, being filled with tents, stacked arms, and the noisy stir and bustle of 968 fighting men. Along the banks of the river tall ingaranas[17] grew, their boughs, still in leaf, intertwining above the bed of the stream. Dozens of swaying hammocks were strung up between the flexible branches, and the men took their ease. The day was calm and peaceful. There was nothing to fear.

Then night fell, and the silence of the night was broken by the dull and measured roll of distant thunder to the north, a thunder that came from the cannon of Canudos.

But the enemy, held tight within the siege lines, would surely have no heart left for adventurous sallies along the roadways. The night, like the day, would be without incident. And, even supposing the jagunços did put in an appearance, they would find an adversary waiting and eager to receive them.

FALSE ALARM

All was quiet as the troops quickly dropped off to sleep—only to be awakened with a start, at 10:00 P.M., every man of them. A shot had been fired on their left flank. One of the soldiers standing guard on the sentry line which had been thrown about the camp had seen, or fancied he had seen, a suspicious-looking figure slipping away in the darkness, and he had promptly discharged his rifle. This, surely, was the enemy they had been longing to meet. As in the case of previous expeditions, he had stolen upon them for a swift, sudden, bold attack.

Then it was that those who had been so eager to measure their strength with the foe had a mysterious, hallucinatory glimpse of what this campaign was really like. They now had a chance to see for themselves, at close range. An indescribable hypnotic fear thereupon laid hold of the battalions, and blaring bugles, cries of alarm, shouts of command, were to be heard on every hand. There was much anxious running about, as startled officers leaped from their hammocks into the river bed below and dashed up the banks in great disorder, bumping into one another, slipping and falling. With swords unsheathed and revolvers drawn, they rushed headlong down the ranks, as the men with a great clatter of bayonets adjusted their weapons and took their place in line. The scene was bedlam itself, with companies and platoons hurriedly and haphazardly forming into squares, as if expecting a cavalry charge—whole detachments with fixed

[17] [The ingarana is the *Pithecellobium racemiflorum* Ducke.]

bayonets, ready to countercharge a vacuum. And among all the companies, platoons, and detachments, lone individuals and small groups running about wildly here and there, trying to find their place in the confused
formation.

For a number of minutes these fighting men were gripped by an emotion they had never thought to experience, as they waited for the enemy's
attack. The brigade now took on the appearance of a long, flashing, turbulent ship's wake, on the bright and tranquil wave of moonlight in which
the whole of the quietly sleeping landscape lay submerged. But it was a
false alarm.

HALF-RATIONS OF GLORY

The next morning their fears were gone, and they were once more the
impatient heroes of old. Marching rapidly and with no further qualms,
they made their way down the trench that is known as the Sargento
River, which now of a sudden overflowed with uniforms. Then they
climbed the barren hill whose slopes on the opposite side descend abruptly
into the Umburanas Valley. There, they were surprised to see, directly
ahead of them and down below, a mile and a quarter away—the village
of Canudos.

This was a relief. There were the two ruined churches, facing each
other across that legendary square—the new church, its towers gone, its
main walls crumbled, split from top to bottom, a veritable rubbish heap;
the old one, likewise ruined and blackened, its façade missing, but a bit of
the shattered belfry still standing, the belfry where that fantastic sexton
so many times had summoned the faithful to prayers and to the battle.
Round about was the compact mass of huts. They were in time; they were
not to be deprived, after all, of those half-rations of glory about which they
were so concerned. And so they made their triumphal entrance into camp,
with the mien of those who are destined to go down in history but who in
reality had come there in search of a bloody but an easy victory.[18]

APPEARANCE OF THE CAMP

The appearance of the camp had changed; it no longer presented the
turbulent aspect of former days. It now was like another village alongside
Canudos. Crossing the dry bed of the Vasa-Barris, the newcomers made
their way through a winding gully. Halfway down this gully, in a wide
concavity to the right, was a huge leather-covered shed, the field hospital;
and, a short distance farther on, they came to the tent of the commander-
in-chief.

[18] See pp. 419–20.

Meanwhile, they had the impression of being in a newly built town. Scattered over the slopes on either side of the road or clustered in tiny valleys, their colors standing out against the grayish hue of the tents, were numerous houses of a novel kind and with a festive air, being wholly constructed of foliage, the roofs and walls green with the boughs of the joaz tree. These dwellings appeared to be singularly inappropriate to those who inhabited them, but they were as a matter of fact the only ones suitable to this region. It was the burning heat, transforming the tents into flaming furnaces, which had inspired this primitive, bucolic architecture.

There was nothing at first glance to reveal the presence of an army. This was more like one of those dubious backlands villages; and the illusion was completed by the "first settlers"—unprepossessing individuals in peasant garb, trailing swords and shouldering rifles, most of them wearing tasseled leather hats, and without shoes or with sandals on their feet; while elsewhere were to be seen tattered women tranquilly sewing in the doorways or going along laden with bundles of firewood. A stranger well might believe that he had lost his way and had strayed here by mistake into the midst of a jagunço settlement—until he had reached the commanding officer's tent farther on. Upon climbing the hillock at the foot of which the general headquarters stood, he would find on the top the engineering commission, housed in a native hut which had not been destroyed; and, by putting his eye to the chinks in the wall—a wall thickened by blocks of stone—he would have a close-up view of the church square a hundred yards away. He was now on the slope at the bottom of which were the stockades along the most dangerous portion of the front, where the Twenty-fifth Battalion was holding the center; this was the "black line," the point at which our forces had penetrated most deeply into the outskirts of the settlement in the assault of the eighteenth of July. Turning to the left, beneath the barrier formed by the discontinuous line of huts that are scattered along there, after going a few paces he would come to First Column headquarters. Descending the southern slope along a winding ledge, he would find, halfway down, a small hut housing the headquarters of the Second Column. This would bring him to the Quartermaster General's tent, with the São Paulo Battalion camped down below, on a sandy plain which in flood season is inundated by the waters of the Vasa-Barris. Continuing on his way, after having crossed the bed of the Vasa-Barris under shelter of the stone breastworks, which ran from one bank to the other and were manned by the Twenty-sixth, he would reach the outermost trench of the siege lines, held by the Fifth of Baía, stationed in a deep gutter formed by the Providencia River. Two hundred yards farther on to the left, high above, on the bulge of the hill near the "Old Ranch House," creating the impression of a hanging bastion, was the Seventh of September Trench.

By thus making the circuit of the intrenchments, the new expeditionaries were able to obtain a clear view of the situation, and, as a result of their inspection, they found some of their former optimism slipping from them. This sector of the siege line was still a small one compared to the size of the settlement, which to them was cause for astonishment. Accustomed as they were to the tiny, dwarfed appearance of backland cities, they were amazed by this Babylon of huts sprawling over the hills.

CANUDOS

Canudos at this time contained—they were later counted, one by one—5,200 dwellings;[19] and, inasmuch as these huts with their vermilion-colored clay roofs were not readily distinguishable from one another, even at those points where they were not huddled together, they came to take on a disproportionate size to one whose gaze had first grown used to the heap of ruins about the square. Seen in perspective, they created a striking impression, which added to the mysterious atmosphere of the place. It was hard to realize that there were so many human lives down there. The closest observation, when a lull in the battle permitted, failed to reveal a single countenance, a fugitive glimpse of a single individual, and there was not to be heard the slightest sound of any kind whatsoever. It was like an ancient necropolis—or, again, with all that jumble of roofs and crumbling walls, an enormous buried-under cata, eaten away with erosions, its surface scarred with pits and caverns.

However, let not the observer show too much of himself above the parapet, or a sudden shower of bullets would quickly enough reveal to him the presence of the population burrowing in those ruins. Let but a single shot be fired, at any hour, over the top of that hill, and there would come the inevitable and prompt reply; for, if the jagunços no longer held the initiative in the matter of attacks, they still responded with all their old-time vigor. The siege might be slowly wearing them out, but they had lost none of their aplomb and made it a point of honor to conceal any signs of weakening. Meanwhile, it was plain that things with them were in a very bad way indeed. This was evident from the ruins beneath which they now had to burrow for safety. The settlement no longer had its garrison of incorrigible "bad men." The population was largely made up of women and children, who for three whole months had been put to the

[19] See p. 475.

ordeal of fire and sword; and many times, above the roar of battle, there would come the sound of piteous wails. Some days before, a shrapnel fired from Mount Favella, after skimming the cornices of the new church, had fallen among the huts near the arbor where prayer services were held. Instantly, there came a heart-rending response, which disturbed even Colonel Olympio's artillerymen, in the form of a prolonged and indescribable chorus of lamentations, a mournful melody of anguish-laden cries, which led that officer, deeply moved, to issue a stern command; whereupon the cannon fell silent.

Thus, doubly blockaded, between the thousands of soldiers, on the one hand, and the thousands of women, on the other hand—between lamentations and warlike shouts, between tears and bullets—the rebels were, from one moment to another, losing ground. That was inevitable. The assurance of victory now spurred our men on to acts of daring. A sergeant of the Fifth Artillery twice ventured to cross the entire square at night, making his way into the ruined house of worship and bringing back a couple of dynamite bombs which had not exploded. A sublieutenant of the Twenty-fifth, some days afterward, rivaled this exploit by setting fire to what remained of the old church, all of which now went up in flames.

The troops which had recently come up to take part in this unequal conflict were aware of these things, and they consequently began to worry once more, fearing that the enemy, being thus *in extremis*, would not have enough fight left in him to enable them to display their own strength and valor. The new iron-clad brigades were fairly panting to put down the insurrection in this, its last convulsive stage. Those who had been there all these months had had more than their share of glory. They were fed up with triumphs, and, now that their subsistence was assured, thanks to the daily supply trains, they deemed it useless to waste any more lives in an effort to hasten the enemy's inevitable surrender. They accordingly remained irritatingly indifferent.

In the intervals between attacks, which were growing longer now, the camp took on the appearance of a well-policed small town. There was nothing about it to suggest the ferocious campaign that was being waged. At the quarters of the engineering commission, General Arthur Oscar, whose free and easy disposition lent an irresistible charm to his company, would hold forth at length on various subjects that had nothing whatsoever to do with the war—pleasing memories of bygone days, hilarious anecdotes, or weighty discussions on political topics. Meanwhile, faithful observers, with a praiseworthy devotion to science, would be taking hourly temperature readings and barometric pressures, invariably putting down a zero for the nebulosity of the heavens as they consulted their hygrometers with faces that were extremely grave. In the military pharmacy students on forced vacations would be laughing noisily and reciting verses; while through the thin walls of all those charming bowers, their foliage spangled with withered joaz blooms, would come the voices and the laughter of those within, who had no fears to disturb their light and carefree hours. The rare bullets that passed high overhead, bounding off the crests of the hillocks, were a cause for no concern. No one paid any attention to them any more. The rhythmic precision with which they cracked or whistled through the air indicated that they were fired by certain sharpshooters in Canudos who had been stationed there to prevent the besiegers from forgetting that the sertanejo was still keeping watch on them. They made no impression, however, even though some of them, lower than the others, would beat against the canvas of the large officers' tents. The same was true of the heavy fusillades, which still broke out occasionally, during the night, when our men were least expecting them.

Life, in short, was becoming abnormally normal, taking on at the same time certain extravagant aspects. The soldiers of the "black line," in the trench farthest forward, would sometimes, in the early hours of the morning, strike up a conversation with the jagunços. The interlocutor on our side would go up to the edge of the trench, and facing the village square, would call out some name, the first that he happened to think of, in a friendly, honest tone of voice, as if he were calling to some old comrade; and invariably, from the mass of huts, or nearer at hand, from the ruins of the churches, there would come a response, with the same homely, slightly ironic twang. A most unusual conversation would then be carried on in the darkness, the two speakers exchanging information on all kinds of subjects, baptismal names, places of birth, their families, living conditions, and the like. Not infrequently, this strange chat would take the form of obscene jokes, and there would be a burst of smothered laughter from the nearest lines. This dialogue would keep up until a divergence of opinion occurred, and then, of a sudden, from side to side, there would be half-a-dozen harsh insults couched in a forceful argot and, after that, a period in the form of a bullet.

The men of the Fifth Police, despite the fact that their earthen breastworks afforded them only an illusory protection, would kill time with serenades (*descantes*),[20] expressive of their longings for the banks of the

---

[20] [The *descantes*, *trovas*, and *tiranas* are old song-poem forms prominent in the folklore of the backlands. The *descantes* were in quatrains and were sung by the boatmen of the São Francisco, the vaqueiros of the Northeast, plantation workers, etc. (see Luis da Camara Cascudo, *Vaqueiros e cantadores* [Porto Alegre: Livraria do Globo, 1939], p. 125).]

São Francisco. If they were interrupted by a fusillade from the enemy, they would boldly dash up to the firing line, discharging their rifles and fighting like demons, terribly, frantically, the rhymes of their favorite *trovas*[21] still on their lips, timed now to the cadence of bullets. Some of them would drop, singing as they fell; and, after the skirmish was over, the others would return to their backlands diversion, languorously intoning their *tiranas*[22] and strumming their banjos, as if all this were one big ranch, with merry pack-drivers taking their noonday ease.

THE CHARLATANISM OF COURAGE

Everyone, the short of it is, was adapting himself to the situation. The daily spectacle of death had bred a disregard for life. Toward the end the veterans would go from one end of the camp to the other, from the extreme right to the extreme left, without taking even the most elementary precautions. As they came out on top of an exposed hillock, they would scarcely quicken their steps as the bullets flayed the earth all around them. They would laugh at those inexperienced newcomers who, in passing points that were under fire, became thoroughly frightened; to see them running, dodging, ducking down, all but squatting, was a terribly comic sight. These novices were unable to refrain from giving a start as a bullet flashed by with a low hissing sound, the insidiously wheedling note of death itself; nor could they restrain themselves from showing their feelings over the most trivial incidents—such as the three or four dying men who were daily carried back from the front lines.

Some of them were merely displaying the charlatanism of courage, a sorry kind of snobbery. Clad in their uniforms, their stripes and buttons glistening in the sun, they would remain in some open place freely swept by the enemy's fire or would stand upright on the top of some unprotected hillock a mile or so from the settlement, by way of estimating the jagunços' maximum firing range. The truth is, this conflict had made them callous. They would tell their new comrades of all the hardships they had endured, taking care to stress the dramatic aspect of things. They would relate the somber episode of Mount Favella with its train of battles and all that they had suffered there, the long days of privation shared by officers and men alike—there was, for example, the case of that sublieutenant who had died when he broke his fast by gorging himself with great handfuls of flour, after having had nothing to eat for three whole days. Then

[21] [A form that stems from the love songs of the medieval troubadours of the Iberian Peninsula.]

[22] [Melancholy love songs, slow in movement, on the theme of love's *tyranny*.]

there was all the trouble they had had chasing wild goats and picking shriveled fruit from the dead shrubs. They narrated all that had happened, in all the minute details. And they concluded by observing that there was very little left to be done; in this war, the grain had been harvested and all that remained was to sweep up the chaff; the enemy, contemptible creature, was very weak; you could hear the death rattle in his throat. All that was happening now was merely a noisy pastime, nothing more.

The men of the Auxiliary Division, however, were not so easily reconciled to the secondary role thus assigned them. Was it for this that they had covered those seventy-five miles of backland territory—merely to look on, as an inoffensive spectator, even though one armed from head to foot, as the rebel settlement little by little succumbed to the slow process of strangulation, without the feverish convulsions of a battle?

III

EMBASSY TO HEAVEN

The blockade of the settlement was, however, incomplete, with an extensive outlet still remaining on the north; and, as a consequence, the enemy was not yet down to his last resources. The Varzea da Ema and Uauá trails were still open, branching out into many bypaths over the plains beyond, in the direction of the broad basin of the São Francisco, passing through a number of obscure little places until they finally reached the insignificant hamlets along the banks of that river, between Chorrochó and Santo-Antonio da Gloria. By these routes the jagunços were able to procure a small amount of supplies, while fresh reinforcements found no obstacle confronting them on their way to Canudos. For, as it happened, these roads ran in what was precisely the most favorable direction, across a huge tract of territory where the backland regions of six states, from Baía to Piauí, meet and overlap. For this reason they provided the best exit that the sertanejos could desire, leading as they did to the very womb where all the elements of the revolt had been generated. If worst came to worst, they represented escape and salvation; the population fleeing along these trails could hardly be pursued for at least the first few miles. The desert—vast and impervious—would give them shelter.

But they were not fleeing, even though they realized that the forces of their adversary were growing in strength, while they themselves were becoming weaker. Their leading fighters were gone now: Pajehú,[23] who fell

---

[23] See pp. 158, 220–21, 301, etc.

in the last battles of the month of July; João Abbade,[24] who died in August; the crafty Macambira,[25] slain but recently; José Venancio;[26] and others. The principal ones left were "Big Peter,"[27] the terrible defender of Cocorobó, and Joaquim Norberto,[28] who was elevated to a post of command for the simple reason that there was no better man available. In addition, there was a scarcity of provisions; and day by day the discrepancy between the number of able-bodied fighting men, which was constantly diminishing, and the number of the women and children, the crippled and infirm, which was steadily increasing, became more pronounced. This greatly hampered the movements of those who were capable of bearing arms and reduced their means of subsistence. True, these weaker members of the community might have made their escape by slipping away a few at a time, along the trails that were still open, leaving the others unencumbered and sparing themselves the supreme sacrifice. This, however, they did not care to do. Of their own volition the weak and disabled, conscious of their uselessness, had devoted themselves to an almost complete fast for the sake of their defenders, whom they would not now desert.

Life in the settlement, meanwhile, had become atrocious. This was shown by the misery, the complete dejection, the terrible state of emaciation of the six hundred prisoners taken. The inhabitants were spending indescribable days of anguish, with the last gateways to life and liberty still open to them. The fact would have remained forever inexplicable had not the source of this admirable stoicism been later revealed by those who had gone through it all. The story was a simple one.

On the twenty-second of August[29] Antonio Conselheiro had died. As he saw the churches fall, the sanctuary crushed, the saints shattered to bits, the candles scattered, the holy relics buried in the debris of the walls; above all—hallucinating vision!—as he suddenly caught sight of the Good Jesus, no longer on the high altar but lying, a sinister figure, on the ground, dismembered by a grenade—as he beheld all this, the Counselor was shaken by emotions too violent for his weakened frame to bear. From that moment he began to die. Refining upon his customary abstinence,

---

[24] See pp. 159, 218–19, 241–42, etc.   [26] See pp. 157–58.

[25] See pp. 158, 319, 342, 387.   [27] See p. 158.   [28] See p. 158.

[29] [The Brazilian editor has the following note: This date, given in the first edition and all subsequent ones, escaped the attention of the author in all his revisions. It is, nevertheless, incorrect. The reading should be "Twenty-second of September," as on p. 469. The Counselor's corpse was exhumed on the sixth of October, and the physician, João de Souza Pondé, who made an external examination of it at that time declared that "it could not have been dead for more than twelve days" (see Dantas Barreto, *Destruição de Canudos* [Baía, 1912], p. 295).]

he refused to touch a morsel of food. And one day they found him within the ruined temple, lying flat on his face, his forehead pressed to the earth, a silver crucifix at his bosom. His body was already cold and rigid in death when it was discovered that morning by "Pious Anthony."[30]

This event, an outstanding one in the history of the campaign, in place of bringing the conflict to an immediate end, as might have been expected, appeared, rather, to have given new life to the insurrection. It may have been due to the sharp wits of one of their leaders, who foresaw the disastrous consequences which might ensue; or, and this may well be believed, it may have arisen spontaneously as a result of mass suggestion, when the pious ones grew disturbed by the apostle's absence (although his public appearances in these latter days had been extremely few)—but, whatever its origin, an extraordinary bit of news was then divulged. The Counselor's vanquished followers gave the following ingenuous account of it:

Antonio Conselheiro had gone on a journey to heaven. When he saw his chief adjutants being killed and the number of soldiers increasing, he made up his mind to appeal directly to Providence. The fantastic ambassador was at this moment in God's presence. He had provided for everything. That was why it was our soldiers, even when they were in the greatest straits, were unable to leave these parts as they formerly had done. It was because they were weighted down in their trenches. It was necessary for them to remain here, on the scene of their crimes, and make the supreme expiation. For the prophet would soon return, with millions of archangels; with flaming swords gleaming aloft, this Olympian band would descend like a flight of heavenly birds, would fall upon the besiegers like a thunderbolt, and then the Day of Judgment would begin.

This was a weight off all their souls; and the true believers prepared for the final act of penance, the greatest of all, the one that was to be their salvation. And none of them noticed that, shortly afterward, under one pretext or another, a number of unbelievers, such as Villa Nova,[31] began abandoning the settlement for parts unknown. These latter were barely in time, the last to make their escape; for on September 24 the situation underwent a change.

THE SIEGE IS COMPLETED

On the morning of that day, while our left wing and the cannon of Favella began a heavy attack, by way of distracting the enemy's attention, Lieutenant Colonel Siqueira de Menezes set out on an expedition of his own, at the head of the Twenty-fourth, Thirty-eighth, and Thirty-sec-

[30] [See pp. 159–60, 468 ff., 475.]   [31] See pp. 159, 458.

ond battalions of the line, under the command of Major Henrique de Magalhães, Captain Affonso Pinto de Oliveira, and Lieutenant Joaquim Potengy; the Amazonas contingent; the right wing of the São Paulo detachment, commanded by Major José Pedro de Oliveira; and a cavalry contingent under command of Sublieutenant Pires de Almeida. These troops now made for the sector which had not as yet been brought within the line of siege, attacking on the way the small bands of jagunços to be found in the outlying houses scattered here and there on this side of the settlement.

This was something on which the enemy had not counted, the sector in question being diametrically opposite the "Old Ranch House" and the farthest distant from the original line of attack. A new suburb had grown up here, "Vermilion Heights" ("Casas Vermelhas"). It had been built following the defeat of the third expedition, and the dwellings looked more like ordinary houses, some of them having tiled roofs. They were not properly fortified, however, for they lacked those trench shelters which were so numerous at other points; and—a disastrous circumstance for the rebels in this emergency—being the most remote from the firing line, all of them were crammed with women and children.

Our troops with the Twenty-fourth in the van, marching along the river bed, fell upon and cleared these houses in a few minutes' time. As generally happens, they were held up in their advance by the terror-stricken womenfolk. The jagunços, indeed, did not at once yield their positions but fell back, fighting as they went, and, in following them, the soldiers became enmeshed in the narrow lanes.

Taking the offensive, the invaders proceeded to stage once more the same inevitable scenes. Forcing their rifle barrels through the mud walls, they fired at random inside, after which they knocked down the huts with the butts of their weapons and threw lighted matches on the kindling heap of miserable furniture and old rags. The fires thus started lighted the way for them as the sertanejo kept falling back in front of them to the nearest convenient hideout. Here and there, one or another of the enemy would put up a stupendous resistance, selling his life dearly. One of them, with his wife and daughter clinging to him, the moment the door was crashed in, threw them roughly from him and leaped to the threshold, where he felled the first assailant that he met with a terrible blow—a sublieutenant, Pedro Simões Pinto, of the Twenty-fourth. A moment later he himself lay stretched out, surrounded by soldiers with drawn swords; and, as he was dying, he let fall a mournful phrase: "At least I got one of them."

There was another who furnished our men some diversion. It was at once an amusing and a horrible episode. Lying in the corner of a room which they had invaded, without the strength even to sit up, was an aged curiboca, extremely emaciated and half-nude, covered only with a sheet. The old fellow was doing his best to fire an ancient fowling piece[32] but was unable even to lift it. Despairingly, he let it fall back in his flabby arms, while his bony face writhed in a grimace of impotent wrath. The soldiers had surrounded him in a moment and now burst into a noisy laugh.

Nevertheless, this desperate resistance, in which even the dying took part, was slowing their progress. Within a short time they had suffered thirteen casualties. Moreover, while the enemy was falling back, he was not fleeing. He remained only a couple of paces ahead of them, in the same house, in the next room, separated by only a few inches of mud wall. They were accordingly compelled to halt. In order not to lose what ground they had gained, they erected a barricade out of furniture and the ruins of the houses. This was the usual and obligatory practice. For in front of them was no neutral terrain. The jagunço was clinging—indomitably—to the opposite slope of the parapet, vigilant, trying out his aim.

TRAGIC STAGE-SETTING

The thunderous echoes of this engagement to the north of them were heard by the men in camp and created great excitement among them. Thronged with the curious, all the huts adjacent to the engineering commission constituted an enormous theater pit from which to view the drama that was taking place. Focusing their binoculars through all the crevices in the walls, the audience stamped, applauded, shouted bravos, and hissed. In their eyes the scene before them—real, concrete, inescapable— was a stupendous bit of fiction which was being acted out on that rude stage to the sinister glow of leaping flames caught up by the northeast wind, the yellowing smoke being shot with fugitive gleams and licking tongues of fire as it bellowed upward in huge puffs. This was the shading of the stage picture, extending from one side to the other and occasionally veiling the whole of it, like the curtain that falls at the end of the act in a tragedy.

At such moments as these the settlement was wholly lost to view, its huts no longer visible, as before the spectators there stretched a smooth gray screen of smoke that hid everything from their gaze. Etched against this background was a circular disk, like a live coal, red and lusterless—a peeping sun in eclipse. Of a sudden, however, the curtain would be torn

---

[32] See elsewhere.

by a stiff gust of wind, and through the enormous rent, from top to bottom, could be glimpsed a triangular bit of the settlement—bands of panic-stricken women and children running southward in great tumult and confusion, their figures barely to be made out against the withered foliage of the arbors near the square. The batteries on Mount Favella were pounding them from in front, and the poor wretches, thus caught between two lines of fire, flayed by bullets, on the one hand, and driven back by cannon, on the other hand, finally ended by diving into the heap of ruins at the back of the sanctuary; or at another moment they might be hidden by the dense clouds of smoke from the slow and inextinguishable conflagration, rolling slowly over the rooftops, hovering along the ground, or swelling upward in spirals with the slow, undulating motion of great silent waves, rising and falling with the wind. For an instant the smoke would clear from the mutilated façade of the new church, affording a glimpse of crumbling wall; then all would be veiled again; and, farther on, a deserted stretch of river bed would next be revealed, or the dissolving smoke wreaths would be seen girdling the summits of the knolls and hillocks.

The curious gaze of those too far away to take part in the battle was fastened upon that fog curtain; and whenever, in this monstrous amphitheater, that curtain became quite impenetrable along the entire circle of crude "boxes," the audience would immediately become uncontrollably obstreperous, the frantic spectators giving vent to their vexation and disappointment by shouting and by waving their useless binoculars in a vain attempt to follow the plot which had been thus unexpectedly cut off from their view.

Meanwhile, the engagement was being abnormally prolonged. In place of the usual intermittent rifle fire there was a lively and heavy fusillade, the bullets crackling with the noisy sound of popping reeds in a canebrake that is on fire. As a result, the anxious onlookers, straining their ears, could not help thinking that perhaps the sertanejos might have broken through our lines to the north. The echoes from the gunfire, reverberating from the hillsides and growing in intensity beneath the thick blanket of foglike smoke, threw them off their reckoning. Those crackling bullets appeared to be near at hand, on their right and in their rear, giving rise to the illusion that the enemy, having made his escape, might be hurling himself pell-mell upon them, in a sudden retaliatory move. Orders were snapped back and forth as the reserve corps formed in line, and there was great excitement and much running about in all directions.

Then came the distant muffled roar of shouts and viva's, and, snatching up their binoculars again, all made a rush for the fortified lookouts. At that instant the wind opened a broad, clean furrow in the smoke, parting it from one side to the other and revealing once more the scene of the drama. Their feelings were vastly relieved, and they burst into loud cheers; for the jagunços were retreating. At last they could see, stretching all the way to the Cambaio Road, a line of vermilion-colored flags. Canudos was completely blockaded.

It did not take long for the news to reach the camp, and swift-riding couriers at once set out for Monte Santo, from which point the news would be telegraphed and spread all over the country.

The settlement was now wholly surrounded by a discontinuous line of trenches, through which, however, it would no longer be possible for a single inhabitant to make his escape. On the east was the center of the camp; in the rear of the "black line" the Third Brigade held the center; on the north were the recently captured positions, manned, respectively, by the Thirty-first, the left wing of the Twenty-fourth, the Thirty-eighth, the right wing of the São Paulo Battalion, and the Thirty-second Infantry, cutting across the Uauá and Varzea da Ema trails; throughout the whole of the northeast sector, scattered garrisons alongside the redan, fortified with artillery, at the extremity of the Cambaio Road; to the south, a line running to Mount Favella and to the dominant Seventh of September bastion.

Even though fragmentary, the closed circle of a real and effective siege line had now been drawn. The insurrection was doomed.

CHAPTER X

LAST DAYS

I

FLOUNDERINGS OF THE VANQUISHED

SOMETHING then happened that was truly extraordinary and wholly unexpected. The battered enemy now appeared of a sudden to have obtained a new lease on life and began displaying an incredible degree of vigor. Even yet the troops that had faced him from the start of the conflict had not really come to know him; or, rather, they knew him only from the glimpses they had had of him, as an astute foe, slipping away among the maze of dugouts and luring them on, indomitably repelling the most valiant of charges, and without an equal when it came to eluding the most unforeseen of attacks. He was beginning to loom as a hero in their eyes.

Hemmed in on all sides by thousands of bayonets, the jagunço was merely stimulated and his resistance stiffened; it was as if all this were no more than a fresh incentive to battle. And battles there were, from the twenty-third[1] on, persistent as never before, at all points along the line, involving the entire circumference of the siege as the enemy fought furiously, blindly, trench by trench. It was like a huge and stormy wave that had broken in a tumultuous whirlpool of battle. Halted, dammed, by the advance trenches to the east, it came flowing back with a gleaming wake of rifle fire in the direction of Cambaio, dashing against the steep slopes which there descend to the river; under the direct fire of our trenches above, it then took a northerly course and burst, foaming, down the bed of the Vasa-Barris until it was shattered on the stockades which formed a dike on that side; whereupon it roared southward, and our men could see it rising and falling, swift and turbulent, within the settlement itself. Having crossed the village, it rose along the bottom of the outlying spurs of Mount Favella—our troops raining fire all the while—and then gave another bound to the east, twisting and writhing noisily, to fall upon the left flank of the Baian Fifth. Repelled here, it once more subsided before the barrier formed by the Twenty-sixth and then drew back from this point to the center of the square, in a serpentine course of many turns and

---

[1] [September 23.]

bends. A moment later it was breaking against the "black line." Barely to be made out now in the fitful light of battle, it again surged northward, against the same points as before; ever repulsed, ever attacking, the eddying wave of jagunços came on and on, with the irrepressible rhythm of a cyclone. And then it stopped. The furious tornado was followed by a sudden and complete stillness; an absolute silence fell upon both camps. The besieging forces maintained their battle formation, but they were given at least a moment's respite.

Then there came the thunder of cannon fire, directed at the new church; and above the ruined cornices of that rubbish heap, parlously clinging to swaying blocks of stone, figures could be seen darting about madly here and there in all directions. In addition to the case shots which burst in a spray of bullets, whole sections of the wall, pounded by the artillery, now fell upon them. This was more than they could endure and they were forced to come down, falling and sliding like monkeys, to seek refuge in the near-by ruins of the "Sanctuary." But they would spring up again, unexpectedly, at some point along the line, would launch an attack and be repelled; they would then attack the neighboring trenches and again be driven back, and so on, until they had completed once again the enormous circle of rotating assaults.

Those who, only the day before, had looked with disdain upon this adversary burrowing in his mud huts, were now filled with astonishment, and, as in the evil days of old, but still more intensely new, they felt the sudden strangling grip of fear. No more displays of foolhardy courage. An order was issued that the bugles should no longer be sounded, the only feasible call to arms being that which the foe himself so eloquently gave. The hillocks were now depopulated, and there was no more swaggering and strutting about in defiance of the enemy's bullets.[2] Men renowned for their courage now crept cautiously along, scrambling through covered passageways, stooping low and bounding across the points which were exposed to the jagunços' fire. Once more, the matter of communications became extremely difficult. The supply trains, the moment they appeared over the brow of the hills along the Calumby Road, were now subjected to a violent attack, and a number of the men in this service fell wounded on the last stage of the haul, at the entrance to the camp.

In brief, the situation had suddenly become quite unnatural. For one thing, it was hard to understand how the jagunços, after all these months of fighting, came to be so well supplied with ammunition. For they were not in the least sparing of it. On certain occasions, when the firing was

[2] [Cf. pp. 427–28.]

heaviest, it was as if a prolonged gust of wind were howling over the camp. At such times one could hear the smooth hiss of Mannlicher and Mauser bullets, the deep, sonorous hum of Comblains, the harsh crack of *trabucos*,[3] sharp as machine-gun fire—projectiles of every species, hurtling over every point of our far-flung lines: over the headquarters tents; over the hilltops, all the way to the sheltered neck of Mount Favella, where the supply-train drivers and the wounded were resting; over all our trenches; over the long, winding bed of the river and the most deeply hidden of the depressions; bursting through the leather awning of the field-hospital shed, causing the patients to start up in a spasm of fear; shattering glass vials in the military pharmacy annexed to the hospital; swooping inexplicably low to graze the leafy bowers and falling within a palm's breadth of the hammocks to startle the exhausted combatants who were snatching a moment's repose; beating like a shower of rocks against the thick walls of the huts that housed the engineering commission and the First Column headquarters; flaying with the whine of a lash the folds of the tents large and small, the huts and awnings everywhere; spraying the hillsides, cracking, ricocheting, bounding off, falling on the schist folds, rending and shattering them to bits, with an incomparable profusion of grapeshot.

The battle was feverishly approaching a decisive climax, one that was to put an end to the conflict. Yet this stupendous show of resistance on the part of the enemy made cowards of the victors.

THE PRISONERS

On the twenty-fourth the first prisoners were brought in.[4] At first, our troops had picked up no more than half-a-dozen terrified children, from four to eight years of age, whom they had found straggling along the road; but a more thorough search of the captured huts resulted in their taking a number of women and wounded men. These latter were few in number and were in a deplorable state indeed. One of them, in a half-fainting condition, supported under the armpits by a soldier on either side, had a scar on his naked bosom which stood out sharply, the mark left by the saber which had laid him low. Another of the prisoners was the aged and dying curiboca who had not been able to discharge his rifle at the soldiers.[5] He had the appearance of an exhumed corpse limping along. Months ago he had been wounded in the abdomen by the splinters from a grenade, and in his belly were two red-bordered cicatrized holes through which his in-

---

[3] [See p. 145.]

[4] [Cf. pp. 406 ff.]   [5] [See pp. 431–32.]

testines had protruded. His voice, a stifled cry, died in his throat. They did not question him but left him in the shade of a tent to continue enduring the agony which he had been suffering for three whole months perhaps.

Some of the women gave information of a revealing character. Villa Nova[6] the day before had slipped away from the settlement, by the Varzea da Ema trail. For some time now they had felt the pangs of hunger, since practically all their provisions were reserved for the fighting men. A still more important revelation concerned the failure of the Counselor to make his appearance for quite a long while. In addition to this, now that all their means of egress had been cut off, the inhabitants of the settlement were beginning to suffer the growing tortures of thirst.

That was as far as their information went. Those who revealed these facts were in so weakened a condition that they were barely able to reply to questions. There was one man alone who did not, like the others, show the effects of the privations they had endured. Sturdily built, of medium height and broad shouldered—a perfect specimen of backland Hercules of the kind to be seen at fairs, with a bony framework that was like iron, and gnarled and prominent joints—he was, everything went to show, a front-line fighter, possibly one of those acrobatic warriors who had clung so agilely to the ruined cornices of the new church. Originally white, he was sunburned all over and his face was spotted with freckles. From his girdle there dangled, to a point below his knee, the empty sheath of a scraping knife. They had captured him in the thick of the fight. Having valiantly attacked and brought down three or four soldiers, he would have made good his escape had he not been knocked silly by a slanting bullet which struck him in the left eye socket. They now brought him, throttled like a wild beast, into the tent of the First Column commander. There they loosened their hold on him, and, as he stood there panting from the struggle, he raised his head, one eye gleaming brightly, the other filled with blood, in a glance that was terrifying. Awkwardly, he stammered a few words which they could not make out; then, taking off his broad-brimmed leather hat, he said something about sitting down. This was a supreme act of insolence on the bandit's part! Powerful hands laid hold of him and brutally tumbled him through the other door. Outside, with no protest on his part, they ran a rope around his neck, then dragged him over to the right side of the camp, where the poor fellow and his sinister guards were swallowed up in the bosom of the caatinga.

[6] See pp. 159, 430, 453.

THE EXECUTION

As soon as they reached the first sheltered spot, a horrible but common-place incident occurred. In such cases the soldiers would invariably demand that the victim shout a *viva* to the Republic, a demand that was seldom complied with. This was but the customary prologue to the cruel scene that was to follow. Seizing the prisoner by the hair, they would bend his head backward to expose his throat and then would decapitate him. Not infrequently, however, the greedy assassins were too impatient to wait for these lugubrious preparations, and matters would then be expedited with a quick thrust of the knife, a single thrust in the lower belly, ripping out the guts.

We had brave men among us who looked forward eagerly to such repugnant acts of cowardice as this—acts which were given the tacit and explicit sanction of the military leaders. Despite their three centuries of backward development, the sertanejos by no means carried off the palm from our troops when it came to deeds of barbarism.

II

DEPOSITION BY THE AUTHOR

It is our purpose rudely to unveil these barbarities by making a deposition in the matter.

The incident which we have narrated was a common enough one, a mere insignificant detail in the whole of things. It all began under the spur of an irritation occasioned by the first reverses which our troops met with and had ended by becoming the coolly accepted practice, a mere trifle from the point of view of the larger exigencies of the war. The moment an able-bodied jagunço, capable of supporting the weight of a musket, had been taken prisoner, there was not a second to be wasted in futile deliberation. Off with his head, out with his guts. One or another commanding officer might put himself to the trouble of making an expressive gesture; but, if he did so, it was so useless as to provoke surprise; it was something the soldier, accustomed to and eager for his task, could well dispense with.

That task, as we have seen, was a simple one. Fasten a leather thong around the victim's neck in the form of a halter or slipknot, then drag him along between the rows of tents; no need to worry about anyone's being shocked by the procedure and no need to fear that the prey might escape, for, at the least sign of resistance or attempted flight, all one had to do was to give a tug on the rope and the lasso would anticipate the work of the knife, and strangulation would take the place of beheading. They would go on until they came to the first deep concavity in the hills, a precaution which in itself was a superfluous formality, and then would stab the fellow to death. At this point, depending upon the humor of the executioners, certain slight variations might be introduced. As is well known, the one thing the sertanejo fears above everything else is dying by cold steel; not from fear of death but from fear of the consequences of this particular kind of death; for they believe that, so dying, their souls will not be saved.

Our men exploited this naïve superstition. They would frequently promise the jagunço the reward of a bullet if he would give them desired information. The information was rarely forthcoming. In the majority of cases the prisoners would remain stoically mute and unshakable—facing eternal perdition. The soldiers would then demand that they shout *viva*'s to the Republic; or for this sorry jest they would substitute mocking insults and cruel allusions, as the brutal and hilarious chorus drove home their barbed jibes. After that they would lose no time in beheading their prisoner or hacking his abdomen with knife thrusts. This obscure, unchronicled tragedy would take place against the somber and impoverished background of the hilly slopes, bristling with stones and cacti; and, with bursts of ghoulish laughter, the killers would then return to camp. There, no one asked them any questions about what had happened; for, as has been said, the episode was utterly and lamentably commonplace. The jagunços themselves, when taken prisoner, knew very well the fate that awaited them. The inhabitants of the settlement knew all about this summary brand of justice, and this it was, in good part, which led to their putting up so frenzied a resistance. In view of all the odious tortures they had suffered in the course of this campaign, they would assuredly have given themselves up to any other adversary, but, in the case of the one who confronted them, they chose to fight until the death.

And when at last, captured and throttled, they were led into the presence of our military leaders, they were by that time already resigned to the deplorable fate that was in store for them. Their bearing was uniformly marked by a strange serenity, a serenity that was hard to explain in view of the many and discordant types of character to be found among them—mestizos of every sort, with temperaments as varied as were the shadings of their skin. Some of these beings on the lowest rung of our racial ladder displayed an incredible haughtiness in the presence of their captors. Let us note an example or two.

There was one Negro, one of the few pure blacks that were there, who, having been captured during the latter part of September, was brought before the commander of the First Column, General João da Silva Barbosa. He was still panting and exhausted from the engagement in which he had been taken and from having been dragged and shoved along by the soldiers. Tall and lean in appearance, his gaunt and slightly stooping frame showed all the rigors of hunger and of battle, his emaciation causing him to seem even taller than he was. His inordinately long hair afforded but a glimpse of his narrow brow, and his markedly prognathous face, all but lost in his cottony beard, was a bruised and filthy mask. He reeled as he walked; and his tottering, infirm step, his woolly head, the scant bit of his countenance that was to be seen, his flattened nose, thick lips, his crookedly protruding teeth, his tiny eyes sparkling brightly in their deep sockets, his long, bare, dangling arms—all this gave him the wizened appearance of a sickly orangutan.

They did not waste any time on him; for he was an animal, not worth questioning. The general of the brigade, João da Silva Barbosa, from the hammock where he lay convalescing from his recent wound, made a gesture, and a corporal attached to the engineering commission, who was famous for such exploits, at once grasped the meaning of it and brought out the rope. Of diminutive stature himself, he had difficulty in adjusting the halter about the condemned man's throat; whereupon the prisoner calmly gave him a hand, fastening about his own neck the noose that was to throttle him.

Near by, looking on at this scene, were a headquarters lieutenant of the first class and a fifth-year medical student. They now beheld a change come over the poor fellow the moment he took his first few steps toward his execution. That begrimed and filthy body, barely supported by the long, withered limbs beneath, now of a sudden took on admirably—and terribly—sculpturesque lines, exhibiting a plasticity that was nothing less than stupendous. It was a statuesque masterpiece, modeled out of the mire. The Negro's stooping frame was now rigid and erect, striking a pose that was exceedingly beautiful in the pride of bearing it expressed: head up, shoulders thrown back, chest out, with all the defiant hauteur of a nobleman of old, as a pair of flashing eyes lighted up the manly face. Resolutely, impassively, he followed where his captor led—silently, his face immovable, his flabby muscles standing out against the bones of his skeleton-like figure, and with an impeccable demeanor. Truly, he was a statue, an ancient statue of a Titan, buried four centuries ago and now exhumed, blackened and mutilated, in that enormous ruin heap of Canudos. It was an inversion of roles, a shameful antinomy.

Yet these things created no impression.

One concession at least they made to that respect which was due the human race: they did not slaughter the women and children. There was, however, a proviso attached to this: the prisoners must not give signs of being dangerous. There was the case of the forty-year-old mameluca who on one occasion was captured and brought to the tent of the commander-in-chief. The general was not feeling well and interrogated her from his campaign cot, surrounded by a large number of officers. The usual questions were put to her, as to how many fighting men there were in the settlement, what conditions were like there, what resources they possessed, and so forth, questions which ordinarily met with an "I don't know!" or a wavering and ambiguous "How should I know?" But this woman was impudent, aggressive, and irascible and very imprudently gave vent to her feelings.

"It's no use asking me all those questions. You know very well that you are done for. You are not besieging us; you are our prisoners. You won't be able to go back as the other expeditions did. The fact is, you are going to be worse off than they were—you're going to remain here, every man of you, blindly groping your way over these hills." These words were accompanied by gestures that were rude and unrestrained and quite unsuited to the occasion.

All this was irritating. She was a dangerous old shrew and deserved no consideration at the hands of the conquerors. As they left the tent a sub-lieutenant and a few privates seized her; and this woman, this demon in petticoats, this witch who was prophesying defeat when victory was near at hand—she was beheaded.

The timid ones were generally spared but were looked upon as inconvenient encumbrances, useless pieces of baggage. This was the case with one old woman who, with her two grandchildren around ten years of age, had been billeted next the slope where the cavalry detachment was encamped. The stunted little ones were so weak that they could no longer stand and had gone back to creeping. They cried terribly from hunger; and the grandmother, driven to despair by their plight, would go from tent to tent begging for leftovers of food; then she would hasten back and, wrapping their bodies in the remnants of old shirts, would lull them to sleep. Busily, tirelessly, she watched over them like this, going here, there, and everywhere in search of an old blouse, a crust from a soldier's knapsack, or a bit of water. Bent over with age and suffering, staggering, reeling from side to side, shaken by a consumptive's hacking cough, she was a sight to move even the hardest of hearts. She was something in the nature of a chastisement, as she came and went like the impertinent and persevering ghost of an old remorse.

Decapitation, our men flatly averred, was infinitely preferable. For this was not a campaign; it was a slaughter-house.[7] It was a matter not of law but of vengeance. A tooth for a tooth. There were the ashes of Moreira Cesar; others must burn. There was the decapitated trunk of Colonel Tamarindo; other heads must fall. Revenge thus knew two poles—fire and the knife. For all this they found justification. There was Colonel Carlos Telles, who once had spared a captive sertanejo. The assassins' ferocity beat a retreat in the presence of this generous-souled hero. But he had paid for it; he had paid for this unpardonable lapse, for the luxury of being kindhearted. The jagunço whose life he had saved had succeeded in escaping afterward, and he it was who had fired the shot which removed the colonel from the scene of action. They believed such stories as these; they made them up, seeking in advance an absolution for their misdeeds. At other times they deliberately exaggerated their feelings. There were their martyred friends who, having fallen into the enemy's treacherous snares, had been ruthlessly slain. Not only that; the jagunços had made sport of their corpses, hanging them up like scarecrows along the road. Their own merciless acts of savagery were thus transformed into acts of compassion for their dead comrades, acts of mourning. Bathed in tears, they washed their hands in blood.

A CRY OF PROTEST

What was more, they had not to fear the formidable judgment of posterity: for History would not go as far as that. Concerned with the fearful physiognomy of peoples amid the majestic ruins of vast cities, against the supremely imposing background of cyclopic coliseums, with the glorious butchery of classic battles and the epic savagery of great invasions, History would have no time for this crude slaughter pen.

The backlands are a refuge for the criminal. Whoever goes along these trails and, by the side of the road, sees a cross standing above the grave of the assassin's victim does not pause to investigate the crime but lifts his hat and passes on. The punitive powers of the constituted authorities assuredly do not extend to these regions. In this case the crime was a public one. The government's chief representative in Monte Santo knew all about it, and he kept silent, thereby covering it with the mantle of a culpable indifference. The offenders knew that they would go unpunished,

[7] See p. 206.

and they were further protected by anonymity and by the tacit complicity of the only ones who were in a position to repress the crimes in question. The result was, all the accumulated rancors burst forth, as a criminal multitude, armed to the teeth and paid to kill, fell upon the wretched backlands populace.

Canudos was appropriately enough surrounded by a girdle of mountains.[8] It was a parenthesis, a hiatus. It was a vacuum. It did not exist. Once having crossed that cordon of mountains, no one sinned any more.[9] An astounding miracle was accomplished, and time was turned backward for a number of centuries. As one came down the slopes and caught sight of the enormous bandits' den that was huddled there, he well might imagine that some obscure and bloody drama of the Stone Age was here taking place. The setting was sufficiently suggestive. The actors, on one side and the other, Negroes, caboclos, white and yellow skinned, bore on their countenances the indelible imprint of many races—races which could be united only upon the common plane of their lower and evil instincts. A primitive animality, slowly expunged by civilization, was here being resurrected intact. The knot was being undone at last. In place of the stone hatchet and the harpoon made of bone were the sword and the rifle; but the knife was still there to recall the cutting edge of the ancient flint, and man might flourish it with nothing to fear—not even the judgment of the remote future.

But, nevertheless, for the light of a future day, let this passage stand, even though it be one marked by no brilliance, uncompromising, angry, unedifying by reason of the subject matter, brutal, violent, because it is a cry of protest, somber as the bloodstain that it reflects.

III

TITANS AGAINST DYING MEN

The battle of the twenty-fourth hastened the end. The attack by our lines closing in from the north on that day was followed by an equally vigorous one from the south, on the twenty-fifth, and a pincers movement was thus effected. It was at this time that the two Pará battalions and the Thirty-seventh of the line were brought into action, coming down from Mount Mario, where they had been camped on a sheltered neck of the hill, in the rear of the Seventh of September Trench. This they did of their own volition, without any orders from general headquarters.

They had weighty reasons for doing so. The fall of Canudos, it appeared

[8] See pp. 20, 143.   [9] [Cf. p. 68.]

to them, was imminent. From the height where their camp was situated, at a re-entrant angle of the slope, they had a clear view of the settlement at every instant; they could see the siege lines tightening down below, while the conflagrations which framed the desolate picture were constantly spreading; the village was being ever more and more reduced to one huge *praça*, a broad open space that was always deserted for the reason that the fighting men of either side were equally afraid of exposing themselves there. Not far away was the redan fortified with the artillery whose thunderous fire was an invitation to action; down below, the constant crack of rifles, incessant fusillades—and there they themselves were, all the while, useless, disdained even by the stray bullets that whizzed overhead, high above them, doing them no harm. From one moment to another, all this might end, and there would be nothing left for them to do but to return home ingloriously, with virgin swords, banners intact, without the precious laurels of battle. The commander-in-chief had made it plain that he did not propose to precipitate events by a futile expenditure of lives when the surrender of the settlement within a few days' time was inevitable. This intention, clearly expressed, in addition to being the more practical attitude was at the same time the more humane. This, however, was a matter that involved the warrior renown of those who had not yet taken part in the fray. Fate, they felt, was playing them a shabby trick by thus forcing them to accept gratis those triumphal wreaths which they were quite sure were being braided for them by their loving mothers, wives, sweethearts, and sisters back in their native states. They were, accordingly, unable to contain themselves and came storming down the slopes.

There then began an engagement which was less of a surprise to those attacked than it was to the rest of our own lines. Breaking out along the slopes of Cambaio, where it was seconded by Colonel Olympio da Silveira's artillery, it quickly grew and spread, with extraordinary intensity. As was later divulged, these impatient heroes, led by Colonels Sotero de Menezes and Firmino Rego, had in mind no less an objective than that of capturing the settlement. Charging down to the river, they fought their way across it without a halt and burst into the deserted square. Scattering out in various directions, they continued charging with their bayonets down the lanes, sweeping them clean, leaping over the smoking rubbish heaps, and trampling the astonished woodsmen underfoot. Then they went on— amid a great outburst of cheering—to fall upon the northern trench and its thunderstruck garrison.

It was a tremendously daring thing to do; but they did not know the sertanejos. The latter, putting up a vigorous resistance, brought them to a halt, hamstrung them, and after a short while stopped them completely. Without being aware of the fact, the jagunços were having their revenge; for there was, indeed, something woefully insolent and irritating in the breathless, impetuous anxiety with which those swaggering military heroes—robust and sound of body, well clothed, well fed, well armed, well trained—thus sought to crush an adversary who for three whole months had been starving, under constant fire, his houses burned, his strength failing, his life's blood slowly ebbing away drop by drop, his courage faltering, his hopes dead, as he day by day succumbed to a process of complete exhaustion. They might give the last bayonet thrust in the breast of a dying man or put a merciful bullet in his brain, but they would, certainly, gain little fame for themselves by such an exploit. However, even this they did not accomplish. The siege lines were narrowed, that is true, but the results achieved did not make up for the sacrifices involved; for the assailants suffered some eighty casualties in all, including Colonel Sotero, who was wounded, and Captain Manoel Baptista Cordeiro, of the Pará Regiment, who was killed.

THE SIEGE CLOSES IN

By way of compensation, so it was said, the losses of the enemy were enormous—hundreds of dead, hundreds of houses captured. As a matter of fact, that portion of the settlement which was still in the hands of the jagunços was now reduced to less than one-third, being restricted to the northern edge of the square and the huts next the church. Eleven battalions (the Sixteenth, Twenty-second, Twenty-fourth, Twenty-seventh, Thirty-second, Thirty-third, Thirty-seventh, and Thirty-eighth of the line, the one from Amazonas, the right wing of the São Paulo Battalion, and the Second from Pará), more than twenty-five hundred men in all, had within the past few days taken nearly two thousand houses and were now closing in on the sertanejos, pushing them up against the slope where the "Old Ranch House" stood on the south, and on the east, up against an equal number of bayonets of the Twenty-fifth, Seventh, Ninth, Thirty-fifth, Fortieth, Thirtieth, Twelfth, and Twenty-sixth of the line and the Fifth Police. This made five thousand soldiers in round numbers, exclusive of those that had been left to guard the camp and the Monte Santo Highway.

In place of a loose and sprawling siege line, the population under attack, crowded into less than five hundred huts, in behind the church, at the bend of the river, was now surrounded by an unbroken circle of twenty battalions; and even this restricted area was being hourly reduced by the conflagrations. While the houses had little wood in their construction on which the flames might feed, the fires nonetheless slowly spread, giving off dense and stifling clouds of grayish smoke, such as might have come from the imperfect combustion taking place in hundreds of Catalan furnaces.[10] These smoke clouds rolled over the rooftops and darkened the skies above, rendering the scene even more monotonous and desolate than it ordinarily was. The artillery on the hills was practically silent now; for the greatest care was required in the matter of firing aim, since the slightest deviation would have led to the cannon balls' dropping upon the assailants themselves.

In spite of this fact, however, the square remained completely deserted. No one made any attempt to capture the houses which bounded it on the north, in a line perpendicular to the arbor.[11] Within these dwellings, and in those which were huddled beyond them, next the church, the last of the jagunços were gathered. The boldest of them still manned the dismantled walls of the house of worship, under the command of leaders of no great renown. These anonymous heroes now prepared their people for death; darting here and there, they spurred them on to a resistance that was really incomprehensible and meanwhile took such measures as might indefinitely prolong the hour of ultimate defeat.

And so it was that, from the twenty-sixth on, these fighting men took turns in leaving the trenches from which they replied to our attacks for other duties which were, it may be, even more important.

DIGGING THEIR OWN GRAVE

They were preparing next to the "Sanctuary" their last stronghold—a wide rectangular excavation. They were digging their own grave.[12] Beaten on all sides, these indomitable warriors meant to fall back, all of them, inch by inch, yard by yard, until they came to this trench which was to be their tomb.

In search of the water which they so badly needed, they were also digging wells, as deep as they could make them. The women and children, the aged and the infirm, collaborated in this backbreaking toil. The ground, however, was so hard that they were not able to go much deeper than a couple of yards in their effort to reach those strata where the last stagnant trickles of river water might still be found. Occasionally, they did find them, only to see the wells sucked dry an hour later by the sponge-

[10] [A furnace for making wrought iron directly from the ore.]

[11] [The arbor where prayers were said (see pp. 160, 243, 425).]

[12] See pp. 474–75.

like avidity of the exsiccated atmosphere. Then it was that thirst truly became a torture for them, in the burning dog-day heat and with all the exertions they were called upon to make.

For this reason, battle became for them a gruesome divertisement, by taking their minds off their greater woes. They now fired in disorderly fashion, up and down the line, at random, with none of that rigorous aim which had marked their fusillades of old, and with an expenditure of ammunition that was capable of exhausting the best stocked of arsenals. Those perched on the new church continued to sweep the hilltops with their fire, while the others at a distance of a couple of paces confronted the battalions which had fought their way into the maze of huts. Brutal episodes now occurred. The field of action was so limited and the lanes so narrow as to make any kind of maneuvers impossible even for the smallest of detachments; and the struggle accordingly took on the exclusive character of a fierce hand-to-hand encounter. Some of the officers as they advanced would unbuckle their belts and throw away their swords and proceed to fight it out with knives.

In the end, however, matters became very difficult for the assailants, with the defenders in that narrow space packed into the houses, filling them to overflowing and putting up a growing resistance. When the enemy did yield at one point or another, the victors would meet with startling surprises; for, even in this grave crisis, the sertanejo was up to his old tricks.

BREASTWORK OF CORPSES

This would become apparent after our men had captured a hut which had been tenaciously defended. The soldiers would rush into it pell-mell, only to find their way barred by corpses, piled one upon another. Unimpressed by this sight, they would go on into the dimly lighted room, and then one of their number would receive a bullet in the back, fired at close range from that pile of bloody rags. Terrified, they would whirl about, and another would get a bullet in the chest. And then, as they cowered there in that tiny room, they would see a fantastic warrior bound up and take to his heels, a warrior who had adopted the irreverent stratagem of fighting from behind a breastwork of the dead.

AROUND THE WATER PITS

The slow progress which the siege had been making was now halted once more. It was the vanquished who, for the last time, thus brought it to a standstill. For the matter of that, the situation did not call for any major effort on the part of our troops, since victory was bound to come of itself. All that they had to do was to hold the positions they had won. With all the points of exit closed and with the inhabitants cut off from the water pits along the riverbank, the surrender of the settlement was inevitable within a day or two at the most—and this was to assume that the besieged in this heat would be able to hold out against the tortures of thirst for so long a time as that.

Hold out they did, for a week longer; for that circle of massed battalions was beginning to be broken intermittently, by the sertanejos, at night. On the night of the twenty-sixth there were four violent attacks; on the twenty-seventh, eighteen; on the following days, one only each night, but it was an uninterrupted one, from six in the evening to five o'clock in the morning.

The object of these attacks was not to open a path by which they might flee. The thing that worried the jagunços was their water supply. Crowded all of them into the southern sector of the village, they were momentarily expecting that the pits or stagnant pools of the Vasa-Barris would be captured; and so, while the majority of their comrades were giving battle, thus attracting the major portion of the assailants to the heart of the settlement, a few valiant ones, unarmed and carrying empty pouches, would come down to the river's edge. Advancing cautiously, they would go up to the few scattered puddles that dotted the river bed, and, filling their leathern casks, would return on the run, bent beneath the weight of their precious burden.

This undertaking, difficult enough in the beginning, gradually became an impossible one. When it was discovered that this was the sole motive of the enemy's attacks, the besiegers from their positions along the riverbank began centering their fire upon the water pits, which were readily visible—small liquid surfaces gleaming in the moonlight, or, in the darkness, giving back the winnowed brilliancy of the stars.

The result was that, when they reached the edge of the puddles, the sertanejos found themselves under fire from all sides. But they kept on coming, occasionally—coming and falling, all of them—one after another. Some of them fell before they reached the dried-up ipueiras, reduced now to filthy mud holes; some were slain as they lay face downward, sucking up the filthy, brackish water; others, as they were returning from their task, bent beneath the laden *bogós*.[13] Their places were taken by still other of their companions who desperately went forth to brave the fire from our lines and to face death itself. Or—and this was what usually happened— they would wait until the energetic and deadly fusillade from our lines had

[13] [Water pouches (cf. p. 145).]

subsided and our men, so they fancied, were off their guard. Our troops, however, had come to know the jagunços' wiles; they knew that these water-seekers would be back in a short while; and so they in turn waited, rifles steadily aimed, their ears keyed to the slightest sound, their eyes unswerving, piercing the darkness, like hunters stalking their game.

Finally, after a few minutes, they would catch sight of blurred figures on the opposite bank, fading into the shadows; they would see them making their way slowly, very, very slowly, down below, creeping along on the ground with the silent, serpentine movement of huge saurians; they would see them, later, crawling along the shady river brink. Our soldiers would make certain of their aim, would let the thirsty ones come up until they had reached the edge of the stagnant pools which constituted the sole decoy in this monstrous man-hunt. Then there would be a sudden blaze of rifle fire! Their aim had been good. Fifteen yards away piercing screams of pain and anger would rend the air, and two or three bodies would be seen writhing beside the wells, as the other jagunços fled in terror, some of them wounded and limping along, while others, throwing all caution to the winds—terrible in their defiance of the infernal, death-dealing barrage—ran swiftly up the banks, leaping over their dying companions.

Occasionally, one of them would be fleet enough to escape and, up the bank at a bound, would be lost from sight amid the rubbish of the huts, bringing to his companions there, at the price of such a slaughter, a few quarts of a dubious liquid contaminated with organic detritus and of a horrible odor, filled with the poison of ptomaines and the phosphates of the rotting corpses which for some time had lain unburied all along the edge of the Vasa-Barris at this point. Incidents such as these came as a climax to the heroism which the backwoodsmen had displayed from the beginning, and, in the end, even their adversaries were deeply moved by it all.

ON THE RUBBISH OF THE NEW CHURCH

Not infrequently, when the entire siege line to the north was ablaze with an unremitting fire—a fire so sustained that it was impossible to make out the sound of individual weapons, amid a roar which was like that created by the sudden opening of a floodgate, with the artillery from the hillsides adding to the din—at such times, some of our men along the center line of the camp, running the risk of being hit by stray bullets from the engagement that was taking place, would become the onlookers at a most extraordinary spectacle, one which eventually evoked in them a sincere and irrepressible feeling of enthusiasm for these brave martyrs, a feeling which they made no effort to conceal. The picture which they now beheld was sufficient in their eyes to render immortal these conquered sertanejos. Each time that they gazed upon it their wonder grew.

There was that sinister church, looming large in relief against the background of the ruined huts; and fearless under the hail of bullets which fell upon them from all sides, their figures lighted by the fugitive gleam of rifle fire, were those rude but indomitable fellow-countrymen of ours, gliding along the walls and over the rubbish heaps, scrambling up the ruined towers or dropping from them, clinging to the swaying blocks of stone like Titans struck by a thunderbolt, and glimpsed by the lightning's vivid flash.

IV

STROLL IN CANUDOS

All in all, it was hourly becoming apparent that the enemy was approaching the point of complete exhaustion. During the day the settlement was silent, wasting away from the stagnation imposed by the blockade. Not even an occasional attack any more. On September 28 the jagunços failed to reply to the salvos of twenty-one guns each with which they were greeted morning and evening. That date well may stand out as marking the conclusion of one of the most virile episodes in our history. It was the end.

In the camp the men were making plans for returning home. Bugle calls were now sounded freely, and one could go from one side to the other in perfect safety. Supply trains and couriers came and went, the latter bearing with them to distant homes the hopes and greetings of the conquerors. Small groups now carelessly roamed the neighborhood, and banquets were arranged on the spur of the moment, while at nightfall, in front of the headquarters of the various commands, the musicians played martial airs.

By this time it was possible to make one's way across practically the whole of the village. On the twenty-eighth the commander-in-chief and the Second Column commander, with their respective staffs, decided to take this pleasant stroll. At first they went along the hilltops to the right of the camp, then turned to the left and came down through a winding gully so overhung with foliage that it had the appearance of a long-covered passageway. They went on until they came to the outlying houses; and there, strewn at random over the heaps of burned beams, rafters, laths, and other debris, they immediately stumbled upon the first of the enemy's unburied corpses. The impression one had at this moment was that of having come upon an ancient necropolis which of a sudden had sprung up out of the ground at one's feet. The ruins added to the general disorder of these tiny chance-built dwellings, facing one another across alleyways that were not more than a yard wide and which were littered with fallen clay roofs. It was consequently necessary to make long and intricate detours; and at each step the officers took—past huts that were still standing but shattered and ready to fall, which the flames had not yet reached—the anguished life that the inmates of those hovels must have led became more and more apparent to their astonished gaze.

The nudity of the corpses was an indication of this. There they lay, in every position imaginable: flat on their backs, face to the heavens; bared bosoms where the medals of favorite saints were to be seen; bodies bent double in the last throes of death; other bodies barely visible beneath the piles of burned wood; still others, crouched over improvised trenches, in the attitude in which death had found them. In all these emaciated, life-less forms and in the tatters that covered them could be read the privations which they had suffered. Some of them were being slowly consumed by fire, although no flames were to be seen, as was revealed by threads to smoke rising here and there. Others had been incinerated, reduced of mounds of white ashes which stood out sharply against the dusty gray of the earth, like huge caricatures crudely scrawled in chalk.

As they went on, it became more and more difficult for them to make their way over the successive rubbish heaps of this frightful dunghill. In clearing the houses, the soldiers had tossed out of doors—thus blocking the alleys with piles of filth—all the broken bits of furniture and other inde-scribable odds and ends: small cedarwood chests; stools and benches and big food cages; hammocks in shreds; liana-stalk cradles and taquara-cane hampers; casks with the bottoms knocked out; old cotton clothing of an indefinable shade; battered iron utensils; broken glass, dishes, cups, and bottles; portable altars of every size and shape; valises made of raw leath-er; worthless sandals; oil lamps bent out of shape; exploded shotgun bar-rels; splintered cattle prongs and wagon bars; blunted knives.

Among all these trash piles there was nothing, not the simplest object, which did not point to a primitive and a woebegone existence. There was a host of rosaries of all sorts, from the simplest variety, made of poly-chrome glass beads, to the most capricious, fashioned of urucuri shell. Equally numerous were the distaffs and spindles, for this was an ancestral custom to which the backland women tenaciously clung, as they did to so many others. In addition to all these objects, scattered over the ground and trampled underfoot were countless others: religious cards and holy relics, charms sewn up in little bags, ancient catechisms, smashed images and grimy pictures of miracle-working saints, crosses and crucifixes, amulets, and filthy scapularies.

Here and there, the officers' party would come to a clearing, a bit of ground that had been swept clean in order to prevent the fires from reaching the trenches. It was easy at such points to make their way into the mass of huts for a closer view. Then they came upon a sentinel who in a low voice advised them to proceed with caution, inasmuch as the jagunço was near at hand, less than three yards distant, on the other side of the stockade.

The visiting officers, from the generals and colonels down to the last man, in their anxiety to avoid an ambush, thereupon dropped to a squatting position and—heroically comic figures that they were—ran along as fast as they could until they had passed the danger line. Having gone down two or three lanes, they came to another trench: motionless soldiers, waiting expectantly, silently, or conversing in whispers. The same scene was then repeated, with hearts and legs leaping as the visitors ran along to the next trench beyond, where they once again found cautious, silent sentries, lying stretched out or with their rifles poised over the protecting breastworks.

After they had gone some fifteen hundred yards, they turned to the left, leaving "Vermilion Heights" behind them; and there they were surprised to come upon a street, the only one in the settlement deserving of the name, Monte Alegre Street as it was called, a long one three yards wide, running all the way across the village and coming out on the square. Along this street were the better dwellings, a few brick and frame houses, among them that of Antonio Villa Nova,[14] where some days before our men had discovered what was left of the munitions captured from the Moreira Cesar column.

Going down this gently sloping thoroughfare, they could see at the far end, on the *praça*, a fragment of the ruined church wall. However, they soon found themselves brought up short by another trench, where a larger number of combatants were gathered. This was the last one in that direction. To go a step beyond it meant certain death. This entire part of the settlement, ahead of them and to the right, was still in the hands of the inhabitants. The adversaries were thus rubbing elbows with each other. Coming through the mud walls of the neighboring huts could be heard the muffled, indistinguishable voices of the population that was burrowing there: hurried, cautious whisperings under those thatched roofs; the scraping of furniture; the sound of footsteps; a noise as of distant cries and

14 [See pp. 159, 430, 433.]

groans; and occasionally—lending a cruelly dramatic note—the shouts, tears, and laughter of little children.

From here, by way of returning to their point of departure, the visitors followed a path to the left, between rows of houses captured in recent days; and it was then that their stroll began to take on a truly terrifying aspect. Throughout the whole of this segment of the siege line, marking the point of farthest advance since the battles of the week before, the soldiers had not destroyed the huts. They had merely removed the inner partitions and the gables; and the mud roofs, which met or all but met, thus came to form one long barrack. The barrier of beams and joists, hampers and furniture of every sort, behind which the battalions were aligned, from here on pursued a long and winding course and disappeared from view thirty yards away, lost in the shadows. On one side were to be seen the soldiers who manned it. In the dark corners at the rear, the bodies of jagunços killed in the last few days were visible; for it was dangerous to burn them amid all the rag piles and wooden splinters that were scattered round about.

The air was filled with the stifling smell of a cave, and it required some courage to go through that tunnel-like passage, at the mouth of which, in the distance, a pallid reflection of daylight was to be seen; for only a couple of steps away, running parallel to it on the other side of those jagged walls, was the invisible trench of the enemy. The slightest bit of carelessness, a glance however rapid over the top of that rubbish-built barricade, was paid for dearly. The truth of the matter is that each side was now practicing the same wiles, inspired by the same kind of hatred. As the conflict drew to its somber conclusion, each was equally afraid of the other, and both were equally anxious to avoid an open combat. Instead, they lured each other on, resorting to the same tricks, as they made a treacherous show of inactivity. Immobilized for a good portion of the time, facing each other, each in the very shadow of his enemy, they both appeared to be afflicted by the same utter exhaustion, as they diligently, insidiously spied on each other. No better setting could have been found than this dunghill of rags and corpses, submersed in the darkness of a cavern, for revealing to soldiers and jagunços alike the most repugnant side of heroism.

The officers went on down this passageway, wrapped in gloomy silence. Soldiers could be seen, ragged and unkempt, without uniforms or caps, with hats of straw or leather on their heads and old worn-out sandals on their feet—in short, clad in the same uniform as the enemy. One could readily believe, indeed, that, with a little presence of mind, a sertanejo, making his way through an opening in that extensive enclosure, would be able to take his place among our soldiers, with his rifle over the top of the barricade, and thus, without being recognized, escape the tortures of the siege. This would have been all the easier by reason of the fact that these were mixed detachments, with men from various battalions. Nor would his obvious ignorance of the duties and necessities of military life have stood in his way, for all discipline had been abandoned. There were no longer any reviews, formations, bugle calls, or commands. As soon as the cartridges had been distributed each one took his place at that breastwork made of old furniture, ready for what might come.

Rations were plentiful now, and, when they were handed out, each one proceeded to prepare his own meal as the opportunity presented itself. Here and there at the rear of the line or in the tiny cubbyholes, perched on tripods of brick or stone, kettles hummed with water for the coffee, pots were boiling, and huge quarters of beef suspended from the rafters glowed red in the darkness, roasting over the braziers. Squatting round about, rifles in hand, were groups of combatants taking advantage of a brief truce to prepare their lunch or dinner. Not infrequently, they would leap to their feet and, tossing aside their jacuba jugs[15] and their slices of roast meat, would make a dash for the stockade, as a sound of firing came from the other side and bullets whined overhead, raining down on the roofs, splintering beams and joists, shattering walls, overturning cauldrons, and scattering soldiers like a blast of wind in the straw. From over the barricade there would come a prompt reply, as those already stationed there fired at random at the partition opposite them, from which the attack had come. Their companions quickly followed their example, and from that point to the far end of the passageway on either side there was one huge nervous spasm as the entire tunnel shook to the sound of rifle fire and a sudden, furious, tumultuous battle began between the adversaries who could not see each other.

A number of soldiers were killed or wounded, and two or three more huts were captured, as our men moved forward all that riffraff of furniture, thereby extending the trench in the form of an advanced salient. Those combatants who had gone farthest in pursuit of the enemy then quickly returned to their original positions, and silence once more fell upon the scene, that same formidable silence which had prevailed before, with motionless soldiers waiting expectantly in ambush alongside that sinister hunting-ground, while at the back, round about the braziers, their companions were busy preparing a light repast—a meal at which, occa-

[15] [*Jacuba* is a savory drink made of manioc flour, sugar, water, etc.]

sionally, tragic guests were present: the assassinated inmates of the huts, stretched out in the corners.

Finally leaving this unprepossessing segment of the siege line, which barred off practically the whole of the northern quadrant, they continued their stroll in the light of day. They now passed sorry-looking gardens with fallen inclosures and trampled beds, with not a bloom in sight and strewn with the same indescribable rubbish piles that were to be found elsewhere. Upon these piles were the bodies of still more victims, with legs sticking up rigidly in the air, bare arms clasped in anguish, palms stiffly flattened or twisted and clenched like the claws of animals—sinister hands, rotting away, extended in ominous gestures of menace or excruciating appeal.

As they went on, they encountered signs of life in the form of skinny curs and famished, mangy hounds, exuding leprosy as they sniffed and clawed at those piles of filth with the eagerness of jackals, some of them even devouring their own dead masters. Most of these dogs fled quickly as the officers approached, but a few ferocious mastiffs, great bony animals, slunk away slowly with threatening growls; for in these visitors they had scented the enemy, the hated and evil intruder.

Going downhill all the time, the party now entered the deep gully below, which, in a direction perpendicular to the course of the river, ran down to the Vasa-Barris, where in the rainy season the waters from the slopes on either side found a channel. The top of the hill, above, where the engineering commission was stationed, marked the extreme boundary of that portion of the settlement which had been captured on July 18. They could now reach camp by keeping on straight ahead, by crossing the moat and going halfway up the hill, past the Krupp battery which was mounted in the rear of First Column headquarters; or they could turn to the right and make a long detour, following the moat along the original line of siege, running downward to the south. There was no danger in this. The houses here were a jumble of ruins along the edges of the erosion furrow that ran down the slope, following the jutting spurs with sharp twists and bends. The majority of these dwellings had been dismantled, but a few had been turned into orderly rooms for the brigades, into headquarters and officers' messrooms. One of them was worthy of note. It was a blacksmith's shop. There were still a few broken sledge hammers and tongs lying around, and there was a stationary forge, originally built of bricks, now in ruins. But the startling thing about this impoverished backlands smithy was the fact that it boasted a luxurious anvil, made of the finest Essen steel—it came from one of the captured cannons of the Moreira Cesar expedition.

Continuing on their way, they arrived at the "black line"—a name which previous events had justified but which was inexplicable to one who came from the somber trenches on the north which they had just left. They now followed the bottom of a ditch until, halfway down it, they came to a broad clear space on their right. This was the square where the churches had stood, calm and deserted now, swept clean, which caused the monstrous house of worship of the jagunços to stand out more brutal and dominant, more ominous-appearing than ever, with its tottering walls split from top to bottom, with its stupendous façade reduced to monolithic blocks, with its crumbling towers, its porch littered with rubbish, and its nave within, dark, empty, mysterious.

A few steps more brought them to the old church, entirely consumed by fire, with only its outer walls left standing. At this point, on their left, was the most wretched of cemeteries, with hundreds of crosses—a couple of stakes bound with liana stalk—marking the site of graves leveled with the ground.

Having crossed the Vasa-Barris, they then threaded their way down the deep trench formed by the Providencia River, whose tortuously winding course led them through the depleted ranks of the Fifth Police, now reduced to a third of their original strength; this brought them out on a hillside clearing, on the slope of Mount Favella. Up above was the Seventh of September Trench, like a balcony overlooking the scene. This was a dangerous point, and they crossed it rapidly, until they came to the trench.

Here, they had a view of the settlement below. It looked different now—shadowed with large dark splotches, the effect of the conflagrations; bristling with planks and beams sticking out of holes in the roofs; jumbled heaps of clay—in brief, a picture of utter ruin and desolation.

Only the narrow strip to the north of the square and the nucleus of huts next the arbor and in the rear of the church still remained intact. The houses were few in number, four hundred in all, perhaps, huddled in that narrow space. And those who were sheltered within them would surely not be able for one hour to withstand the assault of six thousand men.

It was worth trying, at any rate.

V

THE ASSAULT

This was what the commander-in-chief proceeded to do, the fact that the rebels were constantly growing weaker having led him to abandon his plan of waiting for them to surrender in order to avoid a useless expenditure of lives. The principal military leaders having been called together on September 30, plans were laid for giving battle immediately; and, in accordance with those plans, the combat units were mobilized that very night and took up positions for the attack the following day.[16]

The assault was to be launched by two brigades, the Third and the Sixth, under command of Colonels Dantas Barreto and João Cesar Sampaio, respectively. The former detachment was composed of hardened veterans who for three months past had engaged in constant skirmishes with the enemy, while the latter, one of the newcomers, was made up of men who longed to measure their strength with the jagunços. The Third Brigade thereupon left its former position on the "black line," its place there being taken by three battalions, the Ninth, the Twenty-second, and the Thirty-fourth; and, countermarching to the right in the direction of the "Old Ranch House," it was joined there by the other brigade, comprising the Twenty-ninth, Thirty-ninth, and Fourth battalions. The two brigades then moved to take up a position in the rear and along the sides of the new church, which was the central objective of the assault.

This primary movement was supplemented by other, secondary ones. At the moment of the charge the Twenty-sixth of the line, the Baian Fifth, and the right wing of the São Paulo Battalion were swiftly to take up positions along the left bank of the Vasa-Barris, on the edge of the square, and were to remain there until further orders. In their rear the two corps from Pará were to hold themselves in reserve, being ready either to replace or to reinforce these detachments as the exigencies of battle might determine. The action was to begin in the rear and along the sides of the church and from there was gradually to be extended along the line of bayonets drawn up on the riverbank, to the south of the square.

As may be seen, it was a vigorous pincers movement which was thus planned, one in which the other troops, manning the recently captured positions, and those in camp were to participate. The latter were to come into action as circumstances might dictate, or when the enemy, having been repulsed, should start falling back in a body from in front of our trenches.

In addition to all these indispensable preliminaries, there was to be a sustained bombardment in which all the siege guns should take part, centering their fire for the space of an hour upon the small area which it was the objective to capture. Only after the cannon had ceased were the brigades to attack, with fixed bayonets but without firing unless conditions should render it necessary, in which case their aim was to be directed

[16] According to the battalion charts, there were 5,871 men under arms on September 30.

along a meridian line only, in order to avoid firing upon the near-by battalions. When the commander-in-chief should give the order, "Infantry advance!" the Third Brigade was to march in double-quick time to a point left of the church, where it was to take up a position of 150 yards in extent, with two battalions of the Sixth Brigade, the Twenty-ninth and the Thirty-ninth, in its rear, while the Fourth, also crossing the Vasa-Barris, was to attack on the right flank. The rest of the troops, unless unforeseen circumstances should call for other plans, were to remain mere spectators of the engagement.

THE CANNONADING

The bombardment began at dawn on the morning of October 1. The batteries formed a semicircular line a mile and a quarter long, extending from those cannon that were nearest the camp to the ones on the redan at the other extreme, where the Cambaio Road came in; and the fire from all of them was now concentrated upon the last small nucleus of huts. It lasted for barely forty-eight minutes, but it was annihilating in effect. The guns had been carefully aimed the night before that they might be sure not to miss that immovable target. This was to be one last salutary lesson for those impenitent rebels. It was necessary to clear the ground for the assault, in order that there might not be any unpleasant surprises, and this they proceeded to do, promptly and in a deadly, unrelenting manner. There must be no obstacles other than ruins in the path of their bayonet charge, and so they proceeded to manufacture the ruins.

The effects of this terrific punishment were visible to the eye: roofs falling and, of a certainty, crushing those that were sheltered in the tiny rooms beneath; partitions crashing, with splinters and clods of earth flying through the air; while here and there, against the dusty background of the trash heaps, fresh conflagrations could be seen starting—separate ones at first, but soon becoming one huge blaze. Up above, the luminous backlands morning was overcast with a network of cannon balls. For not a single grenade must be wasted. They beat against the broken cornices of the church, exploding in fragments, or bounded off on the "Sanctuary" and the arbor beyond, in broad-sweeping ricochets; they burst in the air; they burst in the *praça*; they burst on the clay rooftops, tearing great gaps in them; and falling through the roofs, they burst inside; they swept the labyrinth of alleyways, blowing the rubbish heaps sky-high; in brief, they ruthlessly battered this last segment of Canudos, from point to point, from house to house. The inhabitants no longer had any barriers or sheltered nooks which might afford them protection. The re-entrant angle formed by the walls of the new church, which had served them as a breast-work against the fire from the Seventh of September Trench, had now been entirely destroyed by the trajectories of the artillery from east and west; and there was nothing left for the jagunços but to suffer the unmitigated virulence of this merciless attack, in which there was not a splinter of steel that failed of its effect.

Meanwhile, the irrepressible screams of anguish were unheard; a fleeing figure here and there or any slight commotion among the inmates of the huts went unnoticed. And when the last shot had been fired and the thunder of the cannons had died away, the sudden stillness which descended upon those battered dwellings was hard to comprehend; it was as if, during the night, the entire population had somehow taken flight.

There was a brief silence; and then a bugle call from the top of Mount Favella. The assault was beginning. In accordance with previously formed plans, the battalions were to converge from three points upon the new church. Without being seen by the enemy, they made their way among the huts or along the thalweg of the Vasa-Barris. One battalion alone, the Fourth Infantry, stood out from the others and was plainly to be seen by the rest of the troops, as, rifles in hand, it marched across the river at a quick step and scrambled up the opposite bank, appearing then at the entrance to the square, drawn up in close-formed ranks.

It was the first time that any troops had arrived there in proper military formation.

THE JAGUNÇOS REPLY TO THE ATTACK

Having accomplished this movement, the detachment in question marched forward heroically. It had gone but a few paces, however, when it was thrown into instant confusion. Some of the soldiers now dropped to the ground, as if they were preparing to fire, to better advantage, from behind the stones of the ruined façade; some fell back without any attempt at formation, while others ran ahead without waiting for their comrades; after which there was a melée of bayonets, with small groups charging at random in different directions and colliding with one another. And, then, the silence which had prevailed up to this point was broken by a sound which resembled the explosion of a mine.

The jagunço was coming to life, as always, suddenly, surprisingly, theatrically, and gloriously, barring the way to the aggressor. The Fourth Battalion, receiving the full fire of the ambushed enemy at the edge of the square, was brought to a halt. The same was true of the Twenty-ninth and the Thirty-ninth, which were fired upon at close range through the walls at the back of the "Sanctuary." On the left, the charge of the Dantas Barreto Brigade was stopped. Strongly attacked on one of its flanks, this brigade was compelled to abandon its original direction and meet the assault, a movement which was imperfectly carried out by three scattered companies detached from the bulk of the battalions. All prearranged tactical maneuvers, the fact is, had to be modified. In place of converging upon the church, the brigades were either halted or dispersed and lost in the narrow lanes.

For about an hour the troops that were viewing the battle from the surrounding hilltops were able to make out nothing beyond the ever increasing din, the sound of rifle fire and distant shouts—a confused uproar from which there emerged the constant, muffled, and as it seemed anguish-laden notes of the bugle. The two brigades had now been wholly swallowed up in the maze of huts; but, contrary to expectation, the sertanejos remained invisible; not a single one of them was to be seen running toward the square. Thus attacked on three sides, they must surely, in fleeing, make for the *praça*, where they would run into the bayonets of our troops that were stationed there, along the center line and the banks of the river; for this, as we have seen, was the prime objective of the assault. The plan failed completely, and this failure was equivalent to a defeat. For the assailants, meeting with a resistance upon which they had not counted, had not only been brought to a halt, but were intrenching themselves, were assuming an attitude directly opposed to the object in view. They were now frankly on the defensive, as the jagunços, rushing out of the smoking huts, fell upon and attacked them.

As it was, they had barely succeeded in taking the new church; and within its ruined nave the soldiers of the Fourth Battalion, standing on piles of debris, were now mingled in confusion with those of the Third Brigade. This success, however, proved unavailing; from one side of them there came a fierce, continuous, deafening fire from the *trabucos* of those warriors crowded into the "Sanctuary." In the meantime the square, to which the defeated enemy was supposed to flee, to be received by our bayonets—the square continued to be deserted.

It was urgent to amplify the original plan of attack by bringing up fresh forces. From the height where the Seventh of September Trench was located, the signal was now given by the commander-in-chief, and immediately afterward the bugle sounded for the Baian Fifth to advance. Jagunço was now to be pitted against jagunço.

The advance of this backlands battalion was not marked by the steady, cadenced rhythm of the usual military quickstep when troops are marching to an attack. Instead, what was to be seen was a long, swiftly moving, swaying line of bayonets which suddenly burst into luminous flame, unfurling a brightly gleaming ribbon of steel from the riverbank all the way to the walls of the church. It was a quick, bewildering movement, characteristic of the jagunços, with nothing of the customary rectilinear formation, but in place of it an indescribable serpentine motion. It was not a charge; it was a thrust. For some moments a flexible line of steel entwined itself about the enemy's sacred bastion; there was a gleam of two hundred bayonets; and the Fifth disappeared from sight, merged with the ruins.

All this had not altered the situation. This ruin-heaped fragment of the settlement, for the capture of which two brigades had appeared to be more than sufficient, had now absorbed those brigades and their reinforcements, as it was to absorb whole battalions more—the Thirty-fourth, the Fortieth, the Thirtieth, and the Thirty-first Infantry. The attacking forces had been doubled, and the din of the invisible battle was rising in a crescendo. The fires were spreading; the entire arbor had been burned; but, amid the dense smoke which darkened the air, the *praça* down below stood out whitely—and without a sign of human life.

LOSSES

After three hours of fighting they had mobilized two thousand men without any effect whatsoever. Our losses, meanwhile, were mounting. In addition to a large number of privates and lower-ranking officers, the commander of the Twenty-ninth, Major Queiroz, and the commander of the Fifth Brigade, Lieutenant Colonel Tupy Ferreira Caldas, were killed.

TUPY CALDAS

The latter's death was the occasion for a rare exhibition of courage on the part of his men. The members of the Thirtieth idolized him. He was one of the few born soldiers. Nervous, restless, and impulsive, his was a temperament that was adapted to impetuous charges and the rude life of the barracks. He had been the commander of the vanguard on the eighteenth of July, and since that day he had emerged unscathed from the deadliest of fusillades. The bullets had spared him; they had grazed him, taken away his hat, flattened his belt buckle. The one that proved his undoing struck him in the arm as he was holding his binoculars to view the assault, and passed through his chest, hurling him to the ground and killing him instantly. The Thirtieth thereupon set out to avenge him. A shudder of fear and of wrath ran through the ranks, and then with a bound the men were out from behind their breastworks and were off on the double-quick down the winding lanes, to attack the fortified huts from which the projectile had come. Not a shot could be heard, but soldiers were to be seen dropping from bullets fired at close range, while their comrades passed over them, throwing themselves against the doors, battering them down with their rifle butts, and forcing their way into the tiny, dark rooms within, only to find themselves locked in a hand-to-hand struggle.

This attack, however, one of the boldest that was made in the course of the entire conflict, like the others, was frustrated by the incoercible tenacity of the jagunços, and the Thirtieth, with numbers considerably diminished, returned in disorder to its former position. Along the entire line there were the same attacks and the same retreats. The final death throes of the vanquished were too much for the iron-clad brigades.

Shortly before nine o'clock our men had the pleasing illusion of victory. As one of the reserve battalions came up, a cadet of the Seventh unfurled the national banner on the crumbling walls of the church. Dozens of bugles sounded, and a resounding *viva* to the Republic burst from thousands of throats. Surprised by this unlooked-for demonstration, the sertanejos ceased firing, and the square for the first time was filled to overflowing with fighting men. Many of the spectators, among them three generals, rapidly descended the hillsides. As they were passing the "black line" down below, they ran into four privates with a couple of captured jagunços. In front of them and all around them men from all points of the line were waving hats, swords, and rifles, running here and there, bumping into one another, embracing one another, and piling tumultuously into the square, amid a delirium of shouts and noisy ovations.

At last, this terrible war was over.

With some difficulty the generals made their way through the surging, shouting throng, toward the arbor, when, as they reached the large lime deposit directly opposite, they were surprised by the whine of bullets overhead.

The battle continued; and the square was once more, of a sudden, emptied, swept clean.

DYNAMITE

Quickly returning to their intrenchments, returning on the run to any sheltered spot they could find, crouching behind anything that might serve as a barricade, slipping along close up to the protecting riverbanks, gripped with fear, bitterly disappointed, singularly downcast just as victory was imminent, made sport of by the vanquished in their death agony, these conquerors of a kind never seen before in history came to realize that this, the enemy's last battered stronghold, would end by devouring them one by one. What did it matter that they had six thousand rifles and six thousand sabers; of what avail were the blows from twelve thousand arms, the tread of twelve thousand military boots, their six thousand revolvers and twenty cannon, their thousands upon thousands of grenades and shrapnel shells; of what avail were the executions and the conflagrations, the hunger and the thirst which they had inflicted upon the enemy; what had they achieved by ten months of fighting and one hundred days of incessant cannonading; of what profit to them those heaps of ruins, that picture no pen could portray of the demolished churches, or, finally, that clutter of broken images, fallen altars, shattered saints—and all this beneath a bright and tranquil sky which seemingly was quite unconcerned with it all, as they pursued their flaming ideal of absolutely extinguishing a form of religious belief that was deeply rooted and which·brought consolation to their fellow-beings?

Obviously, other measures were imperatively called for in dealing with a foe who was so impervious to all the forces of Nature, so schooled in havoc and destruction. Fortunately, they had made provision for such an emergency; they had foreseen this terrifying epilogue to the drama. And so, a certain lieutenant, an adjutant orderly of the headquarters staff, now had them bring up from the camp dozens of dynamite bombs. This was fitting enough; it was absolutely the only thing to be done; for the sertanejos had inverted all the psychology of ordinary warfare; their resistance was stiffened by reverses, and they were strengthened by hunger, hardened by defeat.

It was the very core of our nationality, the bedrock of our race,[17] which our troops were attacking here, and dynamite was the means precisely suited. It was at once a recognition and a consecration.

The firing now ceased, and over the whole of our lines an intense silence fell, one of anxious waiting. Then there came a violent tremor along the circumference of the besieged settlement, running through the camp and suddenly spreading to the distant batteries on the hillsides, covering the entire neighborhood with a vibrant network of seismic curves, crossing and crisscrossing over the ground. The jagged ruins of the churches came tumbling down, walls tottered and fell, and roof after roof went hurtling through the air, creating a mountain of dust to add to the smoke. From within the stricken area came irrepressible shrieks of terror from hundreds of throats, as the mighty thunder of the explosions rocked the earth. It seemed as if all were ended now and this last segment of Canudos had crashed in utter ruin.

[17] See p. 78 and "Author's Notes," Note V.

The battalions that were huddled in the alleyways outside the death zone, where splintered beams and roofs were flying in all directions, were waiting for the thundercloud of flames and dust to subside that they might launch their last attack. This, however, they were not destined to do. Instead, they suddenly fell back. Swept by a heavy and incomprehensible fusillade from the blazing huts and rubbish heaps, the assailants sought refuge wherever they could, at the corners of the lanes, by creeping along in the shelter of the huts, or—and this was true of most of them— by running back to their intrenchments.

And now, from the portion of the village beyond, there came an indescribable sound of weeping and wailing, screams and imprecations, reflective at once of terror and of pain, of anger and exasperation, on the part of the tortured multitude that was bellowing there. Amid the glow of the flames shadowy figures could be seen darting convulsively in and out: women fleeing their burning hovels, carrying their young ones in their arms or dragging them along as they ran down the lanes and disappeared in the maze of huts; figures fleeing wildly in every direction; floundering on the ground, their clothing in flames; bodies burned and writhing in agony, like human firebrands. And overlooking all this stupendous scene, scattered about with no attempt to conceal themselves, leaping over the blazing bonfires, drawing themselves erect on the roofs that were still left standing, were the last defenders of the settlement, shouting and gesticulating in their rude fashion, their profiles barely visible amid the smoke. And then it was that everywhere of a sudden, only a couple of paces distant from the line of fire, sinister physiognomies made their unexpected appearance, begrimed masklike faces, naked bosoms scarred and singed, as the jagunços once more, boldly, insanely, came back to the fray.

THE ENEMY CONTINUES TO FIGHT BACK

These figures, these visages, had come to slay their adversary in his own trenches. For our troops were discouraged, the life had been taken out of them, as the futility of the artillery bombardment, the constant fusillades, and even this last resort to dynamite was borne in upon them. They had lost all unity of action and command. The bugles sounded stridently, discordantly, on every hand, but no one paid any attention to them; it was impossible to obey their signals when the tactical conditions of the struggle varied so, from moment to moment, with every step they took. Detachments from the same company would go forward, fall back, or halt, would break up into smaller units at every corner of the lanes, their members mingling with those from other corps as they attacked the houses or made their way around them, only to break up again and join other groups, repeating the process all over again, with the same advances and the same retreats, the same dispersions at every few paces. As a result, small bands made up of men from all the battalions were soon floundering about without any sense of direction.

MORE CASUALTIES

Taking advantage of the tumult, the jagunços subjected them to a merciless fire. After a short while, those of our men who did not have the shelter of breastworks were to be seen huddled against the walls of those dwellings that were still intact, while others had retired for a considerable distance down the lanes in that part of the settlement which was in our hands. This was in an effort to avoid the danger zone; but that zone was now widening. Men on the other side of the trenches, entirely outside the flaming orbit of battle, now were falling; and, as in those terrible days when the siege was in its first week, the slightest bit of imprudence, such as showing one's self from behind the fragile shelter even for a fraction of a second, was as much as a life was worth.

The captain commissary of the Second Column command, Aguiar e Silva, as a platoon marched by, stepped for an instant from behind the corner of a hut and, by way of spurring on the attack, raised his hat in the air enthusiastically and shouted a *viva* to the Republic. He did not pronounce the last syllables, however, for he was struck down by a bullet in the chest. The commander of the Twenty-fifth Battalion, Major Henrique Severiano, met an identical fate. He was a fine, heroic character. In the midst of the battle, seeing a child struggling in the flames, he dashed through the blaze, took the young one in his arms, and clasping it to his bosom with a kindly gesture, carried it to safety—the one outstanding act of heroism in all that bloody day. But he paid for it. Wounded by a bullet, he died a few hours later.

And so it went. The battle was now taking on a wholly unnatural aspect for either side alike.

IN THE FIELD HOSPITAL

Our losses once more were mounting. The spectators, crowded about the fortified observation posts on the hill at the far side of the camp, were able to form some idea as to the extent of the casualties from the mournful procession of biers, stretchers, and hammocks which passed through their midst, going over the hill. Emerging from the gully down below, the stretcher-bearers would wind slowly upward, making their way around the houses with which the slope was dotted; and, having reached the top,

they would go down the other side to the field hospital, where, at one
o'clock in the afternoon, there were already around three hundred
wounded.

The leather awning which covered the concavity of the hill was unable
to contain them all. The patients were packed in and overflowed onto the
rocks along the edge of the southern slope, where they were to be seen
dragging themselves along and contending with one another for the shade
of the barracks, all the way to the pharmacy annex and the medical
pavilion. Doctors and nurses, far too few in number, ran hurriedly back
and forth, while the wounded of previous engagements, leaning on their
elbows or lying face downward, cast an anxious eye at these new companions in misfortune. At one side, stretched out on the bare ground with the
sun beating down upon them, were the bodies, rigid in death, of a number
of officers—those of Lieutenant Colonel Tupy, Major Queiroz, Sublieutenants Raposo, Neville, Carvalho, and others.

Panting and sweating, the bearers came and went at intervals, bent beneath the weight of their stretchers. They would deposit them and quickly return to the scene of battle; and this funereal bustle threatened to keep
up the entire day, since up to that hour the situation had not changed for
the better and the outcome was still in doubt. The enemy was continuing
his fierce counterattack, and the insistent notes of the bugle all up and
down the lines, sounding the charge, lent a touch of cruel monotony to the
prevailing tumult. Charges were made, one after another, swift and impetuous charges—with platoons, batallions, brigades, huge waves of metal
and of flame, gleaming, rolling, crashing, and thundering against those
floodgates which they were unable to surmount.

The dynamite bombs (ninety of them in all were thrown) kept exploding from moment to moment, but with absolutely no effect. It was, accordingly, necessary to resort to still other expedients, and cans of kerosene were tossed on the houses everywhere, by way of spreading the fires.
This barbarous recourse, however, in its turn proved to be a futile one.

Finally, at two o'clock in the afternoon, the assault came to a standstill; the charges ceased, and the besiegers, frankly on the defensive and
back in their original positions once more, experienced all the disappointment of a defeat. Meanwhile, in stretchers, in hammocks, or carried under
the armpits by their comrades, the wounded continued to go up the hill,
with the bearers, staggering from exhaustion, keeping close to the houses,
leaning against them for support. And over all, over the fortified hilltops,
sweeping and flaying them, over the entire camp, at twilight, at nightfall,
and throughout the night, reaching to every point of the circling siege

line, whistling through the air with every sound imaginable, from that
tiny area where the jagunços now were penned, the bullets kept coming.

It was a bloody and a fruitless combat, costing us 567 men, with no appreciable result. As always, after a while, the noise of battle died down,
until there was only scattered firing to be heard; and the night passed
with our battered troops on the alert, looking forward grimly to fresh encounters, further useless sacrifices, and wasted efforts. In the meantime
the situation of the sertanejos had grown worse. With the loss of the
church they had at the same time lost the last of their water pits. They
were now encircled by enormous fires, closing in upon them from three
directions—from the north, east, and west—penning them in their last
stronghold. Yet, at dawn on the morning of October 2, the weary victors
were awakened by a heavy, sustained, and defiant fusillade.

NOTES FROM A DIARY

On that day. . . . .

Let us transcribe, without altering a single line, the concluding notes
from a "Diary"[18] written as these events were taking place.[19]

". . . . At one o'clock a large number of new prisoners came in—a clear
sign of weakening on the part of the rebels. They were expected. Shortly
after midday a white flag was raised from the center of the last group of
huts, and firing on our side at once ceased. This was the final surrender.
The bugles no longer sounded, and a vast silence enveloped both the battle lines and the camp. The flag, a mere rag nervously waved in the air,
was withdrawn; and, shortly afterward, a couple of sertanejos, emerging
from an impenetrable passageway, presented themselves before the commander of one of the battalions. From there they were conducted into the
presence of the commander-in-chief in the quarters of the engineering
commission.

"PIOUS ANTHONY"

"One of these envoys was 'Pious Anthony,' the Counselor's acolyte and
aide.[20] A tall, light-colored mulatto of erect bearing, he was excessively
pale, lean, and flat-chested. On his brow was the pride of resignation. His
small face, lighted by a pair of intelligent, bright eyes was framed in a
scant growth of beard. He was clad in a tunic of indigo-blue, and, after
the fashion of the community leader, he carried a staff on which he leaned

[18] See pp. 369–72.

[19] These notes, jotted down in the course of the day, in camp, and completed that night, on
Mount Favella, however lacking in accuracy they may be, have the value of spontaneity, reflecting the tumult amid which they were written.

[20] See pp. 159–60, 430, 475.

as he walked. He and his companion, escorted by a number of privates, were followed by a throng of the curious.

"Upon reaching the general's presence, he calmly removed his blue linen cap with the white stripes and tassels and stood there in a properly respectful attitude, waiting for the victor to speak first. Not a syllable of the dialogue which promptly began was lost upon the listeners.

" 'Who are you?'

" 'I would inform the Doctor General[21] that I am Antonio Beato ('Pious Anthony') and that I have come of my own accord to give myself up, because our people don't know what to think any more and they cannot hold out any longer.'

"As he said this, he slowly twirled his cap in his hands, glancing about, quite unperturbed, at the bystanders.

" 'Very well. And the Counselor . . . . ?'

" 'Our good Counselor is in Heaven. . . . . '

THE COUNSELOR'S DEATH

"He then went on to explain that, weakened by an old wound from the splinter of a grenade which he had received on a certain occasion as he was going from the church to the 'Sanctuary,' the Counselor had died on September 22[22] of dysentery, or, as he put it, 'the trots'—an expression so horribly comic as to evoke at once an irrepressible ripple of laughter, despite the painful gravity of the occasion. He did not notice this, however; or perhaps he was pretending not to notice, as he stood there motionless, his face calm and inscrutable, looking the general straight in the eye with a gaze that was at once humble and unflinching. The dialogue continued:

" 'Your people are not disposed to surrender, then?'

" 'I tried my best to get some of them to come with me and they wouldn't, for there's a bunch of them there that don't want to. They're of many ways of thinking. But they can't hold out any longer. Nearly every one of them is ready to bow his head to the ground, out of necessity. Nearly every one is dying of thirst.'

" 'And still you can't bring them in?'

" 'That I cannot. They were ready to shoot me when I left.'

" 'Well, you see how many men we have here, all well armed and well equipped?'

---

[21] This extravagant form of address is literally transcribed, as all those present at this interesting interview will recall. For the matter of that, the entire dialogue as here set down is literal and complete, the only alterations being in the matter of pronunciation, as the sertanejo has difficulty with his *rr*'s and *ll*'s.

[22] See p. 429 and n. 29.

" 'Yes, I'm astonished to see so many!'

"His reply was either sincere, or else admirably calculated; for over the altar boy's face there flitted an unmistakable expression of fear.

" 'Very well, then. Your people can neither hold out nor flee. Go back and tell those fellows to surrender. They will not be killed. I will guarantee their lives. They will be turned over to the government of the Republic. And tell them that the government of the Republic is good to Brazilians. Let them surrender. But without any conditions; I will not hear to any condition.'

" 'Pious Anthony,' however, obstinately refused to undertake this mission. He was afraid of his own companions and was able to offer the best of reasons for not going.

"At this point the other prisoner, who up to then had remained silent, took a hand in the conversation. Here for the first time our men had an opportunity to see a jagunço who looked well fed and who stood out from the uniform type of sertanejo. His name was Bernabé José de Carvalho, and he was a second-line leader. He gave the impression of being Flemish, and it is no exaggerated conjecture to say that he put one in mind of the fact that the Dutch for long years had roamed these northern territories, trading with the natives. His big manly blue eyes shone, and his flat, energetic-looking head was covered with a thick mop of straw-colored hair. These features were by way of being his credentials, as coming from a higher racial stock. He was not an ordinary backwoodsman and was married to a niece of Captain Pedro Celeste of Bom Conselho.

"He appeared somewhat disgusted with his companion, and spoke up boldly, endeavoring to persuade the stubborn Anthony.

" 'Come on, man! Let's go!—I'll have a word with them—leave it to me. Come on!'

"And they went.

PRISONERS

"This mission, however, had a wholly unlooked-for effect. After an hour had passed, 'Pious Anthony' returned, followed by some three hundred women and children and half-a-dozen helpless old men. It appeared as if the jagunços were carrying out one last stratagem of unparalleled cunning, by thus freeing themselves of all these useless mouths to feed from what scant store of provisions they may still have possessed. By so doing, they were in a position to prolong the conflict more at their leisure. 'Pious Anthony' possibly—who can say?—had accomplished a masterstroke. Consummate diplomat that he was, he not only was sparing these wretched beings the torture of flames and bullets; he was at the same time relieving his comrades of an encumbrance which so hampered their efforts.

"A critical study of events indicates that this was, quite possibly, a trick. This is not to overlook the fact that the crafty ascetic who engineered it returned with the others. This was a point in his favor, deliberately and astutely planned, it may be, as indisputable proof of the good faith in which he was acting. But, aside from that, it may be that he was motivated by the aspiration to make a final sacrifice in behalf of the common creed, by thus returning to camp and giving himself up to the consecration of a martyrdom which he, perhaps, ardently desired, with that sickly mysticism that is characteristic of the visionary. There would seem to be no other way of interpreting the circumstance, in view of the fact that the other envoy did not return but remained with the fighting men in the settlement, where he doubtless was instructing them as to the disposition of the besieging forces.

"The entrance of the prisoners into camp was a moving sight. At their head came Anthony, his flabby torso drawn erect, his eyes on the ground, as he walked with the slow and cadenced step that was customary in those solemn processions in which he had been used to taking part. With his right hand he waved his long shepherd's crook, as if it had been an enormous baton with which he was beating time for what was truly a funeral march. The line of prisoners, which formed a long undulating curve along the slope of the hill, kept on in the direction of the camp and, passing First Column headquarters, came to a halt a hundred yards beyond—an ugly cluster of ragged, repulsive-looking human bodies.

"Our men viewed them with a mournful eye. They were at once surprised and deeply moved. In the course of this fleeting armistice the settlement *in extremis* was here confronting them with a legion of disarmed, crippled and mutilated, famished beings in an assault that was harder to withstand than any they had known in the trenches under enemy fire. It was painful for them to admit that all these weak and helpless ones—so many of them!—should have come out of those huts which had been bombarded for three whole months. As they contemplated those swarthy faces, those filthy and emaciated bodies whose gashes, wounds, and scars were not concealed by the tattered garments they wore—as they viewed all this, the longed-for victory suddenly lost its appeal, became repugnant to them. They were ashamed of themselves. They found small compensation for all the battles they had fought, the reverses they had suffered, the thousands of lives thrown away, in this assortment of human derelicts, now their prisoners; and so they could not but look on gloomily as this endless stream of rags and carcasses flowed past them, sinister and pity-inspiring, foul and tragic in the extreme.

"Not a manly countenance among them, not an arm that was capable of supporting a weapon, not a single warrior with heaving bosom, conquered at last. Nothing but women, women, women—ghostlike old women, young girls old before their time, the young and the old indistinguishable in their ugliness, their filth, and their emaciation. And the children—children barely able to stand on their weak, bowed legs, children clinging to their mothers' backs or withered bosoms, or dragged along by the hand. Children, children, children. No end of children and the aged. Few men among them, none but feeble-looking invalids, their swollen, deathlike faces the color of wax, their bodies bent double, swaying as they walked.

"Let us take an example or two. There was one old man, absolutely unable to walk, who had to be supported by some of his companions, thus disturbing the line of march. He appeared to have come against his will. Struggling to free himself, he turned backward and stood waving his tremulous arms in the direction of the settlement, where, of a certainty, he had left able-bodied sons to take part in the last struggle. He alone of all the prisoners wept; the others went on with impassive faces. To these rugged old woodsmen, this cruel calamity in their old age was, when all was said, merely an episode in the tragic life of the backlands. Some of them respectfully bared their heads as they passed through small groups of curious spectators. One, an octogenarian who was not stooped like the others, walked along slowly, pausing every now and then to look back at the church, after which he would resume his march, only to pause once more after he had gone a few paces and gaze again upon the ruined shrine; he kept this up intermittently, all the while telling the beads of a rosary which he held in his hand and praying, for he was a true believer. He was, perhaps, awaiting the great miracle which had been promised.

"Some of the sick were unable to take more than a step or two before they would fall and had to be carried bodily, by the arms and legs, four soldiers to each of them. They did not writhe or groan, but remained silent and motionless, their eyes wide open, fixed as in death. Alongside the others, thin little children ran up and down the line, weeping, calling for their parents who were either there or among the dead down below. Tiny tots were carried on the backs of soldiers, grasping the latter's long hair, uncombed for three months now; and these brave fellows who half an hour before had been risking their lives behind the barricades now did their awkward best to play the part of dry nurses and solve the difficult problem of carrying a child.

"Then, there was the horrible hag, a wrinkled and skinny old witch—the foulest old woman in all the backlands, it may be—who alone raised her head, her angry eyes darting sparks, to look the bystanders in the face. Her tangled white hair, filled with lumps of earth, fell down over her naked shoulders. Restless and agitated, active in spite of her age, she attracted everyone's attention by falling into a broken trot, forcing her way through the wretched group. In her spindling arms she carried a small child, her granddaughter, great-granddaughter, or great-great-granddaughter, perhaps. That child was a horrifying sight to behold. The left side of its face had been torn away some time ago by a splinter from a grenade, and the jawbones, white as could be, now stood out from the crimson edges of the wound, which had healed over. The right side of her face was wreathed in a charming smile—a pitiful half-smile which was at once extinguished in the vacuum, the gash, on the other side.[23] This was the most monstrous sight in all the campaign, to see that old woman reeling along, like one afflicted with locomotor ataxia, down that long line of unfortunates.

"The procession came to a halt alongside the tents of the cavalry squadron, within the four lines of a military square. And then it was, for the first time, that our men had a chance to see the population of Canudos en masse. Aside from those variations due to the imprint of suffering variously borne, there was a rare and striking uniformity in the more characteristic facial features of these prisoners. There were few whites or pure Negroes among them; an unmistakable family likeness in all these faces pointed to the perfect fusion of three races. The legitimate *pardo* type predominated, a mixture of Kafir, Portuguese, and Tapuia Indian—bronzed faces, stiff and straight or curly hair, unshapely torsos. Here and there would be a profile with perfectly correct lines, pointing to the admixture of a higher racial element. And round about them all were the victors, separate and disparate, proteiform types, the white man, the black man, the cafuso, and the mulatto, with all gradations of coloring. There was a contrast here: the strong and integral race thus reduced, within this square, to these indefinable and pusillanimous mestizos, wholly broken by the struggle. Broken and humiliated. From the miserable aggregation there now came plaintive, wheedling voices, asking charity. For they were devoured by the hunger and thirst of many days."[24]

The commander-in-chief on this day had granted the last of the rebels an armistice of a few hours. The effect of this, however, had merely been

---

[23] See p. 407.

[24] [End of quotation from the "Diary."]

to withdraw from the stricken area these useless prisoners. The afternoon was a peaceful one for the jagunços, who waited until the truce was over. When the end of the alloted time was announced by a couple of blank rounds fired by the artillery, followed shortly after by a cannon ball, the defenders of the settlement at once opened a heavy fire on the besiegers, in various directions. The night of the second was a noisy one, filled with lively fusillades.

VI

THE END

There is no need of relating what happened on October 3 and 4. From day to day the struggle had been losing its military character, and it ended by degenerating completely. The last remnants of a meaningless formality were now abandoned: deliberations on the part of the commanding officers, troop maneuvers, distribution of forces, even bugle calls; and, finally, the hierarchy of rank itself was practically extinguished in an army without uniforms which no longer knew any distinctions.

LAST STRONGHOLD

One thing only they knew, and that was that the jagunços would not be able to hold out for many hours. Some of the soldiers had gone up to the edge of the enemy's last stronghold and there had taken in the situation at a glance. It was incredible. In a quadrangular trench of a little more than a yard in depth, alongside the new church, a score of fighting men, weak from hunger and frightful to behold, were preparing themselves for a dreadful form of suicide.[25] They called this "the jagunços' field hospital," but it was in reality a grave. As a matter of fact, there were already more of the dead than the living in the trench; some of the former had been there a number of days already, and their bodies lined up around the four sides of the excavation formed a macabre square within which a dozen dying men, their fingers clenched on the trigger for one last time, were destined to fight an army.

And fight they did, with the advantage relatively on their side still. At least they succeeded in halting their adversaries. Any of the latter who came too near remained there to help fill that sinister trench with bloody, mangled bodies. Sprinkled over the heap of ragged jagunço corpses were the vermilion stripes of uniforms, among them those of the sergeant adjutant of the Thirty-ninth, who had entered the pit never to emerge. A

[25] See p. 447.

similar fate awaited his comrades. They harbored the illusion that this last engagement would be an easy and a fortunate one; all they had to do was to burst through the remaining houses round about and fall upon those famished Titans like a thunderbolt, crushing them.

The terrible exploits that followed are veiled in obscurity for all time to come. Those who undertook them seldom returned. Standing above that ditch, the horror of it all overcame the fury of their attack. There before them, a tangible reality, was a trench of the dead, plastered with blood and running with pus. It was something beyond their wildest imaginings. And they were paralyzed by it.

CANUDOS DID NOT SURRENDER

Let us bring this book to a close.

Canudos did not surrender. The only case of its kind in history, it held out to the last man. Conquered inch by inch, in the literal meaning of the words, it fell on October 5, toward dusk—when its last defenders fell, dying, every man of them. There were only four of them left: an old man, two other full-grown men, and a child, facing a furiously raging army of five thousand soldiers.[26]

We shall spare ourselves the task of describing the last moments. We *could* not describe them. This tale we are telling remained a deeply stirring and a tragic one to the very end, but we must close it falteringly and with no display of brilliancy. We are like one who has ascended a very high mountain. On the summit, new and wide perspectives unfold before him, but along with them comes dizziness.

Shall we defy the incredulity of future generations by telling in detail how women hurled themselves on their burning homes, their young ones in their arms?

And, words being what they are, what comment should we make on the fact that, from the morning of the third on, nothing more was to be seen of the able-bodied prisoners who had been rounded up the day before, among them that same 'Pious Anthony' who had surrendered to us so trustingly— and to whom we owe so much valuable information concerning this obscure phase of our history?

The settlement fell on the fifth. On the sixth they completed the work of destroying and dismantling the houses—5,200 of them by careful count.[27]

[26] See p. 369.

[27] See p. 424.

THE COUNSELOR'S CORPSE

Previously, at dawn that day, a commission assigned to the task had discovered the corpse of Antonio Conselheiro.[28] It was lying in one of the huts next the arbor. After a shallow layer of earth had been removed, the body appeared wrapped in a sorry shroud—a filthy sheet—over which pious hands had strewn a few withered flowers. There, resting upon a reed mat, were the last remains of the "notorious and barbarous agitator." They were in a fetid condition. Clothed in his old blue canvas tunic, his face swollen and hideous, the deep-sunken eyes filled with dirt, the Counselor would not have been recognizable to those who in the course of his life had known him most intimately.

They carefully disinterred the body, precious relic that it was—the sole prize, the only spoils of war this conflict had to offer!—taking the greatest of precautions to see that it did not fall apart, in which case they would have had nothing but a disgusting mass of rotting tissues on their hands. They photographed it afterward and drew up an affidavit in due form, certifying its identity; for the entire nation must be thoroughly convinced that at last this terrible foe had been done away with.

Then they put it back in its grave. Later, however, the thought occurred to them that they should have preserved the head, that head on which so many maledictions had been heaped; and, since it was a waste of time to exhume the body once more, a knife cleverly wielded at the right point did the trick, the corpse was decapitated, and that horrible face, sticky with scars and pus, once more appeared before the victors' gaze.

After that they took it to the seaboard, where it was greeted by delirious multitudes with carnival joy. Let science here have the last word. Standing out in bold relief from all the significant circumvolutions were the essential outlines of crime and madness.

TWO LINES

The trouble is that we do not have today a Maudsley[29] for acts of madness and crimes on the part of nations. . . . .

[28] Extract from the official report of the First Column commander: ". . . . I ordered them to remove the body from its burial place, with the greatest of care, and to take it to the *praça*, where it could be better identified. The fact having been duly established, and attested by affidavit, that this was the body of the notorious and barbarous Antonio Vicente Mendes Maciel (vulgarly known as Good Jesus Counselor), I sent the photographer in order that those who had known him might be certain it was he."

[29] See p. 120.

PRINCIPAL EVENTS OF THE CANUDOS CAMPAIGN

1896

October.—Dr. Arlindo Leoni, magistrate of the Joazeiro District, telegraphs the governor of Baía, asking that measures be taken to guarantee the safety of the town, which, he asserted, was about to be assaulted by the jagunços under Antonio Conselheiro.

November 4.—General Solon, commandant of the Third Military District, grants the request of the governor of Baía for military assistance by dispatching a force of 100 men under command of Lieutenant Manuel da Silva Pires Ferreira, accompanied by a surgeon.

November 7.—The troops set out for Joazeiro, arriving on the morning of the same day; they remain stationed there until the twelfth.

November 12.—The troops leave for Uauá, arriving on the nineteenth.

November 21.—The troops are attacked in Uauá, at dawn, by the jagunços. The latter lose 150 men, while the losses of the former amount to 10 killed and 16 wounded. The surgeon goes insane. Retreat to Joazeiro.

November 25.—A force of 11 officers and 200 men sets out from Baía for Queimadas, under command of Major Febronio de Brito.

December.—Reinforced by 100 additional men from Baía, the troops leave for Monte Santo.

December 29.—They arrive at Monte Santo (543 men, 14 officers, and 3 surgeons).

1897

January 12.—The troops set out for Canudos.

January 14.—Arrive at "Lagem de Dentro." Continue the march. Bivouac at "Ipueiras."

January 15.—They proceed to "Penedo." Bivouac at "Mulungú."

January 17.—Pitch camp at "Vicar's Ranch." Their provisions give out.

January 18.—Crossing of Mount Cambaio. First battle: 4 killed, 20-odd wounded; 115 jagunços killed. Bivouac on the "Little Tablelands."

January 19.—They proceed in force to Canudos. Second battle: 4 killed and 30-odd wounded; more than 300 jagunços killed. Retreat. Catcalls. Third battle at "Bendegó de Baixo": 20 jagunços killed.

January 20.—The retreat to Monte Santo continues.

February 3.—Moreira Cesar embarks for Baía, at Rio, in command of the First Regular Expedition.

February 8.—The expedition arrives at Queimadas (1,300 men).

February 20.—Arrival at Monte Santo.

February 21.—Departure for Canudos (1,281 men).

March 2.—Arrival at "Angico" (11:00 A.M.) and at Mount Favella (1:00 P.M.). Assault on the settlement. Moreira Cesar is mortally wounded.

March 3.—Moreira Cesar dies. Retreat. More catcalls. Death of Salomão da Rocha and Colonel Tamarindo.

April 5.—General Arthur Oscar's order of the day with respect to organization of the forces of the Fourth Expedition: six brigades in two columns (Generals João da Silva Barbosa and Claudio do Amaral Savaget).

June 16.—The Savaget column sets out from Geremoabo (2,350 men).

June 19.—General Arthur Oscar leaves Monte Santo with the First and Third brigades (1,933 men).

June 22.—The brigades of the First Column assemble at "Juá," at night.

June 23.—They go on to Aracaty.

June 24.—Proceed to Jueté.

June 25.—The Savaget column arrives at Cocorobó. First battle: 178 casualties (27 killed). General Savaget is wounded.

June 26.—From Cocorobó to "Macambira"; second battle: 148 casualties (40 killed).

June 27.—General Arthur Oscar and the First Column arrive at Mount Favella: 75 casualties. The Savaget column also arrives at Canudos.

June 28.—Battle and cannonading: 524 casualties.

July 1.—The jagunços assault the camp.

July 13.—Fresh provisions arrive.

July 18.—Assault in force on the settlement: 947 casualties.

July 31.—The Girard Brigade is assembled in Queimadas: 1,042 men and 68 officers.

August 3.—The Girard Brigade leaves Queimadas, commanded by a colonel.

August 10.—It leaves Monte Santo for Canudos, under command of Major Henrique José de Magalhães.

August 14.—Reaches Jueté.

August 15.—Is attacked at "Vicar's Ranch"; loses 91 oxen. Two more brigades arrive at Baía, constituting a division, under command of General Carlos Eugenio.

August 24.—Bombardment of the churches of Canudos by the Witworth 32. The bell falls.

September 6.—The towers of the new church fall.

September 7.—The "Old Ranch House" is captured. The "Seventh of September Trench." The Calumby Road is taken.

September 15.—Battle of "Caxomongú"; two trenches and thirteen pack animals are captured from the jagunços.

September 22.—Antonio Conselheiro dies.

September 24.—The siege line about Canudos is completed, all the way to Mount Cambaio. First prisoners.

September 26.—Four violent night attacks by the jagunços.

September 27.—Eighteen night attacks by the jagunços.

September 28.—The jagunços fail to reply to the cannonading, morning or afternoon; but they keep up a fusillade from 6:00 P.M. to 5:00 A.M. on the morning of the twenty-ninth.

October 1.—Final assault. Ninety dynamite bombs are brought down to Canudos. Death of Tupy Caldas; 567 casualties.

October 2.—More than 300 jagunços (women, old men, and children) give themselves up.

October 5.—Death of the four last defenders of Canudos.

October 6.—Exhumation of Antonio Conselheiro's corpse.

AUTHOR'S NOTES

TO THE THIRD EDITION OF *OS SERTÕES* (1905)

This book having been given to the public without any defense whatsoever on my part, in order that the protests against any misstatements which it may contain might be freely voiced, nonetheless met with a hearty and spontaneous response on the part of my generous-minded fellow-countrymen and the leading organs of the press, a response which I did not go out of my way to seek, and which, as a matter of fact, took me completely by surprise. The very insignificance of those few slips of the pen which the critics have pointed out constitute an eloquent testimony to the soundness of the ideas and propositions which are set forth in the work. This may be seen from the following rapid summary.

NOTE I

Page 2. ".... *unconscious mercenaries.*"
This expression has occasioned surprise. Nevertheless, it should be allowed to stand; and I let it stand. It was not my purpose to defend the sertanejos; for this book, unfortunately, is not a defense but an attack. An open, and I should add, an involuntary attack. In thus assailing, with seeming defiance, those extraordinary representatives of civilization in our backlands who exhibited so lamentable a degree of barbarism toward semibarbarians, I was merely being rigorously obedient to the truth, a truth which cannot be denied, and which no one will deny. If it were not that I feared taking to myself an implied honor which I do not deserve, I should have engraved upon the first page of this work that nobly sincere phrase of Thucydides, as he sat down to write the history of the Peloponnesian War; for I, too, even though lacking in the eagle-eyed vision that was his, have written: "Without giving credit to the first witnesses that I encountered, or to my own impressions, but simply narrating those events of which I was the spectator or concerning which I had assured information."

NOTE II

Page 15. ".... *wholly unprotected against the erosive acidity of the tempestuous rains.*"
This phrase has been termed inexact, and a certain critic has seen in it one of the evidences of my alleged scientific obscurantism (*Revista do Centro de Letras e Artes*, of Campinas, No. 2, January 31, 1903). Inasmuch as time is lacking for an extensive citation of authorities, I shall limit myself to a reference to page 168 of Contejean's *Geology*, a passage having to do with rock erosion: "Des actions physiques et chimiques produites par les eaux pluviales plus ou moins chargées d'acide carbonique—principalement sur les roches les plus attaquables aux acides, comme les calcaires, ..." With regard to the special case of Brazil, see also page 151 of Em. Liais' work on the geological formation of our land, where he describes this phenomenon, which "se montre en très grande échelle, sans doute à cause de la fréquence et de l'acidité des pluies d'orage." Meanwhile, the critic in question proceeds to read me a lesson: "Rains do not cause

erosions by reason of the fact that they happen to contain a few molecules more of niter or ammonium; erosions are due to the resistance of the upper horizontal layer in relation to the softness of the lower ones." An extraordinary kind of geology, this. . . . .

NOTE III

Page 32. ". . . . *the* favellas . . . . *possess, in their leaves, stomata which, expanded in the form of villosities.* . . . ."[1]
I hasten to correct this obvious mistake with reference to so simple a matter. The reading should be: ". . . . the *favellas* . . . . possess, in their leaves, *cells* which, expanded in the form of villosities. . . . ."

NOTE IV

Page 42. "*The fact of the matter is, the morphology of the earth violates the general climatic laws.*"
Another expression with which the critics have found fault. It is challenged by a respectable scientist: "In my opinion, if Nature combats deserts, the geographical lay of the land does no more than modify the extrinsic conditions. If violence means modification, 'to violate' implies disobedience to the pre-established. Thus, beyond the question of a doubt, there is no such thing as a violation of the general climatic laws" (*Correio da Manhã*, February 3, 1903).
An inexplicable refutation, this, and one that is at odds with all the conclusions of modern meteorology! It is sufficient to recall the fact that, inasmuch as the general laws that determine a climate are derived from astronomical relationships, the very undulations of the isotherms, with their undisciplined curves, which, if those laws were respected, would follow the parallels, are an attested instance of such violation. We shall not here undertake to exemplify the predominance which is constantly to be observed of particular or secondary causes in determining the climatic constitution of any country. From Santos, whose equatorial climate is an anomaly in a latitude above the tropic, to ice-covered Greenland opposite the benign coast of Norway, we should be able to find splendid examples. Only recently, in a brilliant work on the psychology of the English, Boutmy drew attention to the fact that their land on the fifty-second parallel has a temperature corresponding to that of the thirty-second parallel in the United States. Whoever on a map will follow the isotherm of zero, starting from frigid Iceland, will find himself going southward, in a capricious curve, in the direction of England, without, however, touching that country; then he will twist back to the extreme north of Norway; after which, he will once more return to the south, and in the cold months will draw near to Paris and Vienna—which thus, despite their much lower latitudes, are linked with the frozen polar region. And the traveler who goes along our coast, from Rio to Baía, in the direction of the Equator—will he not, here too, follow a line that scarcely varies and which in geometrical fashion reflects the constancy of the climate all along the way, as mirrored in the luxuriance of the forests, which turn this vast stretch of seaboard into a garden land? But should he at any point pause and turn westward, along a parallel, the line that astronomically determines climatic uniformity, he will have gone but a few dozen miles when he will come upon habitats that are entirely different. Are not these cases, which we could multiply if we so desired, obvious instances of a violation of the general climatic laws?[2]

[1] [The corrected reading is the one followed in the present rendering: *cellulas* for *estomatos.*]

[2] [It may be of interest to compare the statement of the nineteenth-century Arctic explorer, Elisha Kent Kane (*Arctic Explorations* [London: Cambridge University Press, 1856], I, 174): "This anomalous temperature seems to disprove the idea of a diminished cold as we approach the Pole. It will extend the isotherm of the solstitial month higher than ever projected."]

NOTE V

Page 54. The same critic elsewhere discovers a contradiction; he says: ". . . . on page 70:³ I find the categoric statement: *We do not possess unity of race, and it is possible we shall never possess it.* And on page 616:³ we are told that it was *the very core of our nationality, the bedrock of our race*, which was being attacked at Canudos."

In this mortal leap—616 minus 70 equals 546 pages—one might expect to meet with a few seeming discrepancies. However, anyone who has followed my reasoning with regard to our racial origins, while realizing that we do not in fact possess unity of race, will at the same time recall that, in connection with the various melting-pot admixtures which had been effected, I did encounter in the backlands (sertanejo) type an ethnic subcategory already formed (p. 84) and one which, as a result of historical conditions, had been freed of the exigencies of a borrowed civilization such as would have hindered its definitive evolution (pp. 87–88). This is equivalent to saying that in that indefinable compound—the Brazilian—I came upon something that was stable, a point of resistance reminiscent of the integrating molecule in the initial stage of crystallizations. And it was natural enough that, once having admitted the bold and inspiring conjecture that we are destined to national unity, I should have seen in those sturdy caboclos the hardy nucleus of our future, the bedrock of our race.

The bedrock. . . . . This locution suggests an eloquent simile. The truth of the matter is, our formation, like that of a block of granite, is due to three principal elements. Whoever climbs a granite hillock will encounter the most diverse constituents: here, pure clay, of decomposed feldspar, variously colored; a little farther along, bits of gleaming mica scattered over the ground; and, beyond that, the sand dust of pulverized quartz. But from a distance, the hill has the erratic appearance of a *roche moutonnée;*⁴ while all around is to be seen a mixture of these same elements, with the addition of other, adventitious ones, the whole going to form an arable terrain that is noncharacteristic and extremely complex. Down beneath, however, when the surface layer has been removed, will be found a nucleus of hard, solid rock. The elements which on the surface are scattered and mixed in a highly diversified manner—for the reason that the exposed soil retains even the foreign matter brought in by the winds— are here, down below, rendered firm and resistant, with their proportions stabilized. And so it is, the deeper he goes, the closer the observer will come to the definite matrix of the locality in question.

Precisely the same thing happens with respect to race, as we leave the cities of the seaboard for the villages of the backlands. At first, there is an astonishing dispersion of attributes, from all shades of color to all types of character. There is no distinguishing the Brazilian in this intricate mingling of whites, blacks, and mulattoes, with the blood of all races in their veins, in every conceivable blending. We are as yet on the surface of our *gens;* or, better, if we are to follow out to the letter the comparison which we have begun, we are here treading the nondescript humus of our race. But, as we make our way deeper into the land, we come upon the first fixed groupings—in the *caipira* of the south and the *tabaréo* of the north.⁵ The pure white, the pure Negro, and the pure Indian are now a rarity. The generalized miscegenation, meanwhile, has given rise to every variety of racial crossing; but, as we continue on our way, these shadings tend to disappear, and there is to be seen a greater uniformity of physical and moral characteristics. In brief, we have struck bedrock—in the man of the backlands.

³ [The reference is to the text of the early Brazilian editions; see pp. 54 and 464 of this translation.]

⁴ [Glaciated rock.]

⁵ [General terms for backwoodsman, countryman, rustic (see the "Glossary of Special Terms").]

NOTE VI

Page 161. But we are not yet done with our critic; he has a fresh objection: "If [he says] *what we had to face was the unlooked-for resurrection, under arms, of an old society, a dead society, galvanized into life by a madman*—if this is true, then it is hard to understand how, in connection with the Canudos Campaign, we were attacking 'the bedrock of our race.' "

In speaking of a "dead society," I was referring to an exceptional situation, in which the backlands population had been corrupted by a nucleus of agitators (pp. 161–62). The very comparison made on the same page with identical situations among other peoples points to its exceptional character. In the other case, I was in a manner enunciating a general and permanent proposition, not a temporary and special one reduced to a fragment of space—Canudos—and to a brief interval of time—the year 1897. Nothing could be clearer than this. We shall find a perfect simile in that mysterious isomerism, thanks to which identically constituted bodies, with similar atoms similarly arranged, still exhibit the most diverse properties. Being of this way of thinking—and I trust that the sensitive plants of our scientific milieu will not be too greatly annoyed by this further, fierce attack of obscurantism on my part—viewing things in this light, I see, as all may see, in the *jagunço* the isomeric body of the *sertanejo*. As I understand it, Antonio Conselheiro made his appearance as an "integration of various social traits, vague, indecisive, not readily perceived when lost in the multitude" (pp. 117–18), and not as a simple pathologic case; for this figure of a little great man is precisely to be explained by the unusual circumstance that it affords a striking and suggestive synthesis of all those errors, all those beliefs and superstitions which constitute the ballast of our temperament.

NOTE VII

Page 183. *"Even the caatinga assumes a different aspect. If one were to describe the backlands flora more accurately . . . . one would perhaps do better to refer to this region as the classic land of the caatanduvas. . . . ."*

This statement likewise has aroused controversy. Officious amateurs, trembling for every petal of a botany trampled underfoot by my scientific obscurantism (everlasting shame!) have risen to object to the erroneous doctrine (*sic*) of this book. They inform me, pontifically: "The *caatinga* (bad forest) is the result not of the terrain but of the dryness of the air, whereas the *caatanduvas* are chlorotic growths (sickly forest), resulting from the porosity and lack of moisture of the soil" (*Revista do Centro de Letras e Artes*). A delightful objection, one that begins by rebelling against the Tupi tongue and ends by rising up against the Portuguese language. *Caatinga* (bad forest!). . . . . *Caatanduva* (sickly forest!). . . . . Chlorotic growths. . . . . Chlorosis in a plant signifying, in the vernacular, its "blanching" (etiolation), that is to say, a morbid change due to insufficient light, these must be very unusual forests indeed, seeing that they grow in those regions of Brazil which lie beneath a blazing sun!

As to the celebrated "doctrine," a couple of words as to that. A discriminating study of our flora is yet to be made; it is a problem that awaits a clarifying solution. Having observed that the principal aspect of the *caatinga* (white forest) is that of a rarified and stunted thicket (*cerrado*), while the *caatanduva* (bad, rugged, sickly forest) has the look of an inhospitable scrubland, I set down the phrase in question for the reason that the flora of which we are speaking here, different from that which is prevalent in the backlands, in my eyes really took on the appearance which I have described.

NOTE VIII[6]

There will be found throughout these pages terms which various critics have described as word coinages or unpardonable Gallicisms. However, these critics were not fortunate in their choice of examples, which I shall herewith cite and defend:

Esbotenar—to take off the corners or edges (*Novo diccionario da lingua portugueza*, Candido Figueiredo).

Ensofregar—to render voracious or greedy (*Aulete's Dictionary*).

Preposterar—to invert the order of anything (*ibid.*).

Impacta—the bringing to bear of force (*ibid.*).

Refrão—This is looked upon as a Gallicism. I reply with a citation from a master, Castilho: "Lo, the eternal refrain (*refrão*) which assails our ears."

Inusitado—This also is regarded as a borrowing from the French. Latin: *inusitatus*.

I shall not take note of the others. We might, rather, consider, on page 296, line 3, the deplorable torture of an intransitive verb which successive revisions have not succeeded in freeing from its bondage;[7] and there are other blemishes which call for a more serious weeding-out.

EUCLIDES DA CUNHA

April 27, 1903

[6] [While this "Note" is of especial interest to Portuguese-language readers, it has been thought that it might have some interest for the reader in English as well, for the light it has to throw on the author's style (see the Translator's Foreword, p. x).]

[7] [The page reference is to the Brazilian edition; see p. 230, l. 4, of the present translation: "Those who saw him for the first time found it hard to believe," etc. The original reading in Portuguese was: "Os que pela primeira vez o viam custavam a admittir que. . . . ." The third and subsequent Brazilian editions have the emendation: "custava-lhes admittir. . . . ."]

GLOSSARIES

LIST OF BOTANICAL AND ZOÖLOGICAL TERMS

[NOTE.—In addition to the botanical terms listed here, references will be found in this work to various families, genera, and species, to Amaryllis, Bignonia, Bromeliaceae (bromelias), Cactaceae (cacti), Euphorbia, Gramineae, Lecidea, Mimosacea, Tillandsia, etc. These require no identification.]

BOTANICAL TERMS

Alecrim dos taboleiros.—*See* Tableland evergreen.

Angico.—*Piptadenia rigida* Benth. *Angico* is used for the *Piptadenia* species in general.

Araticú (*araticum*).—Term applied to various trees of the *Annona* spp.

Baraúna (*braúna; garaúna;* also called *arvore preta da mata* and *Maria preta da mata*).—Hardwood tree of the Leguminosae family (*Melanoxylon braúna* Schott.).

Cajó.—*Spondias lutea* L.

Cajú (*cajuys*).—*See* Cashew-nut tree.

Candombá.—Identification in some doubt; perhaps the *cunduma* (*kunduma*), the *Iriartea ventricosa* Mart., a variety of palm.

Canudos de pita.—"Pipe reeds"; hollow reeds of the family Solanaceae. See p. 143.

Caraíba (*carahyba;* also known as *parahyba*).—*Simaruba versicolor* var. *angustifolia* Engl.

Carandá.—Plant of the family Palmaceae (*Copernicia australis* Becc.).

Carnaúba.—The wax-palm (*Copernicia cerifera* Mart.).

Caroá (form in Cunha: *caruá*)—*Neoglaziovia variegata* Metz. See p. 91, n. 68.

Cashew-nut tree.—Cunha identifies as the *Anacardia humilis* (see p. 31). It would appear to be the *Anacardium occidentale* L. Native term: *cajú*. For description of this tree and its underground growth see pp. 31–32.

Catingueiras.—General term (plural) applied to certain hardy plants that grow in the *caatinga* (for *caatinga* see Glossary of Terms).

Chique-chique (*xique-xique*).—Cunha identifies this plant as the *Cactus peruvianus* (see p. 34). It would appear to be the *Opuntia brasiliensis*, or the *Opuntia* in general.

Cocoanut.—*Cocos nucifera.*

Cumanan (form in Cunha: *cunanan*).—Shrub of the family Euphorbiaceae (*Euphorbia phosphorea* Mart.).

Erythrina.—Genus of tropical trees and shrubs of the family Leguminosae.

Gerimum (*jurumum*).—Fruit of the *aboboreira*, which belongs to the Cucurbitaceae, or gourd family (*Strategic Index of Latin America*).

Icozeiro (form in Cunha: *icoseiro*).—*Capparis yco* Mart. Plant of the family Caparidaceae which grows in the scrub-forest region.

Ingarana.—*Pithecellobium racemiflorum* Ducke; also, *Pithecellobium* in general.

Joazeiro (joaz tree).—*Ziziphus joazeiro* Mart.

Juá.—*Solanum balbisii* Dun. The term is applied to a number of plants of the family Solanaceae. In Marajó it is applied to *Solanum toxicarium* Lam.

Jurema.—*Acacia jurema* Mart.; also, *Mimosa schomburgkii* Benth.; also, *Pithecellobium* spp.

Jurumum.—See *Gerimum.*

Macambira (tree).—*Bromelia laciniosa* Schult.

Mandacarú.—Vernacular name in Brazil for species of *Cereus* in general. Cunha identifies as *Cereus jaramacarú.*

Mangabeira.—*Hancornia speciosa* Gomez.

Mango tree.—*Mangifera indica.*

Manihot.—Any of a number of species of Euphorbiaceae.

Marizeiro (form in Cunha: *maryseiro;* cf. *marimari, marimari saro*).—*Cassia* spp.

Melocactus.—Genus of Mexican and South American cacti ("melon thistles").

Mimoso.—Vernacular term for a variety of grazing-grass (genus of Mimosaceae?). Cf. *Panasco.*

Monkshood.—Any species of the genus *Aconitum.*

Mulungú.—The cockspur coral tree (*Erythrina mulungú* Mart.); the term is also applied to other species of *Erythrina.* Habitat ranges from Maranhão to Minas Gerais and Rio Grande do Sul.

Oiticica.—Name given to two trees, one of the family Rosaceae (*Licania rigida* Benth.), which is the commercial variety, the other of the family Moraceae (*Clarisia nitida* Benth. Hook.).

Palmatoria.—*Opuntia vulgaris* Mill.; also *Opuntia monacanthia* Haw.

Panasco.—A variety of grazing-grass (*Aristida setifolia* H.B.K.). Cf. *Mimoso.*

Pitomba.—*Eugenia lushnathiana* Berg.

Quipá.—Creeping vine of northeastern Brazil (*Opuntia inanoena* Schum.).

Quixabeira.—Tree of the family Sapotaceae (*Bumelia sartorum* Mart.).

Red oak.—*Quercus rubra.*

Rhipsalis (pl. *rhipsalides*).—Term applied to several plants of the Cactaceae family, genus *Rhipsalis*, species *Clavata, Pachyptera,* and *Salicornioides* Spreng. The first two species are known under the Portuguese name of *Conambaia,* the last one as *Bico de Papagaio.*

Sapé.—*Imperata braziliensis* Trin.

Silk-grass (*gravatá*).—*Bromelia fastuosa* Lindl.

Siphonia.—*Siphonia* spp., genus of plants synonymous with *Hevea.*

Tableland evergreen (*alecrim dos taboleiros*).—*Holocalyx* spp. (Cesalpiniaceae).

Tamarind tree.—Tropical tree of the bean family (*Tamarindus indicus*).

Taquara (*taboca*).—A tough-fibered cane (bamboo) that grows wild in Brazil; *Guadua* spp.; *Chusquea* spp.

Umbú (*ombú; imbu*).—*Phytolacca dioica* L.

Umburana.—Tree of the family Leguminosae (*Amburana cearensis* A.C. Sm.). To be distinguished from the *imburana* (*imborana*), *Bursera* spp., and the *umbú* (*q.v.*).

Urucurí (palm).—*Attalea excelsa* Mart.

ZOÖLOGICAL TERMS

Boa.—The *sucuri,* or anaconda (*Eunectes murinus*).

Caitetú (*caititú*).—Forest pig (*Dicotyles torquatus*). See p. 38, n. 64.

Cobra.—The venomous reptile, *Naja tripudians.*

Ema.—See *Rhea.*

Jacú.—Bird of the Cracidei family (*Ortalis squamata* Less.). Brazilian term: *araquam.*

Jaguar.—*Felis onca,* found from Texas to Patagonia.

Jungle-cat (*gato do mato*).—Name given to small wildcats that live in the jungle.

Maritataca (also *maritacaca, jaritataca,* etc.).—Carnivorous animal of the Mustelidae family (skunks, weasels, and the like).

Moco.—The rock-cavy (*Cavia rupestris*).

Parakeet.—Small Amazonian parrot of the genus *Chrysotis.*

Puma.—The *Felis concolor.* The Brazilian term is *sussuarana.*

Rhea (Portuguese: *ema*).—The South American ostrich (*Rhea americana*), which ranges from Brazil to Patagonia.

Sericoia (*sericora*).—Species of waterfowl (*Aramides cajanea cajanea*).

Seriema.—Long-legged, crested cariamoid bird (*Cariama cristata*).

Tapir.—*Tapirus terrestris,* or *Tapirus americanus,* common in Brazil and Paraguay.

LIST OF TERMS IN REGIONAL USE

Aboiado.—The cowboy's melancholy song as he drives the cattle home.

Aboiar.—To sing when driving the cattle home. See p. 99, n. 82.

Aguardente.—Brandy; the *aguardiente* of the Spanish-speaking countries.

Aió.—A hunting-bag, made of *caroá* or other fiber.

Anhanguera.—Name applied to certain large-scale *bandeirante* expeditions. Cf. *Bandeira, Bandeirante.*

Araxa.—Poetic name given to the high plains of the interior. Literally, the place where one first sees the sun.

Arrancar.—To stampede (of cattle). See p. 100, n. 84.

Arribar.—To stampede (of cattle). See p. 100, n. 84.

Baiano.—A north-country dance in Brazil.

Bala e onça.—"Rough and ready," "up-and-coming," etc. See p. 103, n. 92. Cf. *Brabo e corado.*

Bandeira.—Armed band in colonial days, composed of adventurers, particularly those of the São Paulo region, who made their way into the backlands in search of gold, silver, diamonds, emeralds, etc.

Bandeirante.—Member of a *bandeira.*

Bogó.—A leather water pouch.

Brabo e corado.—"Rough and ready." See p. 103, n. 92. Cf. *Bala e onça.*

Bró.—A kind of bread (described by the author as "sinister") made of urucuri roots.

Caapora.—A goblin of the plains. Cf. *Sacy.*

Caapuera.—A burned-over tract of forest land, with stunted vegetation; literally, "extinct forest." See p. 43.

Caatanduva.—A tract of scrub-forest land still more desolate than the *caatinga* (*q.v.*); literally, "sickly forest." See p. 35 and the description on p. 43; cf. also p. 183. For etymology see p. 183, n. 30.

Caatinga.—Scrub-forest land. See p. 11, n. 13.

Cabocla.—An Indian woman. See *Caboclo.*

Caboclo.—Brazilian Indian; literally, "copper-colored" (cf. *Tapuia*). See *Cabocla.*

Cabra.—A young fellow ("young buck"). See p. 103, n. 92.

Cafuso.—Offspring of Indian and Negro parents.

Caipira.—Countryman, rustic, of southern Brazil. Cf. *Tabareo;* cf. also *Jagunço, Sertanejo.*

Campos.—See *Campos Gerais.*

Campos Gerais.—Vague general term for open country or country that is not heavily forested; applied in particular to the highland plains of the Paraná Plateau. See p. 7, n. 7.

Candomblé.—African fetishistic-religious ceremony common among the Negroes of Baía.

Cangaceiro.—A bandit. See p. 178 and n. 14. Cf. *Cangaço.*

Cangaço.—The bundle of weapons which a bandit (*cangaceiro*) carries. See p. 178, n. 14.

Canhembora (*cânybora*).—A fugitive Indian. Cf. *quilombola*, a fugitive Negro.

Capanga.—A hired assassin, gangster. (Sometimes means a backwoods Negro.)

Capangueiro.—A gang leader. Cf. *Capanga.*

Cariry.—Brazilian Indian tribe.

Cassuá.—Basket made of liana or ipecacuanha fiber.

Cata.—Tract of land rendered sterile by surface-mining operations. See p. 44.

Cateretê.—A backlands dance.

Catingueiro.—One compelled to contend with the rigors of the *caatinga* (*q.v.*), especially in the early, pioneer days.

Choradinho.—Brazilian dance.

Cipó.—Liana.

Corredeira.—A stretch of river marked by a succession of small waterfalls.

Cruzeiro.—A large cross, built of stones, in a street or public square.

Curiboca.—Offspring of white and Indian. Cf. *Mameluco.*

Cuscuz.—Dish made of the finest flour. See p. 156 and n. 160.

Desafios.—Poetic tourneys ("challenges"). See p. 103, n. 95.

Despontar o dia.—"To take the edge off the day." Phrase applied to the first sip of any drink at the beginning of a party. See p. 102 and n. 90.

Destabocado.—Adjective applied to a strong, capable individual. See p. 103, n. 92. Cf. *Destalado, Temêro.*

Destalado.—Exclamation of surprise evoked by a feat of prowess. See p. 99 and p. 103 and n. 92. Cf. *Destabocado, Temêro.*

Dgi.—Keen-edged tool made of diorite.

Emboabas.—Nickname given to the Portuguese *bandeirantes (q.v.).*

Encamisada.—A camisado. See p. 102, n. 87.

Estancia.—A country estate or ranch, especially (in Cunha) in southern Brazil. Cf. *Fazenda.*

Estancieiro.—Proprietor of an *estancia (q.v.).* Cf. *Fazendeiro.*

Estourar.—To stampede (of cattle). See p. 100, n. 84.

Fazenda.—A ranch, plantation, country estate, ranch house (cf. *Estancia*). Cunha distinguishes between the *fazenda* of the North and the *estancia* of the South (Rio Grande do Sul).

Fazendeiro.—The proprietor of a *fazenda (q.v.).* Cf. *Estanceiro.*

Ferrão de vaqueiro.—Cattle prong. Cf. *Guiada.*

Ficar varios.—To lose one's way on the plains. See p. 183, n. 28.

Friagem.—The cold season.

Fueiro.—A wagon bar (fastened on the side of a cart or wagon to sustain the load).

Furo.—A pool formed by the overflowing of the Amazon. Cf. *Paranamarim.*

Garimpeiro.—A diamond hunter.

Gaucho.—A cowboy of southern Brazil (Rio Grande do Sul), as distinguished from the *vaqueiro (q.v.)* of the North. Cf. the Argentinian and Uruguayan *gaucho.*

Girão.—A food container made of wooden stakes and resembling a hammock, suspended from the ceiling; also applied to a hammock or a litter. See p. 145, n. 148, and p. 262.

Guaiaca.—A girdle or belt in which the pistol, knife, etc., are carried.

Guiada.—The cowboy's cattle prong, some three yards long. See p. 145. Cf. *Ferrão de vaqueiro.*

Hollandilha.—Garment of coarse linen cloth worn by victims of the Inquisition.

Igapó.—A bit of aquatic jungle; a pool overgrown with vegetation.

Igarapé.—A canoe creek or natural channel in the Amazon region, between two islands or between an island and the mainland.

Ipueira.—Marshland, or a lake that is filled only in the rainy season; literally, "dead lake." See p. 11.

Jacaré.—"Alligator knife" (literally, "alligator"), with a broad, strong blade.

Jacuba.—A savory drink, made of rice and roasted maize, sugar, etc.

Jagunço.—This word, originally meaning a ruffian (see p. 148), in Cunha comes to be practically synonymous with *sertanejo*, or inhabitant of the backlands. Cf. *Caipira, Tabareo.*

Logrador (logradouro).—A pasture ground or corral near the ranch house, as distinguished from the *solta (q.v.)*, or "run," which is more distant.

Machete.—A banjo or small guitar. See p. 103, n. 96.

Mal triste.—A leprous infection in cattle; in southern Brazil, a form of hydrophobia.

Maloca.—An Indian village.

Mameluco.—Offspring of white and Indian parents. Cf. *Curiboca.*

Massapê.—Fertile topsoil.

Mate.—Paraguayan tea.

Mocambeiro.—The inmate of a *mocambo (q.v.).*

Mocambo.—Originally, the name given to a hut in a *quilombo*, or runaway-slave colony. Today, the word means, in general, a hovel.

Mutan.—An elevated platform, built in trees or shrubbery, on which the hunter awaits his game.

Orizes.—Brazilian Indian tribe.

Pala.—A *gaucho*'s scarf.

Pampeiro.—A strong, cold, dry southwest

wind off the Argentine pampas; Spanish *pampero*.

Paracê.—Tupi religious ceremony.

Paranamarim.—Channel formed by the Amazon overflow. Cf. *Furo.*

Pardo.—The light- or brown-skin racial type in Brazil.

Parnahyba.—A knife (weapon) with a long swordlike blade. See p. 145.

Passoca.—Roasted Brazil nuts ground up in a mortar with manioc flour, salt, and sugar. See p. 107, n. 99.

Paulista.—A native of São Paulo or the São Paulo region (Rio Grande do Sul).

Peia.—Fetters for a bull, steer, or horse.

Pingo.—A cowboy's pony.

Poeira.—A jail ("dust bin"). Cf. our "calaboose," "jug."

Pombeiro.—A mining prospector; comrade, "partner." See p. 183, n. 127. Cf. *Positivo.*

Positivo.—Comrade, "partner"; expression employed by prospectors in the gold-rush days. See pp. 177 and 183. Cf. *Pombeiro.*

Potyguarras (Potigoarras).—Indians of the Pernambuco and Itamacará regions.

Praça.—A square or public place in a city, town, or village; equivalent to the Spanish *plaza.*

Procás.—Brazilian Indian tribe.

Quilombo.—A runaway-slave colony in colonial days, of which Palmares was the most famous example.

Quilombola.—Inhabitant of a *quilombo* (q.v.), or runaway-slave colony of colonial times. Cf. *canhembora,* a fugitive Indian.

Ralhar na viola.—To play noisily and with dexterity on the guitar. See p. 103, n. 93.

Rengue.—A form of lameness in cattle.

Retirantes.—"Quitters"; those who flee the backlands region in time of drought. See p. 109.

Rodeador.—The leader, or foreman, of the *rodeio (vaquejada),* or roundup. Cf. *Rodeio.*

Rodeio.—A roundup of cattle (cf. Spanish *rodeo*). See also *Vaquejada.*

Roqueira.—Cannon for shooting stone; catapult.

Sacy.—A goblin of the plains. Cf. *Caapora.*

Samba.—The famous Brazilian dance (of Baía).

Sapateado.—Dance marked by the clacking of shoes or sandals (from *sapata,* "a shoe").

Senhores de baraço e cutelo.—"Lords of life and death." A proverbial expression. See p. 122, n. 116.

Serenar na dansa.—To dance very slowly, without making any noise with the feet. See p. 103, n. 94.

Sertanejo. Native of the *sertões,* or backlands. To be distinguished from *sertanista* (q.v.).

Sertanista.—As used by Cunha, this term is practically equivalent to "pioneer" (of the *sertões,* or backlands); also, in general, a student of, or authority on, the *sertão* (q.v.). Not to be confused with *sertanejo,* a backlands native. See p. 174, n. 5.

Sertão (pl. *sertões*).—The interior of the country, hinterland, backlands; the term is applied particularly to the backland region in northeastern Brazil centering in the state of Baía.

Sertões.—See *Sertão.*

Solta.—A cattle "run" at some distance from the ranch house. See p. 96, n. 77. Cf. *Logrador (logradouro).* The word *solta* also means a "loose woman." See p. 156, n. 163.

Solteira.—A spinster, "old maid." See p. 156, n. 163. Cf. *Solta.*

Tabajara.—An Indian of the Ceará region.

Tabarêo.—Originally, an awkward, clumsy military recruit; comes to have the general sense of rustic or backwoodsman. Cf. *Caipira, Jagunço, Sertanejo.*

Taboleirinho.—A "little tableland." Cf. *Taboleiro.*

Taboleiro.—A tableland. Literally, a coffee or tea tray. See p. 7, n. 6.

Tapera.—An abandoned country estate, grown into a wilderness; a "weed patch."

Tapuia (Tapuya).—Brazilian Indian; employed as a generic term, commonly referring to a linguistic stock. Cf. *Caboclo.*

"Teimosa."—Nickname applied to rum or brandy; literally, "the headstrong." See p. 102.

Temêro.—Exclamation of surprise evoked by a feat of prowess. See p. 98. Cf. *Destabocado, Destalado.*

Terras grandes.—The "big lands"; term applied by natives of the backlands to the seaboard and to the outside, civilized world in general. See p. 184, n. 31.

Trabuco.—A species of catapult gun. For description see p. 145.

Tropeiro.—A pack-driver, mule-driver.

Tupi.—Brazilian Indian tribe.

Umbusada.—Savory drink made from the *umbú* tree. See pp. 37 and 100.

Vaqueiro.—North Brazilian cowboy (cf. the *gaucho* of Rio Grande do Sul).

Vaquejada.—A "cow-hunt," on a larger scale than the *rodeio*, or ordinary roundup, with the cattlemen of neighboring ranches joining to assemble and separate the cattle of the community.

Varzea.—A plain bordering upon a river or stream.

INDEXES

INDEX OF NAMES

[NOTE.—References to the Introduction, Preface, and other introductory material are in lower-case Roman numerals; references to the body of the work are in Arabic numerals. Items marked with an asterisk refer exclusively to material other than that by the author.]

INDEX OF SUBJECTS

[NOTE.—References to the Introduction, Preface, and other introductory material are in lower-case Roman numerals; references to the body of the work are in Arabic numerals. Items marked with an asterisk refer exclusively to material other than that by the author.]